The Queer Bible Commentary

The Quest Bible Commentary

The Queer Bible Commentary

Edited by

Deryn Guest, Robert E. Goss,
Mona West and Thomas Bohache

scm press

© Deryn Guest, Robert E. Goss, Mona West and Thomas Bohache 2006

British Library Cataloguing in Publication data

A catalogue record for this book is available
from the British Library

0 334 04021 3/978 0 334 04021 7

First published in 2006 by SCM Press
9–17 St Alban's Place,
London N1 0NX

www.scm-canterburypress.co.uk

SCM Press is a division of
SCM-Canterbury Press Ltd

Typeset by Regent Typesetting, London
Printed and bound in Great Britain by
William Clowes Ltd, Beccles, Suffolk

Contents

Part II: The Second Testament

The Contributors

Rebecca T. Alpert is Chair of the Department of Religion and Associate Professor of Religion and Women's Studies at Temple University. She is the co-author of *Exploring Judaism: A Reconstructionist Approach*, with Jacob Staub; author of *Like Bread on the Seder Plate: Jewish Lesbians and the Transformation of Tradition*; editor of *Voices of the Religious Left: A Contemporary Sourcebook* and co-editor of *Lesbian Rabbis: The First Generation* with Sue Elwell and Shirley Idelson. She is currently at work on a volume about Jews, race and sports. She teaches religion and sexuality, the politics of race and gender, and religion in American public life.

Marcella Althaus-Reid is Reader in Christian Ethics, Practical Theology, and Systematic Theology at the University of Edinburgh Divinity School, Scotland. She is a Latin American theologian and author of *Indecent Theology: Theological Per/versions in Sex, Gender and Politics, The Queer God* and *From Feminist Theology to Indecent Theology*. She writes, 'I call my style of doing theology Indecent because it denounces the status quo and the complacency with power that theologies had in the past, while claiming to be proper or decent. Meanwhile, they ignored that the only decency in theology comes from honesty and a pursuit of justice in all orders of life. If we call theologies in alliance with systems of exploitation decent, then I want to be an indecent theologian.'

Angela Bauer-Levesque has served on the faculty of Episcopal Divinity School, Cambridge, Massachusetts, since 1994. She received her PhD from Union Theological Seminary, and holds the MDiv from the Universität Hamburg. In *Gender in the Book of Jeremiah: A Feminist-Literary Reading*, in *Seeing God in Diversity: Exodus and Acts* and in her teaching, she has emphasized various aspects of social location (gender, race, sexual identity) and their impact on hermeneutics. She is currently working on a book titled *Reading While White: Strategies toward Antiracist Biblical Interpretations*. Angela and her spouse Irma live in Ogunquit, Maine.

Roland Boer is Logan Research Fellow in the Centre for Studies in Religion and Theology at Monash University, Australia. He completed his PhD at McGill University. He has served on the steering committee for Gender, Sexuality and the Bible for the Society of Biblical Literature, and for Critical Theory and Discourses of Religion at the American Academy of Religion. His recent publications include *Knockin' on Heaven's Door* and *Last Stop Before Antarctica*. His great passions are Marxism and bicycles.

The Revd Thomas Bohache has been clergy in the Metropolitan Community Churches since 1988, pastoring congregations in California, Virginia and Delaware. He has undergraduate degrees in classical languages and theology and two Master of Arts degrees in religion from the University of Virginia and Georgetown University. He is currently a doctoral candidate at the Episcopal Divinity School in Cambridge, Massachusetts. Among his publications are an essay queering Galatians in *Take Back the Word*, a queer view of incarnation in *Theology and Sexuality*, and a book on contextual Christologies, forthcoming from SCM Press.

Michael Carden received his PhD in 2002 from the University of Queensland in Australia. His dissertation was a study of the reception of the stories of Sodom and Gomorrah and the outrage at Gibeah in both Christian and Jewish traditions up to the time of the Reformation. Michael has taught in the area of biblical studies and comparative religion at the University of Queensland and introduced a course there on Religion and Sexuality. Michael has also had many years of involvement in LGBT and HIV/Aids community organizations.

The Revd Patrick S. Cheng is an ordained minister with the Metropolitan Community Church. He holds degrees from Yale College, Harvard Law School and Union Theological Seminary. Patrick Cheng is currently a doctoral student in Systematic Theology at Union Theological Seminary. He is the founder and co-ordinator of Queer Asian Spirit, www.queerasianspirit.org, an online ministry by and for LGBT people of Asian descent.

J. Michael Clark is a theologian who has taught at Emory University and Georgia State University. He currently teaches at Warren Wilson College. Michael Clark is founder and later Co-Chair of the Gay Men's Issues in Religion Group of the American Academy of Religion. He is author of *A Defiant Celebration: Theological Ethics and Gay Spirituality*; *Beyond Our Ghetto: Gay Theology in Ecological Perspective* and *A Place to Start: Towards an Unapologetic Gay Liberation Theology*. Dr Clark is co-editor of *A Rainbow of Religious Studies*; *Aids, God, and Faith* and *Homophobia and the Judaeo-Christian Tradition*.

The Revd L. William Countryman is the Sherman E. Johnson Professor of Biblical Studies at Church Divinity School (Berkeley). He received an STB from General Theological Seminary and PhD from the University of Chicago. He is co-author of *Gifted by Otherness: Gay and Lesbian Christians in the Church*. He is author of *Love Human and Divine: Reflections on Love, Sexuality, and Friendship*; *Interpreting the Truth: Changing the Paradigm of Biblical Studies*; *The Poetic Imagination: An Anglican Spiritual Tradition*; *Living on the Border of the Holy: Renewing the Priesthood of All*; *Forgiven and Forgiving*; *The Mystical Way According to John: Crossing Over into God*; *Good News of Jesus: Reintroducing the Gospel* and *Dirt, Greed, and Sex: Sexual Ethics in the New Testament and their Implications for Today*. Revd Countryman is an ordained priest in the Episcopal Church.

Sue Levi Elwell earned her PhD from Indiana University, and has taught courses on Jewish feminism at the University of Cincinnati, the University of California, Los Angeles, and LaSalle University. Ordained by the Hebrew Union College–Jewish Institute of Religion in 1986, she has served congregations in California, New Jersey and Virginia. The Founding Director of the American Jewish Congress Feminist Center in Los Angeles, Elwell served as the first rabbinic Director of Ma'yan, the Jewish Women's Project of the Jewish Community Center on the Upper West Side in New York City. Elwell served as editor, with Rebecca Alpert and Shirley Idelson, of *Lesbian Rabbis: The First Generation* and authored *The Jewish Women's Studies Guide*. Elwell is the editor of *The Open Door Haggadah*, and served as one of the editors of the acclaimed *The Journey Continues: The Ma'yan Haggadah*. Elwell serves as the Director of the Pennsylvania Council of the Union for Reform Judaism.

The Revd Robin Hawley Gorsline is Senior Pastor of the MCC Church in Richmond, Virginia. Dr Gorsline received his PhD from Union Theological Seminary. He is co-editor of *Disrupting White Supremacy from Within: White People on What We Need to Do*. Revd Gorsline is co-founder of People of Faith for Equality in Virginia.

The Revd Robert E. Goss serves as Pastor/Theologian of the MCC Church in the Valley in North Hollywood, California. He received his MDiv from the Jesuit Weston School of Theology and ThD in Comparative Religion from Harvard University. Goss served as co-chair of the Gay Men's Issues in Religion Group of the American Academy of Religion and won the 2000 Templeton Course Prize in Religion and Science. Revd Goss is the author of *Jesus ACTED UP: A Gay and Lesbian Manifesto* and *Queering Christ: Beyond Jesus ACTED UP* (a Lambda Literary Finalist for Spirituality). He is co-author of *Dead, But Not Lost: Grief Narratives in Religious Traditions*. Goss is co-editor of *A Rainbow of Diversities*; *Our Families, Our Values: Snapshots of Queer Kinship*; *Take Back the Word: A Queer Reading of the Bible*; and *Gay Catholic Priests and Clerical Sexual Misconduct: Breaking the Silence*. He is currently working with Justin Tanis on an anthology on leather spirituality.

Deryn Guest received her PhD from the University of Birmingham, UK, where she currently lectures. Her research interests are focused on lesbian, gay, bisexual and transgendered interpretations of the Hebrew Bible. Prior to her academic career, Deryn worked as a Salvation Army minister and she retains a keen interest in the biblical hermeneutics operative within faith communities. She is the author of *When Deborah Met Jael: Lesbian Biblical Hermeneutics* and lives in the West Midlands, UK, with her civil partner Fiona, and their two children.

Holly Hearon is Assistant Professor of New Testament at Christian Theological Seminary, Indianapolis, Indiana. She is author of *The Mary Magdalene Tradition: Witness and Counter-Witness in Early Christian Communities* and editor of *Distant Voices Drawing Near: Essays in Honor of Antoinette Clark Wire*. Dr Hearon received a DMin from Union Theological Seminary and PhD in New Testament from the Graduate Theological Union. Hearon is a minister of word and sacrament in the Presbyterian Church (USA). She has served in parish ministry and as an associate for women's ministry for the Women's Ministry Unit of the Presbyterian Church (USA)

The Revd Tom Hanks received an MA from Garrett Evangelical Seminary and Northwestern University and a ThD in Hebrew Scriptures from Concordia Seminary in St Louis. He has served as a missionary in Latin America since 1963, first with the Latin American Mission as Professor of Hebrew Bible at the Latin America Biblical Seminary in San Jose, Costa Rica (1963 to 1985), and then in Buenos Aires, Argentina (1986 to 2003), with the Universal Fellowship of Metropolitan Community Churches and as executive director of Other Sheep. Dr Hanks is an ordained minister in the Presbyterian Church USA. He is author of *God So Loved the Third World* and *The Subversive Gospel*.

Teresa Hornsby is an Associate Professor at Drury University. Her primary research is in the area of gendered interpretation of Christian scriptures. Recent publications include *Ezekiel Off-Broadway* and *The Annoying Woman: Biblical Criticism after Judith Butler*. Her contribution on Ezekiel includes a brief history of interpretation and an assessment of the usual foci. Her unique contribution is to interpret Ezekiel within a queer hermeneutic: 'the sinner as queer'. 'Sinner' is constructed over and against what is considered 'normal' or 'good' or 'perfect' or 'righteous'. As God is imagined by Ezekiel as masculine, the 'normal' or 'good', etc., is also imagined as masculine. Thus, the sinner, as queer, is also perceived as flawed masculinity.

Theodore W. Jennings is Professor of Biblical and Constructive Theology at Chicago Theological Seminary in Chicago. He received his PhD from Emory University. He is author of *Jacob's Wound: Homoerotic Narrative in the Literature of Ancient Israel*; *Reading Derrida, Thinking Paul: On Justice*; *Beyond Theism: A Grammar of God-Language*; *Good News to the Poor: John Wesley's Evangelical Economics*; *Loyalty to God: The Apostles Creed in Life and Liturgy*; *Santidad biblica*; *The Insurrection of the Crucified: The 'Gospel of Mark' as Theological Manifesto*; and *The Man Jesus Loved: Homoerotic Narratives from the New Testament*. Dr Jennings is an ordained minister in the Methodist Church.

Tamar Kamionkowski is Vice President for Academic Affairs and Associate Professor of Bible at the Reconstructionist Rabbinical College. She holds a BA degree from Oberlin College, an MTS from Harvard Divinity School and a PhD in Near Eastern and Judaic studies from Brandeis University. She is the author of *Gender Reversal and Cosmic Chaos: Studies in the Book of Ezekiel* and of articles on prophetic literature, priestly literature and feminist readings of the Bible.

Christopher King completed his doctorate in early Christian studies at the University of Oxford. His doctoral thesis, *Origen on the Song of Songs as the Spirit of Scripture: The Bridegroom's Perfect Marriage-Song*, was published by Oxford University Press in 2005.

The Revd Tim Koch serves as pastor of the New Life Metropolitan Community Church, in Charlotte, North Carolina. He holds an AB in religion from Duke

University, and his MDiv and PhD are from Boston University, the latter with a specialization in the History and Literature of Ancient Israel. Author of several articles on queer biblical hermeneutics, Tim is also the founder and director of the Rosemary Theological Resource Center, also in Charlotte.

Jennifer L. Koosed is an Assistant Professor of Religious Studies at Albright College in Reading, Pennsylvania. She has published articles in *Semeia*, *Strange Fire: Reading the Bible After the Holocaust* and *Imag(in)ing Otherness: Filmic Visions of Living Together*. She has also recently written a book on Qohelet entitled *(Per)mutations of Qohelet: Reading the Body in the Book*.

The Revd Deborah Krause is Academic Dean and Associate Professor of New Testament at Eden Seminary. She received her MDiv from Eden Seminary and PhD from Emory University. She is author of the commentary, *1 Timothy* and co-author of *New Proclamation Year B: 2005–2006: Advent through Holy Week*. Deborah is an ordained minister in the Presbyterian Church. Her speciality is Feminist-Womanist, Postcolonial and Postmodern Hermeneutics.

Ronald Edwin Long is the author of *Men, Homosexuality, and the Gods: An Exploration into the Religious Significance of Male Homosexuality in World Perspective* and is currently an Assistant Professor in the Program in Religion of Hunter College, City University of New York. A former Fulbright Scholar to what was then West Germany, he holds degrees from Kenyon College and a PhD from Columbia University. Ron has previously taught at Vassar College and Columbia University, and served for many years on the steering committee of the Gay Men's Issues in Religion Group of the American Academy of Religion, also as one of its co-chairs. His essays and reviews have appeared in such publications as *Theology and Sexuality*, *The Harvard Gay and Lesbian Review*, *The Journal of Men's Studies*, *The Journal of the American Academy of Religion*, and *White Crane*.

The Revd Stephen Moore is an ordained minister with the Metropolitan Community Churches. He has served as Senior Pastor of several MCC churches and finally as Pastor of MCC Baton Rouge when Hurricane Katrina hit Louisiana and Mississippi. He led major relief efforts to the New Orleans refugees and provided relief to the LGBT refugees as relief efforts provided little to no services.

Tina Pippin is Associate Professor of Religious Studies at Agnes Scott College in Decatur, Georgia. She received an MDiv from Candler School of Theology and an MA and PhD from Southern Baptist Theological Seminary. Dr Pippin is the author of *Apocalyptic Bodies: The Biblical End of the World in Text and Image* and *Death and Desire: The Rhetoric of Gender in the Apocalypse of John*. She is co-editor of *The Monstrous and the Unspeakable: The Bible as Fantastic Literature* and *Violence, Utopia and the Kingdom of God*.

Ron L. Stanley is a transgendered man living in Dallas. He has a PhD in Old Testament from Southwestern Theological Seminary. He has published several articles on the history of Israel and presented a paper at a regional Society of Biblical Literature entitled 'A Practical Old Testament Theology'. His dissertation was a sociological evaluation of the leadership of the Old Testament from Moses through Nehemiah. His current research interests include the organization of Old Testament theology, theories on the openness of God and queer readings of the Bible. Dr Stanley currently works for the federal government.

David Tabb Stewart is Assistant Professor of Religion and Philosophy at Southwestern University, Georgetown, Texas. He has taught Bible and topics in religion at Stanford University, the University of California, Davis, and UC Berkeley, where he received his PhD in Near Eastern Studies. Prior work on Leviticus includes an excursus in the *Anchor Bible, Leviticus 23–27*. He is currently revising his book, *Ancient Sexual Laws* for publication.

Ken Stone is Associate Professor of Hebrew Bible at Chicago Theological Seminary, where he also teaches courses in Lesbian and Gay Studies. He holds a ThM from Harvard Divinity School and an MA and PhD in Biblical Studies from Vanderbilt University. He is the author of *Sex, Honor and Power in the Deuteronomistic History*, editor of *Queer Commentary and the Hebrew Bible* and has written a number of additional articles on sexuality, gender and biblical interpretation.

Elizabeth Stuart is Professor of Christian Theology and Director of Research and Knowledge Transfer at the University of Winchester, UK. She is the author of a number of books on lesbian and gay and queer theology, including *Gay and Lesbian Theologies*. She co-edits the academic journal *Theology and Sexuality*.

The Revd Justin Tanis was for many years Director of Clergy and Leadership Development of the Universal Fellowship of the Metropolitan Community Churches. Revd Tanis received an MDiv from Harvard Divinity School and a DMin from San Francisco Theological Seminary. He is the author of *Trans-Gendered: Theology, Ministry, and Communities of Faith*. He is active in the Leather Community and is Program Manager for the National Center for Transgender Equality, Washington DC. Dr Tanis is working on a leather spirituality anthology.

The Revd Mona West is the Senior Pastor of the Church of the Trinity MCC in Sarasota, Florida. Originally she was ordained in the Southern Baptist denomination in 1987 and transferred her credentials to the Metropolitan Community Church in 1992. She holds an MDiv and PhD (Old Testament/Hebrew Bible) from Southern Seminary in Louisville, Kentucky. After teaching in colleges in the South, she became the Academic Dean for Samaritan Institute, the school that trained MCC clergy for ministry. Dr West has also served as pastor at Cathedral of Hope and Midway Hills Christian Church (Disciples of Christ), both in Dallas, Texas. In 2000 she published a book with Pilgrim Press titled, *Take Back the Word: A Queer Reading of the Bible*.

Preface

This commentary has been written and published during a time when the topic of human sexuality and religious life is at the forefront of debates concerning human rights, church polity, ordination, marriage, parenting and adoption. At the foundation of these debates are the Jewish and Christian scriptures as again and again a handful of selected texts are made to speak across the centuries in order to provide an authoritative and compelling word from God that will securely ground the discussion in something reliable and unshakeable. But the mooring that the scriptures are thought to provide is not as unshakeable and secure as some might hope. Quite the contrary. This *Queer Bible Commentary* demonstrates, perhaps above all, that these texts will not be bound but, rather, have the ever-surprising capacity to be disruptive, unsettling and unexpectedly but delightfully *queer*. Moreover, this commentary provides ample demonstration that this queerness can be found, not just in a handful of selected texts, but across the board in every text of the First and Second Testaments.

A range of hermeneutical approaches is employed within the commentary as contributors draw on feminist, queer, deconstructionist, postcolonial and utopian theories, the social sciences, and historical-critical discourses as each sees fit. Contributors take seriously both how reading from lesbian, gay, bisexual and/or transgender perspectives affect the reading and interpretation of biblical texts and how biblical texts have and do affect lesbian, gay, bisexual and/or transgender communities. Politically and religiously engaged, disruptive of both sex-gender-sexuality norms and academic conventions, playful and at times purposefully irreverent, here academic and lay readers will find a commentary quite unlike all other commentaries. Rather than a verse-by-verse analysis, typical of more traditional commentaries, contributors to this volume focus specifically upon those portions of the scriptural text that have particular relevance for readers interested in lesbian, gay, bisexual and transgender issues such as the construction of gender and sexuality, the reification of heterosexuality, the complicated question of lesbian and gay ancestry within the Bible, the transgendered voices of the prophets, the use of the Bible in contemporary political, socio-economic and religious spheres and the impact of its contemporary interpretation upon lesbian, gay, bisexual and transgender communities. Accordingly, the commentary raises new questions and redirects more traditional questions in fresh and innovative ways, offering new angles of approach for ancient texts.

Acknowledgements

The editors would like to thank the staff at SCM Press for their support for this ambitious project. We thank Barbara Laing in particular for being such an enthusiastic supporter of the commentary, for her patience and understanding when deadlines needed to be renegotiated and for prompt, efficient correspondence at all times. It has been a pleasure to work with such a commissioning editor. We also thank staff who helped see the manuscript through to publication, in particular Mary Matthews and David Sanders for whose careful work we are indebted. Our gratitude also to Pilgrim Press for permission to include a chapter on the Song of Songs that was previously published under the title 'A Love as Fierce as Death: Reclaiming the Song of Songs for Queer Lovers' in Robert E. Goss and Mona West (eds) *Take Back the Word: A Queer Reading of the Bible*, 2000. We thank all our contributors for being willing to participate in this project and providing such refreshing, ground-breaking new encounters with old texts.

Deryn Guest would like to thank the University of Birmingham for providing one term's sabbatical leave. This valued gift of time provided a much-needed breathing space that enabled me to produce one of the chapters in the commentary. I send thanks to the students of my Que(e)rying Theology module, 2005–06, whose happy (and noisy!) participation in class was always refreshing, and whose celebratory good cheer at the time of my civil partnership was much appreciated. I also wish to thank the women of the Women and Religion seminar group that was initiated during the writing of this commentary. Simply being there as an inspiring and supportive network of friends meant much, especially the words of personal encouragement that were received. Finally I send much love and gratitude to Fiona who provided endless steaming mugs of tea and who continues to provide a seemingly effortless loving bedrock of support that enables me to think and write. I hope the cat was some compensation for these efforts.

Mona West would like to thank the leadership of Metropolitan Community Churches and her clergy colleagues for encouraging and supporting me over the years as a queer biblical scholar and writer. Special thanks go to Jim Mitulski, Bob Goss and Nancy Wilson. I also want to express my humble love and undying gratitude for my spouse of ten years, Deb Elder, who has been my biggest fan and supporter, taking care of our home and pets when I have travelled to present papers and workshops at conferences or spent hours at the computer writing. Without her steadfast love and presence I could not have written a word.

Robert Goss would like to thank publicly the MCC Church in the Valley for participating in my healing process after a soul-deadening tenure battle. The Church is a wonderful piece of 'heaven on earth' – an inclusive, soul-building community. It is for folk like yourself that I continue to write when academic homophobia attempted to silence me. I want to thank all those scholars who wrote on my behalf when I began to despair. I dedicate all the merit accrued from this liberating volume to you. I want to thank all those contributors who worked hard to make this volume possible. Your creative voices help take back the Jewish and Christian scriptures from fundamentalists. Finally, I want to thank my spouse Joseph for a wonderful journey in sharing your love, spiritual passion, dreams of justice and colouring outside the lines. You were there during the frustrating moments of editing and cheerfully encouraging as I wrote two chapters in the last months. My gratitude and enduring love.

Thomas Bohache would like to thank those who have encouraged him to move between the pastoral and academic worlds, especially fellow MCC hybrid Robert Goss and academic advisors Chester Gillis of Georgetown University and Kwok Pui-lan of Episcopal Divinity School. I am also grateful to the Metropolitan Community Church of Rehoboth for being the 'test audience' for many of the ideas I explore in my work that are not ordinarily enunciated from the pulpit – another part of my queerness! I dedicate my work on this commentary to my husband, Tom Laughingwolf Simmons, who is not only my partner in life and ministry but also an accomplished scholar of Native American religion and culture.

Acknowledgements for Scripture Translations

Except as otherwise stated, scripture quotations are from the New Revised Standard Version of the Bible (NRSV), copyright 1989 by the Division of Christian Education of the National Council of the Churches of Christ in the USA. Used by permission. All rights reserved.

Scripture quotations in the chapters for Joshua and The Book of the Twelve Minor Prophets, except as stated, are from the Jewish Publication Society (JPS); and in the chapters for Leviticus, Numbers and Psalms are from the New Jewish Publication Society, *Tanakh* (NJPS); translations in the Exodus chapter are by the author, based on the NJPS.

In the chapters for 1 and 2 Chronicles and The Pastoral Letters, scripture quotations are from the Revised Standard Version of the Bible (RSV), copyright 1946, 1952 and 1971 by the Division of Christian Education of the National Council of the Churches of Christ in the USA. Used by permission. All rights reserved.

Scripture quotations in 'Mark' are taken from The Jerusalem Bible (JB), published and copyright © 1966, 1967 and 1968 by Darton, Longman and Todd Ltd and Doubleday, a division of Random House, Inc. and used by permission.

Scripture quotations in 'Ezra–Nehemiah' are taken from the *Holy Bible, New International Version* (NIV). Copyright © 1973, 1978, 1984 by International Bible Society. Used by permission of Hodder & Stoughton Ltd, a member of the Hodder Headline Ltd.

Translations in the chapters for 1 and 2 Samuel, 1 and 2 Kings, Job, Lamentations, Ezekiel, Romans and Hebrews are by the authors, except as stated; and in the Introduction and Deuteronomy chapter are as stated *in situ*.

Abbreviations

AnBib	Analecta Biblica
AV	Authorized Version
b.	*Babli*, or Babylonian Talmud
BA	*Biblical Archaeologist*
Bib	*Biblica*
BJRL	*Bulletin of the John Rylands Library*
BKAT	Biblischer Kommentar: Altes Testament
BN	*Biblische Notizen*
BR	*Bible Review*
BZAW	Beihefte zur Zeitschrift für die alttestamentliche Wissenschaft
CBOT	Coniectanea Biblica Old Testament Series
CBQMS	Catholic Biblical Quarterly Monograph Series
DH	Deuteronomistic History
ESV	English Standard Version
ExpTim	*Expository Times*
GLBT(I)	gay, lesbian, bisexual, transgender/transsexual (intersex)
HAT	Handbuch zum Alten Testament
HUCA	*Hebrew Union College Annual*
IDBSup	Interpreter's Dictionary of the Bible Supplement
JAAR	*Journal of the American Academy of Religion*
JB	Jerusalem Bible
JBL	*Journal of Biblical Literature*
JFSR	*Journal of Feminist Studies in Religion*
JPS	Jewish Publication Society
JR	*Journal of Religion*
JSOT	*Journal for the Study of the Old Testament*
JSOTSS	Journal for the Study of the Old Testament Supplement Series
KAT	Kommentar zum Alten Testament
KEK	Kritisch-exegetischer Kommentar über das Neue Testament
KHCAT	Kurzer Hand-Commentar zum Alten Testament
LGBT(Q)	lesbian, gay, bisexual, transgender/transsexual (queer)
LXX	Septuagint
m.	*Mishnah*
MCC	Metropolitan Community Church
NIBC	New International Biblical Commentary
NICNT	New International Commentary on the New Testament
NIV	New International Version
NJPS	New Jewish Publication Society version (*Tanakh*)

NRSV	New Revised Standard Version
OBO	Orbis Biblicus et Orientalis
OTL	Old Testament Library
PE	Pastoral Epistles
PWA	person with Aids
RB	*Revue Biblique*
RSV	Revised Standard Version
SBLDS	Society of Biblical Literature Dissertation Series
SBLMS	Society of Biblical Literature Monograph Series
SBT	Studies in Biblical Theology
SJOT	*Scandinavian Journal of the Old Testament*
SNTSMS	Society for New Testament Studies Monograph Series
TynBull	*Tyndale Bulletin*
VT	*Vetus Testamentum*
VTSup	Vetus Testamentum Supplement
ZAW	*Zeitschrift für die alttestamentliche Wissenschaft*

Introduction

Disarming Biblically Based Gay-Bashing

RONALD E. LONG

> The leader, the great man or woman, does not say, 'The end justifies the means.' The great person says, 'There is no end, and even though it may cost me (as it cost Saint Joan her life; as it may cost X, Y, or Z the election; as it may cost the actor the audition), I'm not going to give them want they want, if what they want is a lie.' (David Mamet, *Three Uses of the Knife*)

Biblical tradition reflects the heritage of the prophetic revolution. It is with the prophets of Israel that the practice of faith comes to be associated with the pursuit of justice. 'what doth the Lord require of thee,' asks the prophet Micah, 'but to do justly, and to love mercy, and to walk humbly with your God?' (6.8b). And more pointedly the prophet Amos, 'let justice roll down like water, and righteousness like a mighty stream' (5.24). One would thereafter expect that those who consider themselves among the faithful would be on the forefront of movements for social justice, especially since every Passover the Jew would remember what it would be like to be a slave in the household in Egypt, and the Christian would remember that his or her Lord was executed as an expendable historical no-account. Perhaps there was a time when the churches could be counted on to be in the lead in the advancement of justice. The early Church, indeed, helped to bring about the eradication of the Roman practice of the exposure of infants and to lead the way in the establishment of found-ling hospitals. In modern times, the Church has in contrast more often than not defended the status quo over against change. While voices of individuals like Wilberforce may have been in the forefront in challenging the practice of slavery and Henry Primatt and the Earl of Shaftesbury in defence of animal life over against human cruelty, the bulk of the faithful have as often as not defended the practices they have grown too comfortable with to challenge.

It might come as a surprise that the repository of the 'faith once delivered to the saints' might from time to time change its mind on moral matters, but it has done so throughout history. Although some of us might doubt the moral wisdom involved, 'usury' – the biblical name for the charging of interest, a practice not only forbidden in scripture but seen as thoroughly un-Christian until the Reformation – became with the rise of capitalistic society so reli-giously innocuous that the long history of its proscription frequently passes unnoticed (Jones 2004). Slavery, on the other hand, was long seen as having scriptural warrant. It is only with modernity that slavery became universally recognized as both unscriptural and immoral.

Of course, to the extent Christian bodies take the Bible as the 'Word of God' – although in classical Christian theology, Jesus is the Word, and the Bible the 'Word' in but a secondary and derivative sense – each time the Church has changed its mind regarding specific moral prejudices (here I am using the term literally in the sense of 'pre-judgement') has required a revision and re-evaluation of its scriptural heritage. It has had to ask, 'Does the Bible really say what we have always taken it to say?' 'What are the grounds for it saying what it does?' and finally, 'What authority does textual accuracy or biblical moral reasoning have for the Church in the matter at hand?'

In our own day, movements for the moral equivalence of homosexual and heterosexual love – that which I take to be the issue in GLBT rights and liberation – have caused faultlines to appear not only in society at large, but among, as well as within, denominations as well. The 'traditionalist' – even those who do not really care much about what the Bible might say one way or another on other matters – protests, 'The Bible says it is a sin.' Only close critical attention to the biblical witness, its grounds and its authority can disabuse the traditionalist of his or her biblically based homophobic presumption. Contemporary rhetoric notwithstanding, the theme of homosexual sex is really not very prevalent. While some episodes or passages, like the story concerning the exposure of Noah's nakedness to his son Ham (Gen. 9.18–29) and others, would need to be employed in framing a complete biblical picture of sex, the traditionalist who would hold that homosexuality is invariably sinful normally has recourse to three passages: a twice-repeated Levitical proscription (Lev. 18.22; 20.13); the story of Sodom and Gomorrah (Gen. 19), and the first chapter of Paul's Letter to the Romans. And it is these texts which are chiefly in need of revision and evaluation in the light of the moral status of homosexual love in our day.

The Hebrew Scriptures

Contrary to what contemporary rhetoric might lead one to believe, the subject of homosexual relations occurs very infrequently in scripture, in both the First and Second Testaments. The only explicit prohibition is contained in the Book of Leviticus. In the literal translations of Saul Olyan, Leviticus 18.22 runs:

> And with a male you shall not lie the lying down of a woman; it is *to'eba*.

And Leviticus 20.13:

> And as for the man who lies with a man the lying down of a woman, they – the two of them – have a committed a *to'eba*; they shall certainly be put to death; their blood is upon them. (1994 (1997): 398)

What is clear is that the author of these injunctions – indeed, they presumably derive from a single individual or a single school of thought – is concerned not with what today we call 'homosexuality', but rather with a certain kind of sexual act possible between men. Most commentators agree that what is forbidden here is anal intercourse, the penetration of one man by another. The act is forbidden, no matter whether the act is committed by a heterosexual who turns to a man for want of a woman, or by a 'homosexual'. Two things are to be noted at the outset. First, the text is unconcerned with the issue of lesbian love and sex. Any viable interpretation will have to admit of an explanation for the exclusion. Second, as is frequently said, these passages are 'act-centred', indifferent to the issue of what we today refer to as the homosexual 'condition'. Although widely noted, it is not always clear what the import of this very common observation means. Today, we live in a world where the quality of our relationships, in particular our sexually intimate relations, is very much the focus of our spiritual work and that from which we derive much of our spiritual satisfaction. To be homosexual is to find that one can find sexual and emotional intimacy primarily, generally exclusively, with members of one's own sex. To deny the homosexual a sexual outlet is to deny him or her access to that from which, as a religious culture, we are bidden to find much of our spiritual significance. The Bible as a whole is not really interested in emotional satisfaction. It fixes its religious sights elsewhere. Clearly, then, we should not deny the homosexual access to that on which he or she is otherwise taught to focus unless the biblical rationale for resistance to homosexuality continues to be persuasive. The morally sensitive exegete needs to focus on what lies behind and motivates texts like that of Leviticus 18.22 and 20.13.

Leviticus presupposes a kind of religiosity we might call 'temple religion'. The dramatic setting is Israel in its wandering after the Exodus, prior to its coming into the 'Promised Land'. But the text really reflects the interests of a settled society. The tent is really a stand-in for the temple, the encampment is an analogue for the territory of Israel, and the environs represent Gentile territory. If we can think of these as a superimposed set of concentric circles, then, according to the Hebrew scriptural scholar Jacob Milgrom, Israel – which is in close proximity to the dwelling of God – is called to reflect that proximity in being holier, which is to say 'purer', than the Gentile world (1991: 731 and *passim*). Israel is called to reflect a concern for purity that is not incumbent upon those living in outlying territory. 'Purity' is here being used in a very ancient sense. The modern reader tends to hear 'purity' as a matter of sexual propriety, and certainly not a matter of diet. Milgrom points out, however, that Israel's restrictive diet is a consequence of Israel's attempt to mirror the divine purity, arguing that the restrictive diet involves a 'reverence for life' that answers to the more decisive 'reverence for life' which is the nature of the divine (1991: 735). 'Purity' is thus equivalent to 'reverence for life' – something which is actualized most fully in the divine, relatively so in Israel, and much less decisively among the Gentiles. By extension, then, homosexual anal sex – because it is inherently non-procreative – fails to answer to the call to embody reverence for life (Milgrom 2000: 1567). Milgrom's theory is the college-educated version of the widely held prejudice that homosexual sex is wrong because it fails to be procreative. However, if that were the focus of the biblical author(s), one has to wonder why the text focuses on homosexual anal sex, and not on anal sex in general. Second, one has to wonder why other forms of non-procreative sex, whether homosexual or heterosexual, are not found equally horrific. And, third, it is hard to see how every instance of sex needs be potentially procreative in order to embody an ethic of reverence for life. In other cultures, as diverse as Rome and China, males at least were free to use their genitals as they wished, as long as they also did their reproductive family duty. Such a policy could only be seen to be 'irreverent' if sperm were somehow seen as a scarce natural resource, a view that is not otherwise evidenced in the biblical texts.

From a scholar's perspective, Milgrom's focus on the calling of Israel to be holy – like the God who dwells in the temple is holy – fails, it seems to me, to do adequate justice to the idea of to'eba (the 'abominable', as it is frequently translated). The Book of Leviticus generally sounds the theme that 'abominations' (or, more generally, 'impurities') threaten the nation. An abomination has the capacity so to nauseate the land that it 'vomits' the people forth. There is evidence that, when the Assyrians overran the northern kingdom, they deported at least some of the upper classes of the defeated population (Noth 1960: 261–2). Deportation to Babylon is a well-attested practice of the Babylonians, the successors to the Assyrians who would later defeat the Southern Kingdom of Judah. (Presumably deportation of the provincial leadership minimized the possibility of revolt.) The Book of Leviticus was written after these deportations, and reflects the fear of a new 'exile' for a re-established Hebrew nation. Indeed, much of it can be seen to be the charter for a post-exilic Israel by which it could avoid the possibility of another exile, another case of being 'vomited forth' from the land. But to put the matter exclusively this way is to fail to realize the way in which the God of Israel is implicated in any possible future exile. The temple is literally the 'House of God', a place where God dwells. As such, the temple is a kind of central power-generating plant, for the temple is the place from which God's power radiates, invigorating the land and ensuring the well-being and political integrity of the people. The sickening of the land represents a compromise of the divine power, perhaps even a withdrawal of the divine energy. The presence of impurity, and particularly of that more serious kind of impurity labelled to'eba, threatens to sicken the land by effectively short-circuiting the power of God, perhaps even causing God to withdraw his divine presence.

The note that impurity is somehow nauseating is helpful, for in anthropological consideration, the 'impure' is that within any given culture that strikes the people as somehow sickening, that which makes them respond with an 'Ugh!' Consider the reaction of the contemporary diner who has just been told that what they had eaten was not really chicken, but cat – or the reaction of the movie-going audience to the monkey-brains served as dessert in the film Indiana Jones and the Temple of Doom. L. William Countryman (1988: ch. 2), following Mary Douglas (1966), has offered an account of the logic by which male–male anal intercourse could be construed as a 'sickening' reality. Indeed, in this line of thinking, an 'abomination' results from categorical confusions (as when animals in the 'pet' category are mistakenly taken for 'food') or is itself somehow a monstrous deformity. That which is 'pure' is 'true to type'. Here, something is set up as paradigmatic or (stereo-)typical. Monstrosities are things which either fail in a significant way to be true to type or otherwise combine elements belonging essentially to other types. If a fish like the sea-bass or the salmon is the paradigmatic sea creature, then lobsters and other crustaceans are monstrous formations to the extent they do not resemble the paradigmatic instance. If the cow is the paradigmatic land animal, then a creature like the lowly pig is 'impure' because in essential ways it fails to conform to the ideal of the ruminant. Such impure creatures are thus forbidden to the Israelite table, just as the blemished cow is inappropriate for the sacrificial table. If the cow is ideally of one hue, then the purity of God requires the purest of the pure, the unblemished sacrifice. Accordingly, if male–male anal intercourse is to be found impure, it must presuppose some norm for what is real sex. In this case, it involves a penis in a vagina. Any other kind of sex fails to conform to the standard: anal sex involves the use of the anus in a way appropriate to the vagina, and homosexual anal sex involves an inappropriate gender blending of roles. The result? Male–male intercourse is a monstrous deformation of the real thing. The underlying threat is that of cosmic disorder: monstrous formations threaten to undo the divine order and the world falls apart. But, once again, why is male–male homosexual anal intercourse singled out? Why not prohibit all anal sex, whether heterosexual or homosexual? Why not prohibit all non-vaginal sex?

Saul Olyan (1994) has attempted a mediating position, combining insights typical of Milgrom's and Countryman's approaches respectively. For him, the power of God is not threatened so much by disorder as it is by the explosive mixing of the things of life with the things of death. Anal sex involves an explosive mixture, the deposition of the fluid of life (seminal fluid) in the place of excrement. His theory would be particularly cogent if Leviticus had been written by priests who had come to know the Zoroastrian tradition in which the devilish Angra Mainyu (the enemy of the good god Ahura Mazdha) creates his powerful horde of demons through self-sodomy (Sproul 1979: 142). Yet once again, the issue becomes, why single out only homosexual anal sex?

I suspect there is something deeper at stake here that comes to light when one considers also the story of Lot's hospitality and the men of Sodom. But already, it must be clear that the Levitical horror of homosexual sex loses its force outside the context of what I have called temple religion.

Genesis 19 recounts the behaviour of the menfolk of Sodom after Lot persuades two angelic visitors to the city to stay with him in his house for the night. Following in the narrative of Genesis immediately upon Abraham's appeal to God not to behave unjustly in his dealings with the people of that city, the episode purportedly justifies God's eventual destruction of Sodom and its twin city Gomorrah. But wherein lies the 'sin' of Sodom? During the night in which the visitors stay with Lot, the men of the town surround Lot's house demanding that he produce the men staying with him that they might 'know' them. It is almost universally acknowledged that the word 'know' is being used here in the sense of 'have sex with', so that the men of Sodom are actually seeking to rape and gang bang the visitors. The issue is not whether homosexual sex might be involved, but what 'meaning' the sexual acts have in context. Whatever is going on, Lot finds the prospect of the gang bang of the visitors so horrifying a prospect that he offers them his virginal daughters instead. But it is not so clear that it is the homosexual nature of the sex that constitutes the sin here. Is Lot saying, 'homosexual sex is so wrong, if you must have sex, at least have it with a woman instead even if it is with my daughters'? Or is he horrified that the visitors might be raped? Careful attention to his words leads in yet another direction. He protests, 'do nothing to these men, for they have come under the shelter of my roof' (v. 8). The issue which is forefront in Lot's mind is the violation of his hospitality that the 'abuse' of these men would represent. Indeed, it is not until the Hellenistic period that the sin of Sodom begins to be identified as homosexual sex. This leaves us with the conclusion, in Gray Temple's pointed words, that in Genesis, 'the Sodomites were first and foremost inhospitable; they thought it good sport to humiliate foreign guests' (2004: 58).

That humiliation of the stranger through sex is the theme of Genesis 19 becomes even more compelling when the episode is read together with the structurally parallel story in Judges 19.22ff. In this second story, a travelling Levite is taken under the roof of a local. When the men of the town demand the traveller, the master of the house offers instead his own daughter and/or the traveller's own concubine. Perhaps the prospect of homosexual sex is what is foremost in his mind in making this offer. But the townsmen are apparently indifferent to whether they have sex with the travelling Levite or his concubine. They are not interested in homosexual sex per se. And the Levite himself seems to have found that abuse of his concubine was tantamount to an assault, if not on his person, then on *his* honour, for when they return home – in a move that cannot be other than horrifying for the modern mind – the Levite murders his concubine, cutting her body into numerous parts which he then distributes to the various tribes, presumably as a call to arms. For the modern sensibility, the concubine is the victim here. For the Levite, however, as for those who live in many traditional societies today, the assault on the woman is taken as an assault on his own person. For him, he has been humiliated in the person of his concubine.

The story in Judges highlights in an excruciatingly horrific way the fact that people in traditional cultures experience(d) their identities quite differently than does the modern Anglo-American. For us, we are primarily individuals who join groups – or are thought to have effectively joined a group as in the idea of the 'social contract'. Thus, group membership is secondary to our primary identity. Traditional people tend to see themselves first and foremost as cells of an 'extended' social body, a body politic as it were. Sometimes it is the family or tribe or nation which comprises the relevant body (Countryman 1988: ch. 8; cf. Emerson 1996: 534–7, 551–4). In this story, the concubine is part of the extended body whose head is the Levite. What is done to her is really done to the whole of 'his' body.

Second, the very fact that sex can so easily become an instrument of degradation of the penetrated in both these stories gives indirect evidence for an ancient construction of sex. Sex was first and foremost about power. Sexual penetration was not so much about love or pleasure, but about the assertion of superiority. The penetrator who 'tops' a bottom of either sex is asserting his superiority over the penetrated social underling. And with this, we are very close to understanding why male–male intercourse was so troubling for the Hebraic tradition. If we went no further, we might conclude with Gray Temple that, in ancient Israel, '[s]ame-sex coupling with a peer or a superior robbed the victim of his prerogatives as a "man," rendering him unfit for further life, and it marked the perpetrator as a murderer, hence a danger to the social order' (2004: 60). The interpretation, I believe, is inadequate since it really fails to show why the sexually humiliated man is unfit to live.

The idea that sexual penetration is first and foremost an act of social top-manship derives, it seems to me, from warrior culture (Long 2004). Where war is a matter of penetrating enemy bodies and enemy lines, it is but a short step to viewing the erect phallus as a weapon. Thus, penetration by either weapon or phallus renders the penetrated a pathetic, if not dead, passive. And indeed, the rape of an enemy's womenfolk or, more dramatically, of the enemy himself, an act which effectively unmans him, turning him into a subservient being, has long been the capstone which seals a victory in war (Tombs 2002). To go outside the ancient Near East for a moment, it is not insignificant that, according to Richard Trexler, 'the Nahuatl word for a powerful warrior (*tecuilónti*) means "I make someone into a passive"' (1995: 71). It is the ideology perpetuated in the vulgarisms of our day. 'Fuck', 'screw' and the British slang 'shag' are all, in the main, transitive verbs, implying that the sexual act is one in which someone *does something* to another. In the light of the identification of phallus and weapon, one can make full sense of the Hebraic horror of male–male anal intercourse. To penetrate a man of one's own cohort, or to be complicitous in one's own penetration, by a kind of magical congruence, threatens the body politic. If a cell (an individual) of the warrior band goes into battle having been penetrated, the warrior band is going into battle already wounded. The penetrated male is a defective soldier whose existence threatens the impenetrability of the wider social body, endangering it by making it vulnerable to penetration by enemy instruments of war.

The religious obligation to avoid impurity as defined above makes no real sense outside the ancient context of temple religion in the light of which impurity is understood to pose a real threat to the world order. At the same time, biblical sexual prohibitions which presuppose the ancient understanding of a relation between sex and war are effectively undermined to the extent such an association seems increasingly less compelling, indeed anachronistic. Indeed, we live in a time in which war is much more a matter of blowing people up or firing at people from extended distances than it is a matter of close combat in which soldiers stab one another. Increasingly, the act of penile penetration seems less and less like an act of martial attack. Second, in a world in which women – whose biology mandates their penetrability in procreative sex – become soldiers, the ancient fear that the sexual penetrability of a soldier makes an army or a people vulnerable to attack seems increasingly unpersuasive. Not only is the ancient equation between sex and war passing away. It seems to me that humanity only stands to gain when we finally sever the equation between the two. There may be a time for each under heaven. But we sell ourselves short when we pretend one is equivalent to the other, even as we deny ourselves in the bed when we don't really allow ourselves to love lest we let down our defences. When the authority of a biblical proscription rests upon presuppositions that we no longer find desirable, then it becomes desirable to abandon those proscriptions – unless we can find other compelling reasons to sustain them.

The Christian Scriptures

The early Christian movement seems to have been already well on its way to leaving the religious obligation of Levitical purity behind. The Jesus of the Gospels, of course, asserts that the Sabbath was made for man, not man for the Sabbath (Mark 2.27) – and is regularly shown as taking less than seriously other concrete dictates of the Law. He apparently felt quite free not only to heal on the Sabbath, but to break bread with such 'impure', dirty people as prostitutes and tax collectors. Nor does he choose disciples from groups who would have been known for their observance. However, Jesus had been a Jew and, as Gentiles were invited into the Christian movement, the answer to the question whether Gentiles needed to become Jews first in order to be followers of Jesus the Jew did not seem to be a foregone conclusion. Indeed, Acts 11 records the momentous decision not to require circumcision of Gentile male converts, a move which effectively started the ball moving toward freeing the Christian from the religious obligation of Levitical purity. But again, the consequences of that decision would take some time to sink in, for the issue would raise its ugly head shortly thereafter in the issue of table fellowship with those who did not abide by Jewish dietary regulations. A common table had already become a staple in Christian worship, and Torah-observant Christians felt that, as part of their practice, they should refuse to break bread with those who did not abide by such in their eating habits. Paul, who had sided with Peter on the circumcision issue (Gal. 2.11–14), took a similar stance with regard to Jewish dietary regulations. In 1 Corinthians 8–10, he divides Christians into two camps: the 'weak' and the 'strong', who – for present purposes – we can gloss as the 'weak-' and 'strong-stomached'. The 'weak-stomached' were the Torah-observant Christians who were nauseated by the idea of breaking bread with the 'strong-stomached' who might even eat food offered to idols! Paul decides that the strong are indeed in the right, but recommends a policy of 'Don't ask, don't tell.' In order to keep peace in the household of the Lord, the strong are minimally not to announce their dietary habits in the presence of the weak – and maybe even refrain from the offensive practices entirely, for the sake of the weak – while the weak are not to enquire about the same of the strong. Effectively – and this is the important point – Paul would seem to be relegating observation of purity regulations at least as far as diet is concerned, to a matter of personal preference, removing it from the sphere of the religiously obligatory. The Law is not binding on the Christian as Christian! Only those rules which could find a rationale other than being an offence against purity could rightly be required.

It is this controversy that is the background for Paul's Letter to the Romans, for Paul is addressing a congregation in which there are both Torah-observant and non-Torah-observant Christians. The vocabulary, logic and rhetoric of the letter is notoriously difficult to interpret – and especially Romans 1.18–32, the passage social conservatives love to point to in their attempt to affirm that the New Testament is firm in its proscription of homosexual sex.

Let me first pass over a full survey of the exegetical difficulties to present what I think Paul is actually saying. He begins with a diagnosis of Gentile culture and opines that, at some point in their history, Gentiles abandoned the native recognition of the power and authority of God for idols. For this reason, God 'gives them up' to both impurity and further sin. Indeed, the phrase 'gives them up' functions as a kind of organizing principle. Now it could imply that what God gives the Gentiles up to is punishment rather than sin, and as Gareth Moore points out, being in prison might be shameful, but it is clearly distinguishable from the criminal offence for which prison is the punishment (2003: 89). More likely, however, I think that Paul is saying that, because of their idolatry, God has already resigned them to a disgusting and damnable existence. But is same-sex behaviour something that will merit damnation? In verse 24 Paul characterizes the 'dishonouring of their bodies' – clearly a reference to Gentile homosexual practices – as shameful punishment for Gentile culture's primordial idolatry, indeed an 'impurity' (*akatharsían*), but impurity in his thinking is not necessarily in itself sinful. He interrupts his thought to invoke blessing upon the name of God, then returns to his line of thinking, repeating the verbal phrase 'gave them up', but this time God gives them up to shameful passion (*pathe atimias*). Let me paraphrase. 'Because of their primordial God-forgetfulness and idolatry, God gave the Gentiles up to impurity . . . indeed, the disgusting dishonouring of their bodies that we (!) recognize all about us. Blessed be God! Indeed, he gave them up to such filth . . . by letting them be overtaken by shameful passion.' Note, Paul uses the singular *pathe*, passion. Now the modern reader might be tempted to think that a passion is shameful because of what is desired. But this would be to overlook the popular Stoicism that Paul is here drawing on. To be under the sway of passion – any passion whatsoever – is to be misled. In his or her passion, a person is being led to think that that which they desire is indeed important, whereas in Stoic doctrine, everything but virtue is only – to use the preferred phrasing of Nancy Sherman – an 'indifferent' (2005). What is desirable is a cool head, devoid of misleading passion. To be led around by passion – something that happens to us, something we undergo, rather than choose – is particularly shameful for a man. The male is called to be in control at all times. To the extent that modern gender stereotyping casts the male as more rational than the female, it echoes ancient assumptions. But in modernity, the male is thought more rational – except when sex is in the air. It is the male who is sexually impulsive and, in the back seat of a car, it is the female who is expected to have the presence of mind to be able to say 'no' to the insistent male. The ancients were more consistent. The male was to be in control, cool, calm, and collected – even when sexually aroused. Thus Paul is, in effect, accusing Gentile males of being oversexed, indeed embarrassingly and uncontrollably so. Perhaps, he is saying they are pathetic excuses for men, insufficiently zealous for their masculine dignity.

And what does being so oversexed lead them to do? First, they give up the 'natural use' of women for sex. The translation of *chresis* as 'use' is quite literal and accurate. In the ancient ideology at work here, reminiscent of that at work in Leviticus, the penetrator 'uses' his sexual subordinate. Pleasure is reserved for the sexual top. And Paul is echoing the ambient Jewish presumption that women (more particularly, vaginas) are the appropriate instruments of male pleasure. By contrast, the Gentile male is so typically oversexed that he seeks out other vehicles for his phallic satisfaction. Now Paul does claim the 'use' of women for sexual satisfaction is 'natural'. But what does the word really mean? I submit that Paul is setting up penis-in-vagina as paradigmatic sex, in contrast with which the use of hand, mouth and particularly anus is revealed to be deformed or monstrous sex. But this is the logic behind impurity. Thus, calling something 'unnatural' is the college-educated form of calling something dirty, nauseatingly monstrous. (To be sure, Plato seems to be the first to call homosexual sex unnatural (Ward 1997: 264–9), and he is followed by the Stoics. Whether calling a kind of sex unnatural involves anything other than name-calling is an idea I will return to later in this chapter.) Here, however, it seems to me that by his use of 'unnatural' Paul is simply employing a circumlocution for 'impure'. For Paul, the Gentile male is so oversexed that he finds himself drawn to 'dirty' (can we read 'kinky'?) sex. That is to say, he develops the hots for his own kind, and proceeds to try to 'do the dirty' with them, with the consequence that males come to 'suffer the penalty' in their persons. Now some would argue that Paul is alluding to health consequences following from homosexual sex. I think Paul is thinking of something less elusive. When men seek each other out for sex, some men end up being mounted and penetrated. Because of the oversexed nature of the Gentile male, some Gentile males bear the consequences; they are unmanned, shamefully bottoming – or perhaps being forced to bottom – for their sexual tops.

Romans 1.26 is unique in the biblical literature in possibly speaking of lesbian sex. Literally, Paul writes 'Their (Gentile) women exchange natural use' – yes, he employs the word *chresis* – 'for that which is against nature.' The phrasing invites a variety of different interpretations. (1) Perhaps Paul is saying, in their disgraceful passion, rather than to be 'used' by men, Gentile women seek to 'use' others – perhaps men, perhaps other women – for their own pleasure. (2) Perhaps Paul is claiming that they seek to be 'used' by men unnaturally, that is, seeking to please men in ways other than vaginal intercourse. (3) Wayne Dynes makes a plausible case that in mentioning the practices of Gentile women before speaking of the men, Paul is echoing the order of thought which he would have known from the *Testaments of the Twelve Patriarchs*, itself elaborating on *1 Enoch*'s treatment of female intercourse with the 'Watchers' referring back in turn to the story in Genesis 6.1–4. In Dynes's view, Romans 1.26–7 is to be read as dealing with '[m]an-crazy women, who are even willing to sleep with extraterrestrial beings' as is known from Genesis 6 and 'parallel man-crazy men, who wish to sleep with other members of their own sex' as were the men of Sodom (Dynes 1998). I, for one, do not know what Paul had on his mind. Perhaps we can retain Paul's ambiguity to gloss Romans 1.26 as saying that 'sex-crazed Gentile women seek out kinky sex with strange partners'.

In verse 28, Paul resumes the use of the verbal phrase 'gave them over' – but this time – to what the NRSV translates as 'a debased mind'. From the debased mind flow all sorts of things that are unambiguously sinful, but the sexual practices typical of Gentile culture are not mentioned in the list of such vices. Thus, Paul seems to reserve the word 'impurity' for Gentile sexual practices and 'sin' for a host of other things. It is tempting to think that Paul is here working with the distinction between taste and religious obligation that seems to underlie his discussion of diet and, by analogy, he construes the avoidance of 'sexual' impurity to be a matter of personal (or perhaps even corporate) taste and not religiously obligatory. But assumptions frequently prove errant, and Dale Martin (1995) has convincingly shown that even the Paul of 1 Corinthians had not abandoned working with a sense of morally significant bodily pollution.

Paul's Letter to the Romans is rhetorically complex – even dizzyingly so. After sketching the decline of Gentile civilization in chapter 1, in verse 2.1, Paul directly addresses one who has presumably been nodding his or her head in heartfelt agreement with what Paul has been saying so far only to turn the tables, chiding him or her about judging others when they themselves are implicated in the same faults. There has been much controversy over the years as to just whom Paul might be addressing here. Stanley Stowers (1993 (1997): 103–4) has made what seems to me a very strong case for seeing Paul addressing not a 'Jew' or a Torah-observant Christian in the Roman congregation, but a Gentile who finds himself in concert with what had become a customary Jewish complaint about the lack of self-mastery (as evidenced in same-sex practices) *and* anti-social behaviour evident in Gentile culture. Indeed, I can imagine any number of slaves who might long for an order that freed them from a culture in which a master could expect to be sexually serviced by his servants – same-sexed or otherwise – as was the case in Rome (cf. Jewett 2000: 240)! Free males or young men destined to be adult Roman citizens were forbidden as sexual partners to the Roman. However, the Roman was quite free to use his male servants for sex. Paul would, I assume, be addressing slaves who were not comfortable about serving their masters in such capacities along with any number of otherwise disaffected Gentiles who shared the general Jewish distaste for Gentile culture along the lines Paul has been developing. But having drawn from such Gentiles nodding agreement, Paul turns the tables. 'Who are you', Paul says in 2.1, 'to condemn your fellow Gentiles for their lack of self-mastery and sinful behaviour when you are caught up in the same perverse idolatrous lifestyle/mode of thinking and/or being led around by your passions like them?' However, Paul is eager to argue that such a Gentile need not become a Jew, that is, a student of Torah, in order to achieve the escape that he or she seeks. That is available to him or her in and as the spirit of Christ. The logic of Paul's argument throughout chapters 2 and 3, however, is notoriously complex, indeed convoluted. What he does say can be reconciled, I believe, only on the assumption of two things, (1) that everyone will be judged according to the Law, but (2) that the Law requires different things of Jew and Gentile (cf. Stowers 1994: 139). But we are still left with the question, does the Law thus forbid homosexual sex to the Gentile? Throughout chapter 1, Paul has been trading upon the sympathies of a Gentile reader who is critical of the sexual practices characteristic of his or her culture. I doubt that Paul has simply been playing to the audience; indeed, I think it highly unlikely that he is not in solidarity with his reader in this regard. While not including homosexual relations among the anti-social vices he lists as proceeding from a 'debased mind', Paul nevertheless speaks of homosexual relations among Gentile men as conduct unbecoming, expressive of nothing less than a shameful lack of (manly) self-possession. Now, in my single year as the lone Protestant student in Catholic military high school, Brother Lawrence, my 10th grade religion teacher, affirmed that 'cursing', while not sinful, was nevertheless unbecoming in a Catholic gentleman. 'Cussing' is indecorous, but not something for which one will be damned. However much I might like to be able to conclude otherwise, it seems to me that Paul, in contrast, is using the words 'dishonourable' and 'shameful' in a yet stronger way. In the light of his discussion in Romans 2, he is thinking of such things as being included among the faults for which God will judge the Gentile in the end, things distinguishable from the social vices but likewise things to be avoided, forbidden them by the Law.

Contemporary anti-gay interpreters, eager to counter any suggestion that Paul condoned removing homosexual 'practice' from the class of sins, have sought to reinforce their case by drawing on the lists of vices that Paul includes in 1 Corinthians 6.9 and 1 Timothy 1.10. Not only is vocabulary problematic in this regard, but the move, I believe, proves counterproductive, ultimately working to undermine Paul's authority on homosexual sex. Among the vicious persons that Paul names are in Greek *arsenokoitai* and *malakoi*. Robert Gagnon sees the word *arsenokoitai* as a Pauline neologism, attempting to capture in a single word the Levitical heritage, translating it as 'bedders of males, those [men] who take [other] males to bed', 'men who sleep or lie with males' (Gagnon 2001: 312). However, following the lead of Gray Temple (2004: 77), we can well ask how likely it is that Paul would take such care to find a word that exactly translates a Levitical notion when in Romans his indictment of Gentile sexual practices does not seem to depend upon the letter of the Law? James Miller argues that the term would have been heard as referring to at least one partner (probably the 'active' partner) in a pederastic relation so typical of the times (1997: 863). For his part, Dale Martin observes that, in 1 Corinthians, the term appears on the cusp of vices relating to sex and those relating to economic exploitation, suggesting that the term might perhaps refer to those who use their position or their money to exploit others, principally sexually (1996: 123). Thus, the word could cover the gamut from clients or 'johns' of prostitutes to masters who 'use' their slaves for their sexual pleasure. But, perhaps, we should join Martin himself in his all too uncommon gesture of humility in admitting ignorance, owning up to the fact that the exact meaning of the word is as of yet beyond our abilities to decipher with any certainty. The term *malakos* seems to be less problematic. Literally, the word means 'a soft male', that is, an effeminate male. But effeminacy could be predicated of a Roman male on any number of grounds. Perhaps he was effeminate in demeanour, in which case effeminacy could characterize both homosexually and heterosexually inclined men. Perhaps he was effeminate in the sense of his willingness to be bedded by other men. Or perhaps – and, in Roman perspective, this was apparently the decisive issue – he was effeminate in his inability to control himself. In Roman understanding, as we have already noted, a failure of self-control was a significant compromise of a man's masculinity. By such standards, a womanizer would have been the very model of the 'effeminate male', while the self-controlled 'practising homosexual' could be a paragon of masculinity. Gagnon may be close to the mark when he suggests that the word should be taken as lying 'somewhere in between "only prostituting passive homosexuals" and "effeminate heterosexual and homosexual males"' (2001:

308). Significant is his failure to entertain that the usage of the word might thus roughly correspond to that of the contemporary English word 'sissy', signifying an effeminacy of which penetrability may function as but a symbol. At this point, however, the modern interpreter cannot but become wary of endorsing Paul *tout court*, for who among us would want to make effeminacy in demeanour a sin – any more than we would want to reinforce Paul's ban on long hair for men or his insistence on covering the hair of women?

We are thus led to what I think is the best strategy for dealing with Paul in the context of contemporary debates over the morality of homosexual sex. The Christian interpreter is all too predisposed to want to find Paul both right and authoritative. However, rather than to seek a basis in Paul whereby he can be seen to allow virtuous same-sex activity, I think it is the better part of wisdom to allow that Paul might have felt same-sex sex should be avoided even by the righteous Gentile and show, on the basis of what he does say, why Paul's reasoning fails. Some years ago, Gary Comstock bade the gay and lesbian community to prove itself a 'friend' of religion. He argued that, while friends may support one another, it is the good friend who also chides his or her friend for failing to live up to all that they can be (Comstock 1993: 11, 48). Let me then follow his lead and seek whether there might not be additional grounds upon which one can mount a friendly challenge to, and finally abandon, any putative Pauline homophobia.

Let us begin with the notion of the 'natural'. First of all, it goes without saying that Paul's understanding of sex as a matter of a 'top' using a bottom for his pleasure is hopelessly dated and ethically challenged. Importantly, such a construction condemns the bottom – no matter the sex – to passivity, (ab)use, not to mention a form of sex in which his or her claims to pleasure can be ignored. In modernity, sex ideally involves a contract between equals for mutual pleasure. In contrast, the ancient view is simply ethically deficient and any view dependent upon it compromised. Likewise ethically deficient is a view that sex must conform to a pattern consistent with the use that nature makes of sex. That nature uses vaginal sex for reproduction is too obvious for words. However, not even in nature is reproduction the sole use to which nature puts sex. For example, among the bonobos, a species very close to the human, nature seems to have 'used' sex principally to bond the group socially, and only indirectly for reproduction. The same might very well be said for the human. Besides, to insist that sexual expression be restricted to vaginal intercourse is to condemn unreasonably a large portion of humankind who find that mouth and hand are likewise the instruments of love, whether homosexual or heterosexual, to an ethical hell. From a theological point of view, all too often proponents of natural law – especially those who see nature as embodying 'intelligent design' – make the mistake of identifying a law of nature with the will of God.[1] Nature cannot be the model for ethical human living. We should neither model ourselves after the piranha, nor the chimpanzees who occasionally go

---

1 The works of the Orthodox theologian David Hart (2003: 128–9, 386; 2005) are particularly helpful in this regard, as are the works of the Oxford theologian Andrew Linzey (1993 (1995): 76–92; 1998: 25–32).

berserk, killing and cannibalizing one of their own kind. Trying to pin down a relevant notion of naturalness, the evangelical John Richardson has stated that 'You can use a screwdriver to open a paint tin but that is not the natural use of a screwdriver' (quoted in Bates 2004: 45). Admittedly, opening a tin of paint is not the purpose for which the screwdriver has been designed. But that hardly makes the use of it to open a can of paint immoral. Indeed, if I used a screwdriver to pry open a space so that a friend could extricate the finger that has gotten caught between the window frame and the air conditioner he was installing, I would have to say the 'unnatural' use of the screwdriver was here ethically admirable. Quite simply, the ethical lies in how we use nature, not in our blind subservience to it. And a tradition that looks for the resurrection of the body, a body exempt from the natural conditions that lead to disease, decay and death, should simply know that!

Because Paul uses Gentile homosexual sex as evidence of Gentile lack of self-mastery and self-control, I think he is assuming that, were it not for their excessive sex drive, Gentile indulgence in homosexual practice might very well cease. He presumes that homosexual sex is the result and symptom of slavery to an overpowering sex drive. Here he is on shaky ground indeed. On what basis can he rule out the possibility of same-sex sex which is *not* an indicator of failure in self-mastery, but proceeds from the love of a self-possessed person? Pointed are the words of the gay scholar Dale Martin:

> The burden of proof over the last twenty years has shifted. There are too many of us who are not sick, or inverted, or perverted, or even, 'effeminate,' but who just have a knack for falling in love with people of our own sex . . . The burden of proof is now not on us, but rather on those who insist that we would be better off going back into the closet. (1996: 130–1)

Given that lack of self-control could very well be understood as a Stoic way of speaking of the pathological, the contemporary person who would analogously hold that same-sex desire is 'sick' really has the entire contemporary therapeutic establishment allied against him or her. And perhaps even more pointedly, it would seem to me that both heterosexual love and homosexual love have the same capacity for, as well as the possibility of inhibiting, what Catholics call 'unitivity' and, as thinkers from Plato to André Guindon have observed, both have the capacity for their respective forms of 'procreativity' (Guindon 1986). As such, they deserve to be recognized to be morally equivalent and on a par[2] – even if Plato, it must be remembered, held the 'brainchildren' of homosexual romance to be more noble than what was for him mere biological issue! It follows that it is both fitting and incumbent upon a religious tradition that grew out of horror at the injustice of the murder of its founder on the cross, with the apparent consent of both secular and religious authorities, to be supportive of the needs of the minority over against even the religious establishment. Indeed, it seems to me that, in view of our

---

2 Indeed, the degree to which the Religious Right is driven to draw on spurious 'science' in a desperate attempt to show that homosexual sex is injurious to one or the other parties involved indicates the poverty of ethical argument to the contrary!

contemporary recognition of the spiritual importance of interpersonal 'unitivity', such a tradition should rather err on the side of supporting those whose sexual impulses lead them to form relationships with members of their own sex, rather than to seek to thwart them by law or exclusion from the rites of religion. Paul, in his best moments, recognizes that love for the other seeks their good, that we echo Christ when we adapt ourselves to their needs. And, as Dan O. Via asks, 'Would this not have to mean seeking abundant bodily life for the homosexual since the homosexual orientation is the destiny he/she has been given?' (Via and Gagnon 2001: 36).

Beyond that, and perhaps this is the decisive issue, Paul's understanding of sexual desire is not only dated, but more importantly, theologically deficient. Whatever sympathies we might have for the Stoic analysis of emotion which he seems to reflect – and I confess I admire the Stoic attempt to affirm human agency even in the midst of terrible suffering, something that we who labor under the shadow of HIV cannot lose sight of – nevertheless, the suggestion that sexual desire is somehow something to be got over neglects what is perhaps one of the most spiritually significant impulses that a human being might have. Indeed, in the hands of Paul, sexual desire is reduced to nothing more than an itch which demands to be scratched. Sexual desire is a demand for pleasure that, in his view, is best left unaddressed, if at all possible. 'Better to marry than to burn,' he says in the well-known injunction (1 Cor. 7.9), as if sexual desire is a kind of steam in a pressure cooker that, at least for some, needs an escape valve. Such a view totally overlooks the interpersonal significance that sexual desire actually has. At the same time, and in deference to Paul – who in this at least seems to get things right – the 'purpose' of sex is taken to be pleasure rather than procreation! Relative to Paul's construal of desire, however, I can do no better than to quote the words of the Second Testament scholar and theologian L. William Countryman:

> Flawed as all human eros, it is still the best thing in our makeup, the brightest treasure that God has placed there. And it is by this that God calls us home.
> For love has the power to triumph even over our own abuse of it. It keeps coming back. It keeps sneaking up on us. It keeps breaking us open and showing us new worlds outside the carapaces we have formed around ourselves. It shows us one another and it shows us God. (2005: 56)

And lest it be thought that he is speaking of eros in a non-sexual sense, this:

> We shortchange the sexual expression of eros if we think of it simply as the satisfaction of physical desire. It is much more than that. The desire is rooted as much in the soul and spirit as in the body. And it is supremely satisfied when it enables a genuinely transcendent union with the beloved, a union that belongs as much to soul and spirit as body. (2005: 39–40)

Finally, and perhaps strikingly, even as we must admit Paul's own seeming indifference to the actual words and example of Jesus, still in the words of the Jesus of the Gospel of John, 'A servant is not greater than his master' (15.20).

Now, it is true that the Jesus of the Gospels nowhere makes any explicit statement about homosexuality in general, nor even the specific homosexual 'practices' that might have been commonly recognized in his day. And it is almost always inadmissible to infer anything from silence. In particular, we go wrong to assume that because Jesus is nowhere shown contradicting the biblical heritage that he therefore endorsed it. Indeed, if there is any evidence, it arguably supports the claim Jesus was more accepting of contemporary homosexual practices than was the tradition out of which he came, not to mention the tradition St Paul himself seems to perpetuate despite himself. Theodore Jennings has to my mind convincingly argued that the burden of the evidence points to the idea that there was at least one man with whom Jesus was homoerotically, if not homosexually involved, the man reflected in the title of his refreshingly written book *The Man Jesus Loved* (2003). I have yet to see his argument effectively countered.

Leaving the argument about Jesus' own sexuality aside, however, the story of the centurion and his 'boy' in Matthew 8.5–13 (cf. Luke 7.1–19) may provide an even stronger case for abandoning any alleged unavoidable Pauline identification of homosexual intercourse with sin. The centurion comes to Jesus complaining that his *pais* is ill. Now, the usual translations imply that this *pais* was but one of the centurion's slaves or servants. But, in that case, we would expect the generic Greek word for slave or servant, *doulos*. Instead, we find the Greek word meaning 'boy', the force of which suggests rather a slave who is a sexual favourite (Horner 1978: 122; Jennings 2003: 132–4; Mader 1980), an idea for which 'toy boy' might not be a wholly inappropriate contemporary rendering. It was quite accepted within Roman society for even married masters to use their young male slaves as sex partners. It was the 'use' of male citizens or youthful males who were destined to be part of the adult citizenry that was forbidden to the Roman, not males in general. While some such master–slave sexual relations might have been the kind in which masters simply 'used' a slave for sexual release, we do know from the example of Hadrian and Antinous that romantic emotional involvement did characterize some such relationships, in the light of which a translation of *pais* by 'boyfriend' seems justified, perhaps even preferable. (Indeed, although the Lucan parallel employs the word *doulos* of the ailing young man, rather than *pais*, there it is coupled with the adjective *entimos* ('dear' or 'valued'), a word that can connote emotional cherishing.) Additionally, just as today, we speak of a night out with the boys, the word 'boy' does not necessarily imply anything about the age of the 'boy' (cf. Boswell 1980: 81). What is really noteworthy about the whole incident is that Jesus doesn't bat an eyelash, but is quite content to heal from a distance the centurion's *entimos pais*, something he might hardly have been expected to do if he had any reservations about the moral legitimacy of the relationship. The textual base is admittedly thin, but it may in fact be sufficient to show that, in contradistinction to those who would argue from the silence of Jesus that he concurred with tradition, the preponderance of the evidence we do have supports instead Jesus' break with his tradition on the subject of homosexual sex.

Beyond that, the text has it that Jesus was 'amazed' and confesses, 'Truly, I tell you, in no one in Israel have I found such faith' (v. 10, NRSV). How about that? Strikingly, if there is any merit to the interpretation, it is one who is arguably involved in a homosexual romance and liaison of some sort who embodies an exemplary faith, a faith in comparison with which that of the pious Torah sensitive Jew comes up short! What is this faith that Jesus in Matthew seems to admire so? I think Jennings hits the nail on the head:

> the centurion . . . wanted, he yearned, for healing and wholeness for his beloved. And he would do anything, risk everything, to get it . . . He knows that religious Jews revile the whole idea of pederasty, having no understanding of, or sympathy for, the kind of love he knows; yet he goes out into the street to find a Jewish healer and, risking rejection and ridicule, asks for help for the boyfriend he loves. (2003: 142–3)

Further,

> the important aspect of the story is the concern that draws one to take risks, to become vulnerable in hope, to reach out in yearning for well-being, to refuse to give disease . . . the last word, to suppose that divine power is not on the side of calamity but on the side of wholeness: Jesus calls this outlook faith. (2003: 143)

Faith lies not in accommodating the self to regnant standards of respectability, whether their source be religion or society, but the daringness to act out of love and an irrepressible hope. In his better moments, even Paul knows this and, if pressed, would probably own up to that being what he really means when he speaks of Gentiles' conformance with the Law in their hearts. Of course, he is not here to press. However, the modern moral progressive, whose programme must inevitably involve distinguishing what is essential and salvageable in the faith from that which is purely historically determined and accidental, must press on. And just imagine! In the New Testament, it is arguably to a 'fag' that we are all – whatever our sexuality – bidden to look to recognize what faith is all about.

I want to conclude with a *caveat*. While the homosexual person who is convinced of his or her own moral integrity before God might – and indeed should – argue with those who would use the Bible and the tradition to discredit him or her in the interest of truth, they should take care not to get caught up in self-apology. To be 'gay' is to recognize that range of persons with whom one can be significantly intimate *and* to refuse complicity in a social practice that would treat one's love as somehow less significant than that of a heterosexual. It is that very recognition that can ground a sense of vocation which can sustain the moral fibre it takes to bear the tiresomeness of so much so-called 'dialogue'. Sexuality is so much a part of who we are that those of us who 'come out' feel we have to own up to it in the public arena. For that very reason, it may be the role of GLBT persons, indeed their God-given task, to point the way for society – and for the Church – into a fuller recognition of the significance of sex and sexual desire in human life. That is an onerous task indeed, but not at all one that is insignificant for the future good of all humankind. And I rest confident that, one day, future religiosity, should it not have rendered itself obsolete by moral obtuseness, will find itself no more upset by homosexual sex than it currently is by interest on loans ('usury'), and no less encumbered by anti-homosexual religious propaganda than by religiously based arguments for slavery. Was it not the Jesus of the Gospel of John who promised his followers that a Spirit would come who would lead them into all truth (16.13), even if – we might add – it was a Spirit that took them far beyond what Jesus, a man limited like all men, could have imagined or perhaps even appreciated?

The First Testament

Genesis/Bereshit

MICHAEL CARDEN

Introduction

Overview

As the name implies, Genesis is a book of beginnings. It relates the origins of Israel and the world. It does so through a connected series of stories about the great ancestors, starting with the first humans at creation and ending with the family of Jacob/Israel. As a book of origins, Genesis is concerned with explaining why things are the way they are now, both in a broad and in a more specific sense. In its creation stories, it provides an understanding of the relationship of the divine, creation and humanity. In the stories of the family that would become the people of Israel, Genesis locates Israel's part in that relationship.

As the book of beginnings, Genesis serves as the introduction to the Pentateuch, the five books of Moses, and clearly anticipates what will unfold in the Pentateuch (Gen. 15.12–16). While Genesis opens with a strong affirmation of the goodness of the created order, there is an underlying tragic vision within the book. Once upon a time, humans were in unmediated communion with the divine, but through human action, the divine and human realms are separated. This pattern is repeated in the family stories of Israel's origins. Abraham, Sarah and Hagar live in a world that intersects very tangibly with the divine realms. At the end of Genesis, not only is the divine world separated from humanity in general but it is only glimpsed in dreams by Israel's ancestors. In another way, too, this tragic but aetiological quality manifests at the conclusion of Genesis. The greater part of the family saga of Israel's ancestors relates how they come to and mark their presence in the Land of Promise. However, Genesis ends with them outside the Land. Not only does this foreshadow the end of the Pentateuch where Israel remains outside the Land, but also the end of the Hebrew scriptures as a whole, which close with Israel no longer sovereign in the Land and scattered among the nations.

Historical and cultural locations

We do not know when, where, or by whom these stories were composed and collated to form the book of Genesis and consequently incorporated into the Pentateuch. Scholarship has long regarded the stories of Genesis 1–11 – Creation, Eden, Flood, Babel – as mythological, classifying them as the primordial history. Nowadays, too, the family sagas of Israel's ancestors in Genesis 12–50 are similarly considered to be myth. These ancestral stories are set in the late third millennium BCE; however, no archaeological or historical evidence has been found for the events and characters in these stories. Furthermore, despite the very ancient setting of these stories, most scholarly opinion would see both their composition and collation into Genesis as taking place in the late first millennium BCE during the periods of the ancient Persian or Hellenistic Empires in the Middle East, which preceded and succeeded Alexander the Great (356–323 BCE).

Seen from this perspective, the composition of Genesis and the Pentateuch can be located as part of major religious movements then occurring in the ancient eastern Mediterranean world. The first millennium BCE was marked by the rise and fall of empires and the resulting intermingling of cultures and religions. The Persian Empire was the first to bring together under one rule these diverse cultures. Established under Cyrus the Great in 559 BCE, at its peak the empire would stretch from Egypt and the Balkans in the west to Afghanistan and Central Asia in the east.[1] Questions of universalism and diversity, the One and the Many, come to the fore, together with the allied questions of justice, good and evil, suffering and death. It is this interaction of Babylonian, Palestinian, Assyrian, Egyptian, Syrian, Persian and Greek religious ideas that lies behind the composition of both Genesis and the other Hebrew scriptures. (For a very good analysis and overview of questions of Bible and history see Thompson 2000.)

We do not know in which context the author/s of Genesis understood the text to be read or performed and we do not know the identity of the community or communities to which it is addressed. Clearly part of the agenda of Genesis is to provide foundation for a community based on shared descent from the ancient ancestors. However, given the sheer diversity of Second Temple Judaism, it could be argued that Genesis and the Pentateuch have been crafted for use by multiple communities. Support for this argument can be further evinced by the fact that Genesis and the Pentateuch exist in three recensions, not one – the Masoretic text, the basis of the Hebrew scriptures, the Septuagint or Greek version, still normative in Eastern Orthodoxy, and the Samaritan. Versions of all three have been found at Qumran as well as others that became defunct in the early Christian era. So it is clear that as far back as we have evidence, Genesis has existed in plural form and we have no way of determining which, if any, of these versions has priority. Furthermore, the existence of the extra-biblical or pseudepigraphal scriptures suggests that Genesis may well have had to compete with other accounts of the past to provide foundations for communities claiming an Israelite identity.

Perhaps it is this indeterminate or open quality of Genesis that led Western biblical scholarship from the late nineteenth century to reconstruct both Genesis and the rest of the Pentateuch so it would conform more readily to Western bourgeois expectations. Known as the Documentary Hypothesis, this reconstruction was pioneered by Julius Wellhausen (1844–1918). Employing

---

1 The importance of Persia for the biblical writers is attested not only by Cyrus being credited with the release of the Judaeans from Babylonian captivity and authorizing the restoration of the Jerusalem temple but also by his being declared, in Isaiah, as the divine shepherd and the Lord's anointed or messiah (Isa. 44.28; 45.1, 13).

this approach, biblical scholars divided the contents of the Pentateuch into four primary sources, determined in part by the form of the name of the deity that was employed. These were the J or Yahwist source, the E or Elohist source, the D or Deuteronomist source and P the Priestly source. Having identified these sources, scholars then dated them according to the biblical account of the history of ancient Israel. Thus J was dated to the time of the united monarchy in the tenth century BCE, E to the ninth century BCE northern kingdom of Israel, D to the southern kingdom of Judah in the seventh century BCE, while P was dated to the exilic or post-exilic period of the fifth century BCE. The problem with this colonialist approach to the text was that it was too uncritically accepting of the biblical account of Israelite history. Archaeological research in Israel/Palestine has failed to substantiate the bulk of the biblical account and, as these four proposed sources are dependent on the veracity of that history, archaeology has also undermined this Western reconstruction of Genesis and the Pentateuch.

Nevertheless, these Western scholarly constructions suggest that Genesis was written to address an audience of diverse communities. Within the diversity of ancient Judaism, Genesis and the Pentateuch would become authoritative as the Torah of Moses. If the authors of Genesis did shape the text to address a variety of communities, then that necessity would account for the fact that Genesis and its stories have become authoritative not only for Jewish people but also for Christians, Muslims and others. However, despite this authoritative status, there was not the rigid, literalist approach to reading in the ancient Jewish milieu that is found in Christian and Islamic fundamentalist groups today. Ancient Jewish communities had an active folkloric relationship with these stories. The biblical narratives are often full of gaps, and Jewish readers and interpreters, from the very earliest times, have not been afraid to fill those gaps and expand and develop the biblical stories. By the practice of *midrash*, Jewish people have retold and expanded these stories and continue to do so. Consequently, these expansions themselves become part of authoritative scripture. The Rabbinic Sages say that everything one finds in scripture, every interpretation, was originally revealed to Moses on Sinai. The meanings of scripture are infinite – it is through reading, interpretation and *midrash* that they are uncovered.

Sexuality in Genesis

As the product of an ancient and alien culture, it should come as no surprise that the world of gender and sexuality encountered in Genesis is very alien to that particularly dominant in Western cultures today. While some Genesis narratives have become crucial in contemporary Christian debates on sexuality and gender, the erotic world of Genesis makes a sharp contrast to the conservative Christian 'family values' being promoted as essential to Christianity today. Whereas Western gender and sexuality systems are constructed around a series of binaries – female/male, homosexual/heterosexual – Genesis comes from and reflects a world in which gender and sexuality are constructed as a hierarchical continuum. This hierarchy is one based on penetration. Men are the ones who penetrate and they stand at the top of the hierarchy. Below them are women and below women are eunuchs, female virgins, hermaphrodites. At the bottom are the monstrous – penetrated men and penetrating women. This gender/sexuality system overlapped with other hierarchies. Outsider foreign males and slaves could be subject to penetration by insider males and masters without loss of status to those men who penetrated. Male rape could thus be employed against defeated prisoners of war explicitly to deny them their male status.

Nevertheless within this hierarchy male–female reproductive sexuality was privileged. Family (but not the nuclear family) was crucial to the ancient world, and reproductive sexuality was understood in agricultural terms of seed and soil. The male sows the seed and the female is the field in which the seed is transformed and from which it is then brought forth (Delaney 1991: 30–6). Associated with this understanding is the practice of endogamous or (patrilineal) close kin marriage. As Carol Delaney observes, 'women *are* land . . . fields and daughters are tended and the fruits of this labour are to be kept within the group' (1991: 102). This monogenetic ideology of procreation, and corresponding endogamous marriage systems, are a feature of Mediterranean/ Middle Eastern cultures from prehistory. However, it is important to note that Rabbinic Judaism held to a duogenetic or even trigenetic theory of procreation whereby both female and male and even the deity contributed to procreation.

If women are like fields, then, just as a man can increase his holdings in land, so, too, with women. Polygamy and concubinage are a feature of the ancient world from which Genesis came. While economic factors might mandate monogamy for many, there is no opprobrium attached to polygamy. However, while a man might accumulate many fields, a field can only have one owner. Women are bound to one man to raise up children for him. A man is not bound to one woman and is free to sow his seed within or without marriage. Nevertheless, he must recognize the proprietorial rights of other men over their women. Adultery is always a crime against the husband, not the wife.

It needs to be stressed that the world of Genesis and the worlds that shaped it did not share contemporary notions of heterosexual, bisexual, homosexual. Homoeroticism, same-sex love and desire certainly did exist but were understood very differently. For the ancient world, males were penetrators, and as long as they conformed to that role there was no shame. Shame and stigma were associated with the penetrated male, while the penetrating female could be viewed as especially monstrous. Eunuchs and hermaphrodites were accepted but subordinate to males and females. Virgin women also occupied a similar subordinate ambiguity in the hierarchy. Likewise, a particular ambiguity applied to boys, who occupied a transitional space between the world of women and that of adult men. Pederastic desire could be accepted, but tensions arose from the fact that boys were proto-men. Class and ethnicity were crucial. A slave boy and/or a foreign boy could be a legitimate object of sexual desire and penetration. In classical Athens desire for a boy of one's own class and ethnicity could be legitimate provided no penetrative sex was involved. While girls as proto-women were already legitimate objects for penetration and desire, as proto-women they were 'valuables' to be 'transacted by others' (Delaney 1991: 78). Their value lay in the integrity of their wombs, the property of their fathers and, subsequently, their husbands. However, despite the transactional value of girls and the ambiguity of boyhood, boys are or grow up to be men and seedbearers, upon which family continuity depends, and thus their status within a given community will outweigh that of girls.

These patterns of sexuality and gender still predominate in much of the Mediterranean and Middle East today but are extremely ancient. Such patterns were shared by 'pagan' and 'Israelite'/biblical communities alike, not in strict uniformity but subject to historical, socio-cultural and religious variations.

Reading Genesis

In reading Genesis, I want first of all to render it alien, strange, to defamiliarize it. Many of the stories of Genesis have been appropriated as a basis for conservative gender and sexual codes. The Genesis stories are used to give a trans-temporal and thus essentializing quality to what are often fairly recent normative social constructions. In responding to Genesis, I am presenting it according to the divisions or portions (*parashot*) of the yearly cycle of weekly synagogal readings. I do so to heighten the strangeness of Genesis for Christian readers and to remind them that Genesis is not Christian property. I will also draw on insights from across the religious traditions that value this book, together with contemporary queer and feminist perspectives. It is not my intent either to depatriarchalize or to homosexualize Genesis. Genesis comes from an ancient and alien culture and if there are aspects of that culture that shock and dismay today then so be it. Nevertheless, I will also endeavour to expose parts that are queerer than might have been thought. Obviously my focus will be on questions of sexuality and gender that arise in reading Genesis. These questions are crucial to much of the narrative in the book and I don't believe the author/s of Genesis provide any easy answers. Those answers that are provided are contradictory and open up many more questions. Part of the resources that I will be using in responding to these questions will be to draw on ancient myths of the primal androgyne, the first human who, combining male and female within itself, reflects the primal unity underlying the world. In the history of exegesis of Genesis in Rabbinic Judaism, Christianity and the Middle Judaism from which these two religions were born, there is ample precedent for applying this myth in order to understand the first humans in Genesis. The power of this myth derives from the fact that in the patriarchal gender structure based on a hierarchy of penetration, the middle or intermediate level, due to its very indeterminacy, evoked the primal androgyne. It is the vision of the primal androgynous unity that, serving as a critique of the existing gender hierarchy, will inspire resistance in the form of celibate, gender variant and homoerotic and sexual utopian movements. They provide ways of going back to Eden. Unlike past Jewish and Christian exegetes, I will be suggesting that the myth of the primal androgyne not only lies behind the creation accounts of Genesis but sheds an interesting light on the stories of the matriarchs, especially Sarah.

I aim to approach Genesis as if it is a Trickster, always challenging and undermining the certainties in which I might want to freeze the text. It is this richly ambiguous and pluri-vocal quality of the book that I most appreciate and one that facilitates undermining the certainty of contemporary oppressive readings based upon it. I would/will argue that rather than going to Genesis for unchanging truths of morality, theology, spirituality, it is much more rewarding and liberating to embrace the ambiguity and play with it, question it, challenge it and be challenged by it.

Commentary

Bereshit 1.1–6.8

This first parasha tells of the creation of the world, however, it contains not one but two creation stories. The first in chapter 1 presents a beautifully poetic account of creation out of a watery chaos over six days. These days are structured in matching pairs. The first day God/Elohim creates light and separates the light from the darkness, to form day and night. On the fourth day, Elohim creates the sun, moon and stars, giving rulership of the day to the sun and of the night to the moon. Similarly on the second day, Elohim creates the hard vault of the sky to separate the upper waters from those below, while on the fifth day Elohim creates the creatures of the sea and the birds of the air. On the third day, Elohim separates the dry land from the lower waters and causes all manner of plants and trees to grow. This act is balanced by the creation of all that lives on the land on the sixth day including, of course, humans who are created male and female in the image and likeness of Elohim. Elohim then declares everything in creation to be good and blesses it. On the seventh day, Elohim rests, thus instituting Shabbat.

While on the surface this account seems quite straightforward, in both its beginning and its ending, an apparent simplicity gives way to ambiguity and questioning. As the poetic prologue to Genesis, this chapter seems to warn the reader that all is not necessarily as it seems. The first problem derives from the opening word, *bereshit*. Christians are used to reading 'in the beginning' but that is not the only way to read the Hebrew. The word is in a form that could better be translated as 'the beginning of' so that the opening verse would read 'the beginning of God's creating' instead of 'in the beginning, God created'. Furthermore, David Sheinkin points out that in Jewish esoteric tradition the first three words of Genesis can legitimately be translated in up to twelve different ways (Sheinkin 1986: 52–3).

Ambiguity also surrounds the crowning act of creation, the creation of humanity – 'God said, "Let us make mankind in our image, according to our likeness . . . " So God created humankind in his image, in the image of God he created them; male and female he created them' (Gen. 1.26–7). Eilberg-Schwartz (1991) raises these valid questions: Does God have a body and, if so, is God male or female or both? Given that humans are commanded to be fruitful and multiply, 'Does God have genitals and, if so, of which sex?' (1991: 17). Other questions arise. Does Genesis mandate a two-gender-only system? What of people who are neither male nor female? Finally, is reproductive sexuality the only mandated sexuality in Genesis?

An answer given in Jewish tradition and found also in some Christian accounts (including Origen) is that the first human was an androgynous being that would subsequently be separated by the deity. Jewish Kabbalah understands that Genesis 1 is a textual representation of the Kabbalistic Tree of Life, the map of the ten emanations/Sefiroth of the divine that give rise to creation. The seven days of creation are understood as representing the seven lower Sefiroth of the Tree. The Tree is equally a map of the divine, a map of creation and a representation of the Primal Human. The Tree consists of a male, female and intermediate column. While each Sefirah will present as female or male, it contains both aspects, the one overshadowed by the other. While being androgynous, the Tree of Life also embraces sexuality. Sexuality is not only part of the creative process of the Tree but also the way of restoring the primal union lost in the process of differentiation that is creation. The androgynous ambiguity of the Tree combined with the idealized erotic quest for union that underpins the understanding of the relationships of the Sefiroth means that, while ostensibly 'heterosexual', the divine sexuality does not match the hierarchical subordinating sexuality of ancient (and modern) patriarchies. Consequently, I would argue that the Kabbalistic accounts do not necessarily warrant compulsory heterosexuality but instead provide a space for a more polymorphous and egalitarian sexuality. The Kabbalistic Tree suggests that the androgyne is the model for each and every human, that male and female represent a fluid continuum in each individual that must be brought into harmony. This androgyny is also found in Tantra where the goal of the spiritual quest is to unite Shakti and Siva within the person.

Furthermore, Sally Gross points out that in Rabbinic Judaism there was recognition that not everyone was born male or female. Rabbinic texts use two terms, *tumtum* and *'aylonith*, to designate people of intermediate gender. The first refers to a person 'whose physical sex is indeterminable because there are apparently no genitalia' (Gross www.bfpubs.demon.co.uk/sally.htm), while the second is a woman without a womb. Gross notes also that there are Talmudic references to other intersex conditions. Similarly in Christianity, the hermaphrodite was a recognized human category. The important issue for theologians was the need for the hermaphrodite to avoid sodomy in sexual relationships. The solution was, as Ambrose Paré stated in 1573, 'to choose which sex organs they wish to use, and they are forbidden on pain of death to use any but those they will have chosen' (Paré, cited in Almond 1999: 8). Christian traditions, therefore, know that there are more than two sexes but frame their response in terms of homosexual panic and homophobia. What has changed in recent times is that surgical intervention to assign a gender to newborn intersexed people has taken away the right of choice traditionally accorded the intersex individual. Indeed, such surgical interventions reveal the homophobia and homosexual panic that underlies the reification of the rigid gender binary of male and female in Western Christianity.

The androgyne's trace is found more clearly in the second creation account in Genesis 2–3. The second story begins as a dry land creation with God/ YHWH Elohim creating a human being (in Hebrew *adamah* or groundling) from the ground. YHWH Elohim then plants a garden in Eden and places the human being in it. The human being is told that it may eat of any tree in the garden except for the Tree of the Knowledge of Good and Evil. To eat of that Tree will bring death. YHWH Elohim then proceeds to create all the animals from the ground as potential companions for the human being. Each of them is brought to it and named by it but none of them are suitable companions. Finally YHWH Elohim puts the human to sleep and takes one of its sides to shape into a woman (the original Hebrew is better translated as side instead of rib). YHWH Elohim brings the woman to the male human who rejoices for now he has a true companion – 'This at last is bone of my bones and flesh of my flesh; this one shall be called Woman, for out of man this one was taken. Therefore a man . . . clings to his wife and they become one flesh' (Gen. 2.23–4). These words echo Aristophanes' tale in Plato's *Symposium* according to which humans were originally dyads of three sexes – male, female and hermaphrodite. Because they were becoming too threatening, the gods took action and bisected them. From that point on, humans quest to find their other half, to reconstitute that lost primal unity of male, female and hermaphrodite so that each pairing can become one flesh. Similarly, in Jewish tradition, the human couple of Genesis 2 was understood to originally have been two sides or faces of the one being, which the deity finally separated to form women and men. Perhaps the author of this second account has deliberately eliminated the male and female dyads, leaving only the hermaphrodite in an attempt to eliminate the homoerotic. If so the attempt fails because the hermaphrodite inhabits the intermediate realm of the ancient gender hierarchy. To become one flesh, a husband must give up his gender privilege and with his wife descend to the intermediate level, neither male nor female.

As if to puncture such idealistic vision, the story then relates how death entered the world. The serpent tempts the woman to taste the fruit of the Tree of the Knowledge of Good and Evil. She at first resists but finally eats and the man follows her example. They then become aware of their nakedness and are shamed. They hide from YHWH Elohim, who realizes what they have done. YHWH Elohim curses the serpent and condemns the humans to a life of struggle and pain. It is at this stage that the man, Adam, names the woman, Eve/Hawah, for she will be the mother of all the living. They are expelled from Eden so that they may no longer eat of the Tree of Life to remain immortal. Eden is placed under the watchful guard of the cherubim and thus death becomes part of human life.

This story is really a type of coming of age or puberty story and is as much about the origins of sex as it is of death. As Niditch points out, this story represents a shift into the world of birth and death, 'in which man and woman relate to each other sexually and according to social roles, a world in which they work hard and know the difference between good and evil' (Niditch 1992: 17). In the fate that YHWH Elohim lays on the woman and the man one can see the emergence of the hierarchy by which the man will rule over the female and the dominion the man will attempt to impose upon the earth:

> To the woman [YHWH Elohim] said, 'I will greatly increase your pangs in childbearing, in pain you shall bring forth children, yet your desire shall be for your husband and he shall rule over you.' And to the man he said, '. . . cursed is the ground because of you; in toil you shall eat of it all the days of your life; thorns and thistles it shall bring forth for you; and you shall eat the plants of the field. By the sweat of your face you shall eat bread until you return to the ground.' (Gen. 3.16–19)

The woman will suffer and struggle to give birth and, like her, the earth, the primal mother from which she was born, so effortlessly, will now give forth fruits only through human struggle and toil. Now both earth and woman are in struggle with the man who seeks to impose his dominion over them. It is as if to instantiate this reality that, immediately, the man names the woman, Eve. As Phyllis Trible astutely observes, this verse echoes the naming of the animals by the earth creature in Genesis 2, an act by which the earth creature has asserted both its dissimilarity from and dominion over them. By naming her, 'the man reduces the woman to the status of an animal' (Trible 1978: 133). The name reduces her to a functional utility in relation to the man. No longer now is sexuality driven towards restoring the primal union, but instead it becomes an act of domination and ownership. The man sows his seed in womb and field and seeks to assert his ownership of both and of the harvests he reaps from them.

Is this a Fall? This has been the dominant reading tradition in Christianity, with dire consequences for women, for the earth and for sexuality. Rabbinic Judaism rejects Christian notions of a Fall, and especially the Augustinian doctrine of Original Sin. Nevertheless, Jewish tradition has recognized that in eating the fruit humanity changed. Formerly an external reality, now evil becomes part of human nature and consequently humans are subjected to death. This reality does not mean that humans are damned or totally separated from the divine. They are still charged to find the good and to make the earth heavenly, but the new circumstances mean that humans must find the good within as well as without.

Some Gnostic and other traditions have focused on the story as a coming of age myth. The woman is seen as the Sophia who brings knowledge to humanity. It's certainly possible to read the story in a way that highlights YHWH Elohim setting up the first humans to eat the fruit of the Tree of Knowledge in the first place. Indeed, it is not the serpent but YHWH Elohim who lies. Eating from the Tree of Knowledge of Good and Evil in itself does not bring death. Death comes as a result of the human pair being driven out of Eden and thus denied access to the immortality-bestowing fruit of the Tree of Life. The woman in this story is also the much stronger and more responsible character. She is the one who speaks, and she acts on her own initiative whereas the man is passive and refuses to take responsibility for his action. Instead he blames the woman and even attempts to blame YHWH Elohim for creating her. Many centuries of male exegesis have followed the man in blaming the woman and taking licence to engage in astonishing misogynistic vilification. In so doing they have followed in the man's footsteps, continuing the process of subordination initiated when the man named the woman in Genesis 3.20.

Genesis 3 tells of the transition from a mythical, primal, paradisiacal world of Eden to the conflicted, hierarchical and day-to-day world of ordinary human life. With its sexual imagery of serpent, tree and nakedness, it could well serve as a tale told at puberty, perhaps even for menarche. Being a tale to signify the onset of menstruation and the entrance into the life of pregnancy, childbirth and husbands could signify the central status of the woman in the account. Then again, her confident speaking and acting can signify the mythic realm of Eden in which the rules and conventions of the hierarchical, patriarchal human realm do not apply. But the story does not blame her and, similarly, the story does not blame sexuality. The preceding chapter culminates not only with the creation of the woman as crown of creation but also with the high, mythic, androgynous vision of sexuality as restoring the primal union of one flesh among humans. The story in Genesis 3 recounts the shift from this egalitarian vision of sexuality to the utilitarian and hierarchical economics of procreative sexuality in the patriarchal social order. In that this order is not spoken as a curse by YHWH Elohim upon the humans (it is the earth and the serpent who are cursed), it could be argued that Genesis seeks to endorse the world as it is, or at least that women and men should understand and accept their place in it. However, by explaining human life by means of the shift from a mythic realm of Eden to the world of the everyday, the mythic androgynous realm remains as a dangerous memory critiquing, challenging the patriarchal procreative hierarchy of seed, field and womb.

That sexuality is not seen in Genesis as a primal source of evil can be argued from the strange story that concludes this parasha, the account of the sons of God taking wives from the daughters of men (Gen. 6.1–4). The Nephilim, the heroes of old and warriors of renown, are the offspring of these unions. This story is a trace of a much more detailed myth found in the pseudepigraphal literature, 1 Enoch and Jubilees especially. By this account, angelic beings, the Watchers, sin by surrendering to their desire for the beautiful daughters of men. They take the women as wives with disastrous results. From their unions come the Nephilim who were the Giants and who in death became evil spirits. Furthermore, the unions between the Watchers and human women lead to a corruption of humanity further compounded by the Watchers teaching humans the arts of magic and warfare. This corruption of humanity and the created order is what leads to the Flood. References to this myth in the Testaments of the Twelve Patriarchs compound sexual pessimism with misogyny by portraying the women as seducing the Watchers into sin. However, the brief Genesis version removes all these details and does not pronounce any condemnation on the sons of God, the daughters of men or the Nephilim. When the text moves abruptly to announce that the wickedness of humans was so great that it caused the LORD to grieve and regret creating them, there is no reference to this preceding story, nor in the detailed account of Noah and the Flood that follows.

Noah (6.9–11.32)

With the Flood story the reader is confronted with the spectacle of genocide. The biblical text declares that the earth was corrupt and that all flesh had corrupted its ways, filling the earth with violence. Medieval Christians understood this corruption to be sexual and used the Flood story to abject the erotic. In Judaism, however, violence was understood to mean robbery, representing a complete breakdown of human solidarity. Zornberg points out that the great medieval rabbi Rashi understood that this collapse of solidarity was reflected erotically in a rapacious sexuality that respected no rights of the other. This sexuality of 'colonial expansionism' radically denying the 'existence of other worlds of self and culture' is illustrated by Rashi with the image of the ruler exercising the *ius primae noctis*, having sex with the bride on her wedding night before she sees her husband (Zornberg 1996: 52–3). So while Judaism can also use the Flood story as a cautionary tale concerning sexuality, this reading is more nuanced than Christian ones. Perhaps by invoking the *ius primae noctis* Rashi is subtly critiquing the broader Gentile Christian society. However, the most horrific image Rashi uses to illustrate the breakdown of human solidarity in the Flood generation is that of parents using their own children as bungs – 'pressing them down mercilessly' – to try and stop up the fountains of the deep to block the rising floodwaters (Zornberg 1996: 57). Something of that attitude is reflected in the way homophobia can cause parents to reject their queer children, pushing them away, pressing them down to prevent the rise of an alternative vision to the patriarchal order of compulsory heterosexuality.

In Judaism, too, there is a nuanced view of Noah's character. Genesis says of Noah that he was 'a righteous man, blameless in his generation' (Gen. 6.9), but given that his is the Flood generation, this statement is faint praise. Zornberg points to the fact of Noah's silence which is itself representative of the breakdown of human solidarity leading to the unravelling of creation in the Flood. This 'unqualified apathy' reveals a Noah who 'does not care what happens to others' and 'suffers from the incapacity to speak meaningfully to God or to his fellow human beings' (Zornberg 1996: 58). In the Zohar, Noah is compared unfavourably to Moses who interceded with God to spare the Israelites – 'after God had said to him "and I will establish my covenant with thee" he should have entreated mercy for his fellow men, and should then have offered up the sacrifice which he brought later, in order to appease God's anger against the world' (Zohar I. 68a). In Noah's unquestioning obedience to divine commandments and lack of concern for others, lies the destruction of a world.

Paradoxically, it is the time spent in the ark that will break down Noah's apathy. Zornberg calls the ark a 'laboratory of kindness' in which Noah and his family would learn a concern for others (Zornberg 1996: 63). They must attend to all the needs of all the animals on board. One other point must be made about those on board the ark. The story of the ark came up on a queer religion email list to which I subscribe. Someone posted to the list the complaint that God only saves heterosexual animals in the ark because Noah takes on board only two of every kind, male and female. Does the Flood story warrant heterosexuality as a norm? My response is that while Genesis maintains the physical continuity of life before and after the catastrophe, in the Flood account it is not mandating heterosexuality. The concept was most likely meaningless at the time the story was written. Furthermore, in Genesis 7.1–7 it becomes clear that, like the humans who care for them, the animals are not all represented by a single reproductive pair for each species. The clean animals and the birds are represented by seven pairs, male and female, of each species. Fourteen individuals allow for many more sexual combinations than do two. It might be objected that these extra animals are to allow for the needs of sacrifice. However, the story does not say that Noah killed all the excess in sacrifice. Furthermore, sacrifice is itself a social activity in which case the story is not privileging, let alone advocating, a simple biological reproductionism as the norm.

Nevertheless, the Flood story closes with a strange incident with possible sexual meanings. Genesis 9.18–28 recounts how Noah, as the inventor of wine, lies drunk in his tent so that his nakedness is seen by the youngest son, Ham. Ham tells his brothers, Shem and Japheth, who straightaway respectfully cover their father. Noah awakes and then curses Canaan, Ham's son, for what has happened, while blessing Shem and Japheth. These are the only words that Noah speaks in the whole story. Various explanations have been given of what it was that Ham did to incur the curse on Canaan. Ham has been said to have mocked his father, to have raped him or to have castrated him. Another account bases itself on the incest bans in Leviticus – 'the man who uncovers his father's wife has uncovered his father's nakedness' (Lev. 20.11) – to suggest that Ham saw his mother naked and mocked her or attempted incest with her. Also important to note is the fact that it is Canaan, Ham's son, not Ham who is cursed. The cursing of Canaan prepares the reader for the dispossession and destruction of the Canaanites at the hands of the Israelites following the Exodus. If Ham's fault is a breach of incest taboos then the curse of Canaan represents the first use of stigmatized sexuality to abject the Other.

Lekh Lekha (12.1–17.27)

The first eleven chapters of Genesis constitute the primordial history of the world's origins. From now on the story focuses on the origins and history of Israel. Israel's origins have been located through Abraham in direct lineage from Shem, and before him, through Noah, to the primal human pair in Genesis 2–3. Nevertheless, Israel's origins represent a new beginning in that Sarah and Abraham parallel the primal humans. Sarah, especially, represents a new Eve. However, from the beginning of this parasha, it is also clear that there is something very strange about the relationship of Abram and Sarai, as they are named when we first meet them. When Abram sets out from Haran, the text says that he is accompanied by Lot, his nephew, before telling us that Sarai also journeys with him. Once they arrive in the land of Canaan they then journey to Egypt. In Egypt, Abram passes Sarai off as his sister not his wife.

There is something not very straight about this suite of relationships. Abram is Lot's uncle but Sedgwick points out that the uncle/nephew relationship can represent 'the pederastic/pedagogical model of male filiation' (1993: 60). The uncle represents 'the whole range of older men who might form a relation to a younger man (as patron, friend, literal uncle, godfather, adoptive father, sugar daddy) offering a degree of initiation into gay cultures and identities' (Sedgwick 1993: 59). Ironically, in much of both the Jewish and Christian exegetical traditions, the pedagogical nature of Abram's relationship with Lot is highlighted. Abram and Lot can serve as a reminder that family and kinship relationships are never purely heterosexual but always 'awash with homosexual energies and potentials' (Sedgwick 1993: 71). In Genesis 13, Abram and Lot separate, with Lot moving to Sodom. Jewish tradition has always been very critical of Lot from this point. By leaving Abram here Lot was understood to be rejecting both his uncle and his uncle's god. Nevertheless, Abram still feels enough for his nephew to rescue him when he is taken captive by the forces of Chedorlaomer in the latter's defeat of Sodom. Despite such a clear demonstration of loyalty, Lot will not subsequently return to Abram's tent but will continue to live apart from his uncle, as before, in Sodom. It is only after this final separation that Abram will declare in chapter 15 his longing for a son and heir. However, even here he acknowledges another significant same-sex relationship, this time with Eliezer, a slave born in his house (Gen. 15.3). Despite being a slave, Eliezer is declared to be Abram's heir, a reminder that the pederastic/pedagogical relationship not only crosses lines of age but also lines of class.

The fact that Abram has no direct biological heir is attributed by the text to the fact that Sarai is barren. It is to this relationship between Sarai and Abram that I will now turn because it, too, does not conform to heterosexual expectations. In Genesis 12, in Egypt Abram declares Sarai to be his sister and, in the following parasha, in Genesis 20 he does so once more when they sojourn in Gerar. On both occasions she is taken by the ruler, Pharaoh in Egypt and Abimelech in Gerar, and on both occasions the deity intervenes with great plagues (in Egypt, thus prefiguring the Exodus) and threatening dream-visions (to Abimelech in Gerar) to prevent either ruler having sex with her. On the second occasion, when Abimelech challenges Abra/ha/m as to why he passes off his wife as his sister, he responds that they are indeed brother and sister. While they have different mothers, they have the same father, Terah. Incidentally this form of brother–sister marriage is not condemned under the Mosaic Law. It is also worthwhile considering that brother–sister marriage is the closest heterosexual instantiation of the androgyne ideal, for, in their parentage, they are literally one flesh. While Abraham and Sarah have different mothers, under the monogenetic understanding of procreation those mothers are the fields that nourished them, the fruit of their father's seed. Like the primal humans of Genesis 1–2, Abraham and Sarah are the primal ancestors of Israel and therefore instantiate the androgyne ideal, albeit refracted through a patriarchal monogenetic filter. This androgyne ideal is further reinforced by a strange passage in the Babylonian Talmud:

> Abraham and Sarah were [each of them a] (*tumtum*), as it is said: 'Look to the rock from which you were hewn, and to the quarry from which you were digged'; (Isaiah 51.1) and it is written: 'Look to Abraham your father and to Sarah who bore you'; (Isaiah 51.2). Rabbi Nahman said in the name of Rabbah bar Abuha: Sarah our mother was an (*'aylonith,*) as it is said: 'Now Sarai was barren; she had no child'; (Genesis 11.30) – she did not even have a womb. (*Yevamot* 64a, cited in Gross, www.bfpubs.demon.co.uk/sally.htm)

This Talmudic gloss serves to reinforce the androgyne ideal over monogenetic patriarchy. Not only do Sarah and Abraham represent the androgyne ideal but they each also instantiate it in their own flesh, neither of them being fully male or female.

Nevertheless, as the story of Abraham and Sarah unfolds, it is possible to read in it a struggle between the androgynous vision and the patriarchal impulse. Having separated from his nephew, Lot, and unwilling to allow his relationship with Eliezer to break down class, and possibly ethnic, barriers, Abram is determined to have a son. However, as the text says, Sarai is barren and furthermore, as was demonstrated in Egypt, the deity is in control of male sexual access to her. It is Sarai, however, who takes the initiative, telling Abram to go in to her slave girl and beget a child by her. The child will be counted as Sarai's. The text then relates that he took Hagar, Sarai's Egyptian slave girl, as a wife and that she conceived. Consequently Hagar looks with scorn upon Sarai, who in turn treats her so harshly that Hagar flees into the wilderness. Commentators such as Renita Weems (1988) and Phyllis Trible have rightly pointed out that Sarai and Hagar illustrate the way that women are divided not only by patriarchal agendas but also by ethnic and class divisions. Sarai is barren and so is of lesser value under patriarchy than Hagar, who conceives. However, Sarai is Hagar's mistress and has given Hagar to Abram without consulting her and, despite Hagar's pregnancy, still retains sufficient power to abuse her. The class divide is exacerbated by the ethnic divide, made more poignant by the fact that it is Hebrew and Egyptian. Sarai's affliction of Hagar invertedly anticipates and perhaps even compensates for the subsequent Egyptian affliction of the Hebrews in Exodus.

However, there is another biblical story anticipated invertedly by that of Sarai and Hagar, that of Naomi and Ruth. In this story, an older Israelite woman and a younger Moabite woman, who are mother-in-law and daughter-in-law, bond together as a couple following the deaths of their husbands. It is Ruth who takes the initiative at first by refusing to abandon Naomi when the latter resolves to return to her people. Ruth declares that she will never be separated from her and leaves her own people behind to accompany Naomi to her home-land in Bethlehem. Once settled in Bethlehem the two women seek to have a child under the levirate law. Being still of childbearing age, it is Ruth who will bear the child to Boaz, a kin of Naomi by marriage. Naomi guides Ruth in what to do and the story ends with Ruth giving birth to a son after marrying Boaz. However, in the final scene, Boaz has disappeared, Naomi is holding the baby, and the women of Bethlehem declare that a son has been born to Naomi. They then praise Ruth as being more to Naomi than seven sons. In contrast, in Genesis Sarai arranges events with Abram, without consulting Hagar. In a further echo of Naomi, Sarai imagines Hagar to be having a child for her, how-ever, the context of the narrative makes it clear that the primary purpose is for Abram to have an heir. The child will be Abram's son not Sarai's. The result of the enterprise is to pit the two women against each other. Curiously in the mid-rash to the story in Genesis Rabbah, the parallels to Naomi and Ruth become even clearer. In this account, Hagar was the daughter of Pharaoh, who, seeing what great miracles God had done for Sarah's sake, said: 'It is better for Hagar to be a slave in Sarah's house than mistress in her own' (Genesis Rabbah 45.1). However, Hagar does not accompany Sarai as a slave but comes with all her maids as befits a princess of Egypt. Hagar's willingness to accompany Sarai is indicated by her subsequent association in Jewish traditions with proselytes wanting to become part of the Jewish people. A pun is also made of her name so that it means Reward, but is she a reward for Sarah or is she rewarded by accompanying Sarah, as was Ruth with Naomi? Finally, just as Naomi guides Ruth in securing levirate marriage with Boaz, so the midrash portrays Sarai persuading an at first reluctant Hagar to marry Abraham.

Sarai and Abram represent the primal androgynous pairing and, as if to reinforce that imagery, they are both initially presented as being in same-sex relationships that cross over age, class and ethnicity. However, as the story progresses, patriarchal and heterosexist impulses lead to the shattering of these ties. Hagar and Sarai become rivals for the status of significant wife to the patriarchal Abram. This struggle causes Hagar to flee into the wilderness where she will be met by a messenger of YHWH. As Trible notes, Hagar is the first person to experience such an epiphany (1984: 14). Nevertheless, the experience is ambivalent both for Hagar and for the reader. She is told to return to Sarai and submit to her. But she is told that she will be the foremother of a great multitude through the son in her womb, Ishmael. These are words that the deity elsewhere has spoken to the patriarch, Abram. Hagar then names the deity, El Roi, God of Seeing. Trible calls her a theologian here (1984: 18). The ambivalence concludes with Hagar returning and giving birth to a son for Abram (Gen. 16.15). Has androgyny now collapsed into patriarchy?

In Genesis 17 there is a resurgence of the androgynous. The deity appears to Abram as El Shaddai. Commonly translated as God Almighty, the Brown, Driver and Briggs *Hebrew Lexicon* lists *shaddai* under *shdh*, the root for breast. They suggest that the name could derive from self-sufficiency, or the mountain associations of El/YHWH. Also suggested is the association with rain, the deity as rain-giver (Brown, Driver and Briggs 1906: 994–5). Perhaps El Shaddai could be translated as God the Bountiful (fitting in with the rain-giver motif) or God the Nurturer. I like to think of El Shaddai as literally meaning God the Many-Breasted. Perhaps, El Shaddai represents a fusion of YHWH and his original consort, Asherah. Whatever the background, as El is itself a masculine noun, the name conveys a strongly androgynous image of the divine. El Shaddai proclaims a covenant with Abram who is renamed Abraham, father of a multitude. Abraham will be the ancestor of a multitude and the land of Canaan will be given to Abraham's offspring. Abraham's patriarchal programme is thus accepted by El Shaddai but with two catches. The first is the imposition of male genital mutilation, circumcision, upon all the males of Abraham's offspring. Circumcision is a form of symbolic castration. To be in a covenant with the androgynous El Shaddai, Abraham and his male descendants are symbolically marked as eunuchs.

The second catch relates to Sarai. El Shaddai declares that she will no longer be called Sarai, my princess, but Sarah, princess. She will have a son who will be given to Abraham by El Shaddai. Furthermore El Shaddai will bless Sarah and she will be the ancestor of nations and kings. It is clear then that, while the text presents us with Abraham's concerns for offspring, what is really at issue is Sarah's progeny not Abraham's. Abraham already has a son by Hagar – Ishmael – and after Sarah's death he will father six more by Keturah. However, only one child, Isaac, is born to Sarah. The story of Sarah and Abraham marks a new beginning, but it is Sarah alone who is fundamental for this new start.

Vayera (18.1–22.24)

While Sarah might be crucial to the new beginnings recounted in this narrative, as yet she has had no contact from the divine, unlike both Hagar and Abraham. Consequently exegetes have long recognized that the theophany opening this parasha is an annunciation scene to Sarah of Isaac's conception and birth, in contrast to the previous account in which Abraham is the recipient of this same message. Nevertheless, Jews, Christians and Muslims all agree on the importance of Abraham's hospitality, in which this annunciation is framed. By welcoming strangers, one is also welcoming the divine. For Jews, too, the appearance of the deity models another virtue. Abraham is recovering from his circumcision, the account of which concludes Genesis 17. By appearing to Abraham at this time, the deity models the virtue of visiting the sick.

Martin Luther was particularly struck by the fact that throughout this annunciation, Sarah remains out of sight in the tent. Luther understood this fact to demonstrate that Abraham kept a model patriarchal household in which the woman knew her place. I accept Luther's insight, but unlike him do not find this scenario praiseworthy. Instead, I take it as a sign that the androgynous has collapsed into the patriarchal. The deity at first appears to work within this structure by addressing Sarah via Abraham. However, the focus is clearly on Sarah alone. Abraham is told that when the deity returns Sarah shall have a son. I regard it as significant that it is Sarah who is said to have a son and not that Abraham will have a son born to him. It is Sarah and Sarah alone who counts here. Furthermore, as the episode progresses, Abraham's control over Sarah is broken down. On hearing the promise that she will have a child, Sarah laughs. The deity questions her reaction but does so in an address to Abraham. Sarah then answers the deity directly, and in answer the deity directly addresses her. What begins as an interaction between the deity and Abraham ends as an unmediated interaction between the deity and Sarah.

While the first half of Genesis 18 can rightly be viewed as an annunciation story to Sarah, it takes place within a scenario of lavish hospitality. From verse 18.16 onwards the paradigmatic nature of that hospitality will be used as a contrast to highlight the evil of Sodom and Gomorrah. The story of the wicked cities of the plain and their destruction by the deity that unfolds in Genesis 18–19 has become a foundational myth for Christian homophobia. According to this Christian myth, Sodom and Gomorrah were destroyed because the inhabitants had given themselves over completely to homoeroticism. This 'fact' is demonstrated when the Sodomites besiege Lot's house demanding that his angelic guests be given over to them. The fact that Lot offers his daughters in place of his guests shows that the Sodomites were demanding sexual access to his guests. That the daughters are apparently rejected by the Sodomites has been taken by Christians to prove that the Sodomites were exclusively homosexual. That this incident is then followed by divine intervention and then the complete destruction of the cities by fire and brimstone falling from heaven has been taken as proof that the deity utterly abhors the homoerotic. In contemporary debates about the morality of same-sex love and desire, the genocidal spectacle of Sodom's destruction is frequently cited to warrant not only the exclusion of queer people from the congregation but also the active resistance to our campaigns for social justice and recognition. Sodom is used as an example to illustrate the fate of societies in which queer people are accorded full acceptance and equal rights. Any gain we make in rolling back homophobia is given an apocalyptic cast by the Religious Right's invocation of Sodom.

However, this reading of the story is a Christian homophobic myth. While its origins probably lie in the works of the ancient Alexandrian Jewish philosopher Philo, this Christian myth began its life in the third century CE but took several centuries to become the dominant reading. It is in the eleventh-century medieval West that the reading further metastasizes with Peter Damian's invention of the word *sodomia*/sodomy (Jordan 1997). With this move, and from that point on, sodomy will denote a state and expression of same-sex desire that takes on the quality of a state of nature, or, more appropriately, a state of anti-nature. The Sodomite, the species of human given over to sodomy, becomes a creature in rebellion against both the deity and the divinely mandated natural order. This myth held sway in the Western Christian world until the twentieth century when it finally began to be challenged.

In contrast to this Christian myth, Jewish traditions concerning Sodom and Gomorrah highlighted the evils of hostility towards outsiders and unwillingness to share resources compounded with a cruelty towards the poor, as the sins for which Sodom and Gomorrah were destroyed. To maintain their privilege and wealth the Sodomites corrupt the mechanisms of justice and go so far as engaging in acts of cruelty to keep outsiders away. It is in this light that the siege of Lot's house by the Sodomites is understood in Judaism. The Sodomites demand Lot's guests so that they can assault and humiliate them. The Sodomites do not act out of unrestrained same-sex desire but instead are understood as threatening sexual violence and rape against Lot's guests. This violent act is designed to serve as a warning to all outsiders to stay away from the Cities of the Plain. The parallel story in Judges 19 demonstrates quite clearly what would have happened to Lot's guests if they had been taken by the Sodomites. In the Judges account, a travelling Levite from Ephraim and his concubine are given hospitality in the Benjamite town of Gibeah by an old Ephraimite man, resident there. They are besieged by a mob demanding to have sex with the Levite. The old man intervenes unsuccessfully offering his own daughter and the concubine. To save himself, the Levite then forces the concubine out to the mob, who pack rape her through the night, resulting in her death. The Judges account makes explicit the violence that is threatened in Sodom. Perhaps because it is a woman who dies there, the Judges account has been largely overlooked in Christian tradition. By ignoring the outrage at Gibeah not only have Christians been able to impose their homophobic reading on the account of Sodom and Gomorrah, but they have failed to address the moral issues of rape on which both stories hinge.

This failure is not only evidenced by the confusion of rape with consensual homoeroticism and same-sex love but also by the overwhelming Christian tendency to exonerate Lot for offering his daughters to the mob in place of the angels. In contrast, Jewish tradition has largely, although not unanimously, condemned Lot for making this offer. There is also a Rabbinic reading of the Sodomites' reply to Lot – 'Stand back' (Gen. 19.9) – as their apparent acceptance of his offer but with the intent to take his daughters first and then rape the angels afterwards. By this account the Sodomites here demonstrate a maliciously cruel duplicity in response to Lot's own grossly immoral offer. One can see Lot's offer as demonstrating his own adherence to the ideologies of Sodom (Jewish traditions say that he had been appointed chief justice of Sodom). The threatened rape of the angels is an attempt to feminize them, thus declaring them to be not real men. It derives from the misogynistic order of penetration by which men rule over women but under which a man's masculinity/privilege can be taken away through being subjected to penetration. Lot's offer of his daughters in place of his guests is an attempt to protect the masculinity/privilege of his guests. The women have no rights, no voice, no self-determination in this misogynist order.

The misogynist order prevailing in Sodom and Gomorrah is also shown by the story to rely on homophobic violence. The threatened rape of the angels is an attempt to inscribe outsiders as not real men and therefore queer. But in attempting to inscribe the outsider as queer the Sodomites are also attempting to inscribe the queer as outsider. By doing so they are effectively declaring that they are all straight in the Sodom state. Similarly in the Judges account, the men of Gibeah accept the concubine because she belongs to the Levite. Raping her carries the same significance as raping him. The Judges account has the added import that the attack on the Levite and the concubine represents a breach of ethnic solidarity. The men of Gibeah are treating fellow Israelites as foreigners (resulting in the civil war of Judges 20–1). Thus, rather than reading the attempted rape of the angels (or the Levite) as an instance of homosexual violence, I believe it should be more accurately read as an instance of homophobic and xenophobic violence.

The story of Sodom and Gomorrah is also an account of mass genocide, and therein lies a danger for inverting the Christian account into one of divine judgement on misogyny and homophobia. The virulence of the Christian myth of Sodom is derived very much from this fact of genocide, giving licence to gallows, concentration camp and hate crime. Perhaps the figure of Lot's wife could be taken as a sign of how to respond to genocide, even when (or especially if) perpetrated by the deity. Christians have always given her a bad press. She is portrayed as a backslider, someone who cannot give up the ways of Sodom, hence her looking back. Her turning to salt is understood by Christians as a punishment for that backsliding. In Judaism, while there are certainly similar harsh negative images of Edith/Eris, as she is called, there are also found somewhat different, more positive and sympathetic, understandings of her fate. She looks back out of compassion; she looks back for her other married daughters (one solution to the status of Lot's sons-in law of 19.14) to see if they follow behind. Medieval rabbis combined the image of Edith's compassion with the notion of her rebellion in a potentially subversive manner. Edith does not look back for her daughters alone but is moved with compassion for the hated of God who lacked the faith to save themselves. Because of her compassion her thoughts cleaved to the doomed Sodomites, which meant that the punishment cleaved to her as well. By this reading, it becomes possible to view Edith's fate as an act of martyrdom, an expression of solidarity to protest against the genocidal dimensions of the divine vengeance. As readers, we are also continually looking back on Sodom and, while in awe of the magnitude of the disaster, as we face no risk of being turned to salt, we, too, should stand beside her and condemn the deity's crime.

There remains one final act in this apocalyptic drama, this time involving Lot's daughters. When first we meet them they are silent and powerless. Facing the threat of pack rape and death, they are nothing more than bargaining chips in a conflict among males. Following the destruction of Sodom they accompany their father in his flight to the hills. Believing there are no men left upon the earth they resolve to get Lot drunk so that they can have sex with him without his knowledge or consent. So the image of rape returns when last we see Lot, but this time there is a reversal, a poetic justice perhaps. The daughters, who were offered up for rape by their father, are now in control of events. They speak and act, and when women speak and act in the Hebrew scriptures the reader must sit up and take notice. Their wishes, not Lot's, determine events. As a result, Lot, the patriarch, is rendered powerless and silent; drunk and subject to his daughters, his authority is stripped from him. As powerless women, subject to abuse, they have risen up and asserted their own power. From their actions, they become the foremothers of the Moabites and Ammonites. Thus, the story ends with Lot, drunk and unconscious, the progenitor of two of Israel's enemies, but not only of Israel's enemies. There are messianic implications in the daughters' agency that have long been recognized by both Jewish and Christian commentators. From the elder daughter comes Moab and from Moab will come Ruth the foremother of David. From the younger daughter, as foremother of the Ammonites, will come Naamah, the wife of Solomon and mother of Rehoboam. Both Ruth and Naamah are in the line of the Messiah, who for Christians is Jesus of Nazareth. Thus it could be said that by raping their father, not only do the daughters act to save the human race but they also initiate the line of the Messiah. They can act this way because the deity's intervention has destroyed the interlocking systems of power and privilege under which they were subjected. In the Zohar, it is said that the deity was an accomplice with the daughters here, even making sure there was wine in the cave for the women to get their father drunk (Zohar I.110b–111a).

Following the destruction of the Cities of the Plain, the parasha returns attention to Abraham's household. Once again Abraham passes off Sarah as his sister, this time to King Abimelech of Gerar. Unlike the earlier similar incident in Egypt, this time Genesis gives no account of Abraham consulting with Sarah beforehand. Instead we are told 'Abraham said of Sarah his wife, "She is my sister"' (Gen. 20.2). As befits the patriarchal order, women have no say in their fate. Consequently Abimelech has Sarah brought to him. The deity appears to Abimelech in a dream threatening to kill him for what he has done or, in actual fact, for what he intends to do. In the exchange between Abimelech and the deity, we discover that the deity has ensured that nothing happened to Sarah. The deity says to Abimelech, 'It was I who kept you from sinning against Me . . . I did not let you touch her' (Gen. 20.6). Therefore, whatever Abraham might do, Sarah is under the complete care and protection of the deity. It is almost as if she has been reserved or set aside by and for the deity. While both the accounts of her being endangered by strange men serve to underscore this impression, in this second account alone the deity speaks, declaring that attempts to have sex with Sarah would be 'sinning against Me' (Gen. 20.6), not Abraham. The chapter ends with Abimelech, his wife and female slaves being healed from an affliction described as the closing of every womb of Abimelech's household. Various commentators have read this closing of the wombs as signifying Abimelech being struck with impotency. Thus, once again the text is assuring readers that nothing whatsoever happened between Abimelech and Sarah.

Such assurance is crucial because the next two verses relate the conception and birth of Isaac, which had been announced to Sarah at the beginning of this parasha. In verse 21.1, the divine role is described in very concrete terms. The deity visits Sarah – in the Hebrew the word used, *paqad*, can be translated as visited or attended to/dealt with. In Rabbinic tradition, the word is read as remembered, in line with other accounts of miraculous conceptions in the Hebrew scriptures. However, the use of *paqad* here singles out Sarah from those other accounts where it is not employed. The verse then continues that the deity then 'did for Sarah as he had promised' – the word 'did', a form of *'asah* can also have the meanings of make or effect. Perhaps the latter meaning might be preferred, as Rabbinic exegesis has understood verse 2 as paralleling verse 1. Sarah conceives and bears a son and thus her conception is to be read beside her being visited by the deity, while Isaac's birth is what was done or effected for her through this visitation. What is also striking in this account is the minimal role Abraham plays here. The text goes on to say that Abraham names and circumcises Isaac, but it is actually Sarah who speaks in verses 6–7, not Abraham, punning on laughter, the basis of Isaac's name. In Rabbinic tradition the birth of Isaac is accompanied by many prodigies – barren women conceive, women everywhere spontaneously and copiously lactate, the sick are healed and the blind and deaf regain sight and hearing. But the greatest prodigies are associated with Sarah and Isaac themselves. Sarah is said to have given birth without the pain of childbirth with which Eve was cursed. In this sense Sarah represents the restoration of the primal Edenic androgyne ideal. Her motherhood is both miraculous and a new beginning effected by the deity. She, too, lactates prodigiously and many children are brought to her to be nursed. These children are blessed with righteousness. The prodigy concerning Isaac relates to the uncertainty about his paternity. Rabbinic traditions express considerable anxiety about whether or not Abraham is father of Isaac. While they entertain possible doubts about Sarah's motherhood saying that she was accused of taking in a foundling, it is Abraham's paternity that is truly in doubt. After all, Genesis leaves no doubt that the conception and birth of Isaac is a miraculous event wrought by the deity with Sarah. But does Abraham have any part to play apart from the circumcision and confirmation of Isaac's name? In contrast with the birth of Ishmael, Genesis nowhere says that Abraham and Sarah have sex together. Isaac's conception is completely attributed to the deity. As if to allay such anxieties, Jewish tradition says that Isaac's face was changed miraculously to be the exact copy of the elderly face of Abraham. However, this miracle seems more like a parody – no parent is exactly duplicated in their child. Is this sign El Shaddai's way of mocking Abraham's patriarchal and monogenetic quest?

Nevertheless, Sarah and her newborn son are subject to the patriarchal system. With the birth of Isaac, Abraham now has two wives, both of whom have sons. One option, as glimpsed in the story of Ruth and Naomi, would be for Sarah and Hagar to make common cause and remove the patriarch or at least end his claim over them. But that is not the option Sarah takes. Instead she views Ishmael as a threat to her son, and subsequent traditions have defamed Ishmael, alleging that he threatened to kill Isaac. Sarah tells Abraham to cast out Hagar and Ishmael in language that aims at debasing the pair. She does not name them but refers to Hagar as the slave girl and Ishmael as simply her son. As Trible (1984: 21) points out, referring to Hagar as a slave girl is a degrading of her earlier status in chapter 16 of both maid to Sarai and then wife to Abraham. We are told that Abraham is distressed on account of Ishmael only and not for Hagar. He finally relents when the deity promises that Ishmael will also become a nation on account of being Abraham's son. In so doing the deity completes Hagar's debasement. In the theophany of Genesis 16 she is told that *she* will be foremother of a great multitude but now it is only Abraham's posterity that counts. Similarly when she and Ishmael are cast out into the wilderness and nearly dying of thirst, the deity responds to her son's voice but not to her tears. As before with Abraham, the deity tells Hagar that Ishmael will become a great nation but does not renew the promise to her. The deity, thus, collaborates fully with Sarah in these struggles that reinforce the divisions promoted by the patriarchal order. How much Sarah implicates herself in the process can be seen in the tradition that she strikes Ishmael with the evil eye, which is why he is so weak and helpless in the wilderness. The deity intervenes to rescue Ishmael and Hagar, along with him. They are shown to a well, which, in Islamic tradition, is the well of Zamzam at Mecca. According to Islamic tradition, Abraham and Ishmael will later build the first sanctuary in Mecca.

Despite being instigated by Sarah, the expulsion of Hagar and Ishmael demonstrates the power of the father in patriarchal systems. Fathers in ancient Greece and Rome could determine whether a newborn would be accepted into the household and, therefore, live, or be cast out to a probable death. Abraham has exercised his patriarchal rights over Ishmael and over Hagar, who bore him. Having called upon such patriarchal power, Sarah herself must now face the prospect of Abraham exercising these prerogatives over her son, Isaac.[2] The binding of Isaac, the Akedah as it is known in Judaism, is the culmination of this parasha and is paralleled, without apparent happy ending, in the Judges account of Jephthah's daughter (Judg. 11.29–40). The fate of Bat Jephthah makes explicit what Isaac faces and, in light of the extolling of Abraham across the traditions of the Book on account of this incident, it might be salutary to read Abraham here in light of Jephthah. For Abraham's willingness to murder his son has become paradigmatic of faith, of what it means to be Jewish, Christian, Muslim, while Jephthah's murder of his daughter has been seen, at best, as tragic folly. In contrast the Akedah has a central role in Jewish liturgy, particularly in the Days of Awe, the ten-day period from Rosh Hashanah to Yom Kippur. It is believed that every occasion on which the account of the Akedah is read in the Jewish liturgy guarantees, by recalling it to divine remembrance, the forgiveness of Israel's sins. Furthermore, early Christians clearly drew on the story to interpret and understand the execution and resurrection of Jesus. In Islam the Akedah is commemorated each year with the feast of Eid Al Adha, which ends the annual Haj. Unlike the biblical account, Islamic tradition believes it was Ishmael not Isaac whom Abraham was commanded to offer in sacrifice, following the completion of the sanctuary at Mecca. However, the

---

2 When she prevails upon Abraham to expel Hagar and Ishmael, Sarah refers to Isaac, not as Abraham's son or as the son of the two of them, but as *her* son (Gen. 21.10).

account in the Qur'an (Sura 37.100–13) is ambiguous as to which son Abraham is commanded to sacrifice. Interestingly, Jewish tradition teaches that both Ishmael and Eliezer accompanied Abraham and Isaac on their journey to the mount of sacrifice. Ishmael's presence gives a strongly ironic quality to the biblical account in which the deity refers to Isaac as Abraham's only, beloved son. Isaac is, of course, Sarah's only beloved son.

Comparing the Genesis account of this incident with the Judges account of Bat Jephthah, what also becomes clear is that Isaac is deceived by Abraham as to what is intended. Isaac clearly has his doubts, senses that something is amiss (Gen. 22.7), but is kept in the dark about what will happen. In contrast, Bat Jephthah is told by her father what he has vowed to do and negotiates with him to postpone it for two months so that she might 'wander on the mountains, and bewail my virginity, my companions and I' (Judg. 13.37). Bat Jephthah thus consents to and actively participates in what her father will do to her. Perhaps so that Isaac will not be seen as less than an unnamed young woman, Rabbinic tradition has portrayed an Isaac who actively co-operates in all that Abraham does. Isaac is even portrayed as asking Abraham to bind him tightly so that he will not resist when Abraham strikes him with the knife, or even jerk in such a way that he might be injured and thus rendered unfit for sacrifice. This tradition of complicity is canonized in the Qur'an's account:

> He said: 'O my son! I see in vision that I offer thee in sacrifice: now see what is thy view!' (The son) said: 'O my father! Do as thou art commanded: Thou will find me, if God so wills one practising Patience and Constancy!' So when they had both submitted their wills (to God), and he laid him prostrate on his forehead (for sacrifice), We called out to him. (Sura 37.102–3)

While in both Genesis and Qur'an, the deity intervenes before the blow is struck, other voices are preserved in Rabbinic tradition, in which Abraham appears to be almost indistinguishable from Jephthah. When Abraham is told not to kill the boy, he is distressed, thinking that Isaac has been deemed unfit for sacrifice. In another account, when the knife of sacrifice miraculously dissolves under the tears of the angels, Abraham attempts to slay Isaac using his thumbnail. Whether with blade or thumbnail, there is a tradition saying that Abraham still cuts Isaac, with the boy losing a considerable amount of blood. Other traditions speak of Isaac's soul leaving his body temporarily, and another says that Isaac was actually killed and burnt on the altar but was miraculously reconstituted and restored to life.

Whether it be Isaac, Bat Jephthah or Ishmael, these stories of sacrificed children call to mind the experience of many LGBT people dealing with parental/family homophobia and heterosexualism. Eve Kosofsky Sedgwick recounts

> I've heard of many people who claim they'd as soon their children were dead as gay. What it took me a long time to believe is that what these people are saying is no more than the truth. They even speak for others too delicate to use the cruel words . . . Seemingly, this society wants its children to know nothing; wants its queer children to conform or (and this is not a

figure of speech) die; and wants not to know that it is getting what it wants. (Sedgwick 1993: 2–3).

Whether it be through donning the straitjacket of the closet, or by following spurious 'ex-gay' and reparative therapy programmes, or through suicide, parents offer up their queer children on the altars of homophobia. The heterosexualist society would like to believe that its queer children are fully complicit in this process, that they willingly lay their heads down on the altar and implore their parents to tie the bonds tighter so that the offering will not be marred. The image of Isaac reduced to ashes and then restored anew represents the ultimate fantasy of the child completely transformed, remade in a way to conform to parental and establishment agendas. But the Isaac of both Genesis and subsequent tradition is a figure haunted by his own death. He lives in his mother's tent, unable to leave the Land. His narrative life in Genesis is brief, and for the greater part of it he is passively subject to the agendas of others. At Abraham's bidding, Eliezer arranges the events that will lead to Isaac's marriage, even courting the bride to be. She, Rebecca, will be responsible for determining which son will inherit from Isaac, who by then is frail and blind. Tradition says that Isaac wore Abraham's face, and, in support of that, the only account that Genesis gives of Isaac in his own right is a pale copy of Abraham in (Egypt and) Gerar. The text does not even change the location or the name of the king. As Zornberg reminds us, the sole reality of Isaac's life is the dread fact of 'his ashes . . . piled on the altar'. (Zornberg 1996: 128)

By being offered on the altar, Isaac at last becomes Abraham's son. Reduced to ashes and reconstituted, he now lives out the life Abraham has circumscribed for him. The binding of Isaac, then, can be read as representing the way homophobia and heterosexualism lead parents to sacrifice their children and how it leads to their spiritual or physical death. Furthermore, the traditions in which Isaac (or Ishmael) is fully complicit in the Akedah demonstrate the way internalized homophobia works to make queer folk complicit in the regime of the closet. However, there are many other ways in which societies and parents can offer up their young, and which can also be illustrated by the binding of Isaac. With the rising clamour of war-talk and militarism, I feel compelled to finish this parasha citing the First World War poet Wilfred Owen, and his devastating reading of this story in the poem, 'The Parable of the Old man and the Young'. Perhaps it was Owen's own homosexuality that particularly attuned him to the dynamics of power and death binding Isaac. Before Owen, practically all the readings across the traditions, including that of Kierkegaard, read from the perspective of the father, only acknowledging the son when portraying him as fully co-operative and complicit. Owen's account briefly summarizes events up until Isaac asks Abraham, 'where the lamb, for this burnt offering?' Isaac receives no reply but, instead, he is bound 'with belts and straps' while all around him is built with 'parapets and trenches'. When an angel from heaven intervenes urging Abraham to 'slay the Ram of Pride instead', Owen concludes, 'But the old man would not so, but slew his son, and half the seed of Europe, one by one' (Owen 1999). It must also be remembered that Bat Jephthah dies to further her father's military agenda.

Hayei Sarah (23.1–25.18)

This parasha, entitled the Life of Sarah, begins paradoxically recounting her death. The narrative significance of her death, following immediately after the binding of Isaac, has long been recognized in the traditions. In various accounts, it is her horror at what Abraham has done that causes her death. Indeed, it is Abraham's intent to keep hidden from Sarah what he is planning and what he does. Sammael/Satan, in an effort to thwart Abraham's plans, exposes everything to Sarah. By one account he comes to her and tells her that Isaac has been sacrificed and burnt upon the altar. According to Zornberg, he 'paints for her the horror and pathos of an old, demented father actually killing a helplessly crying child' (1996: 124). Sarah begins to cry and wail and, giving three sobs and then three wails, she dies. In another account, Satan appears to her in the form of Isaac and tells the saga of what has happened. Sarah dies in horror, her only response 'What has your father done to you?' (Zornberg 1996: 125). A variant of this account has it that it is truly Isaac who stands before Sarah and tells her all. She dies in horror at the reality of what has transpired. Perhaps her death can be paralleled to that of Lot's wife who dies in protest against the fires that burn Sodom and in solidarity with the victims. Sarah dies, screaming, 'What has your father done to you?', for the Isaac who confronts her is the reconstituted and made-over child of patriarchal dreams. He wears Abraham's face; he is now Abraham's son, not Sarah's. This fact can account for the absence of Isaac at Sarah's funeral. In Genesis, Abraham alone is portrayed in the account of the funeral. In contrast, when later in this parasha we are told of Abraham's death, the text relates that both Isaac and Ishmael buried their father (Gen. 25.9).

Sarah's death enables two things. First, Abraham can take complete charge of Isaac and so to this end he sends Eliezer back to Mesopotamia to find a wife for Isaac, from among Abraham's kin. Second, he can take another wife (Gen. 25.1). Genesis tells us nothing of her except that she bears Abraham six sons. Rabbinic tradition has identified Keturah with Hagar. On that basis I can use my earlier comparison of Sarah and Hagar with Naomi and Ruth to here highlight the contrasting endings of the two stories. In Ruth's case, while she marries Boaz, at the end of the story he has disappeared (tradition says he died after the wedding night), leaving her and Naomi together with a son, born to Ruth but said to be Naomi's. In Hagar's case, Sarah has died and Hagar is wedded to Abraham, bearing six more sons who, nevertheless, will not be counted as Abraham's heirs. Whether or not they are equated, the status of Hagar and Keturah remains ambiguous. After naming her sons, Genesis refers to the sons of Abraham's concubines. This terminology has been understood to refer to the sons of both Hagar and Keturah and thus to indicate that only Isaac, Sarah's son, will be heir to the promises to Abraham. Ironically this short anecdote about Keturah serves to remind the reader that progeny of Abraham is not the point of this saga but progeny of Sarah. Bound, offered up and reconstituted, Isaac still remains Sarah's only son. He might wear the face of Abraham, but after the Akedah, Isaac has nothing more to do with him, apart from burying him. Abraham has arranged a marriage for Isaac but the woman, Rebecca, who returns with Eliezer, is someone both like and unlike

Sarah. Isaac takes Rebecca into his mother's tent (Gen. 24.66) and the light that went out with Sarah's death 'returned to its place' (Zornberg 1996: 139). For her part, too, Rebecca sees in Isaac 'the anguish at the core of his prayers' and his 'remoteness from the sunlit world' (Zornberg 1996: 142), phrases that so aptly describe the vulnerability and self-alienation of the closet. Isaac has been bound into this closeted space to live a life in copy of Abraham the patriarch but, ironically, to fully copy Abraham he must have a Sarah in his life. Perhaps that is why Rebecca's birth, in a genealogy traced from the fore*mother*, Milcah, both niece and sister-in-law of Abraham (Gen. 11.27–9), is related immediately after the Akedah and before the death of Sarah (Gen. 22.20–3). She enables a return of what Abraham has tried to repress.

Toldot (25.19–28.9)

That Rebecca represents a return of the repressed is signalled very strongly at the outset of this parasha. It begins with the complete elision of Sarah, declaring Isaac to be Abraham's son. As if wanting to eliminate any doubts on that score, the text declares that Abraham fathered or begot Isaac (Gen. 25.19). We are told that Isaac married Rebecca but then we are told that Rebecca was barren. Rebecca's barrenness links her to Sarah and thus, like Sarah, her barrenness represents the resurgence of the primal androgyne in opposition to heteronormative patriarchy. From when we first meet Rebecca she stands out as not conforming to patriarchal standards for women. Her birth is announced in a lineage beginning with a woman. When she first meets Eliezer, she not only responds with a strong generosity (Ostriker 1994: 92) to this stranger's request for water, but she boldly takes charge of the needs of his camels and then confidently offers the hospitality of her family's household (Gen. 24.18–25). Perhaps it is the confident authority by which she performs such hospitality that causes Zornberg to equate her to Abraham and his practice of hospitality at Mamre (Zornberg 1996: 139). But it is to her mother's house that Rebecca takes Eliezer and it is with her brother, Laban, that Eliezer discusses his mission. Rebecca's father is mentioned briefly in verse 50, but he is insignificant in this family, which seems to be based on a matriarchal structure. While her mother and brother attempt to draw out the negotiations with Eliezer, they still defer to Rebecca's wishes in the matter. It is Rebecca alone who decides to return with Eliezer. When she does, she goes in the company of her nurse, and so Rebecca, like Sarah, is in a same-sex relationship, but one that is very intimate and long-standing, also crossing over age and class.

Ostriker implies that there are misogynist traditions of Rebecca psychically emasculating Isaac, that she 'made a fool of him' and 'reached into his testicles' (Ostriker 1994: 91). What these traditions indicate is that Rebecca does not conform to patriarchal norms of the role of women and wives. She acts autonomously and with determination, planting herself in her future (Ostriker 1994: 92). However, these traditions also indicate that Isaac similarly does not conform to these patriarchal norms. Despite, or because of, the Akedah, try as he might, he cannot perform the masculinity expected of him. Indeed, there is a tradition that not only Rebecca but Isaac, too, was barren. So rather than blaming Rebecca, there is a recognition that there is something about Isaac, himself, that prevents him from fulfilling the masculinity expected of him. According to Genesis, Isaac is forty when he marries Rebecca and sixty when she gives birth to Esau and Jacob. Is Rebecca's pregnancy the result of a miraculous conception like Sarah's? I would argue that Genesis 26, concerning Rebecca, Isaac and Abimelech, does not allow such an interpretation. This curious story, in which Isaac passes off Rebecca as his sister when sojourning in Philistine Gerar, resembles the two occasions when Abraham passes off Sarah as his sister. Indeed, Genesis 26 combines features of both these earlier stories. It takes place in Gerar, ruled by a king called Abimelech, just as in the second Abraham/Sarah account. Moreover, Isaac and Rebecca move to Gerar on account of famine, the same reason Abraham and Sarah move to Egypt in the first account in Genesis 12. However, in this account, unlike Sarah, Rebecca is a mother of twins while Sarah is childless in the parallel stories. Furthermore, Rebecca is not saved by divine intervention as Sarah was. Instead, Abimelech, looking out the window, spots Isaac fondling Rebecca. This story, therefore, serves to indicate that Rebecca and Isaac developed a level of physical intimacy enabling them to become parents. It was clearly not an easy process – the twins were not born until after twenty years of marriage; and it was not the intimacy of great lovers – Isaac and Rebecca had been in Gerar 'a long time' (Gen. 26.8) before the ruse was uncovered.

When Isaac and Rebecca met there was a moment of recognition between them. When Isaac saw Rebecca he recognized in her something of his mother, Sarah, but he saw also something of himself in her; he is his mother's son, after all. Rebecca, too, recognizes in Isaac the vulnerability and self-alienation that bespeaks the queer person enmeshed in the closet, and perhaps she intuits this fact from Eliezer, thus accounting for her readiness to leave her kin and travel to a distant land. I believe Isaac and Rebecca can be read as representing two types of queer experience involving heterosexual marriage. Isaac is the closet case who marries to conform to hetero-patriarchal norms, to escape from, suppress or cure his minority sexuality. Rebecca's choice, however, demonstrates that not all queer people rely on marriage to secure the regime of the closet. For many there is the legitimate desire for parenthood and it must also be remembered that for the ancient world and the greater part of our contemporary world, children/family represented social security, care in one's old age. Marriage could also serve as the rite of passage from childhood to adulthood, especially for women. Rebecca is a strong, autonomous woman and, for her, marriage represents escape from her childhood home and an opportunity for her to exercise control over her destiny.

Part of that destiny is to shape the future of this family, of the twins she bears. While pregnant, she has a presentiment of the tragic power she holds. The twins struggle in her womb causing Rebecca to cry out in words whose meaning translators find unclear but, literally rendered, are, 'Why this I am' (Gen. 25.22). Her doubt and uncertainty compel her to consult the deity who replies telling her that her two sons will be two peoples divided, the elder of whom will serve the younger. As the story progresses it becomes clear that it is Rebecca's role to bring this oracle into effect. Zornberg suggests that not only Isaac but Rebecca and the twins are victims of the Akedah (Zornberg 1996:

158). Rebecca's initial confident, adventurous spirit and generosity, leading her readily to leave home and family in the company of a stranger, has been deeply challenged by the anguished remoteness and self-alienation of Isaac, causing her to question 'the value of her life' in light of the 'pain and conflict' she must endure (Zornberg 1996: 159). In the struggle between her sons, she cannot be neutral, and she will also be pitted against Isaac.

Two noteworthy patterns emerge in this family story. Not for the first time, there is an occurrence of a regular pattern of the Hebrew scriptures, the bias against the firstborn in favour of the younger. Already in this family saga, Ishmael, the firstborn of Abraham, has been supplanted by Sarah's son. Now Isaac, doomed by the Akedah's closet to live as a shadow copy of Abraham, the patriarch, must experience the supplanting of his firstborn son, Esau. Zornberg declares Esau to be the real victim of the Akedah and, thus, the 'presenting patient of the family' through whom 'an underlying pathology is . . . expressed' (Zornberg 1996: 160). Esau is red and hairy, an outdoors man, a hunter. Esau represents heteronormative masculinity, the patriarchal ideal, and consequently he is loved by his father, Isaac. Esau is the man Isaac can never be no matter how hard he tries. In contrast, Jacob is said to be 'a quiet man, living in tents' (Gen. 25.27). As was seen in Genesis 18, the tent is the women's space in the patriarchal order. In declaring Jacob to be a man living in tents, Genesis is questioning his masculinity – Jacob is effeminate – perhaps also his sexuality. Certainly Rebecca, his lesbian mother, loves her femmy son and it is her role to circumvent the patriarchal order so that the straight butch, born to rule, is displaced by and must therefore defer to, the swishy, delicate, pretty boy.

The other pattern I find significant here is the fact that Esau and Jacob are twins. The image of the Divine Twins is one of the mythic representations of same-sex love. Same-sex, homo-sexual love can be understood as a marriage of likeness, most clearly signified by the twins (note also the gay subcultural phenomenon of the clone). Same-sex relationships can be understood in terms of sisterhood or brotherhood, and this sororal/fraternal dimension also extends to the tribal bondings of the various queer subcultures. 'We are family' is the tribal anthem expressing the hoped-for realization of a new type of affinity and kinship outside the hetero-patriarchal order. Jacob and Esau have been pitted against each other by the exigencies of this order, and Jacob will flee into exile. As the story progresses, Jacob will return from exile to be reconciled with Esau, who falls weeping on his brother's neck and kissing him (Gen. 33.4). A queerly utopian reading of this reconciliation might be one in which Esau is revealed not as the straight butch but as a gay bear. Jacob and Esau, then, become somewhat like Gilgamesh and Enkidu, the heroic male pair of Mesopotamian mythology. This reconciliation follows the night in which Jacob wrestles with a strange night visitor (Gen. 32.22–32). One Rabbinic tradition identifies this entity with Esau's guardian angel, and Zornberg states that such a figure literally represents the principle of Esau's 'authenticity' (Zornberg 1996: 234). Ostriker presents a highly eroticized version of this wrestling match. Jacob sees in the other a dark – 'the color of black olives' – twin – 'so beautiful' – of himself (Ostriker 1994: 98). While Ostriker baulks at the eroticism of the scene – 'It is not like making love. Unlike. Unlike'

(Ostriker 1994: 99) – her repeated denials cannot escape the fact that wrestling, especially wrestling all through the night, is a powerfully masculine image of male/male lovemaking. In her description they gasp and moan, slipping and sliding against the other face to face, words that evoke the erotics of frottage or inter-femoral sex, an erotics of twinship. Continuing this queer utopian reading, following the erotic reconciliation of the brothers, Isaac, their father, no longer needing to live a false masculinity projected through his favourite son, can finally be freed from the bonds of the Akedah, perhaps to embrace a transgender possibility. Rebecca, who set off on an adventure into the unknown, somewhat reminiscent of the Beauty and the Beast fable, and in a queer twist of that fable, discovers that within the haunted man she has been wedded to is the woman of her dreams, the sister of her heart's desire.

Vayetze (28.10–32.3)

Jacob flees to his mother's kin, a journey retracing the path that Eliezer took many years earlier. That Jacob flees his brother's enmity while Eliezer journeyed according to Abraham's wishes, is one of a number of twists and changes that mark out the two accounts. Eliezer found Rebecca living in an apparently matriarchal establishment. He negotiates with both her mother and her brother, Laban, although it is Rebecca herself who decides her fate. Jacob has found that in this new generation, matriarchy has been replaced with patriarchy. Jacob has come to the house of Laban and all his subsequent negotiations will be with Laban. Jacob meets Rachel at a well, as Eliezer did Rebecca. However, unlike Rebecca, Rachel does not speak throughout this encounter. Furthermore Jacob, not Rachel, repeats Rebecca's actions. Jacob approaches Rachel rather than wait for her to approach him. Jacob opens the well, fetches water and waters Rachel's sheep. It was Rebecca who provided water for Eliezer and his camels. Jacob announces himself as his mother's son but Rachel runs to her father. Provocatively, Ellen Frankel suggests that Rebecca raised Jacob as her daughter, 'schooling him in the traditional ways of women . . . to play the woman's role in the family drama' (Frankel 1996: 50).

Rebecca might have raised her son to not conform to the heteronormative patriarchal male role, but in what follows, it could be argued that Laban puts Jacob through a crash course in patriarchy. Genesis says that Jacob loves Rachel, but in Laban's household women have no say over their fate. They are the property of their father and Jacob must purchase Rachel with seven years' labour for Laban. When the time comes, however, Jacob will find himself deceived in a strange echo of his own deception of Isaac. Instead of Rachel, the younger daughter, Laban has substituted the firstborn, Leah. In this strange twist of the firstborn motif, it might seem that a firstborn has bested the younger. But Leah, who at no time has been consulted about her fate, has been consigned to a loveless union. Jacob still wants Rachel and must agree to work another seven years before Laban will give her to him. Both Leah and Rachel at their weddings have been given maids, Zilpah and Bilhah, by their father. By tradition these two women are half-sisters of Leah and Rachel, being daughters of Laban by his concubines.

In this patriarchal household, the women have no say over their fate – up until now they have not spoken – and are disposed of as merchandise by their father. Consequently, there is no solidarity among them. Jacob loves Rachel but Leah remains unloved. What follows is a bizarre but tragic battle of the wombs. To win her husband's love Leah embarks upon a campaign of child-bearing. In this enterprise, she is not only blessed by the deity who assures easy conceptions, but in her favour, too, is the fact that Rachel is barren. In the patriarchal economy, a woman's value is determined by her productivity, her fieldship. She must produce progeny, sons, to have worth and status in the patriarchal household. Leah will give birth to six sons, each of whom she will name to record her sorrow and triumph. Rachel's barrenness echoes that of Rebecca and Sarah, and as such she echoes the primal androgyne. Is that why Genesis tells us that Jacob, the man raised as a daughter, loves her from when he first meets her? Nevertheless, Rachel does not trust in this love but cries out to Jacob, 'Give me children or I shall die' (Gen. 30.1). Not content with Jacob's protestations that only the deity can help her, Rachel acts to resolve the situation in a manner that again recalls Sarah. She gives her half-sister and maid, Bilhah, as a wife to Jacob. Like Hagar before her, Bilhah is to be a surrogate mother for Rachel. Bilhah has no say in this transaction; she does not speak at all. Rachel names the sons born to her half-sister, arrogantly appropriating them in terms of her own life not Bilhah's. Not to be outdone, and despite the fact that she has, by this stage, given birth to four sons, Leah does the same with her own half-sister maid, Zilpah, who like Bilhah remains silent and passive in this transaction. Their silencing has been continued in Jewish tradition, which speaks of four matriarchs, Sarah, Rebecca, Leah, Rachel, not six.

The reproductive wrangling of the two sisters comes to a climax after Leah's son, Reuben, brings her some mandrakes, in Hebrew, *dudaim*. The weight of opinion is that the plant is the *Mandragora officinalis*, a plant related to the night-shade family. It is also known as the Sodom-apple, the love-apple. In Arab culture, it is known as Satan's apple. The plant is known for its narcotic and magical effects and is reputed as an aphrodisiac. Rachel bargains with Leah that the latter will have Jacob for another night in return for the mandrakes. The text doesn't say why Rachel wants them but the implication is that she wants them either for fertility purposes to help her conceive or perhaps for their aphrodisiac quality to arouse Jacob to the task. After all, does her appeal to Jacob to give her children indicate a sexual difficulty between the two of them as the core of the problem? (Does Rachel, echoing the androgyne principle, bring out the femme in Jacob?)

Surprisingly, given the long rivalry, Leah agrees to Rachel's request. She conceives two more sons by Jacob, but finally 'she bore a daughter, and named her Dinah' (Gen. 30.21). Her birth is the first mention of a daughter in the saga of the Sarah/Abraham lineage. The significance of this fact has given rise to a surprising account of transgenderism. Leah knows that Jacob will father twelve sons. Eleven have been born, six to her, two each to Bilhah and Zilpah, but only one to Rachel. If Leah bears a seventh son then Rachel will be less than her maid. Leah prays that her child will be female and the deity, accordingly, changes the sex of the child in her womb. Dinah was conceived male but had her sex changed to be born as a girl (Zlotowitz 1986: 1310). Furthermore, this transformation, sexual reassignment, is the tangible expression, at last, of female solidarity. Immediately after Dinah's birth, 'God remembered Rachel . . . heeded her and opened her womb' (Gen. 30.22). Rachel conceives and gives birth to Joseph. She has found her place in the patriarchal economy but it has come about not through exploitation of and vying with other women but mutual support and the subversion of the rigid gender norms of patriarchy.

Vayishlakh (32.4 (32.3 NRSV)–36.43)

Jacob has learned and prospered in the house of Laban. He has acquired two wives and two concubines who have borne him eleven sons and, at least, one daughter. He has also acquired 'oxen, donkeys, flocks, male and female slaves' (Gen. 32.5). Chafing under Laban's authority, Jacob sets out to return to Canaan. Surprisingly Jacob consults with his wives as if to seek their consent for his plans, a consent they give (Gen. 31.4–16). This parasha opens with the company encamped on the borders of Seir, Esau's country. Jacob has sent messengers to Esau announcing his good fortune and return, and is now anticipating the reunion with his brother. It is in this context that Jacob wrestles with the night visitor at the ford of Jabbok. Earlier I gave a utopian erotic reading of this incident as signifying a reconciliation of the two brothers as an instance of the homoerotic myth of the Divine Twins. Christians have understood this incident as an encounter between Jacob and the deity because Jacob is here renamed Israel, he strives with God and man (ish), and because Jacob renames the place Peniel, face of God, where he saw God face to face and lived. This Christian identification of Jacob's visitor with the deity can serve to indicate that the homoerotic is a valid ground for divine manifestation. The deity has appeared as a 'man' and spoken to Jacob in a highly charged night of erotic brotherhood. Such an identification fully accords with the incarnationalism intrinsic to Christianity.

  Such an identification has been more problematic for Judaism and in Islam would be considered as shirk, associating the created with the divine. Consequently, this story is not found in the Qur'an. In Jewish tradition, Jacob wrestles an angel, and some identify this angel as Sammael/Satan. Whereas earlier, I proposed a queer utopic account of Jacob's return, Sammael's presence enables a dystopic reading of Jacob's return, which conforms to the process of diminution emerging in this parasha. Zornberg portrays Jacob's wrestling and besting of the angel as a type of failure on Jacob's part in dealing with the question of power. Citing Rashi, she points out that the angel guarantees to Jacob he will no longer have the reputation that 'blessings came to you through insinuation and trickery, but by authority and openly' (Zornberg (citing Rashi) 1996: 228). Jacob must go to Bethel for his 'new modality' to be confirmed by the angel and 'properly defined by God' but Jacob is impatient and prematurely assumes the name Israel 'before he had any authority to do so' and without waiting (Zornberg 1996: 228). Jacob is the pretty-boy nancy who has had to live by his wits, outsmarting all the males confident in the ways of patriarchy. He is fearful of his coming reunion with his brother, fearful he will not measure up. Holding down Sammael, the accusing 'prince of this world' (John 12.31), Jacob demands his blessing, confirming Jacob's power and manliness. The next day

Jacob will go to meet Esau arraying all his achievements ahead of him. He has already sent ahead herds of livestock and now he places before him his concubines with their children, Leah and her sons behind them followed by Rachel and Joseph, ahead of Jacob himself. Esau will have no doubt that his fairy kid brother has become a man. Esau's homophobic shame and outrage at being bested by this pansy collapses in the face of such heteronormative accomplishment and he falls, weeping in relieved joy, on his brother's shoulder.

Jacob's appropriation of/into patriarchy sets the stage for the remainder of this parasha. Jacob's return is followed immediately by the rape of Dinah. According to Zornberg, the rape of Dinah is a direct consequence or illustration of Jacob's arrogation of power. She cites a tradition that Jacob hid Dinah, keeping her in a box so that Esau does not set eyes on her. Zornberg argues that this control of Dinah represents a type of avarice, a hoarding, a locking-up of Dinah in the family (Zornberg 1996: 226). Dinah is a marketable commodity, a womb, and must be kept under male control. Jacob's avarice takes this control to extremes, locking Dinah in a box. A box can be a type of closet, and recalling Dinah's sex change in her mother's womb, an alternative reading would be that Jacob has hidden this very queer child from his very straight brother lest his own sexuality be challenged by association. Dinah's going out is an attempted exercise of personal autonomy, and it is significant that she goes out seeking the company of women. As the transgendered daughter, Dinah represents the androgynous principle, like Sarah and Rebecca before her. Unlike her grandmother, Rebecca, who was raised in a matriarchal milieu, Dinah finds herself in a patriarchal household and a patriarchal milieu. In such a world, autonomous female agency is punished, suppressed. Instead of finding same-sex companionship, Dinah is raped by Shechem. That Shechem is a prince of the land demonstrates that the hierarchies of gender and sexuality operate as part of the hierarchies of class. As a prince of the land, Shechem is a Canaanite giving the story an added edge of inter-ethnic conflict. A prince, he regards Dinah as another of those itinerant, gypsy, Hebrews camped outside the city. A Canaanite, his rape of Dinah can then be subsequently used to justify Israelite possession of other people's lands.

Scholz's translation of the Hebrew account of the rape strongly conveys the 'rapid-fire' violence involved, 'and-he-took her, then-he-laid-her, and-he-raped-her' (Scholz 1998: 165). I am strongly persuaded, too, by her account of what follows between Shechem and Dinah. Most translations tell how Shechem 'loved the girl and spoke tenderly to her' (Gen. 34.3). Scholz argues that the word translated as love is ambiguous and in this context is best translated as lust or desire, describing 'Shechem's intention . . . to treat Dinah as he pleases' (Scholz 1998: 169). Furthermore, instead of speaking tenderly to Dinah, Scholz argues that Shechem 'attempted to soothe the young woman' (Scholz 1998: 171). Nevertheless, Shechem now seeks to possess Dinah, telling his father to get her to be his wife. As with the rape, in what will transpire, Dinah has no say, does not speak. She is the object of transactions between men. For all of the men what counts is their status, privilege, profit and honour. Events spiral out of control, as Dinah's brothers use deception to carry out a hideous vengeance, genocide. The house of Jacob/Israel now casts 'a terror from God' upon the people of the land (Gen. 35.5). As if in response to this eruption of sexual, racial, patriarchal violence, Deborah, the nurse and same-sex companion of Rebecca, dies. She is 'the only servant in the Torah whose death and burial receive notice' (Frankel 1996: 69). All we know about Deborah is that she went with Rebecca on her journey, and it is only now that we even learn her name, so this record of her death and burial testifies to her importance to Rebecca. After Deborah's death, Rachel, who through her barrenness echoes Sarah and Rebecca, dies giving birth to Benjamin. The patriarchal impulse appears now to triumph over the utopian androgynous with the preceding pattern of violence finally emerging within Dinah's family. Her brother, Reuben, 'went and laid . . . Bilhah his father's concubine' (Gen. 35.22). The word here for laid is the same used when Shechem rapes Dinah, so I have retained Scholz's rendering here to show that the Other's (sexual) violence is in no way different to one's own.

Vayeshev (37.1–40.23)

Violence and power now appear dominant in the story. Even the deity has disappeared as a character – 'We are approaching civilisation as we know it' (Ostriker 1994: 111). Nevertheless, in this parasha the androgynous principle, linked again with the motif of the latter-born triumphing over the firstborn, surfaces again in the character of Joseph, Rachel's son. Furthermore, sexual transgression, the story of Tamar, will again play a crucial role, with messianic overtones reminiscent of the account of Lot's daughters that closes Genesis 19. While Joseph is Rachel's firstborn son, she herself is the younger sister, who does not conceive until all of Jacob's wives have had children of their own. So Joseph is both latter-born and firstborn. This intermediate status alone could confirm Joseph as marked by the androgynous, but additionally, his mother, Rachel, is herself androgynously marked through her initial barrenness. But there is another marker – he is the beloved son of Jacob/Israel, beloved 'more than any of his other children' (Gen. 37.3). The text tells us that it is because Joseph is the son of Jacob's old age, but perhaps Jacob sees in Joseph something of his own youth, his long ago abandoned queerness. Jacob further marks out Joseph with a highly embroidered or ornamented tunic, the coat of many colours as the Septuagint describes it. A multi-coloured robe is evocative of the rainbow, now very much established as a queer symbol, but also in many mythologies evocative of the primal creation, thus here it can evoke the primal androgynous human origin. The rainbow is also a sign of hope and, following the Flood, is a marker of peace between creator and creation (Gen. 9.12–17). The rainbow is a bridge that brings together the heavenly and terrestrial realms, and it is the heavenly or Uranian that lies behind the term, urning/urnind, coined by Karl Ulrichs, the nineteenth-century pioneer activist of the LGBT movement as terms for gay men and lesbians. For Oscar Wilde and others of his era, Uranian love was the love felt for a beautiful young man by an older, and it is worth noting that in Islamic tradition Joseph is considered to have been extraordinarily beautiful. The Qur'an records Joseph's story in Sura 12, named for Joseph/Yusuf himself. In Jewish tradition, too, Joseph is the image of his beautiful mother, 'fair of form and fair to look at' (Ostriker 1994: 111). But this is a transgressive, suspect beauty, as Ostriker points out,

Joseph is the darling, a pretty boy ... his father's pet ... the rabbis say he painted his eyes and walked with mincing step. Showing off the coat of many colors, which old Jacob made him. Twirling, hugging himself. A young Hebrew Narcissus. No wonder his brothers hated him. (Ostriker 1994: 111–12)

Twirling, mincing, in rainbow garb and with painted eyes, Joseph is a flaming young queen. No wonder his brothers, particularly the sons of Leah, hate him. In the previous parasha, they have even resorted to genocide to salve their wounded male honour. It is no wonder, then, that they will resent and hate this prettified affront to normative manhood.

Joseph hasn't helped by his bringing a 'bad report of them to his father' (Gen. 37.2) and neither does broadcasting his dreams that he would receive the obeisance of his brothers. It is possible to see in those accounts something of Joseph's assertion of himself in response to the harassment, bullying and intimidation of his brothers. To twice tell such dreams betrays a brazen, sassy, impudence, which can often be a support for someone enduring such oppressive situations. Matters come to a head when Jacob sends Joseph to his brothers when the latter are away pasturing near Shechem. With the help of a stranger he meets on the way, Joseph finds his brothers at Dothan. Seeing him coming, they plot to kill him and throw his body into a pit. Reuben talks them out of killing Joseph and instead they put him alive into a pit. Judah then proposes to sell Joseph to the Ishmaelites and pretend to Jacob that he has been killed. The brothers agree, but Joseph has already been found by Midianite traders who then sell him to some Ishmaelites. The brothers return to their father telling the lie that Joseph was killed by an animal and producing his coat, dipped in goat's blood as proof. Jacob cries out, 'Joseph is . . . torn to pieces' (Gen. 37.33).

Zornberg comments that the account of Joseph's sale is confused and contradictory, giving a 'blurring effect on the actual crime of the brothers' (Zornberg 1996: 266). She continues that Jacob's cry articulates '(w)hat the brothers had wanted to do to Joseph – indeed, what they had done to him' (Zornberg 1996: 266). Certainly, as is noted in the Zohar, the brothers deceive their father in a manner reminiscent of his own deception of Isaac. In his case, he used goatskins but they have used goat's blood (Zohar II.185b–186a). However, Zornberg's observation reminds me of another father–son interaction, the Binding of Isaac. In both Judaism and Islam, there are traditions that Jacob did not believe his sons, either that they were innocent in what happened or even that Joseph was dead. I want to suggest Jacob's complicity in what happened; after all, it was Jacob who sent Joseph out on his own to join his brothers. Interestingly, in the Qur'an's account, Jacob's complicity is strongly suggested. The brothers are portrayed pressuring their father to allow Joseph to accompany them. Finally Jacob relents saying, 'It saddens me that ye should take him away: I fear lest the wolf should devour him while ye attend not to him' (Sura 12.13). Ali comments that 'Jacob did not know the precise plot but had misgivings . . . (i)n saying this he was really unwittingly giving a cue to the wicked ones, for they use that very excuse' (Ali 1938: 553). Jacob could not have missed the brothers' aversion to Joseph's blatant behaviour and certainly understood the import of the dreams. It is said that Jacob 'kept the matter in mind' (Gen. 37.11) and then, immediately after, he sends Joseph to his brothers. Perhaps he thinks that he is exposing Joseph to a form of informal therapy from his peers that will restore his masculine competency and core gender identity. That Joseph is spoken of as torn to pieces recalls Isaac (and Bat Jephthah) reduced to ashes on the altar, to confirm what Sedgwick observes, in her analysis of psychiatric literature on the 'sissy boy' syndrome and its 'cure', 'for a proto-gay child to identify "masculinely" might involve identification with his own erasure' (Sedgwick 1993: 161). But not only in the family, Jacob can also be read here as representative of those authority figures in classroom, workplace, neighbourhood or barracks who, awkwardly embarrassed in their homophobia, turn a blind eye to the harassment and blatant violence that confronts a person publicly, flamboyantly, defiantly in breach of the gender and sexual norms.

Joseph, the blatantly flamboyant queen, has been cast into the pit, torn apart and sent off in captivity, despised and rejected, to Egypt. Genesis then presents us with the story of Tamar, a story of outrageous sexual transgression with messianic results. Significantly, the butt of the story is Judah, the brother who proposed selling Joseph into captivity because there was no profit in killing him (Gen. 37.26). Judah will subsequently emerge as the main protagonist, representative of these brothers in the final chapters of Genesis. Thus, with the apparent triumph of the heteronormative and patriarchal, Judah, as the instantiation of these values, will be challenged, humbled and exposed, and by a woman, Tamar. If, at this point in Genesis, we are approaching civilization as we know it, it is also important to note of Tamar's story that this is the last time the deity acts and is a protagonist in the events, albeit briefly, to kill the first two husbands of Tamar. In so doing, however, the stage is set for Tamar to speak and act, opening up a messianic possibility. Tragically, however, this messianic story has been misread to promote repression of women and erotophobia.

Genesis tells nothing of Tamar's background but introduces her abruptly when Judah marries her to his firstborn son, Er. Just as abruptly, the text says that Er was wicked and 'the LORD put him to death' (Gen. 38.7). Judah then tells Onan, his second son, to go to Tamar and 'perform the duty of a brother-in-law; raise up offspring for your brother' (Gen. 38.8). Onan is quite willing to have sex with Tamar but will not sire a child that will not be counted as his and pulls out his penis each time he is about to cum to spill 'his semen on the ground . . . so that he would not give offspring to his brother' (Gen. 38.9). For this refusal, Onan is in turn killed by the deity. The death of Onan has been used in Christianity to justify the condemnation of masturbation. In the eighteenth century masturbation was even termed onanism to give a biblical basis to a moral panic that would continue through the nineteenth and twentieth centuries. There is nothing in Genesis or anywhere else in the biblical texts condemning masturbation. Linking masturbation to Onan shows the pathological morbidity underpinning erotophobia. Onan is not killed for jacking off in front of Tamar. That Onan's act is one of *coitus interruptus* has meant that the story has also been conscripted in Roman Catholicism to give a biblical basis to its opposition to birth control. As with masturbation, there is nothing in Genesis or elsewhere in the biblical texts, to give biblical basis to an opposition to birth control. Instead, Onan's *coitus interruptus* represents a breach of the old levirate marriage law, by which if a man dies childless, his brother must beget a child for the dead man by his widow (Deut. 25.5–6). Onan refuses to do so, demonstrating a mean, proprietorial, attitude to life. If a child won't be counted as his, then there will be no child. If the child can't be his, how can he profit? Onan is revealed here very much as his father's son because it was Judah who proposed a profitable way of disposing of Joseph. Additionally, Onan's behaviour can be read as an abuse, even rape, of Tamar. We are not told her feelings for Onan, but in what follows it is clear she is determined to raise up progeny for her dead husbands. She consents to sex with Onan on those grounds and, thus, every time he has sex with her only to spill his semen on the ground is an abuse of that consent.

Judah has a third son, a boy, and so Tamar is sent home to her people until he comes of age. Judah, however, is afraid to marry his youngest to Tamar. He wants his line to continue but each of her husbands has died childless. Tamar is not prepared to wait on Judah, but taking matters into her own hands, sets off to find him, posing as a prostitute. Judah sees her and arranges to have sex with her. It is striking that Judah never recognizes this woman with whom he barters and will eventually have sex. Zornberg argues that this failure represents a 'dangerous and even immoral' lack of vision on Judah's part, demonstrating his lack of any 'complex sense of connection and responsibility' (Zornberg 1996: 327). In contrast, Tamar is possessed of a strong sense of purpose and awareness of her connectedness in the world, which has brought her to be bargaining her sexual access with her father-in-law. He offers her a kid from his flock, but she will only accept his signet, cord and staff as pledge items for future redemption.

The importance of these pledge items is revealed in what follows. Tamar conceives, and when news of her pregnancy is brought to Judah he condemns her to be burned. When she is taken to be executed she sends the pledge items to Judah with the message that their owner is the man who made her pregnant. Tamar thus trumps Judah, forcing him not only to release her and confess his own wrongdoing and lack of concern for others but to praise her as more worthy than he. The story ends with Tamar giving birth to twins, Perez and Zerah. Perez is the younger and, in a recurrence of the younger supplanting the older theme, will go on to be the ancestor of the Davidic line and, through that, of the messiah. So for the second and last time in Genesis (and the Pentateuch) transgressive sexuality is crucial for inaugurating the line of the messiah. On the first occasion, when Lot's daughters rape their father, it is the female lineage that is initiated. On this second occasion, Tamar tricks her father-in-law to have sex with her and initiates the male lineage. On both occasions, the lineage depends on the agency and action of women.

The parasha concludes with Joseph brought to Egypt and sold into the house of Potiphar. In coming to Egypt, Joseph has, in Australian parlance for cities, come to the big smoke. The city has long served as a place of refuge for queer people fleeing the confining homophobic environment of family and small hometown. Despite the circumstances that bring him to Egypt, Joseph can be seen as a type of queer refugee from such environments who make their way to the big city with its promised opportunity of cosmopolitan, anonymously tolerant diversity. Joseph is successful in his undertakings for Potiphar and is promoted to be his personal attendant. At this point, Joseph is said to be 'handsome and good looking' (Gen. 39.6). Joseph now comes to the attention of

Potiphar's wife, who demands that he lie with her. Joseph's repeated refusals will lead to her charging him with attempted rape, and Joseph is thrown into prison 'where the king's prisoners were confined' (Gen. 39.20). Prison, where he will display his talents of dream interpretation, will prove to be the avenue for Joseph to enter into Pharaoh's service and be appointed to be in charge of all the land of Egypt.

Potiphar's wife has been used as the archetype of the 'vengeful and conniving woman scorned . . . a means of asserting the male's desirability and innocence' upon whom is projected all sexual desire so that she becomes a 'manifestation of the feminine frightening to men' (Niditch 1992: 28). Her false charge of attempted rape against Joseph has served to cast doubt on the veracity of such claims in real life and supports the notion that the woman really wanted it. However, when read in terms of class, other factors come into play. Joseph can be seen as representing the plight of household servants or domestics who are subjected to harassment and abuse, sexual and otherwise, by their employers. Furthermore, in the ancient world the master of the house had the right of sexual access to all his slaves, male and female. Only after Joseph has been promoted to be Potiphar's personal attendant does Genesis tell of Joseph's beauty. For Joseph, it is risky, indeed, to have sex with his master's wife, but furthermore, to refuse her provides him an opportunity of autonomy, otherwise denied – he does not have the right to refuse Potiphar. The class hierarchy of the household is also manifested by the rape allegation made by Potiphar's wife – in the Qur'an's account she is known as Zulaikha. Clearly, Zulaikha does not share her husband's right of sexual access to the slaves, otherwise she could simply charge Joseph with insubordination.

Nevertheless, I want to suggest another way of reading the story, based on the fact that Joseph's imprisonment is the key to his eventual success. In the Qur'an, Pharaoh only releases Joseph after first hearing Zulaikha admit that the charges she brought against Joseph were false (Sura 12.51–3). As part of her disavowal she declares, 'This (say I) in order that he may know that I have never been false to him in his absence, and that God will never guide the snare of the false ones' (Sura 12.52). This strange statement is perhaps behind subsequent Islamic traditions of a romance between Joseph and Zulaikha, resulting in their marriage after Potiphar's death. I want to suggest an alternative perspective, that Zulaikha and Joseph together invent this story in order to get Joseph out of Potiphar's house. Why does Zulaikha do this? According to Rabbinic tradition, as found in *Pirke de Rabbi Eliezer* XXXVIII, 'the wife of Potiphera was barren' (Friedlander 1916: 288). Zulaikha's barrenness makes her representative of the androgynous principle like Sarah, Rebecca and Rachel before her. In both Rabbinic tradition and the Qur'an, Zulaikha enlists the support of the leading women in her campaign to get Joseph imprisoned. She shows Joseph to them and they cut their hands declaring, 'no mortal is this! This is none other than a noble angel' (Sura 12.31).[3] They will pressure their husbands so

_____

3 In the Qur'an's account she shows Joseph to the women because they have been gossiping about her outrageous desire for him. By displaying him to them she is challenging them to admit that no one could be unmoved by his beauty. My reading is, of course, very different to the Qur'an's account.

that Joseph is eventually imprisoned. According to the Qur'an, Potiphar does not believe Zulaikha's original allegations, which, considering Joseph's flamboyant, mincing effeminacy, is not surprising. According to my reading, then, Potiphar and Zulaikha are in a marriage of convenience, given his high status, and Potiphar wants to keep Joseph for himself. It is through Zulaikha's actions that Joseph is able to escape, albeit through prison. However, it is only through prison that Joseph will come to the attention of Pharaoh and thus fulfil his destiny. The Islamic tradition that Joseph and Zulaikha love each other and eventually marry, I will take as a sign of their solidarity and partnership in this whole enterprise.

Miketz (41.1–44.17)

In prison, Joseph will display his talent for dream analysis, and it is this ability that will eventually bring him to the attention of Pharaoh. Summoned to Pharaoh to interpret the famous dreams of the seven fat cows/ears of grain being eaten by seven scrawny or shrivelled cows/ears of grain, Joseph predicts seven years of abundance to be followed by seven years of famine. Joseph further suggests that Pharaoh appoint someone to superintend all of Egypt so as to ensure the resources of the land are managed to survive the famine. Impressed, Pharaoh appoints Joseph to the task. Pharaoh gives Joseph an Egyptian name and marries him to Asenath, daughter of Potiphar and presumably Zulaikha. How can Zulaikha be barren and have a daughter? In Rabbinic tradition, Asenath is actually the daughter of Dinah, conceived when Shechem raped her. In *Pirke de Rabbi Eliezer* XXXVIII, it is said that Jacob's brothers want her killed in case they got a reputation for immorality. The text is unclear whether they mean Dinah or Asenath (the consensus of tradition is the latter) but it is Asenath that Jacob takes and, hanging from her neck a plate bearing the Divine Name, abandons her in the country. She is rescued by the Archangel Michael, who takes her to Potiphar's house where she will grow up as Zulaikha's daughter (Friedlander 1916: 287–8). This story reveals that both Joseph's father and brothers have fully incorporated patriarchal values – in the ancient world the father had the power of life and death over newborn children, and the exposure of unwanted children was a common practice. As a result of heavenly intervention, Asenath will link the androgynously barren Zulaikha to the lineage of transgendered and androgynously barren women from which Joseph himself is born.

In Joseph's case, however, Genesis provides no such divine interventions. He must rely, instead, both on the assistance and good will of others and on his own wits and skill. In this way he has risen to be, under Pharaoh, governor/vizier of all Egypt. He epitomizes the faggot runaway who made good beyond his wildest dreams in the big city. Despite such success, there still remains the family to contend with, but now Joseph is in a position to confront his old pain. The famine is not only in Egypt but Canaan as well. Jacob sends Joseph's brothers to Egypt to secure food but keeps Benjamin behind, 'for he feared that harm might come to him' (Gen. 42.4). In keeping Benjamin with him, Jacob echoes Abraham and Isaac who passed off their wives as sisters for fear of the Other. The youngest, Benjamin, is still a 'boy' (Gen. 43.8) and son of the beautiful Rachel, brother of the beautiful Joseph. A beautiful youth would certainly be a target for rape or abduction into sex slavery. It's also possible that Jacob does not trust his other sons after what happened with Joseph.

It is these fears that Joseph will exploit in his subsequent dealings with his brothers. There is a cruelty in the way Joseph toys with them. Given what had happened, that might not surprise; however, the cruelty extends to Jacob and Benjamin himself. In Jacob's case, as he sent Joseph to join his brothers, perhaps Joseph holds his father as equally responsible for what happened. In Benjamin's case, though, what unfolds will combine elements of the Akedah and the story of Psyche and Eros. When the brothers arrive in Egypt, they are recognized by Joseph and brought before him. He accuses them of spying and, in their defence, they tell who they are, including the facts that one of their brothers is no more and that the youngest is still in Canaan with their father. Joseph begins demanding that they bring this youngest to him. That a foreign ruler displayed such obsession for the youth could only inspire alarm. The brothers knew, from their attempt to profit from the sale of Joseph, that a beautiful youth was a valuable commodity. Eventually they are released under the proviso that they return with their brother. Simeon is kept as a hostage to guarantee their return. Both Jacob and the brothers are prepared to abandon Simeon, but the famine continues, leaving them no recourse but to return to Egypt bringing Benjamin with them. Jacob must offer up Benjamin, Rachel's only surviving son, to a possible life as the sex slave of a foreign ruler in order that the family might survive the famine. Genesis tells us nothing of Benjamin's feelings in these events. Does he feel dread at the prospect of becoming some rich foreigner's toy boy? Conversely, is he excited to be leaving these backwoods behind for the sophisticated high life of Egypt and a new life of erotic possibilities, not available in the confines of the family tent?

Vayiggash (44.18–47.27)

With his brothers once again before him, Joseph continues his cruel games. This time he has contrived to make it appear that Benjamin has stolen a goblet and will be detained. This parasha opens with Judah appealing to Joseph to let the boy go and keep him as his slave. Before they left their father, Judah had already pledged he would be a surety for Benjamin (Gen. 43.8). Now he will make good that pledge. As Zornberg points out, whatever Joseph's intentions, these events (including the story of Tamar) have forced a moral re-education of Judah. In his speech before his brother, Judah has finally 'redescribed himself in a new vocabulary of intimate relationship: a vocabulary that suggests what it is like to *see* [Zornberg's italics] the other seeing, and not to be able to bear seeing what he sees' (Zornberg 1996: 330). Judah has been shocked out of the complacent sense of privilege the patriarchal hierarchy had inculcated in him and forced to express his connectedness and reverse his role in the abuse of Joseph. With Joseph, all Judah was interested in was the profit that could be made when they got rid of this faggot. Now, before Joseph, he intervenes to speak up for his brother when he is about to be bound in captivity, like Abraham should have done all those years ago for Isaac. And Benjamin? To his surprise, this powerful foreign prince is suddenly revealed as his big faerie brother, lost long ago. Unlike Psyche with Eros, this discovery will not mean sudden separation but restoration.

By revealing himself to his brothers, Joseph sets in train the move of his family to Egypt, thus enabling them to survive the famine. As the story comes to its end the family now leaves the Land of Promise as their descendants will over and over again. On the road to Egypt the deity speaks to Jacob one last time but only, as if in deference to Joseph's reality, through a dream, 'visions of the night' (Gen. 46.2). Imitating Joseph before Pharaoh, the deity foretells to Jacob briefly the subsequent events of the Pentateuch. But while the deity tells Jacob, 'I myself will go down with you to Egypt' (Gen. 46.2), it will not appear again in Genesis.

Vayechi 47.28–50.26

The story ends now with the deaths of both Jacob and, subsequently, Joseph. Before Jacob dies Joseph brings his two sons, Ephraim and Manasseh, to his father to be blessed. By so doing he enables a resurgence of the messianic motif of the supplanting of the firstborn by the younger. Joseph positions his sons so that Manasseh, the elder, will be blessed by Jacob's right hand and Ephraim by his left. However, Jacob crosses his hands to bless the younger with his right and the older with his left. Joseph attempts to correct his father, pointing out that Manasseh is the firstborn and should be blessed with the right hand. Jacob refuses, saying, 'his younger brother shall be greater than he, and his offspring shall become a multitude of nations' (Gen. 48.19). In Jacob's conscious refusal is a declaration that the messianic will not be bound by patriarchal heteronormative hierarchies but will, instead, undo and reverse/pervert them, as did Lot's daughters and Tamar.

After blessing Joseph's sons, Jacob now blesses his own. Over only one does he invoke the androgynous divine, Shaddai. That son is Joseph, the mincing, flamboyant queen with painted eyes. Jacob calls on Shaddai to bless Joseph 'with the blessing of heaven above . . . of the deep that lies beneath . . . of the breast and of the womb' (Gen. 49.25). Frankel points out that Jacob's words over Joseph are 'brimming with female imagery' (Frankel 1996: 89). Perhaps they can be read as a sign that Jacob has fully accepted his very queer son. After Jacob's death, it is the turn of his brothers to be finally reconciled with him. His brothers ask his forgiveness for their crime against him. In part they act out of fear – Jacob is dead and Joseph is still ruler of the land. But Joseph freely forgives and reassures them pointing out that while they intended him harm, the deity used their actions for good, 'to preserve a numerous people' (Gen. 50.20). Surprisingly, while they can never be justified by it, evil, suffering and oppression contain within themselves the perverse seeds of their reversal and undoing, the opportunity to work goodness, justice and liberation.

Conclusion

The world of Genesis is a strange and unsettling one. The stories it contains have been used to justify patriarchy, misogyny, homophobia and erotophobia.

However, one must approach these stories with caution if one wants to use them to justify a particular rule of society or of sexuality. In Genesis, one finds polygamy (calling out for a consciously polyamorous reading of Genesis), surrogate motherhood, incest and close-kin marriage all treated as perfectly legitimate. While Genesis might be the product of a patriarchal world, the women of Genesis do not, in contrast to Luther's hopes, remain silently subordinated and sequestered in the tent. Far from it, they speak and act with confidence, and when they completely breach all patriarchal standards they give an opening to messianic impulses. The characters in Genesis have both mythic qualities and are caught up in a web of relationships in which power is exercised and abused and resisted. Genesis presents not only the world of civilization but also the gaps through which alternative utopian possibilities might be glimpsed.

It comes as no surprise then that Genesis and its stories have been fundamental to a variety of religions. As a result of this appropriation, the stories of Genesis are embedded in textual and literary webs that are diverse, expanding and multivarious. Genesis is thus a politically potent text, with both toxic and enriching possibilities. The Christian weavings of these webs, in particular, have created especially potent and toxic ideo-stories from Genesis on which to base patriarchal, misogynistic and homophobic thought and practice. The contemporary struggles in the Middle East and the so-called War on Terror demonstrate how Genesis has been used to generate new toxic ideo-stories of fascism, racism, imperialism and colonialism.

The use of Genesis for such toxic purposes demands new ways of reading that call such toxic ideo-stories in question. It is what I have attempted to do here, and in doing so I have drawn on the many literary and textual webs that have enmeshed it. With some trepidation, I have drawn in large part on the stories of Jewish, Rabbinic traditions. Trepidation, because I am very conscious of the issues of appropriation involved in a Gentile, like myself, using Jewish texts in such an exercise. With even more trepidation, I regard what I have done as a type of queer midrash. Midrash is fundamentally Jewish, but I use the term in the sense of Alicia Ostriker's description, the use of the imagination to yield from ancient tales new meanings, liberating meanings, to new generations. As she reminds women:

> The texts plainly beg and implore women to read them as freshly, energetically, passionately – and even playfully – as they have been read by men. 'Turn it and turn it,' the rabbis say of Torah, 'for everything is in it.' Besides, they tell us, God has intended 'all the meanings that He has made us capable of discovering.' (Ostriker, 1994: xiii)

As for women, so too for queer people, and so what I have attempted is a queer turning and turning of the many threads that make up the meta-tapestry that is Genesis. It can only ever be a turning and certainly not a definitive queer reading. As I am very aware of the omissions, witting and unwitting, necessarily entailed in this exercise, I hope, instead, to invite, if not provoke, a multiplicity of queer readings across all the traditions and beyond.

Exodus

REBECCA ALPERT

Introduction

The book of Exodus, which in Jewish tradition is called *Shmot*, or 'Names', tells the story of the birth and rise to leadership of Israel's greatest prophet and lawgiver, Moses. It narrates the development of the Hebrew people's journey from Egyptian enslavement through the hierophany at Sinai. It describes the beginnings of the Israelites' forty-year trek in the wilderness, and delineates some of the crucial laws that form the basis of the ethical and ritual codes still followed by Jews, Christians and Muslims today who claim this people Israel as their ancestors.

Of course the authors[1] of the book of Exodus did not have a translesbigay community in mind when this text was handed down. But if we value the Bible as a sacred document, we believe it has something particular to say to us in every facet of our lives, and so it is our task to figure out what this book has to say to us as people who identify as gay, lesbian, bisexual and transgender.

The themes, actors and values present in Exodus have much to say to the translesbigay community. The main themes of the book: exodus and liberation, subversion and rebellion, wandering in the wilderness, and a communal response to revelation, speak powerfully to us. The relationship between God and Moses, and the stories of Moses' brother Aaron (and his priestly family), his sister Miriam, his wife Zipporah, and the midwives Shifrah and Puah and the women of Moses' family who were responsible for his birth and survival, will touch on different dimensions of a translesbigay sensibility. Much of the book of Exodus explores the building of the tabernacle, and we find inspiration in the work of the artist Bezalel and the adornment of holy places. Finally, some of the laws and commandments, especially the Ten Commandments and the often repeated injunction not to oppress the stranger, have a critical resonance for the translesbigay community.

---

1 This work presumes that the book of Exodus was not written by Moses, but was written by members of the Israelite community at a later date, although it bypasses the discussion of precisely when and by whom this book was edited and promulgated. There are many approaches to studying the biblical text from literary to psychoanalytical to historical. The story told here combines aspects of each of these approaches, describing how the followers of Mosaic law understood their early history and how later commentators chose to interpret that story for the purposes of particular faith communities.

Exodus and Liberation

The story of the Exodus from Egypt resonates deeply for translesbigay people, as it has for other oppressed communities. The story formed the backbone of the struggle of African people during their enslavement in the Americas. The Africans who were enslaved found messages in the Hebrew Bible and Christian scripture that gave them hope and comfort. The story of the Exodus became emblematic for them as a symbol of the possibility that like the Hebrew slaves in Egypt, they, too, would be released from bondage. They told the story throughout generations, and created many magnificent musical compositions that used this theme to give them strength in the liberation struggle. 'Let My People Go', and other spirituals, gave the enslaved Africans courage and hope in their struggle (Williams 1987), although African and African American theologians have also questioned the Exodus narrative as a model for their struggles for liberation. Stephen Reid (1986: 162) asks, for example, whether it is 'fair for God to use the poor and oppressed as tools to educate the world', as is the case when God hardens Pharaoh's heart and prolongs the time when the people remain in Egypt in order to show God's greatness?

The Exodus story also forms the basis of liberation theology for Latin American and other revolutionary movements. It has given many on the religious left a language and narrative through which to interpret oppression in contemporary society. Liberation theology assumes that the story of the liberation of the Israelites in Exodus is living proof of a God who cares about the poor and oppressed; to do God's work is to work for the liberation of the poor and those who have not had the opportunity to speak for themselves. The example of a people pressed into harsh labour that is allowed to go free from its oppressors makes a powerful myth and provides hope for any group that experiences oppression, although there are dissenters from this point of view as well, particularly Native American authors who cannot separate the Exodus narrative from the story of conquest of Canaan that follows. While the story has been understood as liberating for many groups, Native writers like Robert Allen Warrior (2000) remind us that the liberation in Egypt resulted in the conquest of Canaan, and that taking others' land is a model that Europeans emulated too well in their conquest of the Americas. And writers like Lyle Eslinger (1991: 43–60) question the theme of liberation in the text. He argues that the goal was not to liberate the Israelites from slavery or subordinate the Egyptians, but to reveal Yahweh as the God of the Hebrews and to prove his power over all creation. Yet liberation theology has also been a powerful tool. In the words of Gustavo Gutiérrez, founder of the liberation theology movement:

> The liberation of Israel is a political action. It is the breaking away from a situation of despoliation and misery and the beginning of the construction of a just and comradely society . . . The Exodus is the long march towards the promised land in which Israel can establish a society free from misery and alienation. Throughout the whole process, the religious event is not set apart. It is placed in the context of the entire narrative, or more precisely, it is its deepest meaning . . . The liberation from Egypt, linked to and even coinciding with creation, adds an element of capital importance: the need and

the place for human active participation in the building of society . . . The Exodus experience is paradigmatic. It remains vital and contemporary due to similar historical experiences which the People of God undergo. (cited in Gottwald 1989: 250)

The theme of liberation resonates for translesbigay people, on both communal and individual levels. In the communal context, we look forward to a time when with whom we choose to have sex and to live and to love, and the ways in which we choose to express our gender identity, will no longer be marked by any members of society as sinful, illegal or disgusting. We may experience the contemporary society in which we live and work as oppressive because it is acceptable for people to express hatred towards us in schoolyards, the media or political speeches, or because we do not have the rights that are commonly accorded to heterosexuals like marriage and adoption, or because we are denied the freedom to express affection for one another comfortably in public spaces. So the theme of liberation that comes through in the Exodus story speaks to us as a model of a time when we can be truly free to express ourselves, and for which we are hoping and working.[2]

The life of the Israelites in Egypt as described in the book of Exodus tells the story not only of a people forced into servitude to a cruel master, but also of a group of people whose identity is being suppressed. The Pharaoh resents the Israelites because they are 'too numerous for us' (1.9). Translesbigay people identify with the Israelites because they were oppressed simply because of who they were. Queers, and others who are labelled 'different' by the powerful in a society, are often resented not as individuals but because in the development of a group identity they are perceived as too numerous and hence a potential threat to the norms of society.

In terms of individual liberation, the stories surrounding Moses' birth and life as a young man in Egypt reflect the experiences of gay people in the process of coming out: first hiding and then revealing identity resonates deeply. Pharaoh's efforts to curtail the power of the Israelites included a campaign to kill all the boys at birth (1.22). In order to save the life of Moses, he was hidden by his family and raised as an Egyptian prince by Pharaoh's daughter. So Moses was not brought up as a Hebrew but as an Egyptian, in an alien culture. Translesbigay people can identify with Moses' experience of being raised by people not like himself. People who are labelled as different by society because of their racial, ethnic or religious orientation usually have a family whom they resemble and from whom they learn about who they are. This is not true for most translesbigay people (or people with disabilities or some adopted children), and so Moses is a model for translesbigay identity as someone who was raised by people from whom he couldn't learn about his identity.

---

2 George Edwards goes so far as to suggest that translesbigay people fit in the framework of liberation theology as those who face economic hardship as well, given the extent of professional discrimination against them, and as such may lay a moral claim to 'God's liberative justice' (1984: 13). Although there may be some truth to these claims, the positive changes in the status of translesbigay people over the past two decades may alter that perception to a great extent.

When Moses grew up, he began to notice the situation of the Hebrews. He 'went out to his kinsfolk and witnessed their toil. He saw an Egyptian beating a Hebrew, one of his kinsmen' (2.11). Moses' reaction was violent; he killed the Egyptian. This event can also be viewed from a translesbigay perspective. Moses was not raised among the Hebrews, and hid his identity. Like many translesbigay people, Moses reached a point where he couldn't tolerate the oppression of his people, and could hide no longer. Moses' name means 'to draw out' (2.10). Although in the biblical text this is a reference to the act of retrieving him from the water where his mother cast him, it is also understood to refer to Moses as the man who drew his people out of bondage. But from a translesbigay perspective, Moses also drew himself out of hiding, as is illustrated in this passage, where he publicly responded to the Egyptian who was oppressing a Hebrew slave, even at the risk of revealing his own identity. Although murder was an extreme response, we see in his strong reaction the behaviour of someone who had to hide his identity and who was drawn out of hiding in part because he was overwhelmed by seeing how badly his people were being treated. As a result, Moses felt compelled to act in a way that risked his own safety in order to help a person with whom he identified and who was being oppressed. For many translesbigay people, the coming out process begins with a realization that being open about our identities gives us the opportunity to challenge oppression of gays and is part of a process of working for our rights in society, as it was for Moses.

The response of those who saw Moses' effort to stand up for his people was not very positive, however. At least two of the Hebrews challenged Moses' intervention, and he had to flee to the land of Midian (2.13). People who are oppressed may resent efforts to liberate them. The period of transition from enslavement to liberation is often fraught with difficulty. Not everyone is ready to confront oppression at the same time, and many people prefer the status quo to making change. The story of Exodus and the story of translesbigay liberation confront this theme as well.

But for those individuals who are ready, like Moses, to draw themselves out and reveal their identities, the story of liberation also resonates. For many of us, the process of coming out echoes not only Moses' experience, but also the experience we assume to have taken place for the Israelites as they prepared to leave Egypt (West 2000). In Hebrew, the word for Egypt is *mitzrayim*, which means 'narrow place' or constricted territory. For many translesbigay people, the closet functions as our own *mitzrayim*, a place of hiding. Coming out of the closet is akin to the experience we imagine the Israelites had when leaving Egypt – the experience of moving from a place of restriction to a place of openness and freedom. As Mona West suggests, the movement of the Israelites from bondage in Egypt to freedom is 'the crucial event in the formation of the identity of Israel' (2000: 74). As people come out of the closet and begin to take on a translesbigay identity, the story of the Israelites leaving Egypt and coming into a new identity as part of a newly created community takes on added meaning. Chris Glaser describes it in this way:

Yet, just as the Israelites came out into the wilderness to celebrate a festival to God, find their holy mountain, and discover their law, so we too come out from the dominant culture and mainstream religion to celebrate our Pride festivals, discover our sacred sanctuaries (our Mount Sinais), and discern our organizing principles (our 'commandments') as a community and as a congregation (in the broadest sense of that term). (1998: 58)

It is no wonder that many translesbigay Jewish people celebrate the holiday of Passover, the festival the Israelites celebrated to God in the wilderness, with great passion. The Passover holiday has its origins in the book of Exodus as the people are commanded to commemorate this event of liberation (12.1), and to tell the story throughout the generations. To do this, the Jews observe an annual custom known as the Passover Seder. At this event that takes place in the home, the story of the deliverance from Egypt is told, and a festive meal is eaten. For translesbigay Jews, attending the Seder with their families of origin may be a painful experience if they are not open to their families about their sexual identity, brought home quite clearly by the theme of the ceremony. Because the Seder is so focused on family, and because it is an almost universally observed Jewish custom, lesbian and gay Jewish groups have made their own families, and put together their own Seders that tell their stories of 'coming out' of their own Egypts into freedom. Some Jews use the moment of Passover to come out to their families. A ritual for coming out includes a blessing that thanks God for the courage to come out, literally to 'go out from narrow places', which in Hebrew is the same as going out from Egypt.[3] More and more, these stories and coming out rituals are beginning to find a place at the Seder table even when translesbigay people are not themselves present. The origin of the custom of putting an orange on the Seder plate, for example, derives from an experience of lesbian Jews in Berkeley, California. It illustrates the ways in which our presence has been accepted and at the same time co-opted for other purposes. When the women in Berkeley asked an Orthodox woman who was speaking to them about women in Jewish law to talk about the role of lesbians in Judaism, she replied that lesbianism in Judaism was like eating bread on Passover; something you're not allowed to do, but not a terrible sin. Feeling like lesbians were treated very negatively in Judaism at the time (the late 1970s), they decided to put bread on their Seder plates as a symbol of the alienation they were feeling. Unlike eating bread during the eight-day holiday of Passover, putting bread on the Seder plate is much more an act of serious rebellion. Because of its strong symbolism, the custom was hotly debated, but incorporated into some lesbian Seders. Soon it became the basis of a story, 'A Crust of Bread on the Seder Plate', included in the Haggadah produced by students at Oberlin College and widely distributed. Lesbians thought telling a story about their oppression would make an effective substitute for the act. Hearing the story, Susannah Heschel, a leading Jewish feminist, decided instead to replace the bread with an orange. But she also replaced the meaning, using the orange to symbolize the oppression of lesbians, gay men and even widows: anyone who was left out of Jewish life. Over time, the custom of putting an orange on the seder plate to remember those who don't fit in the Jewish community, or more commonly to symbolize the plight of women in Judaism,

---

3 See Leila Berner's blessing in Rebecca Alpert (1997: 63).

has remained. The original symbolism of lesbian alienation has been lost. See Alpert (1997: 1–3) and Susannah Heschel (2003: 75).

The process through which the Israelites left, the plagues that God brings upon the Egyptian people, the way God is said to harden Pharaoh's heart against the people leaving, and the drowning of the Egyptian army in the process are all difficult dimensions of this story. While translesbigay people may identify 'Pharaoh' with those people who work against our liberation, we may find ourselves uncomfortable with the suffering of the innocent, and particularly with the intentional destruction of the Egyptian ecology and its people, presumably in order to show God's greatness. It is important for us to remember, as we think of using Exodus as an example of liberation, that it is an imperfect paradigm. It is useful to remind ourselves that in any struggle for change there are consequences that we can't always foresee, and aren't always good. We should be reminded by this story that we need to beware of simple solutions, and remember that even those people who are the 'pharaohs' in our struggle for liberation should be treated with respect and decency. And that even if we cannot always discern or predict what will come of our efforts, we also cannot run away from the work that must be done.

Rebellion and Subversion

A second major theme of the book of Exodus is the rebellious nature of the people during their liberation. They raise grievances about conditions in the desert (15.22; 16.2; 17.3), and express regret at having left Egypt (14.11). And in their greatest act of rebellion, they build a 'golden calf' a molten idol to worship when they fear that Moses has abandoned them (32.1). The people's rebelliousness is often described in terms of their lack of faith in Moses or in this new way of life, their scepticism in regard to belief in the God of their ancestors and an unwillingness to obey the laws they are given.

But looking at the rebellions of the people from a gay perspective, perhaps we can see more in them than these negative depictions of a whining, ungrateful, faithless people. One might rather assume that in rebelling against the authority of Moses, the people provide a model of the critical role dissent plays in a community. Because the people did not slavishly follow Moses, they prove themselves to be people who are thinking for themselves. They are willing to go against a powerful leader, and question his ideas and commands.

As George Coats (1977) suggests, this text raises questions about how we view obedience. He argues that the text depicts a God that persuades humans to obey, but does not coerce them. This God is a ruler who can tolerate opposition. The question we need to ask is always whether we are looking at a rebellion for legitimate claims to justice or not.

In their rebellion, the Israelites provide a model that may help us understand how translesbigay people can function in society. Because we are defined by society as different, and because we do not follow the rules of society about how to go about the processes of sexuality and reproduction, we may be the ones who are willing to ask difficult questions, and not just to go along with the crowd. When a society lacks dissent, voices of difference are stifled, much to the detriment of the growth of a society. Those who rebelled against Moses and challenged his authority remind us of the need for dissent. They gave Moses the opportunity to learn how to lead, and to listen to the people. We cannot underestimate the power of rebelliousness in shaping the social fabric and making sure that all voices are heard.

The Generation in the Wilderness

According to the Exodus story, the generation that left Egypt had to wander in the desert for forty years, because only a new generation, born in freedom, would know how to live in freedom.

Many of us who came out during the early gay liberation movement resemble the wilderness generation. For us, there were no rules about how to live in the world as translesbigay people. We have created community structures and searched for ways to live openly gay lifestyles. We have demanded that we be given the rights and privileges that are automatically given to heterosexual members of society, like the right to express ourselves in public gatherings (parades and demonstrations), freedom from hate crimes, the freedom to marry, to adopt children, and the right to serve in the armed forces. These are the desires of a wilderness generation that is attempting to gain society's acceptance. While these struggles are far from over, we have seen enormous changes over the past three decades. Now, a new generation is making different kinds of demands. More comfortable with their status in society, they are looking towards a world where our rights are not in question, where we do not have to excuse or explain our differences, where we experience sexual freedom. They are less willing to tolerate societal condemnation, and less afraid of being open about their sexuality. They are also more willing to define themselves as queer rather than lesbian, gay, bisexual or transgender. For some of the wilderness generation, the term queer often has negative associations. They are not comfortable using a term in self-reference that has been used by those who have oppressed them. This may be because for the wilderness generation it is not easy to forget the problems of the past, or the very oppressive ways in which gay people were treated in most societies prior to the movement for gay liberation in the 1970s. The term queer resonates differently for people who lived through a time when everyone was hiding and when being labelled queer meant something much more threatening than the current generation could imagine.

The ultimate lesson of the wilderness generation in Exodus is to remember that for each generation the struggle is different. As the wilderness generation has made many openings for translesbigay people, we live with the awareness of a time when being gay meant being happy, homosexuality was a psychiatric disorder, Aids did not exist, and the only gay characters in the media were either observable only through codes to other gay people, or evil characters who needed to be punished or fixed. The new generation did not know that world, and therefore is free in a way that the wilderness generation is not free. In less than forty years, the landscape of translesbigay life has changed dramatically. The new generation is able to envision worlds that are closed to the wilderness generation, and they will determine what translesbigay life will be like in the future, when we hope they will arrive in the promised land.

The Moment at Sinai

The book of Exodus tells the story of the moment at Sinai when the people were asked, even in the face of their rebellions and struggles, to accept the covenant with God and the laws that Moses was promulgating as God's messenger. In that moment, the people make a peculiar statement of assent. They say, literally, *'na'aseh v'nishmah'*, we will do and we will hear (24.7). Of course, by common sense the word order should be reversed; they must hear before they do. Translators have usually responded to this problem by suggesting that they were making some form of emphatic assent, 'we will faithfully do'. But biblical scholar Avivah Zornberg (2001: 308) interprets the phrase differently. We will do and then hear means we are open beyond simply observing the laws to new dimensions of understanding and continued growth. This interpretation leaves room for ever changing interpretations and ways of looking at and doing Torah.

This is a very important dimension for a gay understanding of this text. Translesbigay religious people need to assume that ancient traditions and laws are continually unfolding, and that we need always to be open to new possibilities. We are not limited by the way the law is written at a particular moment, but are aware that things are always evolving and changing. The moment at Sinai provides a blueprint for how we are to deal with future possibilities, and keeps us mindful that while we won't know in advance what they are, we must remain open and ready to listen.

There is also a translesbigay perspective on the meaning of covenant. Because our life commitments to one another are not sanctioned by law, we must take on the responsibility of making binding connections without societal sanction. Although that is burdensome, it also gives us a perspective on making covenants with one another that others may take for granted because their covenants have the weight of law. For translesbigay people to make commitments, we must stay more conscious of the power of the bond that we make, and the echo of the experience of the covenant at Sinai, to become a holy people, is ever present to us.

God and Moses

These themes are very powerful dimensions for a gay approach to the book of Exodus. But can we also find a gay sensibility in the personalities portrayed in the text? The main characters in Exodus are Moses and God. They clearly have a very special relationship. While it has been analysed as a father–son relationship with Oedipal dimensions – see Ilona Rashkow (2000) – there is evidence in the text to support a reading of the relationship as homoerotic.

Avivah Zornberg makes reference to Moses' 'infertile marriage to God' (2001: 256, 357) and marriage is indeed an apt metaphor for their connection. The courtship begins when God reveals himself[4] to Moses in the astonishing scene in the desert at the Burning Bush (3.2). In this moment, we might also envision God as 'coming out', revealing himself as the same God of the ancestors of the Hebrew people, the God of the patriarchs of the Genesis narrative, Abraham, Isaac and Jacob (and, as we would add today, the God of their mates, Sarah, Rebekah, Rachel and Leah). But Moses wants more; he wants God not only to identify as the God of his ancestors. Moses wants God to really 'come out' and tell Moses his name. In this moment God coyly suggests that he is 'Ehyeh-Asher-Ehyeh' (3.13): 'I am who I am', or possibly 'I will be what I will be'. This enigmatic presentation heightens God's mysterious and playful nature, and also allows Moses to be able to see in God whatever he wishes to see. Jewish tradition makes much of God's willingness to reveal even this aspect of his identity to Moses. Jews do not even utter the name of God, and only Moses has the privilege of this very close, personal connection. There is a deep intimacy between Moses and his God that begins in this moment of intensity at the Burning Bush.

The next section describes another encounter between Moses and God.[5] Moses leaves the desert after his first encounter with God at the Bush, and we are told that 'he' is attacked by God, who is seeking to kill him. Zipporah, according to midrash, recognizes that something is happening to Moses in a dream. The midrash suggests that God has attacked Moses, and swallowed all of him except his penis,[6] which Zipporah takes as a sign that she should circumcise her son. While Zipporah acts as the ritual circumciser, the relationship that is consecrated through the circumcision is between God and Moses, not Moses and Zipporah. After the circumcision, Zipporah places the foreskin on 'his' raglaim (this could refer to his legs or his penis, but this is also unclear in the text). Zipporah then refers to Moses as a 'bridegroom of blood'. Although there are many ways to interpret this verse, and we will examine it from a different perspective later when we look at the character of Zipporah, it is plausible to read this encounter as a metaphor of marriage between God and Moses. Moses is once again reminded of his unique relationship to God, who binds Moses to him again through the symbolism of circumcising his progeny and having the bloody foreskin placed on the location of Moses' own circumcision. As Daniel Boyarin argues, circumcision places the male Israelite in the position of the female in relation to God. Boyarin further suggests that for Jewish mystical tradition, 'revelation is an erotically charged encounter' (1992: 496). It is through circumcision that the feminized male can 'open' to

---

4 Although feminist interpretations suggest that God is best understood as beyond gender, there is also no question that throughout much of Jewish and Christian history, God 'the Father' was seen through masculine imagery. I retain this imagery here because the text suggests that the relationship between Moses and God is a relationship between two male characters.

5 Although Moses is never mentioned by name in this section, most commentators and scholars conclude that the 'he' that is mentioned several times in this text is most likely Moses.

6 This is suggested by the medieval biblical commentator known as Rashi.

receive the 'divine speech and vision of God'. Boyarin supports his argument with evidence from the following Rabbinic interpretation of 12.23:

> R. Yose said: Why is it written 'And the Lord will pass over the door' [lit. opening]? . . . That is, the opening of the body. And what is the opening of the body? That is the circumcision. (1992: 496)

The story in the desert then can be read as a continuation of the experience at the Burning Bush, where intimate contact between God and Moses takes place that begins their special, and erotically charged, relationship with one another. The bloody bridegroom episode completes the revelation at the Bush. Moses is ready to receive God as his lover.

The intimate relationship between God and Moses continues throughout the book of Exodus. Moses takes God's 'rod' (4.19), using it as his main weapon in his encounters with Pharaoh (7.8ff.), in fighting against Amalek (17.8), and to provide water for the complaining Israelites (17.5). Ilona Rashkow suggests that the rod/snake, a 'time honoured phallic symbol', represents the authority of the male God. She then concludes that 'the lure for Moses is affiliation with the father/God and the power inherent in his rod, the superiority of masculine identity and masculine prerogatives (2000: 72). But the 'lure' for Moses could be read not as Oedipal but as erotic; holding God's rod is symbolic of Moses' sexual relationship with this powerful male deity.

God cares for Moses, and shows himself to Moses in a variety of ways, spiritual and physical. The point of their greatest intimacy comes in chapter 33, when Moses needs reassurance from God who is disturbed by the people's rebellion in building the golden calf. Here God is said to speak to Moses face to face, 'as one man speaks to another' (33.11). Moses asks for God to reveal his presence to Moses again, and while God refuses to show Moses his face, he agrees to allow him to stand in a cleft of a rock so that when God passes by Moses is allowed to see God's back (33.18). The people see the 'afterglow' of the connection between God and Moses, as he comes down from the mountain with the 'skin of his face radiant' (34.29).[7] Moses' glow is so intense that he wears a veil after his encounters with God (34.33). In Jewish tradition, Moses is the only individual who is described as having been kissed by God, who intimately conversed with God, who was called by God to have this special relationship.

Although Moses is married, and therefore bisexual, we learn little about his wife or his personal relationships with women, and Mosaic law tends to ignore women or put them in a second-class role. For example, although God asks Moses simply to tell the people to prepare for the event at Sinai, it is Moses who adds the detail, 'Do not go near a woman' (19.15). According to Rabbinic legend, he is also reluctant to accept the women's mirrors that they donate for the building of the tabernacle (Frankel 1996: 143). And when his

---

7 The mistranslation of this phrase resulted in the common assumption that Jews have horns, immortalized forever by Michelangelo, whose statue of Moses does have phallic-looking horns protruding from his head; another way of reading Moses' radiant glow.

wife, Zipporah, returns to him, he turns to greet her father, Jethro, and not Zipporah (18.6). And he sends her back to Midian rather than keep her with him on the journey through the wilderness. All human relationships, but particularly those with women, were secondary to the love that existed between Moses and God. The exclusive 'male bonding' in this relationship, the love and intimacy, are indeed a model of the male homoerotic that so often distresses women who wish a similar intimacy with God.

Although God is seen as the masculine partner and Moses the feminine in my interpretation, Ronald Boer's fanciful essay 'Yahweh as top: a lost targum' reads the love between God and Moses differently. In this fantasy, Moses is no longer the feminine, submissive partner who begs God for attention, opens his orifice, and clings to God's rod. Rather, Boer imagines Yahweh as a typical queen who is serving tea elegantly, as Moses, the manly partner, smoking a cigar, is 'dying for a look beneath these furs that Yahweh insist on wearing on this unbearably hot mountain' (2001: 78). Boer's further 'evidence' for God's queenly nature is how much fascination God shows (six chapters in Exodus) with the details of making the tabernacle and the priestly vestments that Aaron will wear (2001: 75–8).[8]

Aaron and Bezalel: The Priestly Tradition and the Tabernacle

Boer suggests that the chapters in the book of Exodus that provide descriptions of the building of the tabernacle and the vesting of the priests (25–31) bear a gay sensibility in their amazing attention to the details of creating a beautiful and richly embellished space. God requests that the people supply magnificent materials for his dwelling place:

> Tell the Israelite people to bring me gifts . . . gold, silver and copper; blue purple, and crimson yarns, fine linen, goats' hair; tanned rams' skins, dolphin skins, and acacia wood; oil for lighting, spice for the anointing oil and fine aromatic incense; lapis lazuli . . . (25.1–6)

The dazzling colourful jewellery and luxurious outfits for the priests mirror gay cultural focus on aesthetic beauty and adornment as well, as this description of the hem of the priest's tunic attests: 'On its hem make pomegranates of blue, purple and crimson yarn, all around the hem, with bells of gold between them round about' (28.33). Advertisers have realized the power of appealing to the gay market through careful attention to design in clothing and décor. The descriptions in Exodus are powerful examples of how these concerns can in fact be connected to the holy. What Aaron and his descendants wore, and the tabernacle that Bezalel designed, are described with the utmost sense of the value of creating beautiful things to give honour to God. Perhaps we can gain

---

8 Ironically, Daniel Boyarin suggests that Freud's efforts to make Moses 'manly and aggressive' in *Moses and Monotheism* is an attempt to refute European notions of 'feminine Jewish [male] passivity, coded as homosexual and experienced as shameful' (1996: 185).

some insight into the sartorial splendour of gay pride parades by finding their roots in the sensibility that built the tabernacle.

The priestly vestments are very ornate, and served as models for the vestments worn by the Pope and other clergy to this day. The wonderfully ornate frocks and tunics and turbans that are described in chapter 28 of Exodus remind us that clothing is an important marker of identity, and what we do when we dress in fabulous clothing may be enhancing 'dignity and adornment' (28.40) as it was for the ancient priests. The lesson taught by priests of old may parallel the lesson taught by those interested in drag and costume today.

Miriam, Zipporah and the Midwives

While the argument for Moses' 'gayness' is made easily, women in the book of Exodus are often seen only as accessories to Moses, not unlike the women today who befriend and support gay men. All the women characters are connected to Moses and their role is to help the great hero. We meet the host of women who saved Moses at birth: his mother, Pharaoh's daughter, the midwives (Shifrah and Puah); his wife Zipporah who saves him through the circumcision, and his sister Miriam who plays a subordinate role to him throughout the text.

Although religious feminists recognize Exodus as a text that subordinates women, they have found ways to read between the lines of the text to provide a feminist analysis. So the midwives, Shifrah and Puah, become important trickster figures as they convince Pharaoh that they cannot stop the Israelite women from giving birth and thus save the male children who were supposed to have been killed, Zipporah's role as circumciser is highlighted, and Miriam becomes a leader in her own right. They often use midrash to accomplish this goal.

A midrash is an exegetical story that helps us read between the lines of the biblical text in imaginative ways, gives us insight into the biblical characters, or resolves the meaning of an unclear passage. While the imaginings of midrash are not meant to provide the actual details of what happened to our ancestors, we are given licence to read our own sensibilities back into the text to make it speak to each generation that is in relationship with the text.[9] This is also a way to create translesbigay readings.

We are told nothing about the lives of the midwives Shifrah and Puah. We do not even know if they were Hebrew or Egyptian (Exum 1983). But they are described as a team,[10] and in our imaginations we could envision them as lovers as well as collaborators. Their act of subverting Pharaoh's rule is in

9 Midrash is a very powerful exegetical tool that has been used throughout Jewish history to explain unclear passages in the text, or to supply readings that help the contemporary reader relate better to the stories they are reading. Many Jews assume that Abraham's father owned a store where he sold idols, and that Abraham, when he apprehended the existence of one God, went into his father's store and smashed the idols. The story exists in midrashic tradition, but, of course, cannot be found in the biblical text. For further explanation, see Melvin J. Glatt (1986).

10 See Exum (1983 n.13), on the various theories about why there were two midwives mentioned.

keeping with the theme of rebellion that is part of what it means to live as a lesbian. We could imagine that their own difference made them understand the importance of keeping alive others who, like themselves, were different. They use the idea that the Hebrew women were different – that they gave birth so fast the midwives couldn't catch the babies at birth – to trick Pharaoh into believing that they couldn't carry out their task. That Pharaoh believes the Hebrews were so different from the Egyptians is an important point in the story, as it reveals the foolishness of those who believe what they hear about people who are not like themselves.[11] Whether Hebrew or Egyptian, Shifrah and Puah are strong, clever, independent women who valued human life and were willing to put their lives on the line to save the lives of those they were committed to bringing into the world.

The midwives were not the only women who are coupled in Exodus. Like Ruth and Naomi, Moses' mother Yocheved and the daughter of Pharaoh work together to raise a child as biological and adoptive mothers. Yocheved both schemes to save Moses, and becomes his wet nurse so that he can be nurtured. Pharaoh's nameless daughter adopts and raises him, and makes sure that he survives. Working together in this way is a wonderful paradigm of the special ways women can connect.[12]

Miriam does not have a love relationship in the biblical text. While Miriam figures prominently in later narratives, in Exodus she is the 'prophet', an independent woman who led the women in song at the sea. This is an image that can be valuable in weaving lesbian elements into the text. After the Israelites cross the sea to freedom, Moses leads the group in a song of praise to God. A fragment of text recalls that when Moses and the Israelite men were finished with their song, 'Then Miriam the prophetess, Aaron's sister, took a timbrel in her hand, and all the women went out after her in dance with timbrels' (15.20). Alice Bach (1994, 2000) imagines that Miriam's brief song has strong parallels to a text by Sappho that emphasizes peacemaking and an anti-militarism resulting from a woman's joy at the destruction not of men but of the 'dominant male culture exemplified and encoded in the language of warfare' (2000: 151).

There are even arguments to suggest that Miriam's song came first, and the song of the men is a response to the women's song, rather than the way it appears in the text we have today (Jantzen 1992). Feminist analysis emphasizes Miriam's strong independent leadership. Carol Meyers (1994a) finds archaeological evidence to support the idea that women were the drummers and musicians in ancient Near Eastern cultures. These ideas remind us that men and women in this sex-segregated society lived separate lives. While the

---

11 Renita Weems (1992) also argues for the importance of the midwives in this story, and sees in it a challenge to the Egyptian assumption of superiority over the Hebrews because they are different. However, Weems concludes that by ending the story with the Hebrew triumph over the Egyptians, difference is only inverted and not subverted as a concept in itself. The implication here is that difference carries with it the assumption of superiority of one group over another. I would argue that difference can also allow for both groups to be understood as valuable.

12 The comparison between the child-rearing of Ruth and Naomi and Yocheved and Pharaoh's daughter is the insight of Athalya Brenner (1986).

women's sphere was marked by a lack of power and stature, it was also a place where women were free to connect to, and to express different kinds of love for, one another. We should remember that lesbian relationships are not interdicted (or even mentioned) in the Hebrew Bible at all. Some might argue this is because these relationships didn't happen. But others suggest that because what women did with one another was not seen as sex (defined as activities that require penile penetration), then what women did together didn't matter to the larger society and was therefore acceptable. Again, using our imaginations, we can envision the lesbian energy of Miriam's song and dance with the women.

Perhaps the most enigmatic text in the entire book of Exodus (and maybe in the entire Hebrew Bible) involves Zipporah. It is the passage in Exodus 4.24–6, discussed above in relation to Moses' circumcision and known as 'the bridegroom of blood' episode. It is impossible to discern what these lines actually mean, because, apart from the strangeness of the narrative, we don't even really know who the actors are or what some of the phrases, like bridegroom of blood, actually meant. But the passage is open to different translesbigay readings.

Somewhere along the route back to rejoin the Israelites in Egypt, Moses and Zipporah stop to rest at a night encampment. Then, we are told, 'God encountered him and sought to kill him'. We do not know who 'him' is; it could be Moses, or it could be one of his sons. Zipporah then takes a flint and cuts off someone's (Moses' or their son Gershom's) foreskin, and touched his (probably Moses') *raglaim* (either legs or penis) with it, and she says, 'You are a bridegroom of blood to me.' Finally, the text tells us, 'he let him alone' and Zipporah added, 'a bridegroom of blood because of the circumcision'. Commentators are baffled by this text, and it has been widely discussed.[13] Some believe this to be an explanation of the strange term 'bridegroom of blood' that occurs only here in the text of the Hebrew Bible. Others think it's meant to explain why the Hebrews chose child circumcision over the more common circumcision at puberty. Others just suggest that the story is strange and inexplicable; an interpolation of an old Midianite tradition.

Ray Shankman, however, gives us some insight into the role Zipporah plays here, and his comments move us towards a translesbigay interpretation. To Shankman, the important element in this story is that Zipporah acts to save Moses' life by becoming the ritual circumciser. She is 'God's handmaiden, the creative catalyst, the agent instrumental in creating the conditions that turn Moses from apparent death to potential life' (1991: 173). Shankman concludes that this act puts Zipporah in the same place as other biblical women; she is a 'helpmate'. But in a translesbigay interpretation of this text, Zipporah is more than that. She has inverted the roles of man and woman. Zipporah takes charge. She is the active partner, and she performs a circumcision (a role that is almost exclusively performed by men). While in a traditional Jewish wedding it is the man who claims the woman as bride, in this instance it is Zipporah who speaks, claiming Moses as a bridegroom, and her words define

13 See Seth Kunin (1996), Julian Morgenstern (1963), Pamela Tamarkin Reis (1991) and Ray Shankman (1991).

the situation. In other words, Zipporah inverts the usual roles of men and women, and in this moment, she is the man and Moses the woman. This unusual text opens possibilities for a new way to approach transgender issues in the Hebrew Bible.

Do Not Oppress the Stranger, for You Were Strangers in the Land of Egypt

The stories and themes of the book of Exodus provide wonderful translesbigay readings, but the heart of the book is the commandments that form the basis of all of Jewish and Christian ethical tradition. The Ten Commandments, and many of the commandments that follow, called the Covenant Code, provide the road map for how we live, and give us a deep understanding of the rules that govern our society and that demand that we create a world based on justice, respect and compassion. The belief in one God, the institution of the Sabbath to provide rest from labour, the creation of right relations between human beings, the respect for others' possessions, and a commitment to honest living provide the basis for a humane society. Translesbigay people are committed to living in a just society that respects these rules.

Yet, in some cases, individual commandments might become the cause for concern. What does it mean, for example, to honour your father and mother (20.12) if they have disowned you because of your sexual orientation? It is necessary for us to look at this commandment in a different light if our parents fail to honour who we are. In Jewish teaching, we are told that we don't have to honour our parents' wishes if they wish us to go against Jewish law. We might also argue that we cannot honour our parents if they cannot honour who we are. Yet the commandment remains to remind us that although our parents may fail to respect who we are, we still need to stay open to the possibility that they can change their minds and hearts, and we must endeavour to the best of our ability to honour their struggle.

Perhaps the most important commandment from the translesbigay perspective is: 'You shall not oppress the stranger, for you know the feelings of the stranger, having yourself been strangers in the land of Egypt' (23.9 and also 22.20). God's command that the people of Israel remember what it felt like to be a stranger and to treat others well on account of that memory brings a powerful message to support the struggle for gay liberation. As Nancy Fuchs-Kreimer suggests, this commandment requires all of us to 'be open to people, ideas and experiences that seem strange' (2000: 150). We must allow ourselves to consider the possibilities that people who are different from us in their manners, customs and ideas deserve to be listened to and encountered.

This commandment refers directly to the experience of the Israelites in Egypt, but it also resonates with Moses' personal experience as an Israelite being raised as an Egyptian, when he went into exile and lived as a stranger in Midian. Moses experienced being an outsider so much that Cheryl Kirk-Duggan asks: 'Does Moses ever feel that he belongs?' (1994: 90). It is not a coincidence that Moses named their son Gershom, which means 'I was a stranger there'. When Moses gives him his name, he adds, 'I have been a stranger in a foreign land' (2.22). And Gershom and Zipporah will also live for a time as strangers among the Hebrew people.

For Jewish, Christian and Muslim readers of the text, this theme of openness to strangers is a reminder that religious communities should work to make sure that translesbigay people do not feel like Gershom, like strangers there. Religious institutions must find ways to incorporate translesbigay people. Translesbigay people in religious communities are keenly aware of how it feels to be a stranger, especially within our own religious communities. Although many translesbigay people are passionately committed to the life of their Jewish and Christian communities, they have had to hide their identities in order to participate. Translesbigay religious people participated for years as congregants, and served religious communities as teachers, musicians and clergy without ever being able to acknowledge their sexual orientations. It is no wonder that translesbigay religious people identify so strongly with this commandment. Treated as strangers for many years, translesbigay Jews and Christians are now demanding inclusion, and beginning to make important inroads. And some Jewish and Christian communities have been welcoming. The welcome in the Jewish community has been, in part, because Jews understand, through experiences of anti-Semitism and because they have lived many times as strangers in many lands, that they must welcome gay people. Welcoming Christians also rely on this verse from Exodus and the teachings of Jesus who emphasized the importance of welcoming strangers and identified with the experience of being a stranger.

For translesbigay readers, the commandment is a caution that we, too, when in positions of power, should not oppress others who are different from us. We cannot always assume that because we have been victimized for our sexual and gender identities that we are always the victims, or the only group that has experienced oppression. We are often in positions where others are strangers in our midst, particularly in gatherings that are predominantly translesbigay, but also in our work lives and even in our religious communities. This commandment is also important for us to observe and to do.

The book of Exodus can open us up to new ways of looking at ourselves in the context of a translesbigay community: as people who came out of hiding to liberation, who belong to or have succeeded a wilderness generation, who have a responsibility both to obey the law and to rebel. We are people who can take courage or comfort from startling connections with Moses and Miriam, Zipporah and Bezalel, Shifrah and Puah. Exodus gives us hope and direction in carving out a unique position for translesbigay people in our world today.

Leviticus

DAVID TABB STEWART

Why Bother with Leviticus? An Introduction

Stuart Burdick, in a letter to the editor of *Bible Review*, asserts under the title, 'Why take Leviticus seriously': 'Leviticus is the work of an ignorant, superstitious author' (2001: 4). The out-of-hand rejection of the book is not a surprise in either the letter-to-the-editor or email wars about the Bible and homosexuality – the dismissal of Leviticus is a common redoubt – and gains power from a common reader response – 'It's dense and boring.' So let me begin with a very queer sentiment: it is my favourite biblical book. But, let me quickly add a disclaimer. I *cannot* 'redeem' Leviticus for queerdom. I *can* report on my reading of the text. The queer reader may find some of these things 'good news' or, perhaps, 'useful', or even artistically pleasing; some neutral in their import; and some 'bad news'.

Arguably, Leviticus is the most important book in the Hebrew Bible – it is the 'lively centre' of the Torah, or Pentateuch, a kind of canon within a canon – and at *its* centre one finds two versions of the 'Golden Rule' (Lev. 19.18, 33–4). It should not be a surprise that within the Christian Second Testament Jesus makes use of both, citing one and using the second to undergird his parable of the Good Samaritan. Nor should it be a surprise that the apostolic decree in Acts 15, rationalizing Gentile participation in the nascent Church, draws its justifications from Leviticus 17–18, nor that Paul would extensively cite the book in Romans, or that the Jacobean tradition would make liberal use of Leviticus in the Epistle of James. Leviticus itself also makes complex use of Genesis and Exodus; it is reused by Deuteronomy and the prophets Habakkuk and Ezekiel. For these intertextual reasons, if no other, the text cannot automatically be dismissed as irrelevant to Bible readers.

Leviticus, of course, is a construction, a one scroll-length section of the Torah. Its story is part of a larger narrative that runs from Exodus 25.1 to Numbers 10.10 (Hartley 1992: xxx). This longer section is mostly assigned to a hypothetical author or authorial school, 'P', for the 'priestly source', but like a novel, it seems to absorb everything in the author's mind. It contains legal insets from other 'sources', such as at Exodus 34.10–26 (from the Jahwist source or 'J'); building and furniture designs; rituals; and miracle stories about the Ark of the Covenant. The result was edited by 'H', the putative author(s) of the Holiness Code (Lev. 17–26; for H as editor of P, cf. Milgrom 1991; Knohl 1995), who added more legal material, tiny fragments of poetic language, and a long song of blessing and cursing (Lev. 26). Any coherence of worldview, then, is achieved in its redacting, or editing. As the redacted work contains multiple voices (and some that might counter the editor's apparent agenda), one should not automatically assume that the views of P are precisely the same as those in the rest of the Hebrew Bible (e.g. the Deuteronomist, or the Jahwist, or any of the later prophets). P and editor H do their own thing. The reader will find differences of nuance and substance.

One can see the work of editors setting boundaries and stitching texts together in how, for instance, Leviticus is set off from Numbers by both the summative statement, 'These are the commandments that the LORD gave Moses for the Israelite people on Mount Sinai' (Lev. 27.34),[1] and the immediately following calendar notice, 'On the first day of the second month, in the second year' (Num. 1.1); or in how a 'ring structure' ties together the proleptic Exodus 40.36–8 with its repetition and expansion at Numbers 9.15–23, bracketing the intervening material of Leviticus 1.1–Numbers 9.14. Likewise, when Yahweh 'called to Moses' at Exodus 24.16, the text uses the same verb, *vayiqra*, as in Leviticus 1.1 – the verb that provides the Hebrew title for Leviticus. But the place from which God calls out changes: from 'the midst of the cloud' on Mount Sinai at Exodus 24.15–18, to 'from the Tent of Meeting' at the start of Leviticus. These two notices enclose the instructions for (and report of) building the cult equipment and sanctuary (Ex. 25–31; 35–40), which in turn encloses the events incident to the golden calf (Ex. 32–4). This second ring structure, setting off the end of Exodus, interlocks with the one ring surrounding Leviticus and the first part of Numbers forming a 'chain link', a common literary trope in Priestly literature (Rendtorff 1996; Stewart 2000). The transfer of the voice and presence of God from the mountain to the ark and its sanctuary provides the unifying 'action' for this long narrative section.

Within the narrative section of Exodus 25.1 to Numbers 10.10 Moses hears the proclamation of the Name in the great theophany of Exodus 34: 'a God compassionate and gracious, slow to anger, abounding in kindness and faithfulness' (v. 6). The routinization of Yahweh as Israel's deity takes shape at the 'Tent of Meeting'. Exodus 33.7–11 grants a proleptic view of the pitching of the tent and Moses' habitual resort to it. Exodus ends and Leviticus begins with a paired set of miracle stories about this tent and its ark, a kind of cult pedestal for the image of divinity. The 'cloud' covers the tent; the divine presence takes residence (Ex. 40.34–8), and Yahweh speaks to Moses out of it (Lev. 1.1). The narrative skein, though very thin in Leviticus itself – and mostly amounting to incipits ('The LORD spoke to Moses, saying' as at 4.1) – is filled out with two additional miracle stories. At the inauguration of the *cultus*, or complex of religious rites, something like a horizontal lightning bolt shoots out from the ark and consumes the inaugural sacrifice (Lev. 9.23–4) and then, in turn, consumes Aaron's sons Nadab and Abihu for making ritual errors that spoil the performance (Lev. 10.1–2). Brief accounts of the stoning of a blasphemer (Lev. 24), the

---

1 All biblical citations in this essay, unless otherwise noted, follow the versification scheme of the Hebrew Bible (sometimes slightly different from Catholic and Protestant English Bibles) and quote the New JPS translation: *Tanakh: A New Translation of the Holy Scriptures According to the Traditional Hebrew Text* (Philadelphia: Jewish Publication Society, 1985).

taking of a census (Num. 1.2), the swapping of the firstborn Israelites owed to God for an offering of money (Num. 3), and the offering of the chieftains on the day Moses finished setting up the tent (Num. 7.1–3), carry the narrative forward.

In a kind of reprise of Leviticus 1.1, we learn that Yahweh's voice actually comes from the empty space just above the ark between the two ornamental cherubim (Num. 7.89). Among Israel's competitors, a cult image might normally have been set in such a spot. But this invisible 'image' of Yahweh seems to be the exact reversal of the androgynous deity of P's account in Genesis 1.27, where man and woman together reflect the image of God. Here the Priestly writer gives no image at all, neither male nor female. The Israelites have exactly fulfilled the command of Leviticus 26.1 not to set up a carved image. God's 'body' becomes a 'cloud' in the imagination. After this, and after the second Passover in the wilderness of Sinai, they renew their long-halted journey as the cloud lifts from the tent (Num. 10.11).

What timeframe does the book of Leviticus cover? 'P' regularly gives chronological notice of its key events. The narrative time of the book must cover about one month: the 'Tent of Meeting' was set up on New Year's Day of the second year after the Exodus (Ex. 40.2, 17); the book of Numbers signals that it begins on the first day of the second month (Num. 1.1). In between seven days are given to the priestly ordination. On the eighth day, these priests inaugurate the *cultus* (Lev. 9.1). That same day Nadab and Abihu die. Leviticus 16.1 gives notice that Yahweh speaks to Moses *after* this event. The Passover quickly follows on day 14 (as recalled by Num. 9.2). The complex of feasts – Passover and Matsoth – ends on the twenty-first day (Lev. 23.5–8). If not a flashback, Moses would then ascend Mount Sinai once again during the final week of the month (Lev. 25.1).

Mary Douglas, known for her work on the Purity Laws in Leviticus (1992), attends to the book's macrostructure. At this level the book reveals a certain cold beauty, perhaps analogous to that of the Crystalline Entity in *Star Trek*. Douglas (1993: 11) argues that Leviticus reflects a kind of ring structure similar to that found in Hesiod. The ring envisions Leviticus as two books – a P-volume (Leviticus 1–16) and an H-volume (Leviticus 17–27). An editor, the Holiness Code Redactor, artfully crafted the whole: Leviticus 17 bridges the two parts; Leviticus 27 latches the end to the beginning. Douglas thus reads the book as a self-standing unity.

In the mind's eye, one can see Leviticus 19, the chapter with two versions of the 'Golden Rule', as a pivot for the whole, nested between two chapters of sexual laws (Lev. 18, 20). Imagine the sculpted frieze above a rank of pillars at the front of a Greek temple. This 'pedimental structure', *per* Mary Douglas's observation of an organizational trope in Herodotus (1999: 60, 237), frames a central panel – like a triptych, or the metaphor I prefer, sets and holds the jewel of the ring. Something similar happens with Leviticus 26 – the blessings and cursings: it is set off by the rules concerning Yahweh's lands and persons in Leviticus 25 and 27. The two jewels in H and their settings – or the two side panels facing a central frieze – balance one another.

Indeed, there is a careful balance of both halves of the book (Lev. 1–16; 17–27): Leviticus 16's Day of Atonement offsets Leviticus 23's sacred times and Day of

Atonement; Leviticus 11–15 and Leviticus 21–2 focus on blemishes and impurities. Leviticus 10 reveals a defilement of the Holy Place; Leviticus 24 focuses on a defilement of the Name. Leviticus 27 latches to Leviticus 1 through the notion of 'things' belonging to Yahweh. One can observe a sort of recapitulation of this whole balanced ring structure within Leviticus 19 itself – again two halves of the chapter held together by verses balancing each other in each part (e.g. the two 'Golden Rules', vv. 18 and 33–4), creating multiple interlocking ring structures.

Such an elegant macrostructure in itself meets some of the questions critics have asked about the odd deployment of topics in the book: How does the blasphemer story in chapter 24, which seems so misplaced, fit here? What purpose do the repetitions of Leviticus 18 and 20 serve? Why does the book have so many fault lines; why is it so disjunctive? The 'macrostructure' offers a possible solution to such riddles.

Forbidden Sex: A Model from Leviticus

It is not only the alleged texts of terror, Leviticus 18.22 and 20.13, that should interest queers and (in)sensitive straights alike, but also the possibility of erasing the homosexual/heterosexual binary that shapes our early twenty-first-century thinking about sexuality in the West. As Ken Stone argues, we might be 'able to allow the biblical text to "make its claims" without excessive interference from modern "interpretative categories"' (2001a: 24). If we do this, we might actually find that the sexual system the text reluctantly yields is wholly different from our sexual landscape; that it contains a notion of multiple genders or gender-continuum; that it 'plays' with gender; that it codes menstrual blood in a surprising way; that it is silent about sex between women but not about women initiating sex; that its interest in seminal emissions does not restrict masturbation; and that the active/passive binarism is mostly absent, though popularly read into the texts by queer exegetes. We might then see how the rabbis, the Second Testament writers, and church fathers and mothers, (mis)read the Bible, and be able to sketch a history of biblical sexuality and its misprision.

If one follows Sedgwick's observations about the dimensions of 'genital activity', one could focus on something other than the 'gender of object choice' to limn out a sexual landscape (1990: 8). Indeed, one might simply look at object choice, or the socio-economic class of subjects, to discover the territories of sexuality. The categories of sexual subject in Leviticus include the Israelite man and woman (18.20, 23), the resident alien (18.26), priest (21.7–8), priest's daughter (21.9) and the high priest (21.13–14). Sexual objects include 'any near kin' (18.6), 'your fellow countryman's wife' (18.20), the 'menstruant' (18.19) and the 'beast', or better, 'quadruped' (18.23). Leviticus 19.20–2 adds the female slave who is 'designated', though not quite fully betrothed or yet redeemed; Leviticus 21.7 delineates women unavailable as wives to priests – women raped (or perhaps former prostitutes) and divorcees – and Leviticus 21.14 adds the widow to the list for high priests and designates 'virgins of his own kin' as the only women available to him.

Implicit here are two systems: one of social class; and one of a hierarchy of beings. The social classes are non-Israelites, (female) slaves, resident aliens, citizen Israelites, priests and their families, and the high priest. If you organize these in concentric circles, the high priests are at the centre with the most restricted group of sexual objects (virgins from the same clan); priests next who may marry widely, even women who are not of the priestly line as long as they have not been raped or divorced; Israelites third, who may marry any woman no matter her sexual history, along with resident aliens who are to be treated as if they were citizens (but of course are not); slaves, who when objects of pre-marital 'adultery' are not condemned to death, nor their lovers executed; and the residual set, non-Israelites. Already there is a surprise. There is a structure that reflects some of the social classes of the ancient Near East. But more, *these laws, within their context, apply only to Israelites and aliens residing in the Land – the Land of Israel* (Lev. 18.27). Milgrom (1993; 1994; 2000) makes much of this. Though he understands Leviticus 18.22 as a prohibition of homosexuality, he argues that it should function as a ban *only* in Israel (and nowhere else, except perhaps in the Palestinian territories). His reading has the virtue of taking the text and its Sinaitic frame seriously. Of course the queer might ask: What are queer Israelis, Palestinians and other residents there to do?

Turning to the objects of desire, a different picture emerges, one of a hierarchy of beings similar to that of Psalm 8.4–9: *'elohim* or 'numinal beings' at the crown; *'enosh* and *bene-'adam* or 'humanity' in the middle; *behamot* or 'beasts' of various sorts at the foot. The forbidden sexual relations of Leviticus 18 can then be laid over this framework as in Figure 1.

Reading the vertical axis of the figure, sexual relations between humans and numinal beings (e.g 'sons of God (*bene-'elohim*) with daughters of men' (Gen. 6.1–4) or something metaphorical such as 'seed passed to Molekh' (Lev. 18.21)) are forbidden. Likewise, the sexual violation of beasts (specifically quadrupeds) by man or woman is disallowed (Lev. 18.23). On the horizontal axis there

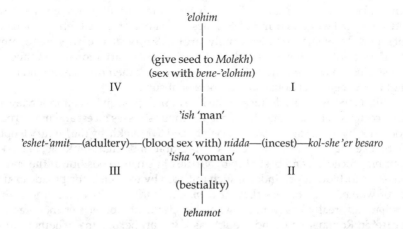

Figure 1. The hierarchy of beings and the forbidden sexual relations in Leviticus 18.

are three forbidden objects of desire: the fellow citizen's wife (*'eshet-'amit*, Lev. 18.20); the menstruant, *not* excluding the menstruating wife (Lev. 18.19); and various relatives, both consanguine (*kol-she'er besaro*, Lev. 18.6–10, 12–14) and distaff (18.11, 15–16), but not restricted to gender opposites. As I'll argue, men 'incesting' male relatives are also in view (18.6, 14, 22). The residual object of desire is a woman, or a man, or an intersexed person not otherwise restricted by the demands of sacerdotal class. Put another way, fornication, or sexual relations between the unmarried, is not specifically prohibited *here*; neither is prostitution, nor lesbian relations, nor relations with those who are intersexed, nor non-incestuous relations between men. This is an argument from silence, of course. But to say these relations *are* forbidden is also an argument from silence. A biblical ethicist must look to other texts, or reason with the texts, to expand the list of things one cannot do.

The quadrants of Figure 1 suggest another set of metaphorical links between the two axes. Folklore studies of Genesis imagine Eve as a mother-goddess – her hinted relations with Cain would represent an incestuous hierogamy (sex between divine beings and humans); (quadrant I; Kikawada 1972; Wyatt 1986; 1995). Freud (1946) and the ethnographers he read, overlay the realm of totemic animals with incest (quadrant II). Nathan's parable (1 Sam. 12.1–12) links the world of animals and human adultery (quadrant III). Idolatry, in the prophets, is spoken of as adultery (quadrant IV). The H-writers give hints that they too can imagine the metaphor of quadrant II. Bestiality (18.23) and daughter-in-law incest (20.12) are linked by the rare word *tebel*, 'confusion'. With regard to the metaphor implied by quadrant IV, Leviticus 18.20–1 links two commands about adultery and a sacrifice to the god Molekh. The writers tease the reader here with the word 'seed' in two senses, 'sperm' and 'offspring'. Whether or not Figure 1 'truly' represents the sexual system of Leviticus, who can say? It is a hypothetical model, a construct, a heuristic device.

The two hierarchical sexualities, bestiality and hierogamy, seem far afield from modern, urban experience and imagination. Hence they both receive scant attention from commentators and exegetes. The former, according to Kinsey, Pomeroy and Martin, is relatively common with rural teenage boys and stockyard workers (1 in 14 US males report one or more lifetime contacts, but reports by women are exceedingly rare (1948: 670–1)). The latter, hierogamy, fills the world's mythologies and has found a new incarnation in UFO abduction stories. So we must allow these ancient writers their due. Their landscape might privilege behaviours we find rare or absurd.

While Genesis casts adultery in the role of the 'great sin', a common view in other corners of the ancient Near East, Leviticus stresses incest and menstrual-blood sex, by virtue of 'air time'; 'passing seed to Molekh' by the literary tropes of 'bracketing' in the centre of its paragraph and 'chain-linking' between chapters 18 and 20; and bestiality by virtue of its trump position at the end of the list of forbidden sex. Indeed, such initiated by women is the parade example of women's sex crimes (Lev. 18.23b). One cannot help wondering if this is what Paul really has in mind when he speaks of women's crimes 'against nature' in Romans 1.26. And though, as I will argue, one male 'homosexual' behaviour is condemned – male–male incest – it is given little play, even when labelled *to'eba*, or 'abomination'. All of the forbidden acts of Leviticus 18 are called abominations in verses 27 and 29. Indeed the word is used 144 times in the Hebrew Bible and covers a number of crimes including unjust weights and measures. A fair reading of Leviticus must acknowledge that, *even if Leviticus 18.22 and 20.13 contained a general condemnation of male homosexuality, this is not the focus of chapters 18 and 20.*

In what follows, I query those texts that address the body, sex, gender and sexuality. I begin with texts that feature or address women; then those that address questions of 'hierarchy' as a form of gender, the notion of multiple genders and transgender; followed by those texts that feature men; and finally two verses that speak of those not queer. Hence, sections 1–10 of this chapter address the following passages and issues:

1 Lev. 12.1–5; 15.19–30; 18.19; 20.18 – the menstruant and birthing mother, her blood, and her sexual partners;
2 Lev. 18.23; 20.15–16 – bestiality;
3 Lev. 18.21; 20.1–6, 27 – passing seed to Molekh and whoring after spirits;
4 Lev. 18.3, 22 – a lesbian presence or absence?
5 Lev. 26.3–39 – reading lesbians into the text as singers and poets;
6 Lev. 21.16–23 – altered bodies: laws for eunuchs and transgendered;
7 Lev. 15.1–18, 31–2 – seminal emissions, wet dreams, and gonorrheic discharges;
8 Lev. 18.6, 14, 22; 20.13 – male homosexual incest;
9 Lev. 13.1–14.57; 26.15–16 – 'scale disease', 'plague', and HIV/Aids;
10 Lev. 19.33–4 – queer eye for the straight.

1. The Menstruant and Her Blood: Leviticus 12.1–5; 15.19–30; 18.19; 20.18

'As for the woman in her menstrual impurity: Do not encroach on (her) to uncover her nakedness' (Lev. 18.19, author's translation). Although H gives menses a possibly negative valence, the P-source accidentally discloses its power. A menstruant, or *niddah*, becomes 'impure' for seven days, ostensibly confining her to her tent (Lev. 15.19). But the condition has the power to subvert the male-dominated social order. Anyone who touches her is unclean until evening. Anything she lies on, or sits on, becomes unclean. Anyone who touches her bed is unclean till evening (Lev. 15.20–3). Her liminal status gives her, consequently, rest from labour, (male) touch, and conjugal 'duties'. Both the Priestly and Holiness writers constrain this power by labelling it 'impurity'. But 'the common fact of menstruation . . . challenges the social order of a male-dominated society and defines and bounds a female subgroup within the society, thereby creating a new and dangerous order' (Buckley and Gottlieb 1988: 28–9).

Treated similarly, blood associated with childbirth also pollutes. Leviticus 12 deals with the parturient, or woman who has given birth. In a passage famous for patriarchal implications, the woman who has given birth to a boy is ritually impure for a total of forty days, a period roughly contiguous with the *puerperium*, the six-week period 'during which the anatomic and physiologic changes brought about by childbirth resolve' (Stables 1999: 655). But for a girl the period is eighty days (Lev. 12.1–5). These periods represent two stages of impurity: 7 or 14 days that communicate a severe pollution (and analogized to that of the menstruant); 33 or 66 days that convey a milder pollution; followed by a sacrifice on day 41 or 81 that terminates her liminal state at evening (Wright and Jones 1992). Magonet speculates that the double period of impurity for a daughter reflects the occasional phenomenon of the 'menstruating baby' or 'false menstruation'.[2] 'Following the withdrawal of the maternal hormones' a newborn baby girl may experience vaginal bleeding, temporary breast development, and lactation. Thus the text may account for the 'equivalent of two "women", each with an actual or potential vaginal discharge'. The mother bears the ritual responsibility for the two (Magonet 1996: 151–2).[3] It is the 'potential' that really counts here. Since the 'menstruating baby' is not inevitable, such cannot be the primary rationale for the ritual cleansing required of *all* mothers who bear female children. The mother must act for her daughter in anticipation of her adult menstruation and child-bearing. One could speculate that its very markedness suggests an analogy to the eighth-day circumcision of the male child mentioned at Leviticus 12.3. Indeed, a particular woman (in another puzzling passage at Exodus 4.24–6), Zipporah ritually acts on behalf of her son (and husband), circumcising the boy. Ilana Pardes' (1992) reading of Zipporah-as-*subject* suggests the possibility of parturient-as-*subject*. The text recollects the woman-as-*mohelet* ('circumciser') when it places the parturient's ritual for a girl in symmetry with male circumcision (Lev. 12.3–5), framing them anew as rites of reproductive potential.

The power of a woman's 'pollution' (Buckley and Gottlieb 1988: 34–6) gives her a special power over her sexual partner: 'If a man lies with her and her monthly flow touches him, he will be unclean seven days' (Lev. 15.24a). Specifically, the woman's husband is *not* exempt. Consider the power of menstrual blood that is able to cut through the heterosexist vision of the 'sacredness' of marriage here and at childbirth (Lev. 12.4–5). The 'one-flesh unity', referred to by one commentator (Patrick 1985: 158), is divided episodically and recurrently. She has the power to pollute her partner for a full seven days – as long as she herself must go aside (Wright and Jones 1992: 205). Perhaps it (only) means that a priest cannot eat his sacrificial portion or enter the sanctuary (as per Lev. 22.3, 5–6), or a husband cannot eat his portion of a votive offering (Lev. 7.19–20), or that any contactee must wash and launder after sunset (Lev. 15.27) – no other consequences are specifically mentioned. But beyond any possible horror of blood, or some practical taboo from prehistoric hunter cultures to

---

2 'As the maternal hormones decline in the body's blood, a clear or white discharge can flow from the vagina during the latter part of the first week of life. Occasionally the discharge will become pink or blood tinged (false menstruation). This normal discharge should not last more than 2 or 3 days' (University of Michigan Health System 2002). The decline of oestrogen in the baby's blood seems to precipitate this vaginal flow somewhere 'between 3 and 10 days after birth' (Children's Hospital St Louis 2003). For the dazzling endocrinal physiology of the perinatal period see Tulchinsky and Little (1994: 423–4); Siler-Khodr (1992: 75); and Stables (1999: 655–61). For a technical discussion of menstrual disorders, see Lott (1998: 69–76).

3 Cf. Macht (1933) for the history of interpretation.

prevent a scent; beyond the opportunity to manipulate everyday encounters, this ability to remove her male partner from at least some (and possibly all) social intercourse holds a figurative power to castrate.

H offers a more extreme penalty for menstrual intercourse than the priestly source above. 'If a man lies with a menstruous woman and uncovers her naked-ness [i.e. has sexual relations with her], he has exposed her source, and she also has uncovered the source of her blood. Both of them must be cut off from their people' (Lev. 20.18, author's translation). Whereas, the male partner must wash and wait (Lev. 15 in the 'P'-stratum), here both participants are 'cut off'. This *karet*-penalty is not a death-penalty precisely – it implies the extinction of the individuals and their family branch: their progeny will die, or they will have no children, and so their name will disappear (Wold 1977; Milgrom 1991: 424). The queer critic might then wonder whether the widespread breaking of this command by heterosexual couples threatens the sanctity of the 'institution of marriage', biblically speaking. On the other hand, a lesbian couple, as Sarah Schulman observes in *People in Trouble*, might practise safer sex by avoiding blood exchange from sexual relations during menstruation (1991: 74, 181). The imagined woman of Leviticus 20 thus has a subjectivity of sorts. She inverts the actions of Rachel who covers her bleeding (Gen. 31.35). This text presumes the menstruant's complicity and consent in exposing her pudenda.[4]

I cannot but feel something paradigmatic about this 'source of blood' – this *maqor* 'spring' – that seems at the centre of H's conception of the sexual uni-verse itself (see Figure 1). More fundamental than vaunted heterosexual marriage, more fundamental than any sexual relationship, it recalls a basic principle from the slaughter rules in Leviticus 17.11: 'The life of the flesh is in the blood.' It recollects the Noahide prohibition of eating flesh with blood (Gen. 9.4–5). Reproductive blood, like shed blood, is handled carefully. The woman's 'source'-as-overflowing-spring is emblematic of womanhood (Prov. 5.18; S. of Sol. 5.12, 15), reminiscent of the four-branched river of Eden, and redolent with fecundity of that lushly moist primeval garden: 'You [Shulamith] are a garden spring,/ A well of fresh water,/ A rill of Lebanon' (S. of Sol. 4.15).

And so behind the *niddah* and Shulamith (and their evocation of Eden) stands the fount, Eve herself, 'the mother of all living' (Gen. 3.20).

2. Beauty and the Beast: Woman as Sexual Subject in Leviticus 18.23; 20.15–16

World folklore is rich in motifs of animal–human possibilities. Animals are tried out as wives; animal suitors approach human women; humans marry people trapped in animal form, or marry a god in the same guise; animal para-mours take human lovers; and a plenitude of animals emerges from the union of a snake with a person (Thompson 1966). So it should not surprise our mod-ern imagination that the Bible would address this. Indeed, Genesis 2.18–24

---

4 It is left to a later reader – Ezekiel – to express horror over the rape of the *niddah* (Ezek. 22.10). His catalogue of excess, and use of the lexicon of violence, implicitly rec-ognizes that a woman might not have consented.

contemplates the possibility of an animal mate as Adam searches through the animal kingdom for a helpmeet. But Leviticus closes the door on this option and throws away the key: 'And with respect to any livestock (or quadruped), do not place your penis in it to defile yourself. And with respect to a woman, let her not stand in front of (any) livestock to mate with it. It is confusion' (Lev. 18.23; author's translation).

The prohibition of male-initiated bestiality has its counterpart in an earlier law in the Covenant Code (Ex. 22.18 (Heb.)), and it is cursed at Deuteronomy 27.21. However, it is not clear whether the Covenant Code and the Deuteronomic cursing liturgy prohibit animal sexual contacts by women. It is a surprise to find a specific prohibition for women (*contra* Levine 1989: 123) because of low incidence. When Kinsey includes dream contacts, fantasies and arousals from general body contact, 3.6 per cent of adult women reported 'encounters' (Kinsey *et al.* 1953: 505, 509). However, only two of his informants actually reported coitus. Considering the reported rarity of female-initiated bestiality, why does H problematize it? 'Woman' is also 'marked' here by virtue of the concatenation of sexual crimes – she is in trump position at the end of the list. In case we were inclined to overlook her act, H adds the diagnostic phrase, 'It is confusion.' This is the first prohibition in Leviticus that addresses the 'active' sexual behaviour of women. She 'stands', enticing the beast. She is an agent departing from 'the properly passive position' (Brenner 1997: 147). Thus in every way – by final position, by diagnosis and by a contrary-to-expectation role – Leviticus 18.23b yields the parade example of 'unnatural' female sexual behaviouur.[5]

The penalty verses in Leviticus 20 underline her behaviour as active:

With respect to the man who lies carnally with livestock, he shall surely be put to death. As for the woman who approaches any livestock (or quadruped) to lie down with it, you shall kill the woman and the livestock (quadruped) – they shall surely be put to death: their bloodguilt is upon them alone. (Lev. 20.15–16, author's translation)

The unique phrase, 'approaches . . . to lie down with', carries the connotation of 'encroach' where there is both physical contact and intent (Milgrom 1970: 16–21). Again the woman initiates contact, and the law now executes the woman and the animal where it was silent before (Ex. 22.18). H explicitly condemns all animal partners to death rendering the issue of animals who initiate or 'consent' mute. Leviticus 20 offers one more clue about the importance of this law, it centres it in the larger inverted structure of Leviticus 20.10–21. 'The center of an inverted structure is the ideological focus of the discussion', writes Hildenbrand (1998: 148; cf. Milgrom 2000: 1744), and so the focus for most of Leviticus 20.

---

5 And thus the probable object of horror in Romans 1.26, 'for their females changed natural relations into what is contrary to nature' as per Eichler (1976: 96–7) and Haacker (1994); but contra Brooten (1996). Readers of Romans 1.27 usually argue that if that verse refers to male homosexuality, Romans 1.26 *must* refer to lesbian sex, an example of *juxta hoc* logic.

The history of the reception of Genesis 3.1–7, the story of Eve and the serpent, gives a hint about why this sexual crime receives such emphasis. The Talmudic rabbis suggest the snake had sexual relations with Eve (*b. Avodah Zarah* 22b; *b. Yevamot* 103b), or at least hoped to marry her (*b. Sota* 9b). Of course, a veil is drawn in Genesis 3 – the text is chaste though suggestive. The phallic serpent leads the way to 'wisdom' in the lush garden's scene of eating – both metaphors of sexual love in the Song of Solomon. At least once in biblical literature knowing the difference between 'good and evil' speaks of bodily pleasures and sensual delights (2 Sam. 19.36). Thus the Genesis story bequeaths to us a certain sexual tension. The humans are naked; the snake, by a pun, is nakedly clever; Eve talks with the serpent. Adam is absent. She eats. In the resolution of the tale, Yahweh finds it necessary to assign her desire an object: 'Your longing shall be for your husband' (Gen. 3.16). If this tale originally told the story of the discovery of sexuality – one that reflects the folkloristic vision of the serpent teaching Eve, and Eve teaching Adam – it has been carefully edited so as not to offend the sensitive reader. One can still notice that Genesis raises the question and gives it emphasis by way of a beautiful literary triptych: 'Adam and the Beasts' on a first panel (Gen. 2.18–24); 'Adam and His Proper Mate' on the central panel (Gen. 2.25); and 'Eve and the Beast' on the last (Gen. 3.1–16).

Why does the Holiness Code make explicit a prohibition against women's bestiality? The implied author of H appears to read Genesis and so the law stems from a certain momentum of exegesis. The stories of Genesis raise the issue of bestial marriage and take up the motif of the 'Woman with the Animal'. That woman, Eve, acts independently of God and man, and the woman of Leviticus 18.23 also dangerously takes initiative. Though the law addresses a male hearer, the text retains traces of a woman's sexual subjectivity.

3. Metaphors that Evoke Sex with Numinal Beings: Leviticus 18.21; 20.1–6, 27

The strange location of the prohibition in Leviticus 18.21 – something about sacrifice in the midst of the sex laws – creates a puzzle. 'From among your progeny (seed), do not dedicate (any) to sacrifice to Molekh' (author's translation). Leviticus 20.2 reinforces this prohibition with a penalty. Perhaps the placement of the command in Leviticus 18.20 is an editorial oddity (so Kilian 1963: 30; Cholewinski, 1976), but what *is* odd is the extraordinary artfulness of the sequence in Leviticus 18.20–1. H creates a kind of staircase with this sense:

> Don't give seed (semen) to a fellow's wife to defile yourself [v. 20]
>> Don't give seed (progeny) to ᴰMolekh⁶ (to defile yourself) [v. 21a]
>>> Don't (give seed to) profane ᴰGod [v. 21b]
>>>> ᴰYHWH [v. 21c]. (author's translation)

The 'art' involves the use of 'seed' in two senses and the counterpointing of three divine names – all of this is to suggest the intentionality of the editing

---

6 Where ᴰ stands for a divinity.

(and so positioning) of Leviticus 18.21. At the centre of the five laws in Leviticus 18.19–23, it is like a jewel in its setting.

If the placement is not inadvertent, what is one to make of its sexual context and connotations? *It pushes off-centre Leviticus 18.22, the alleged prohibition of homosexuality.* Verse 22 is not the most important thing here – verse 21 is. So we must enquire: 'What is more important about passing seed to Molekh than homosexuality?'

A traditional reading understands the passage as forbidding intermarriage with Gentile women. Molekh, then, is a metonymy for a foreigner who is an idolater. A more contemporary reader (Elliger 1966) understands the children sacrificed as the offspring of temple prostitutes. To find temple prostitutes in Israel, though, depends on a commonplace misunderstanding (traceable to Frazer's *Golden Bough*) that sacred prostitution existed in ancient Israel. There is really *very little* evidence for this.[7]

Can we consider a sexual context without resort to (hetero)sexual fantasy? In the end the passage must be about something both idolatrous and sexual. With respect to idolatry, the law forbids sacrificing seed/children to the god Molekh. The very practice of this cult is described as a kind of lust: 'I will cut him off, and all who wantonly follow him to whore after Molekh, from among their people' (Lev. 20.5). The Molekh cult represents a species of *zenut*, the general term for prohibited sexual activity or fornication. Trito-Isaiah tells us that the cult of Molekh has at least some association with fornication (Isa. 57.3). There is also a suggestion in this same passage of infanticide as a postpartum method of birth control: 'the seed of the adulterer and she who fornicates . . . [who are] slaughterers of children in the wadis'. The location of sacrifice – the wadis – evokes child sacrifice to Molekh in a renowned wadi, the valley of Ben-hinnom outside Jerusalem (2 Kings 23.10).

The most important verse of the second paragraph of sexual laws in Leviticus 18, as evidenced by the text's structure, is this prohibition of the destruction of sexual fruit (seed) in worship of another deity. The text argues against a particular idolatry of the day, and a particular ritual in honour of that god.

Now the biblical writers have shown displeasure over actual or threatened sex with divine or numinal beings. Genesis 6.1–4 already has 'dropped beads' about the sons of God (*bene-ha'elohim*) taking the daughters of men (producing giants for offspring). The context implies that this impropriety contributes to the Deluge. Likewise at Genesis 19.1, 5, heterosexual readers, agitated by the demand that Lot send out the visiting 'men' so that the inhabitants of Sodom may know them carnally, forget that these 'men' are angels. What the inhabitants of Sodom do not know, the narrator has revealed to us. Are we to imagine with heterosexual readers that the demand to homosexually rape the visitors is more horrific than the demand to rape angels? Genesis chapters 6 and 19 are reciprocals: angels or divine beings 'take' women; men want to 'take' angels. These texts reveal a violation of the hierarchical chain-of-being – sexual relations between species on different planes. The human and the numinal are not

---

7 Elaine Adler Goodfriend sketches the history of the idea (1992). As early as 1941 Beatrice Brooks cast doubt on this heterosexual fantasy and Mayer Gruber dealt it the death blow (1983; 1986; 1988).

to have sexual relations. Sexual union is reserved for the human with Yahweh, metaphorically speaking. Yahweh *is* a jealous God.

It should not be a surprise then, that 'idolatry' is referred to as 'adultery' by the prophets, or that sacrifice to other deities becomes infused with sexual or reproductive imagery. In the Epistle of Jude, we have at least one Christian reading like this: 'Sodom and Gomorah and the neighbouring towns which practised immorality in the same way the angels hankered after strange flesh' (v. 7). Even the evangelical commentator Bauckham reads it this way: 'As the angels fell because of their lust for women, so the Sodomites desired sexual relations with angels' (1983: 54).

Thus, it cannot be a surprise that the writers of Leviticus pick up the metaphor of sex-with-numina in another context. When speaking of ghosts and familiar spirits, none are to 'whore after them' (Lev. 20.6). If they do go a-whoring, they are to be executed (Lev. 20.27).[8] These verses, and the Molekh passages considered before, underscore what is really at issue. The Holiness writers, using the heterosexist imagery of 'whoring', rail against a new cult or cults competing with, or syncretizing with, Yahwism. Child sacrifice ritual, necromancy and spiritism represent the outward visible signs of the new *cultus*.

In sum, Leviticus gives a sexual charge to its campaign against particular religious practices. Is this new? It is a time honoured polemical gesture to accuse an adversary of sexual impropriety. The queer has not been immune to this. Here is the worst of all charges: infidelity to Yahweh by a driving lust for other gods.

4. Whither the Lesbian? Leviticus 18.3, 22

Returning to the topic of women, what about lesbians? Lesbianism per se is not mentioned or condemned as either *zenut* or adultery in Leviticus or anywhere else in the Hebrew Bible (Patrick 1985: 159). Sometimes lesbianism is imagined to be included in the alleged condemnation of male homosexuality (Lev. 18.22; 20.13) through an argument of symmetry (male and female homosexuality are two sides of the same coin). This is a reading of the twenty-first century focusing on the same genderedness of sexual subject and object. But our texts mark sex where there is a seminal emission, or sex where 'reproductive' blood is exchanged (Lev. 12, 15). Sex without exchange of menstrual blood or semen, the possible provenance of two women, is not marked as polluting. We cannot read silence as condemnation.

Rachel Biale notes that twice in the Talmud *mesolelot*, a term for women enjoying 'some kind of sexual act', occurs (1984: 193).[9] Rashi suggests that the

---

8 This metaphor of 'whoring after' is not only used for ghosts and familiars, but also for Molekh (Lev. 20.5), and satyrs and goat-demons (Lev. 17.5–7). All of these fit under the general rubric of *'elohim*. Whereas other biblical writers legislate genus-level prohibitions of whoring after *'elohim* (cf. Ex. 34.15–16; Deut. 31.16; Judg. 2.17), the Holiness School is interested in the species. Ezekiel (20.31) and the Holiness School (Lev. 26.30) even fall to scatological mockery of these *'elohim* – they are *gillulim* '(dung)balls' or 'dingleberries'.

9 See Jastrow (1989: 995b). The root, 'to sport (euphemism)', is also used for a female-initiated incest, a mother committing 'lewdness with her little son'.

term refers to a kind of rubbing or frottage (Rashi on *b. Yebamot* 76a). *Babli Yebamot* itself discusses the halakha of Rabbi Huna – 'women who are *mesolelot* are disqualified from [marrying into] the priesthood'. But Raba rejects this on the grounds of an unjustified symmetry: 'a bachelor who has intercourse with a single woman thereby renders her a *zonah*, because that [opinion of Rabbi Eliezer] is [only stated in reference] to [sex] with a man but not with regard to [sex] with a woman [where] it is mere licentiousness.' *Yebamot* thus argues that the silence about women carries significance – there is no legal penalty. Likewise, a second passage in *Babli Shabbat* 65a–b recounts that 'Samuel's father did not permit his daughters to . . . sleep together', *not* to prevent *mesolelot*, but rather 'it was in order that they should not become accustomed to a foreign body' and so be more ready to fornicate with a man (Biale 1984: 194–5; cf. Zeidman 1997). It is the woman acceding to man's desire that exercises the rabbis here, not women's desire for each other. Thus with Biale, 'lesbian acts do not constitute transgression or *zenut*' because they are not explicitly prohibited in the Bible; nor are they 'polluting' when there is no exchange of blood.

Zeidman notes that the medieval Jewish philosopher Maimonides, in his legal compendium *Mishneh Torah*, follows the older Rabbinic commentary on Leviticus, *Sifra* (according to *Aharei Mot*), placing lesbianism under the command at Leviticus 18.3. 'You shall not copy the practices of the land of Egypt where you dwelt, or of the land of Canaan . . .' This hermeneutical move, ascribing the behaviour to despised 'others' and lumping it under a generalized command, is made very late in the history of Leviticus interpretation. These early Rabbinic writers and medieval exegetes, as Zeidman notes, ironically 'find' lesbianism in the Bible and then simultaneously 'absolve' women of the worst consequences – death, divorce or exile. One might commend their postmodern reading (they find lesbians in the text). But alas, it allows the earlier rabbis to derogate, and later Jewish men to prohibit their wives from engaging with other women, and to flog those who do (*Mishneh Torah*, '*Issurei Bi'ah* 21.8). So I will look for lesbians elsewhere: as composer and singer of the song in Leviticus 26.

5. On Reading the Lives of Lesbians in(to) the Text: Leviticus 26.3–39

In the longer Priestly narrative of which Leviticus is a part we learn little of the role of women in the cultus (Bird 1987). In Exodus 35.25–6, women spin yarn and goat's hair thread for use in sewing the curtains of the tent. They give donations toward its construction (Ex. 35.29) and, in particular, give mirrors to make the copper laver (Ex. 38.8). The donors were the 'women who performed [some untranslatable] tasks at the entrance of the Tent of Meeting'. Taking the lead from Irigaray's use of 'mimesis', a method that allows one to 'assume the feminine role deliberately', I attempt 'to play with mimesis' here, which

> is . . . for a woman, to try to recover the place of her exploitation by discourse, without allowing herself to be simply reduced to it. It means to resubmit herself . . . to 'ideas', in particular to ideas about herself, that are elaborated

in/by a masculine logic, but so as to make 'visible', by an effect of playful repetition, what was supposed to remain invisible. (Irigaray 1985b: 76)

What acts, from the Pentateuchal narratives, might I reproduce mimetically to recover any further role of women in the cult?[10]

Turning to Miriam, one of the ruling triumvirate in the wilderness with Moses and Aaron, and one of five women in the Hebrew Bible specifically identified as a prophet, she sings, and perhaps composes, a song of victory at the sea. The song repeats the elements of the prose account in Exodus 14 but displaces the victory from Yahweh's use of Moses' arm (Ex. 14.21) to Yahweh's right hand alone (Ex. 15.6). Moses and the Israelites sing the song; the women with Miriam take timbrels and dance (Ex. 15.20). Miriam's authorship may be hinted in a 'credit' line, 'Miriam chanted for them' (Ex. 15.21). This motif – women singing to the victor – appears again at Judges 11.34 (Jephthah's daughter sings to her father), and Judges 5.1 (Deborah the prophet, with her general Barak, sing a victory song that praises women, Jael and Deborah, and mocks the defeated general's mother). Another biblical woman, not a prophet, Hannah also sings a victory song at the Shiloh temple in 1 Samuel 2 after she produces children in her competition with her co-wife Peninnah. In this, all three women participate in a long ancient Near Eastern tradition: women composing (and singing) poems. Enheduanna, Sumerian priest, prophet and daughter of Sargon, the first named, non-legendary author in history, is known for her 'Exaltation of Inanna' (Hallo and Younger 1997: 518–22). Goitein (1988) suggests that this in and of itself provides evidence for the invention of poetry by women. Thus, mimetically, I propose that these women at the entrance of the Tent of Meeting were not washerwomen or janitors, waitrons or cult prostitutes. Like Miriam and her cadre, they are singers, poets, musicians and dancers – a 'fact' that was to remain invisible.

Now, as such, they do not unravel male hegemony. The saviour-women of Exodus – Miriam, the Hebrew midwives Puah and Shiphrah, Pharaoh's daughter, and Zipporah who all rescue the patriarchal hero – uphold the status quo. Nor are they given unambiguous credit: Miriam and Deborah follow the '"path" . . . historically assigned to the feminine: that of mimicry' (Irigaray 1985b: 76). Their songs reflect the preceding prose narratives and they 'sing' with Moses and Barak. Hannah's song resembles a psalm ascribed to David.

Nevertheless, there *is* a song in Leviticus 26.3–39, albeit with inserted prose commentary (cf. Reventlow 1961: 158; Elliger 1966: 364; Cholewinski, 1976: 130), that I propose belongs to Miriam or her ilk – and I will assert here, a *lesbian* Miriam. I assert it because of the singer's strong stand against the tide. She calls for reflection, inverts the formal conventions, and proclaims her critique of the future.

All of the embedded songs are important. They structure and interrupt biblical narrative like an all-cast dance number stops the show in *Oklahoma!* The

---

10 As a male-identified-male with a growing consciousness of the 'internalized voice of androcentrism' (Fuchs 2003: 99), I am aware that any expression of women's voices in a 'document written by men for men' (108) is mediated – so not 'authentic'. Ironically, I find myself recapitulating that mediation as I write.

hearers can think about what has transpired, anticipate what comes next, or reflect on the qualities of lead characters. Such songs start and end the narratives they frame (e.g. the creation hymn of Genesis 1 and Jacob's last will and testament in Genesis 49; Hannah's song in 1 Samuel 2 and David's songs in 2 Samuel 22–3). Sometimes the writer supplies them at pivotal points in the action (e.g. after the victory in the Reed Sea, Exodus 15; David's lament for Saul and Jonathan, 2 Samuel 1). Our poem in Leviticus 26 thus urges us to reflect as Israel establishes its *cultus*; as the nation pauses before leaving Sinai.

This poem of blessings and cursings is unlike a similar one in Deuteronomy 27–8 that closes the Pentateuch. There the Levites declaim (Deut. 27.14). Here it is the unnamed women. Unlike the collections of imprecations in ancient Near Eastern treaties, our song presents the blessings first. It replaces the expected 'blessed/cursed be ye' with a hyperbolic vision and a structure of intensification ('I will go on to discipline you sevenfold', Lev. 26.18, 21, 24, 28). Our poem falls at the end of Leviticus, just before the appendices (as 2 Samuel 22–3 in their location do). It pivots the reader's focus toward the journey through the wilderness to the settlement of Canaan land.

What of the content? There are two visions of the land: one utopian; another dystopian. The former sees a fertile and fruitful land, where one eats their fill and lies down in peace. It is a land where people find sabbath rest – including women and slaves as provided in the Decalogue (Ex. 20.10 [Heb.]). Or in the latter, it becomes a land where 'ten women shall bake your bread in a single oven' (Lev. 26.26) and 'you shall eat the flesh of your sons and the flesh of your daughters' (Lev. 26.29). It is possible that this concern with fertility, food preparation, investment in children and rest from work reflects the quotidian round of most Israelite women's lives. In that respect it might not be so different from the Second Testament parable that takes a similar tack: 'The kingdom of heaven is like yeast that a woman took and mixed in with three measures of flour until all of it was leavened' (Matt. 13.33 NRSV) – a text often read in a way that suppresses the presence of the woman and her baking (Schottroff 1994: 521–5). It is a subject matter that might suggest itself to a person who lived this daily reality and feared the hardships children and women would bear from divine retaliation. Who is our singer? Miriam has sung once; she is a natural candidate to sing again. She is our Israelite Sappho, our Enheduanna.

6. Altered Bodies: Transphobia in Leviticus 21.16–23?

As Deborah Sawyer observes, 'the Bible contains varieties of constructions of gender that compete and contradict across the breadth of the canon' (2002: 10). Thus what appears to be a binary gender system in the D-source (Deut. 22.5) and P-source (Gen. 1.27), male and female, looks like a three-gender system in the J-source (Gen. 2.20–1): male, female and androgyne or *ha-'adam*, 'the human'. Leviticus 21 gives us one more possibility to add to these three. Leviticus 21.16–23 discusses the 'disabilities' that disqualify one from the priesthood (a woman is always disqualified). The list of twelve has much in common with the list of twelve blemishes in Leviticus 22.21–7 that disqualify a sacrifice. Four injuries to animal genitals are problematic: '[testes] bruised, or crushed, or torn, or cut' (Lev. 22.24); one injury to the priest's genitals: 'crushed testes' (Lev. 21.20). Such a priest cannot offer sacrificial food, come near the altar, nor enter behind the curtain to the Holy of Holies. The latter rule would only restrict the High Priest, and none of the rules apply to the non-priest or citizen Israelite. Perhaps this 'male' with altered genitals is too much like a female, and for that reason cannot officiate. However, exclusion by feminization does not explain its co-occurrence with other disabilities like blindness or lameness.

Later mishnaic literature names a fourth category: 'a person of indeterminate gender' (*b. Arakhin* 1.2A; *m. Arakhin* 1.1; *b. Bikkurim* 4.1). The tractate *Arakhin* comments on Leviticus 27.1–10, the consequences of vowing a person (we have one untoward consequence of vowing people in the story of Jephthah's daughter in Judges 11). A person pays a fine to the priests based on the gender and age of the person vowed (in place of sacrificing them or placing them in dedicated service). There is a rough correlation here with what the person could earn doing field work over several harvests – or perhaps we have an ancient price list for slaves. In either case, the problem arises for the rabbis: What if you cannot clearly identify the person's genitals as male or female? That is, what if a person is *androginos*, that is a 'hermaphrodite' (perhaps by congenital adrenal hyperplasia or gonadal intersex syndrome) or *tumtum*, 'one whose genitals are hidden' (concealed by a patch of skin; perhaps cloacal exstrophy?), or 'undeveloped' (perhaps Kallman's syndrome or Mayer-Rokitansky-Kustur-Hauser syndrome?), or 'whose sex is unknown' (Jastrow 1989: 81c and 524c)? Since the command only contemplates a 'man' or 'woman' as the object of a vow, the rabbis must confront the biological reality of intersexed persons (about 1.7 per cent of the population; Fausto-Sterling 1993; 2000: 53). The very fact that *testes* in reliable shape are a biblical standard suggests that a eunuch would fit here, and so might an M-to-F or F-to-M transsexual in transition. Once transition was completed, the M-to-F would be excluded from the priesthood, but perhaps the F-to-M would be included by the measure of ostensible genitals. This 'person of indeterminate gender' fills out the matrix of possibilities one would elucidate through a form of logic: 'Male', 'Female', 'Male and Female', 'not Male and not Female'. If I am right that this last category is also anticipated by Leviticus 21–2, then we have both a biblical and a Rabbinic marker of the four genders: *visible attributes of the genitals*.

These four genders form five sacerdotal classes: (1) male Aaronites who may function as priests and be objects of vows; (2) female Aaronites who may eat of the dedicated food offerings (Lev. 22.10–13) and be objects of vows; (3) androgynous or gender-indeterminate persons born into the priestly class who cannot function as priests or be objects of vows (but can still eat of the prebends); (4) Israelite citizens plus female Aaronites who marry outside the tribe of Levi (they can be vowed, but not eat prebends); (5) Israelite citizens who are androgynous or gender-indeterminate who cannot be objects of vows. Transgendered and intersexed persons sit at the margins of the priestly and common Israelite social classes.

Though the text hints at social recognition, there is a transphobia here in the very exclusion of some transsexuals and intersexed from the priestly class. What is not clear is whether stigma develops from the 'feminization' of a man's body or whether from a kind of handicapism – or at least ableism. In any case, the existence of intersexed people is not completely effaced and there are no rules requiring their celibacy or sex assignment, or forbidding their marriage. As Judith Butler suggests:

> The heterosexualization of desire requires and institutes the production of discrete and asymmetrical oppositions between 'feminine' and 'masculine', where these are understood as expressive attributes of 'male' and 'female'. *The cultural matrix through which gender identity has become intelligible requires that certain kinds of 'identities' cannot 'exist' – that is, those in which gender does not follow from sex* and those in which the practices of desire do not 'follow' from either sex or gender. (Butler 1999: 23–4; emphasis mine)

Has Leviticus *not* heterosexualized desire, allowing the revised gender of someone with altered genitals or 'sex' to 'exist'? While the J-source allows the androgyne an unstable and temporary status (*ha-'adam* before the 'rib' is removed), H permits the eunuch a continuing, disabled status. It is the Deuteronomic writer that is wont to assign masculine and feminine on a putative male and female binary, condemning men who take up the symbolic equipage of femininity – the spindle and distaff – and women who take up the symbols of masculinity – the bow and arrow (*not* cross-dressing; compare Deut. 22.5 with Hoffner 1966). It is Deuteronomy that refuses entrance into the Israelite congregation (not just the priesthood) of males with crushed testes or whose members are cut off (Deut. 23.2, itself an apparent conjoining of Lev. 21.20 and 22.24). Readers should resist the temptation to harmonize Deuteronomy and Leviticus, or let Deuteronomy's laws trump Leviticus. Deuteronomy may read Leviticus (or vice versa), but Leviticus speaks with a different voice – and that voice, though giving little to transgendered persons to celebrate, is marginally less transphobic than Deuteronomy.

7. The Leaking Male Body: Gonorrheic Discharges, Seminal Emissions and Wet Dreams: Leviticus 15.1–18, 31–2

Leviticus 15 discusses gonorrheic discharges, seminal emissions (from masturbation, wet dreams or carnal relations – no distinction is made), the regular discharge of menstrual blood, and menorrhagia (hypermenorrhea), which is the extended discharge of blood from the genitals past menstruation (cf. Lott 1998).

The first of these, male gonorrheic discharges, causes primary and secondary uncleanness. The discharge makes bedding, any object on which a man sits (such as saddles), or any earthen vessel or wooden implement touched by the man, unclean. If some second person then touches, sits on or carries any of these objects, such a one does not escape uncleanness. They must bathe and launder their clothes, remaining unclean until sunset. If the man with a discharge is touched by another person directly, or he spits on them, or he touches an earthen vessel or wooden implement, the results are similar. The toucher, or one spat upon, must launder and bathe and remain unclean until sunset. If the man with gonorrhea himself touches another without having first washed his hands, the touched must bathe, launder and remain unclean until evening. The clay vessel is broken; the wooden implement is rinsed. Break the crockery; rinse the spoon. For those who are thus the objects of primary or secondary contagion, one must ask what being 'unclean until evening' might mean. On the practical level it seems to mean that those from priestly families would fast till sundown, denied the meat of sacred donations to eat (Num. 18.11). Nor can they enter the sacred precincts. Nor can they have relations with sex partners. Whatever other practical consequences there might be is not clear. However, if they fail to carry out proper ablutions they are faced with stiffer penalties.

As to the primary pollution – the direct burden of the man with the discharge – when he becomes healed (penicillin?), he must count off seven days, launder, and bathe in fresh water. On the eighth day he offers two turtledoves or pigeons to the priest, who makes two kinds of offerings – a 'purgation' offering and a burnt offering – and expiates on behalf of the person with the discharge.

One imagines, then, the leaking man reflecting the disintegration of a corpse. Has he taken on himself the image of death? Is this what links the leaking (gonorrhea in Lev. 15.2–12; menorrhagia in Lev. 15.30) and disintegrating bodies (scale disease in Lev. 14.31; the corpse in Lev. 21.1; Num. 5.2; 19.11–20)? It seems that the rituals reinscribe a boundary for the body. The proper body is a bounded one. But this metaphor does not fully hold: Leviticus does not mark the bloody gore of battlefield wounds polluting (Dolev and Nerubay 1982).

I have paid close attention to this abstruse ritual problem because of what comes next: semen emissions and menstruation. Here are other, regular 'leaks'. How are they treated? A student once asked me: 'What does the Bible say about masturbation?' I said, 'Wash.' 'Wash?' he asked, his voice breaking. 'Wash,' I said again. So note that seminal emissions from masturbation, wet dreams and sexual relations are all treated the same way: 'He shall bathe his whole body in water and remain unclean until evening' (Lev. 15.16). Note that the outcome is similar to that of contagion from *secondary* pollution – it draws the most minor consequence. As for laundering, this is conditional: 'All cloth or leather (!) on which semen falls shall be washed in water and remain unclean until evening' (Lev. 15.17). If, with foresight, semen only falls on the body, nothing need be laundered. (One wonders, though, how good is it for the leather to wash it? Follow up with an application of mink oil, please.)

The ritual consequences of carnal relations between a man and a woman (married, unmarried, hired, slave or free, consensual or not) are the same – bathing and the small inconvenience of remaining 'unclean until evening' (Lev. 15.18). I am attempting to speak, of course, from within the ritual world of the priestly writers. Whether or not the twenty-first-century reader takes these rules as normative does not matter: One must still try to see how these rules might have worked within the biblical world. Though the text is not explicit, one could extrapolate the same rule set to ejaculative sex between men, or one lesbian artificially inseminating another.

Now some have argued that masturbation, under the rubric of Onan's seed falling to the ground during sex with Tamar (hence the term *onanism*; cf. Gen. 38), brings condemnation and death. They have not reckoned with Leviticus 15.

The Genesis context is about *coitus interruptus* – an ancient form of birth control practised by the levir (or brother-in-law) who is obliged to raise up heirs for his deceased brother. Onan refused to mar the inheritance of his children by complicating the lines of succession. He drew God's wrath for his heterosexual misdeed, an aggravation above and beyond the 'normal' leaking of the body. There is nothing about masturbation here. But if some reader desires an ethic of masturbation, let them note that the Bible supports showering after sex.

The Levitical purity code parallels menstrual flows with seminal emissions just as it has hypermenorrhea with gonorrheic discharges – with these differences: semen makes you unclean until eventide, touching the menstruant likewise; but lying with the menstruant leaves her partner unclean for seven days. Menstrual blood has more potency than semen.

The closing line of Leviticus 15 tells us that the goal of these passages is to put Israelites on guard against uncleanness, lest by neglect of the matter the miasma from their unresolved polluting acts attaches to the Tent of Meeting, and so they die (Lev. 15.31; cf. Milgrom 1976). The purity code (Leviticus 11–15) does *not* apply to everyone – only to Israelites!

8. Male Homosexual Incest: Leviticus 18.6, 14, 22; 20.13

The two 'texts of terror' for gay men read: 'Do not lie with a man as one lies with a woman, it is an abhorrence' (Lev. 18.22) and, 'If a man lies with a male as one lies with a woman, the two of them have done an abhorrent thing; they shall be put to death – their bloodguilt is upon them' (Lev. 20.13). It should be clear that the second passage depends upon the first. It adds the penalty.

But the first thing to know is that the 'as' does not exist in the Hebrew text. It is supplied by the translators. Now if the 'as' were actually there, it would beg the question of likeness. Is it clear that a man *cannot* precisely do that – lie with a man as with a woman? That anal intercourse is not vaginal intercourse? Or as one wag suggests: only a lesbian could actually obey this law (Travis 2000: 37).

Stripping away this 'as' we are left with something that looks like a technical phrase: *mishkebe-isha*, literally 'lyings of a woman'. The command thus reads: 'Do not lie with a male [the] "lyings of a woman".' So what is that? Elliger suggests pederasty (1966: 241); Milgrom, the homoerotic acts of Jews, ancient or modern, living in the land of Israel (1993; 1994); Daube (1986: 447–8), Olyan (1994: 186) and Boyarin (1995: 336), male–male anal intercourse – Daube relying on the grounds of comparative law; Olyan on philological grounds; Boyarin on the history of Rabbinic interpretation of these verses. Olyan argues that 'lyings-of-a-woman' speaks of 'vaginal receptivity' (185) and so conflates women's sexual experience with that of gay men. It is easy to slip from 'lyings-of-a-woman' standing for one homoerotic act to interpreting it as a metonymy for all. But underneath this lies the deep structure of metaphor – two sorts of intercourse have shared and unshared elements. The metaphor, taking the commonality of a receptive partner, analogizes two *different* behaviours. (Think about it.) This metaphorizing seems to underlie all interpretations of this passage.

Did the writer need to write more than 'You shall not lie with a male' if the intent was a general condemnation of male homosexuality? Unless one posits that the 'lyings-of-a-woman' means nothing, or is a redundancy, it must specify something: anal intercourse perhaps, if we can imagine nothing more to male–female sex than the crude 'pole-in-a-hole'.

If we were to examine all instances of this or similar phrases we find that 'the lying [singular] of a male' means 'defloration of a female' (Num. 31.17, 18, 35; Judg. 21.11, 12); 'the lyings [plural] of your father (a male)' means 'incest with the (step)mother' (Gen. 49.40).[11] Occasionally a plural noun carries a more abstract sense than the singular.[12] The case in Genesis 49 points the way – when 'lying(s)-of-X' is plural, it has the technical sense of incest and not just carnal relations. Oddly the 'lyings-of-your-father' and the 'lying-of-a-male' both refer to sex acts with women. The female 'object' – unmentioned – is absorbed into the subjectivity of the male. That is, the phrase assumes the sexual agency of the male alone. The 'lyings-of-a-woman' still presumes the agency of a male but refers to an act with another male by a kind of literary gender play. Just as the 'lyings-of-your-father' refers to a usurpation of the father's bed by the son, the 'lyings-of-a-woman' metonymically refers to a male as incestuous object – a metonym because elaboration of the incest category has been (primarily) in terms of female objects (Lev. 18.7–16).

The anthropology of a century ago – the anthropology on which Freud relied in *Totem and Taboo* – didn't think of male–male incest at all. Here is a parade example of heterosexism. But the ancients understood the possibility. Hittite Law §189 forbids a man from sexually violating his son (Hoffner 1997). Indeed, a closer reading of the Holiness Code finds a prohibition in both directions: neither should son take the father, nor the father the son. Leviticus 18.6 reads: 'Anyone with respect to his own flesh[-and-blood], do not draw near to uncover nakedness . . .' (author's translation). Who are those of your own flesh? Susan Rattray answered this in 1987 and with it resolved the old conundrum of the apparent absence in Leviticus of a prohibition against a father incesting his daughter. When one reads this verse with Leviticus 21.2, where there is a similar phrase, 'near relations', the matter takes care of itself. Biblically speaking, 'near relations' include mother, father, son, daughter, brother and sister of marriageable age. Rattray observed that Leviticus 18.6 (read with 21.2) forbade incest by the male subject with mother, daughter and blood-sister. What she did not see, and this is where internalized heterosexism can blind us, is that it must also forbid *the incest of the male subject with father, son and brother.*[13]

This prohibition then is reinforced at Leviticus 18.7: 'Do not expose the nakedness of your father [conjunction] the nakedness of your mother.' Now the conjunction is usually translated 'which (is)', again out of heterosexual

---

11 See my full technical discussion in Stewart (2000: 69–74).

12 e.g. *chatan-damim*, 'bridegroom of blood', where the plural for blood, *damim*, has an abstract or technical sense in Exodus 4.26.

13 I might like to add the female subject with mother, daughter and sister. However, the opening phrase *'ish 'ish* probably means 'each and every male' as opposed to 'anyone at all' (Milgrom 2000: 1453, 1533). Joüon allows the phrase the more general meaning (because of a context including women) in one non-legal instance in the P-stratum, Exodus 36.4 (Joüon 1947: § 135d).

presumption. It could just as easily be translated 'and' or 'nor', resolving the one command into two: Don't incest your father or your mother.

That the Bible is agitated about 'uncovering nakedness' – a technical phrase for both incest and sex with the menstruant in Leviticus – is first seen in Genesis 9.21–2, where Ham sees his father's nakedness while Noah is drunk. It is not precisely clear what happens here and it is impossible to believe that the mere seeing was problematic. Why? Nearly every male who reads this will have seen his father's nakedness. Moreover, Noah's response is way out of proportion to a mere seeing: he curses his own grandson Canaan! Collectively, readers from the rabbis to the present have suggested four main theories of what happened. (1) Ham (or Canaan) castrated Noah. The Talmud offers this suggestion and there are analogues in Ugaritic, Greek and Hittite myth. (2) Ham (or Canaan) sexually abused Noah (or maybe his wife). Here is incest. (3) Ham looked and complicated his gaze by mocking his father's sex organ or by staring lasciviously, or by seeking to magically acquire his father's potency. In other words, there is some sort of sexual innuendo. (4) The text doesn't reveal what happened. The implied author is intentionally silent (*per* Ibn Ezra). But doesn't such a silence suggest something too awful and base to mention?

The collocation of drinking and exposing genitals occurs not only with Noah and Ham, but also in the incest of Lot and his daughters (Gen. 19.32–5), in Lamentations 4.21, and Habakkuk 2.15–16. The last gives us a kind of 'riff' on the Noah–Ham incident: 'Woe to the one causing his friends to drink – even making drunk – in order to look upon their genitals' (Haak 1992: 68–9). Why did someone do this? Simply for a peek? Thus it seems modest to assert that Ham's gaze carried lascivious intent.

The echoing of this looking-upon/uncovering-nakedness language in Leviticus 18.6–7 is intertextual, a reuse of prior text. Leviticus references Genesis 9.21–2 as the touchstone from which to build its legal commentary. The Holiness writers extend the abhorrence of incest beyond father and son to a set of new relations – brother–brother, brother–sister, father–daughter, son–mother – always with the agency of the male in view. H forbids incesting affines such as one's stepmother (Lev. 18.8), half-sister (v. 9), stepsister (v. 11), paternal uncle's wife, one's aunt-by-marriage (v. 14), daughter-in-law (v. 15) and the sister-in-law who is your brother's wife (v. 16). Among forbidden consanguines are a man's granddaughter (v. 10), paternal (v. 12) and maternal (v. 13) aunts, and *another male*, one's paternal uncle (v. 14a): 'Do not uncover the nakedness of your father's brother.' One might also read a sort of incest-prohibition into the two-women rules of verses 17–18. The intergenerational rule in verse 17 would exclude a male agent's mother-in-law and stepdaughters. The 'rival sister' rule in verse 18 would exclude the sister-in-law through one's wife, or the sister of a man's female lover.

If Leviticus 18.22 is an incest rule, what does it do? It extends the incest prohibition to all the male relatives of the same degree of relation as those forbidden women in 18.6–18. To wit: among consanguines grandfather, maternal uncle and grandson are verboten; among affines brother-in-law, half-brother, stepbrother, stepson and son-in-law. Thus one can see an ever-widening series of concentric circles delineating incest. At the centre is the father and the heir; next are the near kin, male and female; in the outer circle one finds an extended family of consanguine and affinal kin with a few omissions such as nieces, nephews and first cousins. The community at Qumran will record a further extension to nieces at a later time. These 'circles' of prohibition may also sketch a developmental trajectory, a tendency to expand laws to cover more and more. But that is beyond our purview here.

One must also speak about the diagnostic word, to'eba, often translated 'abomination'. The noun occurs 116 times in the Hebrew Bible and the verbal root 23 times (L'Hour 1964). The term is used in four contexts: idolatrous ritual and magic, sexual prohibitions, food and diet restrictions, and false weights and measures (Weinberg 1977). Thus unjust weights and measures are as abominable as man-on-man incest. Indeed, the homiletic frame to Leviticus 18 asserts that all the behaviours of chapter 18 (male–female incest, lying with two related women, lying with the menstruant, adultery, Molekh worship and bestiality initiated by both men and women) are abhorrent (Lev. 18.26) and among the reprehensible customs of the Egyptians and Canaanites mentioned in verse 3.

To collect these observations: Leviticus 18.22 and 20.13 forbid male-on-male incest within certain degrees of relation. This abhorrent behaviour is one among a number including all the sexual crimes of Leviticus 18. (Thus, a straight man sleeping with his lawfully wedded and menstruating wife is also an abomination.) These 'texts of terror' are *not* a general prohibition against all homosexual relations. One must turn to the pages of the history of interpretation to find *that*. The residuum, homosexual relations between two women and between two unrelated men, is subject to the purity rules covering leaking bodies – washing, laundering, avoiding blood associated with reproduction, and avoiding sancta while polluted.

9. Disease-as-Impurity (Leviticus 13–14) and Plague (Leviticus 26.15–16)

René Girard was certainly not the first to notice that 'the plague is found everywhere in literature' as a metaphor for social disorder, reciprocal violence and all variety of ills that affect the whole community. That, indeed, 'this metaphor is endowed with an almost incredible vitality'. 'The plague', he argues, 'makes all accumulated knowledge and all categories of judgement invalid' because 'all life, finally, is turned into death, which is the supreme undifferentiation' (1996: 155–8). If we who are gay are acutely aware that HIV/Aids is sometimes labelled as 'the plague' (see Tony Kushner (1993) for instance), we are even more aware of how it threatens, as Girard observes, 'the very existence of [our] social life' (1996: 156). It is not just the biological reality of disease, but the 'social construction of the diseased [as] stigmatized other' (Simpson 1997: 18) that threatens us. So the mention of plagues in the Bible must contribute to the 'epidemiology of representations' or 'images of plague that circulate in human culture' (1997: 19).

Vernacular readings of the Bible take plagues as divine punishment with some warrant. David's census of potential warriors results in a plague; the song in Leviticus 26 promises 'consumption and fever, which cause the eyes to pine and the body to languish' if 'you do not observe all my commandments

and you break my covenant' (Lev. 26.15–16). Contextually, the particular commands in view are the making of idols of several sorts, Sabbath-breaking,
and not venerating the Sanctuary (Lev. 26.1–2). Sabbath-breaking may seem
antique to many readers, but within the context of the Pentateuch the Sabbath
is the outward visible sign of the Sinaitic covenant – a big deal. Leviticus 26
details an escalating series of punishments for violation of the essential covenant principles. In the peroration, a particular Sabbath-breaking is in view, the
ecological crime of not allowing the land to lie fallow every seventh year (Lev.
26.34–5). For sex crimes, rather, the Holiness Code threatens exile from the
Land of Israel as a collective punishment (Lev. 18.27–8) and the *karet*, or 'cut-
off' penalty (v. 29) discussed above. Thus, even within the terms of Leviticus,
HIV/Aids *cannot* be read as a punishment for those who live outside the Land;
for those who live in Israel or Palestine, it cannot be read as a punishment for
sexual behaviour.

A second vernacular reading takes lepers as representative of persons with
Aids (PWAs). This, of course, is partially based on the Second Testament depiction of lepers – but *that* has its basis in the supposed discussion of leprosy in
Leviticus 13–14 and Numbers 5.1–4. Perhaps it is too pedantic to observe that
tsara'at in Leviticus is *not* leprosy, or Hansen's Disease, but a collection of skin
conditions that should be translated as 'scale disease' (Hulse 1975).[14] Leviticus
13 concerns itself with the details of priestly diagnosis of the several skin conditions, along with spreading moulds in cloth and houses (the last is a great
problem in some parts of the United States). Leviticus 14 prescribes a ritual for
the person with scale disease *after it has been healed*, and for a replastered house
after it has been purged of mould. The ritual allows the re-entry of a person
into the community or the reuse of a house. As the P-text in Numbers 5 discloses, the person with a skin eruption, or a discharge, or defiled by a corpse
must be put outside the wilderness camp. This last – quarantine outside the
camp – seems to provide a biblical justification for some who are Aids-phobic
to ostracize all those who are HIV-positive. As a minister told me once, he
would not visit PWAs in the hospital because it would 'put his family at risk'.

Now the linking at Numbers 5 of scale disease, seminal and menstrual discharges and corpses leads one to ask, what do these have in common? Milgrom
answers (1991), 'life out-of-place' or death. A person with scale disease looks
like a corpse. Blood associated with reproduction and semen represent 'life'
– and when lost by reproductive organs, 'death'. Things associated with death
pollute; the Israelite *cultus* is about preserving life – particularly, the life of the
Israelite community.

This antique concern of Leviticus with blood and semen as potential pollut-
ants – indeed the very notion of purity rules of any sort – seems untoward to
so many moderns. But if I ask myself, 'Do I put shoes on the table where I eat',
my answer reveals that I do have a purity rule (or two). It's a cultural thing.
Safer sex campaigns represent an attempt to inculcate a new set of purity rules
in queer culture. Thus the first-world queer community, by its experience with

---

14 Hulse observes that *tsara'at* is a scaly condition that could comprise 'psoriasis,
seborrheic dermatitis, [and] fungus infections of the skin' such as 'favus, patchy
eczema, and pityriasis rosea' (1975: 93, 96).

blood and semen, is particularly well-placed to understand and interpret this biblical obsession to the first-world, non-medical, straight community. Ignore us at your peril!

Musa Dube, of the 'Circle of Concerned African Women Theologians', presses us to ask these questions about HIV/Aids instead:

> What *does* the Bible say, if anything, about HIV/Aids? What *should* it say and what *can* it say? How does HIV/Aids affect women and what does the Bible say about *women* and illness? How should we interpret the Bible to empower women, whose powerlessness makes them more vulnerable to infection and forces them to bear the burden of care in HIV/Aids contexts? How should we interpret the Bible to fight against HIV/Aids and to support the infected and affected? (Circle of Concerned African Women Theologians 2003; emphasis mine)

Leviticus says nothing about HIV/Aids specifically, although some have made it say things: ostracize the divinely punished; let them die. Mitulski tells us that an HIV hermeneutic denounces the 'religious impulse to blame the victim' and the 'spiritually toxic notion that God sends illness as a means of teaching humanity a lesson' (2000: 155). How should we interpret Leviticus to empower women who are vulnerable to positive partners? If a husband, or any person at all, does *not* have a right to the menstruant's body, then that one does *not own* any woman's body. She may say (I am speaking of those who accept biblical authority), 'You must obey God and use a condom, or stay away. You must not use your penis for ill.' Or to a lesbian partner, 'We must not exchange blood.' How should we interpret Leviticus to fight against HIV/Aids and support the infected and affected? Mitulski tells us to 'take back the Word to find its message for us [all those with HIV experience]' (2000: 160). Central to that experience is the loss of those who are beloved, facing the prospect of one's own death, grief, emotional and physical suffering, floating guilt, and casting about for hope and renewal.

After Aaron lost two of his four sons, Nadab and Abihu (they had committed ritual errors and died in one day), Moses angrily addresses Aaron's other two sons, Eleazar and Ithamar, about their errors (Lev. 10.16–18). Perhaps Moses was alarmed that events would repeat themselves and all his nephews would die. Aaron starts to explain but breaks down – 'and such things have befallen me!' – If everything had been done right and I had eaten the sacrificial food, 'would the LORD have approved?' he asks (Lev. 10.19). Moses backs off. This is a small and obscure text, but it declares that grief (and anger) can interrupt the most important sacerdotal functions – here the inaugural rituals of the *cultus* – and be approved. Though biblical narrative is laconic in the extreme, here it takes precious air-time to record Aaron's cry of pain in the face of death.

Queerer Than Thou: A Meta-Discourse on Theory

In the most trivial way, as a North American, middle-class, post-fundamentalist, (US) Episcopalian, queer, white boy, academic, my reading of Leviticus is queer because a queer did it. But my reading also attempts to problematize the hegemonic, heterosexist reading of the book. Once when I was talking with a student, she averred that her church's reading of Leviticus 18.22 was actually *better* than the text because it included lesbianism under the ban (even though, she acknowledged, the text did not). So I join Ken Stone in the hope that, rid of heterosexist categories (or cognizant of internalized heterosexism), the biblical text might make its own claims heard, or at least the text mediated through a different subjectivity might show something else of its plenitude (2001a: 24).

However, I admit, this runs the risk of being apologetic, a hermeneutical strategy Koch (2001a) divides into three parts: 'The Pissing Contest' that marshals evidence to show what the Bible really says (I try this); love trumps all (I'll try this below); and 'I *Can* Fit the Glass Slipper!' finding queers included if one just looks hard enough (I try this too!). Koch advocates a non-apologetic approach that flowers out of queer lives and experience. He offers 'cruising' the scriptures as a way of looking for queers there without validating the text's authority. His actual exercise depends on the presence of characters embedded in narratives. Alas! I have so little of that! I'm left only with Yahweh, Moses, Aaron, Nadab, Abihu, Eleazar, Ithamar, an unnamed blasphemer and various unnamed women. Three die so quickly, I don't have time to cruise them; Moses and Aaron have their best scenes elsewhere. Perhaps I could imagine a roundtable where I overhear a clever discussion with Yahweh, as does Roland Boer (2001). What I have is a de-gendered Yahweh talking to Moses, and sometimes Aaron too, from above a box in a tent. Or, I could dispense with the text as a 'recalcitrant witness', and all my work to out-Foucault Foucault (1990) excavating the history of sexual thought in the Bible, and simply jump directly to constructing queers in the text as Boer suggests.

After effacing the tiny presence of lesbians in Leviticus 18.3, 22 allotted by the history of misreading, I do construct some lesbians who avoid blood exchange, would know to wash and launder after artificial inseminations, and recognize an outlaw woman who asserts her own sexual subjectivity. I imagine an Israelite Sappho who composes and sings the song in Leviticus 26. Perhaps her name is Miriam. Surely, also, it is a construction to treat people with injured gonads as fluidly gendered, outside the dualism of men-identified men and women-identified women. But what I may have gained for 'contemporary gay, bisexual and female-to-male transsexual men may actually constitute a significant and more troubling loss for lesbian, bisexual and male-to-female women' (Schneider 2000: 219–20). By rejecting a full-on prohibition of lesbianism, or even lesbian incest, I may simply uphold masculinist presumptions.

Steven Seidman helps me out a bit: Queer theory studies 'knowledges' that organize societies by sexualizing – heterosexualizing or homosexualizing – 'bodies, desires, acts, identities, social relations, knowledges, culture, and social institutions' (1996: 13). Ancient Israel sexualizes the bodies of beasts and numina, clan women and men, other people's wives, and the menstruant. Man's commended body in Genesis 2.24 becomes the forbidden body of Leviticus, leaking reproductive blood, eroticized yet unattainable – as seductive as the serpent's fruit. The commended sex-object for women – the husband-as-ruler of Genesis 3.16 – is, ironically, part of Yahweh's curse on the earth. When will this curse be overcome?

I might, like Adam, *name* some of this biblical sexualizing: 'sanguinality', say, for sex with blood; or the grating-to-the-ear 'hierarchiality' for sex with numina or beasts. Or I might assign genders to numina ('N'), humans ('H'), and beasts ('B'), noting that relations up or down the hierarchy – *hetero*sexual relations – are forbidden. And conversely, same-gender, intra-species relations (e.g. 'H' with 'H') are permitted. For gender 'H', those too close (kin), too claimed (wives), and too leaky (menstruant, parturient or gonorrheic) are the forbidden *homo*sexual objects. It is to such 'straight' *homo*sexuals that I now must turn.

10. An Appeal to the Reader for a Queer Love: Leviticus 19.33–4

In Matthew, Jesus' telling of the parable of the Good Samaritan seems to rely on Leviticus 19.33–4, the law of loving the resident alien as yourself. Embodied in the resident alien is a siglum of the 'other', even the religious 'other'. The Levite and priest who walk by the injured Israelite ostensibly see a problem with corpse contamination if they stop to help. It is Leviticus, of course, that raises this issue: 'None [i.e. no priest] shall defile himself for any [dead] person among his kin, except for the relatives that are closest to him' (21.1b–2a). What is good for distant kin must also be good for the stranger. The priest might imagine that the temporary desanctification from touching the corpse impedes his important spiritual work. The parable implies that such a priest cannot decode the important principles of his own law, nor rank their priority when faced with two conflicting ethical demands. The priest of the story could not see that 'The stranger who resides with you shall be to you as one of your citizens; you shall love him as yourself' (19.34a) is more important than maintaining sanctification at his workplace. Thus Jesus is in concord with this ethical development in Leviticus: One is to love (especially) the 'other' who is near. *Can you, Queer Reader, offer any principle in Leviticus more important than this?*

If one were then to try and extract an ethical principle from Leviticus that might apply in a twenty-first-century setting, then are we not challenged to love the alien resident among us? Those fashion-challenged 'straights' who cannot decorate their homes, nor recognize art beyond sofa-sized paintings, who lack the semiotic skill to decode things camp, who let their bodies fall apart after they marry, or who cannot even dissimulate with 'many of my best friends are homosexuals'; though we must pay taxes for their children to attend school, though we are objects of their loathing and presumed pederasts until proven innocent, though they conspire to advance a heterosexist agenda, though they speak hateful words against us as an exercise in 'freedom of religion', may we meet their violence with nonviolent resistance, and though we harbour scant hope that such 'straights' will test their own behaviour by these texts, may it not absolve queer Bible readers from embracing the power of love for an-'other'.

Suggestions for Further Reading

The reader who wishes to pursue all of the delicious complexities of Leviticus should consider Milgrom's three-volume commentary, part of the Anchor Bible series, a standard work found in college and public libraries. For someone not so obsessive, Hartley, or Levine, or Wenham will do, but all three are hetero-sexist and homophobic. The most important articles on Leviticus from a queer male perspective are those by Olyan and Boyarin in the *Journal of the History of Sexuality*. Tanis's work offers a purchase on transgendered biblical criticism. To understand the strangeness of purity codes, Mary Douglas's *Purity and Danger* offers an accessible starting-point. While Brenner and Bird present examples of feminist readings of the Bible, Butler and Irigaray offer theoretical direction for a future queer-feminist biblical critique as Jagose hints (1996: 119).

Numbers

SUE LEVI ELWELL

Introduction

One of the life tasks of each human being is individuation, finding one's own path, one's own voice, one's own way of being in the world. The infant slowly discovers that she is not her mother, that first source of warmth and nourishment and care. The subsequent years of our lives are spent differentiating ourselves from others. The very first word of the Hebrew Bible indicates how very wrenching separation can be, and scholars and interpreters continue to debate whether scripture opens with 'In the beginning,' or 'When God began to create,' or 'In the beginning of God's creation'. Did matter, or earth, or light or darkness exist before this story begins? And what did it mean to differentiate chaos from order, presence from void, waters from earth, absence of light from a world where God's call for light echoes through space?

For those of us who are distinguished by difference, for those of us whose own first consciousness as individuals was about our difference, we ask: what do these tales of becoming a people mean? The book of Numbers counts the people, again and again. These 36 chapters are very much notes towards a statement of who counts, both who enumerates and who is counted. This book focuses on individuals and how they enumerate or are considered, and it is also about who counts among and with and for – or against – the people Israel. These chapters of counting have an interesting self-consciousness about them as they serve as intermediary chapters of the Israelites' journey narratives, the five books of Moses that begin with Genesis and conclude with Deuteronomy.

Each story in Numbers that focuses on an individual helps the reader move closer to understanding how individuals move towards the possibility of forming a collective. The collective that is formed is not a spontaneous gathering, or a temporary banding together for a single event. Rather, the biblical narrative describes the construction of a corporate identity of individuals bound together by the elusive but potentially permanent bond of faith, a collective that will finally count.

How does this happen? How do the people come together? The book of Numbers begins with setting boundaries, determining who is in and who is out, defining what behaviour is acceptable and what behaviour is unacceptable, considering what actions are tolerable and what actions put one beyond the bounds of the community in formation. These are stories of frightening years, times when the earth swallows up those who challenge the Source of

light and peace. These are times when the ritual of drinking the dust from a
stone floor can either exonerate or convict a woman suspected of adultery.
These are times of transition for a population that had become accustomed to
a life of slavery, a life predictable in its daily punishments and humiliations, a
life that silenced deep hungers and nearly all voices. Now these former slaves
are forced to wander across a harsh and unmarked landscape, stumbling and
halting, nearly paralysed by their fear of the unknown.

How do we read these tales that both lift up and flatten the solitary voice that
calls for justice or fairness or compassion? Some who speak out are rewarded
for their courage; others are punished by death for having sought a different
way. We read these words of rebellion and challenge to authority, and are star-
tled by the unexpected voices of talking animals and insects that become some
of the most powerful metaphors in the Torah.

We who read this text through eyes and life experiences that are both ancient
and new bring new questions and new readings to these words. Too often, we
will not know how to read these tales. We may wish to ignore or challenge, or
simply stop reading some of these stories. The stories will wait for us, until we
are wiser, more patient, less anxious for immediate transparency or applica-
bility. Those who have been reading these texts for many years, many decades,
know the innate luminescence, the power of these stories to be read anew by
each generation. We return to these words because they call to us as does the
sea: enter here. These words can delight, confound and tantalize. It is our task
to learn to swim.

Katherine Doob Sakenfeld comments that 'Numbers is among the most dis-
jointed books of the Bible' (1992: 45). One of the challenges of any reader of
biblical literature is to learn the techniques of the master cinematographer:
knowing when and how to draw back the camera for a wide angle view that
takes in a broad and sweeping picture of the landscape, and when to come in
close for a tight shot, an intimate look that helps the viewer see the macrocosm
of the storm in a drop of rain. The reader of Numbers must often draw the
camera back far enough to see the wide expanse of the arid land across which
Numbers' actors make their way. This journey narrative comes to us in fragments, but the incidents that are reported, when taken together, help us to see
individuals trying to become a people, through stories from a wide variety of
perspectives that can be read as instalments in a drama that only takes shape
after many readings. James Ackerman writes that the editors 'have [arranged]
a sophisticated collage of diverse materials into a new literary context' (1987a:
78). Adriane Leveen notes, 'in the end, through careful combination and dramatic juxtaposition, these distinct texts create a richly layered but coherent
narrative' (2002: 204). Phyllis Trible believes that the wilderness narrative
mirrors the landscape:

> Wilderness symbolizes complaint, confusion and conflict. Moving from site
> to site, the people of Israel murmur, indeed rebel. Their deity replies with
> ambivalence. Gracious acts mingle with kindled anger. Nothing happens
> in an orderly way. Entangled in the wilderness, multiple layers of tradition
> defy source analysis and internal coherence to become much like the chaos
> they report. (1994: 173)

These 36 chapters introduce several strong themes, but the sensitive reader must dig below the surface of the sand again and again to discover the deep rivers of connection that irrigate this desert journey. The band of ex-slaves makes its way across the wilderness, and the idea of stopping and building a society begins to take shape as the journey continues. What will it mean to stop and settle? What might it mean to sleep in the same place for more than one night, to be able to see the light change in one place, to be able to plant seeds and have enough water to drink, to water cattle, and to irrigate a farm? When their minds are clear, and quarrelling does not take all their energy, the wanderers begin to consider the society they hope to create, how they will create boundaries and connections, how they will distinguish themselves from one another and from their neighbours, how they will order their calendar, how they will honour the predictability of the seasons and the vagaries of nature. Throughout these chapters, deep questions of the legitimacy and authority of leadership, both human and divine, are raised, explored and then raised again. What does it mean to be faithful? Who judges the veracity of God's voice and direction?

Because of the diversity of styles and genres included in this book, many scholars attempt to divide the book according to the stages of the Israelites' journey. Some see three distinct sections: the final encampment of the Israelite people as they prepare for their wilderness journey, the actual march from Sinai to Moab, and the encampment at Moab, which includes a preparation for the entrance to Canaan and the anticipation of living as a free people. Others see the censuses in chapters 1 and 26 as clear markers of new and discrete sections, with a mid-section of rebellion and apostasy that begins with chapter 11 and concludes with Beit-Peor in chapter 26. Dennis Olson (1997: 230) names those who are counted in the first census the generation of death, and those who are enumerated in the second census the generation of hope. Chapters 27 and 36 bracket the narrative tale of the daughters of Zelophehad. Chapters 22–4 seem to be a separate unit, focusing on the story of Balaam and Balak. However divided, the time span covered by the 36 chapters of Numbers are years of growth and change, years in which all but a tiny remnant of the generation of the Exodus die and a new generation of faithful emerges. The fidelity of those born in the desert is juxtaposed with the querulous and restless survivors who too often translate their memories of servitude into fury and rebellion against their leaders.

Among the topics and the correlative questions raised in the narratives of the book of Numbers are:

1 The census: who counts? Who is counted and who does the counting?
2 The priesthood: who are the priests and what are their responsibilities?
3 Boundaries: physical and metaphorical, boundaries of behaviour and acceptability:
   a Who sets the boundaries?
   b What does it mean to be a part of/apart from?
   c Who is in, who is out, and why?
   d What are the consequences of maintaining boundaries? Of wandering beyond or challenging them?

4　How are grievances presented and settled in the emerging Israelite community?

5　How does a subjugated minority move from slavery to freedom? What are the stages of becoming a free people?

6　What is the role of leaders in determining the direction and mores of the community?

7　What is the role of God in determining the direction and mores of the community?

8　What is the place of the individual in/vis-à-vis the emerging and dynamic community?

9　What does it mean to be connected to a people?

10　What does it mean to be connected to a land?

Each of these topics can be examined in the light of the experiences of translesbigay people. As queer folk living in heterosexist cultures, too many of us have experienced the 'slavery' of oppression, discrimination and physical attack. Like slaves, we are not allowed to marry, we face considerable barriers to bearing children, and in many places we are not able to adopt legally. Like the women of the Bible, we are prevented from inheriting what is rightfully ours, and we are often denied a voice. Like many minorities, we may be denied access to certain jobs or professions, and may not be able to live in neighbourhoods of our choice. We may experience discrimination based on how we dress, our speech, our affect. Many of us identify with the Israelites of Numbers, for we too are on a wilderness journey whose end we cannot see. The horizontal violence or antipathy that is too often experienced in some translesbigay communities may mirror the inability of the former slaves in Numbers to accept the leadership of Moses or Aaron or the priests.

This enquiry builds on the work of feminist scholars who, in the last three decades, have challenged and changed long-held assumptions about who reads the biblical text, and how, and why. As Tikva Frymer-Kensky writes, 'How can a book that teaches the common divine origin of all humanity and the sacred nature of each human being reflect a social order in which women are systematically disadvantaged and subordinated?' (2002: xiii). Translesbigay readers approach the text with a range of a similar questions, but we focus on our invisibility, not our status in the narrative, for the biblical text presumes binary gender differentiation. Until recently, we assumed that all individuals are born either male or female, and that identity is fixed throughout one's life. So when we read the biblical text, we could only read it through one set of eyes, those of a male or those of a female. However, we are now entering a new world of interpretation. As Laurel Schneider writes:

To presume a stable heteroeroticism and heteronormative social architecture throughout such a complex and multi-authored record of the events, myths and fantasies of a whole people is silly in terms of human history, sociology and what we know from contemporary histories of sexuality. It is also becoming an ill-advised presumption in light of biblical scholarship. Once opened, our eyes cannot be so easily shut, and the world that we imagine, superimposed on so many layers of retrieval, is changed. (2001: 210)

This chapter will examine six specific narratives from the book of Numbers, asking some of the questions enumerated above and raising additional queries and concerns about the possible meanings and understandings of these narratives for translesbigay readers and interpreters. Those narratives are: the story of the Sotah, or the accused wife; the nazirite; the spies; Korach's rebellion; Balaam's prophecy; and the daughters of Zelophehad. Each narrative will be examined in its context, followed by considerations for queer readings of the text.

Sotah: Numbers 5.11–31

The first portion of Numbers that we will examine is the 20 verses that describe the divine pronouncement concerning the ritual trial of a woman whose husband suspects her of adultery. These verses are preceded by purity regulations, stipulating who may reside in the Israelite camp, which imply the priests' responsibility for maintaining the camp's boundaries.

These verses reflect the frame of the book of Numbers, for they go to the heart of the question of who counts. These verses take us into a biblical world where women and men are defined by their relationship to one another: women are men's wives. This narrative is about men's suspicion that their wives have not been 'faithful' to them, and have been with another man. However, the men are not to act on their jealousy. Rather, God speaks through Moses and outlines a clear if unpalatable procedure for determining the guilt or innocence of the accused wife.

This section is known as the rules of 'Sotah', from the root that means to move about, be unsteady, go astray. Traditionally, it is not called 'suspicion of sotah', so embedded in the name of this portion is the guilt, not the innocence, of the subject, not the jealousy of the accuser. This attribution is made in spite of the fact that the word 'jealousy' is repeated in the text a total of ten times (see Levine 2000: 266).

In the Bible, sexuality is almost inseparable from reproduction, and this concern is amplified in the book of Numbers, with its reiteration of counting the souls who will open the way to and build a new society. This section, coming so early in the book, reflects a concern about charting bloodlines, about keeping familial and tribal boundaries clear and controlled.

> Judaism . . . has been very strict in treating men's (as well as women's) reproductive organs and capabilities as 'sacred vessels.' Much of Jewish law concerning sexuality is based on telling men where they can put their penises and when . . . Sotah [this portion] would provide yet another limitation on male sexual prerogative. (Antonelli 1975: 340)

The sotah ritual, which may have never been actually carried out, employs two essential ingredients: earth and water. The suspected woman stands bareheaded and shamed before the priest, who represents the potentially wronged husband. She is then forced to drink water that has been made 'bitter' by the addition of earth from the floor of the tabernacle. If the woman is guilty, her body swells in a distorted parody of pregnancy; if she is innocent, 'she shall be unharmed and able to retain seed'. Preserving and perpetuating the woman's fertility is the primary social concern of this narrative. The woman in the tale is simply a vessel for the people's future.

Feminist scholars have responded to this ordeal by pointing out that the accused woman's 'innocence or guilt was to be established beyond a shadow of a doubt by God. Her fate was not left to a jealous husband, a court of men, an angry mob, or a pagan river god' (Antonelli 1975: 357). Sarra Levine writes:

> Rabbi Toba Spitzer points out that the text, with all its difficulties, must be seen as taking responsibility for male jealousy as a societal problem, and for introducing a societal mechanism for its resolution. Whereas today men kill women in jealous rages – all of which the media represent as normative – in the biblical period jealousy was not an individual problem to be solved by an individual man in whatever way he saw fit. The biblical text attempted to deal with an otherwise impossible problem that could have worked itself out in more dangerous and painful ways. (2000: 267)

What about a woman who is suspected of having an extra-marital lesbian relationship? And conversely, did women who suspected their husbands of any extra-marital relationships have recourse to any kind of parallel ritual? Judith Antonelli addresses these questions:

> The lesbian affair of a married woman was not adultery, nor was the sexual activity of an unmarried woman, whether she was single, widowed, or divorced. Extra-marital sexual activity of a married man was only adultery if his affair was with a married woman. He might be fined or required to marry a single woman with whom he had intercourse, but he would not have committed adultery. This one sided-definition of adultery is a clear sign of male sexual prerogative under polygyny. (1975: 337–8)

The lines are clear: women's sexuality is presumed to be heterosexual. Unmarried women, whether never married, divorced, or widowed, inhabit a different sociological and legal universe than their married sisters. These verses focus solely on the married heterosexual man and his jealousy of his wife's behaviour with another man.

Phyllis Trible's groundbreaking book, *Texts of Terror*, does not include a close reading of this narrative, but claiming these verses as a terror-filled text may help us to understand them anew. Trible writes, 'If art imitates life, scripture likewise reflects it in both holiness and horror. Reflections themselves neither mandate nor manufacture change; yet by enabling insight, they may inspire repentance. In other words, sad stories may yield new beginnings' (1984: 2). So while this passage reinforces the invisibility of non-heterosexual individuals and of homosexual and non-procreative sex, these verses also reflect the attempt of those on their way to create a new nation to apply divine legislation to the too-often destructive human emotions of jealousy and suspicion.

The sotah ritual makes an additional point about who is counted and the implications of failing to count any individual in the tribe. Sarra Levine points out that the erasure of the parchment that includes God's name in Numbers 5.23 – 'The priest shall put these curses down in writing and rub it off into the water of bitterness' – parallels the humiliating ritual the woman has just suffered. Levine writes, 'the act of humiliation itself, according to Jewish tradition, is tantamount to erasure . . . The Torah's decisive statement is that the shaming of women is, in fact, the erasure of God' (2000: 269). Sotah can be read, then, as a protest against the incomplete enumeration of the Israelite people. These verses can be read as a direct and pre-politicized statement of the challenge later posed by Korach: 'for all the community are holy, all of them, and the Holy One is in their midst' (Num. 16.3).

The Nazirite: Numbers 6

The sixth chapter of Numbers describes the particular laws governing those who, by their own free will, set themselves apart from the community in order to devote themselves to divine service. In a narrative that is so concerned with external categorizing and enumerating, this self-designation is particularly interesting.

> If anyone, man or woman, explicitly utters a nazirite's vow, to set himself apart for the Lord, he shall abstain from wine and any other intoxicant . . . Throughout the term of his vow as nazirite, no razor shall touch his head; it shall remain consecrated until the completion of his term as nazirite of the Lord . . . Throughout the term that he has set apart for the Lord, he shall not go in where there is a dead person. (Num. 6.2–6)

The chapter continues, delineating how the nazirite will serve the priest in the Tent of Meeting and beyond, until the end of his/her term of service.

The chapter ends with a tripartite blessing, known as the priestly blessing. Moses is directed by God to speak to Aaron and his sons and to pronounce these powerful performative words in the presence of the people.

The chapter on the nazirite may have particular power for the translesbigay reader, for this portion indicates that anyone who wishes can place him/herself in holy service. There is no evidence in the text of any tests or measurements or qualifications for those who choose this service, or of a particular timeframe for this service – those who are willing to take on these responsibilities seem to be recognized as appropriate to carry out the terms of their 'vows'. This self-naming is unique in the Hebrew Bible, where so often status is derived from familial or tribal or God-appointed relationships. In addition, both men and women can dedicate themselves to this service, and there is no distinction made between them in the regulations of service that follow (Frymer-Kensky 2002: xv). The nazirite calls him/her self, names him/her self. Too rarely have translesbigay individuals named ourselves. We have struggled to find names of our own, names that reflect our pride in who we are, terms that reflect the relationships that sustain us, categories that allow us to draw boundaries of inclusion. Those who claim a particular kind of service, for a month or a year or more, can be transformed by that service, that self-naming, that opportunity to work in co-operation with others who serve a Creator who accepts every offering as a gift.

When read in the context of the two preceding chapters, the priestly blessing that concludes this chapter gains power. If one understands the sotah narrative as protection against the excesses of jealous revenge, and if one reads the nazirite narrative as providing an open door to all those who wish to serve, this simple blessing becomes a divine promise of protection, kindness and compassion, acceptance, and the gift of peace. This blessing includes the wrongfully accused wife, the wife who has gone astray, and even the jealous husband. This blessing embraces those who choose service and willingly give up their rights to enjoy wine, to cut their hair, and to care for the dead – in the name of other kinds of holy service. And this blessing reaches to those who, for whatever reasons, do not choose the rigorous service of the nazir, but who distinguish themselves in other ways.

This blessing is offered to all, those who are traditionally numbered and those whose names and gifts are yet to be counted. 'May God bless you and watch over you. May the Holy One's face shine upon you and be gracious to you. May the Source of Love's presence be lifted up to you and grant you peace.'

The Spies: Numbers 13–14

The Israelites' journey through the wilderness is punctuated with a series of challenges to authority, both the authority of the human leaders and the authority of the Holy One who has appointed those leaders. The book opens with an enumeration of the duties of the Levites, those who serve as the priests, and the narrative repeatedly returns to a delineation of their duties, their responsibilities and the terms of their service. And as the priests' purview is examined, the narrative exposes the mounting challenges to Moses, by the people, by Moses' own siblings, and by the rebels who mobilize around Korach.

'The Lord spoke to Moses, saying, "Send men to scout the land of Canaan, which I am giving to the Israelite people; send one man from each of their ancestral tribes, each one a chieftain among them"' (Num. 13.1–2). The text continues, naming each tribe and the tribal representatives who will embark on this mission, twelve in all, and then Moses' directions:

'Go up there into the Negev and on into the hill country, and see what kind of country it is. Are the people who dwell in it strong or weak, few or many? Is the country in which they dwell good or bad? Are the towns they live in open or fortified? Is the soil rich or poor? Is it wooded or not? And take pains to bring back some of the fruit of the land.' Now it happened to be the season of the first ripe grapes. (13.7–20)

The Israelites have been traversing a wilderness, making their way across empty expanses and arid wadis, trekking day after day under the relentless sun. The scouts are sent out into populated areas with directions to take a measure of the people and their cities. They are also directed to assess the land

and its yield. The first notable encounter in the travelogue reported in the text is in a vineyard where the travellers come face to face with a bunch of grapes so substantial that 'it had to be borne on a carrying frame by two' (13.3). At the conclusion of their forty-day journey, the scouts return to the camp with reports of a land that 'does indeed flow with milk and honey', and, producing a somewhat travel-worn but nevertheless impressive bunch of grapes, they continue, 'and this is its fruit'. 'However,' they warn, 'the people who inhabit the country are powerful, and the cities are fortified and very large' (Num. 13.27–8).

In spite of this report, one of the scouts, Caleb, appeals to Moses to go forth, insisting that they are able to possess the land. The other spies, however, re-emphasize the size of the task, 'All the people that we saw in it are men of great size . . . and we looked like grasshoppers to ourselves, and so we must have looked to them' (Num. 13.32–3). The community is frightened by the majority report, and they cry out for a return to Egypt. Caleb, now joined by Joshua, urges the people to trust in God's promise to bring the Israelites safely into the land. But the people, now diminished in their own eyes, turn their anger on their leaders. In turning aside from the Holy One, they forget that they, and those they fear as giants, are all created in God's image. James Ackerman comments:

> The opening chapters of Numbers have strongly emphasized divine guidance as God dwelt in Israel's midst. The census of six hundred thousand fighting men has also indicated a continuation of God's promises to make Israel a great nation. How could such a multitude feel as small as grasshoppers? Even apart from divine guidance, they could have moved into the Land like locusts. . . . The narrative makes clear that the key to conquest is faith in, and the reality of, the divine presence. (1987: 83)[1]

But for the majority, God's presence is obscured. They see only their own fears.

This narrative yields rich interpretations when read from a translesbigay perspective. The majority of the scouts experience one reality: oversize produce and oversize inhabitants. They are overwhelmed by the seeming enormity of the obstacles to entering the land, and when they look at themselves, they begin to shrink like Alice in Wonderland after she drinks the diminishing elixir. They leave behind the realm of humans and mammals and become

---

1 Adriane Leveen writes: 'These terms of complaint [the utterances of chapter 11] mark the change in the people's fortunes, pouring from their mouths in a rapid torrent until the culmination of the crisis with the suppression of the revolt of Korah and the Reubenites in Chap 16. The peoples' discontented words in ch. 11 are followed by the politically charged argument of Miriam and Aaron against Moses in ch. 12 which involves the medium of speech. They challenge Moses as unique spokesperson for God, asking "Hasn't the Lord spoken through us as well?" (Num 12.2) The spies use words as a weapon of subversion, more destructive even than those murmured by the people or Miriam and Aaron, as they spread evil reports, *dvat haaretz*, (literally 'utterance of the land') among the people in Num. 13.32. Finally, at the lowest point of the narrative, the heated words exchanged between Korah and Moses mark the climax of the lexicon of complaint first begun in ch. 11' (2002: 214).

like insects. Grasshoppers, spindly and green, become indistinguishable from the grass or the rich vineyard floor. Grasshoppers light for a moment and are gone. What is more insignificant than a grasshopper, especially to a giant, who could unwittingly destroy an entire colony of these orthopterous insects by shifting his or her weight?

How often have members of sexual minority groups felt that the enormity of the obstacles to our visibility, or our being taken seriously, or our being considered human, are simply too large to challenge? How many of us have watched ourselves or others shrink into insignificance, or allowed our concerns to diminish, because the barriers to visibility have simply seemed too great? And how easily have we, after time, agreed that we are like grasshoppers, 'And so must we have looked to them' (Num.13. 33).

When the majority takes a stand that seems wrong or exclusive or diminishes the humanity of any individual, who among us has the courage to stand up, as did Caleb and Joshua, and speak out for a different vision, carrying forth a minority report? Who among us speaks in the name of strength and optimism, who among us insists on continuing to see through our own eyes, not to the exclusion of other points of view, but honouring our own experience? Caleb and Joshua speak their truth to the collective, sharing their conviction that the Holy One will accompany them as they enter the land, and that the people will see that the inhabitants are as human and as vulnerable as are the Israelites. Rabbi Lisa Edwards asks: 'As women, or members of minority groups, how often have we taken on the grasshopper image in our own eyes, and assumed that others view us the same way? How often do we fixate on how we look to "them" and fail ourselves in the process?' (2000: 284).

The people cannot hear the minority report, for they have been frightened by the stories of the other, and have lost sight of the spies' original mission: to scout the land that the Holy One is granting to the Israelites. When they 'threatened to pelt [Caleb and Joshua] with stones, the Presence of the Lord appeared in the Tent of Meeting to all the Israelites' (Num. 14.10). Horizontal violence is all too familiar within communities that experience themselves at risk of annihilation, communities that have experienced discrimination and marginalization. Too often, communities that see themselves only through the distorted images of an other turn upon their own leaders, the very ones they need to move from shame to self-worth, from degradation to security. In this narrative, both God and Moses enter the story to protect Caleb and Joshua from physical attack. When the Holy One is angered by the majority's faithlessness, Moses takes the role of the compassionate shepherd, arguing with the provoked Divine and asking for mercy on the people's account, reminding God of the attributes of mercy enumerated in Exodus and Deuteronomy and repeated here: 'The Lord God is slow to anger and abounding in kindness, forgiving iniquity and transgression' (Num. 14.18 and Ex. 20.5–6; Ex. 34.6–7 and Deut. 5.9–10). The Holy One does forgive the Israelites, but tells Moses that 'none of the men . . . who have disobeyed Me shall see the land that I promised on oath to their fathers' (Num. 14.23). The Israelites' punishment for not believing in themselves is great. *Our* punishment for not believing in ourselves, for being blind to our own rights and responsibilities to ourselves and others, might be understood as our inability to enter the next stage of our lives, a time and place when we dream and then create realities that become mirrors of our strength and full visibility.

Korach's Rebellion: Numbers 16–17

By the time Korach is introduced in chapter 16, readers of Numbers have become familiar with the Israelites' despair and God's intolerance of their faithlessness. Korach and 250 chieftains rise up against Moses and his appointed and challenge their authority, saying 'You have gone too far! For all the community are holy, all of them, and the Lord is in their midst. Why then do you raise yourselves above the Lord's congregation? (Num. 16.3). Moses has just endured a similar challenge by his sister Miriam and his brother Aaron (chapter 12) that ended when Miriam was stricken with ghostly scales that created a shroud of her own skin. However, Miriam and Aaron challenged their brother's authority with a question, 'Has the Lord spoken only through Moses? Has He not spoken through us as well?' Korach and his followers assume the question and posit an unambiguous response: 'all the community are holy, all of them'. As leaders and chieftains, it is interesting that they do not use the first person plural, but rather refer to the people as 'them'. This reflects their sense of themselves as apart from as opposed to a part of the very people they are claiming as holy. They come up with the 'right' answer, but for the 'wrong' reason. Interested only in usurping Moses' position as leader, the intent of their challenge is to establish their eligibility for his position.[2]

The Korach story is short and brutal. Unlike the spies of chapter 13, who could not see themselves at all, Korach and his band overestimate their power and influence. In their arrogance, they do not imagine that their public challenge to Moses will incite God to 'bring about something unheard of' (Num. 16.30). Moses responds to Korach by challenging him to a sort of biblical bake-off, warning the rebels that God will serve as the judge in this winner-take-all competition. 'Scarcely had he finished speaking all these words when the ground under them burst asunder, and the earth opened its mouth and swallowed them up with their households, all Korach's people and all their possessions' (Num. 16.31–2). This is a disaster so unique that is reported as if it occurs without a sound. The only noise that the reader hears are the piercing shrieks of the hapless witnesses. The earth closes up, and those who had offered incense are consumed by a raging fire.

Centuries of commentators have attempted to interpret this troubling story, explaining that the sin was 'process', not content, likening the service that Korach calls for 'somehow akin to serving Pharaoh' (Ackerman 1987a: 82), or calling it 'Korach's Riddle' (Pitzele 1996). For the translesbigay reader who has too often been the victim of a system of laws and regulations and jurists and legislators who seem to have arrogated absolute power and decision-making to themselves, there may be significant numbers of us who want to cheer on Korach and his followers, agreeing that he may have failed to utilize

---

2 Elie Wiesel cites Onkelos's commentary: 'Vayakumu b'hutzpah: it is with arrogance, with insolence, that they stand before Moses' (Wiesel 2000: 14).

appropriate channels, but acknowledging the justice of his claim. 'All of the community are holy. All of them.' However, this narrative may remind us of the importance of seeing incidents in context, the imperative of pulling the camera back so that we can view the greater story, the fuller narrative. This incident is seen by some interpreters as the pivotal challenge to Moses' authority in the book of Numbers. God's response to the frightened spies is to clarify exactly who will enter the promised land, delineating the nature of the generation who will create the new society. Korach and all his followers disappear from the earth without a trace, and the way is opened for the survivors to resume their journey. While the book of Numbers includes one more narrative of apostasy (chapter 25), this is a challenge directly to God, not to Moses or to the priests. In fact, many consider the second half of the book, whether marking its beginning with chapter 22 or with chapter 26, as a section that reflects the fidelity of the new generation. Perhaps one or two generations that carry old angers in their hearts must pass away before a new generation can forge a truly just and egalitarian society.

Balaam and his Ass: Numbers 22.21–35

The tale of Balaam and Balak is unique among biblical narratives. This complex and interesting story may have been included in Numbers primarily because of its geographic location; neither the characters nor the events described are directly linked to any of the other stories related in this book. The theme of community boundaries undergirds this tale, for a non-Israelite is approached by another non-Israelite to intervene with the Israelites. This narrative may serve as an example of outsiders' definitions, understanding and approach to avoidance of Israel. Balak, the king of Moab, enlists Balaam to curse the approaching Israelites. However, Balaam fears the God of Israel and invokes the Holy One's direction in carrying out Balak's charge. While the oracles, blessings and curses of these chapters provide rich material for interpretation, our focus here will be on a single incident in this narrative: the episode of the seer Balaam and his ass.

The very first word of this narrative reminds the reader of another tale in which an animal plays a pivotal role. The single verb, *v'yakam*, is the same word that begins Genesis 22. Just as Balaam arises early, so does Abraham on the day that he takes his son Isaac to Mount Moriah, binds him upon an altar as if to prepare a sacrifice, and substitutes a ram for his son. In Numbers 22, the seer Balaam is travelling at God's behest and, like Abraham, encounters a messenger of God (the same Hebrew word, *malach*, is used in Genesis 22). However, unlike Abraham, Balaam is blind to the angel. Rather, his ass sees God's messenger, and 'swerved from the road and went into the fields'. Balaam beats his animal, and when the angel again blocks the ass's path, the animal squeezes her master's foot against a wall, and is beaten a second time. Again the angel blocks the animal's way, and the ass simply lies down, incurring Balaam's wrath once again. 'Then the Holy One opened the ass's mouth.' Balaam's ass is the first animal who speaks in the Hebrew Bible since the serpent beguiled Eve in Genesis 3.1. Both creatures open with a question, but the contrast between the questions is powerful. Where the serpent was wily and intentionally misrepresented its Creator, the ass is direct. 'What have I done to you that you have beaten me three times?' (22.28). The narrative continues:

> Balaam said to the ass, 'You have made a mockery of me! If I had a sword with me, I'd kill you.' The ass said to Balaam, 'Look, I am the ass that you have been riding all along until this day! Have I been in the habit of doing this to you?' And he answered, 'No.' Then the Lord uncovered Balaam's eyes, and he saw the angel of the Lord standing in the way.

Once God intervenes, Balaam turns his full attention to the Holy One, and the ass is all but forgotten by both Balaam and the reader. However, the animal that sees the angel of the Lord and is then, ever-so-briefly, granted the gift of speech, presents an interesting image to the translesbigay reader. In the biblical narrative, there are clear distinctions between human beings and animals. However, animals are the closest of God's creations to human beings, and in this story, the ass is used by the Holy One to 'teach Balaam a lesson'. The seer is blind, and the dumb animal wisely perceives the Lord's messenger. The few words that the ass speaks reflect a sense of the connection between crime and punishment that the seer has failed to consider in his willingness to curse the Israelites. The ass's query provides a mirror to Balaam, who has failed to ask how the Israelites have earned or whether they deserve these curses. The ass speaks with clarity, directness and for justice. The confused prophet curses his faithful companion, and, subsequently, in spite of himself blesses the people who serve the Source of his own confusion. The reversal of roles between the 'dumb' animal and the 'foolish' seer may have particular appeal to queer readers who have long been marginalized or shut out of the narrative of our religious traditions. We are not unfamiliar with topsy-turvy tales where those who are forbidden to love one another become exemplars of devotion and care, or stories of rejected individuals who become builders of families, communities, and agents of world-repair: 'sometimes the only way to glimpse the deep working of desire in imagination is through those stories, tellings and images that cavort with carnivalesque energy on the margins of intelligibility' (Schneider 2001: 214). The tale of Balaam and his ass may be one such story.

The Daughters of Zelophehad: Numbers 27 and 36

The two-part story of the daughters of Zelophehad is a source of consternation for both the historic and the modern reader. The first 11 verses of chapter 27 and the first 12 verses of chapter 36 present a narrative that is unique in many ways. Following the exhaustive male census that begins in chapter 26, the reader unexpectedly encounters the daughters of Zelophehad: named as Mahlah, Noah, Hoglah, Milcah and Tirzah. These five women, who are distinguished by being named, one by one, both in Numbers 26.33 and now once again (27.1), boldly position themselves in the most powerful place and before the leaders of the camp as they 'stood before Moses, Eleazar the priest, the

chieftains, and the whole assembly, at the entrance of the Tent of Meeting'
(27.1–2). They forthrightly state their concerns:

> Our father died in the wilderness. He was not one of the faction, Korah's fac-
> tion, which banded together against the Lord, but died for his own sin; and
> he has left no sons. Let not our father's name be lost to his clan just because
> he had no son! Give us a holding among our father's kinsmen! (27.3)

This carefully constructed speech is attributed to all five daughters, and it
is delightful to consider how they might have orchestrated its delivery. This
simultaneous or synchronized or syncopated speech establishes the sisters as
a unit; indeed, throughout the narratives that refer to them, none of them is
ever given individual status. Like Shifra and Puah, these sisters are referred
to solely in partnership. Like the midwives of Exodus, these five sisters share a
special status as members of a particular collective, in this case, as daughters
of a single father. (We never know whether they are also the daughters of a
single mother, which underscores the invisibility of women in this narrative.)
Not one of these women ever acts, or is acted upon, as an individual (Person
2000: 323).

By referring to Korach's 'faction' against the Lord, the women allude to
God's punishment of the rebels, not to Korach's challenge to Moses, to whom
the sisters now appeal. Their request is not based on their own need for sus-
tenance or security, but posited rather to preserve the honour and lineage of
their deceased father's name. These women understand the structure and
dynamics of their world, and modestly, if circuitously, request their inheritance. Moses consults with the Holy One, who advises him to 'transfer their
father's share to them' (27.6). The text continues with God's citing this example
as a precedent for further legislation for men who die without male issue:

> If a man dies without leaving a son, you shall transfer his property to his
> daughter. If he has no daughter, you shall assign his property to his brothers.
> If he has no brothers, you shall assign his property to his father's brothers. If
> his father had no brothers, you shall assign his property to his nearest rela-
> tive in his own clan. (27.8–11)

Certainly, no men bear sons *or* daughters without wives, but in this patriarchal system, neither wives nor sisters of the deceased are eligible to inherit.
This portion ends with these five women becoming the first rightful female
landowners in the biblical text. As Hara Person writes, 'The daughters of
Zelophehad set a significant precedent. They stepped outside the boundary
and survived (2000: 323). Mahlah and her sisters not only survive, but triumph:
they challenge the system and are rewarded.

A second narrative section continues the daughters' tale. Somehow, the
issue of the daughters' marriages was not considered in the earlier ruling.
Given that biblical culture was based on a binary understanding of sexuality, and that all women were potential brides and mothers, it seems odd that
these women are initially dealt with solely as inheritors and not as sources of
land and wealth for their eventual, inevitable husbands. Chapter 36 rectifies

this oversight. 'The family heads in the clans of the descendants of Gilead
. . . [Zelophehad's family]' come before Moses to ask about the assignation of
Zelophehad's land. They posit: 'Now, if they [Zelophehad's daughters] marry
persons from another Israelite tribe, their share will be cut off from our ancestral portion and be added to the portion of the tribe into which they marry;
thus our allotted portion will be diminished (36.1–3). The clansmen's query
stands in stark contrast to the daughters' earlier request to Moses, which was
about their father's honour, not their own comfort. These male relatives are
forthright in their concern about their own 'diminished portion'. Moses again
consults with the Holy One, and responds to the worried clansmen:

> They may marry anyone they wish, provided they marry into a clan of their
> father's tribe. No inheritance of the Israelites may pass over from one tribe
> to another, but the Israelites must remain bound each to the ancestral por-
> tion of his tribe . . . The daughters of Zelophehad did as the Lord had com-
> manded Moses, [and they] were married to sons of their uncles . . . so their
> share remained in the tribe of their father's clan. (36.6–12)

What initially seemed like a victory, enabling women to inherit family land,
is subsequently understood as a means of keeping their father's tribal lands
intact. Zelophehad's daughters' marriage choices are circumscribed because of
their position as heiresses. Tikva Frymer-Kensky points out that each daughter does own her land for her lifetime, and that if her husband divorces her, she
stays on her land (2002: 22). However, she cannot bequeath it to her sisters or
to her daughters; once she dies, the land belongs solely to her husband and his
heirs, who only include her daughters if there are no sons. Tal Ilan writes,

> one may point out the sensitivity Scripture shows to injustice toward
> women, hastening to correct it. This example, one may surmise, should
> probably serve as a guideline for future Jewish lawmakers who, based on
> the example of Moses, will listen to women's complaints and correct wrongs
> inflicted upon them.

However,

> The biblical daughters-of-Zelophehad amendment was a halfway reform of
> the law. As a general principle, to be applied legally in other cases, it served
> a useful purpose. It pointed the way to the future Jewish lawgivers as inno-
> vators. However, on the question of a woman's right to inherit according to
> Jewish law, its outcome was detrimental. (2000: 179–80)

These two sections point up the challenges of accommodating the exceptional case in a developing system of case law. The sisters, and subsequently
their male clansmen, turn to Moses for answers, and Moses turns to God.
The divine legislation accommodates daughters of landowners who would,
without this ruling, become homeless. This section stands in stark contrast to
the first narrative in Numbers that we considered: the sotah. There, only men
spoke, and the accused woman remained mute and potentially disgraced.

The daughters-of-Zelophehad narrative introduces women of agency, women who, once named as individuals, band together and demand what is rightfully theirs. Considered sequentially, this text may be a source of hope. The absence of the voice of the accused woman is not even noted in the sotah narrative. The power of the sisters' collective voice sets a new legal precedent. The naming of the daughters in the second census may presage their agency. The acknowledgement of the diversity of voices, those of women as well as men, those of daughters as well as sons, provides a fuller and truer picture of the generation of wanderers.

Queer readers, like feminist readers, are left with the discomfiting experience of watching the disenfranchised demand and be awarded rights, only to watch those rights disappear in a patriarchal system that prevents women from owning property, a system that tragically continues to be the norm in too many cultures to this day. Like the experience of many gay and lesbian Americans who seek civil marriage, we have seen the way open in one jurisdiction after another, only to discover legal loopholes, considerations and pre-existing statutes that make all but a very few civil unions invalid in too many of the states and municipalities in which we live. But we are also left with the power of the daughters of Zelophehad, who come out of their mourning, come out of the shadows, bearing their names and their clear sense of justice. Laurel Schneider writes,

> The queerest stories of women in the Hebrew Bible may in fact be those about women who managed to have a voice at all, women who managed to survive and/or overcome with some kind of chutzpah their barrenness, widowhood, slavery, rape, virginity, abandonment, marriage, ugliness, or other signifiers of their male-derivative identity, economic dependence and status. These stories may be more queer tales, in a desexualized sense, than those stories (if such stories exist) that hint at female homoeroticism. (2001: 218–19)

This story has power for the queer reader, because it speaks of a clear sense of identity, collective action, and a challenge to authority. The force of the daughters' claim can remind us that we, as queer readers of this text, must continue to seek out those who share our just claims, including our claim to a text that includes us. Together, with a single, rich and most probably cacophonous voice, queer readers now speak truth to power and demand our rightful inheritance. From the silence of sotah to the speech of the daughters, this text of wandering includes the voices of the formerly silent, and thus points the way towards future journeys where the invisible are seen, the cast-aside recovered, the despised reconsidered.

Conclusion

The book of Numbers constructs a narrative from disparate experiences in the long trek of the Israelites across the wilderness. Too many times, the book itself wanders, and even the most attentive reader fears that she has lost her way. This essay has attempted to map one pathway through the text for the translesbigay reader, aware that any attempt to create a way through this diverse and sometimes treacherous text bypasses incidents and events that some consider essential. The six narratives that provide the focal point of this discussion, taken together, yield several powerful areas of enquiry for the translesbigay reader. A relationship with the divine seems to be imperative to survival in the wilderness, but that relationship must be a right relationship, and the definition of 'rightness' changes and develops as the Israelites' journey continues. In the first narrative we examined, God's justice protects the wrongly accused wife from her husband's jealousy, but the trial that is constructed seems to modern readers unnecessarily cruel and demeaning. The narrative establishes a question of 'who counts' which carries through the book of Numbers. The nazirite, who serves the Holy One, becomes one who counts him/herself, providing stark contrast to the sotah, who is acted upon and lacks all agency. For the modern reader, the priestly blessing, which occurs in this portion, can be read as a gift from the biblical tradition: in our time, a wide range of individuals can share the words of this blessing with others. The story of the spies who see themselves diminish in their own eyes and the eyes of others reminds us to see ourselves through eyes of compassion and possibility. The narrative of the rebellious Korach and his band challenges modern readers to consider the context of our own dissatisfactions and disappointments, and to realize that our leaders reflect collective strength and possibilities as much as they exemplify their own individual shortcomings and blindness. Balaam and his ass provide comic relief in this unrelenting narrative of hunger, impatience and rebellion. The talking donkey serves as a model for the irrepressibility of a direct demand for justice that simply, finally, cannot be ignored. The ass's ability to see God reminds each of us of the possibility of the Holy One's presence at the crossroads of our own lives. The fact that the book of Numbers concludes with the unlikely narrative of the daughters of Zelophehad may indeed be the most powerful statement for the queer reader of these texts. Voices that demand justice, be they animal or human, cannot be stifled or stilled. And even if the final chapter of Numbers keeps the sisters' inheritance within their tribe, their voices have been heard, and legislation has been passed that changes history. As Ackerman says, 'the final word of the book is . . . about tribal integrity' (1987a: 89).

The people continue their journey, but the lessons of this book are incorporated into the continuing story of the Israelite people. Through the book of Numbers, we witness the creation of a delicate fabric of connection that is woven by genealogies, the establishment of a line of leadership, and of a structure of legislation that will serve the people as they go forth. This book takes the reader beyond geography into some of the essential questions that face all developing societies: questions of relationships and essence. These are questions that are at the core of all queer lives. We are left with the possibility that each of us, whatever our gender or sexuality, may indeed find blessing. Some of us will find that blessing by reading this text, by turning it, teaching it, considering it through the lens of our own lives and our own experiences.

Deuteronomy

DERYN GUEST

Introduction

The book of Deuteronomy takes its name from the Greek translation of Deuteronomy 17.18, which says that the king should have a 'copy of the law' provided for him. The Greek translated this as 'second' (*deuteros*) law (*nomos*). Its Hebrew title derives from the usual practice of taking the opening words of a book as its title: accordingly it is known as *debarim* – 'words'. Although Deuteronomy is identified in most English Bibles as the fifth book of Moses (the last of the five books that constitute the Torah), it was originally the opening to a larger work that extends to the end of 2 Kings: the Deuteronomistic History. The book of Deuteronomy is programmatic for this larger work: setting the theological agenda for the story that follows and explaining, in advance, that worship of other deities will lead to political disaster. Set in the time of Moses and cast as his extended farewell speech, the book outlines a series of laws for the Israelites who are about to take possession of the land promised to them by their deity. The book is pervaded by a passionate encouragement to abide by these laws since their ability to remain in the land rests on obedience to them. Failure to abide by the laws will lead to divine punishment and expulsion.

The laws themselves are often noted for their humanitarian elements such as care for the vulnerable and marginalized; or the (idealistic) constraints it puts on those in power (see the law of the king in 17.14–20 for example). However, Cheryl Anderson's (2004) work on the laws contained in Exodus's Book of the Covenant (20.22–23.19), several of which appear again in Deuteronomy, indicates how biblical law codes, often applauded as humanitarian, are actually infused with racist, classist and sexist assumptions. Moreover, she argues that these law codes do not *reflect* pre-existing ideas about sex and gender, but actually *construct* or call into being sexed and gendered identities. Queer readers can build on her work and find new examples of the way Deuteronomy's law codes not only construct male and female bodies, but create clear and rigid boundaries between the two sexes and a set of gendered norms for each.

Date

Since at least 1805, the date of de Wette's influential paper, the book of Deuteronomy has been identified as the book of the law found by the High Priest Hilkiah when the Jerusalem temple was being repaired (2 Kings 22.8–20). This book is taken to King Josiah who, upon hearing the words of the book, tears his clothes in dismay before embarking upon a major programme of religious reform. He deposes priests who had officiated in the cult of Baal and astral worship, takes down the Asherah and burns it in the Kidron valley, breaks down the living quarters of cultic personnel, destroys the horses dedicated to sun worship set up at the entrance to the temple and the roof altars on the temple. He abolishes the Molech cult. The priests of the high places are removed from the regional sanctuaries and brought into Jerusalem; the high places at which they had served are defiled with bones of the dead. He bans wizardry and sorcery. The identification of Deuteronomy as the ancient law book that inspired these reforms makes sense since it calls for the centralization of worship of one deity alone, at one place by one people, together with a demand for the elimination of all things deemed non-Israelite/Yahwistic. The story of 2 Kings 22.8–20 thus infers that Deuteronomy pre-existed the time of Josiah (640–609 BCE), and that the rediscovery prompted the reforms. However, the whole story of 'finding' an ancient law book may well have been constructed to boost credibility for Josiah's actions, created (as the book of law book itself may have been) by a pro-Yhwh, pro-independence party in order to legitimize Josiah's centralization policies. Deuteronomy thus might be *set* in ancient times, *presented* as the farewell speech of Moses, but is actually to be dated to the late seventh century, around 622 BCE.

Evidence for this date is found in Deuteronomy's noted structural similarity with contemporaneous Assyrian vassal treaties. Discovered in 1956, the vassal treaties outline the loyalty contract between the Assyrian king, his successor and his subjects. A treaty would typically commence with a preamble identifying the two parties undertaking the agreement, details of the historical relationship between them, the conditions and injunctions of the treaty, details of where the document would be stored, instructions on its public recital, before closing with the invocation of divine witnesses and a section of blessings and curses that would ensue if the treaty was kept or broken. Deuteronomy certainly appears to have been informed by the vocabulary, themes and structure of a vassal treaty, the main difference being that Deuteronomy posits a treaty (a 'covenant' in its vocabulary) between a deity and his subjects, rather than between a king and his subject peoples. Deuteronomy is thus modelled upon, and informed by, the seventh-century BCE Assyrian treaties, but provides an alternative to them, inviting Israel to bind itself to a deity rather than any earthly king. For an overview of these arguments see Soggin (1976); and for an attempt to determine the connection see Steymans (1995).

Although Deuteronomy may have been substantially compiled from the seventh century BCE onwards, there may well be older oral and written traditions incorporated within it. Certainly the Deuteronomist was familiar with the laws of Exodus 21–3 and 34, but it is difficult to say with any assurance what other source material may have been included or how extensive it might have been. There was also further editing of the text in the years after Josiah's reform. The introduction of chapters 1–4 and epilogue of chapters 29–30 may have been added when the descendants of the exiles were returning to Jerusalem. As Rogerson points out, Deuteronomy's opening chapters position Israel on the eve of entry into the promised land but hint strongly at the exile to come (4.25–8), while the latter chapters presuppose an exilic community on the eve of return to that land. Moreover, the impracticalities of compulsory attendance at the one religious centre (Jerusalem) at least seven times a year, plus the substantial transfer of resources from local towns to a single sanctuary as implied in chapter 12, may be indicative of a time when 'Israel' was the small, post-exilic community of Yehud (Rogerson 2003: 154, 159). Deuteronomy may incorporate older traditions, but it could also thus be seen as a product, ultimately, of the post-exilic period.

Contents

1.1–4.43: a first introduction. Moses reviews the Israelites' progress thus far noting how the Lord has been paving their way, fighting on their behalf. The people are enjoined to learn the lessons of their recent past so that they might live long in their new homeland.

4.44–11.32: a second introduction. Moses urges exclusive worship of Yhwh, singling out the worship of Baal and Asherah as particularly disastrous and potential cause of divine punishment. There is a repetition of the Ten Commandments, emphasis upon the jealousy of Yhwh and the need to love this deity solely.

12–26: Encouragement to uphold various laws.

27.1–30.20: an epilogue detailing the consequence of non-compliance. It states the blessings and curses connected with the maintenance of the laws proclaimed and it appears to addresses a community that has experienced the exile.

32–33: concluding appendices, including the Song of Moses, the Blessing of Moses and a brief note recording Moses' death.

Loving a Jealous God

The command to *love* the Lord their God with all their heart, soul and might (Deut. 6.5) has resonance with the Hittite and Assyrian vassal treaties; particularly the latter (see Mendenhall 1954; Weinfeld 1972). In both Deuteronomy and the Assyrian treaties, subjects are instructed to love the deity/king. This word 'love', however, in its ancient context, refers to allegiance and loyalty. Rather than being drawn from the realm of deeply affectionate, intimate relationships, it is a political term that calls for unstinting faithfulness to one's superior. However, the Israelites need to love/be loyal to this deity because he is a jealous god; and here we *do* have a term that derives from the realm of personal relationships rather than politics. This is not a term that occurs in the vassal treaties. Rather, it is probably derived from Hosea's use of the marriage metaphor to describe Israel's relationship with their God. Jealousy (*qin'ah*), as Tikva Frymer-Kensky comments, is specialized language. She notes how it refers to the 'spirit of jealousy' that overcomes a husband in Numbers 5.11–31 when he suspects that his wife has been unfaithful, and continues:

It is marriage language, and it expresses the attitude of the one whose prerogatives have been undermined: the husband, whose wife owes him exclusive loyalty; and God, whose people owe God the same exclusive fidelity. The other side of jealousy is inconstancy, unfaithfulness, or 'whoring'. (1992: 53)

The focus that Deuteronomy places on the jealousy of God is taken up extensively by the prophets Jeremiah and Ezekiel, who use the marriage metaphor and image of the cuckolded husband to explain why God allowed his people to be punished and exiled from the land in 587 BCE. Imaging the apostasy of his people as the behaviour of an adulterous wife, giving a blow-by-blow account of how Woman/Israel would be stripped, beaten, raped and abandoned, would certainly have caught the attention of the prophets' audiences. The pornographic features of this imagery, noted by Robert Carroll in his 1986 commentary on Jeremiah, has subsequently been taken up by feminists in what has become known as the 'pornoprophetics' debate. An early contributor to that debate – Rachel Magdalene (1995) – points out how its origins might lie in the curses of ancient treaties. Building on the work of Hillers (1964: 1–11, 80–9), she notes that of the 18 variations of treaty maledictions, three specifically threaten (a) that the city would become a prostitute; (b) that it will be stripped; and (c) that wives will be raped. The deity's violent punishment of Woman/Israel is thus depicted as appropriate action for a husband/deity who needs to maintain his own honour and enforce covenantal compliance. If she is right, then Deuteronomy's indebtedness to the Assyrian vassal treaties had far-reaching consequences for the imaging of God's relationship with his people.

When modern religious speakers call for a return to biblical values, or more specifically, call upon the Bible to endorse their idealization of heterosexuality and marriage, they fail to observe the very damaging image of marriage and heterosexuality that is represented in the idea of the jealous deity. Feminists were right to bring the pornoprophetics debate into the open. The marriage metaphor is grounded in real conditions (the punishments that can be enacted upon an adulterous woman). So, although it is 'just a metaphor' that supplied a productive means of humiliating a nation sufficiently to initiate a return to the covenant relationship with the deity, its derivation from the punitive actions that could be inflicted on wives suspected of adultery renders it problematic. Effective it may have been, but it could only gain currency by exploiting a shared conception of the fickle, wanton woman who 'gets what she deserves'.

What feminists have not drawn attention to is the way the idea of the 'jealous' deity also reinforces the heteronormative atmosphere of the scriptures by positing the relationship between God and Israel as one of marriage. In the only lesbian engagement with this debate that I know of, Rabbi Rose suggests that a woman who is both lesbian-identified and Jewish has a different vantage point. Insofar as the marriage metaphor posits the harsh punishment of an adulterous wife, Rose stands outside its remit:

I do not engage in heterosexual relationships. I am not dependent upon and have no reason to be in close proximity to that abusing male . . . A Jewish lesbian stands outside the heterosexual matrix. From that position, I identify neither with the abusive God nor the abused whore-wife. (2000: 147)

So whereas heterosexually identified feminists and womanists might find themselves uncomfortably the target of such metaphors, a lesbian reading provides a critical distance from which to view the metaphor's implications. Rose's response is to challenge the depiction of the deity ('Either I know this God of Israel is not worthy of any fidelity, or this is not God' (2000: 147)). She chooses the latter option, arguing that the image is 'a literary trope written by a man apparently steeped in cultural misogyny' (2000: 147). Reading as an insider/outsider she also takes up a position of solidarity with the abused metaphorical woman. Her identity with the metaphorical woman happens on a number of levels. They are both women, the sexual acts of both have been considered sinful. As a Jewish woman her legacy is one of a people raped and abused from Roman occupation through to the crusades, the inquisition and the holocaust. But as a lesbian reader,

> there may be another dimension altogether . . . I may in fact love this woman, yearning to express this love as a lover might. My interest in the story then changes. I become as rival suitor, offering in my mind the kind of lovemaking I hope would heal. (2000: 150)

Conceding that there is self-interest here, she adds, 'With the appropriate maturity, I understand the situation may require the most absolute chastity . . . In offering my intervention, assistance, and love, however chastely, I express my sexuality once again – and because it is justice making, I can call that very sexuality God also' (2000: 150). She claims that a lesbian reading turns the text on its side (2000: 147). She is in the margin as witness of this domestic abuse scene, she is not *in* it. Her reading position is thus one of standing at a critical distance observing from the sidelines, assessing texts that purport to present the words and actions of God.

In addition to feminist and lesbian readings, the recent application of studies in masculinity to biblical interpretation can be brought to bear on this issue. While the image of Woman/Israel might be grounded in the perceived fickleness and wantonness of women, the image of the deity as cuckolded husband who breaks into flights of testosterone-driven rage is grounded in cultural understandings of masculinity. In his essay on 'He-prophets' David Clines notes how prophets reinforce the strength of their deity and idealize strength as a desirable (male) attribute; how they reinforce notions of male honour; how violent imagery and terminology that includes pornographic and sadist elements is used. He closes with a section on 'masculinity as a problem' arguing that the problem is first that the prophets were not aware of how their masculinity impacted upon their ideas and writing and, second, that the commentary tradition has also been blind to the fact that scriptural texts are written in 'Masclish' (2002: 325). This is especially a problem for contemporary readers who take the Bible as the word of God because they will not easily recognize or accept the view that its message is written in 'Masclish', that culturally laden ideas about masculinity have impacted upon the depiction of a deity who incorporates masculine credentials writ large. Clines leaves his readers with a question: 'How can a "message" that comes in male attire . . . hope to speak to a world that is 53 per cent female (to say nothing of the men in the other 47 per cent who are troubled about traditional masculinity)?' (2002: 325). Queer readers who engage with the ways in which masculinity is constructed and policed, may find it useful to engage critically with this image of the masculine jealous deity who must be 'loved' at all costs.

A further disturbing feature of the Lord's 'jealousy' is the ruthless insistence that all potential sources of unfaithfulness are rooted out. Moses recounts how they battled against King Sihon of Hesbon and King Og of Bashan, capturing all their towns and utterly destroying the men, women and children, leaving no survivor (2.34; 3.6). Later, when anticipating their entry into the promised land, Moses says that Israel must take on the 'Hittites, the Girgashites, the Amorites, the Canaanites, the Perizzites, the Hivites, and the Jebusites' (7.1), 'break down their altars, smash their pillars, hew down their sacred poles and burn their idols with fire' (7.5). Israel must 'devour all the peoples that the Lord your God is giving over to you, showing them no pity' (7.16). The fact that a jealous deity will not withstand any rivals thus provides divine sanction for extreme religious purges. Historically, it is doubtful that any such campaigns actually took place: the stories of conquest anticipated here, and partially fulfilled in Joshua and Judges, have little archaeological support. Moreover, the names of these ancient people act rather as literary foils for the Deuteronomist; they are the symbolic 'other' to the Israelite nation (see Van Seters 1972 and Lemche 1991). Yet the rhetoric remains; and the later instructions regarding holy war in chapter 20 again reinforce sanction for a brutal, pitiless annihilation of the Hittites, Amorites, Canaanites, Perizzites, Hivites and Jebusites (20.16–18). Described variously as 'problematic', 'offensive', 'distasteful' to modern ears, the extent to which appeals to the historical context soften biblical verses that are tantamount to sanctioned genocide is for the reader to judge.

Mercy for the Marginalized

As motivation for keeping the laws that will follow, Moses regularly reminds his audience that they were once in bondage themselves (5.15; 6.12, 21; 15.15; 16.12; 24.18, 22), strangers in a foreign country (10.19), and that they must accordingly take especial care of the vulnerable: the immigrant, the widow and the orphan. One might not be comfortable associating LGBT/Q-identified[1] people with the marginalized, since this reinforces the binary between normative society and its margins, firmly assigning LGBT/Q-identified people outside the norm. Nevertheless, these references evidently struck a chord with early lesbian and gay theologies where the scriptural tradition of bondage in Egypt and living as a marginalized member of society was often associated

---

1 I have chosen to separate Q from LGBT with a forward slash in order to indicate that 'queer' is not an identity label. Although it is sometimes used as an umbrella term for non-straight people, queer strategically upsets the homosexual–heterosexual binary and transcends LGBT categories. Similarly, I used LGBT-*identified* to indicate that it is not necessarily a case of 'being' lesbian or gay so much as having *been positioned* as such or choosing to adopt that label for strategic purposes.

with the experiences of living within the oppression of the closet and of living as a gay or lesbian-identified person in a heterosexist world. Deuteronomy's focus upon God's concern for the vulnerable prompted calls for the compassionate treatment of LGBT/Q-identified people or indeed indicated that God has a special interest and compassion for the marginalized. Dr Rembert S. Truluck's popular website 'Steps to Recovery from Bible Abuse', which is particularly addressed to gay and lesbian-identified people, identifies the seventh of the twelve steps to recovery as 'Find positive supportive scripture', and on these pages we read:

> Being helpless and vulnerable in the face of social and economic pressures has also brought many gay and lesbian couples together. Living 'in the closet' makes most homosexuals 'mute' and defenseless about their deepest feelings and needs. Lesbian and gay couples can identify with the fears and dangers faced by widows in ancient times. Homosexuals can also appreciate the many references in the Bible about legal protection from abuse and injustice against widows, orphans and aliens. Deuteronomy 27:19: 'Cursed is the one who distorts the justice due an alien, orphan, and widow. And all the people said, Amen!'[2]

However, while Deuteronomy may well have a humanitarian instinct, as can be seen in the way it modifies laws prescribed in Exodus 20.22–23.19, the retention of laws relating to slaves continues to reify class differences between the enslaved and the free. Even the seventh-year release scheme, in Anderson's (2004) view, might have been a mixed blessing since those released would probably remain in an economically underprivileged category. The provisions allowed for the widow, orphan and stranger, in her view, are not enough to result in any redistribution of wealth; they may reduce hardship but not fundamentally challenge the causes of it. For all the rhetoric of the Deuteronomist, who optimistically devises laws for the protection of the widow, the orphan and the foreigner, he concedes in 15.11 that there will never cease to be some people who are in need. There is thus a problem with latching on to biblical texts regarding the marginalized, for these texts do not sufficiently problematize the boundary between the privileged and the margins. Accordingly, they do not promise deliverance from the margins; rather they deliver laws that perpetuate it, while injecting sufficient compassion to make life there more acceptable for the privileged and more bearable for the marginalized. If LGBT/Q-identified people want to break free of their stigmatized status, this identification with God's vulnerable ones needs to be reconsidered.

The Valorization of Fertility and Reproduction

In the central section of Deuteronomy (12–26), Moses exhorts the Israelites to follow a range of miscellaneous laws, several of which have an overt relevance for LGBT/Q readers. As noted in my introduction, biblical laws do not only

---

2 www.truluck.com/html/ruth_1_15–18__4_13–17.html

reflect cultural norms and values concerning the respective roles of men and women; they construct them. The following discussion demonstrates how law codes call into being defined sexed and gendered beings. In so doing, they reinforce a binary model of the two sexes with respective roles and privileges that is rigidly heterosexual and complementary. The laws that valorize fertility and reproduction construct males as the active and aggressive pursuers of women. To be a man is to desire, obtain and impregnate women. The same laws construct females as passive recipients of male desire, submissive to the control of their family's males. In so doing, Deuteronomy eliminates from the imagination any other way of relating sexually and any other possibilities for same-sex relationships. The discussion below ends with a note of how this can be resisted.

We begin with the key interest in Deuteronomy's legislature in maintaining the availability of women for the purposes of procreation, giving control of her sexuality to the male members of her community, thereby ensuring that husbands will be the fathers of any offspring. This interest is evident in laws concerning the exemption of a betrothed/newly married man from military service. Deuteronomy 20.7 dictates that a betrothed man should be permitted to go home to ensure that no other man secures his betrothed while 24.5 declares that, once married, a man should be free from military service for one year in order to be with his wife. Such laws place the emphasis clearly upon a man's primary role: that of reproduction. It is also evident in laws relating to female war captives (21.10–14). Any captive woman considered sufficiently desirable is to shave her head, pare her nails, discard her captive's clothing garb and remain in her new owner's house a full month. Only then is he permitted to marry and have intercourse with her. Insofar as the woman is protected from being subsequently sold into slavery should she not satisfy the man, this is sometimes hailed as a set of humanitarian laws. However, in an insightful article, Harold C. Washington says that the above considerations do

> not make the sexual relationship something other than rape, unless one assumes that by the end of the period the woman has consented . . . But to assume the consent of the woman is to erase her personhood. Only in the most masculinist of readings does the month-long waiting period give a satisfactory veneer of peaceful domesticity to a sequence of defeat, bereavement, and rape. (1997: 349)

Moreover, the waiting period during which she has to shave her head and pare her nails was a humiliating experience. The full month is likely to represent the completion of a menstrual cycle so that paternity is assured. So, 'In this instance male sexual aggression is constrained only to secure the claims to paternity, another element of male sexual control' (1997: 351). This desire for sexual control and certainty of fatherhood is also evident in the stoning of adulterers (22.20–2) and the law compelling rapists to marry their victims (22.28–9).

The severe punishments that accrue to anyone that damages the reproductive cycle also demonstrates the valorization of procreation; hence the severe punishment for any genital-grabbing by a female (25.11–12). These verses suppose a situation where a woman's husband is involved in a brawl, and in an attempt to defend her husband, she grabs the genitals of the other man. Her harsh punishment is to have the offending hand severed. Burnette-Bletsch suggests that the harshness of the penalty for the genital-grabbing women is 'because the injury to the man would impede his ability to perform sexually or to sire children' noting how 'Near Eastern laws mandate the amputation of a woman's finger if one testicle is damaged and a more radical mutilation for damage to both testicles' (2001: 234). But it is more than this. Biblical law, as Frymer-Kensky indicates, renders men's genitals sacrosanct:

> all men are now a privileged caste protected by the state, and their genitals, the emblem and essence of their manhood, are now sacrosanct . . . Even the primary husband–wife bond . . . must bow to this diffused authority of 'maleness,' which literally embodies the public realm. (1992: 62)

As for the women, Anderson persuasively argues that such laws construct the female body in three ways: as one that submits to male authority, as one that is destined for sex with men, and as one meant for maternity. Female sexual activity is thus legally circumscribed and geared entirely towards motherhood. Anderson concludes that of all the identities constructed by biblical laws, gender is the 'master-status' identity. It 'underlines other traits such as nationality and class' and therefore 'any challenge to the male dominant/female subordinate gender paradigm is perceived as a threat that would undermine the integrity of the whole group' (2004: 74). Anderson further argues that biblical laws embody male experience and foster the ideology of male domination. In her conclusions she states, 'the problem with these laws is not only that they fail to recognize rape as a crime against the female . . . [but] because they fail, through the repression of the feminine, to consider the female experience at all' (2004: 98).

This failure means that women's relationships with each other and the possibility that ancient women may have found their primary affinities or sources of comfort in their relationships with women is never discussed. However, I have recently argued that a key principle of lesbian hermeneutics would be a commitment of resistance to the common (mis)conception that there are 'no lesbians in the Bible'. I identify three textual strategies that have rendered female homoeroticism invisible: the valorization of motherhood, the image of women as competitive rivals and the injunction to comply with notions of gender complementarity (see Guest 2005: 111–56). A queer commentary on Deuteronomy may be interested in texts that appear to relate especially to lesbian, gay, bisexual, transgender and transsexual-identified people, but it is queer only insofar as it poses a challenge to heteronormative assumptions. I have thus argued that a lesbian hermeneutic has to resist these textual strategies. One way the valorization of motherhood can be disrupted is by reference to the serious costs this meant for women expected to endure multiple pregnancies in the face of adverse circumstances. Brenner's discussion of the skeletal remains at En Gedi indicate that women died younger than their male counterparts. Left to draw her own diagnosis as why this should be, Brenner concludes that childbearing would have been a major contributing factor. For the women in ancient Israel, childbirth meant enhanced status and security in old age and another pair of hands for the labour force, but at a cost to their own health and longevity. So while the Hebrew Bible insists that women yearned for children, their pro-life stance was in reality a 'pro-early death choice' (Brenner 1997: 68). Given this situation it is at least possible that, for practical reasons alone, not all women longed for children. As for those women whose primary affinities and desires were directed towards their female companions, marriage and mother-hood may have been thought of as particularly undesirable and onerous. So a second resistance strategy is to explore what Phyllis Bird calls 'rebellious moments' when women escaped their procreative destiny by choosing (in so far as that was possible) a sacral life:

> Women may take vows that are costly and undertake forbidden pilgrimages as actions of rebellion or flight from oppressive household responsibilities and restrictions. As religiously sanctioned actions they may offer limited relief to women whose options for action were often severely circumscribed. (1987: 410)

Whether there was any scope for Israelite women to escape from the wife/mother destiny altogether by entering into religious life is unclear, but con-sider the role of the *qedeshah* discussed below. The renewed interest in the cult of Asherah and interest in the role of women as musical performers may reveal further possibilities not currently envisaged.

As for the images of women as competitive rivals, it is likely that rivalries did sometimes occur among Israelite women, but the images promote the idea that animosity was a *characteristic feature* of female relationships. But what if wives were not jealous? What if, on the contrary, they felt affection and sympa-thy for their husband's co-wives? What if the women turned to each other for comfort and consolation? A lesbian-identified paradigm takes such questions and explores the *likelihood* of women's love and affection for one another, their common support, the preference of some to be in the company of each other rather than with their husbands. For evidence of this, the scriptural sources offer little help: it is a social-scientific approach that offers useful insights for a principle of resistance. Drawing on a wide range of ethnographies of Middle Eastern societies Gale Yee (2003) indicates how a sex-segregated world provides opportunities for female bonding and support rather than hostile competitiveness. In fact a sex-segregated world might be seen as a blessing, maintained to some extent at women's own request. In such contexts, women draw strength from each other and co-operate in a range of mutually support-ing activities. In the Iron Age village life of ancient Israel, Carol Meyers has pointed out that the labour tasks assigned to women and the adjoining clusters of village houses

> meant that Israelite women had more access to each other than men did to other men. Many repetitive household activities performed by women, such as certain food preparation tasks, would have been done in each other's com-pany. Such regular and intimate contact creates familiarity; and the shared tasks, problems and experiences create a sense of identity. Familiarity and

identity foster the solidarity of the women of a community – the neighbourhood associations visible in the Bible. (1999: 122)

Such feminist studies place the scriptural images of quarrelling, competitive
women in a different light. Read from a lesbian-identified feminist perspective, one might also include evidence of women finding support, solace, sexual
satisfaction and a sense of solidarity in the arms of female partners, facilitated
by the sexually segregated space available to women. It thus expands the realm
of the thinkable and, in bringing female homoeroticism into the light, counters
the suppression of this most routinely erased face of female experience.

The injunctions to comply with sex-gender norms can also be challenged.
Rebecca Alpert (1997) and Ken Stone (2000), for example, have noted how
Genesis 1–3, the key verses that prescribe gender complementarity and the
ordering of male–female relations, have their queer elements that disrupt
the heterocentric rhetoric. For instance, a lesbian-identified reading may well
notice, not without humour, how the instruction that Eve's desire will be for
her husband is contained with the punishments and curses meted out in verses
14–19. Thus, talk of desire for a husband, desire that outweighs the reluctance
to be ruled over, does not appear to have been a feature of the Eden society.
Moreover, a lesbian-identified reading notes that a woman's sexual drive has
to be specifically directed towards a male object, and by ordination of a deity.

Other ways in which the scriptural injunctions to sex-gender complementarity can be resisted include highlighting those occasions where scriptural
women choose instead an overt commitment to each other (as with Ruth
and Naomi). Being prepared to imagine, to think creatively and openly
about the likelihood of women's relations, even when they are not explicitly
recorded in the text, is vital if one is to resist the valorization of wifedom and
motherhood.

Constructing Religious Orthodoxy

Throughout Deuteronomy there is an overriding primary concern with the practice of religion. The Israelites are to worship one deity, in one place and via specific orthodox practices. While Yahwism incorporated far more diversity than the
Deuteronomists are now prepared to allow, the definition of orthodox Yahwism
is a major programme in Deuteronomy, and chapters 22–3 indicate some of the
practices that will no longer be considered appropriate. Worship of Asherah and
practices once tolerated are now firmly associated with the Canaanites. Indeed,
the instruction to wipe out entirely the Canaanites from the land (7.1–2; 20.16–
17) is an effect of the desire to redefine Yahwism. The Deuteronomist presents
this redefinition in terms of a historical *Kulturkampf*, and so persuasive has his
presentation been that scholars for almost a century have understood Israelite
origins in terms of a cultural struggle over and against the Canaanites. In reality,
however, the Israelites and Canaanites may well have shared a common ancestry (see for example Dever 1993; Thompson 1992; Finkelstein 1996), Asherah may
well have been the consort of Yahweh (see Binger 1997; Hadley 2000; Smith 1995;
Dever 2005) and the various 'Canaanite' practices discussed below may once

have been active positive elements of the Yahwistic cult. The discussion below focuses on three prohibitions for Israelite worship: the ban on cross-dressing in 22.5, the ban on eunuchs from the congregation of the Lord in 23.1, and the ban on sanctuary men and women in 23.17–18.

22.5: The ban on cross-dressing

Most English translations of this verse are poor. First, the Hebrew places far greater emphasis upon the masculine subject than many translations recognize. Brenner's translation brings this out: 'There will be no man's clothing on a woman, nor will a man wear a woman's garment' (1997: 145 n. 52). This grammatical emphasis upon the male, in her view, betrays typically male anxieties: 'In spite of the mention of women's cross-dressing, the anxiety is not truly paralleled for both genders. As in previous instances, the safeguarding of male sexual autonomy is of uppermost importance, for it signifies male social supremacy' (1997: 145). Second, as A. D. H. Mayes points out, the sentence reads that there will be no $k^e li$-geber (anything pertaining to a man) on a woman, and $k^e li$ carries a broader range of possibilities than just clothing. The law could therefore prohibit women from wearing 'weapons (1:41), utensils (23:24) as well as clothes' (Mayes 1979: 307).

It was informative to see how many commentaries either omitted this verse from their discussions or afforded it only a few words. Clearly, as Stone (2005) has argued, the question of what biblical texts are 'about' depends to quite an extent on the interests of the readers. In a history of reception that has largely been male, white, middle-class, European/North American and heterosexual, this verse appears to have had no especial relevance. For readers who identify in various ways as transgender or transsexual, it could be a key text. Certainly, website forums indicate that Deuteronomy 22.5 constitutes a text of terror for Christians and Jews who also identify as butch lesbians, or drag queens/kings, or are transsexuals. In the commentaries that do address this verse, commentators present the reason for this prohibition in at least three different ways. First, early Jewish commentators saw it as a way of preventing undesirable sexual activities (homoerotic relations or heterosexual adultery). Rashi, for instance, argued that the prohibition prevented opportunities for men to enter women's areas, and vice versa, and thereby prevented opportunities for adultery. However, a long-held belief present in many commentaries on Deuteronomy is that the ban of transvestism is associated with fear of contamination with the cultic practices of non-Israelites, particularly the Canaanites. This second explanation is grounded in the early twentieth-century scholarship where scholarly portrayals of Israelite religion mirrored the biblical portraits. William Foxwell Albright's *From Stone Age to Christianity*, published in 1940 was very influential in its confirmation of the purity and distinctiveness of Israelite monotheistic Yahwism over and against the paganizing influences of the Canaanite religion, described in very negative terms. Albright's influence can clearly be seen in the work of John Bright's claim: 'Canaanite religion presents us with no pretty picture. It was in fact an extraordinarily debasing form of paganism . . . numerous debasing practices, including sacred prostitution, homosexuality and various orgiastic rites were prevalent' (1981: 118).

These days, scholars no longer take the biblical presentations of Canaanite religion at face value (see Stone 2005: 57–67). Nevertheless, there remains documented evidence that cross-dressing did play a part in some ancient religions. For example, the Assyrian *Ishtar's Descent to the Underworld* speaks of the *assinnu* and *kurgarru* whose

> duties consisted of ecstatic dance, music and plays. They dressed up and wore make up like a woman, and they carved masks and weapons, which they used in their dances and plays . . . Their most typical gear was a spindle (*pilaqqu*) – a feminine symbol – but they also bore swords and other cutting weapons. (Nissinen 1998: 30)

Ishtar, god of love and war, had dual genders – the bearded man and the erotically charming woman – and she is credited with causing the same dual identity to fall upon others in order to keep them in fear. The *assinnu* had been changed in this way and they 'symbolised the androgynous aspect of the goddess not only occasionally in rituals but in their whole life, action and self-presentation' (Nissinen 1998: 31). Whether this was manifested via transvestism or whether men were physically castrated by their cutting tools, or whether they were hermaphrodites from birth, is debatable.

Some readers may be interested in exploring this cultural history. However, it must be borne in mind that while tracing a transsexual or transgender ancestry to ancient times might understandably be popular and have strategic advantages, the very different constructions of gender and sexuality in different places and times seriously undermine such ventures. Certainly, the application of this verse to (post)modern transsexual transition would not have been envisaged by any ancient author. Nonetheless, exploration of these ancient practices remains valuable insofar as it disturbs mainstream ideas about what is normative within religious life and practice.

A third explanation for the ban on cross-dressing is the argument that it is motivated by a concern for sex/gender order and boundaries and the anxieties caused when sex/gender roles are blurred. Chapters 21–5 contain moral directives that centre on notions of purity. As the opening chapters of Genesis, the codes concerning clean and unclean in Leviticus, and these Deuteronomic chapters make clear, purity is a matter of keeping given categories in their rightful place and not mixing them. The command of Deuteronomy 22.5, Patrick Miller notes, has a much 'deeper meaning' that is 'ignored by simply marking it as a prohibition of transvestism'. That deeper meaning is concerned with 'the order and structure of things, the recognition of difference and sameness, and a desire to maintain things as God created them' (1990: 162). Likewise, Patrick (1985: 130) suggests that it was more to do with anxieties of sex/gender confusion and for Goss (2002) also, the prohibition against cross-dressing in Deuteronomy 22.5, the exclusion of eunuchs in 23.1, and Genesis 1.27's division of humanity into gendered categories all combine force to prevent this blurring taking place. As Brenner notes, any activity that disturbs the hierarchic and differentiated world of Genesis breaches the 'natural' created order: 'Gender-bender dressing . . . blots out some visual, easy to recognize sex and hence gender difference (1997: 133). The issue, for Brenner, is thus one of sex distinction and the desire to police the 'visual parameters' of that distinction' (1997: 144). Commenting on Brenner's work, Anderson notes how biblical texts can thus be seen as harmful for men insofar as they produce anxiety as they 'strive to perpetuate artificially created gender differences' (2004: 98).

Whatever the original motivations for the prohibition might have been, the Church today has made use of this verse in its discussion of cross-dressing and transsexuality in the modern world. The Christian Institute's briefing, written as the British government introduced the Gender Recognition Bill in November 2003, used this verse for a predictable condemnation of transsexuality. The Institute also used Genesis 1.27 to clarify in no uncertain terms 'that there are two, and only two, sexes'. Such a shallow proof-texting approach was not so evident in the Evangelical Alliance Policy Commission's report on transsexuality; at least as far as Deuteronomy 22.5 is concerned. Arguing that Deuteronomy 22.5 was intended to 'prevent involvement on the part of Israelites in contemporary Canaanite religious rituals of the day, which involved swapping of sex roles and cross-dressing', the authors of the report state, 'it is probably doing a disservice to reasonable hermeneutics to apply it directly to transsexuals' (2000: 47). However, Genesis 1.27 features strongly as the Alliance's report reaffirms the distinctiveness of the two sexes and the inappropriateness of crossing sex/gender boundaries. Both this report and that of the Christian Institute claim that it simply is not possible to change one's sex and that those who determine to live transsexually cannot live compatibly with 'orthodox' Christianity.

There is arguably more room for manoeuvre in the Anglican publication *Some Issues in Sexuality*. The historical discussion within their opening chapter states:

> the Christian tradition has rejected transvestitism [*sic*] on the grounds that cross-dressing is forbidden in the book of Deuteronomy (Deuteronomy 22.5) and, more widely, on the basis of the belief that the distinction between male and female instituted by God at creation is a boundary that must not be transgressed. (House of Bishops 2003: 14–15)

The report later acknowledges recent theological thinking on the subject and raises the possibility of a different perspective. Section 1.4.14 indicates how Christian discussion has queried whether transsexuals should be helped to come to terms with their 'God-given' birth sex or whether it is 'possible that someone's God-given sex is not identical with their physiology, and that it is therefore legitimate to allow people to change their bodies to allow this true sexual identity to be expressed' (2003: 34). As for biblical prohibitions such as Deuteronomy 22.5 and the prohibition of castration in Leviticus 21.16–23 and Deuteronomy 23.1, the report acknowledges that the relevance of such texts to contemporary transsexual identities is questionable. The report takes refuge in the pervasive belief that Deuteronomy 22.5 'is primarily addressing the need for the people of Israel to avoid copying Canaanite religious practices' while recognizing that it 'may also reaffirm the need to reflect the principle that the distinction between male and female established at creation should be upheld' (2003: 229). However, to this end, Genesis 1.26–7 again features strongly and *Issues* draws heavily on Oliver O'Donovan's 1982 argument for the dimorphic creation of humanity which rejects any idea that one can have a 'real sex' which is other than the one given at birth (1982: 11). Ultimately the chapter concludes with an open invitation to explore the relevance and application of such scriptural texts as Genesis 1–2, Deuteronomy 22.5, Matthew 19 and Acts 8 to Christian views of transsexualism, and, reading very optimistically, there seems to be room for movement here.

23.1: The ban on eunuchs from the congregation of the Lord

Chapter 23 opens with a list of persons banned from entering the assembly of the Lord. It includes bastards, Ammonites, Moabites and the one whose testicles are crushed or whose penis is cut off. The commentarial history offers a number of reasons why 23.1 outlaws the latter two categories from public worship. For some, it prohibits non-Israelite practices. We noted above how Mesopotamian society included eunuchs (*sa-resi*) who had a special relationship to the Ishtar cult. In later material from Syria and Asia Minor there is mention of the *galli* – emasculated priests who served the Syrian goddess Atargatis and the Roman goddess Cybele. Nissinen cites the third-century CE writings of Lucian who claimed (polemically) that a member of the *galli* would castrate himself while in an ecstatic trance state, publicly slashing his testicles with a sword and taking from the crowd and people's houses women's clothing and accessories. Nissinen says that *galli* 'had to live the rest of their lives in a permanently changed social and gender role' (1998: 32). The *galli* thus became a kind of third gender who 'later on, became the target of the promoters of the Christian faith, who saw in them the most outrageous example of the corruptness of the pagan world' (1998: 31–2). But despite being disparaged in some sources, Nissinen believes that, like the *assinnu*, their role was institutionalized and approved:

> They . . . did things on her [Ishtar's] behalf that exceeded social conventions and were forbidden to ordinary people, and their activities were part of the divinely sanctioned world order. As human beings, however, they seem to have engendered demonic abhorrence in others; few would have envied their lot. The fearful respect they provoked is to be sought in their otherness, their position between myth, reality, and their divine-demonic ability to transgress boundaries (1998: 32).

He goes on to speculate that those who looked for this role may have experienced what he calls a 'transvestite need' and that these people

> were better able to express it in that role or that they felt themselves otherwise incapable of fulfilling the requirements of the male role in a patriarchal society . . . Moreover, there may have been persons among them who were transsexual or born intersexed. All this is beyond modern knowledge. Unknown also is whether anyone was forced to become an *assinnu*, for instance, as a mythologically justified means to control overpopulation. In any case we have to do with gender-blending not as an impulse but as a role

that required education and life-long dedication, not simply an act of cross-dressing or castration. (1998: 34)

For some commentators, Deuteronomy 22.1 thus distinguishes Israel and its cult from the practices of surrounding nations. However, a different view is that the prohibition reflects the belief that mutilated bodies ran counter to God's creative purposes. Damaged testicles and lack of a penis necessarily indicated lack of procreative power, and the implication is that such people were not considered to be 'whole'. Deuteronomy 23.1 thus provides a further verse that has the potential to be applied to male-to-female transsexuals (MTFs). However, the Anglican report *Some Issues in Human Sexuality* dismisses the idea that this verse provides a 'prima facie rejection of those who have undergone male-to-female SRS' since Isaiah 56.4–5 removes the ban on eunuchs and because there is acceptance of the eunuch in Matthew 19.12 and Acts 8.26–39. This statement demonstrates one of the common hermeneutic strategies of such documents: allowing biblical texts to offset each other and, by implication, placing greater store by texts found in the Christian scriptures. Such a strategy does nothing to dent the problematic texts of the Bible; it simply reinforces the Bible's status and significance for modern debate and indeed privileges it over other discourses. Moreover, such statements do reinforce the view that Deuteronomy 23.1 does have something to say about transsexuality.

Early lesbian and gay-identified biblical studies/theology further reinforced the view that texts relating to eunuchs were relevant to gay readers. Nancy Wilson (1995), John J. McNeill (1976) and more recently Kader (1999: 89), 'outed' and celebrated the biblical eunuch as a gay ancestor. More recent studies (Kolakowski 1997: 42–3; 2000) relocate the eunuch within transgender and transsexual discourse. The eunuch, in Kolakowski's view, is a specific ancestor to the transsexual and transgendered person, and she objects to any 'form of cultural hogging of tradition, which denies to transgendered people our own history and which marginalizes us' (1997: 48).

In her 1997 article she makes connections between the role and treatment of the eunuch in the ancient world and the derisory way in which transgendered and transsexual persons are treated in the modern world. Deuteronomy 23.1 indicates that the eunuch could not participate in normative religious worship and, despite the overturning of this view in Isaiah 56, the question put to Jesus in Matthew 19.12 indicates to Kolakowski that the eunuch continued to be regarded as deviant to some extent. However, in Jesus' response she finds he took the 'derogatory slang word thrown at him and proudly claimed it as part of his own identity' (1997: 45). The significance of her essay thus lies in the fact that it highlights 'extremely powerful statements of validation and acceptance from Jesus and the early Christian church': a message not of neutrality on the issue, but 'a voice of specific affirmation of us, one which I am not inventing just to feel accepted. We need to take ownership of this radical message' (1997: 47).

However, as Kolakowski would later acknowledge, the biblical portrayal of the eunuch is not always a good thing. In her (2000) discussion of the role the eunuchs play in Jezebel's death, she recognizes that the eunuch plays precisely the anti-woman role that some feminists fear. Janice Raymond's (1979) trenchant accusation that MTFs will do the bidding of the 'rulers of patriarchy' when the latter decide to control and contain the lesbian feminists, can be mapped on to the Jezebel story with an eerie resonance. Given the laws against castration and the inadmission of eunuchs to the assembly or priesthood that one finds in Deuteronomy 23.1, Kolakowski believes it is reasonable to assume a negative attitude to eunuchs. In throwing Jezebel to her death, the eunuchs thus attempt to regain credibility and value for themselves by siding with Jehu over and against the defiant Queen Jezebel. In her words, they function as 'mediators of the gender play between the defiant, seductive and strong Jezebel and the dubiously manly Jehu (the manliest among wimps)' (2000: 107) in an act that may have been a way of 'symbolically regaining their masculinity' (2000: 108). Thus, while she 'would like to think of this story as validating and supporting eunuchs as divine agents' she has to ask whether they are actually 'pawns in the patriarchal oppression of women or . . . tool[s] for belittling men?' (2000: 108). The story of Jezebel thus becomes a most useful tool for discussing the current controversies and conflict between transsexual communities and lesbian feminist communities. Recognizing that transsexuals receive hostility from both straight and lesbian/gay communities, she realizes that Wilson's reclamation of the eunuchs as fully part of the queer community does so at the very risk that Raymond fears. Wilson sees the eunuchs who threw Jezebel to her death as God's agents (1995: 282): not a very attractive interpretation for feminists who might choose to side with the bold Jezebel. Kolakowski thus points out that while some biblical stories can 'redeem and liberate us' . . . we need to be sure when we choose an "affirming" reading that we know whom or what we are affirming' (2000: 110). For both Wilson and Raymond 'eunuchs are spies in every territory, ready to spring into action when the Master calls. It is just that for Wilson the Master is a loving God, while for Raymond the Master is a cruel patriarch' (Kolakowski 2000: 110). This leaves Kolakowski in a difficult and unresolved hermeneutical dilemma:

> Do I accept Wilson's view that the eunuchs are divine agents, and thereby claim a respectable role in God's plan? And if so, am I committing the very act that Raymond fears, that is, throwing the strong, subversive woman out because the patriarchal keeper demanded that I do so? If I reject Wilson's interpretation and argue that this story is indeed a betrayal of the subversive woman by the assimilationist queer . . . am I accepting Raymond's conclusion that my own inclusion into the lesbian-feminist world is a threat to women?. (2000: 110–11)

Finding models for transsexual, transgender, lesbian, gay and bisexual identities is an understandable endeavour. In the wake of Stonewall and the embracing of the popular 'we are everywhere' slogan an understandable surge of interest in locating a gay and lesbian heritage took place. Such projects were politically useful, for if one can demonstrate that same-sex relationships permeate societies cross-culturally and throughout time, and that some of the greatest figures of Western civilization were 'transsexual', 'gay' or 'lesbian', then this undermines accusations that such relationships are unnatural, sick or sinful. However, as scholars began researching history in the wake of early gay liberation politics (c.1970 onwards), what became clear was that although cross-dressing, transitioning and same-sex activities are indeed a cross-cultural observable fact, such choices are not a uniform, universal phenomena but something that has to be assessed in terms of the context in which it is found. As Jeffrey Weeks argues: while same-sex behaviour 'has existed in a variety of different cultures' as 'an ineradicable part of human sexual possibilities', attitudes towards it are 'wholly specific and have varied enormously across different cultures and through various historical periods'. It is, accordingly, 'no longer possible to talk of the possibility of a universalistic history of homosexual behaviour' (1996: 42).

Robert Goss is accordingly very wary of anachronism and labelling biblical figures as lesbian, gay, transsexual or heterosexual, though he does not so much dismiss such approaches as redefine them: 'The question that remains for queer interpretative communities is whether we can see ourselves reflected in Biblical narratives without these modern identity templates' (2002: 214). His second criticism is that such approaches grant the Bible 'too much power to authenticate our lives as queers', placing authority 'entirely in the text as parent' (2002: 214), a criticism also raised by Tim Koch (2001a). Goss prefers an approach that begins with the positive self-evaluation of queer lives as *a priori* – 'queer folks need to come out and recognize the blessing of their sexualities before they engage the biblical text' (2002: 214). So, while a 'befriending the text' approach, that identifies finding solidarity and affinities with 'the poor, the marginal, the lepers, the gender-benders, the strangers or foreigners, the sexual nonconformists such as eunuchs or barren women, or the boundary-breakers' (2002: 215) might be strategically useful for opposing religious homophobia, for Goss, 'real textual subversion' happens when heterosexist presumptions are decentred and this is where the application of queer theory has a useful part to play.

23.17–18: The ban on sanctuary men and women

At face value, Deuteronomy 23.17–18 outlaws the use of revenue procured by commercial sex with the *qadesh* (male) and *qedeshah* (female) for temple purposes. The AV translated *qedeshah* as 'whore' and *qadesh* as 'sodomite', contributing to a long-standing belief that what we are dealing with here are male and female cultic prostitutes, denounced as an abomination to Yhwh. The very prospect of male and female cultic personnel, located at religious shrines and hiring out their sexual services, has produced much scholarly intrigue and speculation. So, who are these figures, what was their role, who engaged their services, and why does verse 18 equate the male figures with dogs and the female with prostitutes?

The words *qadesh* and *qedeshah* derive from the Hebrew word for holy (*qodesh*); something that Burns (2000) reflects well in his references to these people as 'sanctuary women/men'. Deuteronomy 23.17–18 is not the only place these people appear, there are further references to them in 1 Samuel 2.22; 1 Kings 14.24; 2 Kings 23.7, 14; 2 Chronicles 15.16; Ezekiel 8:14 and Hosea 4.13. The reference in 2 Kings 23.7 indicates that the males had their own living quarters within the Jerusalem temple, which again infers their role as cultic personnel. However, it is very difficult to say much else. Commenting on Hosea 4.11–14

all Bird can conclude is that the association of the sanctuary woman with prostitution is part of Hosea's polemic. Accordingly, the reference 'does not give
us any reliable information about the function or activities of these women,
except that they must have been a recognized presence at the rural sanctuaries
in Hosea's day' (1989a: 87).

There have been various attempts to use a range of extra-biblical texts to
shed light on their role. Nissinen wonders whether they might be helpfully
compared with the *assinnu*, *kurgarru* and *galli* discussed above. The *qadesh* and
qedeshah would thus refer to 'those who had assumed an unusual gender role
and expressed their lifelong dedication to a deity' though he concedes that
such 'speculation is based on circumstantial evidence' (1998: 41). There is a
clearer etymological link with the *qds* mentioned in Ugaritic texts: a class of
married, male cultic personnel, mentioned after the category of priests, but
it is difficult to find agreement about the role of these figures and there is no
implication that they were involved in ritual sexual activity. In Mesopotamian
texts, there is a female cultic official referred to as a *qadishtu*, but while recent
evaluations of the relevant texts 'suggests that she assumed various cultic roles
. . . none of these are explicitly sexual' (Goodfriend 2001: 231).

The idea that they were cult prostitutes derives from a series of faulty connections. First, early discussions took place in an academic context where
ancient Near Eastern fertility religion was being reconstructed from available
texts. As Ken Stone indicates in his chapter on Kings in this volume, the old
but influential view that Canaanite fertility religion incorporated religiously
sanctioned intercourse with visitors to the sanctuary (since engaging in sexual
acts prompted the gods to follow suit, resulting in fertility on earth) led to
the view that the *qadesh* and *qedeshah* had a similar role. This view has largely
been abandoned, for the evidence on which it was based never warranted the
interpretation.

Second, Phyllis Bird points out that the idea that these sanctuary men
and women were involved in prostitution derives from the polemic of the
Deuteronomist, who deliberately stigmatizes them by association with the references to the hire of a harlot and wages of a dog. The long-held view that the
qadesh and *qedeshah* were involved in cultic prostitution is thus to misinterpret

> religious polemic as social history, creating a class that corresponds neither
> to the Mesopotamian *assinnus* nor to attested classes or associations of
> prostitutes. The biblical references are polemical constructs that exhibit no
> firsthand knowledge of the institutions they condemn. (2000: 173)

Nonetheless, Bird (2000: 171) does not dispute the possible existence of male
prostitution within Israelite communities. Suggesting that verse 18 is the older
law, aimed not at the sanctuary men and women themselves, but prohibiting
the use of the income derived from male and female prostitution for sacral
purpose, she says:

> If it provides evidence for an accepted (or at least tolerated) form of homo-
> sexual practice, then it is instructive that it is in the form of prostitution, a
> commercial form of sex that in its better-attested female form typically takes

place away from home, among strangers, in taverns or traveler's lodges. If the prohibition of homoerotic relations is primarily concerned with the violation of male honor . . . then the male prostitute, like his female counterpart, provides a safe, though despised, object as one who stands outside the normal system of sexual honor. (2000: 171)[3]

Certainly the reference to the 'dog' in verse 18 has been understood as a contemptuous term for a male prostitute. While it is true that the dog label can indicate loyalty – a faithful servant or devoted follower of a deity – it does also have pejorative connotations. That 'dog' is an entirely understandable derogatory label for a male prostitute has been recently reinforced by Burns. He notes how images of the conquered grovelling before their superior, such as we find on the Black Obelisk where Jehu kneels before Shalmaneser III are dog-like. Here, and in four other noted images, the supplicant figures bend low before their superiors, with head between hands and bottom raised – precisely, says, Burns 'in the position of a dog, fawning but uncertain as to its reception, the head between the front paws, the rear raised exposing the animal's anus' (2000: 7). This image of the dog-like supplicant is pervaded with connotations of inferiority, passivity and submissiveness. Burns then considers Middle Assyrian laws and analogies from Greek and Roman societies where male sexual passivity among free-born men is despised and argues that this pervasive cultural belief lent itself readily to the canine imagery of inferior supplicants. The visual/ideological combination of dog-like posture of a supplicant with raised anus plus the cultural stigma attached to passive submissiveness informed the colloquial references to the male prostitute as a 'dog'.

Burns's hypothesis may be right. The male prostitute may have been stigmatized; that to behave sexually as a woman probably was thought to be dishonouring oneself in the culture of that time. Arguably, however, there needs to be greater critical distance from these contextual beliefs. When Burns says that the Deuteronomic prohibition concerns 'the passive male prostitute plying his sexually liminal trade . . . dubbed "dog" as befitting his fawning passivity and incorrigible perversity . . . His offering, bought with the earnings of this "loathsome trade," was not allowed to sully YHWH's presence' (2000: 8), the scare quotes do not sufficiently distinguish the contextual difference between that time and ours. On the contrary, such comments may encourage a continued reaction of distaste to such practices.

---

3 Karel van der Toorn, who also strongly rejects connections with sacred prostitution, argues that the prohibition is aimed at those who would use the money gained from prostitution for cultic purposes, specifically vow-making. A woman, he points out, may well be dependent upon her husband to make the required payment, but if 'a husband was unaware of his wife's religious pledge or did not agree with it, she found herself in a delicate situation . . . Under such circumstances prostitution might seem to a woman the only solution left' (1992: 511). Prostitution could thus be a source of financial gain for the temple and certainly, verse 18 refers to bringing payment into the temple. However, it seems unlikely to me that this avenue would ever have been made available for married or single Israelite women when the laws concerning her husband's/father's rights and the expectations of her monogamy/virginity were so tightly governed.

Moreover, while Burns's essay is focused entirely on the 'dog' reference he does not follow Phyllis Bird's careful distinction between the *qadesh/qedeshah* and verse 18's polemical references to money earned by 'harlots' and 'dogs'. At the conclusion of his paper he suggests that the AV translation of verse 17's *qadesh* as 'sodomite' might have originally been intuitive, but is now justified by the evidence. This restores the link between the sanctuary man and male prostitute; the very link that Bird (1997b; 2000) has worked so hard to dismiss.

Conclusions

We have seen that a queer commentary, focused upon gender fluidity, the questioning of the two-sex model, the exploration of transgender, transsexual and intersex experiences presses hard against a scriptural text that is most resistant to such explorations and which is used in current religious rhetoric to condemn lesbian, gay, bisexual, transgender, transsexual-identified people and their choices. The Bible is used as ammunition on both sides as each battles for their own interpretation and application. Accordingly, it was interesting to note how the Deuteronomist is keen to eliminate the voice of the false prophet.

When the will of God is mediated through human beings then inevitably societies will have the problem of discerning the true from the false intermediary. The Deuteronomist is anxious that (false) prophets might lead Israel into apostasy (13.1–5) or claim to speak for Yhwh when they do not (18.20). In such a situation, one can well understand the Israelite's puzzlement: 'How can we recognize a word that the Lord has not spoken?' (18. 21). The Deuteronomist resolves this by declaring that a prophet's worth will be established by the success of his prophecies: an interesting notion for our contemporary context where debate regarding the compatibility (or not) of same-sex relationships and Christian and Jewish faith continues to be hotly and vehemently pursued. Those staunchly taking an anti-gay stance believe that they are upholding biblical norms (and thereby the will of God) and protecting the church or synagogue from the surrounding tide of secularizing norms. Donald J. Wold (1998), for example, seeks to convince his readers that the Bible condemns homosexual activity. Arming himself with a formidable knowledge of Egyptian, Mesopotamian, Ugaritic and Hittite texts he brings the full weight of his scholarly credentials to bear on his effort to discern the authorial intention behind such texts as Genesis 19 or Leviticus 18.22. Believing that his methodology allows the plain meaning of scripture to resound, he counters the so-called revisionist ethics, or bad interpretations of those he accuses of distorting and disabling the word of God. For Wold, the plain meaning of scripture means that those enjoying same-sex relationships should be called to repent of their sin if they are to avoid God's condemnation. Yet, those who staunchly take a pro-gay stance on, for example, *How the Bible Really Is Gay Friendly* (Kader 1999) or *What the Bible Really Says About Homosexuality* (Helminiak 1994), argue with equal force that when understood correctly, scripture does *not* condemn modern expressions of homosexuality. Kader talks about being open to God's new revelations, of experiencing 'a genuine encounter with the Holy Spirit', of practising the kind of exegesis that is 'really listening' and 'paying attention' to the good news of the Bible (1999: 15) and to what the Lord is *really saying* to the Church universal' (1999; 126, emphasis added). The scriptures are thus divided between both camps and both claim to have God and the word on their side.

There is little doubt that each camp is equally sincere in their beliefs, but ultimately, despite all claims to the contrary, the attempt to discern the will of God in this area will always be hostage to the interpreter's agenda. Daniel Patte (2002) has made this abundantly clear in his discussion of Romans 1.26–7. At the time of writing, the Anglican Communion is being torn apart by the intense controversy between those fervently opposed to such issues as the blessing of same-sex partnerships or the ordination of practising gay clergy and those who are taking the Church precisely down those paths. The question of who represents the true and false prophet thus has a new specificity for contemporary seekers of the will of God. The Deuteronomist's somewhat passive solution to the dilemma is to declare that time will tell; but one should not let this encourage passivity in the here and now. A hundred years from now perhaps people will marvel that so much ink was spilt in a controversy that was so heated and intense. Certainly, as one looks back to the use of scripture in the abolitionist/anti-abolitionist debate, another occasion where much ink was spilt and the Bible proved to be another battleground for both pro-slavery debaters and the abolitionists (Glancy 1998), I doubt that anyone would argue that the will of God was not ultimately achieved. But it would be foolish to ignore the level of effort, struggle and contestation that eventually brought that resolution, and as I have already argued (Guest 2001), there is far too much at stake for us to sit back and 'wait and see'.

Joshua

MICHAEL CARDEN

Prologue (as I am writing this on aboriginal land, I must first acknowledge the traditional owners of this land)

The first intimation that I might be writing this chapter on Joshua occurred on 26 January, the date on which Captain Arthur Phillip and the First Fleet, with its load of convicts, disembarked at Sydney Cove in 1788 to begin a new British penal settlement. In Australia, that day has been marked as our national day and is known as Australia Day. Originally a holiday was granted, either on that day if it fell on a Monday or on the nearest Monday, as part of the old (and worthy) Australian tradition of the long weekend. In the 1990s, as part of a push to develop a new national pride, the holiday was set on that day exclusively, with a Monday holiday in lieu occurring only when Australia Day fell on a Saturday or Sunday. Nowadays the day is marked by a wide range of public activities, including the now obligatory firework events on the night viewed by mass crowds.

One category of events isn't normally listed in official Australia Day programmes and that is the indigenous rallies and marches held around the country to mark Invasion Day. The First Fleet marked the beginning of the European invasion and occupation of the land and the displacement and elimination of the indigenous peoples. Australia even held to a principle of *terra nullius*, that the land was vacant, that no one had ownership of it at all and that it was there for the taking. That principle was finally struck down by the courts with the Mabo and Wik decisions in the 1990s, major turning-points in the land rights struggles of the last three to four decades. Mabo gave legal recognition of native title to this land, a principle that governments, especially the Howard conservative government, have done their best to subvert. Furthermore, while Aotearoa/New Zealand, Canada and the United States signed treaties with the first peoples of those lands, Australia has yet to sign a treaty with any of the indigenous peoples of this land. As a result of these struggles it has now become a fairly common practice in Australia for many public events – rallies, conferences, performances and so on – to begin with a statement acknowledging aboriginal ownership of the land. Sometimes representatives of the local aboriginal community might open the event with a welcome to the country.

I don't observe Australia Day. I rarely even use the term, preferring the more accurate Invasion Day. If I do anything 'official' on the day I attend the Invasion Day rallies and marches. If we must have the holiday then, I would prefer it if we went back to the older practice of using it as an excuse for a long weekend.[1] I am not an indigenous Australian but one of Anglo-Irish descent. My ancestors came here too long ago for me to even be eligible for a UK or Irish passport, unlike many of my friends who hold (or are eligible to hold) two (or more) passports even if they were born here. Being Catholic, I grew up with the Irish side of my ancestry strongly accented, Irish nuns in the local parish school, an Irish parish priest, St Patrick's day, my grandmother, who had never seen Ireland herself, singing songs of that old isle. I was told many stories of what the English did to old Ireland and especially stories of Protestant persecution of Catholics in the Emerald Isle. Ironically, my English ancestors very likely played a part in the oppression of my Irish ancestors. Irish was the colour of that old Australian Catholic world of my childhood, and we were being taught to hold firm to that faith of our fathers, to be true to it to death.[2] That world would give way, as I grew up, to the coming of the Italians and other Catholic Europeans, Vatican II, ecumenism and then the coming of the Catholic Vietnamese and other Catholic Asians. While I felt a resurgence of that old tribal identity with the onset of the Troubles in Northern Ireland, by then I was facing my homosexuality and was developing a new tribal identity as a gay man. That identity sat uncomfortably alongside my older Catholic, Irish and Australian identities.

And so it was with some trepidation that I turned my mind to writing on Joshua. After all, it's about warfare, invasion and genocide isn't it? Before I made up my mind one way or another, I decided to read it. I found that there was, indeed, warfare, bloodshed, massacre and genocide aplenty. However, as so often happens with the biblical texts, I found something subversive there, a counter-tendency in the face of such warrior militancy. I found that the main concern of Joshua was community and identity, who is and who isn't Israel. It seemed, too, that while the Canaanites were apparently to be extirpated from the land, Joshua knew that to be fantasy. It struck me that Joshua was saying that Israelites and Canaanites were one and the same, all the bloodshed and massacre was only so much smokescreen and metaphor. It also struck me that anyone who reads Joshua as a warrant for genocide, for invading a land and expelling its people, has seriously misread this text. Nevertheless, Joshua uses the language and imagery of invasion, dispossession, ethnic cleansing and genocide and has been implicated in such events in Ireland, the Americas, Australia and the South Pacific, Africa and, currently, Palestine. Consequently, I felt it necessary to begin this chapter with the recognition of such colonial realities and an acknowledgement of the dispossessed. I acknowledge the traditional owners of this land in which I live and that this land was taken from them.

---

1 The greatest irony of this national day is that it as much celebrates continuity with Britain, as it does a particular Australianness. The day was adopted when Australia saw itself a loyal component of Empire and the narrative of Australia Day perfectly fits that imperial ideology. Australia's real national day, the day we became a unified nation, is 1 January, but as it is New Year's day everyone is too hungover to engage in displays of patriotic enthusiasm.

2 The reality of Irish history is very different to that diaspora Catholic narrative of my childhood.

Introduction

Overview

The book of Joshua recounts the entry of Israel into the land of Canaan following the Exodus from Egypt. It is the first book of the Former Prophets (Joshua, Judges, Samuel, Kings) and, therefore, follows the Torah in most Bibles. However, there is a Rabbinic tradition that Moses was the author of both the Torah and Job (*Baba Bathra* 15a). Consequently, the Peshitta (the Syriac translation held as canonical by the Syriac Churches of the Middle East) places the book of Job before Joshua and after the Torah (Freedman 1950: xi). The Samaritans count only the Torah as scripture; nevertheless they also keep a version of Joshua as part of their Chronicles but preserved only in an Arabic version not Hebrew. The main textual versions of Joshua are the Masoretic (Hebrew) and Greek, the latter being canonical for the Eastern Orthodox churches. Greek Joshua is 5 per cent shorter than the Masoretic and both texts 'offer substantially different readings in many places' (Nelson 1997: 22). Manuscript fragments of Joshua found at Qumran position the pericope of Joshua 8.30–5 immediately before Joshua 5.2–7. So it is clear that as far back as we have evidence, Joshua, like other biblical texts has existed in plural form and we have no way of determining which, if any, of these versions has priority.

The book falls into three parts: stories of Israel's occupation of the land (chs 1–12), the division of the land among the tribes (chs 13–21), and the conclusion in which questions of fidelity to YHWH are addressed (chs 22–4). The first part consists mainly of narratives describing Israel's entry into and occupation of the land. While there are some brief narrative elements in the second part, it mostly comprises geographical descriptions and lists. In the final section, there is the narrative of the Transjordanian tribes and the near civil war (ch. 22) followed by concluding speeches and ceremonies (chs 23–4). The two main characters in Joshua are the LORD, YHWH, who is almost always referred to by the divine name and not by other divine titles, and Joshua himself, whose name means Yah saves. Joshua is presented as a leader fully accepted by the deity, and the two collaborate together in full harmony. Yet despite this fact, Joshua is not a prominent figure in the Hebrew Bible overall. He is a minor character in the Pentateuch, even presented as subordinate to Caleb (Num. 14.24, 30). He is omitted from the recapitulations of Israel's history found in 1 Samuel 12, Nehemiah 9, and Psalms 105 and 106. He appears in the opening chapters of Judges and is referred to in 1 Kings 16.34. He appears without comment in 1 Chronicles 7.27, a listing of the descendants of Ephraim. Furthermore, apart from 1 Kings 16.34, the Hebrew Bible makes no mention of any of the events with which Joshua is associated. It is only in later scriptures that one can find references to Joshua and his exploits (for example Sir. 46.1–8; 1 Macc. 2.55; Acts 7.45; Heb. 4.8). While the Qur'an knows of the Israelites' entry into and conquest of the land, it does not name Joshua directly. Islamic tradition knows him as Yusha bin Nun and he is understood to be one of the anonymous helpers of Moses recorded in the Qur'an.

The biblical Joshua's character is in many ways a reflection of the character of Moses. While he is at first referred to as Moses' servant, by the end of the book he is termed, like Moses before him, the servant of YHWH (Josh.

24.29). The crossing of the Jordan echoes that of the Red Sea. Joshua's encounter with the commander of the army of the Lord (Josh. 3.2–5) recalls Moses
at the burning bush (Ex. 3.2–5). According to Nelson, Joshua 'repeats Moses'
function as intercessor' (Josh. 7.6–9; Deut. 9.25–9) and 'holds up his sword
against the enemy much as Moses holds up his arms' (Nelson 1997: 30; cf.
Josh. 8.18; Ex. 17.11). Joshua's role in distributing the land in the second part of
the book (Josh.14–19) is predicated by recalling Moses distributing the land
among the tribes (Josh. 13.8–33). Like Moses, Joshua even takes on a prophetic
role (Josh. 6.26; 7.13; 24.2). This likeness of Joshua and Moses extends to that
between the books of Joshua and Deuteronomy. According to Polzin, much of
Joshua 1 is 'a pastiche of Moses' utterances from Deuteronomy, now put into
the mouths of God, Joshua, and the people' (1980: 75). Thus Joshua 1.3–5a =
Deuteronomy 11.24–5; Joshua 1.5c–7a is very close to Deuteronomy 31.7–8; and
Joshua 1.13–15 is almost identical to Deuteronomy 3.18–20. Hawk declares that
'Deuteronomy constitutes a sort of narrative lens through which the reader
may understand the story Joshua tells' (2000: xxiv). Joshua regularly cites and
alludes to Deuteronomy and regularly employs Deuteronomic vocabulary and
phrasing. Deuteronomic laws will be crucial for some of the events in Joshua
while even the structure of Joshua 'corresponds to that which gives shape to
Deuteronomy's overview of the acquisition of the land in the Transjordan'
(Hawk 2000: xxv; cf. Deut. 2.24–4.43).

In 1943, Martin Noth hypothesized the existence of a Deuteronomistic
History (DH), by which the books of the Former Prophets should be considered together with Deuteronomy as constituting a unified whole: a hypothesis
that has won the support of a broad scholarly consensus.

Noth advanced four main reasons in support of his hypothesis.
Chronologically, the five books work as a single unit. Stylistically, there is uniformity in vocabulary, diction and sentences. As has been noted in the case
of Joshua, the speeches of the main characters seem to parallel those found in
Deuteronomy – the characters all begin to sound like Moses. Structurally, at
various points in the history, the writer presents a speech by one of the leaders
that looks both backward and forward to interpret the course of events and
give direction to the people on what they must do. Finally, there is a theological unity in interpretation of events, 'particularly the writer's concern with
God's "retributive activity" when the people fail to heed demands that God
has made on their conduct' (Rowlett 1996: 32). The underlying theme of this
'history' is the call to obedience to the stipulations of Deuteronomy, 'service
of the one God by an elect people centred around one sanctuary, through obedience to the law in the land which God has given' (Prior 1997: 227). Because
Israel failed to be obedient to the covenant, the covenant failed.

These themes and patterns can certainly be found in Joshua. Not only does
the character of Joshua echo and resemble Moses but he appears as the ideal
model of the later leaders, both judges and kings. Nelson cites various instances
where Joshua is presented as a royal figure (Josh. 1.6–9; 5.10–12; 8.30–5; 23.6)
and observes that 'the figure of Joshua serves as a forerunner for the ideological role played by later kings, and especially for . . . Josiah' (Nelson 1997: 22).
As I have mentioned, Joshua, like Moses, also has a prophetic role and thus
anticipates the role prophets will play in the later stages of this history.

Because of its themes and concluding point in Kings with the end of the monarchies, Noth argued that the DH was written at the time of the exile when Israelite and Judaean history had come to an end. Many other scholars (cf. Rowlett 1996; Nelson 1997) have argued a double redaction hypothesis, whereby the DH was first written in the reign of Josiah to support his 'reforms', centralizing cult and state around the royal sanctuary in Jerusalem. With the fall of the Judaean monarchy to the Babylonians, there was a rewriting and expansion of the DH to maintain community and religious identity in response to the crisis of exile. Other scholars have argued for a post-exilic setting for the composition of the DH. Writing on the book(s) of Kings, Linville (1997) argues that Kings does not require an exilic provenance but could have been written later. In Linville's view, Kings suggests that exile is the normal state of things. The book is addressed to a variety of different communities and thus is working memories of the Israelite past into a systematic whole that would appeal to a variety of communities, and not just one in Jerusalem or elsewhere, who are making claims of a return from exile.[3] If Kings is to be understood as part of an integrated text, from Deuteronomy to Kings, then Linville's observations can certainly be applied to Joshua. Indeed a central concern of Joshua is who constitutes Israel, including the question of whether Israel is to be defined only by residency in the land of Canaan. Joshua rejects that definition.

Historical and cultural locations

These issues of provenance and audience raise questions of history. As I have said about Genesis and the Twelve Minor Prophets, we don't know when, where, why or by whom they were written. Whether it be regarded as its own discrete entity or part of a longer DH, the same can be said of the Book of Joshua. As with Genesis and the rest of the Hebrew scriptures, Joshua is born out of the religious ferment of the Imperial age in the eastern Mediterranean during the second half of the first millennium BCE. But because such historical questions in relation to Joshua are fraught with so much baggage for our world, I will address whether or not there was an invasion of Canaan, as Joshua recounts, and the relationship of Israel and Canaan.

Was there an invasion of Canaan, memories of which Joshua preserves? There are four perspectives that can be and have been held by scholars and non-scholars alike. The first is the traditional view that the biblical account is essentially correct. Israel moved into Canaan *en masse*, defeating the Canaanites through a systematic military campaign and taking over the land. However, archaeological evidence does not support the claim of a large-scale conquest of the land. Most importantly for Joshua, archaeology shows that Jericho had been destroyed two or more centuries before the Israelites are traditionally

---

3 This 'universalist' intent of the DH is further supported by the fact that the Samaritans accepted not only Deuteronomy as scripture but Joshua as part of their Chronicles. It is only in the latter part of the DH that the temple at Jerusalem is identified as the site of Mosaic/Deuteronomic observance. The Samaritans believe their temple at ha-Gerizim is the true location of divine presence. Both Deuteronomy (Deut. 1.29; 27.12) and Joshua (Josh. 8.33) portray it as a mount of blessing.

supposed to have invaded the land and remained abandoned until the seventh century BCE, two centuries after when the biblical narrative says it was resettled (1 Kings 16.34; cf. Josh. 6.26). Other cities recorded in Joshua as having been destroyed by the Israelites – Ai, Kadesh-Barnea, Arad – were likewise uninhabited at the time of a putative Israelite invasion. In the face of such evidence, many scholars adopted the second view that Israel did not move into the land as a people. Instead, separate tribes moved into Israel, sometimes peacefully and sometimes involving military action. In their view, the movement of Israel into the land is best described in Judges 1 (again showing that the biblical texts are never content with just one version of events). Israel only became Israel after it had settled into the land. According to this way of thinking one of the tribes which moved into the land had a tradition of Exodus, another tradition of Sinai, others traditions of Abraham, others of Jacob and so on. These were brought together to form the Pentateuch once Israel was settled in the land and Israel worked out a common history in which Yahweh was understood to be the God of this people.

A third perspective draws on the archaeological evidence that seems to indicate large-scale movement of people into the central hill country of Canaan, and a number of scholars argued accordingly that Israel did not move into the land but that Canaanites became Israelites through a peasant revolt. Canaanite peasants rebelled against the oppression of their Egyptian overlords and the Bronze Age Canaanite city states, which acted as Egypt's surrogates. This peasant insurgency was understood to be reflected in the Amarna correspondence dating from the reigns of Pharaohs Amenophis III and Akhnaton. Some held that a small group of slaves escaped from Egypt and their god, Yahweh, was adopted by the peasants to create a religious federation. Thus

> (t)he Hebrew conquest of Palestine took place because a religious movement and motivation created a solidarity among a large group of pre-existent social units, which was able to challenge and defeat the dysfunctional complex of cities which dominated the whole of Palestine and Syria at the end of the Bronze age. (Mendenhall 1962: 73)

Norman Gottwald (1979) further developed the peasant revolt hypothesis, employing a Marxist perspective that highlighted a class warfare model. In his view, whereas 'the inhabitants of Canaan had El, for their god at first, they adopted Yahweh at Shechem (Josh. 24), who thus became the god of a new society of revolutionary covenanters, the Israelites' (Prior 1997: 234). Nevertheless, there remains no archaeological evidence for either an invasion from the outside or even a peasant revolt within Canaan. So there is now a broad consensus among biblical scholars, historians and archaeologists that no conquest, or any other change in Canaan later portrayed as such in Joshua, occurred. Instead, in this fourth perspective, the biblical texts have created a world of the past into which are projected the issues and concerns of a later community. Thus Lori Rowlett (1996) argues that Joshua is a fiction created at a time of crisis when lines of power are being contested. Thus Joshua was composed in the time of Josiah, when his kingdom was challenged with the decline of the Assyrian Empire and the emergence of the Babylonian Empire. More and more scholars, however, would now argue for a Persian or Hellenistic setting for the compo-sition of Joshua and the rest of the texts of the Hebrew Bible, a position with which I concur.

If there is no evidence of an invasion of Canaan by Israelites in the late second millennium BCE, then the only scenario left is that Israelites and Canaanites are one and the same. Furthermore, Israelite religion and Canaanite religion were also the same or the former has come out of the latter. Indeed the Hebrew scriptures contain many parallels to Canaanite mythology especially as recorded in the clay cuneiform texts unearthed from ancient Ugarit in northern Syria (for the parallels between biblical religion and Ugaritic mythology see Cross (1973) and Wyatt (2005)). Such parallels are part of a broader body of archaeological evidence, which indicates that the religious and cultural background of the biblical texts was similar to the one behind the Ugarit texts. Rather than the biblical portrait of an Israelite/biblical monotheism struggling like an exotic flower to resist the incursions of the (polytheistic) Levantine religio-cultural matrix in which it was planted, this biblical religion/ monotheism was itself a product of that same (polytheistic) Levantine religio-cultural matrix. In other words Israelites were first Canaanites and biblical monotheism was (is) grounded in biblical polytheism (for a good analysis and overview of the problems of how to define ancient 'Israel' see Davies (1995)).

I hold the view that the Hebrew scriptures were composed and collated in the Persian and Hellenistic periods, and are a product of the Imperial age in the eastern Mediterranean. This period was marked by the rise and fall of empires and the resulting intermingling of cultures and religions. The Persian Empire was the first to bring together under one rule the eastern Mediterranean world. Established under Cyrus the Great in 559 BCE, at its peak the empire would stretch from Egypt and the Balkans in the west to Afghanistan and Central Asia in the east. Before Cyrus, the Fertile Crescent had been subject to the Assyrian and Babylonian Empires through most of the first half of the first millennium. Canaan and the broader Levant had been caught up in these imperial progressions from the ninth and eighth centuries BCE onwards. I would argue that the Hebrew scriptures and the associated Greek and Samaritan scriptures, Pseudepigrapha and Qumran literature then are better understood as representing a religious project(s) of engaging with and transforming that older Canaanite–Levantine religio-cultural matrix. This project was part of major religious movements then occurring in the ancient eastern Mediterranean world in the first millennium BCE in response to the upheavals and transformations brought about by the imperial progressions. In this biblical project, elements of older mythology, imagery, ritual and history were taken up and deployed to experiment with, explore and debate questions of universalism and diversity, the One and the Many, together with the allied questions of justice, good and evil, suffering and death. Babylonian, Assyrian, Egyptian, Persian and Greek religious ideas are also deployed as befitted the multicultural imperial background. This project was open-ended, pluralistic. There was no single monotheistic vision but several, and I would argue the project continued even after the construction of biblical canons and the rise of Rabbinic Judaism and Christianity. (For a very good analysis and overview of questions of Bible and history see Thompson (2000).)

Wyatt and other scholars of Middle Eastern mythology have argued that for too long the polytheistic or 'mythic' background of the Hebrew scriptures has been ignored by biblical scholars in favour of a reading that saw them as representing a triumph of a rational monotheism over 'mythic' paganism. While such a view accorded with the theological positions of many biblical scholars, its main motivation lay in 'the attempt to reconcile . . . (Christian and Jewish) belief systems with the rationalist demands of the Enlightenment' (Wyatt 2005: 179). Similarly Margaret Barker has argued that to read the 'Old Testament . . . as the writings of a monotheistic faith which had one God with several names' is to sanitize it 'for the benefit of modern readers for whom mythology, ritual and mystery are too reminiscent of all that has been cast aside with the Reformation' (Barker 1992: 28). Barker is somewhat of a maverick scholar who has attempted to read the Hebrew scriptures (and related texts) without assuming that they reflect or are the product of a long-standing monotheistic faith and culture. While I am critical of some of her arguments, I believe her position opens a space in which 'Israel' can be understood as a face of 'Canaan' and the two no longer viewed as alien antagonists. I believe she brings valuable insights that represent an important corrective to long-term assumptions and that scholarly biblical consensus to which Wyatt refers, and that she enables a richer perspective on the relationship of Yahweh to the broader Canaanite religious world.

Barker is interested in the religious background of the biblical texts and its relation to the temple and religion of pre-exilic Israel. She argues that the figure of Melchizedek in Genesis 14 is a memory of the worship of the Canaanite high god, El Elyon, in Jerusalem in the days of the kings (Barker 1991: 15). According to her reconstruction, El Elyon presided over a council of Holy Ones or heavenly beings who were the sons of Elyon. The chief of these was Yahweh, the Holy One of Israel. As in Ugarit, El Elyon had as his consort Asherah, the mother of the sons of Elyon. Asherah was the Queen of Heaven and was not simply a consort of El Elyon but the female aspect of an androgynous divine principle (Barker 1992: 57; cf. Wyatt 2005: 246–8). She is symbolized by the tree and represents the power of Wisdom that sustains the universe. Elyon, Asherah and the heavenly retinue dwelt in a 'mountain garden where there was fabulous vegetation, the tree of life, the waters of life and the great throne' (Barker 1987: 279). The temple was the central place in the cult and represented this heavenly place. 'Its Eden setting, with throne, cherubim, menorah and great sea, was the place where the movements of heaven were enacted on earth, and its rituals, which derived their authority from the upper world, were assured of effectiveness on earth' (1987: 280). Above all, this was a royal cult. Yahweh and a number of the Holy Ones or angels had charge of individual nations. Thus, the 'successive kings of these nations were the earthly manifestation of the heavenly patron' (1987: 279). Yahweh had charge of Israel, and the king in Jerusalem (the David or beloved, cf. Wyatt (2005: 26)) was understood as the earthly manifestation of Yahweh. In other words, the cult in Jerusalem was typical of royal cults throughout the Canaanite–Levantine region, which were presided over by El (Elyon) and Asherah, with a subordinate deity (e.g. Yahweh, Baal, Chemosh) who was represented by the king. The subordinate deity likewise had a sister-consort. Baal's consort and sister was Anat and, as with El and Asherah, they functioned as the two sides of an androgynous divine principle. There is evidence from the fifth-century BCE Jewish community at Elephantine in Egypt, that Yahweh was likewise paired with Anat (Barker 1992: 56; cf. Patai 1978: 53–8). In the old royal cults (and for the post-exilic polytheistic devotees of Yahweh) Yahweh and Anat would similarly have been regarded as twin parts of an androgynous whole, which also accounts for the transgender aspects of the deity in the Hebrew scriptures.

The Hebrew and associated (Greek, Samaritan, Pseudepigraphal, Qumran) scriptures themselves are evidence of major transformations taking place in the religion of the old Canaanite royal cults of Yahweh in the latter half of the first millennium BCE. In these transformations, Yahweh and El were fused together with Asherah and Anat, while the lesser deities of the Host of Heaven were transformed into angels (and demons). Thus, '(w)hen Yahweh became Elyon, his roles were filled by . . . angels' (Barker 1992: 70). The sheer variety and plurality of these scriptures attest to the fact that the transformations were not a uniform, harmonious process. The texts retain traces of polytheism and henotheism, together with various monotheistic theologies of the pluriform divine (e.g. Wisdom, Angel of the Lord), unitarian monotheistic trajectories,[4] and developing angel/demonologies. The other point of contestation in these texts is the temple:

> The Temple generated strong feelings for many centuries . . . the temple was called a harlot by those who had reason to quarrel with the priesthood of the day . . . Despite such invective, the temple was central to the hopes of even its fiercest critics. This power of the temple must have been rooted in its remotest past, in the time before it became the subject of such bitter controversy. What gripped the minds and hearts of all sides in these disputes was not the actual temple in Jerusalem,[5] but the ideal, the memory of a temple which was central to the heritage of Israel. (Barker 1991: 13)

These contests are very clear in the texts of the Latter Prophets. Furthermore, the ideal in the Deuteronomistic History, of which Joshua is a part, is that of an Israel united around the sole sanctuary of the one god, Yahweh, on Zion at Jerusalem, following the precepts of the Mosaic Law as refracted through the prism of Deuteronomy. This ideal is the standard by which the characters and events of that 'history' are judged, including those in the book of Joshua.

Holy War and the Ban

As I said earlier, Joshua regularly cites and alludes to Deuteronomy and regularly employs Deuteronomic vocabulary and phrasing, while Deuteronomic laws are crucial for some of the events. Most crucial are the laws of war set down in Deuteronomy (Deut. 20) and the Deuteronomic provisions for occu-

---

4 I think what is termed Deuteronomistic by biblical scholars might represent a unitarian theological tendency.

5 Or Ha-Gerizim, Bethel, etc.

pying the land (Deut. 7). Regardless of the fact that these events are fiction, the main imagery in Joshua is that of war, an integral part of which is *herem*, the ban. Deuteronomy envisages war as a holy activity. The warrior camp is a holy place in which the deity is present, and the deity accompanies the Israelites into battle (Deut. 20.4).[6] Priests are present in the camp and their role is to give encouragement to the warriors. Warriors must also be wholly devoted to the forthcoming war. Those who cannot fully devote themselves to battle for a number of reasons are sent home (20.5–8). Rules for the conduct of war require that when drawing near a town, it must first be offered peace terms, and if the town accepts and surrenders then the inhabitants must be spared but subject to forced labour (20.10–11). If however peace terms are rejected, then the town must be besieged and conquered. All its menfolk are to be put to the sword but the women, children and livestock are to be spared so that, 'You may enjoy the spoil of your enemies, which the LORD your God has given you' (Deut. 20.14). However, these rules only apply to those who are 'far' from the Israelites (20.15). For the peoples of the land of Canaan – specifically the Hittites, Amorites, Canaanites, Perizzites, Hivites and Jebusites – there is only one possible fate, extermination (20.17). Deuteronomy 7 gives specific instructions for dealing with the peoples of the land (and adds the Girgashites to the list of those to be annihilated[7]). The Israelites are to make 'no covenant with them and show them no mercy' (7.2). There is to be no intermarriage with them and everything belonging to them, especially their religious objects, are to be destroyed. The chapter concludes warning the Israelites against taking the gold and silver of the Canaanites and not to bring anything abhorrent into their houses, otherwise they 'will be set apart for destruction like it' (Deut. 7.26). In other words, the peoples of Canaan are to be subjected to the ban, *herem*.

This word can also be translated as devoted and connotes something set aside as belonging to the deity and forbidden for ordinary use. Conrad points out that the word *harem* is derived from the Arabic cognate of *herem* and that, as a practice, the ban is not unique to Israel but is attested elsewhere in the ancient Middle East (Conrad 1993: 73). In the Moabite Stone, dating from approximately 830 BCE, the Moabite king, Mesha, records his victory over the house of Omri and declares that all the Israelite inhabitants of Ataroth and Nebo were subjected to the ban, or devoted to Chemosh, the Moabite patron deity. The religious ideology of warfare and the ban that we find in Joshua and the rest of the biblical texts, then, is not peculiarly Israelite but Canaanite or, more broadly, one common to the 'pagan' world of the ancient Middle East. Indeed, Niditch goes further and points out that the ban is reminiscent of human sacrifice. The vanquished are offered to the deity in thanksgiving for victory. The

---

6 Additional provisions in Deuteronomy 23 apply strict purity rules in the camp, for dealing with excrement and nocturnal emissions, to further underscore the sacredness of the camp and the activities of war (23.9–14).

7 According to both Rabbinic and Islamic traditions, the Girgashites emigrated *en masse* from the land to either North Africa or the Caucasus. By some Islamic accounts the Girgashites are the ancestors of the Berbers (Ginzberg 1941: 10; 1956: 177–8; al-Tabari 1991: 98).

'killing of actual humans like oneself . . . in a successful battle' is regarded 'as necessary offerings to God, required if the battle is to succeed', with the ironic implication that the 'enemy is not the unclean "other," but a mirror of the self, that which God desires for himself' (Niditch 1993: 50). Deuteronomy struggles against such notions and seeks to justify the ban as divine justice or as a means of protecting the Israelites from idolatrous contamination (Deut. 7.26; 20.18). In Deuteronomy 13, Israelites who apostatize are also to be subjected to the ban. The net effect of these moves is to turn holy war into crusade, and the desired enemy into the unclean Other.

Both these ideologies should be regarded as abhorrent. However, Niditch points out that the ban as divine justice 'actually motivates and encourages war, implying that wars of extermination are desirable . . . to eradicate evil in the world . . . and to actualize divine judgment' (1993: 77). As she says, it is not easy for humans to kill each other, and dehumanizing the Other makes it easier for people to contemplate eradicating those others. The discourse of othering is the discourse of murder. The Jew becomes Christ-killer and race-poisoner; the Muslim becomes warmongering terrorist and anti-Christ. Whether the Other is termed heretic, infidel, pagan, sodomite, savages, faggots or whore, behind such figures stands the hapless Canaanite. Joshua uses the metaphors of crusade and the notion of *herem*, for both sacrifice and divine justice, but we as readers are not required to endorse them but instead can resist and condemn them. Joshua can be read to illuminate the othering process not just in the text but in our lives (something crucial in a time of a putative clash of civilizations and war between terrorisms).

Commentary

Reading Joshua

Both sexuality and gender are crucial elements in Joshua although sparsely deployed in the book.[8] In my reading of Joshua I will highlight these pivot points in the book. I will draw on Jewish and Islamic traditions and contemporary readings in my engagement with the book. Nevertheless, while sexuality and gender mark pivot points in the story, I will also endeavour to bring out the broader patterns of which they are a part. In particular, I wish to highlight the slippage between Canaanite and Israelite that recurs throughout the book and the associated question of who actually is or comprises Israel. So I am interested, as well, in the othering process in the book. Othering can as much be used to rally oppressed or marginalized communities to resistance as it can to rally dominant communities to attack and oppress. Community-building can often be as much about exclusion as it is about inclusion. Furthermore, as part of the Deuteronomistic History, Joshua is part of a larger tragic narrative in which I believe Israel is set up to fail. The author/s know/s full well how it will turn out, and this knowledge is an important shaper of the Joshua narrative.

---

8 The reader may like to turn to the chapters on Genesis and the Twelve Minor Prophets for what I have to say on sexuality in the ancient world.

Joshua 1: 'After the death of Moses'

Joshua opens with speeches, first from the LORD, then from Joshua and finally from some of the people. As noted earlier, much of the content is recycled from Deuteronomy, establishing the continuity between the two books. The LORD speaks only to Joshua, who is portrayed as the obedient and faithful successor to Moses. Joshua is commanded to mobilize the people for war and to 'be careful to act in accordance with all the law that my servant Moses gave you' (Josh. 1.7). As will be seen these instructions will not be adhered to. Curiously, Jewish tradition records that Joshua had difficulties in applying the Law. He was so ignorant that he was called a fool. When Moses was dying, he asked Joshua if he had any questions on the Law wanting clarification. Aware of 'his own industry and devotion, Joshua replied that he had no questions to ask' and '(s)traightway . . . forgot three hundred Halakot, and doubts assailed him concerning seven hundred others' (Ginzberg 1941: 4). He was threatened by the people because he couldn't resolve their legal difficulties. The deity finally commands Joshua to war so that the people forget their grievance against him. Islamic tradition, too, knows of problems between Joshua and the people. al-Tabari records that the people thought Joshua had killed Moses and, not believing his denials, made plans to kill him. In response to Joshua's prayers, God 'approached in a dream . . . every man who was guarding him and informed that Joshua had not killed Moses' (al-Tabari 1991: 86).

Jewish tradition records another story about Joshua's childhood and youth, ostensibly to liken him to Moses but presenting him as a Hebrew Oedipus. In infancy Joshua was swallowed by a whale, but survived and was spewed forth on a distant coast. As with Moses and Pharaoh's daughter, Joshua was found by strangers and raised unaware of his descent. Grown up, he was appointed executioner and unbeknownst to him executed his own father. By law he was entitled to the wife of his victim and was only prevented from incest by a prodigy – '(w)hen he approached his mother, milk flowed from her breasts' (Ginzberg 1941: 3). Joshua made enquiries into his background and learnt the truth. His mother had exposed him as an infant because her husband, Nun, had had a revelation that his newborn son would behead him. This bizarre story, in attempting to make Joshua a reflection of Moses, serves to highlight the fact that Moses and, apparently, Joshua did not grow up as Israelites. Nun is said to have lived in Jerusalem, then a Jebusite city, while Joshua works for the Egyptian Pharaoh (Ginzberg 1956: 169). Does Joshua grow up as a Canaanite? The motif of incest suggests an element of sexual peril for an Israelite separated from his people and, as it is set in pre-conquest Canaan, might associate the people of the land with sexual irregularities.

Returning to Joshua the book, the final part of chapter 1 presents us with the reality that all the Israelites will not live in the land. Recalling Deuteronomy 3.12–22, Joshua addresses the two and a half tribes, Reuben, Gad and half-Manasseh. He reminds them that while they have settled in the Transjordan and will not live in the land, they must still help their fellows in the invasion and occupation of the land before they can 'return to' their 'land and take possession of it, the land that Moses . . . gave you beyond the Jordan to the east' (Josh. 1.15). While the two and a half tribes reaffirm their loyalty and solidarity with Israel, the pericope underscores the fact that Israel's identity will never be fully grounded in occupation of and residence in the land.

The conquest commences (Joshua 2.1–8.29): Rahab and Achan

The stories of Rahab and Achan bring to the fore all the themes of outsider and insider, the Other and Israel. The boundaries between Israelite and Canaanite shift and blur. The narrative begins with Joshua's response to the LORD's command to cross the Jordan and enter the land. He 'timidly sends out spies to reconnoiter the country and we are immediately alerted that Joshua might not be as strong and resolute' as expected (Polzin 1980: 86). From the very start sexuality is implicated. The spies are sent secretly from Shittim, which as Hawk (2000: 40) reminds us was the place where the Israelite men were led into worship of other gods through consorting with Moabite women. The spies go from there straight to the house of a woman, a prostitute, called Rahab (Josh. 2.1). Her name means wide or broad in Hebrew, and Brenner points out that 'there is a sexual pun here', thus she refers to Rahab as 'The Broad' (2005: 83). The Targum Jonathan translated the Hebrew word for prostitute, zônāh, as innkeeper,[9] and a number of Rabbinic commentators accepted this possibility to argue that she was 'a moral person to whom the spies went for succor' (Kramer 2000: 158). However, it remained a minority position, and Rahab was sexualized to such an extent that in Rabbinic tradition it was said that the mere mention of her name enkindled such lust in men that 'a seminal discharge would immediately ensue' (Kramer 2000: 159). The text itself plays with double meanings because it says that when the spies went to her house they lay (wayyiškĕbu) there.[10] Bird points out that this verb heightens such sexual connotations (1989b: 128). Hawk agrees, noting that the Hebrew Bible employs the verb as 'a common idiom for sexual intercourse' (2000: 40) in a number of instances (Gen. 34.7; 39.7, 10, 12; Ex. 22.16; Num. 5.13; Deut. 22.3; 28.30; 2 Sam. 12.11). Brenner imagines her as a madam running a brothel cum tavern with a flax business on the side (2005: 90).

Rahab, then, represents the complete Other to Israel; she is both prostitute and Canaanite. Most of all, she is a woman. When women speak and act in the Hebrew Bible the reader should sit up and take notice, particularly when it happens in Joshua, itself very much a men's book. Not only does Rahab speak and act but she is in control of events from when we first meet her. It appears that the spies (in Jewish tradition, Caleb and Phineas) have made of their mission an opportunity to enjoy the local bordello. Certainly they have not attempted to cover their tracks because the king of Jericho is told that spies are abroad and straightway sends a force to Rahab's house to apprehend them. Rahab hides the spies amidst the flax on her roof and tells the king's men that the spies have left. She sends them on a wild goose chase in pursuit 'on the way to the Jordan as far as the fords' (Josh. 2.7). Thus far the spies have been silent and passive and Rahab goes up to the roof to parley with them. She gives a speech

---

9 The LXX, however, accepts the sexual meaning and translates it as porne.
10 The NRSV softens this by rendering it as 'spent the night there'.

citing the mighty deeds of the LORD and of the Israelites and declaring that all the people are in dread of Israel in language that cites the song of Moses in Exodus 15.15–16 (Hawk 2000: 44). She then proceeds to praise the God of Israel in Deuteronomic language (Hawk 2000: 45; Josh. 2.11; cf. Deut. 4.39). Having established her bona fides she asks the spies to guarantee the safety of her family 'and all who belong to them' (Josh. 2.13) in return for her aid. The spies agree, swearing an oath guaranteeing the safety of her and her family. She lowers them through the window to safety outside the city walls (into which her house is built) and gives them further instructions on how to return safely. Hawk notes that all of her speech employs imperatives underscoring her control of events. As if to assert their own masculine authority, the spies respond attempting to forswear responsibility for the pact they have made. After all, by making this agreement with Rahab they have broken the stipulation in Deuteronomy 7.2 to make no covenant with the Canaanites. They declare they have been made to swear Rahab's oath and they place further conditions that everyone must remain in her house if they are to be saved and that Rahab must hang a crimson cord on the window (a scarlet one in Freedman 1950: 11). We last see Rahab hanging the cord in her window, obviously determined to keep her part of the bargain. The story closes with the spies telling everything to Joshua and declaring the land is Israel's for the taking.

According to Rowlett, Rahab is a cartoon figure and likens her to Pocahontas, particularly as portrayed in the Disney film of that name. According to Rowlett, Rahab is not 'allowed to speak in a truly indigenous voice', and further:

> The colonizing powers telling the story have given her words to speak in praise of themselves as conquering heroes . . . the woman is regarded as worth saving and assimilating because she recognizes the specialness of the conquerors, making her the mirror which magnifies their own glory. (2000: 75)

Rowlett's observations serve as a healthy caution in reading this story but, while I haven't seen the film in question and have only an outsider's acquaintance with the story of Pocahontas, I believe she more aptly describes that story/film than that of Rahab. Unlike the Pocahontas I meet in Rowlett's essay, Rahab is in control of the situation the whole time and she certainly is not impressed by the Israelite spies (are they impressive at all?). Whatever one makes of her so-called profession of faith, she acts primarily to save herself and her family from a destruction that is clearly pending. Rather than the hyper-sexualized Canaanite mirror magnifying Israelite glory, Rahab could be seen as representing Israel herself. As a prostitute or brothel keeper she is a marginal figure in her society, as attested by the fact that her house is in the city wall. Bird asks whether the crimson cord is 'a permanent sign of an ancient red light district, or only specific to this narrative' (1989: 130). Even today prostitution is a sign of security risk, and I can remember a time when homosexuality was regarded as a marker for possible disloyalty (there are probably still many countries where that applies). Guy Burgess, of the Cambridge spies, is probably the most spectacular example of how marginal sexuality can lead to a shift in loyalties and the crossing of ideological and actual boundaries.[11] Bird goes on to say that the narrator might be drawing a parallel 'between the low or outcast estate of the harlot . . . and the low and outcast estate of escaped slaves beyond the Jordan' (1989: 131). Furthermore the crimson cord recalls the Israelites daubing their doorways with blood to escape destruction on the night of the first Passover in Egypt (Hawk 2000: 41), an impression strengthened when the reader discovers in Joshua 5 that these events take place in Passover time. Rahab might be the absolute Other, but as a type of Israel she places Otherness at the heart of what it means to be Israelite. As the walls of Jericho collapse bringing together inside and outside, Rahab, the woman of the walls, collapses the distinctions between Israelite and Canaanite.

This becomes clear when Israel enters Canaan. Joshua circumcises all the males of Israel (Josh. 5.2–9). According to Hawk, both the mass circumcision and the Passover celebrations that follow are meant to affirm Israelite 'identity as a unique people bound by covenant to YHWH' through 'the performance of rites which mark beginnings but stress continuity with the past' (2000: 78). But the question remains, why aren't the Israelites circumcised? Circumcision was commanded by the covenant with Abraham and, according to the text, the generation who left Egypt were circumcised but those who were born in the wilderness were not (Josh. 5.5). No explanation is offered as to why. Those who came out of Egypt were condemned to perish in the wilderness due to their lack of faith, but did they completely abandon all the precepts of the covenants? Where were Moses and Joshua while this was happening? Rabbinic tradition has suggested that the wandering in the wilderness was too exhausting for circumcisions to be carried out or that they hadn't been properly performed (Freedman 1950: 23). Perhaps the text is suggesting that Israelite identity is a constructed identity and that despite the claims of lineage and genealogy there is no intrinsic difference between Israelite and Canaanite after all.

The final pericope of chapter 5 contributes further ambivalence and uncertainty to the overall narrative, this time even challenging the notion of Israel's exclusive (monotheistic) religion. Joshua is confronted by a heavenly being. While the pericope might be likening Joshua to Moses via the latter's divine encounter at the burning bush, the overall effect is unsettling. Joshua is confronted by a 'man . . . with a drawn sword' (Josh. 5.13). As Hawk observes, the 'appearance of a divine being before the outset of a battle is an element of the war literature of many Ancient Near Eastern cultures' (2000: 83). But isn't Israel's religion different to those pagan religions of the ancient Middle East? Joshua's concern is whether the man is 'one of us, or one of our adversaries' (Josh. 5.13). The man's answer is unexpected and unsettling on two counts. He responds to Joshua with a 'no' – $l\bar{o}$' – (NRSV renders as 'neither'). The man continues that he is 'captain of the LORD's host' (Josh. 5.14 JPS) at which Joshua falls on his face to the ground and worships him. The man then commands Joshua to remove his sandals, 'for the place where you stand is holy' (Josh. 5.15 NRSV). Is the man the LORD, and if so why isn't he identified as such, and

---

11 There is a certain ambiguity to espionage, which gives it a heightened air of sexual outlawry, as evidenced by the figures of Mata Hari and James Bond. Perhaps it is quite in character for the spies in Joshua to head straight for a brothel.

if not who is he? He is clearly a divine being, and later traditions identified him as either Michael or Metatron. But Metatron in later Jewish esoteric texts is none other than Enoch who was taken up to heaven and transformed into a (semi-)divine being. Michael, whose name means the likeness of El/God, is one of the four or seven spirits/archangels who represent powers of the divine. The LORD's host is the Heavenly Host of lesser deities who form the Council of El, God Most High, in both Canaanite and biblical religions. Does this epiphany/theophany represent the resurgence of an older or parallel Israelite religion that the DH might even categorize as Canaanite?

Immediately after this encounter comes the siege and conquest of Jericho by the Israelites in Joshua 6. It is near Jericho that Joshua encounters the divine being, and the account continues the unsettling, alien religiosity of the previous pericope. What is described here is not a military campaign but a (magical) religious ritual. The Israelite warriors march around the city once a day for six days, together with the Ark of the Covenant and seven priests bearing seven horns. On the seventh day, they march around the city seven times with the priests blowing the trumpets. Then follows a 'long blast with the ram's horn' at which 'all the people shall shout with a great shout' (Josh. 6.5). Straightway the walls collapse. When Joshua gives the command to shout, he decrees the ban on Jericho, all that are alive, human and animal, in the city are killed, the city is burnt and 'only the silver and gold, and the vessels of bronze and iron, they are put into the treasury of the house of the LORD' (Josh. 6.24). The mass slaughter of all the living entailed by the ban here is characteristic of the ban as sacrifice. What happens with the fall of Jericho is a sacrificial holocaust, offered up to the LORD, of all human and animal life, just as the city's treasures are placed in the treasury of the LORD. An intimation of the sacrificial nature of what happens can be found in Rabbinic traditions that Joshua imposed the ban because Jericho fell on the Sabbath. Thus 'Joshua reasoned that as the Sabbath is holy, so also that which is conquered on the Sabbath should be holy' (Ginzberg 1941: 8).

Of course, Rahab, her family and all that are within her house are spared. While the text specifically mentions her parents, brothers and sisters, it goes on to include 'all who belong to them' (Josh. 2.13). Rabbinic tradition specifically records that it was not just her family 'but all the families allied to her by marriage' (Ginzberg 1956: 174), and one could assume that if her house was a brothel or tavern all her workers and their families might be included. When we see her taken out of the wreck of Jericho she is accompanied by her 'father, her mother her brothers and all who belonged to her' and the text adds, 'they brought all her kindred out' (Josh. 6.23). So it is not just a small family unit, let alone a Western-style nuclear family, that Rahab has rescued and brought into the community of Israel but a considerable number of people. By her actions alone, many are saved. According to Kramer, 'Rahab's heroism was twofold, saving both the spies and her family . . . God rewarded her, blessing her with special descendants' (2000: 160). It could be argued that she only saves the spies to save her kindred, and for that latter act she becomes a paragon of loving-kindness. She becomes the foremother of the prophetess, Huldah, as well as eight prophets and priests including Jeremiah, Baruch, Shallum and, by some accounts, Ezekiel. As well, she was reputed to have married

Joshua himself and even to have been a foremother of seven kings (Ginzberg 1956: 171). In Christianity, she was married to Salmon and was the mother of Boaz, making her the foremother of David and the kings and Jesus himself (Matt. 1.5). According to James 2.25 she is an example of how one is justified by one's works and not by faith alone. Paradoxically, Hebrews holds her up as an example of how people are saved by faith (Heb. 11.31). I have found no evidence that she has been remembered in Islam.

Rahab has challenged Israelite identity and has begun expanding the boundaries of who is included in Israel. In the face of this blurring of Israelite and Canaanite, Israel resorts to the scapegoat mechanism to generate the solidarity that cannot be sustained by any number of exterminated Jerichos. Enter Achan, who will be the necessary scapegoat. The text relates that he broke the ban, taking some of the treasures of Jericho. He will be uncovered only after Israel is unexpectedly defeated in its attack on Ai. Joshua appeals to the LORD, who responds that 'Israel has sinned; they have transgressed my covenant' and 'have taken some of the devoted things; they have stolen, they have acted deceitfully' (Josh. 7.11). Joshua initiates a process whereby all of the tribes must present before the LORD. The tribe that 'the LORD takes' must present by clan, and then the households of the similarly selected clan until a culprit is determined (Josh. 7.14–15). The text is not clear how this selection process works, but both Rabbinic and Islamic traditions say that it was by lot (Ginzberg 1941: 8; al-Tabari 1991: 96). The apportionment of the land in the second part of Joshua is explicitly carried out by lots, so the use of lots here would be consistent. It would signal that Achan, who is finally singled out (Josh. 7.18), serves a scapegoat role here. Lots are cast in the scapegoat ritual to determine which goat will be for the LORD and which driven out into the wilderness for Azazel (Lev. 16.8). The use of the lot here signals that what is being set up is, in effect, a human sacrifice (cf. Girard 2005: 329–32). Achan resembles Jonah, who is likewise identified by lot as responsible for the storm besetting the ship on which he is a passenger (Jonah 1.4–7). After being identified, Jonah confesses. Likewise Achan confesses willingly when asked to by Joshua (Josh. 7.19–21).

Rabbinic tradition records that Achan does not immediately confess but questions the legality of what has happened, 'Moses has been dead scarcely one month, and thou hast already begun to go astray, for thou hast forgotten that a man's guilt can be proved only through two witnesses' (Ginzberg 1941: 9; cf. Deut. 17.6; 19.15). This Rabbinic challenge highlights the fact that Achan is no less guilty than Joshua and Israel. Joshua has instituted a process in breach of the Law; he and Israel have made covenants with Canaanites and, by taking in Rahab and her kindred, have themselves broken the ban imposed on Jericho. This Rabbinic challenge also picks up on the underlying theme in the DH of Israel's accelerating decline that occurs even before they have entered the land. Achan finally confesses but only to avert a threatened civil war because his tribe, Judah, has rallied to his defence. Through confessing, Achan signals his consent to be sacrificed, thus absolving his killers of blame.[12] He is led away

---

12 Rabbinic tradition says that on account of his confession, he may have lost his life, but retained a place in the world to come (Freedman, 1950: 38).

to be killed along with 'his sons and 'daughters . . . his oxen, donkeys and sheep . . . and all that he had' (Josh. 7.24). Then 'all Israel stoned him to death . . . and raised over him a great heap of stones that remains to this day' (Josh. 7.25–6). Being interred under a great heap of stones evokes further scapegoat associations, recalling the fate of Azazel, who is likewise buried under a pile of rocks in the wilderness (1 Enoch 10.4–5). Hebrew Joshua is ambiguous as to whether Achan's sons and daughters die with him. According to the LXX, he alone perishes. If they are killed with him, then there is another breach of the law, for children shall not 'be put to death for their parents; only for their own crimes may persons be put to death' (Deut. 24.16). Although it has been argued that, 'if the children were also executed, they must have been punished as accomplices' (Freedman 1950: 38).

The place of execution is named Achor, Trouble, and Achan's name is rendered Achar, Troubler, in 1 Chronicles 2.7. However, the name Achan 'derives from no known (Hebrew) root and is attested nowhere else in the Hebrew Bible' (Hawk 2000: 120). Hawk goes on to suggest that the name represents an anagram of the root from which Canaan is derived. Achan thus represents the Other within, in contrast to Rahab who is the Other without. Both are marked with the sign of Canaan. Consequently, they blur the boundaries between Israelite and Canaanite. Rahab is a paragon of loving-kindness who refuses her fate under the ban to be incorporated into Israel with all her kindred. Achan is found guilty of sins that have been by committed by Joshua and all Israel. By confessing, he submits to his own murder and perhaps that of his children. Through his death the Israelites have externalized difference and uncertainty and achieve 'community, united in hatred for one alone of its number' (Girard 2005: 84). The Roman Catholic Church employs the same mechanism by scapegoating gay priests in response to the clerical child abuse crisis. More broadly, too many conservative religious and community leaders who loudly condemn LGBT people have also been found guilty of breaking the same sexual and other mores they proclaim sacrosanct. It is not so much the guilt of the scapegoat but the guilt of the accuser at the heart of the process. Of course, scapegoating is not the preserve of conservative or religious bodies but is a mechanism common to all communities. In many gay and lesbian communities, the bisexual or transgender person has served the same role as have flaming queens, femmes, HIV+ people, lipstick lesbians, bull dykes, radical activists. The scapegoat mechanism is no respecter of persons.

The conquest continues (Joshua 8.30–12.24): 'all Israel, alien as well as citizen'

This section repeats the themes of the blurred boundaries between Israelite and Canaanite together with the ban and associated motif of human sacrifice. I have marked as the boundary between the two sections, the final pericope of Joshua 8, where all Israel is gathered to renew the covenant. The ceremony marks 'both an end and a beginning' (Hawk 2000: 131). Here Israel is described as comprising both citizens (or natives as per the LXX) and aliens (or proselytes as per the LXX). It goes on to repeat the image of Israel's inclusivity by specifically including women and children, as well as aliens, in the assembly.

That women as well as men count as Israelites will be taken up in chapters 13–21, the apportioning of the land. In what immediately follows, in the second part of the conquest story, the question of aliens in Israel and, expressly, the Canaanite nature of Israel is once more accentuated.

The Gibeonites, seeing the Israelite victories, resolve to save themselves by a ruse. They send a delegation to the Israelites. Disguised as travellers from a far country, they seek a treaty with the Israelites because they have heard of 'the name of the Lord your God ... of all that he did in Egypt, and ... to ... the Amorites ... beyond the Jordan' (Josh. 9.9–10). Joshua and the elders finally agree to a covenant and swear an oath to the Gibeonites. This story parallels that of Rahab but now on a mass scale, instead of one woman and her kindred, a whole people, the Hivites of Gibeon, have been incorporated into Israel. Once again, Israel has broken the Law by making a covenant with a people of the land. Once again, the similarity of Canaanite and Israelite is stressed. Rahab was a marginal person like the Israelites. The Gibeonite delegation disguises themselves such that the Gibeonites 'look like the Israelites *would* have looked ... had it not been for the presence and provision' of the LORD (Hawk 2000: 140, emphasis original). In the Samaritan version, this resemblance is underlined by parallels to the Rahab story. When the Israelite spies come to Jericho, like the Gibeonites, they are in disguise, saying they have come from far away, seeking news of Joshua whose renown has come even to their faraway land.

Another parallel to Rahab and Jericho appears when the ban is invoked but in mitigated form. On learning that they have been duped, Joshua and the Israelites confront the Gibeonites, cursing them to slavery as hewers of wood and drawers of water. Joshua then modifies this such that their work will be devoted to the service 'of the altar of the LORD' (Josh. 9.27). Thus, like the treasures of Jericho, the Gibeonites have been taken into the holy place and dedicated to the LORD, in effect the ban, but in this instance being devoted entails life not death. The fate of the Gibeonites strongly suggests that when characteristics of marginality – like minority sexualities, gender non-conformity and physical conditions like epilepsy – are often associated with the sacred as a sign of sacerdotal, medium or shamanic vocation, it is because these characteristics also mark a person for death as potential sacrificial victim (cf. Girard 2005: 12).

That the Gibeonites are now part of Israel is confirmed when the Israelites come to their aid after they are attacked by a league of five kings headed by Adoni-Zedek of Jerusalem. The name suggests that Adoni-Zedek is a descendant of Melchizedek who blessed Abraham in the name of the Most High (Gen. 14.17–24). This ancestral (religious) affiliation places Adoni-Zedek both inside and outside Israel. In some respects he thus parallels Achan. Like Achan, he and the allied kings will be offered up in sacrifice. The Israelites are victorious and Joshua hangs Adoni-Zedek and the four other kings from five trees. In a further parallel to Achan, when the kings are cut down, the bodies are thrown into a cave, with stones being piled up covering the entrance. Then follow accounts of further successful conquests, culminating in a listing of all the kings defeated and killed by Joshua and the Israelites (Josh. 12.9–24). To me this list recalls the Pharaonic victory inscriptions on the walls of ancient Egyptian temples depicting the executions of defeated kings. Apart from the propaganda effect, by being inscribed on temple walls they become a perpetual sacrifice. The list of vanquished dead kings in Joshua 12 conveys the same effect.

Apportioning the land (Joshua 13–21): 'Israel, and the women and little ones and the aliens who resided among them'

As if to puncture the triumphalism of chapter 12, this next section opens with the LORD detailing to Joshua all the areas of Canaan that have yet to be taken by the Israelites. It serves as a preamble to the apportioning of the land, the subject of chapters 13–20. Once more the themes of inclusion and diversity come to the fore, signalled not only by ethnicity but also by gender. The apportionment begins with the lands of the two and a half tribes east of the Jordan, yet another reminder that membership of Israel does not demand connection to the lands of Canaan, west of the Jordan. At the same time the text declares, 'the Israelites did not drive out the Geshurites or the Maacathites; but Geshur and Maacath live within Israel to this day' (Josh. 13.13). As the apportionment proceeds it appears that the Geshurites and the Maacathites are not the only aliens who will live within Israel to this day, along with Rahab and her kindred and the Gibeonites. The Jebusites of Jerusalem (Josh. 15.63), the Canaanites of Gezer (Josh. 16.10) and the Canaanites of Bethshean, Ibleam, Dor, Endor, Taanach, Megiddo and all their villages (Josh. 17.12–13) are also listed. Ethnicity and gender come together at the very outset of the apportionment west of the Jordan. The text relates how Caleb is granted Hebron by Joshua (Josh. 14. 6–15). Twice Caleb is referred to as 'son of Jephunneh the Kenizzite' (Josh. 6.6, 14). The Kenizzites are referred to as a people of the land in the covenant the deity made with Abraham (Gen. 15.19). A Kenaz is also listed as a grandson of Esau (Gen. 36.1; 1 Chron. 1.36) and Kenaz is further listed as a clan name in Edom (Gen. 36.15, 42; 1 Chron. 1.53). Caleb is a heroic figure in the text. Along with Joshua, he was one of the spies Moses sent into Canaan, and he and Joshua were the only two who encouraged the people to go on and take the land. According to Rabbinic tradition, he and Phineas were the two spies Joshua sent to Jericho. In Islamic tradition he was Joshua's successor as well as husband to Miriam (al-Tabari 1991: 91, 118). Is the text saying that Caleb is not a full Israelite but of Edomite or even Canaanite descent? The places he is associated with, Hebron and Debir, fall to the south towards Edom.

The text then begins apportioning Judah's territory but interrupts the account to describe how Caleb took Hebron, before introducing the figure of his daughter, Achsah. Caleb promises her to the person who takes Debir, who turns out to be Othniel, his nephew. Like Rahab, Achsah is a woman who speaks and acts. She comes to her father and asks him for a present, saying, 'since you have set me in the land of the Negeb, give me springs of water as well' (Josh. 15.19). Caleb grants her request giving her the 'upper' and 'lower springs' (Josh. 15.19). Achsah signals that not only men but also women have a share in the community that is Israel – Israel is not just a boy's club. This point is reconfirmed in Joshua 17 when the daughters of Zelophehad step forward to remind Joshua that Moses had ruled that they inherit their father's portion as there were no sons born to him (cf. Num. 27.1–11). Joshua recognizes and confirms their claim, 'giving them an inheritance among the kinsmen of their father' (Josh. 17.4).

As well as employing gender and ethnicity to highlight the diversity and inclusivity of Israel, the account of the apportionment further questions the extent to which Israel will be defined by possession of the land of Canaan. Only the territories of Judah, Benjamin and, to a certain extent, Ephraim are clearly defined. Those of the rest are vague – Simeon seems to be incorporated into Judah. Furthermore the apportionment does not proceed smoothly. The Josephites, Ephraim and half Manasseh, complain of their allotment (Josh. 17.14–18) while the Danites lose their territory completely and have to take another one (Josh. 19.47–8).

Altared endings (Joshua 22–24)

The final section of Joshua resolves the issue of what constitutes Israel quite dramatically to declare that it is not determined by presence in the land but by obedience to the Lord and adherence to the one sanctuary. At the same time, it foreshadows the later loss of the land and dispersal of the people. Most strikingly, it infers that the Israelites are already breaching the covenant and turning away from the Lord. The LXX closes by moving from inference to outright accusation. In chapter 22, the two and a half tribes return home to the Transjordan. While on the way, they erect an altar at the border of Canaan in the vicinity of the Jordan. This act provokes the Israelites in Canaan to declare war on the Transjordanian tribes. However, before opening hostilities a delegation, headed by Phineas, is sent to the two and a half tribes. They accuse the tribes of rebellion against the Lord by building 'an altar other than the altar of the Lord our God' (Josh. 22.19). According to the Deuteronomic vision there is to be only one sanctuary, one altar to the Lord in Israel. Erecting this other altar implies establishing a second, rival sanctuary. The two and a half tribes are compared to the Israelites who apostatized at Peor (Num. 25) and to Achan and are accused of putting all of Israel at risk of the wrath of the Lord. Horrified, the two and a half tribes reject the accusation completely. Poignantly they explain that the altar was erected 'from fear that in time to come your children might say to our children, "What have you to do with the Lord, the God of Israel? For the Lord has made the Jordan a boundary between us and you . . . you have no portion in the Lord"' (Josh. 22.24–5). They are motivated by the fear that their descendants would be prevented by the tribes in the land from worshipping the Lord on the basis that they themselves did not reside there. At issue here is cultic loyalty versus connection to the land as the basis of Israelite identity. As war is averted and a renewed solidarity affirmed between the tribes on both sides of the Jordan, it is clear that cultic loyalty and not connection to the land remains the final determinant of what constitutes Israel.

Sexuality is evoked negatively here by the reference to Peor. It was there that the Israelites had sex with Moabite women and were encouraged into idolatry. Idolatry and abandoning cultic purity are thus made analogous to sexual transgression and infidelity, a strong motif in much of the Hebrew and other scriptures. Women and unbelievers/foreigners are paralleled as a seductive threat to Israelite purity. This intimation becomes explicit in Joshua's speech to the Israelites in chapter 23. He warns the Israelites against intermarriage with the 'survivors of these nations left here among you . . .

they will be a snare and a trap for you . . . until you perish from this good land that the LORD your God has given you' (Josh. 23.12–13). No matter how disturbing these parallels are, Joshua's speech serves to confirm the point of chapter 22 that cultic loyalty, and not connection to the land per se constitutes Israelite identity. Of course, for the author of Joshua, the survivors of 'these nations' might denote people who themselves identify as Israelite but possess a different notion of what constitutes loyalty to the LORD than that expressed in Joshua. In its final chapter, Joshua continues the theme of cultic loyalty this time without sexual imagery. Joshua gives one final address summarizing the Israelite saga and exhorting them 'to put away the gods that your ancestors served beyond the River and in Egypt' (Josh. 24.14). What gods are these? Are the Israelites still worshipping them? When the people affirm their loyalty to the LORD, Joshua apparently rebukes them – 'you cannot serve the LORD for he is a holy God' (Josh. 24.19). It is almost as if Joshua is giving them a chance to give up on the LORD and stay with their 'foreign gods' (Josh. 24.20, 23), because they twice more affirm loyalty before he relents. After making a covenant with the people, Joshua then sets a large stone in the sanctuary of the LORD under the oak there, as a 'witness against you, if you deal falsely with your God' (Josh. 24.27). That stone will always challenge and discomfort the Israelites. Yet there is something strange here. Why is there an oak tree in the sanctuary? Is it a sacred tree? The sacred tree is associated with Asherah. According to Freedman, some commentators had taken it for a sacred tree, but he rejects that, saying that the form of the noun here – 'allāh – is not used elsewhere in the Hebrew Bible. In Rabbinic Hebrew this form of the word means pole, and so Freedman argues that what the verse means is that 'the stone was set up by the tent-pole' (Freedman 1950: 150). However, sacred poles also represent Asherah, while the unpointed consonantal form of the word used here for oak, 'lh, could possibly be read as goddess. There is an ambiguity here consistent with Joshua's earlier questioning of the Israelites' unswerving commitment to unitarian devotion to the LORD. But the Hebrew text leaves it there, going on to relate the deaths of Joshua and Eleazar. Only the Greek text makes explicit what is suggested, by appending to its final verse, 'and the children of Israel worshipped Astarte, and Ashtaroth and the gods of the nations round about them' (Josh. 24.33 LXX). Of course, it could be understood that Israelites have here turned into Canaanites, but the point of this final chapter is that there has been no dramatic change on the part of the Israelites. Thus, Israelites and Canaanites are one and the same. Maybe Canaanite is a term of abuse used by differing Israelite communities against each other. Maybe the invasions of the land that removed the Canaanites are the self-same ones that would remove the Israelites – by the Assyrians, the Babylonians, the Persians, the Greeks and ultimately the Romans.

Conclusion

When I took on this project, I had not given much thought to the book of Joshua, regarding it, as many have done today and in the past, as a disquieting tale of warfare and genocide. While that will always be the surface feature of the book, to make that its main point or, even worse, to use it as endorsement for like behaviour in our world, is to seriously misread it. The book is about the Other, the othering process, deploying sexuality and gender, together with ethnicity and religion to mark the boundaries of community and outsider. Nevertheless, even though it first appears that the Other has been totally exterminated and the borders of community definitely determined, Joshua immediately throws those boundaries into question dissolving the distinction of (communal) Self and Other. Sexuality and gender are crucial elements of this questioning process.

I am concerned that perhaps I have been too generous towards the book. After all, by blurring those distinctions that mark off the Other, Joshua sets up the Israelites for what it knows will come about, the invasion of Eretz Israel by the nations, the end of the kings and the dispersal of the Israelites outside the land among the nations. Ironically, the true othering in the book is of the community's own ancestors and past. Nevertheless, I have come to think that readings of Joshua that seek either to solely condemn or endorse the ideologies of warfare, genocide and the Other in the book do it a disservice. To condemn turns the book into an Other to be shunned; to endorse it makes it a tool for creating the Other. Both perspectives get absorbed in the imagery of the book and miss the subtleties beneath that imagery. Othering is not a phenomenon of the past but something in which we are all and constantly implicated; it is the shadow side of community. Perhaps, Joshua can best serve as a mirror in which we can discover the othering in our own lives and communities, that which is done to us and that which we do to others.

Judges

DERYN GUEST

Introduction

Situated within the larger context of Genesis–2 Kings, the storyworld of Judges opens with the aftermath left by the death of Joshua, who had brought the tribes to the promised land of Canaan and given instructions on how to retain control of the land and live successfully within it. The emphatic nature of those instructions (particularly the injunction to put away all other gods and serve Yhwh alone) serves to heighten the reader's suspicion that their foothold in this land will be precarious, a fear enhanced when the lack of any regular, reliable leadership becomes apparent. The Israelites rely upon a series of saviours to deliver them from the surrounding enemies who, by the will of Yhwh, periodically oppress Israel. An ideal pattern of leadership is provided by the exemplary Othniel, but successive judges degenerate as the book proceeds until, by the end of the book, the Israelites are fighting their own people in civil war. Such things, stresses the narrator, happened when 'there was no king in Israel' (17.6; 18.1; 19.1; 21.25) – a pointer to anticipate the appointment of Saul in the book of 1 Samuel.

Much conventional scholarship has been devoted to historical-critical concerns: the composition of the text, identifying constituent sources and editorial activity, dating its various elements and considering possible authorial intentions. These approaches to the text have their distinctive merits but have tended to focus all attention upon the text as a refractor of history. However, it is necessary to distinguish between the 'period of the Judges' that the Bible creates and the history of Canaan in the early Iron Age (c.1200–1000 BCE) for these two things are not necessarily connected. While it has generally been assumed that any archaeological data relating to Canaan in the early Iron Age will have a bearing on the 'period of the Judges', the current debate relating to Israelite origins has made it clear that no such assumption can be made. Certainly, there is a population here at these chronological and geographical co-ordinates, a population that lived in difficult environmental circumstances and probably engaged in various survival activities; but any presupposition that this Iron Age society relates to an 'ancient Israel' and, specifically, to the characters that populate the book of Judges, is open to justified challenge.

Such awareness opens the text to different, engaging, questions and approaches. If Judges is not a collection of sources recounting history, then who are these entertaining stories aimed at? When were they composed and in what context? What were the pedagogical purposes of the author? More recent approaches to reading Judges focus upon the way the author uses characters, events and plot in order to promote certain messages; notably, that Israel is best governed directly by the deity, but that in the face of Israel's failure to remain faithful, a Judaean king committed to upholding Yahwism is the next best thing; that Israel must avoid tribal disunity, must beware of the dangers of foreign women, and must avoid the worship of other deities (for further elucidation see O'Connell 1996). Scholars differ in their views on the date and audience such messages originally addressed. In my view, Judges might be best understood as directed toward a post-exilic audience by an author concerned to reinforce a community identity and intensify the boundaries between the group he presents as 'Israel' and all other ethnic groups.

In order to advocate this message the author provides carefully constructed, often humorous stories of judgeship that have already been noted for their sexual innuendo. Early commentators such as Wellhausen (1883) and Moore (1895) accounted for the coarse, ribald language by positing its origins in early tenth-century BCE tribal folklore, but these judge stories probably have no such early origins. Tightly woven and interlocking, most of these stories were probably deliberately composed as vehicles for the author's pedagogy – ideologically laden fictions of a creative and sophisticated author, as opposed to remnants of an earthy oral tradition (Guest 1997; 1998). If this is so, then the question of why this author chose to employ such overtly sexualized stories becomes interesting. Certainly, Judges is a sexy book, frequently using euphemism and *double entendre* and non-too-veiled sexual references in order to transmit its messages. Alert to such features, literary, rhetorical and feminist readings have already noted how sex permeates the text, but a queer reading is particularly well placed to take up these notices and explore them further. In so doing, it may well contribute to an understanding of the author's purposes and his context, but it is also alert to the ethical issues the text raises for contemporary readers and any harmful effects it may have for those expected to read from a perspective contrary to their own interests. Attentive to the constructions of race, gender and sexuality at work in the text, this essay accordingly concentrates on three specific narratives from Judges asking what rhetorical purposes such constructions serve for the author and considering the impact such narratives have for contemporary readers, particularly those who identify as gay, lesbian, bisexual or transgender/sexual.

Ehud and Eglon: An Erotic Encounter: Judges 3.12–30

Deviousness and deviancy in the characterization of Ehud

Three elements of Ehud's characterization suggest that his assassination of Eglon is meant to be read figuratively as a male rape scene: the emphasis upon his left-handedness, the several references to his 'hand', and his Benjamite affiliation.

First, verse 15 states that Ehud was 'bound' in the right hand. Interpretations that Ehud was crippled (Soggin 1981: 50; Hamlin 1990: 70–3; Webb 1987: 131) do not convince, because any assumption that Ehud was unable to use his right hand ruins the carefully devised strategy. Ehud has to appear right-handed for the ploy to work (so Halpern 1996; Lindars 1995: 141; O'Connell 1996: 87, 45). The reference to being 'bound' in the right hand is rather a roundabout way of indicating that Ehud was left-handed. Why use this circuitous terminology? In Boling's view, this is due to the belief 'that left-handedness was considered peculiar and unnatural' (Boling 1975: 86). This is consistent with the slipperiness in the range of Indo-European language terms used for the left, a situation Robert Hertz explains 'by the sentiments of disquiet and aversion felt by the community with respect to the left side. Since the thing itself could not be changed the name for it was, in the hope of abolishing or reducing the evil' (1960: 99). In fact Hertz goes on to suggest that even specifically beneficent words, if associated with or applied to the domain of the left 'are quickly contaminated by what they express and acquire a "sinister" quality' (1960: 99), adding:

> The power of the left hand is always somewhat occult and illegitimate; it inspires terror and repulsion. Its movements are suspect; we should like it to remain quiet and discreet, hidden in the folds of the garment, so that its corruptive influence will not spread. (1960: 105)

The left hand *can* be used in a beneficial way, but only when it is turned against the left realm, where 'it excels at neutralising or annulling bad fortune' (1960: 105). In such cases it 'provides for the needs of the profane life . . . it can parry an adversary's blows, its nature fits it for defence' (1960: 108). But even here it cannot be redeemed: 'A left hand that is too gifted and agile is the sign of a nature contrary to right order, of a perverse and devilish disposition: every left-handed person is a possible sorcerer, justly to be distrusted' (1960: 106). Hertz specifically bemoans the case of a warrior trusting his weapon to his left hand with the emphatic 'Unhappy the warrior who profanes his spear or sword and dissipates its virtue! Is it possible to entrust something so precious to the left hand? This would be monstrous sacrilege' (1960: 106).

While one would not wish to endorse such beliefs, it is clear that there is a traditional cross-cultural association of the left realm with the untoward, with weakness, with evil and perversity, but did the Hebrew writer mean to cast aspersions on Ehud's actions by designating him as a left-handed judge? There are several biblical references to the left that have simply neutral values, but there remains some evidence that the left realm could be associated with adverse connotations. In Genesis 48.9–22 Jacob deliberately crosses his hands when blessing Ephraim and Manasseh, so that his right hand lies on the head of the younger child Ephraim. Joseph, outraged, uncrosses Jacob's hands demanding the right-handed blessing for the eldest child, but he fails since Jacob prophesies that the younger brother will be the greater. Also Ecclesiastes 10.2 reads, 'The heart of the wise inclines to the right, but the heart of a fool to the left', and Crenshaw, commenting upon this verse says:

> In ancient Israel the right hand connoted power and deliverance; the right side, moral goodness and favor. Hence the place of honor was on the right side. The left hand usually symbolized ineptness and perversity. Like attitudes reflected in the language of ancient Greece (*skaios*, awkward, *aristeros*,

clumsy) and Rome (*sinister*, sinister), and in modern French (*gauche*, awkward). The moral sense of right and left is also found in *šabb.* 63a, where the two verbs mean to study the Torah properly and improperly. (1988: 169–70).[1]

It is often pointed out that being left-handed is a singularly odd fate for one who has just been described as a Benjamite (literally, 'son of the right hand'); an incongruity immediately suggestive of ambivalence, of things not being as they should be. But while almost every commentator has had something to say about the sense of discomfort that the Ehud narrative provokes, this discomfort has not been linked with his left-handedness, and one is left with a sense of unease about the left-handedness that is not adequately followed through. For instance, for all that Lillian Klein sees his left-handedness in terms of deformity (1989: 115) she acknowledges that 'left-handedness seems to have connotations of being peculiar and unnatural that is upheld by Ehud's actions' (1989: 37). For O'Connell the ambiguity of a left-handed son of the right hand leads the reader to expect 'that there will be something devious about his characterization' (1996: 99), but he interprets this merely in terms of Ehud's unlikely strategy and victory. Meir Sternberg similarly sees Ehud's left-handedness as a negative trait, that renders him a 'sinister redeemer' with 'connotations of ill-fortune' shed only by the divine logic of deliverance (1985: 332, 333) but he ultimately exonerates Ehud.

Second, it is when the focus upon Ehud's left-handedness is connected with the euphemistic use of the word 'hand' that reasons for the ill-defined discomfort come to the fore. 'Hand' is certainly a dominant motif in this narrative. Alonso-Schökel (1961) has demonstrated its status as a leitmotif, an opinion reinforced by Webb (1987: 245 n. 23), Gunn (1987: 115), Lindars (1995: 139) and Amit (1999: 179). But what exactly is implied by this key word? Certainly *yad* can simply mean 'hand', but it also bears the meaning of penis/phallus – a homographic situation that permits wordplay as has been noted by Décor (1967) and Botterweck and Ringgren (1986: 398–426). References where *yad* seems to indicate the penis include Isaiah 57.8, where the prophet chastises the adulterous Israelites for widening their beds and gazing upon the 'hand' of their 'lover'. In the Song of Solomon 5.4 the beloved thrusts his 'hand' into his lover's opening. More questionable references are found in Jeremiah 5.31 and 50.15. Considered in this light, it is possible to see the entire Ehud–Eglon encounter as a deliberately scripted figurative rape scene. Indeed, the notion that Ehud's thrust into Eglon carries phallic connotations has already been noted by Robert Alter:

> Ehud 'comes to' the king, an idiom also used for sexual entry, and there is something hideously sexual about the description of the dagger-thrust.

---

1 There are other examples. Among several terms available in English there is 'cack-handed' meaning excrement-handed, perhaps connected to the Islamic tradition of using the left hand to clean oneself. It is interesting that in Australia a left-handed person can be referred to as a 'molly-dooker', where a 'molly' is an effeminate man and 'duke' is slang for hand.

There may also be a deliberate sexual nuance in the 'secret thing' that Ehud brings to Eglon, in the way the two are locked together alone in a chamber, and in the sudden opening of locked entries at the conclusion of the story. (1981: 39)

Alter himself did not address the possibility that Ehud's left-handedness was an integral dimension of the sexual innuendo, but the fact that it is his *left* hand – the side associated with the untoward – only adds to the potential sexualization of Ehud, who will perform a 'deviant' sexual act in order to deliver his people from the Moabites.

Defending Alter from those who may think of this as a faddish reading, I note Brettler's (1995: 82) comment that a sexual reading of Judges 3.22 existed in the thirteenth century CE indicating, says Brettler, that such a reading is not simply the product of modern, post-Freudian sensibilities, but may be an integral part of the biblical story. Certainly, the fact that this ribald portrayal of an Israelite victory over a foreign leader was capable of provoking considerable offence seems to have been recognized very early, for Josephus tellingly removes the sexual connotations in his rendition of the story. Brenner supposes that he purges the account of the innuendo and humour precisely because he 'recognized the subversive potential of the humour involved' (1994b: 53).

Brettler concurs with Alter's reading, arguing that the emphasis upon the opening and closing of doors ('a set of words that are well anchored in metaphors for sexuality in ancient Israel') and the expression 'come into' so often used of sexual penetration, do warrant his reading of the passage. He adds further weight to Alter's suspicion about the 'secret thing' (i.e. the sword held, we note, in his left 'hand'), saying:

> The possible sexual significance of Ehud's sword in v. 16a, as short and double-edged, namely as a short straight sword, gains credence once we realize that the typical sword of the period had a curved side with which one hacks away at enemies, and thus was much less appropriate as a phallic symbol. (1995: 92)

The fact that the sword is said to be a *gomed* in length contributes further to the sexual connotations of this narrative, for as Guillaume notes, *gomed* has an Arabic cognate meaning 'to be hard'. Moreover, the word translated 'hilt' 'is only known to mean "handle" in a rare Arabic expression' (Guillaume 2004: 27 n. 62) – its more usual range of connotation carries the sense of 'erect'. Guillaume does not offer an alternative translation of the sentence in 3.22–3 but is content to conclude that these verses contain 'saucy language closer to the one heard in army barracks than in the temple' (2004: 27).

Third, the narrator seems at pains to stress that Ehud is a Benjamite. His and his father's names are indicative of this; Benjamite genealogies often have names compounded with the *-hud* element, and his father's name, Gera, is the name of a Benjamite clan. The implication is that, despite his victory, Ehud's actions should be viewed in a negative or at least dubious light. O'Connell (1996: 84, 284–5) for example argues that Ehud's Benjamite status, together with other features of the story, link him with Saul's rise to power and defeat of Nahash of Ammon (1 Sam. 10.27–11.15) and the subsequent battle against Agag of Amalek (1 Sam. 15.1–31). For O'Connell, these connections are part of the deliberate rhetorical strategy of the narrator to taint Ehud with all the derogatory implications associated with Saul and 'depict the disadvantages to Israel of serving under non-Judahite leadership' (1996: 285). Tammi J. Schneider highlights different connections between Ehud and the story of Saul. For her, the narrator may well have 2 Samuel 16.5–13; 19.16–19 in view: passages that tell of Shimei, a son of Gera, who insults David as he flees from Jerusalem in the time of Absalom's rebellion, thereby associating Ehud with a 'remnant of Saul's kingship which will gloat at Kind David's misfortune' (2000: 48). It does seem likely that the narrator of Judges is deliberately using the narrative to foreshadow events that will occur during the years of David/Saul rivalry. What these commentators have not drawn attention to is that in the Hebrew Bible's major homoerotic relationship – that between David and Jonathan – the young prince devoted to David is also a Benjamite. It is at least plausible that the author of Judges had this in mind and that in 20.16's reference to the Benjamites as a tribe of expert 'left-handers' we seem to have a satirical jibe at the Benjamites that gives double pleasure to the assumed Judaean reader who can laugh not only at the Moabites but also at their tribal brothers who gave their loyalties to the wrong king and whose sexuality is questioned.

To summarize, the emphasis upon Ehud's left-handedness, the dominant motif of the 'hand/penis' and the emphasized Benjamite connection all combine to present an Israelite judge who is devious but also deviant in the way in which he carries out his attack. Whether the author intended this dent in his reputation is a matter discussed further below.

The emasculation and rape of Eglon

The object of Ehud's action is Eglon, introduced in 3.12–14 as a king of Moab who had been strengthened by Yhwh to punish Israel. At this point in the narrative Eglon is imaged as a powerful king capable of making alliances with Ammonites and Amalekites and ensuring the servitude of Israel for 18 years. However, once Ehud has been introduced, the characterization of Eglon develops into a scathing portrayal permeated with sexual innuendo. His fatness is pointedly over-stressed (vv. 17, 22); so fat that the dagger thrust into his body is swallowed, hilt included. His fatness has been seen as a cipher for a number of things: gullibility and stupidity (Handy 1992: 236) and/or greed (Klein 1989: 39) for example. Fatness in the ancient world could be an indicator of opulence, but it was also especially associated with effeminate men (see Brenner 1994b: 45 and the literature she cites in n. 20). Eglon is clearly being staged as one obliged to perform the traditional woman's part in a sexual encounter, that is as the one who is penetrated and passive. His fatness is thus not mentioned solely to signify greed or gullibility but to indicate his role in a male rape scene.

As with Ehud, Eglon's very name contributes to this portrayal. Eglon, notes Alter (1981: 39), bears phonetic similarity to 'egel (calf), and given his emphasized fatness (the adjective bari' is also used mostly in connection with cattle), his name and description are evocative of a fatted calf ready, of course, for the slaughter. Calves, however, are not only referred to as appropriate sacrifices for sin offerings (as in Lev. 9.2, 3, 8), they are also symbols of idolatry (cf. the golden calf incident of Exodus 32 and the bull symbol of Baal worship). The name 'Eglon', says Hamlin, thus 'connotes alternatively an object of illegitimate adoration or of sacrifice' (1990: 96). This is well suited for a man who is presented as both sexual object and also sacrificial victim of rape/murder.

The choice of location for the encounter also repays close attention. The NRSV's 'cool roof chamber' assumes a derivation from *qarar* (to be cool). But Tom Jull (1998) points out that given the climate near Jericho, an upstairs room, even if open to the elements, would actually be a very hot room – probably the hottest. He argues therefore that the derivation is rather from the noun *qareh* (literally the 'chance/accidents' of the night) as referred to in Deuteronomy 23.11. What is precisely meant by the 'accidents' of the night is debatable. Jull first entertains the possibility that it was an ejaculation of semen, noting that Leviticus 15.16 accommodates such occurrences. However, given the context of battle that Deuteronomy 23 covers, imagining the fear of death that soldiers might face and the possibility of dysentery in outdoor conditions, he says it could also be referring to defecation. The subsequent injunctions that the man must take his trowel and cover his filth perhaps make this more likely. Whatever the case, Jull argues that the reference to the room in Judges 3.20 could, like *dining* room or *bed*room be named after its function i.e. the *toilet* room. Since the people in this narrative did not have automatic access to this room, he further speculates that it was a toilet area where Eglon could go alone – a royal toilet.

Several commentators puzzle over why Eglon stands when Ehud enters this room. However, commentators have not taken into account the sexual layer of meaning present within this narrative, and there may be an explanation not previously detected. If we bear in mind that the semantic range of *qareh* includes seminal emissions and that this encounter is loaded with male–male sexual innuendo, then Eglon simply needs to stand in order for the figurative penetrative encounter to take place.

In conclusion, it becomes clear that the Moabites, who are all described as 'fat' men at the close of the story (3.29), are the butt of a narrative loaded with ethnic humour and scathing satire. The sexual slur reinforces the generally hostile and racist presentation of the Moabites, as has been noted by Handy (1992), Brenner (1994b), Brettler (1995), Bailey (1995) and Jull (1998).[2] The narrator thus uses sexual practice to create boundaries between self and other. Bailey (1995) in particular demonstrates how foreigners, as the 'out-group', are often distinguished on the basis of their practice of taboo sexual acts. For Bailey, what lies behind the sexual imagery and innuendo is the desire to dehumanize foreigners by labelling them as sexual deviants. Ethnic 'humour' grants the 'in-group' a sense of superiority while pouring contempt and ridicule over the 'other'. Here, in Judges 3, sexual language, imagery and *double entendre* are graphically used in order to ridicule and discredit such foreigners and to legitimize their oppression. This lays a foundation for further derogatory

---

2 Notable exceptions to the anti-Moabite polemic include Deuteronomy 2.9; 1 Samuel 22.3–4; and the book of Ruth.

devaluations of these people that will be 'readily sanctioned, condoned and accepted by the reader, both ancient and modern' (Bailey 1995: 137) and, in the case of this Judges narrative, discredits the Moabites, who are figured as a nation that takes the penetrated role of a woman (note 3.30: 'So Moab was subdued that day under the "hand" of Israel'). Bailey's essay goes on to demonstrate how the commentarial tradition has often repeated the sexual slurs against the foreigner with uncritical abandon, presumably because commentators have aligned themselves with the in-group. The question of whether Ehud has/should come out of this encounter as a heroic figure in the commentarial tradition is thus an intriguing one.

Ehud, the discomforting deliverer

Discomfort with Ehud's victory has been accounted for in various ways. John L. McKenzie is troubled by Ehud's deceit, speaking of Ehud's 'unfair game' and his departure from 'ethical standards' (1966: 123). Polzin says, 'Ehud . . . comes across in the narrative as someone who is repugnant, deceitful, and cruel' (1980: 160). Others, as noted above, are troubled by Ehud's Benjamite connection. Webb, who believes one should put aside moral judgements and just enjoy the 'sheer virtuosity of his performance', nonetheless remains uneasy and admits that 'we cannot explain the choice of "Ehud the Benjamite" with quite the same assurance that we could the choice of Othniel' (1987: 131, 132). Overall, Ehud's exploits are described variously by commentators as peculiar, unnatural, devious, sinister – but perhaps the word they are all looking for is 'queer'.

As commentators flounder amid their desire to praise Ehud as an Israelite hero and their recognition of something unsettling about him, it is interesting to see how unease is overcome by over-stressing the red-blooded, virile, warrior-like manliness of Ehud. Thus, for all that Alter has identified the sexual layer of meaning in this narrative, he still describes Ehud as a 'tough, clever guerrilla leader' (1981: 37), a man of 'bold resourcefulness' and a member of the left-handed Benjamite warriors 'known for their prowess' (1981: 38). Halpern describes him as 'a lefthanded combat ace, a hardened professional warrior' (1996: 59). Amit believes that Ehud is characterized as 'a superb fighter having special talents . . . a daring fighter known for the use of his left hand, who shall exploit this unique physical advantage when bringing the tribute in order to deliver his people' (1999: 179–80). Meir Sternberg, who opposed Alter's reading and firmly rejects any sexual reading of this drama, objects to such readings precisely because of 'the stigma they must put on the most admirable of the judges' (1985: 532 n. 4). Sternberg's comment, and those above, demonstrates a will to maintain Ehud's 'straight' credentials in the face of homoerotic connotations.

Indeed, it is questionable whether Ehud's manliness is being criticized when his actions are considered in the light of the text's cultural context. The fact that he is portrayed as the active initiator, who imposes his 'hand'-thrust into Eglon arguably serves to promote his manliness. Drawing on a range of sources (Dover (1978); Greenberg (1988); Schmitt and Sofer (1992)), Michael Carden notes how in Middle Eastern societies, the male, penetrated by other men, is stigmatised (to use our parlance, is the queer) but not the male who penetrates . . .

There is no shame for a male to bugger other men, his sexuality is not suspect. But for the man who is buggered it is different . . . Male homosexuality (shame) is confirmed by being buggered. (1999: 86–7)

Ehud could thus emerge from this encounter with his masculinity enhanced rather than censured. However, the problem of applying the general ancient ethos to the Ehud narrative is that the Hebrew Bible infamously does not share the general ancient Near/Middle Eastern view. The injunctions of Leviticus and Deuteronomy appear to condemn male–male sex in any circumstances as an abomination, condemning both active and passive partners, so Ehud's deed stands condemned by such laws even if this deed is just the erotic undercurrent of a narrative that, on the surface, simply relates a cunning, military victory. This begs the question of whether this is meant to be Ehud's flaw. All the judges in the text, except the paradigmatic Othniel, are flawed characters. The narratives demonstrate the sovereign freedom of Yhwh to accomplish victory for his people despite, or often via, the flawed human traits of these leaders. Several commentators emphasize Yhwh's use of Ehud as his agent for the victory of Moab. McKenzie notes, 'it was not Ehud who killed Eglon, but Yahweh, who used Ehud as his agent' (1966: 124). Webb says that by the close of the narrative 'Ehud stands unveiled as Yahweh's chosen "saviour". He has been "raised up"; his deceptions have been providentially directed and guaranteed, although even Ehud may not have been aware of it at the time' (1987: 132). For O'Connell Ehud is 'but a foil for the elevation of YHWH as Israel's true deliverer' (1996: 91). For Amit 'Ehud's success is the result of divine providence . . . Ehud's ability to realize his tactics – not only without mishaps but, on the contrary, while relying upon everything that came in his way – is a result of the divine will' (1999: 196). She attributes the 'ribald atmosphere' of the narrative to the need to provide light relief and interest for the reader after the 'heavy introduction and the stereotypical description of the period of Othniel' (1999: 197). It does not, in her view, harm the 'primary message' of the narrative.

Certainly there are other cases in the Primary History where characters flagrantly flout laws pertaining to sexual acts when it is for the good of the nation, with the deity seemingly turning a blind eye, or indeed actively favouring the acts. David Biale notes how the laws of the Hebrew Bible are often suspended or undermined by its narratives, demonstrating this with examples from the stories of Ruth, Abraham, Jacob and David. Even if the laws post-date these narratives Biale rightly points out that we are dealing with an author/editor who chose to leave these earlier narratives intact. He therefore concludes:

The authors or editors who produced the text were surely aware of the flagrant contradictions between the laws and the narratives, but they must have seen those contradictions as serving an important cultural function. The creation of the Israelite nation was seen by these later authors as a result of the suspension of conventions, a sign, perhaps, of divine favor for a ragtag, ethnically mixed people. Far from a disgrace to be hidden, sexual subversion, like a repeated preference for younger over older sons, hints at the unexpected character of God's covenant with Israel. (1997: 17)

He goes on to note that God's place in these subversions and transgressions is as one who 'must step backstage in order to make space for human actors . . . to bend social custom and law . . . God's absence implicitly sanctions these inversions and subversions' (1997: 31). The narrative of Ehud appears to be an example of the pattern Biale has identified. Insofar as he is putting his (figurative) sexual deviance to work for the sake of Israel and insofar as Yhwh is glorified despite the manner in which Ehud carries out his mission, perhaps Ehud is meant to be an exonerated figure. However, such exoneration comes at a cost for contemporary readers who identify as gay men or as transgendered.

Judges 3.12–30 as a text of terror for gay-identified readers

For Trible (1984) it is the absence of the deity that makes the texts she discusses 'texts of terror'. In the case of Judges 3.12–30 the terror of the text lies in the way the narrator positions Yhwh as a character within the storyworld of the text who appears to condone the death/rape of a lampooned character. When the most powerful character within the Hebrew Bible – the deity – has been invoked as a complicit collaborator in this piece of ethnic humour it raises serious ethical questions.

Ethnic humour is only humorous if one is able to share the joke and able to side with the protagonists. It is not funny for the Moabite reader and, as the discomfiture of commentators indicates, the humour has had an enduring uncomfortable edge. Handy has rightly pointed out that it is not enough to recognize the text's genre as ethnic humour; one must also undertake a critical evaluation of the values embedded within that genre:

> We laugh, or smirk superiorly, along with the author as the dumb Moabites 'get theirs', safe in the knowledge that no present-day Moabite Anti-Defamation League is going to object . . . [But i]f it is not alright for modern professors in universities to use ethnic stereotypes in dealing with the student population, faculty, or those outside the bounds of academics, such ethnic stereotypes cannot be allowed to pass unacknowledged in works to which academics must introduce their students. (1992: 245)

I add that it is not only the racist polemic that requires critical examination but also the implications of the narrative for gay-identified readers sitting in university classrooms, or in the seats of churches and synagogues for whom this text has a particularly sharp edge. Its feminization of Eglon not only reinforces the popular construction of gay men as effete and, somehow, less than 'real' men, but celebrates a figurative forced rape/assassination. Modern readers, only too aware of the rape and murder of gay men on our streets by heterosexually identified men, can sense the homophobic violence of this text.

Furthermore, this text assumes that to be caricatured as a passive recipient of anal rape is one of the most derogatory insults that one can direct towards a person/group. The text thus requires a shared contempt for any man who is penetrated by another and for the act itself. It also assumes that people like Eglon *deserve* to be violated/eliminated from society, and let us not play down the immoderate relish with which the narrator seems to savour Ehud's rape/murder of Eglon. Indeed the ideology of the text implies that the deity of the Hebrew scriptures not only condones but is glorified in the violation and elimination of Eglon and, further, that his elimination can bring its reward to the nation carrying out such acts, so long as it is done for appropriate reasons such as patriotic zeal. Brenner's view that the narrative 'is dark and ought not to be to our liking' is offset by her opinion that the narrative exists as a piece of verbal counter-aggression by a people unable to carry out a physical attack against their overlords. As such, she claims it achieves 'a serious critical aim: the subversion of (proverbial) foreign powers who act against Jews and Judaism' (1994b: 50). Her reading is critical and yet implies an admiration for the survival tactics employed by the narrator of this text. As with several other commentators, Ehud is too easily forgiven and exonerated, given a quick box around the ears but then a smiling tousle of the hair for achieving something useful despite the methods used. To sympathize with Eglon's plight is simply not an expected readerly position. Rather, the text invites us to share its deplorable assumption that the rape/murder of individuals and peoples like the Moabites, albeit in a storyworld, is comical. Straight-identified readers who side with the Israelite 'hero' may be able to afford such luxuries, but for the reader who has to read against their own interests, the text's rhetoric and assumptions are problematic and cannot be shared, and although Judges 3.12–30 has never, as far as I know, been listed among the 'texts of terror' for gay-identified people, it is arguably deserving of a place.

Deborah and Jael and lesbian-identified hermeneutics: Judges 4–5

The story of Deborah and Jael continues the use of sexual imagery noted in the story of Ehud and Eglon and again connects sexuality with violence in another murder scene. Again, the narrative is loaded with none-too-subtle sexual innuendo and *double entendre* and again death comes via a sexually transgressive act. However, on this occasion there does not appear to be any same-sex reference; on the contrary, it appears to be an overtly heterosexual plot. Jabin sends his general Sisera into the fray. Deborah sends her chosen man – Barak – to face him. Because Barak fails to respond with immediacy to Deborah's command, she prophesies that Sisera will instead be delivered into the hands of a woman. The erotic death scene is thus one played out between Sisera and Jael (for more discussion of the erotic imagery see Niditch (1989) and Fewell and Gunn (1990)).

Deborah and Jael never meet each other in the text. Although Deborah prophesies that Sisera will be delivered into the hands of a woman there is no implication that she knows who this woman will be. The two women never converse, never compare tactics and do not search each other out in the aftermath of the battle to congratulate each other on their part in the victory. There is no mention of any pre-existing friendship. Only in the Song of chapter 5 does Jael's name cross Deborah's tongue as she praises Jael's actions in verses

24–7. The lack of information about the two women's relationship with each other is not surprising, given that this is not a matter of concern for the narrator of the text, who seems primarily engaged in demonstrating the sovereign freedom of the deity to act in unforeseeable ways in order to achieve the most dramatic of victories on behalf of Israel. A lesbian-identified reading, however, queries whether the two women have been kept deliberately separate, perhaps subconsciously, in order to prevent an excess of anxiety created by the narrative's only too clear demonstration of the results that can accrue when two women act in harness with each other.

I have recently argued that one of the major ways by which the narrators of the Hebrew Bible suppress the reality of female intimate friendship and solidarity is by valorizing the role of women as wives and mothers and by representing women as competitive rivals rather than supportive friends. In that publication (Guest 2005) I suggest that a lesbian-identified hermeneutic must employ strategies of resistance and operate from a hermeneutic of hetero-suspicion in order to counter the general erasure of women's interests and friendships and the particular suppression of female homoerotic relationships. I demonstrate how archaeological evidence can be used to explore the material lives of women, and contest the valorized depiction of wifedom and motherhood; how historical and social-scientific research can be used to explore potential escape routes for women, using cross-cultural analogies where appropriate, to bring to light how women in the surrounding cultures of the ancient world, or in modern pre-industrial analogous societies, find ways of renegotiating their expected destinies. However, while a commitment to a principle of resistance exposes issues of erasure and problematizes absence, its recognition of 'the radical lack of our knowledge about women in antiquity', of the fact that the story 'is nearly entirely missing', that the material we *do* have is an account of 'what men thought about women' rather than a representation of women's authentic lives (Brooten 1985: 67, 65) means that, ultimately, a principle of resistance is insufficient. A lesbian-identified hermeneutic for biblical studies needs also to operate from a principle of reclamation that unsettles the text by focusing upon its queerer elements and by welcoming the use of the critical imagination and midrash which fill in some of the inevitable gaps in biblical stories. To this end, imaginative readings of scriptural stories have a useful part to play and Sara Maitland's (1983) fictional reading of the Deborah and Jael story can make a valuable contribution to this endeavour.

Maitland's rereading assumes a solidarity and intimate friendship between the two women that is hardly present in the canonical account. Her midrash-like story of the victory over Sisera introduces Deborah and Jael as friends who had 'both come a long way to find that friendship, they who never had a friend before' (1983: 1). Both women are married but it seems not to be the 'natural' fulfilment of their desires. Rather their marriages are extraneous to the more primary and fundamental solidarity of friendship that they share with each other. In Maitland's account, one senses that these women have known each other for a long time. They have actively sought each other out to find this friendship. They have a history. Together, they appear to have planned the battle strategy, and, in Deborah's mustering the army, in the prophecy of victory and particularly in Jael's assassination of Sisera, both women find a shared strength and unity that becomes something Other; a thing of fear and unnerving disquiet for the men:

> Deborah and Jael look at each other, they smile at each other – they are friends. They look at the smashed head of Sisera, the blood soaked bedding, the tent-peg still standing upright in the remains, and they grin. They reach out hands, unspeaking, almost shy with excitement, and touch each other very gently. They know their husbands will never want to touch them again. They know who the enemy is. They grin again, and then laugh . . .
> . . . Deborah laughs, Jael laughs, but the men watch in silence. What is the source of the joy that lights up these women? What are the words of the song they will sing together? What power drove the hand that drove the nail? The men cannot avoid seeing the women, they cannot help feeling the hatred and the joy. They are sick with fear. (1983: 4)

Whereas Fewell and Gunn (1990) justifiably argue that Deborah and Jael's actions in the canonical text actually serve a patriarchal agenda rather than subvert it, Maitland's imaginative rereading presents a challenge to that agenda. Both women rejoice in the fear their actions have provoked. They positively bathe in its aftermath. In taking on for themselves roles designated for male heroes they have rendered themselves unfeminine, untouchable and, perhaps, uncontrollable. Earlier in her rereading, Maitland has Barak, unnerved by events that he realizes are out of his control, refer to Deborah as 'that old witch . . . who has stolen from him his triumph and left him shaken with fear' (1983: 3). He refers to Jael as 'that crazy little woman' who has rendered the great Sisera a bloody, smashed wreck of a man. Such derogatory labels reveal the anxiety invoked by these women's joint actions, driven by the recognition that these women are acting outside the control of men.

In 'The Straight Mind' Wittig famously concluded that 'it would be incorrect to say that lesbians associate, make love, live with women, for "woman" has meaning only in heterosexual systems of thought and heterosexual economic systems. Lesbians are not women' (1992: 32). And for Wittig, when the practical resistance of living lesbian lives is put into theoretical action, undermining the heteropatriarchal concept of woman, then the straight mind itself comes under attack. It is thus interesting to see how Maitland's reading of Judges 4 and 5 includes a representation of men who do not know what to do with these women who are arguably not-women. But as far as her female characters are concerned, Deborah and Jael rejoice and are exultant in the face of this male fear. Maitland for example has Deborah gaze upon the slaughter of the battlefield and laugh, and compares this with the gaze with which Deborah has beheld her husband but, up to this point, never felt sufficiently free to laugh. Maitland leaves her readers to find the connection that holds the two things together. Does Deborah look at her husband in the way that a superior commander of forces beholds the result of her efforts – with laughing disdain? Or does she look at her husband with a renewed sense of comedy that she should have such power despite her circumstances? Or is she laughing with the ironic humour that laughs at the incongruity of the battle scene, likening this to the absurdity of her own self living as wife to a husband?

Maitland's reading invites these possibilities but leaves them delightfully open.

Deborah laughs; Jael laughs. Why does Maitland have Deborah and Jael so exultant? Perhaps it is because it at last prevents them from being objects of male possession and desire, leaving them free to enjoy each other's company, free from the interference of their husbands. Whatever the case, the song these women create is, for Maitland, a thing that only women can fully share and appreciate: a song that women sing in remembrance while working. The men sing a phrase or two, but it is never theirs – 'men never came to love and use it' (1983: 1). The song, like the actions it celebrates, disturbs the status quo, it upsets the norms, it destabilizes the 'natural' order of things and this is what makes Maitland's reading such a valuable resource for the lesbian-identified reader. As Monique Wittig (1992: 33–45) has argued, a lesbian reading is one that, by definition, must challenge the roots of heterocentrism and break free from the heterosexual contract to which we are (silently) signed up. Women, she says, need to negotiate a new social contract but can only do so by actively running away and resisting the pervasive political regime that is heterosexuality, for at present there is no utopian place in which one can stand outside that regime:

> There is, on the one side, the whole world in its massive assumption, its massive affirmation of heterosexuality as a must-be, and on the other side, there is only the dim, fugitive, sometimes illuminatory and striking vision of heterosexuality as a trap, as a forced political regime, that is, with the possibility of escaping it as a fact. (1992: 47)

Maitland's brief story has made an important space available in which lesbian readers may begin to question that heterosexual assumption and undertake a new analysis of the relationships and status of women in the Bible. The joy of her imaginative reconstruction lies in its playful yet serious exposure of biblical women who, despite being married, might have resisted their heterosexual script and harboured other loyalties. It demonstrates what can happen when one comes to a text as a lesbian reader and makes that aspect of oneself central to the act of reading, breaking free from the reading script that we have been trained to follow. To do this is not easy. Gerda Lerner's *Creation of Patriarchy* reminds us that women are conditioned to please and we have been trained well in patriarchal and androcentric schools of thought, standing 'within the boundaries of the question-setting defined by the "great men"' (1986: 227). So long as women remain within that paradigm, then the source of a radically new insight is inevitably closed off. A lesbian reading must break free from those straitjackets. Lerner offers guidance on how to do this, one can apply her general comments in a way that would apply especially to lesbian-identified women. It would involve breaking free from the suppression of lesbian existence and its marginalization. Drawing on the work of Rich, whose concept of the lesbian continuum incorporates a diverse range of woman-identified experience (such as 'the impudent, intimate, girl friendships of eight or nine year olds', the relationships among the Beguines, the women of Sappho's school in the seventh century BCE, the 'secret sororities and economic networks reported among African women' and 'Chinese marriage-resistance sisterhoods' (Rich 1987: 54–5)), it would assume that women-identified-women have *always* been involved in the world's happenings, except when deliberately restrained. It would make us ask ourselves, if lesbians were central to an argument, how would it be defined? It would encourage us to use methodologies 'from the vantage point of the centrality of [lesbian] women. [Lesbian] Women cannot be put into the empty spaces of patriarchal thought and systems – in moving to the center, they transform the system' (Lerner 1986: 228). As for stepping out-side the system, this would involve the application of a hermeneutic of hetero-suspicion to all systems of thought and a critical appraisal of all 'assumptions, ordering values and definitions' (1986: 228). Lerner cautions that such work has to be ready to break with our training:

> Perhaps the greatest challenge to thinking [lesbian] women is the challenge to move from the desire for safety and approval to the most 'unfeminine' quality of all – that of intellectual arrogance, the supreme hubris which asserts to itself the right to reorder the world. The hubris of the god-makers, the hubris of the male system-builders. (1986: 228)

Lerner's advice and the example shown by Maitland inspire a reconsideration of the women in Judges and in the Bible generally. Certainly, Maitland's account is based on an imaginative re-creation and never pretends to be an academic paper, but this does not diminish its usefulness for this project. We are left with so few resources for the lost history of women whose primary affections were directed towards other women, that retellings such as Maitland's are important for opening up what is thinkable about biblical women, and that is the crucial first leap of the imagination necessary before one can even think of asking whether there may be any historical evidence upon which a read-ing like Maitland's might stand. Once the leap has been made and the Grand Narrative's cracks are opened, an irrevocable instability is introduced into dis-cussions of biblical women and new avenues of possibilities emerge. To bring Maitland's rereading of this story into a biblical commentary is to begin the work of dismantling the heterosexual imperative that permeates the Bible and the history of its interpretation.

   A queer commentary on Judges should generate research that draws upon anthropological, sociological, archaeological and textual evidence to see if non-heterosexual options were available for women and to redress the pic-ture that we have been given of a society consisting entirely of heterosexual women longing to bear children. A lesbian-identified reading of scripture can move in various directions to destabilize this assumption. It can generate a historical research exercise drawing upon anthropological, sociological and textual evidence along the lines noted above, looking for evidence of women who resisted their script. It can generate a hermeneutic exercise drawing upon lesbian-feminist and queer theories in order to destabilize the heterosexual imperative assumed within the text's construction of 'biblical women'. It could generate an imaginative retelling of the lives of such women, drawing upon the text itself and our own experiences as lesbian, gay, bisexual and transgen-dered persons. These options could, in turn, generate a critical evaluation of how biblical stories are used in contemporary culture to continue the oppression and suppression of such persons. For, as Fewell recognizes, deconstructive readings take us out from an exegesis of texts into the realms of ethics, politics and responsibility:

> Attention to the Other leads to a critique of mainline scholarly traditions, canons, and institutions that have excluded the Other; it leads to a critique of social and political systems that marginalize the Other. In other words, how we read texts affects how we read the world. The opening of texts calls for the opening of politico-institutional structures. This is risky business in a world that encourages the status quo and rewards conformity . . . The moment we shift the question from 'What truth is being claimed and what suppressed?' to 'Whose truth is being claimed and whose suppressed?' we are in the business of politics. We are not only looking for traces, we are listening for marginal voices. We are discovering that the seldom-heard voices have truth to impart and that their truth is often at odds with a text's or an institution's 'party line'. (1995: 127)

Male Rape and the Traffic of Women: Judges 19.22–30

An essay on Judges written for the purposes of this commentary cannot ignore the outrage narrated in 19.22–30. The aggressive demand by 'sons of Belial' of Gibeah to have sexual access to the Levite echoes the demand of the men of Sodom to 'know' Lot's guests in Genesis 19 and has long been interpreted as a perverse homosexual attack upon vulnerable guests in a city. Soggin, for example, refers to 'the theme of homosexual violence, basic to Gen. 19' that is echoed to a limited extent in Judges 19 (1981: 282). The assumption that the sons of Belial were acting upon homosexual instincts has served to deepen the revulsion with which homosexuals and their sexual desires have historically been regarded and facilitated the use of this text as a means of condemning homosexuality.

There have been attempts to disassociate the men's request from any sexual connotation, on the basis that *yada'* can simply mean 'to know'. Thus Kader (1999: 30–7), following Boswell (1980), suggests that the house is surrounded by a mixed mob of ungodly people who want to be acquainted with the Levite as a pretext for their underlying motive of mob violence and murder. Arguing further that the offer of daughters does not make sense if the men are homosexuals, he claims, 'there is no homosexual activity involved in this story at all' (1999: 33). However, Kader's interpretation of *yada'* is not well founded. It is far more likely that the verb *does* have sexual connotations and that the rowdies gathered outside the house *are* demanding to have sexual relations with the Levite. However, this does not invalidate Kader's argument that these are not homosexual men. Studies by Stone (1996) and Carden (1999) that have drawn upon research into the cultural codes of honour and shame prevalent in the ancient world have demonstrated how male rape was used as a means of dishonouring one's male rival.

Honour, shame and the rape of men

In the ancient world, gender performance was of vital importance to a man's ability to maintain and increase his reputation, prestige and honour. A fundamental dimension of that gender performance relates to a man's sexual activities, whether with men or with women. In terms of male–female relations, a man would be expected to be able to take and control his women, impregnate them and guard their chastity so that he could be sure that the children born are his. Since the women fall under his ownership and protection, he was obliged to exert vigilance over them. In terms of male–male relationships, male honour was associated with being the active, penetrative initiator. To engage in same-sex relationships was not dishonouring in and of itself, but unless one was a younger or inferior male, taking the passive role could be looked upon with contempt. The construction of masculine honour was thus founded upon men being the active penetrators in their sexual relationships with men and women alike, and that where the latter were concerned they also had to ensure that their ownership stakes were unrivalled.

Honour was thus never a stable commodity. On the contrary, it was often at stake in a competitive world where one enhanced one's own honour largely at the expense of another man's concomitant dishonour. When Judges 19.22–30 is reconsidered in this light, traditional interpretations are modified in at least two important ways.

First, the practice of referring to the sons of Belial as men with homosexual intent is called into question. The threatened rape of the Levite should be understood as a direct attack upon his ability to maintain his status. In the threatened encounter he would be positioned as the sexual object rather than subject, acted upon and thereby (in the cultural codes of this world) feminized. The approach of the men of Gibeah is one that directly challenges the Levite's masculinity, power, honour and his subject status. To that extent, this narrative has very little, if anything, to do with homosexuality, since this threat is posed by heterosexually identified men intent upon dishonouring a rival male. As Stone (1996: 79–82) notes, the men of Gibeah are challenging the Levite's ability to perform according to his bespoken masculine honour and concomitant reputation and prestige. If he is a 'real man' he will be able to resist their demands.

The particular form that this male rivalry takes – that of threatened male rape – is understandable when the Levite's status is taken into consideration. The Levite and his host are both referred to as living as sojourners/strangers in their lands. As such the Levite is Other and the fate that befalls him is the one that often falls to the Female Other – that of sexual contempt. As Ilse Müllner comments:

In this context, it is incorrect to interpret as homosexual desire the demand made by the men of Gibeah that the other man be handed over for the purpose of violating him sexually. The threat made by the foreign man is made less serious by means of feminization. Thus, being strange is transformed into another form of being Other. And it is this . . . being feminine, that makes it possible for the Gibeah men to get control over the Otherness by means of sexual violence. (1999: 140)

However, one should also note that the men of Gibeah belong to the tribe of Benjamin and that here is another instance of Benjamites using their sexual potential in a 'deviant' manner. Ehud, as we have seen, is somewhat vindicated by the narrator because at least his figurative male rape is directed at a foreign enemy of Israel. However, the men of Gibeah direct their phallic power against an outsider from their own people in a narrative that culminates in civil war. This second connection of male rape with the tribe of Benjamin casts a slur against the tribe as a whole and may be intended to cast further aspersions upon Saul's house and dynasty. It is no coincidence that at the precise point at which the Book of Judges laments the absence of a king, a polemic against the Benjamites is most pronounced. And if there was any doubt about this, the decision made at Mizpah by the assembled eleven tribes, reported in 21.1, makes it perfectly clear – they swore never to give one of their daughters in marriage to a Benjamite.

Second, it resolves the question of why the (assumed) homosexual men of Gibeah could suddenly switch their sexual object-choice and be satisfied with the offer of a woman. The reason why this ever became a scholarly dilemma in the late nineteenth century is due to the assumption that the men of Gibeah were homosexual and the further assumption that homosexuality was an unchangeable condition, as exemplified in K. Budde (1897: 131). Reading the story through that set of presumptions certainly raises awkward questions. However, the rape of the Levite's woman occurs not because she is a (strangely) acceptable second-rate sex object that can be used to satisfy the mob's heightened sexual drives; but because she too is part of the honour–shame system. The Levite should be able to protect his woman from the advances of male rivals. The mob finds her an acceptable substitute since (a) she can be abused in order to dishonour the Levite – insofar as his woman is gang-raped all night long in his place, the prestige of the men of Gibeah is enhanced while the prestige of the Levite is severely damaged; and (b) she and the feminized Levite have become, in Müllner's words, 'interchangeable objects . . . The men of Gibeah are primarily interested in doing violence to the Levite, but they achieve this goal by attacking his wife. Initially weakened by discursive feminization, the violent attack on his wife has a direct effect on him' (1999: 140). This explains why it had to be the *Levite's* woman and not the virgin daughter of the host that is thrown out to the mob. The rape of the host's daughter would not rub off against the Levite.

This narrative thus revolves entirely around male prestige; the woman's honour in and of itself is not a matter of significance for the narrator. Stone is probably right that for the producers of the text, the woman is practically a by-product of a text primarily interested in discrediting the Levite. To this end, Stone and Müllner rightly see her as the conduit for men's dealings with each other, the body upon which the power relations between the men of Gibeah and the Levite and hosts are acted out. This does not mean, however, that commentators should reify this abhorrent disinterest. The feminist work that has already been done on this narrative has taken to task a commentarial tradition that has often ignored the woman's plight, or even worse, suggested that she may have received her comeuppance for deserting the Levite in the first place. Interpretations that draw upon the cultural codes of honour and

shame to demonstrate how this narrative has nothing to do with homosexuality must do more than simply explain the purpose the rape of the woman
serves or demonstrate why she is nothing more than an object of exchange in
an honour–shame complex that renders women the helpless victims of men's
desires. It must actively resist such cultural assumptions. Having rescued the
text from homosexual connotations it needs to also rescue the woman from
her plight. After all, the narrator ultimately chose not to narrate a male rape,
he chose to narrate the rape of a woman. Exum makes this very clear when she
says what we have here is

> a gender-motivated subtext . . . motivated by male fear of female sexuality
> and by the resultant need of patriarchy to control women. In order to illus-
> trate the social and moral disintegration of Israel before the monarchy, the
> narrator of Judges 19–21 tells a story in which the threatened abuse of the
> Levite and the actual treatment of his wife lead to internecine warfare . . .
> Yet the fact that the central act in the illustration is the rape and dismember-
> ment of a woman foregrounds the important role gender plays, on a deeper
> level, in the presentation. Moreover, in the aftermath, women are again the
> objects of male violence.
>
> Something else could have been chosen to illustrate the depravity of the
> times. In fact, the narrator offers another possible scenario: the rape of the
> Levite himself . . . But this is, as we know not what happens. And since it
> does not happen, it obviously – in terms of narrative poetics, in terms of the
> story the narrator chose to tell – was not meant to happen. (1993: 181–2)

Honour, shame and the rape of women

The surrender of the Levite's woman to the mob is part of a much wider gift-
ing of women in a book that describes the giving away of women to men
with alarming regularity and lack of concern. The rape of the Levite's woman
deliberately echoes two earlier exchanges of women in the prologue to Judges
(1.1–3.6). First, Achsah is offered by her illustrious father Caleb as a prize
to the man who can conquer the city of Kiriath-sepher. Shortly afterwards,
the prologue is brought to a close with the general exchange of women
between Israel and the surrounding nations: 'So the Israelites lived among
the Canaanites, the Hittites, the Amorites, the Perizzites, the Hivites, and the
Jebusites; and they took their daughters as wives for themselves, and their
own daughters they gave to their sons; and they worshipped their gods' (3.5–
6). These scenes are deliberately echoed in the epilogue (17–21), where the single exchange of the Levite's woman is followed by a further mass exchange
(four hundred virgins from Jabesh Gilead and two hundred from Shiloh are
taken and given to the Benjamites after civil war has rendered the tribe almost
extinct). In between, Jephthah's daughter is implicitly offered in exchange for
divine aid in conquering the Ammonites (11.30). The Timnite woman given
first to Samson, at the direction of the spirit of Yhwh in order to facilitate
his conquering of the Philistines, is then given to his best man (14.4, 20). The
Timnite woman's sister is subsequently offered by her Philistine father to
placate Samson.

It is noteworthy that this traffic in women per se requires no explanatory and justifying comment from the book's narrator, other than to cast aspersions on any inappropriate liaisons and their consequences. The exchange of women is simply portrayed as social norm within the 'period of the Judges', created by the text.

This narrated reality is entirely consistent with the views of M. Mauss (1967) and Claude Lévi-Strauss (1969), who highlighted the role of giving and receiving women as part of a gift exchange between groups. This system of exchange forges links between kinship groups and, in Strauss's view, ultimately founds civilized society. However, it is a system constructed upon a division of the world into male and female as mutually exclusive categories; a division that, as Gayle Rubin influentially argued, is based not on 'an expression of natural differences' but rather on the 'suppression of natural similarities' (1974: 180). Once the concept of sexual difference is established, it leads to the establishment of complementarity in terms of gender roles. The destiny of women is thus, to a large extent, determined by being born a 'woman'. This movement towards biological determinism is neither natural nor inevitable; rather, the sexing of the universe and concomitant obligatory heterosexuality has *constructed* such a determinism. Readers thus need to recognize that the Levite's woman is not just a victim of general patriarchy, but a victim of the underlying sex/gender system. The criticisms by feminist biblical scholars thus far do not go far enough; in particular, they do not reach the root of the problem, which lies in the creation of a sexed universe and the construction of compulsory heterosexuality. If the feminist critical agenda were to focus more upon exposing the assumptions upon which the exchange of women is based, then a lesbian critique would have much to offer feminist critical readings.

The woman's plight begins in 19.1. Notice that she has little choice in her union with the Levite – the Levite *took to himself* a 'concubine'. The narrator does not pause to consider the desires of the woman in describing this act of appropriation. The sheer regularity of the assumption that women can be taken in this way is telling. For the narrator, the script is a naturalized one. Women belong to men and are there for the taking (the right regulations with the previous owner having taken place). It is small wonder that the querying of the existence of female homoeroticism has hardly taken place. When such an assumption is so routinely and deeply embedded in the narrator's storyworld and, often, in the world of the commentator, it is not thinkable for women to have any long-term primary relationships with each other.

In this particular case, the Levite's taking of the woman seems to be portrayed negatively – not because he took a woman, but because he took a woman from *Bethlehem in Judah*. First, although the verb 'to take' (*laqah*) is regularly used to describe a man's requisition of a woman and would not paint the Levite in any especially poor light, when the previous chapters' use of *laqah* in terms of 'to steal' is permitted to affect our understanding of the Levite's taking of the woman, a negative connotation may be implied. In 17.2 we are told how Micah 'took' his mother's money, in 18.17 we read of how five heavies from the Danites 'took' the idols that had been created with the stolen money, and in 18.20, 27 how the mercenary Levite (himself 'taken') 'took' the ephod, idol and teraphim and went with them. When we read just a few verses later that the Levite took for himself this woman, the connotations of stealing are still strongly present.

Second, Schneider (2000) points out that the repeated formula 'In those days there was no king in Israel, all the people did what was right in their own eyes', cited in full at 17.6 and 21.25 is repeated in a shortened form at 18.1 and 19.1. In each of these shortened appearances, the statement that replaces the regular 'doing what is right in their own eyes' is, she argues, meant to be synonymous, describing a specific example of what this meant in practice. Thus in 18.1 the Danite search for a new territory and in 19.1 the Levite's taking of a concubine from Bethlehem are equated with doing right in their own eyes: that is, doing wrong in the eyes of the deity.

Third, the story of the Levite's woman needs to be read alongside the story of Achsah in 1.11–15, for the two stories clearly mirror each other, and the parallels reveal why the taking/stealing of this woman is portrayed negatively. Achsah was *given* to Othniel by her father Caleb in return for his conquest of Kiriath-sepher. She was a reward for military endeavour, exchanged between two men with Judaean brotherly credentials. The parallels highlight two major differences: (a) Achsah is gifted while the Levite's woman is taken/stolen; and (b) Achsah is exchanged within the tribe while the Levite's woman is taken to the remote parts of Ephraim. In a text that is foreshadowing the rivalry between the Benjamite House of Saul and the Judahite House of David, these geographical notices are not there by accident. Her body is the site on which these two houses can act out their hostilities. As Schneider (2000: 249) sees, she is the personalized symbol of what Judah must protect and what Benjamin could violate – their women. The inference is that this woman from Bethlehem should never have been taken/stolen by a northern Levite who hails from the remotest areas of Ephraim and is a stranger in his own land: he has no right to a Judahite woman.

The woman has no say in any of this. But although she could not resist being taken, she certainly initiates some resistant action during her subsequent relationship with the Levite; action that results in her abandonment of the relationship and a return home to her father's house. Her reasons for doing so are debatable, given the differing textual traditions. The Hebrew text uses the verb *zanah*, telling us that she committed adultery or acted as a harlot. However, the Greek uses the verb *orgizomai*, indicating that she 'became angry with him'. Given that the Levite comes to collect her four months later and speaks kindly to her it seems unlikely that she was found guilty of adultery or prostitution and most translations of this verse work with the Greek and Old Latin texts suggesting she was angry with the Levite. On the other hand, the parallel with the Achsah narrative might give support to the Hebrew text. The Achsah narrative, argues Klein (1993: 57), is loaded with sexual connotations. The use of the verb *bo'* – ('when she *came* to him') – can indicate simply her arrival at her husband's side; but it can also indicate sexual entry, suggesting that Achsah waited for an opportune moment ('when the man is pleasantly weak with sexual satisfaction') to prod her husband to action on her behalf. In so doing the text allows that women can use their sexuality to achieve better things for themselves within certain circumstances – within marriage and with due respect shown (i.e. within the sex/gender system). This would contrast antithetically with the Levite's concubine using her sexuality in an untoward way and committing adultery against him. Whatever the case, the woman's actions result in her desertion of the Levite. And this is the significant consequence for, as Exum (1993) notes, this is tantamount to an assertion of (sexual) autonomy, an assertion that cannot be permitted to stand, even for a Judahite woman. Achsah gets away with her bold requests because of her dutiful and deferent behaviour. Achsah not only complies with her father's rather risky marriage strategy without question, but in dropping from her donkey before him in order to make her request for fertile land, shows utmost deference. The narrator never intimates that the Levite's woman dutifully fulfils her sexual obligation to the Levite or that she shows deference to father or 'husband'. On the contrary, whether we are to read that she cheats on the Levite or that she gets angry with him, her final act is one of abandonment. This act seals her doom:

> The issue . . . is male ownership of women's bodies, control over woman's sexuality. A woman who asserts her sexual autonomy by leaving her husband . . . is guilty of sexual misconduct . . . Women give up autonomy in return for protection by their men from other men. By daring to act autonomously . . . Bath-sheber[3] puts herself beyond male protection, and for this she must be punished. The men who ordinarily would be expected to protect her – her husband and their host – participate in the punishment because her act is an offense against the social order; that is, against the patriarchal system itself . . . As narrative punishment for her sexual 'misconduct', her sexual 'freedom', she is sexually abused, after which her sexuality is symbolically mutilated. (Exum 1993: 179–80)

Exum goes on to suggest that male anxiety lurks beneath the surface of this text; a fear of independent female sexuality. The dismemberment of the body acts as a misogynistic punishment on one level, but also as an assuaging of male anxiety on a deeper level. Dismemberment also represents an attempt to defuse her Otherness and de-sexualize her female body. Exum thus exposes a chilling undercurrent to women's relations with men, as portrayed in the Hebrew scriptures. It is an exposure that should extend beyond a criticism of patriarchy and phallocentric ideology to a criticism of heterosexism itself that places women in this position.

Detoxifying a text of terror

Readings of this narrative by Stone and Carden have done much to 'detoxify' (Carden's term) its potential to be used as a text of terror. Carden's criticism of 'the uncritical use of Western terms to describe non-Western cultural phenom-

---

3 The Levite's concubine has no name, but some feminists have sought to take away this added humiliation of anonymity. Exum names her Bath-sheber (broken daughter) as a way of deconstructing the text: 'naming the woman and making her the focus of our inquiry are interpretive moves that restore her to the subject position the androcentric narrative destroys' (1993: 177).

ena', specifically 'the use of terms that are loaded with stigma, in a Western context, to describe non-stigmatised behaviour in a non-Western context' (1999: 92), needs to be heard. The act of male rape that is threatened in Judges 19 should not be described in terms of homosexuality, for this will only perpetuate anti-gay/lesbian reactions within Christian and Jewish discourse.

Conclusion

As we have seen, the book of Judges is pervaded by constructions of sex, gender and sexuality. For over a century, commentators have recognized the ribald, often coarse sexual language and imagery that pervades the text. However, it is the queer reader who may be best placed to re-explore the many layers of this language and imagery. They are also probably best placed to identify the effects such language and imagery have for readers today. This chapter has had space to explore only three narratives within the text. A fuller queer reading of the text waits to be written.

Ruth[1]

MONA WEST

Introduction

Ruth is one of two books in the Hebrew Bible named after a woman. It is unique in the canon of Hebrew scriptures and Israelite patriarchal society because it celebrates one woman's love for and devotion to another. There has been much debate concerning the legal material in the book and its relationship to the narrative. Two laws seem to be most prominent. The Levirate, which required a living brother to marry his deceased brother's widow and have a son by her (Deut. 25.5–10), is alluded to by Naomi in 1.12–13 and by Boaz in 4.7–10. The *go'el* law requiring a kinsman to buy back (redeem) a relative or his land (Lev. 25) is mentioned throughout the book (2.20; 3.9, 12–13; 4.1, 3, 4, 6, 7). Both Levirate and *go'el* legislations are placed in a unique context when applied to the situations of Ruth, Naomi and Boaz.

Other laws that affect the narrative are gleaning and 'spreading the skirt or cloak'. In chapter 2 Ruth 'happens' into the field of Boaz when she decides to take advantage of the Israelite gleaning law that provides for the poor, the orphaned, the widow and the foreigner (Lev. 19.9–10; 23.22; Deut. 24.19–22). At the threshing floor in chapter 3 Ruth proposes to Boaz by using the phrase *spread your cloak over your servant*. This phrase is symbolic of marriage in Israelite tradition (Deut. 22.30; 27.20; Ezek. 16.8).

It is important to realize that the artistry and message of Ruth are dependent on the interplay of law and narrative within the book. This artistry is lost if the book is approached as a legal treatise or test case for the laws it contains. Instead, the legal material should be viewed as a creative matrix for plot movement and character development. The laws are intentionally ambiguous in order to provide possibilities for the characters to act above and beyond what society requires of them (on this see further Biale (1997)). Laws define their identity and challenge their existence. As each character makes choices that go beyond the letter of the law, that character moves toward more authentic existence within the narrative and within society.

The strategies we find in Ruth are essential to our very survival in a society and a culture that invoke and create laws with narrow definitions of family and procreative privilege in order to exclude us and perpetuate hatred and violence against our community.

---

1 Portions of this essay appeared in the anthology *Our Families Our Values: Snapshots of Queer Kinship* edited by Goss and West (1997).

Coming Out on the Road from Moab to Bethlehem (1.1–22)

In a matter of five short verses, a whole family moves from Bethlehem to Moab because of a famine, the father dies, the sons marry Moabite wives, ten years pass, the sons die, and three women are left widowed and childless. The narrative quickly focuses on the situation of the three women: Naomi, the mother-in-law, and her two daughters-in-law, Ruth and Orpah.

There were only two ways a woman could be valued in this society: as an unmarried virgin in her father's household or as a child-producing wife in her husband's household. Naomi is a widow who also becomes childless upon the deaths of her two sons. As childless widows, Naomi, Ruth and Orpah are women who are worthless and on the margins of ancient Near Eastern society. Naomi recognizes that they have limited options for relationships and for places of 'security' in such a society. Naomi admonishes her daughters-in-law not to follow her back to Bethlehem but instead to try and find husbands in their homeland of Moab.

We are told that Orpah kisses her mother-in-law goodbye and that Ruth clings to her. It is at this point in the story that Ruth 'comes out' and declares her true feeling for Naomi. In words that have traditionally been repeated in heterosexual wedding ceremonies, Ruth speaks to Naomi:

> Do not press me to leave you or to turn back from following you! Where you go, I will go; where you lodge, I will lodge; your people shall be my people, and your God my God. Where you die, I will die – there will I be buried. May the Lord do thus and so to me, and more as well, if even death parts me from you! (1.16 NRSV)

These words and actions present the closest physical relationship between two women expressed anywhere in the Bible. The Hebrew word that describes Ruth's clinging (*davka*) to Naomi is the same word used in Genesis 2.24 to describe the relationship of the man to the woman in marriage. He leaves his father and mother and clings to her, and the two become one flesh.

In her words of devotion Ruth names her relationship to Naomi using words that depict a relationship that crossed the boundaries of age, nationality and religion. Ruth chooses against the odds to stay with Naomi – one worthless woman joining herself to another, and, in her choosing, she refuses to accept the status quo of a society that limits and defines their existence as worthless, empty and marginal based on marital status or reproductive ability.

Ruth is our Queer ancestress. She has gone before us and so offers us an example. In her own way she knew that 'silence equals death'. After all, Orpah says nothing. According to the story she kisses Naomi goodbye and promptly disappears. Ruth, however, goes on courageously to name and affirm our relationships in the face of seemingly insurmountable odds. She provides us with an example of self-determination, refusing to accept a marginalized status based on heterosexist patriarchal definitions of marriage, family and procreation.

Ruth's words to Naomi in 1.16 are words for our community. They are pronouncement, blessing, creed, hymn, poem and declaration, offering paradigms for the ways in which we relate to one another in our comings and goings.

Strategies for Surviving a Hostile Environment (2.1–23)

In chapter 2 Boaz is introduced to the story as a wealthy landowner and a distant relative of Naomi's. After their return to Bethlehem the women are faced
with the day-to-day struggle of providing food for themselves. Israelite law
minimally provided for widows and the poor through an ordinance requiring
some grain to be left in the fields during harvest for the less fortunate to come
behind and glean for their food. Ruth knows of this law and decides to go to
Boaz's field to glean. Boaz notices her and in true patriarchal fashion asks, 'To
whom does this young woman belong?' And the foreman of the reapers has an
interesting reply, 'She belongs to Naomi.'

Boaz introduces himself to Ruth and the two of them acknowledge the relationship that exists between Ruth and Naomi. Boaz says:

> All that you have done for your mother-in-law since the death of your hus-
> band has been fully told me, and how you left your father and mother and
> native land and came to a people that you did not know before. (2.11)

These words of Boaz echo Ruth's words of devotion spoken on the road from
Moab to Bethlehem. Not only does Boaz acknowledge their relationship by
repeating them but he invokes God's blessing on their relationship, 'May
Yahweh reward you for your deeds and may you have a full reward from
Yahweh the God of Israel, under whose wings you have come for refuge.' In
addition to this blessing, as a male in this patriarchal society and the owner
of the field, Boaz offers extra grain for Ruth and Naomi, and he offers Ruth
protection from molestation as she gleans in his fields.

Boaz works out an arrangement with Ruth so that she is able to provide
food for herself and Naomi. He also strategizes with Ruth about how to avoid
sexual violence in a situation where she is at risk. All of this is done so that
Ruth is able to live with Naomi.

Ruth and Boaz provide the Queer community of today with some strategies
for survival in hostile environments. Like Ruth we find ourselves working within minimal laws to provide for our relationships and our well-being – inheritance laws, custody laws, health care laws. And like Ruth we often deal with
the threat of physical violence. The strategy of Ruth and Boaz invites us to join
forces to create communities in which all of us have equal access to goods and
services. Like Boaz, those of us with some privilege (those of us who are white,
male, able-bodied, educated and have economic resources) can use those privileges to resist oppressive structures and go above and beyond the law to ensure
that those less fortunate in our community are provided for. Ruth and Boaz
remind us that even in the midst of hostile environments we are able to create
communities that affirm our relationships, provide protection and sustain us.

We Are Family: Ruth, Boaz and Me! (3.1–4.11)

Ruth and Naomi live together because of the arrangement Boaz and Ruth
were able to work out 'until the end of the barley and wheat harvest'. At the

beginning of chapter 3 Naomi realizes that a more permanent arrangement must be made so that it 'may be well' with all of them. However, keep in mind that up to this point in the story Ruth has done all the strategizing about how she and Naomi will stay together in a society that refuses to acknowledge their relationship as worthwhile. Naomi's strategy which follows in chapter 3 directly involves the well-being and security of Ruth but also includes Boaz as an important member of the 'family' Naomi is about to create.

Naomi is of course aware of the Levirate and go'el laws of Israel, but there seems to be some ambiguity in the narrative concerning Boaz's legal responsibilities as well as his blood relationship to Naomi. The book of Ruth is also filled with terms and language that describe family and kinship. In 3.2 Naomi identifies Boaz as a 'kinsman'. Earlier Boaz was identified as a 'kinsman' of Naomi's on her husband's side, a member of the 'tribe' or 'clan' of Naomi's deceased husband (2.1), and in 2.20 Naomi identified him as 'nearest kin'.

All of these words and laws provide for some interesting narrative possibilities concerning the familial relationship that exists between Ruth, Boaz and Naomi. Naomi works with these ambiguities to create a situation in which she, Boaz and Ruth can form their own family to provide security and well-being.

The encounter between Ruth and Boaz at the threshing-floor is similar to their first meeting in chapter 2. Like gleaning in the fields, Ruth takes advantage of the go'el law and proposes to Boaz by instructing him to spread his skirt or cloak over her because he is next of kin. Ruth repeats the words Boaz spoke to her in chapter 2. The same word for wing in 2.12 (kanap) is used for cloak in 3.9. Ruth claims that Boaz will be the means by which she and Naomi will find refuge under the wing of the God of Israel.

The wheat and barley harvests have ended and marriage is the alternative arrangement she suggests to Boaz. His response to Ruth confirms the nature of the arrangement: 'This last instance of your loyalty is better than the first; you have not gone after young men, whether poor or rich' (3.10).

All of these actions indicate Naomi, Ruth and Boaz's decision to create their own family and define their own understanding of kinship and responsibility to one another within the context of the inheritance and kinship laws of ancient Israel. These actions are similar to the ways in which Queer people of today create families: a bisexual man and two lesbians live together with their biological child; a gay man is a sperm donor for a lesbian couple and is part of the parenting of their child; three gay men live together as lovers and family for twenty years; a lesbian mother and her lover live two doors down from her lesbian daughter and her lover.

Ruth, Naomi and Boaz provide our community with an ancient example of the ways in which we have been creating our families. We find, however, that like us they must overcome some legal barriers in the creation of their family. After Ruth and Boaz decide to marry so that the three of them can be family, Boaz remembers that there is a nearer kinsman, more closely related to Naomi, who by law is required to act as the redeemer.

Once again it is ambiguous as to the exact nature of these laws as they apply to Ruth and Naomi's situation. Within this ambiguity Boaz manipulates the legal situation so that the nearer kinsman abandons his claim to redeem Naomi and her land. The scene at the city gate shows Boaz at his best in the story. He sets up the nearer kinsman by giving just enough information about Naomi and this mysterious land she owns. As the nearer kinsman agrees to redeem the land, Boaz interjects, 'The day you acquire the field from the hand of Naomi, you are also acquiring Ruth the Moabite . . .' Out of fear of damaging his larger inheritance because of Ruth, the nearer kinsman passes on his right of redemption, leaving Boaz free and clear to move ahead with marrying Ruth.

Certainly there are ways that we in the Queer community manipulate laws to overcome barriers that deny the legality of our relationships. We also work the system to make our relationships more permanent and secure. We do this through wills, durable power of attorney and medical power of attorney. We take each other's last names and, in states and countries that allow it, we have civil unions and marry one another. Transgender people are able to manipulate the heterosexist system of 'marriage' when as a result of one member of a same-sex couple transitioning they are able to be 'legally' married. Ruth, Naomi and Boaz would be proud of the ways in which we continue to follow their strategies for creating family and having our relationships recognized!

Blessing Our Unions and Affirming Our Procreative Strategies (4.13–22)

In Ruth 4.13 we are told that Ruth and Boaz have a son. The townswomen of Bethlehem have some interesting things to say in response to this birth. They bless the birth and designate the child as *go'el*. They claim the child shall be a 'restorer of life' for Naomi. They acknowledge Ruth's love for Naomi (the only time the word love is used in the whole story) and they make the outrageous statement that Ruth is more to Naomi than seven sons! To top all this off the townswomen name the child Obed, saying, 'A son has been born to Naomi.'

In their words and actions the townswomen acknowledge the procreative strategy of Ruth and Boaz that produced a son for Naomi. Their blessing redefines procreation as life-giving. Naomi is not the biological mother of Obed, yet the townswomen realize Ruth's relationship to Naomi has been life-giving – procreative.

The Queer community hears the blessing of our unions in the words of the townswomen of Bethlehem. We claim with them that our unions, our love, our families with or without children, are life-giving and procreative. Their words are both blessing and promise: 'Blessed be Yahweh who has not left you this day without family.'

1 and 2 Samuel

KEN STONE

Introduction

The books of 1 and 2 Samuel offer a narrative account of an important period of political transition in Israel's imagined past. At the beginning of 1 Samuel, Israel appears to take the form of a confederation of tribes akin to that found in the book of Judges. By the end of 2 Samuel, Israel has become a kingdom governed by David from the capital city of Jerusalem. The central human figures involved in this transition are Samuel, the judge and prophet for whom the books are named; Saul, who is initially anointed as ruler by Samuel but later rejected; and David, who is anointed by Samuel to replace Saul and who establishes a hereditary monarchy that rules from Jerusalem.

This political transition is represented, however, in theological terms. Israel's god, Yhwh, is often described as intervening in the lives and careers of Samuel, Saul and David. Thus, the realm of politics and the realm of religion are thoroughly intertwined in the books of Samuel. Moreover, matters of sex and gender frequently play a role in this theo-political story. Readers of the Bible who are interested in the relations between sex, gender, religion and politics may therefore find it useful to give close attention to 1 and 2 Samuel.

Form and text

The study of 1 and 2 Samuel provides us with valuable opportunities to remind ourselves of important, but frequently overlooked, facts about 'the Bible'. While it is quite common for people to ask about, or refer to, 'what the Bible says', in fact 'the Bible' does not really exist as a single text with a uniform content or agreed-upon books and divisions. 'The Bible' is rather an abstraction from numerous different, actually existing, 'bibles' that correspond to diverse religious traditions (with conflicting views about the canon), diverse ways of dividing up the Hebrew scriptures and relating them to one another, and diverse traditions of manuscript transmission. Although it is usually not necessary to worry about these complications when reading a biblical text, it is important for readers of biblical literature to be aware that such complications do exist. The books of Samuel offer many reminders of such complications.

For example, evidence from the ancient world such as the lengthy Samuel scroll (known as 4QSam[a]) found among the Dead Sea Scrolls indicates that our two 'books' of 1 and 2 Samuel actually belonged at one time to a single Hebrew book. Indeed, the events narrated in the opening chapter of 2 Samuel follow directly from the events narrated in the last chapter of 1 Samuel. Moreover, printed versions of the standard Hebrew text of the Bible (the 'Masoretic Text') still today do not make a sharp distinction between 1 and 2 Samuel such as we find in most Greek and English Bibles. Rather, the beginning of 2 Samuel is printed on the same page as the end of 1 Samuel, without a significant break comparable to that found between most other books of the Hebrew Bible. The two 'books' are, thus, recognized as one.

The distinction between 1 and 2 Samuel that has now become traditional in many Bibles seems to have originated with the Septuagint (abbreviated LXX), the Greek version of the First Testament, which may have divided the book of Samuel into two parts because the book was too long to fit conveniently onto a single ancient manuscript. Although the Septuagint did divide the book of Samuel into separate sections that correspond to the books we now know as 1 and 2 Samuel, the titles given to these two sections in the Septuagint tradition are actually '1 Kingdoms' and '2 Kingdoms'. At the same time, our two books of 1 and 2 Kings are referred to in Septuagint manuscripts as '3 Kingdoms' and '4 Kingdoms'. This way of referring to the books of Samuel and Kings (as 1–4 Kingdoms) indicates that the persons responsible for the titles of books in the Septuagint recognized that some sort of relationship exists among all four of these books, and not simply between the books of 1 and 2 Samuel.

Modern biblical scholarship has generally confirmed this insight, but in complex ways. Thus, the influential German scholar Martin Noth argued in the middle of the twentieth century that the books of Samuel and Kings, together with the books of Deuteronomy, Joshua and Judges, all belonged at one time to a single work, put together during the Babylonian exile and referred to by Noth as the 'Deuteronomistic History' (see '1 and 2 Kings' in this volume). Noth and other scholars have also suggested, however, that careful analysis of this 'Deuteronomistic History' enables the reader to make distinctions among various earlier sources, with different dates and authors, which are now incorporated into the larger Deuteronomistic work and which transgress the boundaries of our biblical 'books'. For example, many scholars interested in the detection of such sources argue that chapters 9–20 of 2 Samuel, along with the first two chapters of 1 Kings, originally formed or belonged to an older document frequently referred to by scholars as the 'Succession Narrative' or 'Court History', which has been used as a source by the Deuteronomistic History. Although it is not necessary for us to evaluate the strengths and weaknesses of these proposals here (see Gunn 1978; Flanagan 1992), the narrative continuity between the central chapters of 2 Samuel and the opening chapters of 1 Kings, which serves as one piece of evidence for such proposals, does blur the boundary between the books of Samuel and the books of Kings.

Other complications surround the boundary between the books of Samuel and the book of Judges. Christian Bibles follow the Septuagint in placing the book of Ruth between Judges and 1 Samuel, presumably because the story in Ruth is said to take place 'when the Judges ruled' (Ruth 1.1). In the Jewish tradition, however, Judges is followed by 1 Samuel. Continuity between the books is apparent from the fact that Samuel judges Israel (1 Sam. 7.15) and that his tenure as judge is given a formulaic summary (7.13–17) which reminds us of the summaries that wrap up the careers of other judges in the book of Judges.

Indeed, David Jobling, in an important commentary on 1 Samuel, has argued that one can read the early chapters of 1 Samuel as part of an 'extended book of Judges', comprised of Judges 2.11 to 1 Samuel 12 (Jobling 1998: 43–76).

On the other hand, if we focus our attention only on the 'book' of Samuel (comprised of our 'books' of 1 and 2 Samuel), we can also see that this book of Samuel itself incorporates the work of multiple authors. The assumption of multiple authorship not only helps to explain the fact that more than one narrative style exists in our books of 1 and 2 Samuel. It also helps to account for the tensions and contradictions that sometimes appear there as well. For example, although 1 Samuel 7.13 indicates that the Philistines no longer encroached upon Israel's territory during the life of Samuel, the stories of conflict between Israel and the Philistines in chapters 13–15 suggest otherwise. Chapters 13 and 15 of 1 Samuel also provide two, quite different, narrative explanations for God's rejection of Saul. Moreover, while a famous story in 1 Samuel 17 attributes the death of Goliath from Gath to David, 2 Samuel 21.19 attributes the death of Goliath the Gittite (which simply means an inhabitant of Gath) to another figure named Elhanan. The description of Goliath of Gath's spear in these two stories (1 Sam. 17.7; 2 Sam. 21.19) makes it difficult to deny that the stories are actually two separate, and quite different, accounts of the death of the same Goliath, both of which have made it into our 'book' of Samuel. These narrative difficulties and others indicate that 1 and 2 Samuel are composite works, which include diverse and sometimes contradictory traditions that have been gathered together into a single book.

Still further complications arise when we compare various surviving ancient manuscripts of 1 and 2 Samuel to one another. Modern readers often forget that biblical texts existed for centuries prior to the invention of the printing press. Because ancient manuscripts of the Bible were copied by hand in a process that easily led to mistakes, numerous differences in detail can be found whenever comparisons are made between surviving manuscripts. An entire sub-discipline of biblical scholarship, known as 'textual criticism', has emerged in response to these differences; and it has been especially active in the study of 1 and 2 Samuel (see McCarter 1980: 5–11, *passim*; 1984: 3, *passim*; Flanagan 1992). Textual critics evaluate the differences that exist between various ancient manuscripts, and frequently attempt either to determine which surviving manuscripts most likely represent the earlier versions of the text or to reconstruct a hypothetical original version of the text. While most of the differences between manuscripts that make textual criticism necessary are relatively minor, occasionally they can be quite significant. Among all the books of the Hebrew Bible, only a few exist in such strikingly divergent manuscript traditions as the books of 1 and 2 Samuel. Thus it is not quite correct to speak about a single version of 1 and 2 Samuel. Rather, we could refer more accurately to the version of 1 and 2 Samuel that can be found in the Masoretic Hebrew tradition, versions of 1 and 2 Samuel that can be found in various Septuagint manuscripts, versions of 1 and 2 Samuel found in various Dead Sea Scroll manuscripts, and so forth. Modern English translations of 1 and 2 Samuel are usually based on a postulated 'original' Hebrew text that has been reconstructed by textual critics after they have made comparisons among the various surviving versions, yet this reconstructed 'original' text does not correspond exactly to any one Hebrew manuscript that actually exists. For this reason, annotated English Bibles usually contain numerous footnotes in the books of 1 and 2 Samuel, indicating some (but not all) of the places in which translators have decided to follow some manuscript other than the Masoretic Hebrew text in order to produce an English translation. While such notes can be found in other books as well, they appear more frequently in the books of Samuel than in most biblical books. Even biblical scholars do not always agree with one another about the precise shape of the 'original' or 'earlier' Hebrew texts of 1 and 2 Samuel, in spite of the fact that they continue to attempt to reconstruct such texts so that a translation can be made.

Content and history

The books of 1 and 2 Samuel bear the name of one of the primary characters in 1 Samuel, the prophet Samuel. This name for the books is probably related in some way to the tradition found in 1 Chronicles 29.29, which links the written account of the life of King David to the words of the prophets Samuel, Nathan and Gad. It should be pointed out, in connection with this link to biblical prophets, that according to the traditional Jewish division of the canon, 1 and 2 Samuel are classified among the 'Former Prophets', together with the books of Joshua, Judges, and 1 and 2 Kings. However, the division between 1 and 2 Samuel that we find in most of our Bibles today occurs at a point in the story after the prophet Samuel has already died, resulting in the curious fact that our book of 2 Samuel is named for a character who plays no role in that book.

Samuel does play a major role in the first half of 1 Samuel, however; and the opening chapters of the book are focused on the circumstances surrounding his birth and upbringing. Samuel's mother Hannah, discussed further below, is an important figure in these chapters; and she turns Samuel over to the priest, Eli, with whom Samuel lives as he grows up and becomes a prophet. The narrative then turns to a conflict between Israel and the Philistines. This conflict results in the capture of the Ark of the Covenant by the Philistines, the death of Eli upon hearing about the fate of the Ark, and the return of the Ark to Israelite territory under strange circumstances.

After judging Israel for many years, Samuel appoints his sons as judges. When Samuel's sons fail to follow the ways of their father, however, the elders of Israel in chapter 8 demand a king 'like all the nations' (8.5). Although Samuel is unhappy about this demand, Yhwh tells him to accede to it; for the people are not rejecting Samuel but rather rejecting the kingship of God (8.7). Chapter 9 then introduces Saul, son of Kish, a Benjamite who in chapter 10 is anointed by Samuel to rule over Israel. Saul leads Israel during a series of conflicts with such enemies as the Ammonites, Philistines and Amalekites. In chapters 13 and 15, however, Saul is rejected by Yhwh for disobedience. Chapter 16 therefore tells us how Samuel, at Yhwh's direction, meets David and anoints him as king. Much of the second half of 1 Samuel recounts the conflicted relationship between Saul and David. Saul is here betrayed, to some extent, by his son Jonathan and daughter Michal, both of whom love David and help him escape from their father. Saul's tale ends when he and three of his sons, including Jonathan, are killed in a battle against the Philistines in chapter 31.

Although Saul does disobey God and later tries to kill David, a case can be made that Saul is not so much a wicked character but rather a 'tragic' one (see e.g. Exum 1992). The circumstances of his disobedience in chapter 13 are rather ambiguous, and his motives there seem sincere. Although Saul does seek David's life, his first attempt to kill David happens at the instigation of an 'evil spirit' sent from God (18.10–11). Saul continues to seek God's assistance (e.g. 28.6), but God refuses to forgive. Indeed, it almost appears as if God is toying with Saul; for the spirit of God does come upon Saul and causes him to fall into a prophetic frenzy (19.23–4) even after God has rejected Saul.

2 Samuel narrates the story of David from the point at which he is told about the deaths of Saul and Jonathan (2 Sam. 1.1–10). The fact that Saul dies in 1 Samuel 31 may have contributed to the decision to divide 1 Samuel and 2 Samuel at precisely this point, for several biblical books conclude with the deaths of major characters in the narrative (e.g. Jacob and Joseph in Genesis 50, Moses in Deuteronomy 34, and Joshua in Joshua 24). In any case, the opening chapter of 2 Samuel is followed by several chapters that recount a struggle for power between the house of Saul (represented in particular by Saul's son Ishbaal) and the house of David. This struggle culminates first in the proclamation of David as king at Hebron (2 Sam. 5.1–4) and then in the conquest of the Jebusite city of Jerusalem (2 Sam. 5.6–10), which subsequently serves as David's capital. Having established himself as king of Israel, David battles successfully against the Philistines (2 Sam. 5.17–25) and brings to Jerusalem the Ark of the Covenant (2 Sam. 6). He then expresses a desire to build a 'house' – that is, a temple – in which the Ark (which apparently represents the presence of God) can reside. In response to this desire, however, Yhwh, who claims not to have lived previously in a 'house' (2 Sam. 7.6–7), specifies that it will be David's son rather than David himself who will build such a 'house'. This specification then becomes an occasion for Yhwh, through the prophet Nathan, to make an important promise to David. According to this promise, Yhwh will also establish for David himself a 'house'. In the context of 2 Samuel 7, this 'house' promised to David is clearly an inherited dynasty; and, at least in this chapter, Yhwh's promise to the Davidic dynasty appears to be eternal and unconditional (e.g. 2 Sam. 7.13–16). This promise to David, it is important to note, serves as a crucial foundation for many of the messianic hopes that later emerged in both Judaism and Christianity. The remaining chapters of 2 Samuel, several of which are considered in more detail below, go on to narrate subsequent events from the reign of David as king of Israel. Somewhat surprisingly, however, David does not die at the end of 2 Samuel, as we might expect, but rather in the second chapter of 1 Kings. It is partly for this reason that scholars have often read the opening chapters of 1 Kings as part of the story of David that is recounted in 2 Samuel. Moreover, the final chapter of 2 Samuel, though focused upon David, looks forward to the building of the temple that is actually carried out by David's son Solomon in 1 Kings 5–8.

It was once common for scholars to argue that the story of David recounted in 2 Samuel is a reasonably accurate historical account of David's reign. Gerhard von Rad even went so far as to suggest that the 'narrative sequence' found from 2 Samuel 9 to 1 Kings 2 was written in the time of David's son Solomon, and 'must be regarded as the oldest specimen of ancient Israelite historical writing' (von Rad 1965a: 176). Numerous historians of ancient Israel have therefore used the book of 2 Samuel with confidence as a source for reconstructing Israel's history during the time of David, though they have usually acknowledged that this source (like all ancient sources) is written from a particular perspective and is influenced by the political and theological biases of its author.

In recent years, however, a number of scholars have raised critical questions about the assumption that it is appropriate for the modern historian to consider 2 Samuel an example of 'historical writing', or to use it as a reliable source for the modern reconstruction of ancient history. While 2 Samuel clearly does tell a story about Israel's past, literary analyses especially of the so-called 'Succession Narrative' or 'Court History' in 2 Samuel 9 to 1 Kings 2 have emphasized the extent to which the narrative has been put together to form a well-written and entertaining piece of ancient story-telling that builds upon traditional storytelling motifs (see e.g. Gunn 1978; Ackerman 1990). Such literary studies call into question the belief of readers like von Rad that the rich descriptive detail of this text is a sign that the text is an eyewitness account; and they suggest instead that such detail is better understood as a component of literary artistry, which therefore tells us little if anything about either the text's date of composition or its historical veracity. Other scholars have argued, on different grounds, that these central chapters of 2 Samuel were written much later than the time in the early tenth century BCE that they claim to recount, perhaps even later than the sixth-century BCE Babylonian exile (see e.g. Van Seters 1983: 277–91). Moreover, since the final form of the larger narrative complex (Noth's 'Deuteronomistic History') in which the books of Samuel and their older narrative sources are now embedded certainly dates no earlier than the exilic or post-exilic era, compelling arguments have also been made that this later period, rather than the period which the text claims to recount, actually provides us with the socio-historical context in relation to which the entire narrative of 1 and 2 Samuel can most usefully be interpreted (see e.g. Mullen 1993).

Although such matters continue to be debated among scholars (see e.g. Halpern 2001), it is clear that readers of both 1 and 2 Samuel need to be cautious about assuming that the story told in these books gives us an accurate picture of either the lives of the historical figures Saul and David or their reigns as kings of Israel. Indeed, it is striking that no independent evidence, dating clearly from the time in which Saul and David themselves are supposed to have lived, has ever been found to confirm the fact that either one of them ruled over a united kingdom of Israel in the late eleventh/early tenth century BCE. Even their existence as historical figures has never been independently attested. An Aramaic inscription found at Tel Dan (in northern Israel), which may recount the invasion of Israel by the Syrian king Hazael (who appears in 2 Kings) in the second half of the ninth century BCE, is understood by many scholars to include a reference to the 'house of David'. If this interpretation is correct, the inscription constitutes our oldest surviving reference to David, and probably the only such reference that pre-dates the earliest biblical books. Yet the significance of this inscription continues to be debated. Given the fact that it refers at the earliest to events taking place more than a century after the time in which David is supposed to have lived, even on a conservative reading it attests at most to the fact that later rulers of Judah were understood to constitute a 'house of David'. Thus nothing about the existence of David himself, or the period recounted in 2 Samuel, can be deduced from the inscription. Matters are even less clear in the case of Saul. Of course, the paucity of evidence does not necessarily mean that no such persons as Saul or David ever lived. Even some of those scholars who are very cautious about the use of the Bible as a historical source believe that there are sufficient reasons to accept the existence of David, in particular, as a real person (see e.g. Finkelstein and Silberman 2001: 123–45). We cannot, however, simply identify the literary characters Saul and David, or the biblical representation of their reigns in 1 and 2 Samuel, with the supposed 'facts' of ancient Israelite history (cf. P. Davies 1999).

Nevertheless, the books of 1 and 2 Samuel can still be quite useful as sources for our understanding of ancient Israel or Judah. They are valuable not so much because we know that – or can know whether – the characters and events in the books were 'real', but rather because the books shed light on the social and religious views held by its ancient Israelite or Judahite author(s). And, as we shall see, these views include many assumptions having to do with sexual practice, gender and marriage.

Hannah

The opening two chapters of 1 Samuel concentrate on Hannah, the mother of Samuel and, in the words of one commentator, 'the first major character in 1 Samuel' (Jobling 1998: 129). Hannah is introduced as one of two wives of a man named Elkanah, who belongs to the tribe of Ephraim. Elkanah's other wife is named Peninnah.

The fact that Elkanah has two wives provides readers of 1 and 2 Samuel with the first of several reminders that the Hebrew Bible presupposes views of marriage and kinship that are often quite different from those most often held by modern readers. Numerous biblical texts, including many texts in 1 and 2 Samuel, assume the legitimacy of polygyny, a system of marriage in which men may have multiple wives so long as they can afford to do so. Most historians believe that, in practice, only a small number of Israelite men (those who were relatively wealthy) would have been able to support multiple wives. Nevertheless, biblical tolerance for polygyny serves as a useful reminder that claims about continuity between biblical texts and modern 'family values' are often unwarranted.

Like many women in the Hebrew Bible, Hannah is characterized initially as barren (in contrast to Peninnah, who has children and causes trouble for Hannah (1 Sam. 1.6)). After praying for a child and vowing to 'give him to Yhwh' (1.11), Hannah conceives and bears a son, Samuel. When Samuel is weaned, Hannah brings him to the priest, Eli, at the 'house of Yhwh' in Shiloh. There Hannah leaves Samuel, stating that she has 'lent him to Yhwh' (1.28). A famous poem is then put on the lips of Hannah at the beginning of chapter 2. Often called the 'Song of Hannah', this poem, which celebrates reversals of fortune for the poor and oppressed, seems to have provided the author of the

Second Testament Gospel of Luke with a model for the Magnificat, the poem of praise delivered by Mary in Luke 1.46–55. After leaving Samuel with Eli, Hannah goes on to bear three more sons and two daughters.

Much commentary on 1 Samuel concentrates on Hannah's role as mother of Samuel. From this point of view, her actions can be seen as troubling. Thus Danna Nolan Fewell and David Gunn point out that, while Hannah 'is a woman of speech and action', nevertheless she ultimately sacrifices her son (1993: 140).

However, the feminist scholar Carol Meyers has called attention to Hannah's role as ritual or cultic agent. In 1.24, when Hannah brings Samuel to Eli, the Hebrew text tells us that she also brings three bulls, flour and wine for an offering. Meyers suggests that Hannah's vow and sacrifice together provide 'an example of women's religion as it existed at some point early in the history of Israel' (1994: 101). Such religion probably had its primary context in the realm of family or household rather than the realm of temple or public cult, and so has left relatively few traces in the Bible (which is more interested in the public religion dominated by men). In this instance, however, Hannah's vow and sacrificial pilgrimage blur the boundary between private and public realms and allow us to catch a glimpse of women's religion in ancient Israel that is otherwise seldom afforded us.

The Medium of Endor

An even more unusual perspective on women and religion in Israel is offered by the story of Saul and the medium of Endor in 1 Samuel 28. The story takes place during a period of hostility between Israelites and Philistines. These hostilities culminate in chapter 31, when Saul and his sons are killed during a battle against the Philistines. In advance of this battle, Saul, noting the large size of the Philistine army, attempts to consult Yhwh. Yhwh refuses to answer Saul by dreams, prophecy or 'Urim' (apparently a sort of casting of lots which functioned as a means of divination in Israel). Confronted with the silence of Yhwh, Saul asks his servants to find a woman who is a 'mistress of ghosts' (28.7). Although the latter phrase is somewhat obscure, it appears to refer to a woman who consults ghosts or spirits for purposes of divination. When such a woman is located at Endor, Saul goes to her in disguise and asks her to consult a ghost that he will name. The woman is initially hesitant to comply, for Saul has previously forbidden such practices and she fears for her life. However, after Saul swears by Yhwh that she will not get into trouble, the woman asks him to identify the person who will be brought up. Saul identifies Samuel, whose death has already been reported (28.3). When the woman successfully brings him up, Samuel confirms that Yhwh has turned away from Saul and intends to give the kingship to David. Moreover, Samuel tells Saul ominously, 'tomorrow you and your sons will be with me' (28.19).

Although this remarkable story recognizes that divination by ghosts was viewed negatively by particular Israelite leaders (cf. Deut. 18.11), it appears to assume that practitioners of spirit divination were successful in calling up the ghosts of dead persons. It is possible that the association of this practice with a woman in 1 Samuel reflects the exclusion of women, in Israel, from such official religious roles as the priesthood and their consequent relegation to 'peripheral religious culture' (Hackett 1998: 94). Other biblical texts recognize explicitly that women as well as men could practise spirit divination (e.g. Lev. 20.27), and women are elsewhere associated with heterodox religious practices involving sorcery (Ex. 22.18; Isa. 57.3) and soothsaying (Ezek. 13.17–23). Thus the text may offer us a glimpse of ancient Israelite popular religious practices that differ from the orthodox rites and activities promoted by the Bible's writers, most of whom were certainly male.

Yet the narrative is surprisingly neutral in its representation of the medium of Endor (see Jobling 1998: 185–9). Indeed, she seems to be represented somewhat sympathetically in the remainder of the chapter. We are told that Saul, after hearing Samuel's words, falls to the ground out of fear and because he has not eaten all day (1 Sam. 28.20). Seeing Saul's distress, the woman attempts to give him food so that he will be strong enough to go on his way. Saul at first refuses. However, when his servants as well as the woman encourage him to eat, Saul sits up. The woman then slaughters a calf and bakes unleavened cakes for Saul and his servants. The attention given by the text to the woman medium's food preparation is intriguing. Meyers has suggested, on the basis of comparative evidence, that the traditional role of women in food preparation may help to account for their association with sorcery and other religious practices sometimes linked to magic (Meyers 2000: 197). Food preparation tasks offered opportunities for familiarity with the herbs and other substances crucial to folk medical practice, which in turn may have provided the basis for particular sorts of healing activities that we associate with magic. In any event, the kindness and hospitality shown by this woman to Saul provide us with our last glimpse of this early king prior to his final battle with the Philistines.

Sex and Gender in the Representation of the Philistines

The Philistines who kill Saul and his sons play a major role in the books of Samuel and in the book of Judges that precedes 1 Samuel in the Jewish Bible (and in the Deuteronomistic History). They function in particular as fierce enemies of the Israelites, though they are also allied with David for a period of his career. Thus the Philistines most often appear in situations of military conflict. However, military conflict is sometimes represented in the ancient world with phallic connotations. Moreover, ethnic difference and sex/gender difference frequently overlap in the ancient world as in the modern world. Queer readers of 1 and 2 Samuel will therefore wish to note the appearance of sex/gender symbolism in the representation of the Philistines.

It is of course striking that one feature of Philistine men which is frequently stressed in the books of Samuel is the fact that they are uncircumcised (e.g. 1 Sam. 14.6; 17.26, 36; 18.25, 27; 31.4; 2 Sam. 1.20; 3.14; cf. Judg. 14.3; 15.18). More literally, they are represented as those who have foreskins. Although circumcision came to be interpreted as a sign of the covenant between God and Israel at some point in the development of Israelite religion, many of Israel's neighbours (including Egypt and Syria) seem to have practised some form of it at certain times and places. In its origins, circumcision may have been understood in this part of western Asia as contributing to male potency or 'fruitfulness' (Eilberg-Schwartz 1990: 141–76). The Philistines, however, belonged to a group of peoples (often referred to collectively as the 'Sea Peoples') who migrated to western Asia from elsewhere in the Mediterranean/Aegean world. The fact that they (like other Aegean peoples, such as the Greeks) did not practise circumcision probably did make the Philistines stand out in their new location on the coast of Palestine.

When biblical characters refer to the uncircumcised state of Philistine men, they nearly always do so with disdain or in a context of hostility. It is likely that these scornful references presuppose a conflict interpreted in terms of gender symbolism. That is, the Philistines were probably understood as improper examples of manhood. Thus, in an ancient world where military conflict already had phallic connotations, conflicts between Israelites and Philistines may well have been conceptualized in part as struggles to determine which sort of man – Israelite or Philistine, circumcised or uncircumcised – was really more manly.

In order to recognize this possibility, one must note the represented speech of the Philistines in 1 Samuel 4.9. In order to encourage one another to fight Israel more fiercely, the Philistines in that verse twice beseech one another to 'be men' or 'be manly'. They also note that, if they fail to do so, they will become slaves to the Hebrews as the Hebrews have been slaves to them. To fail to be manly, then, is to be subjugated – and so, within the framework of ancient phallic symbolism, to be emasculated (cf. Stone 1996).

It is also striking to note that Saul refers to the uncircumcised state of the Philistines (literally, 'these ones with foreskins') in 1 Samuel 31.4 when, after being wounded, he asks his armour-bearer to kill him. While Saul is worried about the treatment he may receive from the uncircumcised, his request also recalls the appeal of Abimelech in Judges 9.54, who, fearing the shame of being killed by the woman who has mortally wounded him, asks his own armour-bearer to kill him instead. The vocabulary used to refer to 'drawing the sword' and 'piercing' someone with that sword is quite similar in the two verses. Thus Saul's fear might be construed in part as a fear of the shame that accompanies death at the hands of the unmanly – in his case, the Philistines, characterized explicitly in terms of their genital difference.

Other biblical texts, inside and outside the books of Samuel, may also question Philistine manhood by associating the Philistines with women. Saul offers to give his daughter to any man who can bring him one hundred Philistine foreskins as a brideprice. Thus, women and foreskins are literally exchanged (1 Sam. 18.25, 27). In the story of Samson in Judges, which refers twice to the Philistines' foreskins (Judg. 14.3; 15.18), the Philistines must use women to subjugate Samson. On the basis of this story and others, Jobling concludes that both Judges and 1 Samuel 'conflate women and Philistines' (Jobling 1998: 216; cf. 230–1).

Recognition that such gender symbolism is at work in representations of the Philistines may lend plausibility to the suggestion of Theodore Jennings that, in 1 Samuel 5, the Ark of the Covenant and the image of the Philistine god Dagon are engaged in a contest of phallic subjugation. There the Philistines, after capturing the Ark that is associated with the presence of Yhwh, place it in Dagon's temple. In the morning, however, Dagon's image has fallen on its face before the Ark. After Dagon's image is returned to its upright position, it is found on its face yet again, this time with its head and hands cut off from the image. Jennings suggests that the 'forced submission' of Dagon to the Ark in this passage represents a sort of symbolic rape of Dagon by that Ark, comparable to the 'phallic aggression' associated with other ancient deities such as the Egyptian gods Seth and Horus (2001: 58–60). Alternatively, the frequent use of the Hebrew word for 'hand' as a sign of physical, military or political might, combined with the occasional use of the word 'hand' as euphemism for male genitals in both biblical (e.g. Isa. 57.8–10; S. of Sol. 5.4) and Ugaritic texts (cf. Pope 1977: 517), might lead one to conclude that the Philistine god Dagon is in 1 Samuel 5 symbolically castrated rather than symbolically raped. In either case, the contest over manhood between Israel and the Philistines appears to be extended in 1 Samuel to the contest between their male deities.

The polemical use of the rhetoric of sex and gender to construct ethnic difference is not limited, in the Bible, to Israelite representations of the Philistines. Randall Bailey has argued that it occurs several times in Genesis (Bailey 1995); and it clearly plays a role in other biblical texts as well, including for example certain biblical texts that speak about the Canaanites (cf. Stone 2004; 2005). However, as Bailey notes, such rhetoric has a troubling history and plays a recurring role in racial and ethnic oppression. Queer readers of the Bible do well to view with suspicion such biblical texts, and to read with caution the writings of biblical scholars and theologians who cite such texts uncritically as accurate representations of non-Israelite peoples.

David, Jonathan and Saul

The book of 2 Samuel opens, as indicated above, with the delivery to David of news that Saul and Jonathan have died during a battle with the Philistines. The description of Saul's death given to David by an Amalekite in 2 Samuel 1 does not correspond exactly with the narrator's description in 1 Samuel 31, but it is unclear whether this difference results from multiple traditions about Saul's death or from a lie on the part of the Amalekite, who claims to have killed Saul himself (2 Sam. 1.10). The fact that David has himself just returned from a successful battle against the Amalekites (1.1) when he learns about Saul's death may cause us to wonder about both the Amalekite's motivations for claiming to have killed David's enemy, and David's motivations for killing the Amalekite. In the text itself, however, the execution of the Amalekite is attributed (1.14–16) to David's concern for Saul as Yhwh's 'anointed' (an important Hebrew word from which we get the term 'messiah').

Just after the narration of these events, David is represented as voicing a lament 'over Saul and over Jonathan his son' (1.17). The lament itself seems to have existed first outside of the books of Samuel in a text called 'the book of Jashar', known and referred to by the author of 2 Samuel (1.18) and by the author of the book of Joshua (Josh. 10.13). Given the contexts in which it is referred to, this 'book of Jashar' may have been a collection of war songs or poems that has been utilized as a source by the biblical author(s). For our purposes, though, the significance of this excerpt from the 'book of Jashar' lies in its well-known comparison between Jonathan's love and 'the love of women' (2 Sam. 1.26). This comparison has stimulated much reflection on the possibility of a homoerotic relationship between David and Jonathan.

Biblical scholars have often noted, correctly, that the language of 'love' was sometimes used in the ancient Near East to describe political relationships between kings and their subordinates. Thus, quite plausible arguments can be made that texts referring to the 'love' of Saul for David, of Jonathan for David, or of David for Jonathan had in the ancient Near East primarily political rather than sexual or romantic connotations, notwithstanding the fact that such texts may also indicate 'great affection' between the individuals in question (McCarter 1980: 281; cf. 1980: 342; 1984: 77). One should not conclude too quickly that such arguments are automatically incompatible with a 'queer reading'. They do, after all, underscore the fact that terms such as 'love', which modern readers are inclined to give fixed, universal and often heteronormative meanings, actually are used in very diverse ways under the changing conditions of history and culture. Readers who recognize that 'love' between persons of the same sex has meant so many different things, and has taken so many different forms in the past, may be better prepared than other readers to imagine a wider range of meanings and forms for 'love' between persons of the same sex in the present and in the future. Thus, the pluralization of possible connotations for same-sex 'love' can itself be a positive development, from a 'queer' point of view; and recognition of the presence of 'love' in the political lexicon of the ancient Near East contributes, potentially, to such pluralization.

On the other hand, the specific comparison that David makes between Jonathan's 'love' and 'the love of women' ('your love was more extraordinary to me than the love of women' (2 Sam. 1.26)) is somewhat unusual even within the framework of those ancient Near Eastern political 'love' relations to which biblical scholars frequently appeal. Moreover, the comment can be read in relation to a series of narratives about the two men in 1 and 2 Samuel, in which personal affection between David and Jonathan is clear. For example, three times we are told that Jonathan 'loved' David 'as his own life' (1 Sam. 18.1, 3; 20.17). On another occasion we read that 'Jonathan son of Saul took great delight in David' (19.1). When, at a later point in 2 Samuel, David decides to act kindly to surviving members of Saul's house, he explicitly does so 'for the sake of Jonathan' (2 Sam. 9.1). Although, as we shall see, David subsequently allows several male descendants of Saul to be killed (21.8–9), he nevertheless allows Jonathan's son Meribaal (referred to in some versions as Mephibosheth) to remain alive because of the 'oath of Yhwh that was between them, between David and Jonathan son of Saul' (21.7; cf. 9.1–13). The relationship between David and Jonathan is clearly represented, then, as having been closer than a simple political alliance. For these reasons and others, some readers of the Bible argue that a more intimate, and possibly even sexual, understanding of Jonathan's love for David is less forced than the political meaning and would be assigned more frequently to the texts that deal with relations between the two men were it not for the fact that biblical interpretation so often takes place in contexts where sexual relations between men are automatically deemed unacceptable (cf. Horner 1978: 26–39; Fewell and Gunn 1993: 148–51; Comstock 1993: 79–90; Schroer and Staubli 2000; Jennings 2001).

How should we evaluate these arguments? The first thing to note is that the prohibitions against male homosexual intercourse in Leviticus 18.22 and 20.13, while potentially relevant, will not answer our questions about David and Jonathan; for the author of 1 and 2 Samuel does not elsewhere assume the validity of all of the sexual regulations found in Leviticus. For example, the story of David's daughter Tamar, discussed below, indicates that certain forms of incest forbidden in Leviticus are understood by the author of 2 Samuel to be acceptable in at least some circumstances. While the literary context of 1 and 2 Samuel within the larger Deuteronomistic History does encourage readers to evaluate the actions of characters against standards found in Deuteronomy, Deuteronomy nowhere condemns same-sex sexual relations. Moreover, the fact that David's relationship with Jonathan or David's relationship with Saul may indeed have had political connotations does not rule out a sexual component to either relationship. Quite the contrary, most of the sexual relationships that appear in the books of Samuel do have political connotations, as we shall see.

Careful literary analysis of 1 and 2 Samuel has led some scholars to conclude that Jonathan is, in his relationship to David, characterized in ways that one would more likely expect from one of David's wives. Thus Jobling suggests that Jonathan's narrative purposes are identical to those of David's wives Michal and Abigail. These narrative roles are 'to love David, to do practical things to save and help him, and to prophesy his coming kingship' (1998: 162). Adele Berlin suggests, from a different point of view, that when one compares the characterization of the siblings Jonathan and Michal one discovers that 'the characteristics normally associated with males are attached to Michal, and those usually perceived as feminine are linked with Jonathan' (Berlin 1983: 24). As different as these interpretations are, they rest upon a shared recognition that Jonathan's literary characterization seems to involve a certain amount of gender reversal or transgression.

The fact that both David and Jonathan marry women and father children tells us nothing at all about the possibility that they may have had some sort of sexual relationship with one another as well. It is clear that, in other parts of the ancient Mediterranean world such as Greece, sexual relations between males were not automatically considered incompatible with marriage to women or with parenting. Indeed, Theodore Jennings has capitalized on some of this comparative evidence from antiquity to suggest that not only relations between David and Jonathan, but also relations between David and Saul, and even between David and Yhwh, are represented in the books of Samuel in terms of a 'warrior eroticism' comparable to that found, for example, in ancient Sparta (2001: 38, 47, *passim*). At the very least, such an argument shows that the relations David and Jonathan have with women are no impediment to a reading in terms of male homoeroticism. Indeed, it is only the modern differentiation between 'the homosexual' and 'the heterosexual' as two distinct types of person that makes such an anachronistic objection sound at all plausible.

It may also be anachronistic, however, to assume that the deep affection Jonathan and David clearly have for one another in the text would automatically signify a sexual relationship in the ancient world. After all, the range of interpretations that seem plausible to us can be constricted not simply by our attitudes toward sexuality, but also by the forms of same-sex friendship with which we are familiar or that our society makes available or encourages today. It may seem self-evident to many modern readers that one's sexual relationships, whether heterosexual or homosexual, are also the relationships in which intimacy and affection are most deeply expressed and in which one finds close companionship. Yet most of the explicit references to sexual activity in 2 Samuel have nothing at all to do with emotional intimacy or affection but are concerned instead, as we shall see, with power, property or procreation. Thus it is quite possible that David's lament over Jonathan actually testifies to a world in which the lives of most people were characterized by, on the one hand, ongoing sexual relations with persons of the opposite sex; and, on the other hand, affectionate and emotionally intimate relations and companionship with persons of the same sex which, however, did not necessarily entail sexual intercourse.

In the end, then, it is neither necessary nor possible to reach a single, definitive conclusion about the nature of the relationship between David and Jonathan. Rather than insisting only upon a sexual interpretation of David's lament for Jonathan, a queer reading might call attention to multiple ways of understanding the text and use those multiple interpretations to raise questions about the reasons why particular readers tend to be drawn to certain conclusions rather than others. The attempt to answer those questions will necessarily involve an exploration of the assumptions about sex and gender underlying the books of Samuel, assumptions that are in many cases quite different from our own.

The Politics of Sex, Marriage and Power in the Books of Samuel

More than most books of the Bible, 1 and 2 Samuel reveal to us a world in which sexual and marital relations frequently do have significant political connotations (cf. Hackett 1998: 96–9). These connotations are clear already in the stories of Saul and David in 1 Samuel. In chapter 18, for example, Saul offers to give his daughter Merab to David if David will serve in Saul's army 'and fight the battles of Yhwh' (18.17). This offer originates as a scheme, on the part of Saul, to make it more likely that David will be killed by the Philistines. However, David's reply indicates that he understands the offer positively, not because of love for Merab but rather because of the positive effects of being a king's son-in-law (18.18).

After Merab is given to another man instead, Saul decides to offer David his other daughter, Michal, instead. Although the narrator reports that Michal loves David (18.20), we are told nothing about David's feelings for Michal. Instead, we learn again that David is pleased about the possibility of becoming the king's son-in-law (18.23, 26). Both David and Saul make decisions about Merab and Michal primarily in terms of their own individual and political self-interest. While Michal's love for David is mentioned once, the desires of Merab and Michal seem not to play a large role for either David or Saul in their negotiations about David's marriage.

The matter of David's marriages resurfaces in the early chapters of 2 Samuel. 2 Samuel 3, for example, narrates events that take place after the death of Saul and Jonathan, but prior to David's ascension to the throne. This period is characterized by a political and military struggle between David and the house of Saul, which after Saul's death is represented in particular by Saul's son Ishbaal (referred to in some versions as Ishbosheth) and Saul's cousin and military commander Abner. 2 Samuel 3.1 describes this struggle by noting that 'David was growing stronger but the house of Saul was growing weaker'. Immediately after this political comment, however, the narrator tells us that six sons were born to David by six different wives (2 Sam. 3.2–5). Although many English Bibles obscure the relationship between these passages by introducing a paragraph break between them, it is likely that the latter passage (3.2–5) is an expansion and illustration of the point made by the former (3.1). That is to say, the multiplication of wives and sons on David's part is understood to correspond to, and even to demonstrate symbolically, his increasing military and political strength.

In order to recognize the symbolism at work here, we have to note the extent to which the narratives in 1 and 2 Samuel presuppose what anthropologists refer to as a relationship between gender and 'prestige structures' (Ortner and Whitehead 1981). In most societies, the criteria used to determine a person's prestige include beliefs about gendered behaviour. One's reputation, and hence one's status, can depend in part on the extent to which one acts or fails to act in conformity with culture-bound beliefs about 'manly' or 'womanly' behaviour. When we examine these beliefs carefully, we find that they almost always include assumptions about sexual activity. In many parts of the modern West, for example, it is still commonly assumed that young men will 'naturally' desire frequent sexual activity with women; and, in certain contexts, numerous sexual conquests can increase a young man's prestige in the eyes, especially, of other young men. Such behaviour is viewed positively because of the assumption that the man in question is just 'acting like a real man'. Of course, the consequences of sexual activity with multiple partners are usually quite different for a woman's reputation and status than for a man's. In both cases, however, sexual practice is evaluated in relation to culture-specific assumptions about proper gendered behaviour; and this evaluation affects the prestige that a person is granted by others who share those assumptions.

Although such evaluations often take place at the implicit rather than the explicit level, careful attention to biblical literature allows us to uncover some of the assumptions about gender, sexual activity and prestige that existed in ancient Israel and influenced the writers of such books as 1 and 2 Samuel (Stone 1996). So, for example, it was apparently important for men to avoid too close an association with activities or behaviour thought to be more appropriate for women. Thus, when David delivers a series of curses on the house of his general Joab, one of those curses declares that Joab's house will always have within it men who handle the spindle (2 Sam. 3.29). Such work with a spindle seems to have been associated in Israel with women, and it is therefore considered shameful when carried out by men. In order to grasp the connotations of David's curse, we might imagine, as a very rough parallel, a modern situation in which one man would curse another man by declaring that descendants of the cursed man would always include male 'sissies'. In both the ancient and the modern cases, such a curse presupposes that it is shameful for a man to act in a way that members of a particular culture might imagine to be 'effeminate'.

At the same time, it appears to have been particularly important, in Israel, for kings and other powerful men, not simply to avoid supposedly 'womanly' activities, but also to demonstrate positively that they were, in the words of one anthropologist, 'good at being a man', that is, capable of acting in such a way as to 'foreground' one's 'manhood' in culturally determined ways (Herzfeld 1996: 16). Such 'manly' capabilities apparently included the ability to get and support multiple wives and concubines, and to sire many children, especially sons. Thus, when 2 Samuel 3.2–5 tells us that David at Hebron sired six sons by six different women, this information does not serve simply to give us more background information about David and his home life. It functions rather as an explanation for the fact, noted in 3.1, that David was growing stronger. The text presupposes that its audience (which probably consisted, in the ancient world, mostly of men) will believe that a man who is 'good at being a man', so far as acquiring wives and siring sons is concerned, will probably also be a capable military figure and will garner prestige and support from other Israelite men. It is therefore significant that one of the wives of David mentioned in 2 Samuel 3, Abigail, was formerly the wife of one of David's enemies, Nabal (1 Sam. 25); and it is possible that a second wife of David mentioned here, Ahinoam, is the same Ahinoam who formerly was married to another one of David's enemies, Saul (1 Sam. 14.50), particularly in light of an oracle given to David in 2 Samuel 12 that will be discussed further, below. The vanquishing of David's enemies, and the multiplication of his wives, appear to go together. David's sexual potency is related to, and contributes to, his political and military potency.

Moreover, this representation of David contrasts intentionally with the representation of Saul's son, Ishbaal, in the verses that follow. In Israel as in other ancient Near Eastern nations, men who could afford to do so – and especially kings – sometimes acquired women other than their wives as sexual partners (cf. Marsman 2003). These 'concubines' were in some cases slave women, and in some cases free; but in either case they were, apparently, understood to be members of a man's household and not simply casual partners. Now 2 Samuel 3.6–11 recounts an incident in which Ishbaal confronts Abner over sexual relations with a woman named Rizpah, who had been one of Saul's 'concubines' prior to Saul's death. This confrontation over Saul's concubine is no trivial dispute over a 'personal' matter. Complex issues having to do with the politics of sex, gender and power are again presupposed by the text (cf. Stone 1996: 85–93). In ancient Israel as in many other societies, including some societies still today, men are expected to guard with vigilance the sexual purity of the women of their household (cf. Gilmore 1987). After Saul's death, Ishbaal presumably is understood to have become responsible for assuming this role with respect to the women of his father's household; and Ishbaal's honour and reputation as a man depend upon his ability to fulfil this duty successfully. The narrator never tells us explicitly whether Abner has actually had sexual intercourse with Rizpah, but it is clear that Ishbaal suspects Abner of having done so. If, indeed, Abner has had sexual contact with the concubine of Ishbaal's father without

Ishbaal's consent, this contact will have constituted a usurpation of Ishbaal's authority. Although such usurpation would be, at any time, a serious challenge to Ishbaal's gendered prestige, it takes on additional political connotations at a moment when the gendered prestige of Ishbaal's political rival, David, is also increasing. Ishbaal's future as king of Israel is by no means secure, for at this point in the story dynastic succession by Saul's male descendants is possible but not certain. In order to attract supporters, Ishbaal must therefore show himself to be the sort of leader and man who can garner a positive reputation among those Israelite men who are his potential followers. He can only do so, however, by acting according to the ways in which an Israelite man of power and prestige is expected to act, in the realm of sex and marriage as in other realms. Thus, Ishbaal confronts Abner about Rizpah, a woman for whose sexuality Ishbaal is now expected to have oversight.

Hearing Ishbaal's challenge, however, Abner responds angrily by affirming not simply his previous loyalty to the house of Saul, but also his ability to give to David the throne of Israel, something he now decides to do (3.9–10). In the face of such a response, Ishbaal is silent and afraid (3.11). This is hardly how an Israelite audience would have expected a good king to act. Ironically, then, Ishbaal has, by confronting Abner, lost the very thing that he was trying to establish through that confrontation: recognition of the sort of 'manly' power and authority that is likely to persuade other men to accept him as king. It is therefore not surprising that two of his own captains subsequently turn against Ishbaal and assassinate him (4.1–12).

The recognition that sex, gender and marriage have political connotations in the books of Samuel also helps us to understand the role played in 2 Samuel 3 by Saul's daughter, Michal. When Abner attempts to establish an alliance with David, David asks in return that Abner and Ishbaal bring to him Michal, who by this point has been given to another man named Paltiel, son of Laish. David explicitly reminds Abner that he has previously given Saul either one hundred or two hundred Philistine foreskins as 'brideprice' (cf. 1 Sam. 18.27; Ex. 22.15–16; Deut. 20.7; 22.28–9). In the narration of that earlier incident, of course, David himself had recognized the great honour that would accrue to a man able to acquire as wife, not just any woman, but the daughter of a king (1 Sam. 18.18). Thus, when he asks now for the return of Michal at the beginning of 2 Samuel, David's motives are probably not motives of personal love and affection. Indeed, a subsequent incident in 2 Samuel seems to indicate that the relationship between them has become rather strained (2 Sam. 6.16, 20–3). David, then, asks for the return of Michal in 2 Samuel 3 because he recognizes that, in his quest for political power, the reacquisition of a king's daughter as wife will enhance his own position and prestige.

The relationship between matters of sex and gender, and matters of political power, that we find in 2 Samuel 3 is again apparent in 2 Samuel 5. In the latter chapter, David is first proclaimed king in Hebron and then rules 'over all Israel and Judah' (5.5) from a new capital in Jerusalem. The chapter as a whole is clearly another description of David's increasing power and reputation, including as it does information about public support for David's kingship (5.1–5), military success under David's leadership against the Jebusites and the Philistines (5.6–9, 17–25), and gifts for David from the powerful Phoenician king Hiram (5.11). The narrative sequence functions to illustrate the fact, noted in verse 10, that 'David kept growing stronger, for Yhwh God of Hosts was with him'. In the middle of this narrative, however, we are told that 'David took more concubines and wives in Jerusalem after he came from Hebron, and to David were born sons and daughters' (5.13). This information about David's ability to acquire still more women, and to sire still more children, is not extraneous to the chapter's narration of power and prestige but rather integral to it. David's 'potency' as Yhwh's chosen king is once again a major point of the story.

Already in 1 Samuel and the opening chapters of 2 Samuel, then, we can see that many of the assumptions about sex, gender and marriage presupposed by the book are rather different from assumptions about sex, gender and marriage that are prevalent today in most religious communities that make use of the Bible. The significance of sex and marriage has nothing to do, in 1 and 2 Samuel, with mutual intimacy or companionship. There is in fact no actual word for 'marriage' used in the books of 1 and 2 Samuel at all, or elsewhere in the Hebrew Bible for that matter (cf. Berquist 2002). Rather, women are 'taken' (2 Sam. 5.13) by powerful men such as David, in part because the ability to get multiple wives and concubines, and to sire multiple children (especially sons), is thought to be a sign of power and divine favour, a sign that can be seen by other men and that will, it is hoped, elicit from those other men respect and loyalty.

David, Bathsheba and Uriah

The ability of powerful men to 'take' women is not, however, unlimited in the books of Samuel or elsewhere in the Bible. This fact is apparent in the story of David, Bathsheba and Uriah that begins in 2 Samuel 11. The story opens in the spring when, according to the narrator, kings usually go out to battle. In this particular year, however, David has sent his armies against the Ammonites while remaining at Jerusalem (2 Sam. 11.1). The contrast that the text sets up between the usual practice of kings, and the practice of this king in this year, serves as a hint to the reader that all will not go as it should in the story that follows; and it may raise questions as well about David's continued ability to embody culturally prescribed norms for the 'manly' behaviour considered appropriate for kings.

From his roof, David sees a beautiful woman bathing and enquires about her. Soon he learns that 'This is Bathsheba, daughter of Eliam, wife [literally 'woman'] of Uriah' (2 Sam. 11.3). It is very unusual in the Hebrew Bible to find a woman identified in the same verse as both the daughter of one man and the wife of another. Normally, one of these descriptors will be found but not the other, since in ancient Israel a woman was understood to move at the point of marriage from a position under the authority of her father to a position under the authority of her husband. Commentators have scratched their heads over this double identification, sometimes concluding on the one hand that Eliam must have been a significant figure since he is mentioned unnecessarily, but noting on the other hand that Eliam does not play any clear role elsewhere in the story of David (McCarter 1984: 285). However, the unusual double identification of Bathsheba as both a wife and a daughter may actually serve the literary function of emphasizing the fact that David does not have automatic sexual access to her. Male sexual activity with women was not necessarily restricted, in Israel, to a man's own wives and concubines. Sexual activity with a prostitute, for example, is nowhere forbidden in the biblical laws and seems to be accepted in a number of biblical narratives, in spite of the fact that some prophetic and wisdom texts appear to view prostitutes with suspicion (see Bird 1997a: 197–236; Brenner 1997: 147–51). Yet sexual intercourse between one man and the wife of another man is considered a very serious offence; and, in the case of such intercourse, both partners are, in principle at least, punishable by death. While sexual relations between one man and the unmarried daughter of another Israelite man do not lead to the same punishment, the man who initiates such relations probably was required to pay her father a 'brideprice' and acquire her as a wife (cf. Deut. 22.28–9). Within Israel's system of marriage, the acquisition of another man's daughter normally required negotiations with her father. By specifying that Bathsheba was both a 'wife' and a 'daughter', then, the text underscores the existence of obstacles in the way of David's sexual desire for her.

These obstacles do not stop David, however, who simply 'sent messengers and they took her' (2 Sam. 11.4). Although some commentators (e.g. Hertzberg 1964: 309) have blamed Bathsheba in part for this incident by suggesting that she bathed upon the roof in order to seduce David, it is important to note that nothing is said in the text about Bathsheba's desire or consent. Indeed, the fact that her consent is nowhere recounted contributes to the argument made by some scholars that the story of David and Bathsheba can be read as something like a literary 'rape' (cf. Exum 1993: 170–201). Once she becomes pregnant, however, Bathsheba does inform David of the pregnancy; and at that point in the story David attempts to cover his misdeed.

David first recalls Uriah from the battlefield (where he is fighting the Ammonites as part of David's army), enquires about the situation faced by his army, and then urges Uriah to 'go down to your house and wash your feet' (11.8). David's language is suggestive, for the word 'feet' is in some biblical texts a euphemistic reference to the genitals. Thus, David may be hinting that Uriah should have sexual relations with his wife. Uriah, however, does not go home; and, when David asks him the next day why he has not done so, Uriah replies that so long as the Ark of the Covenant and the army of Israel are camping in the fields he will be unable to go to his house 'to eat and to drink and to lie with my wife' (11.11). Uriah's language is interesting, for it makes use of an association between eating, drinking and sexual relations that also occurs at other points in David's story and elsewhere in the Bible (cf. Stone 2005). Since Uriah will not go home to drink, David himself drinks with Uriah the next day until Uriah gets drunk. David's apparent belief that Uriah is more likely to have sexual intercourse with Bathsheba when Uriah is drunk reflects a link found elsewhere in biblical literature between male drunkenness and sexual activity (see e.g. Gen. 19.30–8). When Uriah still refrains from going home, however, David has to resort to more drastic means in order to cover his crime. He arranges for his army to pull back from Uriah on the battlefield, so that

Uriah is killed. After Bathsheba has mourned for her husband, David has her brought to the palace where she becomes his wife and bears his son.

Yhwh, however, displeased with David's actions, sends the prophet Nathan to tell David a story about a rich man and a poor man. The rich man has many sheep and cattle, but the poor man has only one ewe lamb that 'eats', 'drinks', and 'lies with' him (2 Sam. 12.3). These verbs, notably, are the same verbs used by Uriah earlier when he refuses 'to eat and to drink and to lie with my wife'. According to Nathan's tale, when a traveller visits the rich man, the rich man does not wish to use any of his own sheep and cattle to feed his visitor. Instead, he takes the poor man's ewe lamb and prepares it as food. Although this story angers David, Nathan delivers an oracle from Yhwh which quickly makes it clear that the story is a clever parable about David's own actions vis-à-vis Uriah and Bathsheba. Indeed, the specification by Nathan that the poor man's lamb was 'like a daughter to him' (12.3) may hint at the significance of the parable, for the Hebrew word for 'daughter', *bat*, is also the first element of Bathsheba's name.

Explication of this parable sheds a great deal of light on the assumptions about gender, power and marriage that undergird many biblical texts, including 1 and 2 Samuel. It is significant, for example, that Bathsheba and the wives and concubines of David can all be represented symbolically as food animals; food animals that are owned and stolen by men. While readers of the Bible disagree as to whether or not it is entirely accurate to characterize the position of women in Israel as 'property', it must be acknowledged that even the Ten Commandments group wives together with slaves, cattle and other property as things belonging to one man which another man might wish to acquire (Ex. 20.17). What we find in the Bible, then, is the sort of marriage and kinship system that the anthropologist and queer theorist Gayle Rubin has referred to as 'the traffic in women' (Rubin 1974). Rubin, building on the work of several other anthropologists, has pointed out that marriage and kinship function in many societies as part of a kind of exchange system, in which the circulation of women and other goods among men serves to create, mediate and strengthen alliances among those men. Within such marriage systems, hostile or exploitative relations between men can also be mediated by women, who serve – like animals and other property – as goods over which men bargain, fight and conspire. Studies such as Rubin's shed a great deal of light on biblical literature, which does characterize marriage and alliance in terms of the giving and taking of women among men (see e.g. Gen. 34.8–24; Deut. 7.3; cf. Schwartz 1997: 133–42).

According to the logic of the parable told by Nathan, then, David's sexual contact with Bathsheba amounts to a kind of theft. The victim of this theft is apparently understood by the text to be, not Bathsheba (in spite of the fact that her own consent to David's sexual advances is never narrated), but rather Uriah, the man who has certain 'rights' to Bathsheba's sexuality. Moreover, the fact that David and Uriah are characterized, respectively, as a rich man with many animals and a poor man with only one animal indicates that the theft is seen as particularly bad, not because the thing stolen is another human being, but rather because a man with many resources – that is, many women – is exploiting a man with few resources – that is, only one, much-loved woman.

Significantly, however, the practice of giving and taking women is not itself characterized negatively. In fact, Yhwh, speaking through Nathan, indicates that he (and Yhwh is clearly characterized as a male deity in 1 and 2 Samuel) has himself participated in the male 'traffic in women'. For according to Nathan's oracle, Yhwh previously gave to David 'the house of your master and the wives [or 'women'] of your master' (2 Sam. 12.8). The women that Yhwh has earlier given to David are not identified by name, but in context we apparently have, here, a reference to a wife or wives of Saul, since Saul has been mentioned in the previous verse. The wives in question may well include Ahinoam, referred to above, since she is the one wife of David who shares a name with a wife of Saul (see Levenson 1978; Levenson and Halpern 1980; Hackett 1998). The fact that the women are not named helps us to recognize that their significance in this male-oriented oracle lies primarily in their impact on the male characters who get and take them. But if the identity of the women given to David remains vague here, the characterization of Yhwh as the one who takes women from one man and gives them to another man is clear. Since most readers of the Bible today are, presumably, troubled by the treatment of women as goods that circulate for the benefit or detriment of men, it is unsettling to find that biblical literature represents the God of Israel as participating in this very treatment, at least on certain occasions. Moreover, Yhwh goes on to say through Nathan that, although David had acted secretly with respect to Bathsheba and Uriah, nevertheless now Yhwh 'will take your wives [or 'women'] before your eyes and give them to your neighbour, and he will lie with your wives [or 'women'] before this sun . . . I will do this thing before all Israel and before the sun' (2 Sam. 12.11–12).

The 'taking' of David's women that Yhwh determines to carry out is, as we shall see, a significant part of the 'calamity' or 'distress' that Yhwh also says he is going to raise up from David's 'house' (2 Sam. 12.11). However, the full extent of the 'calamity' that results from David's actions with respect to Bathsheba and Uriah is even greater than this. Already before the end of chapter 12, the son that is produced by David's union with Bathsheba dies; and still more trouble occurs among David's offspring in the very next chapter.

Amnon, Tamar and Absalom

Although, as we have seen, the use of the Hebrew word for 'daughter' in Nathan's parable alludes to the first element of Bathsheba's name, nevertheless this reference to a 'daughter' probably serves also as a link between the story of David, Uriah and Bathsheba in 2 Samuel 11–12, and the story of Amnon, Tamar and Absalom in 2 Samuel 13. For in 2 Samuel 13 Tamar is, like Bathsheba in 2 Samuel 11, made to submit to a man's sexual desires and caught up in a relation between two men that results in the death of one of those men. Whereas chapter 11 is simply silent about Bathsheba's desires or consent, however, chapter 13 makes it clear that Tamar resists the sexual intercourse to which she is forced.

Chapter 13 opens by noting that 'Absalom son of David had a beautiful sister, and her name was Tamar, and Amnon son of David loved her' (2 Sam. 13.1). The fact that Absalom's name appears prior to those of Amnon and Tamar, even though he will not play a role in the story until verse 20, indicates that the text is concerned not simply with the events that transpire between Amnon and Tamar but also with the effect of those events upon Absalom. Tamar, who is Absalom's full sister but only a half-sister to Amnon, functions in this story as a point of conflict between the two half-brothers. Amnon, we are told, 'loves' Tamar but makes himself sick over the fact that, since she is a 'virgin', he cannot have sexual relations with her. At the suggestion of his friend Jonadab, however, Amnon carries out a plot to obtain her sexually. Pretending to be sick, Amnon asks his father David to send Tamar to him to 'prepare two cakes in my sight, and I will eat from her hand' (2 Sam. 13.6). When Tamar, at David's command, arrives at the house of Amnon, the text describes in detail the way in which Amnon watches Tamar while she carries out her task of food preparation. This description sets up another striking association between food and a female sexual object, which may cause the reader to recall that David's sexual relations with Bathsheba have already been represented symbolically, in the previous story, as the turning of a lamb into food. When Amnon sends everyone out of his room and attempts to force Tamar to have sexual relations with him, Tamar protests that 'it is not done thus in Israel' and that Amnon's 'disgraceful' action would bring upon Tamar 'shame' (2 Sam. 13.12–13). Although biblical incest laws rule out sexual relations between a man and the daughter of his father (Lev. 18.9), presumably the 'shame' and 'disgrace' to which Tamar refers do not result from incest; for Tamar indicates that David would give Tamar to Amnon if Amnon asked him to do so (2 Sam. 13.13). The problem seems rather to be that Amnon is forcing a virgin princess to have sexual relations without going through the steps normally required in Israel for a man to obtain a woman from her father.

In any case, Amnon refuses to heed Tamar's objections and goes on to rape her. Once Amnon has done so, however, the narrator tells us that 'the hatred with which he hated her was greater than the love with which he had loved her' (2 Sam. 13.15). When Amnon orders Tamar to leave, she objects by noting that, in sending her away, Amnon is committing a greater misdeed than the one he has already committed by raping her. The logic of this objection may be revealed by Deuteronomy 22.28–9, which tells us that if a man rapes a 'virgin' he is supposed to marry her. While modern readers are rightly unsettled by the notion that a woman would be made, or would be represented as desiring, to marry the man who rapes her, it is important to remember that, in the world of ancient Israel, where a great deal of symbolic weight was placed upon the ideal that a wife should be sexually pure prior to marriage (see Deut. 22.13–21), a woman who had been raped may very well have had a difficult time finding another husband. Indeed, the narrative of 2 Samuel nowhere indicates that Tamar herself was ever later married, implying instead that she remained in the house of her brother Absalom (2 Sam. 13.20).

While David is said to be upset about these events (13.21), it is not David but Absalom who eventually responds to them. Two years after the rape of his sister, Absalom invites Amnon to a sort of sheep-shearing celebration and, when 'the heart of Amnon is merry with wine' (13.28), has Amnon killed. For this act Absalom has to flee to a place called Geshur for three years, apparently to escape the wrath of his father. Although David eventually decides, as a result of intervention by his general Joab and a Wise Woman from Tekoa, to allow Absalom to return to Jerusalem, the rupture between David and Absalom that follows the murder of Amnon is one of a series of events that culminate in the rebellion of Absalom against the reign of his father and, eventually, in Absalom's death.

Among those biblical texts that describe or refer to violence against women, the story of Tamar's rape is unusual in that it actually incorporates a speaking voice and point of view attributed to the female object of violence herself. Because the text not only recounts Tamar's objections but also represents her grief after she has been mistreated by Amnon (13.19), the narrative lends itself to interpretations that underscore the horrific effects of Amnon's actions upon Tamar (see e.g. Trible 1984: 37–63). It is clear, to be sure, that the story of Tamar functions within the overall narrative of 2 Samuel primarily as an illustration of the trouble that Yhwh causes to emerge in David's house and as an explanation for the series of events that lead to Absalom's rebellion. Nevertheless, her story can also be read as a testimonial to those victims of sexual violence, especially women, whose distress goes so often unheard and who struggle, like Tamar, with their own shame (2 Sam. 13.13).

Absalom's 'Public Sex'

Absalom eventually initiates a revolt against his father from the city of Hebron (2 Sam. 15.7–12). The choice of Hebron is ironic; for it was apparently from Hebron that David himself first marched against, and then seized control of, Jerusalem during his own quest for the throne in opposition to the House of Saul (cf. 2 Sam. 5.1–10). Absalom's rebellion seems to attract a good bit of support, for according to one of the characters in 2 Samuel 'the hearts of the Israelites have gone after Absalom' (2 Sam. 15.13). Even one of David's trusted counsellors, named Ahithophel, joins the conspiracy. Thus, David, his officials and the members of his household eventually have to flee the city of Jerusalem. Ten of David's concubines are left behind, however, to look after David's house (15.16).

When Absalom and his followers enter the city of Jerusalem, Absalom asks for advice from Ahithophel. Ahithophel recommends in response that Absalom 'go in to your father's concubines, the ones he left behind to watch over the house, and all Israel will hear that you have made yourself a stench to your father, and the hands of all who are with you will be strengthened' (2 Sam. 16.21). The suggestion to 'go in to your father's concubines' is, in biblical terminology, a recommendation to have intercourse with them. Thus, when the narrator goes on to tell us that 'they put a tent for Absalom on the roof, and Absalom went in to the concubines of his father before the eyes of all Israel' (16.22), we are reading about a very public sexual act. The passage is yet another one of those biblical texts in which male characters use their sexual relations with women to jockey for prestige and power vis-à-vis other male characters. Absalom's sexual activity with the concubines of his father constitutes a sort of message to other male Israelites, in whose eyes Absalom hopes to shame David by demonstrating publicly David's inability to control sexual access to the women of David's household. Within the games and power struggles of manhood, as 'manhood' is understood in the ancient Mediterranean and Near Eastern world, such a demonstration amounts to a kind of symbolic castration. In that respect, in fact, it parallels an earlier instance in 2 Samuel in which another enemy of David, the Ammonite king Hanun, taunts David into military conflict by performing symbolic actions that challenge David's manhood indirectly (2 Sam. 10.1–6). While Hanun's attempt at symbolic castration takes the form of shaving the beard and cutting the skirts of David's representatives, Absalom's attempt takes the form of a demonstration that David is incapable of guarding with vigilance sexual access to the women of his household. Absalom hopes to show thereby that David is not 'good at being a man', and hence not good at being a king, either; but that Absalom is his more powerful superior – and, hence, a more appropriate and 'manly' king of Israel.

Although Absalom eventually fails in this quest for kingship (see 2 Sam. 18.9–17), and although David is elsewhere represented as the chosen king of Israel's god (see e.g. 1 Sam. 16.1–13; 28.17; 2 Sam. 7.8; 12.7), it is important to note that Yhwh is actually the one who causes this incident to take place. As we have already seen, Yhwh, through the prophet Nathan, has not only given multiple women to David prior to this point but has also said explicitly to David, in 2 Samuel 12.11, that 'I will take your women before your eyes and give them to your enemy, and he will lie with your women in the sight of this very sun'. Whereas Yhwh warns David in 12.12 that 'I will do this thing before all Israel and before the sun', the narrator notes in 16.22 that Absalom's sexual relations with David's concubines take place 'before the eyes of all Israel': what Yhwh predicts in chapter 12, Yhwh brings about in chapter 16. Ironically, then, it is Yhwh rather than Absalom who actually initiates something that we might call 'public sex' in 2 Samuel.

It is important to keep texts such as this one in mind when debates take place today around the Bible and sexuality. Very often it is assumed that the Bible tolerates only a rather limited range of types of sexual activities, and that this range corresponds more or less to notions that are still widely held about 'traditional' 'Judaeo-Christian' sexual morality. Members of religious communities that utilize the Bible as a theological resource sometimes conclude that the only sorts of sexual relations of which the god of the Bible could possibly have approved would be sexual relations between a man and a woman in the context of a monogamous marriage. Stories like this one, however, show that such assumptions are inaccurate; and that a surprisingly wide range of sexual activities either receive divine approval (as do both David's collection of multiple wives and Absalom's 'public sex' with the concubines of his father) or are otherwise accepted by the writers of biblical literature (as are both polygyny and prostitution in a number of texts). 'Queer' readers of the Bible who are aware of this fact may be better prepared to reflect on the possibility that contemporary communities of faith which utilize the Bible could once again provide a space for multiple forms of sexual activity – including, perhaps, forms of 'public sex' (cf. Stone 2005: 68–89).

On the other hand, it is important to be clear about the fact that biblical representations of sexual contact such as this one certainly do not provide us with models for contemporary emulation. After all, the women with whom

Absalom has sexual relations never are described as having given their consent. One can quite plausibly conclude that what we have in 2 Samuel 16 is a representation of rape, which is understood within the logic of the narrative of 2 Samuel as having been initiated by God. When considered from that point of view, the story in 2 Samuel 16 is arguably one of the most disturbing texts in the Bible and needs to be evaluated critically on the basis of the fact that it incorporates (as does much of 1 and 2 Samuel) obviously patriarchal notions about the sexual use of women. In this instance, moreover, such views are not simply presupposed by the narrator or held by male human characters, but are projected onto the male divine character, Yhwh. Inasmuch as Yhwh uses the rape of ten women to humiliate, and thereby punish, David, Yhwh seems no more concerned about the actual fate of those women than are Absalom, Ahithophel, or for that matter David (who weeps bitterly over the fate of his son Absalom (2 Sam. 19.1) but simply secludes his ten concubines as widows for the remainder of their lives, avoiding sexual contact with them because, presumably, they are now considered damaged goods (2 Sam. 20.3)).

Such texts require contemporary readers, then, to engage in a kind of double reading. On the one hand, such a reading would use the strangeness of the ancient text as an invitation to interrogate critically some of our own modern assumptions about sex, gender and the Bible. In the case of 2 Samuel 16, for example, and of numerous other texts from 1 and 2 Samuel that also represent sexual activity, such a reading would unsettle the assumption that biblical views on sexual practice (which are in any case multiple and sometimes contradictory) are identical to views on sexual practice espoused by those modern religious readers who claim to be 'biblical'. It would also unsettle the common assumption that such controversial matters as 'public sex' could never find a place within 'Judaeo-Christian' traditions by demonstrating that such matters have a place already within the texts that lie at the roots of those traditions. On the other hand, such a reading would highlight as well the necessity of evaluating critically even so important a text as the Bible, from the point of view of values that are important to us today. Such values ought to include, in this instance, the full and equal humanity of women and the need to prevent sexual violence and coercion. Freed from the illusion that modern sexual ethics can ever be derived in a simplistic, literalistic fashion directly from the biblical text, we may be encouraged to take responsibility for our own ethical positions instead, developing those positions *in dialogue with* the Bible but never hiding our own ethical choices by pretending that such choices have been determined for us in the distant past *by* the Bible.

Rizpah's Challenge to the Powerful

Challenges to David's kingship and authority, such as those launched by his son Absalom and, at a later point, by the 'scoundrel' Sheba son of Bichri (2 Sam. 20.1–2), are all put down successfully in 2 Samuel. It has often been noted, however, that the story of David is told in such a way as to underscore the fact that many of David's Israelite enemies are killed without David himself having to become directly involved in their deaths. Thus Saul, Abner, Ishbaal, Absalom,

Amasa (20.8–10) and Sheba (20.20–2) are all removed as real or potential rivals to the throne of Israel, but David himself does nothing to bring about their deaths. Indeed, he is even represented as mourning the deaths of Saul, Abner and Absalom. The recurrence of such deaths in 2 Samuel, and of the specification that David was not directly responsible for the deaths in question, has led some scholars to suggest that 2 Samuel was written in part as an 'apology' for David, which is attempting to counter the perception of David as a ruthless king who may have been responsible for the murder of his enemies (see e.g. McCarter 1984: 64–5, *passim*; Halpern 2001: 73–103).

There are, however, some individual deaths in 2 Samuel for which David is clearly made responsible, even if someone else does the actual killing. One such death is that of Uriah, which we have already discussed. Another example is found in 2 Samuel 21, in a little-known story that may prove useful for a queer reading. Particular attention needs to be paid in this story to the role played by Rizpah, the concubine of Saul over whom Abner and Ishbaal have earlier quarrelled.

Chapter 21 opens with the report of a famine in Israel that lasts for three years. Responding to an enquiry from David, Yhwh reveals that the famine has been sent because of bloodguilt resulting from an attempt by Saul to exterminate the Gibeonites. The Gibeonites, a non-Israelite people, live in the midst of the Israelites in accordance with a treaty described in Joshua 9. Although Saul's actions or intentions against the Gibeonites are not described outside of 2 Samuel 21, it appears that Yhwh is punishing Israel for the fact that Saul has violated the agreement with the Gibeonites, an agreement to which Israel had sworn 'by Yhwh the god of Israel' (Josh. 9.18). Thus, David determines to act in such a way as to expiate Israel's bloodguilt. While the Gibeonites apparently do not have the same rights to blood vengeance that are accorded to Israelites, David hands over to them two of Saul's sons (whose mother is Rizpah) and five of Saul's grandsons (whose mother is Merab, the daughter of Saul who was at one time promised to David (1 Sam. 18.17–19)). All seven of these members of the House of Saul are executed by the Gibeonites by being impaled 'on the mountain before Yhwh' (2 Sam. 21.9), though Jonathan's son Meribaal is allowed to remain alive (21.7).

If we read this story in a straightforward way, David's motives for handing over the sons and grandsons of Saul to the Gibeonites seem not only acceptable (within the framework of biblical views on bloodguilt) but even divinely approved. It is important to note, however, that once again David's potential rivals to the throne are being eliminated. Though the text attributes no ulterior motives to David, the deaths of Saul's male descendants can only make David's reign more secure. Apart from Meribaal, there are now, so far as we can tell, no other male descendants of Saul left alive. Meribaal, moreover, is himself lame (2 Sam. 4.4; 9.3); and, given the role of military conflict and the likely importance of ideals of 'manly' behaviour and bodily wholeness in the chieftaincy-like form of kingship that we find throughout the books of Samuel (cf. Flanagan 1981), it is rather unlikely that Meribaal will be considered a legitimate contender for the throne. Thus, it is easy to read this chapter with much suspicion about David's actual reasons for bringing about the deaths of the sons and grandsons of Saul.

Rizpah, however, spreads sackcloth on a rock and keeps birds and wild animals away from the bodies of her sons and those of Merab. According to the narrator, she remains there 'from the beginning of the harvest until the water fell on [the bodies] from the sky' (2 Sam. 21.10). Although the precise meaning of this temporal reference is not altogether clear, it is possible that we are to understand here a span of several months, from the spring barley harvest to the rains in November. Thus, her actions on behalf of those she loves are quite remarkable, and are motivated by the biblical assumption – especially clear in the book of Jeremiah for example – that improper burial is horrifying, perhaps shameful, and possibly a result of divine judgement (see e.g. Jer. 7.33; 8.1–2; 9.21; 16.6; 22.18–19; 36.30). In that respect, Rizpah has been compared by some biblical scholars (e.g. Fewell and Gunn 1993: 161) to Antigone, the female character who seeks a proper burial for her brother in the famous Greek tragedy by Sophocles that bears her name.

When David hears about the actions of Rizpah, he not only allows the bones of the seven impaled Saulides to be buried; he also retrieves and buries the bones of Saul and Jonathan, whose bodies had much earlier been desecrated by the Philistines before being taken away and cremated by the inhabitants of Jabesh-gilead (1 Sam. 31.8–13). Only at this point does the text note explicitly that God once again has regard for the supplications of Israel (2 Sam. 21.14). It appears, then, that the actions of Rizpah serve to persuade David to give Saul, Jonathan and Saul's sons and grandsons a proper burial, in the territory of their tribe Benjamin and in the tomb of Saul's father Kish (2 Sam. 21.14). Although Rizpah presumably has relatively little official power and has, instead, been the silent object earlier of quarrels between powerful men, her determination and devotion here inspire – or perhaps shame – the very king who has brought about the deaths of her two sons so that he changes his course of action and treats the bodies of his enemies with honour. While we naturally wish that we knew more about Rizpah than the male-centred text of 1 and 2 Samuel allows us to see, her ability to influence David's actions nevertheless serves as a useful reminder to those who stand outside the channels of official power today that bold and persistent action can sometimes have far-reaching effects, even perhaps changing the behaviour of those who wield significant authority and whose goals and interests appear to be quite far-removed from one's own. Such a reminder is important indeed for queer readers of the Bible.

1 and 2 Kings

KEN STONE

It may seem unlikely at first that the books of 1 and 2 Kings would be of any particular interest to lesbian, gay, bisexual or transgendered readers. Indeed, the presence within the books of Kings of numerous difficult names, obscure historical references and complex formulae for specifying the duration of the reigns of rulers can be daunting obstacles for all but the most committed interpreters of these books. Nevertheless, careful study of the books of Kings has much to offer the queer reader who is concerned, not simply to find supposed biblical references to homosexuality, but also to understand the interrelations between sexual practice and a range of other issues, including religion, politics, marriage and especially ideologies of gender.

Content and Context

The books of Kings claim to narrate the story of Israel from the end of the reign of King David, and the subsequent reign of David's son Solomon, through the respective histories of the two divided kingdoms that result from a split in Israel after Solomon's death. This story continues through the destruction of the northern kingdom of Israel (or Samaria) under the Assyrians in 722/1 BCE and, subsequently, the destruction of the southern kingdom of Judah under the Neo-Babylonians in 587/6 BCE. However, the narration of this story does not take the form of a straightforward reporting of political history. While the reigns of some rulers (such as Solomon, Hezekiah and Josiah) receive a great deal of attention, other rulers are discussed in much less detail or even referred to only in passing. The primary criteria used to determine the amount and types of emphasis given to the reigns of particular rulers are not the conventional criteria of political might and wealth (though attention to such matters is certainly not lacking). Rather, the story of Israel's past that we find in the books of Kings is shaped especially by a particular theological perspective and motivation.

Recognition of this characteristic of the books of Kings played an important role in generating one of the most influential hypotheses to emerge from modern biblical scholarship. In the mid-twentieth century, the German biblical scholar Martin Noth argued that the books of Kings were actually part of a much longer document, consisting of the biblical books of Deuteronomy, Joshua, Judges, 1 and 2 Samuel, and 1 and 2 Kings. Noth referred to these books collectively as the 'Deuteronomistic History' (sometimes referred to as the 'Deuteronomic History') and argued that the present form of these books was due largely to the activity of a single author/editor. Noth called this author/editor the 'Deuteronomist' or, in abbreviated form, 'Dtr' (Noth 1991). While certain passages from the Deuteronomistic History – for example, many of the theological speeches and prayers inserted into the mouths of major characters (e.g. 1 Kings 8.14–9.9) – were attributed by Noth directly to the hand of Dtr, Noth also suggested that Dtr made substantial use of various types of earlier sources, incorporating some of those sources directly into the Deuteronomistic History and weaving the incorporated sources together with Dtr's own compositions. Some of Dtr's sources are referred to in the Deuteronomistic History itself, including for example 'the book of the daily deeds of the kings of Israel' (e.g. 1 Kings 14.19) and 'the book of the daily deeds of the kings of Judah' (e.g. 1 Kings 14.29). Most biblical scholars understand these 'books of daily deeds' to be comparable to the annals or chronicles known to us from the archives of other ancient Near Eastern nations. However, Dtr also appears to have relied upon other types of source material, including oral and written legends about the activities of such prophets as Elijah and Elisha.

While Dtr was, in Noth's opinion, attempting to produce a reliable account of Israel's past, still Dtr did not hesitate to select, modify or even create material in order to construct a relatively coherent story of Israel's past that would also achieve the theological purposes which motivated Dtr to put that account together. In order to identify both those theological motivations and a likely date for Dtr's project, Noth pointed out that the book of 2 Kings – which, according to Noth's interpretation, concludes the Deuteronomistic History as a whole – ends rather abruptly during the Babylonian exile of the former inhabitants of Judah, when the Judahite king Jehoiachin is released from prison and admitted to the presence of the Neo-Babylonian ruler Evil-merodach (2 Kings 25.27–30). As these events took place around 562 BCE, Noth believed that the Deuteronomistic History must have been produced very shortly after that date, during the Babylonian exile. By placing Dtr's work in the time of the exile, Noth was able to come up with a motivation for Dtr's activity. In Noth's view, Dtr wrote the Deuteronomistic History to give a theological account of Israel's past that would explain why and how it came to be that Yhwh's chosen people were defeated and taken into captivity by the great Mesopotamian empires of Assyria and Babylon. Briefly, Dtr argued that Yhwh determined this fate for Israel when its people, and especially its rulers, failed to live up to the obligations of the covenant between Yhwh and Israel that are specified in the book of Deuteronomy. Chief among these obligations was the commandment to worship no other god besides Yhwh (Deut. 5.6–10).

Noth's arguments for an exilic 'Deuteronomistic History' that owes its present form largely to the work of a single author/editor have not gone unchallenged or unmodified. For example, a number of scholars have suggested, since the time of Noth, that an earlier version or 'edition' of the Deuteronomistic History was written prior to the Babylonian exile (probably during the reign of King Josiah described in the book of 2 Kings) and then updated at the time of the exile. Other scholars have proposed that the Deuteronomistic History was actually produced through a series of successive revisions during and after the exile. All of these theories rely, with varying degrees of plausibility, on the reconstruction of hypothetical layers and sources from the material found in the books of the Deuteronomistic History. While such theories need not be adopted uncritically, they do underscore certain features of the books included within the Deuteronomistic History – including the books of Kings – that ought to be kept in mind by readers. The project of narrating Israel's past that we find in the books of Kings should not be mistaken for an objective account of Israelite history, such as a modern historian might attempt to produce. Rather, the story of Israel contained in the books of Kings is part of a larger theological argument that is written to persuade its readers to accept a certain interpretation of Israel's past and of Israel's relationship to its god, Yhwh. The version of this story that is found in our Bibles is a composite work that was put together long after most of the events recounted there are supposed to have taken place. Although some of the characters found in the books of Kings are known to have been real historical figures, other characters and many of the narrated events found in 1 and 2 Kings are derived from traditional and legendary materials utilized as sources by the author or authors. What we find in the books of Kings is therefore a story that moves sometimes closer to, and sometimes further away from, the sort of account of the past that we would recognize today as 'historical'. The primary motivation for this story is in any case not straightforward reporting, but rather theological argument. This motivation helps us to understand why the reigns of several kings of Israel and Judah, including a few kings who appear to have been quite important from a strictly political point of view, are recounted with little attention to detail apart from a verdict about the willingness or (more often) failure of the kings in question to live and rule according to the theological and religious guidelines specified in the book of Deuteronomy. Such theological evaluation is of central importance to Dtr and strongly shapes the story that we find in the books of Kings. It presupposes a rather strict view of divine justice, which assumes that God eventually blesses or curses a people such as the Israelites in accordance with its faithful obedience, and the obedience of its rulers, to covenant stipulations. And, as we shall see, this theological interpretation of Israel's past is structured and communicated rhetorically on the basis of, among other things, ideological assumptions pertaining to sex and gender that need to be examined critically.

But recognition of the theological motivations and ideological presuppositions underlying the structure and arguments of 1 and 2 Kings should not lead us to ignore the heterogeneity that also characterizes these books. Multiple voices do sometimes appear in the books of Kings. Even when a single voice dominates it is possible to read the narrative against the grain in order to uncover dissident points of view and ways of living that must also have existed within ancient Israel. Since 'queer' readers, who have often been asked, or forced, to conform our sexual and gendered lives to particular interpretations of political, social and religious reality, know all too well the importance of acknowledging alternative perspectives and modes of life, we ought to read the books of Kings with special attention to the multiple points of view that can be detected there.

Solomon and the 'Theo-Politics' of Sex

The book of 1 Kings opens near the end of King David's reign and recounts a struggle for the throne of Israel that involves two of David's sons. As an introduction to this struggle we are told in the first chapter that David, now an old man, cannot keep warm. Consequently, his servants locate a beautiful virgin named Abishag who will serve the king by, among other things, lying with him to keep him warm (1 Kings 1.1–3). The narrator specifies, however, that David does not have sexual relations with Abishag (1.4). This observation is more than a statement about David's chastity. Like the writers of many ancient (and modern) texts, the biblical authors expected kings and other prestigious men to be characterized by 'manly' behaviour, that is, behaviour which conformed to certain social and cultural expectations about gender. Power and prestige were more likely to be granted to men who successfully demonstrated such behaviour, not only through such activities as military prowess but also through sexual practice. Thus, in ancient Israel as in other parts of the ancient world, a man's sexual potency and his political power were often interrelated (Stone 1996). A king's power was signified by, among other things, the size of his harem and the ability to sire children (especially sons); and the story of David's rise to power in the books of Samuel is written in such a way as to emphasize the fact that the number of David's wives and sons increased as his power and political significance increased (e.g. 2 Sam. 3.1–5 (see '1 and 2 Samuel' in this volume)). It is clear that the opening chapter of 1 Kings presupposes the narratives about David found in the books of Samuel, including those narratives that do link David's sexual potency to his political potency. Thus, the notation in 2 Kings 1.4 that David does not have sexual relations with Abishag, while perhaps misunderstood by some modern readers as a statement about David's virtue, actually calls attention to the impending end of David's reign by underscoring his inability or disinclination to have sexual intercourse. Physical impotence hints at political impotence. For precisely that reason, David's son Adonijah asserts in the very next verse (1 Kings 1.5) that he will be the next king of Israel. As this incident at the very beginning of 1 Kings indicates, sex, gender and politics are inextricably intertwined throughout the books of Kings; and they frequently are linked to theological matters as well.

However, Adonijah's bid for the throne does not go unchallenged. Encouraged by the prophet Nathan, one of David's wives, Bathsheba, manages to elicit from David a promise that her son Solomon rather than Adonijah will succeed David as king of Israel. Bathsheba's motives are probably not altogether altruistic. The role of 'queen mother' appears to have been one of the most powerful positions available to women in the patriarchal world of Israel and the wider ancient Near East (see Andreasen 1983). Bathsheba can only fill this position if Solomon is named king. The mother of Adonijah, however, is one of David's other wives, Haggith; and if Adonijah is named king, then Haggith rather than Bathsheba will be 'queen mother'. It is at least possible, moreover, that Bathsheba and Nathan rely on deception to achieve their goals. Although Bathsheba tells David that he has previously sworn to her that he will make Solomon king, no such promise from David actually appears in the books of Samuel or Kings prior to this point. Perhaps Bathsheba is taking advantage of the failing memory of an ageing king to advance her own position and that of her son. In any case, her attempt to have Solomon named king is successful.

Solomon initially allows his rival and older half-brother Adonijah to live, though he specifies that Adonijah's continued survival depends upon worthy behaviour (1 Kings 1.52). When Adonijah later is executed at Solomon's command, the circumstances leading to his execution underscore once again the political connotations of sex and marriage. After David's death, Adonijah approaches Bathsheba and asks her to request from Solomon that Abishag be given to Adonijah as a wife. Solomon, as David's successor, has apparently inherited the right to determine the sexual fate of the young virgin formerly associated with his father. However, when Bathsheba does approach her son on Adonijah's behalf, Solomon responds angrily to Bathsheba's request by saying that Bathsheba might as well ask Solomon to give his kingdom to Adonijah and Adonijah's supporters (1 Kings 2.22). Although Adonijah acknowledges explicitly that Yhwh has given the throne to Solomon (1 Kings 2.15), Solomon clearly believes – or pretends to believe – that Adonijah is acting dishonourably here, whether by insinuating himself closer to the throne through marriage to a woman (Abishag) associated with the previous king or by manipulating Solomon's relationship with his mother, who was herself also associated with the previous king. In either case, Adonijah's attempt to secure marriage with Abishag becomes for Solomon an opportunity to have Adonijah killed and to punish two of Adonijah's primary supporters, the priest Abiathar and the general Joab, by demotion and execution respectively. Another potential threat to Solomon's rule, a kinsman of the former king Saul named Shimei who previously has caused problems for David, is also put to death at Solomon's command (1 Kings 2.36–46). Thus, the first two chapters of 1 Kings narrate the process by which Solomon secured his claim to the throne of Israel.

Just after recounting these events, the narrator of 1 Kings notes that Solomon made an alliance with the Pharaoh, or king of Egypt, which was cemented by a marriage to the Pharaoh's daughter (1 Kings 3.1). Although historians question the veracity of this account (e.g. Redford 1992: 311), the report does underscore the political nature of marriage in much of the Hebrew Bible. Whereas marriage is usually understood today as a matter of love and commitment, marriage was in Israel and other parts of the ancient world frequently a means by which men solidified their relations with other male heads of households, specifically by giving and receiving one another's daughters (cf. Gen. 34.9–10). Among kings, such marriages were often an opportunity to solidify ties with other monarchs. In 1 Kings 3, then, the author of Kings is beginning to emphasize the legendary wealth, influence and reputation of Solomon by stating that even so powerful a monarch as the Egyptian Pharaoh found it beneficial to enter into an alliance with him. Whether or not such an alliance is plausible historically, it is consistent with the biblical characterization of Solomon's reign as a period of international co-operation, as evidenced for example by the contributions made by Hiram, king of the important Phoenician city of Tyre, to the temple that Solomon builds for Yhwh in Jerusalem.

Solomon's reputation, however, is based not only on his ability to achieve political alliances with other powerful kings, or on the fact that he builds a magnificent temple for Yhwh, but also on the wisdom that Solomon asks for and receives from Yhwh. This wisdom is illustrated in 1 Kings 3.16–28 by the story of two prostitutes who live together and who come before Solomon so that he can settle a dispute. In the night, one of these women has accidentally caused the death of her infant son and then exchanged her dead child for the living son of the other woman. When Solomon declares that the child will be cut in half and divided among the women, one woman gives her assent to this decision while the other woman prefers to give the child to her rival rather than allow the boy to be killed. Consequently, Solomon is able to discern that the woman who expresses more compassion for the child, even to the point of allowing her rival to keep the infant, is actually the boy's mother.

Although this story may be based on earlier folk traditions, in its present context it obviously functions as a demonstration of Solomon's renowned wisdom. The literary effect of this narrative in ancient Israel almost certainly depended upon the characterization of these two women as prostitutes. However, prostitution holds a somewhat ambiguous status in the Hebrew Bible, which makes that effect rather difficult to gauge (see Bird 1997a: 197–236; Brenner 1997: 147–51). Female prostitution (in the strict sense of sexual intercourse exchanged for some sort of payment) seems to have been tolerated in ancient Israel, as in other parts of the ancient Near East, so long as the woman involved in such an exchange was not living under the authority of a father or husband. Certainly there is little biblical evidence that men who had sexual relations with prostitutes were understood to have committed a crime or a sin, even when such men also had a wife or wives of their own. In the text of 1 Kings 3, the narrator gives no explicit indication that these two women were viewed negatively as a result of being prostitutes, and the mother of the living child is characterized explicitly as compassionate (1 Kings 3.26). On the other hand, female sexuality is frequently viewed with great suspicion by the male authors of the Hebrew Bible; and the Hebrew term that is translated as 'prostitute' in this story actually comes from a verbal root that is often used in the Bible to refer negatively to a range of female sexual activity considered promiscuous or improper, irrespective of whether or not an exchange of payment is involved. When all the evidence is taken into account, then, it appears that, although prostitution was tolerated, prostitutes were themselves sometimes viewed with ambivalence in ancient Israel, as they still often are today, even by the men who purchase their services.

The women in this particular story clearly are living without fathers or husbands and so stand outside the patriarchal social norms cherished by the wisdom tradition that Solomon here represents. In that respect, the situation in which these women find themselves may have been understood by the story's ancient audience as an example of the social chaos inherent in the lives of women who lived outside of the patriarchal family. Since one function of wisdom in the biblical wisdom tradition is to establish order in the face of chaos, the story aims to demonstrate Solomon's wisdom partly by showing his ability to resolve a difficulty that has emerged from the dangerous and chaotic realm of non-normative female sexuality.

It may be useful, though, for us to try to imagine the story, not from the point of view of the wisdom tradition which is making use of the women's status as prostitutes to underscore Solomon's wisdom, but rather from the perspective of women in ancient Israel who were actually prostitutes. While such women may have been viewed with ambivalence, it is quite likely that their motivations for taking up prostitution were in most cases economic. Women who were unmarried and unable to live with male relatives probably had few options available to them for eking out a living. Since the sexual activity of most women was sharply circumscribed by law and by the vigilance of their husbands and male kinsmen, it was precisely those women unattached to men who were most likely to exchange sexual intercourse for payment in order to survive. Ironically, such women may have been able to exercise a certain amount of agency in their day-to-day lives that was unavailable to most other Israelite women. Yet this agency came at the price of a rather precarious existence characterized by an uncertain future. In such circumstances a son was an invaluable asset, since a son could take care of a mother in her old age. This picture of the social context of Israelite prostitution casts the actions of both female characters in a slightly different light. The deceptive prostitute can be understood as acting out of desperation rather than greed, for her survival may depend upon the son she has lost. At the same time, the compassion of the living child's mother is further underscored; for she is willing to give up the son who could provide for her in the future in order to ensure his own survival. Such attention to the socio-economic realities of Israelite prostitution also allows us to see that Solomon is being characterized, in this story, in terms of the traditional ancient Near Eastern and biblical mandate that the wise and good king must ensure justice for those who occupy marginal social positions.

It is striking to note that another major test of Solomon's wisdom in 1 Kings also involves a challenge, though not an explicitly sexual one, from a woman. While the news of Solomon's wisdom brings visitors to his court from many nations (1 Kings 4.34), the foreign visitor who receives the most attention in the narrative is the Queen of Sheba (1 Kings 10.1–13). This queen (who probably comes from the southern Arabian Peninsula (cf. Cogan 2000: 310–11, 315)) is at first sceptical about Solomon's wisdom and attempts to test it with difficult questions. When Solomon successfully answers all of her questions, however, she acknowledges his wisdom explicitly and gives to Solomon large gifts of gold, spices and jewels. Even more significantly, the non-Israelite queen praises Yhwh by name and acknowledges that it is Yhwh who has placed Solomon on the throne 'to do justice and righteousness' (1 Kings 10.9). It is notable, however, that Solomon does not marry the Queen of Sheba, who returns to her own land.

In contrast to this representation in chapter 10 of Solomon's ability to cause a non-Israelite woman to praise the Israelite god, the narrator tells us in chapter 11 how non-Israelite women led Solomon to follow non-Israelite gods. The report that Solomon had seven hundred wives and three hundred concubines coheres with the prediction in Deuteronomy that kings will attempt to have many wives (Deut. 17.17). However, as the story of David shows, multiple wives and concubines were considered permissible and perhaps even commendable for a king (though the staggering quantity of wives attributed to Solomon may be a way of differentiating Solomon from his father). The text of 1 Kings 11 seems not to be concerned so much about the total *number* of Solomon's wives;

but rather emphasizes the fact that Solomon had many *foreign* wives, who lead Solomon in his old age to follow non-Israelite gods. In addition to the Pharaoh's daughter, Solomon is said to have 'loved many foreign women', including Moabites, Ammonites, Edomites, Sidonians (Phoenicians) and Hittites (1 Kings 11.1). Alluding to a passage from Deuteronomy 7.3–4, the text specifies that Solomon loved women from nations with which God had forbidden intermarriage precisely because 'they will turn your hearts after their gods' (1 Kings 11.2). Solomon's own narrated actions then are used to underscore the wisdom of this divine interdiction, for in spite of his close association with Yhwh Solomon is said to have worshipped or built places of worship for the gods of 'all his foreign wives' (1 Kings 11.8), including specifically Phoenician, Ammonite and Moabite gods. In this way Solomon becomes the first of many Israelite kings who, according to the books of Kings, brought disaster upon the Israelites by allowing or encouraging the worship of deities other than Yhwh. In the case of Solomon, who has been explicitly warned about the devastating consequences of following other gods (1 Kings 9.3–9), such disaster takes the form of a division in Israel between the northern and the southern tribes and a decision that Solomon's son will rule only the latter. Yhwh does agree 'for the sake of David your father' (1 Kings 11.12) to wait until after Solomon's death to bring about this division, but already during Solomon's life the northern kingdom is promised to one of Solomon's officials named Jeroboam, a member of the important northern tribe of Ephraim. While the primary cause given for political disaster is Solomon's worship of other gods, the worship of other gods is itself said to have been caused by sexual liaisons upon which the author of Kings frowns. This rather dismal conclusion to the story of Solomon's reign is one of a number of biblical passages that associate religious apostasy and subsequent divine punishment (often in the form of political disaster) with sexual or marital relations between Israelite men and foreign women. Elsewhere in 1 Kings, this association reaches its most complete form in the stories about Jezebel, as we shall see below. However, the book of Nehemiah later refers to Solomon as a negative example when arguing against intermarriage between Jews and 'foreign women' (Neh. 13.23–7).

It is important to remember that the interpretation of Israel's past found in 1 Kings is being made hundreds of years after the time when Solomon is supposed to have lived. Although some scholars have questioned the existence of Solomon as a historical individual (given the lack of attestation to him or his reign in the surviving evidence), most scholars continue to believe that some such person probably did exist (cf. Knoppers 1997). It is clear, however, that the biblical account of his reign in 1 Kings is greatly exaggerated, and represents something like a literary 'golden age', in relation to which the subsequent division and diminution of Israel can be interpreted as divinely willed punishment (cf. Finkelstein and Silberman 2001: 123–45). This golden age is characterized by riches, impressive building projects, political alliances with other nations, a greatly inflated geographical scope for the nation of Israel, a large population and plenty of food and drink. Such a golden age could have been looked back upon simply as a peaceful time of religious, sexual and ethnic pluralism. Instead, a negative perspective on interethnic marriage is being used as a framework within which both Solomon's reign and Israel's subsequent political calamities are interpreted. According to this interpretation, Israel was at one time a mighty nation; but it began to lose its exalted status precisely when its ruler was led astray by sexual partners who are, for ethnic and religious reasons, viewed with suspicion. Queer readers of the Bible, whose sexual and domestic choices are also linked rhetorically by contemporary moralists to divine judgement and political disaster, have good reason to be suspicious of this 'theo-politics' of sex at work in the story of Solomon.

Rehoboam and Jeroboam

Solomon's building projects were not completed without human cost. According to 1 Kings 5.27 (5.13 in English), Solomon subjected the Israelites to 'forced labour'. Chapter 9, by contrast, indicates that Solomon conscripted non-Israelites who were living in the land of Israel into forced labour but allowed Israelites to serve as soldiers and officials (1 Kings 9.15–23). However, the latter picture is contradicted by the narrative of the reign of Solomon's son, Rehoboam; for, according to 1 Kings 12.3–4, 'all the assembly of Israel' came to ask Rehoboam to lighten the 'hard labour' and 'heavy yoke' that Solomon had placed upon them. Whereas chapter 9 states that the Israelites were not themselves subject to Solomon's forced labour, chapters 5 and 12 indicate that they were; and a reference in chapter 11 to the 'hard labour of the house of Joseph' under Solomon suggests the same thing (1 Kings 12.28). Recognition of these sorts of tensions in the text of Kings is important, for such contradictory assessments serve as evidence for both multiple authorship of individual biblical books, and the fact that dissenting perspectives on Israel's past existed already at the time the Bible was being put together.

In response to the demand made by the Israelites, Rehoboam seeks the advice both of the elders who had served his father and of certain younger men who are now serving him. But whereas the elders counsel Rehoboam to respond kindly to the people in order to retain their loyalty, the young men argue that Rehoboam should respond scornfully, letting the people know that 'my little finger is thicker than my father's penis' (1 Kings 12.10 (cf. Brenner 1997: 37; Cogan 2000: 348–9)) and that Rehoboam's own yoke will be even heavier than the yoke of his father. When Rehoboam follows this foolish advice, all of the tribes of Israel except for Judah (Rehoboam's own tribe) and Benjamin break away from Rehoboam's kingdom and form a new nation of Israel under the leadership of Jeroboam. These events constitute the beginning of the period of Israel's story often referred to as 'the divided monarchy', during which the northern kingdom of Israel and the southern kingdom of Judah exist as two separate nations. A major turning-point in the political history of Israel, then, is marked in 1 Kings by a striking instance of sexual rhetoric that plays upon the symbolic association between male genital size and the dynamics of dominance and submission.

Although the division of Israel into two kingdoms and the installation of Jeroboam as ruler in the north are represented in 1 Kings as actions taken by God, nevertheless the subsequent story of Israel found in the books of Kings is clearly told from a point of view more sympathetic to the southern kingdom of Judah than to the northern kingdom of Israel. The narrator gives all of the northern kings a negative evaluation, and the primary reason for that negative perspective is apparent already in the account of Jeroboam's reign. Worrying that worship in the southern Jerusalem temple will lead the northern Israelites to return to Rehoboam for political leadership, Jeroboam makes two calves of gold and sets them up in Bethel and Dan, two towns located respectively toward the southern and the northern borders of the northern kingdom. Jeroboam also participates in additional religious practices that are much disliked by the author(s) of Kings, including worship at so-called 'high places' and the appointment of priests who are not from the tribe of Levites (1 Kings 12.31). As a result of such actions, Jeroboam comes to represent northern apostasy; and a number of subsequent Israelite kings are criticized by the books of Kings for failing to 'turn from the sins of Jeroboam'.

Divine displeasure with Jeroboam and his religious practices is made clear in an oracle delivered during Jeroboam's lifetime against one of the places of worship that he established, specifically, the altar at Bethel. The delivery of this oracle in 1 Kings also becomes the occasion for one of the strangest stories in the entire Hebrew Bible. According to 1 Kings 13, an anonymous prophet from Judah referred to as a 'man of God' is sent to Bethel while Jeroboam is offering incense there. This man of God predicts the destruction of the Bethel altar by the much later Judahite king, Josiah (cf. 2 Kings 23.15–18). When Jeroboam invites the man of God to eat with him, the man of God replies that Yhwh has forbidden him from eating food or drinking water on his journey, or from returning to Judah by the same route on which he travelled initially. However, an 'old prophet' from Bethel also invites the man of God to come home and eat with him. After the man of God explains again what Yhwh has forbidden, the old prophet retorts that he, too, is a prophet; and that 'an angel told me by the word of Yhwh, "Bring him to your house so that he will eat bread and drink water"' (1 Kings 13.18). The narrator states explicitly, for the benefit of the reader, that the old prophet is lying. Once the man of God gets to the old prophet's house and eats and drinks, however, the word of Yhwh comes to that same old prophet, who announces that the body of the man of God won't make it back to the man of God's ancestral tomb since he has disobeyed Yhwh's commandment. When the man of God nevertheless sets out for Judah on a donkey belonging to the old prophet, a lion kills the man of God on his journey. Following a rather bizarre scene in which both the lion and the donkey continue to stand alongside the body of the man of God, the old prophet retrieves the man of God's body, brings it to the old prophet's own home in Bethel, and places it in the grave of the old prophet. After mourning the death of the man of God, the old prophet commands his sons to bury his own bones with those of the man of God since the man of God's prophecy against the northern altar will surely come to pass.

This very unusual story is striking for the way in which it departs from many preconceptions about theological and moral coherence. The man of God who initially delivers an oracle for Yhwh is killed for disobedience in spite of the fact that he is misled by another prophet and apparently assumes that that prophet does speak for Yhwh. The lying prophet, on the other hand, does eventually deliver Yhwh's oracle of judgement to the man of God and then mourns for the very person whose death has been brought about by the prophet's own lies. Like a number of other incidents from the books of Samuel and Kings, the story has an almost folktale-like atmosphere about it. It stands alongside other stories from the books of Kings that are difficult to reconcile with modern theological orthodoxies, including for example stories of a prophet who sends bears to maul boys who are making fun of the prophet's baldness (2 Kings 2.23–5), prophets who prophesy falsely because Yhwh has put a lying spirit in their mouths (1 Kings 22.23), and a disciple of the prophets who orders another disciple to strike him and causes a lion to kill the second disciple when the latter disciple refuses (1 Kings 20.35–6). Most scholars believe that such tales, which frequently involve prophets, originated from oral legends much older than the literary documents in which the stories now appear (see e.g. Long 1984: 150–1). In its present context, however, the story of the man of God and the old prophet functions to underscore divine displeasure with the places of worship built in the northern kingdom.

Although the books of Kings take an especially dim view of the northern kingdom of Israel and of its kings, the southern kingdom of Judah and many of its rulers also receive negative evaluations for adopting religious practices deemed unacceptable by the Deuteronomistic narrator. Already in the account of Rehoboam's reign, we are told about a number of religious phenomena adopted in Judah that the narrator considers unacceptable (1 Kings 14.22–4). Two of these phenomena in particular bear closer examination by readers interested in biblical approaches to gender and sexuality.

Goddesses and *Qedeshim*

The books of Kings oppose Israelite worship of all deities other than Yhwh. Indeed, it is part of the argument of 1 and 2 Kings that Yhwh brought about the destruction of the kingdoms of Israel and Judah by, respectively, the Assyrians and Babylonians, in order to punish the Israelites for worshipping such deities. Our contemporary knowledge of the deities in question has been greatly enhanced by the study of non-biblical evidence from the ancient Near East, such as the important collection of texts discovered in the remains of the ancient Syrian city of Ugarit. Among the gods referred to in 1 and 2 Kings, the one known best by most readers of the Bible is certainly the male deity Baal, whose worship is opposed by numerous biblical texts including, in particular, the prophetic books of Hosea and Jeremiah. Opposition to Baal in the books of Kings is clear especially from the narratives that concern the northern prophets Elijah and Elisha. However, Baal worship is practised in the books of Kings not only by northern kings such as Ahab and Ahaziah, but also by the southern king Manasseh. The severity of the threat of Baal worship in the eyes of the biblical writers may result in part from the fact that very similar functions were attributed to Baal and Yhwh by their respective adherents. For example, both Baal and Yhwh were storm gods credited with control of the rainfall and of the fertility of the land that results from that rainfall. Numerous biblical poems use vocabulary and images to speak about Yhwh that are quite similar to, or even identical with, the phrases and images applied to Baal in other ancient Near Eastern texts. In addition to Baal, the books of Kings refer to Israelite worship of such male gods as the Moabite deity, Chemosh, and the Ammonite deity, Milcom, who are frequently mentioned together (e.g. 1 Kings 11.5, 33; 2 Kings 23.13); and the god Molech, whose worship seems to be associated by the biblical writers with child sacrifice (2 Kings 16.3; 21.6; 23.10).

However, the books of Kings and a number of other biblical texts also refer to goddesses who were worshipped in Israel. These goddesses include Astarte, a deity associated in the Bible with the Phoenicians (1 Kings 11.5, 33; 2 Kings 23.13) but well-known also from the Ugaritic literature and related linguistically to the famous Mesopotamian goddess, Ishtar. Still more important for an understanding of biblical literature and Israelite religion, however, is the goddess Asherah (see Olyan 1988; Binger 1997; Hadley 2000). The Hebrew word 'asherah appears quite a number of times in the books of Kings. In some of these instances, the word refers to the goddess Asherah who is also known to us from Ugaritic texts. So, for example, we read about an object made for Asherah by Maacah, the mother of Asa king of Judah (1 Kings 15.13); and about four hundred prophets of Asherah who eat at Jezebel's table along with four hundred and fifty prophets of Baal (1 Kings 18.19). Although in these two instances Asherah is associated with queens, King Manasseh of Judah also makes an image of Asherah and places it in the Jerusalem temple (1 Kings 21.7). In other instances, however, where the Israelites are said to have made or built 'asherim (e.g. 1 Kings 14.15, 23; 2 Kings 17.10), the reference appears to be to a cultic object other than an image, perhaps a sacred pole of some sort. These objects were probably associated initially with the worship of Asherah, though some scholars argue that the presence of these sacred poles does not necessarily imply the worship of the goddess herself and that such objects could also be used in the context of the worship of Yahweh. In any case, the author of 1 and 2 Kings clearly takes a negative view of both the goddess and the sacred poles. Yet the argument of the books of Kings itself testifies to the fact that Israelite religion included the worship of Asherah, for the recurrence of such worship is one of the pieces of evidence that the author uses to explain why Yhwh was angry enough with the Israelites to bring about the destruction of Israel and Judah.

Our understanding of the worship of Asherah has been increased, but also complicated, by archaeological finds. At two different sites, excavators have discovered inscriptions that include references to Yhwh and 'his asherah'. Scholars have been unable to reach a consensus about the best understanding of these inscriptions. While some scholars argue that the inscriptions refer only to cultic objects such as those mentioned in some biblical texts, other scholars argue that the inscriptions understand the goddess Asherah to be the consort or sexual partner of Yhwh (e.g. Dever 1990: 140–9). Though the latter interpretation certainly goes against the religious sensibilities of many people of faith, it is important to note that Asherah was, outside of the Bible, clearly a sexual partner of the great god, El. The name 'El' is applied in the Bible to Israel's god, and various features of El that we find in extra-biblical sources correspond to biblical representations of the divine. Thus, the Israelites appear to have identified Yhwh early on with El and to have assimilated many of El's characteristics to Yhwh. The relationship between Yhwh and Asherah needs to be understood in the light of this association between Yhwh and El. When all of the evidence is taken together, it is not at all unreasonable to conclude that at least some of those Israelites whose views are opposed by the books of Kings understood Asherah to be the sexual partner of the male Israelite god, Yhwh, just as certain Ugaritic texts understand her to be the mistress of El.

In addition to the worship of gods and goddesses other than Yahweh, a number of other religious phenomena that existed in ancient Israel are referred to negatively by the books of Kings. One of these phenomena has received a great deal of attention from scholars interested in biblical views on gender and sexuality. Several passages from the books of Kings tell how various kings in Judah either tolerated or expelled from the land certain figures referred to as *Qedeshim* (1 Kings 14.24; 15.12; 22.47; 2 Kings 23.7). In English translations of Kings, the words referring to these figures are rendered as 'male temple prostitutes' (NRSV), 'male prostitutes' (NJPS) or even 'Sodomites' (AV). The same Hebrew terminology appears in Deuteronomy and Job, and feminine forms of the word appear in Genesis, Deuteronomy and Hosea (where they are rendered by English translators as 'temple prostitute' (NRSV) or 'cult prostitute' (NJPS)). None of these translations is literal, however, and all of them cover up an important question of interpretation.

The word *Qedeshim* (singular *Qadesh*) comes from a Hebrew root that is very common in the Bible, and its general range of meaning is not at all difficult to translate. The root literally refers to things that are holy or sacred, and so a very literal translation of *Qedeshim* would be, simply, 'holy persons', 'sacred persons', or 'consecrated persons'. The question that confronts interpreters, however, is whether it is possible to know more about the function of these religious professionals so as to understand why the books of Kings find them so distasteful. Unfortunately, the books of Kings do not give us any answer to this question, and it is impossible to reach a conclusion from the contexts of those passages in Kings in which *Qedeshim* appear.

Now it has long been argued that both the *Qedeshim*, who are referred to in the books of Kings, and their female counterparts the *Qedeshot* (singular *Qedeshah*), who do not appear in Kings but are referred to in a handful of other biblical passages, participated in sexual intercourse with men either as a religious act that was thought to contribute to the fertility of the land or as a form of prostitution that raised money for the temple or in order to fulfil a religious vow. This conclusion was based in part on three biblical passages outside of Kings where the *Qedeshim* or *Qedeshot* are referred to in passages that also refer in some way to prostitutes or to female sexual promiscuity. Scholars who support such a conclusion have also appealed to certain ancient texts written in Greek or Latin which claim that adherents of particular deities, especially in Western Asia, sometimes functioned as prostitutes or participated otherwise in religious sexual intercourse. Based on the popularity of this way of understanding the function of the *Qedeshim*, Christian advocates for lesbians and gay men have sometimes argued that biblical texts which forbid male homosexual intercourse (e.g. Lev. 18.22; 20.13) may actually have been written to oppose intercourse between Israelite men and the *Qedeshim*, and so are irrelevant to modern debates about other forms of homosexual contact.

However, these arguments, though often made out of gay-friendly motives, are problematic in several respects. The Semitic root underlying the words *Qedeshim* and *Qedeshot* does not itself have any sexual connotation whatsoever, either in its biblical occurrences or in non-biblical ancient Near Eastern texts where cognate forms of the word appear in other Semitic languages. When the cognate terms are used outside of the Bible to refer to religious professionals, moreover, there is no hint that sexual relations formed any part of the duties of these professionals. Two biblical passages (Deut. 23.18; Hos. 4.14) of the three that seem to associate the *Qedeshim* or *Qedeshot* with prostitution do so in a context that is clearly polemical, and probably reflect nothing more than the tendency, common among the biblical writers, of using prostitution and sexual promiscuity metaphorically to symbolize detested religious practices. A somewhat more difficult case involves Tamar, the daughter-in-law of Judah, who is referred to by others in the book of Genesis as both a 'prostitute' and a *Qedeshah* (Gen. 38.21–2). The association of Tamar with both of these words is taken by some readers to be evidence that the *Qedeshah* had some sexual function. Since the ancient Near Eastern evidence does not give us any plausible reason to identify the functions of *Qedeshim* and *Qedeshot* with sexual activity, however; and since no other biblical passage unambiguously makes such an identification either, the passage in Genesis is itself the text most in need of an explanation. Although a full consideration of that passage is impossible here, several recent interpretations demonstrate that it is not necessary to understand the role of a *Qedeshah* in a sexual fashion in order to make sense of the story of Tamar (see e.g. Westenholz 1989; Frymer-Kensky 2002: 264–77). There are even fewer reasons to conclude that the *Qedeshim* so disliked by the author of Kings participated in sexual activity as part of their religious activity. Indeed, the only conclusion that we can draw from Kings about the *Qedeshim*, apart from the fact that they are religious functionaries who are evaluated negatively by the Deuteronomistic narrator, is that they may have been associated at some point with women who participated in weaving as part of their devotion to Asherah (2 Kings 23.7); and even this association appears in an obscure passage from which historical conclusions are difficult to draw (see Bird 1997b).

The older view that *Qedeshim* and *Qedeshot* were 'cult prostitutes' is actually a by-product of the attempt by some readers of the Bible to make an absolute distinction between Yahwistic religion and so-called 'fertility religions', which are often said to have been practised among Israel's neighbours. However, many of the notions about ancient 'fertility religions' that were held by older generations of scholars are now considered dubious, including the idea of widespread cultic sexual intercourse. While the phrase 'fertility religion' is still sometimes thrown about, it produces more confusion than clarity when it is used either to understand the details of ancient religious practices and beliefs or to compare biblical religion with the religions of Israel's neighbours. Indeed, careful attention to the evidence for ancient Near Eastern religions, as well as to the biblical texts themselves, reveals that Yahwistic religion was itself a kind of 'fertility religion', in the sense that the worshippers of Yhwh attributed to him the very same gifts of fertility – rain, agricultural produce, childbirth – that the worshippers of other ancient Near Eastern deities such as Baal attributed to their gods (see Hackett 1989; cf. Stone 2005: 57–67, 111–28).

Moreover, when readers of the books of Kings encounter references in the text to goddesses, *Qedeshim*, and other unorthodox religious phenomena, it is important to reflect carefully on the fact that the books of Kings as we have them are engaged in a polemic against alternative religious points of view. By arguing so vehemently against these alternatives, the books of Kings demonstrate that the actual practice of Israelite religion was much more diverse than the orthodox vision promoted by the biblical writers (cf. Ackerman 1992), just as the actual practices of Judaism and Christianity today are much more diverse than proponents of certain orthodox versions would prefer. Yet our ability to reconstruct the range of religious practices found in ancient Israel is hampered by the fact that our primary evidence – the Bible – is intolerant of many of those practices. Lesbians, gay men, bisexuals and transgendered persons are only too aware of the dangers that can result from accepting uncritically a picture of particular practices and people that comes from someone opposing the practices and people in question. So also we must be cautious about the conclusions that we reach while reading accounts of Israelite religious pluralism produced by opponents of that pluralism, including the accounts found in 1 and 2 Kings.

Jezebel

Among those figures associated with the religious pluralism that is opposed by 1 and 2 Kings, few have been more strongly vilified, in both the biblical texts and later interpretations of those texts, than Jezebel. Like the foreign wives of Solomon, Jezebel, a Phoenician, is blamed explicitly by the narrator of the books of Kings for causing her Israelite husband to do evil (e.g. 1 Kings 21.25). Yet Jezebel's bad reputation has long outlasted the reputations of most other characters in 1 and 2 Kings. Still today, in much of Western culture, the name 'Jezebel' is synonymous with female evil; and it often carries strongly sexualized connotations that exceed even the negative portrait of her found in the Hebrew Bible (see Pippin 1994).

According to 1 Kings 16.31, Jezebel was a daughter of the Phoenician king Ethbaal, and wife of the northern Israelite king Ahab, who inherited the throne of Israel from his father Omri. Jezebel's father-in-law, Omri, seems to have been, historically, one of the most important kings Israel ever had; and he deserves more attention than he is normally given by readers of the Bible or the Bible itself. In distinction from such biblical heroes as David and Solomon, Omri is referred to in non-biblical sources that testify to the impression he and his dynasty made on other ancient Near Eastern rulers. An important inscription from Moab known as the Mesha Stele tells of military successes that Omri had over the Moabites, and Assyrian inscriptions continued to refer to Israel as the 'land of Omri' after Omri himself was dead. The books of Kings, however, are not particularly interested in Omri's power and influence but rather stress his wickedness, claiming that he was more evil than all the kings who came before him (1 Kings 16.25). Few details are given about this wickedness, though the claim that Omri 'walked in all the ways of Jeroboam' (1 Kings 16.26) probably indicates that worship continued at the cultic sites of

Bethel and Dan under Omri. However, the narrator of 1 Kings does refer to the city of Samaria built by Omri (1 Kings 16.24) and claims that, after Omri's death, his son Ahab built a temple in Samaria for Baal. Archaeological excavations have confirmed not only the existence of Samaria but also that the fact that it was, relative to the standards of its time and geographical location, an important and wealthy city. It is also clear from the remains of Samaria that the Phoenicians influenced the Israelites in such matters as architecture. The marriage of Ahab the Israelite and Jezebel the Phoenician probably should be understood as evidence of a strengthening of political alliances between the Israelites and the Phoenicians. But while good relations between Israelite and Phoenician kings are referred to without any negative connotation as far back as the time of David (2 Sam. 5.11), the story of Jezebel has the effect of casting Phoenician influence on Israel in a negative light by stressing the evil nature of Jezebel's impact on both socio-political and religious matters during her husband's reign.

Jezebel appears in the books of Kings primarily in those sections of the book that focus on the prophets Elijah and Elisha. Some of the references to Jezebel are brief but nevertheless emphasize her wickedness. So, for example, an account in 1 Kings 18 of Elijah's dealings with a servant of Ahab named Obadiah refers in passing to a time 'when Jezebel was killing the prophets of Yhwh' (1 Kings 18.13; cf. 18.4). Jezebel is said to have supported four hundred and fifty prophets of Baal and four hundred prophets of Asherah (1 Kings 18.19), and after Elijah slaughters the prophets of Baal he is forced to flee when Jezebel threatens to take his life (1 Kings 19.1–3). Such passages represent Jezebel largely as a religious zealot, comparable to Elijah himself in both her devotion to particular gods and her hostility toward the prophets of other gods. Since Jezebel worships Baal and Asherah rather than Yhwh, however, the Yahwistic author of Kings casts Jezebel's religious intolerance in a negative light, whereas the religious intolerance of Elijah is viewed positively.

But if numerous passages refer to Jezebel's religious zeal, 1 Kings 21 concentrates instead on her great political influence. This famous story concerns Naboth the Jezreelite, who owns a vineyard that sits beside one of Ahab's palaces. When Ahab offers to buy Naboth's vineyard, Naboth turns down the offer on the grounds that he has inherited the land from his fathers. In an amusing scene, Ahab, 'sullen and vexed . . . lay down on his bed and turned away his face and did not eat food' (1 Kings 21.4). This representation of Ahab as a pouting and rather passive king contrasts with the picture of Jezebel in the same story as an active and determined character, capable of achieving her goals. Hearing the reason for Ahab's dejected behaviour, Jezebel admonishes Ahab to 'exercise kingship over Israel', orders him to 'get up, eat bread,' and assures him that she will get Naboth's vineyard (1 Kings 21.7). By writing letters in Ahab's name and sealing them with his seal, she is able to cause the officials in Naboth's town to bring false charges against Naboth and have him stoned.

On one level, this story is a stinging indictment of the ways in which those with political power manipulate the judicial process for their own gain and exploit those with less power. In that respect, the relevance of the story has not diminished over the centuries. Yet the story itself is also structured in such a way as to manipulate its readers by playing upon gender stereotypes. Against the widespread assumption, common in the ancient world and not unknown even today, that men are properly active and women properly passive, the narrative represents Jezebel as an active character and her husband Ahab as a passive one. The negative characterization of both Jezebel and Ahab is thus achieved and heightened through a sort of gender reversal. Ahab becomes a weak and 'unmanly' figure who consequently is unable to 'exercise kingship' in an appropriate fashion, whereas Jezebel becomes a strong and manipulative figure who usurps her husband's political position in order to accomplish misdeeds that are both religious and socio-economic in nature. Ahab in fact comes to regret the actions taken against Naboth (1 Kings 21.27), whereas nothing comparable is said about Jezebel. Rather, Jezebel is blamed explicitly for instigating Ahab's evil actions (1 Kings 21.25).

The story of Jezebel's role in the matter of Naboth and his vineyard reveals an awareness that at least some women could wield considerable power and influence even in the patriarchal world of Israel and the ancient Near East, though perhaps only under extraordinary circumstances. Yet such female power and influence are represented quite negatively in this story. Recently it has been argued, on the basis in part of linguistic evidence, that the story of Naboth's vineyard in 1 Kings 21 may actually have been written much later than was previously believed, during the post-exilic Persian period of Judah's history (Rofé 1988). If this suggestion is correct, then the characterization of Jezebel as an evil foreign woman who led her Israelite husband into wickedness may have been intended to address a particular socio-historical context. It is clear from a number of biblical books that the matter of intermarriage between foreign women and the men of Judah was a source of much controversy in Persian-period Judah. The representation of Jezebel as an especially evil foreign woman, who led her Israelite husband Ahab into idolatry and other forms of wickedness such as the murder of Naboth and the theft of his vineyard, may have been written in part to dissuade the men of Judah from taking foreign wives (cf. Camp 1998a: 110).

Today Jezebel's negative reputation often has connotations that are more sexual than religious or socio-economic. To refer to a woman as a 'Jezebel', in the contemporary world, is to speak negatively about her ability to manipulate men through sexual means. Yet this understanding of Jezebel's wickedness has a very weak foundation in the biblical texts, where the emphasis in almost entirely on her religious and socio-political deeds. The sexualizing of Jezebel's bad reputation may have its origins, in part, in words attributed to Jehu, the military commander who is anointed by Elisha after Ahab's death to exterminate Ahab's dynasty and take the throne of northern Israel. Before killing Ahab's son King Joram (or Jehoram), Jehu speaks to Joram about 'the whoredoms of Jezebel your mother and her many sorceries' (2 Kings 9.22). In fact the word 'whoredoms' in this passage is probably a metaphorical reference to Jezebel's support for the worship of Baal and Asherah, grounded in the prophetic tradition of speaking about Israel's religious infidelity in the symbolic language of female sexual infidelity. However, more literal interpretations of this reference to 'whoredoms' may have contributed to Jezebel's subsequent reputation as a sexual seductress. Already in the New Testament book of

Revelation we find an association between Jezebel and 'fornication' that may involve a more literal understanding of Jezebel's reputation for 'whoredoms' (Rev. 2.20–3). While this reputation far surpasses any foundation for it in the Hebrew Bible itself, the biblical tendency to conflate religious apostasy and female sexuality certainly contributes to the sexualizing of Jezebel's misdeeds that seems to have taken place among later readers of the Bible.

This sexualizing of Jezebel's character may also build upon a certain interpretation of the biblical description of Jezebel's death. When Jezebel learns that Jehu has arrived in Jezreel, she paints her eyes with a black powder and fixes her hair before looking out of the window to speak to him (2 Kings 9.30). These actions have sometimes been construed by readers as evidence that Jezebel intends to allure Jehu sexually. Such an interpretation is implausible in the context of the story as a whole, however, since Jezebel immediately insults Jehu by associating him with an earlier usurper of the Israelite throne named Zimri, who was only able to hold the throne for seven days before committing suicide when faced with the forces of Jezebel's father-in-law Omri (cf. 1 Kings 16.8–20). Far from attempting to seduce Jehu, Jezebel, dressed in royal finery appropriate for a queen mother (cf. 2 Kings 10.13), is demonstrating her 'self-assurance and courage' (Cogan and Tadmor 1988: 112; cf. Camp 1998a: 110; Long 1991: 129; Cohn 2000: 70), taunting Jehu defiantly by suggesting that his coup d'état will ultimately fail. At Jehu's command, however, several eunuchs throw Jezebel down to Jehu where she is trampled by Jehu's horses. When Jehu, after eating and drinking, gives orders to bury Jezebel, those who proceed to carry out the task find that dogs have eaten all of her body except for her skull, feet and hands, in accordance with a prophecy made earlier by Elijah (2 Kings 9.10). In the context of 1 and 2 Kings, the brutal end of Jezebel serves as a kind of warning to those Israelites or Judahites who may have been tempted to step outside the boundaries of the version of exclusive Yahwism promoted by the Deuteronomistic tradition. The subsequent sexualizing of Jezebel's reputation, however, serves as an important reminder to us of the widespread tendency to conflate wickedness and sexuality, a tendency that has roots already in the Hebrew Bible but is carried much further in the later development of Judaism and especially Christianity.

The Widow of Zarephath and the Woman of Shunem

Jezebel is not the only female character who plays a significant role in the cycle of stories that centre on Elijah and Elisha. Already in 1 Kings 17, in the same chapter in which the reader of Kings is first introduced to Elijah, we read about a widow living in the Phoenician town of Zarephath who, though nearly without food herself, supports Elijah with food and water. This narrative incident follows immediately after the account of Elijah's being fed by ravens (1 Kings 17.6), and is one of a number of tales from the books of Kings that deal with miraculous feeding. In this case, the Widow of Zarephath's jar of meal and jug of oil do not go empty though she continues to feed Elijah long after her supplies should normally have been depleted. It is not surprising to find that this Widow of Zarephath initially has little food and is preparing for the death of herself and her son (1 Kings 17.12), for widows were in Israel and throughout the ancient Near East recognized as a vulnerable class (see Hiebert 1989). In a time of drought and famine such as we find in this section of the books of Kings (cf. 1 Kings 18.1–2), widows would almost certainly be among the first persons affected. However, the fact that Elijah is fed by both ravens and widows in chapter 17 may not be accidental. Elsewhere in the Hebrew Bible, Yhwh is characterized explicitly as one who feeds young ravens when they cry out for food (Ps. 147.9; Job 38.41). So, too, Yhwh, who 'gives food to the hungry', is the one who 'restores' widows (Ps. 146.7, 9). Thus, the narrative of 1 Kings 17 seems to underscore the fact that Yhwh miraculously causes Elijah to be fed by some of those very figures – ravens and widows – who are, themselves, normally dependent upon Yhwh for food. When this same widow's son subsequently becomes deathly ill, Elijah revives the boy by stretching himself upon the boy's body three times and pleading with God for the boy's life.

Some of the motifs found in the story of Elijah and the Widow of Zarephath in 1 Kings recur in 2 Kings in connection with Elijah's successor, Elisha. In 2 Kings 4.1–7, for example, two children of a prophet's widow are saved from debt slavery when Elisha causes large supplies of oil to be produced miraculously out of a single jug so that the widow can sell oil and pay off her debts. This brief narrative incident clearly makes use of the motif of a widow's miraculously bountiful supplies of oil, which appears first in the tale of Elijah and the Widow of Zarephath.

Still other motifs from that earlier tale are found in the much more striking story of the Shunammite woman, which follows immediately after the incident involving the prophet's widow. The Shunammite woman is referred to in the text as a 'great woman' (2 Kings 4.8), which probably is a way of indicating her wealth. Like the Widow of Zarephath, this woman from Shunem supplies food to a prophet. She is not a widow, however; but she is far more active and insightful in the text than is the man referred to simply as 'her husband' (2 Kings 4.9). It is she who proposes that a room be built on the roof of their house so that Elisha can stay with them. Although the woman is old and has no son, Elisha causes her to conceive in return for her hospitality. Like Abraham and Sarah, then, the Shunammite woman receives a son under miraculous circumstances in exchange for the food provided to a messenger of God (cf. Gen. 18.1–15). When this son subsequently dies, the Shunammite woman sets out to find Elisha in spite of discouragement from her husband. While Elisha initially sends his servant Gehazi to the woman's house under the mistaken impression that Gehazi will be able to revive her son, the woman insists all along that she will not return home without Elisha himself. Eventually her determination pays off and Elisha returns to the woman's house. In a rather strange scene, Elisha lies upon the boy, placing his own mouth on the boy's mouth, his eyes on the boy's eyes, and his hands on the boy's hands until the boy becomes warm. Eventually the boy returns to life, sneezing seven times and then opening his eyes before Elisha calls his mother into the room.

The story of the Shunammite woman continues in 2 Kings 8, where we learn that she and her household left the land of Israel at Elisha's command in order to avoid a seven-year famine sent by God. After seven years have passed, the woman returns from the land of the Philistines just as Gehazi is telling an unnamed King of Israel (usually assumed to be Jehoram) about Elisha's miraculous resuscitation of her son. In response to complaints made by the woman concerning 'her house and her field', the king gives her a eunuch and commands that 'all which is hers' be returned to her along with the revenue produced by her field from the time she left Israel (2 Kings 8.5–6). Remarkably, this language seems to indicate that the Shunammite woman rather than her husband is the owner of their property. Indeed, her husband is not mentioned in this chapter at all, yet the text gives no indication that her son has inherited property from his father. While the allotment of property to women is not completely unknown in the Hebrew Bible (cf. Num. 27.1–11; 36.1–12; Judg. 1.12–15), it is rarely mentioned. Whether this woman's story hints that female ownership may have been more common in Israel than the biblical texts indicate, or whether it simply offers us a picture of an exceptional case, the narrative representation of the Woman of Shunem stands in some tension with the assumptions about gender, household and property that we most often find in the Hebrew Bible.

It is interesting to compare and contrast the Widow of Zarephath and the Woman of Shunem with Jezebel. The story of the Widow of Zarephath shows that Phoenician women are not automatically reduced in the books of Kings, as is the Phoenician princess Jezebel, to symbols of wickedness. Like the Queen of Sheba, the Widow of Zarephath acknowledges Yhwh explicitly (1 Kings 17.24); and this acknowledgement, together with her acts of hospitality, serve to characterize her positively within the Yahwistic perspective promoted in the books of Kings, in spite of the fact that she is not an Israelite. So, too, the story of the Woman of Shunem shows that strong women, who are willing to confront both prophets and kings and to act independently of their husbands in order to achieve particular goals, are not automatically stigmatized in the biblical texts. While there can be no doubt that both the social world which produced the books of Kings and the writings of the narratives themselves were dominated by men, still, such stories as that of the Shunammite woman serve as an important reminder that multiple gender roles and possibilities for gender role reversal exist even in the most patriarchal of societies. At the same time, it is important to note that the Woman of Shunem eventually finds herself falling at Elisha's feet and bowing to the ground before him (2 Kings 4.37). In the final analysis, then, we have to acknowledge that even so strong a figure as the Shunammite woman is known to us only through a story constructed to glorify Yhwh and Yhwh's prophets. Although, as we shall see, at least one woman does serve as a prophet of Yhwh in the books of Kings, most of the prophets found in these books are, like Yhwh himself, characterized as male (cf. Shields 2000).

Cannibal Mothers, Judahite Queens, and Female Prophets

Several female characters who appear in the books of Kings, in addition to those already mentioned, do so in contexts that also cause us to wonder about either the range of views held about women, or the range of social roles played by women, in ancient Israel. Included in 2 Kings 6, for example, is a little-known tale that may shed light on biblical assumptions about motherhood. The story takes place during a campaign waged by King Ben-hadad of Aram (Syria) against the northern kingdom of Israel. Ben-hadad's siege of Israel's capital, Samaria, leads to a severe famine within the city. During the famine, a woman tells Israel's king (who is not named in the text but is assumed by many scholars to be Jehoram) that she and another woman have agreed to eat one another's sons together, on two subsequent days. On the first day, the son of the woman who is now speaking to the king is cooked and eaten. On the next day, however, the other woman hides her son and refuses to allow him to be eaten. Thus, the first mother calls upon the king for help; and the king, in response, tears his clothes (revealing the fact that he is wearing sackcloth, a sign of humble petition, underneath) and determines to kill the prophet Elisha (2 Kings 6.31). The king appears to believe that he can no longer trust in Yhwh, given the fact that Yhwh has allowed such horrific circumstances to take place (2 Kings 6.33); and so the prophet associated with Yhwh is chosen to take the blame.

This story, like many biblical texts, raises a number of questions in the mind of the reader without giving us enough information to answer such questions completely. Perhaps most strikingly, we are never told about the outcome of the situation that has transpired between the two mothers. Once the first mother recounts her story to the king, the two women are never mentioned again. Their story seems to function primarily to represent the severity of the situation in Israel, and secondarily to represent the inability of the king to remedy the situation. The ultimate fates of the two women and the surviving son appear to lie outside the interests of those who told the story in its biblical form.

It is not accidental, however, that the narrator uses an example of maternal cannibalism to indicate the severity of the famine in Samaria. Other biblical books also use such imagery in order to underscore the potentially devastating consequences of famine, including, most notably, the book of Deuteronomy, which provides the criteria utilized in Deuteronomistic books such as 2 Kings for interpreting Israel's story (Deut. 28.53–7; cf. Lev. 26.29; Jer. 19.9; Lam. 2.20; 4.10; Ezek. 5.10). Within the books of Kings as a whole, moreover, this story follows a series of other tales in which a number of different women (for example, the prostitute who is recognized as true mother by Solomon, the wife of King Jeroboam in 1 Kings 14, the widow of Zarephath, the Shunammite woman) have been represented as trying, in one way or another, to save the life of a son. The recurring appearance of such figures no doubt reflects an assumption that maternal care for children is the norm for women's behaviour. Against the background of this widespread assumption and the series of stories about maternal concern that have already appeared in 1 and 2 Kings, the tale of the cannibal mothers stands out as a horrific 'countertype' (Camp 1998a: 114). While the structure of the story may remind us, in particular, of the tale of two prostitutes who come before Solomon in 1 Kings 3, the actions of the mother who speaks to the king in 2 Kings 6, and who has already cooked and eaten her own son, stand in sharp contrast to the mother in 1 Kings 3 who was willing to give up her son so that he might live. This sharp contrast between the actions of the mothers in the two stories leads some scholars to argue that 2 Kings 6 is trying to show us just how terrible things have become in Israel by drawing a picture of a 'topsy-turvy world', in which 'all expectations concerning maternal nature' have been disrupted (Lasine 1991: 29, 42). The literary impact of the narrative depends in part, then, upon the reader's holding a particular set of assumptions about probable and exceptional maternal behaviour, assumptions that are not unrelated to beliefs about gender.

On the other hand, the male-centred gender priorities that seem to have shaped the text of 2 Kings are sometimes carried further in the interpretation of this story. Gina Hens-Piazza has pointed out, for example, that scholars who study this text nearly always concentrate on its implications for the characterization of the king and his reign, rather than on the mothers themselves, even while acknowledging that the story's characterization of the king manipulates assumptions about maternal behaviour. Moreover, it is widely assumed that the mother who speaks to the king is asking for him to force the other mother to surrender her son. Yet the first mother does not actually say this, and it is possible to read her appeal to the king otherwise. For example, she might be calling on the king to remedy a terrible situation in which mothers are reduced to such circumstances simply in order to live. Indeed, Hens-Piazza suggests that, however ineffective the king might be, it is only the 'mother's audacious confrontation of the king with her own lamentable straits' that 'finally stirs the king to act' (2003: 92). Hens-Piazza, then, uses the tale of the cannibal women as an opportunity to encourage reflection on the ways in which our understanding of the biblical text can change when greater attention is given to its so-called 'minor' characters, among which we most often find female characters in particular.

Gender assumptions also influence both textual representations and readers' interpretations of female characters who play a more central role than do the cannibal mothers. We have already seen the ways in which both text and reader have influenced the impression left by the character Jezebel. Another character viewed quite negatively by the author of Kings, and associated with the same royal dynasty as Jezebel, is Athaliah, Queen of Judah. Athaliah, the only woman who rules alone in either Judah or Israel, is the daughter either of Omri (2 Kings 8.26) or Ahab (2 Kings 8.18) of Israel. Because the term 'daughter' can probably mean 'granddaughter' as well, it is likely that Ahab rather than Omri should be understood as Athaliah's father. Since Ahab was married to Jezebel, it is at least possible that Jezebel was the mother of Athaliah; and many scholars simply assume that this was the case (e.g. Cogan and Tadmor 1988: 98). Yet the text of 2 Kings never explicitly associates Athaliah with Jezebel, and we have no reason to believe that Ahab had only one wife when such kings as David and Solomon clearly had multiple wives and concubines. It is difficult to escape the impression, then, that scholars insist on identifying Athaliah with Jezebel in large part because Athaliah, too, is seen negatively and is associated in the text with both murder and the worship of Baal.

Though Athaliah is a princess from the northern kingdom of Israel, she marries King Jehoram of Judah and gives birth to Jehoram's successor in the southern kingdom, Ahaziah. She is thus Queen Mother during the one year of Ahaziah's reign (cf. 2 Kings 8.26). When Ahaziah is killed by Jehu (2 Kings 9.27), however, Athaliah seizes the throne of Judah by having 'all the royal seed' put to death (2 Kings 11.1). The reference to 'royal seed' is probably a reference to male children only, since Ahaziah's sister, Jehosheba, is clearly still alive in the next verse (11.2). Jehosheba takes Joash, who is her nephew and Ahaziah's son, from among the 'sons of the king' who are about to be put to death; and she hides him for six years while Athaliah rules over the land of Judah. Athaliah, as mother of Ahaziah, is necessarily the grandmother of Joash. Thus, the text's implication that Athaliah would have killed her own grandson, were it not for the actions of Jehosheba, probably manipulates assumptions about gender and appropriate maternal behaviour in much the same way that the story of the cannibal mothers does. That is, Athaliah is characterized all the more negatively by virtue of her desire, not simply to kill male members of the royal family, but even to kill her own grandson. When that same grandson is made king and Athaliah is finally put to death (2 Kings 11.15–16), the reader is therefore more likely to approve.

It is important to note, however, that in spite of her negative representation in the text, Athaliah is able to hold the throne of Judah for six years. This length of time surpasses the duration of the reigns of several other kings of Israel and Judah, including that of her own son, Ahaziah. It is clear, then, that Athaliah's rule must have had supporters; and that she was, in certain respects at least, a successful sovereign. While the grandson who replaces her does rule for a much longer period of time, his survival is due in part to the fact that he pays tribute to the Syrian king who is marching on Jerusalem (cf. 2 Kings 12.18–19). In the end, moreover, Joash is assassinated by his own courtiers (12.21–2). Thus, it is not altogether clear that he was actually a more effective monarch than his grandmother. Of course, the text of 2 Kings also attempts to associate Athaliah with the worship of Baal, and the end of her reign with resumption of proper Yahwistic religious practice (see e.g. 2 Kings 11.17–20). Within the framework of religious assumptions that shape the book of 2 Kings, such associations are reason enough for her removal from the throne. Yet Athaliah's name is clearly a Yahwistic name, which probably means something like 'Yhwh is great' or 'Yhwh is exalted'; and it turns out that her grandson Joash does not entirely live up to the standards of Deuteronomistic orthodoxy, either (cf. 2 Kings 12.4). Thus, the Bible's much more negative portrait of Athaliah probably results in part from the fact she, alone among all the Judahite monarchs, and in distinction from her grandson, does not belong to the Davidic dynasty to which the throne of Judah has been promised. And we cannot help wondering whether her negative reputation may have been influenced as well, to some degree at least, by the fact that she was not simply a powerful non-Davidide but also, quite clearly, a brave and powerful woman (cf. Brenner 1994a: 28–31).

Would the author of 2 Kings have been more positively disposed toward a female Judahite monarch who was both a member of the Davidic dynasty and a practitioner of Deuteronomistic orthodoxy? It is difficult to answer this question with certainty, since no such cases exist. It would, however, be incorrect to assume that the book of 2 Kings always represents powerful or authoritative women in a negative light. An important female character who plays quite a positive role is the female prophet Huldah, referred to in 2 Kings 22.

Huldah's story appears in the narration of the reign of King Josiah of Judah, who, along with his great-grandfather Hezekiah, is represented as one of the few kings who attempt to reform life in Judah along lines approved by the Deuteronomistic History. Josiah's reform is sparked by the discovery in the temple of a book or scroll that, when read to the king, leads him to tear his clothes and to order the priest Hilkiah and several other officials 'to enquire of Yhwh on my behalf and on behalf of the people and on behalf of all Judah, concerning the words of this book that has been found' (2 Kings 22.13). In response to Josiah's command, Hilkiah and the others seek out Huldah, who is referred to explicitly as a female prophet (22.14). Huldah, moreover, begins her reply with the traditional prophetic formula, 'Thus says Yhwh, God of Israel' (22.15); and she proceeds to deliver a prophetic oracle.

Because the Hebrew Bible refers to female prophets so infrequently, it is easy to assume that such prophets must have been rare in ancient Israel. The only other clear cases, apart from Huldah, are Miriam (Ex. 15.20), Deborah (Judg. 4.4) and Noadiah (Neh. 6.14). An unnamed woman in Isaiah 8.3 is referred to with the same terminology, but it is unclear in her case whether we are to understand a female prophet or a prophet's wife. It is important to note, however, that when such female prophets are actually mentioned by name, the text gives little if any indication that an unusual phenomenon is being discussed. Certainly there is no such indication in the case of Huldah, either in 2 Kings or in the parallel version of her story found in 2 Chronicles 34. Moreover, evidence from the ancient Near Eastern city of Mari, one of our most important non-biblical sources for understanding ancient Near Eastern 'prophecy', indicates that women as well as men were understood to participate legitimately in prophetic activity in the ancient world, even if they did so less frequently than men.

In 2 Kings 22, the words of Huldah are apparently understood to confirm the truth of the written document that has motivated Josiah to 'enquire of Yhwh' in the first place. As Claudia Camp points out, Huldah interprets that document by assessing its relevance for her contemporary situation, and she 'authorizes' it by affirming and explaining that relevance to her listeners. She and her story are thus crucial for the study of the development of notions about scripture, inasmuch as her 'validation of a text . . . stands as the first recognizable act in the long process of canon formation' (Camp 2000a: 96; cf. Camp 1987). When her words are reported to Josiah, moreover, he reads to an assembly in the temple 'all the words of the book of the covenant' (2 Kings 23.2) and initiates a series of religious reforms that are clearly seen by the author of 2 Kings as consonant with the will of Yhwh, and as representing something like the religious high point of Judah's history after the division of Israel into two kingdoms. Thus, notwithstanding the fact that she is not always emphasized, or even necessarily remembered, by readers of the Bible today, the significance of Huldah for the story told by the books of Kings can hardly be overestimated, even if we receive less information about her than we might wish to have.

Ironically, though, the truth of Huldah's oracle is disproven by the text of 2 Kings itself if it is taken too literally. Huldah, speaking for Yhwh, tells Josiah at one point that 'I will gather you to your fathers and you will be gathered to your grave in peace' (2 Kings 22.20). Yet Josiah, far from dying 'in peace', is killed during a military confrontation with Pharaoh Neco, king of Egypt (23.29). Although this is not the only example of a biblical prophetic oracle, accepted as true and inspired by Yhwh, which fails to be literally and completely fulfilled (cf. Carroll 1979), such instances of failed prophecy can be disconcerting for readers who approach the Bible as authoritative scripture. It is no doubt partly for this reason that such cases are generally ignored. In this instance, however, the fact that Huldah's prediction does not literally come true tends to cause commentators to accept its authenticity as 'a genuine political prediction delivered prior to the events it refers to' rather than a much later interpretation (Brenner 1994a: 60; cf. Gray 1963: 661). Thus, Huldah's positive reputation as an inspired prophet of Yhwh was apparently strong enough that the incongruity between the literal wording of her oracle and the actual nature of Josiah's death was allowed to stand in the final version of the books of Kings. When, at a later point, the author of 2 Chronicles felt the need to resolve this apparent contradiction while retelling Josiah's story, that author does so, not by changing Huldah's words, but rather by inventing a rationale for Josiah's unexpected demise (cf. 2 Chron. 35.20–4). Huldah's positive reputation seems to be confirmed, moreover, by later Jewish traditions which claim that certain gates on the Temple Mount were referred to as the 'Huldah Gates'. Clearly, then, her gender did not prevent Huldah from being held in high regard. And, while it is true that we learn very little about Huldah apart from prophetic activities that she carries out in relation to the king, this is true as well of certain male prophets in the books of Kings (e.g. Nathan) who bring the word of Yhwh to Israel's rulers.

It is nevertheless striking that no other female prophets appear in the books of Kings. Whether we conclude from Huldah's singularity that female prophets were in fact rare in ancient Israel, or whether we conclude that the male-centred focus of the books of Kings has resulted in a skewed picture of a historical situation in which female prophets were actually rather common, the scarcity of women in roles of religious authority in the Bible has surely had a negative impact on the ability of women in Judaism and Christianity to be accepted as religious leaders.

Eunuchs in the Books of Kings

Gender assumptions do not only shape the representation of female characters in the books of Kings. We have already noted the ways in which such assumptions are used in the characterization of David as an elderly king with flagging powers. But while kings and prophets are the most prominent characters found in the books of Kings, other sorts of characters appear as well. 'Eunuchs', for example, play a crucial narrative role in the closing scenes of both the story of the Shunammite Woman and the story of Jezebel. In 2 Kings 8.6, the king of Israel assigns a eunuch to the Woman of Shunem when he orders that her house and field be restored to her with profit. And, at the end of the very next chapter, Jehu, who will shortly become the new king of Israel, orders 'two or three' eunuchs to throw Jezebel down from the window at which she taunts him (2 Kings 9.32–3). These two references are, in fact, only two among several texts from the books of Kings in which the Hebrew term most often translated as 'eunuch' appears. Since some writers (e.g. Wilson 1995) have suggested that eunuchs might serve as a useful point of identification in the biblical texts for lesbian, gay, bisexual and transgendered readers, it is important for us to give some consideration, in a queer reading of the books of Kings, to the status of eunuchs in ancient Israel and in the Hebrew Bible.

The Hebrew word normally translated as 'eunuch', *saris*, is derived from an Akkadian term that literally means something like 'he who is at the head', that is, 'he who is chief'. Thus, the word itself refers literally to an administrative function rather than a state of the genitals. Although non-biblical evidence shows clearly that some of the officials referred to with this Akkadian terminology were castrated males (cf. Cogan and Tadmor 1988: 112), scholars of the ancient Near East have long debated whether all of the figures to which the language is applied should be understood in that way. Similar questions have been raised in relation to occurrences of the word *saris* in the Hebrew Bible.

Most of the biblical instances of the word *saris* occur in contexts where castration is neither confirmed nor ruled out explicitly. In certain passages, however, contextual clues are called upon by scholars who are trying to decide whether the translation 'eunuch' is appropriate. In at least one biblical text, the term is applied to an official who is clearly married – specifically, Potiphar in Genesis 39.1. Potiphar's marital status seems to many scholars to rule out the likelihood that Potiphar ought to be understood as a 'eunuch' in the conventional sense of that term. Whether such a conclusion is the only valid conclusion to reach is, perhaps, a point that could be debated in the context of a reading of the Genesis story. Isaiah 56.3–5, on the other hand, refers to the *saris* in a context in which the more common understanding of 'eunuch' is nearly certain. Encouraging the *saris* to refrain from saying 'I am a withered tree', the author of Isaiah 56 proclaims that the *saris* who obeys the covenant obligations of Yhwh will receive 'a monument and name better than sons and daughters, an everlasting name' (Isa. 56.5). The context indicates that the oracle speaks to a person who would normally not have sons and daughters. Thus, most scholars agree that the *saris* in Isaiah 56 is best understood as a 'eunuch', as are certain figures referred to outside the Bible with the cognate Akkadian term. The passage from Isaiah stands in some tension with, and may even render obsolete, Deuteronomy 23.2, which indicates that no one with crushed genitals will be allowed into the 'congregation of Yhwh'. For our purposes, though, the importance of the Isaiah passage is its relatively clear indication (consistent not only with the Akkadian evidence but also with long traditions of translation going back to the Septuagint) that *saris* can in Hebrew signify a 'eunuch'. Thus, we might conclude from Isaiah that *saris* should be understood as a 'eunuch' unless there are good contextual reasons for suspecting that another translation would be better in a particular passage.

When scholars use context to argue for or against 'eunuch' as the best translation of *saris*, however, gender ideology may influence the shape of the argument. Although it appears from both the biblical and non-biblical evidence that a number of different administrative tasks could be assigned to eunuchs, in several instances they are represented as interacting with the queen or other women in the royal household. In these cases, scholars nearly always translate *saris* as 'eunuch'. In the book of Esther, for example, where eunuchs are mentioned quite a number of times, seven eunuchs carry messages back and forth between the Persian king and Queen Vashti (Esth. 1.10–12, 15); the eunuch Hegai is in charge of the women of the harem (Esth. 2.3) and gives advice to Esther (Esth. 2.15); the eunuch Shaashgaz, who is in charge of the concubines, receives the women who spend a night with the Persian king but are not chosen as queen (Esth. 2.14); and the eunuch Hathach, one of several maids and eunuchs who serve Esther, plays the role of messenger between Esther and Mordecai (Esth. 4.4–11). In each of these cases, eunuchs 'serve as mediators between the sexes' (Beal 1997: 37). Their structural functions in the text, like their bodies, therefore arguably blur the boundaries between male and female. While the book of Esther also mentions eunuchs who serve the king but have little or no explicit interaction with the women of the court (e.g. Esth. 2.21–3), the frequency with which the eunuchs are referred to in connection with Esther, Vashti and the royal concubines underscores the likely importance of the role of eunuchs as figures who interact significantly with queens and other royal women. No doubt the fact that it was considered unlikely that eunuchs would have sexual relations with these women made them especially appealing as candidates for such a role. Thus, it is no surprise to find that eunuchs are close enough to Jezebel to throw her down at Jehu's command in 2 Kings 9, or that the king of Israel assigns a eunuch to the Shunammite woman in 2 Kings 8.

However, eunuchs serve other roles as well in the books of Kings. In 1 Kings 22.9, for example, the king of Israel sends a eunuch – later called a 'messenger' (1 Kings 22.11) – to the prophet Micaiah son of Imlah in order to summon Micaiah before the king. This reference is a more controversial one, for it has often been doubted that we have to do here with a literal 'eunuch'. The word, however, is again *saris*; and 'eunuch' is certainly a justifiable translation (see e.g. Cogan 2000: 487). In 2 Kings 18.17, the Assyrian king Sennacherib sends to King Hezekiah in Jerusalem a delegation that includes 'the Rabsaris', that is, 'the chief eunuch'. Non-biblical texts from the ancient Near East indicate that such 'chief eunuchs' participated on other occasions in Assyrian military matters (Cogan and Tadmor 1988: 229–30). However, the term 'Rabsaris' in 2 Kings 18.17 is sometimes translated into English with language (e.g. 'commander-in-chief' (Gray 1963: 613; Fretheim 1999: 202)) that obscures the linguistic connection to our biblical terminology for 'eunuchs'. While such translations might be based in part on the conclusion that terms most often translated as 'eunuch' actually had multiple meanings in the ancient Near East, we also have to consider the possibility that readers simply find it difficult to associate eunuchs with military tasks. In a similar fashion, translators sometimes use the word 'officer' to render into English the *saris* who is in charge of soldiers in 2 Kings 25.19 (e.g. Gray 1963: 700). But the fact that we, today, may find it hard to imagine a eunuch in a military role should not be allowed to determine, by itself, our interpretation of the ancient evidence. Rather, the range of functions given to persons with the title *saris* in the ancient world ought to become an occasion for critical reflection on the gender assumptions – and especially the assumptions about masculinity – which are at work when readers are surprised to discover the possibility that eunuchs may have participated in the ancient world in military expeditions. Of course, it is quite possible that the word *saris* did have, in Hebrew, a range of meanings that we cannot entirely reconstruct.

Nevertheless, questions of philology and translation can never be separated entirely from questions of politics; and there is surely a particular politics of gender at work in the decision made by many translators that a 'eunuch' simply cannot have been involved in military matters.

On the other hand, the negative attitude taken toward eunuchs in Deuteronomy 23.2 does indicate that eunuchs were frequently viewed by others with ambivalence. This ambivalence has left its mark on the books of Kings. An oracle found in 2 Kings 20.18 (as well as in Isa. 39.7), in which Isaiah tells King Hezekiah of Judah that some of Hezekiah's sons or male descendants 'will be eunuchs in the palace of the king of Babylon', clearly has negative connotations; for it appears to assume that no one would wish for one's descendants to be eunuchs.

It may well be the case, then, that the very feature of eunuchs – their sexual ambiguity – which made them attractive candidates for the role of mediator between male and female, also produced discomfort among those in the ancient world, including the authors of certain biblical texts (e.g. Deut. 22.5), who felt that distinctions between male and female needed to be kept clear and unambiguous. Queer readers of the Bible know only too well the potentially pernicious effects of such discomfort, which often impact negatively the lives and experiences of those who are thought to embody sex/gender ambiguity. Thus, it is no surprise that some queer readers have found in the vague biblical references to eunuchs an occasion for creative reflection on 'gay and lesbian tribal identities' (Wilson 1995: 126).

At the same time, other readers have raised critical questions about the assumption that biblical eunuchs offer particularly valuable points of identification for queer interpreters of the Bible. A focus upon the sexual/gender dimensions of a eunuch's status can lead us to ignore other important dimensions of the eunuch's identity or of his role in the biblical text (see Henderson 2003). The contribution of eunuchs to the horrible death of Jezebel in 2 Kings 9 might lead us to wonder about unintended consequences of positive identification with them, particularly for those transgendered readers who wrestle with the charge of betraying feminism (see Kolakowski 2000). And, of course, the fact that ancient eunuchs apparently lived lives that were most often 'sexually and socially circumscribed' may cause us to doubt their usefulness as models for those of us who are struggling for sexual freedom and social equality (Koch 2001a: 174). It is likely, then, that biblical references to eunuchs, such as those found in the books of Kings, will continue to generate a wide range of responses from queer readers of the Bible.

Conclusion

The books of Kings were written primarily to provide a theological interpretation of Israel's past, and especially of the circumstances that brought about the destruction of a people who understood themselves to be chosen and set apart by Yhwh (cf. 1 Kings 8.53). It would be a mistake to assume, then, that such books will always prove to be directly focused on the concerns of queer readers today. Nevertheless, in the course of telling a theological story about events that we would today call political, the books of Kings rely at multiple points on images and assumptions relating to sexual practice, gender and marriage. While hasty or simplistic accounts of those images and assumptions need to be avoided, an investigation of them serves as a useful reminder that sex, gender and marriage have always been thoroughly implicated in both religion and politics. It is therefore no surprise that sex, gender and marriage continue to be objects of both religious and political disputes today.

1 and 2 Chronicles

ROLAND BOER

Chronicles reminds me a little of East Sydney: men as far as the eye can see. Men in couples, men in night-clubs and bars, men finely muscled and flabby, moustached and clean-shaven, tall serious men in long black jeans and boots, men cruising other men up and down Oxford Street, men sleeping together in all manner of formations and places. And if East Sydney was one of the first gay ghettoes in the city, Chronicles is one of the first men-only utopias. Now, a cursory glance through Chronicles, with its endless genealogies and details of temple construction and ritual, will hardly give the impression of a utopia, and so I will need initially to track over the territory I have covered before, teasing out the features that make this a utopian text. However, as with the earlier gay ghettoes and their overwhelming presence of men – you could go for weeks and not see a woman – a feminist criticism is that this male-only world relies on the silencing of women. In fact, such a ho(m)mosexual world, to borrow a term from Luce Irigaray, is but a microcosm of the reality of the world at large. Men do in fact dominate and control at every level, and the systemic exclusion of women from the gay ghetto of Chronicles shows in stark relief the unwanted truth of patriarchal domination. Gay men just do it better than breeders, except that now we find ourselves in a distinctly dystopian place. At least so the criticism goes, and more than one feminist has pointed out to me, after a particularly effusive embrace from a gay man, that gay men greet each other more enthusiastically than they do women. So the Irigarayan criticism will form the second part of my essay. But there is a third moment, a response to this criticism in which I return to utopian theory to point out that any depiction of utopia is doomed to fail, that it will never hold together, showing up cracks and flaws all over the place. But I want to go a step further and argue for a utopian hermeneutics of camp. And Chronicles, in all its deathly seriousness, gives itself over to camp all over the place, in the overwhelming machismo, the genealogies of men begetting men, and above all in the attention to the finest detail of temple organization and decoration . . . in short a text full of queers doing their thing. As far as dystopia is concerned, the inappropriate excess of camp is the dialectical flaw in which dystopia itself fails, where a genuine utopian possibility begins.

Uchronian Chronicles?

Elsewhere I have argued in some detail that Chronicles may be read as utopian, or rather uchronian, literature (Boer 1997: 136–68). To put it briefly, Chronicles narrates a different past in order to open up the possibility of a different future – the basic definition of uchronian literature. I will leave open for now the questions that immediately pile on top of one another: a better future for whom? Is it possible to speak of utopia in an ancient text like Chronicles? As far as I am concerned, this is a false question, since any interpretive act on a text like the Bible will be anachronistic: it is not that this is a necessary admission of failure, but rather a necessary feature of interpretation itself.

In fact, I am saying nothing new, at one level at least, in suggesting that Chronicles presents a picture of an ideal or utopian Israel in opposition to the strongly dystopian lines of the narrative representation in the Deuteronomistic History. By contrast with the Deuteronomist History, which presents an increasingly apostate people and leadership, Chronicles has a much more positive picture of both people and kingship, for whom the exile to Babylon then becomes something of an unfortunate interlude. In conventional biblical scholarship such a position has been cast in terms of eschatology or messianism – the closing of the book with 'let him go up', the ideal figure of David as messianic precursor and so on (see Braun 1979: 59–61; DeVries 1986; Whitelam 1989; Williamson 1977: 135; 1982: 24–6). In presenting an ideal past, with the obedience or disobedience of king and people functioning as a trigger for immediate divine favour or disfavour, with the priests as the actual rulers, Chronicles also generates a hope for a future in which such an ideal state will be realized (that it comes close to the Hasmonean era is no accident). At this level, I have merely shifted the terminology from eschatology to utopia. However, a small shift like this, innocuous in itself, inevitably ends up having a whole series of ramifications that leads to a completely new situation. Let me use a political example: the recognition of gay and lesbian couples as married. In today's world, especially the West, marriage seems ever more fragile. More and more marriages end in divorce, heterosexual couples live together without getting married, less and less is the domestic unit based on a sexual and legal couple. Rather than gay and lesbian couples seeking the sanction of the state in terms of marriage for same-sex partners, would it not be easier to campaign for the abolition of marriage as such? As a relatively small change to an institution that is fading anyway, as a recognition of what is already happening, would it make any difference? Yet, the ramifications would begin to run in all sorts of directions – social structure, the judiciary, economic structures and so on.

What then are the consequences of suggesting that Chronicles should be read as utopian, or rather uchronian, literature? The immediate problem is determining what utopian literature might in fact be, and here I draw on the work of Louis Marin, Fredric Jameson and Ernst Bloch. Briefly, the formal features of a literary utopia include the following: a structural contradiction between narrative and description of the utopian place, contradiction between the description itself and any efforts at graphic representation, and a dialectic of disjunction and connection between the constructed utopia and outside world, in particular the society from which the writer originates (one wants a very different world, yet not too different, since then the possibility of passing from this world to the utopian one becomes too problematic). Above all, we find neutralization, which may best be characterized in terms of a resistance to Hegel: rather than understanding the dialectic as a process of breaking into something new, of opening out a new direction from the bind of the contradiction itself, neutralization runs in a different direction. It allows the contradiction free reign, letting it replicate itself in a wild and utopian abandon. Here I rely on Louis Marin, but it seems to me that neutralization is a very fruitful category for exploring the possibilities for what might lie beyond heteronormativity, but also for understanding the function of camp. As for content, utopian literature normally deals with alternative worlds (utopia) and/or alternative histories (uchronia), and I locate Chronicles primarily in the latter category. All of which gets us beyond the simple determination of utopia by means of the political positions of authors and readers; in this case utopian texts would be produced by those with whom we agree politically and dystopian by those with whom we disagree. Rather, narratives are not simply dystopian or utopian: they often embody both, but in tension, cracking up the story.

What I will do for the remainder of this section is summarize a much longer argument. Let me begin with the tension between narrative and description, which we find interspersed throughout Chronicles. The narrative sections deal explicitly with the kings of Israel and Judah after the division of the kingdom, beginning with Saul in 1 Chronicles 10.1, running through intermittently to the end of the scroll (1 Chron. 10.1–11.9; 12.38–14.17; 15.25–16.3; 16.43–18.13; 19.1–23.5; 28.1–29.30; 2 Chron. 1.1–17; 5.1–9.12; 10.1–36.23). These stretches of narrative are broken up by descriptions of various organizational features of both kingship and the cult, usually cast in terms of lists of cultic arrangements and administrative elements (1 Chron. 11.10–12.37; 15.1–24; 16.4–6, 37–42; 18.14–17) and organizational elements relating to the temple and Solomon's succession (1 Chron. 23.6–27.34; 2 Chron. 1.18 (2.1)–4.22). Solomon's wealth is a list on its own (2 Chron. 9.13–21). The other major category in the realm of description is of course the genealogical list in 1 Chronicles 1–9. By 1 Chronicles 9, however, the genealogical material shifts strongly back to the organization of the cult, where the list of names functions not only in a genealogical capacity but also for various tasks around the sanctuary.

In itself there is nothing remarkable about the difference between narrative and description in Chronicles, and I am not the first to point it out. Yet, in utopian literature narrative is a necessary prop: narrative enables the writer to get to utopia in some way, but the major purpose is to describe utopia itself. The problem here is that even the best description, even the most innovative lists, will overcome the resistance of even the most resilient insomniac; and so narrative is that formal device that holds attention, that keeps the eyelids from drooping. So also Chronicles has often been regarded as the poorer literary product beside Samuel–Kings, indeed beside Genesis–Kings as a whole, precisely because of its predilection for large slabs of lists and descriptions, administrative directions and cultic details.

However, within the whole realm of description itself there is a further tension, namely that between description and any efforts at graphic representation. In Marin's study, *Utopiques*, perhaps the best example is the discrepancy between the description of the city itself, particularly the organization of neighbourhoods, and the graphic representation of those neighbourhoods. Out of a whole range of possible examples in Chronicles, let me select but one, the description of the measurements of Solomon's temple in 2 Chronicles 3.3–4: 'These are Solomon's foundations for building the house of God: the length, in cubits of the old standard, was sixty cubits and the width twenty cubits. The vestibule (*ha'ulam*) that was in front of the length, across the breadth of the house, was twenty cubits, and the height one hundred and twenty'. Compare 1 Kings 6.2–3: 'The house that King Solomon built for Yahweh was sixty cubits long, twenty wide and thirty cubits high. The vestibule in front of the temple of the house was twenty cubits long, across the width of the house. Ten cubits was its width in front of the house'.

What interests me here is the vestibule. While in Kings it is ten by twenty cubits on the ground plan, in Chronicles we have a different set of measurements: 20 cubits across and 120 high. But that would make the vestibule twice as high as the length of the whole temple, a massive phallic tower that would leave the temple itself merely a support like a somewhat angular pair of balls. Surely not! Especially for the commentators. Suffering an acute case of collective penis envy, the unanimous agreement is that 2 Chronicles 3.4a has been corrupted in some way (but of course). As far as utopian literature itself is concerned, I suggest that the idea of a vestibule six times as high as its width, even twice as high as the length of the full temple, indicates a representational flaw: the whole temple is skewed, upended and 90 degrees off its line, thrust upward like a new tower of Babel that stresses the vertical dimension of Chronicles' theocracy. A high-rise temple for Solomon would indeed be novel, but I suggest that it is one of the best examples in Chronicles of the breakdown of descriptive language in the realm of utopian construction.

A third feature of utopian literature is the tension between conjunction and disjunction, the necessary difference from this world and yet the need to maintain some connection, some means of transition. The most obvious conjunction, at least on a literary level, is with Genesis–Kings, especially Samuel–Kings. Overlapping, meshed in and yet diverging, Chronicles usually ends up in some comparison or other with Samuel–Kings. Yet we find a very different world in Chronicles, one that sets it apart from that in Samuel–Kings, a disjunction that shows up all the more sharply after countless rereadings.

Perhaps the best way to characterize such a pattern of conjunction and disjunction is through the dual motifs of alternative worlds and alternative time. In doing so, I want to take Darko Suvin's definition of utopian literature as apposite for Chronicles itself:

> Utopia is the verbal construction of a particular quasi-human community where sociopolitical institutions, norms, and individual relationships are organized according to a more perfect principle than in the author's community, this construction being based on estrangement arising out of an alternative historical hypothesis. (Suvin 1979: 49)

Or in short, 'cognitive estrangement'.[1] The 'alternative historical hypothesis' is the key here, for Chronicles presents a historically rather than transcendentally different world. Further, Chronicles is less an explicit presentation of the Israelite world as it should have been or even how it should be, but rather an analogy, a parable, of the potential of the society out of which the work comes. And the explicit content of such an analogy is that of an alternative world and alternative history.

The various pieces of the alternative world of Chronicles have been put together time and again by commentators: the deity, ideal kingship, a 'democratization' that effaces material differences, and the cult. Let me focus on the first and last points. The content of such a world begins with a deity who is very much present in the daily activities of at least the more important people (such as kings). The difference from other texts in the Hebrew Bible is the sheer efficiency and predictability with which Yahweh operates, so much so that he becomes highly mechanical, a sort of physical force with a moral bent. It is as though Chronicles has carried through the idea of Yahweh as a moral agent to its logical conclusion: that which is deemed good is rewarded immediately, and that which is evil is, after warning (2 Chron. 16.7–10; 24.19–22; 25.15–16; 26.16–21), punished promptly.

In a way that is comparable to what has happened to Yahweh in Chronicles, the cult achieves an intensification and centrality that is comparable only to Leviticus; yet here the cult is so interwoven with every other significant aspect of Chronicles that my inclination is to see it as the crucial organizing feature of this text as a whole. What I mean here is the loading of an immense amount of literary energy onto the question of the administration and practice of the cult: apart from the suggestion that it reflects the situation from which the text arises, it is perhaps worth entertaining the possibility that it is a case of the return of the repressed. That is to say, with the long-term removal of the Judaean ruling classes from effective power – governing only by proxy under Persian and Hellenistic empires – the energies normally directed to this task find themselves unconsciously re-channelled into the minutiae of religious observance and ordering. It is precisely these minutiae that interest me: like the genealogical lists, there is something in the very act of producing the detail of cultic organization that, like an analogy or a parable, lifts the construction of an alternative world beyond the ostensible content to another level. Like

---

1 Suvin argues that utopian literature is a subset of science fiction, but that is another argument. See also his longer definition: 'The science fiction narrative actualizes a different – though historical and not transcendental – world corresponding to different human relationships and cultural norms. However, in science fiction the "possible world" induced by the narrative is imaginable only as an interaction between two factors: the conception which the collective social addressee of a text has of empirical reality, and the narratively explicit modifications that a given science fiction text supplies to this initial conception. The resulting alternate reality or possible world is, in turn, not a prophecy or even extrapolation but an *analogy* to unrealized possibilities in the addressee's or implied reader's empirical world; however empirically unverifiable the narrative agents, objects or events of science fiction may be, their constellation in all still (literally) significant cases shapes a parable about ourselves' (Suvin 1979: 49).

obsessive behaviour in Freudian theory, it is as though the meticulous detail of worship and sacrifices, of temple plans, building and furnishing, the organization of the roles of priests, Levites, singers, gatekeepers, officers and judges is a visible manifestation of a wish-fulfilment that remains repressed. I want to suggest that the meticulous detail of the cult, of the temple and its personnel, is but a figure for work itself, particularly the work required to build a properly alternative world.

In the end, however, the alternative world of Chronicles bends its path to that of time, of alternative history. My focus on alternative histories also taps into the philosophical dimension of utopian reflection: an alternative construction of the past breaks the acceptance of the present and future as irrevocable. The future now becomes a place of an alternative vision based upon a different construction of the past in question. That Chronicles constitutes an alternative history to that found in the Deuteronomistic History, particularly Samuel–Kings, hardly needs to be argued, although for many enticed by the historiographical logic of historical criticism, the value of Chronicles lies in its ability to provide evidence for historical reconstruction (which then becomes yet another construction of the past in question).

I take but one example, the accession of Solomon to the throne. Even before Solomon, David occupies a huge slab of text (1 Chron. 11–29), to be followed by the man himself (2 Chron. 1–9). As is so often the case, the story of David is extremely enticing, but I will resist the seduction on this occasion, diverting my attention to the comparable succession narratives. According to Samuel–Kings, Solomon's accession to the throne is troubled from the beginning: not only is he born of a woman with whom the king had committed adultery, but he is also not the firstborn and therefore not the natural successor to the throne. The succession itself splits the royal court in 1 Kings 1, pitting military commanders, priests and sons against each other. Bathsheba wields her influence on an aged David who has lost his virility, and Solomon secures his reign with a series of murders (2 Kings 2). After the building and dedication of the temple (2 Kings 6–8) the attention shifts to Solomon's debts to Hiram, the forced labour, his immense wealth and the effort to impress the Queen of Sheba. His downfall comes with a mix of libido and religion, his many wives being the cause of Solomon's religious syncretism and subsequent troubles with rebels (1 Kings 11). The break-up of the kingdom then owes much to Solomon's excesses. It is in fact David who becomes the paragon of piety in the remainder of Kings, rather than Solomon.

The contrast in Chronicles couldn't be sharper: Solomon is the divinely chosen heir to the throne. In 1 Chronicles 22.9–10 (and also 1 Chron. 28.6–7) David reports that Yahweh promised a son who would bring peace (Shalom/ Solomon) and rest to Israel, and who would build the temple. The transition from David to Solomon is a calm affair, full of David's wise presence and blessing, rather than his ineffectual and aged presence in the text of 1 Kings 1. When the transition to Solomon's reign finally takes place – after interminable speeches and arrangements by David – 1 Chronicles 29.22–5 has the people of Israel accept him with one accord and without a murmur of protest (this is so over-the-top that we can hardly read it without a sense of caricature, something I will develop in my discussion of camp below). In contrast to the problems

Solomon faced in the early chapters of Kings, 1 Chronicles 29.24 indicates that 'all the leaders and the mighty warriors, and also all the sons of David, pledged their allegiance to King Solomon'. Absalom, Adonijah, Abiathar the priest and Joab the commander – not to mention all the sons of David that celebrated with Adonijah (1 Kings 1.9) – all seem to have been forgotten, or at least their efforts to have Adonijah put on the throne after Absalom's abortive revolt have been banished from the story: 'A view of Solomon's rise more divergent from that of Kings can hardly be imagined' (Braun 1986: xxxiv). In the account of Solomon's reign there is no rise and fall, as in the account of Kings, but rather a brilliant culmination in the honour of the visit of the Queen of Sheba (2 Chron. 9). The division of the kingdom that follows Solomon's reign becomes the fault of a rebellious Jeroboam rather than the result of Solomon's kingship. For the Chronicler Solomon's reign was filled with pious devotion to Yahweh, wealth and international recognition. There is no suggestion of apostasy or syncretism. The final section on Solomon's reign finishes with a grand summary of his reign, including vast imperial claims: 'he ruled over all the kings from the Euphrates to the land of the Philistines, and to the border of Egypt' (2 Chron. 9.26). What we have here is a distinctly alternative history.

The question that remains, however, is how the alternative history of Chronicles enables a different perception both of the present and of the future. What are the consequences of altering an accepted construction of history? The major issue is the building and organization of the temple: the less blame that applies to David and Solomon, the more the process of temple construction is enhanced. Saul's death becomes an occasion for the enthronement of David and an example of retribution for sin. Even the census (the one negative act on David's part, although it is now Satan's fault (2 Chron. 21.1)) is an occasion for repentance and the location of the temple site. The more David has to do with the organization of temple personnel and the planning of the temple, the smoother the succession of Solomon, the less scandal associated with Solomon, then the greater the temple itself becomes. And I have already hinted at the importance of the temple itself, although specifically in association with the work involved in building and operating the temple. I want to suggest that the temple is a figure, an analogy, for the sort of collective existence that is only glimpsed in Chronicles: the image of everyone, without distinction, working hard and together is an image that projects beyond the specific hierocratic content of Chronicles to a possible collective life for which the temple is the enabling figure.

At a more general philosophical level, Chronicles may be understood as a document that draws on memory of the past in order to construct the picture of a possible and hoped-for future. But this may be taken a step further into a more proper dialectical relationship: it is a particular memory that Chronicles wishes to construct as a basis for the future hope, a memory that differs considerably from the other official memory. Chronicles thus attempts a break with the accepted picture of the past in the Deuteronomistic History in order to write its own narrative of that same past so that it may have a different basis for the future. It challenges, erases and rewrites the established patterns, providing an appeal to alternative collective memories – embodied particularly in the genealogies – for the hope of the future. By rewriting the past, Chronicles breaks the inexorable ideological connection between the past and present way of things and thereby sets up the future, based now upon a new past, as a place of radical difference from the present rather than its simple continuation.

Or, a Ho(m)mosexual Chronicles?

Thus far I have by and large argued before, although a queer reading lies hidden within such an analysis, peeking out every now and then only to duck down again. And we'll have to leave it there for a little longer, satisfied with a glimpse of hip, or leg or butt every now and then. For what I need to do first is recount a systematic criticism of my argument for a utopian Chronicles that comes from an Irigarayan-inspired reading of Chronicles. In short, because Chronicles provides us with one of the best examples of the way in which men construct their worlds through the occlusion and silencing of women, it is rather a dystopian text. It is not just that women do not speak – we do in fact find the unnamed mother of Jabez, the Queen of Sheba, Athaliah and Huldah speaking, although only in the world of men – but that at a deeper level the silencing of women is the foundation of the world of Chronicles.

There are a number of elements to this criticism, which is being developed most fully by Julie Kelso by means of Luce Irigaray (Kelso 2003; see Irigaray 1985a; 1985b; 2002). Both psychoanalyst and philosopher, Irigaray takes Lacan's statement 'Woman does not exist' absolutely seriously. In other words, women do not enter the Symbolic like men, do not rely on the Oedipus complex in order to construct a world of language, society and law that makes sense to them. Their Symbolic is vastly different from that of men. For men, women remain very much part of the Real, which cannot be represented in any way but is at the same time constitutive of the world that is. The Real is that which is left out, the extraneous item that keeps a fragile social structure together, the unbearable truth that cannot be named, and so on. Rendering the Symbolic inherently unstable, the Real is that which both keeps it in place and threatens to bring about its collapse at any moment.

For Irigaray the philosopher, the whole tradition of Western philosophy relies upon that silencing of women, the sheer exclusion that does not allow any space for representation. Kelso suggests that Irigaray has neglected the Hebrew Bible, being perhaps subject to a European tradition that sees a long if highly troubled history that runs through from ancient Greece to modern Europe. Making use of some key Irigarayan strategies, especially the notion of two modes of interpretation (rather than a method), one that is critical and the other that seeks another path for women, reading for the 'silence' of women, and the idea of the *practicable* (the setting of analysis: its topography and arrangement), Kelso argues that Chronicles is a dystopian text for the following reasons.

At particular points Chronicles shows forth a consistent strategy of appropriating the maternal body. Unable to produce life, lacking a womb, men appropriate the ability to create in a variety of other ways, from the 'creative' activity of art and literature to religious systems. Not only is Chronicles, as a literary text produced by a scribal elite some time ago, an example of this process, but this appropriation also turns up in the details of the text. Two examples will suffice. First, in the genealogies we find an endless list of men producing men, with the occasional exception, such as Keturah, Abraham's 'concubine' in 1 Chronicles 1.32, or Tamar in 1 Chronicles 2.4, or Ephrathah in 1 Chronicles 2.24, or Caleb's concubines in 2 Chronicles 2.46–9. Even in these cases, the women produce sons for men, but the overwhelming formula for the genealogies makes use of *holi'd*, translated variously as 'was the father of' or, in a still classic translation, 'begat'. So we get 'A *holi'd* B, C, D . . .' Semantically there is nothing particularly exceptional about the formula, for does not a man 'beget' a child, become the father of a child? But here the 'exceptions' I cited, where women are in fact named, become important. These 'exceptions' indicate that at a basic level the *holi'd* formula leaves the mother entirely out of the process. Where the mother's name does appear, we find *yaledah*, 'she bore', the Qal form of which the mother is the direct subject, the son the object and the father the indirect object. And so we get, 'X bore Y for A' (see 1 Chron. 2.19, 21 and so on), or just 'X bore Y' (see 1 Chron. 2.17; 7.14). However, with *holi'd* we have the Hiphil, 'A caused to bear B'. But the question then becomes: whom did he cause to bear? The mother is the obvious answer, but the formula itself effaces her presence, attributing the verb for giving birth to the man. So much so that when the mother's name does appear in the formula, the syntax breaks down. Thus, in 1 Chronicles 2.18 we have the curious sentence: 'Caleb the son of Hezron begat (*holi'd*) Azubah, his wife, and Jerioth'. Or is it that 'Caleb the son of Hezron begat by means of (*'et*) his wife, Azubah and with Jerioth'? It is unclear here whether the *'et* is a marker of the direct object – in which case Caleb begets his wives – or the preposition 'with'. Is *holi'd* transitive or intransitive? 1 Chronicles 8.9 and 11 suggest not, for here the indirect object, the wife, is prefaced by *min*, whereas the names of the sons have the direct object marker *'et*. In fact, overwhelmingly *holi'd* is transitive and *'et* the marker of the object, a son or sons, as 1 Chronicles 5.30–9 (ET 6.4–15) indicate. The confusion over *'et* in 1 Chronicles 2.18 is an indication of the problem, for the only way a woman can be present in the *holi'd* formula is indirectly, an uncomfortable addition to a process that by and large excludes them. The various uses of the verb 'to bear' (*yld*) count as the most direct instance of the appropriation of the maternal function by men, as though men had wombs themselves, generating themselves, auto-generative.

The second example comes at the beginning of the narrative proper, namely Saul's death. Beginning abruptly, with no lead-up whatsoever, we arrive on Mount Gilboa in the last minutes of Saul's life as the Philistines press upon him. Nearly every commentator looks to 1 Chronicles 10.13–14 to point out that it must assume something from Samuel–Kings – Saul's unfaithfulness, in particular consulting a medium rather than Yahweh. But the point that Kelso makes about this beginning to the narrative proper, after the long stretch of genealogies in 1 Chronicles 1–9, is that it is both an extraordinarily violent beginning – Saul and his sons all die, in fact 'all his house' perishes – and one in which Saul's own body becomes feminized. As for the second point, Saul is broken up: the Philistines take his head and his armour, putting them up in the temples; the Israelites come and take the corpse (*guphah*) of Saul and the corpses (*guphot*) of his sons and bury them under the oak at Jabesh. Or rather, they bury their 'bones' (*'atsmot*) (1 Chron. 10. 12–13). But the word for body here is curious: *guphah*, attested only here, suggests an emptied out vessel, a cavity or vacant space without the messy entrails and putrefaction of *gewiyah* (in the parallel text of 1 Sam. 31.12). For Kelso, we have here an appropriation of the womb precisely at the moment of narrative beginning, one that is intimately connected with the hollowed-out space of the temple that lies at the centre of Chronicles. The narrative cannot get under way, cannot be born, without a linguistic appropriation of the maternal body. From Saul's womb-like body the narrative of the Davidic kingship is born. But what of the question of violence? Apart from the point that this is a displacement of the violence by which the bodies of women are wrenched into the service of men, the grisly end of Saul is on a par with the violent myth of creation in which a male god kills his female protagonist and then breaks up her body to 'create' the world: the most obvious example is the battle between Tiamat and Marduk in *Enuma Elish*. In the case of 1 Chronicles 10, this creation gets the narrative under way, and, more importantly, creates the world of Chronicles itself.

Kelso deals with other elements in Chronicles, particularly the temple – whose measurements are made with cubits, *'ammot* (which Kelso connects with *'am*, mother), and whose enclosed space is a transferred and appropriated womb that is the centre of the masculine world of Chronicles – and the rare moments in which women do speak. But her argument hinges on Irigaray's rereading of Lévi-Strauss's argument that women are the exchange objects in all socio-economic systems. From the patterns of barter to the role of money in capitalism, it is women who are exchanged between men as a means of ensuring their world. And so Irigaray coins the term ho(m)mosexual for that world, no matter what its permutations. The brackets are crucial here, for the crossover between hommosexual and homosexual – men in control and men having sex with each other – is in line with Irigaray's argument that there is nothing subversive or revolutionary in the struggle for gay and lesbian rights, for the fundamental changes sought in a social system that continues to repress and oppress gays, lesbians and bisexuals. For Irigaray, these changes in fact realize the deeper pattern of the world as it is, showing the uncomfortable truth of that world (hence the resistance to gay and lesbian liberation).

It is not for nothing that gay, lesbian and bisexual political activists and theoreticians find Foucault more amenable than either psychoanalysis or Irigaray, for Irigaray's position on the ho(m)mosexual lacks adequate recognition of the long and often contradictory political struggles in which gays and lesbians have been engaged. Nor does she recognize sufficiently the problem that the categories of 'man' and 'woman' themselves raise for contexts outside capitalism, their very different constructions in distinct social and economic systems. To be fair to Irigaray, however, she would find that heteronormativity is in fact another way of speaking about the problems she seeks to address, and it would be possible to argue that her search for a very different way of speaking about the relations between men and women – as two genres, two universals, with two legal systems – can be interpreted in terms of gay and lesbian politics. It is unfortunate, then, that she speaks of such a programme in terms of sexual difference, or that heterosexuality has not as yet existed, or that her models operate by means of the sexual and social relations between men and women. It seems to me that while she works towards a very different formulation, she cannot dissociate heterosexuality so completely from heteronormativity. It is similar to ingenious moves that Lacanians make when they argue that the phallus is not the penis.

However, all that I have said thus far falls within the category of critique, a necessary but preliminary Irigarayan step in engaging with texts like Chronicles. For Irigaray there is another dimension or mode, one that laments a world dominated by men – a world in which women have been forgotten and silenced – but that refuses to discard it in anger. Rather, a very different level of engagement takes place, one that seeks a possible way forward. Most obviously, this engagement shows up in Irigaray's style, which moves beyond critical analysis to a poetic and lyric style. But above all, it is a mode of engagement that does not yet know its own way of operating. Or, to put it more directly in terms that are familiar from Chronicles, Irigaray, and Kelso following her, seeks a genealogy of and for women, one that concerns the forgotten and foreclosed relationship between mother and daughter. In the end Irigaray is a utopian thinker and writer, although of a somewhat different ilk from Chronicles. Thus, she seeks out paths to situations that do not yet exist.

Although the content is different, the utopian gesture is very similar to that of Adorno (see Adorno 1990; Adorno and Horkheimer 1999; Bloch and Adorno 2001) and of Fredric Jameson (1981; 1982; 1988). Although she refuses to describe herself as a utopian thinker, she speaks of 'militating for the impossible'. So also Adorno and Jameson, for whom any representation of utopia, any blueprint, is doomed to fail, for we do not yet possess the language to speak of such things. What, then, is utopian literature, if the possibility of imagining something so very different will fail the moment it happens? For Adorno and Jameson, the key lies with the gesture itself and not the content, the effort itself to imagine a world different from the one we know, rather than merely variations on this one (for instance, corporations will continue to exist, or money, or indeed heterosexuality).

The Utopian Hermeneutics of Camp

Without dismissing Kelso's arguments regarding Chronicles, I want to pick up Irigaray's notion of militating for the impossible along with Adorno's and Jameson's suggestion that what counts is the gesture itself rather than any explicit content. Irigaray is a feminist and Adorno and Jameson Marxists, but what these approaches share with gay and lesbian criticism is that they are not merely theories, but also political practices, that the theory itself arises from and informs the politics in which they are engaged. At this level, I suggest, we should understand the role of camp, which I want to read quite deliberately as a utopian hermeneutics.

In my earlier discussion of utopian theory I stressed the features of literary utopias, tracing them in Chronicles. But utopian theory is also inescapably tied up with dialectics, although in two related senses. First, drawing from Ernst Bloch, it is a hermeneutical strategy whose task is to locate the utopian moment where it is least expected, in the negative moment, the despised, crass, vulgar and reactionary. Bloch's great work, *The Principle of Hope* (1995), is a vast exercise that runs from the most ancient mythology through to the popular genre of detective fiction, with a deep inspiration from the Bible and Goethe's *Dr Faustus*, all in the search for utopian glimmers and hopes. And he relies on the dialectical position that the negative, dystopian moment will give out to a utopian possibility despite itself. This is one of the senses in which I understand camp, and I would like to think that Bloch would smile in his grave were he to learn of my enlisting of camp in his utopian hermeneutics.

Second, I want to bring Bloch's dialectics into contact with Louis Marin's notion of neutralization. As I noted earlier, neutralization is not the process of resolving contradictions in classic Hegelian style, of seeking the modes in which texts and other ideological products attempt a resolution of real social contradictions, all the while showing signs of such attempted solutions; rather, neutralization allows the contradictions to have their play, to run out in unforeseen directions. If we take camp as such a process, then it gives free reign to other possibilities that may then be read in terms of utopia. This means that camp is not merely an aspect of the interpretation of cultural products, a predilection for film and its stars, fashion and music that is aesthetic rather than political. Rather, camp has a distinctly political edge, a cultural strategy that makes pleasure a political issue, one that looks forward to a very different world – utopia, if you like.

As for camp itself, it is both a strategy of interpretation and a form of cultural production. Susan Sontag first identified camp as a distinct strategy, albeit desexualized, depoliticized, privatized and with the connotations of homosexuality minimized (see the reprint in Sontag 1994: 275–92).[2] While Sontag argued that Camp (capital C) is an unintentional 'sensibility' rather than an 'idea', the study of camp has sought to turn the tables on conventional readings of camp: whereas the gay, lesbian and bisexual dimensions of camp were seen as one aspect (and a small one at that), subsequent critics have argued that camp is primarily a queer activity that has been co-opted by straight society (see Robertson 1996: 4). For Al La Valley, camp generates a 'sense of too-muchness, the excess, or inappropriateness, produces a sudden self-consciousness in the viewer, but one that needn't dissolve the basic meaning of the gesture' (La Valley 1995: 63). As a reading strategy, camp appropriates and redefines in terms of gender and sexuality cultural products that come from earlier moments of production but have lost their cultural force (and so Chronicles lends itself readily to camp). While there has been some debate over the territory and ownership of camp – gay male (Meyer 1994), feminist (Robertson 1996) and/or straight (Creekmur and Doty 1995) – all agree that it is ultimately a queer strategy: 'camp has the ability to "queer" straight culture by asserting that there is queerness at the core of mainstream culture even though that culture tirelessly insists that its images, ideologies, and readings were always only about heterosexuality' (Creekmur and Doty 1995: 3).

So what would a camp reading of Chronicles look like? Let me focus on

---

2 For the debate over Sontag's essay, see Meyer (1994: 7), Miller (1989), Moon (1989), Michasiw (1994), Babuscio (1977) and Kleinhans (1994).

three instances: the machismo of David's mighty men, the genealogies and the issue of cultic correctness. David's 'mighty men' (*hagibborim*) muscle their way through 1 Chronicles 11.10–47 full of bristling machismo. Their feats are so extraordinary that one would rather they just flopped their dicks out and measured them instead – much less trouble and somewhat less dangerous. Except that they seem to do this too, wielding swords and huge spears with admirable precision. My favourites here are not so much Jashobeam or Abishai, who slaughter 300 each – although Jashobeam does do it 'at once' (*bepha'am 'ehat*), conjuring up images of a grand thrust of his spear that decapitates 300 men at one go. Rather, Benaiah and the three unnamed water-bearers take my fancy. Benaiah topples a massive Egyptian (five cubits tall) by sauntering up to him, wrenching the massive spear from his hand and then poleaxing him with it. Penis envy has nothing on this story, except that the giant Egyptian must have bought his spear from the same shop as Goliath, namely the 'Weaver's Beam' (1 Chron. 11.23; see 1 Sam. 17.7; 2 Sam. 21.19). Not that they seemed to help all that much, since their owners don't last very long. But Benaiah's great claim to fame is as the lion killer: in what must be one of dumbest acts imaginable – was he acting out a dare? Stoned out of his mind? – he leaps into a pit full of snow and takes on a lion (1 Chron. 11.22).

But when all the violence is done, when the lions and Philistines and various other enemies are extinct, the campest story of the lot must be the glass of water. The three big ones, the mightiest of the mighty, the condoms stuffed with walnuts, respond to David's wistful wish: 'O that some one would give me water to drink from the well of Bethlehem which is by the gate' (1 Chron. 11.17). Given that the aforesaid well was a good distance away, and that it just happened to be behind Philistine lines, I can't help but think of David as somewhat callously seeking the ultimate test of loyalty. Such a pitiful wish, really, such a small thing to ask: so the three men – in Chronicles we know of Jashobeam and Eleazer, while in 2 Samuel we know of Shammah as well (2 Sam. 23.11) – simply smash their way through enemy lines, calmly draw out some water with one hand while fighting off hordes of Philistines with the other and carry the glass back to David without spilling a drop. But David, in (mock?) awe of their feat vows he can't touch a drop of it: 'Far be it from me before my God that I should do this. Shall I drink the lifeblood of these men? For at the risk of their lives they brought it' (1 Chron. 11.19). So he pours it out as a libation to God. Overcome with his extraordinary act of self-denial, the extreme sacrifice for his men, he binds them ever so tightly to himself.[3]

High camp? I don't think we can read these vignettes in any other way. There is, to return to Al La Valley (1995) for a moment, an inappropriateness, an excess, a sense of too-muchness in these narratives of mighty deeds and tall tales, particularly Benaiah's lion in the snow and David's dry throat. But then

---

3 I have never been able to get out of my head the thought that the big guys must have been thoroughly pissed off, not because of David's waste of the water itself, but because his act of self-denial is hardly on a par with their act of getting the water itself. Unless of course they had spilled a good deal of blood in it from Philistine-inflicted wounds, in which case David's 'Shall I drink the lifeblood of these men?' is perhaps a little more literal than we might have imagined.

what comes through is their extraordinary dumbness, for they can't figure out whether they belong to the Two, the Three or the Thirty. There is the obvious stupidity of taking on 300 enemies single-handed, leaping into a pit with a lion, or getting a drink of water from a well behind enemy lines. But at a more subtle level, they can't seem to organize themselves, particularly in a text in which organization and its description is a crucial element. Is Jashobeam the head of the Thirty, as 1 Chronicles 11.11 has it, or of the Three (2 Sam. 23.8)? But then Eleazer thinks he is just behind Jashobeam among the 'three mighty men' (2 Chron. 11.12). Abishai seems to feel that he is in fact chief of the Three (1 Chron. 11.21), except that he 'had no name among the three' (1 Chron. 11.20). A chief without name, perhaps, or one who snuck into the three without renown. But then we read: 'Among the Two was he more renowned than the Three, and he became their leader, but unto the Three he did not come' (1 Chron. 11.21). Abishai has no idea where he is, or whether he can indeed count at all. Benaiah, on the other hand, did 'have a name among the three mighty men' (1 Chron. 11.24), or did he? For although he was more renowned than the Thirty, he doesn't seem to have attained to the Three after all (1 Chron. 11.25). Confused? Well, so am I and so is the narrator, but above all so are the men themselves. It is a little like a football team in which someone with half a brain makes such a difference, directing the play, knowing which direction to run and kick. But without such a key player, the team mills about in confusion, not quite sure about anything really. This is the stuff of camp, of brawn but no brain in mass confusion. One trembles at the prospect of one of them, Benaiah, being appointed over David's bodyguard (1 Chron. 11.25). After all, what can you expect from men 'whose faces were like the faces of lions, and who were as swift as gazelles upon the mountains' (1 Chron. 12.8b)?

What, then, of the genealogies, of men begetting men in a grand sequence from Adam until the present? I can't get out of my mind the image of the utopian space of Chronicles filled with pregnant men waddling about, wondering how in the world they are going to give birth to the sons they are carrying, unless of course we are going to grant them medical know-how that borders on the science fictional. At a lesser level we might imagine them producing sons out of thin air with a wave of the hand or perhaps of the penis, a version of spontaneous generation that maintains the mystery of the Hiphil of *yld*, a causing to give birth without any sense of the process itself. Except that this is a little too close to the way breeder men see their role in giving birth anyway.

Yet the moment of high camp appears late in the genealogies. In the midst of the priestly genealogies, especially the organization of the Levites in 1 Chronicles 9, we come upon the queerest of verses:

Some of them had charge of the utensils of service, for they were required to count them when they were brought in and taken out. Others of them were appointed over the furniture, and over all the holy utensils, also over the fine flour, the wine, the oil, the incense, and the spices. Others, of the sons of the priests, prepared the mixing of the spices, and Mattithiah, one of the Levites, the firstborn of Shallum the Korahite, was in charge of making the flat cakes. Also some of their kinsmen of the Kohathites had charge of the showbread, to prepare it every sabbath. (1 Chron. 9.20–32)

This is the first time we stumble across such material – however much we might have been conditioned by the detail on the Levitical gatekeepers in 1 Chronicles 9.17–27 – but it will emerge as the major item on camp in Chronicles. Now, gatekeeping can, without too much effort, be seen as an important task: the tent and then later the temple would need its bouncers to keep out the general riff-raff. But we need to ask, what are they in fact protecting? The brilliant and unbearable presence of God in the tent itself, especially the Holy of Holies that even the high priest entered on one day of the year? Possibly, but the text reads otherwise: the bouncers protect the crockery and cutlery, furniture, fine flour, wine, oil, incense, spices, flat cakes and showbread. Further, each of these items has its own Levites in charge, down to overseeing the mixing of the spices. Less interior decoration, although that will come soon, the tabernacle becomes a department store, or perhaps a café with its gay waiters and cooks. The picture is incomplete without the singers, who were freed from any other service since they seem to have sung day and night, or at least they were on duty to do so (1 Chron. 9.33). So, as the various Levites mixed the spices, cooked the flat cakes, arranged the furniture, supervised the correct ordering of the holy crockery and so on, they were surrounded by the singers and choirs bursting forth into song 24 hours a day.

Only a few verses at the close of the genealogies, and yet the question of correct and detailed cultic organization will become the leitmotiv of Chronicles camp. By 1 Chronicles 23 the text moves into full-scale temple organization, utilizing the 38,000 Levites who were at least thirty years old (1 Chron. 23.3). And even with this number, their resources seem stretched, for David then decides that the twenty-plus age group would assist the priests (1 Chron. 23.24). Their tasks: cleaning, cooking the showbread and wafers and baked offering (scones and muffins?), mixing the various oils and singing at every opportunity (1 Chron. 23.28–31). The allocations continue: strumming lyres and harps, ringing cymbals, and vocalists (1 Chron. 25), gatekeeping (1 Chron. 26.1–19), watching over the treasuries (1 Chron. 26.20–32), and the mass organization of monthly rosters that included most of the people; even the muscle men of 1 Chronicles 11 lend a hand (1 Chron 27).

As for the building of the temple itself, David turns out to be a deft interior designer, a gift he passes on to Solomon. Thus, in the detailed instructions David leaves to Solomon, written down no less than by the hand of Yahweh (1 Chron. 28.19), David slips into camp: gold and silver lampstands, tables and bowls, pure gold forks and basins and cups, a golden altar of incense, down to what must be his crowning achievement, the golden chariot for the cherubim on the ark of the covenant (see 1 Chron. 28.15–18) – the pre-industrial revolution version of the train set, I guess. Not to mention the endless fine, coloured and precious stones scattered throughout the temple (1 Chron. 29.3). Afraid he will be outcamped, Solomon rises to new heights with the temple itself. Apart from the dimensions of the temple, and the massive weight of gold that adorns every nook and cranny, Solomon excels himself with the veil of the Holy of Holies, made 'of blue and purple and crimson fabrics and fine linen' (2 Chron. 3.14), embroidering cherubim onto it himself. (Well, not quite, but I like the idea of Solomon sitting at his embroidery day and night.) He decorates the tops of the pillars with necklaces of gold and pomegranates, and then becomes so attached to them he names them Jachin and Boaz (2 Chron. 3.16–17). And the list continues: finely wrought and carved washbasins, lampstands, pots, shovels, forks, tongs, snuffers, firepans, and of course flowers (2 Chron. 4.1–22). As 2 Chron. 9.10–11, 13–28 suggests, Solomon had a liking for the fine things in life: to a collection that ranges from lion arm rests to peacocks, we might add soft fluffy bathrobes and matching slippers.

I could go on, but the nagging question underlying all of this attention to fine furnishings and correct table settings becomes clear only later. In the narrative of the break-up of the united kingdom after Solomon, Abijah, the son of Rehoboam, addresses the rebel Israelites and Jeroboam from Mount Zemaraim. The issue comes down to cultic correctness, but note the form such correctness takes. After pointing out Jeroboam's cultic laxness, Abijah says:

> But as for us, Yahweh is our God, and we have not forsaken him. We have priests ministering to Yahweh who are sons of Aaron, and Levites for their service. They offer to Yahweh every morning and every evening burnt offerings and incense of sweet spices, set out the showbread on the table of pure gold, and care for the golden lampstand that its lamps may burn every evening; for we keep the charge of Yahweh our God, but you have forsaken him. Behold, God is with us at our head, and his priests with their battle trumpets to sound the call to battle against you. (2 Chron. 13.10–12a)

The signs of faithfulness to Yahweh include the vital elements of offering sweet spices, setting out the showbread on the gold table and ensuring that the golden lampstand keeps burning. The catch is that Abijah is deadly serious, and yet I can see him standing atop the mountain in his finely wrought linen robe, washed and neatly pressed, hair and beard trimmed, washed, combed and oiled not long beforehand, the tassels and bells at the hem of his robe jingling slightly as he berates the Israelites for their waywardness. Forget devotion of the heart, faithfulness and justice, what counts is that the appearance, aroma and ordering of the cult is correct down to the finest detail.

All this inappropriate excess renders Yahweh not a place-holder of the void but a key participant in the camp of Chronicles. For does he not require all of this, from golden forks to baked bread, at the hands of his obsessive priests and Levites? So much so that we come, finally, upon a camp battle scene during the reign of Jehoshaphat. Faced with the marauding Ammonites, Moabites and men of Mount Seir, Jehoshaphat enquires of Yahweh what he must do (2 Chron. 20.1–17). No ambush or pincer movement, no introduction of the phalanx or heavy artillery (well before its time), what they must do is sing, prophesies the Levite Jahaziel! Temple worship moves out into the battlefield, and the choir becomes the front line. Facing the enemy, Jehoshaphat 'appointed those who were to sing to Yahweh and praise him in holy array' (2 Chron. 20.21). We even have a snippet of the song: 'Give thanks to Yahweh, for his steadfast love endures forever' (2 Chron. 20.21). Fully decked out, in holy array, the basses, tenors and sopranos kick in, as the harps keep the bass line, the cymbals the beat and the lyres the lead. And Yahweh takes over the battle so that the Ammonites, Moabites and men of Mount Seir ambush and slaughter one another. Music with bite, song with an edge, battle as a musical! All Judah need do is gather the spoil and head for home, still singing (2 Chron. 20.24–8).

As I have pointed out already, these are not mere moments of camp, not glimmers of possibility in a text that runs elsewhere. Correct observance of the cult is a, if not the, key feature of Chronicles. Upon such observance hinges Yahweh's punishment or blessing, in the well-known 'immediate divine retribution'.[4] Incense mixed incorrectly, a golden basin out of place, a false note sung – these unforgivable sins among many others would bring his immediate wrath, usually in terms of rampaging foreigners, strange diseases, loss of those valuable sons the men laboured so valiantly to produce and gruesome early deaths. Of course this means that Yahweh is the *raison d'être* of camp in Chronicles, a cantankerous old queen who will fly off the handle at the smallest provocation.

In the end, I have been able to outline only the possibilities of camp in Chronicles without going into the necessary depth that is so much more delectable. However, in my response to Kelso's argument I don't want to suggest that camp detoxifies the misogyny of Chronicles. By contrast, it is a form of utopian hermeneutics, one that belongs in the same arena as Irigaray's 'militating for the impossible'. And a camp reading of Chronicles faces the negative – here the unremitting misogyny of the text – not in order to seek a dialectical resolution, nor to seek the redeeming elements that we can then appropriate for ourselves, as though we were panning for gold, grasping the granules of precious metal left after the sand and dross have been washed away. Rather, I have opened up the text in order to let it run away in different directions, making the most of Chronicles' excesses, where it goes far too far. For it seems to me that the cultic gravity and over-the-top masculinity of the text gives out to the playful overindulgence of camp.

---

4 First identified by Julius Wellhausen (1994: 203–10), 'immediate divine retribution' is often the source of negative assessments of Chronicles' theological sophistication. I am not so sure. To spell it out: the divine response to obedience or disobedience is immediate blessing or punishment, particularly by the kings and often exhibited in terms of cultic correctness (see, for example, 2 Chron. 29–31). The inevitable punishment that follows disobedience may be averted by repentance after a warning. See further Boer 1997: 148–50.

Ezra–Nehemiah

RON L. STANLEY

The book of Ezra–Nehemiah[1] is not one of the places in the Bible queer people often turn for support or encouragement. In fact, this book is not one that is read often under any circumstances. As primarily a book of history, Ezra–Nehemiah tells the story of the rebuilding of the city of Jerusalem and the rebuilding of the Jewish community. But this book also tells the story of leadership – both successful and unsuccessful. Two primary figures, Ezra and Nehemiah, emerged to lead the Jewish people as they resettled Judah, but only one had any measure of success. Nehemiah, the Persian king's eunuch cup-bearer, was able to successfully lead the Jews to rebuild the city walls, resettle the city and pledge to follow the covenant. It was the eunuch – the sexual outcast – that was able to lead the people to successfully restore the city and community. Perhaps there is more in the book of Ezra–Nehemiah for the queer community than was first assumed.

Basic Commentary

Ezra–Nehemiah can be divided into four parts that correspond to the return and subsequent activities of the people. These activities include rebuilding the temple, rebuilding the community, rebuilding the city walls, and finally: religious renewal, reform and the struggle to be faithful. The first three stages follow a basic pattern: an initial return of people to Jerusalem, opposition to reconstruction by outsiders and the eventual defeat of the opposition (Throntveit 1992).

The first return and rebuilding of the temple

Ezra–Nehemiah opens with a decree from Cyrus the king of Persia proclaiming that the Jews could return to Jerusalem and rebuild the temple. This is consistent with what we know of the Persian Empire and their policies toward

---

1 Although most English translations divide the books of Ezra and Nehemiah into two distinct books, the earliest Hebrew manuscripts treat the books as one. The first division of the books was done by the early Christian Church and it was only in modern times that this arrangement made its appearance in Jewish circles. For this commentary, Ezra–Nehemiah will be treated as one book, albeit compiled from various sources. See further H. G. M. Williamson (1985: xxi–xxiii).

conquered peoples. Persia's attitude was dominated by 'a sense of political expediency' that saw religion as one way to gain support and keep peace in the empire (Janzen 2000: 631). At the same time, the Persians were not above destroying temples or levying high taxes in areas involved in attempted revolts – from the Persian's perspective, the return of the Jews and the rebuilding of the temple in Jerusalem was a purely practical matter for the stability of the region.

For the Jews, however, it was a spiritual matter. God had finally allowed them to return home from the Exile. They celebrated in Jerusalem by observing the Feast of Tabernacles and resuming the daily sacrifices. They also began the rebuilding of the temple. But the Jews were not without opposition. The enemies of Judah and Benjamin began to actively campaign against the Jews and the rebuilding almost as soon as they arrived in the area. They tried to discourage the people of Judah and make them afraid to rebuild. Their enemies hired counsellors to work against them and made false accusations to the Persian kings, accusing them of planning to revolt. All of this caused the Persian king to stop the work in Jerusalem – the whole purpose of allowing the return and rebuilding was to keep peace in the area.

After a short period of time, Haggai and Zechariah appeared in Jerusalem and encouraged the people to start work again. The enemies of Judah took notice immediately and again sent word to the king. The Persian king ordered a search of court records containing the decree giving the Jews the right to rebuild. When the edict of Cyrus was found, King Darius not only ordered that no one interfere with the rebuilding but also provided materials for the project. Thus, in the sixth year of the reign of Darius the temple was completed and the people celebrated with the Passover and the Feast of Unleavened Bread.

The second return and rebuilding of the community

With Ezra's arrival in Jerusalem, the text provides a lengthy introduction detailing his lineage as a priest all the way back to Aaron the brother of Moses. According to the narrator, he was also a teacher 'well versed in the law' (Ezra 7.1–6). And he travelled from Babylon with a letter from the Persian king giving him great authority in Judah. Most notably, Ezra was given the ability to request provisions from the royal treasury for the temple and to appoint magistrates and judges and to punish any who did not obey the law. In short, Ezra was given broad powers to act on behalf of the king – particularly in relation to Jewish law.

The actions taken by Ezra once he arrived, however, do not stack up to what he was commissioned to do by the king. He did deliver the king's orders to the governors around Judaea so that they would provide supplies when needed, but the rest of the directives to Ezra from the king were largely left undone. Ezra was not the leader of the people that he could have been. First, Ezra had to be told about the intermarriage of Judaeans with foreigners around them, and it was a leader in the community, Shecaniah, not Ezra, who offered a solution to the problem. Shecaniah even had to encourage Ezra to take action on the matter: 'Rise up; this matter is in your hands. We will support you, so take courage and do it' (10.4). Second, there is no record that Ezra fulfilled his role as a teacher of the law until much later. It is only after the walls of the city were completed under Nehemiah that we have any record of Ezra reading the law to an assembly of the people. If this was one of his central tasks, why did several years pass before he began? And third, the only record of officials appointed in Jerusalem relates to those appointed by Nehemiah. It appears that even with the backing of the Persian king, Ezra was reluctant to take a leading role with his people and did not accomplish all that the king sent him to do.

The third return and rebuilding of the walls

Nehemiah the eunuch

The third return took place under the leadership of Nehemiah. Nehemiah was the cupbearer for the Persian king Artaxerxes I.[2] Classical sources give detailed descriptions of royal cupbearers and their responsibilities. Naturally, one of the primary duties of the cupbearer was to taste the king's wine and food to guard against poisoning (Xenophon, *Cryopaedia* 1.3.8–9). However, early sources also indicate that the cupbearer often had many other responsibilities. Tobit mentions a cupbearer who was 'keeper of the signet, and in charge of administration of the accounts, for Esarhaddon had appointed him second to himself' (Tob. 1.22). This man was not a mere servant or waiter who delivered the king's food. This was a man who enjoyed the privilege of the king's favour and made decisions on the king's behalf. Furthermore, Yamauchi mentions six traits that a cupbearer was likely to possess including the 'unreserved confidence' of the king and the ability to control who had access to the king.[3] This close rapport with the king squares well with Nehemiah's conversation with Artaxerxes concerning Jerusalem and provides valuable insight into the skills Nehemiah would have acquired as a cupbearer.

It is also known from ancient sources that most cupbearers were eunuchs. Cyrus, the earliest of the Persian kings, began the practice of employing eunuchs in the royal house. He believed that a man would never be loyal or trustworthy if he loved his family more than the one he was to protect. Therefore, he supposed that eunuchs would be the most loyal of all servants since, without a family, they would be most loyal to the one that could give them riches and honour. Cyrus resolved that all of his personal servants would be eunuchs and practised that throughout his reign (Xenophon, *Cryopaedia* 1.3.8–9). That this practice continued after Cyrus is attested to by Ctesias, who was a physician in the court of Artaxerxes II (404–359 BCE). Ctesias stated that during his time in the royal court all the cupbearers were eunuchs (Yamauchi 1980: 298). Thus, with evidence from both before and after the reign of Artaxerxes I, it is unlikely that the situation would have been any different during the days of Nehemiah. While the book of Ezra–Nehemiah never specifically calls Nehemiah a eunuch, it is very likely he was.

---

2 That Nehemiah served Artaxerxes I (464–24 BCE) is generally accepted since an Elephantine papyrus dated to 407 BCE mentions the sons of Sanballat the governor of Samaria and an adversary of Nehemiah (Yamauchi 1980a: 291).

3 Other traits included training in etiquette and wine selection, a handsome appearance, and good listening skills (Yamauchi 1980: 296–7).

Nehemiah's status as a eunuch is significant because it made him a sexual outcast among his people. While he enjoyed an important position in the Persian court, the status of eunuchs in Hebrew life was very different. Deuteronomy 23.1 states that 'No one who has been emasculated by crushing or cutting may enter the assembly of the Lord.' The eunuch was essentially cut off from the aspects of life that were the centre of Judaism – worship and family. At the same time, it is likely that Nehemiah and others were aware of the work of the prophet Isaiah some 300 years before their time. Isaiah prophesied concerning eunuchs: 'For this is what the Lord says: "To the eunuchs who keep my Sabbaths, who choose what pleases me and hold fast to my covenant; to them I will give within my temple and its walls a memorial and a name better than sons and daughters; I will give them an everlasting name that will not be cut off"' (56.4–5). Isaiah essentially took away the stigma attached to eunuchs – both the stigma relating to their physical body and the stigma relating to their lack of children. Isaiah thus elevated the covenant and its adherence over any supposed external or physical indicators of spirituality. It is likely that Nehemiah's numerous prayers for God to 'remember' him (5.19; 13.14, 22, 31) look back to the promise given through Isaiah.

Rebuilding the wall

After Nehemiah's return to Jerusalem he surveyed the work that needed to be done and immediately took charge of the situation. He enlisted the leaders and the people to help in rebuilding the walls of the city. Of course, there was opposition. Local governors, Sanballat, Tobiah and Geshem, were alarmed that someone was promoting the welfare of Judah and they began to ridicule the Jews and the work they were doing. Nehemiah replied only that God would support them and that their enemies had no part in Jerusalem. As the Jews began to close the gaps in the wall, their enemies became more bold and planned to attack them. When Nehemiah heard this, he and the Jews prayed and posted guards. Nehemiah was never distracted by the taunts of his enemies – not even when his life was threatened. Nor he did not let the people get distracted. Instead he offered practical solutions to their concerns so that eventually half of the people worked while the other half stood guard and the wall was completed in 52 days.

Nehemiah was very successful as a leader of his people. He sought and was granted permission to return to Jerusalem from the Persian king. The king also granted him soldiers for the journey and the ability to request provisions for rebuilding. Nehemiah led the people around Jerusalem to rebuild in spite of opposition, and the city walls were quickly repaired. In addition, Nehemiah helped restore the community itself by providing leadership concerning charging interest to kinsmen, marrying foreign women and keeping the Sabbath. In short, Nehemiah's leadership was far reaching and decisive.

Renewal, reform and the struggle to be faithful

When the walls were finished, Nehemiah led the people to resettle the city and appointed men to guard the gates. The people asked Ezra to read the law to them and they celebrated the Feast of Booths. While listening to the law, the Jews again realized they had foreigners living in their midst and had them removed. The people also made a binding agreement between themselves and God to keep the law from that time forward. After this, the wall was dedicated and the people worshipped God for all that had been accomplished. But remaining faithful was still a struggle. Shortly after this, while Nehemiah was away, a foreigner was allowed to have a room in the temple, and the supplies that were to be given for the priests were neglected. When Nehemiah returned, he reminded the people of their commitments and they returned to keeping the covenant. Other than his role in the worship celebration, Ezra was curiously absent in all of this. For further detail see Allen (2003), Blenkinsopp (1988), Clines (1984), Gordon F. Davies (1999) and Grabbe (1998).

Nehemiah and Ezra as Leaders

Leadership is a topic that has been widely discussed over the past few decades. In businesses, charities, schools and even churches, the question of what makes a good leader has been asked frequently. Much more than this, however, people want to know what makes an outstanding leader – what makes one leader merely adequate for the task while another leader is seemingly able to move mountains? Sociological studies have sought to answer this question based on observations of exceptional leaders and their followers. Researchers have found that certain situations and certain individual characteristics can lead to the emergence of highly successful leaders. A brief discussion of these findings will be helpful as we discuss Ezra, Nehemiah and other First Testament leaders.[4]

Often, highly successful leaders arise in the midst of a crisis. The crisis can be either physical or ideological but often contributes to a society's willingness to accept an unconventional leader. These leaders frequently come from outside the immediate situation and are able to address the concerns of their contemporaries in ways that other leaders have been unable or unwilling to pursue. The crisis, when combined with the qualities present in the potential leader, results in a willingness for others to follow.

Moving beyond the situation in which a leader emerges, researchers have searched for universal qualities common to successful leaders, but have found that the variations in personal characteristics were so great that one particular personality type seems unlikely (Conger 1988: 19). What has emerged is a constellation of traits common among successful leaders (Conger 1988: 35). Any given leader will not possess every trait identified, but will have enough traits to attract and keep the attention and loyalty of his or her followers.

Willner (1968), Conger (1988) and Bass (1990) have each identified character traits which seem to be most common among extremely successful leaders. These behaviours include being expressive, self-confident, insightful and

---

4 Portions of this section are based on the author's dissertation, R. Stanley, 'Charismatic leadership in ancient Israel: a social-scientific approach' (unpublished doctoral dissertation, Southwestern Baptist Theological Seminary, 2001).

energetic. Communication skills give the leader the ability to communicate a 'powerful, confident and dynamic presence' (Bass 1990: 190). An ordinary leader may possess the necessary skills but fail in his or her task because of an inability to communicate vision and drive. Ordinary leaders may inspire admiration and respect, but extraordinary leaders inspire devotion and even blind faith (Willner 1968: 6). The self-confidence found in most outstanding leaders is revealed in a 'stubborn self-confidence and faith in the movement's prospects of victory and success' (Tucker 1968: 87). This trait may be the quality that is most important in garnering followers. People in the midst of a crisis are often plagued by anxiety and often easily respond to a leader who can inspire them to believe in the possibility of deliverance. Such self-confident leaders are able to inspire exceptional trust from their followers even in the face of setbacks and failure as their presence of mind and composure under stress never falters (Bass 1990: 191).

Successful leaders also typically possess an unusual amount of insight and energy and a profound sense of vision. They are believed to have a unique ability to understand the current situation and respond appropriately. They also possess insight into the values, goals and needs of the people, and tailor their plans to fit the situation. Also, when compared to other leaders, highly successful leaders tend to show a higher energy level and an extraordinary degree of vitality. Their actions and decisions are significantly stronger than others and they make extensive use of role-modelling to demonstrate how their goals and vision can be achieved, as noted by Willner (1968: 67), Bass (1990: 191) and Conger (1988: 34). Vision, in this sense, refers to an idealized future goal that the leader wishes to achieve. By providing goals and methods of achieving them the leader gives a sense of tremendous challenge and motivation to his followers. The leader describes the current situation as unacceptable – in this sense they strive to create dissatisfaction – a critical step in every successful change process. Less successful leaders tend to either downplay the negative aspects of the current situation or fail to effectively articulate why it is unacceptable. The successful leader presents his vision as the most reasonable alternative. And while his goals are often idealistic, this leader portrays them as both realistic and attainable (Conger 1988: 31).

Next, the successful leader often has several possible social identifications. In other words, the individual, by virtue of his or her previous experiences, may be identified with several different groups or segments of society. This results in a flexibility that adds to the influence of the leader by appealing to a broader spectrum of people than might be possible for others. This type of leader has the advantages of multiple perspectives on the world and is able to communicate with members of different segments of society (Willner 1968: 51).

The last personal characteristic is present in religious belief systems where the follower's attention may be focused on the transcendental authority the leader represents (Downton 1973: 212). In this instance, followers are more concerned with the authority behind the leader than with the leader himself, making the individual characteristics of the leader less important. Thus, a leader may be followed solely because of the belief that he or she speaks for God.

These same behaviours and qualities that move supporters to extremes of love, veneration and admiration of a leader, may also move opponents to extremes of hatred and animosity. A leader cannot inspire trust and respect from everyone, in fact they may inspire 'opposition and hatred in those who strongly favor the old order of things' (Bass 1990: 187). In essence, those in positions of power with a vested interest in the old order of things will be unlikely to support the leader and their reforms and thus become openly negative and hostile.

Finally, leaders and their followers must take steps to assume the continuation of their influence. At some point the crisis will pass or the leader move on. If steps were not taken to ensure the continuation of the new system it too will pass from the scene. The leader and/or followers must put a more routine bureaucratic system in place in order to ensure the continuation of the message and mission. This may even include the emergence of oral and written traditions which help ensure continuity with the original leader's vision (Bass 1990: 198).

Nehemiah and Ezra

Nehemiah is quite often looked to as the most explicit model of leadership in the First Testament, yet when reading the Bible it is Ezra that appears to have been given the more honoured position. Ezra is given the longest and most colourful introduction in the book of Ezra–Nehemiah: 'Ezra son of Seraiah, the son of Azariah . . . the son of Aaron the chief priest – this Ezra came up from Babylon. He was a teacher well versed in the Law of Moses, which the Lord, the God of Israel, had given. The king had granted him everything he asked, for the hand of the Lord his God was on him' (7.1–6). This lengthy introduction traces Ezra's lineage back to Aaron the high priest, describes him as a great teacher of the law and places him in the favour of both God and king. In addition, this interruption is particularly uncharacteristic of a narrator who rarely interrupts the flow of the story in Ezra–Nehemiah. Nehemiah's introduction – 'The words of Nehemiah son of Hacaliah' – by comparison, not only looks anaemic, but returns to the more normal silence of the book's editor (Eskenazi 1988: 136). The introduction is short and unenlightening and it is the only introduction Nehemiah is given. The reader is left to gather information about Nehemiah from the story as it unfolds. It is only later that we find that Nehemiah is the cupbearer to the king of Persia; that he is a dedicated man of God concerned about his home and people; that he has earned the confidence and favour of the king, and is able to use his position in the court to help his people in Jerusalem. The fact that Nehemiah is a eunuch is left out completely.

If Ezra is emphasized more by the narrator, how do the two men compare as leaders? Both Ezra and Nehemiah arrived in Jerusalem in the midst of a crisis and with the support of the Persian king. Ezra's letter from the king appointed him to teach the law of God, restore the temple and appoint judges and magistrates to administer the justice. The confidence of both the king and the narrator in Ezra creates the expectation of a great figure emerging on the scene (Eskenazi 1988: 137). But in this, Ezra only disappoints. Even with the confidence the king has shown him, Ezra is too timid to ask for protection for the journey. In spite of the powers given to him to teach and implement the law of God, the obvious problem of intermarriage had to be brought to his attention and the solution had to be suggested by someone else. Ezra even had to be encouraged to help with the solution (Ezra 9.1–10.4). In short, Ezra's leadership ability seems to be severely lacking.

Ezra's lack of leadership ability can be clearly seen when compared to the list of successful leadership characteristics discussed earlier. He did enter Jerusalem at a time of crisis and possessed a measure of authority given to him by the Persian king. Those who followed Ezra tended to focus on the divine authority given to him by his position as a teacher of the law and descendant of Aaron. However, Ezra does not appear to have had a driving vision for the community or the self-confidence to communicate with the people on important issues. Ezra was expressive only in his grief over the sins of the people and seemed unable to move beyond the grief to a solution. Of the eight characteristics commonly displayed by successful leaders, Ezra displayed only two – he sought to conserve the religious order and he was expressive of his grief over the people's sins. Finally, Ezra was ineffectual enough that he had no opposition.

If Ezra shows a decided lack of leadership ability, Nehemiah is one of the model leaders of the First Testament. Nehemiah was serving in the Persian court when he heard of the crisis in Jerusalem and he immediately took action. He prayed for his people and himself and determined to approach the king for help when the time was right. Nehemiah spelled out his vision for the rebuilding of Jerusalem in a way that even the king was persuaded to help him. Upon arriving in Jerusalem, Nehemiah showed his insightfulness by touring the damaged city walls at night before he addressed the people so that he would have firsthand knowledge of the city's condition. Nehemiah's relevance to the people is seen in his first task – rebuilding the walls of the city. The people were spread out across the countryside because the city was not safe. Nehemiah's determination to rebuild the walls was directly relevant to the people, who would be able to live there again.

The people followed Nehemiah because what he wanted to do was relevant to their lives and he inspired them to believe it could be done – this was in spite of the fact that he was a eunuch and sexual outcast. It was common knowledge at the time that the Persians preferred to have eunuchs serving in the palace. Many of the young men taken captive by the Babylonians were made eunuchs and trained to work in positions of government service, education and business. Nehemiah was no different. In addition, as the king's cupbearer he was well trained in court etiquette and is likely to have controlled who had access to the king. He had firsthand exposure to political intrigues and their resolutions, making him well aware of the possibilities of deception and manipulation. Nehemiah would have also been a good conversationalist who was knowledgeable about the kingdom. It is likely that no one had more access to the king or spent more time with him. Thus, Nehemiah would have acted as a sounding board or confidant of the king. Finally, the king placed the utmost confidence in his cupbearer and would have rewarded him with gifts and riches.[5] All of these skills, skills that were a direct result of his training and work as a eunuch, were integral to his success as a leader in Jerusalem.

First, Nehemiah was expressive and self-confident – skills he honed in the Persian court. He was accustomed to speaking with people of varying influence and was able to make his positions known. He was unafraid of confronting hard issues even among his own people. Even though he could be considered one of the officials of the city, Nehemiah knew and understood the situation of the common man. When the people complained that the nobles and officials were charging high interest on loans for food and basic necessities, Nehemiah was outraged. He confronted the offenders and demanded they stop and return what they had taken. He even summoned the priests and made the officials take an oath to do what they had promised. Unlike Ezra, Nehemiah did not need anyone to tell him how to solve the problem, nor was he afraid to take action.

Second, Nehemiah's energy and commitment to the task was contagious. When the people were threatened, and even his own life was threatened, he continued to work. Even when fellow Jews advised Nehemiah to hide in the temple he refused to stop working. Threats of attack or slander did not slow Nehemiah down. Following his example, the people worked and stood guard day and night. At times, they worked with one hand while they held their sword in the other. They went as far as to sleep in their clothes with their weapons at their side. Watching Nehemiah and the way he handled the opposition, the people were inspired to continue the work.

Finally, like most strong leaders that seek to make a profound change in a society, Nehemiah faced tough opposition. From the moment he made known his vision to restore the city walls, there were those that wanted him to fail. Sanballat, Tobiah and Gesham led the fight against Nehemiah and the Jews and their determination to rebuild the walls. They waged a campaign of ridicule and slander, and when that did not work they threatened violence. However, even this did not deter Nehemiah. He merely strengthened the guard around the city and had the people watch for attacks while they worked. Nehemiah did not let threats intimidate him or his people. Instead, he laid out a plan to deal with their enemies that allowed them to continue their work.

With all of this, it is obvious that Nehemiah was a strong, successful leader of the Jewish people. He led the people to restore the city to the point that they could return and live in safety. He had the vision and the drive to see through what other leaders had only meagrely attempted. The training he received as a eunuch enabled him to step into the leadership role in Jerusalem and see the job through to completion. His status as a eunuch or sexual outcast never appears to have arisen as an issue among the people in Jerusalem. It may be that they remembered the prophecy of Isaiah and granted Nehemiah the same grace that Isaiah spoke of. There is no doubt that he led them in worship – a situation that would have been impossible prior to the Exile. It is also likely that Nehemiah was such a strong and charismatic leader who addressed concerns that they considered essential that his sexual status became a non-issue.

---

5 Nehemiah's prosperity is evident in the loans he was able to make after returning to Jerusalem (Neh. 5.10).

Conclusion

Nehemiah's leadership can be favourably compared with that of Moses and David: each leader addressed a crisis in society that made the people more willing to follow them; each was a visionary and had specific plans for the people and was able to communicate those plans in a way that gained support for the effort; each was insightful when it came to solving problems; and each leader was confident both in themselves and in their call from God. When placed side by side with Moses and David, who are almost universally acknowledged as great leaders, Nehemiah rises to the same status. He was as successful and resourceful as Moses and David, and the restoration of the city walls and resettlement of the city lasted well into the future. Thus, Nehemiah deserves to be remembered alongside other great leaders in the First Testament. He deserves to be remembered for what he was – the eunuch who was able to lead in rebuilding the city when no one else could.

Esther

MONA WEST

Introduction

Esther is one of two books in the Hebrew Bible named after a woman (Ruth being the other). It is not a work of history – there is no evidence of a Persian queen named Esther – but is a fictional story or historical novel, much like the book of Jonah. There is no mention of traditional Jewish themes such as covenant, law, dietary regulations, or even the name of God.

Its mention of Ahasuerus (Xerxes 486–465 BCE) in chapter 1 indicates that the setting of the story is the Jewish Diaspora in Persia. The version of Esther found in the Hebrew Bible as part of the Writings was probably written during the Hellenistic period between 400 and 200 BCE. Later in the Hellenistic period the Hebrew text was translated for Greek-speaking Jews and additional material was added to give more detail to the story and make the book more religious. These Greek additions to Esther can be found in the Apocrypha.

Esther is also the only book in the Hebrew Bible to explain the origin of a new Hebrew festival. One of its primary purposes is to explain the origin and the details of the observance of the Jewish feast of Purim – the only Jewish feast not mentioned in the Torah. The other reason Esther exists is to make people laugh.

In her recent commentary Adele Berlin agrees with a variety of scholars who claim that Esther has a comic spirit bordering on the carnivalesque. Berlin claims, 'The book of Esther is the most humorous of the books in the Bible, amusing throughout and at certain points uproariously funny' (Berlin 2001: xvii–xviii).

But often the inclusion of a book in the biblical canon can limit the full range of readings of that book. Somehow, because Esther is considered scripture, readers feel they must find something holy, or instructional, thus limiting a full appreciation of the book as comedy. Berlin wants to 'press' the comic aspects of the book, not as incidental, but as the 'essence of the book' (2001: xvii).

The way she does this is to show how Esther exaggerates life in the Persian court – not to critique it, but to provide a backdrop for hilarious comedy. Esther's presentation of the Persian court and Jewish life in it are not meant to be historical presentations, even though they are realistic. More than being realistic, they are conventional (Berlin 2001: xxx).

Esther and Camp

In her essay 'Camping around the canon' Elizabeth Stuart wants to move readers beyond just finding the comic in scripture to claim laughter as a hermeneutical tool. But not just any laughter, laughter produced by a camp reading of scripture (2000: 28). Camp not only includes humour, it uses the tactics of parody to provide subversive critique and when applied to scripture it produces a 'drag reading of scripture – a performance designed to subvert dominant readings and understandings' (Stuart 2000: 30).

Camp, drag and queer theory all use performativity to critique dominant conventions in a society or to sabotage binarisms such as male/female which are used to maintain a certain social order (Cleto 1999: 12–15). In particular, camp exaggerates dominant conventions to the point where they are exposed as conventions rather than seen as absolute norms. Tactics employed by camp include parody, exaggeration, boundary-crossing, occupying spaces, and miming privileges of normality (Berlant and Freeman 1993: 196).

The exaggeration in Esther serves not only to entertain, but to expose the conventions of power in the Persian court and to sabotage the gender binarism of male and female, as well as the constructed identities of Jew and Persian in the Diaspora.

Cross-dressing also figures prominently in the book of Esther and in the tactics of camp, drag and queer theory. Jopie Siebert-Hommes has pointed out that clothing in any given society 'expresses a person's cultural identity, or indicates the status, power or gender of the wearer' and clothing plays a major role in these areas in the book of Esther (Siebert-Hommes 2002). In a structuralist reading of Esther, David J. A. Clines has also noted the significance of the 'code of clothing' as it relates to power (Clines 1998: 5–7).

Marjorie Garber, in her book *Vested Interests: Cross-Dressing and Cultural Anxiety*, indicates that cross-dressing challenges the binary notions of male and female – 'whether they are considered essential or constructed, biological or cultural' (1992: 10). The way cross-dressing offers a critique of this kind of binary thinking is to create what looks like a 'third term'. She goes on to emphasize,

> But what is crucial here – and I can hardly underscore this strongly enough – is that the 'third term' is *not a term*. Much less is it a *sex* . . . The 'third' is a mode of articulation, a way of describing a space of possibility. Three puts in question the idea of one: of identity, self-sufficiency, self-knowledge. (1992: 11)

Crucial to the book of Esther will be the way clothing – in particular cross-dressing – is a third mode of articulation for Jewish identity in the Diaspora.

Eunuchs in the book of Esther are also a third mode of articulation. Will Roscoe has identified eunuchs in ancient Mediterranean societies as 'state third-gender roles' (1997: 56). He calls them 'state' because they function in the realm of civic and state institutions. They are considered 'third-gender' because these ancient societies attributed to them 'both secondary sex characteristics and psychological traits, labeling them in ways that distinguished them from both men and women' (1997: 64). Persians in particular preferred eunuchs as military officers and chief officers of state because as castrated males they could not complicate dynastic succession by fathering children (Roscoe 1997: 64). Other characteristics of third-gender roles included intermediaries for the emperors, confidants and servants who lacked competing loyalties, and scapegoats for social or political ills (Roscoe 1997: 70).

Kathryn Ringrose in her study of eunuchs in the Byzantine Empire indicates that Byzantine society was intentional about constructing eunuchs as a third gender category. This was done through castration at a young age, rearing children born with ambiguous sexual organs as eunuchs, and gendering young eunuchs into 'patterns of behaviour considered to be "normal" for what it determined would be their gender category' (Ringrose 2003: 5).

These eunuchs were 'perfect servants' since they had no ties to family or offspring. In addition to being servants, agents or proxies for their employers, other characteristics included the ability to move freely across social and gender boundaries, as well as distinctive physiological and behavioural traits (Ringrose 2003: 5).

Eunuchs appear in half the chapters of the book of Esther as servants or agents of the Persian king. Many are mentioned by name, and their ability to cross social and gender boundaries allows them to play key roles in the plot of the story. It is the king's eunuch, Hegai, who instructs Esther in the application of her make-up and clothing in order to make a Jewish maiden into a Persian queen in drag.

Exaggeration

Feasting, fasting and violence are exaggerated elements in the story of Esther that lend themselves to a camp reading for the purpose of exposing conventions of power in the Persian court. There are nine banquets (drinking parties) that provide the context for these exaggerations as well as the structure for the plot (a banquet is the setting in which major events occur).

Banquets one, two and three

Exaggerated extravagance dominates two of the three banquets found in chapter 1. In the opening verses King Ahasuerus gives a banquet for all his officials and the entire armies of Persia and Media. We are told that the king 'displayed the great wealth of his kingdom and the splendour and pomp of his majesty' (v. 4).[1]

The next banquet lasts seven days and is given for the people of the capital city Susa. The location is in the court of the garden of the king's palace. The description is opulent: white cotton curtains and blue hangings tied with cords of fine linen, marble pillars, couches of gold and silver on a mosaic pavement of porphyry, marble, mother-of-pearl and coloured stones. Drinks were served

---

1 All references are from the NRSV.

in gold goblets, of different kinds, and drinking was by flagons. (A décor that would not go unnoticed by a gay male reader who happens to be a 'queen'!)

In stark contrast to the exaggeration and elaborate description of the first two banquets, we are told that Queen Vashti 'gave a banquet for the women in the palace of King Ahasuerus' (v. 9).

On the seventh day of the people's banquet the king sends for Vashti wearing the royal crown, wishing to add her to the collection of opulence. But Queen Vashti refuses to come, and this enrages the king. Sages are consulted and it is decided that a decree must go out to all the land announcing that Vashti may never again come before the king, and furthermore her position as queen will be given to someone else. The rationale for the decree is clearly stated in verses 17–18:

> For this deed of the queen will be made known to all women, causing them to look with contempt on their husbands, since they will say, 'King Ahasuerus commanded Queen Vashti to be brought before him, and she did not come.' This very day the noble ladies of Persia and Media who have heard of the queen's behaviour will rebel against the king's officials, and there will be no end of contempt and wrath!

The first three banquets, through their exaggeration, parody gender and power in the Persian court. The king attempts to show his power with the extravagance of his ability to throw parties for his officials, his armies and all the people of Susa (all assumed to be male, since Vashti's banquet is for women only) to find that his power is usurped with one woman's refusal to come before him. Vashti's refusal threatens male power to the point that it must be legislated: 'So when the decree made by the king is proclaimed throughout all his kingdom, vast as it is, all women will give honour to their husbands high and low alike' (v. 20).

The decree itself becomes exaggerated, 'sent to every province, in its own script and to every people in its own language, declaring that every man should be master in his own house' (v. 22).

The parody continues in that the very decree grants Vashti her wish – not to come before the king – and does the very thing the men are trying to prevent: spreading the news of Vashti's rebellion.

Banquets four and five

In chapter 2 the king gives a banquet upon the election of Esther as the new Queen of Persia. Even though it is called 'Esther's banquet' it serves to re-establish male power. The king has a queen again who is the most desirable and beautiful of all the virgins that had been brought before him. Yet this queen is not all that she seems. She is a closeted Jew, with a strong relationship to her cousin Mordecai who lives outside the Persian palace.

The banquet in chapter 3 is really a private drinking party between the king and one of his officials, Haman. Its description is chilling: 'The king and Haman sat down to drink but the city of Susa was thrown into confusion' (v. 15). The banquet is an occasion for exaggerated violence that has just been decreed. Haman has plotted to annihilate all Jews of Persia as an act of revenge against Mordecai, who would not bow down to him because he was a Jew.

While the banquet itself is not extravagant, the violence it celebrates is. This exaggeration of violence begins the critique of the construction of Jewish identity in the Diaspora – identities that become ambiguous with the role of Queen Esther in the sixth and seventh banquets and the remaining eighth and ninth banquets given not by the Persian king, but the Jews!

Banquets six and seven

These banquets are found at the centre of the book and are the occasion for the climax of the plot and the reversal of the fortune of the Jews. When Esther learns of the plan to annihilate the Jews she sends word to Mordecai who sends word back encouraging her to go before the king, to come out as a Jew and to plead for the life of her people. Esther sends another message to her cousin expressing concern that if she goes before the king unbidden she will be put to death. Upon receiving this news Mordecai sends back a reply that has become one of the most famous quotes from the book:

> Do not think that in the king's palace you will escape any more than all the other Jews. For if you keep silence at such a time as this, relief and deliverance will rise for the Jews from another quarter, but you and your father's family will perish. Who knows? Perhaps you have come to royal dignity for just such a time as this. (4.13–14)

Esther sends a request to Mordecai asking all the Jews of Susa to fast for three days on her behalf, while she and her maids also fast. The Jews were already fasting as a sign of their mourning over Haman's decree. This exaggerated fasting is a prelude to the feasting that is about to take place in order to expose Haman's plot and rescue the Jews.

On the third day of the fast Esther comes before the king, wins his favour and invites him and Haman to a banquet that she has prepared. Esther has prepared a feast, while she has been fasting. Jews fast, Persians feast. The fact that Esther is the only character in the story that does both underscores the ambiguity of her identity.

The first banquet that Esther gives for the king and Haman is a prerequisite to the second in which she will plead for the life of the Jews. In the short span of one night and one day between banquets Haman builds a gallows for the Jew Mordecai and the king remembers a valiant act performed by Mordecai that saved the king's life.

In a campy, comic scene, the day before he is to attend Esther's second banquet, Haman shows up at the king's palace. Thinking that the king wants to honour him for some valiant act, Haman lavishly describes what should be done for the man the king wishes to honour. Insult is added to injury when the king commands Haman to bestow the very honour he thought would be his upon Mordecai. This exaggerated scene is a prelude to the reversal of fortunes that will begin to take place between Mordecai and Haman and the Jews and their enemies.

On the second day of her second banquet Esther comes out as a Jew to the king. She also exposes Haman's plot, which results in his being hanged on the very gallows he had built for Mordecai. The king gives Haman's house to Esther and she in turn sets Mordecai over it. Mordecai is also given the king's signet ring, which had belonged to Haman. Fortunes continue to be reversed as Esther and Mordecai are given the same power Haman had from the king, to write a decree that gave the Jews the power to defend themselves and to destroy, kill and annihilate all people who would attack them.

Banquets eight and nine

The exaggerated violence that had once been against the Jews is now against their enemies. Just as the king and Haman had feasted at the legislation of violence against the Jews in the fifth banquet, the Jews in every province and in every city make festival and holiday on the occasion of an identical decree against their enemies (8.9–11).

After mass killings of their enemies the Jews in the Persian provinces made the fourteenth day of the twelfth month of Adar a day of feasting and gladness. The Jews in Susa who had also killed their enemies celebrated on the fifteenth day. These days of feasting were legislated by Esther and Mordecai to be held every year and were called Purim.

Cross-Dressing

Clothes indicate insider and outsider status as well as positions of power in the Persian court. When Mordecai hears of Haman's decree to have the Jews annihilated, he tears his clothes and puts on sackcloth and ashes. He and the Jews fast, wear sackcloth, weep and lament. He is able to go throughout the city clothed in this way, but may not enter the king's gate clothed with sackcloth (4.1–3). Sackcloth is clothing that signals outsider status and powerlessness.

From inside the palace Esther sends Mordecai a change of clothes, but he refuses to remove his sackcloth and instead sends a copy of Haman's decree to Esther, asking her to intervene on behalf of the Jews. Esther's response indicates the in-between place she finds herself with regard to Persian power. She is indeed inside the palace, but unable to go before the king inside the inner court unless summoned. To do so would mean death.

When Mordecai convinces her to take the chance and go before the king, Esther declares a fast herself, although she cannot don sackcloth. Instead she puts on royal robes and stands in a place within the palace where the king is sure to see her. Esther the closeted Jew is the fasting, Persian queen in royal robes. She is a queen in drag.

The camp performance of the role reversal between Haman and Mordecai (6.1–11) is heightened with the cross-dressing of Mordecai. Mordecai, the condemned Jew who had been parading around the city in sackcloth and ashes, is now adorned in royal robes by the very one responsible for the death sentence against the Jews. An outrageous scene unfolds with Haman leading Mordecai in his royal robes and crown through the city on a horse proclaiming, 'Thus shall it be done for the man who the king wishes to honour.'

Mordecai's cross-dressing is complete in chapter 8 when he is described as a member of the king's court wearing royal robes of blue and white, with a great golden crown and a mantle of fine linen and purple (a description very similar to the opulence found in chapter 1).

Not only does clothing signify power and status in the Persian court, in the book of Esther it confronts notions of identity. The cross-dressing of Esther and Mordecai sabotages the binarism of Jew/Persian. In a materialist and deconstructionist reading of the book, David J. A. Clines claims that Esther sends a confusing signal to Jewish audiences by refusing to present an overthrow of the Persian government. Instead the hero and heroine of the story co-operate with Persian power, and deliverance is achieved by denying one's Jewishness (Clines 1998: 10–12).

The message is confusing if the binarism of Jew/Persian is maintained. A camp reading of Esther, however, sabotages and confronts the binary notions of Jew and Persian identity in the Diaspora. In their cross-dressing, Esther and Mordecai create a third mode of articulation, a space of possibility that does not belong to one or the other of the constructed identities. Marjorie Garber reminds us that cross-dressing is a disruptive act, creating category crisis that permits border crossings from one category to another (1992: 13–16).

Jewish stories set in the Diaspora (such as Daniel) emphasize Jewish piety, kosher eating, and devotion to God as means by which one's Jewish identity is kept intact in a foreign land. None of these themes is found in Esther. Instead, what we find is exaggerated feasting, fasting, violence, law-making, and cross-dressing. Esther's function as a Diaspora tale is in its camp.

Eunuchs

No commentary (especially a queer one) on the book of Esther would be complete without an emphasis on the role of the eunuchs. They are 'perfect servants' to the plot of the story. In chapter 1, seven eunuchs are named (Mehuman, Biztha, Harbona, Bigtha, Abagtha, Zethar and Carkas). They function as go-betweens in the battle of the sexes that dominates the opening scenes of the story.

The eunuch Hegai is a queen-maker in chapter 2. He is the one who instructs Esther and positions her to be noticed by the king over all the other women. Also in chapter 2, Mordecai's discovery of an assassination plan by two eunuchs, Bigthan and Teresh, puts him and Esther in a favourable position with the king as the plot continues to unfold. The hanging of these two eunuchs on the gallows is a foreshadowing of Haman's demise.

At the crucial scene in the middle of the book in chapter 4, eunuchs along with Esther's maids will tell her of the mourning of her people. And as Mordecai pressures Esther to come out as a Jew on behalf of her people the only way they are able to communicate is through the messenger efforts of the eunuch Hathach. In chapter 6 the king's eunuchs usher Haman into Esther's second banquet, at which his evil plot to kill the Jews is exposed.

In chapter 7 Harbona, one of the king's eunuchs, suggests Haman should be hanged on the very gallows he had built for Mordecai. Harbona will be the last eunuch mentioned in the book, but his suggestion of the hanging becomes the gateway for the reversal of fortunes of the Jews that will dominate the remaining four chapters of the book.

The eunuchs in the book of Esther function as a 'third term' or more precisely as a 'third mode of articulation'. Their ability to cross boundaries of gender, power and physical space articulate spaces of possibility for the plot. They are able to move between male and female worlds in the story. They can move freely across physical boundaries that other characters cannot, such as the king's gate and threshold and into the king's presence. Finally, they are able to move across information boundaries. For all of the story's decrees and messages, the eunuchs seem to be the only ones with all the information in the story. Indeed they are the ones with the real power.

Job

KEN STONE

The book of Job is widely acknowledged to be one of the most difficult of all biblical books to translate and interpret. Although the book has relatively few allusions to matters of sex and gender, it is a valuable resource especially for readers of the Bible who come to it holding views, or engaged in practices, that are considered 'unorthodox' – including lesbian, gay, bisexual and transgendered readers. In order to recognize the potential importance of Job, however, it is necessary to move beyond widespread assumptions about the book such as the assumption (encouraged by a hasty reading of the Second Testament book of James) that the figure of Job is a biblical model of 'patient' suffering (cf. James 5.7–11). Even a cursory glance at Job's speeches will show that Job, the character, is anything but 'patient'. What we have in the book of Job is not an endorsement of patience in suffering but, rather, something like a dialogue, or even an argument, about human suffering and the role played therein by God and by human piety. The stakes of this argument, and the potential relevance of such stakes for 'queer reading', only become apparent when one pays careful attention to the book's literary form as well as its content.

Authorship and Literary Structure

The book of Job gives us few hints about its authorship or the precise time period in which it was written. Indeed, many scholars doubt that a single author was responsible for the book of Job at all, since the book contains several distinct sections that appear to articulate diverse points of view.

An initial distinction in literary form can be made between the book's narrative framework and the longer poetic sections that are found between the two parts of that framework. The narrative introduction (Job 1.1–2.13) is no doubt the best-known portion of the book of Job, and it probably serves as the source for Job's image as a 'patient' sufferer. Shortly after three of Job's friends arrive 'to console him and comfort him' (2.11), however, the book's literary form changes dramatically. Beginning in chapter 3, we find 39 chapters that contain some of the most complex poetry in the Bible. In addition to being characterized by a literary form quite different from that found in the narrative framework, these poetic sections of the book also articulate points of view that stand in tension with the narrative framework. Indeed, many of the poems stand in tension with one another as well, since they are spoken by different characters who hold distinct points of view. At a minimum, we have in the poetic section of the book speeches attributed to Job (in chapters 3, 6–7, 9–10, 12–14, 16–17, 19, 21, 23–4, 26–31 (an independent Wisdom hymn appears in 28)); his three friends, Eliphaz (4–5, 15, 22), Bildad (8, 18, 25), and Zophar (11, 20); a mysterious figure known as Elihu (32–7); and, eventually, the Israelite deity Yhwh (38–41). Moreover, the speeches of Yhwh do not wrap up the book. Rather, the narrative frame resumes with an account that also seems in some ways to contradict other parts of the book (42.7–17).

How can readers of the Bible approach such a complex and difficult text? Carol Newsom has made a compelling case for reading the book of Job as a 'polyphonic text'. Literally, to refer to something as 'polyphonic' is to say that it is comprised of 'many voices'. Writing in part under the influence of the Russian literary theorist Mikhail Bakhtin, Newsom underscores the fact that 'many voices' in the book of Job contest and interrupt one another; and she argues that, even by the end of the book, 'the conversation remains not only unfinalized but unfinalizable' (Newsom 2003: 29). This feature of the book of Job serves for Newsom as an indication of the way in which we might most profitably read it, for '[t]he proper response to such a book . . . is to inject oneself into the conversation, but with the awareness that the final word can never be spoken' (2003: 30). In order to 'inject' ourselves into the book of Job, however, we need to look more closely at the heterogeneous voices participating in the conversation.

The Narrative Introduction

The book opens with a tale about a man named Job 'in the land of Uz' (1.1). The name 'Job' appears as an ordinary human name in other ancient Near Eastern texts, but its occurrence elsewhere in the Bible alongside Noah and 'Daniel' (Ezek. 14.14, 20) may indicate that the character Job is based on a heroic, legendary figure from the ancient world. 'The land of Uz', on the other hand, is unknown to us outside the Hebrew Bible. While some scholars have attempted to locate an actual 'Uz' either in Edom or further to the east (see Pope 1973: 3–5), the name could well be a fictional location for a tale that had its origins in ancient Near Eastern folklore, or that is being set intentionally in some vague location long ago and far away from the world of the author (cf. Habel 1985: 86). In either case, it seems clear that Job is not an Israelite; and neither 'Israel' nor 'Judah' are ever mentioned in the book. We are dealing, then, with a biblical book that has as its main human character someone who stands outside, or at the margins of, certain dominant (e.g. 'Israelite' or 'Judahite') emphases of the Hebrew canon. This feature of the book should not go unnoticed by readers of the Bible who find themselves positioned today at the margins of religious tradition, for it shows that even the Bible can make space for voices and ideas that do not fit neatly within the orthodox mainstream.

Job is characterized in the opening narrative as a wealthy and prayerful man who is described by God as 'blameless and upright, fearing God and turning from evil' (Job 1.8). This positive representation of a pious rich man is sometimes taken as one of several indications that the book of Job as a whole may have had its origins in a social matrix of relative wealth and privilege (see Clines 1995a: 122–44; Newsom 1998: 141–3). However, Job's piety, though viewed positively by God, is assessed rather more cynically by a figure known as 'the satan', who suggests that Job's good character and behaviour result largely from the fact that God has put a 'fence' around him (1.10), thereby preventing Job from being subjected to distress.

This 'satan' figure should not be confused with later Christian ideas about 'Satan', which for the most part post-date the Hebrew Bible. 'The satan' is not, in the book of Job, a proper name. As the use of the definite article ('the') indicates, 'the satan' is a term for a function or an office, which literally means something like 'the accuser'. 'The satan', who wanders about on the earth, apparently plays a role somewhat akin to that of prosecuting attorney when he returns to the court of divine beings that is referred to with the phrase, 'sons of God' (1.6). We find ourselves, then, in the world of ancient Near Eastern mythological ideas associated with the divine council.

Although the satan is widely understood to be evil, the book of Job does not necessarily represent him that way. It is actually God, in fact, who brings Job to the attention of the satan (1.8). When the satan suggests that Job will curse God if his good fortune is taken away, God allows the satan to do whatever he will with Job's possessions. Job then loses most of those possessions, including his children. Yet Job still does not speak negatively about God (1.22). Rather, as God points out to the satan, Job 'still maintains his integrity' (2.3). The satan, in response, asks for and is given power over Job's physical condition. Forbidden by God only from killing Job, the satan then 'inflicts' Job with terrible boils from the sole of his foot to the top of his head. This choice of affliction is rather ironic, since, according to Deuteronomy 28.35 (which uses very similar language), God will 'inflict' those who fail to obey God's commandments with just such boils. The irony highlights a fact that Job himself appears to struggle with in later portions of the book, which is the fact that his fate contradicts covenantal notions of reward and punishment such as those emphasized by biblical books like Deuteronomy.

The satan, then, never acts independently of God, who seems in the narrative much less interested in Job's well-being than in winning a wager. Job is caught up in forces of which he is partly unaware and over which he has no control. Although the result, for Job, is devastating, the narrator presents these events with no hint of a radical dualism between good and evil forces. God and the satan are, rather, working together; indeed, God actually acknowledges that the satan 'incites' God to do things (2.3). Much later in the book, the narrator will even identify God rather than the satan as the one who brought 'all the evil' upon Job (42.11). For modern readers, such an unusual representation of God and the satan may seem to come surprisingly close to the unorthodox notion, articulated in another context by the Danish writer Isak Dinesen (who was much interested in Job), according to which 'God and the Devil are one' (Dinesen 1989: 19).

The Role of Job's Wife

An exchange occurs at this point in the narrative between Job and his wife, who has not previously been mentioned. Job's wife is generally treated by readers as a negative character, and Job's own response to her indicates that he understands her words negatively, as words suitable for 'foolish women' (2.10). Such language no doubt reflects the patriarchal context that produced the book. The biblical Wisdom tradition, after all, which gave us the book of Job, often articulates ambivalent or dualistic attitudes toward women on the part of its male authors (cf. Stone 2005: 134–5).

Nevertheless, the actual speech of Job's wife – restricted to a single verse (2.9) – is very ambiguous. Her first words to Job are nearly identical to words that God has also used about Job: 'you still persist in your integrity'. She then gives Job a command that is most often rendered into English as 'curse God and die'. However, the Hebrew verb that appears here, *barak*, is very common in the Hebrew Bible and is normally translated 'bless'. It does seem in certain texts to have nearly an opposite meaning, closer to 'curse' or even 'blaspheme' (e.g. 1 Kings 21.10, 13). Indeed, by the time Job's wife speaks, the narrative has already used the verb with both its positive (e.g. Job 1.10, 21) and its negative (e.g. 1.5, 11; 2.5) connotations. Thus, the precise meaning of the word in the mouth of Job's wife is not altogether easy to decide.

Partly because of the way in which Job responds to his wife, her words are usually translated with the simple imperative, 'curse God and die'; and her role in the book is understood largely as a negative contrast to Job. Yet her speech can also be understood in other ways. Ellen van Wolde, for example, suggests that the speech of Job's wife (who has, after all, also lost her children) functions in the book as a 'catalyst'. It urges Job to stop being passive and causes him to reflect actively on the choice between positive and negative assessments of God's relation to undeserved suffering, positive and negative assessments that correspond to the contrasting meanings of the verb Job's wife uses (Van Wolde 1995: 203–6). From this point of view, the words of Job's wife are not simply a negative foil for Job's piety. Rather, her speech marks and perhaps leads to an important transition in the book, from the pious but passive Job found in the narrative to the assertive and unorthodox Job of the speeches.

Job's First Speech

After sitting with his friends in silence for seven days and seven nights, Job utters the speech found in chapter 3. The attitude of Job presupposed by this chapter seems already quite different from that earlier, pious passivity in the face of cosmic forces, which has been challenged by his wife. Far from simply accepting his suffering, Job now curses the day of his birth in a passionate poem that, like the lament in Jeremiah 20.14–18, suggests that it would have been better never to be born than to endure the suffering that he is currently undergoing. Job's 'lament', however, more clearly than Jeremiah's, makes this point partly by appealing to mythological language and imagery associated in the ancient Near East with creation. This language and imagery anticipates themes that will resurface later in the book, especially in the speeches of God. To cite only one example, in 3.8 Job longs for a cursing of his day of birth by 'those skilled in rousing Leviathan'. 'Leviathan' is a mythological sea monster, associated with the forces of chaos against which ancient Near Eastern gods sometimes do battle in order to create the cosmos. Whereas Job refers to Leviathan here, God refers to Leviathan in his response to Job later in the book (41.1–11), in the context of speeches that also make significant use of the themes of creation and nature. Both Job and God seem to recognize, then, that nothing less than the nature of creation and the cosmos is at stake in the book's dialogue.

However, Job's use of creation imagery in chapter 3 has the effect of characterizing Job's experience as a kind of undoing of creation. Job's suffering leads him to wish, rhetorically, that the day of his birth would be covered in darkness (3.3–10). This 'darkness' should be understood in relation to the primordial darkness that was believed to have existed prior to God's creative, ordering activity (cf. Gen. 1.2). Such darkness seems to be closely associated with Leviathan in the ancient Near East (cf. Day 1985: 44–8). By calling up darkness and referring to the rousing of Leviathan, Job rhetorically stirs up the very forces of chaos that God subdued at the creation of the cosmos. Thus, in a reversal of the common ancient Near Eastern view of creation as an establishing of order against forces of chaos, Job's language allows us to glimpse the chaotic disorientation which radical suffering introduces into the presumed orderliness of human existence.

Of course, one may wonder what Job's allusion to an undoing of creation says about the one who creates. Job does not, at this point, make the sorts of direct accusations against God that appear later in the book. A rhetorical question in 3.23, however, does refer to Job as 'one whom God has fenced in'. This reference recalls ironically the satan's remark, in 1.10, that Job is upright precisely because God has put a 'fence' around him. Although the 'fence' in 1.10 has positive connotations of protection, here in chapter 3 the connotations appear to be entirely negative: because God has 'fenced in' Job, Job cannot find his way. Already we begin to see that Job is being led by his experience to turn conventional piety on its head. 'Fenced in' by God, Job has good reason to conclude this speech by asserting that 'I am not at ease, and I am not quiet; I have no rest, and turmoil comes' (3.26).

Job's Friends

Job's initial speech in chapter 3 is answered, in chapters 4 and 5, by a speech from his friend Eliphaz. This speech is merely the first of eight sections of the book in which Job's friends Eliphaz, Bildad and Zophar respond to Job's outbursts. Although these friends make a number of different points, their efforts seem to be directed in particular at persuading Job to accept an orthodox perspective on his suffering and God's role in it. Already in his first speech, for example, Eliphaz appeals to rather traditional notions of divine retribution, asserting that God punishes the wicked and doubting that the innocent or upright will suffer calamity. In the opinion of Eliphaz, moreover, suffering can be a form of divine 'discipline' that ultimately works for the good of the one who is chastened (5.17). Such themes are also stressed by Job's other friends. Bildad, for example, seems certain in chapter 8 that since God is just, those who sin are punished and those who are blameless will not be abandoned by God. When he comes back to these themes in chapter 18, Bildad's insistence that the wicked are punished sounds very close to an accusation that Job himself must have been wicked in order for such calamities to overtake him. Zophar, too, is convinced that if Job puts away wickedness, his life will go well (11.13–20); for it is the wicked who suffer distress and lose their possessions (20.4–29).

Moreover, as Job continues to complain about his fate, to assert his innocence, and to question God's actions, Job's friends become more and more assertive in their own insistence that Job's critical interrogation of God is itself wrong. Eliphaz not only refers to Job's talk as 'speech with no use and words without worth' (15.3) but also accuses Job of undermining piety with iniquities of the mouth and crafty language (15.4–6). Rather than questioning God's ways, Eliphaz believes, Job should put himself in God's service, allowing himself to be instructed by God and meditating on God's words (22.21–2).

It is important to note that many of the assertions made by Job's friends sound like thoroughly orthodox statements. Indeed, their view of divine retribution – that God punishes the wicked and blesses the righteous – coheres well with many passages from the Bible, especially in Deuteronomy, the 'Deuteronomistic History' (see '1 and 2 Kings', this volume), several of the prophetic books, and even the book of Proverbs (which is usually understood, as is Job, to be standing in the 'Wisdom tradition'). Yet, toward the end of the book of Job, God states explicitly that Job's friends have not spoken about God 'correctly' in the way that Job has. This statement indicates that the purpose of the book of Job is not to reaffirm the orthodoxy that Job's friends represent. The views of those friends are allowed full expression, and no doubt many people of faith find the orthodox arguments of the friends compelling even today when those arguments are heard outside the context of the book of Job. In the end, however, the arguments of Job's friends – the 'representatives of older, settled, traditional faith' (Brueggemann 2003: 294) – are rejected by the very God whom those friends imagine themselves to be defending.

The Speeches of Job

Like his friends, Job seems to have started out assuming that we live within a moral order regulated by a just God, a moral order in which those who live properly will prosper and those who live improperly will reap negative consequences. It is easy to conclude, on the basis of such a worldview, that the person who suffers must have done something wrong in order to bring adversity on herself or himself. Although Job's friends apparently conclude exactly that about Job, Job knows that he is innocent. His experience of undeserved suffering therefore provokes a crisis, and Job responds to this crisis with some of the most emotionally vivid language in all of scripture.

In sharp contrast to the popular reputation of Job as a man who was patient in suffering, the poems attributed to Job reveal a speaker who is unafraid to make accusations against both a God who allows or causes undeserved suffering, and other humans who prefer orthodox platitudes to an honest airing of the complaints of those who suffer. Such humans include Job's friends, whose attempts to reprove Job and steer him back onto orthodox paths are dismissed by Job as unending 'windy words' (16.3), spoken by 'treacherous' (6.15) people who assume they know the truth but actually 'crush [Job] with words' (19.1). Job is clearly not prepared to sit back quietly while others make statements that he believes to be untrue.

However, most of Job's complaints are directed at God. Picking up on ancient Near Eastern and biblical images of God as a warrior, Job asserts that God has attacked him with 'arrows' (6.3). In Job's view, God treats him in much the same way that God treats 'Sea' and the sea dragons (7.12), those forces of chaos against which ancient Near Eastern deities more traditionally do battle. Job's experience of suffering feels like a full but undeserved assault upon him by no less an opponent than God:

> I was at ease, and [God] shattered me,
> he seized me by the neck and scattered me,
> he set me up as his target,
> his archers surround me.
> He cleaves open my kidneys, and has no compassion,
> he pours out my gall on the ground.
> He bursts out upon me again and again,
> he rushes upon me like a mighty warrior.
> . . .
> My face is red on account of my weeping,
> and on my eyelids is a deep darkness,
> yet there is no violence in my hands,
> and my prayer is pure. (16.12–14, 16–17)

Here, and at several other points in Job's speeches, we have the articulation of a theological experience that is not often discussed by readers of the Bible: the experience of God as enemy (e.g. 13.24). As far as Job is concerned, it would be better to be dead than to be treated in this way by God. Thus, while we often imagine that biblical prayer asks for God's attention, Job demands instead that God leave him alone for a while, 'long enough for me to swallow my spit' (7.19). When Job wants to find God, he cannot (23.8–9); but at other times God is nothing less than Job's 'adversary' (16.9). Job's friends are horrified by such rhetoric, of course, which seems to them inappropriate as language about God. But, Job shrewdly asks, if it is not God who does these things, then who does them (9.24)?

While we may be uncomfortable with notions of 'God as enemy' and are rightly cautious about adopting such language literally, we have to acknowledge that there do seem to be times in human experience when nothing less than cosmic forces appear to be arrayed against us. Job is undergoing just such an experience. At the root of Job's anguished laments and complaints is recognition that his own experience contradicts the moral order presupposed by his tradition – and, we need to remember, presupposed or even asserted by much of the Bible. But although it is Job's personal experience which causes him to question traditional points of view, his perspective does not remain restricted entirely to his own situation. For example, he comes to recognize that, while he is suffering and yet is innocent, others who are wicked are actually prospering (21.7–26; 24.1–25). Indeed, it seems at times to Job that God actually turns over the earth to the wicked and thwarts justice while simultaneously mocking the situation of the innocent (9.23–4). Such insights are, for Job, more disturbing than any actual punishment for having committed an offence; for if he were guilty of some wrong he would at least be able to understand his situation and know that God has acted justly. However, Job knows instead that he is not guilty and continues to maintain his integrity (27.1–6). In a final, moving discourse in chapters 29–31 (which follows the wisdom hymn that has apparently been inserted in chapter 28), Job recalls his former state, contrasts that state with his present suffering, accuses God of cruel animosity (30.21), and asserts once again his innocence.

Whereas the speeches of Job's friends are compatible with much that passes for conventional orthodoxy, the speeches of Job are much more radical. Still today, readers are often shocked by the boldness of Job's language, which at several points sounds heretical or even blasphemous. Yet it is important to recognize that Job's language also stands within a recognizable tradition of biblical thought. In form and in content, Job's speeches recall the tradition of biblical lament or complaint found in numerous psalms, in the book of Lamentations, and in a few other biblical texts such as scattered sections of Jeremiah. As several scholars have noted (e.g. Billman and Migliore 1999; Brueggemann 1995: 67–111), contemporary people of faith often fail to take this tradition adequately into account when making use of the Bible, to the detriment of both our perceptions about the Bible and our experience of the life of faith.

However, a 'queer reading' of the Bible, in particular, might benefit from closer attention to the biblical lament tradition. Some attempts have been made along these lines in the context of reflection on Aids/HIV (see Stone 1999; West 2001) but the potential value of the biblical laments probably extends even further. For although the lament tradition is something of a minority tradition in the Bible, it is a central component of what Walter Brueggemann calls 'Israel's countertestimony'. This 'countertestimony' is comprised of various portions of biblical literature that interrogate core assumptions about God and the life of faith which are attested elsewhere in the Bible. Among the claims made by some of these texts, including laments that give voice to the experience of undeserved suffering (such as the laments of Job), is the bold claim that Yhwh has failed to live up to agreements made elsewhere in scripture. To be sure, even among such texts the speeches of Job seem to stand out as something like 'the extreme expression of Israel's countertestimony about Yahweh, who is now shown to be unreliable' (Brueggemann 1997: 388). Yet there are other texts of lament or complaint (e.g. Pss. 44; 88; cf. 22.1–2) that do approach Job's speeches in their bold articulation of 'the incongruity between the core claims of covenantal faith and the lived experience of . . . life' (Brueggemann 1997: 378). Of course, lesbians, gay men, bisexuals and transgendered persons are only too familiar with a certain amount of 'incongruity' between 'lived experience' and particular 'core claims' of religious tradition; but are often unaware that parts of the Bible give voice to just such 'incongruity'. Thus, the speeches of Job and similar texts have much to offer a 'queer reading' of the

Bible, partly because they authorize the honest assertion of one's integrity and experience, even in those moments when orthodox tradition and its defenders vigorously oppose such assertion and denounce it as wicked or foolish.

The Speech of Elihu

Between the final words of Job's speech in chapter 31, and the reply to Job from God that begins in chapter 38, stands the speech of a figure named Elihu. Prior to this point, Elihu has not been mentioned in the book of Job at all. The narrator states that Elihu has waited to speak because the other participants in the dialogue are all older than he. However, many scholars explain the unexpected appearance of this speech in chapters 32 to 37 by suggesting that the Elihu poems were written after the other speeches, by an independent author who was dissatisfied with the responses to Job from Job's friends that appeared in the earlier book of Job (see e.g. Pope 1973: xxvii–xxviii; Newsom 1996: 558–9; 2003: 201–2, *passim*). Substantively, Elihu's speeches do not add a great deal to arguments that have been made already in the book. Elihu makes many of the same points that Job's friends have made, insisting that God repays the wicked for their sins, criticizing Job's rebellious language, and expanding upon the theme of redemptive suffering. However, Elihu, unlike Job's friends, frequently addresses Job by name and tends to quote specific pieces of Job's speeches so as to refute them. His fourth and final speech, in chapters 36 and 37, seems, in its reflections on the role of God as creator, to look ahead to the speeches of God that begin in chapter 38. These features of Elihu's speeches can be interpreted as evidence that their writer was reading the book of Job carefully, and chose to respond to the dialogue found in the book by entering that dialogue actively, literally writing his own response into the book.

Thus, while a few scholars do consider the Elihu speeches to be an integral part of the book's overall literary structure (see e.g. Habel 1985), the case for viewing the Elihu speeches as a later insertion is strong. Yet the conclusion that the Elihu poems were added at a later point need not result in a negative evaluation of the function of Elihu in the book of Job. Recognition of the process that probably led to the inclusion of these speeches in the book may provide us instead with hints about the value of active response to the book. As Newsom notes, 'Elihu represents the position of all readers', since, as a voice that was added later to the book, he 'comes to a conversation that has begun without him and yet at which he finds himself present' (2003: 202). Even readers who are not entirely convinced by the specific arguments that Elihu makes can affirm the model that Elihu gives us for participating actively in the debates about suffering and the divine which are initiated in the book of Job.

The Speeches of God

Beginning in chapter 38, God – more specifically, Yhwh – speaks to Job 'from the storm' (38.1). This divine response clearly constitutes, in some way, the climax of the book of Job. Yet the focus of Yhwh's reply is quite unexpected, for Yhwh does not seem to respond directly to Job's questions and complaints. For example, while Job has asked God to let him know about the transgressions he must have committed in order to deserve his fate (e.g. 13.23; cf. 10.2), Yhwh neither affirms nor denies that Job has done anything wrong. Rather, in two vivid poems that consist largely of a series of rhetorical questions, Yhwh directs Job's attention elsewhere.

Partly because of this shift of focus, the precise meaning of Yhwh's reply, and the significance of that reply for the issues that are being debated by Job and his interlocutors (and, subsequently, by readers of the book), have been the topic of much disagreement. Edward Greenstein has even referred to these speeches as 'a readerly Rorschach test' (1999: 302) because of the tendency of readers to draw from the speeches such diverse conclusions. Nevertheless, an interpretation of the significance of the speeches can and must be attempted.

The fact that Yhwh speaks to Job out of a storm perhaps hints, from the beginning of chapter 38, at something that becomes more and more clear over the course of Yhwh's speech: the image of God and of divine activity evoked by these chapters is both spectacular and unsettling. At first glance, Yhwh may seem to be doing little more than putting Job in his place. 'Who is this,' Yhwh demands in 38.2, 'who darkens counsel with words without knowledge?' The implied answer, of course, is 'Job'; and, after warning Job (in language that has both gendered and adversarial connotations) to 'gird up your loins like a man' (38.3), Yhwh proceeds to interrogate Job with a series of questions that emphasize distance and distinction between Job and God: 'Where were you . . . ?' 'Have you entered . . . ?' 'Can you . . . ?' 'Do you know . . . ?' etc.

In terms of content, Yhwh's discourse largely focuses on matters of creation. As one might expect from an ancient Near Eastern creation text, the early parts of Yhwh's speech evoke a cosmos in which the created order and its foundations are established in part by the restraining of such mythological forces of chaos as 'Sea' (38.8, 16), the 'Deep' (38.16), and 'Death' (38.17). The process by which such restraints are put in place is frequently represented, in the ancient world, as a kind of struggle or even battle between the forces of chaos and a deity, most often a male deity (though the warlike goddess Anat also sometimes plays this role). Biblical literature frequently appeals to the fund of images that were associated with this 'chaos battle' (see Batto 1992; Levenson 1988; Day 1985). Here, though, in a gender-related twist on the more common patterns in which those mythological images appear, language about a 'womb' (38.8) and a 'swaddling cloth' (38.9) is used in such a way as to make one imagine God to be something like 'the midwife who births the sea and wraps it in the swaddling bands of cloud and darkness' (Newsom 1996: 602). This picture of God as something like the mother of the forces of chaos already indicates that Yhwh's speeches, while making use of traditional creation imagery, may be taking that imagery in directions for which conventional piety does not prepare Job – or us.

Such a possibility seems to be confirmed in 38.39 when, at the beginning of a lengthy reflection on the world of animals, Yhwh asks Job whether he is able to 'hunt prey for the lion, or satisfy the appetite of young lions'. Yhwh's point, here, is clearly that Yhwh rather than Job is the one who finds prey for the lions. The idea that God feeds the lions is not in itself surprising and is, in fact, found elsewhere in the Bible, specifically in Psalm 104 (Ps. 104.21). However, as Greenstein (1999: 307–8) points out, whereas Psalm 104 apparently understands God's concern for the animals within a wider framework that also includes God's concern for human beings, Yhwh's speech to Job affirms that God is busy hunting with the lions while giving no indication that God is very much concerned about the fate of individual human beings. Indeed, since the lion was sometimes understood in the Bible as a hunter of sheep and hence an opponent of shepherds, Yhwh's concern about prey for the lion may hint that God is aligned more closely with the foes of human beings than with humans themselves (cf. Newsom 1996: 609).

In chapter 39, moreover, after observing that God but not Job knows where mountain goats and deer give birth to their young, the divine speech associates Yhwh with several other animals whose specific characteristics seem to oppose them to human civilization and order. The wild ass, for example, is understood elsewhere in the Bible to wander about alone (e.g. Hos. 8.9) and to be at odds with others, as its association with Ishmael in Genesis indicates (Gen. 16.12). Job himself has earlier used the wild ass in the desert to symbolize the chaos brought about by the wicked (24.5). In Job 39, Yhwh acknowledges that the wild ass both scorns the city and ignores humans who attempt to master it (Job 39.7); yet simultaneously he takes credit for setting the wild ass in opposition to human domestication and giving it the barren steppes and salt wastes as a home (39.5–6). The wild ox, too, is described in terms of its unwillingness to accommodate to human desires and constraints (39.9–12).

Still further outside the realm of human comprehension and control is the ostrich, described in 39.13–18. The book of Isaiah indicates that ostriches were understood in ancient Israel to inhabit ruins and deserts, along with other strange creatures such as jackals, hyenas, and the mysterious goat demons (Isa. 13.21; 34.13; 43.20). Thus, in biblical imagery, ostriches represent something like the antithesis of human civilization and order. Job, in fact, has earlier described himself as 'a brother of jackals and a companion of ostriches' (30.29) in order to indicate, in a moving passage, the chaotic state to which his suffering has reduced him. Moreover, the book of Lamentations underscores an ancient (albeit erroneous) perception of ostriches as poor parents (Lam. 4.3), which would seem to oppose them symbolically to the concern for progeny and kinship so common in the Hebrew Bible and so often associated, still today, with 'family values'. Yhwh's speech to Job accepts this ancient notion about ostriches as poor parents, and even elaborates upon it in more detail (39.14–16). Yet it also asserts, shockingly, that the ostrich has these supposed characteristics precisely because God made it that way (39.17). Thus God is associated here not with human values but rather with values understood to stand in opposition to that which humans consider good and proper. This strange creature of God, far from being subject to human beings or fitting neatly into functional human categorizations, flaps her flightless wings wildly (39.13) and 'laughs at the horse and its rider' (39.18).

Of course the horse, too, is one of God's creatures, as Yhwh goes on to remind Job. It is Yhwh who creates this mighty animal; and, in fact, the horse is described with language that in the ancient Near East is associated with deities themselves, so that the horse appears here as 'a magnificent godlike

figure . . . a warrior god poised for battle' (Habel 1985: 347). Such an association between God and the horse is rather frightening, however, once one recognizes that those qualities of the horse underscored in the poem (39.19–25)
have to do precisely with the horse's excitement for battle. The possibility that
God, too, might be characterized by just such blood lust seems to be hinted at
further in the subsequent sketch of the eagle (39.26–30), which soars at God's
command (39.27); for its young 'suck up blood, and where the slain are, there
it is' (39.30).

The picture of nature drawn in God's first speech is therefore hardly that
of a peaceful, harmonious realm. The animal world appears rather as a wild
and raucous space, in which some creatures naturally serve as prey for others
and human values seldom prevail. The fact that this realm is associated so
closely with God seems to hint at the notion that God, too, may act according
to principles which humans cannot fathom, and indeed sometimes even in
frightening ways.

This possibility becomes even more likely in Yhwh's second speech, beginning in 40.7; for here God speaks of the two mighty beasts, Behemoth and
Leviathan. In some older translations and commentaries, Behemoth and
Leviathan are understood respectively as the hippopotamus and the crocodile.
However, our greater knowledge of ancient Near Eastern symbol and myth,
and of the impact of such symbol and myth on biblical literature, now leads
most commentators to conclude that Behemoth and Leviathan, though perhaps modelled in part on real animals, are in fact mythological beasts, 'liminal
creatures' that 'represent the frightening and alien "other," bearing the terror
of the chaotic in their very being' (Newsom 1996: 615; cf. Day 1985: 62–87).

These frightening creatures are, however, also closely associated with God.
The association is perhaps more obvious in the case of Behemoth, since Yhwh
states that Behemoth is just as much a creation of God as Job himself. Literally,
in fact, Yhwh calls Job's attention to 'Behemoth which I made with you' (40.15).
Such an assertion is potentially disquieting, for it raises the possibility that
God is as concerned about Behemoth as with humankind and treats it in a similar fashion. Indeed, Behemoth is not just any creature but literally, according to
40.19, 'first of the ways of God'. This enigmatic statement is often understood
to mean simply that Behemoth is the greatest of all creatures, or the first to be
created; and both interpretations are possible. Yet it may also point toward
some priority of interest, as if Behemoth (whose name is literally formed from
the plural of the Hebrew word *behemah*, 'beast') actually has a greater claim
on God's time and attention than Job. Behemoth's explicit association with
'the ways of God' also reminds us that this speech is shedding light on Yhwh
as well as on Behemoth. Since the poem emphasizes Behemoth's spectacular
strength, fearlessness and potency (note how a euphemism seems to refer to
Behmoth's erect penis in 40.17 (see Pope 1973: 323–4; Habel 1985: 565–6)), it
is God's awesome nature rather than God's intimate involvement with individual human beings that is here underscored. Creation imagery is thus used
once again by Yhwh in an unexpected and even troubling fashion. As Timothy
Beal notes, the encounter with Behemoth produces not a sense of 'order and
harmony' but rather awareness of 'a kind of dangerous otherness in creation'
(Beal 2002: 50), a 'dangerous otherness' partly associated with God.

The climax of God's speeches, however, occurs in the lengthy poem about Leviathan in chapter 41. Job, of course, has invoked Leviathan in his very first speech (3.8); but Yhwh's emphasis on Leviathan in the last speech of the dialogue seems designed rhetorically to call into question the wisdom of any such invocation on the part of mere humans:

> Can you draw out Leviathan with a fishhook,
>   or with a rope press down his tongue?
> Can you put a cord through his nose,
>   or with a hook pierce his jaw?
> ...
> Will you play with him like a bird,
>   or tie him down for your young women?
> ...
> Can you fill his skin with harpoons,
>   or his head with fish spears?
> Put your hands on him, think of the battle!
>   You will not do it again! (41.1–2, 5, 7–8 (Heb. 40.25–6, 29, 31–2))

In the light of Job's earlier reference to Leviathan, such rhetoric can be read as implying here that Job has in his speeches been treading onto territory with which he is unfamiliar, and might be wise to avoid.

Another clear implication of Yhwh's questions, of course, is that while Job cannot engage Leviathan, Yhwh can. Scholars note that the Leviathan traditions are used in the Hebrew Bible with two, rather different, emphases: an emphasis on Leviathan as the creature or even 'plaything' (Levenson 1988: 17) of God (e.g. Pss. 104.26); and an emphasis on Leviathan as the opponent of God or the gods in divine battles against forces of chaos (e.g. Ps. 74.14). The speech of Yhwh in Job 41 does seem to presuppose familiarity with the latter tradition of battle, for 41.25 (Heb. 41.17) refers explicitly to the fears of the gods when they are confronted with Leviathan; and in some ancient manuscripts 41.9 (Heb. 41.1) does so as well. Clearly, then, the awesome power of Yhwh is being underscored in the passage, inasmuch as Yhwh's ability to do the things with this fearsome creature which Job cannot – drawing out Leviathan with a fishhook, pressing down his tongue with a rope, putting a cord through his nose and so forth – is presupposed by Yhwh's rhetorical questions. Yhwh may well be asking how Job, who cannot engage mighty Leviathan, dares to do battle with a god who can (cf. Day 1985: 83, 87).

But is Leviathan represented here only as Yhwh's enemy? Does Yhwh stand only over against forces of chaos such as Leviathan? The implication of 41.5 that God is able, not only to battle Leviathan, but also to play with him 'like a bird', indicates that the association between Yhwh and the forces of chaos may be more complex than any absolute opposition will allow. We cannot help being reminded of the assertion in Psalm 104.26 that God 'formed' Leviathan 'to play'. Indeed, in Hebrew, God in Job 41.3 (English 41.11) literally asserts that Leviathan is 'for me' or is 'mine'. Moreover, most English translations obscure a disorienting oscillation between third-person and first-person personal pronouns in the Hebrew text of 41.1–3 (English 41.9–11) that make it difficult to differentiate Leviathan from Yhwh. Thus, as Beal shrewdly observes, in the divine speech about Leviathan, 'the identity of the monstrous blurs with that of God, and vice versa. God identifies with the monster over against all challengers' (Beal 2002: 51–2). Given this identification, it is perhaps less surprising that the speeches of Yhwh end, not with a description of God's successful battle against Leviathan (a description that would reassure readers of God's intention and sovereign ability to overpower all those forces of chaos that threaten to overwhelm us (cf. Levenson 1988)), but rather with an admiring description of Leviathan that culminates in the utterly unexpected image of Leviathan as a king (41.34 (Heb. 41.26)). Whether God is always able, or even necessarily always desires, to subdue this magnificent king of chaos remains unspecified.

What are we to make, then, of the image of God that emerges from the speeches of Yhwh in chapters 38–41? At the very least, we find in these complex passages a representation of divine involvement that is centred elsewhere than on human beings. To the extent that the speeches of God allow us to locate a sphere for divine activity, they point us in the direction of creation. It is almost as if God is saying to Job and his friends: If you truly want to understand me, look to the world of nature. Here we find a world that is complex, beautiful and even playful. It is a world that only a truly powerful God could sustain, a God tender enough to notice young birds crying out for food but mighty enough to engage Behemoth and Leviathan. Yet the world evoked in God's speeches also sometimes seems, much like the ostrich, to be at odds with human wisdom and order. Here we find a world of carnivores and monsters, a world of bloodthirsty young eagles and snorting war horses, a world of creatures that cannot be tamed and secrets that cannot be found out, a world in which beauty and brutality are difficult to disentangle.

Of course, such a close association between God and the beautiful but brutal world of nature contradicts assumptions that have been made by both Job and his friends. From radically different sets of experiences, both Job and his friends have presupposed that a just God, overseeing a moral order, ought to be busy ensuring that suffering falls on the wicked rather than the righteous. God is understood to be a just judge who responds reliably to human moral conduct. The chief difference between Job and his friends is that Job, unlike his friends, recognizes correctly that this desired moral order is not in fact working in his case; and he is not afraid to say so bluntly, in spite of the implication that God is unjust and in spite of protestations from his pious companions. Yet as Dinesen perceptively notes, the divine speeches seem to portray God less like a judge than an artist, eager to revel in display of the artist's creation (Dinesen 1942: 291–2; cf. Keller 2003: 132). Humans are part of this creation, but are not represented as having any special claims on the creator. Such a perspective on creator and creation thus opens up the possibility that suffering is a tragic, but to some degree inevitable, feature of human existence as it is of animal existence (cf. Farley 1990: 106–10). More ominously, the speeches of God ask us to reflect on the terrifying possibility that the realities of the world we inhabit, and of 'the uncanniness and contingency of nature', undermine altogether the urge for moral order and purpose that characterizes Job, his friends and very often ourselves as readers (Connolly 1993: 12, *passim*).

Returning to the Narrative

Yhwh's speeches do not, however, end the book of Job. The last segment of poetry in the book of Job is found at the beginning of chapter 42, where Job answers Yhwh briefly. Job's response does not include the curse against God that the satan seems to have anticipated in the narrative introduction. On the other hand, the meaning of Job's actual reply is not altogether clear. The reply consists, in part, of two quotations from the speeches of God. It also includes acknowledgement of God's power (42.2) and of Job's lack of understanding and knowledge (42.3). Exactly what one believes Job to have failed to understand depends, of course, upon the significance one grants to the speeches of God that have just concluded. Yet the most difficult portion of Job's reply to translate and interpret is probably the final verse (42.6), which NRSV renders as, 'therefore I despise myself, and repent in dust and ashes'. Numerous interpretations of this obscure statement have been offered by commentators (see, for several possibilities, Newsom 1996: 628–9). Does God simply reduce Job, here, to silence and shame? The possibility is a troubling one, especially in light of the contribution of certain religious ideas to the inculcation of toxic shame (see Pattison 2000). It is possible, grammatically, to construe the text in other ways, so that Job is not despising himself but rather rejecting or abandoning his 'dust and ashes', in other words, his state of being in mourning. Even if the precise translation and significance of Job's words in 42.6 remain obscure, however, Newsom suggests that the various parts of Job's brief statement, taken together and read in the context of the speeches that precede them, probably indicate that Job now sees 'a world in which the vulnerability of human existence can be understood, not in terms of divine enmity, but in terms of a creation within which the chaotic is restrained but never fully eliminated' (1996: 629). We are vulnerable to suffering not because of some inherent flaw in ourselves that we must 'despise', but rather because we live as mortals in a vast but contingent world where some potential for tragedy always remains.

At this point, though, the book suddenly reverts to the narrative voice that appeared in the introductory chapters. Although both Yhwh and Job have indicated in their speeches that Job did not understand the things about which he spoke, the narrator reports that Yhwh first rebukes Job's friends and then says to them, twice, 'you have not spoken of me what is right, as has my servant Job' (42.7b; 8b). This divine assertion sounds very much like a contradiction of the dialogue between God and Job that has just been completed. While the reader who has examined the speeches of Yhwh in 38–41 can hardly be surprised to learn that God does not side with Job's orthodox friends, the affirmation of Job is much more unexpected. Having just concluded that Job spoke without knowledge and understanding, the book uses the voice of God to insist that Job rather than his friends has rightly spoken about God. Moreover, beginning in 42.10, Yhwh appears to act exactly like the judge that Job has earlier hoped for and that his friends believe in, but which God has so far refused to play. Job's fortune is restored in excess of that with which he started, he receives sons and daughters to replace those lost earlier, and he is granted a long life.

For some commentators on Job, the tension between this narrative conclusion and the poems that precede it can only be read as a sign of clumsy editing, which resulted when the dialogues of Job were framed with, or inserted into, a didactic folk narrative. Irrespective of the process by which the book of Job was put together, however, there are other ways of construing the significance of this return to the narrative frame. Among other things, we are reminded of Newsom's suggestion (2003) that we ought to read Job as a 'polyphonic' book. In a sense, the resumption of the narrative frame reminds us that even God's speeches and Job's reply cannot be understood, finally, to have resolved altogether our questions about suffering, piety, creation and the divine. The ongoing nature of the dialogue between the narrative portions and the poetic portions of the book of Job serves as an invitation to us to join the debate.

Moreover, the incongruity produced by the transition from poetic dialogue to narrative conclusion may well be understood as an important, albeit unsettling, part of the book's message. One can after all read the speeches of God as indicating that all attempts to limit the divine within human notions of order and consistent behaviour will finally fail. What better way to make this point than to describe the very deity who has rejected anthropocentrism, and eschewed the role of judge, as turning once again to human affairs and dispensing judgements and rewards? The shift in divine perspective does seem rather absurd, and the inconsistency in divine activity can seem somewhat frightening. Yet absurdity has already been perceived in the ostrich, created by God without wisdom; and fright has already been inspired by Leviathan, with whom Yhwh seems partly to identify. Perhaps one can see here a challenge to the Wisdom tradition that produced the book of Job. The Wisdom tradition seems to have assumed that the wise person could, through a careful examination of the world and of experience, discern the orderly structures that undergird this world created by God. According to this perspective, the wise person who not only discerns such orderly structures but lives life in conformity with them could expect to be blessed. The book of Job does not abandon entirely its Wisdom tradition. It continues, for example, to emphasize the examination of creation and of human experience. Nevertheless, the book of Job also offers a challenge to rigid versions of its own Wisdom tradition inasmuch as it asserts that human assumptions about consistency and moral order are finally inadequate for grasping the complex realities within which many of us are born, live and die. A literary representation of inconsistency on the part of God, here at the end of the book, is entirely compatible with that challenge. Human beings do, after all, sometimes experience in life absurdities and sudden changes of fortune, which can cause people of faith to wonder whether God really acts consistently over time. These realities of chance, fortune and misfortune are not always captured well by systematic theology. They are sometimes captured better in literature, however, as in the unexpected shifts that structure the end of Job; or as in the words of one of Dinesen's characters, who, attuned to the tensions and absurdities of the world, suggests that 'to love [God] truly you must love change, and you must love a joke, these being the true inclinations of [God's] own heart' (Dinesen 1934: 355).

This invocation of a joke, in relation to a book focused in part on the deadly serious question of radical suffering, may seem perverse; but it is worth thinking about further. Several biblical scholars have suggested that the prose conclusion turns the book of Job into a 'comedy'. By using the word 'comedy', such scholars do not necessarily mean to imply 'laughter'. Indeed, sometimes they distance themselves explicitly from any implication of laughter (e.g. Whedbee 1977), pointing out that they are using the term 'comedy' in its classical sense to refer to a literary genre in which matters are resolved, in the end, in an affirmative direction. Some insight may be gained when one imagines the narrative conclusion of the book of Job in terms of this classical literary category, though one must ask whether too much emphasis on comedic resolution runs the risk of obscuring the dynamic dialogue set in motion by ongoing tension between the various parts of the book. However, to draw too sharp a line between the book of Job and actual laughter may not do justice to certain images found in the book. After all, as Newsom points out, laughter is explicitly said by Yhwh to characterize several of God's creatures, including the ostrich (39.18), the war horse (39.22) and Leviathan (41.29). While Job is never himself described as laughing, Newsom notes that a series of 'playful names', with connotations of sensuality and even delights of the palate, which Job gives to his three 'beautiful' daughters at the end of the book (42.14–15) can be read as 'a form of laughter – not heedless or anarchic laughter – but human and therefore tragic laughter' (Newsom 2003: 258; cf. Keller 2003: 124–40). Lesbians, gay men, bisexuals and the transgendered are often ourselves associated with laughter, of course, as discussions of camp humour make clear. Elizabeth Stuart has therefore suggested that 'laughter', and even 'camp laughter', needs to be included in any queer 'hermeneutical toolbox' (Stuart 2000: 28). Although such humour can sometimes be read as a form of cynicism, it might also be understood in a very different sense as an affirmation of hope and resistance, and a determination to celebrate and dance, even in a context where mighty forces sometimes seem to be arrayed against us. From that point of view, a 'queer reading' may find much to appreciate in the way in which the book of Job, by juxtaposing the speeches of God and the merry narrative conclusion, 'gestures toward the human incorporation of tragedy into the powerful imperatives of desire: to live and to love' (Newsom 2003: 258). For the ability to acknowledge explicitly the tragic dimension of life, while still affirming with a laugh one's hopeful determination 'to live and to love', is a sign of queer resistance indeed.

In Lieu of a Conclusion

Taken as a whole, the book of Job ultimately refuses to be captured by a single, clear and consistent conclusion. It is not an orderly treatise, but rather a cacophonous argument, incorporating multiple points of view and conflicting positions. How could it otherwise do justice to its topic? It does, after all, probe such difficult matters as radical suffering; the nature of God; the motivations for piety; justice and retribution; chaos and creation; beauty and brutality; and the tension between our individual experiences and emotions, on the one hand, and the rigid categories given to us by tradition and society, on the other hand. Rather than offering us a single perspective on such matters, the book of Job opens an argument and invites us to join.

In spite of the difficulties involved in reading it, the book of Job has much to offer a 'queer reading' of the Bible. Indeed, its complexities and its contradictions, and its unorthodox challenge to other parts of biblical tradition, can even be understood as having certain parallels to 'queer' lives. For lesbians, gay men, bisexuals, transgendered persons and others know only too well that the neat, ordering principles given to us by society and religious tradition often fail to do justice to the messy realities we experience in relation to such matters as gender and kinship, sex and friendship, the complexities of the body and the vagaries of desire. Thus, like Job, we are often compelled – and rightly so – to assert the integrity of our own experiences over against the platitudes of orthodox authorities or even other parts of the Bible. Our experiences in relation, for example, to Aids/HIV have taught us only too well that affliction will often be wrongly interpreted by others as divine retribution. On this point, the affirmation of Yhwh that Job spoke rightly, rather than his orthodox friends, is important indeed. Yet such experiences also show us, much as God shows Job from the whirlwind, that mortal humans embedded in a beautiful but strange world can never eliminate entirely the realities of chaos and tragedy.

The acknowledgement by the God speeches that creation is not always orderly and neat also has other important points of contact with queer resistance to heteronormativity. For example, religious opponents of homosexuality or of transgender inclusion sometimes attempt to ground normative views of heterosexuality, heterosexual marriage or binary notions of sexed bodies in creation itself, either by appealing to natural law or by appealing to orderly creation stories such as that found, for example, in Genesis 1. Yet the God speeches in Job recognize that creation is a much more complicated and even chaotic realm than humans usually wish to admit. Much that is seen there remains strange, and cannot be reconciled with human values, beliefs and orderly schemes. A reader who learns this from Job will be less surprised to discover that attempts to ground heteronormative structures in creation have necessarily ignored numerous complexities and ambiguities that surround the supposedly 'natural' and orderly matters of sex, gender and bodies (cf. Fausto-Sterling 2000; Butler 2004; Bagemihl 1999).

In its incorporation of multiple and contradictory perspectives, the structure of the book of Job also cautions us against settling on static or tidy conclusions and encourages us to structure our communities so as to include diverse points of view. If we come to recognize, with Job, that the world around us is too vast and too complex to conform to our own, all-too-human, rigid ordering principles, we may be less inclined to insist dogmatically that other human beings so conform their lives (cf. Connolly 1993). And even when our individual and collective lives, like the book of Job itself, fail or refuse to resolve all conflicts and tensions, they can be put together in such a way as to end with an affirmation of hope, laughter, life and beauty without thereby denying the existence of chaos and pain.

Psalms

S. TAMAR KAMIONKOWSKI

Introductory Remarks[1]

The book of Psalms, also known as the Psalter and *Tehillim*, is a collection of 150 poems which were composed over the course of several hundreds of years and which include a variety of literary genres and socio-religious settings.[2] Thus, we can speak of this collection as a book insofar as it was eventually compiled into a set, 'authoritative' collection. Yet, in focusing upon particular psalms, we must remember that there can be vast differences in style, perspective and theology from psalm to psalm. The book of Psalms is unique among the books of the Bible in that these writings represent the voices of individuals speaking with and about the God of ancient Israel. This collection is also distinctive in that these poems have played a central role in both private prayer and public worship for Jews and Christians throughout the centuries.[3] Still today, many people turn to the Psalms in times of distress and in times of joy.

Given the centrality and continued popularity of this book among contemporary religious communities, it is of central importance that we consider how this religious resource speaks or might speak to individuals who challenge heterosexual normativity. Do psalms speak a universal, gender-free language? Or do psalms communicate particular gender and sex norms? Additionally, do one's gender identity and sexual orientation have an impact on how psalms are read?

In this chapter, I will begin with a general overview of biblical scholarship on the book of Psalms. The rest of the chapter will be divided into two main sections, dealing with queer theory and translesbigay identity respectively. The first section will be the primary focus of this study. In *Take Back the Word*, Robert Goss and Mona West advocate 'approaching the Bible as our friend' (Goss and West 2000: 5). In other words, their task is to claim that the Bible has something positive to offer people of faith. The first section of this chapter is neither positive nor negative, but seeks to explore the complexities of same-

---

1 Translations of the biblical Hebrew text are taken from the NJPS unless otherwise indicated.

2 The primary critical commentaries are Delitzsch (1880–1); Briggs (1906); Buttenwieser (1938); Weiser (1962); Dahood (1965–70); Craigie (1983); Allen (1983); Kraus (1988; 1989); and Tate (1990).

3 See Holladay (1993) for a history of the development of the Psalter and its use throughout the centuries, primarily among Christians.

sex gender relations in the psalms. Whether this is affirming or alienating is for each reader to determine. Among the central claims that I make are that there are some psalms that are indeed gender-free and universal. However, these psalms are rare and constitute the exception rather than the norm. The majority of psalms exhibit predominantly binary thinking and do not allow for grays and fluidity. Thus, even if gender is not an element in a psalm, it is most likely present in some latent or implied form. I will further argue that the psalmists and the God of the psalms reflect the viewpoints and perspectives of stereotypical masculinity. Given the maleness of God (in these texts) and of the psalmists, I then ask what happens when we read the psalms with male-to-male relationships at the forefront of our minds? What models of male-to-male intimacy are presented? The answer to this question will be as diverse as the types of psalms in the collection of 150.

In the second section of this chapter, I will shift from a queer reading of the psalms to a translesbigay liberationist perspective. I will briefly consider how some of the central motifs that run throughout the book of Psalms might be read as translesbigay positive. I will conclude with a consideration of a few sample psalms that could be recontextualized to serve as inspirational texts for translesbigay individuals today.

A final introductory word is necessary here. Although this is a queer reading of the book of Psalms, women are glaringly absent. My research has led me to conclude that in an historical context, the psalms were written by men, for men, to a male God. I do not argue against those who have suggested that the psalms can be reclaimed by women,[4] but my analysis focuses on uncovering and exposing dimensions of gender and sexuality as they are embedded in the texts. From this perspective, I have certainly not found any examples of female-to-female intimacy presented in the book of Psalms.

Historical Critical Scholarship: A Brief Overview

It is now commonly believed that the book of Psalms came into existence through a series of gradual steps over the course of hundreds of years. Some of these psalms originated in the Premonarchic Period (e.g. Pss. 29 and 82), others originated in the North after the split of the kingdoms (e.g. the Psalms of Korach and Asaph),[5] some are connected to the Temple in Zion (e.g. Pss. 24 and 122) and a number of psalms reflect the period of exile or even the early Second Temple Period (e.g. Ps. 137). Individual poems were written for various occasions and then they were gathered into small collections like the Psalms of Ascent and the Psalms of Korach. These small collections were then connected to other collections and brought together into larger groupings like the Elohistic Psalms. At some point during this process, superscriptions were added to the psalms and the final 150 were divided into five books (mirroring

---

4 Bail (1998) reads Ps. 55 through the lens of possible female authorship. This excellent article brings new insights to this difficult psalm.

5 Rendsburg (1990) offers a compelling argument for the Northern origins of 35 psalms.

the Five Books of Torah),[6] each concluding with a formulaic doxology. The final establishment of 150 in the Hebrew Masoretic text must have been rather late since the Dead Sea Scrolls fragments and Greek versions attest to significant differences and variations (Sanders 1967; Flint 1998).

Since the groundbreaking work of Gerald Henry Wilson on the shaping of the Psalter in the mid-1980s, there has been great interest in the compositional history of the psalms as a literary whole. That is, many scholars today are interested in the ordering of the psalms, their relationship to one another, and the book as a whole (e.g. Wilson 1985; Goulder 1982, 1990, 1996, 1998; McCann 1993). Matthias Millard, for example, seeks out themes of despair and hope that run throughout the work and argues that the editors compiled and arranged the psalms in a manner that would give expression to grief and hope during the exilic period (Millard 1994). Robert L. Cole reads Psalms 73–89 (Book III) as one organic text through the lens of rhetorical criticism, looking for unifying features through repetition and parallelism (Cole 2000).[7]

The current interest in the final shaping of the Psalter marks a sharp shift from earlier interest in the authorship and provenance of individual psalms. During the early stages of critical studies, after the traditional ascription of the psalms to King David was questioned, late nineteenth- and early twentieth-century biblical scholars focused on determining the actual authors and dates of the texts. The psalms were seen as spontaneous outpourings of individual poets who wrote from personal life experiences; thus, a sensitive modern reader could determine the actual experience of the psalmist and could date the text based on linguistic clues and historical references (e.g. Buttenwieser, 1938). At this early stage of critical study, scholars believed that these poems were only secondarily incorporated into public worship. Thus, individual poems written for purely artistic reasons were only secondarily given a liturgical place.

In the early decades of the twentieth century, Hermann Gunkel changed the direction of psalms studies for ever.[8] He noted that the psalms exhibit a high level of stereotypical language that could easily be classified into various types. He asserted that this stereotypical language was explicable only on the supposition that the psalms had been written, from the start, within the context of public worship and inspired by private artistic reflection. The first type of psalm, according to Gunkel, was the Hymn, which he characterized as generally enthusiastic and filled with praise for God. He posited that these were originally used primarily in public worship contexts, but that some hymns were later written by individuals simply to express their devotion to God. The second type of psalm was the Communal Lament, recited at times of public calamity like natural disasters or military threats. Gunkel identified a

---

6 See Sarna (1993: 15–19) for a discussion of the division of the book of Psalms into five books and its earlier Jewish liturgical use.

7 Also, Hossfeld and Zenger (1993) have published a commentary on the book of Psalms taking the canonical shape of the book as their interpretive starting-point.

8 Gunkel's earliest significant work on the psalms appeared in the encyclopaedia *Die Religion in Geschichte und Gegenwart* (1927–31) and then in his full-blown study, *Einleitung in die Psalmen* (1937). His work is now most accessible in English through *The Psalms: A Form-Critical Introduction* (1967).

group of psalms that he called the Individual Laments in which an individual poured out his personal grief and appealed to God for rescue. He believed that these psalms were used for private prayer and not public worship. Similarly, Gunkel believed that the Thanksgiving Psalms were also used by private individuals who would express their thanks to God. Wisdom Psalms were deemed to be those poems that have affinities with general wisdom literature. Gunkel also developed the category of the Royal Psalms, those texts related to the cult and the monarchy. Since Gunkel's work, almost all biblical scholars have accepted these categories as basic starting-points from which other research is conducted.

Sigmund Mowinckel took Gunkel's quest for the original *Sitz im Leben* a step further than his predecessor by suggesting that many of the psalms were employed in an annual enthronement festival which would have included a procession of the ark-throne of YHWH, some kind of dramatization of YHWH's primeval battles with the enemies of creation and a final celebration of YHWH as king of Israel and the world (Mowinckel 1962). Mowinckel's work engendered a host of scholarly responses and debates regarding the original settings for these poems. The two most important scholars who have made contributions to the form-critical study of the psalms in recent years are Claus Westermann, who has examined the theological function of various genres (Westermann 1980, 1981) and Erhard Gerstenberger, who has argued for a tribal, family-oriented *Sitz im Leben* for many of these texts (Gerstenberger 1998, 2000).

Currently, most scholars would agree that the book of Psalms contains an assortment of texts, some private and some public, which reflect a variety of settings that we cannot determine with any certainty. It is also agreed upon that at some point these poems entered into the post-biblical world of liturgy and lost their associations with their original settings. For example, regardless of the posited original setting and use of Psalm 23 as a song of thanksgiving at the temple (Kraus 1988: 305–6), it is now known as a psalm of mourning for both Jews and Christians. Regardless of how we categorize Psalm 90, it is now a part of the Jewish liturgy that welcomes in the Sabbath each week.

The early questions raised by the work of Gunkel and Mowinckel gave rise to specialized topics of interest in Psalms studies. I mention only briefly here some of the topics that may have a bearing upon a queer reading of the psalms. Mowinckel's association of many psalms with the royal cult has led to many studies on the representation of kingship and royal theology in the psalms (e.g. Eaton 1986; Brettler 1989; Ollenburger 1987; Starbuck 1999). The identity of the enemies, which dominate so many psalms of various genres, has stymied scholars for years. It has been suggested that the enemies may be national military enemies, witches, psychological demons, the ruling elite or openly antagonistic peers (Birkeland 1955; Anderson 1965–6; Delekat 1967; Croft 1987; Sheppard 1991; Lamp 1989). As a result of more interest in literary studies among biblicists, there are recent studies that apply methods of new literary criticism to the book of Psalms.[9] Also, renewed interest in biblical

---

9 Mandolfo (2000) approaches the psalms through dialogic criticism and an interest in how the psalms may have been voiced, or performed. Tanner (2001) argues that interpreters have used intertextuality through the centuries in reading the psalms.

theology has given rise to a host of theologically oriented studies on the book of Psalms. These studies, primarily produced by Protestant biblicists, attempt to link biblical scholarship with concerns for the life of the Church. Among the most prominent writers in this area are Brueggemann (1984), Kraus (1986) and Miller (1986). In more recent years, a number of Jewish scholars have published interpretations of the psalms that address Jewish theological and spiritual need. See for example Magonet (1994), Polish (2000) and Chiel and Dreher (2000).

This brief introduction to scholarship on the book of Psalms has only touched upon the most prominent studies in this vast field of enquiry. The actual literature on this biblical book is massive and is represented by varied methodologies and points of entry. Although recent trends focus on the canonical shape of the final book and literary criticism, this study will utilize the questions and concerns of form-critical studies. Having considered queer theory side by side with the book of psalms, I believe that the most fruitful intersection of the two can be found in asking specific questions about specific psalms that fall into general types.

Introduction to a Queer Reading of the Psalms

It came as a great surprise to discover that there is no literature on the psalms from the perspective of queer theory that I was able to find, especially given the flourishing literature in both areas. All the conventional methods of academic research, from on-line searches to roaming library stacks, to enquiries with colleagues led me absolutely nowhere! There is less than a handful of academic articles on feminist readings of the psalms. There has been some work among Christian churches to develop inclusive lectionaries and there are a few Jewish and Christian translesbigay synagogues and churches that are creating new psalms for new life experiences; but there are almost no analytic, gender-sensitive readings of the book of Psalms.[10] (More than one colleague laughed sympathetically as I admitted that I had volunteered to work on the psalms.)

Ultimately this should not come as a shock. The complex and often erotic biblical narratives of Ruth and Naomi, David and Jonathan, and God and the community of Israel, or his 'bride' Jerusalem, have a lot of interesting raw material from which to work. By contrast, the characters of psalms poetry are much more oblique, and without characters, how can we talk about gender and sexual identities? The most unambiguous character is God, but the human speakers are very difficult to identify as are the enemies or occasional friends to which they refer. Queering the psalms therefore entails a careful combing through the 150 texts for clues about gender through characters that are difficult to identify in broader strokes.

In contemporary communities of worship, the psalms tend to be read in a gender-neutral manner. Generally, modern readers do not think of God or the

---

10 The exceptions are Brettler (1998), Clines (1995b) and Bail (1998).

human speakers in the psalms as particularly male.[11] This is not surprising. The masculinity of the speaker's voice is much subtler than that of the biblical male characters and prophets. A psalm that addresses God in the midst of suffering can easily be construed as universal. All people suffer from physical and social ills. Loneliness, pain and paranoia cannot be claimed by any single gender identity.[12]

Likewise, a psalm that praises the works of creation and that celebrates nature and all life within it is not limited to particular gender identities. For example, it is easy to understand how Psalm 148 can be taken as a universal, gender-free poem by lay readers and many scholars as well. In other words, there is nothing in the call to the heavens and earth and to all of creation that is particularly gender-oriented. The only hints of gender in this psalm are the masculine grammatical markers for God and echoes of the *Chaoskampf*[13] motif. Assuming that most readers are not aware of the *Chaoskampf* background, they can easily engage with this psalm as a universal praise for the works of creation, especially when the grammatical masculine markers are removed from the English. Note how a recent inclusive version renders Psalm 148:

Hallelujah! Praise God from the heavens; praise God in the heights! Praise God all you angels; praise God, all you multitudes in heaven! Praise God, sun and moon; praise God, all you shining stars! Praise God, you highest heavens, and you waters above the heavens! Let them praise the name of the Most High, for God commanded and they were created. God established them forever and ever; God fixed their bounds, which cannot be passed. Praise God from the earth, you sea monsters and all deeps, fire and hail, snow and frost, stormy wind fulfilling God's command! Mountains and all hills, fruit trees and all cedars! Wild animals and all cattle, creeping things and flying birds! Sovereigns of the earth and all peoples, royalty and all rulers of the earth! Young men and women alike, old and young together! Let them praise the name of God, for God's name alone is exalted; God's glory is above the earth and heaven. God has raised up a horn for God's people, praise for all the faithful, for the people of Israel who are close to God. Hallelujah! (Gold *et al.* 1995: 534)

The psalm goes out of its way to be as inclusionary as possible by setting up a series of merisms. The poetic pairing of 'creeping things and flying birds'

---

11 There are a number of 'inclusive' translations of the book of Psalms that intentionally remove all gendered references to God in the texts. This is based on the modern belief that God is neither male nor female and that the gendered basis of the Hebrew language created many unnecessary male grammatical markers. Although this may be a useful technique in encouraging universal readings of these texts, these translations end up downplaying the problematic elements of the text. This is certainly not useful in analytic, critical readings of the psalms. See Gold *et al.* (1995).

12 This is not to suggest that there are not specific gender-based kinds of sufferings or reasons for suffering. The pain of childbirth is biologically bound. Military language tends to reflect the experiences of men, and so on.

13 This term refers to the mythological battle between YHWH and the forces of chaos (other gods) which resulted in the creation of the ordered world.

indicates all animals; likewise, 'old and young together' means not just the old and young, but people of all ages. In this context, the appearance of 'young men and women alike' could be rendered as a call to all people, regardless of sexual orientation.

Admittedly, after reading through all 150 psalms for those that are the most universal, I ended up with a list of only 21 that I felt comfortable putting into this category. The more I reviewed those 21, the shorter the list became. In other words, as I began to look for gender clues, I found them in the most unlikely places.

Binary Thinking

One way of looking for clues about gender in any work is by considering to what extent binary thinking dominates the text under scrutiny. A text can hint at its attitude about gender identity and sexuality if it presents a strong dualistic worldview. Proponents of queer theory, alongside other postmodernists, have argued that the cultural myth of stable male and female genders and heterosexual and homosexual identity and behaviour are rooted in the larger problem of binary thinking. Given that the cast of characters in the book of Psalms is limited, it may be worthwhile to consider if the psalms exhibit a strong tendency toward binary thinking. If they do, it will be suggestive of a general worldview in which traditional gender and sex binaries are supported.

Psalm 1 sets the tone for the entire book of Psalms and instructs the reader how to relate to the psalms in general. This text provides two paths for living from which one can choose: the way of the righteous or the way of the wicked. In a highly structured poem, the reader is invited into a world of binaries. One can and must always choose between two options. One option is the correct path and leads to full acceptance in society: 'He is like a tree planted beside streams of water, which yields its fruit in season, whose foliage never fades, and whatever it produces thrives' (v. 3). The other way leads to marginalization: 'the way of the wicked is doomed' (v. 6b). The definition of 'righteous' is the one who accepts the teachings of God ('the teaching of the LORD is his delight, and he studies that teaching day and night' (v. 2), or put differently, one who accepts the normative, dominant culture.

The rest of Psalms essentially presents competing claims to right and wrong, to good and bad. The petitioner in the laments often asserts his innocence by saying, 'I'm not "them" or the "Other".' God is praised for being able to distinguish between the insider and outsider, the just and the unjust. For example, Psalm 5 alternates every two verses between statements asserting that God hates the wicked, but loves the righteous. The petitioner thus makes his case by aligning himself with A (the righteous) and not B (the wicked). Psalm 7.10 states this theme succinctly: 'Let the evil of the wicked come to an end, but establish the righteous; he who probes the mind and conscience is God the righteous.' There are good guys and bad guys, and it is God who tells us who is who.[14] Psalm 26 similarly invites God to probe the psalmist's mind to see

---

14 Psalm 11.5 expresses the same sentiment.

that he is not one of 'them'. The binary is not always set between the good and bad, but through other dual pairings as well. Psalm 9.6–7 points to another common binary – that between permanence and impermanence. The enemies are fleeting, but God is everlasting.

Given the strong polarities in thinking, between good and evil, righteous and wicked individuals, we might be justified in expecting the same kind of binary thinking with respect to gender and sexual identity, even if gender and eroticism are not at centre stage in this collection of poetry.

Masculinity in the Psalms

The gender identity of the elusive Psalms characters are clearest in the royal psalms, where the primary relationship is between the heavenly king and the earthly king. These texts establish male hegemony and define maleness as embedded in military power and physical strength and domination over others. The king is depicted primarily as a warrior as is YHWH. Psalm 18.8–14 provides a typical description of the God of the psalms:

> Then the earth rocked and quaked; the foundations of the mountains shook, rocked by His indignation; smoke went up from His nostrils, from His mouth came devouring fire; live coals blazed forth from Him. He bent the sky and came down, thick cloud beneath His feet. He mounted a cherub and flew, gliding on the wings of the wind. He made darkness His screen; dark thunderheads, dense clouds of the sky were His pavilion round about Him. Out of the brilliance before Him, hail and fiery coals pierced His clouds. Then the LORD thundered from heaven, the Most High gave forth His voice – hail and fiery coals.

The human king emulates his father (Ps. 18.33–8):

> the God who girded me with might, who made my way perfect; who made my legs like a deer's, and let me stand firm on the heights; who trained my hands for battle; my arms can bend a bow of bronze. You have given me the shield of Your protection; Your right hand has sustained me, Your care has made me great. You have let me stride on freely; my feet have not slipped. I pursued my enemies and overtook them; I did not turn back till I destroyed them.

Even in contexts that are not primarily battle scenes (where testosterone traditionally runs high), the maleness of God is explicit. He is described as a king in over a dozen psalms. Psalm 47.3 describes God as the 'great king over all the earth'. The poet of Psalm 95 extols God as 'the great king over all divine beings' (Ps. 95.3).[15] Apart from explicit imagery of God as king, he is often depicted as a father to his people. Psalm 103.13 describes God as a father. Psalm 68.6 speaks

---

15 God is explicitly described as a king, *melek*, in the following passages: Pss. 10.16; 24.7–10; 29.10; 44.5; 47.3, 7, 8; 68.25; 74.12; 84.3; 89.19; 95.3; 98.6; 145.1; and 149.2.

of God as the father of orphans. In Psalm 89.27, the king describes God as his father. And apart from explicit descriptions of maleness, most psalms imply a male God through traditional male settings.

David J. A. Clines (1995b) has argued that the psalms consistently depict piety in exclusively male terms. He studies the psalms from the perspectives of the rhetoric of war, the ideology of honour and shame, the representation of enemies, the role of women and the value placed on strength and height among other categories. He concludes that piety, according the book of Psalms, is about attaining power and honour. He asserts that whether the psalms are the work of a single or multiple authors, the psalmist(s) is a warrior who is obsessed with his honour and lives a life of confrontation with enemies. As Clines remarks at the end of his paper, he welcomes the day when commentaries or textbooks on Psalms will include subtitles such as: *Theology of the Book of Psalms: God Helps You Kill People*. Or alternatively, *God Will Make a Man of You*.

In an in-depth study of a handful of psalms (especially Ps. 128) that mention women, Marc Brettler similarly concludes that the psalms represent male interests and perspectives. In each case, he suggests that women are portrayed marginally, and that at best, a few psalms could arguably be gender-neutral, such as Psalms 65 and 142.

From a feminist perspective, these observations do not bode well for a positive, affirming reading of the book of Psalms as a work that speaks equally to all individuals. Women are rendered invisible, or at best marginal. Nonetheless, from a translesbigay perspective, particularly from a gay male perspective, the psalms offer a complex and rich picture of a variety of male-to-male relationships. Some of these relationships may be affirming to contemporary translesbigay readers while other models presented in these texts may be problematic or even offensive.

Male–Male Intimacy

The psalms express a range of emotions, from hate to love, from resignation to stubborn perseverance. These emotions are set within a male world in which a male petitioner converses with his male God. The goal of the communication is always greater intimacy and connection between the male human being and the male deity. However, defining the nature of the intimacy is complex and fraught with difficulties.

Understanding the male-to-male dynamics in these texts requires us to suspend our own assumptions, shaped by twenty-first-century Western culture. In this regard, the insights of Eve Kosofsky Sedgwick can be helpful here. In defining 'desire' Sedgwick writes: 'I will be using "desire" in a way analogous to the psychoanalytic use of "libido" – not for a particular affective state or emotion, but for the affective or social force, the glue, even when its manifestation is hostility or hatred or something less emotively charged, that shapes an important relationship. How far this force is properly sexual . . . will be an active question' (Sedgwick 1985: 2). Sedgwick further points out that homosocial, that is same-sex bonding, may or may not be on a smooth continuum with homosexuality. As Sedgwick observes in modern society, men often bond through shared homophobia. This is an example of same-sex bonding that is at odds with homosexuality, another form of same-sex bonding. It is one of Sedgwick's goals to point out that each historical moment and cultural complex plays out his continuum in various ways.

The concept of a continuum for homosociality and homosexuality is a helpful model for queering the psalms. Defining various psalms as homosexual or even sexual feels nearly impossible given the paucity of information on homosexual identity or even behaviour in the biblical periods. We can argue that a psalm is charged with the language of desire between men and that the language may sometimes be erotic; but this language does not tell us enough to draw conclusions about identity or behaviour. In fact, I contend that these psalms were written by men with wives and families, and that these men played out their expected roles as men in society. Thus, we have here examples of men engaged in heterosexual, family-based behaviour, who also express and maintain intimate relationships with their male God (if not other men).

A queer reading ought to emphasize, as much as possible, the maleness of the characters while reading all the psalms, not just the explicitly male ones. What happens when we read psalms with a male-to-male lens? What kind of model of male–male relationship emerges from these texts? Given the variety of genres and epochs from which these texts emerge, there is no single consistent reading that can fairly be gleaned from the 150 psalms without over-generalizing to the point of meaninglessness. A study of psalms reveals that some texts present homosocial bonding in a manner that supports patriarchy and glorifies stereotypical masculinity. Others present homosociality and homosexuality on a fluid continuum. In other words, there is no single model of male-to-male intimacy in the psalms.

A number of texts describe intimacy between two males through the model of father–son relationships. The love between the two players is described literally as a father–son relationship. 'You are My son, I have fathered you this day. Ask it of Me, and I will make the nations your domain; your estate, the limits of the earth. You can smash them with an iron mace, shatter them like potter's ware' (Ps. 2.7–9). Psalm 89.20–9 reads:

> I have conferred power upon a warrior; I have exalted one chosen out of the people. I have found David, My servant; anointed him with My sacred oil. My hand shall be constantly with him, and My arm shall strengthen him. No enemy shall oppress him, no vile man afflict him. I will crush his adversaries before him; I will strike down those who hate him. My faithfulness and steadfast love shall be with him; his horn shall be exalted through My name. I will set his hand upon the sea, his right hand upon the rivers. He shall say to Me, 'You are my father, my God, the rock of my deliverance.' I will appoint him first-born, highest of the kings of the earth. I will maintain My steadfast love for him always; My covenant with him shall endure.

In this relationship, the dominant human king mirrors the dominance of his heavenly father. Thus, although the human king is clearly subordinate to the heavenly king, what is emphasized is the mirrored dominance and power; the human king is not described as subordinate to his 'father' in any significant way. In fact, the father confers power onto his son. I believe it is reasonable to conclude that the homosocial bonding here reinforces the dominance of men over women and presumably men over other men. It is this model of homosociality that is commonly assumed by readers of these military psalms.

It is easy to notice gender in psalms that express hypervirility, or at least speak explicitly about kings and battles. However, there is a range of other psalms in which male homosocial and homosexual bonds are not at odds with each other, texts in which male bonding is not achieved at the expense of others. These psalms are completely overlooked by most readers of Psalms because gender is subtler in these texts. We noted earlier that in contemporary communities, readers tend to de-emphasize any signs of gender that exist in the psalms. The psalmist becomes the universal gender-neutral human and God's maleness is overlooked. However, a queer reading of the psalms could choose to highlight the gendered players rather than to downplay them, even in those texts where the gender play does seem subtle.

Once we open our eyes to male eroticism, we discover that it is indeed embedded in the texts. For example, Psalm 25.15a expresses the desire for the divine gaze, the desire for the body of God, 'My eyes are ever toward YHWH.' While Psalm 73.25 beautifully expresses the male psalmist's desire for God above any other lover or intimate friend on earth, 'Whom else have I in heaven? And having You, I want no one on earth.' Psalm 36.8 articulates the desire that a community of men have for the 'top' male, a desire to be cared for and protected, a desire to 'drink from the river of thy delights' (RSV). These highly charged, erotic same-sex verses are overlooked both because readers have not traditionally looked for erotic tones and also because these lines are often embedded in other contexts. Nonetheless, on some unconscious level, the power of the intimacy here, in hidden corners, has drawn male readers to these texts. These psalms provide a safe veil by which to express love for a male God.

Psalm 84: A Crush on God[16]

Psalm 84 is typically described as a pilgrimage hymn and the psalmist is identified as an Israelite on pilgrimage to Zion (cf. Tate 1990: 355–7).

> For the leader; on the gittith. Of the Korahites. A psalm. How lovely is Your dwelling-place, O LORD of hosts. I long, I yearn for the courts of the LORD; my body and soul shout for joy to the living God. Even the sparrow has found a home, and the swallow a nest for herself in which to set her young, near Your altar, O LORD of hosts, my king and my God. Happy are those who dwell in Your house; they forever praise You. Selah. Happy is the man who finds refuge in You, whose mind is on the pilgrim highways. They pass through the Valley of Baca, regarding it as a place of springs, as if the early rain had covered it with blessing. They go from rampart to rampart, appear-

---

16 My analysis of these psalms is not comprehensive in detailing all of the philological and form-critical issues; for the purposes of this study, I am interested only in the features directly pertinent to a queer reading of these texts.

ing before God in Zion. O LORD, God of hosts, hear my prayer; give ear, O God of Jacob. Selah. O God, behold our shield, look upon the face of Your anointed. Better one day in Your courts than a thousand anywhere else; I would rather stand at the threshold of God's house than dwell in the tents of the wicked. For the LORD God is sun and shield; the LORD bestows grace and glory; He does not withhold His bounty from those who live without blame. O LORD of hosts, happy is the man who trusts in You.

Marvin E. Tate summarizes this psalm as follows: 'Ps. 84 bears witness to a strong and living faith which longs for the "living God" (v. 3) and the context of holiness, life and love in the temple courts and beyond' (Tate 1990: 362). Hans-Joachim Kraus writes:

> The psalm bears witness to the longing of an OT singer for the place of the presence of God. A love for the sanctuary that encompasses and fills all of life wants to awaken the song . . . But the sanctuary as an immanently sacred place is not the object of love . . . At the center of the psalms stands the *'ēl hay* . . . Only with him can one find protection, security, satisfaction, and good fortune – life in the fullest sense of fulfilled existence. (Kraus 1989: 170–1)[17]

These commentators are certainly picking up accurately on the intimacy and intense longing in this psalm, but by putting blinders onto gender, several significant aspects of this psalm are overlooked. There are a number of features in this psalm that bring male-to-male longing to the forefront.

First, although we have pointed to the general male orientation of all the psalms, Psalm 84 emphasizes the maleness of both the psalmist and the deity. God is referred to as 'my king' in verse 4. The term *'adōnay sᵉbā'ôt*, translated variously as Lord of Hosts, Lord of Armies, or the like, appears four times in a psalm of only 13 verses. This is rather exceptional given the fact that only one other psalm has so many occurrences of this term, Psalm 80. One explanation for the use of this epithet for the deity is that this term reflects the cultic name of God on Zion (Kraus 1989: 85–6; cf. also Mettinger 1982). However, most scholars agree that the association with the temple does not fully explain the meaning of the term and they usually connect the epithet to an expression of God's military prowess as the warrior rider on his chariot or warrior king leading the armies (Galling 1956: 146; Freedman 1960: 156).[18] While the appearance of the name YHWH is enough to conjure up male images, *sᵉbā'ôt* evokes images of hypervirility and intense stereotypical masculinity.

More significantly than the terms used for the players are the words uttered by the petitioner to the One he loves. Verses 2–3 set the tone for the rest of the psalm. The poet begins: 'How beloved[19] are your dwelling places, O YHWH of

---

17 Dahood (1965–70: 280) connects the imagery of the living God to the image of God as the 'Fountain of Living Water' in Jeremiah 17.13.

18 For a comprehensive bibliography on this term, see Zobel (2003).

19 I choose to use the translation 'beloved' over JPS's 'lovely' because I believe that the former term focuses more on the feelings of the speaker, while the latter term sets the attention onto the object of love.

warrior might' (my translation). With these words, the poet begins to express
love for the presence of his male God. This first verse sets up both the unambiguous maleness of God and also the primary theme of love. The second
verse further develops and defines the central concern of love. 'My entire being
longs, yea pines for the presence of YHWH' (my translation). Said in any other
context, this line would certainly be understood as a declaration of love and
longing within a romantic, erotic setting. The verb *ksp* is a rare verb appearing
only five times in the entirety of the Bible. Although it is used in a variety of
contexts, it clearly expresses desire and longing on an intense level. The phrase
kāleʿtâ napšî is unique to Psalm 84, although the verb is used with *rûᵃh* (Ps. 143.7)
ʿenayim (Ps. 119.82, 123) to express the notion of intense yearning to the point
of pain. Our poet desires the presence of God with desperation, the feelings
of a man for his lover. The B colon of the verse further clarifies the nature and
object of desire. The psalmist's longing and desire is felt not only through his
emotions and will (*lēb*), but through his body (*bāsar*). He experiences physical
desire, and the ultimate object of his desire is 'the living God'.[20] The phrase 'to
rejoice with one's body' raises an interesting question of interpretation. Kraus
argues that heart and body indicate the 'human being in its totality' who gives
out a 'shrill sound' in yearning for God's nearness (1989: 168). Briggs best represents standard critical commentaries in asserting that the heart and body
reflect the body and the soul (1906: 224). In verses 9–10, the psalmist expresses
his desire to be seen by his 'top'. And then he recites his pronouncement of
love, better one day with you than a lifetime with anyone else. The maleness
of the characters and the physicality of the desire make this not only a psalm
of pilgrimage uttered by an Israelite, but a psalm of male erotic longing for
physical intimacy with his male God (similar language is used in Psalm 27.4
and in Psalm 42).

When Konrad Schaefer concludes his commentary on Psalm 84 with the
line: 'In a word, the poet is in love with the temple', he is only partially correct.
The man is in love with his male God and the temple is simply the stage for
the intimate rendezvous. As I stated in my introduction to the book of Psalms,
the hypothetical setting for each psalm has historically had a major influence
on its interpretation. Since most historical-critical scholars have posited that
this psalm was a song of pilgrimage to be recited at the gates of the temple,
the interpretive focus has naturally been on the anticipation and longing for
entrance into the courtyards of the temple. By contrast, Rabbi Samson Raphael
Hirsch reads this psalm in the context of Diaspora Judaism. For Hirsch, this
psalm expresses the pain of living in exile and at a great distance from the
Land of Israel. In this context, the psalmist asserts his ability to stay connected
to God even in full knowledge of the great distances between them (Hirsch
1966: 98–102). I am simply suggesting that we set this psalm within the context
of one man's longing for another. Read in this light, we have a beautiful example of a man longing with all his body and soul to gaze upon the love of his life.
All he seeks is a glimpse from the object of his desire and he also deeply yearns
that the 'man-God' whom he adores will notice him in return. It is interesting
to note how some translations make every effort to move away from this kind

---

20 This rare term appears only in Joshua 3.10; Hosea 2.1; Psalm 42.3 and our psalm.

of a reading. For example, Richard S. Hanson translates the first couple of lines from Psalm 84 as follows: 'How pleasant are your encampments, O Lord of Armies! My spirit has longed, yes, yearned for the courts of the Lord. My mind and my flesh sing out the Living God' (Hanson 1968: 76–7). Compare the tone of Hanson's translation to Stephen Mitchell's adaptation: 'Lord, how beautiful you are; how radiant the places you dwell in. My soul yearns for your presence; my whole body longs for your light' (Mitchell 1993: 37).

Psalm 63: A Love Poem

The superscription to Psalm 63 attributes the following poem to David when he was in the wilderness of Judah. Traditional Jewish texts suggest that David was escaping the persecutions of Saul. David sang a song (a *mizmor*) because he was glad to be in the Wilderness of Judah within the Land of Israel and not in the Diaspora. Critical thinkers, having challenged the superscriptions, offer other theories about the context for Psalm 63. The psalmist could be a king (Dahood 1965–70: 96) or an individual who has taken refuge for a night in the sanctuary and prays for the defeat of his enemies (Kraus 1989: 18–19), or a person in anticipation of a pilgrimage festival (Broyles 1999: 260). Psalm 63 is commonly referred to as a psalm of vigil (McKay 1979; Ceresko 1980). As Tate aptly notes, given the great number of contexts that have been suggested for this psalm, 'We would be wise to follow their trail and read the psalm with whatever contextual imagination proves meaningful, being careful to accept the discipline of good exegesis and literary analysis' (Tate 1990: 126).

The 'contextual imagination' for the present study is a queer one. A queer setting for Psalm 63 puts the language of desire and bodily images at the centre of analysis. This is a psalm about love and desire and physicality. Although the last few verses have the typical call to God to defeat the enemies, the main part of the psalm contains no specific petition to God or complaint. These are the words of a man who has gotten a glimpse of his God and wants more. The vocabulary of desire and of the body is central throughout the poem. Following are two translations of verses 1–9. The first is the NJPS translation and the second is my own.

A psalm of David, when he was in the Wilderness of Judah. God, You are my God; I search for You, my soul thirsts for You, my body yearns for You, as a parched and thirsty land that has no water. I shall behold You in the sanctuary, and see Your might and glory. Truly Your faithfulness is better than life; my lips declare Your praise. I bless You all my life; I lift up my hands, invoking Your name. I am sated as with a rich feast, I sing praises with joyful lips when I call You to mind upon my bed, when I think of You in the watches of the night; for You are my help, and in the shadow of Your wings I shout for joy. My soul is attached to You; Your right hand supports me.

God, you are mine! I desperately search for you, my whole being thirsts for you, and my body is faint from desire for you, as a parched and dry land without water. I gazed upon you in the holy place, looking upon your virility and palpable presence. Your love is better than life itself, let my lips praise you! I bless you as long as I live, I lift up my hands in your name. I am satisfied, as with a rich feast, my mouth praises you with joyful lips. As often as I think about you in my bed, I turn you over in my mind throughout the hours of the night. For you have been my help and in the shadow of your wings I shout for joy. My being pursues you, even as your right hand holds me fast.

The psalmist begins by claiming ownership of his beloved: 'you are mine',[21] he exclaims. He then immediately expresses his intense desire for closeness with his lover. The rare verb, *šḥr* is poetically paired with *'wh*, a synonymous word for desire in Isaiah 26.9. This term for desire may also be connected with the nominal form for 'dawn'. So, with one word, the poet is able to express that feeling of overwhelming longing that comes over a person in the early hours of the morning while just waking up from sleep.[22] The psalmist then could have used the more common verb *'wh* whose subject is always *nepeš* but instead he chooses to use the language of thirst for his beloved.[23] This anticipates the imagery of the desert that follows in the next verse.[24] After describing general longing, and then a thirst, the psalmist uses a very rare term, *kmh* coupled with *bāsar* to express the pinnacle of his desire. The hapax legomenon *kmh*, is a cognate to Arabic 'pale of face'. Most commentators translate this verb as faint and take *bāsar* as a synonymous parallel with *nepeš*, that is, alternative ways of expressing one's whole being. Alternatively, we could take *bāsar* in its more embodied, literal sense, that his physical body aches with desire. The use of rare terminology here with *šḥr* and *kmh* may reflect the rarity of expressions for passionate longing from one male to another.

Why does the psalmist long so intensely for his beloved? Because he caught a glimpse of him and he wants more. The double verbs *ḥzh* and *r'h* put an emphasis upon gazing and physicality. It is the psalmist's experience of having seen God that arouses his desire. Most commentators interpret *ḥzh* in its technical sense, meaning a vision experienced in some kind of ritual setting (cf. Kraus 1989: 19; Tate 1990: 127). Mark S. Smith posits an ancient Near Eastern background of solar divine experiences and argues that 'it is possible that the experience of the dawn after the night vigil helped to evoke the perception of the luminescent dimension of the divine presence. "Seeing God" thus represents the culminating experience in the temple' (Smith 1988: 181). However,

---

21 Contra Kraus (1988–9: 18) and Dahood (1965–70: 85), who read the second ms pronoun with what follows; 'you, I seek'.

22 Traditional Jewish texts interpret *šḥr* as conscientiousness and diligence in prayer.

23 Similar language is used in Psalms 42–3 which has been connected to Psalms 63 and 84 by many scholars through themes of desire and the temple. See Culley (1994), who notes that a sacred site enables a special encounter between the individual and deity.

24 Note that the preposition *beth* often expresses locality; thus, he longs 'in' a desert (Weiser 1962: 453). Kraus (1989: 18) emends the *beth* to *kaph* while Tate (1990: 124) retains the *beth* and interprets it as a *beth essentia*, citing G-K 119i. Dahood (1965–70: 96) takes the *beth* as comparative.

this interpretation and ones similar to it further avert the gaze away from God. Our reading here takes the words in a more literal fashion, assuming that the individual does indeed want to gaze upon the object of his affections.

After a few verses of praise to God, the psalmist returns the scene to his bed, where he is prone to think most intensely about the object of his affections. As the poet winds down his personal words before formulaically concluding with an appeal for the destruction of enemies, he utters, 'My soul is attached to you, your right hand supports me.' The first part of the phrase initially sounds like the famous passage from Genesis 2.24 where a man clings to his wife. The phrase is also used in Deuteronomy 4.4 to describe Israel clinging to God.[25] However, in our passage the verb *dbq* is followed by the preposition *'aḥ°ray*, and not the more common *beth*. The combination of this verb with *'aḥ°ray* occurs in only four other instances in the Bible. In each case, the context is military and the verb implies some kind of pursuit in battle. The poet's use of this phrase in the context of Psalm 63 is therefore quite striking and puzzling. Either he is using the phraseology in an anomalous form or he is trying to indicate the psalmist's active and fiery pursuit after his beloved.[26] In any case, he concludes his words with another unique phrase, 'your right hand supports me'.

In the larger context, the psalmist seeks not only to gaze upon and be intimate with his beloved, but also to secure protection and refuge. This is expressed through the language of steadfast love (*ḥesed*) and *ṣel kānāp*. However, the petitioner does not approach God in a formal manner as a subject might approach his king, but rather through language of intimacy, love and passion. The interpretative context of traditional and modern critical commentators moves us away from this fact and focuses more on the psalmist's desire for refuge in the temple.

In my study of Psalms 84 and 63, I have drawn attention to gender references, language of desire, and physicality. These elements have been overlooked by biblical scholars, who either have been more interested in the original cultic settings for these texts or have been influenced by the Western philosophical tendency to split the body and mind.

Attention to gender and desire impact our readings of the psalms in a number of ways. First, it can make us all aware that reading the psalms as gender-neutral and universal is simply one way of interpreting the psalms and that it is not the inevitable or correct reading. Second, gay men in particular, or any men seeking to challenge heterosexual normativity, may now have a new avenue by which to explore their relationship with the divine. Finally, a queer reading of the psalms uncovers heretofore hidden spaces for multiple models of intimacy among men. None of the psalms are unambiguously homoerotic, but there are latent homoerotic elements embedded in the language. These psalms present, at minimum, examples of homosociality, that is, bonds between men that are charged to some extent with eroticism. That

---

25 The verb with the preposition *beth* is common in Deuteronomic language and always seems to imply clinging.

26 It is also possible that had the author used the more common *beth*, there would have been two *beth* prepositions next to each other on the line. Poetically, this may have felt too awkward.

the eroticism is veiled may be a result of complex ancient cultural and theological tensions. Howard Eilberg-Schwartz has pointed out that 'humans are
understood as created in the image of God, yet God has "no-body" – neither
others with whom to interact nor a fully conceptualized body with which to
do it' (Eilberg-Schwartz 1992: 17). Since the psalmists long for connection and
intimacy with God, a problem exists: if human beings express desire and
intimacy through the body and God is bodiless, how is one to be intimate
with God? I believe that the veiled language of desire and love in these psalms
struggles with this problem. The psalmist longs to gaze upon his beloved God
in the sanctuary, but if he indeed could, what would God look like? Again,
returning to the insights of Eilberg-Schwartz, God is clearly masculine in
the Hebrew Bible, but God is ambiguously male. With tensions such as these,
thinking only within the framework of the homo–hetero binary limits and
oversimplifies our understanding of these complex poems.

Voices from the Margins

Another approach to the psalms from a translesbigay perspective involves a
more sociologically positive reading of the book. To this point, we have dealt
with analysis and queer *theory*, but we can also approach the book to see what
it has to offer queer *identity*. The use of the psalms in this way is a liberationist
approach. This methodology seeks to use the psalms as a positive reaffirming
religious resource for the support of translesbigay lives.

Beyond academic circles, the psalms have a rich and vibrant life among various Jewish and Christian communities. They function today in the form of
prayer, in both private and congregational worship. An observation of contemporary uses of the psalms in dialogue with queer theory raises two interesting areas for further exploration. Given the limitations of this study, I will
only call attention to these areas in the hope that others may further develop
these ideas. First, we can search for translesbigay positive themes that run
throughout the Psalms[27] and second, we can recontextualize psalms to create
new Translesbigay Psalters.

The book of Psalms, when taken as a whole, expresses general perspectives
that can be construed as supportive for the challenges that translesbigay communities face. A great number of psalms represent the voices of the oppressed
and the marginalized. Both through individual suffering and through ancient
Israel's national experience of exile and displacement, the psalms present a
rich record of the perspectives of the 'Other'. The psalms explore what it feels
like to be ostracized and abandoned by friends and family. The psalms represent the experiences of depression and spiritual emptiness. The psalms give
expression to the feeling of being abandoned by God. In expressing a theology
from the perspective of oppression and marginalization, the translesbigay
community may find ancestral antecedents for its contemporary experiences.

Psalm 10 represents the perspective of an individual who is oppressed by

---

27 Phyllis Trible (1973) first introduced this method of liberating texts in her ground-
breaking work 'Depatriarchalizing in Biblical Interpretation'.

a powerful elite. The oppressors use lies and deceit to hurt the psalmist, who claims his innocence. Psalm 12 likewise accuses oppressors of using their fraudulent words to oppress the innocent yet marginalized. In this text, God is called upon as the force that is ultimately on the side of the marginalized and who supports the victim with words of truth. Psalm 22.7–19 describes the perspective of the sufferer in poignant and powerful language:

> But I am a worm, less than human; scorned by men, despised by people. All who see me mock me; they curl their lips, they shake their heads. 'Let him commit himself to the LORD; let Him rescue him, let Him save him, for He is pleased with him.' You drew me from the womb, made me secure at my mother's breast. I became Your charge at birth; from my mother's womb You have been my God. Do not be far from me, for trouble is near, and there is none to help. Many bulls surround me, mighty ones of Bashan encircle me. They open their mouths at me like tearing, roaring lions. My life ebbs away: all my bones are disjointed; my heart is like wax, melting within me; my vigor dries up like a shard; my tongue cleaves to my palate; You commit me to the dust of death. Dogs surround me; a pack of evil ones closes in on me, like lions they maul my hands and feet. I take the count of all my bones while they look on and gloat. They divide my clothes among themselves, casting lots for my garments.

In these texts, God is generally turned to as the only one who ultimately hears the words of the outcast. Psalm 142.5–7 is paradigmatic of this attitude: 'Look at my right and see – I have no friend; there is nowhere I can flee, no one cares about me. So I cry to You, O LORD; I say, "You are my refuge, all I have in the land of the living."' Psalm 34 tells the story of an individual, down and out, who finds support in God alone. These psalms teach the translesbigay community that even in times of oppression, even when those closest to us turn away, the ultimate life force, God, is on our side. As Walter Brueggemann (1995: 104–7) has argued, the lament psalms are not merely religious texts that offer a cathartic experience; rather, they are also political and social documents that note injustices. They claim that there is something wrong in the world and that God should step in to correct the wrong.

Furthermore, these texts, set at the social margins, teach that complacency is not acceptable. In each of these texts, the outcast individual demands a divine response to his or her predicament. The psalms do not encourage individuals to sit contentedly on the margins; rather, they guide the marginalized person from a place of victimhood to empowerment. In the psalms of lament, the speaker often demands God's presence and insists that God change the situation. Although the speaker is down and out, he never fails to demand God's intervention. In Psalm 6, for example, the petitioner addresses God through a series of imperatives, challenging God to rectify the situation and to acknowledge that the petitioner's current suffering is unjust. The petitioner, in the midst of pain and tears, does not call out to God in a quiet plea, but rather screams out in indignation: 'My whole being is stricken with terror, while You, LORD – O, how long!' (v. 4). In other words, here I am suffering, so where the blank are you?!

Ken Stone makes a similar point in his consideration of the usefulness of the psalms of lament in the age of Aids. He argues that like Aids activism, psalms laments set physical suffering within the context of the social arena. The psalms recognize that other human beings often further contribute to an individual's suffering. Most relevant to this study, he writes,

> perhaps most importantly, the willingness of the laments to accuse God of complicity in human suffering underscores the unacceptability of such suffering in an uncompromising and astonishing fashion, calling into question any theological discourse that is willing to construct a comforting God while refusing to confront the difficult question of evil. (Stone 1999: 25)

In other words, Stone argues that the laments teach us that human pain must be taken seriously, but that this should not lead to despair. They offer a healthy balance of attention to pain with avenues for hope. Mona West has similarly explored the positive uses of the book of Lamentations for the queer community, particularly in confronting the Aids epidemic (West 2001). She shows how Lamentations provides a voice for remembrance and mourning, but also resistance to the acceptance of victimhood.

Reading the laments as religious documents that resist victimhood while acknowledging suffering is rooted in Jewish approaches to suffering. So it is no accident that Jon Levenson, a Jewish biblicist, explores the dialectic between hymn and complaint in the psalms:

> the dialectic of this vision does not allow for an unqualified acceptance of the pessimism that attributes to innocent suffering the immovability of fate. The absence of the omnipotent and cosmocratic deity is not accepted as final, nor his primordial world-ordering deeds as confined to the vanished past. Present experience, which seems to confirm these propositions, is not seen as absolute. Rather, it is seen as a mysterious interruption in the divine life, an interruption that the supplications of the worshipping community may yet bring to an end. The failure of God is openly acknowledged: no smug faith here, no flight into an other-worldly ideal. But God is also reproached for his failure, told that it is neither inevitable nor excusable. (Levenson 1998: 24)

In this manner, the psalms provide an invaluable resource to the translesbigay community. One of the theologies of the psalms teaches that individuals who experience marginalization and ostracism can express their suffering in a clear and bold voice; and most importantly, can demand from God (and society) a world of truer justice and compassion.

Contemporary Translesbigay Psalters

Marc Brettler argues that women in antiquity may have recited the psalms in various liturgical contexts even though the texts were written by men and for men. Brettler points out that Hannah recited a royal psalm that had many irrelevant or even inappropriate verses as she prayed to God concerning her infertility. As suggested by this example, Brettler goes on to demonstrate, through multiple analogies, how 'The pray-er effectively brackets the irrelevant or even the offensive sections, while concentrating on the part that is appropriate to the issue at hand, no matter how small the reference to that issue might be within the larger prayer' (Brettler 1998: 47). As Brettler and other scholars of Jewish liturgy show, psalms often entered into Jewish liturgy through very tenuous connections.[28] Brettler concludes that even if the psalms were written by a male elite, 'this would not exclude women from reciting the psalms or from participating in various forms of Israelite prayer' (Brettler 1998: 56). Marchiene Vroon Rienstra's *Swallow's Nest: A Feminine Reading of the Psalms* (1992) is based on the assertion that the psalms speak to women in powerful and intimate ways.

In *Daring to Speak Love's Name: A Gay and Lesbian Prayer Book*, Psalms 133, 84, 100, 117 and 65 are adapted and modified for use in celebrating lesbian and gay relationships within a Christian context (Stuart 1992: 28–31). Psalms 69 and 130 are included in rituals of ending relationships (Stuart 1992: 101–3). Interestingly, other biblical passages and contemporary poetry are found in much greater abundance than psalms passages.

Daring to Speak offers one example of a successful attempt to recontextualize Psalms. Even if there are no psalms that unequivocally speak to the experiences of translesbigay people, there are psalms that can be used for particular life cycle ceremonies or experiences unique to queer folk. There is precedent for this use of the psalms from the biblical period to the present.

Psalm 139 can easily be adapted as a coming-out prayer. This psalm proclaims that God fashions each person in the womb and that we are who we are because of God's intentions. ('It was You who created my conscience; You fashioned me in my mother's womb' (v. 13)). The text teaches us that we cannot escape who we are because, simply put, it is impossible to run away from oneself. No matter where we run, there we are ('Where can I escape from Your spirit? Where can I flee from Your presence? If I ascend to heaven, You are there; if I descend to Sheol, You are there too. If I take wing with the dawn to come to rest on the western horizon, even there Your hand will be guiding me, Your right hand will be holding me fast' (vv. 7–10)). So, we ought to stand proud ('I praise You, for I am awesomely, wondrously made' (v. 14)) and know that God stands with us when bigotry and oppression overwhelm us. This psalm could easily be used in an individual or communal setting for coming out.

Psalm 31 could be recited by an individual who has experienced ostracism and pain through the coming-out process. The suffering in this psalm is intense and long-lasting: 'I am in distress; my eyes are wasted by vexation, my substance and body too. My life is spent in sorrow, my years in groaning; my strength fails because of my iniquity, my limbs waste away' (v. 11). The poem speaks of suffering at the hands of those who were once close to the petitioner: 'Because of all my foes I am the particular butt of my neighbours, a horror to

---

28 The weekly haftarah readings, that is selections from the Prophets that accompany the weekly Torah reading in Jewish liturgy, were often chosen simply on the basis of a one-verse connection or very loose thematic relationship.

my friends; those who see me on the street avoid me. I am put out of mind like the dead; I am like an object given up for lost. I hear the whisperings of many, intrigue on every side, as they scheme together against me, plotting to take my life' (vv. 12–14). Like the parents who essentially ignore or even banish their translesbigay children, this petitioner turns to God as the One who will be there in times of distress and who will hold up this falling individual. Even when family and friends may turn on us, God is always on our side.

Psalm 133 is perfect for a Gay Pride parade that brings together not only translesbigay folk, but also their family, friends and allies. All together, everyone asserts that dwelling together in peace is the ultimate good for all involved. 'How good and how pleasant it is that brothers dwell together' (v. 1). Blessings come through acceptance and love.

Psalm 82 could be recited at a protest rally. It condemns those in power for abusing their power and playing God. It challenges a corrupt leadership to stop showing favour to those who stand for bigotry and prejudice. It challenges a corrupt leadership to advance the cause of those on the margins of society. And it reminds those leaders that they will ultimately fall because the power of justice outweighs crooked forces.

Conclusions

Considering the psalms through the lens of queer theory has resulted in a conclusion that I did not anticipate at the outset of my research. Whatever the real lives, particularly sexual lives, of the ancient Israelites and biblical writers, the psalms are indeed queer. By this I mean that the psalms do not present a stable, single-minded perspective on same-sex bonding. The psalms may fall into relatively clear-cut form-critical categories, but same-sex relationships are presented complexly and fluidly. The male biblical writers could address God as a distant sovereign, intimate father, lover or judge. The writers could imagine God as exceptionally virile and as relatively benign. God could be remote and intimate. This makes the psalms queer, for these poems defy easy categorization as they depict same-sex love. They offer multiple models of male bonding, which are often at odds with one another. To summarize, an initial study of the psalms in their ancient contexts leads me to conclude that they present unstable and complex models for same-sex intimacy.

That the psalms are queer does not mean that they are necessarily translesbigay-friendly or feminist in their orientation. In order for these psalms to be constructively useful for translesbigay and/or feminist readers, they must often be recontextualized. For this reason, the second part of my investigation, on translesbigay identity, focused more on contemporary needs and the validity of recontextualization as a valid method of reading.

Amidst the many uncertainties and difficulties posed by this study, what can be declared unequivocally is that the psalms continue to speak powerfully to many different types of individuals and communities. No single group can claim exclusive access to this rich body of religious poetry. Their words, whether affirming or challenging, joyful or painful, continue to compel people of faith.

Proverbs

ELIZABETH STUART

Undoing

In her book, *Undoing Gender*, the queer theorist Judith Butler points out that there is something particularly frightening about an open future. Human beings as individuals and grouped in cultures tend to feel immensely threatened by the loss of a sense of certainty about how things are and, perhaps more importantly, how they must be. The response to this threat is to act to 'foreclose futurity' (Butler 2004: 180). In such a context the asking of certain questions becomes dangerous because to do so is to threaten to destabilize the future by introducing elements of doubt which may ultimately undermine the current political structures and render the future cloudy and fearful. In a context where political or social circumstances have blown the future open there is often a rush for what Butler calls a 'foundational fix' (Butler 2004: 181). This foundational fix is a cultural reverse-gear, which seeks to reaffirm through a process of moralism how things are, or more accurately, how things were. Butler notes that such foundational fixes are not the prerogative of the right or the conservative but are equally evident in the worlds of the left and radical theorists (and, we might add, theologians).

What is it that this foundational fix seeks to pre-empt? Butler's answer is that what we fear is an undoing of the 'I', whether that is on an individual or corporate basis. But, as Butler points out, being undone is an aspect of relational humanity which it would be and is disastrous to avoid. Desire and grief testify to the fact that we are undone by each other:

> grief displays the way in which we are in the thrall of our relations with others that we cannot always recount or explain, that often interrupts the self-conscious account of ourselves we might try to provide in ways that challenge the very notion of ourselves as autonomous and in control . . . This relation to the Other does not precisely ruin my story or reduce me to speechlessness, but it does, invariably, clutter my speech with signs of its undoing. (2004: 19)

We use the language of possession and autonomy even as we are in the process of being dispossessed by that which we lay claim to. This is the paradox and complexity of being human or perhaps even of being simply embodied. Mourning, desire, fear, rage make us ec-static, beside ourselves. We experience something of our pre-'I' state, the state in which we arrived dependent, vulnerable, unsure and porous. As embodied persons we are always something more than ourselves, always for something more than ourselves, which means that 'ourselves' are always under interrogation and on the brink of dissolving.

We are, therefore, forever on the brink of unknowing. Foucault (1991) drew attention to the clear relation between knowledge and power and to the need to be attentive to the apparatus of coercion in knowledge. When we are so attentive we are confronted with the limits of knowledge and stand on the edge of the unknowable and therefore in close proximity to the unreal. Social transformation is contingent upon the willingness of some to risk destabilizing concepts of what is real and knowable with their unreality. It is about daring to risk fantasy, of learning to imagine, articulate and embody the impossible. As Butler puts it, 'possibility is not a luxury; it is as crucial as bread' (2004: 29). This is the task of queer politics, to act as a resistance movement to the cultural lurches towards foundationalism, knowing and integration which inevitably ossify into oppressive 'truths' which underpin systems of exclusion. The task of queer politics is to persistently undermine 'reality' with its outrageous fantasies, forever positioning all that is obvious, natural and evident on the precipice of unknowing and unreality.

For Butler the paradox of being human is that it is the character of our existence to be ec-static, to be dependent upon others and therefore to be in the grip of the very forces queer politics seeks to undermine. However, to be ec-static is to be orientated away from oneself, from the anchor of the 'I', and therefore it is also to be constantly on the edge of being undone from those forces, of realizing their unreality and being plunged into a state of unknowing. This is a place of terror but also a place of hope. It is the space in which fantasies are born, visions are seen and prophecies trip from the mouth. It is also the place of the rush to the foundational fix and therefore is a space of competing forces and difficult tension, power-struggle and sometimes violence. It is a space in which the melancholia of a culture which forecloses all kinds of love in the process of creating the categories by which we relate and regulate each other is simultaneously reinforced in reaction to the terror by some but also allowed by others to turn into genuine mourning and therefore into undoing (2004: 159–60).

This space always exists; but in a cultural context in which the future is rendered radically uncertain, it expands and encroaches upon cultural consciousness to a much larger degree and the stakes and consequences of the tensions of what is being worked out in that space become vital, sometimes even a matter of life and death.

Butler avoids any deep engagement with the religious and the theological, which is extraordinary considering her interest in mourning, the future, kinship identity and performance, not to mention her close engagement with Hegel and Foucault. This avoidance of deep engagement with religion deprives Butler of so much to underpin her theory and to bring it to some sort of *telos*. And, as I have argued elsewhere, in terms of Christianity it deprives her of a community under a divine mandate to be queer, to make cultural trouble, to perform humanity subversively for the sake of different reality and greater cause, the kingdom of God (Stuart 2003).

This reading of the book of Proverbs is a reading from the perspective of a queer politics of undoing as outlined by Butler. Into the world of the ancient

Jewish wisdom tradition bursts queer politics shaking the foundations perhaps of established readings but more interestingly, perhaps, identifying Proverbs as a space in which the competing cultural tensions of foundational fix and undoing are evident and played out. It seems to be widely accepted that the book of Proverbs in its current form is post-exilic and therefore reflects a time of extraordinary social and theological upheaval in the life of Israel. The future had been rent asunder and rendered radically uncertain by the deconstruction of the 'certainties' upon which the nation had built itself: election and promise. The nation was in danger of dissolution. The book of Proverbs perfectly reflects the conflicting impulses of a culture in danger of dissolution: the rush towards a foundational fix and the taking advantage of a cultural context of fissure and dislocation to live in a space of undoing and to play with concepts which have hardened into truths.

The Queer God

The most distinctive feature of the wisdom tradition is the character of Hochma/Sophia/Wisdom who bursts unapologetically into the book of Proverbs in 1.20 literally shouting in the street. Her appearance cuts a swathe through what I shall called the propositional proverbs with which the book begins, disrupting their flow, dissolving their controlled 'natural' advice of a father to a child or a teacher to a pupil, with a loud cry and explicit threats to those who will not heed her. She demands attention with her thunderous, raucous voice. And then she disappears again as dramatically as she arrived and the measured tones of the sage return for a while. In 3.14–20 she is described as being more precious than jewels, with ways of pleasantness and paths of peace, the tree of life, the one by whom the Lord founded the earth. Then Hochma herself returns shouting again in chapter 8 and reveals her origins:

> The Lord created me at the beginning [or me as the beginning] of his work,
> the first of his acts long ago.
> Ages ago I was set up, at the first, before the beginning of the earth. (8.22–3)

Here then we learn that we are dealing with something theologically disruptive, the undoing of the divine. The melancholia which resulted from the Israelite denial and suppression of the goddess is turned in the literal wake of the Babylonian exile by some, at least, into a mourning which allows the pre-exilic dominant theology to be undone and the divine to be reconstructed. Here we are presented with a female figure who is somehow with the Lord at the beginning, somehow brought forth before creation and somehow coexisting with him like a child or master workman, separate and yet intimately connected.

Divinity is undone and queered by Hochma. The reader is left confused by her revelation. The gender of God is no longer entirely clear. A solo performance in creation is suddenly revealed to be a team effort. Divinity is broken open to reveal plurality at its heart and thus ceases to be a stable, solid foundation to cling to in a cultural earthquake. Rather it is revealed to be unpredictable, surprising, as likely to be encountered shouting on street corners and at the city gates as in the temple or court and not of one gender. The destabilizing of the divinity both reflects and precipitates the destabilizing of the 'I'. Israel is a nation now unsure of itself and of its God. And this uncertainty is related to the issue of divine absence. Post the Babylonian exile, where exactly is God? This was a question addressed by many sections of the Israelite people. It is answered differently in the separate parts of Proverbs. But here the answer is that God is the heart of human activity. She has built her house among the people and prepared a feast to which she invites all (9.1–6). She is the expression of the divine delight in humanity (8.31). This is a God who is immanent and at the heart of human experience, the most difficult and dangerous God of all, who becomes tangled (sometimes hopelessly) in our own hopes and desires. But she is also an inclusive God, with an open invitation to eat at her table. Yet as we shall observe, locating Hochma at the heart of human experience and open to all does not make her any less easy to grasp or any less mysterious.

Carol Newsom (1989) is undoubtedly correct to point out the patriarchal context of Proverbs 1–9 and to draw attention to the way in which Hochma's voice is positioned in Proverbs to bolster the patriarchal values enshrined in the surrounding discourse. Of course the context is patriarchal. Butler is clear that we cannot create virgin space beyond the oppressive contexts in which we live, move and define our being, but we can subvert those spaces by performing the scripts of those contexts subversively. Hochma can at least be read as a subversive performance of divinity, a God of the streets.

This subversiveness of Hochma's performance is best appreciated in the context in which she burst forth in and from the text. For around her is built the tomb of the foundational fix. In the bulk of the book the sense of the divine absence is suppressed beneath a body of knowledge, arranged in such a way as to be easily memorized and absorbed. The deity is not a key player in these texts, only referred to indirectly. The foundational fix is based upon a nostalgia for king, court and sage, for a nation which knew who and what it was, a nation clear about and confident in its God. Positioning the nation as a son or pupil in need of clear instruction whose well-being and right-relationship with God and with others is dependent upon obedience and morality provides an alternative to purity as the means to police the borders of belonging, and the family offers an alternative to the temple as the location in which these boundaries are enforced or breached. The divine is domesticated and mystery is banished at the door; in its place is the banality of common sense in a patriarchal, familial context. The social order is reinforced through the twin forces of nostalgia and obedience. And while it is perfectly possible to read the figure of Hochma as simply the personification of that which is made foundational, it is also true that in the very performance of personification the foundations are simultaneously undermined.

Hochma is wisdom in drag. She is the excessive performance of the wisdom outlined in the main body of the text, and so excessive is the performance that previous understandings of wisdom are blown apart. She is the prudent, excellent and wise wife whose virtues are extolled in Proverbs played to excess, taken from the closeted environments of the family and into the street. She performs her outrageously enlarged character on the street corners and at the city gates, the busiest places in town. There she simultaneously seduces and threatens. She makes outrageous claims as to her origins. She dresses herself up in such a way as to remind her listeners of the goddesses they were taught to fear and spurn in order to be who they are. She is Maat, Ishtar and Hathor and all the goddesses Israel was warned about. She is Asherah, the tree of life, whose fruit humans were barred from eating, and here she is claiming not only pre-existence but also an equal hand in creation. She is the wise woman of ancient Israel writ large and dangerous. To some extent then, Hochma is a caricature, a drag act, an excessive performance which could (as all drag can) be read as a degrading and violent performance of wisdom and the wise woman, a parody intended to diminish. But, as Butler has consistently argued, drag is always valuable for exposing the understandings of gender operative in a particular culture, and for offering the possibility of its rearticulation. Hochma rearticulates many different things: she rearticulates the wisdom tradition as something broken loose both from the court and from the family; and open to all in the public spaces of common life, knowledge is presented less as proposition and more as relationship, a knowledge of intimacy represented by images of eating and drinking. Hochma also rearticulates the construction of the wise woman and wife by being loud, bold, challenging and demanding. Finally, she rearticulates the divine. By taking the feminine into the divine she allows Israel to escape from its melancholy and mourn the loss of the feminine and also the loss of the male, for by taking the feminine into the masculine both are transcended and deconstructed in the process. Hochma, therefore, takes gender further than Butler is able, into the space of the divine, the only space where gender is not, a space beyond our knowledge. We can only totter on the brink of this space, confused and confounded by the tensions, dualisms and contradictions that brim up when melancholia turns to mourning and the undoing begins. Hochma may have been employed to bolster the foundation, but in fact she is its undoing.

Hochma offers 'a journey without direction, uncertainty and no sweet conclusion'. These are words spoken at the beginning of Derek Jarman's disconcerting passion narrative, *The Garden* (1990). Jarman made this film in the full horror of the Aids crisis when facing his own death. He and the gay community were in the process of being undone by a future which was as uncertain as it was certain in terms of inevitable mortality. Jarman's film is of particular interest because of its similarity to Proverbs in many respects. Jarman's film also shimmers with the absence of God. Despite being peppered with strange apocalyptic images, *The Garden* lacks any linearity and therefore any kind of eschatological dimension. There are no easy answers, no history to wait upon; no clarity as to the content of hope and what 'life' before or after death ultimately may consist of beyond the image of the meal, and the viewer is left disconcerted by a narrative which makes no 'sense'.

Hochma/Sophia herself appears in *The Garden* arising behind a table of woman disciples, a mysterious figure somehow conceived to operate behind the scenes of the unfolding tragedy of the death of two gay men to bring it to a just conclusion, unlike the figure of Christ who appears disengaged and impotent in the face of homophobic violence and murder.

Jarman can be seen to stand in the wisdom tradition in his decision to embrace the undoing, mourn the suppressed with the same result, queering God in the process.

Hochma is revealed here as in Proverbs as an impossibly queer figure.

Nothing like a Dame

But even queerer than Hochma is the figure that is positioned against Hochma, the strange or foreign woman, often referred to as Dame Folly in English versions of the text. She makes her first appearance shortly after that of Hochma in chapter 2. Wisdom, we are told, will save from 'the strange woman, from the adulteress with her smooth words, who forsakes the partner of her youth and forgets her sacred covenant; for her house leads down to death and her path to the shades' (2.16–18). Whereas Wisdom offers life, this strange woman offers only ruin and unending death and her house is to be avoided at all costs (5.1–23). Chapter 7 describes in graphic detail the seduction of a young man by this strange woman: 'She is loud and wayward; her feet do not stay at home; now in the street, now in the squares, and at every corner she lies in wait' (7.11–12).

She goes out to meet the young man who has foolishly wandered into her neighbourhood and takes him to her home. Later we are told that the strange woman is 'loud . . . ignorant and knows nothing'. She sits at her door or on a seat at the high places of the town, calling out to those who pass by offering stolen water and the secret bread of Sheol (9.13–18), an explicit contrast with the depiction of Hochma in 9.1–5.

What is most interesting about the Strange Woman is that the contrast drawn between Hochma and herself is not all that absolute, as Claudia Camp (2000b) has observed. In fact they are remarkably similar. Both are portrayed as loud, confident and seductive women who claim public spaces to proclaim their message and both issue invitations to their open homes (which are positioned on the sacred space of the hill) to all to come and feast. The Strange Woman may indeed be read as an alternative view of Hochma. It is not that she is the evil twin but the same person viewed from a radically different angle. To those whose instincts are to cling to foundations when the future fractures open, Hochma may well have represented a wild, seductive wisdom associated with foreign gods, or more precisely, goddesses, which threatened to seduce Israel into foreign and ultimately death-dealing ways. Perhaps what we have here represented are two responses to a massive cultural shift operating in tension with and responding to each other. Hochma acts up even more in response to the representation of herself as a prostitute. She is indeed promiscuous in her offering of herself and her feast. She plays the role that others have created for her, parodying it to her own ends. It is not just that she is wisdom in drag; it is that she is the feared Strange Women also dragged up and rearticulated to subvert the very purpose of the character in the first place. The gateway to death in a foundational mentality is the gateway to life in those who are prepared to live with undoing. The Strange Woman is depicted as seducing the young man into the mouth of the abyss. He is lured into a state of unknowing and undoing. But Hochma too offers such a state, for she offers the divine, and she offers it to all and at the heart of human life. She offers an experience of immanence which is no less mysterious for being so. She offers an encounter with that before which there are no options but undoing and unknowing and she offers it in an expansive, inclusive and immanent experience. Thus Hochma represents a mystical approach to the divine, and in the mystical experience the dualisms between death and life, light and darkness, knowing and unknowing are dissolved and the bridge between humanity and divinity becomes a terrifying unstable one to cross over a treacherous chasm.

The full experience of wisdom as mystical encounter with the divine is therefore only possible if the figures of Hochma and the Strange Woman are held together and are allowed to perform as a double-act or perhaps more accurately as one excessive, ec-static character whose offer, unknowing and undoing, is both centrifugally attractive because it promises the end and fulfilment, the *telos*, of all desire (hence the use of explicit sexual imagery to describe the human encounter with wisdom in Proverbs) and stomach-churningly terrifying because it demands a willingness to be undone now, to live one's own undoing in the streets, in the political spaces, the city gates, and the sacred spaces, on the hill. Undoing is not for a next life and it is not the sole prerogative of the divine. The location of Hochma at the heart of a nation's life reveals that it is possible to engage in transformative social practice precisely because the divine is active at the heart of human engagement.

The encounter with the women of wisdom in Proverbs is then an experience of the carnivalesque as defined by Bakhtin (1964). What is being parodied is the foundational fix, the refuge in propositional knowledge, the very concept of knowledge as the defining characteristic of a community and highway to the divine. Many of the characteristics of the carnivalesque are evident in the performance of the women of wisdom. First, there are two voices, Bakhtin's minimum requirement for existence. Second, there is the ec-static experience of being outside the dominant culture, which was the essence of the post-exilic experience inducing a crisis of national identity. Third, there is the emergence of the suppressed voices of marginalized groups. In the case of Proverbs, the women of wisdom may represent the suppressed voice of the divine feminine, the wise woman and/or the mystical. In the space of the carnival, genuine dialogical encounters between dominant and oppressed voices is possible and this may be represented by the two women of wisdom here. In the space of the carnival they are revealed to be one not two. Fourth, there is extravagant juxtaposition in the form of the two women and, indeed, in the juxtaposition of the personification of and knowledge of wisdom and the performance of the grotesque in the figure of the Strange Woman who exposes both the fear and attractiveness of Hochma. Bakhtin (1964: 177) believed that the purpose of the carnival was to extend the narrow sense of life. This extension is what makes life bearable; it allows a greater participation in it, particularly by those whose voices are marginal. It is thus ultimately and ironically a system to reinforce the current social system. However, the ultimate *sitz im leben* of Proverbs may have been a context in which the social system was fractured and open post-exile and therefore much was up for grabs. In this context the carnivalesque becomes less of a safety-valve and more of a space in which different possibilities for dealing with the future can be played out and the fears induced by these different possibilities faced. The resistance of this carnival is not so much a resistance to a dominant social order as a resistance to the future as it would develop based upon present constructions. It is a carnival at the cross-roads of a culture and that is why the women of wisdom position themselves at the street corners in town (1.21; 7.8) and, indeed, at the crossroads (8.2). The concern being expressed in the wisdom carnival is the direction that Israel may go.

Two types of wisdom interact with and critique each other in the book of Proverbs, and both are responses to cultural crises: one decidedly and quite complexly queer, one seeking a nostalgic foundational fix; one leading to the edge of knowing, one securing in the concrete of knowledge. The complex-ity of the text is further reinforced by the figures of Hochma and the Strange Woman, who leave the reader quite bewildered, not least because the content of acceptance of their invitation(s) is not entirely clear. We are told that it is the way to life/death and worth seeking and waiting for, but what it is that is to be revealed remains opaque except for the revelation of Hochma's part in crea-tion. In its current form one is obviously supposed to read the propositional wisdom material as the content, but a queer reading in exposing the fissures in the book makes such a reading difficult or impossible. So we are left with the presumption that the acceptance of the invitation involves an undoing which propels us into the realm of the mystical. One can begin to see how the Hochma tradition could eventually give birth to groups such as the Therapeutae and Therapeutrides of Alexandria, described by the philosopher Philo in his *De Vita Contemplativa* as ascetic communities of Jewish men and women devoted to Sophia who lived apart from mainstream Alexandrian life in contemplation and prayer coming together for a joyous weekly liturgy and feast and spend-ing the rest of the time in study of the deeper meanings of sacred texts which they seem to have regarded as having a soul enclosed in the literal mean-ing of the words. The book of Wisdom is often regarded as having perhaps its origins, or at least a common theological context, with these communities. And this exposes a paradox of the wisdom tradition. On the one hand, from Proverbs onwards this tradition is presented as an inclusive one, open to all, a street-theology; but, on the other hand, it becomes quickly evident that the pursuit of Hochma/Sophia is costly and demanding. It takes effort to be queer, to be constantly letting oneself be undermined and undone, and while that path may be open to all and, as it were, naturally followed by many on the social (and theological) margins, the burdens of Hochma are great.

She is Family

Of course, the main body of material in Proverbs is not concerned directly with either of the two women of wisdom but consists of various collections of propositional proverbial material. The queer eye immediately focuses on the familial nature of much of this material. Whereas a feminist reader may be heartened by the location of wisdom within the authoritative space of the woman, the queer reader is more suspicious. The reader is constructed as the son, the recipient of the father's (or more likely teacher's) wisdom and is exhorted to listen and respect the teaching of both his parents (1.5; 15.20; 17.25; 23.20, 22). Parents are encouraged to discipline their children (19.8; 23.13–14). Mothers are instructed not to neglect their children (29.15). Good wives are lauded as the 'crown' of their husbands (12.4), a quarrelling wife decried as 'a continual dripping of rain' (19.13), and contentious wives are decried (21.9). The whole book ends with a detailed description of the ideal wife in the Words of Lemuel (31.10). Furthermore, the one who lives alone is described as 'self-indulgent, showing contempt for all who have sound judgement' (18.1). The way of the wise is therefore associated with the family, and the patriarchal family at that. There are no proverbs about husbands, and daughters are only mentioned once in pejorative terms as constantly demanding and never satisfied, like the barren womb of Sheol (30.15). Those outside the family structure (and there evidently were some of those) are portrayed as being foolish. Wisdom is therefore collapsed into family life in much the same way as beleaguered late twentieth-century Christianity collapsed discipleship into heterosexual marriage and family life. This was, of course, motivated by a fear that these institutions were under threat and recognition that the Church was losing many of its power-bases in Western culture. The emphasis on the familial in these sections of Proverbs may be read with queer eyes to reflect not only the fear induced by the potential undoing of the nation but also a fear that the family too was in danger of being undone and with it one of the cornerstones of religious and national identity. And who we might ask are those who live on their own? Who might choose or be forced to live beyond the confines of the family in a context in which regeneration and reproduction became a compelling issue to the extent that the priestly authors wrote (hetero)sexuality and reproduction into the creation narrative (Genesis 1.27–8)? It is possible that these people might have something to do with Hochma/the Strange Woman. Those who live outside the structure of the family are often constructed as sexually voracious and socially dangerous, as Hochma/the Strange Women are in the early sections of Proverbs. It may be possible that the figure of Hochma emerged from a group of post-exilic Jews, proto-Therapeutae, who took the radical step of eschewing family life in the pursuit of Hochma.

But it has to be noted that even in the propositional sections of Proverbs, family life is not always romanticized and the raw brutality and tension of relationships are realistically represented (though always from a male perspective). It is recognized that neighbours and friends are sometimes more important than kindred (27.10). And, indeed, friendship is valorized at several points: 'Some friends play at friendship, but a true friend sticks closer than one's next of kin' (18.24). There is recognition then in Proverbs that kinship is sometimes experienced most significantly and authentically between those not bound by marriage or blood.

So even in its attempt to locate wisdom firmly within the family structure, Proverbs hints at fissures and alternative possibilities. A queer reader might conclude that the family in Israel at this time was in as much danger as the nation and in need of shoring up. Some of that trouble may have been related to the role of women. At times of national crisis when structures falter and the future fissures, women are often able to assume roles and responsibilities closed off to them in normal circumstances. The ideal wife described in detail in chapter 31 is an active, strong woman in absolute control of the household and its well-being and future. Though she 'opens her mouth with wisdom and the teaching of kindness is on her tongue' (31.26), there is no space in her life for contemplation or even religious observance. In her case 'fear of the Lord' seems to consist of a ferociously active life in which there would be no time to seek out Hochma and sit at her gates. In chapter 9 Hochma herself is portrayed as super-active, she builds her own house, slaughters beasts, prepares the wine, orders her female servants, but the purpose is different. The purpose is to enjoy an inclusive feast, to create a new kinship made up of all who will accept the invitation and be willing to lay aside 'immaturity/simpleness, and live and walk in the way of insight' (9.6). The portrayal of the ideal wife may well be one designed to counteract movements by women away from the home and family life into a life defined by the search for Hochma, the search for insight and spiritual maturity, movements which also may be reflected in the condemnations of female devotion to goddesses in the prophets Jeremiah (7.18; 44.19) and Ezekiel (13.18, 23), who seem to testify to the existence of female-led and focused cults within Israel at the time of the exile and afterwards. Furthermore, the focus in this material on obedience to parents may also suggest a fear that the family is crumbling and that children are choosing paths which may ultimately undermine the foundations of Israelite identity, paths which may involve seduction by the Strange Woman/Hochma.

Wisdom as constructed in this propositional material has no doctrinal content. The nature of the divine is not discussed; in fact it is strangely absent. What is presented is a collection of proverbs which constitute reflections upon the nature of humanity and ethical guidelines for a nation's life. The absence of an underpinning theology actually serves to give the author a divine voice. By mentioning the divine very little, the divine is assumed to be the authoritative voice behind the narration, and hence the teaching acquires the status of revelation. The reduction of theology to anthropology and ethics is a familiar response to crises in culture and theology. Liberal Protestant theology took this route in reaction to the shaking of the foundations wrought by the Enlightenment, prompting Barth to respond that God is wholly other and beyond the reckoning of natural forms of knowledge. Various forms of radical theology have taken this stance in response to the demise of metaphysics, including the Death of God and Sea of Faith theologies. And many feminist and lesbian and gay theologies have followed suit. This is an understandable response. If the divine is collapsed into human ethics, the possibility of realizing the divine life becomes real because it depends upon human effort. Difficult, mind-numbing questions about where and what God we are dealing with can largely be avoided, and consequently it becomes easier to persuade others of the validity of one's approach. Locating the divine in the particularities of human experience can also be extremely empowering, particularly to those whose voices are excluded from other theological approaches. In a cultural context where divinity and natural identity appeared to be unravelled, or at least in the process of unravelling, and the future has become uncertain, trusting in an ethical system at least places the future in the hands of human beings and gives a sense of control. The problem with collapsing divinity into the human experience is that because there is no such thing as universal human experience we are in fact talking of quite specific human experience, which results in the marginalization and silencing of other types of experience. Furthermore, the divine can all too easily be invoked to bolster systems which do violence to others, and religion is reduced to mythology, simply reinforcing existing horizons. God ceases to be the God of surprises, the God of the parable who blows our horizons to pieces, and becomes instead a mirror to humanity reflecting itself back at twice its size. There is nothing in such a theological scheme to precipitate an undoing or good mourning. Rather the cultural tendency is towards melancholy, neurosis and fear of Otherness. In Proverbs the two women of wisdom represent this Otherness, and two strategies to neutralize the threat they pose are evident: assimilation (Hochma) and demonization (the Strange Woman).

A similar sense of control is given by a confidence in the natural order to underpin this ethical system. Such a confidence is patently evident in Proverbs. The divine is understood to reward the wise and punish the foolish and wicked. The righteous do not go hungry (10.3), they live longer than the wicked (10.27) who are prone to misfortune and ruin (13.10). For example,

The eye that mocks a father and scorns to obey a mother
will be pecked out by the ravens of the valley
and eaten by the vultures. (30.17)

The divine underpins a foundational order in which the wicked and foolish do not get away with it and the wise are recompensed with a good, stable life. The problem with this approach, of course, is that it is based upon the unsteady and shifting foundations of human constructions of what constitutes the good and it is a patently false and dangerous approach to the way things are. Anyone who lived through the onset of the Aids pandemic in the USA and Europe will know the violence of the kind of logic that interprets current circumstances as a divine judgement upon character. It leads to the easy division of a community into the good and the wicked and justifies violence, demonization and scapegoating.

The propositional sections of the book of Proverbs seek to foreclose the future by completely collapsing the divine into human experience with no room for mystery or difference that Hochma and the Strange Woman provide, and very particular human experience at that. The family becomes the location and chief horizon for wisdom. This wisdom is propositional, providing a foundation upon which a society may be maintained and policed. It creates a mythological framework in which the wicked and the wise are clearly identified by their circumstances and the future is guaranteed by the righteous living the life of wisdom outlined in the various collections of material brought together here.

Refusing to be Son

The queer reader refuses to be the son addressed in this material. S/he positions herself as difficult pupil, the son who causes pain to his parents (as many do) by refusing to play the role outlined in the text. S/he seeks to undo the foundations and the melancholia buried in them, by mourning those who the text may seek to exclude; those who followed an alternative type of wisdom, those who dared to live outside the family and construct different types of kinship and who are labelled 'wicked' as a result. S/he mourns those who live 'good' lives and yet do not receive their reward in this life. S/he mourns the absent divine who is not allowed to make trouble and queer the pitch but is made a hostage to human ethics and thereby ceases to be Other. The queer reader is the non-ideal wife and the daughter of the family who subvert the natural order and the ethical system attached to it by causing trouble. The queer reader refuses to memorize the text, conscious of its repetitions which suggest a certain despair and redundancy, and therefore the queer reader rejects the foreclosure of the future which the text attempts. This is not to say that s/he rejects all of the teaching or fails to appreciate the wisdom contained in some of it. S/he is aware that she cannot step outside the confines of the text altogether. But the queer reader's task is to undo and to be undone, to assume an ec-static relation to the text in order that the grip of melancholia may be lessened.

Two-Timing

The queer reader is 'naturally' more attracted to the drag show! Hochma is a fabulous figure, the personification of undoing, a disruptive, dangerous, demanding divinity, who in her public performances rearticulates the concepts of wisdom, deity and gender. We call her 'she' but we are not clear if she is a she or he is in drag. We are not quite clear what lies inside her gates or what her food will taste like when we sit down at her feast. In the figure of the Strange Woman we confront our fears and the fears of others regarding Hochma, that in the end we will be seduced into nothingness, into the abyss, into death, into an ultimate undoing where 'I' and 'we' shall cease to exist, the ultimate fear of what the future may bring. We sense that a relationship with Hochma/the Strange Woman involves the undoing of domesticity constructed as such a powerful desire in Proverbs and in our own cultural context. We sense that Hochma will confront us with Otherness and foreignness and with ideas that will challenge and undo our own. We dread the possibility that she will make us mourn our losses and banish the melancholy that holds together our identities. We all become Freudians, afraid that the womb may also be the tomb, and in the process of laying hold of the life she promises, Hochma may also bring us death. We fear that Hochma will cause all kinds of trouble for us. And this is how it must be. We need to hold together Hochma and the Strange Woman.

The danger of being a disciple of Hochma is that she is such an open sign that it is easy to project one's own desires and self into her and there allow them to become petrified into 'truth'. The Strange Woman constantly disturbs the pool of wisdom, allowing us to constantly undermine and undo ourselves and refuse foreclosure of the future and with it the possibility of continual social transformation. We need to two-time Hochma and the Strange Woman in order to retain the possibility of transformative politics and to prevent queer becoming a foundational-fix of its own.

Karl Rahner noted that, 'Revelation does not mean that mystery is overcome by gnosis bestowed by God, even in the direct vision of God; on the contrary, it is the history of the deepening perception of God *as* the mystery' (1999: 269). Hochma hectors and seduces us into the mystery of God by passing close to us, by suddenly appearing in the public spaces of our lives, bewildering us with her performance of the divine and summoning us into her mysterious house. But what lies beyond the meal is unclear; life and death, darkness and light; the dazzling darkness of the mystics. In the figure of Hochma (and the Strange Woman) God refuses to be easily named or understood and therefore ultimately avoids manipulation and control. It is this mystical dimension that guarantees the persistence of queer undoing. It is what Butler needs to make her theory work. God renders us all fag-hags stirring up a yearning which is simply incapable of being contained within Western constructions of desire and which is fuelled by its apparent lack of attainability. But only the divine can prevent the prospect of ultimate undoing and a radically open future leading to despair by holding out to queerness the possibility of a *telos*. There is a greater point than social transformation for queerness and an ultimate target for it and that is the divine life. The divine is queer and summons us all into queerness.

Like a drag queen at a carnival, Hochma passes by, disconcerting those who line the streets to watch. She promises a different way of being, a different type of God, a lot of mourning but therefore a lot of laughing because real grief frees laughter for ever. She offers a lot of undoing but also a lot of insight and maturity. She offers a journey without maps, a journey only the queer can take.

Ecclesiastes/Qohelet

JENNIFER L. KOOSED

Qohelet is queer. Consequently, commentators have always looked at it askance. For example, the two Anchor Bible Commentaries on Ecclesiastes open in nearly identical ways: 'Ecclesiastes is the strangest book in the Bible . . .' (Scott 1965: 191); and 'There is perhaps no book in the Bible that is the subject of more controversies . . .' (Seow 1997: ix). Others write commentaries peppered with the words: 'strange', 'peculiar', 'radical', in other words, queer. Queer name, language, genre, form, structure, content, place in the canon – nothing in this biblical book fits straight.

Michael Warner, in his introduction to *Fear of a Queer Planet*, defines queer politics in a number of ways, the first of which is 'dissatisfaction with the regime of the normal in general' (1993: xxvii). In terms of sacred scripture, Qohelet is a canonical book that constantly challenges the very notion of canon (from the Greek, a measuring rod against which to judge rules, standards, norms). It is within the tradition but also a constant thorn in the side of the tradition, goading it on like nails firmly fixed, the words of the wise (Eccles. 12.11). James Crenshaw writes, 'Qohelet's radical views render his teachings an alien body within the Hebrew Bible' (1988: 52). Because Qohelet is in the tradition, its challenge is one of the insider/outsider. It contests the very notion of normal categories, taking up the rod and whipping its canonical partners, reshaping the very notion of what constitutes biblical theology and ethics.

But focusing too much on queer theory as 'strangeness' may run the risk of desexualizing queer theory. It is not just any type of strangeness that makes something 'queer' in contemporary parlance. The word indicates a sexual and/or gendered strangeness. Someone or something labelled 'queer' is one who does not fit within the tightly scripted norms of heterosexuality in terms of gender identity and/or sexual practice. In this sense, then, can Qohelet be said to be 'queer' or is Qohelet able to be read 'queerly'? To be queer in this sense, must the adjective refer to the sexual practices described in the book, or to the sexual practices of the author of the book, or to the sexual practices of the reader of the book? Where are Qohelet's queer meanings located?

On the surface, at least, there are no descriptions of sexual practices of any kind. Yet, many commentators have sensed an undercurrent of sexual desire that has shaped their understanding of both the book and the author. On the surface, at least, there is no signature, no firm detail to anchor the words on the page to a particular person with particular desires and practices. Yet, most commentators have sensed a distinct individual identity in the book and have conflated this sensed personality with the author behind the book. Thus, much has been written about the life of the author, including speculation on the author's sex life. Qohelet has been called queer before.

One of the most prestigious commentary series in biblical studies is the Anchor Bible Commentary with which I began this chapter. An anchor is a heavy metal device, which is thrown over the side of a ship, designed to catch in the sand below in order to immobilize the ship against the water's currents and waves. Is the Anchor Bible intended to perform the same service? Is it meant to provide a strong and fixed counterweight to an interpreter's wayward readings? The adjective 'queer' as used in this chapter modifies not only 'Qohelet', but also 'commentary'. As a queer commentary, my readings will be wayward, unmoored from standard academic forms and models, perhaps even drifting too far into uncharted territory. But new discoveries only come from such unruly explorations.

The Narrator Who Dare Not Speak His Name

I do not know Qohelet's name. The superscription of the book declares that what follows are 'The words of Qohelet, the son of David, king in Jerusalem' (Eccles. 1.1).[1] But 'Qohelet' is not any kind of name known before or since its appearance here. Hebrew is a consonantal language that builds up its meanings on the foundations of trilateral roots. 'Qohelet' is a form of the root *qhl*, which means in *nifal* 'to be gathered together, congregate'; and in *hifal* 'to convoke an assembly'. The form in which the word appears in Ecclesiastes is otherwise unattested in any other Hebrew text. Most commentators (the notable exception being Brown, Driver and Briggs's masterful lexicon) identify the form as a feminine *qal* participle, meaning something like 'Gatherer' or 'Assembler'.

Personal names are textual markers of gender identity. In most cultures, male and female names are carefully demarcated. In the Hebrew Bible, men's and women's names never cross-dress. The name is feminine in form; yet, Qohelet is always assumed to be male.[2]

Assuming for now that Qohelet is a biological male, albeit one who has a feminine side, who then does this male speaker desire? I follow him to his various places, scrutinize his every word, look for any indication of his desire. There is one mention of a wife (Eccles. 9.9: 'Enjoy life with the wife whom you love . . .'), but no clear indication that this verse is a reference to a particular woman, let alone the woman of the author or speaker. Within the context of the passage, it is general advice. Qohelet addresses women one other time, in 7.26: 'I found more bitter than death the woman who is a trap, whose heart is

---

1 All translations are from the NRSV unless otherwise noted.

2 There is some evidence that during the Persian Period, certain titles had feminine endings. For example, see Ezra 2.55, 57; and Nehemiah 7.57, 59. Qohelet may be a title as well, but it only appears with a definite article twice (and one of these instances is with emendation). The word functions more as a proper name than a title in the text (as might the above examples from Ezra and Nehemiah; the translators of the NRSV, for example, simply transliterate the words in question, thus leaving them open to function either way).

snares and nets, whose hands are fetters; one who pleases God escapes her, but the sinner is taken by her.' These negative comments are often understood to be in tension with Ecclesiastes 9.9. How can one call women bitter, like death; yet also commend enjoying life with the woman one loves? In order to resolve this seeming contradiction, commentators have devised several strategies. Either Qohelet really does believe that one should love one's wife (9.9) but he hates his own (7.26) for some justifiable reason (always justifiable according to androcentric commentators, women always deserve the hatred they elicit); or the adverse, Qohelet may love his own wife but hate women in general (as if he were saying, some of my best friends are women); or Qohelet commends marrying generally but is himself a confirmed bachelor.

In terms of the latter option, in the history of life in the closet, bachelors are often anything but . . . the uncle who never married, the single cousin with the male room-mate who always comes to family events. Qohelet could be a bachelor in this sense – a man without a wife; one who prefers the company of other men.

The former option can also lead us down queer avenues. In the history of life in the closet, married men are often anything but heterosexual. Some commentators establish that Qohelet hates his own wife, and then explore the reasons for his antipathy. Frank Zimmermann in his book *The Inner World of Qohelet* believes that Qohelet hates his own wife and all women by extension, because she is an adulterer who belittles his masculinity. Qohelet's feelings toward women are not all his wife's fault. Qohelet's sister and mother also bear the blame. They turned him into the neurotic, impotent, latent homosexual he is by the time he writes his story.

Zimmermann is relying on a psychoanalytical definition of homosexuality that regards adult same-sex attraction as a misstep in normal sexual development. Even further, Qohelet's homosexuality is an aspect of his neuroses and is therefore connected to his mental illness. Zimmermann understands all of the queer (read: strange) features of the text as indicators of the queer (read: homosexual) nature of the writer. In particular, the contradictions and inconsistencies in the text are the result of 'the complex neuroses that gripped and overpowered him, neuroses which he tried to ameliorate through a series of compulsive actions intended to drain off the pressure and the drives that surged within him' (1973: xiii). Qohelet's normal heterosexual development was derailed by early sexual trauma: 'some traumatic experience seared him and destroyed his normal heterosexual relationships with women' (1973: 30).

The root of Qohelet's problem is his mother. Zimmermann writes, 'Qohelet's hostility to women could stem only from one primal source: the unwholesome, hostile relationship with his mother which is in the background of the text' (1973: 29). She is the root of his problems, but the precise nature of this early trauma is unknown and thus open to speculation. Zimmermann lists common sources for sexual trauma in an adolescent boy, including his divorced or widowed mother remarrying within a year, or catching his mother in the act of adultery. It is also quite possible, according to Zimmermann's psychoanalytical perspective, that Qohelet slept next to his sister on the floor of his parents' bedroom. He was thus a witness (audibly if not visually) to his parents' sexual encounters. As he grew into puberty, he began 'exploratory sex play' with his sister to which she did not object (1973: 31). Since his sister was then his first sexual experience and thus his first love object, his normal sexual development was crippled by the guilt, shame and anxiety of desiring such a forbidden partner.

Qohelet suppresses the memory of his early trauma. Incestuous desire and experience results in hatred for women, which is connected to homosexual orientation, all of which is embedded in a host of neuroses (1973: 46). Qohelet has been called queer before, but this type of queer reading relies upon and reinforces stereotypes about gay men: they are gay because of their mothers, they are neurotic, they are inclined toward abusing children, they hate women.

A reading like Zimmermann's would recommend a psychoanalyst's couch in order to pinpoint and then verbalize the early trauma. The goal of such a talking cure would be Qohelet's ability to engage in normal heterosexual intercourse with his wife, and thus live a happy life of family fulfilment. Zimmermann published his book in 1973, the very year the Board of Directors of the American Psychiatric Association voted to remove homosexuality from the Diagnostic and Statistical Manual of Mental Disorders. The membership of the APA concurred in their 1974 vote. In some ways, Zimmermann was obsolete before his book reached the library shelves. Yet, in other ways, his definition of homosexuality continues to haunt the medical establishment and certainly is a core belief among some conservative and evangelical religious denominations.

> When I was 17, I dated a skater. He went to a different school; his hair fell in silky straight locks over his eyes; my hair was cut at an angle; I did not see him often. Then, suddenly, he was in the mental ward of Children's Hospital and I was the only non-family member who was allowed to see him. The largest scar on my body is on my left knee, round and pale like a full moon glowing through a foggy night. He had cut his wrists. I later found out that his parents had caught him with his boyfriend. They locked him up in the hospital, and allowed me to see him several times a week. Although I did not know it at the time, I was a pawn in their 'normalizing' plot. He had tried to teach me how to skate: I am flying down the hill in front of his house, standing on the board, not understanding how to meld my body into the board, to move with it and have it move with me, at the bottom of the hill I fall, gravel and dirt embed in my palms and knees. In the bathroom off the kitchen he holds a towel soaked red, bloody against my lacerated skin.

Zimmermann's method establishes links between the words on the page and the author's life (in and out of the bedroom). Whereas his interpretation is unusual, his general method is grounded in standard historical-critical methods of peering behind and through the words in order to reconstruct the author(s) and context. Although extreme, Zimmermann's reading demonstrates that such reconstructions rely more on interpreters' assumptions than on historical evidence. The profiles of Qohelet have been as numerous and as diverse as the people who have written them; which leads to the ironic situation of readers proclaiming that the sense of identity in the text is strong, yet there is no consensus on the contours of that identity. Identity thus becomes an empty category, filled in with the projections of the commentator. The text is a mirror, not a window.

Who do you see when you look into the book?

Qohelet can be read as a metacommentary on the nature of identity and the interconnections between identities and texts – both the author's and the reader's. By using autobiographical language ('I'), the text poses as an interface between the author and the reader. Yet, because the text is fragmented, contradictory, inconsistent, confusing and disturbing – what kind of interface is it? Rather than being a book reflecting someone's particular identity, the text ends up refracting the identity of the reader in multiple and unpredictable ways. The mirror cracks from side to side.

I see the inconsistencies of my own identity; the contradictions of my own sexed and gendered self.

According to Steven Seidman, the first phase of queer politics and theory (1969–73) 'departed from previous homosexual theory that mirrored dominant medical-scientific ideas by conceiving of homosexuality as symptomatic of an abnormal psychic condition characteristic of a segment of humanity' (Warner 1993: 115). Such 'oppressive identity models' buttressed by the sciences (Warner 1993: 109) were challenged, along with the claims of objectivity and neutrality that are the hallmarks of scientific enquiry. By trying to forge a single identity for the speaker in the book of Qohelet, Zimmermann uses psychiatry and historical-critical biblical method to argue for a single though very disturbed individual whose homosexuality is a key mark of his neurosis. My queer reading begins by challenging his claims of scientific knowledge, as well as the claims of objectivity voiced by most interpreters of Qohelet.

Seidman goes on to outline what he sees as the second phase of queer politics and theory (the remainder of the 1970s): the ethnic identity model. Gay and lesbian identity is not chosen; it is as much a part of a body as its sex or the colour of its skin. The gay and lesbian movements split into two but still developed along similar trajectories. 'In particular, there was an emphasis on community building around the notion of a unitary lesbian and gay identity' (Warner 1993: 116). Certain types of gay and lesbian culture flourished under this model, and it became the basis for advocating gay rights in ways commensurate with the women's rights and the civil rights movements.

But these communities only flourished by suppressing that which (or those who) did not fit:

Specifically, individuals whose experiences and interests were not represented in the dominant gay identity constructions criticized the ethnic model as exhibiting a white, middle-class bias. Simultaneously, the ethnic identity model was under attack by constructionist scholars who underscored the immense sociohistorical diversity of meanings and social arrangements of same-sex desire. Finally, the emerging prominence of post-structuralism provided a language to deconstruct the category of a gay subject and to articulate the dissenting voice. (Warner 1993: 117).

Queer identity is not singular. First, there are differences, conflicts and tensions between gay men and lesbians. Among gay men and lesbians, race and class multiply the differences and further undermine any notion of an essential, stable 'gay' identity. The phenomena of bisexuality, S/M sexual practices, and the presence of transsexual and transgendered persons in the queer community further complicate the matter. Anyone's identity, particularly one's sexual identity, is more complex, fluid and multifaceted than any essentialized or 'ethnic' notion of identity allows. In addition, just because someone identifies 'queer' does not mean that any one political or social perspective can be assumed. Jacqueline Zita writes, 'one significant challenge postmodern queer theory brings to sex and gender studies is a critique of sexual identity as a monolithic unity based on dichotomous categories' (1998: 132; see also K. Stone 2001a: 20–8).

What have you assumed about me?

Unlike Zimmermann, this is what I mean when I call Qohelet queer. I situate Qohelet's queerness within poststructuralist discourses on identity, and a politics of difference. Echoing Roland Boer, I too avow that I am attracted to reading queerly because such a posture allows me to 'discover a wealth of divergent sexual constructions in any one text' (1999: 15). Above all, I experience a perverse pleasure, gaiety if you will, in writing in ways a biblical scholar is not supposed to write.

Queer identity has at the very least demonstrated that people are not always what they seem. One's public face can be quite different from one's private self, and one's sexual orientation, actions, identity and desire may even be hid from close friends and family. Anyone who has experienced the closet knows that identity is too multifaceted to be simply read – either from a conversation, a friendship, or a text. Even a biblical one. I began this section by noting that I do not know Qohelet's name. Every enquiry into the identity of the speaker yields more mysteries and more obfuscations, which leads to my suspicion that Qohelet is trying to hide something. So what if Qohelet appears to be a male voice and discusses wives as if he does or could have one? Could not any female-to-male transsexual, or closeted gay man, or bisexual husband do the same? In the words of Ted Gott, 'Some of my queerest fucks have sported baby-restraints in the back seat' (as quoted in Boer 1999: 13).

Strike a Pose

Qohelet is a cross-dresser. Whether he is dressed in women's clothing or whether she is dressed in men's clothing, I cannot quite tell. S/he has mastered the art of putting on and taking off gender. Qohelet first signals his/her cross-dressing in the opening line: 'The words of Qohelet, the son of David, king in Jerusalem'

(Eccles. 1.1). What kind of name is 'Qohelet'?[3] As aforementioned, 'Qohelet' is usually identified as a feminine *qal* participle. The letter *tāw* at the end of the word signals the feminine form. Despite this, Qohelet is always assumed to be male. I have found only one commentator who attempts to capture the gendered nature of the Hebrew by translating the name as 'female-gatherer': 'The words of (the) female-gatherer, son of David, king over Israel in Jerusalem' (Ginsburg 1861: 245). There is no gender consistency in the book of Qohelet, not even in the superscription. Is Qohelet like Hapshepsut, the female Pharaoh who put beards on her statues and used a masculine pronoun in her inscriptions? Or is Qohelet like a drag queen, a man who assumes a woman's name?

Despite the feminine form of the name, the verbs are all masculine – save one. Ecclesiastes 7.27 reads with emendation, 'See, this is what I found, says [singular, masculine] the Qohelet . . .' However, in the Hebrew Masoretic Text, the verse actually reads thus: 'See, this is what I found, says [singular, feminine] Qohelet . . .' The difference is in the placement of a *hê*. If the *hê* appears at the end of the verb, it renders the verb feminine. If the *hê* appears instead at the beginning of Qohelet, the name becomes a title. The gender of Qohelet is destabilized in more than just name.

Drag culture has been the subject of documentaries, and has achieved a certain acceptance in mainstream entertainment. Yet, drag is also a site of controversy among cultural critics and theorists of gender, race and class. Those who cross-dress do demonstrate that gender identity is a performance that can be taken on and off (Butler). In addition, as bell hooks writes, 'Cross-dressing, appearing in drag, transvestitism, and transsexualism emerge in a context where the notion of subjectivity is challenged, where identity is always perceived as capable of construction, invention, change.' As such, these experiences are 'subversive places where gender norms were questioned and challenged' (hooks 1992: 145). Yet drag, especially as entertainment, can reinforce negative stereotypes about women rather than liberate all from gender roles and expectations. The potential misogyny inherent in certain performances is also noted by hooks (1992: 146). It is perhaps no coincidence that the gendered slip of the tongue, the flash of drag in 7.27 comes in the exact centre of a passage that condemns all women.

> Qohelet looks me straight in the eye and remarks, 'I found more bitter than death the woman who is a trap, whose heart is snares and nets, whose hands are fetters; one who pleases God escapes her, but the sinner is taken by her. See, this is what I found, says the Teacher, adding one thing to another to find the sum, which my mind has sought repeatedly, but I have not found. One man among a thousand I found, but a woman among all these I have not found' (Eccles. 7.26–8). I watch a drag show in Philadelphia where some

---

3 Martin Luther's translation of 'Qohelet' as 'Preacher' has been widely influential, but it is anachronistic. The LXX translates the Hebrew into the Greek word *Ekklesiastēs*, from the word *ekklēsia*. In this time period, *ekklēsia* means broadly 'assembly', thus *Ekklesiastēs* means a member of such an assembly. In early Christian communities (as reflected in the Gospel of Matthew, for example), *ekklēsia* became defined more narrowly as 'church', thus leading to the understanding of *Ekklesiastēs* as 'preacher'.

of my friends are performing. I stand in the back of the club, drink in my hand, angry. When the audience laughs at some feminine gesture, exaggerated, I cringe. Yet, I am also riveted by these beautiful white men; these men who look masculine without make-up and in men's clothing; these men who are completely transformed by some paint, a wig, and a dress. Is it really that easy to become a woman? Is it really that easy to become me?

From the documentary *Paris is Burning*, Pepper Labeija looks at me his viewer and remarks, 'I have been a man and I have been a man who emulated a woman. I have never been a woman. I have never had that service once a month; I have never been pregnant. I could never say how a woman feels. I can only say how a man who acts like a woman or dresses like a woman feels. I never wanted to have a sex change. That's just taking it a little too far . . . once it is gone, it is gone. A lot of kids that I know they got the sex change because they felt, oh I have been treated so bad as a drag queen, if I get a pussy (excuse the expression) I will be treated fabulous. But women get treated bad. They get beat; they get robbed; they get dogged. So, having the vagina, that doesn't mean you are going to have a fabulous life – it might, in fact, be worse.'

Gender performance is not the full extent of Qohelet's drag. Qohelet declares him/herself King, a son of David who is

(Pepper Labeija speaks again: 'Those Balls are more just like our fantasy of being a superstar . . .')

the most famous and powerful king of Israel. This turns out to be a guise as well, just like her masculinity, just like his femininity. Our clothes, our movements, our hair – these signify more than gender. Class is also performed by such signifiers. The drag balls that emerged among African-American and Latino gay men in Harlem in the 1980s, for example, were not just about dressing as a woman; they were also about desiring wealth, a wealth often associated with whiteness. Competition categories included Town and Country, High Fashion Evening Wear, Opulence

(Venus Xtravaganda declares, 'I would like to be spoiled rich white girl').

Qohelet emerges onto the Ballroom floor and the MC calls out 'Act like you own everything.' As he dances across the room, his robes swishing in time to the music, his fantasy takes shape: 'I made great works; I built houses and planted vineyards for myself; I made myself gardens and parks, and planted in them all kinds of fruit trees. I made myself pools from which to water the forest of growing trees. I bought male and female slaves, and had slaves who were born in my house; I also had great possessions of herds and flocks, more than any who had been before me in Jerusalem. I also gathered for myself silver and gold and the treasure of kings and of the provinces; I got singers, both men and women, and delights of the flesh, and many concubines'. (Eccles. 2.4–8)

Jennie Livingston's film *Paris is Burning* is 'a graphic documentary portrait of the way in which colonized black people (in this case black gay brothers, some of whom were drag queens) worship at the throne of whiteness . . .' (hooks 1992: 148; see also Zita 1998: 184–201). Race as we construct it did not exist in the biblical world. People were aware of the differences in skin colour, but people were not classified and categorized by those colour differences. After all, most of the people in the biblical world were quite dark. But ethnic differences regardless of skin colour do play a role in the biblical world, and ethnic differences can exacerbate conflict in biblical stories. This ethnic element is present in Qohelet's dragging as well.

The female-gatherer claims to be the son of David – which would date the text to the tenth century BCE. Yet, an analysis of the words spoken point to a much later date. The vocabulary and the grammar indicate that the text was written either in the Persian or the Hellenistic period. The tongue betrays a context that the meaning of the words tries to hide. During the Persian and Hellenistic eras, there was no Israelite or Judaean king in Jerusalem. Rather, the people of Israel were a colonized people, ruled by foreign kings and emperors. By dragging kingship in this era, one is not dragging a king of one's own ethnicity, but rather taking on the trappings of the foreigner because that is where power resides.

In fact, the words in chapter 2 are aping not actions and inscriptions of ancient Israelite kings – at least none of which we know. The words in chapter 2 are aping the words and actions of West Semitic and Akkadian kings and their inscriptions. Choon-Leong Seow archives the words and phrases which Qohelet uses in his performance as an Akkadian ruler: 'I am Qohelet' (1.12); 'I have been king' (1.12); 'I built' (2.4); 'I made' (2.6) (Seow 1995: 281–3).

Soon after Qohelet's royal fantasy, the royal drag is dropped and Qohelet seems to appear as an official in the king's court (Eccles. 8.2–4). And then at the end, Qohelet is revealed as a sage, a teacher (Eccles. 12.9). Generally, the commentators believe the words at this point. Qohelet is a sage and the royal identity is the fiction covering over the real. But what is real and what is fantasy on the dance floor of the ball? After all, Qohelet spends most of his book lamenting his inability to find wisdom – his fantasy is to hold her fast and to become wise. His fantasy is not just to be a king, but also to be a sage. Another category judged in the balls is 'School boy/School girl'. Between the man and the woman, between the Israelite and the Akkadian, between the king and the sage, the space between the fantasy and the real blurs.

Dorian Corey is the elder sage. She is painting her face, putting on thick, long false eyelashes, adding her epilogue to *Paris is Burning*, her final 'pleasing words . . . words of truth plainly' (Eccles. 12.10): 'I always had hopes of being a big star. As you get older, you aim a little lower. You say, well you still might make an impression. Everyone wants to leave something behind them, some impression, some mark upon the world. And then you think, you left a mark on the world if you just get through it. And if a few people know your name, then you left a mark. You do not have to bend the whole world. I think that it is better to just enjoy it. Pay your dues, and enjoy it. If you shoot an arrow and it goes real high, hurray for you.'

Butch or Femme?

Despite the fact that the word Qohelet is feminine in form, the author is always presumed to be male. Even feminist scholars, who question the assumption that all biblical texts were written by men, classify this text as a masculine one (Brenner, for example). But what kind of man is he? Is Qohelet a burly, aggressive, testosterone-filled man? Or is he effeminate, impotent and inclined toward feminine occupations? Both of these characterizations of Qohelet's masculinity (or lack thereof) have been interpreted from the exact same text: Ecclesiastes 3.1–8.

Generally labelled a poem about time, some interpreters have sensed erotic and violent (even erotically violent) undercurrents to its comprehensive catalogue of human experience. For example, Athalya Brenner calls Ecclesiastes 3.1–8 an 'M' text, specifically, it is a 'male poem of desire' (Brenner and van Dijk-Hemmes 1993: 133). By this she means that the narrative voice is masculine. Although she does not necessarily equate the masculine voice of the speaker with the maleness of an author, she does sometimes slip into this identification. She bases her assessment of the speaker's masculinity on 'the ejaculatory and thrusting nature connoted by key expressions' (1993: 151). To reach this conclusion, Brenner focuses specifically on verse 5. This verse affirms that there is 'a time to throw away stones, and a time to gather stones together; a time to embrace, and a time to refrain from embracing' (Eccles. 3.5).

As the central pair in the poem, it is the key to Brenner's interpretation. Rejecting the simple literal meaning of throwing and gathering stones, Brenner links the first part of the verse to the second and together the sexual connotations emerge. Brenner is not the first to look beyond the literal meaning of stones. She takes her cue from rabbinical sources such as *Qohelet Rabbah* and *Yalqut Shimeoni*. Both of these texts read the casting of stones as a man having sex with his wife. Gathering stones then has the opposite meaning: to refrain from sex. Stones may be a euphemism for sexual intercourse, or even for testicles. Although neither the rabbis nor Brenner are explicit on this point, 'throwing stones' could be a reference to the thrusting of the hips necessary for penetration and the continuing pleasurable back-and-forth, which results in orgasm.

Whereas the rabbis interpreted gathering stones as abstaining from sex, Brenner is not convinced. Rather, she speculates about the meaning, seemingly puzzled since throwing stones is so obviously and aggressively masculine, and gathering stones is not. Yet, her puzzlement is based upon stereotypical constructions of masculinity, and the heterosexist assumption that the body this M-speaker wants to penetrate is female. If throwing stones is thrusting one's hips, then maybe gathering stones is clasping and caressing a lover's testicles, pulling them toward you, invitingly. Perhaps Qohelet likes to fuck and be fucked.

I am not supposed to like to be overpowered, penetrated, fucked. But I want you to crush me; I want to feel your weight, pressing me down, taking me. I know that you could take me by force; I know that you do not because you will not; I feel your restrained power. I see the tension in your muscles, the danger behind your eyes, it radiates from your skin. Your power makes me tremble, and your restraint makes me strong. I want you to crush me; I want to feel your weight, pressing me down, taking me.

It is also possible that the gender positions in the poem shift and change – a male voice throws stones and a female voice gathers stones together. After all, other interpreters sense more femininity in the catalogue of the times than masculinity. Zimmermann, for example, reads Ecclesiastes 3.1–8 as more evidence that Qohelet is effeminate, emasculated, gay. Qohelet's homosexuality is not just manifest in his hatred of women and his desire for other men, but also in his transgression of normal masculine activities. The poem of the times encapsulates all of his violent, sexual and gendered neuroses.

The phrases upon which Zimmermann focuses are 'a time to kill', 'a time to throw away stones' and 'a time to sew'. Regarding the first, it is evident 'that Qohelet has hostile, aggressive, criminal impulses' (1973: 10). At whom, then, is Qohelet so murderously angry? The clue is in the next focus verse: a time to throw stones. Zimmermann rejects any allegorical or metaphorical meaning for this verse. Instead, he takes it literally and asks under what circumstances would the speaker want to throw stones and at whom? Women caught in adultery are stoned, according to the Torah (Deut. 22.22). Qohelet suspects his wife of adultery and he wants to kill her for it. As discussed above, one of the primary hallmarks of Qohelet's queerness for Zimmermann is his hatred for women. But there are other clues in the text as well, and one within this very passage. Qohelet writes that there is 'a time to sew'. Now, if Qohelet were a professional tailor, he might sew. But he is not (Zimmermann believes that Qohelet is a court official, 1973: 10). 'Why should a man advocate what is essentially a feminine occupation . . . ? This too is a compulsive action, an index of the latent homosexuality of Qohelet' (1973: 11). Just as Brenner relies upon certain stereotypes for her reading, Zimmermann does as well.

A third possibility exists – not every body is clearly male or clearly female. A third body type exists, destabilizing our neat categories: the hermaphrodite.

One can be born a hermaphrodite. There are people like Herculine Barbin, born with both male and female genitalia, raised as a girl in a convent. Her queer genitalia was only discovered when she fell in love with another girl and they embarked upon a sexual relationship. Michel Foucault asks in his introduction to her remarkable memoirs, 'Do we *truly* need a *true* sex?' (vii). In Herculine Barbin's case, being forced into categories not of her own making led to suicide. Such a case could, perhaps, have only happened in the nineteenth century when a girl could live for over 20 years without anyone else seeing her naked body. Nowadays, when a child is born with ambiguous sexual organs, decisions are made and operations are performed to force the unruly body into proper sexed categories. Modern medical culture responds to Foucault's question with a resounding Yes.

Consequently, nowadays, hermaphrodites are more likely to be self-made. Men take hormones in order to grow breasts. Sometimes their male–female bodies are a transitional state during the process of sex reassignment. Sometimes the ambiguous body is the goal.

Hokhma removed my cap and jacket; I started undoing her blouse. Large, dark areoli surrounded huge nipples on her breasts. My woolen shirt came away, my slightly smaller breasts falling out into her hands. But her hands didn't stay there, for they moved down my back, undoing my belt and loosening my pants. When she felt my cock, she laughed and in anticipation. 'This will be fun,' she said . . .

My hand slipped up her skirt, pulling it up as I eased beneath her panties. The skirt unclipped and fell away and I slid the panties down. Beneath was a rapidly rising penis supported by the hairiest balls I have ever seen. My dream lover . . .

(Boer 1999: 84–6).

Is Qohelet a man who likes both active and passive roles during sex; is Qohelet not one speaker but two both male and female; is Qohelet a hermaphrodite?

What does your body look like when you look into the mirror of Qohelet?

Between Men

Qohelet advocates companionship: 'Two are better than one' (Eccles. 4.9a). Should these verses be read in conjunction with Qohelet's statement about enjoying one's wife (Eccles. 9.9), in which case he is speaking of male–female partnerships? Or is he advocating companionship between men? If he is advocating companionship between men, is it platonic only or is there a homoerotic, homosexual or homosocial tenor to his words?

The first clue may come in the first phrase of the passage: 'Two are better than one.' Already, things are a little strange because the syntax is not proper. In the typical numerical sayings, the numbers progress in order, from lesser to greater (Seow 1997: 181). In the reversing of the sequence, Qohelet queers the grammar. Is it because he is hinting at the queerness of the content through the queerness of the form? One reversal may not a queer boy make, but the cumulative effect of the oddities of this passage suggest that there is more than one way to read the companionship lauded by the speaker.

The passage continues, explaining Qohelet's reasoning. Better are two than one 'for if they fall, one will lift up the other' (Eccles. 4.10a). Again, Qohelet's grammar is questionable, even nonsensical. The verb is *yippōlû* – a third-person plural of the verb *npl* 'to fall'. The clear, literal meaning of the word is that both have fallen. How, then, can one help the other up if both are down? Some interpreters (Driver and Galling; see Seow 1997: 182) recommend emending the text to set it straight. Others stop short of such drastic coercive measures and instead suggest that despite what the words say, they should be understood differently: 'if either one falls' (Seow's suggestion; 1997: 182). The manuscript tradition (LXX, Syriac translations, Vulgate) is all over the map with this word, probably because other scribes noted the same difficulties we do today and tried to smooth them over. The situation that is most often imagined by the commentators is that of two men, walking together in the wilderness, one falling into a pit (Seow 1997: 189), perhaps even into a trap set for animals. Luckily, the one who falls has a companion who can pull him up and out of such an unfortunate circumstance.

Another reading lies right at the surface. When two people fall together in English, they are experiencing the emotional vertigo of mutual love: 'they fell in love'. The verb 'to fall' can be used idiomatically in Hebrew in ways that suggest a similar meaning. Several uses of 'fall' carry an erotic connotation: one can fall on someone – which either means a violent attack (Gen. 43.18), or it means an affectionate embrace (Gen. 33.4). One can fall into bed (Ex. 21.18) – and two falling into bed would certainly imply a sexual encounter. And one can fall before someone else, as in the case of the idol Dagon falling repeatedly before the ark of the Lord (1 Sam. 5.2–5), an incident where the violent sexual connotations have recently been drawn out by Theodore W. Jennings, Jr (2001: 58–9). In these idiomatic uses of 'falling', two falling together are better than one, and they certainly do aid each other in getting (it) up.

All of this is, perhaps, stretching the meaning of the Hebrew words on the page. Perhaps. But read now the next verse: 'Again, if two lie together, they keep warm; but how can one keep warm alone?' (Eccles. 4.11). The two who lay together may be a male and female pair – in fact, 'the two' can be understood in this way throughout the passage. Because of the way in which Hebrew is gendered, any group of people that includes at least one man is rendered masculine. However, it is rarely regarded that way in the commentaries because of the content of the surrounding verses. In the previous verse, Qohelet has these two roaming around together (perhaps roaming around the wilderness together – though as stated before, the precise nature of their falling is unclear), and in the next verse (verse 12) they are fighting together. Both of these situations imply if not require a male–male couple. If the surrounding verses are almost universally understood to be referencing two men, then why suddenly switch here to a heterosexual pair? A passage that discusses two men who travel together, fall together, and then keep each other warm is highly suggestive of queer sexual activity.

An interpreter reading through a straight lens may protest – perhaps these two men are simply protecting themselves against the chill of the desert. If they are roaming around in the wilderness, the evenings can get quite cold and the best survival strategy is for each to augment his own body's heat with the heat of the other. However, one who is reading through a queer lens can not help but raise an eyebrow at the picture of two men lying down together creating heat. The Hebrew verb 'to make heat' is *ḥmm*, and it is used in other contexts to refer to animal heat, the heat of conception. For example, when Jacob brings the sheep down to their watering places so that they would breed in front of his various rods to produce striped, speckled and spotted young, the sheep *yeḥĕmū* – literally 'make heat' (Gen 30.38–9). Since the result of their 'making heat' is progeny, 'making heat' clearly refers to sexual intercourse here.

The rabbis who paraphrased Qohelet into Aramaic noted the erotic undertone to these two 'making heat' and clarified the sex of the participants by adding the phrase 'a man and his wife'. The Aramaic tames the Hebrew. I have also heard this verse read at heterosexual wedding ceremonies. It has slipped into opposite-sex contexts of love and devotion, just like the passionate speech spoken by Ruth to Naomi. Although often unspoken and sometimes denied, there is an erotic spark in these words of Qohelet.

> The first time I saw two men kiss, I was at a party. They were there, up against the wall, at the edge of the dancing, music and lights pulsating in a savage syncopated rhythm. I had moved off the dance floor myself, wet with sweat, needing air. And that is when I saw them across the room. One had crushed the other up against the wall, holding his shoulders back, pinning him. Their bodies were moving, slowly and deliberately, their tongues exploring, ravenous and wild. I could not turn away; I could not catch my breath.

At the beginning of this passage (Eccles. 4.9–12), the numbers did not add up. At the end of this passage, proper arithmetic fails again. Like Thomas Hanks quips concerning the writer of the Gospel of Matthew and the queer maths in his genealogy, 'our publican either can't count straight or (like a thoroughbred queer) decides not to' (2000: 188). The same can be said for our sage; Qohelet just cannot add straight. In the passage, the two companions are now beset by those seeking to do violence to them (not an unfamiliar scenario for same-sex couples). The two together have a better chance of surviving the attack, whereas one alone might be overpowered. The final phrase – 'A threefold cord is not quickly broken' (Eccles. 4.11b) – has left some interpreters scratching their heads. How can two suddenly turn into three? Seow reviews the puzzlement of mathematically inclined scholars, but believes that the verse simply indicates that there is strength in numbers (1997: 189). However, taken together with the numerical problem that introduces the passage and with the oddities of grammar and content in the verses in between, another interpretation emerges. Qohelet affirms that two do not always add up in the expected way, things are not always what they seem, and that there is more than one way of understanding the companionship between men.[4] Through hint, innuendo and allusion, Qohelet is advocating queer associations between men.

Forward, Never Straight

> We are driving home from the Michigan Womyn's Music Festival and I am angry. My driving companions have decided to carry the festival over into the day and across the state: they played guitars in a restaurant parking lot; they flashed their breasts at surprised pedestrians; they quizzed a truck stop waitress about MSG and animal by-products in the food on the menu. But more infuriating, my ex-girlfriend is hitting on the other woman in

---

4 There are also allusions to the *Epic of Gilgamesh* in the queer equations that frame the passage. A passage of the *Epic of Gilgamesh* also culminates in a saying about 'a three-stranded rope' (Seow 1997: 181). The *Epic* then is an intertext, and it too is about companionship between men. Even though both Gilgamesh and Enkidu have their fair share of heterosexual conquests, both of them find true, passionate, death-defying companionship not with women but with each other.

the car, a woman I had a crush on myself. I listen moodily to their playful banter. Meanwhile, I am giving her directions while she is driving and she keeps quipping, 'forward, never straight' whenever I tell her to 'go straight' through this light or that intersection.

The book of Qohelet contains two verses which proclaim that what is not straight cannot be made straight. Verse 1.15 reads, 'What is crooked cannot be made straight' and verse 7.13 reads, 'Consider the work of God; who can make straight what he has made crooked?' Of course, the word 'straight' does not have the same colloquial meaning in biblical Hebrew as it does in contemporary English, and 'crooked' is not generally used as a synonym for 'queer' in any language I know. Nevertheless, by allowing a little language play, various interpretive possibilities are opened. Words are always in conversation with their multiple meanings as they cross time, languages and cultures.

Even though 'crooked' does not mean 'queer', queers are often called perverted and this is one of the possible translations of the verb *'wt*. For example, in Job 34.12 Elihu proclaims that 'Of a truth, God will not do wickedly, and the Almighty will not pervert justice.' Rereading 7.13, translating the verb according to the use of the word in Job: 'Consider the work of God; who can make straight what he has perverted?' Who can make straight what God has made queer?

This phrase in Qohelet is possibly an aphorism, or the perversion of an aphorism. Searching the cross-cultural wisdom parallels, a similar saying is found in the Egyptian text *The Instruction of Anii*. In the Egyptian version of the saying, however, the crooked *can* be made straight (see Crenshaw 1988: 74, 133; Seow 1997: 122). Qohelet disagrees. Qohelet is the counter-voice to rehabilitation ministries, though the modern-day movement is staffed largely by evangelical Christians and not ancient Egyptians. Perhaps if they read Ecclesiastes more closely, they would channel their moral outrage into other projects.

By the time we pull into my driveway, the hour is late and I am seething. My ex-girlfriend helps me take my bags to the door. I turn on her. The weekend had been full of controversy: male-to-female transsexuals and sado-masochistic lesbians protested their exclusion, the latter even hiring a plane to fly over the festival scattering leaflets. My hair is long; I am thin; I listen to the wrong kind of music; I wear the wrong type of clothes. I am told: gain weight, cut your hair, I don't understand you Ohio dykes. I care that I am late returning home; I care that my family may be worried; I care that I had things to do today. These angry, hurried, hushed words spoken standing under the late night summer sky are the last words I ever speak to her.

The Metrosexual

What else besides 'queer' would you call someone who opposes the traditional platitudes about God and the social order, and instead wants to replace such traditional piety with a good party; someone who thinks that one should pay proper attention to dressing well, styling one's hair, and smelling good?

Chapter 9 opens with a long tirade:

All this I laid to heart, examining it all, how the righteous and the wise and their deeds are in the hand of God; whether it is love or hate one does not know. Everything that confronts them is vanity, since the same fate comes to all, to the righteous and the wicked, to the good and the evil, to the clean and the unclean, to those who sacrifice and those who do not sacrifice. As are the good, so are the sinners; those who swear are like those who shun an oath. (Eccles. 9.1–2)

This litany of the saintly and the sinful ends with the radical leveller called death. Death for Qohelet (as with the rest of the ancient Israelite tradition) means at most a descent into Sheol – a shadowy place where 'there is no work or thought or knowledge or wisdom' (Eccles. 9.10). If there is any consciousness at all, and that is a debatable question, it is a most dreary state indeed.

Qohelet calls the entire biblical system of ritual and morality, including clean and unclean, ultimately meaningless, even arbitrary. As Seow points out (1997: 303), this biblical passage resonates with the Babylonian text *I Will Praise the Lord of Wisdom*, in which the human inability to know the divine mind is even more explicitly stated:

I wish I knew that these things were pleasing to one's god!
What is proper to oneself is an offence to one's god.
What in one's own heart seems despicable is proper to one's god.
Who knows the will of the gods in heaven?
Who understands the plans of the underworld gods?
Where have mortals learnt the way of a god?
He who is alive yesterday is dead today.

None of our most basic categories, not even love and hate, not even good and evil are meaningful. All of what we know is ultimately undermined by death.

The laws prohibiting male–male anal intercourse appear only in the purity codes in the book of Leviticus (Lev. 18.22 and 20.13).[5] Most of the purity legislation involves the categories of 'clean' and 'unclean'; these categories are not to be equated with 'good' and 'evil'. They are ritual categories and not moral ones. In fact, there are many activities that are good, even commanded by the law, yet these activities make one unclean (like burying a dead body, or giving birth to a child). But there are some purity laws that do at least imply moral condemnation – anal penetration between men, for example. If one engages in it, there is no mechanism for moving back again from unclean to clean; there is nothing but censor and death. The state of the matter is quite clear in Leviticus, but Qohelet asks who knows what is love and what is hate, what is clean and what is unclean in the eyes of God? Qohelet confounds our normal binary oppositions, our smug pronouncements of morality, our categories of meaning.

---

5 There are no laws prohibiting any type of female sexual activity with other females.

In the face of such questions, Qohelet has the following recommendation: 'Go, eat your bread with joy and drink your wine with a glad heart, for God has already approved your actions. At all times let your clothes be white and do not lack oil on your head' (9.7–8). In other words, throw a party, get drunk, dress well, and style your hair. Whereas Qohelet's primping regime and social calendar may signal a queer identity, with the success of the TV programme *Queer Eye for the Straight Guy*, we know that such activities are not just for gay men anymore. This lifestyle has been embraced by a certain type of straight man known as the 'metrosexual'. The queer theorist and cultural critic Mark Simpson coined the term in 1994 ('Here Comes the Mirror Men', in *The Independent*), though it did not receive widespread usage until after another article by Simpson in 2002 ('Meet the Metrosexual' in Salon.com). Although Simpson uses the term to describe a straight, gay or bisexual man, it is more commonly employed in the manner of Alexa Hackbarth. Lamenting the D.C. dating scene from her perspective as a straight woman, Hackbarth writes, 'A metrosexual . . . is a straight man who styles his hair using three different products . . . loves clothes and the very act of shopping for them, and describes himself as sensitive and romantic. In other words, he is a man who seems stereotypically gay except when it comes to sexual orientation' (Hackbarth 2003).

> You are vain. You gaze in the mirror, constructing and reconstructing your identity with every curl of your hair, with every stroke of the make-up brush. I watch you as you watch yourself and you laugh at my querying expression: 'Vanity of vanities! All is vanity.' I know that when we go out tonight, people will have trouble reading us. It has happened before: we are hit on by both men and women; another asks me if you are gay; some-one else thinks my best friend is my lover, not you. I smile. I knew it would be like this after that first morning after that first night. You walked out of my shower, hair wet, towel lazily wrapped around your warm naked body. You asked: Where's your face soap? I did not, of course, have any. You were honestly puzzled, aghast really at my recklessness: don't you know that regular soap dries out the face's delicate skin? I shrugged. You grabbed my hand and brought it up to your soft cheek, across your smooth brow: I guess I shouldn't even ask if you have any moisturizer. You are vain, but romantic in your self-reflection, beautiful in your self-obsession. With you, I am tak-ing and taken, dominant and passive, hidden and exposed. We intertwine into each other, so much so that I can no longer tell where my reading ends and yours begins. You are vain; I am more.

Qohelet embraces a metrosexual aesthetic, whether gay or bisexual or straight. Rather than devoting himself to religious ritual and righteous living, Qohelet devotes his Saturdays to shopping, taking a trip to the beauty parlour to get a new hair style and to stock up on various products, preparing for a night of clubbing – all with divine sanction. Qohelet is another customer in God's beauty parlour (Moore 2001) and he recommends we make an appointment as well.

Adrift at Sea

Where does this leave us? A conventional commentary would have provided the reader with information about Qohelet's history of interpretation, date, authorship, themes, integrity, structure and genre. It would have addressed such central questions in Qohelet scholarship as how many authors and redactors were involved with its production; is it influenced by Hellenistic philosophy or is it a Persian period text; what is the best translation for *hebel*; can the riddle of its structure be solved? A conventional commentary would have anchored interpretation in the solid ground of historical and literary criticism. The reader of Qohelet and this commentary might need to send out an SOS and hope for rescue from the Coast Guard, or better yet, the Navy.

Rather than grapple with interpretation, my queer commentary offers the reader six vignettes which explore the polymorphous possibilities of certain words, verses and passages, and which explore their intersections with my own life and sensibilities. It addresses such central questions as does Qohelet like to dress up; what does the speaker do in bed and with whom; what does his hair style tell us about his sexuality and gender; is identity, even a textual one, simple and stable? My commentary does not pretend to be comprehensive, and my six readings are not all necessarily consistent with one another. But who is singular within themselves, transparent to the world around them, simply and straight-forwardly read?

Song of Songs

CHRISTOPHER KING

Many Jews and Christians often wonder how the Song of Songs was included in the Hebrew Scriptures. Its erotic content makes erotophobic Jews and Christians blush with embarrassment over its celebration of the sexual and social outlaw. Christopher King reads the Song of Songs from a queer perspective, noting how it celebrates transgressive eros and exalts a passionate love for the outsider. The man falls in love with a chosen outsider, the Shulamite, and their illicit love is expressed fully between equal partners. Their love reflects an ethic of intimacy rather than gender complementarity. How often queers have heard the rally cry of creationist homophobia: God made Adam and Eve, not Adam and Steve! For King, the Song affirms not only the sexual outlaw but queer ways of loving, desiring and connecting sexually with others.

In 1996, my partner and I celebrated our tenth year together with a ceremony of holy union and blessing, a public eucharistic liturgy to complement a simpler private ritual of covenant that we had shared in the first year of our relationship. Among the scriptural readings that we chose for the occasion were appropriate passages from the Song of Songs, the great poem of the Hebrew scriptures praising a passionate love affair. For me, the liturgy of the word reached its high point with these formidable words from among those passages, words that also stand at the zenith of the whole Song of Songs:

> Bind me as a seal upon your heart,
> a sign upon your arm,
> for love is as fierce as death,
> its jealousy bitter as the grave.
> Even its sparks are a raging fire,
> a devouring flame.
> Great seas cannot extinguish love,
> no river can sweep it away. (8.6–7a)

It astonishes me even now that so few words could sum up so much of our story. The text tells of our deep sense of covenant interconnectedness ('bind me as a seal . . . sign'), a deeply interior unity of life ('upon your heart') that also demands public expression ('upon your arm'). Here is a love 'as fierce as death'. It is both the 'dear love of comrades', which Walt Whitman knew to knit all queer folk together in one vast tribe, and also the particular death-defying love that has given my partner and me the courage to stand together against the perils of living with HIV. 'Great seas' could not swallow up our love during the years that I studied abroad. A 'raging fire', a 'devouring flame', perhaps even a 'flame of God' (*salhebetyah*), this love urges us to live every day with passion for each other and, ultimately, for all of God's people.

What we found in the Song of Songs was an affirmation of love that matched our own experience in poignancy and power. But I must now ask difficult questions. What right did we have to seize upon this poem as a statement, even a vindication, of *queer* love? Does the Song of Songs legitimately belong to two gay men? Can the Song of Songs belong to queer people at all?

At first glance, the Song of Songs might seem to be the biblical book most friendly to a queer-positive reading. Whatever its original genre – whether love poem, covenant allegory or hierogamic hymn – the Song of Songs builds its whole symbolism on a fervent, unashamed enthusiasm for human eros. And, indeed, when read with a fully honest, open-eyed hermeneutic, the Song of Songs yields the Bible's most potent balm for healing one of the great spiritual wounds of Christianity: the inherited fear of sexual desire. At every turn, the Song of Songs upholds embodied human eros as a genuine good, whose true measure is, not its conformity to some external standard of 'nature', but only its capacity to bring joy to the hearts of man and woman.

But it is precisely on this point that the queer reader, however devoted to the Song of Songs' all-lovely lovers, must be alert to a roadblock on the way to a queer interpretation, for we must not forget that the Song of Songs' zeal for embodied, passionate love is directed entirely to that love as shared by *woman and man*. Of all the dimensions of the Song of Songs' narrative context, the one that remains most visible to us today is its situation in a world suffused with the images and reality of opposite-sex desire. Queers seem to be left entirely out of the picture. How, then, are queer believers to 'take back' such a text as this?

A Paradigm for Queer Identity and Action

The discussion will aim to show that, in fact, queer people of faith need not perceive the Song of Songs as unfriendly scriptural terrain, for as we shall see, even if the Song of Songs' two lovers (whom I shall call the Shulamite and her Beloved) are a woman and a man, the text is not principally concerned with extolling the virtues of *heterosexual* love per se. Rather, it celebrates the gift of human love itself, apart from any external measure of its worth – its procreative value, its conformity to natural law, its place in the right relationship of the sexes. Thus loosed from the fetters of an exclusive heterosexism, the Song of Songs can be seen to set forth a paradigm for queer identity and action. It only remains to be seen how this is so.

Both black and beautiful: The chosen outsider and transgressive desire

In the first moments of the Song of Songs, a theme appears that encapsulates so much of the queer experience: the Shulamite as focus of a problem of identity, marginalizing discourses, fascination and repulsion. The first time that the Shulamite speaks specifically about herself, she identifies herself as the object of a collective gaze that is, paradoxically, both enthralled and repelled:

> I am black and beautiful,
>   O daughters of Jerusalem,
>   like the tents of Kedar,
>   like the curtains of Solomon. (1.5)

Whether the Shulamite addresses her listeners here as a dark-skinned territorial foreigner (like Moses' Cushite bride in Ex. 12), as a well-tanned worker in field and vineyard, or even as a lingering apparition of the black goddesses of antiquity, hers is an outsider's voice, speaking as a privileged alien to jealous hometown girls (the 'daughters of Jerusalem'). She is as exotic and elusive as the black shelters of desert nomads ('tents of Kedar'). Yet, she has come as close to the privileges coveted by Jerusalem's social insiders as the 'curtains of Solomon' are to the intimacies of the king's bedchamber.

The Shulamite enters the 'daughters'' field of intense awareness only when they learn of her sexual affair with the coveted Beloved. Once initiated, this love affair alters public perception of the Shulamite. True to Foucault's model, the public 'gaze' of the city daughters fixates on her most distinctive feature (i.e. her blackness), further exaggerating their perception of her as a social 'other':

> Do not gaze at me because I am dark,
>   because the sun has gazed on me. (1.6a)

The Shulamite recognizes that because of her relationship to the Beloved, she has become the subject of a discourse that intensifies her experience of marginality. Having begun merely as a social outsider, she now becomes a taboo person, at once fascinating and forbidden.

The paradoxical convergence of blackness (i.e. outsider status) and beauty (i.e. desirability) in the Shulamite, then, disturbs and puzzles the 'daughters of Jerusalem'. Simultaneously jealous and disapproving, they cannot comprehend what drives the Beloved to pursue this dark-skinned outlander. Or, rather, perceiving the primal allure of the Shulamite with fearful clarity, they cannot risk bringing to conscious awareness its appeal for themselves. Theirs becomes deeply a problem of interpretation – how to reconcile her 'blackness' with their own conflicted mimetic attraction to her beauty.

Significantly, this bedazzling blackness has also been perceived as a hermeneutical problem by the classical Jewish and Christian allegorical readings. In the Christian patristic allegories, for example, the Shulamite's 'blackness' becomes a perpetual sign of her sin. Not surprisingly, this sin is frequently construed to be of a sexual kind, as spiritual *porneia* or adultery against Christ. Indelibly inked into her 'flesh', into her existential density of presence, this black coloration becomes a full-body tattoo narrating her seasons of sexualized spiritual waywardness. Indeed, for Origen, the Shulamite's moral waywardness is the circumstantial cause of her 'blackness'. She has been deeply tanned because she has walked in crooked paths, skew-wise to the rays of the divine Sun of justice. We stand in a similar danger, Origen insists: 'For how can those who are crooked receive that which is straight? We ought, therefore, to hasten to straight ways and to stand fast in the paths of virtue, lest the Sun of Justice, who rises straight overhead, should find us crooked and turned aside, and looking askance at us, we should become black.'[1] Such paths of virtue and vice do not, Origen thinks, exist outside the soul. Rather, they denote the soul's own internal processes of growth or degeneration. They are the soul's own form of life. What else does this mean except that in her infidelity to Christ, the Shulamite – as the primordially unchaste Bride of Christ – is, or rather was in some now-repented life, an ontological deviant. For Origen, the Bride was quite literally 'queer' in her former lifestyle.

For the queer community, it should seem particularly apt that many Christian allegories associate the Shulamite's blackness with the disobedience of the Jews. In these readings, the Shulamite as 'black' denotes the Jews as an intractable, disobedient people. As 'beautiful', predictably, the Shulamite appears as the Church, particularly the Gentile Church, now redeemed from her particular waywardness. In this way, the phrase 'black but beautiful' comes to denote two communities: a straight, righteous community of insiders and a deviant, intractable cluster of outsiders. For these allegories, the move from 'black' to 'beautiful' involves a conversion, a renunciation of an aberrant past.

In seeing something deviant or 'queer' in the Shulamite, the Christian allegorical tradition proves its astuteness, for the Song of Songs does indeed portray her as sexually dangerous and socially 'other'. Yet, because this tradition sits ill at ease with the very notion of deviance, it construes the Shulamite's beauty as standing in tension with her blackness. This fact explains the Christian fathers' preference for the disjunctive rendering of the Hebrew phrase *sehorah 'ani ve-na'vah* as 'black *but* beautiful'. By insinuating such a contrariety into the relation between 'black' and 'beautiful', this interpretive tradition reinforces those dualisms that queer folk openly and vocally challenge – between sexuality and spirituality, between freedom and nature, between deviance and goodness, between outcast and insider.

Yet, in the more satisfactory reading of the verse, the Shulamite is 'black and beautiful'. Blackness and beauty appear as complements, not antagonistic qualities. Thus, what the classical allegories do not see, indeed what they labour to obscure, is the causal link established by the Song of Songs between the Shulamite's blackness and the Beloved's attraction to her. This 'blackness', the most visible sign of her outsider status – her sexuality, freedom and deviance – now becomes the most dazzling quality in her multifaceted beauty. The Song of Songs does not let the Shulamite's queerness vanish away into the consensus normality of the collective. It defends her 'otherness' as a more sublime standard of perfection.

As a class underling or territorial alien, the Shulamite's social location as outsider makes her a prohibited object of the Beloved's erotic favour. Yet, the Beloved showers her with his passionate attention in spite of this prohibition. Indeed, he pursues her largely because of his attraction to the very feature

---

1 Origen, *Commentary on the Song of Songs* 2.2.

that is the deepest sign of that prohibition. The Song of Songs, therefore, does not speak abstractly of passionate desire but of a specific sort of desire – a yearning and a pursuit whose object is not an insider but someone on the social margins, not a neighbour but the forbidden other. Thus, the romance of the Shulamite and the Beloved begins with the violation of a fixed social boundary. Their love affair, like that of all queer lovers, is essentially transgressive.

Indeed, so transgressive is the eros felt by the lovers that it propels them altogether beyond the ordinary routines of moral decision-making. The Song of Songs does not portray the sexual trespasses of the Shulamite and Beloved merely as matters of individual preference. This is no 'lifestyle choice' for the lovers. Why, then, do they risk the pursuit of a dangerous, socially explosive love affair? The answer is both simple and, for the Song's queer reader, manifest: *they are driven to it by the sheer desirableness of one other.*

With the Shulamite's lover, this erotic compulsion finds a poetic outlet in the language of inebriation and festal excess:

> I eat my honeycomb with my honey,
>   I drink my wine with my milk.
>
> Eat, friends, drink,
>   and be drunk with love. (5. 1b)

This love not only fulfils beyond mere satisfaction. It entices the lover with its luxuriance, drawing him irresistibly into a drunken whirl.

The Shulamite, too, is tormented – but deliciously! – by a desire over which she has utterly no control:

> Upon my bed at night
>   I sought him whom my soul loves;
> I sought him, but found him not;
>   I called him, but he gave no answer.
> 'I will rise now and go about the city,
>   in the streets and in the squares;
> I will seek him whom my soul loves.'
>   I sought him, but found him not.
> The sentinels found me,
>   as they went about in the city.
> 'Have you seen him whom my soul loves?' (3.1–3)

The Shulamite's longing eros for her Beloved brings on an acute delirium, a 'fever' or 'faint' (5.8) of lovesickness. It disturbs her sleep, drives her by night to the city streets, and leads her almost unwittingly into those dangerous brushes with the law (the 'sentinels').

Standards, rationales, social norms, codes of conduct, and reflective moral reason – all these scatter before the heat of the lovers' desire like so many clouds in the noonday sun. Nowhere in the Song of Songs does the Shulamite or the Beloved seek out any external grounds or justifications for their love affair. Nor does the Song of Songs try to interpret their love affair in light of any such rationales. The lovers ask no questions of right and wrong. Even the classical pieties surrounding fecundity, procreation and sexual duty to the family disappear from the Song of Songs (cf. vv. 1.6; 8.5, 12). In short, the lovers altogether transcend the limits of socially constructed 'nature' (as *physis* – the 'way things ought to be') in pursuit of a higher 'nature' that is truer to the vision enlivened by their desire.

In the final analysis, the Song of Songs presents us with an insight already known and spoken out loud by queer folk: *Reciprocal desire is a law unto itself.* In the Song of Songs, neither 'nature' nor gender can finally lay claim on the allegiance of truly well-ordered desire. Only a mutually beheld allure, an attractiveness that opens up the possibility of a coequal response between lovers, holds the last word in matters of love, sexuality and human eros. Ultimately, then, eros – passionate yearning for union with the beauty of another – reigns supreme in the moral universe of the Song of Songs. When true to its own energy, eros requires no justification and needs make no defence for its movements.

My beloved is mine, and I am his: Subversive equality and erotic autonomy

The Song of Songs does not uniquely grace the Shulamite with beauty, nor is it only the Beloved who expresses a desire for union with such beauty. Rather, the fervent love of the Shulamite and her Beloved is fuelled by a real parity of desire, an erotic symmetry arising from their reciprocal share in a loveliness that is irresistible. Each lover is, in other words, drawn to a 'sameness' – an essential similarity – seen in the beauty, the sexiness, of the other. The dynamism might be heterosexual, but its structure is definitely homoerotic: *an attraction of sames.* By unveiling this 'queer' dimension in the love life of the Shulamite and the Beloved, the Song of Songs not only champions the dignity of queer passion but upholds it as a model for any love worth pursuing.

The Song of Songs lets us witness this deep reciprocity, this 'sameness', in the exchanges of the lovers themselves. The Shulamite, for example, says of her Beloved:

Let him kiss me with the kisses of his mouth!
For your love is better than wine,
. . .
therefore the maidens love you
. . .
    rightly do they love you. (1.2–4)

His appearance is like Lebanon,
    choice as the cedars.
His speech is most sweet,
    and he is altogether desirable. (5.15b–16)

Concerning the Shulamite, we hear the Beloved say:

If you do not know,
O fairest among women,
follow the tracks of the flock
and pasture your kids
beside the shepherds' tents. (1.8)

You are beautiful as Tirzah, my love,
comely as Jerusalem,
terrible as an army with banners.
Turn away your eyes from me,
for they overwhelm me! (6.4–5a)

How fair and pleasant you are,
O loved one, delectable maiden! (7.6)

The mutual likeness of beauties is one of the emphatic themes of the Song of Songs. Each lover acknowledges the other's beauty to be all-surpassing. And each holds out this beauty as the deepest proof that the desire is legitimate.

This attraction is seen where the Beloved and the Shulamite, drawn in desire to one another's beauty, are caught up in an exchange of mutual adoration. The Song of Songs is largely a record of this dialectic, and it reaches a particularly brilliant visibility in passages such as these:

Ah, you are beautiful, my love;
ah, you are beautiful;
your eyes are doves.
Ah, you are beautiful, my beloved,
truly lovely. (1.15–16)

As a lily among the brambles,
so is my love among maidens.

As an apple tree among the trees of the wood,
so is my beloved among young men. (2.2–3)

In a circling dance of acclamation, the lovers declare their pleasure in one another's beauty. In this way, their mutual attraction flows like an alternating current from the fundamental 'sameness' of their shared desirability. So intense, indeed, does this mutual perception of 'sameness' become that the Shulamite and the Beloved begin to see one another as 'brother' (8.1) and 'sister' (4.9–12; 5.1–2), a recognition of a shared likeness that can be expressed only in metaphors of family resemblance.

Love and lovemaking in the Song of Songs, therefore, become a 'union of sames'. In this union, the lovers attain an experience of synergistic merging that heterosexist ontologies usually reserve for 'opposites' alone, whether genital complements or gender polarities. Certainly, the Shulamite and the

Beloved do not lose their identity as female and male, but the Song of Songs refuses to appropriate this difference as a category with any ultimate social, moral or metaphysical significance. The text thus purifies their love affair of the hierarchicalism and differences of power typical of traditional relationships between men and women. And by implication, it levels the very basis for making moral distinctions between kinds of human love, desire and sexual relation. The Song of Songs allows us to see that, morally speaking, queer love – precisely because it is love – is the 'same' as heterosexual love.

It is not surprising, then, that the Song of Songs holds up as one of its preeminent values the coequality of erotic response. In the moral world of the Song of Songs, this equality seeks its principle in the lovers' erotic autonomy, in the power to choose to live sexually as one wills. We see this autonomy in the actions and words of both the Shulamite and the Beloved.

The Beloved reveals his autonomy through his freedom of movement, a constant coming and going that signifies his independence from confinement:

> The voice of my beloved!
>   Look, he comes,
> leaping upon the mountains,
>   bounding over the hills. (2.8)

This mode of autonomy is erotic inasmuch as it allows the Beloved to visit the Shulamite by night for secret trysts ('My beloved is like a gazelle / or a young stag. / Look, there he stands / behind our wall, / gazing in at the windows' (2.9)) or to withdraw from her so as to tantalize her sexually ('I opened to my beloved, / but my beloved had turned and was gone. / My soul failed me (5.6)).

The Shulamite, by contrast, does not enjoy this same physical liberty; she is kept at home behind walls, curtains and lattices (2.9) and forced to tend the family vineyards (1.6). Nevertheless, she maintains a stance of inner liberty, laying bold claim to free erotic agency:

> Solomon had a vineyard at Baal-hamon;
>   he entrusted the vineyard to keepers;
>   each one was to bring for its fruit a thousand pieces of silver.
> My vineyard, my very own, is for myself;
>   you, O Solomon, may have the thousand,
>   and the keepers of the fruit two hundred! (8.11–12)

In Solomon's vineyard, the Shulamite finds a symbol of her own fecund sexuality. Yet, whereas Solomon disposes of his vineyard and its fruits as his own property, the Shulamite asserts exclusive rights to her sexual energy. Her 'vineyard' with its fruits is her 'very own', for herself. The Shulamite, in other words, will not allow the reader to regard her as another's sexual possession or as a mere vessel for procreation. She is, by her own strength of resolve, free to love as she chooses – free to love as she is compelled by the innate directives of her own passion.

To follow the example of the Shulamite is fundamentally a 'queer' choice, for she cheerfully disregards any extrinsic norm whereby her choice to love as she pleases might be condemned. The Shulamite fearlessly and joyfully proclaims her erotic autonomy and her freedom from procreative mandates. In so doing, the Shulamite holds out a liberating message not only for women but especially for the queer community. It is a simple message that is, nevertheless, difficult for sexism of any kind to assimilate: *When moved by reciprocal desire, men and women have the right to love as they will, whom they will, when they will, and how they will.* A more revolutionary word of sexual freedom could scarcely be spoken, yet here we find it exemplified in a sacred text that, with respect to its mystical value, lies at the heart of the biblical canon.

The erotic autonomy of the Shulamite and the Beloved does not restrict their capacity to relate to each other unselfishly. On the contrary, it enables them to recognize and freely to pursue the mandate latent in their desire for one another. It makes possible a genuine self-offering in which each belongs fully to the other:

> My beloved is mine and I am his;
>   he pastures his flock among the lilies. (2.16)

> I am my beloved's and my beloved is mine;
>   he pastures his flock among the lilies. (6.3)

Notice the pure reciprocity in these two passages. No hierarchy or asymmetry of power can be inferred from them. If the Shulamite had said only, 'I am my beloved's and my beloved is mine', some superiority in the status of the Beloved could be inferred from her word order. Yet, the Shulamite has already underscored her own prior possession of the Beloved: 'My beloved is mine and I am his.' Each owns the other in precisely the same degree and proportion, in accordance with their ability to honour one another's personal autonomy and erotic freedom.

The lovers' mutual exchange of desires, then, becomes a mutual gift of selfhood. Not only do the Shulamite and the Beloved give themselves to one another without holding back; they also each receive their own new and truest identity from the other's gift of desire: 'I am my beloved's, / and his desire is for me' (7.10). Who does the Shulamite declare herself to be? She is her beloved's. In other words, she experiences the Beloved's desire as an activity *pro me*, an erotic grace-gift in which her new identity comes into being. The Song of Songs, therefore, presumes aetiology of the human self in which true identity grows, not from obedience to iron-clad laws of natural morality, but from pursuit of one's profoundest desire for union with another.

The Song of Songs knows the queer truth that love, desire and sexual life are given for the full blossoming of human persons, their growth unfolding in and through soul-and-body union with others whose likeness – 'sameness' – they also bear. And the integrity of the developmental process, so the Song of Songs implies, depends upon all persons having the fullest freedom to follow eros where it leads, for only unconditional erotic autonomy makes true and complete self-offering possible in the first place. It is this liberty to love as one wills that queer people of faith must finally claim as a fundamental principle of human well-being and, truly, of salvation itself. With justification, then, queer men and women of faith may take heart that the Song of Songs so completely sanctions the vision of human selfhood and relationship implicit in queer desire itself.

To My Mother's House: Social Oppression and the Struggle for Reconciliation

In their relation to each other, the lovers are 'same', not 'opposites' in polar complementarity. They have voluntarily surrendered any differences of power or status that might inhibit their union. Yet, paradoxically, in the course of eschewing difference, they have made themselves 'different' – deviant – in the public eye. Pursuing a vision of equality in desire and reciprocal self-offering, they have made themselves vulnerable to exclusion as outsiders, as 'queers'. Like queer folk of today and every age, then, the two lovers in the Song of Songs do not enjoy the benefits of public, cultural, or social sanction. On the contrary, their love is expressly forbidden and opposed by the custodians of the social economy.

Three representatives of this public economy dominate the social universe of the Song of Songs: the city sentinels, the Shulamite's brothers, and her mother. Each of these parties has its own reasons for disapproving of the love affair that the Song of Songs praises as exemplary. For these civil and familial powers, the public fictions of purity, property and filial duty hold greater authority than the truth articulated in the passion of lovers. We shall examine these in turn, for each illuminates the oppression that queer women and men face today. And in the responses of the Shulamite and her Beloved, we find an appropriate pattern for queer response.

On the fringes of the Shulamite's social experience are certain 'sentinels', night watchmen whose violence she will suffer and survive. She first encounters these men as she roams the streets, deliriously seeking her lover (3.1–3). When the Shulamite first describes this meeting, she innocuously remarks that the sentinels merely 'found' her. Later, though, she reveals the more violent truth behind her euphemism:

Making their rounds in the city,
    the sentinels found me;
they beat me, they wounded me,
    they took away my mantle
    those sentinels of the walls. (5.7)

The very men who ought to protect the Shulamite have savagely attacked her. Not only have they thrashed, bruised, and perhaps raped her, they have also stolen her outer garment, exposing her body to the physical elements and, more seriously, unveiling her shame to the elemental forces of public scorn.

But what accounts for such enormous brutality? Presumably, the sentinels have mistaken the Shulamite for a prostitute, walking the streets in search of a john. She is thus marked as a sexual outlaw and so becomes a target of the law's enforcers. Acting as guardians of public decency, then, the sentinels find in the Shulamite a fitting victim for a violence that, so the text implies, is itself sexually charged. In this way, the Shulamite becomes a scapegoat for the sexual hypocrisies of the 'city' that the sentinels police; their ruthlessness merely brings to fruition the germinal envy that we have already felt simmering beneath the Jerusalem daughters' 'gaze'.

In the Shulamite's experience of victimization, we can find an almost exact correlate of the queer experience of 'bashing', for the queer community is truly a 'peculiar people', a tribe of sexual outlaws. Its members, consequently, in so many ways suffer the wrath of the collective towards those whose sexual identity it simultaneously vilifies and envies. This wrath takes its most explicit form in acts of verbal abuse and physical violence – taunts, threats, beatings, killings – but it is also endemic to the structures of heterosexist society itself. All this brutality is most often unleashed upon queer people when, like the Shulamite, we dare to reveal our sexual selves, our queer desire, in public places, on the 'streets', inside the city 'walls'.

Queer folk must remember that by taking the Shulamite's side in these struggles with violence, the Song of Songs also condemns the agents of violence. Heterosexism with its fear, rage and wrath will not find any justification in the Song of Songs. The Shulamite's response to this violence, moreover, is a model for the queer reader. Rather than suppressing her own voice or internalizing the shame that her attackers try to heap upon her, the Shulamite speaks her outrage 'out loud'. Through the Song of Songs itself, she tells every reader the truth about her mistreatment. The Shulamite never loses heart, never ceases to persist. And in spite of all her suffering, she continues to pursue her love with confidence in its perfect justice (3.4; 5.8).

If the Shulamite must endure the grave brutality of the sentinels, she must also cope with the anger of her brothers, her 'mother's sons'. The Shulamite's brothers are angry with their sister because she claims sole property rights over her sexual 'vineyard'. But her brothers do not acknowledge her prerogative:

My mother's sons were angry with me;
   they made me keeper of the vineyards,
   but my own vineyard I have not kept! (1.6b)

The Shulamite sets the family vineyards, which she has faithfully cultivated, in ironic counterpoint to her sexual 'vineyard'. The family property – that she will tend well and true, but, she declares, she would rather risk incurring her brothers' anger than lose her rights over her own erotic property. Her tone is teasing, but her sense is deeply serious.

Where the Shulamite and Beloved see their love affair as a shared feast of bodies, of beauties and of desires, the 'brothers' perceive it only as a violation of the family's stake in the body and the fertility of the Shulamite. Thus, they are angry because she has not 'kept' her sexual property to herself. She has offered it freely to her Beloved, in keeping with the parity of erotic power that each acknowledges in the other. Once the brothers know of this, their imagination runs wild:

Catch us the foxes,
  the little foxes,
  that ruin the vineyards –
for our vineyards are in blossom. (2.15)

These 'foxes' are the many lovers that the brothers fear have ruined the Shulamite's virtue and, more centrally, her value as a family commodity. The brothers' anxiety is as palpable as their avidity.

The reader, of course, knows that the Shulamite is possessed by a single-minded fidelity to her Beloved. Yet, the brothers cannot conceive of a sexual liberty that is not also fundamentally promiscuous. Their response to the Shulamite's misbehaviour is predictably restrictive:

If she is a wall,
  we will build upon her a battlement of silver;
but if she is a door,
  we will enclose her with boards of cedar. (8.9)

Had the Shulamite acted as a 'wall' in defence of her virtue (and their interests!), the brothers would have honoured and dignified her, though their honour sounds more like pedestalizing, their 'battlement of silver' more like a gilded cage. Yet, they now fear that she has become a 'door', opening to all comers. Their solution to this apparent problem is to 'enclose' their sister 'with boards of cedar'. They intend, in other words, to confine her in ways that will restrict her freedom to love as she chooses.

In the interaction between the Shulamite and her brothers, queer readers will find a mirror of their own experience. The 'brothers' reflect the image of all those social and cultural forces that would subdue human eros to their own interests – whether social stability, economic security or the continuity of family lines. Queer women and men, however, have renounced the myth that these interests are ultimately compelling. We have, in fact, abandoned the very notion that eros needs to be subdued at all. It is a move that not only opens us to charges of promiscuity but that also makes us vulnerable to those regimes of control (e.g. repressive laws and customs, shame-inducing mores) put into place by those whose interests we threaten.

Finally, at the centre of the social universe of the Song of Songs is the mother of the Shulamite. Throughout the Song of Songs, the Shulamite hints at her estrangement from her mother. At first, for example, she can only dream of taking her Beloved home and finding parental welcome there:

I would lead you and bring you
  into the house of my mother,
  and into the chamber of the one who bore me. (8.2)

The Shulamite even fantasizes of having the mother's permission to share the same bed with the partner that the Shulamite herself has chosen. It is an intimate desire felt today by many queer men and women, who too often know the pain of hearing words of rejection – 'Not under my roof!'

The 'mother', the 'mother's house', and the 'mother's breast' all embody the parental blessing, the domestic security and bliss, that the Shulamite has put at risk by pursuing an illicit love affair. But why should the Shulamite fear her mother's rejection? It is because the mother prizes her daughter's purity. She is attached to it as to an ideal:

> My dove, my perfect one, is the only one,
>   the darling of her mother,
>   flawless to her that bore her. (6.9a)

The Beloved recognizes here that his 'perfect one' (the Shulamite) is also her mother's flawless darling. She is perfect and pure to each: to the mother, because she is domestic and chaste; to the Beloved, because she is sexually desirable, available, and wild.

These two sets of reasons, however, simply cannot be reconciled. For the Beloved, the Shulamite's perfection consists precisely in the ready sexuality that, for her mother, is incompatible with the purity of a dutiful daughter. Were the mother to learn the truth about the nature of the Shulamite's desire for her Beloved – and certainly of their sexual trysts – she could never again view her daughter in the same way. 'Coming out', as it were, would shatter the mother's pristine image of the Shulamite. The mother would then face a choice that the Shulamite fears; she may either reject her daughter, or she may adjust her own values and accept a new and more truthful image of her daughter.

The Shulamite presents to queer folk a model of persistence, boldness and endurance in seeking out her love. Yet, even though she spurns and defies all social restrictions upon the free pursuit of her love, she does not remain locked into a fixed gesture of rebellion. On the contrary, she longs to return in reconciliation to her mother's house, hand in hand with her beloved:

> O that you were like a brother to me,
>   who nursed at my mother's breast!
> If I met you outside, I would kiss you,
>   and no one would despise me.
> I would lead you and bring you
>   into the house of my mother,
>   and into the chamber of the one who bore me. (8.1–2a)

Given the Shulamite's social matrix and family ties, public intimacy with her lover would make her an object of derision. Were her Beloved only a 'brother' – a kinsman with whom she may freely associate – she could meet him in the streets, kiss him, and take him home to her mother. Their degree of kinship would, of course, make an erotic love life untenable, but the Shulamite's dream of public acceptance and domestic reconciliation briefly overshadows such considerations.

At first glance, the Shulamite might appear merely to be indulging in wishful thinking here. She shows no clear determination to pursue a definite plan of action. But, earlier in the text – at a point that actually speaks of a later event

– we discover that the Shulamite does, at last, find the courage to bring her Beloved home:

Scarcely had I passed them [the sentinels],
    when I found him whom my soul loves.
I held him, and would not let him go
    until I brought him into my mother's house,
    and into the chamber of her that conceived me. (3.4)

The Shulamite's hope, then, is to win from her mother (and perhaps from her estranged brothers, her 'mother's sons') the gift of acceptance and reconciliation. She acts boldly to fulfil her hope. Surviving the violence of the sentinels, she lays hold not only upon her courage but also upon the Beloved himself, leading him – against his will? – to her mother's house.

In the 'mother', queer folk will see the face of all those persons and communities – loved ones, parents, churches – whose accepting embrace we long for and whose rejection we dread. Queer men and women know well how painful and embittering it can be to suffer rejection by parents or by whole communities of faith. Equally, with the Shulamite, we know how intense can be the urgency for the 'mother's' full acceptance, for full admission to the households of faith and family. The Song of Songs develops a realistic portrayal of such rejection, of such pain, and of such urgency for acceptance. And to queer readers especially, it offers a paradigm for a fearless and truthful ministry of reconciliation towards all those 'mothers' whose love does not yet know how to comprehend our desire.

This discussion has only begun to explore the positive implications of the Song of Songs for queer women and men. True, the Song of Songs celebrates the love, desire and sexual life of a man and a woman. Yet, it praises it for reasons that ought to prove deeply challenging to anyone who hopes to find in it any support for heterosexist mores, for through the words and examples of its characters, the Song of Songs sustains a moral worldview in which:

The sexual and social outlaw is a preferred object of loving desire and sexual interest.

Beauty alone is a sufficient motive for love, desire and sexual union.

All persons have the right to love as they will according to the dictates of reciprocal desire.

An ethic of intimacy, rather than gender complementarity, ought to be central in human love relationships.

Authentic eros must be grounded in a certain homoeroticism, an attraction of 'same'.

The human person is essentially erotic in nature.

Love and sexual life are most perfectly expressed in love between fully equal partners and in fully mutual self-offering of body and soul.

Persecution or oppression of the sexual outlaw is unjust and morally wrong.

The sexually marginalized person has a responsibility to work courageously and persistently for justice, tolerance and acceptance.

The astonishing fact that the Song of Songs celebrates socially transgressive eros ought already to secure its status as a valuable biblical apologetic for queer identity. But more than this, the Song of Songs exalts a love that, like the love of queer women and men, presumes not only the inherent worth of human desire but also its moral sufficiency as a motive for the fullest union of life between human beings. Such love will, inevitably, cause social friction and discord. These difficulties, however, arise not because queer eros is inherently unjust. On the contrary, they arise because it is so acutely just that it calls the social constructions of nature, culture and law to a painful but healing crisis.

The Song of Songs sets this eros as our ideal – a passionate love that prefers the outsider, that is entranced by sexual difference, that answers the call of beauty without vacillation, and that honours the authority of its own strength. Knowing this, queer folk have every reason to take up the Song of Songs with confidence that it affirms our own ways of loving, desiring and bonding sexually with others. Indeed, we have every cause to take up the Song of Songs as a banner of our love, which is truly as fierce as death.

Isaiah

TIMOTHY KOCH

And I said: 'Woe is me! I am lost, for I am a man of unclean lips, and I live among a people of unclean lips; yet my eyes have seen the King, the LORD of hosts!'

Then one of the seraphs flew to me, holding a live coal that had been taken from the altar with a pair of tongs. The seraph touched my mouth with it and said: 'Now that this has touched your lips, your guilt has departed and your sin is blotted out.' Then I heard the voice of the Lord saying, 'Whom shall I send, and who will go for us?' And I said, 'Here am I; send me!' (Isa. 6.5–8)

Introduction: Coal (Mining) as Hermeneutical Metaphor

In considering this passage from Isaiah's prophetic call, let us place ourselves in the position, not of the 'man of unclean lips' – surely a role that many LGBT persons are perpetually cast in – but in that of the *seraph*! Let us consider this scene from the perspective of the winged angel, whose job it is to select the appropriate coal from the altar and somehow cauterize Isaiah's sinfulness. What is involved here is selecting the one coal from among many, the one that is yet 'live', can be handled by tongs, and will do the job necessary. This is the seraphic task of those of us engaged in biblical studies on behalf of the LGBT community: to choose the right coal for the right situation.

I myself come from coal-mining country in Southwestern Pennsylvania. My grandfather was a coal miner who, from his adolescence and for several long decades, descended into dangerous bituminous mines before dawn, and emerged from those same mines (often after dark) bringing up coal for 'the Company'. It was hard, dangerous work, and, in fact, my grandfather contracted and eventually died from Black Lung Disease. Coal mining is part of my family and culture, and it provides a powerful metaphor for my work in queer biblical scholarship. As with coal mining, studying biblical texts is best undertaken to unearth *useful* resources for our lives. And although the *processes* we as LGBT persons use of surveying, digging, extracting and refining may be shared with many others who study the Bible, *we* are the ones to decide where we will survey, what we will dig for, what we want to extract from these texts, and how we will refine them for our use.[1]

---

1 It is when we cede our own authority to 'the Company' (e.g. the Church, the Academy, our Tradition) to decide how, when, where and why we will mine a biblical

Let us consider the following, abbreviated geological survey of land in Western Pennsylvania that was mined in the nineteenth and twentieth centuries, beginning from the earth's surface and extending downwards:

Tionesta sandstone, 50 feet.
Coal and bituminous shale, 3 inches.
Brown and blue shale, 1 to 3 feet.
Limestone chert (ferruginous), 2 feet.
Coal, 12 inches.
Light coloured shale, 6 to 8 feet.
Argillaceous sandstone, 2 feet.
Light coloured shale, 12 to 13 feet.
Bituminous shale and coal, 4 feet.
Blue sandy shale, 6 feet.
Flaggy sandstone (argillaceous at top), 75 feet or more. (see Hazen 1908)

What is immediately apparent is this: if one is looking for coal, there are numerous other materials (sandstone, shale, limestone) that one has to break through to get to the coal, and minerals – of use in other contexts – will be of no interest to one seeking to mine coal. Just because you say to me, 'Yes, but what about the blue sandy shale? You just can't ignore that! What are you going to do about it?!' I am not thereby required to drop my search for coal to deal with blue sandy shale! If someone else wishes to mine shale, then so be it.

To make this perhaps a little clearer in the field of biblical studies: if I am seeking something useful for LGBT persons that might be found in the Bible, then of necessity I will be doing *highly selective work*, and I may or may not be particularly interested in and/or willing to spend time on everything that I encounter; moreover, because what I want may well be embedded in other materials, I *need* my own energy for my own work. So just because someone else wants me to 'reconcile' Leviticus 20 or Romans 1 with my homosexual lifestyle, I am not obligated to postpone my work on Isaiah until I adequately acquit myself to their satisfaction. In fact, as with the coal miner and the shale, I have the full option to clear away and/or blast through others' agendas that get in the way.[2]

---

text and to choose what we will look for, what we will disregard and how we will use these resources, that we find ourselves at risk. For example, we spend extraordinary energy in trying to find biblical texts that will indicate that it is acceptable for us to be homosexual, or, failing that, in attempting to demonstrate that biblical texts condemning homosexuality are misconstrued by others. Because this is not an agenda of our own choosing, we end up breathing in amazing quantities of toxic gas, our strength is sapped, and our homes are no better heated in the end . . . and for what? So that others can continue to tell us that we are *still* wrong and must conform ourselves to (their version of) the biblical texts or resign ourselves to an eternity in hell?!

2 OK, OK: this is not perhaps an 'environmentally friendly' approach if extended to the actual process of coal mining (which was, in fact, never a very environmentally friendly endeavour at its best). But I simply cannot imagine my grandfather or his company feeling the least bit morally or ethically bound to fill their trolleys with sandstone or with slate because coal-phobes wanted them to have to deal with those materials instead!

This somewhat protracted discussion is important, I believe, even when the task at hand is to offer a brief commentary on just one biblical book (in this case, Isaiah). We, as LGBT persons, come with our own questions, our own need for resources, our own limited energies; when we regard biblical texts as *resources* for us (like coal) and not as some kind of Answer Book that will tell us definitively how to live our lives, whether or not we are acceptable, and what the Divine does or does not think of us, then we are free to focus on obtaining true value from the text and to disentangle from others who either do not share a similar freedom or do not wish us to be free in this way. What is more, we can begin to see Bible-bullying when and where it occurs and name it as the attempt to subvert our own agenda through intimidation, force and coercion.[3]

Of course, this presupposes that we come with our own questions for the text, not, as we are often instructed to do, coming to the text in order to be questioned. So what *are* we seeking, and why turn to the prophetic literature in the Hebrew Bible, specifically to the book of Isaiah? Beyond the fact that a few of its verses are cited by bullies to condemn us, the Hebrew Bible is a readily accessible and ultimately viable source of hope, power, inspiration and joy for us, even for those who do not consider themselves members of any organized religion, but who can appreciate powerful poetry, provocative prose and meditations upon life and death. We can find our own concerns, emotions, goals and fears reflected throughout these pages; we can find role models, cautionary tales, ribald stories and points to ponder that can illuminate our own journeys.

Moreover, prophetic literature is, among other things, 'Justice Literature'. It is literature of protest, of indignation, of strategy, of calls for the end of hypocrisy – particularly 'in the name of God' and as practised by religious persons and institutions. Time and again, the prophets of ancient Israel issue a 'Word from the Lord' that places the welfare of humanity and creation over ritual observances: a poignant message for LGBT persons who are kept out of clergy, priesthood or rabbinate because of fears that we might defile the sanctity of these religious bodies. And, indeed, prophetic literature is utterly *dramatic*! Where else can we find holy and revered figures who use their naked bodies, their tears, their clothing, pubic hair, whining, and their own sense of public displays and performances as ways of obeying God's directives and reaching the lives of their fellow countryfolk? See, respectively, Isaiah 20; 2 Kings 8; Jeremiah 13; Isaiah 7; Ezekiel 9; and Ezekiel 4, among many other references to dramatic prophetic activity.

And, more germane to our considerations here, is the book of Isaiah. Located first among the major prophetic books in both the Hebrew and Christian Bibles, and occupying a special place in both Jewish and Christian thought, study and

---

3 And bullying it is. Consider the threats used: hell, denial of tenure, denial of or termination of clerical status, marginalization of scholarly work, castigation in the popular press, even picketing at public events. See the insightful study by S. Harris and G. F. Petrie (2003). By setting aside Pissing Contests about what the Bible 'really means', we can move on with creating the world that we want to inhabit. For a discussion of such 'contests', see T. R. Koch (2001b).

piety, the book covers in its 66 chapters a vast number of themes, and offers perspectives ranging from condemnation of its audience to the hope of a glorious, new future. Its messianic and apocalyptic aspirations have fuelled Jewish and Christian imaginations, hopes and fears for millennia. And more than a few queer women and men have thrilled to Handel's *Messiah*, with its liberal use of texts from Isaiah. Perhaps for me as a queer Christian and biblical scholar, I find that the dominant themes of newness and renewal – of a new song and a new creation, and a new way of doing business, handling relationships and carrying out religious activity – so prevalent in the latter sections of this book are what bring me back to Isaiah and afford to me and to others a vision for a loving future world, a vision without which we all perish.

Some Very Basic Isaiah Scholarship[4]

One of the very first things that is put forward when the book of Isaiah is considered critically (that is, textually, literarily and historically), is how it offers ample evidence of multiple authorships and redactions over a long period of time, spanning centuries. It is not unusual to hear or read of 'First Isaiah', 'Second (or Deutero-) Isaiah' and even 'Third Isaiah'; these designations provide a convenient shorthand for describing three distinct strands of style, concern and historical connections within the entire book. The corresponding divisions are typically, if not very carefully, marked off as Isaiah 1–39; Isaiah 40–55; and Isaiah 56–66.

Some of those who have dismissed (if not ridiculed) attempts to divide the book of Isaiah in this way accuse scholars of lacking faith in the possibilities of predictive prophecy, essentially arguing that the only reason scholars want to talk of First, Second and Third Isaiahs is because they cannot allow that the original Isaiah ben Amoz could have prophesied events with such specificity (particularly with respect to the Persian leader, Cyrus) several centuries into the future. Joseph Blenkinsopp, in his Anchor Bible commentary, offers this rejoinder:

> For the majority of critical scholars this view of the matter [of multiple authors writing in different periods of time within the book of Isaiah] is not, as conservative polemicists argue, dictated by a disposition to rule out the possibility of predictive prophecy. Critical commentators for whom this is still an issue would probably want to ask why inspiration should be denied to *anonymous* biblical authors. And in the most debated case, the authorship of chs. 40–66, predictive prophecy would mean, for example, that Isaiah, active in the eighth century BCE, was comforting his people in view of a disaster – the fall of Jerusalem and deportation – that was still a century and a half in the future, a not very plausible scenario. (2000: 82, emphasis original)

---

4 Excellent resources, including thorough bibliographies of Isaianic studies and scholarship, can be found in works such as J. N. Oswalt (1986, 1998); B. S. Childs (2001); G. M. Tucker (2001); C. R. Seitz (2001); J. Blenkinsopp (2000, 2002 and 2003).

For those scholars (and their number approaches a critical consensus) that affirm multiple, original authorships of various parts of Isaiah, there are yet further discussions that sound rather like 'What parts belong to which Isaiah?' One example to illustrate the complexity of this issue can be drawn from Susan Ackerman, who assigns chapters 1–12 and 28–32 to First Isaiah; sets aside chapters 36–9 as essentially copied from 2 Kings; places chapters 34–5 with the oracles of Second Isaiah found in chapters 40–55; and identifies chapters 24–7 with chapters 56–66, under the rubric of Third Isaiah. This still leaves chapters 13–23 and 33; the former, Ackerman sees as largely being composed contemporaneously with First Isaiah (though not in line with his thought), and chapter 33 she identifies as 'a late composition' close in time to Third Isaiah (1998: 169).

What can be distilled from these efforts is that there are at least three major strands of thought, perspective and theology woven into the pages of the book of Isaiah. In incredibly broad terms, one strand of Isaian prophecy ('First Isaiah') addresses Judah during the time of the divided monarchy and prior to the fall of Israel to Assyria and Judah to Babylon, and warns strongly against transferring dependence from God to foreign alliances and political manœuvring. The second strand speaks to the impending return from exile of the people of Judah, and the new peace that will result in the reconstituted nation. The work attributed to a Third Isaiah addresses a people *after* their return from exile, when they have found poverty, famine and death – rather than a land newly flowing with milk and honey; here, God is sought out for a miraculous, even apocalyptic resolution to the people's misery.[5]

A Queer Reading of Isaiah

In this chapter, I suggest that queers need not make a choice of which way to read, understand or construe the book of Isaiah. I do believe that we will most often find it useful to be informed by the scholarship that identifies the various stages of development in this book, but not bound by it in how we mine the pages of its text. In taking this approach, we are in good company. Christianity has lifted isolated pericopes, verses and even half-verses from this book, irrespective of their original context and the intent of *any* of the three or more Isaiahs, and formed complex theologies therefrom. Consider this one example

---

5 Even with this barely distilled discussion of the strands of this book, we must remember that we nevertheless have in our possession a *single* book, called Isaiah, that is canonical in its final, redacted form for both Jews and Christians. This has led other scholars to ask questions of this text that are related to how the whole of it is composed, what themes recur throughout the text, and what are the means by which the redactors sewed up all the pieces together. Katheryn Pfisterer Darr, in her work, *Isaiah's Vision and the Family of God*, operates from the assertion that those who begin reading at Isaiah 1.1 and continue straight on through to Isaiah 66.24 ('sequential readers') 'discover unfolding themes, motifs, etc., that are likely overlooked in the course of purely pericopal readings' (1994: 169). Darr's work focuses specifically on children, women and birth imagery as it functions metaphorically – and therefore *strategically* – across the book of Isaiah.

from the seventh chapter of Isaiah: the prophet is sent to King Ahaz to tell him
not to fear the king of Aram and the king of Israel who have plotted together to
attack Judah. Ahaz is invited by God to ask for a sign, and demurs. This proves
annoying to God, who decides to give Ahaz a sign nonetheless:

> Look, the young woman ['virgin', in AV] is with child and shall bear a son,
> and shall name him Immanuel. He shall eat curds and honey by the time
> he knows how to refuse the evil and choose the good. For before the child
> knows how to refuse the evil and choose the good, the land before whose
> two kings you are in dread will be deserted. (Isa. 7.14–16)[6]

Christians have plucked a 'virgin giving birth to a child called Immanuel'
from any reference to Ahaz, curds, honey or the king of Aram and Israel,
and applied it wholesale as a predictive-prophecy-come-true about Jesus of
Nazareth. Why should we as queers not feel a similar freedom to pluck from
these texts (as well as any attendant scholarship) those nuggets which may
prove useful to us?

My Queer Reading of Isaiah

What follows is what I in my own context – as a gay man, a Christian pastor, a man
living with Aids in the early twenty-first century in the Southern United States
– look for as I dig down into the book of Isaiah, and I offer this as an example
rather than as a blueprint, believing that your (and our) aspirations, your needs,
and your questions are the best maps to guide your (and our) excavations.

The three richest veins that I have identified in my own survey of the book
of Isaiah are, I believe, of immense value to the LGBT community that self-
identifies as spiritual: the prophetic unmasking of political tactics; manifold
and unlimited images of divinity; and transgressive images of humanity. The
book of Isaiah names in unvarnished, even arch ways the techniques employed
by those in power (governmental and/or religious) who would seek to keep
an unjust hold upon the people. Beyond this, Isaiah is replete with new and
creative, informing and even shocking ways of describing the actions, movements and motivations of God in our world – something beyond the 'same ol',
same ol'' of Father/Judge/Rock/Fortress/Creator. The more openness we can
experience in envisioning the divine – such as is found throughout this biblical book – the more we can come to value our own expressions, utilize our
own experiences, craft our own 'worship language' and even find joy in our
God-by-whatever-metaphor-we-know-God. With respect to the human community, I am particularly interested in the ways of blurring and transgressing
the oppressiveness of societal roles – of gender-based and proscribed images
– and of any bending of or reframing of how we describe, experience and live
out our lives as omni-gendered people.[7] Isaiah is filled with surprises along

---

6 Unless otherwise noted, all citations of the book of Isaiah are from the NRSV.

7 For the introduction of the phrase 'omnigender' into our discourse, see V. R.
Mollenkott (2001).

these lines. By accessing a multiplicity of ways for organizing human identity and human community, we build both capacity and innovation into our own efforts for liberation and toward creating a world with greater respect, vision and, even, *joy*!

Prophetic unmasking of political strategies

Ah, you who drag iniquity along with cords of falsehood,
who drag sin along as with cart-ropes,
who say, 'Let him make haste,
let him speed his work
that we may see it;
let the plan of the Holy One of Israel hasten to fulfilment,
that we may know it!'
Ah, you who call evil good
and good evil,
who put darkness for light
and light for darkness,
who put bitter for sweet
and sweet for bitter!
Ah, you who are wise in your own eyes,
and shrewd in your own sight!
Ah, you who are heroes in drinking wine
and valiant at mixing drink,
who acquit the guilty for a bribe,
and deprive the innocent of their rights! (Isa. 5.18–23)

As in much prophetic literature, one finds in the book of Isaiah a decrying of hypocrisy, of oppressive social, economic and religious practices, and of faithlessness. What is so powerful for LGBT persons in this book is the way in which Isaiah so clearly names ancient strategies of manipulation and control that are very much in evidence today, tactics frequently employed by those in religious and/or governmental power to our detriment. By 'outing' these tactics, this ancient literature can empower us to see, to name and ultimately to change these practices in our own place and time.

The above passage, from the fifth chapter of Isaiah, serves to make this point; each of these denunciations speaks to dynamics all too familiar to us in the twenty-first century. The first discusses those who cart around utter lies while claiming to be seeking God's judgement and justice. How many times do people who claim to be doing God's will bring out and parade a set of lies about us, *en masse*?! Consider typical lies such as the threats homosexuals pose to children; the equation of homosexuality with the inability to make moral choices about our sexual expression (e.g. that if we affirm sexual relations between same-gendered persons, then we will next be saying that incest, paedophilia and bestiality are also acceptable as 'just other variations'[8]); and

---

8 Robert Gagnon, Associate Professor of New Testament at Pittsburgh Theological Seminary, seems particularly fond of making this point.

the biggest lie of all: that our love is an abomination. These lies are dragged out and disseminated, in particular by those claiming to be 'on the Lord's side'.

The second of these indictments, against those who 'call evil good and good evil', point to one method that patriarchal systems use to maintain dominance, what Mary Daly names as *reversals*.[9] In short, this is a technique of saying that 'up' is 'down' and that 'green' is 'red', with the result that persons begin to doubt their own sanity and, in time, find it easier just to believe the unbelievable – rather than to be branded a liar, an idiot, a security threat, or a pervert. Centuries ago, Isaiah was already naming this very phenomenon.

This technique of reversing the truth and stating publicly that what is so is not (and vice-versa) is particularly problematic for the LGBT community, and it is imperative that we name it for what it is. We are told that what is normal and natural to us is ab-normal and un-natural. How many efforts at cultural assimilation on the part of LGBT persons have resulted from our own internalization of these reversals? How many suicides, how many ill-fated marriages, how many acts of violence have resulted from this very basic and very *base* reversal of our own sense of self-in-community?

Further, political and religious statements speak of homosexuals destroying the morality of peoples and nations, rather than the reverse; of groups that are threats to national security, rather than the reverse; of the freedoms of religious conservatives being trampled upon by the courts, rather than the reverse. What the book of Isaiah offers us is a reminder that this pervasive technique is nothing new – and that naming it as such, publicly decrying it, and demonstrating to others (so that they can learn to question, to consider, to identify reversals) is a potent means of unravelling oppression.

The third group that the prophet identifies in the above passage are those who are 'wise in [their] own eyes' and are 'shrewd in [their] own sight'. These are the ones, today, who have created their own committees, organizations and even broadcast networks so as to position themselves as putative sages, commentators and experts on matters of the day. They fashion themselves as a Family Focus Council, and then begin to offer 'wisdom' on matters affecting *all* families, including advising and even threatening presidents over potential Supreme Court nominations. It is not enough to simply roll one's eyes at this strategy; Isaiah passionately and publicly calls it out and denounces it!

As for the fourth group that falls under prophetic condemnation in this passage – those who are 'heroes' and 'valiant' when it comes to alcohol but whose ethics when it comes to justice are anything but heroic – what comes to mind are those who are adept at offering people a 'buzz' without concern for the rights of the innocent and the culpability of the guilty. These are the ones who can incite a crowd to protest places where abortions are performed, to break the windows of Jewish shops and homes, to lynch, to bait, to bash. What they offer is a heady cocktail of emotion: protecting the rights of *our* unborn children; the purity of *our* bloodline; the future of *our* nation; the safety of *our* women; the

---

9 See especially M. Daly (1973). Daly points out mythic examples, such as Adam giving birth to Eve and Zeus to Athena; a more contemporary example was the declaration that, in 2003, Iraq posed an imminent threat to United States security, when just the opposite was the case.

sanctity of *our* religion . . . while caring little if any about what might happen when *our* customers 'leave the bar'. How often have churches that whipped their people up into a frenzy over abortion disavowed any responsibility for shootings or bombings at clinics? How often have organizations proudly proclaimed vehemently anti-LGBT rhetoric and then distanced themselves from the beatings and murders of our people by those who got drunk on their very words? And how often have governments – political and ecclesiastical, local and national – overlooked the abuses committed by these purveyors of 'hatred highballs', primarily because they pay protection money to these governing politicians to be allowed to operate?

What keeps this from becoming hopeless is that it continues to be possible to recognize, identify and unmask these strategies and tactics, just as Isaiah did. Metaphor, poetry, spoken word, public performance: all of our passionate art has a place in the effort to open the eyes and ears and hearts of our fellow people. Isaiah's words help us to know that we are not alone, that we are not mistaken, that we are not crazy. And it is this knowledge that will help us not to 'grow faint or be crushed / until [we have] established justice in the earth' (Isa. 42.4).

Manifold images of the divine

It will be said on that day,

> Lo, this is our God; we have waited for him, so that he might save us.
> This is the Lord for whom we have waited;
> let us be glad and rejoice in his salvation. (Isa. 25.9)

There may be no other biblical book, with the possible exception of the Psalms, that I find myself over and over again feeling, 'Yes, here: here in these pages is a God worth waiting for – *this* God, the One that emerges in these 66 chapters – is the One I would willingly worship, the One who might just possibly be able to save this world and me along with it!'

And it is precisely because the God that is worshipped, feared, extolled, depicted and sought after in the book of Isaiah simply and utterly defies easy generalization or even categorization. What can be made of a God who is 'high and lifted up' and whose 'train filled the temple' in Isaiah 6, and then who, in chapter 23, becomes pimp to the city of Tyre? Or of the God who is a spurned-lover-turned-vengeful (Isa. 5; 65) and yet also the mother-nurse of Israel (Isa. 66)?

Consider this amazing set of descriptors in just five verses drawn from Isaiah 44:

> Thus says the LORD, your Redeemer,
>   who formed you in the womb:
> I am the LORD, who made all things,
>   who alone stretched out the heavens,
>   who by myself spread out the earth;

who frustrates the omens of liars,
  and makes fools of diviners;
who turns back the wise,
  and makes their knowledge foolish;
who confirms the word of his servant,
  and fulfils the prediction of his messengers;
who says of Jerusalem, 'It shall be inhabited',
  and of the cities of Judah, 'They shall be rebuilt,
  and I will raise up their ruins';
who says to the deep, 'Be dry –
  I will dry up your rivers';
who says of Cyrus, 'He is my shepherd,
  and he shall carry out all my purpose';
and who says of Jerusalem, 'It shall be rebuilt',
  and of the temple, 'Your foundation shall be laid.' (Isa. 44.24–8)

Here, God is redeemer, mother, craftsman, artist, trickster, genius, employer, divine, city planner, climate-controller, international politico and architect.

And it is *this* God that is indeed worth waiting for, this God who is not only capable of any number of roles and activities and points of entry into the life of the world, but the God who can only be described metaphorically, apprehended through the prism of our own daily experiences.[10] This is no hidden, inaccessible deity that is only approachable by the consecrated and ordained few: this is an utterly democratic God, one who is ribald and majestic, peevish and painstaking, manipulative and nurturing! Nowhere is it easier to see ourselves as made in the image of such a God! Nowhere is there such opportunity for demanding that 'the book' on how to describe God and how to articulate our worship of the Divine One not be closed – ever.

One is left with the sense, after mining Isaiah, that the supply of imagery for God is virtually inexhaustible, elastic and manifold. And thus it becomes easy to understand the presence, in this same book, of numerous and lengthy warnings and diatribes against idolatry (especially chs 42, 44, 46). Any kind of iconic encapsulation of God is necessarily a truncation, a distortion and an act of fruitless hubris. Can it be any less a form of idolatry to require that God be worshipped according to a *verbal* iconography, such as any insistence on casting God solely or necessarily as 'Father'?

Transgressive images of humanity

It is, one may argue, one thing to assert that God can 'rightly' be understood in manifold, even seemingly contradictory ways, for God is the I AM. Yet does this open up new possibilities for human beings who likewise defy easy categorization, who do not fit into stereotypical (even iconic) roles, human beings who are, well, *queer*?!

---

10 Much great work on metaphor in religion has been produced. Of particular value is S. McFague (1982).

The book of Isaiah begins conventionally enough, with those who have disappointed God described as rebellious children (Isa. 1.2). The description of apostate Israel rings with a familiarity tedious to many LGBT persons:

> Ah, sinful nation,
>   people laden with iniquity,
> offspring who do evil,
>   children who deal corruptly,
> who have forsaken the LORD,
>   who have despised the Holy One of Israel,
>   who are utterly estranged!
>
> Why do you seek further beatings?
>   Why do you continue to rebel?
> The whole head is sick,
>   and the whole heart is faint.
> From the sole of the foot even to the head,
>   there is no soundness in it,
> but bruises and sores
>   and bleeding wounds;
> they have not been drained, or bound up,
>   or softened with oil. (Isa. 1.4–6)

We are so often described as sinful, iniquitous, evil, corrupt and outside of God's pleasure. We are thought of, still, as people who deserve it when we are beaten (there are those who even now maintain that Matthew Shepard got what he deserved, that he was 'looking for it' when he agreed to go off with his murderers in their truck). Others will and do say we are 'sick in the head' in terms of suffering from a 'personality disorder' and/or that we are lacking in moral strength – either because we cannot or do not resist our impulses or because we have not progressed psychologically into full adulthood. Some might, more charitably, consider us as 'wounded' by our early environments (domineering mother, absent father; abusive authority figures), *yet* they point out that we refuse to be healed . . . that we are content to have our wounds undrained and undressed, and our hearts unsoftened.

But, note: this 'works' to condemn us only if *we* are the ones cast as rebellious children, either by others or (sadly) by ourselves. Familiar arguments, yes. But applicable to us? It is well worth considering how the rest of the book of Isaiah deals with ideas of what, to press some kind of term into application here, we might well refer to as *gender dissenters*. By this, I mean those who, like all LGBT persons and a significant number of others (to greater or lesser degree), do not fit in with established, gender-based social norms and expectations.[11] By mining the book of Isaiah for instances of gender dissent/social *queerness* (especially when treated positively), we find a veritable mother-lode – even

---

11 For an engaging, entertaining and scholarly work that is worth a look, see S. Maddison (2000).

though we need to dig down to those last 11 chapters, frequently dubbed as 'Third Isaiah'.[12]

By the time we have reached this stratum, beginning with chapter 56, we are entering into what Paul Hanson calls 'an eschatological ideal of the community and its destiny, and of Yahweh's relation to that community' coupled with 'a pervasive polemical element' in support of this vision (1979: 42). One of the key elements found in this ideal, in this vision located in Third Isaiah, is the bending of gender rules and roles, and the social status associated with them.

Several passages will suffice to demonstrate the overturning of norms and expectations related to sexual roles. First, as several LGBT theologians have already noted, the status of eunuchs – of those who, for physical, religious and/or preferential reasons do not or cannot procreate – is not only respected, but elevated *and promised a posterity* in Third Isaiah (see especially N. Wilson (1995: 120–34), and H. Moxnes (2003: 72–107)). God declares through the prophet:

Do not let the foreigner joined to the LORD say,
    'The LORD will surely separate me from his people';
and do not let the eunuch say,
    'I am just a dry tree.'
For thus says the LORD:
To the eunuchs who keep my sabbaths,
    who choose the things that please me
    and hold fast my covenant,
I will give, in my house and within my walls,
    a monument and a name
    better than sons and daughters;
I will give them an everlasting name
    that shall not be cut off. (Isa. 56.3–5)

The responsibility of 'being fruitful and multiplying' is not a prerequisite either to God's good favour or to being remembered from generation to generation!

Later, we find the free expression of delight in the prophet's experience of God's blessing, as if he were marrying God – either as the bridegroom or as the bride. Consider this verse from Isaiah 61:

I will greatly rejoice in the LORD
    my whole being shall exult in my God;
for he has clothed me with the garments of salvation,
    he has covered me with the robe of righteousness,

---

12 However, one does find instances of the queering of the standard relationships among animals and between animals and humans (wolves living with lambs, the calf and lion together, the cow and the bear as well; then, there is the vegetarian lion and the infant playing with snakes); this queering of boundaries, detailed in Isaiah 11, is actually set forth as a *vision* for the peaceful reign to come! Additionally, though tangential to this discussion, one finds here in Isaiah (as in Hosea) the use of sexual relationships *as prophetic activity*; in Isaiah 8, the prophet has sex with a prophetess and the child that results is given a God-ordained, significant name foretelling the impending desolation at the hands of Assyria. Worth exploring, along these lines, is K. Stone (2002).

as a bridegrooms decks himself with a garland,
    and as a bride adorns herself with her jewels. (Isa. 61.10)

This imaging of God as marriage partner (alternating with God as father) continues throughout Third Isaiah, and the prophet has no problem casting himself (and the nation) as partner.

Other images, no less striking, are utilized in Third Isaiah that go beyond bending gender roles and expectations. Isaiah 54 begins with an invitation for the barren woman to sing, to shout, to rejoice and to enlarge her tent (vv. 1–3), an activity usually reserved for and accompanying the birth of (additional) children; in Isaiah 60.16, the people are given this promise: 'You shall suck the breasts of kings'; and in Isaiah 66, we find a vision of a woman giving birth without labour (vv. 7–9), an undoing of the curse of Genesis 3.16.[13] The sweep of these images and the implications for what the 'new heavens and the new earth' (Isa. 66.22) shall look like are breathtaking. This eschatological vision represents a freedom that is exhilarating, and a reframing of righteousness that is within the purview of all – without respect to physicality, nationality or sexuality.

What are we to make of this vision of the righteous and peaceful future? The answer suggested in the latter parts of Isaiah is that we are to make of it what we will! There is a fluidness that is as available to all of us as the free water being promised in Isaiah 55.1 to all who thirst: here is an eschatological hope for social organization that is free from the constrictions of gender roles and has within it the seeds of a democratization of all persons from all nations – notwithstanding the not-surprising requirement in the text that all persons be worshippers of Yahweh. Yet, before this is itself written off as a 'my religion trumps all others' eschatology, perhaps we should take stock of how this vision redefines who and how this Yahweh is! This is a Yahweh that is *not* interested in the form either of the religion (Isa. 58.1–7) or of the physical plumbing of the person (as in the cases of the eunuchs and the barren women), nor even of a person's country of origin (Isa. 56). This is a Yahweh unlike the one(s) around which a great deal of ancient Israel's religious, political and social organization had grown.

The power of this today is not to be underestimated. There is in particular a 'Christian God' in America (and elsewhere) around which a great deal of religious, political and social organization has grown – a god who is portrayed as being overwhelmingly concerned about defining which religious forms are true or acceptable; who is proclaimed as dictating the reproductive (not to mention sexual) capacities and rights of human beings; and whose blessing is to be either granted or withheld according to whether or not individuals, groups and nations subscribe to these standards. Unless 'abstinence-only' is being taught, *this* god's nation shall not fund sexual education of youths; unless abortion rights are not mentioned, *this* god's nation shall not fund

---

13 In expelling her from the Garden, God declares to Eve, 'I will greatly increase your pangs in childbearing; / in pain you shall bring forth children, / yet your desire shall be for your husband, / and he shall rule over you' (Gen. 3.16). When Isaiah 66.7–9 is placed alongside the virgin birth of Isaiah 7.14, it certainly seems that no part of the curse laid upon Eve need be in place in the Isaianic eschaton.

reproductive services for women; unless non-condemnatory attitudes toward homosexuality are removed, *this* god's nation shall not provide funding for the care of persons with Aids.

If there is something vital to be taken from Isaiah, in particular for the LGBT community, I would suggest that it is that Yahweh, the God whose word is given to the prophet Isaiah (be it the first, second or third time around), defies and undermines any attempts to link true righteousness and peace-making with the carrying out of any ideological, ritualistic and/or theo-political agenda. These, no less than statues made of wood or gold, are idols – and the God of these pages of Isaiah eschews any and all identifications (let alone equivalences) with them.

Into Our Future: Creating 'Fourth Isaiah'

If we as a community of spirited persons – as those who seek to live and love boldly, even *fiercely* – want to participate in effecting a transformation throughout our world, then it is time to come out and into our own as what I will here call 'Fourth Isaiah'.

That is, we too must open ourselves to receiving a Word from the Lord . . . or, if you prefer, a Vision of justice and of loving relationships for our planet. We can, and I believe shall, come to understand ourselves as worthy and capable, simply by virtue of having been given the yearning for such a future. Yet, with this Word or this Vision comes, as for all Isaianic prophecies, a pronounced discomfort that challenges the (including our own) status quo. Our sacred cows have to be offered up, be they political ideologies, convictions about religion, even our own self-understandings. All Isaiahs, no matter how scathing or consoling they are about past and/or present situations, are nonetheless seized with a vision of a future that defies conventional wisdom, that rejects the most finely tuned social agendas, and that opens into new, uncharted and certainly *dramatic* territory.

So why bother with Isaiah at all? Why should we not just declare a new and separate manifesto, one more appropriate to twenty-first-century LGBT persons? Why not, instead of trying to tack ourselves onto an ancient biblical book, simply publish our own Vision Statement for the World as Issued by Spiritually Sensitive and Justice-Minded LGBT Persons and Our Allies? I would suggest that it is for the same reasons that we are fortunate enough to have this beautifully cobbled-together book of Isaiah, woven from these clearly diverse strands, instead of, say, three separate books: Isaiah, Harry and Claire.

It is, I believe, because the vision of *each* Isaiah is self-consciously connecting itself to the history, the tradition, the wisdom and teachings of the larger community – as well as to that community's sinfulness and shortcomings. The choice was made deliberately to place each 'Isaiah' into one *incredible* tapestry of the search for righteousness and justice for the world! Not only can we and, I would argue, should we, as Fourth Isaiahs, self-consciously connect ourselves and our vision to this tapestry (with the pain as well as the comfort that this entails), we then also begin making an essential and lasting contribution for everyone who is and who is yet to come, a Work of Art that is not just woven to what has come before but which in turn becomes a take-off point for the Fifth, the Sixth and all subsequent Isaiahs! So be it.

ex-vyuu.nu, b a xi d w .o _yci H o .ume a Work of A_ that is tropiut wonu to
wh.it has come before, but which in truth concises a .plac.ot .point to the f th
the xxib and all .i .n :quent Cara.ld.So b'd'i

Jeremiah

ANGELA BAUER-LEVESQUE

When translesbigays turn to the book of Jeremiah, what do they/we find? What
may this ancient Near Eastern exilic text from the sixth century BCE, with a
very different worldview and understanding of society and thus corporeality,
possibly reveal that is relevant for translesbigays in the twenty-first-century
CE Western world?

The book of Jeremiah is not one of the biblical books commonly pulled out
in discussions about 'sexuality and the Bible', nor about identity formation of
any kind. Rather, the most commonly quoted passages from the book echo
psalms of lament ascribed to the prophet. Yet a translesbigay perspective may
uncover some unexpected dynamics within these so-called 'lamentations of
Jeremiah' and in some other places throughout the book.

Historical and Literary Settings

The majority of scholars locate the initial layer of the book of Jeremiah in
the seventh century BCE with two later editorial stages during the exile and
post-exile (Brueggemann 1998; Lundbom 2004: 582–5; O'Connor 1992). Only
a few read the book as a predominantly post-exilic reflection on that earlier
time leading up to the exile (Carroll 1986: 65–82). In either case, the historical
realities described in the book tell of an at first impending, and later actual
war and destruction, of various ways of responding to the crisis as a people
and its leaders, and of differing evaluations by the next generation of what
had led to the calamities in which the contemporary audiences in and around
Jerusalem found themselves. Like most prophetic literature in the Bible, the
book of Jeremiah testifies to the trials and tribulations and conflicts between
and among the man Jeremiah, the Israelites/Judahites male and female, and
their God YHWH (portrayed mostly as male yet sometimes as female) as they
search together and separately to make sense of their experiences of war and
violence, chaos and attempts at resistance, defeat and daily life. A collection of
poetry and prose, the 52 chapters of the book lack a clear chronological order,
including several repetitions of historical events in poetic and narrative sections, complicated by the various textual origins of the Masoretic text and the
Septuagint. Thus, the composition history of Jeremiah continues to be debated
among scholars, with the leading theories either following an assumption of
three sources and authors (Duhm 1901; Mowinckel 1914) or a proposal of two
scrolls (Holladay 1986, 1989), or an understanding of various editors (Carroll

1986; more narrowly Rudolph 1968). Alternative interpretations of the book have mostly dealt with the literary text in its final form. Feminist and womanist readings focus on female imagery, gendering of power dynamics, sexual violence and 'porno-prophetics' (O'Connor 1992; Brenner 1993a, 1995, 1996; Jost 1995; Exum 1996: 101–28; Weems 1995; Bauer 1999), while a recent postcolonial interpretation highlights various sections of Jeremiah as resistance literature (Davidson 2002). From a queer perspective the fluidity of gender dynamics in Jeremiah and the instances of power exchanges with sexual connotations are to be foregrounded, yielding suggestive insights and offering various points of entry and intrigue with/in the book of Jeremiah.

Jeremiah 1.1–6.30

The book opens with a prologue and two cycles of judgement oracles replete with gendered imagery. Right after the superscription (Jer. 1.1–3) which locates the prophecy historically and geographically, the first words out of YHWH's mouth literarily surround such a metaphor. The womb (Heb. *beten* and *rehem*) belongs to God and provides the locus for Jeremiah's call: 'Before I formed you in the womb (*beten*) I knew you, and before you came forth from the womb (*rehem*) I set you apart, a prophet to the nations I appointed you' (Jer. 1.5). The Hebrew text remains ambiguous as to its use of the definite article without a pronominal designation thus allowing for the connotation of maternal aspects in YHWH (cf. Trible 1978: 35–6). Commentators uncomfortable with such a reading introduce Jeremiah's human mother into the text (Carroll 1986: 97; Breuer 1988: 3). Maternal imagery will function differently for various translesbigay readers depending on our respective identities and socializations. It is the unexpectedness of this gendering of the divine I that draws attention, enwombing and calling the prophetic You 'to pluck up and to break down, to destroy and to overthrow, to build and to plant' (Jer. 1.10). The pregnant imagery of the opening quickly gives way to metaphors of bride, prostitute, wife and promiscuous woman in the first cycle of judgement oracles (Jer. 2.1–4.4). Assuming a heteropatriarchal mindset, the writer juxtaposes Israel as loving bride (Jer. 2.2–3) with Israel/Judah as prostitute and promiscuous woman (Jer. 2.20; 2.25–8; 2.29–37; 3.1–5, 6–10; 3.19–20) in characterizing the prophet calling the people to repent. The 'loving bride' is portrayed as 'pure' and 'innocent' attaining saintly qualities (Jost 1995), while male Israel is pursuing unacceptable ('defiling', 'no good') love interests and female Israel is prostituting herself on heights under trees – ancient places for goddess worship – and is showing the supposedly uncontrollable sexual libido of a cow camel and a female wild ass. Regardless of their various gifts and failings, the focus is on presumed sexual activities. To translesbigay ears such accusations sound familiar. Oppressive dualisms and animalization function to other and lessen the accused then as now. At the same time, the back and forth of gender designations for the people may inadvertently suggest modes of deconstructing the same such system. The presence of such a judgement oracle points to the historical realities of a folk religion existing alongside the official YHWH cult (cf. Jost 1995; Ackerman 1989), as the later passages regarding worship of the Queen of Heaven also attest (Jer. 7.16–20; 44.15–25). Meanwhile, the choice of imagery has pornographic qualities (Brenner 1993a, 1995, 1996; Exum 1996: 101–28), perversely reversing typical heteropatriarchal dynamics by accusing the female of sexual aggression run amok. The judgement proclaimed is divorce (Jer. 3.1–5). While the metaphor of a raped woman may function as a metonym for society's body broken by war (Keefe 1993), the clutter of sexualized images weighing so dominantly on the negative side continues to perpetuate the sex-negative influence of the Bible.

In the next cycle of judgement oracles (Jer. 4.5–6.30) the call to repentance morphs into inevitable judgement as the gendered imagery shifts some. The prophet addresses the Israelites as 'Daughter My People' and 'Daughter Zion' in a trans-gender move identifying himself with Jerusalem portrayed as female. This becomes more explicit in Jeremiah taking on a female voice in a brief lament (Jer. 4.19–21) (cf. Kaiser 1987) crying 'My belly! My belly! I writhe in labour' (Jer. 4.19). The metaphor of woman in labour pain signifies the calamity of the inhabitants of Jerusalem under siege as the experiences of war find bodily expression in an m/f trans-gendered prophet succeeded by the image of a made-up street walker (drag queen?), who instead of her lover meets her murderer (Jer. 4.29–31) (cf. Bauer 1999). Both metaphors suggest vulnerability unto death, uttered as threat and judgement and continuing into the next chapter where also the children are included in the accusation (Jer. 5.7–9) and the impending death (Jer. 6.2–3, 11; 6.23–4).

From a pregnant God to a pregnant prophet, from a call to prophesy to a call to repent, this first section of the book embraces gender-fluid images and traditional sexualized power dynamics with pornographic dimensions, all mixed together.

Jeremiah 7.1–25.38

Gendered imagery in this section, during which impending disaster turns into actual destruction, provides further points of entry for queering Jeremiah. While those interested in portrayals of strong women will turn to Jeremiah 7.16–20, Judahite women leading worship of the Queen of Heaven, and Jeremiah 9.16–21, professional mourners and teachers leading ceremonies, those interested in potential sexual dynamics between YHWH and Jeremiah will turn to Jeremiah 20.7–13.

Following right after Jeremiah's temple sermon (Jer. 7.1–15), women who by contrast are not identified by their lineage (not 'daughter of . . .', 'wife of . . .') but simply *nasim* 'women' are described as leaders in rituals venerating the goddess, here called Queen of Heaven. They bake special ritual cakes (Jer. 7.18) and can be understood as cult officials at the temple (Jost 1995; cf. Ackerman 1989). The Queen of Heaven has been identified with various goddesses including the Assyrian Ishtar and the Canaanite Astarte; she is probably a conglomeration of various local goddesses at the time. The phenomenon of women practitioners in such folk religion is confirmed by other exilic prophets such as the women weeping for Tammuz in the book of Ezekiel (Ezek. 8.14). Alternative worship practices existed then as now, and were also condemned as heresy by the 'orthodox' religious establishment as represented by the prophet, and consequently threatened with judgement of destruction of the entire creation (Jer. 7.20). The litany of condemned practices without distinction includes the sacrifice of children (Jer. 7.31). Again, the resonances to contemporary accusations witnessed by translesbigays are eerily close (e.g. Pat Robertson's famous 1995 quote that 'The feminist agenda is not about equal rights for women. It is about a socialist, anti-family, political movement that encourages women to leave their husbands, kill their children, practise witchcraft, destroy capitalism and become lesbians'; or Jerry Falwell's well-known quote after 9/11 along similar lines). Comprehensive destruction cannot be averted (Jer. 8.4–17). Short of death, what remains is the option to find an outlet in lament and mourning and the longing for healing and wholeness (Jer. 8.18–23). The jeremiad for a balm in Gilead has become a comfort song for various oppressed groups through the centuries.

What follows is an example of an alternative reality. In another jeremiad (Jer. 9.16–21), YHWH through the prophet Jeremiah calls the wise women keeners to intone their laments. The prophetic oracle contains the only messenger formula addressed exclusively to women in all of the First Testament: 'Hear, O Women, the word of YHWH' (Jer. 9.19). The divine command requests the women to teach their daughters a lament and their female companions a dirge. The word I translate 'female companion', in Hebrew rᵉʿutah, has the connotation of close friend, neighbour and lover. These women have the task of keeners to sing, to teach and to lead in wisdom (Jer. 9.16–17). The word employed contains the root hkm, which many Bible translations make invisible, talking instead about 'skill', though the identical root is rendered 'wise' when applied to men (Jer. 9.22–3). To this day, the official role of leaders in rituals of grieving in most cultures belongs to women. Here in Jeremiah these female leadership roles are consonant with earlier ritual leadership (cf. Bird 1997a: 81–120), and further make sense when considering the conditions of households during war time when male members are absent (cf. Meyers 1983). For translesbigays this passage may be of interest for its subversion of traditional culture and the possible mention of same-sex companions.

An exhortation to prepare for Exile (Jer. 10.17–25) closes the section. Notably, heteropatriarchy appears dislocated in such a situation, as binary constructions of reality have not served the people in crisis.

The following chapters (11.1–20.18), where reversal of the situation/repentance is proclaimed as no longer possible, portray the prophet in an identity struggle in terms of his/her relationship to the people and to God. The loci for such expression in first-person speech are predominantly the so-called 'Confessions of Jeremiah' (Jer. 11.18–23; 12.1–6; 15.10–21; 17.14–18; 18.18–23; 20.7–13(18)). Meanwhile, destruction is described in the porno-prophetic metaphor of a woman, stripped naked and raped with the consent and even participation of YHWH (Jer. 13.20–7) (Bauer 1999: 100–9). The passage joins familiar imagery of labour pain (Jer. 13.21) and rape (Jer. 13.22, 26). 'On account of the greatness of your iniquity are your skirts uncovered and your heels/genitals violated' (Jer. 13.22). The punishment is announced as a result of the people's iniquity. Addressed as female, they are to be violated sexually. The action described is one of exposing and violation. Both verbs, 'to uncover' and 'to treat violently', have active forms but occur in the niphal, a Hebrew passive tense. The niphal form of *glh* is attested elsewhere in contexts of sexual violence (cf. Isa. 47.3; Ezek. 16.36, 37; 23; 29) but the niphal form of *hms* is a *hapax legomenon* (Jer. 13.22). The direct objects both have sexual connotations. Both 'skirts' and 'heels', like 'feet', are euphemisms for genitals (cf. Isa. 6.2; 7.20; Ezek. 16.25). Thus, the punishment is rape. The victim is identified, yet the rapist is not. The passive forms of the verbs allow for the agent of the sexual assault, the perpetrator, to remain unnamed. The people gendered female here are told that their own apostasy is responsible for their being raped. For anyone who has had any experience with sex crimes, this is a familiar dynamic. The victim is being blamed. Indeed, here in Jeremiah the condition of the rape victim (and not the perpetrator) is described as beyond repentance. And to drive this point home even further, Jeremiah employs racialized rather than gendered imagery: 'Does the Ethiopian change his skin or the leopard his spots? Then also you are able to do good having been taught to do evil' (Jer. 13.23). Using the impossibility of changing one's skin colour as an illustration, the oracle moves to assert that the people have reached a condition beyond repentance. Explicitly racial imagery compares the people Israel to more southern and thus darker-skinned Africans. Then in a second racist move those Ethiopians are made less than human by being equated with wild animals. Thus the rhetoric furthers the shaming of the audience. Ideology of race intertwines with ideology of gender. Racialized and gendered metaphors meet (and reinforce each other) in this prophetic indictment of the people (cf. Bailey 1995). Then, in a second avalanche of accusations and punishments, images of sexual violence multiply. YHWH continues to address the people: 'And also I myself shall strip your skirts over your face so that your shame is seen' (Jer. 13.26). Brutally, the deity promises to join the violation of the female as YHWH threatens to violate Israel as female sexually. The Qal perfect leaves some room for ambiguity as to whether or not the action has already taken place, as suggested by the perfect, or is threatened in the future, as suggested by the narrative sequence. Through the deity's activity, her shame is exposed. But rape is not the end of it. Public humiliation extends the violence against the female.

While female readers are challenged by the familiarity of such threats, gay and trans male readers with experiences of effeminization may also connect to reverberations of rape. The mindset of the authors does not shy away from involving the deity as perpetrator.

The language of violence and destruction makes me shy away in this instance to explore dimensions of s/m power dynamics in this interaction. In Jeremiah's last 'confession' (Jer. 20.7–13(18)) the prophet cries out: 'You seduced me, YHWH, and I was seduced, you overpowered/(raped) me, and you prevailed. I have become a laughingstock all day long, everyone mocks me' (Jer. 20.7). Gendering the players involved in this interaction determines the kind of reading produced for translesbigays and others. If one chooses to see a connection to Jer. 4.19–21, where Jeremiah takes on a female/trans persona, the lament suggests another accusation of rape – the verb root *hzq* has connoted thus elsewhere (cf. Deut. 22.25; 2 Sam. 13.11, 14) – with God being accused of seducing and raping the prophet (cf. Heschel 1962: 113–14; Bauer 1999: 114–16). Another option would be to assume homosexual rape there, though the overall tone of the book does not move in that direction. Staying with a male–male encounter (cf. Carroll 1999), another way of reading connects overpowering and humiliation with a sense of possession by and adoration of the one who overpowers (Jer. 20.11–13) with bottom/top interchanges of s/m, 'as a kind of ritual S/M encounter between the male deity Yahweh and his male devotee' (Stone 2004b). I find this an intriguing reading from a gay male perspective; for female identified readers, even those interested in exploring dynamics of domination and submission, the predominant identification of YHWH as male does not support such an exchange. While Jeremiah's succeeding death wish (Jer. 20.14–18) lends itself to sexualization again, the invocation of the maternal womb connects back to the beginning of the book (Jer. 1.5) in a highly ambiguous layering of primal instincts (Freudian allusions abound!).

The section closes with a summary of the people's fate, sexualized, gendered, in pain both of labour/birth and of destruction/death in a way underscoring the tenor above (Jer. 22.20–3). From strong woman-identified women teachers to a possible gay male s/m ritual encounter, translesbigay readers find a plethora of images to explore.

Jeremiah 26–52

The second half of the book of Jeremiah changes in style in that the proportion of narrative passages and poetry is reversed compared to the first half. Most of the Deuteronomistic prose retells the historical events mentioned earlier and elaborates on the prophet's encounters with people and king(s). In terms of gendered and/or sexualized imagery, it is again found predominantly in the poetic sections, especially the section known as 'the Little Book of Comfort' (Jer. 30–1). Wartime terror and panic are symbolized by male warriors in labour pain, as the prophet proclaims, 'ask and see if there is a male giving birth! Why do I see every warrior male with his hands upon his loins like a woman in labour?' (Jer. 30.6). Traditional interpretations have read this effeminization of warriors as the ultimate mockery and degradation (cf. Holladay 1989). Yet a trans reading might find this description of agony akin to actual experiences of gender fluidity, which can also be observed in the following chapter (Jer. 31). There the recollection of a dancing and drumming Maiden Israel planting and building (Jer. 31. 4–5) recalls the maternal ancestor Miriam at the Sea of Reeds (Ex. 15.20–1) as well as aspects of the prophet's call (Jer. 1.10) (cf. Meyers 1991). A New Exodus is prophesied (Jer. 31.2–6), as the strong woman-identified women mourners and musicians (cf. Jer. 9.16–21) find their grief transformed into joy. The maternal ancestor Rachel joins the chorus when her weeping for her children is transformed as well (Jer. 31.15–22). Maternal imagery for YHWH, with a 'trembling womb' promising in first-person speech 'motherly compassion' on Israel portrayed as son (Jer. 31.20), contributes to an eschatological theology of empathy, culminating in a promise to 'rebellious daughter Israel'. Again gender fluidity stands out in this promise: 'For YHWH has created something new on earth: Female surrounds warrior-male' (Jer. 31.22). The New Creation is one of gender reversal yet again, possibly trans reality for all. And if such an interpretation goes too far even for translesbigay readers, I maintain that a reversal of or at least a challenge to the gendered status quo is proclaimed here in ambiguous language, whatever meanings get attached to such.

Traditional interpretations in Bible translations and commentaries tend to belong to one of three categories: (a) the reversal of the status quo is promised in the woman offering protection to the man (e.g. Holladay 1989: 193); (b) the woman takes on a different role in sexual activity as more aggressive (e.g. Carroll 1986: 601, 605); (c) the woman becomes a man, based on a different verb form (e.g. Luther; Rudolph 1968: 198–9), without really addressing any F to M trans dynamics. Meanwhile, feminist interpretations suggest new roles for women in a peaceful society, more active participation in family planning and other possible role changes (Bozak 1991: 104; O'Connor 1992: 176) or explore literary echoes of innovation and continuity (Trible 1978: 47–8). In any case, the interpretive possibilities of differently gendered realities are inviting and not yet fully explored, suggesting a theological trajectory from Exile to Eschatology, from present experience to future expectation.

The new gendered realities climax in the promise of a New Covenant (Jer. 31.3–14) that comes in the form of a marriage contract with somewhat changed role expectations (Bauer 1999: 145–8). Given the gender fluidity within this chapter, translesbigay readers might make connections to contemporary discussions on marriage (cf. Bauer-Levesque 2004).

Yet the book of Jeremiah continues turning back from eschatology to exile, from promises back to judgement, including another indictment of veneration of the Queen of Heaven (Jer. 44.15–25; cf. 7.16–20) in which women lead in such strength that no redaction of the book could leave them out (cf. Jost 1995: 218–20). The subsequent oracles against the nations (Jer. 46–51) echo earlier imagery of sexual violation applied to Babylon (Jer. 51.2, 47) or women's birth pangs applied to Moab's warriors (Jer. 48.41), and to all of Damascus (Jer. 49.24), and to the king of Babylon (Jer. 50.43). Similar interpretations regarding gender dynamics suggest themselves, leaving the reader with a sense of a prophetic book that crosses gender lines back and forth again and again in trying to make sense of the historical reality of a people led into exile as summarized again in the final chapter (Jer. 52).

Scenes of/for Audiences and Readers

So what difference can queer reading strategies make for interpretations of the book of Jeremiah? Considering the various audiences for the book ancient and contemporary, what is at stake?

Historically, the prophecies of Jeremiah addressed a primarily male audience in and around Jerusalem in the years leading up to the Babylonian exile and beyond, as well as audiences in the sixth and fifth centuries when editorial stages may have taken place. How did those gendered and sexualized images function for them? One can only speculate about the effectiveness of rhetorical strategies that publicly shame the addressees into changing, by means of misogynous, effeminizing and racist accusations. In a cultural system of honour and shame, shame functions to reclaim group boundaries, to keep people 'in line'. Shaming is to evoke feelings of inadequacy and inferiority, to evoke rejection and exclusion from community and diminished social status. In a closed system of hetero-binaries, males are forced to identify with feared female sexuality and fantasies of sexualized violence, culminating in being forced to confront a God portrayed as male and thereby urged into female positions in a culture of assumed heterosexuality (cf. Eilberg-Schwartz 1994: 137–62). Threat and shaming, together with the power of the office, the prophetic and/or the divine, may perhaps result in compliance. Yet compliance is not repentance, which requires conviction or conversion. Threat and shaming instead evoke resentment and fear and possibly begrudging action.

Strikingly, the similarities to contemporary situations are bound to resound for translesbigay readers in particular. And yet, there are different scenes. As power dynamics are constructed variously across the queer rainbow, gay men will find affinity to other passages than trans folk, and further differently for F to M than for M to F and in-betweens, while lesbians depending on their locations vis-à-vis power exchanges erotic and otherwise – the fine line between pleasure and pain – might yet read differently again. On one level, each their own! On another level, however, where do all these discoveries of gender fluidity, same-sex dynamics, erotic s/m lead us given the power of scripture in various cultures?

While these new scenes and exchanges excite me, I need at the same time to recall the destructive functions of uses of the Bible to claim power, whether proof-texting from the right or from the left. Analogies between ancient texts and contemporary contexts are limited, indeed. Almost needless to say, scripture has been misquoted and biblical literalism defaulted to, as if values of biblical times and values of faithful peoples in the twenty-first century were identical. Quoting the Bible as prescriptive inevitably raises the question as to whether we want to get back to the male head of household owning his wife, children, slaves and cattle. Again, maybe we are still closer to that than many of us want to believe. Thus ethical principles are called for in how we use scripture in general and the richly layered images in Jeremiah in particular as we forge scenes of engagement.

Enjoy responsibly! It's the Bible after all.

Lamentations

DERYN GUEST

Introduction

The book of Lamentations consists of five psalms of lament permeated by
a whole gamut of emotions: bitterness, anger, distress, grief, despair and
loss mingled with a tentative but tantalizing glimmer of hope mid-book.
Traditionally read against the background context of the siege and destruction of Jerusalem in 587/6 BCE, commentators have interpreted these evocative
laments as the work of a, or several, psalmists who are coming to terms with the
devastating losses of that event. Evidence for this view lies mainly in the grisly
vividness of the laments thought to derive ultimately from the oral tradition
of eye-witness accounts (Westermann 1994: 61–2) and the several references
that appear to tie in with the siege and subsequent exile: the references to the
destruction of Jerusalem (especially 2.1–9), to her 'lovers' who have failed her
(1.2, 19 and possibly 4.17), correspondences to the desecration and pillaging
of the temple (1.10), frequent mention of famine (1.11; 2.11, 12, 19–20; 4.4, 9–10;
5.6, 19), the mention of compassionate women boiling their children in 4.10 (cf.
2 Kings 25.3), talk of the people of Jerusalem wandering among the nations
and going into captivity/exile (1.3; 5.18), of the remaining citizens being left to
meander around desolate ruins (1.4; 2.10; 5.18), and the lack of any awareness
of recovery or restoration. Certainly, a sixth-century BCE context would appear
to account well for the images of assault, the sense of abandonment, the language of accusation and acrimony, and the qualified acknowledgement of sin
and punishment offset by the unwillingness to accept full responsibility for
that punishment.

However, although the scholarly consensus has been that Lamentations is
best read against this background,[1] the possibility that Lamentations can be
read against a historical context other than that of the early mid-sixth century BCE has been raised. J. Morgenstern (1956, 1957, 1966), for example, has
argued for an early fifth-century context, while M. Treves (1963) and T. Lachs
(1966) have suggested a mid-second-century BCE Maccabean setting. Although
these views have not been widely accepted they do demonstrate how the
text's poetic language and imagery militates against locating a clear historical
context. As poetic formulations, these psalms of lament belong to an ancient

---

1 Gottwald (1954) and Hillers (1992: 3–6) all, with minor variations, opt for an exilic
setting, although Hillers does add the important qualification that 'much of the language of the book is universal and nonspecific' (1992: 15).

cultural tradition of lamentation that has conventionally drawn upon formulaic images and stock-in-trade language.[2] Thus, images that appear to reflect historical events may actually be conventional images used in this genre to depict distress, anger, resentment and despair (see Mowinckel (1962) and Ackroyd (1979: 49)).

This is not to suggest that the poems of Lamentations did not have their point of origin in some historical catastrophe. Rather, it is suggested that the form in which these laments are cast inevitably involves conventional formulaic language, hyperbole and images that transcend any *specific* event and historical context.[3] Two useful corollaries ensue from this: first, it puts the focus back on the profundity of the laments themselves and the way in which they deal with the perennial issues of human pain and its concomitant emotions, such as distress, despair, anger and resentment. Second, it frees the interpreter to consider the continued reading of Lamentations within worshipping communities and the application of this text to new contexts and experiences. Thus, Lamentations is read in Jewish services on the 9th Ab in commemoration not only of the fall of Jerusalem, but in memory of subsequent experiences of oppression such as the expulsion of Jews from Spain in 1492 and the Holocaust. In the Christian tradition, portions of Lamentations are used in the Matins-Lauds services for the latter days of Holy Week, applied as they are to the hostilities directed against Jesus of Nazareth prior to his crucifixion and, by implication, applied to subsequent experiences of oppression suffered by his followers.

---

2 Similarities between Lamentations and the Sumerian lament tradition have long been noted; see Kramer (1959), Kraus (1968: 9–10), Gadd (1963: 61) and Westermann (1994: 11–23). Similarities with the balag laments of ancient Mesopotamia are particularly striking. Cohen's (1988) translation of 39 balag laments, which he claims ultimately reach back to at least the second millennium BCE, describe the destruction of cities, the defiling of temples and the suffering of a populace. Insofar as the balag laments also describe acts of pillage and disaster, attribute the disaster to the deity, emphasize the merciless nature of this outbreak of the deity's fury which embraces all, attempt to assuage/cope with this wrath, and are permeated with emotive references to general bitterness, affliction, eyes flowing with water, the orphanage of children, and widowing of wives, these laments share strong thematic affinities with the book of Lamentations.

3 According to McDaniel, 'The experience of most cities in the ancient Near East under siege, and their fate upon subsequent defeat, were usually the same. Poets writing on the general theme of war and defeat, though at different times and at different places, would likely refer to the hunger, famine, pestilence, the social disintegration during the siege, the destruction of the city, the spoils taken by the victor, and the captivity of the conquered following defeat' (1968: 200). McDaniel here is seeking to demonstrate how difficult it is to make a case for literary dependence, but his comments also demonstrate how difficult it is to locate the precise event being described. Destruction of cities, defeat, captivity, hunger and famine, death and despair, were endemic to ancient Near Eastern life and the theological questions these experiences raised remain relevant to the human predicament in general as is evidenced in their continued usage in both synagogue and church. This is an issue explored in more detail by Provan (1990), who rightly questions whether we can reconstruct, with any certainty, the specific concrete reality that motivated the writing of these laments.

Commentaries that specifically address the contemporary believing community regularly apply the text to ongoing experiences of oppression and explore how far this text offers advice to believers on how to deal with experiences of being seemingly abandoned by a punitive deity. Thus Robert Davidson notes how 'it is a mistake to confine them [laments] to that week. Their healing power is open to all who are prepared to live through tragedy and grief and to share it with God and their fellow believers' (1985: 172). Other contemporary interpretations place their focus upon the text's usefulness as a resource for working through specific situations of pain. Alice Miller (1991) uses Lamentations to inform her work on child abuse, finding in Lamentations' voices of outrage, resistance and protest a useful sanction for objection against child cruelty. Paul Joyce (1993) reads Lamentations in terms of working through bereavement and reactions to the experience of dying as explored by Yorick Spiegel and Elisabeth Kübler Ross respectively. Tod Linafelt (2000) discusses Lamentations in terms of 'survival literature', exploring the afterlife of Lamentations in Jewish survival literature as writers attempt to make their peace with Zion's outcries. Mona West (2001) has demonstrated how the text's voices of remembrance and mourning can provide a useful resource for dealing with issues surrounding Aids. Ken Stone's (1999) work on reading psalms of lament in the age of Aids does not deal specifically with Lamentations but his work can nonetheless be applied to this text.

This chapter offers a further contribution to this cultural afterlife of Lamentations by assessing the usefulness of Lamentations as a resource for those who have had to endure a history of heterosexist acts and discourse.[4] The chapter is organized around features noted at its outset – first, the text's images of assault; second, its exploration of the experience of abandonment; and third, the images of accusation and acrimony, where the qualified acknowledgement of sin and punishment is offset by unwillingness to accept full responsibility for that punishment. These three headings are used to explore contemporary experiences of the heterosexist intimidation of Jews and Christians who are regularly 'under siege' within society generally, and often within their faith traditions specifically, because of their decision to identify as lesbian, gay, bisexual, transgender or queer (LGBT/Q).[5]

---

4 I find Wilton's definition of heterosexism useful. She states that heterosexism is: 'To regard heterosexuality as being better, more normal, more natural or more morally right than homosexuality' (2000: 6). This definition strikes at the heart of a common double-standard strategy where those who would distance themselves from any associations with overt homophobic discourse, acts or attitudes still consider that the majority's adherence to heterosexual unions indicates that this is the more 'natural', 'normal', and perhaps 'better' practice.

5 I have chosen to separate Q from LGBT with a forward slash in order to indicate that 'queer' is not an identity label. Although it is sometimes used as an umbrella term for non-straight people, queer strategically upsets the homosexual–heterosexual binary and transcends LGBT categories. Similarly, I used LGBT-*identified* to indicate that it is not necessarily a case of 'being' lesbian or gay so much as having *been positioned* as such or choosing to adopt that label for strategic purposes.

Images of Assault

Images of assault pervade the book of Lamentations. When the book opens it is all over; we are simply confronted with its terrible aftermath in the form of the bereaved Woman/Zion sitting in isolation weeping long and hard into the night. This personification of Woman/Zion as a betrayed, beaten, raped, publicly humiliated woman captures the imagination all too vividly and is problematic.[6] As the subsequent verses unfold, we see how she has been made to bear the brunt of the deity's unabated fury as the psalmist rehearses the details of the assault in a variety of vivid images. The literary technique of parataxis, combined with the use of hyperbole and rhetoric, recreates in tortured detail a blow-by-blow account of the assault.

What is noteworthy is the way that Lamentations spends practically all its time detailing this experience of assault without moving on to any sustained hope or thanksgiving – developments that normally feature in psalms of lament. Rather, Lamentations allows the speaker and hearer to dwell on 'the complex cluster of emotions – sorrow, anger, guilt, hope, despair, fear, self-loathing, revenge, compassion, forgiveness, uncertainty, disorientation' (Dobbs-Allsopp 2000: 785). The psalmist thereby encourages the users of these laments to express *fully* the emotional distresses of their experience. Indeed, when scholars discuss the possible purposes of Lamentations several believe the psalmist was deliberately providing an opportunity to give vent to the full horror, terror, distress and agony that has been experienced, providing an invaluable vehicle through which to remember and recount the diverse aspects of the assault. Thus, for Hillers, 'Lamentations was meant to serve the survivors of the catastrophe simply as an *expression* of the horror and grief they felt. People live on best after calamity, not by utterly repressing their grief and shock, but by facing it, and by measuring its dimensions' (1992: 4).

The reason why four out of the five laments use an acrostic form has also been supposed to reflect a desire to express grief in full. As Gottwald comments:

> in naming the whole alphabet one comes as close as man [sic] may to a total development of any theme or the complete expression of any emotion or belief . . . The author . . . wished to play upon the collective grief of the community in its every aspect, from 'Aleph to Taw', so that the people might experience an emotional catharsis. (1954: 29–30)

Whether this was the intention behind the use of the acrostic or not, Lamentations certainly does dwell upon diverse features of the assault and urges survivors to cry out from the depths of their pain and to give vent to grief, distress and despair. By so doing, Lamentations fulfilled and fulfils the fundamental need for people who have suffered assault to be given opportunity to voice their painful experience of that oppression.

What, then, might this text offer modern LGBT/Q-identified readers? The International Lesbian and Gay Association (ILGA) lists 42 countries where

---

6 For discussion on the damaging nature of this personification see Seidman (1994), Exum (1996: 101–28) and Guest (1999).

homosexuality is illegal.[7] Criminalized 'homosexuals' are liable to a range of penalties. In those countries where Sharí'a law prevails, execution still remains a real threat.[8] In others, imprisonment is more likely to be prescribed, with sentences ranging from ten days to 20 years, depending upon the country, plus fines. However, being held for trial and subsequent imprisonment can bring its own additional terrors of torture and rape. Moreover, in regions where the rhetoric of government and religious authorities is virulently anti-gay/lesbian, this can indirectly lead to state-tolerated murders in regions where perpetrators can act with relative impunity. The Amnesty International report *Crimes of Hate, Conspiracy of Silence. Torture and Ill-treatment based on Sexual Identity* pulls no punches:

> Around the world, lesbians, gay men and bisexual and transgender people are imprisoned under laws which police the bedroom and criminalize a kiss; they are tortured to extract confessions of 'deviance' and raped to 'cure' them of it; they are killed by 'death squads' in societies which view them as *'desechables'* – disposable garbage. (Amnesty International 2001)

It is not within the remit of this chapter to cover the full range of discriminatory and punitive practices that are applied across the world. A variety of organizations are committed to documenting instances of such practices and providing up-to-date reports.[9] Such reports can be examined for evidence of the ways in which state-sponsored discourses construct, position and criminalize the 'homosexual', and the repercussions for the individuals who are thus positioned.

This section of the chapter draws on the instances of assault that have been documented in Comstock's (1991) review of surveys. His review demonstrates that men and women who identify (or who are identified) as LGBT/Q have experienced being chased/followed, being the target of thrown objects, being spat at, being punched, kicked or beaten, being assaulted with a weapon or being raped and have been murdered, and their homes have been the object

---

7 In Africa: Angola, Benin, Burundi, Cameroon, Cape Verde, Djibouti, Ethiopia, Guinea Conakry, Liberia, Libya, Malawi, Mauritania, Mauritius, Morocco, Senegal, Sudan, Swaziland, Togo and Tunisia. In Asia/the Pacific: Afghanistan, Bangladesh, Brunei, Pakistan, the Solomon Islands and Western Samoa. In Europe: the Chechen Republic. In the Americas: Barbados, Grenada, Nicaragua, Puerto Rico, Saint Lucia, Trinidad and Tobago. In the Middle East: Bahrain, Iran, Lebanon, Oman, Qatar, Saudi Arabia, Syria, United Arab Emirates and Yemen.

8 Countries where homosexual acts remain subject to the death penalty include Mauritania, Sudan, Afghanistan, Pakistan, the Chechen Republic, Iran, Saudi Arabia, Yemen and possibly the United Arab Emirates (source: http://www.ilga. org/Information/legal_survey/Summary%20information/death_penalty_for_ homosexual_act.htm)

9 Organizations such as Amnesty International, the Lesbian and Gay Immigration Rights Task Force, the International Lesbian and Gay Association, the National Gay and Lesbian Task Force, Queer Resources Directory, Behind the Mask (lesbian and gay affairs in Africa) maintain websites with relevant, detailed documentation. For a review of the global context see West and Green (1997) and Donnelly (2003).

of vandalism and arson. It is not surprising that the effects of living in such a heterosexist environment can be manifested in low self-esteem, depression, self-harm and ultimately suicide. It is particularly worrying to note that young people at school who identify (or are perceived to be) gay or lesbian face regular harassment from their peers and, in some cases, their teachers. This harassment ranges from name-calling, public ridicule and teasing, theft of belongings or ostracism, to, in some cases, actual physical violence. According to Ian Rivers one in three young people face such harassment and, in the UK, '40% of those young people may go on to self-harm or attempt suicide, a figure that is supported by research in the United States and Canada' (2000: 19).

Survivor literature generally speaks of the need for survivors of any calamity or oppression to give verbal or written expression to the experience of pain, and this is where Lamentations offers a useful resource. While there is obviously no direct analogy between heterosexist oppression and the situation that prompted the writing of the ancient text of Lamentations, the virtue of its stylized imagery is that its poetic form readily lends itself as a timeless resource for expressing the distresses of different situations, times and locations.[10] It is in this sense that the features of the surveys reviewed by Comstock find a resonance in the book of Lamentations.

Lamentations, for example, contains several images of being chased and harried. Not only are there specific references to being pursued (1.3), being harried like a hunted bird (3.52), chased by enemies swifter than eagles and ambushed in the mountains (4.19); but when linked with the predator imagery of the deity becoming like a lion or bear lying in wait, or an archer waiting to ambush (3.10), there is an overall feeling of being *relentlessly* hunted down. Moreover, the avenues of escape have been closed down: the claustrophobic impression of being utterly trapped is present at 3.7–9 in references to the deity building a wall around the victim, twisting the victim's paths and walling them up with hewn stone.

Survey reports of being publicly spat at echo the portrayal of Woman/Zion as the object of general public derision as passers-by clap their hands, hiss/whistle and shake their heads, gape and gnash their teeth, relishing her public humiliation (2.15–16; 3.46). These gestures, like spitting in the modern day, are expressions of contempt, mockery and intimidation.

The surveys reported experiences of being the target of thrown objects and being assaulted with a weapon. In Lamentations it is none other than the deity who casts a net for the victim's feet (1.13), who bends a bow like an enemy and whose arrows find their mark in the victim's kidneys (3.12–13).

The surveys report incidents of being punched, kicked or beaten, and Lamentations contains images that could enable a reader to give voice to these experiences. Using hyperbole typical of the lament genre, the representative

---

10 Thus, although Joyce's article on 'Lamentations and the grief process' uses insights from the world of pastoral psychology to inform his interpretation of the text, he also recognizes that, conversely, the text can be used to inform our contemporary experiences of loss (1993: 317). He rightly cautions against any uncritical, loose application of the principle of analogy, yet as his article demonstrates, he finds that a self-critical, careful use of analogy can bear rich fruit.

speaker of chapter 3 speaks of how his flesh and skin is wasted and how his bones have been smashed (3.4–6), how he has been forced to eat gravel, been bent in the dust and sated with wormwood (3.15–16). There is talk of being forced to wear a yoke around the neck (1.14). The virgin daughter Zion has been trampled as a wine press (1.15). She declares that her innards turn to liquid (1.20; 2.11) and speaks of the deity's fire burning deep within her bones (1.13).

Even the experience of rape reported by Comstock can be voiced by using the cries of Woman/Zion (5.11) and by considering the metaphorical rape of Woman/Zion herself evident in 1.10 where a 'hand' (a term used euphemistically for the penis) is spread over her 'desirable things' as the nations enter her 'sanctuary'. When in 2.7 we read that the walls of her citadels are given into the 'hand' of the enemy, the personification of Zion as a woman allows for a reading that sees her body being given over for rape.[11]

Finally, Lamentations reverberates with the sheer unpredictability that gays and lesbians face in their everyday life. Tamsin Wilton speaks of the damaging effects of living in a British society that honours the President of Stonewall Angela Mason with an OBE, yet is simultaneously rife with anti-gay prejudice and violence: 'One of the hardest things for lesbians and gay men to live with is unpredictability. There is no way of knowing when you get up in a morning whether today will be one of those days when everyone you meet returns your smile, or whether you and your partner will be spat at in the street' (2000: 6).

The book of Lamentations thus contains much conventional lament language and imagery that provides a rich, timeless, generic vocabulary of assault that can be applied subsequently to specific instances of oppression and its concomitant physical, psychological and emotional distress. A focus on overt physical assaults should not come at the expense of exploring the mental stress that derives from being in relationship with a deity and belonging to a religious tradition that, in the eyes of many people, condemns to severe judgement anyone engaging in homoerotic relations. The psychological stress that this induces for many LGBT/Q-identified Jews and Christians requires an outlet just as much as the expression of experiences of physical assault. Many of the emotional reactions that generally accompany such experiences are covered in Lamentations: bitter weeping (1.2; 2.11; 3.48–9), misery (1.21), faintness/illness (1.13, 22), churning innards (1.20; 2.11), sighs (1.11, 21), disquiet and deep unhappiness (3.17–18), and the sense of utter humiliation and disgrace (1.1–3, 8–9; 3.14; 5.1).

However, these reactions are also accompanied by expressions of outrage and disbelief. The fact that the people have lost not only their religious centre – the temple – but the faithfulness of their God who, the psalmist claims, has organized and taken pleasure in the assault, is not only a cause of great hurt but also of bewilderment. Cognitive dissonance seems to permeate the text of Lamentations.[12] This is evident in the number of reversals present within

---

11 For further details on the rape imagery see Mintz (1982) and Guest (1999).

12 Gottwald believed that the key to this text's theology lay in the cognitive dissonance caused by the disparity of God's behaviour with Israel's recent repentance and reform under King Josiah. For him, the tension between theological expectation (based

the text. Previous symbols of his positive, guiding presence have now unexpectedly become hostile and destructive. Thus, God's right hand, the hand of support and strength often used on behalf of Israel, protecting them from adversity, alarmingly, takes its stand as a formidable foe, armed with bow and arrow. Cloud and fire that have previously been symbols of a guiding and protecting presence are turned against the people: God is hidden in a cloud and burns destructively (2.1–4). One quickly gets the sense that the unthinkable has happened, that God has acted entirely unpredictably and excessively.

Faced with such a prospect, lament psalms are invaluable resources, for they offer speakers the words and images to confess their sense of radical dissonance:

> They are speeches of surprised dismay and disappointment . . . sharp ejaculations by people accustomed either to the smooth songs of equilibrium or to not saying anything at all because things are 'all right.' They are the shrill speeches of those who suddenly discover that they are trapped and the water is rising and the sun may not come up tomorrow in all its benevolence. And we are betrayed! (Brueggemann 1995: 19)

In Lamentations, as with several psalms of lament, the fact that the betrayal has come from the deity is perhaps the most bewildering and worrying feature. In response to this dissonance, Lamentations approaches the deity at times with outrage, sometimes with remorse, and certainly with incredulity that *Yahweh's* people should have been so assaulted and abandoned. In 2.20 the psalmist reminds the deity that this is *Israel* who is the object of wrath, assaulted to a greater extent than has ever previously been known, even greater than the sudden fate that came to Sodom (4.6).

Herein lies the reason why this text may be such a vital resource for those who identify as lesbian, gay, bisexual or transgendered Jews and Christians. These laments bewail the way a people have been betrayed by their religious leaders, abandoned by their deity to a miserable existence where they are subject to the gloating derision of onlookers, bereft of the one structure that gave them not only pride and stability but a means of access to God – the temple. Oppression of LGBT/Q-identified Jews or Christians has often been legitimated by reference to the very scriptures to which one gives allegiance, and by reference to one's own deity who is invoked as prosecutor. The temple – be it church or synagogue – may as well be deemed lost insofar as certain branches of those religions have closed their doors to (openly practising) lesbian, gay, bisexual and transgendered-identified members. The legacy of this is a sense of radical dissonance. The dissonance is so strong that it threatens

---

on a supposed widespread acceptance of the Deuteronomic doctrine of retribution) and the actual reality of catastrophic destruction lies at the heart of the text (see 1954: 50–1). Albrektson suggested rather that the dissonance lay in the widespread belief in the inviolability of Zion, the guarantee of the deity's protection and security, and its actual destruction (1963: 219). Moore (1983) has rightly criticized these attempts to locate a 'key' to Lamentations. However, cognitive dissonance does appear to lie at the heart of this text and pervades its chapters.

to force individuals down two equally distressing paths: either stay with one's religious faith, live a life of secrecy or celibacy and bear the consequences;[13] or abandon one's faith, losing the religious community that goes with it.

Certainly, abandoning one's faith could be seen as a liberative option. Turning one's back on an oppressive god, scriptures and a condemnatory community could be applauded as an affirming, positive action. However, such drastic action can also leave its scars, and insofar as such a decision may lead a person to abandon the idea of faith and religious life *in toto* it impoverishes individuals further, forcing them to choose from a very young age 'between the integration of their self and sexuality and the god presented to them by church, family, culture. Put quite simply, either God goes or the person goes. This huge conflict creates a spiritual lacuna' (Lynch 1996: 204).

However, several gay-affirmative books on raising self-esteem, on counselling, aiding spiritual well-being, on LGBT/Q-identified people in health and social care settings, contain chapters on counteracting the effects of one's religious upbringing (which in itself indicates the significance of religion for the well-being of gay-identified people), helping them to renegotiate their religious lives rather than abandoning them. What is of interest is the way such literature points to the urgent need for clients to express their hurt and their anger. This is an important stage in coming to terms with the way their scriptures and their deity have been wielded against them. Lynch, for instance, notes how several of his clients present with the damaging effects of 'Bible bingo'.[14] As part of the healing process, the provision of a safe space and target for the expression of deep emotional distress is very important if the client is to be able to move forward. Similarly, Dominic Davies, who warns that the effects of bottling up anger can be very damaging, leading some to drug abuse, alcoholism, depression, low self-esteem and suicide, concurs that 'safe, contained "anger rituals" can prove extremely effective in moving clients away from depression and suicide or self-harming tendencies' (1996a: 32).

Lamentations could be used as a resource for this much-needed expression of anger and distress, thereby laying a basis for finding a way back to one's spiritual life without passively accepting the punitive judgement and opprobrium that has been conventionally heaped upon the head. Precisely how Lamentations was originally used is not known, but the five psalms offered

---

13 The consequences of enforced closeted existence are now well documented. Nugent, for example, notes how Roman Catholic teaching has an insidious effect on openly gay priests. A gay priest is in the difficult position of being required 'to live as a public minister of a Church that condemns homosexual acts in strong language while attempting to speak compassionately among homosexual people. There is a considerable inner dissonance generated when a person in this position is asked to articulate views that he does not accept and that he is at times powerless to publicly oppose or reject' (1997: 366). It is not surprising that McFarlane's (1998) review of the experiences of lesbians, gay men and bisexuals in the mental health services reveals that attempts to be Christian, Jewish or Muslim *and* lesbian, gay or bisexual lead to the discomforting experience of living double lives or having split personalities (1998: 22–5).

14 By 'Bible bingo' Lynch refers to the 'selective and destructive use of Biblical (or Talmudic or Koranic) passages to back arguments for a patriarchal, heterosexist and homophobic world view' (1996: 201).

the singers some kind of sanctioned time and place to give expression to all the hurt and pain, grief and bitterness, sense of betrayal, anger and recrimination, a basis for renegotiating one's relationship with this deity. Brueggemann claims that psalmists 'had already understood the psychotherapeutic importance of fully expressing hurt and rage' (1995: 54), implying that this was a recognized and acceptable part of religious life. This is the great strength of Lamentations today: it provides a public, canonically sanctioned opportunity to give voice to human pain and to address God from a position *within* the religious life of the people. The canonical existence of Lamentations indicates the strong desire to stake a claim to be heard through communal rituals of mourning, grief, confession and complaint.

However, as far as contemporary lesbian, gay, bisexual and transgendered-identified persons are concerned, that recognition has hardly been afforded. Apart from those congregations that have set up their own gay-affirmative synagogues or churches, many Jews and Christians belong to synagogues or churches where they dare not reveal their sexual preferences and certainly are not free to express their emotional responses to the oppressive environment in which they live and (perhaps) worship. The situation implied in Lamentations is that *all Israel* is invited to share in the expression of outrage and distress. The catastrophe has overwhelmed all, and *all* have a stake in the cultic response.[15] If LGBT/Q-identified Jews and Christians are not to be alienated entirely from their religious communities they too need a place where they can communally find expression for their experiences. And just as the ancient psalmists found their way back to their deity through radical liturgy, so too LGBT/Q-identified Jews and Christians need to be offered cultic spaces in which to work through their experiences and renegotiate their relationship with God. The church/synagogue ignores this at its peril: 'In the past, the response of lesbians and gay men has been to tend their wounds, limping away from the oppression of Christianity in particular and religion in general' (Lynch 1996: 202).

Images of Abandonment

While Lamentations encourages an outpouring of bitterness and grief in response to the experiences of assault, it simultaneously confronts a deep sense of abandonment. Woman/Zion sits in lonely existence and in her solitary state weeps long and hard into the night. In a forlorn gesture she spreads her hands in appeal to others but receives no comfort. Indeed, the conspicuous lack of any compassionate solidarity is emphasized in the repeated references to its absence (1.2, 9, 16, 17, 21; 2.13). Her loneliness is exacerbated by the fact that people she might have relied upon for help, betray and turn against her. Her pleas to old friends, lovers and onlookers are fruitless. Her 'lovers'

---

15 Moore notes how the book has 'an astonishingly complete spectrum of non-metaphorical terms for nearly every age, sex, and class of humanity. Babes, sucklings, children, boys, young men, young women, mothers, fathers, and old men are portrayed in the book suffering differing degrees of trauma. Slaves, priests, prophets, widows, orphans, princes, and kings are there as well' (1983: 546).

offer no consolation, all her friends are treacherous. But perhaps most significant is the realization that the deity has also turned against and deserted her. Woman/Zion demands recognition and recompense from God, but these demands are not satisfied. For all that there is a window of hope mid-book (3.22–41) and other glimmers in 4.22 and 5.21, the experience of abandonment is most painfully evident in the tortured closing verses of the final chapter: are the people destined to be forgotten, forsaken for the length of days? Has the deity, exceedingly angry, utterly rejected them?[16]

The fear that the recital of the laments may not even reach a deity who hides behind a cloud, makes its usage within the cult all the more important. These laments are prepared to contemplate the unthinkable. When liturgy can go this far, when there is freedom to express one's worst fears, then there is truly therapeutic space for the expression of grief and loss, and perhaps, eventually, healing. Here again, Brueggemann's insights are instructive. His proposal that the function of the psalms of lament is to move people through a sequence of orientation–disorientation–reorientation stresses that there needs to be an *utter breakdown of old certainties*, a fully explored experience of rage, bitterness and distress before there can be any useful reorientation. It is telling, he says, 'that these psalms use the words "pit/Sheol/waters/depths," for in therapy, one must be "in the depths" if there is to be new life' (1995: 21). He therefore stresses the absolute importance of Psalm 88, 'for it is a word precisely at the bottom of the pit when every hope is abandoned. The speaker is alone and there is as yet no hint of dawn. Psalm 88 is the full recognition of collapse' (1995: 21–2).

Like Psalm 88, Lamentations, in all its bleakness and full exploration and acknowledgement of distress, offers a profound space in which to voice the experience of the 'depths'; of the deep dislocation that abandonment creates. In this, Lamentations can again be a useful resource for the LGBT/Q-identified Jews and Christians who may have felt abandoned by their deity, given their abandonment by the religious communities that purport to represent that deity's will. Lamentations squarely faces that trauma. And although there are acknowledgements that the people must have sinned to provoke such a frenzied and brutal attack, importantly, the psalmist does not feel that their conduct merits the overkill. Rather, that the deity has reacted, as the prophets suggest, like a raging cuckolded husband, who has taken revenge upon the adulterous wife in a most humiliating, vicious and violent fashion. Any attempt to soften, explain away or redeem this metaphor has potentially damaging consequences for contemporary women.[17]

---

16 The Rabbinic tradition of repeating verse 19 after verse 22, thereby offsetting the dismal and sombre end to the book, only endorses the acute awareness of the unbearable bleakness of 5.19–22.

17 Texts such as Hosea 1–3; Jeremiah 2–5; Ezekiel 16; 23; and Isaiah 47 have been scrutinized as part of an ongoing 'porno-prophetics' debate; a debate that challenges the way in which the image of an adulterous metaphorical woman is used to describe Israel's sin and justify God's violent excesses. See, for example, Setel (1985), Galambush (1992), Magdalene (1995), Weems (1995), Sherwood (1996), Brenner (1997), Dempsey (1998, 2000). The debate explores the damaging effects this metaphor may have had (and continues to have) upon readers of these texts. See for example Fontaine (1997), Fortune (1983, 1987), Scarf (1983).

If there is any saving grace for Lamentations it is that it does not contain a submissive Woman/Zion who concedes defeat and runs back to her 'husband'. On the contrary, her resilient challenges to God, her strident insistence that God should answer to the brutal treatment of her and her people, means that the deity is not let off the hook. Woman/Zion registers the complaint and waits. As in Psalm 88, where the psalmist 'addresses what is apparently an empty sky and indifferent throne', the psalmist's 'stubborn resolve' remains

> not because there are no alternatives, but because Israel will not concede that the conversation of prayer belongs wholly to Yahweh or happens wholly on Yahweh's terms. Israel has a stake in the conversation and is 'part owner' of the process of prayer. Israel will not be driven from the conversation, even by Yahweh's lack of response, and will not yield its claim to the silent sovereignty of Yahweh. Israel determinedly and self-assuredly knows that this prayer is the meeting ground where life occurs and will wait there for a response from Yahweh, if need be, 'until hell freezes over'. (Brueggemann 1995: 56–7)

The LGBT/Q-identified Jews or Christians learn from this that there need be no either/or 'take it or leave it' relationship with their faith. There is no 'open and shut case' in regard to how the relationship with God operates or on what basis. They too have a stake in this relationship and they can bring their hurts, distresses, anger and bewilderment before this deity and stake their claim to be heard and to have their situation remedied. Their complaint, once registered – and registered in its uttermost – is, in fact, the only basis upon which the fertile ground of renewal can be sown. This is not a 'tail between the legs' return to an abusive partner but a refusal to accept the hurt that has been dealt out and a steadfast demand that the abuser acknowledges the infliction of pain and acts to put things right. The disorientation part of Brueggemann's sequence allows for a thorough review of the relationship between God and worshipper that is exhaustive and utter. Any resumption of the relationship has to be on these terms. As such, it is inevitably radical. Within the period of dislocation the people can refuse to accept the judgement or treatment that has been dealt to them, they can complain stridently about God's justice and initiate a period of waiting for the *deity's* repentance.[18] If that deity elects to hide behind a cloud, then the lamenter stands beneath that cloud and refuses to be bowed, refusing to be abandoned, refusing to accept the judgement, refusing to be cut off, maintaining the vigil; being present to God even within the experience of the deity's most profound absence, awaiting a hearing.

Many LGBT/Q-identified Jews and Christians have already been through this transitional period and have begun the work of renewal and reorientation. Theologians are blazing the way forward. Gay-affirmative synagogues and churches are listening to, and expounding, God's new word to the people. This is consistent with the view, often found within many liberation theologies, that readers have to find their own acceptance or rejection of scriptural

---

18 For a profound discussion on waiting for the deity's repentance see Blumenthal (1993).

judgements and renegotiate their own path to God, often through a period of much dislocation and complaint. The focus that has been given to taming the gay texts of terror illustrates the sense of disorientation that such texts continue to instil upon gay readers and indicate why our relationship with them, and with the deity they claim, has to be renegotiated. Thus Gary Comstock advocates an approach where 'Christian Scripture and tradition are not authorities from which I seek approval; rather, they are resources from which I seek guidance and learn lessons as well institutions that I seek to interpret, shape, and change' (1993: 4). Comstock describes his deity as one in whom he has made a commitment and invested dearly, but with whom he insists on a 'mutual exchange of critique, encouragement, support, and challenge' (1993: 11). Such renegotiation is an important part of the healing process as we gain 'confidence to snatch back the Bible from those who locked it away' and learn 'to read it through our own eyes rather than through the eyes of others' (Stuart 1997: 41–2).

So, staying in relationship with God and with the larger religious community need not necessarily be seen as colluding with one's oppression, or not adequately shaking off an oppressive regime (though it can be that). Alison Webster acknowledges the dilemma: to leave the church, says Webster, when religion is such a significant mover behind socio-political Western life, can be a 'serious tactical error' (1995: 165). Indeed, it can indicate a 'form of collusion with the unimaginative, anti-religious and fundamentalist forces which use the power afforded by their political supremacy to define who God is, what Christianity is, and what is ethical and unethical' (1995: 183). But she also recognizes that

> not to leave is also a collusion with the forces of patriarchy, for our precious energies are wasted in trying to 'change things from within'; or even in just holding on to a basic belief that we have the right to exist. Continued engagement of any kind could be interpreted as legitimation of what patriarchal Christianity stands for. (1995: 183)

Against this dilemma, Webster advocates maintaining a plurality of options – some might leave, some might stay and we should uphold the legitimacy of the decision as to where one fights one's battles. Absolutely so. Webster has a vision of Christianity as a 'creative quest' whereby the 'unconversion' experiences of her contributors are 'not stories of losing religion at all, but reflect the discovery of a form of religions which is more authentic than the forms of Christianity that they left behind' (1995: 180).[19]

Elizabeth Stuart also argues that Christianity's influence on Western society is so deeply embedded that the absence of a queer voice would be counterproductive and would effectively 'hand over huge amounts of power to the oppressors' (1987: 15). Such sentiments are echoed by several of the speakers in Peter Sweasey's *From Queer to Eternity* who argue that they will stay because Christianity is such a political force in the world: Diana Reynolds

---

19 For an example of one who has moved forward in such a way see the work of Clark (1989, 1997).

deliberately chooses to fight from within by opting to be ordained knowing she was lesbian. She says,

> Until we have a real cross-section of society represented, the Church will never be the body of unity that it's supposed to be . . . So we have to stay: if we don't, it will never change . . . I see my ministry as a revolution in the Church. (Sweasey 1997: 72)

For Mike Fox, it is a question of helping the next generation:

> If you don't stay within the institution then what happens to those who do? . . . If people like me desert the Church and don't try and change it through our example, then the people who are coming up after us who face the same problems will have no one to turn to, and we will be making the misery worse. (Sweasey 1997: 72)

Sweasey, following Goss (1993), sees such people as frontiers-people, pioneers, operating as thorns in the side, catalysts for change. By staying within established traditions we 'steal their trump card', for the ranks of religious believers include queers along with the homophobes. 'Instead of saying we don't want to play your stupid game, we're saying, we're already playing, and what makes you think you can set the rules here?' (Sweasey 1997: 79). Such a stance is important, for many individuals are still experiencing 'Sheol', fearing that their sexual orientation may have cut them off from any relationship with their God. Anti-gay theology and exclusive religious communities are confirming that abandonment and using it to urge such people to acknowledge that their sexual choices render them liable to the wrath of God (see Wold's (1998) work for example). Such fear drives individuals into the damaging arms of anti-gay/lesbian ex-gay ministries.[20] Even though there are now many support groups available within the Jewish and Christian traditions, and a rapidly expanding corpus of pro-gay theological literature available, testimonies still indicate that people feel betrayed by religious leaders and experience considerable pain and distress when attempting to come to terms with a God who is repeatedly invoked as their accuser and punisher. It is therefore imperative that gay theology and religious communities do not ghettoize themselves but continue to dialogue with the theologians and communities that remain committed to a heterosexist agenda.

Images of Accusation and Acrimony

The book of Lamentations encourages its readers to recount hurts and grievances and issue their complaints to God who, to all appearances, has been an overbearing, abusing and over-punitive deity. It is blatant and strident in its complaint, but only relatively recently has this been upheld as a healthy,

---

20 On the damaging and largely unsuccessful methods of ex-gay ministries see Haldeman (1994) and the references cited there, and Morrow (2003).

legitimate and profoundly helpful mode of theological address. Previously there has been a tendency, particularly evident in Christian circles, to see the lament as an embarrassing and theologically unsound mode of address. Claus Westermann identifies 'a noticeable tendency . . . to devalue the lament or to speak of it with depreciatory reserve' (1994: 81). He cites several explicit devaluations – as in the work of Brandscheidt (1988) and Rudolph (1962) – together with some less blatant yet no less devaluing comments in the work of Kraus (1968) and Childs (1970: 595). Westermann argues that the fault lies not with interpreters themselves but with the fact that

> lamentation has been severed from prayer in Christian piety throughout the history of the church. In the Old Testament lamentation is an intrinsic component of prayer, as is shown in the Psalter with its high percentage of psalms of lamentation. In the Christian church, on the other hand, the lament no longer receives a hearing . . . One of the consequences of this state of affairs is that, in Christian interpretations of Lamentations, the laments are simply not allowed to be laments. (1994: 81–2)

To view the lament as a healthy, wholly appropriate form through which to address God requires, first, the recognition that humans find it very difficult to move on from any distressing situation without being given time and space in which to grieve and be angry (as noted above); and second, that this is a *sanctioned* mode of address without which one cannot move to a reorientation of faith and relations with God.

To some extent, the discomfort associated with lamenting before God may be especially felt by LGBT/Q-identified Christians and Jews who, despite a history that has featured considerable reasons to lament, have not, until recently, rehearsed their remonstrations in any sustained detail, and may have sympathy with those who try to forward a gay-affirmative agenda in more subtle and socially acceptable ways.

Yet there have been moments of bold resistance in our history. The much-celebrated moment of resistance outside the Stonewall Inn on 28 June 1969 provoked subsequent political action undertaken by the Gay Liberation Front, the Gay Activists Alliance, OutRage and Stonewall. Since that moment, resistance to oppression has been voiced strongly and ACT-UP! campaigns have visibly and physically given form to that resistance. However, the activists' methods are not always supported and their campaigns create ripples of nervousness in some quarters of gay communities. The voicing of grievance, and the public action undertaken to confront the authorities perpetuating oppression and discrimination, can seem too loud and brazen, too public, too immodest in the demand for equality and liberty.[21] Such anxieties serve institutionalized heterosexism, playing into heterosexism's compulsion to keep this 'love that dare not speak its name' ashamed and silent.

---

21 This discomfort is recognized in Woodman and Lenna's four-stage coming out model, discussed by Dominic Davies (1996b). At the stage of identity confusion, anger may be expressed against those who are enjoying an open lesbian or gay life, who are being 'blatant', and those who are at this stage may think, as Davies puts it, that such flaunting of sexual choice is 'giving the rest of us a bad name' (1996b: 74).

It may be the case that such nervousness has also beset LGBT/Q-identified Jews and Christians, given the emphasis in those traditions (particularly for Christians in the writings of Paul) on sobriety, humility and modesty, deference to authority, and 'proper' behaviour. The tradition that feminists have long been resisting as patriarchally oppressive, holding women to a submissive inferior status and role, the tradition that held slaves in their assigned place as inferior beings who must offer obedience to their masters, is also *hetero*patriarchally oppressive. Not only does the strong heterosexist ethos of the scriptures appear to vindicate societal opposition to same-sex preferences, but more subtly, the emphasis upon 'proper' behaviour, gender roles, and above all deference and modesty, works against the desire to be vocally and actively resistant to that ethos. Commitment to these qualities could easily tie faithful people to a more apologetic model of action that seeks not to offend or disrupt, not to embarrass or humiliate, but to politely request *privileges* rather than demand *rights*. When the Church puts its emphasis on those passages of scripture and forgets, neglects or ignores its heritage of complaint and resistance, the Church serves the status quo and the god of the status quo.

However, within Lamentations there is little evidence that the psalmists feared offending anyone – least of all God. On the contrary, Woman/Zion is urged to voice her distress and call the deity to account for the devastation God has poured out upon her. LGBT/Q-identified Jews and Christians need not allow religious qualms to put them off being acrimonious with God. Rather the Church (in particular) needs to attune itself once more to this right of complaint and re-accommodate the lament into its liturgy. Only by so doing will worshippers be able to develop and mature as equal covenant partners with their deity. As gay theology moves forward, the need is to do 'theology without apology', to be unashamedly 'unrepentant, self-affirming and practising' as Gary Comstock's book titles (1993, 1996) put it, for as Goss says, 'There is no apologizing in an authentic gay/lesbian liberation theology' (1993: xvii). For this, Alpert's description of an 'encounter approach' is helpful. An encounter approach is one where readers are encouraged to 'encounter the text directly with our emotions and our self-knowledge, allowing it to move us to anger and then beyond anger to action' (1997: 38). Alpert describes how, in the case of Leviticus 18.21, the encounter brings a sense of pain, anger, humiliation and terror:

> We imagine the untold damage done to generations of men, women, and children who experienced same-sex feelings and were forced to cloak or repress them. We reflect on those who acted on those feelings and were forced to feel shame and guilt and to fear for their lives. We remember how we felt when we first heard those words and knew their holy source. And we get angry – at the power these words have had over our lives, at the pain we have experienced in no small part because of these words. (1997: 44)

But there are ways of using this anger creatively:

> if we can, we grow beyond the rage. We begin to see these words as tools with which to educate people about the deep-rooted history of lesbian and

gay oppression. We begin to use these very words to begin to break down
the silence that surrounds us. (Alpert 1997: 44)

This is one of the reasons why I can now see my way clear to reconsider the
merits to retaining Lamentations where once I called for its removal from the
canon. It stands as a relic of oppression, a trace of history that influenced pernicious views of women, waiting to be re-encountered by those who resist its
personification of Woman/Zion and its damaging effects. And as Rabbi Rose
has insightfully and creatively suggested, a lesbian-identified reader may be
precisely the interpreter best placed to do this.[22]

What, then, is to be done with the admissions of guilt that are found in
Lamentations, and with the acknowledgements that Israel has sinned and
to some extent has been justly punished (1.8, 14, 18; 4.22)? There are two
things to note here. First, while there are acknowledgements of guilt within
Lamentations and moves towards repentance, this is no biddable, acquiescent,
subservient, grovelling repentance, but one that is forged through a resistant, outraged, full and frank confrontation of God and God's behaviour, and
one that exposes and objects to the inadequacies of God's representatives on
earth, the priests and prophets (as in 4.13–15). Woman/Zion is urged to cry
aloud with streaming tears and without rest, to cry out regularly throughout
the night, pouring out the heart and lifting hands to Yahweh (2.18–19). The
anxiety relates rather to the waiting time required to reinstate relations: 'ekah'
(how/why or perhaps a distressed 'Ah') moan the psalmists at the beginning
of three of the chapters (1.1; 2.1; 4.1, 2).

Second, Robert Davidson wisely cautions his readers against a naive acceptance of the psalmist's projection of guilt:

Lamentations . . . can look at what happened to Jerusalem and say, rightly, it
was richly deserved. But this is not always true of life. There are tragedies in
life in face of which people say, 'I wonder what he – or she – did to deserve
that?'; and the only honest answer is 'nothing'. The Old Testament elsewhere
is aware of this. Nowhere is it more passionately argued than in the Book of
Job. (1985: 175)

---

22 As a woman who is both Jewish and lesbian-identified, Rose sees herself as being
inside the addressees of the text, but also outside. As lesbian-identified she can look at
the adulterous wife/Israel metaphor without considering herself addressed by it. This
is not to say that she does not identify with the image of Woman/Zion. However, her
identity with the metaphorical woman happens on a number of levels. They are both
women, the sexual acts of both have been considered sinful. But as a lesbian reader
'there may be another dimension altogether. I may more than identify with this woman
qua woman and her sexuality qua female sexuality, with the attendant impulses to
intervene and save her. I may in fact love this woman, yearning to express this love as a
lover might. My interest in the story then changes. I become as a rival suitor, offering in
my mind the kind of lovemaking I hope would heal' (2000: 150). Conceding that there is
self-interest here she adds, 'With the appropriate maturity, I understand the situation
may require the most absolute chastity . . . By assisting the abused woman, I enact again
the rebellion-towards-freedom/justice by which I freed myself. In offering my intervention, assistance, and love, however chastely, I express my sexuality once again – and
because it is justice making, I can call that very sexuality God also' (2000: 150).

Ken Stone makes a similar assessment:

> It is not difficult to think of biblical passages which state or imply that disaster and distress are divine responses to sinful activities formerly carried out by those who suffer. Thus, the Bible – which is already used to justify discrimination against lesbians, gay men, bisexuals and transgendered folk – can also serve as a powerful rhetorical weapon for those who interpret the HIV virus as a sign of perversity. (1999: 16)

His work on the lament psalms values the resilient way in which the psalms accost God and call God to account for not alleviating excessive human suffering. But the most significance usefulness of the psalms' complaint to God lies in their emphatic declaration of the 'unacceptability of such suffering in an uncompromising and astonishing fashion, calling into question any theological discourse that is willing to construct a comforting God while refusing to confront the difficult question of evil' (1999: 25).

When reading Lamentations in the light of heterosexist discourse and actions, one needs to be wary of passively adopting those accusations of blame and taking on responsibility for the concomitant feelings of guilt that are fired out from the text. Blaming oneself or feeling guilty about the abuse one has suffered is a common experience – whether one has been sexually abused as a child, raped, been subject to war crimes or any other such experience. It is vital, however, that the survivor is not left in this condition but moves towards the ability to assert their innocence. It would be all too easy to accept the heterosexist ethos of the Hebrew and Christian scriptures and concede, for all the unfairness of the condemnation that is often heaped upon heads, that we have brought it upon ourselves by wishing to live lives that appear to be so contrary to the will of God. This temptation needs to be resisted robustly.

The move towards healing usually involves a rethinking of previous relationships. Therapist literature indicates how survivors need to choose whether or not, or on what renewed terms, they will remain in relationship with the people who committed the assault, or were witnesses to it and did little to help. L. Davis (1990) encourages her clients to set new boundaries, limits, ground rules, when in recovery. The book of Lamentations does not take us into that renegotiation period, but leaves us in the period of dislocation and dissonance, standing beneath the received judgement and registering protest. For the original singers of Lamentations and for its contemporary readers, this text provided/provides a most valuable resource to begin that period of recovery. Basic trust had/has been broken and the survivors needed/need to find a way back into the covenant relationship that sets new boundaries and ground rules through giving vent to the experiences of assault and abandonment and working through the stages of accusation. Healing begins here.

Ezekiel

TERESA HORNSBY

The erasure of the subjugated makes the dominant possible. (Laurel Schneider)

[S]tructures [of meaning] depend on what they dismiss/define as 'other.' Doing so displaces the mastery of those structures and renders legible the trace of the text's 'other.' (Ellen Armour)

In a standard article on the book of Ezekiel, one would expect the author to begin with a discussion of all the various points of contention about the writing: When was it written? To whom was it written? From where was it written? Why was it written? What are the major themes? Is it a unified composition? In this essay, I will address these issues only because it is expected. I, as a queer responder to the book of Ezekiel the prophet, must question whether any of these issues are relevant. Even if these issues could be resolved, which they cannot, ever, a queer reading would not be overly concerned with how modernist-thinking historicist scholars sought to categorize, compartmentalize and legitimize potentially subversive writings of Ezekiel, a primary character in a narrative about exile.

Organizing the book of Ezekiel into the categories of time, ownership and landscape serves only to support and maintain existing power centres – an endeavour that could be understood as antithetical to queer theory. More, to use Ezekiel to define concepts such as 'exile' or 'prophesy', or even 'queer', excludes concepts and stifles thinking. However, such an exercise is requisite for acceptance into an academic work, and, without those credentials, queer scholarship may never make it past the front door. Indeed, many readers may have picked up this publication hoping to learn more about Ezekiel's historical context and about 'the person' Ezekiel rather than Ezekiel as a literary character and what the book of Ezekiel might suggest for my contemporary readers. The first part of this chapter will reiterate what other scholars before me have said. My own readings will commence in the second part. I will explore relationships between Ezekiel's prophecies and queer performance art, and, finally, consider the word 'exile' in light of Derrida's *pharmikon*. Queer theory often enters a party on the arm of a more traditional guest.

Historicist Ezekiel (What, Where, When, Who)

Historical biblical scholars tend to place Ezekiel's prophecy between about 593 BCE and 571 BCE (Kamionkowski (2003: 1–29); Greenberg (1967); Darr (1992); Blenkinsopp (1990); Eichrodt (1970)). This means that Ezekiel began his diatribes after King Jehoiakim of Judah rebelled against Nebuchadrezzar, the Babylonian king. The rebellion failed and Nebuchadrezzar took control of Jerusalem and deported anybody who was anybody to Babylon – which included, it is assumed, Ezekiel. This was around 597 BCE and Ezekiel did not begin prophesying until four years later – perhaps it was because the exiles seemed pretty hopeful that Egypt would help the Judaeans rebel and then they would all be able to come home. However, Zedekiah, Nebuchadrezzar's newly appointed king in Jerusalem, lacked a spine and, eventually, completely submitted to Babylon in 597. To be fair, Zedekiah, again relying on Egypt for assistance (not unlike the 'Bay of Pigs' invasion) rebelled in 589–8. Nebuchadrezzar quickly took Jerusalem, captured Zedekiah, blinded him and took him to Babylon. Nebuchadrezzar's men destroyed Jerusalem and the temple. Any representatives of 'the people', including the chief priests and military leaders, were executed.

Most modernist scholars separate the book of Ezekiel into three primary divisions:

Chapters 1–24 are 'Oracles of judgement against Jerusalem'.
Chapters 25–32 are 'Oracles of judgement against Judah's neighbours'.
Chapters 33–48 are 'Oracles of salvation and hope'.

Ezekiel's Judgements have several themes, but a primary one is that the Israelites were always ingrates. Even from the time of Moses, they never properly worshipped Yahweh. Also, because of dealings with foreign powers, they are whores and adulterers (idolaters) – see Galambush (1992).

His misogynist assumptions and stereotypes about how 'whoring', adulterous women deserve humiliation, dismemberment and death, are problematic, to say the least (see Guest (1999); Weems (1995); Shields (2001: 129–51); Camp (1998b: 81–104)). This particular theme, that Jerusalem is an unfaithful wife who merits physical and emotional abuse, has been a focus of feminist biblical scholarship on the prophets in the last few decades (see Setel (1985); Exum (1996: 101–28); Galambush (1992) and Weems (1995)). While other prophets use this theme (e.g. Hosea, Jeremiah), Ezekiel's version is particularly harsh and explicit. Without a doubt, 'Ezekiel' believes he has 'the truth' about God: God is in control always; God will destroy Israel (and Jerusalem); all this destruction is brought about because of Israel's wickedness and disobedience to God; and God is always just – no matter what and no matter where (Darr 1992: 185).

Who Is This Guy?

Tamar Kamionkowski's recent work, *Gender Reversal and Cosmic Chaos*, provides an excellent and concise history of interpretation for Ezekiel. Regarding Ezekiel's composition and dating, she sees three divisions within the scholarship. The first, pre-1924, is characterized by a wholehearted acceptance of the book as a logical and cohesive unit (Kamionkowski 2003: 10). The second division is from 1924 to 1982, marked by Gustav Hölscher's conclusion that only a small fraction of Ezekiel was authentic to the prophet, and by Walther Zimmerli, who attributed Ezekiel to a school of disciples (Kamionkowski 2003: 11–12). The final era of Ezekiel scholarship began in 1983 with Moshe Greenberg's first volume of *Ezekiel* in the Anchor Bible Commentary series. Greenberg gives serious attention to matters of literary cohesion and relationships between form and meaning, while maintaining a focus on historical contexts. Feminist critiques of Ezekiel's misogyny and pornography, particularly in chapters 16 and 23, emerge during this third era of Ezekiel scholarship.

Thus far in Ezekiel's interpretive history, the scholarship is historicist and assumes for the most part that there is an Ezekiel apart from the literary character. Some conjure up 'facts' about his occupation, his social class, his intellect, his childhood; others say that we know hardly anything about 'the man' Ezekiel. The assumption that there is a historical truth about the man behind the text is one that is foreign to queer theory. I wonder if we could offer a fourth division to Kamionkowski's schema: poststructuralist works which understand that 'meaning' occurs at the intersection between reader and text. Ezekiel, as far as any modern reader knows, exists only in her or his mind as an interpretation of words on a page. I can make Ezekiel into any type of person I choose: he can be crazy, brilliant, ridiculous, poor, illiterate, angry – there are no limits.

Consequently, Ezekiel has been interpreted a number of ways – all of which would support an author's notion about Truth, God, the World, and all things capitalized. For example, von Rad sees genius in Ezekiel: he is not only a prophet, but a Theologian (von Rad 1965b: 223); Ezekiel is coolly, didactically detached (1965b: 223); he has his foundation in the priesthood, and thus, according to von Rad, he is one who 'depends on [the sacral tradition], and yet free from it' (1965b: 225). Von Rad also claims that we see for the first time, in Ezekiel, a sense of an individual working out his salvation with God. In Christian triumphalism, he writes,

> In ch. xviii Ezekiel is dealing with people who were suffering because the divine dispensation took no account of the individual, and who opposed the old collective idea according to which the generations form a greater organic body, which is also a single entity in the sight of God. They deny God's right to punish them for the sins of their fathers. The prophet helps them to think these problems through, and tries to comfort their troubled hearts by saying that every life is in a direct relationship of its own with God. (1965b: 231)

For von Rad, Ezekiel is an innovator: 'He was the first prophet consciously to enter this new sphere of activity, which may be described as a "cure of souls," provided we remember that it corresponds to the New Testament, i.e., Christian, *paraclesis'* (von Rad 1965b: 231).

What a Queer Ezekiel has to Offer

I salute the historicist tenacity for order. Ezekiel's endless lists of diatribes against foreigners are difficult to read without nodding off, and many scholars have spent their lives dissecting them. Yet, Ezekiel can be wrestled away from the tedium and can offer splendid and fabulous readings for all of us. His visions are fantastic and fabulous works; it is worth wading through the muck. From the 'wheel within a wheel' to the 'valley of the dry bones', the images of Ezekiel have become a part of modern vernacular. Not only are the visions fantastic spectacles, Ezekiel often inserts himself into the fantasy. In other words, Ezekiel gives us performance art pieces – embodied declarations, carnal protests which parallel the best of today's modern performance art pieces (Ezek. 4.1–11; 5.1–12; 12.1–20; 24.15–17).

Performativity and performance/embodiment

In a poststructuralist understanding, the text of Ezekiel becomes a site where meanings come together and are organized by the readers' interaction with it; it is a constructed organizing entity that participates in the creation of meaning. The text and the reader create meaning through 'interpreting events and making sense of experience' (MacDonald 1995: 2). Whether the text is visual, tactile, aural, auditory, hallucinatory, etc., Mieke Bal claims the common ground is narrative. She writes, 'Narrative as a mode of implicit argumentation is the line which runs through my work on all these different bodies of writing. Narrative as a mode of representation is a tool of manipulation, a figure of rhetoric . . .' (1994: 263). Likewise, Julia Kristeva understands texts to be written, dramatic, musical, visual or auditory as well (Grosz 1990: 252). The aggregation of acts coalesces into a single act, a performative symbol that is open to interpretation. To approach Ezekiel's prophetic performances as 'body as text' is a dandy example of queer theory in motion.

I can easily imagine watching Ezekiel perform in an off, off-Broadway experimental lab theatre project. I would watch this lone performance artist, similar to those I have seen before (Karen Finley, Annie Sprinkle, Bill T. Jones) turning his body into a symbol. He writes words of mourning on the front and back of a scroll and then eats it (2.10–3.3). The stage is dark and quiet as Ezekiel binds himself in strong rope and sits mute (3.24–6). He then places a steel plate between him and 'the city', lies on his left side for an extraordinarily long time and then on his right side for an extraordinarily long time (4.1–4). Then he bakes bread, on stage, and uses some sort of excrement. He eats the bread while he is lying on his side. He eats the same amount of bread every day at the same time – it is a very long performance (4.9–13). Finally, Ezekiel takes a sharp sword and shaves his head and face. He weighs all the hair and divides it into three equal parts. He strikes one part with the sword, one part scatters with the wind, and he keeps part of the hair in his robe and burns the rest (5.1–4).

What reviews the *Village Voice* would give him! The performance would not get rave reviews for originality – the repetition, the excrement, the excessiveness, the presence of ordinary, private acts publicly performed are common fodder in the world of queer performance art. That Ezekiel's prophetic performances and queer performative art are so similar is not coincidence. Both seek to express concerns that emerge from the fringe and counter power centres. Performance seems to hold a privileged place especially in the post-structuralist, queer discourses that seek to circumvent the linguistic.

There is a strong move in recent queer theory toward expressing queer concerns through the genre of performance (for example, see Pellegrini (1996); Hart (1998); Sedgwick (1990) and Phelan (1993)). One of the basic claims that performance theorists are making is that performance can be more disruptive of gender norms than written text. There seems to be an underlying assumption that performance is a more 'transgressive' or subversive form of signification. There are several reasons given to support this claim. First, some argue that performance exists in a non-categorizable space (cf. Phelan (1993); Elwes (1990); Bell (1994)). This claim would presuppose, of course, the existence of categorizable objects.

For example, Catherine Elwes claims that when a person, particularly anyone whose sexuality has been labelled 'obscene' in a particular culture, becomes the speaking subject of a performance, she or he refuses

> easy categorisation and begins to put together what patriarchy has pulled apart. A performer may be sexual, but she is not a stripper, she may act but she is not an actress . . . [S]he escapes categorisation into existing disciplines with their attendant pigeon-holing for women. (Elwes 1990: 174)

Here, Elwes is claiming that performance in itself defies categorization as a genre. It may involve speaking, but not necessarily. Performance not only defies genre categorization, some claim, but also may be understood as occupying the same interstitial location, as Elwes describes above, in its relationship between the sign and its referent. There is a relentless claim in many of the new queer theory works on performance, particularly performance art, that performance retains a direct relationship with the signifier because of the presence of a flesh-and-blood body. (Lynda Hart does not make this claim; in fact, in *Between the Body and the Flesh*, she specifically argues against the essentialist placement of the body in performance, see 1998: 84–123.) There is an assumption that the presence of a body somehow trumps or negates those texts that are merely representative of the spoken or written word.

In contrast to the claim that there is a non-referential, extra-symbolic body in a performance, I would agree with those (such as Hart and Butler) who claim that performance *creates the illusion* that the Real is being actualized through the presence of flesh-and-blood bodies. Often, the value of the performance is connected to its authenticity, its parody of the 'real'. According to Hart, watching a performance piece should elicit the question from the spectator, 'Is this real? Is this really happening?' But Hart astutely observes that when the distinction is blurred between what is 'real life' and what is art, that is, when the performance is 'too real', those who watch and interpret become mighty uncomfortable.

In order to explore the disruption that a performance brings when it so completely erases any distinction between the Real and acting, Hart analyses the 'non-review' by Arlene Croce, the primary dance reviewer for *The New Yorker*, of Bill T. Jones's dance performance, 'Still/Here'. Hart cites the following reasons that Croce gave for not seeing the performance: '(1) "Still/Here" incorporated videos of people with Aids who talk about their illness; (2) in doing so, the performance "crossed the line between theater and reality" ...; and (3) the combination of points one and two has made critics like herself "expendable". It is almost as if Croce believed that by attending the performance she herself would be annihilated' (Hart, 1998: 131).

In the analysis of Croce's article, Hart is intrigued at Croce's refusal to see the performance. From Croce's review, it is clear that she does not think the piece is art because it is too 'real'. Hart suggests that Croce senses threat or danger in admitting, not representations of disease and sex into the performance, but 'real' disease and sex. Hart understands that what has happened in the interpretation of 'Still/Here' is that when Croce refuses to allow the performance piece to be called art, she is in fact refusing it entrance into the Symbolic. Hart writes, 'What Croce's actions and language signify is her participation in the dominant order's refusal to allow Aids and its representations to enter into discourse' (1998: 132). Further, Hart describes what is occurring in Croce's 'non-review' as an example of what Tim Dean calls 'social psychosis': Aids is encountered not only as the discourse of the Other in a return of the repressed that constitutes the repressed as such (the structure by which we understand a neurotic subject); it is encountered also in the real as a consequence of its wholesale repudiation by a society that refuses to admit a signifier for Aids and is therefore analysable according to the structure by which we understand a 'psychotic subject'. What Hart is saying, simply, is that Croce (as an interpreter) is threatened by Jones's performance piece because she recognizes the 'realness' of it:

> Croce keeps her distance from Bill T. Jones and his representations of people who are terminally ill – 'I have not seen Bill T. Jones's "Still/Here" and have no plans to review it.' But she does review it. She re-views it, without first viewing it, as an unspeakable, extradiscursive act, a dance that cannot be symbolized, a dance that falls out of her repertory of the symbolic ... When Croce says that Jones's performance was too realistic, she doesn't mean dramatic realism – the illusion of reality – she means life. (Hart 1998: 133)

By refusing to call it art, Croce is refusing Aids signification in the dominant discourse (because Aids is a discourse of an Other). Thus, the process is self-reproducing: because Aids (as a conflation of sex and death) poses a threat to the dominant discourse because it is a discourse of an Other, it is refused signification. Then, death and sex become real, and in their 'realness' become threatening to the symbolic order. By this construction, the Real, then, is something that threatens the production of the symbolic order, is something that is refused signification by that order, but remains necessary in the determination of the primary discourse.

There seems to be some credence, then, in the claim that there is a 'real-ness' present in some types of performances: it is a realness defined as that which opposes the Symbolic. As Hart argues, the performances that register discourses of an Other seem to have direct bearing on the production of social norms. What is threatening about performance, then, is not anything onto-logically specific to performance, nor is it due to the presence of a flesh-and-blood body, but the perceived threat comes from the flesh and blood body in performance combined with the presence of an Other. Karen Finley notes that it is not when she performs 'bold and painfully graphic' speeches about 'the horrors of sexual abuse, governmental indifference to Aids, incest, rape, and a host of other issues that address race, class, gender, and sexual minorities', that has generated the greatest controversy (Hart 1992: 8). Rather, the elements that have been labelled the most 'obscene' in her performances are when, in one, she smears chocolate all over her body, and in a piece called 'Yams Up My Granny's Ass', Finley smears yams on her buttocks. Hart notes that in the interpretations of Finley's performances, 'the image – conveyed through the physical action – subsumed the speech' (Hart 1998: 130).

Yet, any political, or aesthetic, or theological point becomes entirely ignored in a rush to judgement by hostile interpreters because of the presence of physical excesses. For example, there are scenes in which urine is supposedly thrown on the audience (it is not really urine; the container was switched off-stage); there is a piece in which HIV-infected blood (not really) is put on a rag, attached to a clothes line and passed over the audience; there are perform-ances of body cuttings (therefore, real bleeding) and self-inflicted (real) muti-lations. All of these have been harshly criticized precisely for their use of the body's refuse.

In addition to the participation of the flesh-and-blood body in a perform-ance communicative of an Other's discourse, there is at least one other aspect of or a type of performance that tends to draw negative criticism and is often labelled 'not art'. The performances of Janine Antoni and Alison Knowles, for example, often draw such criticisms.

In one performance called 'Specific Lunch' Knowles invites the viewer to prepare and eat a tuna sandwich on wheat toast with lettuce and butter, no mayo, a large glass of buttermilk, or a cup of soup. Antoni, in a piece called 'Loving Care', mops the floor with her hair, which has been dipped in Loving Care hair dye. Like Ezekiel shaving, she is doing a mundane activity (mopping the floor/shaving) but doing it in an unusual, almost bizarre fashion. Other performances, such as 'The House' performed by the Gob Squad, and 'Object Lesson Part III', by Ailie Cohen, merely present ordinary household items and invite the audience to ponder the strangeness of everyday objects.

These performances may be mimetic of everyday events. The piece may be nothing more than 'the appearance of the insignificant, meaningless natural behaviour of daily life presented apparently with no other message than the acts themselves parading nakedly' (Pywell 1994: 26). Geoff Pywell notes that the staging of everyday, mundane events works to show that common things are never exhausted of their meaning; the presumed simplicity of ordinary acts is itself a fiction. Thus, performance again muddies any distinction, if there is one, between reality and acting.

However, the blurred distinction between what is 'real' and what is 'acting' in Jones's performance does not appear to be the same 'realness' that is portrayed in the performance pieces I am describing here. Here, in Antoni's pieces, for example, is not the stark realness that death and disease represent, but the desolate and unsettling realness of banality. But I would argue it is the same 'real' in that its font of subversion is in its potential for disruption, which in turn elicits rejection by the Symbolic (as is evident in the work of the interpretations). In other words, both types of performances are perceived to be subversive; they are labelled 'too real' and are rejected as being 'not art' by critics. Regardless of the severity of the event, whether it is the actual presence of disease or a woman ironing clothes, any assumed division between theatre and reality dissolves. The dissolution of this boundary removes all that one imagines to protect himself or herself from whatever maleficence is causing the weeping, bleeding or any excessive behaviour. Thus, the security of the spectator and, by implication, the order of the spectator's world, is perceived to be threatened by both types of performances. What is it, then, that both hold in common apart from their identical (negative) reception in the critical interpretations?

I have already pointed out the similarities of the presence of a flesh-and-blood body participating in a performance that dissolves perceived distinctions between what is real and what is art. Perhaps, additionally, it is the out-of-placeness of behaviour that further compels severe criticism. The ordinary events of urinating or bathing oneself, or the simple gestures of ironing or cooking or reading, take on a sense of surrealism, that is, a subverting of reality, when removed from the private sphere into a public display. When ordinary objects merely become noticed, they become exceptional. Pywell writes,

> A tent, like [an] apple or [a] sink, is, after all, such an ordinary thing, so very unexceptional . . . Only when, through happenstance, a mundane thing is attached to some otherwise unconnected human significance does it become precious. By definition, it then leaves the ranks of the ordinary and becomes something else. (1994: 79)

Thus, the simple act of noticing an object or a gesture makes that thing or action extraordinary. Calling attention to the ordinary can take on many forms. If an ordinary event, such as braiding one's hair or washing one's hands, is performed to excess – beyond what is considered to be necessary, merely adequate or functional – the gesture becomes exceptional and, in some cases, disturbing (Pywell 1994: 83).

Thinking about queer performance art gives me insight into Ezekiel's prophetic performances. It is easy to see in his actions the distinguishing features that were present in the performance pieces that have been labelled deviant and/or obscene, or just annoying: he is a strange/familiar person doing strange/familiar things with his body.

Yet, what we have is a linguistic text describing the embodied symbolism of Ezekiel. In the translation of performative into linguistic, the function of language is to displace or conceal the body because performance threatens to disrupt the symbolic order (particularly the production of gender norms). The queer performer or a performance inclusive of excess or parodic repetition, such as Ezekiel's, can signal an intrusion or transgression into the defined and bordered social mores of any culture. Such performances disrupt or threaten to destabilize the orderliness of societal norms (maintained by language) much in the same way Ezekiel's prophetic performances do. The problem is, we do not really have Ezekiel's abject body, but the linguistic arrangement of those acts it performs. Judith Butler makes this clearer for us (really, she does).

As I demonstrate above, poststructuralism posits there is no such thing as a 'real body' – even the performance is a linguistic text. And, as a text, the body is placed squarely within the dominant culture. Another debate arises then around this question: are some texts, some bodies more subversive than others? Are Ezekiel's prophetic performances of eating dung and shaving his head more destabilizing than, say, the lamentations of Jeremiah?

On the one hand, Kristeva would argue that when Ezekiel bakes bread made with excrement and eats exactly the same amount at exactly the same time every day (4.9–13), his acts become abject, that is, bodies marked by contact with human refuse are relegated to the fringes, displaced, and called unclean. Ezekiel's body exists in a semiotic place – a place perhaps not outside the dominant order, but closer to its boundaries. The word 'closer' here is pivotal because the idea of a gradation or of degree in naming the relationship between the symbolic body and the 'real' body, or a pre- or post-linguistic body, marks the primary distinction between Kristeva's work on the abject and Judith Butler's.

Briefly, Kristeva's work on the abject was initially understood just as Butler describes it: it places the abject body *outside* language. New Kristevan scholars, such as Kelly Oliver, Ewa Ziareck and Martha Reineke, argue that Kristeva does not place the abject outside the symbolic. Kristeva understands such bodies to be situated very near the borders, or the margins. Here, one must wonder, 'The borders between what?' For Kristeva, who is following Lacan here, there is clearly a 'pre-linguistic', non-constructed body as well as a post-linguistic (which usually means psychotic to Kristeva and Lacan). Thus, the borders are what separates the symbolic, linguistic order from that which exists outside that order. Kristeva, according to her most recent interpreters, places the abject body at the edge of language, right up against the borders. Even in this rereading of Kristeva, she and Butler would still not agree.

Kristeva understands different bodies to be at different stages of constructedness. She implies that those bodies bearing the marks of abjection are not fully involved in dominant order (and particularly, its gendering processes) but may resist, up to a point, participation in that order and even disrupt its production. In other words, Kristeva understands that bodies are constructed in degrees and, thus, some bodies more fully participate in the perpetuation of the paternal ordering of gender. Reineke describes Kristeva's abject bodies as follows: 'For Kristeva, the abject is ambiguous and wholly incoherent in its very form, or non-form. An inassimilable nonunity, the abject is a primary mark of the not-yetness of a subject who is in process and on trial' (Reineke 1997: 43).

Butler, as I read her, does not posit an 'outside' at all. Butler calls for us to 'cure ourselves of the illusion of a true body beyond the law' (1990: 93). For Butler, even the flesh-and-blood body that bleeds or lactates is no less a socially constructed product than any other thing that exists; the abject body participates equally in the maintenance and perpetuation of gender norms. Butler does, however, posit a possibility of subversion, though it is a subversion that remains firmly 'inside' the gendering process. She writes, 'If subversion is possible, it will be a subversion from within the terms of the law, through the possibilities that emerge when the law turns against itself and spawns unexpected permutations of itself' (1990: 93). The possibility of gender norm subversion within the patristic order may be brought about, according to Butler, through parodic repetition of those actions considered to be gender normatives.

Gender norms are sustained through repetition in that it

both conceals itself and enforces its rules precisely through the production of substantializing effects. In a sense, all signification takes place within the orbit of the compulsion to repeat; 'agency,' then, is to be located within the possibility of a variation on that repetition. If the rules governing signification not only restrict, but enable the assertion of alternative domains of cultural intelligibility, i.e., new possibilities for gender that contest the rigid codes of hierarchical binarism, then it is only within the practices of repetitive signifying that a subversion of identity becomes possible. (Butler 1990: 145)

Thus, according to Butler, gender norms can indeed be subverted by doing the very thing that creates them: performing them again and again. The parodic or excessive repetition of norms exposes, claims Butler, 'the illusion of gender identity as an intractable depth and inner substance' (1990: 146). Butler's statements here about parodic or excess repetition could confirm the third argument offered by those proponents of performance as subversive (the first being an assumption of incategorization and the second being the presumed presence of a 'real' body): the portrayal of everyday events in excess works to disrupt and displace ordinary space.

Reading Ezekiel with Butler's perception of performance would place particular emphasis on the fact that Ezekiel embraces a form of the ridiculous. His mimicry of ordinary events even unto the absurd transposes those acts into subversions. The excess of Ezekiel is precisely the thing that makes the performance an effective disruption of societal norms. This disruption, as Ezekiel must understand it, is a matter of life and death – to permit 'business as usual' is to sanction death, captivity and exile of his own people. Ezekiel's withdrawal from the linguistic, that is, his muteness and his performances, is an effort to withdraw from the dominant culture. However, protecting and maintaining gender norms becomes first and foremost the priority of language. So, of course, any subversion that Ezekiel may claim is subsumed again by the literary text and becomes, again, a part of the dominant order.

The value of using a performance model in an analysis of Ezekiel is that it allows one to acknowledge that the performances of prophetic acts can be disruptive without placing the subversive or queer body outside the dominant culture; indeed, it is impossible to do so. One of Butler's critiques of Kristeva is that those experiences which Kristeva labels abject, such as lesbian or maternal, make those women 'intrinsically unintelligible' (Butler 1990: 87). Butler makes a space for the subversive within the workings of culture. Reading the prophetic acts through Butler's lens, Ezekiel, in his performances, disrupts the social normative by parodying familiar events. However, though his performance draws attention to and works to break down the norms he is mimicking (to be secluded, to be bound, to be defiled), he ultimately suffers those fates. The interpretations of the events, indeed, the historical sexist, homophobic, racist readings of Ezekiel, become the vehicle through which language toils to organize and appropriate.

Exile/naked

Another subject to which modernist historical critics attend is the idea of exile. Theo/logically, the exile has provided, among other things, an arena to talk about a Judaism that was not connected to a particular place. It has also been an oft-used metaphor for the displacement and sufferings of various peoples. However, the Babylonian exile was indeed, as Andrew Mein has written, 'a time of almost unparalleled crisis for the Jewish people' (2002: 1).

Kamionkowski suggests that the exile was such anguish and chaos that only an extreme metaphor could even begin to paint the agony the men of Jerusalem felt. Kamionkowski argues that Ezekiel's metaphor was one of gender reversal – women became men and men became women. She asserts that through the base metaphor of *a weak man is a woman*, Ezekiel produces a more *real* image of the profound loss, shame, vulnerability, shock and despair that the men of Jerusalem must have experienced within the exile. It is, she claims, a far more effective metaphor than simply a metaphor of marriage used elsewhere in the prophets. Kamionkowski claims that by metaphorically turning a woman (YHWH's wife in Ezekiel 16) into a man (she becomes active, powerful, violent, sexual), Ezekiel is explaining why the men of Jerusalem feel like women (passive, powerless, victimized, emasculated). Kamionkowski finds strong evidence for this literary motif of emasculation in Mesopotamian literature and in the Bible. She asserts that by screwing around with gender roles, Ezekiel is painting a picture of a world that is in complete chaos – men are women and women are men – but YHWH is nonetheless in charge. It is, as Kamionkowski writes, 'all part of God's plan to set things back in order' (2003: 152).

Kamionkowski's work is important to a queer reading of Ezekiel because it reminds us of two things: first, assigned and rigid gender roles form the bedrock of 'the norm' and seek to ensure stability; all behaviours that do not conform to those expectations are queer, therefore subversive and utterly chaotic. Second, her work reminds us that any metaphor of marriage that places YHWH as husband and Israel (or Jerusalem) as wife is homoerotic and, therefore, a queer metaphor. Both Kamionkowski and, previously, Howard Eilberg-Schwartz have recognized an emasculation and/or a feminization of males in prophetic rhetoric. To understand Ezekiel's metaphor as simply one of a marriage completely anaesthetizes the hopelessness, the shock and despair of being violently displaced from the homeland. Kamionkowski's reading of gender reversal in Ezekiel gives the reader more access to an understanding of status reversal, homelessness and vulnerability. The world of the Jerusalem men has become a queer place, and only queer metaphors will do.

Kamionkowski writes,

> Ezekiel 16 is not simply an expression of covenant theology in the packaging of a marital metaphor. Rather, this text is about the collision between an image of God as the sustainer of order and the reality of chaos. Gender is used to express this crisis because gender was considered to be one of the most absolute expressions of God's ordering of the universe through distinctions and separations. A king may be overthrown by his subjects and a son may rebel against his father, but men must always be men and women must be women. (2003: 9)

Of course, the onerous weight of exile cannot be expressed linguistically, even with queer metaphors. Ezekiel's effort to do this involves the evocation of every experience of every person. He must reach, as Kamionkowski claims, for metaphors that suggest that the world is a mess; everything from the foundation up is completely undone. From the images of a baby dying in its birth fluids, from the fields full of bones of the dead, to women lusting after men with horse-sized penises, Ezekiel embodies emotions that impress upon the reader/listener the agony of displacement. All of these images are bound together by one word: Exile.

glh

There is no single word that is consistently translated as 'exile'. Rather, the prophets, primarily Ezekiel and Jeremiah, weave together the images of exile with the root glh. The word is translated consistently throughout the Hebrew Bible as 'to be naked' (e.g. Gen. 9.21); 'to strip naked' (e.g. Ezek. 16.36); 'a revelation of God' (e.g. 1 Sam. 2.27; 3.7; 3.21); 'captivity' (e.g. Judg. 18.30); 'exile' (2 Sam. 15.19); or 'a captive' (e.g. Jer. 39.9). Brown, Driver and Briggs (1906) list its primary meanings as 'to uncover, to remove, to become clear, to reveal oneself, to become naked, to go forth, to emigrate' (1906: 162–3). Ezekiel's embrace of glh is broad; he leans hard upon almost inexhaustible connotations of the word. And we, as readers, hold on to bits and pieces of meaning without understanding that each occurrence of the word should evoke all of its possible meanings at once. For example, on the one hand, Herbert Haag recognizes only the 'godly meaning', which he understands as 'revelation'. He writes,

> The root meaning of glh is undoubtedly 'to unhide' or 'to disclose', thus to make free and visible that which, hidden and closed, is bound and concealed. Here, the image-laden language in the Hebraic goes in two directions. It can remain a concealed thing to people because it is itself concealed [by some entity], or because the human ear and eye is bound [in or by some entity] and therefore cannot apprehend its object. (1960: 252)

On the other hand, Resa Levitt Kohn notices that the phrase *galah 'ervah*, 'uncover nakedness', occurs 24 times in the Hebrew Bible: 17 of these are in the Levitical sexual codes and 5 are in Ezekiel chapters 16, 22 and 23. She looks only at sexual connotations for *glh*.

While both scholars are writing specifically about the same root word, Haag focuses on the theological connotations while Kohn gazes upon the physical. Neither recognizes the extensive range of meaning and the ambiguity *glh* offers Ezekiel's readers. Hans-Jürgen Zobel (1975) suggests that the root *glh* is related to a Ugaritic root *gly*, a verb of motion 'to enter', and is similar to a Phoenician root 'to reveal, to uncover'. He sees a connection between 'uncovering the land' and exile: the land is revealed and thus open to entering (penetration). Knowing that 'entering' is a common euphemism for sexual intercourse in the Hebrew Bible, it is logical, he claims, that the phrase *galah 'ervah* in Ezekiel 16.36, 37; 22.10 'means either "to commit fornication" . . . or "to rape"' (1975: 479). Thus, in this sense, exile becomes a consequence of rape and fornication. To see relationships between the body, the land and sexual penetration is requisite in order to understand the exile through Ezekiel's text. But that's not enough; there is also a theological dimension through which God is present and redemptive. It is through these three divergent abstractions that Ezekiel constructs *exile* as a whole.

Though *glh* is scattered throughout the Hebrew Bible and occurs some 190 times, there is a concentration in two places: in Leviticus (17 times) and between Ezekiel chapters 16 and 23 (14 times). As I have already noted, those instances in Leviticus are found entirely within the sexual codes. If the Levitical codes define social boundaries as physical boundaries, as many (following Mary Douglas) claim, Ezekiel's use of P's phraseology in chapters 16 and 23 should cause the reader to think about nasty sex. As the priests in Leviticus tell us what *not* to do lest we dissolve all boundaries and cause all hell to break loose, Ezekiel is showing us what *has* happened and that indeed, all hell has broken loose. It is, to quote the priests and Ezekiel, an abomination.

Ezekiel begins chapter 16 with the image of a bastard baby left totally vulnerable in a field. As the baby grows her bosoms, becomes beautiful, naked, and confused, God 'reveals' himself to her. He adorns her with gifts, luxuries, necessities, and she is not grateful. She 'opens herself' to everyone else: to Egyptians with large penises; to Assyrians; to Chaldeans. Already, those who know Leviticus 18 and 20 are hearing abominations. In verses 36 and 37 Ezekiel uses the root *glh* in the following sequences: God tells the woman Jerusalem that, since she has 'exposed her naked body', he will 'strip her naked'. The description continues with the dominant theme of being naked and exposed (see vv. 37–52).

Ezekiel uses *glh* again in 21.24 to connect the 'uncovering of nakedness' to being 'taken by force' by the enemy. He makes this connection between nakedness and exile even more explicit in 22.10 when he lists, in order, nearly every 'abomination' from Leviticus 18: uncovering a father's nakedness, having sex with menstruating women, having sex with neighbours' wives, with daughters-in-law and with sisters. Leviticus clearly tells Ezekiel's readers that if they do these things, 'the land will spit them out' and they will 'be cut off from the people' (v. 29). There is nothing new in a thesis that Ezekiel, as well as other prophets, were arguing, that Jerusalem fell and its people were exiled as a result of various adulterous/idolatrous abominations. What we have missed, however, is the third leg of this stool: *glh* not only connects exile to exposed nakedness and penetration, it becomes the remedy, the means through which Ezekiel restores the people to God.

As chaos abounds, Ezekiel embraces *glh* because it summons, simultaneously, notions of being bound and unbound, of having one's eyes and ears opened, of God revealed. According to Thomas Raitt in *A Theology of Exile*, Ezekiel's ideas of exile envelope more than fear and rage. He shifts, according to Raitt, into the 'oracles of hope' – Ezekiel integrates a juxtaposition (deconstructs a binary) of judgement and salvation. Though the description of God's forgiveness after punishment is not new for the prophets, Raitt claims that Ezekiel's idea of forgiveness is one not at all based on merit but on God's grace. He sees the exile as a 'good thing', as something that forces one away from the familiar, the secure. Raitt writes,

> Exiled people are attractive to God. They know that the events of the past are a judgement. By that judgement they are stripped of facades. They are forced to be mobile, to travel light, to stand naked before god. They have no enduring worldly roots, no enduring worldly security. They are vulnerable . . . No agenda binds them. God loves exiles. They are ready to receive him as he is. They are a good risk. (1977: 229)

Though Raitt doesn't say much about God exiling the people to begin with, he does make the connection between being naked, open and vulnerable to being open to God's presence.

As remedy and as poison, Ezekiel's *glh* becomes Jacques Derrida's *pharmikon*. It is poison in its connotations of violation, vulnerability, rape, emasculation; it is remedy as it becomes the occasion for God's presence. Concerning *pharmikon*, Ellen Armour writes that in ambiguity, 'those structures [of meaning] depend on what they dismiss/define as "other". Doing so displaces the mastery of those structures and renders legible the trace of the text's "other"'. (1999: 71). In Ezekiel, God's revelation through exile is inextricably interdependent with sex and the naked body. In other words, God's goodness and justice are inseparable from and defined by the queer body: the whoring, promiscuous and rebellious body. Ezekiel cannot talk about God's redemption and love without images of sexual debauchery.

Glh is a word of slippery ambiguity that invokes, all at the same time, God revealed, God's people exiled, naked vulnerability, and being fucked. For Ezekiel's reader, the exile is infused with an idea that captivity, as it is often symbolized by bound bodies, is a condition of being completely naked and vulnerable to penetration, while being inextricably and simultaneously involved in a revelation of God. Ezekiel's performances, visions and metaphors all play upon various nuances of *glh* in order to construct some understanding of what it means to be exiled.

Conclusions

All we can learn from Ezekiel is what we already know. As queer people (and every single person is queer in one way or another) we find ourselves in Ezekiel. Some of us know what it is to have visions that seem impossible yet salvific; some may recognize a yearning to ruin or obliterate our enemies; some come to Ezekiel knowing the extremes to which we would go to save ourselves and to save our people. Some of us may come to Ezekiel simply hoping that God hears us no matter where we are, and 'the name of that place forever shall be, "The Lord is There"' (Ezek. 48.35). We expose ourselves to God.

Daniel

MONA WEST

If queer theory is about the politics of resistance and the indeterminacy of identity (and it is) then Daniel is one of the queerest books of the Bible. There is much about the book's composition for instance that resists 'normative' categorization. It is among the Writings in the Hebrew Bible and included in the Prophets in modern Christian canons. Rather than a prophetic book, however, scholars have identified it as an example of apocalyptic literature.[1]

The first half of the book consists of six stories set during the time of the Babylonian exile right at the time of the Persian conquest in the sixth century BCE. The function of the stories or tales was to embody the exilic prophecy of Jeremiah 29.7 – co-operation with foreigners so that in their prosperity Jews would prosper (Collins 1993: 51). The last half of the book consists of four visions set during the Hellenistic period of Jewish persecution in the second century BCE, whose purpose was to impart an apocalyptic understanding of the historical situation of persecution resulting in God's final victory (Collins 1993: 60).

Daniel's queerness continues in its very language. The Hebrew portion of the text can be found in chapters 1.1–2.4a, while chapters 2.4b–7.28 are written in Aramaic. Then there are the Greek additions to the stories: the Prayer of Azariah and the Song of the Three Young Men; the story of Susanna; the story of Bel and the Dragon.

Not only is the book queer in its composition, but the book's main character resists any fixed category of identity. As an apocalyptic work, the pseudonymous authorship of the book is assigned to an ancient worthy in order to give the stories and visions credibility and authority. The book of Ezekiel mentions an ancient worthy known as Daniel who was known for belief in the face of danger, and wisdom in the face of foolishness and is 'one who knows secrets' (Ezek. 14.14; 28.3). The earliest reference to a figure named Daniel can be found in Ugaritic literature which dates to around the fourteenth century BCE and describes a king who was a righteous man who gave judgements for widows and orphans (Collins 1993: 1–2).

These early references to a legendary figure known as Daniel do not identify him as Jewish, but in the context of the book, Daniel is cast as a pious Jew

---

1 John J. Collins (1993) claims that Daniel is one of the earliest examples of historical apocalyptic characterized by a periodization of history, revelation through symbolic visions, an interpreting angel, a pattern of crisis–judgement–salvation which transcends the bounds of ordinary history and pseudonymous authorship in which an ancient respected figure gives authority and credibility to a written work.

who survives foreign captivity and persecution. A traditional interpretation of the book underscores that Daniel's Jewish piety is what sustains him during his captivity, but more than his piety, it is his ability to interpret dreams – to cross boundaries between the human and supernatural world – that gains him favour with the Babylonian king.

This ability to cross boundaries is one of the major characteristics of being a eunuch. In chapter 1 of the book the king tells his chief eunuch to take the Jewish captives Daniel, Hananiah, Mishael and Azariah and make them eunuchs.[2] In the Babylonian and Persian periods eunuchs were court officials charged with the administration of the king's household. They were often military officers and chief officers of state because as castrated males they could not threaten dynastic succession. They were considered a 'state third gender' because they functioned in the realm of civic and state institutions and third gender because secondary sex characteristics and psychological traits identified them in ways that were different from men and women (Roscoe 1997: 64).

Making one a eunuch in ancient society included more than castration. Eunuchs were identified by their dress, mannerisms and even the food they ate.[3] Chapter 1 of the book indicates that the king of Babylon set out to make Daniel and his three friends eunuchs – perfect servants[4] of the kings court:

> Then the king commanded his palace master [chief eunuch] Ashpenaz to bring some of the Israelites of the royal family and of the nobility, young men without physical defect and handsome, versed in every branch of wisdom, endowed with knowledge and insight, and competent to serve in the king's palace; they were to be taught the literature and language of the Chaldeans. The king assigned them a daily portion of the royal rations of food and wine. They were to be educated for three years, so that at the end of that time they could be stationed in the king's court. (Dan. 1.3–5)[5]

---

2 The term *saris* is used in 1.3 to describe the king's chief eunuch. The term is used elsewhere in ancient Near Eastern literature and the Hebrew scriptures to refer to servants of the king's court and castrated males who have been made so as a result of being a prisoner of war (Collins 1993: 134).

3 Kathryn M. Ringrose (2003) has done extensive research on the ways in which eunuchs were constructed as a third gender category in the Byzantine empire. Following the practices of other ancient societies, this third category of 'perfect servant' was achieved through castration at a young age, the rearing of children with ambiguous sexual organs and gendering young eunuchs into patterns of behaviour considered to be 'normal' for their gender category.

4 The term 'perfect servant' is from Ringrose: 'I maintain that the fundamental features around which a gender was constructed for eunuchs were the separation of eunuchs from reproduction and family obligations and the aptness of eunuchs for what I will call "perfect service." The idea of "perfect service" as focal point for the social construction of gender is not something I have found in other studies of the topic. Eunuchs existed outside of the dominant social values and institutions of family, offspring, and procreation. This made them ideally suited to serve as servants, agents, and proxies for the masters or employers, male or female. They moved freely across social and gender barriers and were not precluded from a wide range of roles often deemed unsuitable for the persons whom they served' (2003: 5).

5 All biblical citations are from the NRSV unless otherwise stated.

The interpretive tradition has also turned this ancient legendary figure, Daniel, noted for wisdom and righteousness, into a eunuch. There is a clear tradition in the Rabbinic literature that identifies Daniel and his three friends as eunuchs – and there is also a Rabbinic tradition that resists this interpretation, on the basis of the prohibition that eunuchs are not able to participate in temple worship (Deut. 23.1). Early Rabbinic interpretations always couple Daniel with Isaiah 56.3–5, expressing the problematic nature of eunuchs in the post-exilic community (Collins 1993: 135–6).

The most remarkable 'regendering' of the legendary narrative tradition of Daniel can be found in the reading of the book during the Byzantine Empire. Kathryn Ringrose traces the interpretation of the identity of the book's hero from court servant to holy man from the fourth to the eleventh century CE in its reading by Byzantine authors. The earlier tradition of Byzantine interpretation of the identity of Daniel by St John Chrysostom, patriarch of Constantinople from 398 to 404 CE, downplayed Daniel's identity as a court eunuch reflecting negative views about court eunuchs in that society at that time. In his commentary on the book of Daniel, Chrysostom emphasized instead Daniel's identity as a prophet and an ecstatic holy man.

By the eleventh century Daniel had made the 'A list' of court eunuchs in the Byzantine Empire with the quote from Theophylaktos of Ohrid, 'What is Daniel to you?' (Ringrose 2003: 87). This was the result of a tenth-century interpretation of Daniel by Symeon Metaphrastes in which Daniel is praised as a court eunuch who is also a holy man (Ringrose 2003: 92). Ringrose concludes, 'Thus the figure of Daniel provides an important example of the way in which the court eunuch was assimilating attributes of the ascetic holy man, uniting these two very different images in one single individual' (2003: 88).

As a court eunuch and holy man Daniel is uniquely gendered to serve in the king's court not only as a 'perfect servant' but as one who has 'insight into all visions and dreams' (1.17). Daniel and his three friends were 'ten times better than all the magicians and enchanters' in the whole kingdom (1.20). Daniel was able to cross boundaries not only between the human and spiritual worlds but between the Babylonian and Jewish worlds. Even though he and his friends are persecuted for their allegiance to their Jewish god, they gain favour in the king's court through Daniel's ability to interpret dreams. The king even fasts on Daniel's behalf (6.18).

For queer readers of the book of Daniel, these characteristics of court eunuch and holy man reawaken the ancient silences of queer spiritual ancestry. In his book *Coming Out Spirituality: The Next Step*, Christian de la Huerta traces the spiritual heritage of queer people throughout the cultures of the world. He claims that queers have functioned in many societies as holy people, priests, priestesses, shamans, go-betweens, keepers of the sacred, and boundary crossers.[6] In many cultures queer holy ones are characterized as 'eternal youths' signifying 'innocence of spirit' and a 'perennial youthfulness of soul' (de la Huerta 1999: 20). Likewise, Daniel is portrayed as an eternal youth. He is identified as a child or youth in chapter 1 and, as a eunuch, was considered eternally youthful (Ringrose 2003: 89). As a eunuch Daniel was a gender go-between,

---

6 See especially chapter 1, 'Walking between worlds', pp. 1–44.

which uniquely equipped him not only to mediate the world of gender but also the spiritual and physical worlds. According to de la Huerta, gender variant people throughout the world have been mediators of the sacred.[7]

In her book *Our Tribe: Queer Folks, God, Jesus, and the Bible,* Nancy Wilson identifies the 'tribal gifts' that queer people offer to today's society, and among them are the 'shamanic gifts of creativity, originality, art, magic, and theater'. She claims that queer folk are the 'mediators of conflict and culture. In some ways, we are those who *intercede,* who create the pathway for change, for moving into the next era' (Wilson 1995: 51). She goes on to recount an experience at the 1991 gathering of the World Council of Churches in Canberra at which she and other queer clergy from Metropolitan Community Church functioned in this capacity by organizing a sacred vigil to protest the Gulf War. She recounts,

> When the Bishop of Baghdad (Baghdad, Iraq, that is) came forward that morning to be anointed by Bishop Browning, the room just broke open in solidarity with our pain and helplessness. Some were too overcome to keep anointing. They collapsed in sobs on the floor, in their chairs. People wept, prayed, hugged . . . Gay and lesbian delegates to the WCC came forward for anointing . . . The tent was filled with the power and presence of God . . . (1995: 53)

Wilson goes on to call narratives in the Bible about eunuchs 'gay and lesbian tribal texts' claiming that eunuchs and barren women are 'our gay, lesbian, and bisexual antecedents' (Wilson 1995: 124). She ends her work with 'The roll call of eunuchs', in which Daniel figures prominently (1995: 284).

As an apocalyptic work the message of the book of Daniel is ostensibly one of political resistance. The tales in the first six chapters promote co-operation with the enemy for the sake of survival, and the visions in the last four chapters promote God's ultimate triumph over evil beyond the present world.

How might one queer this message of Daniel? Should this 'normative' message of co-operation and ultimate triumph be resisted by queer readers? Like the character of Daniel, in addition to being sacred intermediaries, queer people have also had a history of political and cultural oppression. Like Daniel, queers have used their 'eunuchness' – their ability to cross boundaries, to pass as heterosexual in a heterosexist society, and their ability to gain access to power structures and systems through their 'shamanic gifts' of art, creativity and theatre – to survive cultures that discriminate and are often violent toward them.

---

7 For example the Lugbara tribe of Eastern Africa honours the *agule* ('like men') and the *okule* ('like women') who serve as intermediaries or mediums. He mentions also the *galli,* a class of transgender holy ones who worshipped the goddess Cybele, the ancient Russian *enarees* ('the unmanly ones'), third-gender priests associated with the goddess Artimpasa, and of course the North American *berdache* or 'two spirited ones' of Native American tribes who were thought to have special powers because of their ability to cross gender boundaries (de la Huerta 1999: 31–9). De la Huerta builds on the earlier work of Judy Grahn (1984), who traces the ancestry of queer people through words, phrases and cultural attributes, often emphasizing the role queer people play as spiritual intermediaries.

Urvashi Vaid, a queer activist in United States culture, cautions against a 'virtual equality', which is a conditional acceptance by the dominant culture that circumvents true liberation of all oppressed peoples. She claims:

> The notion of mainstreaming homosexuality has been the dominant object-ive of legions of gay and lesbian activists since the 1950's. The mainstream has a seductive appeal to those of us who were taught our entire lives that we are sick, immoral, sinful, and depraved. Mainstreaming means integra-tion, social acceptance, political attention, and credibility. To be mainstream is to be part of a majority, to be safe, respectable maybe even respected. (Vaid 1995: 202)

There is a difference between gaining access and wielding power, and queer political resistance must 'strive beyond personal gain to an institutional trans-formation, beyond mainstreaming ourselves into the center to transforming the mainstream' (Vaid 1995: 80).

So in the end is there a queering of the queering of Daniel that must be done by queer readers? Do we embrace our queer ancestor, the ancient wor-thy Daniel, as a way of 'transforming the mainstream' while at the same time resisting the message of co-operation/mainstreaming, and even the passive notion that in the end God will ultimately triumph over evil empires?

The Book of the Twelve Minor Prophets

MICHAEL CARDEN

Introduction

Overview

The book of the Twelve contains the body of writings associated with the Minor Prophets – Hosea, Joel, Amos, Obadiah, Jonah, Micah, Nahum, Habakkuk, Zephaniah, Haggai, Zechariah and Malachi – as opposed to the three Major Prophets – Isaiah, Jeremiah and Ezekiel – each of whom are associated with their own book. Most Christian readers are accustomed to regard this literature as 12 short books, concluding their Old Testaments. However, in the Jewish tradition, the collection of the Twelve comprises one scroll and has long been considered as a single book, 'a different kind of book from Isaiah, Jeremiah and Ezekiel, but . . . a book nevertheless' (Redditt 2001: 49). In recent years, Western (Gentile) biblical scholars have begun reading the Twelve as an edited whole. Other scholars still, however, focus their attention on the individual prophetic figures that make up the Twelve, while many of those who read the Twelve as a unity believe such a strategy supplements the more traditional individually focused readings of the Minor Prophets.

Nevertheless, when read as a unity, a number of patterns and themes emerge in the Twelve. Structurally, the book shares with Isaiah a pattern of opening in an Assyrian past but concluding in a Persian present. Prophets are portrayed as figures in that Assyrian past while the Persian present is marked by the emergence of messenger figures. Unlike Isaiah, which focuses on the southern kingdom of Judah and Jerusalem, the Twelve has a focus on the northern kingdom of Samaria/Ephraim although it shifts to a Jerusalem present. Both Haggai and Zechariah are set against the rebuilding of the Jerusalem temple and advance its claims to priority over the sanctuaries of the north. With Malachi, Jerusalem's claims to supremacy are no longer at issue, but instead it is Jerusalem itself which, like its former rivals, has lost its way and must return to the Lord (Mal. 3.7).

It is this theme of faithlessness punished and a remnant restored that dominates the Twelve. Disturbingly, the book uses both erotic and sexual-violence imagery to illustrate the themes of faithlessness and punishment. Free autonomous women's sexuality is a marker used to abject apostasy and rebellion while patriarchal male sexual violence against women signifies divine punishment of faithless Israel. The book of Hosea, in particular, has been the focus of much feminist analysis of the dynamics of 'porno-prophetics' found throughout the Latter Prophets. Nevertheless, such imagery gives rise to surprising queer moments of slippage. Israel is represented as faithless wife and lover, and yet the book most likely addresses a male audience. This marriage metaphor of husband YHWH and wife Israel places the men of Israel in a highly ambiguous gender space. They are recast as wife/woman of the divine husband. This gender ambiguity does not only apply to Israel, YHWH's male wife. On a number of occasions in the Twelve, especially the final chapter of Hosea, this ambiguity turns back upon and undermines the masculine certainty and authority of the divine itself.

Historical and cultural locations

I remind the reader of what I had to say about Genesis, that we don't know when, where, why or by whom it was written. The same can be said of the book of the Twelve. As with Genesis and the rest of the Hebrew scriptures, the Twelve is born out of the religious ferment of the Imperial age in the eastern Mediterranean during the second half of the first millennium BCE. While the Twelve begins with Hosea in an Assyrian past, in Haggai and Zechariah the reader enters a Persian present in which the Jerusalem temple is being rebuilt. However, the conclusion, Malachi, gives no clear temporal references except for the fact that the temple is standing and operating in Jerusalem. Malachi's placement in the Twelve suggests a present after the rebuilding of the Jerusalem temple, but whether it is in Persian or Hellenistic times cannot be determined.

While Genesis and the Pentateuch are highly ambiguous about the communities they address, the Twelve provides some clues as to the audience it addresses. Unlike the three Major Prophets, the Twelve has very strong northern kingdom concerns. However, it uses these concerns to advance the superior status of the temple in Jerusalem. It is no longer Bethel or Samaria where YHWH dwells and speaks but Jerusalem. Moreover, it is clear from Malachi that, while the Jerusalem temple is the house of YHWH to which all the nations will come and worship, this day will not happen until there is a change in the authorities who administer and perform the temple functions. While they might acknowledge the temple in Jerusalem, the community or communities addressed by the Twelve do not accept the groups in control of it.

Prophets, prophecy and prophetic books

The biblical prophets have been read in many ways. In intertestamental times they were understood as foretelling significant events of the time. This approach was employed by the Qumran community to interpret scripture. Similarly, early Christians saw the life of Jesus as fulfilling the words of the prophets. Many fundamentalist Christians today continue to read the prophets as a means of understanding current events. In Judaism, prophets have been understood as commentators on Torah. For biblical scholarship over the last century, however, prophets have been considered to be 'first and foremost "proclaimers"' (Sawyer 1987: 1). Consequently, the goal of scholarship was to discover the *ipsissima verba* of the prophets and thus to find the men behind the books. Beginning with Wellhausen, biblical scholars have understood the prophets to be more concerned with the events of their own time rather than predicting the future. Prophets were seen as ethical teachers who somehow transformed the religion of ancient Israel. That this scholarly project was shaped by Christian preconceptions is demonstrated by Wellhausen's declaration that the 'Law is later than the Prophets' (cited in Sawyer 1987: 2). With the writing down of the law came the writing down of the prophets, thus spelling the 'death of prophecy' (Wellhausen, cited in Conrad 1999: 13).

As was the case with the Torah (and Moses is the archetypal prophet of the Hebrew scriptures), prophetic texts were torn up in order to discover the authentic words of the prophets. As Conrad notes, scholars 'have been preoccupied with the notion that the prophet, buried in the written tomb of the text, needed to be resurrected, to live again' and, thus, 'by dissecting (prophetic books) . . . the spoken word could be heard once more' (Conrad 1999: 13). It was postulated that initial collections of prophetic sayings were set down in the prophets' lifetimes and that these minor written collections were subsequently added to until eventually there emerged the final prophetic book. Scholars entertained concepts of ancient prophetic schools and of prophetic disciples who, cherishing the words of a Micah, a Joel, or an Obadiah, added material to these collections, over the centuries, to apply them to their own times. This approach can be seen in its extreme form in Wolfe (1935), who posited no fewer than 12 redactions of prophetic materials to eventually form the book of the Twelve, not to mention further scribal alterations after its formation. With Wolfe's scenario, one can only wonder what relevance the prophets might have had to the books that bear their names, particularly as most of the books are not really interested in presenting any biography of the individuals whose names they bear. How can one ascertain anything about a Joel, who has been dated by scholars to both Assyrian and post-exilic times, in order to determine his 'authentic words'? Indeed, out of all of the Twelve, it is Jonah who is the most fleshed-out by way of biographical details and who alone appears in the historical narratives of Samuel–Kings (see 2 Kings 14.25).[1] Yet, clearly, Jonah is a fictional work.

Further complicating the quest for prophetic originals are the intertextual linkages shared by the books of the Twelve. One major linkage is the pattern in which the ending of one book of the Twelve and the beginning of the following one often share significant vocabulary. The most striking example is Joel 4.16, 'the LORD will roar from Zion', which is reproduced as coming to pass in Amos 1.2, 'the LORD roars from Zion'. There are also other intertextual links and shared motifs among the Twelve such as the striking image in Joel 4.10 of turning ploughshares into swords, reversing the swords into ploughshares of Micah 4.3 and also Isaiah 2.4. Indeed, the text of Micah 4.1–5 is itself a quote from Isaiah 2.2–4 (or vice versa).

---

1 Unless Obadiah be identified with the Obadiah of 1 Kings 18, who is not there identified, however, as a prophet.

Twelve books or one scroll in two editions?

It is these intertextual connecting features of the Twelve that have led many scholars to argue that the Twelve should be read as one book. As already noted above, this position accords with Jewish tradition. In the second century BCE, Jesus ben Sirach refers to 'the bones of the Twelve Prophets' (Sir. 49.10) in a context suggesting that the 'Twelve had already taken shape as one book' (Redditt 2001: 49). Both 2 Esdras 14.44 and Josephus (*Against Apion* 1.8), in speaking of the books of scripture, appear to count the Twelve as one book. The Church Father, Origen, who was well acquainted with Rabbinic exegesis, also appears to have regarded the Twelve as one book (Sweeney *et al.* 2000: xvi). The Twelve is clearly counted as one book in the Talmud, but there is an ambivalence because it is also stated that 'the books are to be separated on a scroll by three blank lines, only one less than for books counted separately' (Redditt 2001: 49).

Ambivalence could almost be a defining characteristic of the books making up the Hebrew scriptures. Genesis exists in not one but three recensions, the Hebrew Masoretic, the Greek Septuagint and the Samaritan, while other ancient recensions have been found at Qumran, with no way of determining which one of these has priority over the others. Similarly, there are two versions of the Twelve, which date back to antiquity, the Hebrew Masoretic and the Greek Septuagint (LXX). The obvious difference between the two is in the sequence of prophets. The Masoretic order is as follows: Hosea, Joel, Amos, Obadiah, Jonah, Micah, Nahum, Habakkuk, Zephaniah, Haggai, Zechariah, Malachi. In contrast, the LXX order differs in the sequence of the first six prophets: Hosea, Amos, Micah, Joel, Obadiah, Jonah, then continuing, as in the Masoretic order, Nahum, Habakkuk, Zephaniah, Haggai, Zechariah, Malachi. The LXX became the canonical First Testament for the Eastern Orthodox Church.[2] The Western Church, following Jerome, did not accept the LXX as authoritative, but adopted Jerome's Latin Vulgate translation of the Hebrew and its ordering of the Twelve. Most Hebrew and Greek manuscripts from Qumran appear to present a proto-Masoretic text of the Twelve. However, in the surviving portions of one scroll, 4QXII[a], which only contains parts of Zechariah, Malachi and Jonah, Jonah clearly follows Malachi. It is possible, then, that 'a third major version of the Twelve existed in antiquity' (Sweeney *et al.* 2000: xix), which concluded with Jonah not Malachi.

According to Sweeney, when read as a whole, the LXX focuses first on the experience of the northern kingdom of Israel and its destruction – Hosea, Amos, Micah – as 'a model for the experience of Jerusalem/Judah and the nations' (Sweeney *et al.* 2000: xxix). Joel marks the shift to the nations, who are metaphorically portrayed as locusts threatening the land. Obadiah, Jonah and Nahum shift attention to Edom and Assyria and the divine judgement they suffer, in the case of the latter despite being offered the opportunity for repentance. Habakkuk, Zephaniah, Haggai and Zechariah focus on Jerusalem and its experience of punishment and restoration. Finally, Malachi sums up

---

2 In the LXX, too, the Twelve preceded Isaiah in the ordering of the prophetic books.

the themes of the Twelve, identified by Sweeney as 'the potential divorce . . . between Israel and YHWH; the polluted state of the Temple, priesthood, and land; the Day of YHWH; and the called for renewed adherence to the covenant' (Sweeney *et al.* 2000: xxxi). Sweeney argues that, in contrast to the LXX, the Masoretic version of the Twelve puts the central focus on the role of Jerusalem and its relationship to Israel and the nations. Thus Joel follows Hosea, which spoke of the looming punishment of Israel but not of Jerusalem, in order to introduce the threat to Jerusalem and the eventual day of YHWH and divine sovereignty at Zion. In Amos, Israel and the sanctuary at Bethel, together with all the nations, are threatened with the vengeance of YHWH, who roars from Zion. Obadiah proclaims the submission of Edom at Zion, while Jonah highlights Nineveh's repentance, enabling it 'to survive and ultimately destroy Jonah's homeland' (Sweeney *et al.* 2000: xxxiii). While focusing on the destruction of Samaria, Micah also points toward the coming rule of YHWH at Zion. Nahum presents the punishment of Assyria and then the sequence focuses on the destruction and restoration of Jerusalem and the temple as the sign of YHWH's universal authority. Malachi concludes, pointing to the coming day of YHWH 'when YHWH's messenger will ultimately return as the basis for an appeal to observe YHWH's Torah' (Sweeney *et al.* 2000: xxxv).

Sweeney uses these thematic elements of the Hebrew and LXX editions of the Twelve to hypothesize their historical background and the steps of their redaction. Conrad, however, is not interested in such questions. Recognizing that the Twelve, like other prophetic books, functions as a collage, Conrad wants to 'understand the Twelve as it is – not how it came to be' (Conrad 1997: 66). Working with the Hebrew edition, Conrad identifies two parts to the book. The first, Hosea to Zephaniah, is set in the period from Uzziah to Josiah as kings in Jerusalem, the period of the Assyrian rise to power and supremacy. The second, Haggai to Malachi, is set in a Persian present, when there is no longer kingship in Jerusalem. In the first part there is confusion over the identification of prophets, only Habakkuk being clearly identified as one. The second part clarifies the prophetic status of these earlier figures in Zechariah, where the individuals who spoke in the first part are identified as former prophets. Conrad also reads the Twelve intertextually with Isaiah, arguing that, just as Isaiah presents the vision in Isaiah 1–39 as a book within the larger scroll, so too the Twelve presents the prophets Hosea through to Zephaniah as books within the larger scroll. These prophetic words from the past 'are understood as having been fulfilled' in a time 'when Persian kings are in power' (Conrad 2000: 86). Haggai and Zechariah are themselves prophets 'who gain authority in their own time because they stand in continuity with the former prophets' (Conrad 1997: 74). Angel/messenger figures are presented in the first part of the Twelve as a memory from Jacob's time, whereas the second part abounds with messengers, culminating in Malachi, 'my messenger'. Conrad argues that the Twelve 'pictures the rise and fall of a prophetic past and the reinstitution of an angelic/messenger presence' (Conrad 1997: 67). The appearance of messengers coincides with a call to return 'to the way things used to be when messengers spoke to the fathers, for example with . . . Jacob at Bethel' (Conrad 2000: 87). The appearance of messengers represents the blurring between the celestial and the human, and even the divine and the human. This blurring arises from the rebuilding of the temple, which itself marks a blurring of 'the distinction between heaven and earth' due to the 'localized presence of Yahweh' as the 'master of the whole earth' (Conrad 2000: 87). While Conrad is working with the Masoretic edition of the Twelve, his insights can apply quite easily to the LXX.

Sexuality and the Twelve: seed, soil and the marriage of heaven and earth

I remind the reader of what I said, in my introduction to Genesis, about sexuality in the biblical world. The same applies with the Twelve. As the product of an ancient and alien culture, it should come as no surprise that the world of gender and sexuality encountered in the Twelve is very alien to that particularly dominant in Western cultures today. Whereas Western gender and sexuality systems are constructed around a series of binaries – female/male, homosexual/heterosexual – the Twelve comes from and reflects a world in which gender and sexuality are constructed as a hierarchical continuum. This hierarchy is one based on penetration. Men are the ones who penetrate and they stand at the top of the hierarchy. Below them are women and below women are eunuchs, female virgins, hermaphrodites and boys. At the bottom are the monstrous – penetrated men and penetrating women. Men can penetrate everyone in the lower levels of the hierarchy without loss of status. This gender/sexuality system overlapped with other hierarchies. Outsider foreign males and slaves could be subject to penetration by insider males and masters without loss of status to those men who penetrated. Male rape could thus be employed against defeated prisoners of war explicitly to deny them their male status.

Nevertheless, within this hierarchy male–female reproductive sexuality was privileged. Family (but not the nuclear family) was crucial to the ancient world and reproductive sexuality was understood in agricultural terms of seed and soil. The male sows the seed and the female is the field in which the seed is transformed and from which it is then brought forth (Delaney 1991: 30–6). Associated with this understanding is the practice of endogamous or (patrilineal) close kin marriage. As Carol Delaney observes, 'women *are* land . . . fields and daughters are tended and the fruits of this labour are to be kept within the group' (1991: 102). This monogenetic ideology of procreation, and corresponding endogamous marriage systems, are a feature of Mediterranean/ Middle Eastern cultures from prehistory. However, it is important to note that Rabbinic Judaism held to a duogenetic or even trigenetic theory of procreation whereby both female and male and even the deity contributed to procreation.

If women are like fields, then, just as a man can increase his holdings in land, so, too, with women. Polygamy and concubinage are a feature of the ancient world from which Genesis came. While economic factors might mandate monogamy for many, there is no opprobrium attached to polygamy. However, while a man might accumulate many fields, a field can only have one owner. Women are bound to one man to raise up children for him. A man is not bound to one woman and is free to sow his seed within or without marriage. Nevertheless, he must recognize the proprietorial rights of other men over their women. Adultery is always a crime against the husband, not the wife.

It needs to be stressed that the world of the Twelve and the worlds that shaped it did not share contemporary notions of heterosexual, bisexual, homosexual. Homoeroticism, same-sex love and desire certainly did exist but were understood very differently. For the ancient world, males were penetrators, and as long as they conformed to that role there was no shame. Shame and stigma were associated with the penetrated male, while the penetrating female could be viewed as especially monstrous. Eunuchs and hermaphrodites were accepted but subordinate to males and females. Virgin women also occupied a similar subordinate ambiguity in the hierarchy. Likewise, a particular ambiguity applied to boys, who occupied a transitional space between the world of women and that of adult men. Pederastic desire could be accepted, but tensions arose from the fact that boys were proto-men. Class and ethnicity were crucial: a slave boy and/or a foreign boy could be a legitimate object of sexual desire and penetration; in classical Athens, desire for a boy of one's own class and ethnicity could be legitimate provided no penetrative sex was involved.[3] While girls as proto-women were already legitimate objects for penetration and desire, as proto-women they were 'valuables' to be 'transacted by others' (Delaney 1991: 78). Their value lay in the integrity of their wombs, the property of their fathers and, subsequently, their husbands. However, despite the transactional value of girls and the ambiguity of boyhood, boys are or grow up to be men and seedbearers, upon which family continuity depends, and thus their status within a given community will outweigh that of girls.

These patterns of sexuality and gender still predominate in much of the Mediterranean and Middle East today but are extremely ancient. Such patterns were shared by 'pagan' and 'Israelite'/biblical communities alike, not in strict uniformity but subject to historical, socio-cultural and religious variations. What they share, though, are their origins in agricultural experience. The earth, the land, the soil is feminine, mother, womb. The sky is the masculine realm – rain and dew are understood as analogous to semen. Sky is heaven – *ouranos* in Greek – and as Benko notes, for the ancient world 'heaven and earth love each other . . . and there is continuous intercourse' between them from which 'not only did life begin', but it 'continually renews itself' (Benko 1993: 90). Ancient cosmologies told how earth gave birth to heaven 'to cover her everywhere over and be an ever-immovable base for the gods' (Hesiod's *Theogony*, cited in Benko 1993: 89). In Athens, marriages were dedicated to heaven and earth, Ouranos and Gaia, whose primal union was understood as the prototype of all marriages. However, the ancients believed a primordial catastrophe occurred causing the separation of earth and heaven. In Greek mythology they are forced apart by Kronos after Gaia gives birth to Okeanos, while in Sumerian mythology the primal unity of heaven and earth is ruptured by Enlil, the air-god. In Egypt, the genders of earth and heaven are reversed, earth being the male deity, Geb, and heaven the female deity, Nut. They, too, were separated primordially when the god of the air, Shu, 'forced himself

---

3 It is such considerations of sustaining ethnic/class solidarity that, I believe, could lie behind the Levitical proscriptions of male–male anal sex (Lev. 18.22; 20.13).

between the two and lifted up Nut' (Benko 1993: 88). Benko further points out that the pagan genderings of heaven and earth are also found in the biblical literature. Consequently 'things that pertain to the celestial sphere are usually masculine and those representing earthly dimensions are feminine . . . God is the father figure and also the husband, Israel, the wife' (Benko 1993: 90).[4]

While such imagery is fundamental to the Twelve, it is also linked to the ancient ritual of the sacred marriage, *hieros gamos*. According to Kramer, the 'Sacred Marriage Rite was celebrated joyously and rapturously all over the Ancient Near East for some two thousand years' (Kramer 1969: 49). Kramer argues that it was first developed in Sumeria as a fertility ritual to ensure both agricultural productivity and human procreation. He notes that a 'well-nigh obsessive veneration of . . . the fertile field and the fecund womb . . . pervades the Sumerian literary compositions, their myths and hymns' (Kramer 1969: 50). However, Harman is critical of notions that sacred marriage is purely a fertility ritual in every context. He points out that sacred marriages in India serve either to 'establish structured relationships between a deity and a group of people' or to 'establish or reaffirm relationships among deities as those relationships are perceived by devotees' (Harman 1989: 364). Benko points out that, in the Graeco-Roman world, while sacred marriage was 'no doubt . . . a fertility ritual . . . meant to ensure good harvest' it also 'pointed toward the great mystery of the union of Earth and Sky' thus symbolizing 'the joyful restoration of the cosmos to its undifferentiated state' (Benko 1993: 68). Thus sacred marriage represented 'a sacramental henosis . . . a return to unity with God, being completely filled with and absorbed into the divine' (Benko 1993: 69). Benko further argues that these sacred marriage themes and motifs manifest most startlingly in the cult of Cybele, the Great Mother of Anatolia, through the self-castration of male devotees, the order of Galli, who dedicated themselves fully to her service. As Benko observes, castration 'changes a man into a condition which is "neither male nor female"', thus becoming 'an androgynous person . . . returned to the primordial state of undifferentiation' (Benko 1993: 78). Through castration, the Galli surrender their patriarchal penetrative maleness, locating themselves on the middle rung of the gender hierarchy.

These sacred marriage themes of blurred boundaries can be found in the Twelve. As noted earlier, Conrad recognized a blurring of divine and human, of earth and heaven with the appearance of messengers at the end of the Twelve. The messengers signify the 'localized presence of Yahweh' as the 'master of the whole earth' (Conrad 2000: 87) in the temple at Jerusalem. The Twelve begins with Hosea, which, in a role similar to that of Genesis in the Pentateuch, serves as the introduction to the Twelve, anticipating what will unfold. Hosea opens

---

4 The image of primal androgynous unity of heaven and earth is found at the beginning of the second creation story in Genesis. Creation begins in the days before YHWH Elohim 'sent rain upon the earth' (Gen. 2.5), before the separation of earth and heaven. Instead, the creative process begins with the self-moisturing or self-fertilizing of the earth by which 'a flow would well up from the ground and water the whole surface of the earth' (Gen. 2.6). Only then does YHWH Elohim form the ground creature, *adam*, from the fecund ground (*adama*) and, subsequently, 'all the wild beasts and all the birds of the sky' (Gen. 2.19). The ground creature is, itself, in both Jewish and Christian traditions, created as an androgynous unity of female and male.

with imagery of a marriage gone wrong (from the patriarchal perspective) but closes with a queerly ambiguous vision, as will be seen, that serves to blur the distinction not only between heaven and earth but also between male and female. That sacred marriage can represent a breakdown of gender binaries is found in this passage from the Zohar:

> When they (the masculine and the feminine) unite, they look as if they were one body. From this we learn: the masculine by itself is like only one part of a body, and the feminine also. But when they join together as a whole, then they appear as one real body . . . The *matronita* united herself with the king. From this, one body resulted. Thence comes the blessing of this day. (Zohar III.296a)

Reference to the Zohar is a reminder that sacred marriage themes repeatedly recur in Jewish mystical traditions. According to Weinfeld, sacred marriage, together with the sacred tree, stands at 'the centre of Jewish mysticism . . . the Kabbalah literature revolves around the ideas of *hieros gamos* and the sacred tree' (Weinfeld 1996: 515). Sacred marriage in Kabbalah is understood as the union of the Holy One (of Israel) and the Shekhinah, the feminine, immanent aspect of the divine. Weinfeld presents some provocative imagery from Jewish tradition of the erotics of the temple in relation to this divine union, which I believe might give a useful perspective for reading a book such as the Twelve, in which the restoration of divine presence in the temple is of paramount concern.

Weinfeld begins by examining the theme of sacred marriage in pious Jewish life. For ultra-Orthodox Jews, every religious act should be accompanied by the formula, 'This is done for the sake of the union of God and his Shekhinah' (Weinfeld 1996: 517). Sex between husband and wife is recommended for the night of Shabbat because that is 'the time when the consort is united with the King' (Zohar II.89a–b). Saying the Shema – 'Hear O Israel – the Lord is One' – realizes the real unity of God, because then

> the Matron adorns herself in order to enter the chamber together with her husband. All the upper numbers (the Sephirot from *Hesed* to *Yesod* that are of masculine type) unite with a unique desire to be 'one' without separation. Then her husband concentrates in her entrance into the chamber to be all alone with her, to become 'one'. (Zohar II.135a)

As with daily pious practice, so, too, the temple and its rituals of sacrifice were understood to have the primary purpose of effecting the union of the Shekhinah and the Holy One. This union is even named the Holy of Holies (Zohar II.231b). The Holy of Holies in the temple is understood to be the divine couple's bedchamber, the 'place of communion for the Holy One and the Shekhinah' (Weinfeld 1996: 518). Most extraordinary is the portrayal of the high priest's worship in the Holy of Holies at Yom Kippur. He enters

> the Holy of Holies in order to unify the holy name, to unite the king with the consort . . . At his entrance . . . he heard the voice of the wings of the cheru-

bim being lifted up for intercourse. When the wings subside the cherubim copulate calmly. (Weinfeld 1996: 518)

This image of the copulating cherubim derives from the Talmud, where it is said:

> Whenever Israel came up from the festivals, the curtain (of the Holy of Holies) would be removed for them and the Cherubim were shown to them, whose bodies were intertwined with one another and would be thus addressed: 'Look! You are beloved before God as the love between man and woman'. (b. Yoma 54a)

Even when drawn, the curtain of the Holy of Holies was erotically charged. The poles of the Ark of the Covenant behind the curtain (see 1 Kings 8.8) pressed against it and 'protruded as the two breasts of a woman, as it is said: "my beloved is unto me as a bag of myrrh that lieth between my breasts"' (b. Yoma 54a, citing S. of Sol. 1.13). The temple and its rituals, then, are understood to be the location not merely of a general divine presence but the very place in which the cosmic sacred marriage of the Holy One and the Shekhinah is effected.

Seen in such a light, then, the destruction of the temple is both a cosmic and erotic rupture. It marks the separation of the Holy One and the Shekhinah, who cries bitterly seeing the defilement of her bedchamber and laments the loss of her husband. As Israel is exiled and dispersed among the nations so, too, the Shekhinah is in exile, wandering upon the earth, longing to be reunited with her Holy One. Thus, in Jewish tradition, rebuilding the temple is not simply a matter of restoring a place of worship. Rebuilding the temple signifies the restoration of the only place in which can occur the sacred cosmic union of the Bride and Bridegroom, the union that 'brings harmony to the whole universe' (Weinfeld 1996: 517).

It could be argued that such imagery of Bride and Bridegroom and their union in sacred marriage is too irredeemably heterosexual to be of any use for queer people. My response would be to question whether sacred marriage accords with contemporary notions of heterosexuality. Recalling Benko's observations concerning the Galli (not to mention the Zohar citations above), I would argue that sacred marriage celebrates the restoration of the undifferentiated and androgynous unity of primordial time. The Galli represent that reality in their own flesh and in doing so they located themselves in the middle rung of the ancient gender hierarchy. As I said introducing Genesis, this middle or intermediate level of the patriarchal hierarchy, due to its very indeterminacy, evoked the primal androgyne. Ironically, then, sacred marriage, through its vision of the primal androgynous unity, can serve as a critique of the existing patriarchal gender hierarchy, even inspiring resistance in the form of celibate, gender variant and homoerotic and sexual utopian movements. Perhaps that is why, in Isaiah's vision of the restored temple, eunuchs are promised a 'monument and a name better than sons or daughters . . . an everlasting name which shall not perish . . . in My house and within My walls' (Isa. 56.5).

Reading the Twelve

When I read the Twelve I am not interested in trying to ascertain historical details of the prophets portrayed there. I don't believe there ever was a Hosea or an Amos or a Nahum or Haggai. Even if there was, we won't find out information about them from the Twelve. Just as the Twelve won't provide historical information about these characters, I also don't expect it to provide historical information about events in Iron Age Palestine or concerning the rebuilding of the temple in Jerusalem in the Persian period. The prophets in the Twelve are characters that foretell events in their future, but their words of prophecy are ignored and not understood until a later time after the events they predict. There is very little narrative in the Twelve – only Jonah provides a detailed narrative with identified characters to frame the prophet's words. The greater part of the Twelve consists of speech, most of which can be attributed to YHWH or the particular prophet, but there are passages of speech where it is uncertain who speaks. Most of this speech is in poetic form, often stylized as psalms, oracles and curses. House, arguing that Zephaniah should be understood as a prophetic drama, provides a translation divided up into dramatic acts and scenes, with two characters, Yahweh and the prophet (House 1988: 118–26). My own position is that the entire book of the Twelve can be read as a dramatic piece, a script or a libretto, and, like House, I have allocated different parts to different voices, primarily YHWH and the prophets/messengers. However, while I am mostly in accord with House in identifying the voices in Zephaniah, many other passages in the Twelve are not so easily identified. The narrative sections in Jonah and elsewhere (mostly the introductory superscriptions on each book) I have allocated to a narrator voice. Taking a cue from ancient Greek drama I have also allowed for the possibility of a chorus speaking some sections, giving an almost liturgical, responsorial quality to certain passages. Indeed, I suspect the Twelve could function well as a type of liturgical drama. Despite this dramatic scoring, there are still passages where it is unclear just who speaks, thus providing a rich opportunity for ambiguity.

In the commentary that follows, I will read this drama alert to the images of sexual violence and the use of sexuality to abject the Other. Given the marriage metaphors and the temple focus, however, I will also draw on the sacred marriage motif and its androgynously queer vistas in my reading. In doing so, I am not declaring that the Twelve is a sacred marriage ritual, or that sacred marriage was practised in the Jerusalem temple or that the composers of the Twelve set out to promote an androgynous alternative to the patriarchal hierarchy. Yet Jewish tradition has clearly portrayed the temple, and divine presence there, employing the images of sacred marriage and androgyny. Weinfeld also argues that these sacred marriage motifs in Jewish mystical and other traditions form a continuity with sacred marriage practices and beliefs in the ancient world. All of these themes and motifs are presented most dramatically in the opening book or act of the Twelve, Hosea. Consequently, Hosea receives the most detailed discussion in the commentary that follows.

Commentary

In the commentary, I will follow the Masoretic order of the Twelve but will also make occasional observations to the LXX ordering. I will employ the chapter/verse divisions of the Hebrew Bible, which vary occasionally from most English translations, with the exception of the Jewish Publication Society (JPS) translation, the Tanakh. Except where otherwise indicated, all citations will be from the JPS translation.

Hosea

Introduction

The book of Hosea serves as the introduction and overture to the Twelve. The name, Hosea, means 'May YH (the LORD) save' and is related to the names Joshua/Jesus and Isaiah. Hosea presents themes of divine vengeance and punishment disturbingly commingled with divine love and tenderness. The book addresses itself to Israel and Judah although, because its setting is in the northern kingdom, Israel (Ephraim) is the main addressee. The book opens with the presentation of marital breakdown, from the husband's perspective, as a metaphor for the relationship between Israel and its deity. The husband, Hosea, represents the deity, and his violent, threatening, yearningly obsessive appeals to Gomer, the wife who has spurned him, anticipate the threatening oracles against Israel that follow in the greater part of the book. Gale Yee breaks the book into three sections, chapters 1–3, the marriage of Gomer and Hosea; chapters 4–11, the oracles against Israel; chapters 12–14, an eventual reconciliation between Israel and the deity, reprising marriage imagery from the beginning (Yee 1998: 207). In contrast, Sweeney postulates a structure in which Hosea 1.1 and 14.10 frame a book in two parts: Hosea 1.2–2.2, 'an anonymous narrator's report of YHWH's initial instructions to Hosea to marry the harlot Gomer' and Hosea 2.3–14.9, 'the presentation of Hosea's speeches to Israel that outline judgement against Israel . . . and call for Israel's return to YHWH' (Sweeney *et al.* 2000: 13). In my reading I will combine these approaches, beginning with a brief discussion of the superscription, then following Yee's thematic divisions, informed by Sweeney's understanding of Hosea's structure.

Superscription (1.1)

The superscription to Hosea dates the events to the reigns of the kings Uzziah, Jotham, Ahaz[5] and Hezekiah in Judah, and Jeroboam in Israel. As Conrad (1997) observes, this pattern of citing specific reigns in the superscription is found in Amos, Micah and Zephaniah together with Haggai and Zechariah. With the latter two, however, the superscriptions are dated to a specific day, month and year of the Persian king, Darius, giving the audience 'the impression . . . that one is moving into a better known world' (Conrad 1997: 68). The earlier prophets are merely dated to the reigns of kings of Judah – Uzziah (together with Jeroboam in Israel) for Amos; Jotham, Ahaz and Hezekiah for Micah; Josiah for Zephaniah. That these earlier datings are so broad indicates to Conrad that the reader is put in a 'vaguely remembered past' (Conrad 1997: 68), a past marked by Assyrian ascendancy. The superscriptions not only date the books they introduce but also provide a chronological structure for the other books – Joel, Obadiah, Jonah, Nahum, Habakkuk, Malachi – whose superscriptions do not contain any dating. Superscriptions then serve as a structuring and linking device for the Twelve. Conrad notes too that a similar pattern is employed in Isaiah, which dates itself in its superscription to the reigns of Uzziah, Jotham,

---

5   The superscription to Isaiah similarly situates its chronology of events as opening in the reigns of these Judahite kings.

Ahaz and Hezekiah in Judah. These kings then appear in the sequential unfolding of the narrative sections of Isaiah 'to situate the first 39 chapters in a chronological timeline measured by the reigns of the Judaean kings' (Conrad 1997: 68). Jeremiah and Ezekiel also date themselves with reigns of Judahite kings. The Twelve is unique in that it opens with Hosea's superscription also citing the reign of an Israelite king to locate itself, and further uses the reign of an Israelite king to mark its chronology in Amos. This usage serves to signal that, unlike Isaiah, Jeremiah and Ezekiel, the Twelve is concerned with not one but two entities who are (descended from) Jacob/Israel and share the Torah of Moses. Hosea's main focus will be on the northern entity Israel/Ephraim; however, the southern one, Judah, while on the sidelines, is never offstage. This fact will be important for viewing what is the opening scenario not only of Hosea, but also of the Twelve as a whole.

The prostitute and the prophet (1.2—3.4)

Immediately, the text presents the disturbing metaphor of the prophet's marriage[6] to the prostitute to represent the relationship between YHWH and Israel. Hosea is told by YHWH to take 'a wife of whoredom and children of whoredom; for the land will stray from following the LORD' (Hos. 1.2). The text then relates how Hosea marries Gomer bat Diblaim, who gives birth to three children. All three are given names that represent YHWH's complaints against Israel. The first is named Jezreel, both the site where Jehu killed Jezebel (2 Kings 9.30–3) ending the Omride dynasty in Israel and a name meaning 'God sows' or 'God scatters' (thus being both a blessing and a curse). The other two are named Lo-ruhamah, Not Accepted/Pitied, and Lo-ammi, Not My People. All of these events are presented as a short narrative in chapter 1 and 2.1–2. In Hosea 2.3, the voice suddenly shifts to the first person, as the prophet addresses his children, voicing complaints about their mother. The prophet's voice modulates into that of YHWH, and the figure of Gomer becomes that of unfaithful Israel, a shift that takes place between verses 8 and 13. This introductory section ends in chapter 3 with a return to the prophet's voice relating how he has been told by YHWH to love an adulterous woman and details of the contract and payment he uses to ensure her sequestration.

This prophetic drama presents a vision of a patriarchal marriage crisis, in which the husband struggles to retain control of his wife. Hosea/YHWH speaks of his love for Gomer/Israel, but it is a love framed in violence. Hosea threatens to strip her naked and make her 'like a wilderness' (2.5). He will cut her off from her lovers with walls and thorny hedges and take back the 'grain and wine and oil' (2.10) he bestowed on her. As the prophet's voice warps into YHWH's the language of violence continues more strongly. Israel's nakedness will be uncovered and she will be exposed to her lovers. Her vines and fig trees will be laid waste and all her festivals will be ended. Free autonomous female sexuality is

---

6 Hornsby questions whether the relationship of Gomer and Hosea should be understood as a marriage. Instead she argues that what is presented is a portrait of 'a jealous client of a prostitute who desires to possess an autonomous, strong woman' (Hornsby 1999: 124).

a marker representing apostasy and rebellion while patriarchal male sexual violence against women signifies divine punishment of faithless Israel.

It would come as no surprise that feminist/womanist responses to Hosea have denounced the pornographic objectification of Gomer, and the apparent legitimation of male violence against women and patriarchal control of women. Male desire, and by extension divine love, is portrayed as hegemonic, seeking 'to control and dominate an objectified other' (Hornsby 1999: 118). The vengeful yearnings of Hosea/YHWH imagine a marriage model of ruthless monogamy, with the woman silently submissive, prisoner to the male. By implication, sexually autonomous women, especially prostitutes, are deemed 'worthy of extreme punishment' and thus 'inspire murderous rage' on the part of males (Hornsby 1999: 117).[7] Not only must this model of marriage and desire be rejected as lethal to women, but also the image of the deity for which this model is a metaphor.

Sherwood describes Hosea as a problem text, comparing it to the problem plays of Shakespeare, and points out that feminists and womanists have not been alone in finding it a 'disturbing, fragmented, outrageous and notoriously problematic text' (Sherwood 1996: 11). In particular, it is the figure of Gomer and the divine command to Hosea to marry her that have generated the most responses. Sherwood surveys a range of readings and interpretations of Hosea 1–3 from the second century to the twentieth and observes that most attempt to tame her and to 'dilute, rather than exploit, the mismatch of the marriage' (Sherwood 1996: 79). Indeed, Gomer often disappears as a character – in the Targum Jonathan's rendering of Hosea 1.2–3 she is turned into fig-leaves (Sherwood 1996: 43).[8] Nevertheless, as Sherwood points out, the power of Hosea 1–3 is precisely the fact that 'the marriage is an outrageous mismatch with dangerous implications' (Sherwood 1996: 80). The character of Gomer, therefore, is crucial to this power, highlighting the fact that Hosea 1–3 is a multiply transgressive text.

Most provocatively, through Gomer, Israel is represented as faithless wife and prostitute, and yet the book most likely addresses a male audience. This marriage metaphor of husband YHWH and wife Israel places the men of Israel (or any community claiming a lineage from that Israel) in a highly ambiguous gender space. They are recast as wife/woman of the divine husband. As Stone observes, not only does this image mobilize male fears of not being a proper male but it reinforces those fears 'by utilizing the image of a sexually promiscuous woman, an image that is threatening in part because, within a certain framework of cultural assumptions, control of female sexuality is partially constitutive of manhood' (Stone 2001b: 130). Nevertheless, it is possible for androcentric readers to identify primarily with Hosea, reading themselves as the wronged husband rather than as the adulterous wife. As Sherwood has

---

7 Hornsby makes these points to critique the dominant feminist reading of Hosea 1–3 as a domestic violence scenario. Hornsby's reading sets out to retrieve Gomer as an independent woman rather than the victimized wife, a reading she argues maintains the patriarchal dynamics of the text.

8 The name of her father, Diblaim, means 'cluster of figs'. Gomer's own name means 'to finish' or 'to complete'.

shown, it has been a consistent position of many biblical scholars 'to express their solidarity with the suffering of Hosea the victim' (Sherwood 1996: 57) such that he even becomes a foreshadowing of the suffering Christ. Another problem for interpreters has been the fact that the marriage of Gomer and Hosea 'is literally a "marriage made in heaven"' (Sherwood 1996: 80). YHWH commands Hosea to marry this woman. This divine command is given twice (Hos. 1.2 and 3.1) much to the consternation of critics who 'sense that Yhwh [sic] is transgressing his own standards of purity and separation' (Sherwood 1996: 81). So even though androcentric readers might identify with Hosea the prophet, Hosea the text can still throw up awkward and disturbing moments of disjunction. Sherwood, herself, proposes a feminist deconstructive approach that emphasizes that 'the marriage is Gomer's as well as Hosea's' to thus invert a 'text and tradition that has always presented the woman as a problem for patriarchy' (Sherwood 1996: 255). This position, of reading from Gomer's perspective, takes 'the woman as a standard for judgement' and explores 'how the premises of patriarchy are a problem for her' (Sherwood 1996: 255).

From a queer perspective, I am struck by several points of dissension or slippage that arise from the text's insistence on ruthless monogamy and a morbidly patriarchal heterosexuality. First, while so much discussion has focused on Gomer's promiscuity, it would appear that no one has questioned the assumption of YHWH's monogamy. Gomer represents Israel, YHWH's wife, but is she YHWH's only wife? Where does Judah fit in this marital drama? Hosea opens citing the reigns of not one but four kings of Judah to locate its events chronologically. Judah is referred to again in Hosea 1.7 and 2.2. While this latter verse imagines a merging of Judah and Israel into one entity, this is yet to happen. As the drama unfolds, therefore, the audience is presented with Gomer/Israel as YHWH's wife but with the knowledge that there is also Judah, YHWH's other wife. When read in the context of introducing the Twelve as a whole, the issue of YHWH's monogamy in Hosea 1–3 is made even more problematic. The Twelve contains visionary declarations that all the nations 'will go up to the Mount of the LORD' (Micah 4.2) and 'attach themselves to the LORD and become his people' (Zech. 2.15). If Gomer/Israel is promiscuous through attachment to Baal, what of YHWH's desire to be attached to all these other nations, in addition to Israel and Judah? Of course, it could be argued that for the ancient audience of this drama, monogamy was only expected of women. Polygamy was permitted for men and they could also keep concubines. So perhaps YHWH is presented as a polygamous patriarch, or, in his desire to be attached to all the nations, perhaps YHWH echoes Solomon with his 700 wives and 300 concubines (1 Kings 11.3). Indeed, when taken literally, the monogamous marriage metaphor for relationship with the divine cannot be sustained but collapses under a vision of divine promiscuity far in excess of what a patriarch or potentate could aspire to.

The motif of sacred marriage itself serves as a point of slippage undermining the patriarchal heterosexuality that Hosea/YHWH seeks to impose on Gomer. Hosea complains that it was he 'who bestowed . . . the new grain and wine and oil' (Hos. 2.10) on Gomer. Grain, wine and oil are the fruits of the earth, the consequence of the union of heaven and earth, 'of the reunion of the Holy One, blessed be he, and the Shekinah' (Weinfeld 1996: 523). Grain, wine and oil are used both in Hosea and throughout the Twelve to signify divine blessing, 'attributing to YHWH characteristics frequently associated with the deities of so-called fertility religion, including Baal himself' (Stone 2001b: 123). I would argue that this move arises from the sacred marriage motif at work throughout Hosea and the Twelve. In my discussion of sacred marriage above I suggested that it lent itself to an androgynous and non-hierarchical, rather than a patriarchal, vision of sexuality. This vision erupts at the end of Hosea 2, just as it will do more queerly in the final chapter of Hosea. As the vision in Hosea 2 develops, it collapses the boundary between YHWH and Baal – 'you will call [Me] Ishi and no more will you call Me Baali' (Hos. 2.18). The word Ishi, in the JPS translation, is the Hebrew 'my husband' or 'my man' while Baali can mean 'my Baal', 'my husband' or 'my Lord/master'. In this sentence YHWH both appropriates Baal (Israel did not understand that Baal was YHWH all along) and offers a vision of a non-hierarchical relationship (YHWH will no longer be called my Baal/Lord but my man). Use of the word Ishi here also evokes the primal Eden and the first humans who come into being following the separation of the original androgynous earth creature. *Ish* and *Ishshah* are the words used to designate the separated male and female parts of this primal androgyne (Gen. 2.23), whose relationship following their separation is egalitarian and not patriarchal until they eat the fruit of the Tree of Knowledge. This evocation of Eden in verse 18 is then reinforced by a vision of a new and fertile harmony in Hosea 2.20–4. There will be a new covenant with all living things by which war and its instruments will be banished from the land. YHWH and Gomer/Israel will be reconciled in a new relationship that signals a new order of cosmic harmony, in which the deity 'will respond to the sky and it shall respond to the earth; and the earth shall respond with new grain and wine and oil' (Hos. 2.23–4). Intriguingly this image replaces the marriage dyad of earth and sky with a triad of deity, earth and sky, as if to say that even notions of exclusive couples are inadequate to match the erotic vision contained in sacred marriage.

Sherwood rightly warns against seeing the contrast between Baal and YHWH in 2.18 as the invention of a new level of intimacy with the divine not found in rival cults. She points out that critics who do so,

> while accurately following the text . . . are also dupes of its all-too-convincing rhetoric. Yhwh's [sic] new role as 'husband' highlights his mimicry of Baal's sexuality and emphasizes the deconstructive irony that the God who condemns the woman and her lovers ends by seducing Israel in the desert and playing the lover himself. (Sherwood 1996: 235)

By highlighting the shift in verse 18, I do so not to let Hosea/YHWH off the hook for the morbid patriarchal heterosexuality which threatens and tries to repress Gomer/Israel. Instead, my goal is to highlight the way that image cannot sustain itself. The audience discovers that Baal was really YHWH all along. Furthermore, after being presented with an image of patriarchal marriage gone wrong, it is given a vision of a final erotic reconciliation, a new erotic community, that can only become reality by the abolition of patriarchal marriage and maybe even of marriage itself.

Oracles against Israel (Hosea 4–11)

The vision of a new erotic community that closes Hosea 2 can be seen as the first of three attempts (the other two being Hosea 11 and 14) by the divine to manifest a new way of being that breaks down the hierarchical, patriarchal order. But this order has not yet been displaced and so the voice of the divine falls silent. Instead, the prophet speaks reprising the divine command to 'befriend a woman who, while befriended by a companion, consorts with others, just as . . . the Israelites . . . turn to other gods' (Hos. 3.1). As I noted earlier, there has been much critical argument about whether this woman is Gomer or someone else and as to whether the deity would command such a relationship. I don't believe the deity in Hosea (or the rest of the Hebrew scriptures) is an upholder of Western bourgeois 'family' values, so I am not troubled by the question of the number of women in Hosea's life. Nevertheless, I regard the prophet's account here as a recapitulation of the narrative account of Hosea and Gomer in Hosea 1.2–2.2. The Hebrew scriptures are not averse to repetition, and Hosea's account here serves to bracket and seal off the divine vision that closes chapter 2 and, thus, to reorient the audience to what will follow. In a sense, the text does to the divine vision what Hosea/YHWH threatens to do to Gomer, 'to hedge up her roads with thorns and raise walls against her' (Hos. 2.8).

Having represented the image of YHWH as patriarchal husband preparing to punish the harlot-wife Israel, the prophet now begins a series of oracles condemning Israel, calling for it to repent and threatening punishment if it ignores these warnings. As in Hosea 2, for the greater part of these oracles, the voice of the prophet becomes submerged in the divine voice. In these oracles sexuality is used to abject Israel in an inversion of sacred marriage motifs. Particularly targeted are the priesthood and sanctuaries of Israel, in particular the ancient shrines of Bethel, also called Beth Aven (house of vanity), and Gilgal. That these are ancient Israelite sanctuaries and not the sanctuaries of rival deities should come as no surprise. One of the main issues in the Twelve is the central status of the sanctuary in Jerusalem, displacing all others. To forward this agenda, all rival shrines, no matter how venerable, are to be defamed. They will be attacked as engaging in corrupt practices, abandoning the ways of their forefathers and worshipping other deities. Nevertheless, in Hosea 2.18, YHWH has already declared himself to be the Baal worshipped in these sanctuaries, making spurious the allegation that they had abandoned him. Indeed, what Hosea and the rest of the Twelve does is to base this claim on the subsequent destruction of Israelite and Judahite monarchies at the hands of the Assyrians and Babylonians. That both Israel and Judah suffered this fate means that occasionally Hosea's threats against Israel include mention of Judah. While Judah, like Israel, brought down divine punishment, this punishment served to clear the way for the establishment of a new era of divine presence in Jerusalem, but not in the allegedly completely corrupted sanctuaries of the north.

Consequently, Hosea begins his oracles declaring that in Israel 'the earth is withered: everything that dwells on it languishes' (4.3). When earth and heaven unite, the earth is fruitful and productive, so this image signals a cosmic rupture. Shifting into YHWH voice, Hosea immediately turns on the priesthood, declaring, 'My people is destroyed because of [your] disobedience! Because you have rejected obedience, I reject you as my priest' (4.6). The corruption of the people caused by the corruption of the cult is portrayed in sexual language. The people have 'forsaken the LORD to practise lechery' and a 'lecherous impulse has made them go wrong', straying from 'submission to their God' (4.10, 12). This is a metaphorical lechery because cultic corruption is the real issue, 'They sacrifice on the mountaintops and offer on the hills' (4.13). Nevertheless, it results in a dire image of social chaos, 'their daughters fornicate and daughters-in-law commit adultery' (4.13). Hosea's audience is male, and this image of the unleashed eroticism of their daughters is used to impugn Israelite patriarchal masculinity. In a world of seed and soil, a daughter's womb is a valuable commodity, over which a father keeps strict control. But now that they have abandoned YHWH, they have lost control of their daughters, while their sons have lost control of their wives. No longer can the patriarchal household guarantee that the fruit of its wombs is the harvest of its seed. YHWH will also no longer maintain Israelite patriarchal authority; the daughters and daughters-in-law will not be punished and their behaviour is not at issue. Sexual morality is not the issue against Israel but the means to shame and abject Israel. A warning then follows to Judah to avoid the corrupt and corrupting influence of the northern shrines, the implication being that Judah's fate was the result of being led astray by northern influences.

These images are maintained in Hosea 5, which opens by attacking both the priests and the royal house of Israel. Israel/Ephraim is said to have 'fornicated' and 'defiled himself' (5.3), paying 'no heed to the LORD because of the lecherous impulse' within its people (5.4). As the oracle progresses, Judah is linked with Israel/Ephraim. When Israel and Ephraim fall, 'Judah falls with them' (5.5). Not just Israel, but 'the officers of Judah' will face the wrath of YHWH, who is both 'rot to Ephraim' and 'decay to the House of Judah' (5.12), and will come 'like a lion to Ephraim' and a 'great beast . . . to Judah' (5.14). Violent abuse linked with marriage, echoing the abuse of Gomer, reappears in Hosea 6. In the opening verses, a chorus declares, 'let us return to the LORD' who 'attacked' and 'wounded' but 'can heal . . . and . . . bind us up' to 'make us whole again' (6.1–2). There follows a call to become obedient to YHWH so that 'He will come to us like rain, like latter rain that refreshes the earth' (6.3). Rain is the semen of heaven in the sacred marriage of heaven and earth, so YHWH comes to Israel as husband, a husband who has violently abused Israel, his spouse. Following this chorus, YHWH expresses a brief lament for both Ephraim and Judah before reverting to the language of warning and threat in ever increasing violence culminating, in Hosea 10.14–15, with images of invasion, the slaughter of mothers and babies and the extinguishing of the Israelite monarchy.

YHWH's brief lament for Ephraim and Judah in Hosea 6.4 can be taken as a sign of a deity struggling with itself. Speaking of Hosea 1–3, Sherwood maintains that 'struggle is implicit' in those chapters, which contain 'imagery that is at odds with itself and that deconstructs its own assertions' (Sherwood 1996: 231). I would argue that her observation is true for Hosea as a whole. Just such a moment of struggle and resistance occurs in the dramatic rupture of Hosea

11 and its striking parental imagery of the deity. Gale Yee says of this chapter that 'the metaphor expressive of God now is the one of the caring parent rather than the loving husband . . . Israel is . . . the rebellious son instead of the adulterous wife' (Yee 1998: 213). She notes that the text does not call the deity either mother or father and that most of the activities portrayed could be performed by either parent, 'although one can argue that the primary caregiver during childhood is the mother' (Yee 1998: 213). However, Helen Schüngel-Straumann argues that the central image of chapter 11 is that of YHWH as mother not father. She points out that

> Hosea loves to work with contrasting pairs. Whereas in the image of God as husband and Israel as unfaithful wife he distributes the male–female polarity in such a way that God is on the male and Israel on the female side, in Hosea 11 and elsewhere YHWH as mother is contrasted with her child, who is depicted as male ('youth', 'son' as in 1.1). (1995: 215)

Most of her argument is based on the linguistics of key Hebrew words in Hosea 11.3–4. She observes that verse 3, which opens with an emphatic I-statement, 'begins a listing based on three verbs, all referring to the way one deals with an infant, a nursling' (Schüngel-Straumann 1995: 200). In particular, she argues that the first verb *tirgaltî*, which, as it contains the root *rgl* (foot) is commonly translated as 'teach to walk' (as in the NRSV),[9] is better understood as meaning to suckle or nurse. She bases her argument on the fact that the verb does not have this meaning anywhere else in the Hebrew scriptures and that furthermore there is a similar Arabic root that means suckle, nurse. Indeed, Jerome translated *tirgaltî* with *nutricius*, 'which can mean "the one who brings up" but the same word is used for "nurse, feed"' (Schüngel-Straumann 1995: 200). Similarly, she argues that the word in verse 4b, *leḥēyhem*, commonly translated as 'cheeks' (again, as in the NRSV), is more correctly translated as 'breasts', that meaning being found in other Hebrew texts such as Ruth 4.16 (Schüngel-Straumann 1995: 202). On the basis of these and other linguistic arguments she renders Hosea 11.3–4 as, 'But it was I who nursed Ephraim, taking him in my arms. Yet they did not understand that it was I who took care of them. I drew them with cords of humanity, with bands of love. And I was for them like those who take a nursling to the breast, and I bowed down to him in order to give him suck' (Schüngel-Straumann 1995: 195–6).

The application of this maternal imagery to the deity is not the only striking feature of Hosea 11 because it combines this image with a 'rare glimpse of the emotional turmoil of God on the verge of destroying the son' (Yee 1998: 213). She points out that under Deuteronomic law both parents had the right to condemn a rebellious son and hand him over to be stoned. In verses 8 and 9 the audience is presented with a graphic image of the deity grappling with such a decision and finally resolving not to destroy Ephraim. Again Schüngel-Straumann mounts a linguistic case that it is YHWH the mother that is presented to the audience by the text. Furthermore, by doing so the text specifically challenges the image of YHWH as husband that has heretofore dominated

---

9 However, the JPS renders it as 'pampered'.

Hosea. It is that latter point that I will pursue here. Schüngel-Straumann translates these verses as:

> How can I give you up, O Ephraim? How can I hand you over, O Israel? How can I give you up like Admah? How can I treat you like Zeboiim? My heart recoils against me, my womb is utterly inflamed within me. I cannot execute my burning wrath, nor can I utterly change (what is within me), so as to destroy Ephraim. For I am God and not a man, holy in your midst, and I do not come to destroy. (Schüngel-Straumann 1995: 195–6)

When the deity declares that it is not a man, the Hebrew word used is ʾîš, having the meanings of husband or male human. Schüngel-Straumann argues that here Hosea is deliberately contrasting divine behaviour with masculine behaviour (1995: 212). She points out that if Hosea wanted to contrast divine and human behaviour, the text would have employed ʾādām, a word used elsewhere to denote more broadly human qualities and behaviours. In particular, ʾādām has already been used in Hosea 11.4 to denote the human 'way of behaving' that mother YHWH employed in rearing Ephraim/Israel (Schüngel-Straumann 1995: 212). Consequently, ʾîš is used to denote specifically masculine or even husband-like behaviours. By rejecting such behaviours and such a role and by identifying YHWH's relationship with Ephraim/Israel so strongly in terms of mother and son, Hosea 11 continues the collapsing of the marriage model that was a feature of the first visionary counter-voice in the latter part of Hosea 2. By changing the deity's gender, Hosea 11 also anticipates the complete collapse of both marriage and gender categories that, I will argue in the next section, is the dominating motif of the final rupture that closes Hosea in chapter 14.

Vision of final reconciliation (Hosea 12–14)

This final section opens not with language of reconciliation but with the language of threat and menace instead. Hosea 12 also draws on the stories of Jacob, retelling them 'as a parable of rebellion and reconciliation' (Marks 1987: 228). Jacob is Israel's eponymous ancestor who is named Israel following his struggle 'with a divine being' (Hos. 12.4, recalling Gen. 32.22–32). It is Jacob who spoke with the deity at Bethel and there established the sanctuary (Gen. 35.14–15). In the course of the Twelve it is Bethel that will be supplanted by Zion as the dwelling place of YHWH (Zech. 7–8). Violence and denunciation continue in Hosea 13, which dramatically inverts the maternal image of chapter 11. Now the deity prepares to attack Israel 'like a bear robbed of her young' to 'rip open the casing of their hearts' (Hos. 13.8). Imagery of death and violence is piled up, culminating in the brutal imagery of war and spoliation, 'They shall fall by the sword, their infants shall be dashed to death, and their women with child ripped open' (Hos. 14.1).

With this scene the homicidal impulse seems exhausted, arousing once more a counter-voice. This counter-voice at first appears to endorse the ideology of domination and punishment. It begins as a call to 'return . . . to the LORD your God' (Hos. 14.2) in the prophet's voice, followed by a choral plea for forgiveness, led by the prophet. The deity then responds in language of ever increasing eroticism drawing on sacred marriage motifs. Israel will be taken 'back in love' (Hos. 14.5), following which,

> I will be to Israel like dew, he shall blossom like the lily, he shall strike root like the Lebanon tree. His boughs shall spread out far, his beauty shall be like the olive tree's, his fragrance like that of Lebanon. They who sit in his shade shall be revived: they shall bring to life new grain, they shall blossom like the vine, his scent shall be like the wine of Lebanon. Ephraim [shall say]: 'What more have I to do with idols? When I respond and look to Him, I become like a verdant cypress.' Your fruit is provided by Me. (Hos. 14.6–9)

Grain, wine and (olive) oil are signs of the joyous union of heaven and earth and represent the 'luxuriant growth of Israel in the land' (Yee 1998: 214). Just as striking is the erotic imagery of dew and lily. Dew in the sacred marriage motif is the semen of heaven. By being like dew to Israel and causing him to blossom, YHWH describes the relationship with Israel as a sacred marriage. However, what is striking in these verses is that it is a sacred marriage of two males. Unlike the opening chapters in which Israel is depicted and addressed as a woman, in these verses Israel is clearly addressed as a male, revealing the implicit homoeroticism of the marriage metaphor applied to a male community to portray its relationship with its god. Making the homoeroticism explicit, naming this relationship to be a male marriage, serves to collapse the metaphor's potential to support heteronormativity. The homoeroticism of this image might even prove liberating for gay and bisexual men,[10] but what about lesbian and bisexual women or women as a whole? As Ostriker observes, drawing upon Eilberg-Schwartz's analysis of the homoerotics of Israel's relationship with the deity, do women pose 'a threat . . . to the male–male love relationship between men and God', thus requiring that 'actual women must be excluded altogether from the circle of immediate spiritual relationship' (Ostriker 2000: 51)? Is this the real impulse behind the exclusion of women from ministry, most prominently in the very queer milieu that is Roman Catholicism? Does the collapsing of the sacred marriage motif here into the homoerotic serve to sustain the violence against Gomer, not as the figure of the brotherhood of Israel, but as a woman representing all women?

I raise these questions because I believe the sacred marriage motif can be used to critique the patriarchal heteronormative ideologies in the text. I believe that in these final verses there is an excess, as in Hosea 11 and the final verses of Hosea 2, that serves to collapse these ideologies and open up queer possibilities. To achieve this effect, the excess must be not androcentric but androgynous, collapsing not only heteronormativity but all rigid gender categories. Is there an androgynous dimension to Hosea's final image of male marriage between Ephraim/Israel and YHWH? The androgynous dimension can be found, and it comes from a surprising source: ancient goddess traditions. Marie-Theres Wacker lists Hosea 14.9, the verse closing this scene

---

10 I confess that when I first saw this homoerotic possibility it came as a joyful surprise to me.

of reconciliation, as one that includes traces of not one but two goddesses. She points out that Wellhausen believed that the Hebrew of 14.9b, 'when I respond and look to Him', could be improved to read 'I am his Anath and Asherah' (Wacker 1995: 224). The Hebrew reads 'anî 'ănātî wa'ăšûrennû, which Wellhausen proposed should read, 'anî 'ănātô wa'ăšērāto. She notes that Wellhausen's proposal has been taken up by a number of scholars. Weinfeld himself employs it in his essay on Jewish sacred marriage traditions to underpin his reading of these verses as part of a sacred marriage motif underpinning Hosea. He argues that the 'purpose of the passage is clear: the God of Israel provides fertility, and not the idols' and therefore the standard reading of this verse would 'hardly suit the context' (Weinfeld 1996: 525). Wacker, on the other hand, argues for maintaining the traditional formulation, but allowing for an ambiguity that would 'suggest an awareness of sound play on the words "Anath" and "Asherah"' (Wacker 1995: 226). One problem for such a reading, she suggests, would be whether the names of these goddesses would have been known and used by Hosea's audience, which she assumes to have been an Israelite one from the eighth and seventh centuries BCE. On that basis she argues that the evidence is firm for Asherah but weak for Anath. As I have already stated, I don't believe that Hosea addresses an eighth-century Israelite audience but a much later one in the Persian or Hellenistic period. This dating strengthens the case for wordplay involving both the goddesses, because Wacker notes that the best evidence for awareness of Anath comes 'from the Egyptian post-exilic (Jewish) military colony Elephantine' (Wacker 1995: 226).

The fact that goddesses are present in this scene through the ambiguity of sound play is reinforced by the imagery of trees in the verses. The sacred tree is very strongly associated with ancient goddesses, in particular Asherah, and such references are found elsewhere in Hosea itself. Wacker argues that the clearest evidence of the goddess through wordplay in Hosea is found in Hosea 4.13, which refers to burning incense in oak and poplar groves under the terebinth 'ēlah. As Wacker observes, the word translated as terebinth 'is a homonym with the feminine form of El, God – that is, Elah or Elat: goddess' (Wacker 1995: 228). In Hosea 14, Ephraim/Israel is likened to the Lebanon tree and the olive tree and in verse 9 there is the image of the 'verdant cypress'. Israel as tree takes the place of the goddess, as wife to the god, YHWH. However, is YHWH god or goddess? In Hosea 11, the audience is presented with YHWH the mother. Does YHWH now become wife to the wife, Ephraim? This gender blurring is maintained in verse 9 and its evocation of Anath and Asherah. According to Weinfeld, YHWH here appropriates the fertility powers of these goddesses as YHWH's powers. He renders the verse: 'Ephraim what more have I to do with idols? I am his Anath and his Asherah. I am like a luxuriant cypress, your fruit is proved by me' (Weinfeld 1996: 525). In Hosea 2, YHWH declared that he is the Baal who has been worshipped in Israel, and now, in Hosea 14, YHWH declares that she is both the Anath and Asherah who bring fertility to Israel. The tree imagery, here applied to YHWH, reinforces that identification of YHWH as goddess. But there is a further ambiguity in verse 9 that becomes evident comparing Weinfeld's version with the JPS translation cited earlier. Weinfeld puts these words in YHWH's mouth whereas in the JPS it is Ephraim who speaks. Most other English translations attribute these words to YHWH but the Hebrew is ambiguous on this account (this ambiguity is retained in the King James version). I would argue that the ambiguity allows both possibilities. Allowing both YHWH and Ephraim to speak these words together to each other facilitates the queer collapsing of rigid boundaries arising from the visionary excess in the sacred marriage motif. Furthermore, not only does this permit the collapsing of the heteronormative patriarchal marriage model into the homoerotic but it also collapses the apparent privileging of the male. What at first sight is a male union, exclusive of the female, reveals the union of women, even a union of goddesses.[11]

Coda

As the curtain descends on this the final scene of the first act of the Twelve, the narrator steps forward saying, 'He who is wise will consider these words; he who is prudent will take note of them. For the paths of the LORD are smooth; the righteous can walk on them, while sinners stumble on them' (Hos. 14.10). The audience is cautioned to use wisdom in discerning what has been said. This verse can be taken to warn against relying on the superficial, surface meaning of the words but to seek out the depths of the imagery for all their rich possibilities.[12]

---

11 Commenting on this verse, Gale Yee points out that in Proverbs 3.18, Woman Wisdom, 'the female personification of God's own wisdom, is also described as a life-giving tree' (Yee 1998: 214). She uses this insight to see in this verse a collapse of the male/husband aspect of the deity into a feminine supportive dimension of the divine.

12 Gale Yee sees the call to wisdom here as further support for the evocation of the feminine divine, Woman Wisdom, through the metaphor of the tree in the previous verse (Yee 1998: 214).

Joel

The book of Joel follows Hosea in the Masoretic order of the Twelve. The book
gives no information on Joel the prophet, except in the opening superscription, where he is said to be the son of Pethuel (Joel 1.1). Joel is nowhere even
said to be a prophet. The name itself is generally taken to mean YHWH is God
(El). What is important in Joel is the text not the personage and, in its opening
superscription, it declares itself to be the 'word of the LORD that came to Joel'
(Joel 1.1). Unlike Hosea, the superscription gives no date as to when or where
this word was delivered. However, as it unfolds, the word is clearly located
in and addressed to a Jerusalem setting. The only clue to its date is from its
placing in the Twelve. In the Masoretic order, Joel comes between Hosea and
Amos, setting it roughly in their time around the eighth century BCE. In the
LXX order, Joel marks a shift in focus away from the northern kingdom, and,
by being located before both Jonah and Nahum, is situated in an Assyrian
present. However, Joel makes no clear reference to Assyria, Babylon or Israel
and neither does it make reference to kings or even the monarchy in Judah.
These absences in the text have led many commentators to locate the book in
the Persian period.

The central theme of Joel is the coming day of YHWH, a time of divine intervention and judgement establishing a universal reign located in Jerusalem,
where YHWH will live together with faithful Israel. In both its Masoretic and
LXX positions, Joel's clear affirmation of the centrality of Jerusalem in the
divine scheme is a declaration that the promises of reconciliation and restoration to Ephraim/Israel that conclude Hosea (as well Amos and Micah) will not
include the temple sanctuaries of Bethel or Gilgal. YHWH will countenance
no rival to the shrine on Mount Zion. As an act of the Twelve, Joel contains
two clearly marked parts or scenes. In the first (Joel 1.2–2.27), there is a graphic
account of Judah and Jerusalem struck by a locust plague and a drought. Both
are taken as signs of divine punishment of Judah for breaching its covenant
with the deity, and thus the people are called to repentance. For the most part,
this scene is related in the prophet's voice, although on occasion it slips into
divine mode as in the final verses (Joel 2.25–7), proclaiming reconciliation
between the people and YHWH. This reconciliation provides the springboard
for the second scene (Joel 3.1–4.21 (2.28–3.21 in most English translations)),
announcing the coming day of the Lord. This apocalyptic event is proclaimed
in a mostly divine voice promising the restoration of Jerusalem and the divine
judgement upon and punishment of her enemies. Such judgement and punishment come in the form of a final battle between YHWH and the nations.
YHWH's triumph over the Gentiles avenges 'the outrage to the people of
Judah, in whose land they shed the blood of the innocent' (Joel 4.19).

The surprising military imagery in these final verses links back to the
description of the locusts in the first part of Joel. In chapter 2, the locust plague
is portrayed very much as an invading army, whose 'vanguard is a consuming fire, their rearguard a devouring flame' (2.3). In their relentless advance,
they 'have the appearance of horses' and 'gallop just like steeds' bounding 'on
the hilltops with a clatter as of chariots' (2.4). When they strike, they behave
just as a hostile force capturing a city: 'Like an enormous horde arrayed for

battle . . . They rush like warriors, they scale a wall like fighters . . . They rush up the wall, they dash about in the city; they climb into the houses, they enter like thieves by way of the windows' (2.5, 7, 9). The locusts, too, are like the Assyrians elsewhere in the Twelve sent by YHWH to punish Israel. They are YHWH's army at whose head 'the Lord roars aloud' and their coming represents 'the day of the Lord most terrible – who can endure it' (Joel 2.11). Behind this blend of military imagery describing the natural calamity of a locust plague, I see an evocation of the sacred marriage theme announced in Hosea. War and invasion are YHWH's punishment of errant Israel whose breach of the covenant has ruptured the harmony of earth and heaven that depends on the union of YHWH and Israel. This rupture is represented by the imagery of drought. Without the lovemaking of earth and heaven, no rain has fallen and thus 'the watercourses are dried up and fire has consumed the pastures in the wilderness, . . . all the trees of the countryside' (1.19–20). The ravages of drought have meant that 'the seeds have shrivelled under their clods' with the result that 'the new grain has failed' (1.17), 'the new wine has dried up, the new oil has failed . . . the crops of the field are lost . . . the fig tree withers, pomegranate, palm and apple – all the trees of the field are sear' (1.10–12).

In response to these calamities, the people are called to repent and purify themselves in an extraordinary gathering comprising everyone from the old to the 'babes and the sucklings at the breast' (Joel 2.16). As if to underscore the gravity of the situation and once again recalling marriage motifs even the bridegroom must 'come out of his chamber, the bride from her canopied couch' (Joel 2.16). No human marriage can proceed when the cosmic marriage of heaven and earth, deity and people has broken down. In response to these acts of repentance and the tearful prayers of the priests, YHWH declares that the rupture has been healed and the restoration of blessing in language evoking the fruits of the union of heaven and earth. The people will be given 'the new grain, the new wine and the new oil' and they 'shall have them in abundance' (2.19). The invading army will be expelled from the land and the drought will end. In a series of reversals, the pastures are made lush with grass, trees bear fruit, threshing floors are piled with grain, and wine and oil overflow their vats. YHWH has made fertile the earth by giving 'the early rain in his kindness' and 'now he makes the rain fall [as] formerly – the early rain and the late' (2.23). The scene ends with the declaration of the union of divine of heaven and earth in terms of divine presence on the earth: 'you shall know that I am in the midst of Israel: that I the Lord am your God and there is no other' (2.27).

The second scene of Joel functions as a response, almost a commentary upon the first. Spoken mostly in divine voice it takes themes and images from the first and reworks and even inverts them. Thus having declared the divine presence in Israel's midst, YHWH gives a graphic portrait of what that means for the people of Israel. There will be an outpouring of YHWH's spirit 'on all flesh' (3.1), including Israel's sons and daughters, old men and young, even female and male slaves. They shall prophesy, dream dreams and see visions. Nevertheless, despite the inclusivity of such a vision, an inclusivity matching the extraordinary gathering of the people in 2.16, YHWH then announces that this presence will not be universal but will be restricted to Jerusalem and Mount Zion. There will be gathered a remnant of survivors who acknowledge

and are acknowledged by YHWH. Then follows a scene of judgement upon the
nations portrayed as a battle between YHWH and the nations for the people
of Israel. Whereas in the first scene, the locust army and, by extension, the
invading armies have acted at YHWH's behest, here YHWH disavows responsibility for the invaders. It was not YHWH but the nations who 'scattered . . .
My very own people, Israel . . . divided My land among themselves and cast
lots over my people' (Joel 4.2–3). Now there will be a reversal as the people of
Judah are brought back to Jerusalem while the sons and daughters of their cap-
tors are sent to faraway lands in captivity. Continuing the pattern of reversal,
Joel then proclaims the call to battle at the Valley of Jehoshaphat (YHWH will
judge) in words that reverse the peaceful imagery of Isaiah 2.4 and Micah 4.3.
Ploughshares will be turned into swords and pruning hooks into spears (Joel
4.10). A further reversal occurs when YHWH destroys the nations in battle.
In Joel 2, the natural agricultural calamity of the locust plague is depicted in
language of war. Now the victory over the nations is conveyed in agricultural
terms, 'Swing the sickle for the crop is ripe; come and tread for the winepress
is full, the vats are overflowing! For great is their wickedness' (4.13). A rich
harvest and an abundance of wine are normally signs of divine blessing, but
here they become metaphors of divine vengeance.

The final verses of Joel return to the theme of divine presence pronounced at
the end of the first scene (2.27). However, now it is defined in restricted terms
as applying only to Jerusalem and Judah. Egypt and Edom will be a desolation
and a waste (4.19) while Zion will be YHWH's holy mountain and Jerusalem a
holy city (4.17). The effect of divine presence on the land of Judah is described
in highly erotic terms that evoke sacred marriage and the union of heaven
and earth. The 'mountains shall drip with wine, the hills shall flow with milk,
and all the watercourses of Judah shall flow with water' (4.18). Divine presence flows copiously (orgasmically?) fructifying the land, which lactates like a
maternal body. Even the arid valley of Acacias is watered by a spring issuing
from 'the House of the LORD' itself (4.18). This temple spring not only conveys divine presence but echoes that primordial androgynous unity of the
self-moisturing, self-fertilizing earth in Genesis 2.6. By doing so, however, the
image undermines itself by its excess. In Genesis, this fecund quality of the
land is a characteristic of all the earth, whereas in Joel it is restricted to Judah.
By engaging in paroxysms of bloody vengeance and abjuring responsibility
for these events, has the divine YHWH diminished itself?

Amos

As the third book of the Masoretic version of the Twelve, Amos develops and clarifies some of the themes of Joel. In particular, Amos develops the theme of the day of YHWH, presenting it as the time of Israel's punishment. The outcome of this process will be the divine restoration of the Davidic state. Amos closes quoting Joel's final verses describing Judah as a site of divine presence, to highlight the fact that this restored Davidic rule will be linked to the Jerusalem sanctuary. Consequently, 'Amos points specifically to the Beth El sanctuary as a major problem that turns Israel away from YHWH and that must be removed' (Sweeney et al. 2000: 191). The day of YHWH entails the complete destruction of the northern sanctuaries, as well as the northern monarchy.

The name Amos carries the meanings of weighty or a burden and the book presents Amos as a 'sheepbreeder from Tekoa' who is sent by the deity from Judah bearing oracles and warnings of impending punishment to be proclaimed in and against Israel. As an act of the Twelve, Amos consists of three main scenes. The first is a series of oracles against the nations that culminate in denunciations first of Judah and then of Israel (Amos 1.2–2.16). The denunciation of Israel is both the climax of these oracles and the longest one. The second section (Amos 3–6) is a lengthy series of admonitions against Israel warning of the destruction that will come. Finally, there is a series of visions pointing towards the final doom and destruction of the Bethel sanctuary (Amos 7.1–9.10) followed by a final vision of the restoration of Israel under Davidic rule centred in Judah (Amos 9.11–15). This final section also contains a brief narrative relating a confrontation between the prophet and Amaziah the priest at Bethel (Amos 7.10–17). This narrative, together with the superscription in 1.1, is the only attempt at giving some details of Amos, the character. The central point about the character, after whom the book is named, is that he denies personal prophetic status or connection to any prophetic lineage. Instead, he is simply an animal herder or breeder who has been sent by YHWH to deliver YHWH's prophetic messages specifically condemning Israel (7.14–15). This information is not designed to develop the character of Amos but instead to highlight the fact that 'in Amos's day (and in Hosea's) there were no messengers at Bethel as there were in the days of Jacob' (Conrad 1999: 67).

It is this agenda of defaming Bethel and the other northern sanctuaries that causes Amos to make an interesting move in its warnings and admonitions. In Hosea, the issue is the worship of other deities resulting in the erotic rupture of Israel and YHWH; consequently, disaster faces the land and its people. Amos, however, argues that while the sanctuaries of the north were once blessed with divine favour, this favour has been withdrawn and has instead been bestowed on the 'booth of David' (9.11). The reason for this divine desertion is not idolatry but injustice. The priests and rulers of Israel have trampled 'the heads of the poor into the dust of the ground' and made 'the humble walk a twisted course' (2.7). Bethel is no longer a site of divine presence but an arrogant oppressor of the poor, a plunderer of the ordinary people. The priests have turned it into a profitable concern to maintain their own wealth and power rather than to maintain the divine presence. Such disdain for all but their own self-interest has even caused them to make 'the nazirites drink wine' and to order 'the prophets not to prophesy' (2.12). While they go through all the motions of cult and sacrifice, they are only concerned with their own profit and comfort and not with the deity or the well-being of the people. Consequently YHWH declares,

> I loathe, I spurn your festivals, I am not appeased by your solemn assemblies. If you offer Me burnt offerings – or your meal offerings – I will not accept them; I will pay no heed to your gifts of fatlings. Spare Me the sound of your hymns, and let me not hear the music of your lutes. But let justice well up like water, righteousness like an unfailing stream. (Amos 5.21–4)

The coming punishment will especially target the rich and powerful, who will see the destruction of their 'ivory palaces' and 'great houses' (Amos 3.15). Nevertheless, while Amos threatens the destruction of the oppressors it remains unclear as to the fate of the oppressed in the midst of such a disaster.

Because Bethel is denounced in terms of its injustice and oppression of the people rather than in terms of idolatry, as per Hosea, Amos makes little use of the erotic and sexuality in its discourses of threat and condemnation. Nevertheless, traces remain both of sexual abjection and of the sacred marriage vision. While Amos mostly attacks the elites of Israel rather than Israel as a whole, in verse 5.2 Israel is personified as 'Maiden Israel' recalling Gomer/ Israel of Hosea. Israel's crimes are described mostly in terms of the oppression of the poor; however, sexual abjection appears briefly with the accusation that 'father and son go to the same girl, and thereby profane my Holy Name' (2.7). The masculinity of Israel's ruling males is called into question through their women. Thus when these elite men 'defraud the poor' and 'rob the needy' it is at the behest of their wives, the 'cows of Bashan ... who say to your husbands, "Bring, and let's carouse!"' (4.1). This surrogate rule by women's whims and desires reverses the patriarchal order, emasculating the men and spreading oppression throughout the land. Similarly, in his confrontation with Amaziah, Amos declares that as part of the priest's punishment, his wife 'shall play the harlot in the town' (7.17). It is unclear how much agency she is supposed to have in this behaviour and perhaps it doesn't matter. At issue is Amaziah's degradation through her fate, not her own. At the same time that she 'plays the harlot' Amaziah's children will be killed and his land confiscated, all of which represents the stripping away of Amaziah's patriarchal authority and masculine potency. Sacred marriage is also evoked in verse 4.7 where YHWH declares, 'I withheld the rain from you', causing drought as a warning sign that divine presence no longer dwells in Bethel. It appears again in the closing vision of Joel quoted at the end of Amos (9.13).

Nevertheless, Amos's language is more that of class war than of misogynistic abuse and sexual abjection. This fact, however, requires reading Amos with even greater suspicion. While Amos denounces the power elites and, most fiercely, those who maintain the northern cultus, it reads more as a takeover bid than a liberation manifesto. Amos advances the cause of Jerusalem and restored Davidic rule rather than the ending of oppression of the poor *per se*. In the final vision, YHWH declares, 'I will set up the fallen booth of David: I will mend its breaches and set up its ruins anew' (9.11). David's city is Jerusalem which 'shall possess the rest of Edom and all the nations once attached to My name' (9.12). Not only does the reference to Edom foreshadow Obadiah's celebration of Edom's fall and the appropriation of its land in the next (Masoretic) act of the Twelve, but it also contextualizes the oracles against the nations in the opening scene of Amos. All of the nations, Damascus, Gaza, Tyre, Edom, Ammon, Moab, Judah and Israel, could be said to form part of David's patrimony once attached to YHWH's name. The partial quote from Joel's final vision of Jerusalem restored, 'the mountains shall drip wine and all the hills shall wave [with grain]' (9.13), furthers the link with the oracles against the nations, which are themselves introduced with a quote from Joel 4.16 but now come to pass, 'He [Amos] proclaimed: The LORD roars from Zion, shouts aloud from Jerusalem' (1.2). These two quotes from Joel's final vision of Jerusalem restored serve as the framework for the oracles, admonitions and visions that comprise Amos and identify its agenda as promoting Jerusalem's sacerdotal/ imperial claims under the guise of national liberation.

Amos warns us to be wary of those who use the rhetoric of justice and liberation to advance their own expansion and power. Such imperial power-plays do not invalidate the principles of justice and humanity but co-opt them. This co-option is a two-edged sword. While an empire might claim the moral high ground in asserting and expanding its power, it acts only in its own power interests and not in the cause of justice. Most recently, while there were very good moral reasons for overthrowing the regime of Saddam Hussein, they had nothing to do with the US invasion of Iraq nor its continued occupation of that country. Indeed, by disregarding global opinion and by its willingness to put at risk the tenuous international structures built up over time to advance international co-operation and justice to further its own narrow interests, the USA stands condemned by the very principles it invoked for its cause. Thus, to prevent future ruthless and reckless action by the USA, or any other power, requires even more determination to build an international order based on justice and democracy, not less. A similar case applies here with Amos and the Twelve. The condemnation of injustice and oppression might mask an attempted power grab by a priesthood based in Jerusalem against their rivals in the north. Nevertheless, the divine has been identified in these texts as demanding, 'Seek good and not evil, that you may live and that the LORD, the God of Hosts, may truly be with you . . . hate evil and love good and establish justice in the gate' (Amos 5.14–15). If the deity is portrayed above all as a supporter of justice, can the victors in these power-plays ever feel safe, particularly if they pay only lip-service to the notion of justice in the same way they accused their rivals of doing?

Obadiah

At 29 verses long, Obadiah is the shortest book in the Hebrew Bible. The name means 'servant of YH(WH)' but the text says nothing concerning this figure. In fact he is only named once in the superscription that simply announces 'the prophecy of Obadiah' (1.1). Spoken mostly in the divine voice, Obadiah proclaims, if not celebrates, the coming destruction of Edom (Esau). In its Masoretic placement, Obadiah links directly back to Amos, which closes naming Edom alone among all the nations who shall be subjected to the restored Davidic rule (Amos 9.12). This destruction is represented as retribution for Edom having committed 'outrage to your brother Jacob . . . on that day . . . when aliens carried off his goods, when foreigners entered his gates and cast lots for Jerusalem, you were as one of them' (1.10–11). Most commentators take this outrage to be Nebuchadnezzar's sack of Jerusalem. Edom is understood to have either collaborated in this event by blocking the flight of Judahite refugees and turning them over to the Babylonians or at the very least to have later joined in the looting of the city after it fell to Nebuchadnezzar. While both Kings and Chronicles depict a long history of hostility between Edom and Judah, its northern neighbour, they make no mention of any Edomite role in the fall of Jerusalem to Nebuchadnezzar. Outside of Obadiah, the only other reference to such Edomite complicity is in Jeremiah 49. In fact, Obadiah 1.1–4; 1.5–6 and 1.9 are almost verbatim quotes of Jeremiah 49.14–16; 49.9–10a and 49.7 respectively. Obadiah thus reads as an improvising adaptation of Jeremiah's oracle against Edom (or vice versa).

The greater part of Obadiah consists of denunciation of and gleeful threats against Edom. However, verse 15 announces the coming day of the LORD. As in Joel and Amos, a faithful remnant will be vindicated and restored to Zion, which 'shall be holy' (1.17). In contrast, for Edom this day of the LORD will mean their complete annihilation. Unlike Israel, which has endured its own near annihilation at the hands of YHWH, no Edomite remnant will remain to survive this divine vengeance. Obadiah celebrates a vision of total genocide. It closes with a vision of the Israelites returning from exile and settling the now depopulated lands of Edom, the Negev and the rest of the Davidic patrimony.

Jonah

Both as a character and as a book, Jonah makes a strong contrast to the rest of the Twelve. First, Jonah is alone in the Twelve in being clearly identified with a character in the historical narratives of Samuel–Kings. In 2 Kings 14.25, Jonah is identified as a prophet from Gath-hepher in Israel. His prophecy concerning the restoration of 'the territory of Israel from Lebo-hamath to the sea of the Arabah' is brought about by Jeroboam II, in whose reign both Hosea and Amos have been dated by their superscriptions. Second, alone of all the books of the Twelve, Jonah presents its audience with a consistent narrative. This is a story about a prophet, not, with the exception of the prayer in Jonah 2, a presentation of the prophet's words. Third, in this story the audience is presented with an astounding series of inversions or reversals of stock prophetic motifs.

Jonah is a prophet who is commissioned to go and 'proclaim judgement' (1.1) upon the great Assyrian city of Nineveh and not, as with the other prophets, on Israel or Judah. In response, unlike the other prophets, Jonah takes flight (Jonah means 'dove') in the opposite direction, to Tarshish. Not only does he flee from Nineveh but 'away from the service of the LORD' (1.3) and consequently his journey takes him not to Tarshish but to the depths of the sea in the belly of a fish. But not even in 'the belly of Sheol' (Jonah 2.3) can a person find escape from YHWH (Amos 9.2). Jonah must finally accept his commission. On arriving in Nineveh he only 'speaks five Hebrew words . . . and thereby instigates the most frantic reform ever heard of . . . the sinful city instantly and completely turns itself around' (Ackerman 1987b: 238–9). Consequently, Nineveh is spared by the deity, much to Jonah's grief, who cries out, 'LORD, take my life for I would rather die than live' (Jonah 4.3). As an Israelite prophet, Jonah knows that Assyria 'will then go on to bring destruction, humiliation on his own people' (Sherwood 2000: 126). In the Masoretic order of the Twelve this destruction follows on immediately and graphically from Jonah in Micah and thus, despite the comic pattern of reversals that make up the text, there is in Jonah a deeply tragic subtext. This tragic quality is reinforced by the strong statement of divine mercy for all of creation with which Jonah closes, 'And should I not care about Nineveh, that great city, in which there are more than a hundred and twenty thousand persons who do not yet know their right hand from their left, and many beasts as well' (4.11). This statement makes a strong contrast with the genocidal fantasy that closes Obadiah and completes the pattern of reversals that make up Jonah,[13] but it also causes one to ask, if so for Nineveh why not for Israel/Ephraim/Gomer?

It is these patterns of excess, paradox, reversal and inversion that have given Jonah's story a rich interpretive history in Judaism, Christianity and Islam (for a fascinating account of Jewish and Christian interpretation, see Sherwood 2000). In both Matthew 12.38–42 and Luke 11.29–32, Jonah's three days in the fish are made a prefiguring sign of Christ's three days in the tomb. Subsequently,

---

13 The deity's words to Jonah about the need to spare Nineveh reverse the scenario in Genesis 18, for example. In this account, Abraham speaks out against the deity's decision to destroy Sodom and Gomorrah and bargains with the deity to finally spare the cities if there are ten just men found there.

for much of Christian history, Jonah operates as a Christ figure. However, a grim supersessionist reading of Jonah was pioneered by Augustine, picked up by Luther, and later, following the Enlightenment, fully developed into a toxic Christian anti-Jewish trajectory. This trajectory plays off a progressive Christian universalism (imperialism?) against an alleged Jewish, retrogressive particularism, focused on the character of Jonah. This rivalry sets up an 'antagonism between Jonah the book and Jonah the character' in which Jonah, the prophet, 'represents the envy and jealousy of Jewishness' (Sherwood 2000: 25). Jonah, the book, on the other hand, or, more particularly, its author becomes a proto-Christian who is attacking Jewish exclusivism, legalism, ritualism and hatred of the Gentiles. As a proto-Christian, the author is 'compassionate, benevolent and rational' while Jonah 'becomes iconic of tyrannical dogma and narrowness' (Sherwood 2000: 27).

In contrast to Christian impulses to singularity, Jewish readings of Jonah mostly conform to general Jewish interpretive traditions that are 'emphatically textual, physical, quizzical, prone to bringing everything (even the deity) into the realm of questions, and prone to multiply contradictions and empathies so that texts ricochet in all directions' (Sherwood 2000: 103). In one such direction, Jonah is representative of the successful prophet *par excellence*. According to the *Pirke de Rabbi Eliezer*, Jonah is already known as a lying prophet in Israel because he was sent by the deity to preach doom to Jerusalem, a doom that was then averted by divine mercy. When commanded to preach doom to Nineveh, Jonah knows that as 'the nations are nigh to repentance, . . . they will repent', therefore, 'is it not enough for me that Israel should call me a lying prophet; but shall also the nations of the world (do likewise)' (Friedlander 1916: 65–6). In other accounts Jonah's concern is not only for his own reputation but also for that of YHWH. The nations will see that Jonah has proclaimed a message of doom from YHWH that does not eventuate and, thus, they will be led to doubt YHWH's power. Jonah here epitomizes the problem of the prophet whose warnings are heeded to give him a 'success rate in annulling his own prophecies . . . second to none' (Sherwood 2000: 120). The *Talmud Yerushalmi*, however, questions the efficacy of Jonah's words. It portrays the Ninevites' repentance as 'a pantomime farce, a "repentance of deception", a cynical exercise in divine blackmail (instant repentance: just add sackcloth)' (Sherwood 2000: 107). The Aramaic Targum to Jonah less excessively portrays the Ninevites' repentance as a temporary phenomenon from which they soon fall back into their previous evil. Curiously, in that the LXX became the First Testament of the Eastern Church, its ordering of the Twelve, in which Nahum follows Jonah, would give weight to these Jewish doubts of Ninevite sincerity. However, the theme of repentance in Jonah, despite its excesses in both text and reception, has given it a prominent place in the synagogue liturgy, being read as the afternoon service Haphtorah on the Day of Atonement. There is another grimmer perspective on Jonah, which I have already alluded to, based on the role of Nineveh/Assyria in the overall scheme of the Twelve and of the Hebrew Bible. Jonah 'went to sea to drown himself because he would rather commit suicide than co-operate in Israel's potential destruction' (Sherwood 2000: 121). Even the dichotomy of universalism and particularism takes on a cruel twist from this perspective. By being spared, Nineveh can become useful to the deity as the instrument of divine vengeance against Israel. However, Nineveh's wickedness requires the deity to send a prophet to call the Ninevites to repentance, 'precisely so that they could be used to harm Israel' (Sherwood 2000: 128). In its sinful condition, Gentile Nineveh is not worthy enough to be used by the deity as an agent to destroy sinful Israel. [14]

Human repentance and divine grace and mercy are associated with Jonah's story in Islam and are the dominant themes of the tenth Sura of the Qur'an, which is named after him. However, his story is only directly referred to in verse 98 of this Sura, extolling the example of 'Jonah's people', the repentant Ninevites, for believers. More detailed accounts of Jonah's story are found in Suras 37.139–48 and 68.48–50. Both recount Jonah's flight from his prophetic mission and being swallowed by the fish. Rather than the repentance of the Ninevites being the model for believers, it is Jonah's own repentance in the belly of the fish and subsequent delivery from the fish to dry land by the deity that is the focus for the believer. Jonah's example is also used to demonstrate the guaranteed response of the deity to genuine prayer and repentance in Sura 21.87–8. While no mention is made in these verses of his sea journey or being swallowed by the fish, it is invoked in the title given to Jonah here, 'the Man in the Fish' (Sherwood 2000: 3), 'Dhu al-Nun' (Wheeler 2002: 168).

Jonah's interpretive history is a richly complex and highly contested one, to which could be added the vast world of popular culture where Jonah surfaces in Melville's *Moby Dick*, Orwell's essays, and even an episode of *Northern Exposure* (Sherwood 2000: 146–7). Jonah's story is one that invites constant rereadings and appropriations. Sharon Bezner's queer reading (2000), despite its US-centrism, is one such revelation. The terrain of Jonah is translated to the United States, in which 'the great gay city' (Bezner 2000: 162) of San Francisco is made to correspond to Nineveh while Jonah is an elected leader of the Christian Coalition. Told by God to go to San Francisco and cry out against it for its wickedness, Jonah goes immediately to the airport and takes a plane to New York.[15] God sends a mighty wind against the plane and Jonah is dutifully cast out of the plane to be swallowed by a big bird provided by the Lord (Bezner 2000: 163). In response to his prayer from the belly of the bird, God then 'spoke to the bird, and it set Jonah down upon the ground' (Bezner 2000: 164). For Bezner, Jonah represents a particular type of Christianity that embraces a theology based upon divine wrath. Such Christians 'have backed themselves into a corner that does not allow them to reach out to homosexuals' (Bezner 2000: 165). This rejection stems from a 'fear that God's love includes

---

14 In contrast, Sherwood, herself, reads the extravagant repentance of Nineveh from the perspective of Jonah's placement in the Masoretic order of the Twelve. Jonah is followed by Micah's visions of the Assyrian destruction of Israel and invasion of Judah (also prefiguring the subsequent Babylonian destruction of Judah). She argues that Jonah makes the Ninevites comic figures and deflates the enemy with the 'extremely therapeutic . . . image of sackcloth-swathed Assyrians, fasting and getting down on their knees before the Judaean God' (Sherwood 2000: 267). While that argument might work for an audience in Jerusalem/Judah/Judaea, I doubt that it would be of much value for an audience in Bethel/Israel/Ephraim.

15 As an Australian reader, I have some quibbles over whether New York adequately translates the end-of-the-earth quality of Tarshish.

everyone, which means that they would lose their righteous status' (Bezner 2000: 165). God's call to Jonah becomes an opportunity for him to examine himself and rethink his homophobia and self-righteousness. He relents and goes on to San Francisco preaching judgement on the city. The 'queer people of San Francisco believed God' and the leader of the Gay and Lesbian Alliance broadcasts a statement declaring a fast and a time of self-examination. In this statement, sexuality is not the issue:

> While we have always known that our queerness does not keep us apart from God, we have failed to recognize that our lack of service to others, or hateful words to each other, and our self-absorption have kept us apart from God. We invite you to make a commitment to turn from these unhealthy areas of your life, and to replace them with actions of love and caring. (Bezner 2000: 167)

In the face of this massive turning around, not from queer sexuality but from lack of respect and care for the other, the deity relents and spares San Francisco, much to Jonah's chagrin. With a slight borrowing from the Good Samaritan story, Bezner closes her version of Jonah with the deity challenging the prophet in the words of Jonah 4.10–11, changed to refer to queer people not Ninevites. In her closing reflection, Bezner observes that Jonah challenges the religious right to recognize the fact that they do not determine whom God loves and to bring their hearts and actions into accord with the divine generosity. She poses the same challenge to queer people vis-à-vis the religious right 'to examine what we would do . . . in Jonah's place . . . (w)ould we be able to let go of a theology of revenge in order to embrace a theology of God's inclusive love that welcomes the religious right?' (Bezner 2000: 169).

I agree with Bezner's concern and I respect the way she has produced a reading that can both affirm the religious worth of queer people and challenge us to recognize the humanity of our religious opponents. Nevertheless, a problem remains in her proposed inversion considering a queer Jonah sent to proclaim a similar message of judgement to the religious right. This problem stems from the fact that Jonah is part of the Twelve. Assyria will subsequently destroy Israel. Like Jonah, I would think very hard before proclaiming such a message to the Westboro Baptist Church or the Vatican, if I thought that as a result they would then be able to destroy queer people.

I will close my discussion of Jonah tendering a queer possibility that I have recognized in the first three chapters. I believe Jonah's flight from and subsequent acceptance of his mission can be read as an allegory of coming out. Jonah opens with the prophet challenged to take a message of judgement to Nineveh. Instead he flees to the other end of the world, taking ship to Tarshish. While on board he hides himself in the hold. When thrown overboard, he is swallowed by a fish and is engulfed in 'the deep' (2.6). Ackerman observes that

> The narrative . . . seems to be depicting Jonah's flight from YHWH's presence as a descent to the underworld . . . The great fish is aligned with the ship's hold, Tarshish, and perhaps the Temple in Jerusalem – shelters that offer the illusion of security but in fact result in a deep sleep that brings one

down to the city of Death. Jonah made the traditional equation between the City of Nineveh and the City of Death; but the story suggests that the opposite is potentially true. (Ackerman 1987: 235, 239)

This language of flight in quest of an illusory security strongly evokes the experience of the closet. The mention of the temple serves to remind me that for many people the closet is embraced on religious grounds. Ex-gay movements and reparative therapy strongly attest to that fact. To embrace these regimes of the closet in flight from one's sexuality does not bring life but death. By finally relenting and accepting his commission, Jonah acknowledges that 'the world . . . offers no eternally secure shelters . . . the ship and the fish spew one forth' (Ackerman 1987: 241) – the deity brings him 'up from the pit' (Jonah 2.7). Jonah goes on to Nineveh to proclaim his message. As a result a wonderful thing happens. Rather than mock him or condemn and victimize him, the Ninevites accept his message. Instead of a place of doom, Nineveh is revealed as a site of divine blessing and Jonah becomes 'the best of the prophets' (Sherwood 2000: 120). Likewise, as Rebecca Alpert observes, 'there is no holy way . . . to be closeted . . . (w)hen the connection between the sexual self and the rest of the self is cut off, we cannot walk with God' (Alpert 2000: 172).

Micah

If Jonah presents the audience with satirical excess, in Micah[16] the audience is confronted by horrific catastrophe. Although presenting itself as a prophet's visions of future judgement, Micah functions to make present that calamitous judgement or, rather, judgements. For not only does Micah present the Assyrian destruction of Samaria/Israel/Ephraim but also the invasion of Judah, and both calamities serve to foreshadow and represent that final disaster, the destruction of Jerusalem by Babylon. In its Masoretic placing, after Jonah's carnival, Micah strikes its audience a shocking blow. In its LXX placing, it both culminates the Israel section of the Twelve and 'emphasizes the paradigmatic role of the punishment of . . . Israel for Jerusalem and Judah' (Sweeney et al. 2000: 339). In both placings, it heralds the destruction of the northern kingdom by dating itself in the superscription by the reigns of Judahite kings only.

The text can be divided into three main scenes. In the first (Micah 1.2–3.12), themes of denunciation and punishment predominate. Condemnation of Samaria (1.2–8) is followed by a lament over Judah (1.9–16). Micah 2 condemns injustice and those who oppose YHWH before offering a vision of a new Israel. Judgement is pronounced as Micah 3 opens and condemns rival prophets before describing the eventual destruction of Jerusalem. The second scene (4.1–5.14) is concerned mostly with visions of hope. Its opening visions of an eschatological restoration of Zion (4.1–8) shift back in time to a vision of Jerusalem under siege (4.9–14). There follows an oracle of a ruler to come, appointed by YHWH to be a shepherd to the people (5.1–5), words of hope concerning the remnant of Israel (5.6–8) and an oracle of judgement against the nations (5.9–14). The final scene (6.1–7.20) makes a shift from denunciation to hope. It opens announcing YHWH's lawsuit against Israel (6.1–8) before condemning the injustice of the northern kingdom (6.9–16). The final chapter opens with a lament over injustice (7.1) and then suddenly shifts into visions of the recovery and rebuilding of Zion (7.8–17) to close with a final hymn of praise to YHWH (7.18–20).

There is no clear narrative in Micah, and the book is noteworthy for its ambiguity and its sudden shifts in mood and voice, the latter shifting not only from prophetic to YHWH mode but also giving utterance to several other unidentified figures. These ambiguities are 'further compounded by the difficult Hebrew structures: ambiguous referents, odd and difficult phrases, and frequent switches in gender and person, addressor and addressee' (Runions 2001: 19). Erin Runions highlights these features in her translation of Micah (Runions 2001: 120–81). For example, in Micah 7.11–12 there is a shift in gender of the addressee from feminine to masculine, 'A day (is) for building your (fs) walls. That day borders are distant. That (is the) day, and he will come unto you (ms) from afar, Assyria and the cities of Egypt' (Runions 2001: 177). Is the feminine 'you' whose walls are to be built the same 'you' unto whom he will come? Apart from the first person, all Hebrew verbs have both gender and number. Micah employs dramatic shifts in the gender and number of both

---

16 The name is a shortened form of Micaiah and means 'Who is like YH' and could function as either a question or a description.

verbs and pronouns to heighten ambiguity: 'In Gath do not tell (mpl), certainly do not weep (mpl), in the house for (of) dust . . . roll (fs) (I roll) in the dust. Pass (by) (cross over) (fs), to/wards (for) you (mpl)' (Micah 1.10–11, Runions 2001: 127). Imperatives addressing a masculine plural shift to address a feminine singular before shifting back to a masculine plural 'you'. Do all these verbs address the same person/s or are there different addressees here?

In contrast to other approaches that come to Micah seeking to make 'the various parts of the book cohere' to a 'prefixed notion of the original, correct and unified text', Runions accepts and works with the shifts and ruptures in the text to consider the effect they might have on the reading process, 'resituating the reader with regard to her own subjectivity' (Runions 2001: 24). In particular, she draws on Homi Bhabha's work on subjectivity and the negotiation of cultural difference to analyse the shifts in the text and their impact on the reader's ideological positioning in and by the text. Central to her analysis is Bhabha's notion of hybridity in the colonial context – the dual effect of an imperfect cultural imitation that both justifies and unsettles dominating ideologies. She argues that hybridity can be read in Micah 'through the text's imperfect repetition and re-presentation of the images that make up the readers ideological pinning points' (Runions 2001: 213).

Hybridity emerges in the presentation of cities, especially Jerusalem and Samaria, which, through the shifting imagery, are presented as ambiguously gendered figures. Runions observes that the figure of Zion is 'consistently crossing lines between "active male, triumphant ruler" and "passive, suffering female nation"' (Runions 2001: 213). The shifts in passive/active can be seen in the imagery employed in Micah 3.10–12, while in Micah 4.8 there is a dramatic gender shift. The verse opens addressing Zion with the masculine you and then immediately addresses her as Daughter of Zion (Runions 2001: 154, 214).[17] In the case of Samaria, Runions identifies a blurring of the masculine/feminine in the one clear instance of sexual abjection found in Micah 1.7–8. Here, the image of prostitution is used to abject Samaria but not by likening Samaria to a prostitute. Instead, 'Samaria enacts a kind of economic, even pimping, behaviour that tends to be considered a "male behaviour" in discourses on gender, and a kind of economic activity . . . uncharacteristic for a female figure in the Hebrew Bible' (Runions 2001: 214). Nevertheless, Runions points out that the text is frequently emended so that Samaria appears more as prostitute than a pimp (the JPS version does so but not the NRSV). What I find interesting is that Jerusalem and Samaria form a kind of hybrid, in Micah, reminiscent of Jekyll and Hyde or Dorian Gray and his portrait. Samaria is Jerusalem's 'horrific counterpart' (Runions 2001: 214) and her destruction is both a warning to and a vindication of Jerusalem as well as a representation of

---

17 Another instance of male–female hybridity, although not of cities but ancient emissaries of the divine, could be found in the reference to Moses together with Aaron and Miriam in Micah 6.4. In citing the Exodus, this verse echoes a similar reference to this event in Isaiah 63.11–12, in which only Moses 'the shepherd of His flock' is named. Micah adds not only Aaron but Miriam as well, highlighting the both-gender quality of those 'sent before you' (Micah 6.4) by YHWH to redeem Israel from bondage in the past.

Jerusalem's own subsequent destruction by the Babylonians in the context of the Twelve, whose audience is located in a post-Babylonian present.

The hybridity of cities gives rise to a highly significant instance of hybridity, 'the female–male Yahweh–Zion' (Runions 2001: 211). The blurring of gender imagery referring to Zion/Jerusalem is further compounded by sudden shifts blurring the boundaries between YHWH and Zion. These blurrings are particularly prominent in Micah 4.8–14, where not only does Zion shift from mother to warrior but, by further juxtaposing this shift with YHWH's own warrior activity, 'Zion appears . . . so much like the phallic-male-hero-Yahweh . . . that . . . the two might be seen to merge into one divine figure' (Runions 2001: 240). According to Runions what helps facilitate this merger is the fact that the linking of birth/fertility and warrior imagery for Woman Zion is paralleled in ancient goddess representations, most prominently in the worship of Ishtar, Astarte and Anath (Runions 2001: 239). The reference to Anath recalls her submerged appearance alongside Asherah at the end of Hosea, a text in which YHWH explicitly merges with Baal. In support of Anath being the figure behind Zion, Runions cites arguments that both 'Asherah and Anat were . . . assimilated to the Yahweh mythos, the one to account for his love, the other to account for his rage' (Runions (citing Jacob Rabinowitz) 2001: 240). The implied hybridity of Zion–Anath permits the merger of Zion–YHWH, breaking the boundaries of male and female, human and divine, heaven and earth. This hybridization in Micah 4 is a process based on the shifts in the Hebrew text, much of which cannot be adequately translated. Nevertheless, Runions points out that most translations of the final part of 4.13 serve to actively hide the ambiguities that allow the merger of Zion and YHWH. It is unclear who speaks this verse although it is clearly addressed to Zion. Most translations (including the ancient LXX, Aramaic Targum and Syriac) render it as addressing Zion, 'You will devote their riches to the LORD, their wealth to the LORD of all the earth' (JPS). If Zion offers riches to YHWH then the two are being clearly demarcated for the reader/audience. However, the Hebrew literally reads, 'I will devote . . .' suggesting that 'this could be the voice of someone else preparing Zion for battle' (Runions 2001: 157). It is not Zion then but the speaker who will offer to YHWH. This unidentified speaker addressing Zion, therefore, cannot be YHWH, as the second person translation might imply, and in that context is also not Zion, facilitating the ambiguity in attributing the warrior role, thus blurring the boundary between Zion and YHWH.

One other instance of hybridity identified by Runions is that of the 'oppressed-oppressing people' (Runions 2001: 211). Israel is both the nation under threat from or subjugated and scattered by great powers and, by the evocation of past events like the Exodus, the conquering and colonizing power that will destroy the people of the land. Runions observes that this ambiguity 'might also resonate with the reader's own ambivalence with respect to colonization and justice . . . wanting to do justice, yet being part of a larger system that makes this difficult; trying to "give things back", yet being caught up in a system in which they are ultimately benefiting' (Runions 2001: 232). Runions speaks specifically in terms of the dynamics of neo-colonialism, but this ambivalence concerning oppression and liberation pertains to the fact that all of us are positioned in interlocking, multi-faceted webs of oppression and power, including the hierarchies of gender, race, ethnicity, class, religion, abil-ity, age, caste and sexuality, to name a few. Micah challenges its audience to 'do justice . . . to love goodness and to walk modestly with your God' (Micah 6.8). Perhaps wisely, Micah does not give a blueprint of how to live according to those precepts but leaves it up to the audience to work that out themselves. Rebecca Alpert has offered a response from her location as a Jewish lesbian focusing on 'some of the problems facing Jewish lesbians today' (Alpert 2000: 170). I think it appropriate to conclude this discussion of Micah with a brief summary of how she takes up Micah's challenge.

She begins with the final point, walking with God, arguing that it challenges a person to full self-acceptance and honesty, recognizing that 'all human beings are holy' (Alpert 2000: 171). This position forms the basis for an ethics of coming out. Coming out and accepting her sexuality is the means whereby the lesbian can 'walk in direction of self-acceptance' (2000: 172). Coming out includes a public dimension of visibility facilitating change in social attitudes and giving the lesbian a new liberating possibility of personal honesty in her life. The conspiracy of silence that is sustained by the closet breaks down 'when we stop demanding one another to keep secrets' (2000: 172). Nevertheless, an ethics of coming out does not support outing others against their will. Outing is an arrogant act that usurps the right to self-determination of other lesbians. The second part of Micah's precept, Alpert interprets as loving well, which she argues calls lesbians to build and sustain loving and supportive relationships. For Jewish lesbians in particular, these relationships include those with their families of origin and the broader Jewish community. Loving well means tak-ing responsibility for transforming relationships in a manner that 'will enable the Jewish and lesbian communities to thrive' (2000: 177). There is a reciprocity here too. The Jewish community must eventually take responsibility for lov-ing its lesbian members well. Finally, Jewish lesbians 'cannot make a choice between accepting ourselves, caring for our circle of loved ones, and doing jus-tice in the world' (Alpert 2000: 177). Alpert argues that doing justice depends on being able to accept one's self and to form loving relationships. It is only in this way that the Jewish lesbian can reach out beyond herself to demand and create a world of justice for everyone. Thus Micah's precepts are, for Alpert, a set of goals to work toward, not just for lesbian Jews but all Jews, yet provid-ing 'a model for the transformation of Judaism from a lesbian perspective that derives from our interpretation of the biblical text' (2000: 181). I would add that Alpert has provided a model that can be applied by queer people in the other communities of faith sharing her connection to this biblical text.

Nahum

The name, Nahum, means 'comfort' but the text speaks words of hatred, abuse and delight in divine retribution. These poetic visions described as the 'Book of Prophecy of Nahum the Elkoshite' present for the audience the destruction of Nineveh and Assyria in two main scenes. The first scene (1.2–2.1) opens with a poem celebrating, in a series of parallelisms, the power and vengeful fury of the deity (1.2–8). Nineveh is then warned that it will face this divine fury (1.9–11) and the scene closes with words of comfort to Judah, announcing YHWH's resolve that 'as surely as I afflicted you, I will afflict you no more' (1.12). Conrad's thesis is that a major theme in the Twelve is the end of prophecy and 'the restoration of messenger/angelic presence as in the days of the ancestor Jacob' (Conrad 1997: 79) to be located in the restored temple at Jerusalem. Interestingly, Nahum's address to Judah ends with the image of a figure crossing the mountains bearing a message of good news and peace (Nahum 2.1). Nahum might be a book of prophecy but nowhere does it depict or refer to the prophet or any prophetic figure. Instead it presents a shadowy herald calling on Judah to celebrate for 'never again shall scoundrels invade you' (2.1). This herald figure could be read as foreshadowing the future return of messengers to Zion.

In the second scene (2.2–3.18), Nineveh's destruction is performed with first a poetic description of the final battle and fall of the city (2.2–13), followed by YHWH's curse on Nineveh (2.14–3.7), to conclude with a song of taunting derision over the ruined city (Nahum 3.8–19). While these scenes exulting in war and destruction are particularly disturbing, they contain a number of images, some of which are curious, especially in the context of the Twelve, while others are particularly offensive and challenging for projects affirming women and queer people. Most curious for Conrad's reading of the Twelve is that the end of Assyria means that it loses the power to control messenger activity, 'the sound of your messengers shall be heard no more' (2.14). This image closes chapter 2, a chapter opening with the image of a figure bearing good tidings to Judah, presumably from YHWH. Assyria's loss is heralded by Judah's potential gain. The imagery of locusts as applied to Assyria in Joel briefly reappears in Nahum's final verses. Rather than representing menace as in Joel, here it is used to disparage and mock Assyrian power, 'your guards were like locusts, your marshals like piles of hoppers which settle on the stones on a chilly day; when the sun comes out they fly away, and nobody knows where they are' (3.17). Nineveh's fall is marked by the exile of a female figure, Huzzab, and 'her handmaidens' (2.8). Some have seen here a reference either to the queen of Assyria or to the Ishtar of Nineveh but it also echoes the imagery of female Israel led off to exile earlier in the Twelve. The city as female is also seen in the description of Assyria's former victory over and despoliation of Egyptian Thebes, No-amon. Like Israel/Samaria before her, No-amon 'was exiled, she went into captivity, her babes, too, were dashed in pieces' (3.10).

While No-Amon's portrayal might move an audience to sympathy, the portrayals of Nineveh itself as a woman are designed to shame and vilify the city and encourage an audience's *schadenfreude* through misogyny and male privilege. The horror of female sexual autonomy is invoked when Nineveh/Assyria is referred to as a harlot and the growth of its imperial power described as ensnaring 'the nations with her harlotries' (Nahum 3.4). Female sexual power is imbued with occult power. Assyria is both harlot and 'winsome mistress of sorcery' (3.4). The use of this imagery to describe imperial conquests and the oppression and spoliation of peoples can only be condemned as misogynist and erotophobic. However, it is followed by an even more misogynist and offensive image, that of the deity as bragging rapist triumphantly subjugating the abused Nineveh (3.5–7). Such imagery has been applied earlier in the Twelve, in reference to Israel, but in these circumstances the text itself has sometimes reversed or critiqued the images of abuse. Not so in Nahum and there is no comfort, no lament here. There exists no alternative but to condemn YHWH's character in Nahum and the text's relentless celebration of both sexual and other violence. To condemn YHWH here is to be reminded that, as Jewish tradition has long recognized, we 'can oppose God as long as it is in defence of God's creation' (Sherwood 2000: 127, her italics). Perhaps, as in Nahum, where the deity is portrayed as both rapist and murderous, plundering warrior, our opposition is required for God's own redemption and hence our own.

Habakkuk

First Israel/Ephraim, then Assyria, now, in Habakkuk, the focus of the Twelve shifts clearly to Judah. Most importantly the text announces that YHWH is 'raising up the Chaldeans' (Hab. 1.6) or Babylonians as an instrument to punish Judah. Sweeney believes that Habakkuk can be read as wrestling 'with the question of divine righteousness insofar as it identifies YHWH as the one who sent the Babylonians against Judah in the first place' (Sweeney *et al.* 2000: 453). This grappling with issues of divine righteousness might be implied in the name, Habakkuk, which 'may be based upon the Hebrew root *ḥbq*, 'to clasp, embrace" (Sweeney *et al.* 2000: 454). The text of Habakkuk engages with these issues in a strongly performative, if not liturgical, manner. It commences with a dialogue between Habakkuk and YHWH (Hab. 1.2–2.5), which is followed by a series of five woe oracles (2.6–20). It concludes, in chapter 3, with a psalm complete with musical directions. This concluding psalm celebrates the power and awesome majesty of the deity. YHWH is presented as a warrior figure and storm-god before whom 'pestilence marches . . .' while 'plague comes forth at his heels' (3.5). Despite the fact that the Babylonians will march on Judah, the psalm declares that finally the warrior YHWH will 'come forth to deliver Your people, to deliver Your anointed' (3.13). Confidence in this final outcome causes the speaker to resolve, 'I wait calmly for the day of distress, for a people to come and attack us', even though 'my bowels quaked, my lips quivered . . . rot entered into my bone, I trembled where I stood' (3.16). Conrad argues that the dialogue of prophet and deity in Habakkuk 1.2–2.5 suggests a distance between the two speakers, in which the former is not really able to understand divine intentions (Conrad 1999: 68). This distance from the deity is reinforced in the final verses of the concluding psalm utilizing sacred marriage agricultural imagery. In a series of absences, recalling those that the deity threatens to wreak on Gomer in the opening scenes of the Twelve (Hos. 2.10–11, 14), Habakkuk announces that the fig trees and grapevines are not fruiting, that the 'olive crop has failed and the fields produce no grain' and even 'the sheep have vanished from the fold' (3.17). There is no marriage between earth and heaven; the deity is no longer present among the people. In the face of such absence and distance, the audience is prepared for the doom that will befall Jerusalem.

Zephaniah

Habakkuk closes anticipating the coming day of distress. In Zephaniah that day arrives and is announced with YHWH's grandiose determination to 'sweep everything away from the face of the earth . . . man and beast . . . birds of the sky . . . fish of the sea . . . and I will destroy mankind from the face of the earth' (Zeph. 1.2–3). More specifically, however, YHWH will 'stretch out My arm against Judah and . . . all who dwell in Jerusalem' (1.4). As I pointed out earlier introducing this commentary on the Twelve, Paul House (1988) has argued that Zephaniah is best understood as a prophetic drama presenting a dialogue between two main characters, Yahweh and the prophet. This dialogue can be divided into three main parts.[18] In the first, the day of YHWH is announced, threatening divine judgement upon all the earth and on Judah (1.2–18). Most noteworthy about this first section is the return of the motif of the people's idolatry, in particular the worship of Baal (1.4), the cause of divine anger in Hosea. This Baal worship is now established in Jerusalem, along with the worship of 'the host of heaven' and 'Malcam' (1.5). In the second section (2.1–3.7), the audience is presented with an admonition and exhortation to Judah, followed by a series of condemnations of the surrounding nations, the Philistines, Moab, Ammon, Assyria and Cush. This section ends with Judah arraigned and condemned. Most notable here is that Judah's condemnation gives specific mention to its officials, judges, priests and prophets (Zeph. 3.3–4). The day of YHWH has brought the overthrow of Judah, the destruction of Jerusalem and the temple, bringing about the end of prophecy. This fact is signalled in the introductory superscription in Zephaniah 1.1. While Zephaniah is given a lengthy genealogy he is nowhere described as a prophet. Instead, he is a figure to whom the 'word of the LORD' came.

The final section of Zephaniah (3.8–20) is a promise of salvation and the restoration of Zion. The central figure here is the remnant of Israel, 'a poor humble folk' who 'shall find refuge in the name of the LORD' (3.12). This remnant has already made brief appearances in the exhortation and condemnations of the preceding section. It first appears in that section's opening appeal to the 'humble . . . who have fulfilled His law' to 'seek the LORD' in order to 'find shelter on the day of the LORD's anger' (2.3). Then, in the ensuing condemnations of the nations, Ammon and Moab are warned that they will be plundered and possessed by 'the remnant of My people . . . the remainder of My nation' (2.9). Now, in Zephaniah's third and final scene, the audience is told that despite the destruction wrought by YHWH on Judah, a remnant of the people has been preserved. This preservation of the remnant might lie behind the name Zephaniah, which can mean either 'YH has hidden' or 'YH has treasured'. Indeed, YHWH's final soliloquy makes very clear to the audience that this remnant is counted as something very special by the deity, 'I will gather you, and . . . I will bring you [home]; for I will make you renowned and famous among all the peoples on earth, when I restore your fortunes before

---

18 House, likewise, divides Zephaniah into three 'acts' (1.2–17; 1.18–3.5; 3.6–20) consisting of eight 'scenes' (House 1988: 118–26). As will be seen, my threefold division only slightly varies from his.

their very eyes' (3.20). Nevertheless, such divine favour and blessing incurs weighty responsibilities as well as privileges, and these will preoccupy the last three acts of the Twelve.

Haggai

With Haggai (the name means festive), the audience is propelled into a Persian present. The first nine books of the Twelve were concerned with the kingdoms of Israel/Ephraim and Judah and their destruction by foreign enemies. In a highly dramatized manner, the Twelve presents these events as forming a divine programme designed to produce a new community, a remnant of survivors chosen by the deity to live in the special site of divine presence, Jerusalem. It is important to note that it is not the institution of monarchy that is the focus of the Twelve's presentation of history. Instead, it is the temple, the place of divine presence, that preoccupies the Twelve. Originally, it was the temples in the north, most prominently Bethel, that were favoured by the divine presence but eventually this presence was relocated to Jerusalem due to the corruption of the north. However, this fact was not recognized in Israel, where the people still remained attached to the old sanctuaries. For this they were punished and the kingdom destroyed. Nevertheless, Israel's corruption infected Judah, driving away the divine presence and necessitating Judah's destruction as well. A remnant was preserved from this ruination because Zion/Jerusalem remained the place of divine favour. The remnant's role is to restore Zion as a place of divine presence, a place where heaven and earth unite. It comes as no surprise then that the final acts of the Twelve are each located in the temple on Zion. Signifying the return of divine presence, prophets will be transformed into messengers.

This transformation will be the central motif of Zechariah, and Haggai's role in the Twelve is to prepare the audience for what will follow. It does so in several ways. Most obviously it marks the shift to the Persian present portrayed as the time when the remnant has been restored to Jerusalem. The precise dating in the superscription – 'the second year of King Darius, on the first day of the sixth month' – reinforces this shift with an immediacy that contrasts with the distant long-ago quality of the events of the first nine acts of the Twelve. The audience is also introduced to some of the main characters who feature in these final acts of the Twelve: Joshua, the high priest; Zerubabel, the governor of Judah; and Haggai himself, who is introduced in the superscription as a prophet (1.1) but will be transformed into a messenger (1.13). His transformation foreshadows that of Zechariah in the next act and the culmination of the Twelve in the speech act of Malachi, 'my messenger'. Finally, Haggai sets the stage for the rest of the Twelve in that, in this act, the rebuilding of the temple literally begins. Haggai's sole prophetic role is to rebuke Joshua, Zerubabel and the people for not already attending to the temple's reconstruction. Temple reconstruction has been accorded lower priority than restoring Jerusalem and bringing the land into production. This latter enterprise has not been successful. The people 'have sowed much and brought in little' (1.4). Utilizing sacred marriage imagery, Haggai declares that because the temple remains in ruins 'the skies above you have withheld [their] moisture and the earth has withheld its yield, and I (YHWH) have summoned fierce heat upon the land – upon the hills, upon the new grain and wine and oil, upon all that the ground produces' (1.10–11). The land cannot produce until heaven and earth are reunited. While the temple is in ruins, there is no place for the divine presence to be brought down upon the earth and thus no way that the sacred marriage of earth and heaven can take place.

Unlike their ancestors of old, the people and their leaders 'gave heed to the summons of the LORD their God and to the words of the prophet Haggai . . . the people feared the LORD' (Hag. 1.12). Temple reconstruction begins and immediately Haggai is transformed into a messenger, signifying that divine presence has come to earth. In verse 1.12, Haggai was referred to as a prophet, but in the following verse he is referred to as a messenger, 'and Haggai the LORD's messenger, fulfilling the LORD's mission, spoke to the people' (1.13). The first words this transformed figure speaks announce the restoration of divine presence, 'I am with you – declares the LORD' (1.13). The deity speaks through Haggai, being brought to earth in his body. In this divinized human, the boundaries of earth and heaven, of human and divine, have blurred, if not even been abolished. As messenger, Haggai represents in his body the union of heaven and earth that will come to pass in the restored temple. This union of heaven and earth not only entails the abolition of the boundaries of divine and human but also female and male, a reality the Galli signified by their castration. Does Haggai mark his transformed status as messenger on his body in a similar way? Does Haggai's messenger status represent the fulfilment of Isaiah's promise to eunuchs that in the restored temple they would be given 'a monument and a name better than sons or daughters . . . an everlasting name which shall not perish . . . in My house and within My walls' (Isa. 56.5)?

Zechariah

When the people accept the divine commission to rebuild the temple, the prophet Haggai, who delivered the commission, is transformed into a messenger of YHWH. His transformation is a sign of the divine presence that will be fully realized in the restored temple. In Zechariah, the process of rebuilding the temple is instantiated in the apprenticeship and transformation of the prophet Zechariah into a messenger like Haggai. Indeed, the superscription's dating of the events that will unfold make Zechariah and Haggai contemporaries. Traditionally, Zechariah has been understood as Haggai's younger contemporary, with both of them sharing the mission of inducing the temple's restoration. The text of Zechariah is generally understood to consist of two parts. Such is the contrasting difference of these two parts, that, for much of biblical scholarship, they have been understood to bear little or no relationship to each other. Most commentaries will therefore speak of Zechariah and Deutero-Zechariah. Zechariah is associated with the first part of the text, chapters 1–8, which is mostly spoken in the first person by the character of Zechariah and recounts a series of eight extraordinary night visions. In these visions many scholars have seen the shift from prophecy to apocalyptic. The text itself declares that the days of prophecy have ended (7.7). However, those days are recalled[19] as a warning not to repeat the mistake of Israel, who in those days ignored the prophets and their warnings (Zech. 7.14). Biblical scholars have understood Zechariah to be having visions of the heavenly realm, in which he consorts with angels who explain what he sees and give him messages from YHWH to the people. Deutero-Zechariah is the hypothetical figure responsible for the second part, chapters 9–14, in which a totally different scenario is found. There are no visions or angelic figures and Zechariah is no longer named. Instead what is presented is a series of oracles proclaiming the doom of the nations and the restoration of Judah and Ephraim (Zech. 9–11), followed by the trials and restoration of Jerusalem, culminating in the establishment of a universal divine sovereignty based in Jerusalem. These oracles also signal the end of prophecy (Zech. 13.2–5).

Conrad, however, challenges most of these assumptions in his reading of Zechariah (1999). I find his perspective very convincing in that it takes into account both the final form of Zechariah as a unified text and the role it plays as part of the Twelve. Most significantly he points out that the Hebrew word translated as 'angel' in Zechariah is the same word translated as 'messenger' in Haggai and elsewhere (Conrad 1999: 30). Consequently, Conrad reads angels in Zechariah as earthly messengers, not heavenly beings, and with that perspective argues that the messenger who speaks to Zechariah and guides him through the visions is none other than Haggai himself. The last reference to a messenger in the Twelve was Haggai's own transformation into a messenger in the preceding act (Hag. 1.13). From that perspective, what Zechariah sees in the first section of the book are not visions into the heavenly realm but instead are the 'sights and symbols associated with the restoration of Jerusalem and the construction of the temple' (Conrad 1999: 41). Under the

---

19 Zechariah means 'memory of YH' or 'YH remembers'.

guidance of Haggai, Zechariah is finally transformed into a messenger and he is portrayed in the end answering questions posed by representatives sent up to Jerusalem from Bethel (Zech. 7.2–3).[20] This transformation of Zechariah represents the completed restoration of the temple. The two oracles in the second part of Zechariah are further pronouncements of the prophet turned messenger. These are addressed to Israel, the people of the old northern kingdom, and advocate its attachment to Judah and Jerusalem. Most radically, Conrad argues that Malachi, which literally means 'my messenger' and is the concluding act of the Twelve, is a third and final oracle of Zechariah the messenger (Conrad 1999: 41).

From a queer perspective, what particularly strikes me about Conrad's reading is the relationship between Haggai and Zechariah. As Zechariah's guide, Haggai is initiating Zechariah into the ways of the temple and its messengers. The way of initiation is strongly associated with age variant same-sex relationships. These relationships of an older and a younger person, historically, have been the most common form of both male and female same-sex relationships. It has sometimes been argued that age variance substitutes for gender difference and its dynamics of polarity/hierarchy in opposite-sex or heterosexual relationships. While that might be the case in many instances, I would argue that age variant same-sex relationships viewed from the perspective of initiation work in a completely different way. As a (mutual) mentoring relationship one says to the other, 'What you are now, I once was; what I am now, you will become.' So from a starting-point of apparent difference, the relationship works on a dynamic of attaining ultimate sameness. For the same dynamic to work in opposite-sex relationships, one partner would have to change gender to match the other, not the normal goal of heterosexual bonding, particularly under patriarchy. This homoerotic way of initiation seems oddly appropriate for the theological dynamics of Haggai, Zechariah and Malachi in the Twelve. According to Conrad, messengers represent the blurring of human and divine that takes place when heaven is brought back down to earth through the temple. From that perspective, Zechariah's initiation into messengership is a process of divinization under the guidance of Haggai. The best model for understanding the relationship of a person with the deity in this process is that of the age variant homosexual relationship. The deity, incarnate in Haggai, can truly say to Zechariah, 'What you are now, I once was; what I am now, you will become.'[21]

---

20 Conrad is following an emendation of Zechariah 7.2 here as found in the NRSV translation by which Bethel sends Sharezer and Regem-melech 'to entreat the favour of the Lord' in Jerusalem. In the JPS translation the mission from Bethel disappears, being rendered 'when Bethel-sharezer and Regem-melech and his men sent to entreat the favour of the Lord'. However, in a footnote it allows an alternative reading whereby Bethel-sharezer sends Regem-melech and his men. Nevertheless, the great medieval exegete Rashi allowed for a reference to Bethel, the place, in this verse.

21 Does this model of incarnation and divinization lie behind the homoerotic motifs in John's Gospel (cf. van Tilborg 1993)?

Malachi

The temple is rebuilt, the apotheosis is complete and Zechariah has become 'my messenger', Malachi. The voice that speaks in this denouement to the Twelve is YHWH's alone, albeit through a human mouth. Nevertheless, Malachi does not declare but debate. Zechariah has closed with extravagant imagery of a world in which Jerusalem is at the centre because YHWH, the acknowledged ruler of the world, lives there. In Malachi, however, while an echo of triumphant universalism can be found in Malachi 1.7, it is clear that this divine rule has not yet come to pass. YHWH alone might speak but the audience is addressed in a series of 'six disputation speeches' (1.2–5; 1.6–2.9; 2.10–16; 2.17–3.5; 3.6–12; 3.13–24) containing 'three basic elements . . . a thesis statement attributed to the audience, a counterthesis advanced by the prophet, and a section of argumentation . . . designed to support the . . . counterthesis' (Sweeney et al. 2000: 716). The speeches address the following issues: 'How have you shown us love?' (Mal. 1.2), 'How have we scorned Your name?' (Mal. 1.6), 'Why do we break faith . . . profaning the covenant of our fathers?' (Mal. 2.10), 'By what have we wearied [Him]?' (Mal. 2.17), 'How shall we turn back?' (Mal. 3.7), 'What have we been saying among ourselves against You?' (Mal. 3.13). These speeches are addressed to an Israel, as identified in the superscription, which Conrad argues is the same Israel as that addressed in the speeches in response to the questions from Bethel's representatives found in Zechariah 7–14. Malachi is Zechariah's final oracle to the representatives of Bethel, the age-old temple of the north. The six issues addressed in Malachi can be condensed to three: the divine love for Israel, Israel's turning away and then its final turning back. They recur again and again as issues in the Twelve and were dramatically performed in its opening scenes in Hosea 1–3. The reappearance of Bethel in Zechariah is a reminder, too, that, while the Assyrians swept away the northern kingdom, the northern sanctuaries have survived intact along with Jerusalem. Their survival thus challenges the often repeated claim of the Twelve, indeed its central theme, that Jerusalem alone is the place of divine presence. Nevertheless, in Malachi's third speech, a slippage takes place from Israel to Judah and Jerusalem (Mal. 2.11). While the Twelve clearly argues the supremacy of Jerusalem that displaces the YHWH sanctuaries in Israel/Ephraim and elsewhere, this northern Israel has frequently acted more like Jerusalem's own Dorian Gray portrait in which appear all the Jerusalem community's faults. Conrad observes that Malachi is addressed to 'those who appear to challenge the temple ideology seen through Zechariah's eyes . . . leaders in the north . . . as well as . . . opposition from within Jerusalem itself' (Conrad 1999: 203, 44). In Malachi, the temple might have been rebuilt, with prophecy ended and messengers returned as in the long distant past, but Israel and Judah, Bethel and Jerusalem have merged. Thus in the final scene of the Twelve, the audience is confronted by Malachi/YHWH petulantly threatening to gather together a new remnant of the righteous and then unleash them in a genocidal fury to 'trample the wicked to a pulp' (Mal. 3.21). In the last two verses, though, it is YHWH who appears to turn around from this violent fantasy, as if realizing that threats alone can no longer suffice. As the lights go down and the curtain descends, YHWH promises to send the prophet Elijah as the promised messenger (Mal. 3.1) to bring about a final reconciliation that 'will avert YHWH's plans to destroy the land entirely' (Sweeney *et al.* 2000: 750).

Conclusion

It is against Jewish custom to end the books of scripture with words of doom. So, as Malachi's final verse tells of YHWH's destruction of the land that Elijah's coming is designed to avert, the Twelve closes with the repetition of the penultimate verse in which YHWH promises to send Elijah before the 'awesome, fearful day of the LORD' (Mal. 3.23). Even so, the final echo is still of that fearful, dreadful day. Thompson observes that, too often, traditional readings of 'the prophetic texts . . . awaken murderous Elijah's and Jonah's for God's sake' (Thompson 2000: 397). Queer people are more often the targets, literally and rhetorically, of such murderous intents. It strikes me that, as the final act of the Twelve, Malachi presents a conclusion dominated by doom and violence. Violence infects the few references to divine love presented to the audience in Malachi's opening speech. The destruction and continuing desolation of Edom/Esau is the only evidence tendered of the deity's love for Israel, by which YHWH 'accepted Jacob, and . . . rejected Esau' (Mal. 1.2–3). Furthermore, Conrad points out that, in both Zechariah and Malachi, a reader can't help but be struck by an overwhelming impression of divine 'anger . . . out of control' (Conrad 1999: 203). Throughout the greater part of Malachi, the deity speaks a language of complaint, of threat and of menace so that it is not really a surprise that the final words should speak of the complete destruction of the land. It makes a complete contrast with the ending of Hosea and its queer erotic rhapsody celebrating the final reconciliation of heaven and earth, human and divine. This erotic rhapsody echoes, too, in the endings of Amos and Joel, while both Micah and Zephaniah conclude celebrating the divine love that will be bestowed on the surviving remnant on the day of restoration. Zechariah and Malachi represent that day, but there is no love, no rhapsody, only menace and the threat of yet another day to come. It is as if all the sufferings of Israel/Judah in the days of the Former Prophets have been invoked, not to celebrate a final reconciliation and restoration, but instead to continue a programme of vilification and abjection of opponents who have frustrated the full realization of the day of the LORD. The deity who speaks in Malachi is not the divine lover of Hosea 14 but the abusive husband of Hosea 2, thus giving licence to the lethal readings of these texts.

To counter these lethal readings, perhaps Malachi can be read ironically. The Twelve can be understood as a series of experiments in divinity and what it means for humans to be in relation to that divinity. These experiments are 'interpretations of known tradition' (Thompson 2000: 387) and exist in a critical tension with each other. One aspect of that tradition is the sacred marriage motif and the associated themes of the merged divine/human, celestial/terrestrial realms. Malachi is the divinized Zechariah in which the audience meets an all-too-human deity, obsessed with the petty details and power politics of the temple. Thus Malachi stands as a final ironic interpretation of what it means to bring the divine down to earth. Through presenting a satirical vision of dystopia, it cautions its audience against taking at face value the claims of those who claim to speak with a divine authority, particularly if that authority can be backed by more mundane terrestrial power. Malachi can be read as a figure of fun warning against submitting to anyone – priest, prophet, politician – who makes demands in the name of God or country or family or liberty or democracy. However, lest one ask, like Peggy Lee, 'Is that all there is?', the concluding verses pull the rug out from under this divine caricature. Malachi declares that the day of the LORD is yet to come. It will only come about through making justice and bringing about harmony and reconciliation. The audience is told to remember and observe the Law of Moses and promised that Elijah will be sent to bring about a final reconciliation before the Day of the LORD. The Law of Moses represents justice while Elijah represents the process of reconciliation. In subsequent Jewish tradition, he is the helper, healer and bringer of peace. Furthermore, Conrad points out that Elijah is the 'prophet/messenger who . . . blurred the distinction between heaven and earth' (Conrad 1999: 204). By citing Elijah, therefore, the Twelve closes critiquing Malachi's angry messenger of doom, and reinforcing that critique by subtly evoking the sacred marriage motif of the merging of heaven and earth.

The Second Testament

Matthew

THOMAS BOHACHE

In a postmodern, secular world, why is it necessary to read or interpret the traditional Christian Bible? I agree with the postcolonial biblical interpreter R. S. Sugirtharajah's evaluation of this very question:

> The answer lies with those who are busily using biblical texts to define a narrow vision of biblical faith, especially in the aftermath of September 11. This includes a Scripture-spouting president of the world's only superpower who combines patriotism with a sense of divine mission. In Bush we have an overtly pious Christian leader whose vision of the world is determined and restricted by a single and simplistic reading of the Bible, thus erasing its indeterminacy and ambiguity. It is precisely this which makes it worthwhile to turn to its pages to make it clear to all those who adhere to a narrow understanding of the Bible that it is a book not with one message but with many, and that biblical texts often emit conflicting signals. (Sugirtharajah 2003: 2)

That the Bible has not one message but many is demonstrated by the diversity of interpretations one sees today as people explore the text through the interpretive lens of who they are as readers – black, brown, yellow, red, white; female, male, transgendered, intersexual; straight, gay, lesbian, queer; rich or poor; lay or clergy; mainstream or marginalized; academic or non-specialist. Contemporary readers have discovered not only that God meets them in their circumstances in the pages of scripture, but also that these same circumstances assist them in reclaiming excised or silenced voices from the biblical past.

I approach the Gospel according to Matthew in several different ways: first, as a white, affluent, well-educated male living in the most powerful country on Earth; second, as a person born, raised, and educated in the Roman Catholic Church; third, as a person of queer consciousness, specifically a gay male who came into awareness of my sexuality during the turbulent 1970s. The first two means of self-categorization locate me as a person of privilege, one who *is* right and *has* rights just by virtue of where I live or how I look or what creed I espouse. The third way of describing myself, however, places me on the margins in many respects, not the least of which is that my country and church of origin do not recognize my social location as one deserving of a say or a place at the table. A refugee from Catholicism, I have found a home in the Metropolitan Community Churches, where sexual orientation is only an issue because it is the social, political and spiritual location from which we prescind as people of faith. I am not (yet) a refugee from the United States; rather, with other queer people (among whom I include not only gay, lesbian, bisexual and transgendered people, but also our straight supporters who, in a presumptively heterosexual society, are truly queer) I am among the colonized – those who live under the hegemony of heterosexuals, heterosexuality and heteronormativity. As such, we colonized queers, despite our best efforts, nevertheless submit to those in power, who dictate an entire way of life according to their own privileged agendas, never questioning whether their perquisites are divinely ordained or humanly constructed.

In this respect, to be queer in the heterosexually dominated United States (or indeed the entire industrialized Western world) in the twenty-first century is not so vastly different from being a Jewish peasant in Roman-occupied Palestine in the first century of the Common Era. The field of Second Testament studies has been enriched of late by social-scientific and cross-cultural studies which show that the Jewish people at the time of Jesus had been colonized and were oppressed on a day-to-day basis by the Roman empire. Moreover, local elites, in order to ensure their own prosperity, further oppressed their own people in a variety of ways. When one approaches Matthew's Gospel against this background, utilizing a 'hermeneutics of suspicion', one is able to glean from the text insights that have been glossed over by the readings of those in power and thereby develop a 'hermeneutics of remembrance or reclamation' that becomes a 'hermeneutics of proclamation'[1] for today's disempowered. This chapter seeks to do so for the queer community.

The Imperial Context

The geographical territory which had once been the biblical kingdoms of Israel and Judah was conquered by a series of foreign empires beginning around the eighth century BCE. The northern kingdom (Israel) was the first to topple, followed eventually by the southern kingdom (Judah). The historical and prophetic books of the Hebrew Bible speak about the political and military chaos that allowed first the Assyrians and then the Babylonians to subjugate these kingdoms. Indeed, the Babylonians so devastated the land and the people that Solomon's temple at Jerusalem was razed to the ground and the Judaean aristocracy carried off to Babylon, its royal family having been killed. After the Babylonian empire succumbed to the Persian empire, some of the Jews (as they had begun to be called during their exile in Babylon) were allowed to

---

1 A 'hermeneutics of suspicion' assumes that the whole story has not been told by traditional interpretations of a text; it 'reads the silence' for clues to develop a 'hermeneutics of remembrance or reclamation' to detect voices of the oppressed that may have been previously ignored, either deliberately or unintentionally. The reader is then able, through reclaiming what has been left out, to advance a 'hermeneutics of proclamation' that reveals fresh interpretations which include the marginalized. These terms are adapted from feminist liberation-critical studies, originally popularized in Second Testament studies by Elisabeth Schüssler Fiorenza (Schüssler Fiorenza 1983 and 1992a) and utilized in Matthean scholarship by Elaine Wainwright (Wainwright 1994b: 638–9).

return to their native land and rebuild their temple. The high priesthood was restored and sacrifices allowed to resume – all under the supervision and control of foreign overlords, originally the Persians under Cyrus the Great, but later the Greeks, who had gained control of the entire eastern Mediterranean basin through the expansionist agenda of Alexander the Great. During a brief period of one hundred years, the Jews gained self-rule through the efforts of the Maccabees, who were able to overthrow Alexander's successors and establish a theocracy in Judaea under the Hasmonean family.

In the meantime, while the Jews were so occupied, another foreign power had amassed a vast empire in the Mediterranean world. First under its Senate and then under a series of triumvirates, the Republic of Rome had extended its military and political power, supplanting the Hellenistic Empire established by Alexander but in disarray since his death. In 64 BCE, in order to secure the eastern borders of its ever-increasing empire, the Roman army conquered and annexed Syria and then, the following year, turned its attention to Judaea. Up to this time, the Romans had not interfered in the Jewish state; however, they saw an opportunity to broaden their power base in the region when the Hasmoneans began to quarrel over who was to rule. After a three-month siege, the Roman army subdued the city of Jerusalem, captured the temple and declared one of the rival Hasmoneans high priest by force of arms. However, in a move that was to have long-term repercussions, Rome stripped the family of political rule and installed as administrator a foreign-born Jew named Antipater. Thus, Palestine (as the Romans called the biblical kingdoms of Israel and Judah) became a vassal state of the Roman empire in 62 BCE.

Nevertheless, Rome's style of oversight was different from that of the Jews' previous conquerors. After the initial military onslaught, the Romans would put in place a ruler whom they could depend upon to administer the jurisdiction as their puppet (for example, Antipater, the two Herods, and Archelaus in Matthew's Gospel); when this failed, the Romans would appoint one of their own career military men as governor or prefect (such as Pontius Pilate). In this way, Rome attempted to appear benevolent to its subject peoples, permitting a semblance of self-rule and a façade of peace, all the while maintaining tight control through military occupation, the exacting of tribute and harsh reprisals in case of insurrection – all of which would have been commonplace occurrences in the world of Jesus of Nazareth.

The Roman empire reached its zenith under Octavian Caesar, Julius Caesar's adopted son, who fought for control of Roman leadership after his father's assassination and, upon the defeat of Mark Antony and Cleopatra, assumed sole authority over the Roman empire, adopting the titles *augustus* ('the revered one') and *princeps* ('first man') rather than *imperator* ('emperor'). In this way Augustus (as he was known from then on) began to empower the fiction that he was simply 'first among many' instead of a tyrant and, through the works of court poets such as Virgil and Horace, that his rule was a period of prosperity for the entire Roman empire after decades of civil war, a time lauded as the *Pax Romana* ('Roman Peace'). Jesus was born during Augustus' reign (27 BCE to 14 CE); his ministry and execution occurred during the reign of Tiberius, Augustus' stepson and successor (14–37 CE). Matthew's Gospel was most likely written some fifty years later during the reign of Domitian (81–96), whose father Vespasian and brother Titus had been responsible for destroying the Jerusalem temple in 70 after a decade of Jewish rebellion.

I do not believe that Matthew's Gospel (or any of the Second Testament, for that matter) can be read properly without an understanding of what was happening politically, socially, economically and religiously. Indeed, I contend that Matthew's Gospel, like John's Gospel,[2] is composed on two levels: its first level is what it purports to relate (the events of Jesus' life), while its second level is what is occurring at the time of composition (life in Matthew's community). Thus, the readers and hearers of the Gospel would have been aware of not only Jesus' context but also their own; additionally, they would have remembered the overall context of Jewish history. Each of these contexts is about imperialism, colonialism, subjugation and domination; and it is through this lens that I interpret the Gospel according to Matthew as a twenty-first-century white, American male of queer consciousness. Just as Matthew's audience would have received the words of the Gospel amid the memory of slavery, occupation, exile, oppressive taxation and government-approved murder, so too today's queer reader comes to this Gospel mindful of the queer history of church- and government-sponsored burnings, false imprisonments, executions, fag-bashing and lesbian-baiting; as well as prejudice and exclusion at all levels of society, unequal treatment under the law despite equal taxation, and daily mental colonial occupation at the hands of a heterosexist society.

The Author and the Audience

It is impossible to discern whether the author of the Gospel according to Matthew was a woman or a man. It is a virtual certainty that the author was *not* the former tax collector and disciple of Jesus, unless he was quite old at the time of its composition, sometime in the 80s of the Common Era. Several regions have been proposed for the location of its composition, but most scholars accept Syria, possibly the city of Antioch, as its place of origin. Because of the Gospel's emphasis on teaching, some have suggested that its immediate context was a school setting (Witherington 1994; Deutsch 1996). Since the author seems familiar with Jewish language, history and culture, it is probable that s/he was writing to a community composed predominately of Jews (Harrington 1991; Meier 1979). Scholars are not in agreement as to whether the members of Matthew's community were Jewish Christians who had already separated from Judaism, or Christian Jews who still located themselves within the ancestral faith but saw Jesus' teaching as one interpretation of Judaism among several vying for authority subsequent to the destruction of the Jerusalem temple. I believe that the latter argument is the more convincing, inasmuch as it accounts for the major conflicts in the Gospel as an interfaith struggle (Saldarini 1994). Moreover, when viewed according to postcolonial theory, this struggle takes on the character of what sociologists call 'horizontal violence', when, under the control of an oppressive power, marginalized groups turn on each other (Freire 1970); one sees this in the queer community

---

2 For the idea of a two-level drama in John, see Martyn 1968.

when those 'in the mainstream' blame the more exotic subcultures or 'fringe' groups within the community for our failure to obtain equal rights.

Recently Warren Carter, in two major studies, has demonstrated how Roman imperialism may be employed as a hermeneutical key for reading Matthew's Gospel and its portrayal of Jesus and early Christian origins.

> I read Matthew's gospel as a counternarrative. It is a work of resistance, written for a largely Jewish religious group. It 'stands and/or speaks over against' the status quo dominated by Roman imperial power and synagogal control. It resists these cultural structures. (Carter 2000: 1; citations omitted)

If one assumes Antioch as the place where Matthew's Gospel originated, Carter's theory is quite compelling. Antioch was the capital of the Roman province of Syria and the residence of its governor, the Roman emperor's representative. The governor had a large staff and palatial living quarters in the city, along with four military legions at his disposal, which could be dispatched to maintain order wherever they were needed. It was from Antioch as a strategic military site that Roman legions and mercenaries were sent to Galilee and Judaea to subdue rioting during the Jewish War of the late 60s. The Jewish historian Josephus notes that, at the culmination of the war in 70, Antioch was the scene of the general Titus' military triumph following his conquest of Jerusalem; this triumph featured displays of booty and slaves taken during the siege. Primary sources also reveal that five Roman emperors visited Antioch between the time of Jesus and the time of the Gospel's composition. In addition to such overt imperial presence, municipal buildings, religious temples, taxes, coinage and daily rituals would have impressed upon the city's Jewish community that they were a subjugated minority under the control of Rome. Indeed, the coins minted after the conquest of Judaea – which Jews in the Empire would have had to use on a daily basis – were imprinted with the words *Iudea Capta* ('Judaea Captured') or *Iudea Devicta* ('Judaea Conquered'), along with likenesses of the Emperor Vespasian on one side and Livia Augusta (Augustus' wife, worshipped as a goddess after her death) depicted as the goddess Pax ('Peace') on the other (Carter 2001: 35–46). Additionally, the art of the period often depicted captured Judaea as a nude, female supplicant, a frequent imperial/colonial trope (Lopez 2004; Donaldson 2002).

Moreover, the resident population of Antioch would have had daily economic reminders of the Roman imperial mechanism. The majority of the city's inhabitants was from the poor artisan class who barely had enough to survive; the city was overcrowded as a result of an influx of peasant refugees who had fled the countryside when either they had lost their ancestral farms due to outrageous taxation or their farms had failed from overwork due to production needs of the Empire's wealthy elite. Though they lived in Antioch at the end of the first century, Matthew's audience would have seen their own economic and political woes reflected in the stories contained in the Gospel about life in Galilee fifty years earlier.

Carter thus sees Matthew's Gospel as a response to political, religious, economic and social conditions in imperial Antioch: 'The Gospel challenges the perception that Rome should rule the world . . . [and] relativizes Rome's claims, demystifies them, reveals their shortcomings, and boldly dares to announce Rome's certain demise in the yet-future establishment of God's empire . . .' (Carter 2001: 53). He encourages the reader to imagine a tension between the 'authorial' audience and the 'actual' audience: the authorial audience reads the narrative of Jesus' ministry against its daily experience of empire, while today's actual audience brings into play 'our own experience as we engage the gospel' (Carter 2000: 6). I submit that a contemporary queer audience brings to its reading of Matthew the experience of living in the worldwide Heteronormative Empire in which the political, religious, economic and social affairs of daily life remind us of the hegemony of the heterosexual majority. Nevertheless, as Carter cautions, an actual reader must also note the ways in which Matthew's community differs from ours. For example, Matthew expects the audience to accept the demonization of Jewish leaders, the invisibility of women as subjects and agents and the importation of imperial language into the text (as in the Great Commission in Matthew 28). 'As an actual audience, we can understand, but reject, what is expected of us as the authorial audience' (Carter 2001: 6).

Finally, Carter's methodology is useful for our queer reading of Matthew, inasmuch as he articulates the community being addressed as a group 'on the margins' of society. First, as Jews in a largely Gentile city, and second, as those professing Jesus as Messiah in the midst of other Jewish groups who did not so acknowledge Jesus, the Matthean community is made up of marginalized people. Carter, following liberation hermeneutics, contends that marginalized people read texts and situations differently because, first of all, the marginalized live 'in both worlds', the dominant culture and that of their own group; furthermore, these worlds exist 'in tension' with different values and commitments. 'To be marginal is to exist out of the centre, on the edge, at the periphery [and] in some opposition to the dominant or central reality'; on this periphery, they foster and maintain their own 'commitments, practices, and worldview' as alternatives to those of the dominant or central world, while still existing in that world (Carter 2000: 45; citing Lee 1995: 42–7).

It is this 'in-both, over-against, alternative existence' that brings queer interpretation, exegesis of the imperial locus, and postcolonial theory into congruence in my reading of Matthew. As I will demonstrate below in my 'queering' of portions of Matthew, queer readers strike a balancing act between the straight world, which colonizes our daily lives, and our own queer imaginings, in which we are free to dream of the world as it should be, which is precisely what Matthew's community did as they came together to read or listen to stories of Jesus' alternative empire.[3]

---

3 Janice Capel Anderson refers to this as the response of the 'actual reader' of Matthew, which she contrasts with the 'implied reader' whom the author had in mind but whose reactions might not be those of an actual reader. For example, she notes that actual women readers would react differently to androcentric bias in the text than an implied or intended readership that was male. In the same way, actual queer readers see nuances in the text that a heterosexual implied reader would not even consider (Anderson 2001: 45–7).

A Note on 'Queering'

The remainder of this essay will be a commentary on specific portions of Matthew's Gospel from a queer perspective, a process which I – along with other queer scholars – call 'queering'. As noted above, I use the term 'queer' in an inclusive sense to refer to all who are disempowered in a heteronormative world, whether they self-identify as gay, lesbian, bisexual, transgendered, straight, questioning or none of these. According to such thinking, the word 'queer' empowers diversity because of its imprecise and hard-to-pin-down meaning. Moreover, 'queer' has both an adjectival (descriptive) and verbal (active) sense. When something is 'queer', it is uncommon, out of the ordinary, unusual, and non-conforming to the dominant culture. One who is 'queer' may be seen as transgressive, unorthodox, radical, in-your-face or against-the-grain, because in imperialist straight society s/he navigates in intentional opposition to a seemingly fixed current. Likewise, to 'queer' something harks back to its Old English meaning of to 'spoil' or 'stir up', in order not to settle for the easy answers of the status quo. Thus, to 'queer' a scripture is to render it unusual and non-normative, to shake it up and see how it might be reconfigured, or even, as the queer theologian and activist Robert Goss has maintained, to 'spoil what has already been spoiled' by generations of sexist, racist and homophobic biblical interpretation (Goss 1993). As I have written elsewhere, 'a queer hermeneutic . . . will not only *"queer"* but it will *"query"*': It must be a questioning and a turning over of layers of heteropatriarchal tradition to reveal what lies beneath' (Bohache 2003: 25).

Genealogy, Birth and Flight

In discussing the Infancy Narrative in Luke's Gospel from a queer perspective, I have stated:

> Those who do historical Jesus research dismiss the Infancy Narratives in Luke and in Matthew as containing nothing historically reliable about Jesus' conception or birth; they point out the inconsistencies, the mythological elements, and the sheer unbelievability of a virginal conception. . . . Rather than dismissing this story as a fanciful creation of the early church, I would read it with a queer hermeneutic of stirring up, possibly spoiling, and imagining what God has to say to queers through this story. (Bohache 2003: 24–5)

In that essay, I utilized the Lucan stories of the Annunciation, Visitation and Nativity to show how queer readers might view the traditional story of Jesus' incarnation in a non-traditional way in order to see our own queer embodiment as an incarnation of the Christ Spirit. In doing so, I did not address the historicity of the Infancy Narratives, because for me a biblical story does not have to be grounded in historical fact in order to contain God's revelatory truth.

This will hold true for all of the queerings in this essay. I prefer, with the Second Testament scholar and historian Richard Horsley, to 'take the gospel whole' (Horsley 2003: 72), treating it as a complete piece of literature – written *for* a specific group, *for* definite reasons, *in* a particular way, *because of* a concrete context. To dissect the Gospels into a series of sayings by a 'talking head' Jesus without an historical or literary context (as, for example, the Jesus Seminar does) is counterproductive if one is seeking to interpret Jesus' context so that it may inform our own. This is in keeping with the current 'reader-response' methodology in Second Testament studies (e.g. Moxnes 2003), which seeks to ascertain not necessarily what Jesus actually said or did, but how the first followers understood what he said and did and communicated it to subsequent generations. This type of criticism, unlike the older form, source and redaction criticism, sees Matthew as a unified whole, a finished literary work with a point of view of its own and, as we shall see, a definite stance toward what was taking place in the imperial world of its composition.

Matthew begins with an extended genealogy (Matt. 1.1–17) which locates Jesus in the line of King David according to patriarchal lines of succession. The normal flow of the generations is interrupted, however, at four places, where a woman from the Hebrew Bible intrudes into the genealogy. These women are Tamar, who became pregnant by her father-in-law Judah (Gen. 38); Rahab, the prostitute who assisted Joshua in taking Jericho (Josh. 2; 6); Ruth, the Moabite who seduced Boaz in order to secure for herself a son (Ruth 2–4); and Bathsheba (referred to by Matthew only as 'the wife of Uriah'), who became pregnant from an adulterous affair with King David (2 Sam. 11).

Interpreters have accounted for these intrusions in various ways, suggesting that the women were 'sinners', preparing the way for Jesus, who was to save the people from their sins; or 'foreigners' (non-Jews), anticipating the acceptance of Christ by the Gentiles; or parties to sexual liaisons that were 'unusual' for Hebrew patriarchal culture, foreshadowing Mary's abnormal conception (Harrington 1991: 32; Brown 1977: 71–4). The feminist biblical scholar Jane Schaberg has demonstrated, however, that male scholars have reached these conclusions unnecessarily. Instead, she suggests that we should view these women not simply as negative foils, but rather as 'lead[ing] Matthew's reader to expect another, final story of a woman who [like these four women] becomes a social misfit in some way; is wronged or thwarted; who is party to a sexual act that places her in great danger; and whose story has an outcome that repairs the social fabric and ensures the birth of a child who is legitimate or legitimated' (Schaberg 1987: 32–3). Schaberg concludes that Mary is just such a woman. A contextual reading of the story of Jesus' conception and birth in Matthew 1.18–25 reveals all of the components Schaberg has gleaned from the First Testament allusions.

A queer reading of Matthew's genealogy will capitalize on the inclusion of these four women – and the fifth, Mary. Each of the four women from the Hebrew Bible, in her own way, is queer in that she stirs up heteropatriarchal expectations and spoils the system that would keep her down: Judah has attempted to deprive Tamar of her rights under the system of levirate marriage, and so she tricks him into impregnating her himself in order to obtain her due; Rahab, no doubt used and objectified her whole life by men, as prostitutes are to this day, determines her own destiny by capitalizing on her status as a sex worker to save her life and that of her family; Ruth, widowed and childless and wishing to maintain her covenant to her beloved Naomi, seduces Boaz and thus obtains a legitimate place in Naomi's family; Bathsheba, raped by King David's male gaze and widowed as a result of his determination to have her at any cost, becomes his queen and gives birth to King Solomon, memorialized for his infusion of womanly Sophia-Wisdom. Each of these queer acts sets the stage for the queer act that will occur in connection with Mary's pregnancy.

Matthew, unlike Luke, tells the story of Jesus' conception and birth through Joseph's eyes rather than Mary's; in Matthew's version, Mary remains a silent character, a virtual victim who is acted upon rather than acting for herself. Nevertheless, the Matthean genealogy carefully refrains from saying that Joseph 'begot' or 'fathered' Jesus: 'and Jacob [was] the father of Joseph the husband of Mary, of whom Jesus was born' (Matt. 1.16). Joseph's role in Matthew's genealogy and birth narrative is exclusively that of Mary's husband; Jesus is *born* 'from Mary'. It is tempting to read Matthew's infancy narrative alongside Luke's and supply information from one to the other (much as contemporary cribs show Lucan shepherds and manger animals alongside Matthean magi). However, there is no evidence in the text that Matthew and Luke had any knowledge of each other's stories; scholars believe that the infancy stories first circulated in oral tradition and were then incorporated by these two evangelists and redacted according to their narrative purposes (Albright and Mann 1971: xxxvii–xxxviii, xlii, 6).

A feminist or queer analysis of the infancy stories would seem to prefer the Lucan story because Mary is the actor who speaks her truth passionately in the Magnificat of Luke 1.46–55 and gives her *'fiat'* to God's plan. Nevertheless, I believe that Matthew's birth story can also be queered if one looks beyond what we are accustomed to seeing in a heteronormative reading. We are told that Mary somehow becomes pregnant while she is 'betrothed' to Joseph but before they lived together. If Joseph were the father of Jesus, this would be a non-issue: the couple would simply marry earlier than planned; perhaps Joseph would have to pay some sort of remuneration to Mary's father as recompense for the premature intercourse. Because Matthew does not even present that option but instead notes that Joseph intends to 'dismiss her quietly', the normal conclusion would be that Mary had engaged in illicit sex outside of marriage/betrothal; the punishment for this could have been death (see Deut. 22.23–7[4]). Joseph's male pride would have been assuaged by the public shaming and possible execution of his unfaithful fiancée. However, we are told that Joseph is 'righteous' (Greek *dikaios*), legal jargon indicating that Joseph adhered to the law and was a blameless man in the sight of God. There is a real irony here: technically, the 'legal' and 'blameless' (ergo 'righteous') thing to do would have been to have Mary – and her child – put to death according to Hebrew law. Joseph, however, influenced by the Spirit of God, does the 'unrighteous' thing – he marries the woman who appears to have betrayed

---

4 There is not enough ancient evidence to ascertain whether this penalty was in fact carried out in Palestine in the first century.

him – and is thereby called 'righteous' by the evangelist.[5] In this way, Joseph subverts heteropatriarchal expectation; he spoils the spoiled system of sexual double-standard that would demand a woman's life. As a result of his queer act, Mary and Jesus are neither ostracized nor put to death, but allowed to live and prosper: God's Messiah is born because of a man who acts outside of his heteronormative role. Joseph, by not doing what his society expects of him, can be a model for queer people of faith who, following God's directive, choose to act contrary to society's demands – by marrying illicitly, by having children in non-traditional ways, by forming intentional, non-biological families.

Doing God's will is not without its costs, however. The story of the magi and the flight from Herod in Matthew 2.1–23 raises the spectre of fear and positions Matthew's narrative in the context of everyday terrorism in Palestine under the Roman empire. While some biblical scholars dismiss this story as a myth or a plot device to explain how the Holy Family got from Bethlehem in Judaea to Nazareth in Galilee (Brown 1977: 188–9, 225–9), Richard Horsley has asserted that there is no reason to see this story as fictitious. Historical elements in the text such as King Herod and the presence of magi, both of which can be verified from extra-biblical sources, suggest that Matthew 2 would be more properly classified as a 'legend', for, unlike myths, legends are historical artefacts that have been embellished over time (Horsley 1993b: 11–13, 17–19).

Herod the Great, son of Antipater, was named King of the Jews by the Roman Senate under the sponsorship of Mark Antony. His Jewish subjects hated and resented him, however, because of his foreign birth and his partiality to the Romans. Upon his accession to the throne there were riots throughout Palestine, particularly persistent in Galilee, which took three years for the Roman army to quell. Herod was seen, no doubt correctly, as a sycophant to the Romans, first Antony and then Augustus. Inscriptions indicate that he adopted for himself such titles as 'Admirer of Caesar' and 'Admirer of the Romans'. His admiration took the form of massive building projects in every portion of his realm, including monuments and entire cities in honour of Caesar; in Jerusalem, Herod built the royal palace Antonia (named for Antony) and undertook a refurbishment of the Jerusalem temple so extensive that the Herodian temple surpassed its splendour at any other point of its existence (Horsley 2001b: 143–4).

Herod's homage to his Roman benefactors was financed, however, on the backs of his Jewish subjects, who were taxed outrageously in order to pay for the public works and building projects undertaken by this king; these taxes were assessed over and above the tithes and offerings required of observant Jews by the temple priesthood. Additionally, once Palestine became a vassal Roman state, there was a tribute exacted by Rome; one of the purposes of the

---

5 Schaberg looks at this story in another way, raising the possibility that Mary had been raped. Evidently, in the case of rape, Hebrew law allowed either a termination of the betrothal or a continuation with the marriage (Schaberg 1987: 45ff.). However, rape was incredibly difficult to prove; in ancient patriarchal society, as often today, a woman was assumed not to have been raped but to have welcomed seduction. It is much more likely that without Joseph's intervention Mary would have been ostracized or put to death.

census mentioned in Luke 2.1 was to enrol each citizen so that a 'head tax' could be charged (Horsley 2001a: 125). Under Herod's rule, the ancestral land of the Jews may have looked more beautiful and 'prosperous', but the Jewish people themselves suffered from overcrowding in the towns, exhaustion of the land due to overplanting, famine, poverty, disease and drought. Under the socioeconomic system in place during the Roman empire, it is estimated that the imperial governors and the local aristocracy (referred to in the Gospels variously as the chief priests, Sadducees and Herodians) made up the smallest portion of the population, yet consumed the majority of the resources; the peasants, artisans and landless poor made up the vast majority of the population (Crossan 1991: 43–6).

This was the situation at the time of Jesus' birth. Palestine was a powderkeg of political tension, colonial disappointment and disempowerment, and messianic hopes; in Galilee especially the crowds would rally behind political pretenders, crowning them messiahs and kings (Horsley 2003: 35–7, 45–52). Herod's means of subduing insurrection and disloyalty was incredibly harsh. An insecure ruler, he put to death hundreds perceived to be traitors. 'Herod, in fact, instituted what today would be called a police-state, complete with loyalty oaths, surveillance, informers, secret police, imprisonment, torture, and brutal retaliation' (Horsley 1993b: 47). His insecurity was only matched by his paranoia: history records that he was responsible for the deaths of his brothers, his mother, at least one of his wives and several of his sons (Harrington 1991: 41–2; Garland 1995: 26–7). It is against this political background that Matthew's story of the magi's visit to Herod must be read.

The magi are referred to in biblical commentaries and popular stories as 'astrologers', 'wise men', 'magicians' and 'kings' from the East. None of these designations is precisely correct; in actuality, they were probably a combination of all of these descriptions. Scholars believe that they were from the Parthian empire, Rome's enemy to the east of Palestine, against whom Herod and his successors guarded the frontiers on Rome's behalf. Zoroastrian clerics, they probably did watch the heavens for manifestations of light; as seers who interpreted these lights, they were advisers to their rulers. Because of some obscure references in the sources, there is speculation that at one point the magi took control of their country as theocratic rulers (Horsley 2001b: 155–8). The lesbian religious leader Nancy Wilson has even suggested that they may have been eunuch priests who would then have been three 'queens' (Wilson 1995: 131–2)! Their appearance on the scene has been sentimentalized in story and song, their treasure chests and star made much of, and their importance to the narrative explained by anti-Semitic interpreters as an example of 'pagan' openness to Jesus Christ, in contrast to the 'faithless Jews' (represented by King Herod) who rejected their Messiah.

There is something wrong with this picture, however. The story of the magi must not be trivialized or sentimentalized. It is not a charming fairy tale about foreign visitors who arrive a little late for Christmas, but is rather a 'text of terror', for 'no one sings in Matthew's infancy narrative as they do in Luke's; instead they weep' (Garland 1995: 30). As Horsley notes, it is a story with strong historical underpinnings, a realistic depiction of jealousy, paranoia and blood lust on the part of a king who is insecure about his power and will go to any lengths to remain sovereign. The fact that these magi seek the new 'king of the Jews' takes this story into the political realm. A ruler already paranoid would have been terribly threatened by travellers from the very empire he is charged with keeping at bay not only appearing in his palace but asking about a new king, when Herod himself is the only king of the Jews. His tricking of the magi and the subsequent slaughtering of all Jewish baby boys under the age of two could easily have happened, as confirmed by Josephus, who details the death squads that Herod sent out without much provocation.

This is where it becomes important to remember that Matthew's audience would have read or heard this narrative on two levels. On one level, this is a horrendous story of innocent slaughter taking place during Jesus' infancy and threatening God's Chosen One. On a second level, Matthew's audience, encountering this story in the 80s, would have been reminded of the mass carnage suffered by the Jews at the hands of the Romans during the Jewish War just twenty years previously. Palestine was decimated by this war; Herod's marvellous temple was razed, never to be rebuilt. Jews outside of Palestine, hearing of the flight of Joseph, Mary and Jesus to Egypt, would have been mindful of refugees in their own day. (There but for the grace of God go I?) Moreover, the journey of the magi would have resonated even deeper with the Matthean audience of the 80s, when they recalled an actual journey that took place in 66 at the height of the Jewish War: the Roman historians Suetonius and Pliny relate the story of King Tiridates of Armenia (himself called a *magus* by Pliny) who travelled to Rome *accompanied by his magi* to receive his crown directly from the emperor Nero as part of a treaty with Rome (Horsley 1993b: 56–7). The searching of the Matthean magi for a newborn king who was to 'save the people' would have been viewed in stark contrast not only to the brutal Herod in the story but to the entire Roman imperial machinery at the time of the Gospel's composition: 'The obeisance they render is not worship of a divinity, but an act of homage and submission to a political ruler' (Horsley 2001b: 158).

The evangelist's words would penetrate his/her audience's memory of genocide. First, Joseph named the baby 'Jesus' (Matt. 1.21), which could be translated into English as 'Deliverance' – proof that there will be divine deliverance and salvation no matter what happens politically; to name a child Deliverance under the bondage of empire is a radical act, a queer act! Second, Joseph and his family returned home after Herod's death, even though they were still afraid on account of Herod's successor (Matt. 2.20–2) – proof that life will go on, even though tyrannical, colonial, imperialist rule continues. Third, they settled in Nazareth in Galilee (Matt. 2.23), a place known to be politically volatile – a sign that one must never avoid the tyranny in hopes that it will go away but must persevere; or, in the words of Musa Dube, postcolonial feminist biblical interpreter from Botswana, 'To be in the struggle for justice and liberation is, therefore, to be in *a luta continua*, the struggle that always continues' (Dube 2000: 197).

The slaughter of the innocents and the flight of the Holy Family to Egypt and their eventual return should resonate strongly with queer readers. Domestic terror such as this is not unknown in our contemporary world, as seen in the government-sponsored death squads of El Salvador, Nicaragua and Guatemala, and in the loss of civil rights in the USA subsequent to the terrorist attacks of September 11, 2001. Every day we are confronted with right-wing propaganda in a culture of fear created by a president who, like Herod, is insecure in his power and scapegoats the gay and lesbian community. Queers are reminded of the government-sponsored genocide in the 1980s and 1990s, when nothing was done to help the thousands of people suffering with Aids because they were seen as expendable elements of the population. Nevertheless, queers also, like Matthew's community, receive good news from this Gospel story, for it assures us that in the midst of such political and social upheaval God's Christ continues to be born – Deliverance! God's angels still surround us and encourage us to venture out of closets of loneliness, despair and degradation – God is with us! God's star still rises in the East and assures us that all is not lost, if we will follow God's leading beyond society's notions of what is appropriate or salvific or even Christian. Who knows? Right this minute, there may be a child being born in the back alley of a bazaar in Baghdad or Khandahar who will lead the world to knowledge of lasting peace and justice. Will s/he live or be slaughtered by imperial forces? What if queer people of conscience lobbied to let all such children live? How queer would that be?

Baptism and Temptation

After telling us that Jesus settled in Nazareth in Galilee (2.23), Matthew skips ahead to the beginning of Jesus' public ministry (3.13). Why does Matthew leave out Jesus' formative years? No one knows; the best answer may be that given by John Shelby Spong, who reminds us that a person's origins do not become important until s/he does something noteworthy in later life (Spong 1992: 59). Nevertheless, for queer readers of Matthew who wish to read the silence, the omission of Jesus' childhood and teenaged years gives us permission to dismiss early years that do not bear remembering – family traumas, schoolyard baiting, verbal and physical queer-bashing, the feeling of 'not fitting in' or that our first crushes were somehow shameful. Jesus prefaces his public ministry with two events that can inform a queer reading of Matthew – baptism and subsequent temptation in the wilderness. The gay mystic Andrew Harvey sees Jesus as God's Divine Child, a model and guide for each of us in order that we might become divine children; in describing Jesus as a sort of 'avatar', Harvey delineates eight thresholds through which all human beings must progress, the first two of which are Baptism and Temptation (Harvey 1998: 93).

Jesus was baptized, an event that each of the canonical Gospels records in its own way (Matt. 3.13–17; Mark 1.9–11; Luke 3.21–2; John 1.32–4). I agree with Harvey that baptism is the first threshold Christians must cross in our faith journey.[6] In a queer context, I believe baptism symbolizes the 'coming out' process, whereby gay and lesbian persons finally come to terms with who we

---

6 I believe that the newness baptism represents can be encountered by everyone, Christian or non-Christian, queer or non-queer, but, because 'baptism' is a term with uniquely Christian symbolism, I do not presume to claim its significance for those on other paths to the divine. In my opinion, one of the dangers of Christian theology and missiology is its claim to 'the Truth', what some have rightly labelled 'Christian imperialism' (Gillis 1998: 28).

are and seek to shed the homophobia that has accrued in our psyches during the formative years. The coming out process 'cleanses' the queer person so that s/he is able to preach good news without the impediment of past baggage. Nor is it limited to gay/lesbian queers: I believe that every person who is 'queer' according to my earlier definition has to 'come out' and be 'baptized' into non-heteronormativity; my own father is a wonderful example of a heterosexual man who 'came out' as the father of a gay son and is now a champion of homosexual rights in church and society; but, like my own coming out, his was a process that did not happen overnight.

A Roman Catholic theologian, Ronald Rolheiser, has asserted, 'To submit to love is to be baptized' (Rolheiser 1996: 173). A queering of Jesus' baptism will indeed see the queer person as submitting to God's love, despite what history, contemporary events and God's churches tell us. God's love, for all people, never lets us go. Until we recognize it and, yes, submit to it, we will not be able to succeed as authentic persons who are children of God. Coming out as an act of self-love is not only a baptismal sacrament but a threshold we must cross in our journey to self-actualization. Moreover, we cannot hope to touch others by word or act as Jesus did (what the medieval theologian Meister Eckhart called 'being other Christs'; see Fox 1988: 121) until we are willing to have enough love for ourselves to share all of who we are with others. This is the love that casts out all fear (1 John 4.18) – fear of rejection, fear of marginalization, fear of physical injury. It is a love rooted in faith that God loved us enough to create us as we are; we should thus love God enough to submit to his/her love for us.

A second threshold queers must cross as we learn from the life of Jesus is temptation (Matt. 4.1–11). Matthew tells us that as soon as he was baptized, Jesus was 'led by the Spirit into the wilderness to be tempted by the devil' (4.1). As soon as he had acknowledged God's love for him and been called God's Beloved Child (3.17), he was subjected to forces that would tear him away from that love. And so it is with God's beloved queer children: often, when we have achieved a measure of success in our coming out process or our quest for liberty, forces gather around to weaken our self-esteem, rob us of our divine birthright which is God's unconditional love and non-judgement, and strip us of whatever progress we have made. This is exactly what 'the devil' (a metaphor for the human evil in our world) tries to do to Jesus. S/he offers him material comfort, physical safety, wealth and power if he will but turn away from God and bow down to the ungodly. Queer lives encounter these forces daily. Politicians and even our own leaders suggest that perhaps we should settle for civil unions rather than marriage; bosses and church leaders urge us to be less flamboyant or strident in order to get ahead; family and partners dangle economic and erotic pleasures before us – if we will agree to somehow back away from the love of self that knowledge of God's unconditional love engenders in us. The message for all people, but especially queer people of faith, is that one cannot enjoy the release of baptism into God's love without the lure of temptation from outsiders. With Jesus, we can draw from the power of the divine love in order to vanquish those other forces and continue onward toward the message and the ministry that God would have us share with others.

Message: The Reign/Rule/Empire of God

It is virtually undisputed that the core of Jesus' message was what most Bibles call 'the kingdom of God', a translation of the Greek words *hē basileia tou theou*. Matthew tells us that Jesus started his ministry by proclaiming, 'Repent, for the kingdom of heaven has come near' (4.17). (Matthew uses 'heaven' for 'God' as a circumlocution, in keeping with the Jewishness of this Gospel; Judaism does not pronounce or write the Divine Name.) I prefer to translate the word *basileia* with verbal 'action' words such as 'reign' or 'rule' because this shows that God's *basileia* is active and immediate among us, not a specific place where we go at some appointed time. For me, the word *basileia* carries both a temporal and spatial connotation: Jesus was telling the crowds, 'The *place* and *time* of God's power is *here* and *now*.' That was indeed good news for people who had been held in bondage by a series of foreign governments and by a native aristocracy and priesthood in cahoots with the forces of empire. Moreover, we must take literally the Greek verb *metanoieō*, which modern Bibles render 'repent', but which actually means to 'change one's mind'. Jesus was empowering for the colonized of his day a change of mind involving how the oppressed saw themselves, their oppressors, and God's love. Jesus' announcement of the Reign of God was meant to let people know that no other ruler or government or religion or hierarchy could hold sway over their lives; only God could. When they changed their minds and realized they were not helpless victims but God's beloved, they would be able to do something about changing their lives, both internally and externally. For contemporary queer people, this proffering of the Reign of God through Jesus' preaching affirms for us that, although we may be second-class citizens in much of the world, although we are unable to marry and may have our children taken from us, although in many places it is a crime to express our love, nevertheless in the Reign of God (the place where *God* rules) there is freedom and liberation for all people. Queer empowerment requires each of us to proclaim this good news to all we meet. By queering the status quo – stirring it up and spoiling it – we can help to make that Reign of God a more present reality day by day.

In today's world, especially in light of political events during the last decade, perhaps it is even better to translate Jesus' primary way of speaking about God's control as 'the Empire of God' (Carter 2000: 119) or 'God's imperial rule' (Funk 1994: ix), for to do so acknowledges the politico-religious context within which both Jesus himself and Matthew's audience lived. The anti-imperial subtext in Jesus' message would have been particularly apparent in Galilee, where all four evangelists relate that Jesus began his ministry (Matt. 4.12; Mark 1.14; Luke 4.14; John 2.1), for Galilee was a hotbed of anti-imperial sentiment and the setting for several messianic movements: 'Jesus launched a mission of social renewal among subject peoples . . . [and] acted to heal the effects of empire and to summon people to rebuild their community life' (Horsley 2003: 105).

It is no accident that the famous 'Sermon on the Mount' (Matt. 5–7) – where a significant amount of Jesus' teaching occurs in Matthew – is situated by the author immediately after s/he states not only the location of Jesus' ministry (politically volatile Galilee) but also its content (the Empire of God). These clues alert the reader that Jesus' teaching in the Sermon on the Mount should be read from a postcolonial perspective; in other words how would people at the margins of society receive his message? When looked at in this way, I believe that Jesus' message as conveyed by this evangelist is also able to inform a queer reading; if the author meant Jesus' message to be especially relevant to the marginal and colonized of his day, might it not be similarly relevant to those marginalized and colonized by heteronormativity in today's world?

The Beatitudes (Matt. 5.3–12): Both Luke and Matthew record 'beatitudes' ('blessings') as a way of showing how Jesus mediated God's love to the crowds who followed him. Scholarly consensus indicates that these two evangelists probably used a common source (labelled 'Q' by scholars for the German *quelle*, 'source'), editing it to suit their different theological agendas. Some scholars claim that Luke preserves the original sense of these beatitudes and that Matthew 'spiritualizes' them; for example, Luke writes, 'Blessed are you who are poor' and 'blessed are you who are hungry now' (Luke 6.20–1), whereas Matthew has Jesus say, 'Blessed are the poor in spirit' and 'blessed are those who hunger and thirst for righteousness' (Matt. 5.3, 6). These scholars suggest that Matthew 'domesticated' the radical message of social change spoken by Luke's Jesus, changing it into a promise of intangible spiritual comfort to arrive sometime in the future (Harrington 1991: 82–3). Such an interpretation, however, flies in the face of the imperial context in which Matthew composed this Gospel.

A different interpretation has been suggested by William Herzog. Utilizing the cross-cultural social-scientific work of James Scott and Paolo Freire, Herzog notes that oppressed people often speak in 'coded' language which differs according to whether the speaker is 'on stage' (in public or among the oppressors) or 'off stage' (in private or among other oppressed); the public record of the oppressed may therefore be examined for a 'hidden transcript' that reveals their actual, inner feelings (Herzog 2000: 194).

I believe that this is how Matthew's Beatitudes should be viewed. Matthew, writing in the imperial context of (perhaps) Antioch, with its daily reminders of imperial oppression and the not-so-distant memory of Jewish decimation by the Romans, may have been led to couch Jesus' socially revolutionary rhetoric in softer language, less blatantly offensive to imperial rulers and their minions; or, Jesus himself may have spoken in such a codified 'hidden transcript', and it is Luke who made changes to, in effect, 'decode' it.

Clearly, Jesus' reference to God's *basileia* would have set up the audience to anticipate what follows in an anti-imperial fashion and interpret it against the status quo: 'God wants the best for you (but the Romans don't); God wants you to be prosperous and free (but the Romans don't); God loves you (but the Roman's don't).' When oppressed people speak or write in this way, when confronted they can innocently say, 'I don't know what you're talking about' or 'I didn't mean it that way,' but the hidden transcript is there for other oppressed people to recognize. We see this in the queer community – 'in' jokes, words or phrases that mean something different to queers than to non-queers, non-normative readings of novels, plays or films, and so on. The inferences are there but coded, and one needs to be part of the intended audience to break the code and engage in what one might call 'homotextuality'.

Torah interpretation (Matt. 5.17–48): Matthew's examples of how Jesus interprets the Torah may be looked at in similar fashion. Reading the Sermon
on the Mount through the lens of the Reign of God, one is able to see Jesus'
remarks concerning what the law says about murder, adultery, divorce, swearing, revenge, or treatment of enemies in a new light – as a way of telling the
marginalized of his own day (the peasants of Galilee) and the audience of
Matthew's day (those still colonized by Rome) that the normative way of
interpreting God's commands is not the only way. William Herzog contrasts
a 'great tradition' emanating from Jerusalem with a 'little tradition' that circulated in the villages of Galilee. The great tradition, represented in Matthew
by those Judaeans in league with the Roman government, sets great store by
codified law and the trappings of ritual, while the little tradition, represented
by Jesus and his followers, reflects the continuing importance of oral tradition
as 'resistance to the imposition of the great tradition backed by temple state,
client kingship, and Roman rule' (Herzog 2000: 99). Moreover, this was not a
strictly religious struggle, inasmuch as those who wielded religious power
were those who had gained political and economic power through alliances
with empire.

According to this little tradition, all of God's laws and human behaviour
must be gauged according to God's love, which is perfect. Jesus in Matthew
commends the crowds to become perfect as God is (5.48) – to reach that amount
of love that will fulfil God's law. 'The "kingdom of God" language used by
Jesus . . . is the way life and society would be if a compassionate God were in
charge or imitated instead of Roman governors, client kings, and the Temple
establishment' (Nelson-Pallmeyer 2001: 174).

Jesus' Torah interpretation is what ultimately brings him into conflict
with other Jewish teachers. Matthew's day shared commonality with Jesus'
in that there was no one, definitive Judaism, but several vying for attention
and respectability. This is reflected in Matthew's Gospel, in which Torah and
temple are major issues of controversy in Jesus' confrontations with scribes,
Pharisees, Sadducees, and others, who believe that they should be the sole
arbiters of the ancestral faith. This would have resonated with Matthew's
Christian Jewish community as it struggled with other Jewish communities
over how to view Torah; that is, whether proper interpretation and fulfilment
of the law was through Jesus himself or the rabbis (the spiritual successors
of the Pharisees), who sought to control Jewish practice and policy after the
temple was destroyed. This is why Matthew's Gospel is able to be used in
an anti-Semitic fashion by readers who are not careful to place it in its context: it is tempting to see stark contrasts (Jesus, right, vs. Pharisees, wrong;
Christianity, good, vs. Judaism, bad; letter of the law, bad, vs. spirit of the law,
good; Christian freedom, good, vs. Jewish legalism, bad; etc.), instead of recognizing the characteristics of an interreligious dispute in which no one group
is absolutely right or wrong (see Saldarini 1994: 44–8, 87–90). One sees this
today in the queer community in the often acrimonious debate between 'religion' and 'spirituality', in which any sort of organized faith tradition is viewed
as homophobic and inimical to genuine spirituality, or eastern traditions are
automatically judged more liberating than western ones. What should be central in any spiritual discussion is the Love that God/the Divine/the Ultimate

(whatever we choose to call 'It') has for all people. This Love must manifest Itself in justice, equality, liberty and empowerment, or it will be perverted; this is the message of all of the world's great religious teachings, including Jesus'. If one carefully examines each of the verses of Matthew's Sermon on the Mount, it is plain to see this Love motivating each statement of Jesus about how best to fulfil God's Torah.

Matthew's Gospel features other blocks of teaching material outside of the Sermon on the Mount which add to Matthew's overall portrayal of God's Reign/Rule/Empire as Jesus' central teaching and contribute to a queer reading of this Gospel. For example:

Parables: Jesus described the Reign of God in the figurative language of parables, utilizing familiar images from everyday life. The *Galilean parables* in Matthew 13 are directed toward peasants who labour far from the Jerusalem temple and its politico-religious elite, yet are expected to pay tithe, tax and tribute, often exhausting themselves and their fields in the process. Warren Carter notes that, by the time the audience encounters these parables, it already knows a great deal about the nature of God's Empire:

- It is manifested in Jesus' words and deeds.
- It is God's gracious gift, initiative and action.
- It resists, rather than endorses, Rome's empire.
- It is divisive; some welcome it, while others, especially the elite, resist God's claim.
- It is disruptive and disturbing, reversing previous commitments, imperial structures, practices and priorities, while creating a new way of life which counters dominant social values.
- It conflicts and competes with the devil's reign.
- It is present in part, but for many life remains unchanged.
- Its present manifestation will be completed when God's Reign is established over all, including Rome's empire. (Carter 2000: 280)

Each parable confirms one of these aspects of God's imperial rule and by implication contrasts it with that of Rome: 'The focus on God's empire and its eventual triumph over all things implies the demise of Rome' (Carter 2000: 281). Moreover, previous hints about the nature of God's *basileia* alert the audience to expect the unexpected. May this not be said also of the type of 'queerings' that this commentary presents? In the same way that such new biblical interpretations stir up and spoil the status quo, are disruptive and disturbing, welcome to some and not to others, and present a view of how life could be when the empire of heteronormativity has fallen, these parables of Jesus queer the status quo of Roman hegemony in the world of rural Palestine.

Thus, when one looks at the Parable of the Weeds and Wheat (Matt. 13.24–30), one would expect to be told that the weeds and wheat should not be allowed to grow together. Instead, Jesus tells his listeners that they should not be disturbed until they are fully grown, and then the harvesters will make the separation. What does this tell us about the Reign of God Jesus announced? That room is left for surprises and for unexpected outcomes! Someone labelled a 'weed' in early life may eventually turn out to be 'wheat'; our own ideas of what constitutes wheat and weed may even change over time. This is in congruence with Jesus' remarks elsewhere about not judging others (Matt. 7.1–5), and is essential for a queer theology of becoming, which recognizes God's presence in our lives as dynamic, progressive and non-static, thus confirming contemporary views concerning the fluidity of all sexuality (Mollenkott 2001).

Matthew immediately follows this parable with the parables of the Mustard Seed (13.31–2) and the Leaven in the Flour (13.33), both of which confirm the unsettling, unpredictable nature of God's Reign. The mustard seed is 'the smallest' of seeds, yet grows to gigantic proportions and is able to become a home for diverse birds. This accords with Jesus' description of the *basileia* as a generous offer on God's part, open to all and welcoming of disparate groups. (See below regarding Jesus' enactment of this inclusivity in his healings, exorcisms and feedings.) Moreover, John Dominic Crossan has noted that the mustard seed was even considered dangerous, for it was uncontainable and could ruin a field – 'a pungent shrub with dangerous, take-over properties' (Crossan 1995: 65). In the same way, leaven, while necessary for baking, is also potentially subversive and dangerous to the end-result, for too much of it ruins the bread. Leaven is a corrupting agent that transforms the dough even as it corrupts (Carter 2000: 291). This dangerous, unstoppable, subversive quality is what Jesus compares to God's Reign. This reign will 'run amok', ruining Roman power and the perquisites of the Jewish aristocracy as it shares God's abundance with everyone in its wake. Then and now, it 'queers' the status quo (corrupting its corruption?), as it stirs up and spoils what has been spoiled by human greed and unfaithfulness to God.

The *Judaean parables* (Matt. 20–21, 25), on the other hand, while they are no doubt still directed toward the poorer elements of society, are nevertheless designed to be overheard by those in power who are living at the expense of the poor. Therefore, one detects in the Judaean parables an element of harshness and judgement not found in the Galilean stories. Moreover, as Jesus' imagery becomes more strident, he knowingly moves closer and closer to his death in Jerusalem as a political insurgent. Thus, these parables must be examined for how they contribute to the Romans' and religious authorities' fear and suspicion of Jesus, with a view toward how they can further inform a queer reading of Matthew's Gospel.

The parable of the Vineyard (Matt. 20.1–16) demonstrates that in God's realm all are to be treated the same. Jesus compares God to a householder who treats all employees equally, even though they have different levels of seniority and have performed differently. Such egalitarianism complements the rest of Jesus' ministry, both word and deeds, in its indictment of a society in which the imperial rulers and those local elite who serve them control the majority of the wealth and material possessions, while those who are the most numerous have the least. 'Instead of using wages to reinforce distinctions, [the householder] uses them to express equality and solidarity' (Carter 2000: 397). God's generosity is thus held up as the standard by which human behaviour is to be measured; moreover, God, like the householder, urges human beings not to begrudge each other the bounty of God's Reign, where there is enough for everyone: 'Friend, I am doing you no wrong [by being generous to another]' (Matt. 20.13). Moreover, it illustrates the 'alternative household' that

Jesus advocates in his preaching and activities (Carter 2000: 376–7; Moxnes 2003: 45; see further below). A queer reading of this parable encourages us to see God's unconditional love as so amazing and open-ended that humans should not become involved in trying to measure it out or gauge its worth; we should all see to our own relationships with the Divine, whatever they may be, and leave the rest up to God. It is directly after this parable that Jesus tells his disciples that 'the Human One' will be handed over to the religious authorities for condemnation and then to the presiding government to be executed (Matt. 20.18–19). In using the ambiguous term *huios tou anthrōpou*[7] (usually rendered 'Son of Man'), Jesus is indicating not only his own treatment but also the treatment that the prototypical human person receives when s/he does God's will and opposes the status quo. For queer readers, this reinforces the importance of speaking our truth in hostile situations no matter what.

Another, much more disturbing, story about agricultural life is the parable of the Tenants (Matt. 21.33–41); however, Jesus here does not specifically compare the owner of the land to God. There are two ways of interpreting this parable: (1) The more traditional reading is to see the vineyard as representing Israel, which has been parcelled out to the Hebrew people for production; the slaves and the heir are those who represent God – the prophets first and then Jesus – while the 'wicked' tenants are those Jews who have not kept covenant with God. According to this interpretation, 'the Jews' (that is, the non-Christian Jewish leaders who oppose Matthew's community) rejected God's gifts and God's heir and will be punished accordingly by having control of Israel taken from them. Matthew is thus directing this parable against those Jews who have not accepted Jesus' way of fulfilling the Torah, as part of the Matthean Christian Jewish community's ongoing struggle with non-Christian Jews (Saldarini 1994: 58–60).

(2) An alternative way of reading the parable is according to the notion of subversive speech, hidden transcript, and counternarrative, as Warren Carter and William Herzog understand these terms. When seen in this way, the story becomes a codified way of referring to the peasant uprisings that were occurring in Palestine as a result of excessive production demands and exhaustive taxation. The vineyard is the ancestral land of Israel that has been overrun by foreign empires; the 'owner' of the vineyard, rather than referring to God, may be seen as referring to Rome itself, encroaching on peasants' lands and making excessive demands upon them; the slaves and heir sent as representatives may be seen as the Herodian aristocracy and the priests who demand their share of the produce and keep track of the land's production for Rome. According to this reading, Jesus is alluding to the peasant rebellions of his time as the logical outcome of imperial and aristocratic greed; the owner of the vineyard, far from referring to God, stands for Rome, who systematically and quickly crushed such peasant uprisings with armed force (Horsley 1993a). The

---

7 This phrase is a Semitism imported into the Greek from Hebrew and Aramaic, where it was used as a circumlocution for 'I' or in a generic sense for 'human being'; scholars disagree as to Jesus' use of this term, some believing that in addition to these two commonplace uses, he also used the phrase to refer to a divine being such as the One referred to in Daniel 7.14. (See Wink 2002.)

'wretches' who are put to a miserable death (Matt. 21.41) are the poor peasants, and the use of the word 'wretch' shows Jesus' solidarity with them. When read in this way, the Matthean postscript to the parable (Matt. 21.42–4) makes sense: Jesus tells the listeners that 'the stone that the builders rejected has become the cornerstone'; rather than stretching this scriptural reference to refer to Jesus himself, it may now be seen as referring to the entire peasant population of Palestine that has been rejected and subjected but is 'amazing' in God's eyes. More importantly, Jesus' statement that the vineyard (Israel) will be taken away from 'you and given to a people that produces the fruits of the kingdom' may now be seen as referring to the wresting of Israel away from imperial rulers and Herodian retainers that have decimated it and its return to the people of God's own choice (Nelson-Pallmeyer 2001: 256–8; Herzog 1994: 178–83).

The second interpretation would be more attractive to a queer reading of the parable, for a queer reading would see Jesus as stirring up the status quo, fighting for the victims who cannot fight for themselves, and punishing those who have dared to assert their colonial power over others in a world that should belong to the liberating love of the Divine. Additionally, such a reading logically explains why it is at this juncture that the chief priests and Pharisees begin to search for ways to arrest Jesus (Matt. 21.45–6): their well-being was being threatened by this upstart prophet from Galilee, who was inciting the crowds to further insurgent activity.

In a queer context, the connection is obvious: our future well-being (both physical and spiritual) depends upon how we treat others in the here and now. Those gays and lesbians in positions of privilege who collude with the hetero-elite powers-that-be are to see the error of their ways; they, like the Jewish sycophants whose prosperity came at the expense of the peasant people, will have to account to the Divine for how they used their God-given talents and did or did not reach out to the suffering 'human ones' in their paths. This is why I believe it is so important for queer people of every orientation to come out – so that the oppressors may know who we are, how we live, where we work and play, how we are different from the token visible 'A-gays' who have been co-opted by the system – that we are not and will never be like everyone else. We might be able to 'pass' for a short time, but not in the long run. No oppressed group can ever hope to gain the respectability of 'normalcy', for those who make up 'the normal' have never laboured under oppression; if tomorrow, all of the marginalized were suddenly 'free', they would still have generations of bondage behind them, informing their context (see Warner 1999). In this regard, Jesus' call to 'change your mind' since the Reign of God is at hand is a call to leave respectability behind and to enter, in the words of the Norwegian queer biblical scholar Halvor Moxnes, 'queer space' (Moxnes 2003: 91).

Family and eunuchs: In recent years, several scholars have noted that in his *basileia* message Jesus opposed the traditional patriarchal family and encouraged an alternative family. Recognition of this is essential for a queer interpretation of Jesus and the Gospels, especially Matthew's, which includes the mysterious saying about 'eunuchs',

... for the 'traditional family' is the bulwark not only of patriarchy but also of heterosexism. A gay-affirmative theology and ethics has the responsibility

of challenging the hegemony of a system of values and structures that produce and reproduce heterosexism and homophobia. . . . [T]he Jesus tradition,
as we have it in the Gospels, transmits a fundamental critique of marriage
and family values. (Jennings 2003: 172, citing Ruether 2000: 25–8)

The patriarchal family was the basic unit of both the Jewish community and
Roman imperial society. The male head-of-household ('father') had absolute
power over the members of his family, their property and possessions, including slaves. Caesar, as the emperor of the entire Roman world, was the ultimate
'father', for all power descended from him and moved outward from him at
his pleasure. Thus, there was a system of brokered power through which those
under Roman rule lived daily. For the Jews, this was confirmed by their sacred
scriptures, which gave power of life and death to the father of the family and
(male) heads of the tribes (Carter 2000: 376–7).[8]

Jesus' message of the Reign or Empire of God was a signal that all would
not be business-as-usual for either Rome or Israel. Matthew 19–20 contains
sayings and stories that address the three primary relationships of households
in Jesus' time: husbands–wives, fathers–children, masters–slaves. 'But while
the chapters utilize this household structure, they do not endorse this cultural
norm. Rather, siding with some other minority cultural views, the two chapters subvert this hierarchical and patriarchal structure by instructing disciples in a more egalitarian pattern' (Carter 2000: 376–7). Thus, in his teaching on
divorce (Matt. 19.3–9), Jesus counsels mutuality between a husband and wife,
rather than affirming the traditional laws of divorce that favoured the husband. Jesus asserts the importance of children, who in ancient societies were
particularly powerless, by saying that 'it is to such as these that the kingdom
of heaven belongs' (Matt. 19.14). The parable of the Vineyard (Matt. 20.1–16),
discussed above, shows a master behaving beneficently toward his slaves.
Moreover, when Zebedee's wife asks Jesus for the pride of place in his 'kingdom' for her two sons (Matt. 20.20–3), he dismisses her, refusing to assume the
role of father over his followers. Instead, he makes a pointed criticism of the
Roman hierarchical order by telling his disciples that they are not to 'lord it
over' one another as the Gentiles do; on the contrary, they are to be in service
to one another – 'whoever wishes to be first among you must be your slave',
just like the Human One, the quintessential human person (Matt. 20.24–8).
While it is true that Jesus does not condemn the institution of slavery, he does
point out by his use of slave/servant language that there is nothing shameful
or inferior about being a slave; in fact, Jesus could even be saying that until the
patriarchal world passes away it would be preferable to be a slave than to be
in power.

Additionally, the author of Matthew's Gospel has adopted anti-familial
statements of Jesus from both Mark's Gospel (Matt. 12.46–50; 13.53–8; 19.27–30)

8 Of course, for every rule there are exceptions; thus, one sees female leaders in
Judaism such as Esther and Deborah. Their power, while important for showing
women's participation in Israel, only serves to highlight that the majority of rulers,
priests and scribes were male and that the Jewish cultus and society were patriarchal
in nature.

and the sayings source Q (Matt. 10.34–6). Jesus states unequivocally that he is not just creating an alternative household but is out to destroy the traditional home, for in God's Empire, unlike Rome's, traditional arrangements of power and brokerage avail one nothing; God's Empire is all about the type of service which is freely given, not for what one will receive in return, but because it is the right thing to do.

For Jesus' queer audience, it becomes clear that Jesus affirms the loyalty to justice and truth that supersedes the traditional family. In God's 'kin-dom', non-traditional relationships are given pride of place, for they are often more authentic because they are not in thrall to patterns of domination (Isasi-Díaz 2003: 163). Like the earliest followers of Jesus to whom Matthew was speaking, queer readers must join the 'Empire of Heaven' instead of (for them) the Roman empire or (for us) the 'empire of heteropatriarchy'. Theodore Jennings believes this is why Matthew insists that in God's Empire God is the only father allowed (Matt. 23.9); earthly fathers pervert God's will (Jennings 2003: 184). Thus, a postcolonial queer reading of Jesus' message according to Matthew requires a reordering of priorities that those who labour in the service of empire cannot accomplish.

In this examination of Jesus' call to form alternative households, the work of Halvor Moxnes is invaluable. Moxnes reads Matthew according to a 'politics of space', demonstrating that Jesus' physical movements in the Gospels mirror his inner, ideological movement. Jesus deliberately withdraws from the patriarchal household and gives up his male prerogatives; his leaving home in Nazareth is a turning away not only from his biological family but from the hegemony of patriarchy. He and his disciples are 'displaced persons' by virtue of their egalitarian and non-conformist relationships to one another and their deliberate flouting of traditional gender roles (Moxnes 2003: 72–3); the men are itinerant preachers who do not support the family, while the women among them take care of them from their own financial means. Jesus has left 'male space' and entered what Moxnes dares to call 'queer space' (2003: 89–90). Thus, Moxnes confirms what I have been saying throughout this discussion on Jesus' notion of God's Reign, which for Moxnes is 'queer in the sense that it questions identities and blurs distinctions' (2003: 113).

Matthew is the only evangelist to include Jesus' saying about 'eunuchs' in his remarks about marriage. When the disciples suggest that because Jesus' policy on divorce is so stringent, perhaps it is better not to marry, Jesus replies:

> Not everyone can accept this teaching, but only those for whom it is meant. For there are eunuchs who were born that way, and there are eunuchs who have been made so by others, and there are those who have made themselves eunuchs because of the rule of heaven. Let anyone receive this message who can. (Matt. 19.11–12; author's translation)

Queer scholars have pointed out that two of the three categories of eunuch enumerated by Jesus are fairly easy to figure out: those who have been made eunuchs by others are those men who have been castrated, perhaps because of enforced prostitution, slavery and/or conquest of war. Those who have made themselves eunuchs might be those such as the priests of the Mother Goddess (known as the *galli*) who castrate themselves or those who deliberately refrain from procreation (Wilson 1995: 128–9; Jennings 2003: 148–50). But what about those eunuchs who 'were born that way'? Essentialists who believe that it is possible to locate 'gay people' throughout history would say that this refers to those whom we call homosexual. Though I am not a strict essentialist, I do know that I did not intentionally choose my sexual orientation; however, recent studies have shown that sexuality is much more fluid than we might expect and cannot be so easily categorized and labelled (see Queen and Schimel 1997). Could Jesus not be referring to a broad category of people who, from their birth, have not 'fitted' the predominant expectations of gender and sexuality? In effect, Jesus in this saying about eunuchs has not only entered queer space, but has 'queered' the discussion of marriage. Theodore Jennings concurs with this conclusion:

> The saying of Jesus is scandalous, linking together hermaphrodites or persons who engaged exclusively in same-sex practices, men castrated for purposes of prostitution, and persons who castrated themselves in religious frenzy. Like many of Jesus' sayings, this one is shocking in daring to link the reign of God with apparently absurd or outrageous behaviour. . . . The saying in Matthew's Gospel . . . associates followers of Jesus who have renounced family structures with stigmatized or marginalized groups in the hellenistic world . . . (Jennings 2003: 153)

Moxnes goes further and suggests that 'eunuch' in Matthew's contextual world could have been a slur levelled against those young men in the Jesus Movement who left home and household and followed him, thus 'putting themselves "out of place"' and 'represent[ing] a provocation to the very order of the community' (Moxnes 2003: 72). He notes that, although there is strong evidence that Matthew 19.11–12 is a saying of the historical Jesus, these verses have not been discussed much by Jesus scholars, perhaps 'because the image of *eunuch* threatens common presuppositions about Jesus as a male figure' (Moxnes 2003: 72). I believe that Moxnes has hit on an essential concept for a queer understanding of Jesus: today there are many for whom the word 'queer' is a volatile word, since it originated as a slur among our opponents, but activists and others have reclaimed the word and use it proudly. In the same way, according to Moxnes, the word 'eunuch' originated as a derogatory epithet applied to Jesus and his company by their opponents to cast aspersions on their masculinity, but instead, 'Jesus picked up the word and accepted it' (Moxnes 2003: 75). This is another example of coded speech on the part of Jesus, signalled by the remarks which bracket Matthew's eunuch saying: 'Not everyone can accept this teaching, but only those for whom it is meant' and 'Let anyone receive this message who can.'

Sean Freyne has recently demonstrated that the hallmark of Jesus' Judaism was his concentration on the compassion of God, the goodness of God's creation, and his acceptance of the inclusive Israel envisioned by Isaiah, while his opponents preferred the more exclusive priestly and scribal interpretations of God and Israel found in Leviticus, Deuteronomy, Ezra and Nehemiah. According to Freyne, it was this radical dream of an inclusive, reconstituted

Zion that drove Jesus to travel to Jerusalem and his ultimate death (Freyne 2004: 110–21). Matthew's Gospel repeatedly portrays Jesus as fulfilling prophecies from the book of Isaiah. His saying about eunuchs mirrors Isaiah's statement of inclusivity for those returning from exile:

> Do not let the eunuch say, 'I am just a dry tree.' For thus says God: To the eunuchs who keep my sabbaths, who choose the things that please me and hold fast my covenant, I will give, in my house and within my walls, a monument and a name better than sons and daughters; I will give them an everlasting name that shall not be cut off. (Isaiah 56.3–5, adapted)

Thus, Matthew 19.11–12 is one more example of Jesus' message of inclusivity toward those who were marginalized,[9] which is reflected even more in his physical acts of ministry, to which we now turn.

Activity: Exorcisms, Healings and Feedings

Jesus' message of the arrival of God's *basileia* is acted out in his public demonstrations of God's unconditional justice-love through exorcisms, healings and feedings. I do not propose a comprehensive discussion of these three elements of Jesus' ministry activity; rather, I will comment upon several instances from Matthew's Gospel that clarify the radical inclusivity of such Christic practices and their ramifications for a queer reading of Matthew.

Exorcism: Exorcism is really a type of healing in which a supposed evil occupant is driven from its human subject. Many bodily disorders with physical-emotional symptoms now classified as mental illnesses such as schizophrenia and multiple personality disorder were perceived in the ancient world as the result of demon possession. Matthew mentions several instances of Jesus casting out evil spirits from possessed persons (Matt. 4.24; 8.16; 9.32–3), but the most extensive treatment of exorcism is found in 8.28–33, which Matthew has adapted (and shortened) from Mark 5.1–20, the story of the Gadarene demoniac. Unlike Mark, Matthew provides few details about this event or the persons involved. Matthew's purpose in including this story is to show that the demons recognize Jesus as God's Son; they know that the time of their reign has come to an end with the presence of Jesus (Garland 1995: 101–2). The act of exorcism on Jesus' part demonstrates that the Reign of God that

---

9 The Lutheran pastor and biblical scholar Frederick Gaiser has asserted that Isaiah 56 may be used by today's Christian Church to speak 'a new word' of inclusivity to a Church which is being torn apart by conflicts over homosexuality. He explains that the community which produced Isaiah 56 championed inclusion of outsiders, contrary to the followers of Ezra and Nehemiah, who were attempting to reconstitute Israel as an exclusivist sect and using Deuteronomy in the Torah to do it. However, '[e]ventually, both the universalistic perspective of Isaiah 56 and the protectionist view of Ezra and Nehemiah found their way into the biblical canon, leaving the community of God's people, now as then, struggling with the dialectical tension between openness and exclusion . . . [but] God's word will prevail – *even if that entails abrogating a previous divine word*' (Gaiser 1994: 283, 287; emphasis in original).

Jesus has come to announce is in contradistinction to the reign of demons or evil spirits. Moreover, it is offered to those whom others might think of as the most expendable – those who rage out of their minds and live among tombs. To a contemporary audience, Jesus' gracious act is a reminder that those who appear to have the least and be the least materially speaking – the homeless, PWAs, drug users, street thugs, prostitutes and hustlers – are just as deserving in divine terms. A postcolonial reading of Matthew sees his exorcisms as a way of overcoming the evils of imperialism and colonialism that seem incurable.

Healings: Throughout his Gospel, Matthew demonstrates Jesus' availability to heal all sorts of people. Two Matthean healing narratives, however, specify the radically inclusive nature of Jesus' healings, even across boundaries of gender and sexuality.

Matthew 8.5–13 tells the story of a Roman centurion who approaches Jesus to request healing for what most translations render as his 'servant'. However, the Greek calls the one in need of healing the centurion's 'boy' (Greek, *pais*). Theodore Jennings, in his excellent exegeses of homoerotic texts in the Second Testament, has stated, 'Within the Greek-speaking world the term *pais* was regularly used of the male beloved in a same-sex relationship' (Jennings 2003: 133, citing Dover 1978: 16); in some segments of the contemporary queer community, one still hears references to 'a man and his boy'. Moreover, in antiquity it was not uncommon for a master and a slave to be in a pederastic relationship (Lawrence 1989: 70–1; Nissinen 1998: 71). In light of these historical conventions, it is difficult to see this story as the centurion merely requesting healing in order to save a beloved servant, as traditional exegesis has held (Harrington 1991: 114–15). Clearly, the centurion cares deeply for his 'boy'; though a Gentile, he has come to a Jewish healer for relief, admitting that he is not 'worthy' for Jesus to come into his house. According to a queer hermeneutic, might this not be an example of possible shame on the part of the centurion for the type of relationship in which he was involved – one that ancient society frowned upon and refused to canonize with respectability? In fact, it is plausible that Jesus here is tacitly approving a same-sex relationship. Queer interpreters are able to read between the lines and see not only an example of same-sex devotion, but also an instance where Jesus could have condemned the practice of homosexuality but did not; that Matthew intends to highlight this status of master and 'boy' is evidenced by the fact that Luke 7.1–10, which derives from a common source, refers not to the centurion's 'boy', but to his 'slave' (Greek, *doulos*). Moreover, Jesus not only heals the centurion's boy but remarks that he has not found such faithfulness among his own Jewish people (Matt. 8.10).

Matthew 15.21–8 relates a similar story in which another non-Jew, this time a Canaanite woman, is rewarded for her perseverance in her quest for healing for her daughter. Matthew's version of this story even has Jesus himself go so far as to utter a racial slur, comparing Gentiles to 'dogs': 'Jesus answered, "It's not fair to take food meant for children and throw it to dogs." The woman replied, "Indeed, Lord; yet even dogs eat crumbs from the owner's table"' (Matt. 15.26–7; author's translation). Once again, Jesus commends the 'great faith' (Matt. 15.28a) of one who is a non-Jew. However, Jesus seems reluctant at first to minister to this Gentile woman; instead, she must be assertive in getting the treatment she deserves. For this reason, the story has become a favourite among minority biblical interpreters. A queer interpretation of this story remembers that often the Christian Church, like Jesus in the story, is reluctant to give queer folk our just deserts; frequently queer activists must resort to extraordinary means to get a hearing, as in the demonstrations by ACTUP and QueerNation during the height of the US government's non-responsiveness to the Aids crisis (Goss 1993: 147–9). Moreover, Matthew's notion of 'dogs' receiving 'crumbs from the owner's table' carries homotextual connotations, since 'dogs' was used as a term of opprobrium not only of pagans in general but especially of those who committed homosexual acts in the religious service of the Goddess (Jennings 2003: 135). So a queer reading of this encounter with Jesus must take into account this double meaning. Just as feminists see power in the fact that the only person to best Jesus in an argument was a woman and the only person who Jesus says has 'great' faith is a woman (Wainwright 1994b: 650–4), so too queer interpreters must take pride in the fact that when dogs are mentioned as being entitled to crumbs (i.e. a place in the Reign of God), Jesus does not protest but agrees and commends for her great faith the one who suggests this. This saying about the crumbs proves that everyone eats from God's table.

The Jewish feminist Matthean scholar Amy-Jill Levine is reluctant to make too much of the ramifications of Jesus' reaching out to 'unclean' Gentiles, noting that this is another way in which Christian scholars portray Jesus' supersession of Judaism (Levine 2001a: 71–2). Instead, Levine points out that the story of the Canaanite woman, along with the stories of miraculous feeding which bracket it, all discuss bread, which is a symbol of inclusivity. There is bread for all in Matthew, and the feeding miracles include women and children (Levine 1992: 259). In this way, Matthew once again urges his Christian Jewish community to include those who are different, as they struggled to cope, on the one hand, with looming separation from non-Christian Jews and, on the other, with Gentiles joining their ministry (Saldarini 1994: 73). A queering of Matthew sees hope in this radical inclusivity that pushes the justice of God beyond human conventions and comfort levels and will thus even overcome the predisposition of many toward intolerance and homophobia.

Feedings: The theme of nourishment raised in the story of the Canaanite woman is made explicit in the two instances of miraculous feedings that precede and follow her story (Matt. 14.13–21 and 15.32–9). Through these stories, Matthew demonstrates that whenever God's justice-love is at large in the world through acts of radical inclusivity, people's needs are met, for the hospitality of God is infectious. The Empire of God as preached and enacted by Jesus is a place and a state of mind and heart where all people are welcome, where all people are ministered to, and where all people have enough, in contradistinction to Rome's empire of hierarchy, scarcity and fear. Thus, John Dominic Crossan points out that Jesus' 'open commensality' is the determining element of both his message and his danger to the status quo (Crossan 1991: 341–4; see also Borg 1984: 93ff., and Schüssler Fiorenza 1983: 137). One of the major complaints of Jesus' critics was that he ate with those he shouldn't; his radical egalitarianism at table was threatening to those elements of Judaeo-Roman society that fostered separation between people as a way of preserving the imperial status quo. A queer sensibility that seeks to stir up and spoil the status quo of imperial heteronormativity will, like Jesus our Christ, be welcoming of everyone; we who have been kept from many tables, both literally and figuratively, dare not keep others from the table. Our oppressors love it when we give in to horizontal violence and do otherwise! In this regard, one of the most disquieting and painful issues that I see within the queer community is the intolerance and divisiveness found among various segments of our community; for example, rich, privileged 'A-gays' often discriminate against drag queens, the transgendered, leatherfolk, and those whose sexuality is considered 'kinky' or 'bizarre'. Those who are in long-term 'committed' relationships cast aspersions upon those who are single or non-monogamous, while those who are HIV-negative sniff judgementally at those who 'end up' HIV-positive because of their alleged 'promiscuity'. Like Jesus, we must offer God's hospitality to all, especially those whom society renders 'impure'. In our quest for a place at the table, we must never become the 'new Pharisees' in the lavender togas.

Passion and Death

No one knows exactly why Jesus decided to go to Jerusalem. Doctrinal theologians tell us that Jesus submitted to death to provide atonement for human sin. However, there is no real, clear evidence of this in the Gospel texts. I believe that Jesus, encouraged by the Galilean crowds' response to his message of God's Empire, was motivated to travel to the 'symbolic source' of the peasants' difficulties – Jerusalem, where the temple elite colluded with the Herodian courtiers and the Roman provincial government. When he arrives in the city, he is welcomed by the crowds, and the reader experiences the triumph and joy of Jesus' entry into the city of Jerusalem on what would later be known as Palm Sunday (Matt. 21.9–11).

From a queer perspective, the Palm Sunday story empowers us to action – collective action, like the crowds who, in partnership with Jesus, stormed the city of Jerusalem to 'act up'. Like the crowds on Palm Sunday, we must not be silenced. Like Jesus, we must accept our prophetic, Christic role to criticize, change and replace systems and structures in church and society that perpetuate all kinds of oppression, not just homophobia and heteronormativity. We must be in solidarity with all who struggle for equality – women, people of colour, the poor, the aged, the young, the differently abled, and those of questionable gender or sexuality. In doing so, we must constantly ask ourselves what it means to 'come in God's name', what it means to speak and to act 'in God's name'. Do we use God's name in vain, for our own violent and sinful agendas, such as those who bomb abortion clinics in God's name or fly planes into buildings in Allah's name or advocate 'killing a queer for Christ'? Or do we use God's name to lift up the lowly as Mary envisioned in her Magnificat, to create justice and liberation as Mohandas Ghandi and Martin Luther King advocated, and to proclaim good news and the year of God's favour as Jesus did?

This is how the life and ministry of Jesus become paradigmatic for his time and ours: he demonstrated what God was like. He showed in his person a perfect God-consciousness and revealed in his words and his deeds the face of God – One who is with the oppressed, One who tells good news in the midst of bad, One who lifts up and carries those who are crucified by their peers. And because the people saw God in this Jesus, they called him the Son of God and, many years after his death, came to believe that Jesus himself was God. A queering of Jesus Christ recognizes that when we emulate Jesus, we become sons and daughters of God and create God in our midst through the incarnation of the Christ in our bodies, minds and spirits (Bohache 2003).

The events of the last week of Jesus' life are well known and are recorded by all four of the canonical Gospels. Jesus experienced a humiliating and painful death before he was resurrected to new life. In the same way, queer people often encounter humiliation, discrimination, physical and emotional torture and even death; and these travails sometimes inadvertently produce goodness in their wake. The importance of the cross for queers is the possibility of meeting God in our pain and receiving ultimate transcendence; Andrew Harvey sees these painful experiences as cathartic for our Christic becoming (Harvey 1998: 94–5). I concur with Jürgen Moltmann and Robert Goss that God was suffering with Jesus on the cross, that God did not plan the crucifixion but could not necessarily stop it, and that our hope as Christians comes from how God reacted to the crucifixion of Jesus and reacts to contemporary crucifixions (Moltmann 1998: 1–5; Goss 1993: 76–7).

In this regard, the interpretive moment – the hermeneutical key, if you will – for my queer reading of the crucifixion is the death of Matthew Shepard, a gay college student in Laramie, Wyoming, who was beaten, tied to a fence, and abandoned to die alone in the wilderness. I believe that Matthew Shepard is the most famous example of the crucifixions gays and lesbians have endured for generations. Eyewitnesses stated that Matthew looked like a 'scarecrow' on that fence (Ingebretsen 2001: 178–9), but looking through postcolonial eyes I believe he resembled the crucified left by the side of the road in Roman Palestine for others to look upon and know what happens to those who do not know their place in the imperial world. His humiliation and suffering were meant, like the scarecrow, as a warning for queers to 'keep away' from decent people, and, like ancient crucifixions, as an example to queers of what might happen if they 'flaunt' themselves on heteropatriarchal territory.

Nevertheless, despite the horror of his execution, I contend that there was something redemptive above Matthew's experience, inasmuch as it did not go unnoticed, as other atrocities against homosexuals have. The horror and brutality of his death, the perpetrators' insistence that he 'had it coming' because he had 'come on' to them, and the media circus created by homophobic hatemongers at his funeral, served to bring the issue of queer-bashing into the public consciousness, and some steps have been taken to preclude this from happening again. The gay playwright Terrence McNally, in the introduction to the printed version of his play *Corpus Christi*, makes explicit the christological link between Matthew and Jesus: 'Jesus Christ did not die in vain because His disciples lived to spread His story. It is this generation's duty to make certain Matthew Shepard did not die in vain either. We forget his story at the peril of our very lives' (McNally 1998: vi). Like the women who watched Jesus' death from a distance, we mourn these modern-day martyrs, yet also are prepared for the resurrection God has in store for all oppressed and marginalized people.

Beyond Death

The queer theologian Robert Goss has asserted that Easter was the moment when God made Jesus queer. This is when God 'queered' or 'spoiled' the spoiling of God's Son by raising him from the dead. This is when God stirred up the status quo by vindicating the deaths of political martyrs for all time and saying 'no' to the oppressions associated with discrimination in all its forms: 'On Easter, God made Jesus queer in his solidarity with us. In other words, Jesus "came out of the closet" and became the "queer" Christ' (Goss 1993: 84). For Goss, the queer Christ is a Christ who is *for* queers and *is* queer himself, by virtue of representing all of the oppressed throughout history who have been brutalized, killed or simply rendered invisible. This is true atonement, standing in for all of the hurts and slights that have afflicted God's queer sons and daughters for millennia (Goss 1993: 85).

This queer Christ not only bursts forth from the empty tomb, leaving behind the graveclothes of homophobic violence and compulsory heterosexuality, but also is resurrected in each of us as we accept our queerness – our divine birthright to imagine, to stir up and to spoil in God's name. In a strictly queer context, the Christ that God queered on Easter looks at the deaths of queer women and men from murder, Aids and suicide, and invites us to proclaim, 'Never again!'

In describing the birth, message, ministry, death and triumph of a poor peasant preacher who saved others through his willingness to become Christ for them, Matthew's queer Gospel stands alongside other liberatory texts of Judaism and Christianity that need to be queered and queried so that their full meaning may come forth for all to hear.

Mark

MARCELLA ALTHAUS-REID

It was the third hour when they crucified him . . . The passers-by jeered at him . . . (Mark 15. 25, 29, JB)

'A homosexual has been killed in Quilmes.' Every so often, the news about the violent death of gays came with macabre rejoicing . . . the sensationalist headlines from the newspapers . . . (Perlongher 1997: 35)

'They killed a faggot.' This is the title of one of the stories of Néstor Perlongher, the *neo-Barroso*,[1] queer Argentinian writer who wrote stories deconstructing sexuality and poverty in Buenos Aires. This is a story of love, poverty and hope of resurrections, as the dreams of the poor. Perlongher took the words for his title *Matan a una Marica* from the headlines of a tabloid newspaper from Buenos Aires. Curiously, these words preserve a certain ambiguity. *Matan a una marica*[2] can be translated as 'They kill a faggot', and also as a present tense functioning as a very recent past tense: 'They killed a faggot.' That ambiguity of the title adds to a sense of presence and continuation of the text which is almost ontological.

Perlongher's story is centred around the news of a body being found on a road. Probably 'she' was a transvestite. Probably 'she' went with other girls to the Panamerican Highway which divides the capital city from the suburbs of Buenos Aires to engage in prostitution, or in the Sao Paulo slums but then . . . What happened? It could have been a fight or simply that she was attacked. Perlongher describes the body lying in full transvestite regalia, now broken and dirty, as a scene from a cruci/fiction. There lies in the muddy road the love for shiny scarves and polka dot blouses à la Marilyn Monroe. There you can see the refined femininity of long, colourful earrings and the high-heeled shoes adorned with ribbons. All that made her, the loving hands which sewed

---

1 Néstor Perlongher was an Argentinian poet and professor of anthropology whose activism in the 'Movement for Homosexual Liberation' in Buenos Aires and his work on poverty and queer issues won him international recognition. He called his style *'neo-barroso'*, playing with the words 'neo-baroque' and *'barroso'* (muddy) in Spanish.

2 The word *marica* is used in the slang of Buenos Aires for gays. Originally, *marica* is an old-fashioned diminutive of the female name 'Maria'. Other variations include the words *mariquita* or *maricón*, even *mariposa* (butterfly). Although this last term is not related etymologically, it is used because of the term 'mari' present in the word. It is then the association with the name Maria which confers 'gayness' to the terms. One could argue that there is a relation between those nicknames and the influence of Mariology in the understanding of gender formations in Latin America.

her blouse and assembled the earrings from bits and pieces which looked good together, and her love for life, now lying covered by blood and dirt from the road. Who killed her? Was it the São Paulo police, in one of their *razzias* against transvestites? The cruci/fiction style of writing of Perlongher reaches a climax as he describes the messianic panic of one policeman when looking at the quality of the girl's make-up and torn clothes: she reminds him of someone he saw on the cover of a magazine. 'Damn it!' – he exclaims as he discerns the identity of the innocent – 'The *loca* was famous' (*loca*: a Spanish term for a mad, crazy person, which is used with sexual connotations). An indecent transvestite lay there as an innocent victim of a system of sexual violence. Transvestites are *locas*; they represent something liminal which has crossed borders and has dislocated the almost spatial ideology of heterosexuality.

The transvestite, the *loca* from Perlongher, lies in the mud and blood with 'her' torn clothes, and it is by something in those torn clothes (colour, shine, transparency, the production of femininity) that she is identified as someone who was somehow a minor celebrity, and should not have been killed. Perhaps she had a brief appearance on some local television show, or perhaps she was interviewed for a tabloid newspaper about human rights and sexuality. Somehow she belonged to a small celebrity circuit. Her death may raise voices; it may not be just another killing committed with impunity. It may create questions and problems. By her death, she may succeed then in calling attention to the killing of so many 'girls' like herself. She may even contribute to the girls' redemption, and finally, a transvestite may be able to get a job, have a decent life, love and be happy. But at the moment the preoccupation is what to do with the body. The body should disappear. And some other transvestites, some girls who were friendly with her, might come and ask, Have you seen our friend? Where have you put her body? But the body will never be found, for she has ascended to heaven. Like the Magdalene asking 'What have you done with the body of my beloved?' the answer will remain mysterious. The name of the transvestite will become legendary. One day the girls will be using medals with a younger and flattering portrait of one who has not died. They have killed a faggot, but she will come back. Cruci/fictions: messianic deaths.

Drag

In patriarchal Argentina, transvestites are at a crossroads of public worship and church and state tactics of extermination. They are adored when acting in public theatres as the famous and admired Florencia de la V and the late Chris Miró, but they attract police as well as religious brutality. Perlongher's narrative on the death of an innocent transvestite forms a close parallel to the scene of the crucifixion of Christ described in Mark 15. Jesus' clothes become the centre of attention. This is Jesus in drag, dressed in a royal purple cloak with a crown of thorns. He is the subject of laughter and derision, just as the transvestite of the Panamerican Highway in Buenos Aires or in the Brazilian slums attracts laughter and derision for her gender-fucking, that is, for crossing borders of dress codes and dislocating identities. And there are also Jesus' own torn clothes, muddy clothes that are taken by the soldiers, not even choosing what they wanted but receiving as the result of gambling, distributed on the throw of the dice. And then there is a Roman officer musing to himself, 'Truly this man was the Son of God!' (15.39). Or as Perlongher would put it, 'Damn it! The *loca* was famous.' Perhaps a famous dancer or perhaps a human rights activist. Or perhaps both. And her body would become the secret of the centuries to come, the *Mysterium Tremendum* of Otto, on which Derrida reflected by saying that the secret is what makes people tremble (Derrida and Ferraris 2001). And people will tremble sensing the mystery of a queer holiness.

The Queer Reader and the Bible

The starting-point of these reflections is the assumption of a queer christological project such as the one developed by Robert Goss in his book *Queering Christ* (Goss 2002) and my own work on Bi/Christ, which is in permanent dialogue with Goss's own project. The basic assumptions that we are making here are:

1 Reading Christ in the scriptures cannot be an exemplary but a revelatory reading. A reading that unmasks that of God in Christ's own intimate chaos of love, messianic public expectations and contra/dictions, that is, the voices of subversion in an otherwise well-tamed text.
2 Reading Christ should not become a conclusive task. Revelation is not compatible with the closure produced by authoritative (and authoritarian) readings of the scripture. What we are looking for is a permanent displacement of references, a quicksand scenario as the alternative for a reading of the different of God in Jesus, beyond the ideological configuration of heterosexuality.
3 Reading Christ needs to relate to Jesus' sexual practices. By that we understand Jesus' practices of solidarity with love and a praxis of social justice, outside a dualist mind/body separation.
4 Finally, we need to read the life of Jesus with the same eyes that we read stories in the tabloids about homosexual people being killed. Unless we can locate Jesus' passion in the real life of people we will not be able to understand the meaning of incarnation nor the subversion of bodies that resurrection implies.

A Gay Lost His Job: Counting the Killings of a Queer Man in Mark's Gospel

One of the mistakes we may commit is to read the text from Mark as a progression: the young preacher of conversion, the itinerant healer, the prophet arrested and put to death. Surprisingly, the early manuscripts of Mark contain no narratives of resurrection after the crucifixion scenes. We shall return to this point, which in itself is hermeneutically significant, but for the moment let us focus on a different, non-progressive dynamics of reading which can liberate the queering of this text. I should like to begin by saying that Jesus' crucifixion was not his only death, just as the transvestite in the story of Perlongher was not killed only by police. The *trava* (transvestite/transsexual in the argot of Buenos Aires) suffered in life many deaths by ostracism, by being abandoned by her family, by being denied a job, by being denied her right to her own identity and to love, and to have a good life with dignity.

Jesus' life according to Mark is also signed by a multitude of deaths. These are the deaths of a queer man. First of all, Jesus is a man who has departed from his family. In a way, he lost his family and social location. Second, he suffers from economic death. How? He is a poor man, rendered invisible by the economic power of his time, a nobody. And finally, torture and death by crucifixion ends his messianic mission. The crucifixion made him redundant. He becomes an unemployed God, a devalued, misunderstood God outside the market. In everything Jesus did, God's abundant presence was there but nevertheless, for society he was a failure.

First Deaths: A Gay Alone

The Gospel of Mark starts with action. Mark shows Jesus doing things rather than simply saying things. It is Jesus' actions and not just his words which will lead to his ruin. There are no supernatural stories of miracle births. There are no loving scenes of mother and child. Whatever happened in his childhood is omitted by Mark. The beginning of the 'good news' is his actions, not his words. The most significant passage is not the ritual of baptism, but the narrative of the temptations. Jesus is a man who seems to be making his own way alone, struggling with dark temptations. We do not know what they are, but if we include the reference from Matthew 4, they relate to many things, including even suicidal thoughts. This is an isolated man who is hungry, unemployed (the temptation of bread. He has no money to buy it, neither has he a family who will provide for him). This is a man who is wondering if anyone in the entire universe would care if he threw himself from the pinacle of the temple, which also seems to be a kind of religious protest. Why was the temple building part of his obscure thoughts at that moment? Were the temple authorities, traditions and regulations driving him mad? And finally, there is this plea for public recognition, to be part of something, loved and respected by society, present in the metaphor of the vision of the cities of the world at his feet, that is, befriending him. Whatever the point of this inner struggle, that isolation and crisis which precedes his public ministry or the kind of voluntary work he felt he needed to do to honour his own identity, was tied to a call from God in his society. Interestingly, in this story, it is not a family that is behind Jesus. It is not the stereotype of the man who with great effort must leave family and friends to become a priest. No, Jesus here is already a man who has been separated from his family and friends, whose call comes already in his inner struggle in search for his own divine identity.

However, the desert is not an image of isolation in itself, but of isolation in the sense of a location where many people who did not fit in with society were to be found. Not only a Jesus with suicidal thoughts of jumping from temples but also other strange people lived in the desert, notably John the Baptist. In any case he was isolated but not alone in the sense that communities such as that at Qumran and other unsettled spirits were also gathering at the margins of Jerusalem's authority. Interestingly, after that period of isolation and crisis, almost a nervous breakdown, we see Jesus searching for companions. He returns from these 'temptations' looking for new friends or a family – as a queer person usually does: you go to places, you speak with some people and, with luck, you start a circle of befriending and love. That is precisely what Jesus did in engaging with the four fishermen. Reading from a queer perspective this is an uplifting text. It is a remedy for melancholy, a text of instant rapport in the kind of encountering that happens among people who recognize themselves as different. Were the fishermen also men accustomed to the isolation that happens in the lives of people when their affectivity has become religiously and/or socially repressed? Why this instant rapport, this immediate desire for togetherness that happened among them? It is like a cruising scene: one minute they did not know who they were, and the next they are walking together like old friends. Later in the text we shall read more about this man Jesus who was called a friend of sinners. Who were those fishermen? Did they know each other already from other occasions? What did these men do when looking for a moment of relaxation?

These queer questionings are important because they help us to think about the original location of Jesus' good news from Mark's perspective. The temptation, the crisis and the meeting of new friends which resolved the crisis is then followed by a curious text concerning 'an impure spirit' (Mark 1.21–8). A heterosexual reading, obsessed with dualist assumptions and a polarized organization of the world, tends to emphasize a Jesus who is pure and meets the impure or the just who meets the sinner. However, the constructions of sin or purity used in these cases is far from clear. The fact is that what strikes us about the text is that 'impure spirits' obey him. Using a bisexual reading perspective, we find ourselves confronted here with a continuation of a narrative thread concerning a man without family, hungry of many things and now coming out. This 'coming out' is carried through with forcefulness.

Shut Up and Leave Him Alone!

The account here continues the narrative of friendship/isolation. It is located in the synagogue of Capernaum. The scene is one of transgression: an impure man is sitting in the temple. Impurity, in the scriptures, is a very corporeal category. That is the reason why it needs to be associated with body disfunctions, such as leprosy, blindness and, of course, menstruation. Impurity is without doubt what exceeds the normativity of the body as religiously constructed and it is important to recognize that 'impurity' is not a given but rather is a legal category imposed upon a person. There is a little scene in this text in which Jesus is presented in general as a scandalous young man. There are frequently outbursts, shouting, calls for explanations and heated exchanges associated with Jesus' appearances, and this is no exception. The impure man reacts strongly when he sees Jesus. The words used are 'I know you' and 'Do you want to destroy us?' A queer reading needs to begin by setting aside any supposed intonation of the words, whether angry or ironic we simply do not know, and the mythical representation of what was declared 'impure' in that man. What we have is the following: the 'impure man' receives a response from the by now assertive Jesus saying: 'Shut up!' and 'Leave this man alone.' But who is Jesus addressing in these words? To the impure spirit who possessed the man (as in a case of dual personality)? Or to someone in the synagogue? Whatever it was, the man concerned seems to have had a strong reaction. Now, he also shouts, but we do not know what he says. Did he in turn say 'Shut up yourself, and leave me alone?' What a magnificent scene of deliverance from prejudices this may be! Not only a lesson to the homophobics of the synagogue but a lesson to the man himself who also becomes suddenly assertive. And to confirm our queer suspicion, someone else present is quoted as saying, 'What is this? . . . Even the impure spirits obey him . . .'

Is there a link here? Is the impurity mentioned as a religious construction of the different, the queer category which links all these texts together? Is the friend of sinners the friend of impurity? In that case we need to reconsider what we call impurity in the Bible. After this, we have several stories of impurity and of Jesus loving and 'healing' the impure people in society. However, the impure of society have good relations with Jesus (3.11–12). Finally this cycle of isolation, self-discovery and the beginning of a popular movement among the impure leads us back to where we began, the scene of the man who did not have a family. This is the dramatic moment when his mother and brothers come to claim him back for his natural family: but Jesus has already found a new spiritual kind of family. These things happen all the time.

Jesus had survived the death of isolation, experienced resurrection and came back to life from his suicidal crisis by an act of taking responsibility for what was different in him. Thereafter he found many others who suffered as he previously suffered. And he found love.

The Economic Deaths: Jesus, Unemployed

Some time ago a friend told me her story. She had been happily working in a firm, until the rumour began to circulate that she was gay. Little by little, her job became more difficult. The secretaries treated her with discourtesy. Her colleagues ignored her or made obscure but hurting remarks in her presence. One day she could not find her own desk chair! It had been removed and she had to get a chair from another office. After describing a long sequence of humiliations and suffering she finally said to me, 'and then, you see, they tried to kill me'. I must have stared at her in incomprehension. To kill her? Surely not. But she continued her explanation. She became depressed and as a consequence her contract was not renewed. Having lost her job, she could not find another. As her savings were used up she moved from flat to flat, convinced that in the end she would be living on the street. She did not have a family to help her and could see no way to survive. Yes, economic killing exists, people become destitute and die.

Was Jesus also killed economically by the system at that time? The wandering preacher, the man who lives his life among the marginalized is not a man with a proper job. It is not original to say that Mark's Gospel is one of the most 'economic' texts in the Second Testament. Fernando Belo, in his pioneering work on materialist exegesis, drew attention to the links between Jesus' preaching on the kingdom of God and productivity relations (Belo 1981). Belo's most revealing exegesis is his reading of the narrative of the feeding of the multitudes, which presents Jesus as a compassionate but impoverished messiah. It is clear in this text that he does not have anything for himself and therefore nothing to share with the crowds. Jesus is not simply the presence of God among the marginalized: more than that Jesus represents a truly marginalized God.[3]

The Redundant God

It may be correct to say that God in Christ was a God with an identity crisis, in all the good and revelatory meaning of the term 'crisis'. That is, a God putting Godself under judgement, a self-judgement involving a type of quest identity for Jesus, was at the same time a becoming messiah and an unfinished God. Let us reflect on two important theological points here. First, the killing of a queer as part of an expiatory sacrifice performed in society, and second, the issue of the redundant God. Was the killing of Jesus an attempt to eliminate that difference which Jesus presented in the idea of God? The messiah was made redundant by the death on the cross. Whatever it was, God Godself was no longer needed. But was God (and God in Jesus) a queer God?

At this point in the narrative we find Jesus more or less at the same point where he began his public life. The queer man of God came out and somehow conquered: he conquered hearts and his community was becoming strong enough to present a different or alternative lifestyle. It was a kind of Stonewall resistance which developed from synagogues to private houses. However, and as with Stonewall, resistance can also be violently killed. Now we see a Jesus who seems to have lost a few friends, a Jesus without a loving companion. This is a Jesus who is greeted with kisses and a show of affection, but who is also betrayed, deserted and denied. The whole cycle of public humiliation, tortures, laughter and derision ends with this poor, fragile young God dying a miserable death on the garbage dump of his city.

Cruci/fictions: Jesus in the Tabloids

Imagine a tabloid headline: 'A queer man of God was crucified yesterday . . .' Why was Jesus killed? What threat could this man have represented to anybody? It is difficult to see. In his story *Matan a una Marica*, Perlongher elaborated on the issue of the need of the expiation sacrifice of the queer. The killings of homosexuals in Argentinian society have within them a necessity of biblical proportions, manifesting the purifying rituals of the different in society. In the

---

3 I have already elaborated this point in my article 'The Divine Exodus of God' (Althaus-Reid 2001b).

tabloids, the killing of queers is a genre in itself, designed to produce a mixture of moralization and amusement in the readers. They are a kind of reasoned killing, which becomes part of a discourse of 'expected deaths', since death is portrayed as the consequence of a sexually transgressive lifestyle. The tabloids reflect the need to provide the public with the exemplary deaths of gays. They go to great lengths to trivialize these crimes as part of a self-justificatory strategy. If we see the killing of Jesus as a crime committed against a sexual dissident, there are some parallels which we may wish to consider. For instance, sexual dissidents are portrayed as ones who seek their own death. For the gay man or woman to deserve their own death is not enough. They need to be portrayed as going out looking for it. Jesus knew what was coming. He could have avoided going up to Jerusalem, once there he could have avoided confrontation, or having left the city he need not have gone to a hillside where he knew his enemies would catch him in the act with his friends. Even accounts in the tabloids of the killing of gays tend to be so deprived of reality that they have the appearance of coming from a comic strip. The horror of the events is glossed over or denied. So it is that in the taking of Jesus the scene is not without comic elements. First there is the description of the company of soldiers creeping up the slope with a variety of swords and weapons to deal with a handful of men who apparently cannot keep their eyes open. Almodovar could not have devised a funnier scene for one of his films. Jesus himself seems to mock them for the exaggerated display of arms. And then there is the incident of the young man who, curiously, was wearing nothing but a piece of linen cloth. As the soldiers attempted to apprehend him he dashed off naked like a streaker, leaving the soldiers holding the sheet. Were they annoyed or did they all collapse with laughter? Queers can be very funny, and our attention is distracted from the true horror of the moment.

Perlongher comments how, in the gutter press, queers seem to be portrayed as prone to do the kind of wrong things which provoke crimes against them, as when they insist on going to places where they should not be seen. Either they love someone too much, or they are too lonely to be prudent. Or too often they have simply a kind of obstinate loving behaviour which attracts fateful crimes against them. The death of a queer in the tabloids never seems real enough. These are texts which produce lesser deaths, like Jesus' own death. Is that the reason why the cross appears so easily as inexpensive jewellery? If Jesus had been electrocuted instead of crucified, would there be a large switch on the altar? If he had been decapitated according to the custom of the ancient world, would Christians carry swords? The death of Jesus has been trivialized not by the tabloids but by the theological gutter press of homophobia.

The most important thing to remember in all this is that with this crime a queer man of God was eliminated. The messianic position was declared redundant. This was a messiah who announced a strange, queer God among those made impure and outcast by the social order of the time. A God who was more than can be expressed, who exceeds all categories of definition and control is a queer God indeed. At the end of Mark's Gospel there is no resurrection narrative. The last words refer to 'fear'. Those women who went to perfume the corpse with spices (Mary, Mary of Magdala and Salome) did not find Jesus' body. Instead they found a man who told them 'he is not here . . . and you will see him in Galilee . . .' But they said nothing. They were afraid.

Queering theology, we can see that in fact Jesus died and was resurrected throughout the whole narrative of the Gospels. Resurrection is an ever present theme. But the queer reading of the scriptures is not progressive: it is transgressive. We see how the category of resurrection appears every time that Jesus is made redundant. When he loses his family and place in society even the council of priests discuss publicly issues concerning his identity and his being-in-the-world, just as at the 2003 Lambeth conference gays were discussed *ontologically* for press consumption. And ultimately, God is declared so redundant that, forgetting himself, Jesus cries to God for the oblivion of the cross. In reality, the cross is the attempt to kill once and for all the multiple resurrections of a queer Jesus, to fix him once and forever on a stable cross so that no queer God would do what queer Gods do, that is, to exceed the border limits of a fatigued heterosexual foundational epistemology which has reduced religious experience and human love. But will the queer Jesus resurrect? I belong to a community of people who think that yes, the resurrection of the queer God is not only possible, but already a reality. The queer God is present in every group or individual who still dares to believe that God is fully present among the marginalized, exceeding the narrow confines of sexual and political ideologies. For God comes out from heterosexual theology when the voices from sexual dissidents speak out to the churches, daring to unveil sexual ideologies from theology, and daring to love with integrity in a world where love has also become a commodity. In fact, in every community of excluded people and in every inch of the struggle for sexual and economic justice, the queer God manifests Godself with full glory, power and grace.

Luke

ROBERT E. GOSS

Early traditions relate that Luke was a companion of Paul, a physician from one of Paul's churches, and his Gospel may be viewed as the development of Pauline Christianity in a Gentile world a generation later. Luke addresses a theology of a divine plan of salvation history in three periods: the prophets, the time of Jesus, and the story of the post-Easter Jesus movement. His theological periodization of salvation history shifted the focus of attention from the imminent expectation of the world's end and the return of Jesus the Christ to serious problems: oppression and poverty. He portrays more than any other Gospel Jesus as a Hebrew prophet sent into the world for the salvation of all people, Jews and Gentiles. His intent is to depict how salvation expanded beyond Judaism to the Gentile world. This is the queer intent of God, the unconditional gift of salvation to all, the expansion of salvation from heterosexuals to queer folks.

I explore Luke's Gospel as a resistant reader – an exegetical activist, a pastor, and a queer theologian. Queering has come to represent a dislocation or transgression of fixed categories. The biblical scholar Halvor Moxnes uses 'queer' as the best term to characterize Jesus: 'To use the term "queer" of Jesus describes the unsettling quality about him' (Moxnes 2003: 6). This is particularly true of the Lucan Jesus, who destabilizes the symbolic world, turning it inside-out and transgressing social boundaries to create a queer utopia, the reign of God. The prophet Jesus creates an alternative, out-of-space symbolic world or, in others words, a queer universe.

Whether Theophilus, friend of God, was actually a patron, a male lover of Luke, friend, or a composite figure of the reader, I interpret him as the queer community: churched and unchurched, 'normal' and 'non-normal' gays and lesbians, transgendered folks, feminists, bisexuals, intersexuals, and all gender-variant folk and sexual outlaws. Scandalously, they are all included in the story of God's queer salvation history in Jesus. Theophilus is described as 'excellent', for he is an excellent lover, representing the queer community. 'Theophilus' is a queer lover, and I read Luke with the hope that Jesus the queer prophet will inspire twenty-first-century Christianity to embrace the gendered and sexually different, the broken-bodied and the marginalized.

Mary: Queer Prophetess and Mother of Jesus

The tradition of remarkable births was part of the tradition of Israel and the Graeco-Roman world. Both the Matthean and Lucan infancy narratives are products of Christian reflection towards the end of the first century CE. God shatters the normativity of heterosexual patriarchy. While traditional churches read this text as the narrowing-down of women's roles or the idealization of women's subordination, the centrality of women in the story of God's liberative action is revealed. The angel Gabriel announces to Mary a prophetic commission that God is with her and that she will bear a child, who will be the Child of God. Mary stands in contrast to Zechariah, a rural priest and a male, whose doubt and unbelief leads Gabriel to strike him dumb. Mary the queer prophetess sings how God will upset the social world, bringing down the mighty and elevating the lowly. God's action will queer the world by turning it upside-down, for Mary will bear a child who will queer the world, disrupting the social world (2.34).

The story of Mary and the birth of Jesus becomes a paradigm of queer empowerment, a story of 'queer self-acceptance and a coming out into our creativity to the birth of the good news of Christ' (Bohache 2003: 27). Mary welcomes the message as many translesbigays receive the news in safe churches that God is with them. Thomas Bohache writes, 'For Mary, that great thing is conceiving the Christ in her body. For queers, that great thing can consist of allowing Christ to take Christ's place within us' (Bohache 2003: 26). Unmarried Mary lives in a culture where she is the sexual property of her father or her betrothed husband, for she has no independent status within Judaism. Mary becomes an exemplary disciple who actively responds to the word of God. She is a lowly peasant woman, who cannot enter the inner temple, yet her status is exalted over a priest like Zechariah, who can enter the temple.

The post-apostolic idealization as Virgin Mother robbed Mary of her humanity and sexuality. The theologian Marcella Althaus-Reid describes how the story of Jesus' conception has become the 'myth of a woman without a vagina' (Althaus-Reid 2001a: 39). Mary is honoured for her non-sexuality and her subordination to a male God, and the myth has been sacralized into a 'theo-ideology' that has harmed and oppressed women:

> Mary is not part of history since she has broken the historical nexus of women as non-menstruating, conceiving outside the realms of sexuality and procreating by unnatural means . . . No young girl thinks 'perhaps if I am humble enough God will have sex with me'. (Althaus-Reid 2001a: 43, 54)

Mary has little in common with real erotic lives and bodies of women. Male church leaders have idealized Mary and made her into an oppressive sexual code for women by robbing her of children. Althaus-Reid is critical of the ideologies of the Spanish conquerors, who employed the white lady to subjugate the indigenous peoples of the Americas, and the vanilla mariologies of recent feminists. If we are to make Mary 'indecent', Althaus-Reid suggests that we make 'Mary, Queer of Heaven and Mother of Faggots', by reclaiming her sexuality and reconnecting her to women's experience. Likewise, in his 'Christmas Letter 1941', the poet W. H. Auden writes to his male lover, Chester Kallman:

> Because mothers have much to do with your queerness and mine,
> Because we have both lost ours, and because Mary is a camp name;
> As this morning I think of Mary, I think of you. (Mendelson 1999: 182)

Queerness remains at the heart of the stories about Mary.

Underlying presumptions of heterosexuality are questioned. Althaus-Reid remarks, 'Having sex with a woman cannot be taken as a proof of God the Father's heterosexuality, nor should Mary's pregnancy be related to a heterosexual conception of womanhood' (Althaus-Reid 2001a: 67). God is queer by transgressing the boundaries of sexual traditions. God neither ravishes nor engages in penetrative sex with Mary but overshadows her. God is more indecent than the 'Spermatogenic' God of decent theologians, who justify a heterosexist natural law of sexuality through the conception of Jesus. Actually, God is more akin to queers, the sexual outlaws who break cultural codes of decency and sexual restrictedness. God is a 'faggot', for God creatively pursues the conception of Jesus outside the bounds of vanilla religiosity. But Mary is queer as well, for compulsory heterosexuality rules out sexual pleasure within women by subordinating it to male pleasure:

> she (Mary) is the woman who has had 'seven times seven' clitoral sexual pleasure. Let us say that she may have conceived by pleasure in her clitoris; by self-given pleasure, perhaps. In this way, lust and love may then be re-linked together in the same way that love and solidarity for justice, in Patriarchal Liberation Theology, has been reconnected effectively. (Althaus-Reid 2001a: 73)

Restoring Mary's sexuality brings freedom to women, for she breaks with her patriarchal culture and male heterosexual economy of reproduction. If a reader holds to the exclusive divine paternity of Jesus, then Mary queers the patriarchal economy that understands women's bodies as not belonging to themselves. She is free to answer as an equal; she has ownership of her body and remains an active agent in making a decision for herself (Schaberg 1987: 143). Elisabeth Schüssler Fiorenza notes that Mary's freedom of choice models 'women's right to choose' (Schüssler Fiorenza 1994a: 169). Heteronormativity fears independent women and their reproductive freedom. Like Mary, many lesbians break the economy of compulsory heterosexuality by choosing to become pregnant in a variety of methods.

Virginia Mollenkott understands that if the virginal conception of Jesus is to be taken literally, then the parthenogenic birth means that Jesus was conceived chromosomal female. She cites a study by a biologist, Edward Kessal, who observes, 'The female embryo Jesus of the Virgin Conception and Incarnation became the two-sexed infant of the Virgin Birth who was the androgynous Christ, bearing both the chromosomal identification of a woman and the phenotypic anatomy of a man' (Mollenkott 2001: 105). That Jesus was then intersexed undercuts all theological claims of those churches that restrict ordination to males based on the maleness of Jesus. Mollenkott follows the traditional interpretation of virginal conception but throws a 'queer' monkey wrench into the literalist theo-ideologies surrounding Mary and the masculinity of Jesus. If Jesus is then intersexed, then his intersexed gender becomes problematic for those churches that base ordination on his maleness.

The Visitation becomes more realistic when it is placed in the context of Roman occupation and sexual violence. A betrothed, pregnant thirteen-year-old Mary travels 'with haste' to seek out another woman, a cousin Elizabeth.

In contrast to the traditional gloss of Mary wanting to share her joy, Schaberg (1987) points out that the Greek idiom 'with haste' carries the overtones of alarm, flight and anxiety. She is alone, shamed and frightened, seeking out understanding and comfort from her cousin. Mary ran for her life from patriarchal violence since the penalty for the seduction of a betrothed woman was, at worst, 'stoning' or the lighter sentence of divorce. Elisabeth Schüssler Fiorenza comments, 'it is the young pregnant woman, living in occupied territory and struggling against victimization and for survival and dignity' (Schüssler Fiorenza 1994a: 187). Thomas Bohache stresses that Mary finds safety in sharing her pregnancy with a pregnant Elizabeth. Her cousin reminds her of Gabriel's earlier message that 'God is with you', and Mary sings a song of liberation for the queer community and for all oppressed peoples and for all queers forced to experience sexual shame. Thus, the story of single, pregnant, unwed girl becomes a story accessible to many women's experience but also to translesbigay experience. God is with us and will reverse cultural shame, bringing life and empowered hope.

The birth of Jesus comes after a difficult journey and no room at the inn. The queer mother gives birth to Jesus in the stable:

> A queer appreciation of the Nativity is the realization that Christ will be born, no matter how perilous the journey, no matter that folks might not receive us, once we have agreed to give birth to the Christ in self-empowerment and creativity, Christ will be born. Much of the world will have no knowledge that we have given birth to this Christ; most will continue to go about their business and their oppressing of others. (Bohache 2003: 27)

Bohache's incarnational theology affirms that translesbigay Christians also give birth to the queer Christ and that they need to manifest the Christ to the queer community. The nativity prefigures the future dislocation of the queer Christ into queer bodies of followers.

Jesus and the Queer Reign of God

Jesus preached the 'reign of God', a rich, polyvalent symbol from Jewish biblical and apocalyptic theology. Jesus' notion of the reign of God is a queer symbol, turning upside-down and inside-out some conservative Jewish theological traditions to make them more universal and inclusive. When Jesus preached the reign of God, he did not preach a transcendent, other-worldly reality. God's reign is immanent, present, and queerly in our midst. It challenges ethnic and political loyalties; his message would be understood as challenging the political interests of various Jewish factions and ultimately the Roman empire.

Jesus is a boundary-breaker, transgressing the purity codes of fundamentalists and challenging proto-heterosexual hegemony. He uses provocative riddles, parables and symbolic acts to challenge religious normativities. Michael Warner defines queer as a transgressive paradigm, representing 'a more thorough resistance to the regimes of the normal' (Warner 1993: xxvi). There is no question that right from the birth of Jesus to the resurrection there is queer dynamic in Luke's portrayal of the activity of God and Jesus. For Jesus, God's reign is out of place; it is socially provocative, politically explosive, and thoroughly queer. It challenges many forms of cultural restrictedness, hegemony and patriarchal cultural normativities. In Luke 17.21, Jesus proclaims that God's reign is 'among you'. Jesus preaches the good news that God is attentive to the needs of people and that God is presently active, changing lives, creating human wholeness, and transforming the world. God's reign cannot be limited to Jesus' metaphorical language in his teachings, parables and proverbs. It is just as active in his parabolic actions, healings and exorcisms, table-fellowship, inclusiveness, and stop-the-temple action in Jerusalem. Luke depicts Jesus as a queer prophet, performing dramatic actions with a queer and camp flair. God's reign will take shape in servant leadership, voluntary poverty and care for the destitute, hospitality, and compassionate action. God will create a queer space; transgressing gender normativities, creating new families, and turning upside-down the symbolic world of many Jewish religious factions.

Discipleship: leadership as servanthood

Jesus called men and women to a discipleship of equals, and in his patriarchal culture of the Roman world, Luke certainly tones down the original freedom of women as disciples. Jesus called disciples to a shared egalitarianism, voluntary poverty, servant leadership and inclusiveness. There was single-mindedness to discipleship in the reign of God. To the disciple who wants to bury his dead father, he says, 'Let the dead bury their own dead' (9.60). God's reign takes precedence over the obligation to bury one's father. Jesus' saying shocks his audience as to the urgency of discipleship for God's reign, for it cannot wait even 24 hours.

Jesus models God's reign as one who serves at table. He defines the greatest as not the one who sits at the table but the one who humbly waits on table. He invites imitation of his own service at table (22.27). He calls male disciples to cross gender roles and economic roles; they are to act as females and slaves, giving up their roles as dominating males. He reprimands his disciples about ambition, imitating leadership modelled on patriarchal Gentile leadership (22.24–5). Humility (14.7–11) and servanthood are the tools for his critique of political and economic relations of domination modelled by the Romans and their co-opted Jewish leadership. Good disciples are leaders who use their power and economic resources in service to those without power and riches. True greatness as servant leaders comes from recognition of the worth of the least (9.47–8). It also comes from the practice of voluntary poverty, giving without the expectation of a return, hospitality and compassion.

Voluntary poverty and the destitute

Luke's Gospel has been called the 'Gospel of the poor' since it advances the notion of 'God's preferential option for the poor'. Jesus calls his disciples to renounce wealth and share their wealth voluntarily with the poor. He calls Simon and the sons of Zebedee to discipleship, and they leave everything to follow him (5.11). Discipleship requires the intentional giving up of possessions (14.33) and familial relationships (9.61–2). It is interesting that Jesus does not call the destitute to discipleship but calls his disciples to a voluntary poverty and a sharing of their wealth as almsgiving with the destitute (12.33). Disciples, willingly embracing poverty, are called 'blessed', for they will have a share in God's reign. Jesus and his closest followers lived from a sharing of goods – a common fund supported by Galilean women (8.1–3).

The love of money is incompatible with service in the reign of God. Luke attaches the Jesus saying to the parable of the Dishonest Servant, to deflect the obvious interpretation of Jesus sanctioning the clever but dishonest actions of the servant. Jesus says, 'No slave can serve two masters; for a slave will either hate the one and love the other, or be devoted to the one and despise the other. You cannot serve God and wealth' (16.12–13). Luke calls Pharisees 'lovers of money' (16.14), and the lovers of money are incompatible with the economy of the reign of God. Riches can numb and blind people to the needs of the destitute, and this becomes apparent in Jesus' parable of the Rich Man and Lazarus (16.19f.). Not the rich but the poor are close to God.

Jesus warns his disciples that the cares, riches and pleasures of life can choke the call to discipleship. The story of the call of the rich young ruler (18.18f.) is an example of the unsuccessful call to discipleship. The rich ruler was unwilling to give up his social-economic status and to sell all that he had for distribution to the indigent. The rich are confident, enjoy material favour and social status, and have no need for God's comfort. Riches become an obstacle to becoming a disciple. On the other hand, Zacchaeus, a tax farmer and outsider, becomes the model of giving (19.1–10). He stands as a foil to the rich young ruler, for he gives half of his wealth to the destitute while paying back fourfold to anyone who is defrauded. Jesus acknowledges Zacchaeus, that salvation has come to his house and that he is now a son of Abraham.

Jesus envisions a utopian community of sharing where no one is wanting and where the care of the poor has priority. He envisions such an alternative vision of community of compassion in the reign of God. While Jesus visits the rich and even accepts their hospitality, he calls them to share their wealth with the poor. He calls attention to the widow who gives her all (21.1–4) and contrasts her with those who give from their abundance. Disciples are encouraged to give without the expectation of receiving something in return (6.35). Halvor Moxnes notes that Jesus models a new notion of benefaction:

> Thus, this model of economic interaction has important consequences for social relations. It is a form of giving which makes other people free. It does not bind in servitude or gratitude to other people. (Moxnes 1988a: 157)

In the reign of God, wealth is not transformed into social power and status over other people. It frees both the benefactor and recipient to understand the gratuitous generosity of God, who gives without the expectation of return.

Hospitality

Queer folk love brunches, meals together and partying. Our queer meals – whether impromptu 'pot lucks' or elegant gourmet meals – are a means of speaking, conceiving and conducting social relationships. Food and food behaviours are part of a cultural complex; they serve social and cultural functions other than nutritional need. They build and express social relationships and cultural values; their etiquette may imitate family values and express alternative visions of relationships and families. Queer meals are often open to lovers, children, friends, friends of friends and former lovers. John McNeill observes that hospitality is a queer virtue, quoting Henri Nouwen's definition as 'that virtue which allows us to break through the narrowness of our fears and open our home to the stranger with the understanding that salvation comes to us in the form of a tired traveler' (McNeill 1988: 97). For McNeill, queer hospitality is expressed in the parable of the Good Samaritan, where the Samaritan is a gay drag queen who picks up a man mugged on 42nd Street in New York City and who is passed by a Catholic priest and social worker (McNeill 1988: 96). But let's queer the text further than McNeill does. Imagine that the mugged man is the Catholic Cardinal or a televangelist such as Pat Robertson. The surprise comes in the love shown to someone who has actively persecuted the queer community and set up a climate of social violence. It communicates the intentional shock of the Samaritan parable and Jesus' injunction to love one's enemies. God's reign is radically inclusive, and Jesus tells his audience to imitate the compassionate Samaritan, a hated and despised outcast of his day. Queer hospitality, likewise, finds God present in the stranger, the enemy, or the homophobic religious leader.

Meals are Jesus' metaphors for the reign of God, expressive of God's inclusiveness. Jesus' rules of hospitality are thoroughly queer; he does a 'queer make-over' of Jewish eating customs and values to envision God's reign. Jesus loved to party: he contrasts himself with the ministry of John the Baptist: 'For John the Baptist has come eating no bread and drinking no wine, and you say, "He has a demon"; the Son of Humanity has come eating and drinking, and you say, "Look a glutton and drunkard, a friend of tax collectors and sinners"' (7.34). Jesus associates with tax collectors and sinners, those excluded from the hope of salvation. He shares the hope of forgiveness with sinners (7.50; 11.4; 15.7, 10; 18.9–14; 19.1–10). His meals were out-of-place feasts for Jews with strict agendas of holiness/purity, for they transgressed holiness/purity etiquette and were suggestive of something new, out-of-bounds relationships. God's forgiveness of sins subverted the temple system of offering sacrifice for reconciliation with God.

What are the rules of hospitality of Jesus' meals? He queers the rules of etiquette on invitations by detailing who not to invite: friends, relatives, rich neighbours, and anyone who can return the favour of the invitation (14.12). Invited guests are replaced by the unwanted: the poor, the crippled, the lame and the blind (14.13–14). The list of invitees is repeated in the parable of the Great Dinner where the host asks the servant to go out into the streets and invite the throw-away people to the dinner (14.21). Here Jesus even shocks some queer hosts by inviting the non-superstars, those with less than perfect bodies, and the queer nobodies. There is neither the capacity for reciprocity nor the possibility of furthering one's status within the in-crowd. The social order is reversed in God's coming reign, for Jesus' festive meals split families, set family members on different sides, and invite all sorts of suspect people with deviant social locations and queer jobs. Outsiders then become insiders, and former insiders become outsiders. These meals metaphorically express God's promiscuous invitation of grace, compassion for all, and inversion of hierarchy. For John Dominic Crossan, Jesus' meals broker an egalitarian vision of God's reign:

> Jesus' kingdom of nobodies and undesirables in the here and now of this world was surely an egalitarian one, and, as such, it rendered sexual and social, political and religious distinctions completely irrelevant and anachronistic . . . But the radical lack of social differentiation remained as a permanent challenge to all specifications, interpretations, and actualizations of the Kingdom proclaimed by Jesus. (Crossan 1991: 298)

Such an egalitarian vision creates a problem for competing Jewish factions with their own politics of holiness and their attempts to construct fences and barriers around God's grace. God's unconditional grace still remains 'out of place' or disruptive for most churches where doctrine, sanctioned conduct and 'pure hearts' ('no erotic desires') are necessary for receiving communion. The Metropolitan Community Churches continue Jesus' queer table practices by an open communion. At MCC services, celebrants proclaim an open communion invitation: 'This table does not belong to MCC; it belongs to God. Everyone, whether you are a member or not, whether you are practising Christian or not, is welcomed to receive communion.'

Compassionate action

Anointed with the Spirit at his baptism, Jesus begins his prophetic ministry, declaring the prophetic verse Isaiah 61.1 has been fulfilled today. For Luke, God has anointed him as a charismatic prophet to preach the good news to the poor, proclaim release to the captives, bring recovery of sight to the blind, free the oppressed, and proclaim a year of God's favour. He breaks social and physical boundaries to heal and mend lives. Luke highlights God's compassion in Jesus' ministry. In the 'Sermon on the Plain', Jesus announces: 'Be compassionate as your God is compassionate' (6.36). Marcus Borg notes that ' . . . compassionate bore the connotations of "wombishness," nourishing, giving life, embracing; perhaps it also suggested feelings of tenderness' (Borg 1984 (1998): 102).

Jesus speaks and lives the compassion of God by addressing the poor and the rich alike, healing the suffering, and creating an inclusive community. Healings and exorcisms are prominent in Jesus' ministry. Luke's Gospel appears to stress the sufferings of those people seeking healing. Traditionally, Luke was understood to be a physician, and that impression emerges from the portrayal of Jesus as compassionately healing the ill and exorcising the possessed. For Luke, Jesus makes whole those who are ill and restores them to a new society: God's reign. Since the sick are not part of the realm of the healthy, they must be kept apart or excluded. Jesus expresses God's compassion for those physically suffering, even defying the Sabbath laws to heal the sick (4.31–7; 6.6–11; 13.10–17; 14.1–6). Jesus argues that the Sabbath is a day of restoration and wholeness, and what better day to heal and make people whole. The Sabbath is about showing God's compassion.

One major parallel between the healings stories of Jesus and the contemporary queer is the revulsion of bodies. Why do translesbigay bodies elicit such phobic responses? Why do diseased bodies in first-century CE Palestine elicit such phobic responses? In both cases, the fear of pollution is symptomatic of a society anxious about social boundaries. What crosses or blurs boundaries is potentially dangerous and definitely polluting to society, then and now.

The climate of exclusions is horrendous in both first-century CE Palestinian and contemporary cultures. This is apparent to many queer folk who have lived through the worst ravages of the Aids pandemic. Juxtapose the healings of lepers in Luke (5.12–16; 17.11–19) with the following story of a young man with HIV:

> One gentle young man from North Carolina seemed to evaporate into pure spirit as his body withered and his eyesight dimmed into blindness. In the last year of his life, he was fed by his mother, morning, noon, and night, from her back doorstep. (Brantley 1996: 217)

Jesus was willing to touch and engage lepers while the mother fed her blind HIV son on the doorstep but kept him outside of the home. Modern Christian purity codes are often as lethal and inhumane as past codes. On Christmas Eve, a wealthy Episcopalian church (many such stories are found in other denominations as well) in St Louis discovered that a priest, Charles, a personal friend, had Aids when he was hospitalized with pneumacytis carinii. They packed his belongings from the rectory and placed them on the sidewalk. A community of faith welcomed Charles into its Friday services:

> For queer Christians, the face of God is imaged in the many faces of people living with HIV illness within their own community and outside it . . . They discovered a God who is deeply embodied in their social world, a God who suffers when they suffer. . . . God really suffers with HIV people, their illness, and their social afflictions. (Goss 1993: 135)

God's compassionate solidarity with the sick and the possessed transgresses the physical and social boundaries that exclude them from society.

The anthropologist Mary Douglas argues that the maps of the physical body are replicated within the social body. The norms that regulate and classify the physical body form a microcosm of the normative maps that govern the social body (Douglas 1966; Neyrey 1991). Jesus cared for the morally unclean as much as he cared for the physically unclean. He is just as flagrant with the moral codes of purity as he is with his physical transgressions by touching the dead and lepers and healing a menstruating woman. He ate with morally suspect people: tax collectors, prostitutes and sinners (5.27–32; 7.29–31; 15.1–2; 18.4–14; 19.1–10). Jesus was a queer prophet, out of place in his adherence to holiness/purity codes. Compassionately, he welcomed outcasts into God's reign, proclaiming that God had drawn new maps of purity and holiness.

Queering God's Reign: Gender-Benders, Families and Sexuality

If the churches spent as much time on sexuality as Jesus did in his minis-try and words, the churches would be a lot healthier than they are on sexual morality. They often read the Christian scriptural texts to justify the subordi-nation of women to men, traditional family values or heterosexual marriage, and the demonization of homosexuality. Support for all three positions falters in reading Luke, for Jesus queers gender codes, patriarchal families and resur-rected life.

Non-conformist women

Luke participates in the patriarchal codes of Graeco-Roman ideology, but he inherits from the Jesus tradition the 'discipleship of equals'. There has been a storm of dispute by scholars on the reading of women in Luke's Gospel. Some scholars have claimed that Luke has a positive view of women while others maintain that he has a negative view of women as leaders in the Jesus move-ment. For example, Luke omits the story of the outspoken Gentile woman who wins an argument with Jesus (Mark 7.24–30). There are no stories of women's call to discipleship recorded in the Gospels; they remain at the narrative fringes of the Gospels. Yet Luke has to accommodate to the historical presence of women in the Jesus tradition, and there are more women visible in Luke but gener-ally silent. Schaberg and other feminist scholars have noted how Luke portrays women as models of submission to male leadership (Schaberg 1992: 63).

Women accompany Jesus; they support him financially. There is an insider group of women (8.2–3), who provide for Jesus and his male disciples out of their means (8.13). Women disciples journey outside the confines of their homes, accompany him to the cross, and are the first witnesses to his resur-rection. Women spatially break the cultural categories of women as respect-able daughters, wives and mothers. Luke portrays only women disciples at the foot of the cross, but they remain nameless. Halvor Moxnes writes about the women who followed Jesus as 'irregular women':

> They were most likely not bound in marriage, or they had some freedom within the relationship to leave their husbands. They were not childbearing, or had reached the stage of life when they were free because of their age. Thus, their sphere of possibilities had opened up. (Moxnes 2003: 100)

These women are more than 'irregular', perhaps transgressive women who were able to follow Jesus just as his male disciples were. They are liminal, if not culturally disrespectful women, crossing the gender-threshold into male space. Jesus notes that barren women are 'blessed' (23.29), and barren women are shamed in the Jewish gender codes. Here Jesus reverses the status of bar-ren women in the reign of God. Irregular, even transgressive women, populate God's reign and they form the core of Jesus' female disciples.

The story of Martha and Mary (10.38–42) has germinated a very productive discussion on whether it supports women's leadership role or submission to male leadership in the Jesus movement and later missionary activities of the

Church. Mary is silent and passively listening to Jesus while Martha is fussing and distracted in her service (*diakonia*), and some feminists understand this as Luke's undermining women's leadership and justifying women's passivity in listening to Jesus. There are two readings resistant to the female submission to male leadership. Warren Carter understands that Luke's usage of *diakonia* does not specify domestic service but 'designates a commissioned spokesperson or agent, a "go-between" who ministers on the behalf of God' (Carter 2002: 222). Martha is not distracted with kitchen duties as traditionally preached but with her duties that included care for followers, teaching and preaching. She is fussing over what she needs to do while her partner in ministry Mary is sitting at the feet of Jesus. Her problem is with what she perceives as Mary's slackness. Jesus' loving reprimand is a reminder to take some time out, not be anxious, and just chill out like Mary. The work will get done. A queer reading might build on the liturgical nature of the text. Mary intrudes on male space, receiving a theological education that authorizes her leadership. She is one of those irregular women following Jesus, preparing herself as a disciple. Irregular women are paradigms of discipleship in Gabriel's annunciation to Mary, Martha's sister, and the women at the tomb.

Gender-variant males

Jesus' male disciples transgress masculinist codes and inhabit a liminal gender space in the ancient world. Moxnes envisions the male followers of Jesus as eunuchs, 'constructing a no-man's land' (Moxnes 2003: 91–107). The male role is identified as patriarchal householder. For Moxnes, Jesus was the prototypical, non-householder; he had no home and remained an itinerant preacher of God's reign: 'Thus, his masculinity was threatening. He did not behave as a "real man." He was out place' (Moxnes 2003: 96). Jesus was out of place in the masculine ideology of both Graeco-Roman and Jewish cultures; he refuses his role as a lesser male in hegemonic masculinity within his culture and rejects marriage (or at least, the canonical sources do not mention any marriage) to sire male heirs. Without heirs, his lineage would not be continued. He abandoned family name, power and status. Furthermore, Jesus broke the patriarchal gender and procreative stereotypes of his culture, and he called men, not into counter-masculine structures such as banditry but into the liminal, gender space of God's reign.

Jesus called his male disciples from their households, albeit to an inferior masculine position in the Galilean social world. His male disciples left homes, possessions and families. Moxnes describes male discipleship as a 'versatile masculinity' (Moxnes 2003: 96). His male disciples accepted voluntary poverty, servant leadership and an inclusive hospitality. The call to discipleship (9.60, 62) supersedes family obligations, for they left families, wives and children to create a new family. Jesus had no concern for what has come to be known as traditional family values: 'Truly, I tell you, there is no one who has left house or wife or brothers or parents or children, for the sake of the kingdom of God, who will not get back very much more in this age, and in the age to come eternal life' (18.29–30). Jesus called his male disciples to a queer space, a dislocation from male gender roles in his society.

Queer families in God's reign

One of the most fanciful fictions of the religious right is the notion that Jesus is the architect and founder of 'traditional family values' (Ruether 2000: 4–7). In fact, much of the Gospel traditions is anti-family, looking to alternative structures to the patriarchal household. In 8.19–20, Jesus' mother and biological brothers cannot reach him, but he is told of their presence. He responds, 'My mother and brothers are those who hear the word of God and do it' (8.21). Spatially, his mother and brothers are outsiders, and those listening to him are insiders in the reign of God. All obligations to parents, wives and families are abandoned for this liminal gender space of God's reign. Traditional family values are emphatically rejected.

Jesus disrupted traditional households: he announces, 'Whoever comes to me and does not hate father and mother, wife and children, brothers and sisters, yes, and even life itself, cannot be my disciple' (14.26). Jesus created a new, alternative household of God: 'Families in God's reign are reconstituted, a non-biological household of equal disciples. Jesus queered the Jewish household to create families of choice' (Goss 1997: 8). Jesus' queer household of God gave men and women a new freedom by subverting hierarchy and allegiance to the patriarchal household. The patriarchal household was the model for state authority, for it represented masculine hegemony over women, children, slaves, lesser males and workers. God's reign belongs to children (18.16), and they model what it means to be a disciple (18.17). Political hierarchies are turned upside down in the reign of God. Thus, God's household challenged Galilean village authority, Herod Antipas, the Jewish priestly elites, and the Roman conquerors.

Homoerotic relationships

The Q story of the centurion appears not only in Matthew 8.5–13 and Luke 7.1–10 but also in John 4.46–54. Most scholarly opinion finds the Matthean story the version closer to the original source. The presumption of heterosexuality has, however, blinded heterosexual scholars and clergy alike to the true nature of this healing story. How could a model of faith be in a pederastic relationship? A number of authors read a homoerotic relationship between the centurion and his boy (Horner 1978: 122; McNeill 1995: 132–6; Williams 1992: 60–3; Hanks 2000: 48; Jennings 2003: 131–44).

Luke uses the term servant (*doulos*) in place of youth (*pais*) in Matthew's version. With the pervasiveness of pederasty in the Graeco-Roman world, any first-century CE reader would instantly understand the relationship between the Roman centurion and his boy as pederastic. Robin Scroggs writes,

> The practices of pederasty emerged out of the dominant social matrix of the day. In some quarters, pederastic relations were extolled, in almost all quarters condoned . . . it is important to keep in mind that the Graeco-Roman pederasty was practiced by a large number of people in part because it was socially acceptable, while by many other people actually idealized as a normal process in the course of maturation. (Scroggs 1983: 27)

Tom Hanks notes, 'In light of the common practices of Roman soldiers, it is best understood as a sexual relationship' (Hanks 2000: 47–8). John McNeill also points out that the centurions were not allowed to marry during their period of military service. The centurion found physical comfort from his slave (McNeill 1995: 134). But Luke uses the word 'slave' rather than the suggestive term 'youth'. Luke notes that the centurion's slave was precious or dear (*entimos*). Verstraete and more recently Walters have underscored the nature of homoerotic relationships and arrangements between Roman free-born men and their slaves (Verstraete 1980: 227; Walters 1993: 29).

The slave was ill, close to death. The centurion sent some Jewish elders to Jesus. They say, 'He is worthy of having you do this for him, for he loves our people, and it is he who built our synagogue' (7.4b–5). Not only is the Roman centurion in a homoerotic relationship, but he is generous to the conquered Jewish community. He differs from the normal Roman occupiers. He has earned the respect of many of the Jews within the community because he has shown respect for their religion, and in his generosity he has contributed and built a synagogue.

Jesus goes to heal the centurion's boy lover, but the centurion again sends friends: 'Lord, do not trouble yourself, for I am not worthy to have you come under my roof; therefore I did not presume to come to you. But only speak the word, and let my servant be healed' (7.6b–7a). Jesus' reaction is not condemnatory. In fact, he says that there is no greater faith in Israel. Did Jesus understand the nature of the centurion's relationship with his slave? Graeco-Roman pederastic relations were not uncommon in the Hellenistic and Roman enclaves in Galilee and the surrounding region. Jesus did not choose to condemn the homoerotic relationship between them. He did not tell the centurion that he had to be celibate or to marry a woman. Nor did he quote the verses in Leviticus to condemn male-to-male anal intercourse.

Donald Mader observes, 'a segment of the early church in which the Q document and Matthew arose, was not concerned, when confronted by a responsible, loving pederastic relationship, but rather held it subordinate to the question of faith' (Mader 1992: 231). This story undermines the contemporary religious right, who maintain that you cannot be queer and Christian. Jesus acknowledges that there is no greater faith in all of Israel than in this Roman centurion actively involved in a responsible homoerotic relationship. It is ironic to remember that Catholics are taught to remember this man in a homoerotic relationship as they recite at the reception of communion: 'Lord, I am unworthy that you come under my roof, but just say the word and my soul shall be healed.'

Sex in the resurrected life

The story of the Sadducee test in Luke 20.27–40 appears earlier in Mark 12.18–27 and a parallel account in Matthew 22.23–33. It is a passage where the Sadducee critics challenge Jesus on the notion of the afterlife. They propose to Jesus the example of a woman who has been married seven times and ask him, 'In the resurrection, therefore, whose wife will the woman be? For the seven had married her' (20.33). Jesus responds, 'Those who belong to this age marry and are given in marriage; but those who are considered worthy of a place in that age and in the resurrection from the dead neither marry nor are given in marriage' (20.34–5). Then Jesus gives the reason for no marriage in the resurrected life: 'Indeed they cannot die any more, because they are like angels and are children of God, being the children of the resurrection' (20.36). 'Like angels' was understood as 'sexless' by centuries of Christian thought that transformed angels from sexual beings in the intertestamental period to sexless, disembodied spirits, and this was used to justify the superiority of the celibate elite. The biblical scholar William Countryman, however, writes on Jude,

> Think . . . of the little letter of Jude, where it appears that early Christians were teaching that you needed to have sex with angels in order to gain high standing in heaven. Jude refers to this teaching only in veiled ways, but that is what he's attacking. Of course, his readers knew the Hebrew Bible (mostly in Greek translation), and they knew the story in Genesis 6.1–4 about angels having sex with human women and the offspring being giants. Jude refers to that story and also to the story of the men of Sodom who in the same manner as these angels 'went after strange flesh' (Jude 7, referring to Genesis 18). (Countryman and Riley 2001: 35–6)

Countryman is well aware that in first-century CE Christian thought angels were understood to be sexual beings, not the sexless constructions of angels in later eras. Jesus' phrase 'like an angel' indicates that there is no marriage and family in God's coming reign. God abolishes the institution of marriage, which is understood as a property right and ownership of women. But traditionally, ecclesial exegetes have understood that this text abolishes not only marriage but also sexuality, because of its narrow interpretation of marriage for the purpose of procreation. But nothing merits such a reading of the abolition of sexuality, and a queer reading can restore sexuality to the coming reign of God. Certainly, Jesus attacked marriage as the patriarchal possession of women in marriage and the patriarchal family, on which the Jewish and Roman political order of domination was based. Jesus is asserting the abolition of patriarchal marriage in the coming reign of God.

A queer reading might likewise affirm that there is no marriage and patriarchal family, but it also might assert that there is sexuality without procreation in the coming reign of God. But there is no more marriage because they cannot die and are like angels. In God's coming reign, there is no need for marriage and procreation when you live forever in resurrected bodies. Jesus' eschatological vision does not preclude erotic desire and sexuality.

Turning the Fundamentalist World Upside-Down

In Acts 17.6, the Jews charge that the missionaries of the Jesus movement have turned 'the world upside-down'. The charge is levelled against the post-resurrection followers of Jesus, yet their practices find their foundation in the social and religious challenge of Jesus in Luke's Gospel to fundamentalist Jews with differing holiness agendas. At the proceedings before Pilate, Jesus is charged, 'He perverted (queered) the nation . . . ' (23.5). Jesus disrupted the symbolic universe of many Jewish factions. It is his symbolic action in the temple that forces the powerful priestly elite to seize him and bring him before the Romans.

Purity codes are symbolic maps of what constitutes holiness and wholeness on the level of the social and physical body. Jerome Neyrey and other biblical scholars have produced impressive analyses of the purity maps of first-century CE Palestinian Judaism, based on Mary Douglas's work (Neyrey 1991: 273–304):

> The idea of dirt implies a structure of idea. For us, dirt is a kind of compendium category for all events which blur, smudge, contradict, or otherwise confuse accepted classifications. The underlying feeling is that a system of values which is habitually expressed in a given arrangement of things has been violated. (Douglas 1966: 51)

In the Levitical codes, there is a strong link between purity and holiness, and this link became more intensified during Second Temple Judaism. Dirt is 'matter out of place'; social disorder that extends to all the maps or classification systems applied to society, the body and people (Neyrey 1991: 274). Various Jewish groups – the Sadducees, Pharisee groups, the Qumran community and its lay adherents – had their own particular politics of holiness and cleanliness.

Jesus shared the symbolic universe of Second Temple Judaism, but he also challenged particular symbolic maps of purity/holiness. He founded a countercultural, religious renewal movement whose agenda was the reign of God. For example, Jesus is portrayed in conflict with particular Pharisees on issues of tithing, the washing of hands, proper preparation of meals, and eating with suspect people. His blatant disregard for the table holiness/purity concerns sets him on a collision course with conservative Pharisees. Jesus' missionary instructions to the seventy disciples ignore the boundaries of the dietary laws and purity codes (10.7–9). He touches unclean bodies of lepers, places his hands on a corpse, comes into contact with menstruating women, allows himself to be kissed by a sinful woman, and heals a crippled woman on the Sabbath. From a conservative Pharisaic perspective, Jesus trampled their cultural maps of purity/holiness. This becomes readily apparent in the story of Jesus' dinner with Simon the Pharisee when a sinful woman intrudes upon the purity of the meal and bathes Jesus' feet with her tears, drying them with her hair and anointing his feet with ointment. Impurity was so contagious for some Pharisees, and it drove Simon crazy at this obscene gesture of an unclean woman.

She shows Jesus hospitality by washing his feet and gratitude by anointing his feet whereas Simon displays neither hospitality nor gratitude. Jesus tells a parable of two debtors where one is forgiven more than the other, and he asks the question: 'Now which of them will love him more?' (7.42). Simon is portrayed as an inadequate, uptight, purity-scrupulous host while the unclean and loose woman shows Jesus hospitality in the fashion of God's reign. She, a loose woman, and not the Pharisee, manifests God's reign and hospitality. The social order is reversed with God's coming reign. It is the shock of the parable of the Great Supper that is now enacted (14.16–24).

Throughout Luke's Gospel, Jesus challenges restrictive maps of holiness/ purity for more porous and promiscuous maps. God's reign is queer by mixing up gender and social divisions, overturning hierarchies, and breaking down holiness/purity boundaries. Jesus' actions disrupt the symbolic maps of his culture, and his disruption in the temple has lethal consequences.

Stop the temple action

Luke downsizes Jesus' provocative 'Stop the temple action' from Mark 11.15–17 to Jesus driving out vendors who were selling in the temple precincts. He sanitizes Jesus' political action for his Graeco-Roman readers. He portrays Jesus teaching daily in the temple, engaging the chief priests, scribes and elders in a series of conflicts: the questioning of Jesus' authority, the parable of the Wicked Tenants, the question of taxes, and resurrection. The conflict stories end with the foretelling of the destruction of the temple and the parable of the Fig Tree.

Jesus' demonstration was directed against the wealthy priestly aristocracy and Jerusalem elites, their exploitation of the poor and their exclusion of 'throw-away' people, and their participation in the Roman imperial system. He antagonized the guardians of Jewish religious and political values with his transgressive actions. The chief priests and the Jerusalem elites took the initiative in arresting Jesus and bringing him before Pilate and Herod. They charge Jesus with 'perverting our nation' (23.2, 14). They perceived Jesus' action as threatening to and contemptuous of the temple. Such a challenge to the temple clergy and the Jerusalem elites had to be decisively met. From one perspective, Jesus' demonstration within the sacred space of the temple failed and directly led to his arrest, legal proceedings and execution. Jesus' staged demonstration models transgressive practice for queer Christians.

Jesus is the model of transgressive queer actions such as ACT UP's demonstration against St Patrick's Cathedral and Cardinal O'Connor's sacrilegious disregard for queer people living with Aids more than a decade ago (Goss 1993: 147–9) or the more recent Marriage Rebellion in San Francisco and other cities to issue marriage licences to same-sex couples. Jesus invades sacred space, indicting the temple leaders that they have lost their sacred mission of representing God's care for the marginalized. He calls for a change of heart as many queer demonstrators have repeated in front of meetings of the Catholic bishops and Southern Baptist Conventions. Jesus' non-violent challenge called for a change of heart and abandoning a politics of exclusion and violence.

Jesus' utterance has prophetic relevance: 'My house shall be a house of prayer, but you have made it a den of robbers' (19.46). Fundamentalist and evangelical churches, political action groups of the Christian right, the Mormon and the Catholic Churches have poured millions of dollars into state referendums to define marriage as one man and one woman. These restrictions hurt millions of same-sex couples and their children. These homophobic church leaders have truly robbed queer people of legitimizing their relationships, also denying families the right to medical insurance and other married partner benefits. These churches are 'dens of robbers' in harming millions of queer families and their children.

The Last Supper

The Last Supper begins a process of dislocating the body of Jesus, and Graham Ward calls this dislocation of the body of Christ an 'ontological scandal' (Ward 2000: 82). Jesus' body becomes dislocated, or to speak in purity terms, it becomes 'out of place'. The rubric of breaking the bread prefigures the breaking of his body in the crucifixion. But within God's economy in Luke's Gospel, the meal foreshadows the melding of Jesus' body with other bodies as he becomes the cosmic Christ.

Many biblical interpreters follow the tradition of interpreting the Last Supper as a Passover meal while others compare it to a Hellenistic symposium meal. Nevertheless, such interpretations redirect the attention from the real scandal that some Jews would experience in such correlation of an unclean body with bread. This is apparent in the registered offence of some pious Jews in the 'bread of life discourse' where Jesus' shocking speech invites listeners to eat his flesh and drink his blood (John 6.60–1). John's Gospel notes how repugnant Jesus' comparison is to his audience. The real scandal of the Last Supper is its violation of the food laws for Jewish fundamentalists, committed to scrupulous observance of the dietary instructions. Jesus identifies his body with the unleavened bread and his blood with the cup of blessing, and he further blurs the blessing of the bread and cup with his anticipated death. Food, death and life are blended into his symbolic actions. Eating human flesh and drinking blood literally violates the purity laws, and its metaphorical usage would be equally shocking to conservative Jewish views of holiness/purity. Second, Jesus is portrayed as touching unclean bodies and engaging in indiscriminate relations with all sorts of unclean people. His body is polluted, if not contagious, and he offers his defiled body as food. All these boundary transgressions would disrupt the holiness/purity codes of the most conservative Jewish factions.

What Jesus does in the Last Supper anticipates final disruption of the holiness/purity systems. Jesus establishes new maps of holiness where God is loosening the holiness boundaries for a more inclusive, covenant community. It will become a new map of bodies incorporated into the body of Christ, a displacement of Jesus' physical body broken on the cross and ultimately God's transgression of all purity systems with the displaced body of the Christ. The male body of the Christ will be displaced from its physical gendered performance into pan-gendered bodies: male, female, transgendered and intersexual (Loughlin 1998; Ward 2000).

The death of Jesus

The death of Jesus was the ultimate act of defilement. The Gentile colonizers crucified him outside the city. Spatially, the crucified Jesus is outside the walls of Jerusalem and the precincts of the temple. In Deuteronomy 21.23, it is acknowledged that a man hung on a tree is 'cursed'. Dead bodies and dying bodies are polluted, for the dead do not belong to the world of the living. An unburied, dead body is a site of pollution; it is 'out of place' because it is not buried. Jesus' death on the cross remains an offensive scandal for many Jewish adherents to a politics of holiness/purity. It represents a polluted death at the hands of defiling Romans, and his identity as a prophet of God is spoiled from a Jewish perspective. A couple of decades earlier, Paul understood that the death of Jesus was a 'stumbling block for Jews' (1 Cor. 1.23), and he reworked the crucifixion into a demonstration of God's wisdom and triumph.

Jesus' death, however, remains an act of transgression of the purity codes but not through his own action. The lines between the dead and the living become porous, and in the ultimate queer act, God abolishes the division between the living and the dead with the resurrected Christ. The monstrous death of Jesus becomes a scandal to confuse the clearly drawn categories of purity/impurity.

Crucifixion breaks Jesus' body as he broke the loaf of unleavened bread to share with his disciples. His broken and abused body becomes embodied in all other broken and abused bodies. This translocation of Jesus' body into all bodies is completed in the Easter faith of the disciples where they recognize Jesus in the proclamation of the good news, the breaking of the bread, and in the communal body.

In Matthew Shepard's death, many Americans saw a repetition of the crucified Christ: two gay-bashers beat him, hung him on a fence as a message to other queer people, and he died. During Matthew Shepard's funeral, Revd Anne Kitch 'evoked the image of Jesus as another man whose body was broken, torn, and abandoned on a wooden cross' (Ingrebretsen 2001: 184). The queer community automatically translocated the crucified Christ into the body of Matthew Shepard hung on a fence. For example, playwright Terence McNally wrote,

> Beaten senseless and tied to a split-rail fence in near-zero weather, arms akimbo in a grotesque crucifixion, he died as agonizing a death as another young man who had been tortured and nailed to a wooden cross at a desolate spot outside Jerusalem known as Golgotha some 1,998 years earlier. They died, as they lived, as brothers. Jesus Christ did not die in vain because His disciples lived to spread his story. It is this generation's duty to make certain Matthew Shepard did not die in vain either. (McNally 1998: vi)

The American cultural critic Edward Ingebretsen observes how Matthew's death and the fundamentalist Christian protesters from Fred Phelps' Westboro Church at the funeral reawakened a crisis within Christianity on the significance of Jesus' death and the nature of the sacred. The scandal is that the abjected, murdered gay youth becomes a 'bearer of sacred memory', refigured in the image of the crucified Christ while the protesters do violence in the name of the cross (Ingebretsen 2001: 181). Ingebretsen recognizes that Christ's bloody flesh was bodied forth in the crucified body of Matthew Shepard. The monstrous 'homosexual' becomes the crucified site of God's grace as once before the queer man from Galilee had.

Easter: The Queer Christ

More than a decade ago, I wrote, 'To say Jesus the Christ is queer is to say that God identifies with us and our experiences of injustice . . . Jesus the queer Christ is crucified repeatedly by homophobic violence' (Goss 1993: 84–5). My theological affirmation of the Queer Christ's solidarity with queer folk and all oppressed peoples began to spell out the risen Christ's compassionate and embodied identification with the marginalized, the poor and the oppressed. God's embodied and compassionate solidarity embraced the crucified and abjected body of Jesus. Graham Ward's notion of Jesus' displaced body, combined with a theology of God's compassionate identification with the oppressed, provides a theoretical and practical framework for imaginatively reconceiving God's salvific economy in Jesus the Christ.

Resurrection is God's ultimate queer surprise. It is the metanarrative for all the parables by which Jesus shocked his audience: the Prodigal Son, the Good Samaritan, and the Great Supper. What God did in the resurrection of Jesus, God was doing from the beginning of creation and in the ministry of Jesus. It is the coming out of God as unconditional love and grace. It is the complete translocation of Jesus' dead body. God creates new embodiments of the Christ. Perhaps the greatest dislocation is how God places queer folk back into the story of the ongoing presence of the risen Christ.

Irregular women as witnesses to the empty tomb

Several women disciples – led by Mary Magdalene, Joanna and Mary the mother of James – go to the tomb, a place of death and pollution. They bring spices to anoint the dead body of Jesus, but when they reach the tomb, they discover the rock rolled away and the tomb empty. Jesus' body is missing, and the empty tomb represents that death is overcome. Two messengers proclaim the good news: 'He is not here, but has risen' (24.5b). At the tomb, the women are first to receive the message of Jesus' resurrection and act as the first disciples to spread the good news to the male disciples. Some of the male apostles are dismissive of the women, for they do not believe them or even check out the stories of the women. After all, they are emotional women, and their story is an 'idle tale', pure nonsense. Yet the female disciples have a mandate from the angels to go back to the despondent male leadership, and they have the courage, the humility and the freedom to witness to the good news that Jesus is risen.

While the female disciples are open to the power of the good news of Jesus' resurrection, they are not accepted as credible witnesses. Peter is the only one to be moved by their words, and he runs to the tomb to check out their story and is amazed at the empty tomb. This seems to be in keeping with Luke's evaluation of Peter as the premier apostle. How often are the stories and faith witness of irregular women – queer women – trivialized or even ignored by many denominational churches which refuse to recognize the ministry of queer Christian women. Many have been denied ordination or placed on trial for being a 'practising homosexual'.

Que(ry)ing Emmaus for the Church

The story of the queer disciples at Emmaus has long been recognized in faith communities (Martin 2000; Kelly 1994). In his video series on queer spirituality and sexuality, Michael Kelly provides a queer reading of the story of Emmaus. The two disciples are outsiders, not huddled and secreted with the male leadership in Jerusalem. They may have left in sadness and disgust over the community's failure to be present to Jesus in his agony and death.

The two disciples are despondent, grieving at the loss of Jesus, but they are joined by a stranger who walks with them, and the disciples speak of their hopes and dreams, betrayals and deadly loss. They expressed to him how they have given their hearts to Jesus, his message and practices and how they hoped that Jesus would set them free. Unlike the male apostles, the two disciples on the road report how astounded they were by the words of the women returning from the tomb. They were not dismissive of the women's story but puzzled and perhaps confused. The two disciples are separate from the mainstream male leadership in Jerusalem; they are queer outsiders, perhaps even two lovers. They raise the women's story with the stranger because they are processing the death of Jesus with the women's proclamation of the empty tomb. The two disciples tell their story to the stranger on the road. It takes a stranger to hear the story of two outsiders.

The disciples are open to hear what the stranger has to say to the truth and integrity of their experience. The stranger goes into the scriptures to explain that Jesus had to queer all religious expectations and that through his ministry, suffering and death, the Christ entered into glory. God has not disappointed them, for God raised the queer Christ. Their queer experience finds hope in God's vindication of Jesus' queer ministry and death. Their hearts were once again set on fire as when they first heard Jesus' proclamation of the good news. The despondent community of the male apostles did not enkindle the fire of hope. The stranger speaks to their estrangement and exile, but they are also emotionally open to speak about the pain of their lives. Many translesbigay folk feel out of place within many churches since those churches have taken Jesus away from them, crucified him, and preach the news of not worshipping God with their bodies.

The two queer disciples invite the stranger to stay with them for the night; they have a natural gift of queer hospitality. Their bodies yearned for his presence, and as outsiders they intuitively recognized him embodied in their own experience. They invited him into their lives. He gives thanks, breaks the bread, and gives it to them. Their eyes were opened; their lives changed. They complete the ritual of the bread, recognizing Jesus in the midst and in their own life experiences. The disciples recognize their lives in the bread. Jesus takes bread, blesses their experiences of brokenness, pain, exile and alienation, and transforms the bread of their lives into his body. The breaking of the bread creates them into church, calling them to become the eschatological body of Christ. The risen Jesus is not the possession of the community but abides in the word of scripture, in the bread broken, and queer embodied lives.

The presence of the risen Christ is repeated in queer lives of faith and struggle, even in contemporary times:

> In Michigan, a man named David wanted his union of twelve years with Jon blessed by a representative of God before they died. David lay on the couch while Jim, a gay Presbyterian minister who also has AIDS, moved his hands to the silent sounds of peace. He spoke nourishing words of bless-ing on these two lives bound by God's grace: 'Those, whom God has joined together, let no one put asunder . . .' And then as the minister began to cele-brate Communion for those who were present, he spoke the familiar words: 'This is my body, broken for you . . .' and that was the point at which David died. 'Do this in remembrance of me.' (Brantley 1996: 217–18)

The story of Jesus is not finished; it is remembered and repeated in the queer lives of countless humans. The risen Christ is encountered in the outsider, in two HIV+ gay lovers whose marriage is blessed and celebrated by a gay minis-ter with Aids. Each time a Christian celebrant fractures the bread in faith, the risen body of the queer Christ is disseminated into pieces of the blessed bread and devoured by queer Christians. The queer Christ becomes recognizable in a multitude of queer bodies and lives.

Michael Kelly notes how queer folk have to look for the risen Christ out-side the community. As they discover him outside the community, they have the responsibility to journey back to the community. Their healing, openness and reflection lead them to follow the trajectory of the irregular women at the tomb. With courage and renewed lives, they leave their exile to tell the story of how Jesus was found in their queer lives and stories, and of how the breaking of the bread made them into a community, empowered by the risen Christ. The risen Christ's breaking of the bread makes the two queer disciples into church. Each time queer followers gather together in faith and remember the meal that Jesus celebrated, they create a queer Church.

Here is the important insight of Kelly's queer reading of the story. The queer Church travels back to the mainstream Church, bringing the message of the power of Christ's resurrection discovered in their embodied, erotic experi-ences. They embody the risen Christ, and the recognition of their embodiment of the queer Christ motivates them to return to the larger community to bear witness to the queer Christ in their own lives. They now have the power to transform the despondent and disembodied community, to change the hearts of its members so that they can recognize the presence of the risen Christ embodied in queer disciples. It is only their embodied return that prepares the community to welcome and hear the risen and embodied Christ in their midst.

Luke comprehends the stories of irregular women and the two outsider dis-ciples as the catalyst for the apostolic community to recognize the presence of the risen Christ within its midst. Outside women and men find the pres-ence of the Christ at the empty tomb, in exile, in their vulnerability, in the scriptures and the breaking of the bread, and in the truth of their erotic lives. The Christian churches can only be reawakened to embodiment of an erotic spirituality as it listens to the stories of women and queer folk. The churches can be resurrected to an embodied Christ who is enfleshed in the erotic lives of women and queer folk. The story of Jesus the Queer Christ will continue in queer lives; they will translate that story into the diverse languages of the many queer sub-communities in Acts and into the future.

John

ROBERT E. GOSS

Most scholars do not dispute the location of the Gospel of John at Ephesus or some similar large urban centre in Lebanon or Syria. A late first-century date is proposed for the final composition of the Gospel, approximately 90–110 CE. Scholars take John 9.22 to refer to the expulsion of the Jewish Christians from the synagogues and date the Gospel sometime after 90 CE. The Gospel narrative claims the text was written by the beloved disciple who was an eyewitness to the events of Jesus' public ministry. The fourth evangelist believed that he was inspired by the Holy Spirit to remember and narrate the events of the Gospel (John 14.26; 15.26).

A major feature of John's Gospel is its Christology. The pre-existent Word becomes flesh in Jesus (1.14). God comes out in Jesus, revealing the nature of God as divine lover. Roger Haight succinctly defines Christology as 'the reaction and interpretation of Jesus' (Haight 1999: 30). In the Gospel of John, the Christology is from the perspective of from on high. Jesus is portrayed as one who descends from heaven and reveals the nature of God. Thus, the portrayal of Jesus is that of the exalted Christ who reveals God as parent and who is one with God.

By the third century CE, John's Gospel was recognized as the spiritual Gospel because it differed from the three canonical synoptic Gospels in its portrayal of Jesus and because of its symbolism. It was the highly sacramental or symbolic way the story of Jesus is presented that was noticed by early Christian writers. In his *Ecclesiastical History*, Eusebius quotes Clement of Alexandria: 'Last of all John, perceiving that the external facts had been made plain in the gospel, urged by his friends and inspired by the Spirit, composed a spiritual gospel' (O' Day 2001: 26). The evangelist writes a Gospel with the internal facts. The Fourth Gospel addresses the internal life experiences of the reader, and it aptly (but not exclusively) addresses queer life experiences in coming out, discovering the grace of their true selves and integrating the message of God's coming out in Jesus.

Central to John's Gospel is the theme of God's coming out in Jesus. 'Coming out' is understood by many as a sacrament (Glaser, Goss, Heyward, Perkins, West). Mona West describes coming out as a 'break-in moment in our spiritual growth': 'Break-in moments are those moments of invitation that happen throughout our life in which we catch glimpses of something more, something bigger in which we participate' (West 2005). The Metropolitan Community Church pastor/writer Chris Glaser understands that coming out is a sacrament, a ritual that reveals the sacred in queer lives. It is a central theme in the Jewish and Christian biblical traditions:

But coming out is a recurring if not central theme of the Bible, easily recognizable to those familiar with the experience and process of coming out as lesbian, gay, bisexual, transgender . . . This links our own experience with that of our spiritual ancestors as well as opens us to the universality of life-giving and life-changing coming out process for every human being. Just as coming out to God opens up the chosen or called in the Bible to God's own coming out, so our vulnerability creates a welcome sanctuary for God's self-disclosure. (Glaser 1998: 49)

God's coming out in Jesus in surprising ways offers a challenge. It helps some folk in the Gospel to let go of past conceptions and traditional images and opens them to new possibilities of life and transformation. Other characters – like Nicodemus, some disciples, and opponents – do not welcome God's coming out in Jesus. They refuse to accept the possibility of God embodied in Jesus and becoming an embodied word of grace.

This theme of coming out enables queer folk to appreciate God's coming out in Jesus and the struggles engendered in the narrative. God's coming out in Jesus resonates with queer life experiences. Many of us have experienced coming out as a double-edged sword, an experience both of grace and self-acceptance and of rejection from a judgemental society. The signs source (chapters 1.19–12.50), often speculated by Johannine scholars as an earlier written source or a missionary tract to persuade Jews that Jesus was the Messiah, provides queer readers with an opportunity to look at themes of the coming out of God in Christ. For many queers, coming out is a gracious invitation to see the divine in our lives but also is a painful, even conflictive experience.

The second aspect of God's coming out in Jesus is to reveal God as lover. It follows from queer folk's struggles to come out. Coming out involves authentic living, making visible one's love. Robert Williams observes, 'The urge to come out, to overcome oppression and self-loathing, to celebrate who I am, is the siren call of God, the Divine Lover – the most promiscuous of all lovers' (Heyward 1989: 120). God's love can not be boxed, controlled or regulated. It manifests itself in the most unexpected ways, in the most unexpected people. The divine invitation to come out of the closet is to leave behind old patterns and to live authentic lives. Jesus models such a coming out of God for queer people of faith.

Jesus and his disciples are from the light, but his opponents are from the dark. They cannot recognize Jesus as God's coming out. Jesus says, 'You are from below, I am from above; you are of this cosmos, I am not of this cosmos' (8.23). Essential to John's retelling the story of Jesus is this particular Christian community's conflict with elements of the Jewish community in the post-temple era. From John 9, it seems that the high Christology of John's community led to its expulsion from certain synagogues. Jesus' opponents keep asking, 'Where are you from?' They are unable to answer those existential questions for themselves and thus assume a hostile position to Jesus and the blind man whose eyesight has recovered. The Fourth Gospel's appeal to despised groups such as Samaritans further antagonized the community with fundamentalist Jewish leaders who were concerned to maintain tight boundaries on the Jewish community. The Johannine community feels isolated in a hostile world, envisioning itself as a light in darkness. For the community, the Gospel offers reassurance that they are not alone in the world and that they are loved by God.

It is natural for queer Christians to identify with the sectarian dimensions of the Johannine community and similarly read of the story of Jesus. Like the Johannine community, the queer Christian community persevered in its faith despite its exclusive and hostile denominational churches. Queer Christians spread the good news to the translesbigay community and reach out to the marginal and the oppressed. They preserve the memory that Jesus was at home with the outcast and the oppressed and that Jesus came out as the embodied Word of God. Yet many could not accept the coming out of the Word because it was too scandalous, too embodied, and too gracious.

The Fleshy Word: Queer Fluidity

Embodiment has been a major problem for Christians through the ages. Body negativity developed with the syncretism of Christianity with body-despising philosophies of the Graeco-Roman world and the development of Christian asceticism. Christians have barely tolerated the body. Years ago, I was struck how incompatible the Christian anti-body theologies were to the Fourth Gospel. God's embodiment in the human Jesus is a fleshly event. Rosemary Haughton wrote, 'Christianity is, far more than any other, a physical religion, which is one reason why many spiritually minded people find it gross and fleshy, and try to refine and "spiritualize" it. But it is inescapably "fleshly," being founded in the human flesh of . . . Christ' (Haughton 1969: 38).

John's Gospel develops the most profound Christological reflections upon Jesus that we encounter in the Christian canon of scriptures. By far, John is the queerest of all the Gospels. It weaves the gender fluidity of Jesus as the embodiment of Divine Wisdom with Jesus as God's revelation. Jesus is the supreme manifestation of God's Word and embodiment of Divine Wisdom. It expresses an alternative to the male imagery of God (Johnson 1992c). Martin Scott argues:

> The point of John's Wisdom Christology is precisely that Jesus Sophia is not mere man, but rather the incarnation of both the male and the female expression of the divine, albeit within the limitation of human flesh. (Scott 1992: 72)

For Scott, Jesus exhibits the feminine traits of the Sophia Wisdom model of God, but his maleness complicates the feminine aspects of Wisdom. Collen Conway notes that Jesus in John's Gospel as he relates to God as Father is 'obedient, submissive, can do nothing on his own' (Conway 2003: 179). Jesus is omnigendered, fluid in gender expressions with relation to various characters and God. He takes on a submissive role as a slave or a woman to wash the feet of his male disciples; he is penetrated by the patriarchal Roman system, nailed to the cross. His flesh is penetrated by the phallic system of patriarchal conquest and rule. Jesus as embodiment of God's Wisdom suffers the abuse that many women have faced from a patriarchal system of power and violence.

The Latina bisexual theologian Marcella Althaus-Reid develops her Bi/Christology on the passage on John 1.14: 'the word became flesh and pitched a tent among us':

> Only a Bi/Christ category which happens to be so unsettled, that no mono-relationship could have been so easily constructed with it. Bi/Christology walks like a nomad in the lands of opposition and exclusive identities, and does not pitch its tent forever in the same place. If we considered that in the Gospel of John 1:14, the verb is to have 'dwelt among us' as a tabernacle (a tent) or 'put his tent amongst us,' the image conveys Christ's high mobility and lack of fixed space or definitive frontiers. Tents are easily dismantled overnight and do not become ruins or monuments; they are rather folded and stored or reused for another purpose when old. Tents change in shape in strong winds, and their adaptability rather than their stubbornness is one of their greatest assets. (Althaus-Reid 2001a: 119–20)

Certainly, the incarnate Word is a coming out of God. John's Prologue places the story of Jesus within the story of God, providing a cosmic context for Jesus' mission to bring light and the revelation of God. It also sets the theme of the mobility and fluidity of God's embodied Word. God's Word is fluid, and those fundamentalists with fixed and literalist religious conceptions will oppose the Word: 'He came to what was his own, and his own people did not accept him. But to all who received him, who believed in his name, he gave power to become children of God' (1.11–12). God comes out in Christ: 'I am the bread of life; I am the light of the world; I am the good shepherd; I am the vine and you are the branches; I am the resurrection and the life; I am.' In each of these statements, Christ comes out, and his own people did not accept him. Queer folk readily comprehend this resistance to coming out; they understand religious hostility and even lethal fundamentalist opposition to coming out. The first-century CE 'Religious Right' were just as recalcitrant and antagonistic as their contemporary Christian successors.

Coming Out into the Light

The Prologue of the Gospel sets up the coming-out motif. The light is revealed but rejected. There is no question that Jesus' unconventional behaviours flaunted and even challenged fundamentalist Jewish notions of religious practice. He transgresses fundamentalist piety and overthrows rigid religious practices. He associates with the disreputable, the marginal, the outcasts and sinners of his day. Jesus finds himself in conflict with rigid Pharisees, the chief priests installed by the Roman occupiers, and the Roman administrative government.

There are a series of witnesses and opponents to the light. The first witness to God's coming out in Christ is John the Baptist. For our queer community, John the Baptist is a 'hairy leather bear' in the gay sense of the word (Perry 1991: 247–8; Boisvert 2004: 53–68). He is not worthy to loosen his sandals, 'shine his boots', as a boot shiner at a leather event might translate. The Baptist steps out of the closet of ordinary cultural space into the wilderness, a liminal space:

> The Baptist's call was also a call to conversion, and his sign was that of water, of renewal and the beginning of life. He stands guard over our comings out, the very first and all the ones we must subsequently face in the harsh course of our lives. He protects and reaffirms our difference, for it is only truth – he who came to speak for it, and to bear witness to it. (Boisvert 2004: 64)

With passionate zeal, the hairy bear Baptist witnesses to God's coming out in the Christ. He names Jesus the 'lamb of God'. He speaks for those alternative males – who transgress the masculine codes, both ancient and contemporary, and who look to a new moral and sexual order that does not dominate women and unconventional males. Jesus draws male disciples from this counter-cultural movement led by a hairy leather bear. He will proclaim that God has come out in himself, through signs, his dialogues and particular encounters with people.

Nicodemus comes to Jesus during the night. He is the archetypal closeted Christian. From the Gospel's usage of darkness and light, coming at night denotes a negative, for he represents the darkness that does not perceive the light. Nicodemus is not a believer though he is both fascinated with Jesus' signs but afraid to be seen with him during the daylight. He is, at best, lukewarm to Jesus' message. Jesus upbraids him for his secrecy and his unbelief. The closeted Nicodemus is caught up in fear, and he fails to hear Jesus' words of grace: 'For God so loved the world that God gave the only begotten child, that whoever believes in the child should not perish but have eternal life.' Nicodemus fades back into the closet. Nicodemus appears twice more in the Gospel (7.50–3; 19.39–42), and he is still on the margins, not willing to fully declare himself to the world.

Nicodemus remains closeted as a believer in the text, coming to Jesus in the middle of the night. The gay author James Alison writes,

> Jesus does not pander to Nicodemus coming to him at night, allowing himself to be flattered by the attention. He knows the desires by night which are in contradiction with the desires of the day are signs that both are distorted. He gives it to Nicodemus straight: there is no such thing as a closet disciple. (Alison 2001: 217)

Jesus speaks to Nicodemus of being born again. This spiritual birth is a realization that desires by the night and desires by the day need to be integrated into a spiritual whole. The integration of one's sexuality with spirituality, the fleshly and the spiritual, requires a coming out, a rebirth. The queer Christian disciple enfleshes spirituality and does not deny embodied dimensions of desire and passionate longing.

Jesus fails to be sympathetic to this closeted disciple, who maintains the religious status quo and whose fear paralyses him from taking the next step to coming out as a disciple. Nicodemus is much like closeted clergy failing to come out and stand up with queer folk. But Jesus has some impact upon

Nicodemus. Later in the Gospel, he timidly stands up to the authorities who try to arrest Jesus by asking a question of due process (7.51). At the end of the Gospel, Nicodemus and Joseph of Arimathea, another closeted official, bury Jesus secretly. Did he have any regrets as he buried the body of Jesus? Nicodemus buys the equivalent of 75 pounds of burial spices. Does the action suggest his unbelief in the resurrection? Or does it reveal his regrets in not following Jesus more boldly? Clearly, Nicodemus is afraid of the communal consequences in making a decision to come out as a follower of Jesus.

How often has this scenario been re-enacted in closeted clergy burying gay men who died because of HIV! Instead of representing Christ, they have mimicked Nicodemus in the closet. Like Nicodemus, they failed to side with the truth and those who witness to the truth. They have failed to speak up against the homophobic pronouncements of hatred and violence of ecclesial leaders. They failed to see the Christ embodied in the faces of gay men who have died. Did Christ appear to Nicodemus? Did Nicodemus finally develop a backbone to come out as a disciple as last? How will closeted clergy face their fallen HIV+ brothers at the resurrection of the dead? With remorse? With profound regret?

If we read the story of Nicodemus as a closeted gay man, it is easy to read the Samaritan woman as a lesbian who has practised serial monogamy and is now living with her sixth lover. Unlike Nicodemus, she encounters Jesus during the day. There are no pretences or hypocrisies or closetedness. She readily admits to her relationships, and unlike Nicodemus, she embraces her embodiment of fleshly desires. The Samaritan woman engages in dialogue with Jesus through curiosity; her fleshliness does not become an obstacle as the religiosity of Nicodemus. She is willing to engage him out of boldness, and Jesus speaks to her about the living water. Without hesitation or a moment's fear, she asks for this water. That living water bubbles into her life, and she goes back to her village leaving her water jug behind but not unchanged. She now has the living water and becomes a disciple preaching the word. She outs Jesus as God's prophet and herself as a disciple to the Samaritans.

The outsider as a lesbian woman and a Samaritan hears the word and does not reject the light, but religious insiders fail to grasp the word and fall short of becoming disciples. How often have churches judged women like the Samaritan woman harshly, never following the example of Jesus who does not judge her harshly but extends a gracious invitation to become a disciple.

Light and darkness have been a constant theme woven into the Gospel text. John 8.12 foreshadows chapter 9 – whose dramatic structure and dialogues seem to intuit a classical drama. The opening verses (1–7) are a theological dialogue on sin and blindness. Whose sin is the cause of the blindness? Jesus takes the initiative and heals the blind man from his oppression. He does not respond to the faith of the blind man. The blind man engages in an initial dialogue with the Pharisees where the seeds of conflict with Jesus are revealed. It is in the ensuing conflicts with the interrogations of the Pharisees, the religious fundamentalists of the text, sandwiched around an encounter with Jesus (vv. 35–8) that the healed blind man comes to faith in hearing the revealing word of Jesus. The Pharisees in the narrative throw the healed man born blind out of the synagogue. They cannot tolerate that he has come to faith through a different path from their own. They have figured out religious experience and defined if very narrowly, not factoring the truth that God's grace is wild: 'The wind blows where it wills' (3.8). Grace breaks away from narrow definitions and surprises us with newness and transformation. This story is a dramatic reminder that churches are seldom comfortable with the lived experience of their people. Exclusionary practices such as expulsion from the synagogue were a communal mechanism to isolate someone whose experience was different rather than taking the time to listen and appreciate the coming of faith of the man born blind. John 9 ends with the man born blind able to see and come to faith while the Pharisees who have sight are unable to escape their fundamentalism and are blinded by their animosity. They lack the freedom to see in new ways the action of God through Jesus.

Jesus curiously never meets the parents of the blind man, who steer a very middle course when interrogated by the antagonists. Out of fear, they equivocate between their blind son now healed and the religious fundamentalists. They realize that to answer is siding with their son and that this meant religious exclusion. Thus, they opted to testify to their son's blindness from birth and now to his ability to see. How often have parents been forced to choose between their children who come out and their church with its narrow ethical definitions and rituals of exclusion and coercion! Because of undue pressure and the moral dogmatism of churches, parents have sent their children into concentration-camp-like, ex-gay programmes to cure their children of their homosexuality.

This story has been re-enacted numerous times in the exclusion of translesbigays from ecclesial communities. But the tolerance of this story has been re-enacted in communal forms of intolerance to communities of wild grace. For example, the Catholic archdiocese expelled the Metropolitan Community Church (MCC) New Orleans from its rental property Project Lazarus because MCC supports the coming out of translesbigays and the blessing of same-sex unions. The new fundamentalist Pharisees in Christianity maintain their purity codes around heterosexual conformity and expel those who deviate from their regulations. They have inadvertently created communities of wild grace where the Spirit lives and challenges them to break down their exclusionary fences.

The resurrection of Lazarus has been interpreted as a coming-out story (Glaser 1998: 10–11; Perkins 2000; West 2003). Queer folk can easily re-image the narrative as a coming-out story. Lazarus, the beloved disciple (see below), dies and is entombed. Because of his love for Lazarus, Jesus performs a sign, bringing him to life. He calls Lazarus to come out from the death of the tomb. From an African American gay social context, Ben Perkins writes,

> In John 11, Jesus calls to Lazarus, shouting for him to come out of the tomb. Lazarus is called forth to life. For queer individuals, the parallel is unmistakable: we are called out in a process that moves us towards a greater integrity in our relationship to self and others. (Perkins 2000: 199)

Perkins uses a hermeneutics of reimagination to reinterpret the story as a coming out for queer folk where the dead Lazarus is called to life by Jesus and the community must unbind him. Lazarus cannot release himself from the bindings alone; he needs assistance from the community. Jesus' love becomes the miracle that brings Lazarus from the tomb and releases him from his bindings for life. Lazarus finds new life and a renewal of relationship with his sisters and other friends.

Mona West reads the Lazarus story from a lesbian perspective. Her focus of attention is on Martha, not Lazarus; the story is about Martha's coming out as a disciple of Jesus.

> She (Martha) is invited to move beyond a mere confession of faith and to accept the radical fullness of Jesus' grace. Her conversation with him thus not only forms the theological heart of the story; it is also at the theological heart of the coming out process for Christian lesbians and gay men. (West 2003: 154)

It is Martha's decision to trust Jesus and roll away the stone, and Martha comes to a new level of awareness and living as a disciple of Jesus. Thus, the story of Lazarus' resurrection is the coming-out event that marks Jesus by the religious authorities for death. That story is repeated so often in contemporary lives of many queer folk.

These stories of God's coming out in Christ provide the fuel for the escalating antagonism between the religious authorities and Jesus. Institutional religion can be lethal in rationalizations to protect the nation and civilization; it closets human sexuality and spirituality through narrow definitions, dogmatic regulations and violent exclusions. Jesus' opponents complain: 'What are we to do? This man is performing many signs. If we let him go on like this, everyone will believe in him, and the Romans will come and destroy both our holy place and our nation' (12.47–8). Similar complaints are echoed from the pulpits of many churches about queer folk.

Gender and Sexuality

The woman characters in the Fourth Gospel are empowered women. Mary, the Mother of Jesus, speaks with confidence at the wedding feast of Cana. The colourful Samaritan woman at the well becomes an apostle to the Samaritans. Martha and Mary have a very special affection in the life and ministry of Jesus, and they seem to exercise leadership in the community of followers at Bethany. Martha confesses Jesus as Messiah and Son of God and comes out as a disciple of Jesus. The Gospel depicts women as preaching, confessing their faith and anointing – thus preserving the inclusion of women ministering in the Jesus movement. Finally, Mary Magdalene becomes the apostle of the resurrection. Adele Reinhartz summarizes a feminist perspective on John's Gospel:

> Its portrayals of women, the absence of gender as an explicit category in the discursive material, and the emphasis on love as the operative term in interpersonal relations all suggest a positive evaluation of the Gospel from a feminist perspective. (Reinhartz 1994b: 595)

The gospel provides some of the strongest representations of women in positive light in the Christian scriptures.

There are two additional stories that address the issue of gender and sexuality. The first is 7.53–8.11, the woman caught in adultery. Many scholars agree that this story was an interpolation into the Gospel. It fits well into the theme of judgement in chapters 7 and 8. Raymond Brown has suggested that the narrative may well be an old story about Jesus and that it travelled independently of the four Gospels and was not included in the Gospels 'until there was a change in the church's reluctance to forgive adultery' (Brown 1997: 377). The ascetical movements in the early Christian churches may have ignored this fragment because it portrayed Jesus as too lax in his treatment of the woman brought for judgement. Christian ascetics – starting from Paul – were very suspicious of the body and sexuality. They took a far more harsh position than the founder of their religious movement.

The narrative fragment about the adulteress has been accepted as scripture from the third century to the present in most Christian churches. The story provides a powerful indictment of condemning attitudes toward sexuality and a double-standard patriarchal culture that targets the woman for punishment and not the male participant. The religious authorities try to catch Jesus in a trap, expecting his compassion to violate the law condemning adultery. Jesus announces to the religious lynch mob of fundamentalist scribes and Pharisees: 'Let anyone among you who is without sin be the first to a throw a stone at her' (8.7). He subverts the fundamentalist lynch mob, pointing to their unreflective double-standard and forcing them to make a decision about themselves. Jesus demonstrates his moral superiority and thus widens the gap between himself and the religious fundamentalists. I remember in class, one student told how she left Christianity because a young 14-year-old girl got pregnant in her church and had to stand up in a worship service to confess her sin while the future father did not. Churches have targeted women, sexual outlaws and sexual minorities with their inquisitions, their sex panics and attempts to strictly regulate sexual behaviours.

The Christian Church has developed a virulent erotophobia; it has nearly equated sexuality with sin, following Pauline sources. Let the erotophobic zealots of the Christian churches – too often prone to condemn the sexual lives of queer folk – listen to this story, noting that Jesus neither was obsessed with sex nor regulated the sexual lives of people as the churches attempt to do. Jesus tackled the far more pressing issues of social injustice and exclusion while the churches often ignore contemporary social issues for sexual issues: pre-marital sex, homosexuality, transgender issues and bisexuality.

The second story is about Jesus' last meal with his disciples, where he performs a queer action. He strips off his outer garments, and performs the menial but intimate action of washing the feet of his disciples. He transgresses both class and gender roles, taking the role of a slave and/or female in the performance of the action (Jennings 2003: 162–6). It is this convention-breaking behaviour that he models for the disciples who are instructed to do likewise for one another. 'So if I, your Lord and Teacher, have washed your feet, you also ought to wash one another's feet' (13.14). Peter is baffled by Jesus' ritual action of foot-washing. How can Jesus model such behaviour of a slave or a woman? It is degrading for a free man; it is unmanly.

That women are not explicitly mentioned in attendance does not mean that there were no women disciples there. The presupposition of some churches that only the twelve were present has been used to justify male ordained leadership. Women disciples were present at many events in Jesus' ministry and were always mentioned. Disciples mentioned in attendance at Jesus' Last Supper must be construed as referring to men and women disciples.

Often, the Christian Church has connected this passage with ritual purification or baptism. I take the symbolism expressing both aspects, but I have often read this text with the book of Ruth in mind, where she uncovers the feet of Boaz. The Hebrew idiom of 'uncovering the feet' is an idiom for uncovering the genitals. I read this symbolic action of washing the feet as Jesus' symbolic purification of human genitals and his recognition of the original blessing and purity of human sexuality. Peter's resistance and alarm at the foot-washing have remained a symbol of the Petrine institutional church failing to recognize the purity of human sexuality. The Petrine church has fought the notion that human sexuality is a gift from God to all human beings of all sexual orientations and gender identifications. Only when Jesus insists on the foot-washing does Peter reluctantly acquiesce. This may be quite an unbiblical reading of Jesus' action for many scholars who have trained in a heterosexist reading of the scriptures. However, it fits with the translesbigay community's recognition of the goodness and original blessing of their sexuality despite Petrine orthodoxies which have condemned their sexuality, their love lives and their families of choice.

The first point I want to make is that Jesus takes up the duty of either a slave or a female, who washes the feet of guests. I use the word slave because it is a more accurate translation of the vanilla version, 'servant'. The word slave makes many modern readers squeamish because of the violent legacy of American racism and the slavocracy prior to the Civil War. But the Christian scriptures abound with slave imagery for its leadership (Martin 1990). It disrupts the class and gender hierarchies, and it communicates a notion that leadership does not belong to itself but to the community. Jesus exemplifies to his disciples what leadership is. His body belongs to the community. His symbolic action is egalitarian, not hierarchical; it is humbling and lowly service to the community of disciples.

Excursus: The Jews

When Christian followers began to tell the story of Jesus, they were conscious of wanting to prove that Jesus was innocent and unjustly executed. As they separated their identities from various Jewish factions, there was a shift of blame from Pilate and the Romans to the Jewish leadership. In the Gospel of John, the term 'the Jews' (*hoi Ioudaioi*) occurs 75 times, and it is frequently used as a negative term for those Jews who are in opposition to Jesus. It indicates a stage in which early Christian self-definition became antagonistic to its Jewish origins. The Jewish enemies of Jesus are depicted as opposed to God and associated with the devil (8.31–59). Moreover, there is conflict between the Johannine community and particular elements of the Jewish community. There are a number of stories that indicate that the Jews who believed in Jesus as the Messiah were either forced to leave or excluded from the synagogue. Those Jews in opposition to Jesus have Satan as their father (8.44). The Jews represent the world that rejects the light. In 9.22, we read the verse, 'the Jews had already agreed that anyone who confessed Jesus to be Messiah, would be put out of the synagogue.' On the other hand, Jesus and his followers participate in the Jewish rituals and festivals. The Gospel contradicts itself if the term 'the Jews' is taken as referring to all Jews.

It is unfortunate, even tragic, how the evangelist used the term 'the Jews' to blur the distinction between the Jewish people and the elements of the Jewish temple leadership who were in opposition to Jesus. It was the Jewish leadership, installed by the Roman occupiers, who were hostile to Jesus and his revelation.

Centuries later, Christians identified the Jews as responsible for the death of Jesus. Queer folk are particularly sensitive to anti-Semitism. Christian history has long persecuted Jews together with sexual minorities. There were probably some of the co-opted Jewish elite and fundamentalists who opposed Jesus, and there were particular Jewish groups antagonistic to the Johannine community in its Christology and challenges to their Jewish practices and beliefs. The textual portrayal of the Jews as plotting Jesus' death and persecuting his followers does not include all Jews and all Jewish groups. There were many Jews in Jerusalem who mourned the death of another Jewish man at the hands of the cruel Roman occupiers. Elaine Pagels writes,

> 'the Jews' have become for John . . . a 'symbol of human evil' . . . John's decision to make an actual, identifiable group – among Jesus' contemporaries and his own – into a symbol of 'all evil' obviously bears religious, social, and political implications. (Pagels 1995: 104–5)

The conflict of the Johannine community with particular groups of Jewish opponents justifies neither the thousand plus years of Christian identification of Jews with human evil nor anti-Judaism, pogroms, ghettoes, persecutions, murders, or the Nazi death camps.

The Jewish scholar Ellis Rivkin suggests that in our textual interrogations, we change the question from 'who crucified Jesus' to 'what killed Jesus'. He writes, 'It was not the Jewish people who had crucified Jesus, and it was not the Roman people – it was the imperial system, a system that victimized Jews, victimized the Romans, and victimized the Spirit of God' (Rivkin 1991: 257). Common practice within my own church is to change the term 'the Jews' in John's Gospel to the Jewish elite or temple aristocrats, meaning the elite priest class installed by the Romans. This shifts the blame back to the Roman system of conquest and occupation and their installed quislings.

Farewell Discourse: Jesus' Instructions to Out Christians

About one-fifth of the Gospel is devoted to Jesus' farewell discourse (13.31–17.26) at his last meal. It starts with a liturgical fragment: 'Now the Son of Man has been glorified and God has been glorified in him. If God has been glorified in him, God also will glorify him in himself and will glorify him at once' (13.31–2). The farewell discourse starts with this liturgical fragment and ends with the priestly prayer of glorification in chapter 17. Jesus announces the end of incarnated existence. Death will bring the end of the incarnation but also inaugurate the coming of the Holy Spirit. The farewell discourse is the heart of the Gospel, the most important discourse given to prepare the disciples for Jesus' departure and his bestowal of the Holy Spirit. It is an instruction to the post-resurrection disciples on how to live in the world full of conflict and antagonism. It is in this important section of the Gospel that the beloved disciple is introduced for the first time and given prominence. I interpret Jesus' farewell discourse and prayer as instructions to his disciples on how to come out and live out in the world. The Johannine community suffers similar antagonisms and hostilities to out queer folk.

Jesus' last discourse is like a Graeco-Roman farewell message or testament where the speaker announces his imminent departure, recalling his life, urging his audience to supersede his words and deeds, and consoling them. Jesus is in the world but not of the world, and he has a transcendent, other-worldly quality of the resurrected Jesus, as he speaks his farewell message. Drawn to Jesus' call to discipleship, they discovered God in Jesus and in one another.

He starts off with a new commandment (13.34) for his disciples to love one another as he loved them. The new commandment presupposes a communal egalitarianism and is critical of hierarchy. This commandment to love one another is expanded later in 14.15 and 15.15 where Jesus calls his disciples 'friends'. He speaks of the indwelling of God and himself: 'I am in the Father and the Father in me' (14.20). He tells his disciples not to be saddened because this indwelling will live in them (14.19–20). God will send the Paraclete ('one standing alongside, or defender'), an advocate to defend them and console them. The Paraclete dwells in all the disciples who love Jesus and keep his commandments. The Paraclete will sustain the disciples in a hostile world and teach them the meaning of Jesus' words. The disciples become lovers of God and one another; they become agents of God's incarnational presence through the Spirit.

Chapters 15 and 16 expand on the themes of the previous chapter. Jesus uses the metaphor of the vine and the branches to describe the vital connection that he will maintain with his disciples after he has departed. Out Christians will bear fruit that is pleasing to God. He proclaims his commandment: 'Love one another as I have loved you' (15.12). This love for one another includes a willingness to lay down their lives for one another. The world will be hostile to out Christians. That Jesus has come out and spoken openly makes the rejection of out Christians sinful (15.22). In the high priestly prayer (chapter 17), Jesus prays that they may be one as he and God are one, and he sends them out into a hostile world to bear witness to the truth.

Jesus' farewell discourse makes clear that the disciples cannot love God, Jesus, or one another separately. The poet Thomas Traherne writes, 'Wouldst thou love God alone? God cannot be beloved.' Bill Countryman comments on this verse:

> And the human capacity to love – the capacity that grounds both the possibility of union with God and the possibility of union with another human being – this capacity is not multiple. There is not love directed towards God and another towards the beloved. In the same way, the love directed toward God and the love directed toward the beloved do not mean that our capacity to love is divided. As Traherne writes, God 'must be loved in all the ways with an illimited love, even in all His doings, in all His friends, in all His creatures.' (Countryman 2005: 40)

We cannot compartmentalize the love of God and the love of the beloved. Loving God does not preclude the love of fellow disciples and humanity. They are inseparable.

Jesus' farewell discourse is addressed to queer Christians, living in a hostile world. Just as the blind man was thrown out of the synagogue, the Johannine community was thrown out of the synagogue for its Christology. Queer Christians have been expelled from their churches because of their same-sex love.

The Beloved Disciple

It is in the farewell discourse that we are introduced to the Beloved Disciple. There is a physical intimacy between Jesus and the Beloved Disciple. He is cuddling with Jesus (13.23), laying his head on Jesus' chest. In the farewell discourse, Jesus indicates that his love for the disciples is one of friendship. But the physical proximity of the Beloved Disciple and his private conversations during the meal single him out. The Beloved Disciple carries on a form of pillow talk. He is not a friend like the other disciples, for he is Jesus' beloved.

Scholars have long disputed whether the Beloved Disciple is John son of Zebedee, Thomas the Twin, Mary Magdalene, Lazarus, or a symbol of the community. For some queer writers, the evidence points to Lazarus (Williams 1992; Wilson 1995: 141–5; Goss 2000: 208–9). Jennings does not rule out the possibility of Lazarus but maintains that the evidence is inconclusive. Elizabeth Stuart understands the Beloved Disciple to be representing perfect intimacy with Jesus (Stuart 1995: 171). The Beloved Disciple serves as a witness to Jesus, and he seems to understand Jesus better than any other in the Gospel. The implication within the text is that he is the author of the Gospel, and his particular intimacy with Jesus gives authority to the Gospel.

For nearly two millennia, men attracted to the same sex have intuited a homoerotic relationship between Jesus and the Beloved Disciple (Goss 2002: 113–39; Jennings 2003: 75–91; Boisvert 2004: 200) They have correctly read the relationship between Jesus and the Beloved Disciple as a rare instance of homoerotic desire, finding moments of grace and self-acceptance in this relationship. Van Tilborg writes about the reluctance of heterosexist scholars to entertain a pederastic model of the teaching relationship between Jesus and the Beloved Disciple:

> The reason that scientific exegesis did not connect the relationship of the teacher Jesus to his beloved disciple with this typical educational background is, probably, that sexuality is present in the majority of the concerned texts or at least not far off. The love for the *pais* in the context of education and training has sexual connotations in Greek and Hellenistic thought and action that cannot be brought in line with the asexual text of the Johannine Gospel. (Van Tilborg 1993: 79)

There is an intimacy between Jesus and the Beloved Disciple that stands out in the Gospel, and gay men have understood the Fourth Gospel from the contexts of their homoerotic lives. Jennings hopes that gay readings of the disciple that Jesus loved would open biblical scholars to reconsider the biblical materials from a new perspective: 'Perhaps one day, even those who have been steeped in the Christian story can read with open eyes the story of Jesus and the man he loved' (Jennings 2003: 91). Jennings claims that the Gospel publicly affirms they were lovers (2003: 64).

The Beloved Disciple has the most prominent role in the Fourth Gospel. He acts as an intercessor between Jesus and Peter and is lying on Jesus' breast during the farewell meal. The Beloved Disciple is fully in love with Jesus, faithful to him and courageously remains with Jesus in his death vigil at the foot of the cross. Jesus looks upon the Beloved Disciple as his replacement within his family and entrusts his mother to the Beloved Disciple's care. When Mary Magdalene tells him that Jesus' body is missing, he runs to the tomb and awaits Peter before going into the tomb. Jennings points out the Beloved Disciple's hesitancy because he is traumatized from the death of Jesus and is not prepared to see Jesus' mangled corpse (Jennings 2003: 29). The Beloved Disciple is the first one to draw the conclusion of Jesus' resurrection while he is noticing the grave clothes wrapped in the empty tomb. He understands himself as remembering and interpreting the words of Jesus in faith, the function of the Paraclete. He helps the community to faith by writing down the story of God's coming out in Jesus.

Ted Jennings anticipates an objection that Jesus and the Beloved Disciple were lovers and that this limits Jesus' love for his disciples (Jennings 2003: 94–6). Jesus' physical intimacy and particular love for the Beloved Disciple do not prevent or limit his love for the other disciples and those marginalized by fundamentalist religion. Clergy will be the first to witness how their physical intimacy with a spouse opens their love, and does not limit their love for others. Particular intimacy does not limit a love for humanity.

For many queer folk, the Beloved Disciple serves as a reminder how faithful we have been to the Christian tradition despite its exclusions, its violence and its crucifixions of our folk. We have remained faithful to a tradition whose institutions have consistently rejected us and targeted us for cultural assault. The gay writer and scholar Donald Boisvert speaks about how meaningful the image of Jesus and the Beloved Disciple is: 'It is, however, a beautiful image, a deep and touching affirmation of our central place as gay men in the heart of God' (Boisvert 2004: 2000). We may not be loved by the churches but we certainly have a place in the heart of God.

Aids, the Passion and Death of Jesus

Judas betrays Jesus to the temple police whose earlier attempt to arrest Jesus (7.32, 45) failed. He is taken to Annas and Caiphas, but the focus of the narrative is outside on Peter and his threefold denial. This is contrasted with the devotion of the Beloved Disciple whose love and courageous devotion to Jesus leads him to the foot of the cross. John places him with Jesus' mother and the women at the foot of the cross during their death watch.

The Jews bring Jesus to Pilate for a verdict and execution. Pilate informs the Jewish leadership: 'I find no case against him' (18.38). He attempts to broker a solution by offering to the lynch mob of fundamentalist antagonists release of a prisoner at Passover. The vocal fundamentalist mobs choose Barabbas over Jesus. The Fourth Gospel suppresses all Roman initiation and complicity in the death of Jesus. Pilate is absolved of his guilt in his dialogue with Jesus, and in fact, shifts the blame to the Jews: 'Your own nation and the chief priests have handed you over to me' (18.35).

On the cross, Jesus manifests God's coming out as lover and compassionate sufferer for the world. Hatred, fundamentalism, homophobia, misogyny, racism, and all such, placed Jesus on the cross.

In John 19.26–7, at the crucifixion, Jesus looks on the Beloved Disciple as taking his place. Jesus places his mother in the care of the beloved and the Beloved Disciple in the care of his mother: 'Woman, behold your son! . . . Behold your mother!' Goss writes:

> I have often witnessed the repetition of this adoption event (between the Beloved Disciple and Mary) at the death beds of gay men dying of Aids with their lovers and their families. It is the powerful entrusting of unfinished business in the face of death and personal tragedy. Gay lovers and mothers of deceased gay men have reenacted the narrative too many times, forming a human quilt to share their grief and a community seeking solace in the midst of tragedy. (Goss 2000: 213)

Jesus chooses his successor within his family. It is symbolic of his succession within the Christian community. The Beloved Disciple and the mother of Jesus create a new family of choice, accepting responsibility for continuing the ministry of Jesus' coming out in the moment of death. Here in the last moments of his life, Jesus establishes a family of choice, based on his homoerotic relationship with the Beloved Disciple. Many mainline and fundamentalist Christian churches play the role of the Romans, crucifying Christ, and attempt to destroy homoerotic families of choice. Their campaigns not only to block same-sex marriage but to repeal all legal recognitions of civil unions and domestic partnerships are mean-spirited, aiming to hurt families. They attempt to undo domestic partnership benefits that provide medical coverage for many millions of children of gay and lesbian parents. The altar of heterosexuality must be preserved from the wild grace and unconventionality of Jesus' life and his message. Jesus answers, 'It is finished!' His body is broken by a political and religious system that had to stamp out God's wild grace. It was too dangerous to let be. God cannot be tied down, controlled, or regulated.

Queer folk have had to learn to create a culture of love and compassion in the face of death from Aids, breast cancer, violence and the oppression of their human rights. We see the reality of bodily and social death on a regular basis. But as Christians we realize that we are not alone. Death is not the absence of God but involves the active presence of God. God does not abandon as God did not abandon Jesus. God was very present in Jesus until his last breath. Then God's wildness came out in its full surprise and glory. God's resurrection of Jesus is the queerest event in history since the creation of the universe.

Mary Magdalene: The Apostle of the Resurrection

Jesus is crucified near a garden. The erotic theme overflows into the resurrection narrative, reflecting themes from the Song of Songs. The Gospel (19.40–2) states that Jesus' dead body is anointed with aloes and myrrh – an unusual combination of spices that also occurs in the Song of Songs 4.14. (Carr 2003: 163). John 20 is full of allusions to the Song of Songs (Carr 2003: 164–7); and these resonances strengthen a reading of the Gospel as depicting the longing of a lover for union with Jesus the Christ. It is found in the portrayal of the Beloved Disciple's physical intimacy with Jesus, the instructions on love to the disciples at the farewell discourse, and the garden scene where Magdalene searches for the absent Jesus.

John stresses that the resurrection takes place on the first day of the week. The Gospel stresses that resurrection is a continuation of creation. God broods over Jesus and raises him to springtime life. In the morning, Mary goes to the tomb and finds the rock rolled back. She runs to tell Peter and the Beloved Disciple that Jesus' body has disappeared. She returns with the two and has a visionary experience of two angels. During the farewell discourse, Jesus predicts that the disciples will weep and grieve. Mary mourns the loss of Jesus' body (20.11, 15). She seeks his whereabouts from a stranger that she mistakes as a gardener. In the Good Shepherd discourse, Jesus claims to know his disciples by name (10.3). The risen Jesus calls Mary by name, and it is the only instance of Jesus calling a woman by name in the Gospel. Mary Magdalene reaches out to touch Jesus, and he responds, 'Do not hold onto me . . .' (20.17). There have been all sorts of speculations about his words – from Mary holding onto the human side of Jesus, who needs to ascend to God, to the resurrected Jesus appearing naked. There are resonances with the unnamed woman searching for her lover in the Song, and these highlight the 'intimacy and love between the believer and the risen Lord' (Schaberg 2004: 334). Magdalene represents the disciple with a passionate longing for Jesus. This has been played in popular literature of the intimate relationship of Mary Magdalene with Jesus, in such books as *The Woman with the Alabaster Jar* (Starbird 1993) and *The Da Vinci Code* (Brown 2003).

Mary Magdalene is clearly the apostle of the resurrection. She experiences the empty tomb and the risen Jesus appears to her in the garden. But unlike the other disciples, she witnesses the ascension of Jesus in John. She is represented as the believer who sees Jesus ascend to God. Jane Schaberg claims that Mary was the first great interpreter of Jesus and the resurrection, not Paul. Mary was the original successor to Jesus' leadership in the community. This tradition of Mary's priority as apostle and leader is, however, upstaged by the arrival of the Beloved Disciple. The Beloved Disciple is superior in faith because he believes first by seeing Jesus' grave clothes in the tomb. His testimony forms the basis of the written testimony (20.30–1), and his authority is superior to Mary's authority (21.24). The disciples later receive the Holy Spirit from the glorified Jesus who has ascended. Some have argued that the appearance to Mary was inferior because it was the risen but non-glorified Jesus who appeared to her. Whatever the case may be, the process of upstaging the priority of Mary's status continued in orthodox Christianity's demeaning of her status as the apostle of the resurrection, by conflating her with the narrative of the prostitute anointing the feet of Jesus. Opposition is found in the non-canonical *Gospel of Mary* and the evolution of the Mary Magdalene legend (Schaberg 2004).

Resurrection and the Dangerous Memory of God's Coming Out

All the appearance accounts in John's Gospel reveal that Jesus has risen from the dead. No one who experiences the presence of the out God remains entirely the same. God's coming out in Christ inevitably changes folk who come to believe, such as the Samaritan woman, Martha, the Beloved Disciple, Mary Magdalene and Thomas. They become transformed and, in turn, become agents of change. Elizabeth Stuart understands resurrection as a metaphorical way of delineating how queer folk come out of their self-crucifixions in the closet and death of self-hatred and internalized homophobia. Closeted bodies are 'often hunched, closed against the world, eyes cast down, the voice is reluctant and weak. The skin is cold, clammy, with no life in it, no response, just the shadow of death' (Stuart 1995: 50). Closeted bodies are entombed like Lazarus; they are dead bodies and dead to their own spirit. Jesus ends the closet; God raises Jesus from the death of the closet and ends the entombment of bodies. Stuart speaks about the freedom queer folk experience bodily as they emerge from the closet tomb:

> The body opens up like a flower: the head is lifted up, the voice becomes stronger, the flesh becomes warmer. I witness resurrection. The resurrection only occurs because someone has rolled the stone away, someone has loved the person to life. (Stuart 1995: 50)

God has loved Jesus the Christ to life, and God continues to love queer folk to life. Coming out is about changing lives and changing society. The ultimate break-in moment, even more so than the incarnation, is the resurrection of Jesus. It is God's coming out in full glory and compassion. From the perspective of the Fourth Gospel, resurrection is part of Jesus' life from the beginning.

Jesus' resurrection is about changed lives. Magdalene stops her grieving and announces to the disciples that she has seen the risen Jesus (20.18); the Beloved Disciple writes a Gospel to bring people to faith and help them remember in the Spirit the words and actions of Jesus as the Christ. Peter is triply commissioned to 'feed my lambs, feed my sheep' in chapter 21. The disciples closeted themselves behind locked doors. The risen Jesus appears in their midst. The Christ breathes the Holy Spirit upon them, reminding them of his farewell instruction on how to carry on in the world and how they are to forgive sins in the name of God. Thomas's doubts are relieved when the risen Jesus instructs him to place his hand in the wound in his side. Thomas makes a confession of faith as the risen Jesus gently rebukes him for his lack of faith. Faith and mission are interrelated. Jesus' resurrection involves a life-giving mission, empowering the disciples to concrete actions to make God's presence manifest and out in the world and to change the world's culture from violence to love.

All Jesus' disciples came to the vivid realization and life-changing experience that Jesus revealed God through his life and person. His life, words and actions, death and resurrection reveal God as God truly is: unconditional love and compassion. God saves Jesus from final death, and this reveals the nature of God as a resurrecting God. Resurrection is the final coming out of God. God's unconditional love reaches out for outcasts and for outsiders. God comes out of the fixity of religious traditions and boundaries. God ultimately reveals God's self as thoroughly queer, outside the box, outside the narrow conceptual frameworks and practice of the grace regulators, and transgresses all human expectations with the surprise of 'outness' in the risen Christ and the concrete manifestation of changed lives.

The Fourth Gospel narrates, 'Now Jesus did many other signs in the presence of his disciples, which are not written in this book' (20.30). The Beloved Disciple understands himself to be performing the Paraclete's function in writing the Gospel. It is the writing of the story that elicits faith in Jesus as the Christ of God. But the story does not end. It continues as the Holy Spirit continues to make present that story in the lives of believers. God's coming out is about retelling the story of Jesus in the lives of queer folk. Many queer folk have been driven out of their churches, and some churches have had to come to terms with queer folk in their midst. They experience the resistances, the lethal hostilities, the graces of acceptance and love, the keeping alive of the memory of God's embodiment in Jesus and themselves, and the commandments to love. Despite the opposition of many churches and cultural hostility, queer Christians find in their erotic lives a link to one another, to the Jesus who came out in the Fourth Gospel, and to the out God. By coming out in faith, we rise before we die, and the story of the Beloved Disciple continues in our 'out' relationship with the Christ. And the churches face the decision to accept the visible presence of the Christ in the presence of queer folk or to form a lynch mob and crucify the Christ once more enfleshed and out in queers.

Acts of the Apostles

THOMAS BOHACHE, ROBERT GOSS, DERYN GUEST AND MONA WEST

At the end of the process of gathering all the pieces together for final publication, the editors had a serendipitous opportunity to collaborate on a queering of Acts – like the early Church, a convergence of scholarship and queering from the perspective of the Hebrew and Christian scriptures. It allows the reader to view four queer strategies of reading particular texts in Acts. Despite the differences, there is a remarkable unified vision that emerges from their writings. Queer Christianity may be the most exciting and challenging movement since Luke wrote about the nascent Jesus movement under the queer inspiration of the Holy Spirit becoming an inclusive community of men and women, Jews and Gentiles. Queer Christianity exists as a contemporary reminder that queer inclusion is possible just as the rocky road to Gentile inclusion evolved in early Christianity. Contemporary Christianity can be authentic to the inclusive vision in Acts as it opens its doors to recognizing the Holy Spirit is alive in GLBTQ Christians.

Pentecost Queered

THOMAS BOHACHE

Acts of the Apostles, the companion volume to the Gospel of Luke, is not one that I have concentrated on during my ministerial career. I much prefer to talk about Jesus and how the integrity of his life and his solidarity with all of creation can lead GLBTQ people toward acceptance of our authentic, divinely gifted selves, along what I call 'the Christ Way'. Nevertheless, in light of recent turmoil in several Christian denominations regarding the suitability of queer persons for marriage, parish ministry and the episcopacy, I believe that it is time for me to rethink my position on Acts.

Acts, as a continuation of what the author had begun in Luke, has much to say to queer readers, but we must be willing to boldly place ourselves in the story. We cannot approach this scripture with the attitude some of us carry that we should accept whatever crumbs of toleration Christian churches cast our way in the guise of 'welcome'. On the contrary: one may read the Gospels with a sense of inclusion because of Jesus' own persona, words and deeds and might choose to ignore epistles which contain less-than-affirming passages because, after all, they were just some correspondence reflecting the authors' opinions. When it comes to Acts, however, we are dealing with a record of the beginnings of the very Christian Church with which we are attempting to cope in today's world. Consequently, here in this book of scripture, if anywhere, we must locate ourselves if we are to remain Christian.

Jesus was the primary character of Luke's Gospel; he is portrayed as a loyal Jew attempting to mount a restoration movement in Israel. To demonstrate this, Luke begins and ends the Gospel story in the Jerusalem temple, the primary manifestation of God's covenant with Israel. However, by the time the two volumes of Luke–Acts were composed, the Romans had already destroyed the temple. Instead, Luke was witnessing the incipient Christian Church spread out from Jerusalem, as the followers of Jesus proclaimed him as the continuation of salvation history. By the time Acts opens, Jesus' work is done and he has ceased to function as a character except in remembrances; the mission of 'the Way' (9.2) is the responsibility of his followers, under the power and direction of the Holy Spirit. If one adheres to a Trinitarian belief system, one may see a process unfolding in the divine's dealings with humanity. The Hebrew Bible tells of creation and covenant by God the Source; the Gospels detail the life, death and resurrection of Jesus as God's representative, the Saviour; and Acts and the epistles describe how the earliest Christians are empowered by the Holy Spirit as Sustainer.

My primary warrant for any queering of scripture lies in my understanding of Spirit. Spirit is the very essence of God that is ever-present: It soared over the waters at creation (Gen. 1.1), was breathed into humans (Gen. 2.7), inspired rulers and prophets both male and female (the historical and prophetic books), descended in a special way upon Jesus of Nazareth (Mark 1.10 par.), was breathed out upon his followers as the Risen One wished them God's *shalom* (John 20.22), and, in the Pentecost story, dynamically took up residence in the earliest Christians to guide their destiny. If we are Christians who believe that Christ's Spirit has validity in today's world and that we are a part of the communion of saints who have gone before us, queer people must see ourselves in the Acts of the Apostles – indeed, we must claim the etymological mantle of 'apostles' as those who are sent to share the Good News. Thus, I read the Pentecost story in Acts 2.1–21 as a demonstration of divine hospitality and inclusivity in earliest Christianity.

Jesus assured his followers that he would send the Holy Spirit, through whom they would be able to do greater things than Jesus himself. In John's Gospel, this Spirit is breathed out upon the disciples as they remain barricaded in a room out of fear (John 20.22). They receive this Holy Spirit, but John does not take the next step and explain how this Spirit empowers the first Christians to action. Perhaps this is because John is the 'spiritual' or 'introspective' Gospel by means of which individual believers are able to commune with God. The book of Acts, however, is a book of action, missionary activity, and, above all, community; thus, in story after story we encounter the first believers *communally* bearing witness to the Risen Christ and the Spirit he has bequeathed to them *as a group*. The overarching message we obtain from Acts is that Christians can only be Christians in community, that we will only make a difference in the world by sharing our goods in common and in a spirit of unity (4.34–5). Unfortunately, the powers of empire were to diminish this communal, almost socialist, sensibility as later books of the Second Testament and other church documents sought to bring the nascent church into greater conformity with and assimilation into the Roman empire. It is here that queer readers can learn from Acts: we can resist those who would have us assimilate into the empire of heteronormativity and realize that our uniqueness, our queerness and our difference make us special bearers of Christ in a hurting world.

In this regard, the Pentecost story is paradigmatic, for it shows the believers gathered together in one place, receiving the Holy Spirit as a group, and yet manifesting that same Spirit in different and diverse ways in order to advance God's one, unified Reign of inclusion and unconditional love. Whereas the disciples in John's account of the giving of the Spirit were able to keep it to themselves, those assembled on the day of Pentecost were unable to do so; on the contrary, they were driven out into the streets of Jerusalem proclaiming God's mighty deeds of power to all they encountered (2.4). Since there were many pilgrims in Jerusalem, of diverse nationalities and languages, the Spirit's strategy was to allow every person to hear the Good News in their own language – or, perhaps more accurately, as they needed to hear it. This is the way in which the Pentecost story becomes queer: it testifies that God's message of inclusion and wholeness will be heard in diverse ways through diverse messengers; it is one truth that is able to be shared in many different ways according to the hearer's individual needs.

Thus, the diversity in the GLBTQ community(ies) reflects the very Spirit of God. As part of our Christian legacy, we are entrusted and empowered to bring the Good News of God's love and Christ's liberating power to every corner of our world, in different words, through differing scenarios, in various costumes, and with multiple props. Accordingly, the Spirit is heard among gay senior citizens who seek to live together in a retirement community. The Spirit is seen when young queers transgress the boundaries of gender and sexuality and refuse to be categorized. The Spirit is described in the language of leather and S/M, in the hilarity of drag shows, and in the solemnity of same-sex weddings. Queer persons individually and collectively open their mouths and proclaim spiritual truth 'as the Spirit gives them ability' in whatever venue they find themselves – bar, bathhouse, women's space, 12–Step group, synagogue, church, mosque, ashram, sex club, rodeo, book group, coffee house, university or seminary classroom. And our warrant for doing so is Peter's explanation of the Pentecost phenomenon as fulfilment of the promises God made through the prophet Joel:

> In the last days it will be, God declares, that I will pour out my Spirit upon all flesh; and your sons and your daughters shall prophesy, and your young shall see visions, and your old shall dream dreams. Even upon my slaves, both men and women, in those days I will pour out my Spirit; and they shall prophesy. (2.17–18, paraphrasing Joel 2.28–32)

God does not declare here that only some flesh – straight flesh or monogamous flesh or celibate flesh or 'decent', acceptable flesh – will receive the Spirit.

God says *all* flesh; this means flesh that is gay, lesbian, bisexual, heterosexual, transgendered, omnisexual, asexual, differently sexual, conservative and progressive, monogamous and single and polymorphously perverse – each encountering the divine in our circumstances and hearing the Spirit in our own language, leading us into the inclusive Reign of God through Christ. Nor does God declare that the Spirit will only be manifest among rich white men in positions of power. On the contrary, God's assurance is quite specific that the Spirit will be poured out on men and women, sons and daughters, male and female slaves, young and old, dreaming dreams and seeing visions, prophesying about the divine presence in this world. The first disciples ministered in multiple languages to people of many nations of different colours practising various religions. Yet together they felt God's presence and power, and the Spirit gave them ability without distinction to glorify God in their very diversity. Can we do any less in today's world?

Perhaps today's Queer Movement is the new Pentecost. Perhaps contemporary society and its culture wars and sex wars are God's attempt to 'get a word in edgewise' so that the human race may prosper and survive beyond the narrow restrictions of current fundamentalisms. Perhaps queer people of faith can be at the forefront of a new understanding of how the divine works. Undoubtedly people will sneer at us as they did the first disciples (2.13), accusing us of being drunk or crazy, demon-possessed or sexually addicted, but the opportunity is before us to change the world by our testimony, by our example, and by our embrace of Spirit.

A powerful way to accomplish this sort of witness is through the medium of 'sexual storytelling', which requires a bold willingness and an outrageous audacity to share our innermost selves – which are, in fact, sexual selves – so that others might touch the face of God. I concur with queer postcolonial theologian Marcella Althaus-Reid that it is essential that sexual minorities grace the world with our sexual stories; for we can only embrace the wholeness of God's *shalom* if we not only are in touch with our authentic selves but also risk sharing them. This is what it means to speak to others 'in their own language'; often, the language of sexual storytelling is able to 'penetrate', as it were, in ways that traditional evangelism cannot. Thus, Althaus-Reid reminds us:

> Why do a theology of sexual stories? Is that not too particular, or too concerned with the 'private realm' of a person? The answer is no, because sexuality does not stay at home, or in a friend's bedroom, but permeates our economic, political and societal life . . . Without a theology of sexual stories, the last moment of the hermeneutical circle, that is, the moment of appropriation and action, will always have a partiality and a superficial approach to conflict resolution . . . That is the point of telling sexual stories: they are always tentative, unfinished, as is a sexual Jesus. They open our eyes to different networking strategies and also to sources of empowerment. (Althaus-Reid 2001a: 130–1)

Likewise, GLBTQ people's faith journeys are not mere 'addenda' in the story of Christianity, but can and must be told as modern-day Acts of the Apostles.

Moreover, in taking the risk to share our sexual selves with others, we are not being prurient, voyeuristic or inappropriate; rather, we are removing the 'dirtiness' from the erotic and the sexual that erotophobic Christianity has lodged there over centuries. In this way, a healthy sexuality shared openly and honestly ceases to be a dirty little secret and instead mirrors God's delight in all aspects of creation. Thus, as the gay theologian Robert Simpson has asserted, the telling of sexual stories is not just good for theology but for pastoral care in our churches:

> In other words, without recognition of the correlation between sexual stories and the development of appropriate forms of pastoral action, the Church's pastoral practice will often fail to be supportive and effective in addressing real needs . . . The sharing of personal details foster[s] the growth of intimacy, develop[s] a sense of trust and [leads to] deep conversations about a variety of subjects including experiences of discrimination, illness, life after death, and even the mystery of God. (Simpson 2005: 100)

When we share sexual stories we say to our listener, 'I've been there. I'm no better than you, and you are better than you think! Your sexual energy and its erotic expression in thought, word and deed are gifts from God!' In daring to describe the ways in which sex allows us to represent God in this world, GLBTQ people undo ecclesiological perversions, stimulate a hermeneutic of participation, and allow the Spirit to blow where it chooses. I call this a 'politics of holy voyeurism', whereby we reclaim the genre of 'Acts' for a queer future.

Elsewhere I have described how each of us is embodied to be, in the words of Meister Eckhart, 'other Christs' (Bohache 2003: 21–3). We are 'christed' – anointed, as Jesus was, to bring good news, release captives and proclaim God's Jubilee Year (Ringe 1985). Likewise, we bear the divine Spirit simply by virtue of being human: not only is God's Spirit breathed into us at birth, but it blows into our midst and beckons us into Christianity. This Spirit opens the doors and windows wide, blows out negativity, despair and inhospitality, and says, 'Come on in! We've been waiting for you!' Each of us carries unique spiritual gifts (1 Cor. 12) without which the Church cannot survive. In an effort to control and restrict institutions like marriage, the priesthood and the episcopacy, churches may build walls, lock doors and shut windows, but the Spirit will always keep blowing the walls down and the doors and windows open, until every part of God's Spirit is together and our world becomes the unconditional dwelling place of *shalom*. This is why the Acts of the Apostles, as the beginning of the Christian story, must become *our* story.

The Controversy of Gentile Inclusion

ROBERT E. GOSS

In Acts 2.44–7, we find a picture of this Spirit-led group of Jesus' disciples, setting up an alternative community: 'And all who believed were together and had things in common, and they sold their possessions and goods and distributed them to all, as any had need.' Acts 4.34–5 notes that many sold their homes and lands, and brought the proceeds to the apostles for distribution to those who had need.

These portrayals of an idealized community were soon rocked with cultural and theological dissensions. In Acts 6, the Hellenists complained against the Hebrews that their widows were neglected in the daily distribution of food. Immigrant Jewish widows from the diaspora would have a greater cultural and social disadvantage than the Hebrew widows. Conflict arose probably from social and cultural differences between the Hebrews and Hellenists. The twelve called the whole of the community together, and the community selected seven Hellenists to wait on table and distribute food to the Hellenist widows.

There has been much speculation on who these Hellenists were. Acts labels Hellenists as appointed to the seven deacons and as a group led by Stephen. There seemed to be foreign groups of Jews who settled in Jerusalem, were Greek-speaking and maintained a Hellenistic Jewish culture. These groups stood in cultural contrast to the Aramaic-speaking Jews. Both Greek-speaking and Aramaic-speaking Jews were shaped through different cultural experiences and languages. The Jesus movement in Jerusalem became divided among the two factions.

At an early stage in the first generation of the post-resurrection Jesus movement, the Hellenist faction of the Jesus movement was driven out of Jerusalem. Gerd Theissen has suggested that the Hellenist and the Jewish factions came into open conflict over the role of the temple. The Hellenist followers of the Jesus movement may have proclaimed that the Jerusalem temple would soon become open to the Gentiles (Theissen 1999: 253). The conflict between Hellenist Jewish followers of Jesus and Hellenist Jews takes shape immediately after the commissioning of the seven Hellenist deacons.

Stephen, renowned for miracles and his ability to debate, emerged as the natural leader of the Hellenists. This newly appointed deacon took on opponents in two separate Hellenist synagogues in Jerusalem. Like ACT UP activists, he harangued Greek-speaking Jews in a passionate debate, and his opponents perceived Stephen as a threat to the temple and the Mosaic law. Stephen's provocative and confrontational style, reminiscent of Jesus' disturbance in the temple, ran contrary to the Aramaic-speaking members under the leadership of James, Peter and John. Peter and his community worshipped peacefully in the temple and gathered together to break bread (2.46).

Greek-speaking Jews charged Stephen with blasphemy: 'This man never stops saying things against this holy place and the law; for we have heard him say that this Jesus of Nazareth will destroy this place and will change the customs that Moses handed on to us' (6.13–14). In his speech before the Council of the Synagogue, Stephen makes a declaration of independence from the bureaucratic temple cult, and his final provocative vision of the Son of Humanity at the right side of God elicits a response of blasphemy from the crowd. The articulate and fiery deacon is dragged outside and is stoned in the presence of a young Pharisee, Saul.

Stephen's death marks the beginning of the spread of the Christian movement. The Hellenists left Jerusalem to expand their movement in Samaria and set up a community in Antioch. Philip preached in Samaria, and the Antioch community began to win over Gentile converts to their movement without requiring male converts to be circumcised. Circumcised Jewish Christian and uncircumcised Gentile Christians worshipped side by side with equal rights.

The Jerusalem faction – led by James the brother of Jesus, Peter and John – maintained the circumcision of Gentile males as a precondition for admission to the Christian community. The leadership of the Jerusalem community resisted the opening of the movement to Gentiles. Acts depicts James, Peter and John as resistant to opening the Jesus movement to Gentiles. On the other side, Stephen, Philip, the Hellenists, and later in Acts Paul and Barnabas, maintained that baptism became the decisive rite for the acceptance of Gentiles into the Christian community and that eating together was absolutely necessary. Ultimately, Peter and Barnabas are the moderates on both sides of the controversy, and they find a solution to accept Gentiles into the Christian movement.

The Story of the Ethiopian Eunuch

MONA WEST

The story of the Ethiopian eunuch in the book of Acts narrates the conversion of the first Gentile to Christianity. It is a significant story for queer people of faith because the eunuch is a sexual minority in the context of Jewish religion during this time. And up until this point in the Acts narrative the only way to become a Christian was to convert to Judaism first.

The reason the eunuch is considered a sexual minority is because Deuteronomy 23.2 specifically prohibits eunuchs from the worshipping community of Israel: 'No one whose testicles are crushed or whose penis is cut off shall be admitted to the assembly of the LORD.' The text in Acts indicates the eunuch is returning home to Ethiopia after having been to Jerusalem to worship. It is possible the eunuch could have been what is known in the book of Acts as a 'God-fearer': someone who believes in the ethical principles of the Torah and who reveres the God of the Jews, but does not follow the law in its entirety, nor submit to circumcision (Fitzmyer 1998: 449).

The eunuch is identified as a court official of the queen of Ethiopia. Katherine Ringrose indicates that this Ethiopian eunuch is a perfect biblical example of what she has identified as a 'perfect servant' (Ringrose 2003: 206). She uses the term to refer to eunuchs as a third gender made so by castration and distinguished by certain patterns of dress, speech, physiological traits and overall affect. They were highly revered and trusted as court officials, serving kings and queens. They were considered 'perfect' servants because they had no allegiance to family and could not jeopardize the dynastic lineage by their own offspring. They were able to move across gender and social boundaries and were often considered holy men because of their ability to access spiritual realms as well (Ringrose 2003: 5–6).

In the story, the Holy Spirit tells Philip, who has just had a successful preaching campaign in Samaria, to go south to the road that leads from Jerusalem to

Gaza. Philip obeys and encounters the Ethiopian eunuch on this road. Having returned from Jerusalem, the eunuch is riding in his chariot, reading a passage from the prophet Isaiah out loud. Philip overhears him, and at another prompting of the Spirit, he asks the eunuch if he understands what he is reading. The eunuch replies, 'How can I, unless someone guides me?' (8.31a).

The passage is from one of the Servant Songs in Isaiah 53.7–8, in which the servant is humiliated and denied justice. The perfect servant who is revered in his own land of Ethiopia but cut off from the worshipping community of Israel is seeking to understand the suffering servant of Israel whom Isaiah talks about.

The eunuch invites Philip into his chariot and Philip interprets the Isaiah passage in light of the good news of Jesus. Philip's opening of the scripture opens the understanding of the eunuch, and when they encounter a body of water on their journey the eunuch wants to be baptized as a Christian and Philip baptizes him.

Queer people of faith would read this story as our own. We are kept from full participation in the Church because of what is perceived as our outsider sexual status. We have been denied ordination and communion. Our relationships are also not blessed by the Church. At best we are allowed to attend worship if we 'leave our sexuality at the door'. We are allowed marginal participation in the body of Christ if we adopt a 'don't ask, don't tell' policy, or if we promise not to be a 'practising' homosexual.

Like the Ethiopian eunuch, we have struggled to make sense of scripture, to find our place in it, when others would use it to condemn us. The good news for us is that there have been those 'Philips' who have interpreted scripture in ways that have been empowering for the queer community. Father John McNeill calls Philip the patron saint of the queer community for this very reason (McNeill 1995: 143). McNeill goes on to say, 'The eunuch rides on into history "full of joy." I like to think of this eunuch as the first baptized gay Christian' (McNeill 1995: 143). Justin Tanis identifies the Ethiopian eunuch with transgendered folk: 'neither the gender of the eunuch nor the gender variance is pivotal to his inclusion or exclusion in the community, but rather his desire to be baptized and included' (Tanis 2003: 79).

The Servant Song that Philip interpreted for the 'perfect servant' that day on the road from Jerusalem to Gaza is located very close to another prophecy in Isaiah that deals specifically with eunuchs:

Do not let the foreigner joined to the LORD say, 'The LORD will surely separate me from his people'; and do not let the eunuch say, 'I am just a dry tree.' For thus says the LORD: to the eunuchs who keep my sabbaths, who choose the things that please me and hold fast my covenant, I will give, in my house and within my walls, a monument and a name better than sons and daughters; I will give them an everlasting name that shall not be cut off. And the foreigners who join themselves to the LORD, to minister to him, to love the name of the LORD, and to be his servants, all who keep sabbath, and do not profane it, and hold fast my covenant – these I will bring to my holy mountain, and make them joyful in my house of prayer; their burnt offerings and their sacrifices will be accepted on my altar; for my house shall be called a house of prayer for all peoples. Thus says the LORD GOD who gathers the outcasts of Israel, I will gather others to them besides those already gathered. (Isaiah 56.3–8)

In this messianic prophecy, all eunuchs will one day be perfect servants of the LORD, able to minister and preside at the altar. Philip proclaimed to the Ethiopian eunuch that that prophecy had been fulfilled in Jesus. It took the Church in the book of Acts several more 'acts of the Holy Spirit' before they finally got the message that 'God shows no partiality, but in every nation anyone who fears him and does what is right is acceptable to him' (Acts 10.34). But there is still an undercurrent in the book of Acts that resists such an inclusive gospel. We see it at the Jerusalem Council in chapter 15.

Queer people of faith must continue to claim the experience of our spiritual ancestor, the Ethiopian eunuch, and we must continue the work of our patron saint Philip in spite of a Church that has forgotten this story from the book of Acts.

Cornelius Story, Paul and Barnabas, and the Council of Jerusalem

ROBERT E. GOSS

An angel of God appears in a vision to Cornelius, a Roman centurion and God-fearer. The angel tells where Peter is staying in Joppa. Cornelius sends two slaves and a devout soldier to search for Peter. Peter, likewise, has a vision from God of a sheet floating down from heaven with all kinds of four-footed creatures, reptiles and birds. God instructs Peter to kill and eat, but Peter protests that he has never eaten unclean food. God responds, 'What God has made clean, you must not call profane.' As Peter is contemplating his confusing vision, the emissaries from Cornelius arrive. He accompanies them to the house of Cornelius. Peter is pushed by God into preaching to Cornelius and his household, and while he is speaking, the Holy Spirit is poured upon Cornelius and his household. They break into tongues. Peter recognizes that Cornelius and his household received the Spirit, and he baptizes them in the name of Jesus the Christ.

When Peter returns to Jerusalem, the circumcised believers, the Aramaic-speaking community of the Jesus movement, criticized Peter for eating with uncircumcised men. Peter narrates his story and finally ends with the comment: 'If God gave them the same gift that God gave us when we believed in the Lord Jesus Christ, who was I then that I could hinder God?' (11.17). The Council of Jerusalem – under the leadership of James the brother of Jesus – begrudgingly acknowledges the inclusion of baptized Gentiles. Luke portrays the inclusion of the Gentiles as not the invention of the Church but the responsibility of God who bestows the Spirit upon uncircumcised Gentiles.

After the conversion of Paul, the Antioch community commissions both Paul and Barnabas as missionaries to other lands in Asia Minor. They find opposition in the synagogues to their preaching and turn to a Gentile audience where successful converts are made (chapters 13–14).

Crossan and Reed write about the issue in Antioch:

When a Christian Jewish assembly and a Christian Gentile assembly existed in the same city and wanted to eat together in the celebration of the Lord's Supper, were kosher restrictions necessary for everyone or unnecessary for anyone? Should the Gentiles change and accept kosher or the Jews change and avoid kosher? The custom in Antioch was the latter option – kosher was not observed by anyone at joint meals. (Crossan and Reed 2004: 219)

This was intolerable to the Jerusalem authorities of the Jewish Christian community. When the two missionaries return to Antioch, they discover Jewish Christians from Judaea who are insisting that male Gentile converts must be circumcised to be saved: 'Unless you are circumcised to the custom of Moses, you cannot be saved' (15.1b). The Antioch community appoints Paul and Barnabas to go to Jerusalem to make their case.

Some of the Pharisee followers of Jesus maintained that baptized Gentile males needed to be circumcised and keep the Mosaic law (15.5). Through the plea of Peter and the stories of Paul and Barnabas about what God was doing among the Gentiles, James responds. As the pillar of the Jerusalem church, James maintains that it is within God's plan to include the Gentiles. He proposes a law for Gentile converts: Gentiles are to abstain from things polluted by idols, from fornication, and from animals not slaughtered according to the Mosaic law. James commanded them to follow kosher rules at the Lord's Supper. Though there is no need for male circumcision of Gentiles, they are to practise kosher rules at joint meals.

Paul plays such a leading role in Acts that it is really the story of Paul with a long preface about Peter and the chief apostles and disciples. Acts uses the pre-Pauline history to set up the continuity of the Gentile mission and to stress that Christian Gentiles do not have to become Jews. The rest of Acts is how Paul spreads Christian mission to the four corners of the Roman empire and to Rome itself.

The scandal of Gentile inclusion

Acts portrays God's radically scandalous inclusion of the Gentiles. Non-Jews barely comprehend how eating non-kosher is sinful for observant Jews and how grave an offence it was to be in the presence of or eat with a Gentile:

To be a Gentile was, in the eyes of Jews and Jewish Christians alike, the same thing as being a sinner, since the Gentiles did not have the law, since they were by definition unclean, polluted, and idolatrous. They first had to repent of being Gentiles and adopt the purifying and transforming practices of God's covenant people, the Jews, before they could become Christians. And yet the experience of Peter and Paul led them, and eventually many others, to the realization that, even as a Gentile, one could come to know God, to worship God, and to receive and show the Spirit of God. To be a Gentile did not by definition mean to be a sinner. (Siker 1994: 230)

Jeffrey Siker has pointed out that there is a parallel with the moral revulsion of contemporary fundamentalist and evangelical Christians to homosexuals. Siker refers to the Cornelius story:

> But just as Peter's experience of Cornelius in Acts 10 led him to realize that even Gentiles were receiving God's Spirit, so my experience of various gay and lesbian Christians led me to realize that these Christians have received God's Spirit as gays and lesbians and that the reception of the Spirit has nothing to do with sexual orientation . . . I once thought of gays and lesbians as Peter and Paul thought of 'Gentile sinners,' but now with Peter, I am compelled to ask, 'Can anyone withhold the water for baptizing these people who have received the Holy Spirit just as we have?' (Siker 1996: 146)

Like law-observant Jewish Christians, many fundamentalist and evangelical Christians deny that there could be 'gay Christians' or 'lesbian Christians', let alone 'transgendered Christians' or 'queer Christians'. Such denials revive old Jewish purity codes, now conflated with homosexuality. Jerome Neyrey defines purity:

> Purity, then, is the orderly system whereby we perceive that certain things belong to certain places at certain times. Purity is the abstract way of indicating what fits, what is appropriate, and what is in place. Purity refers to a system, a coherent and detailed drawing of lines in the world to peg, classify, and structure the world. (Neyrey 1991: 275)

Compulsory heterosexuality has become the new purity map for homophobic Christians. Married heterosexual relationships are pure while all other forms of sexuality are seen to be abhorrent, sinful and an abomination. It generates the moral revulsion of many Christians against LGBTQ folk. Like their Jewish and Jewish Christian predecessors, phobic Christians adhere to their purity maps of gender and sexuality, producing a homophobic (biphobic and transphobic) 'Creationism' that allows for no deviance in the fundamentals of gender and sexuality. Jerry Falwell states, 'homosexuals are brute beasts . . . part of a vile and satanic system that will be utterly annihilated, and there will be celebration in heaven' (Hill and Cheadle 1995: 69–70). Christian fundamentalists satanize queer folk and project their own fears upon them as a group. Purity maps – whether in Acts or today – are powerful moral fences that protect fundamentalists from listening to moral and religious differences from themselves. Contemporary fundamentalist Christians fail to listen to genuine sexual variations and gender differences. It becomes blindness, preventing them from discerning the presence of the Holy Spirit in queer Christians.

  Peter and Paul called Jewish Christians from their moral revulsion at associating with and eating with uncircumcised Gentile males to embrace Gentile Christians as brothers and sisters. Such church movements as Open and Affirming and More Light Movements have taken steps towards inclusion; they have attempted to discern the Spirit of God in queer Christians. These are the first steps towards full inclusion that recognize that if churches baptize translesbigay children, it is incumbent upon them to recognize their holy unions and their call to ministry. Full inclusion is nothing less than full recognition of God's Spirit in queer Christians.

The conversion of Saul from rigid fundamentalism

Acts introduces a young Pharisee, Saul, holding the garments of the mob stoning Stephen and looking on approvingly. The Catholic biblical scholar Jerome Murphy O'Connor describes Saul as 'an immature religious bigot working out his personal problems' (Murphy O'Connor 1996: 69). Young Saul supported the high priest, the temple and a unified view of Jewish practice. He became super zealous in persecuting the nascent Christian community. Many folk have intuited that Saul was ill at ease with himself, and some have suspected that he was attracted to men (Spong 1991: 115–27; Theissen 1983/87: 26, 241; Goss 2002: 123–4). Sidney Tarachow presents a suggestive psychoanalytic portrayal of Paul as erotically attracted to men (Tarachow 1955). If that be the case, could Saul have been attracted to Stephen? Stephen had those same brash, provocative and bold qualities that Saul possessed. Was he simultaneously repelled and physically attracted to Stephen? Saul had to 'repress with the aid of the law, his libidinous impulses, with a clearly homosexual component, in order to keep these from his consciousness' (H. Fischer quoted in Theissen 1983/87: 236). How did Saul feel when the crowd pelted Stephen with stones and the dying martyr had a vision of the Christ at the right side of God? Did Stephen's self-confidence, faith and courage impact Saul? Was Saul unconsciously attracted to the freedom of the good news – a freedom from the law – that Stephen preached?

Theissen maintains that Saul unconsciously envies Christianity for its freedom from the law and its theology of grace (Theissen 1983/87: 236). Stephen's death called into question Saul's mechanism of psychological repression. It explains Saul's over-identification with the Pharisee interpretation of the law and his obsessive aggression against a small splinter group that moved away from the normative values of the majority of Jews. After the death of Stephen, Saul persecuted the 'devout' Hellenists who buried Stephen (8.2–3). Acts has Saul approaching the high priest and asking for letters to the synagogues in Damascus to apprehend members of this Hellenist group that described itself as 'the Way' (9.1–3). Acts portrays him as the most zealous and fanatic enemy of the Church. In Galatians 1.14, Paul writes, 'I advanced in Judaism beyond many among my people of the same age, for I was far more zealous for the traditions of my ancestors.' Gerd Theissen notes how Paul in Romans 2.1 says that 'we condemn in others what we do ourselves' (Theissen 1983/87: 241). In other words, his fundamentalist zeal for the Pharisee values and the support of the temple forms the basis of his earlier projection mechanism and scapegoating Stephen and the Hellenists. What is apparent in young Saul is a fragile ego, buttressed by an over-identification with Pharisaic values and obsessive need for validation from the law. He is unable to listen to anything other than his own beliefs. His identity is formed from strong group authority that restricts his options and his ability to think outside of narrow theological boundaries.

On the road to Damascus, Saul is struck by a light from heaven and falls to the ground. A voice speaks: 'Saul, Saul, why do you persecute me? . . . I am

Jesus, whom you are persecuting' (9.4b–5). Acts 9.3–16 gives a third-person account, but in Acts 22.6–15 and 26.12–18, there are two first-person accounts in Paul's speeches. Did Saul see in the light a heavenly figure or did he see the face of Jesus in a flashback of dying Stephen's beatific face? In 1 Corinthians 15.8–9 and Galatians 1.12, Paul speaks of his revelation of God's child, the risen Christ. Bruce Chilton writes,

> He (Paul) had been mortally opposed to Jesus' followers, but his own vision proved that they were right and he was dead wrong. Jesus spoke to Rabbi Paul the persecutor, a man as alien to God as a person could be. That showed that God also wanted to uncover the divine Son within Gentiles, whose alienation from God was not the result of their own actions. (Chilton 2004: 54)

Saul before his conversion was a zealous Pharisee, who unquestioningly supported the temple and the high priest. He understood Stephen and the Hellenist Jewish followers of Jesus as enemies of the temple, the central institution of first-century CE Judaism. Saul was a rigid personality, fearing loss of control; he was dogmatic and aggressively persecuted the Hellenists. He had rigid gender notions, and these are reflected in Pharisaic residues in his later writings (1 Cor. 11.2–16). Men with long hair and women with short hair confused his Pharisaic purity codes. And certainly homoerotic relationships troubled the purity codes by 'exchanging natural intercourse for unnatural' (Rom. 1).

We experience people similar to 'Saul' in our contemporary experiences of fundamentalist Christians with internalized homophobia. Since queer Christians cannot produce on demand 'road to Damascus' visions of the risen Christ to engage Christian fundamentalists, what other strategies remain to us? Many queer Christian leaders and clergy have tried the route of education through 'homosexuality and the Bible' classes and talks. How do we help fundamentalists move from group thinking to find individual authority in their consciences, to listen to differences, and not surrender to clerical authority and facile and selective uses of the authority of the Bible? When we look to Saul for some clues as to how to deal with a fundamentalist-style personality with strong internalized homophobia, it is a relationship with the risen Christ and the gospel of freedom that attracts Paul. He is attracted to Stephen but shares the synagogue mob's panic attack. Stephen's witness impacts him; it is the Christian experience of the freedom of the gospel and the inclusion of outsiders. Queer Christian strategies of nonviolence, witness to the freedom of the gospel, a vision of an inclusive Christ and a community of service, and a comfort with diversity and plurality may have a powerful effect upon fundamentalists and enable them like Saul to see the risen Christ in our faces.

The Conversion of Lydia

DERYN GUEST

The story of Lydia's conversion related in Acts 16.14–15 is just one among several brief references to the participation of women in the early church movements. Luke's work is one of our primary resources for knowledge about their roles. However, the details provided are, as Schüssler Fiorenza (1992b: 788) has noted, just the tip of the iceberg, its presence indicating what is absent beneath the waters, submerged in historical silence. Accordingly, we need to apply a strong hermeneutic of suspicion and employ the critical scholarly imagination if we hope to do justice to any reconstruction of their lives and leadership responsibilities. Feminist biblical scholarship has produced a substantive body of research that restores balance to traditional histories of the early Church. Much, if not most of this work, however, has been conducted within a heterosexist frame of reference with few writers considering how far women who lived and travelled together in the first century CE might have found in their ministries a welcome escape route from expected destinies of wifedom and motherhood. One of the notable exceptions is the significant essay by Mary Rose D'Angelo (1999), who suggests that the references to Tryphaena and Tryphosa (Rom. 16.12), Euodia and Syntyche (Phil. 4.2), Mary and Martha (John 11/Luke 10.38–42) have been edited by both the writers and interpreters of the Christian scriptures so that mention of their relationships and work accommodates accepted norms regarding the role and place of women. Yet in her view such partnerships 'reveal a commitment between women that, in the light of early Christian revision of sexual mores, can be seen as a sexual choice' (1999: 442). D'Angelo is rightly cautious of claiming any lesbian ancestry not least because the organization of women's lives probably did not accord to a homosexual/heterosexual binary, though there is contextual evidence of female homoeroticism in the first century CE. Rather, she draws upon Rich's (1987) influential concept of the lesbian continuum that incorporates strong female–female commitments within its scope regardless of whether or not one can know about their erotic relationships. D'Angelo's work helps to open the heterosexual frame in which scholarship has been conducted and consider alternative possibilities.

It is precisely this ability to think outside the heteronormative frame that the film critic Alexander Doty encourages. His treatment of film classics notes how audiences routinely assume the heterosexuality of characters unless they are specifically labelled otherwise; when in reality the assumption has no real basis. Doty would no doubt approve of the operational gaydar of Nancy Wilson (1995) and Tim Koch (2001) who have already identified Lydia as a woman with great dyke credentials. The basis for this happy recognition lies primarily in the reference to Lydia as a seller of purple. Purple, together with its shades of lavender and pink, has long had a specific resonance for people within lesbian and gay communities; lesbians were criticized as the 'lavender menace' during second-wave feminism; lavender was used as a code for a homosexual screen presence during the early to mid-twentieth century; the pink triangle was the sign of a homosexual in Nazi Germany. Precisely when and where the connection was first established is probably lost to obscurity (Judy Grahn's (1983) attempts to trace it back to Sappho are highly speculative). Nonetheless, the reference to Lydia's selling of purple thus scores an immediate 'hit' with both Wilson and Koch, and further resonances follow. Koch notes the overt lack of reference to any male relations, how Lydia appears to be running her own business and household, and how she goes out to join a group of women gathered at the riverside on the Sabbath. Finally, he and Nancy Wilson (1995: 158) both comment on the fact that the route from Troas to Samothrace, to Neapolis and then Philippi where this scene is located (Acts 16.11), lies in the immediate vicinity of the Isle of Lesbos. Koch declares, 'If this doesn't at least suggest (let alone scream) "dyke", what does?!' (2001: 19).

The felicity with which both Wilson and Koch make such connections can be likened to critical treatments of lesbian and gay sensibility. The film critic Vito Russo, for example, notes how the stigma that was attached to homosexuality necessarily constructed a lesbian or gay sensibility:

> Gay sensibility is largely a product of oppression, of the necessity to hide so well for so long. It is a ghetto sensibility, born of the need to develop and use a second sight that will translate silently what the world sees and what the actuality may be. It was gay sensibility that, for example, often enabled some lesbians and gay men to see at very early ages, even before they knew the words for what they were, something on the screen that they knew related to their lives in some way, without being able to put a finger on it. (1987: 92)

In fact, Wilson's basic approach, despite its somewhat essentialist framework, does not seem to be so very far away from the statement of the acclaimed critic Sally Munt, that

> we are particularly adept at extracting our own meanings, at highlighting a text's latent content, at reading 'dialectically', at filling the gaps, at interpreting the narrative according to our introjected fictional fantasies, and at foregrounding the intertextuality of our identities. If we accept that language is unstable, then within its heterosexuality we must also be able to find its homosexual other. A lesbian reader's literary competence brings to the text a set of interpretative conventions for decoding and encoding which is rich in its own historical, cultural and linguistic specificity. (1992: xxi)

Koch refers to his approach as a 'cruising methodology'. A cruising methodology is one of encounter where a text is brought alive to the reader due to some correlation between it and one's own experience. For Koch, such encounters are not tangibly different to encounters 'along a roadside, in a bar, in an internet chatroom' (2001: 21). In all such cases a cruising method is one grounded in a reader's erotic knowledge which allows him or her to pursue that which catches the eye. And, as Guest (2005) has suggested, such a method provides a very useful initial starting place for engaging with scripture. As they stand, the connections are loose and flimsy and do not, without a more detailed level of discussion, convince. But as examples of the imaginative flair of LGBT readers, who can find queer elements in the apparently straightest of texts, they provide welcome disruptions to the heteronormative atmosphere of biblical interpretation; and perhaps this is their greatest strength – freeing up biblical studies from the dominance of heterocentric interpretation and introducing a new reader-response community to the academy and to lay readers. They also help to produce further cracks in the heterocentric interpretations of the Jesus and early Church movements. Too often a handful of selected texts that appear to condemn same-sex relationships are allowed to construct an anachronistic hetero-homosexual binary within the scriptures themselves and within the social world that produced them: a binary that simply is not there. While it is not possible to pose simplistic direct links with LGBT identities today in order to reclaim a gay ancestry, it is important to break down the implicit and deep-seated assumption that there is a direct link between *heterosexual* people today and the sexuality of the biblical characters. Lydia's story does offer us the tantalizing glimpse of an economically apparently independent woman who likes to spend her Sabbaths in the company of women at the riverside. Historically, we will never know anything more than Luke tells us, but hurray for the details he did mention, without which no hit would probably have been ever scored, and no tip of an iceberg ever become visible.

Romans

THOMAS HANKS

Introduction

Among his opponents and fellow Jews, mainly married, whom he was soon to face again in Jerusalem, with almost fatal consequences, Paul's law-free Gentile mission created suspicion about his manhood and that of his mainly unmarried co-workers (see the evidence from 1–2 Corinthians presented by Jennifer Larson, 2004: 85–97; also Jennifer Glancy, 2004: 99–135). Hence, in Romans 1.24–7 Paul first echoes the traditional Jewish propaganda line against Graeco-Roman homoeroticism, which he had imbibed from his youth (Wisdom of Solomon 14.24–7) and assimilated in the form of interiorized homophobia. This approach would have reassured Paul's potential allies in the Roman house churches that not all rumours arriving from Jerusalem were true. However, once the party line had been echoed, Paul first springs a trap on judgemental readers, showing that those who condemned common pagan idolatry and deviant sexual behaviour (2.1–29) were even more guilty than the Gentiles who applauded it (1.32). In the succeeding chapters Paul then proceeds to deconstruct the Jewish homophobic propaganda line, showing:

- that the queer Jesus' shameful experience of being crucified was in fact the decisive revelation of God's liberating justice (3.21–6); then
- that behaviour 'against nature' was precisely what God himself engaged in when ingrafting believing Gentiles into the olive tree of Israel (11.24; by referring to Gentiles as uncircumcised 'by nature' Paul makes the very rite of circumcision itself a human cultural imposition, an act 'against nature'; 2.27; see 2.14); and finally
- that behaviour traditionally condemned as 'unclean' (1.24) had now been cleansed (14.14, 20).

In chapter 16 Paul wisely avoids reducing his gospel to any narrow 'identity politics' of a single oppressed group. The three married couples are warmly greeted and affirmed without any sense that such support might threaten or endanger the stability, felicity and sanctity of the many sexual minority partnerships and living arrangements. The apostle had made quite clear elsewhere that he thought those who decided to become heterosexual and get married had settled for something less than God's best (1 Cor. 7), but he would not condemn them for their weakness. If they would be co-labourers in his law-free Gentile mission, their handicap would be graciously overlooked.

Although many imagine that Paul sought to condemn all male slaves subjected to same-sex and anal intercourse (the dominant interpretation of Rom. 1.27), that definitely could not qualify as 'good news to the poor', since slaves (male and female) commonly were expected to satisfy their owners' sexual desires (Williams 1999: 30–8; Glancy 1998: 481–501; Lebacqz 1987: 21–2, 42–3). Had Paul really intended to demand that Christian slaves be willing to face the death penalty rather than fulfil their sexual obligations to their masters, he surely would have made that clear when he gave them his instructions concerning Christian sexual behaviour later in the epistle (13.11–14). However, Paul's epistolary exhortations address agents who are free to fulfil them, such as Christian males tempted to visit prostitutes (see 1 Cor. 5–7). For Christian slaves to be 'free from sin' (Rom. 6) and free from the wrath of God (Rom. 5.9) did not imply that they became free from fulfilling their sexual obligations to their owners. The common interpretation of Romans 1.27 as condemning all males involved in any kind of 'homosexual act' in effect has Paul proclaiming God's wrath against the poor, the oppressed, victims of violence and rape, and not just their oppressors.

Twelve Young Trees that Make a New Forest

1   Although virtually ignored by first-world scholars, José P. Miranda long ago demonstrated that sin in the Bible, and in Romans in particular, is to be understood in terms of oppression/injustice (1971/74: 169–99). Hence Paul repeatedly refers to oppression/injustice in central affirmations in the opening section (1.18, 29; 2.8; 3.5) and does not refer to 'sin' until 2.12. Lately, the interpretation of Romans in the light of Roman imperial oppression (Horsley 1997; 2000; Wright 2002) takes Paul's understanding of sin as 'injustice/oppression' more seriously. The prominent place of oppression in Romans (1.18, 29; 2.8; 3.5) is paralleled in 1 Corinthians (6.8–10), where Paul's vice list similarly is headed with the reference to oppression (*adikía*), implying that the only homoerotic acts condemned in the following list are those characterized by exploitation, injustice and violence (rape), all especially experienced by slaves (Hanks 2000: 105–8; Glancy 1998; 2002).

For centuries Romans 16, with Paul's numerous greetings, was ignored by commentators as rather dull and scholars argued that Paul couldn't possibly have known so many individuals in a city he never visited. In the latter decades of the twentieth century, a wave of feminist studies brought to light the amazing role of women in leadership attested in the chapter, which led to discerning a remarkable contrast between such authentic Pauline material and the more traditional patriarchal perspectives of the later deutero-Pauline letters (the household tables of Colossians and Ephesians and the pastoral letters, especially 1 Timothy 2.8–15; see 1 Corinthians 14.34–5, now rejected as a textual gloss). Feminist investigations were soon followed by studies in the socio-economic mode, which demonstrated the high proportion of slave names in the list of those greeted. Of the 28 believers greeted, at least 12 and perhaps as many as 26 bore names commonly used for slaves, some of whom may have been liberated by the time Paul wrote, but in most cases would still represent the poorer and marginalized classes, and under Roman law slaves could not legally marry (see the Appendix, p. 604; Lampe 2003: 183).

In my studies of Romans 16 (Hanks 1997: 137–49; 2000: 88–94), I have taken the liberation reading a step further, pointing out that the saints whom Paul greets in the Roman house churches were not only mainly poor/slaves, and led by women, but also overwhelmingly sexual minorities: out of 28 persons greeted and 38 named, only three are married couples, as would be expected among immigrants and slaves, while the rest of Paul's friends apparently are sexual minorities like Jesus and Paul himself (this continues to be overlooked; see Clarke 2002: 103–25). Even two of the three married couples Paul greets break with the patriarchal pattern and like the unmarried persons might well be described as gender-benders. Moreover, when Paul writes Romans he is not living with a woman, but has Timothy as his closest companion and they are housed in Gaius' bachelor pad with six other single males (Rom. 16.21–4). Paul's friendship pattern thus reveals him to have an option for the poor and to be some kind of feminist liberation theologian with a message subversive to the dominant patriarchal family ideology. These remarkable deposits of exegetical dynamite buried for millennia at the end of Romans beneath dull lists of names led me to argue that contemporary readers with traditional prejudices need to study Romans backwards, beginning with chapter 16 and proceeding in reverse order to chapter 1 (Hanks 2000: 80–1, 94). Similarly, Stephen Moore recently concluded that for his purposes 'I shall have to outflank the letter's defenses and steal up on it from behind' (2001: 135).

Both for the unmarried Paul and for his largely unmarried friends, the memories of David's covenanted love relationship with Jonathan and Jesus' relationship with the Beloved Disciple would have been especially strong and appealing. As a repressed homosexual, Paul would be most naturally attracted to traditions focusing on pairs of males, so it is not surprising that Romans reflects heavy continuity with such traditions and avoids focusing on heterosexual couples: Romans 5.12–21, Adam and Christ, but no Eve; Romans 4: Abraham and David, but no Sarah or Bathsheba, etc. The royal function of the 'Son of David' is to bestow Abrahamic blessings on 'all the Gentiles' (15.11), not just the married heterosexuals.

2   In her doctoral thesis, Elsa Tamez, Latina theologian, demonstrated that 'justification' in Romans refers particularly to God's gracious acceptance and vindication of the poor and oppressed (1991), and in a later work focuses on the prominence of women leaders among the congregations of the poor (1998/99). Recognizing Paul's teaching on *sin* as (imperial) oppression, and *justification* as the acceptance and vindication of the marginalized poor, women and sexual minorities, enables us to see that the Good News of the revelation of God's *justice* (Rom. 1.16–17) refers especially to the kind of *liberating* justice experienced by Israelite slaves in the Exodus. For Paul in Romans, then, divine justice is to be understood as liberating justice, starting from the experience of oppression, and not primarily as a maintaining of 'law and order' (euphemisms for imperial oppression and violence; Hanks 2000: 9–11).

Contemporary gender studies take us a step further, unmasking the patriarchal ideology that is both presupposed and partly subverted in Romans.

As Stephen Moore points out: *'Righteousness* [liberating justice] *in Romans is essentially a masculine trait* . . . the very mark of masculinity' (2001: 163, italics his). Sinfulness (injustice, oppression, violence) then, is the lack of masculinity, the loss of self-mastery, 'essentially a feminine trait in Romans' (163). Thus in Romans 1.24–7 the apostle describes 'unclean' persons who allow masculine reason to be dominated by the passions and lusts that were characteristic of women (according to patriarchal ideology); similarly in 1.28–32 masculine reason does not rule, but feminine passions dominate, as covetousness (*pleoneksía*) leads to oppression (*adikía*) and violence against neighbour.

On the other hand, males are the active sexual penetrators, while females (according to traditional patriarchal ideologies), are to be passive and receptive (Brooten 1996: 11; Long 2004: 26–7, 142–4). Thus, God is imaged as passively feminine when hospitably accepting and receiving unclean Gentiles into the divine household (God's people) and Paul seeks to mould the Roman house churches in the image of the divine feminine when he insists that they should hospitably 'receive' and accept one another despite ethnic differences (Rom. 14.1; 15.7; cf. the more masculine image of God 'inserting' the Gentiles into the Israelite olive tree in 11.14, 20). The apostle's male-like penetration of Caesar's empire by the establishment of subversive communities acknowledging Christ as Lord (1.1–15; 15.14–33) constitutes the dialectical counterpart to the hospitable house churches and their welcoming God.

3 Only when we scrutinize the entire letter to the Romans, are we in a position to understand the controversial 1.18–2.16 text *in its context*, which is the first principle of sound hermeneutics for interpreting any literature. Previous commentaries and studies have suffered a great deal by failure to apply this principle. Learned commentaries on the entire letter commonly become shockingly superficial when treating specifically 1.24–7 (Wright 2002; Esler 2003a; Lohse 2003), while studies of 'homosexuality' in 1.24–7 commonly fix on extensive Jewish and Graeco-Roman background materials, but neglect to interpret the text in the light of the context of the letter itself and Paul's personality profile (repressed homosexual) – and thus miss the amazing deconstruction that takes place (Brooten 1996; Gagnon 2001).

Modern commentators increasingly recognize that Romans 2.1–16 constitutes a rhetorical trap, 'a sweeping "sting operation"' (Gagnon 2001: 278; see Edwards 1984: 98–9; Countryman 1988: 121; Byrne 1996: 70). However, although isolated elements are acknowledged by a few writers, previous commentators do not note how Paul deconstructs three of the four major negative elements regarding Gentile sexuality in 1.24–7, while he acknowledges as a continuing norm for the church *only* the prohibition against coveting, the tenth commandment of the Decalogue, since such excessive ill-directed desire fails to fulfil the norm of love for the neighbour, harms the neighbour and destroys communities (Rom. 13.8–10; see 12.1–15.13).

Dale Martin (1995) and David Fredrickson (2000: 207–15) have demonstrated that in Paul's negative rhetorical portrayal of Gentile sexuality in 1.24–7, his *primary* concern is not with the gender of the sexual partner but with the *excessive* desire, passion or 'covetousness' that breaks the tenth commandment of the Decalogue (Ex. 20.17; Deut. 5.21) – not *'disoriented* desire' but *'inordinate* desire' (Martin 1995: 342). In Graeco-Roman culture, *epithumía* (excessive desire, covetousness; 1.24), like sin in general, commonly was viewed as characteristically feminine, the loss of masculine self-control of the passions by reason, even resulting in softening and feminizing a man's soul and even his body (Rom. 1.27b; Glancy 2003: 247–9). Woman-like indulgence in such excessive desire also results in loss of masculine honour, the other major concern in the text ('bodies dishonoured', 1.26; 'passions of dishonour', 1.27; 'the unseemliness working', 1.27).

Repeatedly Paul returns to this major concern of dishonourable passions at key points in the later chapters (6.12–13; 7.7–8; 13.8–10, 13). Such excess of desire leads to acts that harm the neighbour (in abuses of power, injustice, oppression; see 1.18; 6.12–13), rather than the love that builds up communities (13.8–10). Thus, when the apostle returns to treat human sexuality and the appropriate norms for conduct, the key negative term that describes what is to be avoided is *aselgeiais*, excesses (13.13). Significantly, each of the other three concepts referred to in connection with Gentile sexuality is carefully deconstructed as the letter unfolds – only the condemnation of covetousness, excessive desire leading to acts that harm the neighbour, remains standing as a norm for believers in the didactic portion of the letter. As Thomas Hubbard points out, evidence from the Greek vases has led some scholars to see 'the active/passive polarity as fundamental to the significance of pederasty as a social institution' (2003: 10, with reference to Dover 1978: 84–91, 100–9; Halperin 1989: 15–40; Winkler 1990: 45–70; and frequently attributed to Foucault 1986). However, 'for Foucault, the fundamental dichotomy is between being active (i.e. in control) or passive (i.e. controlled) in relation to one's own appetites' (Hubbard 2003: 10, note 8; see Hubbard 1988 and Davidson 2001).

Only when we give due weight to the rhetorical trap Paul lays in 1.18–32, to be sprung in 2.1–16, and also carefully analyse each of the four elements in Paul's rhetorical condemnation of Gentile sexuality in 1.24–7, observing what the apostle does with each of these elements as the letter unfolds (deconstructing three and maintaining only one as normative for the churches), can we properly interpret 'the author's intention' (to use the term still defended in evangelical hermeneutics) regarding the homoerotic activity referred to (male–male anal sex) in 1.27.

The proper interpretation of Romans 1.24–7 in the context of the entire letter, as normative for church praxis today, thus requires that we give full weight, first recognizing

- the rhetorical trap constituted by the relation of 1.18–32 to 2.1–16;
- the deconstruction of three elements in the negative rhetoric of 1.24–7; and
- the prohibition of excessive desire, of the coveting that results in harm to neighbour, which remains standing and is subsequently developed, being linked to love for neighbour as normative for behaviour in the house churches in Rome (13.8–14).

The two transcendent norms that remain standing (avoid the coveting that leads to harm, love the neighbour) were perfectly appropriate for the large number of slaves in the Roman house churches. Although slaves could not avoid providing the sexual services commonly demanded of them, they could fulfil the norm of love for neighbour that avoids harm, injustice, oppression and violence. This perception thus unmasks any notion of an 'ethical absolute' against 'homosexuality' as totally oblivious to the socio-economic-historical context and hopelessly anachronistic. Paul's construction of norms for sexual conduct condemn the covetous, oppressive sexual demands of slave owners, but insist on love for neighbour as the *unique* norm that fulfils the divine intent in Moses' law. This teaching is coherent with his proclamation of a gospel that is good news to poor slaves, who commonly could not conform to all the cultic cleanliness code of Leviticus. In recent centuries we have seen fundamentalist-type churches move from incessant citations of Paul to enslave women and *defend* slavery, to forgetting that Paul often addressed churches largely consisting of slaves – and the incessant citations of Paul to promote homophobia and attack 'homosexuals'. Modern paraphrases that substitute 'servants' for the more literal 'slaves' and then add the neologism 'homosexuals' to Paul's theological vocabulary greatly facilitate the disappearance of slaves from our hermeneutic grid and promote violence against sexual minorities.

4   Paul immediately begins his deconstruction of 'against nature' (*para phusis*, 1.26) in chapter 2 by making circumcision itself a cultural imposition, an act *against* nature that God himself commanded (2.27)! As commentators universally recognize, Paul refers to nature (*phusis*) in its most common meaning in 2.27, when he refers to the Gentiles as those who are 'not circumcised *by* nature'. Even Robert Gagnon admits that Paul in effect says that the cutting of the foreskin in the act of circumcision is an act 'against nature' (2001: 372, note 34) – and hence when God commanded Abraham and his male offspring and slaves to be circumcised, he was commanding them to undertake an act 'against nature' (Gen. 17). The NIV, rushing to protect evangelical readers from falling into such heresy, disguises the deconstruction process by translating Paul's 'by nature' as 'physically' (2.27), so the reader misses the link Paul established with the phrase 'against nature' in 1.26 and 11.24 (cf. the NIV '*do* by nature', instead of '*Gentiles* by nature' in 2.14). As Tom Wright points out, 'All males are "naturally uncircumcised" in the sense that they are *born that way*' (2002: 448, note 73). Wright, in fact, concludes that, except for the reference to an abstract nature in 1 Corinthians 11.14 (male and female hair length), all the other Pauline usages refer to the status people have *by birth or race* (even Rom. 1.26). Moreover, the earlier, more ambiguous text (2.14) is best translated:

For whenever Gentiles who do not *possess* Torah *by nature* (*phusei*) the things of the Torah *do*, these, though not having the Torah, are a law to themselves.

The two recent major evangelical commentators recognize that Paul uses 'by nature' in the same sense ('by birth') in both 2.14 and 27 (Schreiner 1998: 123; Wright 2002: 441–2; earlier Cranfield 1975/79; *pace* Gagnon 2001: 371, note 32). Wright points out that Paul always uses *phusis* in an adjectival phrase ('*Gentiles by nature*', 2.14), not adverbially ('by nature *do*'; 1996: 145, citing Achtemeier 1985: 45).

Finally, as Eugene Rogers and Elizabeth Stuart emphasize, in 11.24 Paul deconstructs his rhetoric about sexual acts 'against nature', affirming that God himself acted 'in excess of nature' by grafting unclean Gentile branches into the pure olive tree (Israel). Such divine action that transcends 'nature' obviously, was to be celebrated (Rom. 11.32–6; 15.7–13), not condemned. Bernadette Brooten in a footnote cites Daniel Helminiak's reference to Romans' two references to *para phusin*, but dismisses its significance as 'methodologically problematic . . . because the two contexts differ so sharply' (1996: 246, note 88). The differing contexts, however, are precisely what give weight to the deconstruction.

On Paul's use of 'against nature' in Romans 11.14b, Eugene Rogers comments, 'Gentiles are so foreign to the God of Israel that Paul can say that God acts "contrary to nature," *para phusin*, in grafting them in. A phrase more liable to provoke . . . is difficult to imagine. Does Paul mean to compare God's activity to homosexual activity?' (1999: 64). Elizabeth Stuart adds, 'Paul's use of this phrase in Romans 11.24 is shocking considering his previous use of the phrase earlier in this letter to describe, not homosexual people, but Gentiles who characteristically engage in same-sex activity, a characteristic that distinguishes them, not from heterosexuals, but from Jews . . . . Paul is making the outrageous claim that God stands in solidarity with these Gentiles; God like them acts against, or more accurately, in excess of nature' (2003: 96).

Rogers concludes that just as God saved flesh by taking it on in Jesus' incarnation (Rom. 8.3), and then defeated death by dying (Rom. 8.11), so God saves the Gentiles, who act in excess of nature (Rom. 1.26–7), by an act in excess of nature (Rom. 11.24; Rogers 1999: 65, cited in Stuart 2003: 96). Countryman observes, regarding Rom. 11.24:

> The inclusion of the Gentiles in the Christian community represents a break with the preceding order of things as substantial as God's handing over of the Gentiles to their unclean culture . . . The constant, in both cases, is an assumption that there was a clear Gentile identity that God has altered not once, but twice: first in punishing the Gentile foundational sin of idolatry, and now, a second time, in incorporating Gentiles in the Christian community for reasons entirely of God's own grace. Both acts were 'unnatural' acts. (2003: 196; see also p. 174)

5   William Countryman (1988: 114; 2003: 196) and Daniel Helminiak (1995/ 2000: 80–4) also note how Paul deconstructs his rhetoric against sexual acts 'against nature' (1.26–7; 11.24) but emphasize an additional fundamental point: the way Paul's rhetoric regarding sexual uncleanness (1.24) is similarly deconstructed later in the letter (14.14, 20). In a later work Countryman maintains and strengthens his original basic position: 'The language is certainly pejorative; and yet it stops short of actually saying that this aspect of Gentile culture is intrinsically sinful or deserving of God's wrath. Paul's argument is rather that God has 'handed over' the Gentiles to their disgusting culture as punishment for another sin, idolatry' (2003: 174; similarly 1988). Because of Paul's use of a perfect participle in Romans 1.29 (represented by 'having [already] been filled with . . .' in the translation above), Countryman concludes (174–5) that the

Greek syntax implies a three-stage process that in effect reverses the order of the last two paragraphs of the text, 1–2–3 becoming 1–3–2:

1 Gentiles abandon their creator and turn to idols (1.18–23, 25);
3 they commit all manner of injustice and oppression (vice list, 1.29–31);
2 God abandons/punishes them with 'a culture that was disgustingly unclean from a Jewish perspective (1.24–8)'. (2003: 174)

Countryman points out (2003: 174): 'Same-gender sexual acts are treated here not as sinful but as consequences of a prior sin' (2003: 177). The Greek syntax in 1.29, as well as the linguistic trap in 2.1–16, thus both support the conclusion that Paul's intent in Romans 1.18–2.16 is not to zero in on homoerotic sex and create some new 'ethical absolute' against homosexuality.

Countryman's reordering of the chronology in 1.18–32, as implied by the Greek syntax in 1.29, results in a twofold emphasis on the *sin* of oppression/injustice (*adikía*, 1.18, 29; see 2.8) preceding the reference to the *uncleanness* of the sexual acts in 1.24–7). The same prioritizing of the sin of oppression occurs in the vice list in 1 Corinthians 6.9–10, where the references to 'softies' (lacking self-control) and 'male-beds' (arrogant penetrators of boys) occur as illustrations of the abuse of power (*adikía*) that heads the list of condemned behaviours (Hanks 2000: 108). In the biblical literature the idolatry condemned (as in Rom. 1.18–23, 25) commonly is that of cruelly oppressive empires, so writers like Paul naturally link the idolatrous worship that rationalizes the oppressive behaviour with sexual abuse (Hanks 1982/83; 1992). These factors would suggest that in so far as the Gentile 'unclean' sexual behaviour involved acts that were also sinful, the reference would not be to loving consensual sexual acts between adults, but to abuses of power, as in rape (Sodom), paedophilia and the sexual exploitation of unwilling slaves.

Countryman (2003: 201) points out how the earlier general instruction on believers' praxis prepares the ground for the later deconstruction of uncleanness: 'What love commands is enough to satisfy the Law, even if it does not fulfil its letter [13.8–10]. The latter interpretation allows for the fact that Paul is about to *bracket the Torah's purity requirements.*' Concerning 14.14 he then observes: 'It would not be a mistake to call this *the central affirmation of Romans.* I do not say that it is the central affirmation of Paul's faith; chapters 7–8 may give us a closer view of that. But it is the principle that Paul sees as necessary to any resolution of the conflict over food purity in the church at Rome' (2003: 205; cf. Schmidt (1995: 74–5) and Gagnon (2001: 273–7) for unsuccessful attempts to refute Countryman and Helminiak). Countryman concludes:

The Letter to Romans has a large and coherent structure. . . . The larger part of it . . . is constructed in the form of *two extended, parallel entrapments.* In these, Paul hopes to neutralize potential opposition by showing those who assume an easy superiority to people of the opposite ethnicity that they have no real claim. . . . The two 'entrapments' (1.18–32; chaps 9–11) came to be read as theological set pieces on the evils of homosexuality and Judaism, respectively, instead of playing their rhetorical function of entrapment for two distinct groups of Christians who prided themselves on their ethnicity and looked down on those who differed [2003: 211–12; see Boswell 1980 on anti-Semitism and homophobia]. . . . It is deeply distressing that Romans 1 and 9 have come to be read as affirmations of Christian cultural prejudices, whether against same-gender sexual partners or against Jews. Passages that began as entrapments for the proud have now become bulwarks of our pride. . . . It is obscene that what began as an exercise in exposing the self-confidence of the proud has so long been an excuse for Christian arrogance and violence against gay-lesbian people and Jews. (Countryman 2003: 217)

Romans 1.18–32 + 2.1–16 constitutes the first entrapment where Paul sets up those Jews and others like them who felt themselves superior to the common 'unclean' Gentile culture. The trap is set in 1.18–32 in the rhetorical denunciation of the idolatry, injustice and unclean sexual practices, and then sprung in 2.1–16 (actually extending to 8.39). Romans 9.1–29 + 9.30–11.36 constitutes the second entrapment, where Paul sets up those Gentiles and others like them who felt themselves superior to traditional Jews. The trap is set in 9.1–29 (with the concluding reference to Sodom in 9.29 playing a role similar to 1.24–7 in the first entrapment. The trap is then sprung in 9.30–11.36 with the teaching that the branches broken off eventually will be restored. The springing of the trap actually extends to 15.13 with the teaching that all things have become clean (14.14, 20).

In addition to deconstructing Paul's rhetoric against 'uncleanness' in Gentile sexual behaviour (Rom. 1.24), his bracketing of Pentateuchal purity requirements in 14.14, 20 may be perceived as specifically deconstructing the prohibitions of male–male anal sex (Lev. 18.22; 20.13, echoed in Rom. 1.24–32; Hanks 2000: 91; cf. Long 2004: viii, 90–4; Brooten 1996: 283–96). In effect, Paul's laying of his rhetorical trap in 1.18–32 leads readers to assume he is simply echoing Leviticus, while the springing of the trap (2.1–16) and declaring of all things clean (14.14, 20) make clear his conclusion that Jewish purity legislation was not literally binding on the Roman churches.

6   Much attention has been given to Second Testament and Pauline cultural-anthropological perspectives on honour/shame (Moxnes 1988b: 207–18; Brooten 1996: 208–12; Jewett 1997: 25–73). Few recognize, however, that this perspective signals the third element in Paul's deconstruction of Romans 1.24, 26–7 (Hanks 2000: 92). Just as each verse focuses on unclean excess desire, three times we find a similar emphasis on the shameful consequences of excess desire, which indicate a lack of self-control and discipline:

- 'to be *dishonoured in their bodies among themselves* . . .' (1.24)
- 'females . . . passions of *dishonour*' (1.26)
- 'males . . . the *unseemliness* working' (1.27).

However, in Paul's gospel Jesus' crucifixion – the most shameful experience in antiquity – is the central element (Rom. 3.21–6)! Thus Paul later deconstructs his earlier rhetoric with the presentation of Jesus' shameful crucifixion (together with the resurrection) as central to God's redemption and liberation of the cosmos. In evident anticipation of the later emphasis on a crucified Messiah, Paul has already declared himself 'not ashamed' (1.16) of his gospel. The apostle proceeds to encourage the humble members of the house churches in Rome (overwhelmingly sexual minorities, mainly slave-class, led by women) to assert their human dignity as God's sons and heirs and learn to 'boast' of culturally shameful experiences. The threefold references to shame in 1.24, 26–7 almost seem to find echo in the three references to appropriate boasting in 5.1–2, 11, where humble, marginalized church members, formerly falling short of the glory of God, are now justified (3.23; 5.1). Troels Engberg-Pedersen points out that Paul uses the term *kauchasthai* (boasting) 'in a reinterpreted manner that almost makes it a term of art for the new relationship with God' (2000: 222).

7   Matthew Kuefler (2001: 384, note 55) credits the Adventist scholar James E. Miller (1995) for reopening the case for the earlier patristic interpretation of Romans 1.26 as heterosexual: 'Therefore God gave them up to dishonourable desires, for even their females have turned from the natural use [*chresin*, intercourse] to the *unnatural* [use].' Significantly, the text does *not* speak of 'changing' male sexual companions for female (cf. 1.27), but only of acts that are termed 'unnatural', that is, according to the dominant sexual ideology since Plato, sex that avoids procreation (Ward 1997: 263–84; Kuefler 2001: 383, note 55). Most probably, therefore, Romans 1.26 speaks of Gentile women who offer themselves to men for anal sex, to avoid procreation (Miller 1995: 1–11). Kuefler mistakenly describes Miller as 'the *only* scholar to recognize the phrase does not refer to sex between women' (2001: 384, note 55); however, in addition to the church fathers until about 400 CE (Van de Spijker 1968; Tomson 1990: 94; Stowasser 1997; Fredrickson 2000: 201; Hanks 1997; 2000: 90–1; Helminiak 2000: 86–90; Bryan 2000: 86–7; Swancutt 2003: 196, 209–10, note 36; Schaeffer 1998: 43–4).

Still holding that Romans 1.26 refers to female homoeroticism are Bernadette Brooten (1985a: 287–90; 1985b: 61–87; 1996: 248–53); Martti Nissinen (1998: 108); Robert Gagnon (2001: 297–9); Stephen Moore (2001: 143–4); and Robert Goss (2002: 200–2). Surprisingly, Brooten gives as her first and 'primary reason' (1985b: 85, note 85) for taking Romans 1.26 as referring to female homoeroticism her perception that '(1) the "likewise" (*homoios*) of Rom. 1.27 serves to specify the meaning of Rom. 1.26' (1996: 249; followed by S. Moore 2001: 143–4). However, the link between Romans 1.18–32 and the prohibitions of male–male anal sex in Leviticus 18.22 and 20.13, which Brooten emphasizes, make it much more likely that the link between Romans 1.26 and 27 lies in the similar *acts* of anal sex, rather than in our modern construct of 'homosexuality' (Miller 1995: 1–3; Brooten 1996: 248, note 99). Moreover, the Greek term (*homoios*) simply indicates some element of similarity, 'similarly' (any non-procreative, 'unnatural' sexual act), not just identity ('being similar *in some respect*, likewise, so, similarly') (Danker 2000: 707–8).

Brooten's second argument at first glance appears more weighty: '(2) other ancient sources depict sexual relations between women as unnatural [a list of seven follows; see below]' (1996: 249–50). Stephen Moore manages to expand

Brooten's list from seven to twelve and summarizes Brooten's argument succinctly, arguing that:

> Explicit castigations of either activity [anal or oral sex] as being contrary to nature are lacking in Graeco-Roman sources (even including Jewish sources), whereas sexual relations between women are denounced as unnatural by an impressive array of authors over a long span of time, including Plato, Seneca the Elder, Martial, Ovid, Ptolemy, Dorotheos of Sidon, Manetho, Pseudo-Phocylides, Tertullian, Clement of Alexandria, John Chrysostom – and Artemidoros. (Moore 2001: 143–4, citing Brooten 1996: 241–53).

Brooten does affirm that 'The type of sexual relations engaged in by women most often called "contrary to nature" (*para physin*) in the Roman world is sexual relations between women' (1996: 251). However, she also recognizes that 'the shapers of Paul's culture saw any type of vaginal intercourse, whether consensual or coerced [rape], as natural' (1996: 250). Moreover, David Fredrickson points out that, while some Greek sources refer to the wife's 'use' (*chresis*) of her husband, we have no examples of 'use' in descriptions of female homoeroticism (2000: 201, note 15).

The citations from the authors Brooten and Moore cover a span of some eight centuries and very few are contemporary with Paul. Most significantly, the understanding of Romans 1.26 as referring to heterosexual anal sex is the only one attested in the church fathers for the first 300 years after Paul wrote! (See Clement of Alexandria, Augustine, etc.) Therefore, with regard to the patristic evidence, Diana Swancutt concludes: 'The dearth of explicit references to women as the sex objects in Rom. 1.26 indicates that *a careful rereading of the patristic evidences presented by Brooten (303–62) is in order*' (2003: 209, note 34; italics mine).

What Brooten and Moore overlook is that, despite lack of explicit references to anal or oral sex as 'unnatural', according to the sexual ideology dominant since Plato, *all sexual acts that were non-procreative were categorized as 'unnatural'* (Ward 1997: 263–84; Kuefler 2001: 383–4 note 55). Swancutt says of Brooten's position: 'Her main argument, that "ancient sources depict sexual relations between women as unnatural" (250) works only if ancient sources *only* depicted sexual relations between women as unnatural. But the bottom line is that they do not (and when they do discuss same-sex intercourse, it is the psychic and/or physical manliness of one of the women that is deemed unnatural)' (2003: 209, note 36).

Ancient sources refer to sex euphemistically and the condemnation of all non-procreative sex as 'against nature' was widespread for centuries. Not until John Chrysostom and Ambrosiaster (late fourth century) does anyone (mis)interpret Romans 1.26 as referring to relations between women ('lesbians')! Consequently, we must conclude that the Second Testament, like the Hebrew Bible (Lev. 18.22; 20.13; Gen. 19, Sodom) and the Koran, contains no mention nor prohibition of relations between women ('lesbians'). Nor is female homoeroticism mentioned in other legal materials from the Ancient Near East (Wold 1998: 115–17), and the ancient sources refer only to male cult prostitutes serving men, never to female cult prostitutes serving women (Gagnon 2001: 145).

Traditional apologists forget that women exist, since 'homosexuals' obviously include lesbians – and Romans 1.26 (properly interpreted) makes clear that *the Second Testament nowhere condemns 'homosexuals'*. In the other three relevant Second Testament texts, as in Leviticus 18.22 and 20.13, *only males are described*, and the condemnations have in view a specific abusive male sexual *act* (anal sex), not *persons* of a certain sexual orientation (1 Cor. 6.9; 1 Tim. 1.12; Jude 7). Were it really Paul's intention in Romans 1.26 to create a new universal ethical absolute suddenly consigning all practising lesbians to condemnation, why do he and other Second Testament authors in all the other texts (following Leviticus) limit themselves to male–male anal intercourse and say nothing about female homoeroticism?

Recent studies of 'homosexuality' in the Bible commonly begin with 1.27 and then anachronistically read our modern concept of homosexuality back into 1.26. However, for Paul's readers, following Paul's order, the female's partner was obviously male, but the apostle must then specify in 1.27 that the males abandoned the natural partner for an unnatural one (Miller 1995: 2). Brooten (1996: 249, note 99) critiques Miller for not taking into account all the ancient sources she cites in her earlier articles, but Bryan (2000: 86–7) cites Brooten's 1983 article as supporting the conclusion that 1.26 does *not* refer to female homoeroticism (attributing to Brooten the conclusion of Miller, whom he does not cite!). Already in lectures taped in the 1960s, the late Francis A. Schaeffer recognized that Romans 1.26 'does not speak of homosexuality' (1998: 42–3).

Mathew Kuefler aptly comments, 'In her otherwise superlative book on sexual activity between women in antiquity, Brooten (1996: 195–302), is mistaken in her assertion that Paul condemned sex between women in this passage' (2001: 383, note 55). Following Miller, Kuefler points out that, unlike the case of the men in 1.27 (exchange of partners), 'of the women it is only said that they have turned "from natural intercourse" . . . "to unnatural practices"' (2001: 383). Following Roy Bowen Ward (1997: 263–84), Kuefler concludes that 'unnatural' implied 'all types of nonprocreative sex'.

Kuefler refers to Brooten's citation of the *Apocalypse of Peter* (ca. 135 CE) in the earliest version (Ethiopic): 'These are they who cut their flesh [castration], sodomites and the women who were with them', which refers only to male homoeroticism and castration (Schneemelcher 1992: 2.631). He finds additional support in Brooten's perplexity that the *Apocalypse of Paul* (ca. 200–300 CE) also refers only to male homoeroticism, 'the iniquity of Sodom and Gomorrah, men with men [anal sex]' (Brooten 1996: 314; Schneemelcher 1992: 2.733).

8   In his important pioneering study, Robin Scroggs concluded (1) that ancient writers referred almost exclusively to male–male homoeroticism ('virtually nothing in the texts about female homosexuality', 1983: 140), and (2) since the dominant expression of male homoeroticism in the Graeco-Roman world was exploitive pederasty (an adult male penetrating an adolescent boy, especially household slaves, slaves in brothels and call boys), this must be the practice condemned by Jewish and Christian writers, including Paul. Although some have accepted Scroggs's argument, more common has been the reaction of Martti Nissinen: 'The reference to women [Rom. 1.26] itself indicates that Paul's criticism should not be restricted to pederasty, although it is definitely

one of the phenomena in the background' (1998: 10; similarly Brooten 1996: 7, 253, note 106; Gagnon 2001: 347–61). However, if (as we have argued) Miller is correct in concluding that Romans 1.26 does not refer to female homoeroticism, but rather to women who offer themselves to men for 'unnatural' (anal) sex, Scroggs's arguments about Paul's rhetoric in Romans 1.27 referring to abusive pederastic relations retain their basic validity. Given Paul's emphasis on oppression and idolatry in the context (1.18–23, 25, 28–32), perhaps we should say that Paul's rhetoric is targeting sexual abuse, but pederasty, as the most familiar example, would be mainly what he and his readers had in mind. Recent studies, of course, continue to break down common stereotypes and complicate the more simplistic generalizations of the pioneering works in the field: 'The texts . . . reveal a much wider diversity of relationships in terms of both age and status' (Hubbard 2003: 5).

9   Following Simon Jan Ridderbos (1963), Kuefler develops the case for interpreting both Romans 1.26 and 1.27 as referring specifically to cultic prostitution (2001: 255–60) and thus considers Bernadette Brooten mistaken when she says 'Roman-period sources on homoeroticism do not focus on cultic prostitution' (1996: 253, note 106). Despite some recent scholarly denials, Kuefler insists that the cultic prostitution and male cultic prostitutes (qadesh/qedishim, 'holy ones'; kelebh/im, 'dog/s') referred to in biblical texts really existed and were not just the literary invention of late biblical authors (2001: 255–6, 381, notes 44–50; see 'holy ones' in Deut. 23.17–18; 1 Kings 14.24; 15.12; 22.46; 2 Kings 23.7; Job 36.14). He argues that various biblical texts reflect common elements of cultic prostitution related to fertility cults: castration of priests (Deut. 23.1); sexual penetration of males (Lev. 18.22; 20.13); transvestism (Deut. 22.5); and the prohibition of wearing mixed cloth of linen and wool, the type worn by cultic prostitutes (Deut. 22.11; Lev. 19.19). Kuefler thus points to considerable evidence that refutes Brooten's dismissal (2001: 245–73 and 382–4 notes).

Kuefler also argues that Romans 1.26–7 makes further reference to cultic prostitution in the puzzling climactic reference to the males as having 'received in themselves the due penalty for their error' (1.27e). Some have seen a reference to venereal disease (Williams 1999: 180–1), while others have argued that the 'error' is the idolatry denounced in 1.23, 25, the penalty being enslavement to unclean sexual practices (1.24, 26–7; Scroggs 1983: 115–16). Kuefler concludes that the penalty is rather the self-castration practised by the eunuch priests: 'Since the priests of the goddess acted like women they deserved the castration that turned them into women' (2001: 257).

10   Recent studies point out that in Romans 1 Paul appears to manifest considerable indebtedness to Leviticus 18.22 and 20.13. As Saul Olyan demonstrated, the only sexual act prohibited in the Leviticus texts was male–male *anal* penetration, not other homoerotic expressions (1994: 179–206; Brooten 1996: 61–2). Nothing is said against oral sex, intercrural penetration (between the thighs), mutual masturbation, and so on. Much less does Leviticus speak of a group of *persons* of homosexual or bisexual orientation (modern scientific concepts), but refers only to a specific male sexual act. If we use Leviticus' teaching as a source for modern norms, therefore, we cannot say that it condemns 'homo-

sexuality' (nothing here about lesbians nor the sexual orientation of persons involved), but it simply prohibits male–male anal intercourse (without condoms). This would not require any great degree of self-denial or discipline for the vast heterosexual majority; but even for persons of homosexual or bisexual orientation it constituted wise counsel throughout human history until availability of prophylactics (condoms), in the late twentieth century. Daniel Boyarin has shown that Jewish rabbis in the early centuries CE also recognized that Leviticus prohibited only male–male anal penetration (1995: 333–55).

Although Bernadette Brooten pointed out the similarities between Romans 1 and Leviticus (18.22; 20.13) and recognized that Leviticus only proscribed male–male anal sex, not female homoeroticism, she would have done well to acknowledge this fact as evidence *against* her interpretation of Romans 1.26 as referring to female homoeroticism (1996: 61–2; 282–3). Having spoken of females who offer themselves to males for anal sex (1.26), Paul turns to males in Romans 1.27, and (*following Leviticus*) refers to males who have 'left' the use of females in order to engage in anal sex (without prophylactics) with other males. Hence, neither Leviticus nor Paul condemn 'homosexuality' (nothing about lesbians nor the sexual orientation of the males involved). What links Romans 1.26 and 1.27 (*homoios*, 'similarly/likewise', 1.27) are the *acts* of anal sex, not our modern concept of 'homosexuality'. Before effective prophylactics became widely available, anal sex was highly dangerous to health, facilitating the transmission of many diseases (before Aids; hepatitis, etc.). So, for any who seek in Romans divinely inspired transcendent norms that are miraculously relevant to the modern context, we may say: *Paul simply teaches safer sex.*

11 Since Paul's rhetoric in Romans 1.24–32 echoes the prohibitions in Leviticus 18.22 and 20.13 against male–male anal sex, readers might think he makes these prohibitions ethical absolutes for the churches. However, Paul not only lays rhetorical traps for arrogant, judgemental readers (2.1–16; 9–11), but also deconstructs popular legalistic use of the Hebrew Bible, culminating with a thunderous and shocking affirmation: *For the end (telos) of the law is Christ so that there may be liberating justice resulting in a new just status for everyone believing* (10.4). This text has long been taken as of fundamental importance in Paul's theology, but especially since the Reformation interpreters have been sharply divided regarding Paul's intended meaning in using the word 'end' (*telos*):

- Goal, fulfilment – Especially traditions that stress *continuity* between the Hebrew Bible and the Second Testament: the early Church (almost universally, citing Matt. 5.17–20); Luther, Calvin and especially evangelicals in the Reformed-Calvinistic and Anglican traditions (Rom. 2.17–29; 3.27–31; 7.7–14; 8.3–4; 13.8–10).
- Termination, cessation – Especially the theological traditions that emphasize the *discontinuity* between the Hebrew Bible and the Second Testament (most Lutherans, Baptists and Dispensationalists; see Rom. 7.6; Gal. 2.19; 3.25; 4.1–7; 2 Cor. 3.7–11, 13–14). Tom Wright complains: 'This reading has become extremely common at a popular level, and one is used to hearing it quoted as an excuse for any and every form of *antinomianism*' (2002: 656), but

critics of the first position, with equal justice, commonly accuse supporters of perpetuating various forms of *legalism*.

- Both fulfilment and termination – Increasingly, modern authorities opt for a more nuanced or dialectical position that sees the law abolished as an *external* authority and system, but fulfilled as *internalized* by the Spirit in the New Covenant and of continuing value as inspired Scripture (2 Tim. 3.14–17; 1 Cor. 7.19), a source of wisdom and guidance when used discerningly and selectively (emphasizing justice and love, but not making circumcision, Sabbath observance, Jewish cultic requirements and ethnic markers binding on Gentile believers). The common translation 'end' (*telos*; NRSV; NIV; ESV) preserves the ambiguity of the Greek. What is terminated is the function of the law as a dividing wall (with ethnic markers) separating Jews and Gentiles (see Eph. 2.11–22).

Although Romans 7 commonly is considered the great Pauline treatment of Torah, the terminology actually occurs first in Romans 2.12–27 (*nomos*, Torah 18 times + *anomos*, without-Torah, 2.12, 12; just-ordinances 2.26; letter 2.27, 29) and with greater frequency (22 times; cf. Romans 7, only 18 times). In Romans 2 Paul begins to deconstruct both the legalistic use of the law (2.12–29) and popular philosophical use of '(against) nature' (2.14, 27). If God is love (1 John 4.16, 23) and all humans are created in God's image (Gen 1.27; James 3.9), we should not be surprised to read that Gentiles, not having Torah by nature, at times fulfil Torah by showing love to the neighbour (Rom. 2.14; see Jesus' parable of the Good Samaritan).

The fact that the only references to Torah in Romans 12–16 are the two references that speak of love as fulfilling Torah (13.8, 10) is evidence that, although Paul may *selectively* cite Torah for Christian instruction (Brooten 1990: 89), he basically draws on other sources for instructing the new communities in how they should live. (See also the references to the 'just ordinances', *dikaíoma*, of Torah fulfilled in those who walk according to the Spirit, 8.4; similarly 2.26.) Thus in Romans 1.8–15 and 15.14–33 the apostle makes clear his project of taking his law-free gospel throughout the world (even unto Spain) and of establishing communities consisting mainly of law-free Gentile believers in the God of Abraham – which would undoubtedly include countless 'unclean' sexual minorities, as was the case in the Roman house churches.

12   In addition to confirming the conclusion (Kuefler 2001) that Romans 1.26 does not refer to lesbian sex, but rather to females performing 'unnatural' (non-procreative) sexual acts with males, Diana Swancutt (2003) argues that the entrapment in Romans 2.1–16 refers to Stoic judges in Rome, who prided themselves on their wisdom and lifestyle ('according to nature'), while hypocritically indulging in sex with other males:

Greek and Latin authors from the first century BCE to the third century CE roundly charged Stoics with hypocrisy for asserting that they were perfect and uniquely qualified to rule, judge, and guide affairs of state. They also criticized the basis of the commonplace, the Stoic tenet that the universe, or nature (*physis*), was the source of their efforts. [2003: 218] . . . The charge of Stoic hypocrisy based on effeminacy and unnatural sex had an august history . . . Denouncing even unnamed Stoic judges as transvestites, sexual passives, or pederasts who effeminated their students was a typical way to strip authority from Stoic claims to live naturally and lead Rome well. (2003: 223; see 215–33).

Such behaviour was hardly a first-century innovation: 'Stoic founder Zeno [333/2–262/1 BCE] was known to chase his [male] students and encourage androgynous dress' (Swancutt 2003: 230).

Commentators commonly identify Romans 2.1–16 as a rhetorical trap for hypocrites who condemn the idolatrous, oppressive behaviour of 1.18–32, although themselves guilty of the same behaviour. Outlines invented by editors and commentators, however, encourage readers to imagine a major break at the end of 1.32, with a fresh start on a new subject in 2.1–16. By creating such a gap, scholars mislead readers into reading the pejorative rhetoric of 1.18–32 as Paul's main emphasis, with the rhetorical trap in 2.1–16 a kind of afterthought of secondary importance – whereas Paul's intention obviously was to make the pejorative rhetoric of 1.18–32 preparatory to the climax of the following rhetorical trap. After condemning Gentile idolatry and oppression (Rom. 1.18–31) and those who approve such behaviour (1.32), in Romans 2.1–29 the apostle – like the prophets Amos (1–2) and Nathan (2 Sam. 12.7) – springs a rhetorical trap, 'a sweeping "sting operation"' (Gagnon 2001: 278) to catch others who disapprove. Since in texts like Amos 1–2, the preparatory rhetoric against surrounding nations denounces their violence, rather than their 'homosexuality', scholars never confuse the preparatory texts that lay the trap for the prophet's main emphasis.

In the Greek, Romans 2.1 is addressed to 'O man' (*o anthrope*, repeated in 2.3) and is directly linked with the preceding context (*Dio*, 'Wherefore'), while the address directed to a Judaean interlocutor in 2.17–3.8 is distinguished from the preceding context with the particle *de* ('but'). In addition, the reference to God's wrath manifest against all idolatry and oppression (*adikia*, 1.18) is echoed in the references to the God's impartial final judgement in chapter 2, where again human oppression provokes God's wrath (2.5, 8); although most commentators suppose that Paul here begins to address Jews, who become explicit only in 2.17–3.8.

Moreover, without ever referring to Robert Gagnon's influential works (2001; 2003) that make the purported 'complementarity' of male–female heterosexual relations the linchpin to interpreting biblical teaching on sexuality – and particularly for condemning all same-sex relations – Swancutt shows that such a concept of 'complementarity' is quite modern, developing only in the nineteenth century and replacing traditional patriarchal, hierarchical ideologies of male superiority.

Ancients did not interpret Rom. 1.18–32 as an exegesis of Gen. 1–3 representing the 'natural complementarity between women and men' as moderns understand it. Complementarity, . . . a 'natural' compatibility between men and women that extends beyond procreation (the ancient view) into other realms such as work and social intercourse, is a modern concept born in nineteenth- and twentieth-century American discussions of women working outside the home. (2003: 207, note 30; citing A. Kessler-Harris, *Out to Work*, Oxford: Oxford University Press, 1982; and R. Rosenberg, *Beyond Separate Spheres*, New Haven: Yale University Press, 1982; see also Rudy (1997: 116–20).

Finally, Swancutt explains what Paul refers to when he speaks of the 'requital' visited upon the Gentiles for their 'error': 'the males, leaving the natural use of the female, burned with passion for one another, males with males committing the shamelessness and *receiving back in themselves the requital/penalty due their error* (Rom. 1.27). The error (*planes*) of the Gentile males was idolatry (18–23, 25) and the 'requital/penalty' was not some venereal disease (Gagnon 2001), but the feminization of their bodies, which Philo of Alexandria (Paul's contemporary) designated 'the *disease* of effemination' (*Spec.* 3.37–41). As Swancutt summarizes this common patriarchal view:

> By taking up gender-bending behaviours, such as receptive sex, cosmetics, and haircoiffing, the boy abandoned his male sex-nature and shifted genders, *becoming* an androgyne deserving death for the disgrace it brought on its person, home, country and fellow humanity. (2003: 200)

In addition to the complicating hermeneutical factor of Paul's preparing a rhetorical trap for arrogant readers (in 1.18–32) and then springing it on two types of victims (in 2.1–16 and 2.17–29), Gerd Theissen concluded that Paul appears to have been a repressed homosexual (1983/7:26). Both Paul's repressed homosexuality and his intention to catch judgemental readers in his rhetorical trap complicates modern efforts to decipher the 'intention of the author' in Romans 1.18–2.16. A century after Freud, when the existence of the 'subconscious' has become almost as axiomatic as the law of gravity, can we continue to speak of the 'intention' of the author (as if he/she only had one)? If Paul's repression of homoerotic desires was accompanied (as it is commonly) by a continual need to repress anger at society's prejudices (and the Creator's all too mysterious ways), we may better appreciate why the wrath of God against all injustice and Jesus' death (as an expiation of sin that results in the propitiation of divine anger) is so central to his message (1.18). When the apostle's rhetoric first echoes common homophobic prejudices (1.24–7) but then proceeds immediately to a powerful deconstruction process of three of the four key elements, is the whole process consciously 'intentional' – or perhaps the fruit of his subconscious working of God's liberating Spirit?

Excursus: Philip Esler: Sodom and Gomorrah in Romans 9.25–6 – a lost rhetorical opportunity?

Picking up on the reference to the vessels of mercy who are 'called' to share in divine 'glory' (9.23–4; cf 8.30), Paul cites two texts from Hosea where the eighth-century northern prophet similarly emphasized God's gracious and efficacious 'call'. However, while Hosea spoke of the restoration of the northern tribes after their judgement and exile at the hands of the Assyrians (722 BCE), Paul takes these phrases in a wider sense as referring to Gentile believers coming to form part of the people of God (Wright 2002: 643).

Even more surprising, Paul – whom many accuse of being hopelessly rigid in gender matters – first images all Israel (males included) as God's beloved *wife*, thus stripping the males of their superior status (Rom. 9.25 and Hos. 2.23; cf Rom. 1.27), but then immediately transgenders God's wife into '*sons* of the living God' (females included; Rom. 9.26 and Hos. 1.19). Obviously, as Bernadette Brooten emphasizes (1996: 252), when his rhetorical purpose required it, Paul pontificated gender rigidity (1 Cor. 11.14–16), but in other contexts he could gender-bend as flamboyantly as any modern queer.

9.27–9 Having followed Hosea's lead and first transgendering males into God's 'wife' and then transgendering females into God's sons, Paul still is unable to let gender matters rest, and so proceeds to yoke together two citations from the prophet Isaiah, concluding with a flourish about antiquity's most infamous gender-benders, the males of Sodom and Gomorrah (who had attempted gang rape of two visiting angels): Israelite males, having been transgendered into God's wife, and her females, transgendered into God's sons, are allowed to rest free from Paul's surgical interventions for a couple of verses (as 'sons', 9.27b). Although universally ignored by commentators, Paul's climactic reference to Sodom and Gomorrah, which concludes this first section (9.1–29), is important for three reasons.

- First, unlike ecclesiastical and political homophobic rhetoric so popular for centuries, Paul carefully avoided any reference to Sodom and Gomorrah in his rhetoric when he condemned Gentile sexuality in 1.27 (male–male anal sex).
- Second, he incorporates Isaiah's reference to Sodom and Gomorrah as an example of devastating divine judgement (as is most common in the Hebrew Bible), not as a cheap shot caricaturing and denouncing male homoeroticism. In this way, Paul follows the example of Jesus, who used the destruction of Sodom and Gomorrah as an example of divine judgement and to condemn inhospitality (Matt. 10.11–15 // Luke 10.8–12). In Romans 9.29 Sodom and Gomorrah remind readers of a divine judgement so severe that it left no remnant. Paul thus prepares the way for his climactic exhortation to the Roman house churches to practise hospitality and be *inclusive* (14.1; 15.7).
- Third, Paul's choice of the text from Isaiah to introduce Sodom and Gomorrah into the argument would remind biblically literate leaders in the Church how Isaiah refers to the judgement against Sodom and Gomorrah (1.9) only to immediately spring a rhetorical trap against the leaders of Jerusalem (Isa. 1.10), whom the prophet proceeded to denounce for their violence ('hands full of blood', 1.15) and as guilty of injustice and oppression (1.17; recall Paul's similar tactic in Rom. 2.1). Both Pharaoh (Rom. 9.17) and Sodom and Gomorrah (9.29) thus represent the kind of violent oppressive behaviour that properly provokes God's wrath (1.18).

The reference to Sodom and Gomorrah that climaxes Romans 9.1–29 thus continues the subversion and deconstruction of apparently homophobic rhetoric of 1.24–7 (followed by the rhetorical trap of 2.1–16) and at the same time anticipates the exhortations to tolerance, mutual acceptance, hospitality and inclusivity in 14.1 and 15.7. As William Countryman concludes:

> Paul . . . adds a second quotation from Isaiah that includes a threatening comparison between Israel and Sodom and Gomorrah (9.29). No doubt, Paul is fully conscious of the irony of this comparison, since by his time, the example of Sodom was part of the Jewish polemic against Gentile tolerance of same-gender sexual relationships. Paul makes no reference to the Sodom story in his own treatment of same-gender sexuality in chapter 1; but here, with Isaiah, he turns it against the Jewish nation. (2003: 193)

Esler, however, proposes a radically different reading (2003c: 4–16). He points out that scholars have sought to identify some particular 'major metaphor' underlying Romans 1.18–32:

- Adam's fall (Hooker 1960 and others);
- A 'decline of civilization narrative' (Stowers 1994 (1996); Martin 1995 and others);
- The Sodom tradition of Genesis 19 (Esler 2003c).

Each hypothesis can explain certain features of the text but all are contradicted by other features, which suggests that Paul may be working without any 'major metaphor'. Perhaps as in the case of the famous 'I' of Romans 7, a combination of influences best explains the complexity of features. Thus, in the case of Esler's hypothesis, he is able to point to several similarities and parallels with the Sodom tradition. However, the following differences seem even more striking:

- When Paul refers to same-sex acts (Rom. 1.27) he makes no mention of Sodom, but later, when he makes the only reference to Sodom in all his writings (9.29), he says nothing about same-sex acts. Same-sex acts and Sodom thus do not appear to be linked in Paul's mind, as we would expect, given their common linkage in Jewish intertestamental literature. In fact the two themes seem to be intentionally separated by a rather wide gulf with eight chapters functioning as a kind of sanitary cord or firewall to keep readers from relating, confusing or equating them.
- Paul's only reference to Sodom (Rom. 9.29) follows the common Hebrew Bible pattern, and says nothing about same-sex acts, but simply cites Isaiah's reference to Sodom as a paradigm of severe divine judgement (Isa 1.9).
- The Sodom narrative in Genesis 19 refers only to the males of the city (who attempt gang rape of the two visiting angels); however, in Romans 1 Paul refers first (1.26) to women engaging in sexual acts 'against nature' (probably anal sex with males to avoid procreation). Scholars remain puzzled about the priority Paul gives to women's unnatural acts, but the problem is only heightened, not solved, if Paul's 'major metaphor' is the Sodom narrative. Esler thinks Ezekiel's six references to the 'daughters of Sodom' (16.46, 48, 49, 53, 55) explains Paul's prioritizing and emphasis on women, but this seems rather far-fetched.

- Esler finds his closest parallels to Romans 1.26–7 not in the Hebrew Bible, but in intertestamental texts such as *Naphtali* 3.2–4, but Paul overwhelmingly cites the canonical books of the Hebrew Bible and (unlike Jude) largely ignores the intertestamental traditions.
- Like the Hebrew Bible, other New Testament references to Sodom (Jude 7 excepted) avoid any link with sexual offences, but refer to Sodom simply as a paradigm of severe divine judgement, or focus on the sin of refusing hospitality (Luke 10.12; Matt. 11.23–4). Jude's exceptional reference to the sexual expression of Sodom's sinfulness reflects the narrative in Genesis 19, where the gender of the two visitors is not the issue, but the attempt to rape 'strange/other [angelic] flesh'. Paul's separation of male–male anal sex (Rom. 1.27) from his single reference to Sodom (9.29) thus fits the pattern of Jesus' teaching and that of the Hebrew Bible about Sodom, not the unique reference in Jude 7 that focuses on the sexual expression of Sodom's sin.
- Paul speaks of God's wrath revealed from heaven (Rom. 1.18), but Genesis 19 and other First Testament references to Sodom make no reference to God's wrath. For Paul God's wrath is provoked by sins of idolatry and oppression, the abuse of power (1.18–23, 25, 28–32), as in the Hebrew Bible (Ex. 22.21–4). The sexual sins referred to in this context (1.24–7) are thus to be understood as occurring in idolatrous contexts (pagan temple prostitution) and involving abuses of power that harm the neighbour (Rom. 13.8–10). If Sodom were one of the metaphors behind Paul's thinking in Romans 1, it would only be as a symbol of such idolatry and violent oppression (see Jerusalem as 'Sodom and Egypt, the city where the Lord was *crucified*', Rev. 11.8). Were Esler correct, of course, it would only strengthen the case for understanding the rhetoric of Romans 1.24–7 as directed against acts of oppression and violence (attempted gang rape of angels), not against expressions of love between consenting adults.

Conclusion

In *Homosexuality and Civilization* (2003), Louis Crompton has written what many recognize as the most significant work in this area since John Boswell's *Christianity, Social Tolerance, and Homosexuality* (1980). Although Crompton cites Boswell mainly to indicate minor disagreement or correction, he overwhelmingly confirms Boswell's major (but universally neglected) thesis: that anti-Semitism and homophobia developed as parallel prejudices, especially in the late Middle Ages (1150–1400 CE; Boswell 1980: 15–16).

Boswell's critics, who are legion, have been obsessed with what they judge to be errors and deficiencies in details of his historiography and biblical exegesis. However, they universally overlook or ignore his fundamental point. In the biblical field, for decades academics of all persuasions have been falling over backwards to defend the Second Testament against any charge or suspicion of anti-Semitism/Judaism, while at the same time blithely propagating the notion that St Paul in particular is responsible for centuries of homophobic violence against sexual minorities. Crompton repeatedly shows how inquisitional torture and violence promoting the legal killing of Jews and sodomites remained characteristic of Western 'civilization' (Europe and the Americas) until the early nineteenth century.

Highly dubious exegetical conclusions in works like that of Robert Gagnon (2001) continue to make their impact, even with academics who should know better, despite blatant pseudoscientific notions of 'curing' homosexuality with scandal-ridden 'ex-gay' treatments. However, although the promoting of 'ex-gay' quackery is an all-too-visible elephant in the china shop in works like Gagnon's, the other elephant – *invisible* – is the *total ignorance evidenced of the churches' complicity in promoting the legal burning of Jews and 'faggots'*. Crompton grapples sympathetically and profoundly with that great mystery for Jewish and Christian believers:

> It is an irony of history that the two cultures which have done most to shape Western civilization should have adopted antithetical views on homosexuality at almost the same time. In the sixth century before Christ, Greece produced the homoerotic poetry of Solon . . . . But in the same century a few hundred miles away in ancient Palestine, a law was incorporated into the Hebrew scriptures which was ultimately to have a far greater influence and indeed, to affect the fate of homosexuals in half the world down to our own day . . . the so-called Holiness Code in Leviticus . . . about 550 BCE. (2003: 32; see also pp. 48, 130)

Concluding his study when executions for 'sodomy' finally cease in Europe (1803), Crompton seeks to analyse the data in his leitmotif:

> Looking back over twenty-four centuries, what pattern can we see in the dozen societies we have examined? Most striking, certainly, is the divide between those that called themselves Christian and those that flourished before or independently of Christianity. In the first we find laws and preaching that promoted hatred, contempt, and death; in the second, varying attitudes, all of them (barring Islam, which like Christianity, inherited the lethal tradition of the Hebrew Scriptures) to a radical degree more tolerant . . . Executions in England, which reached their peak in the early nineteenth century, were the result of centuries of campaigning by clergy who called up the nation to 'exterminate the monster'. (2003: 536, 538)

Crompton does not write without sympathy and appreciation for Christianity:

> The debt owed by civilization to Christianity is enormous. How can we not be grateful for its works of compassion, its service to education, and its contribution to the world's treasury of great art, architecture, and music? . . . Christianity has proved itself a creed with a conscience, not lacking in men and women of good will. Even in the case of homosexuality there have been Christian Christians, though they are still a prophetic minority disconcerting the church officialdom. (2003: 547–8; 130)

Crompton's approach, however, commonly evidences a fundamental methodological weakness. For instance, he provides an excellent account of Emperor

Justinian's 'reign of terror' (527–65 CE) involving the torture and castration of several Christian bishops who slept with men (2003: 142–9), but indicates his disagreement with Boswell for insisting that early Christianity was not really hostile to homosexuality (144). However, while Boswell may minimize hostility, why accept Crompton's decision to acknowledge Justinian as really representing 'Christianity', rather than the tortured castrated bishops? Since heterosexuals represent an overwhelming majority of the population and commonly dominate the power structures of institutions, it is not surprising the Christian institutions commonly conform to the worldly pattern (despite Rom. 12.1–2). But if the norm for identifying authentic 'Christianity' be Jesus' praxis and teaching or even the canonical Second Testament books (including Paul), why not accept the bishops who were persecuted and tortured as representing the Christian norm, rather than the cruel emperor, with whose brutal laws, as Crompton concludes, 'the medieval world was inaugurated' (2003: 149)?

The lesbian scholar Bernadette Brooten in her magisterial work makes quite clear her view of the implications regarding Paul:

> I have argued that Paul's condemnation of homoeroticism, particularly female homoeroticism, reflects and helps to maintain a gender asymmetry based on female subordination. I hope that churches today, being apprised of the history that I have presented, will no longer teach Rom. 1.26f. as authoritative. (1996: 302)

Robert Gagnon basically agrees with Brooten's exegetical conclusions, but differs theologically and politically:

> Those who engage in same-sex intercourse act contrary to God's intentions for human sexual relations. . . . Same-sex intercourse is strongly and unequivocally rejected by the revelation of Scripture. (2001: 487)

Authors like Gagnon, who would perpetuate the homophobia of the medieval world – backing off somewhat reluctantly and totally inconsistently from Leviticus' requirement of the death penalty (20.13) – gather support and comfort from the conclusions of Brooten and others who interpret Paul as condemning all homoerotic relations.

Without in any way pretending to treat or resolve the issue of Pauline and biblical authority in general (which would require another volume and many excellent works are available), I have sought to develop the case initiated by other 'Third Way' theologians that locate the problem not so much in Leviticus and/or Paul, but in the misinterpretation and misuse that has been made of such portions of scripture. Furthering this approach, Ted Jennings now provides us with a powerful companion volume to *The Man Jesus Loved: Homoerotic Narratives from the New Testament* (2003) in *Jacob's Wound: Homoerotic Narrative in the Literature of Ancient Israel* (2005). Here he shows that the Bible is not homophobic, but is a 'profoundly, positive, homoerotic text' (comment by Rolando Boer on back cover). In a third projected volume Jennings will seek to establish 'that Christian homophobia derives not from either Paul or

Leviticus but from the tradition going back to Plato and carried forward by certain stoics and then into an Alexandrian tradition of reading derived from Philo, Barnabas, Clement and so on' (personal correspondence, 31 July 2005). As in the cases of distorted biblical citations to support racist slavery, monarchy against democracy, and inferior status for women, this, I believe, is the way forward, both for the edification of the Church and for justice in society.

Appendix: Romans 16. Poor slaves, women leaders and sexual minorities in five humble house churches in Rome

Paul refers to some 38 persons in Rom. 16.1–16 and 21–4 (women, slaves, sexual minorities)

Key: */*? = common name for slaves and liberated slaves (mainly poor)
(J) = Jew

16.1–2 Phoebe, bearer of the letter from Paul in Corinth, deacon/minister (masculine form in Greek); benefactor of Paul and others → under 3 Poor
16.3–16 Greets 28+ persons in some five house churches: vv. 1–5a, 10, 11, 14, 15

Only three married couples (six persons)
PRISCA (J) and AQUILA (J) (vv. 3–5a);
See 2 Tim. 4.19; Acts 18.26; cf. 1 Cor. 16.9; Acts 18.2
Andronicus*? (J) and Junia (J)*, both 'apostles' (v. 7a)
Philologus*? and Julia* (v. 15a)

Six single women, etc., five of the six commended for their work for the church
Mary*? (J?) (v. 6a), worker for the church
Tryphaena* + Triphosa* (v. 12a, sisters), work for the church
Persis* (v. 12b), 'the beloved . . . who worked much'
The mother*? of RUFUS (v. 13b), 'like a mother to me' (hospitality)
The sister*? of Nereus (v. 15b)

16+ single males: only one is designated a worker; Paul calls three his 'beloved'
Epaenetus*? (v. 5), 'my beloved'
Ampliatus* (v. 8), 'my beloved'
URBANUS (v. 9a), 'our fellow-worker in Christ'
+
Stachys*? (v. 9b), 'my beloved'
Apelles*? (v. 10)
The slaves* of de Aristobulus' house (died 48–9 CE) (v. 10b)
Herodion* (J) (v. 11)
The slaves* of Narcissus (died 55–7 CE) (v. 11)
RUFUS (v. 13); cf. Mark 15.21
Asyncritus*?, Phlegon*?, Hermes*, Patrobas*?, Hermas*? + brothers (v. 14)
Nereus* (v. 15)
Olympas*? (v. 15)

16.21–24 Greetings from eight male companions living with Paul in Gaius' house
(total nine)

Timothy (J) (v. 21a)	Lucius (J), Jason (J) and Sosipater (J) (v. 21b)
Tertius (v. 22), Paul's secretary	Gaius (v. 23a), the host
Erastus (v. 23b), the city treasurer	Quartus (v. 23b)

Summary. Romans 16 refers to 38 persons (including Phoebe and Paul)

32 apparently unmarried (sexual minorities: single persons, divorced, widows, etc.)

6 married persons (three couples)

10 women, eight of them leaders: one deacon (Phoebe); Prisca; one apostle (Junia); five workers

12–26 slaves or liberated slaves (mainly poor); PRISCA and AQUILA clearly are not slave names (details, Lampe 2003: 153–83).

11 Jews: six of those 28 greeted in Rome were Jews; five (Paul + four) of the nine in Corinth

1 and 2 Corinthians

HOLLY E. HEARON

I read these letters of Paul from a location represented by the intersection of multiple identities. As a biblical scholar and professor I strive to hear Paul within the context of his socio-historical setting, attentive to the filters imposed by my own social location; as a lesbian feminist I am often suspicious of Paul as well as ways in which Paul has been interpreted and find myself reading against the text in an effort to hear an authentic, life-giving word; as a Presbyterian minister I struggle to engage Paul as one who continues to speak a vital, liberating word for the life of the Church today. In an effort to hold these identities in dynamic tension, I offer here a reading that consists of multiple voices. One voice attempts to faithfully represent Paul; another reads with Paul, listening for how his argument continues to challenge readers today; a third voice resists Paul: sometimes aligning itself with the unspoken voice of the Corinthians, sometimes calling attention to ways Paul manipulates the reader. I have chosen this strategy because I believe it reflects the legitimate way in which GLBTI communities have learned to question both the text and its interpreters and, at the same time, to reclaim the text as a liberating, life-giving word for their communities. I do not think we can hear one voice without hearing the other, not only because all are a part of our experience, but also because each voice offers a positive challenge to the others. Attentiveness to all of these voices is necessary to our survival. I also attempt to employ voices which reflect the multiple ways in which GLBTI communities may hear and respond to the text. As a part of this effort, I employ 'GLBTI' rather than the more generic 'queer' throughout. I believe it is important to recognize our diversity even in our unity and to realize that much is to be gained from the dialogue that emerges when we bring all of these voices together.

Introduction

The city of Corinth visited by Paul dates from 44 BCE. An earlier city was destroyed in 146 BCE while resisting Rome's advances against Greece. Julius Caesar, recognizing Corinth's strategic location on a major trade route, re-established the city, populating it with veterans of the Roman army and freed slaves. The result was an ethnically and religiously diverse population estimated to have reached 80–100,000 by the end of the first century CE. Although the earlier city was known as a 'city of ill-repute', there is no reason to assume this ascription applied equally to the new Corinth. Nonetheless, as a cosmopolitan centre, Corinth can be expected to have enjoyed the benefits and vices that attract people to urban centres. Corinth eventually became the capital of the region known as Achaia. An inscription identifies Gallio as proconsul of this region in 51–2 CE. According to Acts 18.12–16 Paul was in Corinth during this time.

Paul identifies himself as the 'father' of the church in Corinth, which consisted of a cluster of house churches (4.15). He spent some considerable time in Corinth before moving on, and continued his relationship with the community through letters and subsequent visits. The two surviving letters belong to a more extensive correspondence between the Corinthians and Paul, most of which has been lost. The Corinthian letters are distinctive because they allow us to experience Paul's relationship with a single community over time and because, of all the Pauline letters, these two are the most grounded in the nitty-gritty of daily life. It is in these letters that we learn about early practices surrounding the Lord's Supper, glimpse into the worship life of the early Church, encounter efforts to work out various relationships between sex and spirituality, uncover problems associated with a collection for the poor, and witness competition among apostles.

1 Corinthians

The letter called '1 Corinthians' was preceded by at least one letter written by Paul to the Corinthians (5.9) and another written by the Corinthians to Paul (7.1), both no longer extant. In addition to this correspondence, Paul has received 'reports' from 'Chloe's people', who may or may not be a part of the Corinthian community, but who report that conflicts have arisen in Paul's absence. 1 Corinthians, then, picks up somewhere in the middle of an ongoing conversation.

Defining the body

Following a short prayer of thanksgiving (1.4–9), in which he praises the Corinthians for their speech, knowledge and spiritual gifts, Paul introduces the body of the letter with an appeal to the Corinthians to be of 'the same mind and the same purpose' (1.10). The resisting reader may be prepared to stop here and go no further. Many members of GLBTI communities will recognize this rhetorical strategy as a ploy to silence opposition by the suppression of differences for the sake of unity: for the good of the country, the church, the family or community. It is this line of argument which has promoted policies such as 'don't ask, don't tell' and which effectively curtails efforts at constructive debate in favour of maintaining the false peace of the status quo (a situation in which many denominations currently find themselves). Those who live on the margins cannot help but see the shadow side of this positive appeal: unity of mind and purpose regards all opposition as petty and insignificant in comparison to the greater good as defined by the dominant group, who hold that position by virtue of numbers and/or power. In 1 Corinthians, Paul wants his voice to be the unifying voice, by virtue of his authority as an apostle and as the one who proclaimed the gospel to them: 'I am not writing this to make you ashamed, but to admonish you as my beloved children. For though you might have ten thousand guardians in Christ, you do not have many fathers' (4.14–15).

According to Paul, 'Chloe's people' (who may be either slaves or freed persons belonging to the household of this woman) have reported that there are quarrels among the Corinthians. Paul ascribes these quarrels to factions within the community who have, in Paul's words, aligned themselves under the banners of Paul, Apollos, Cephas or Christ (1.12). This is likely to be Paul's way of describing the situation rather than a reflection of how the Corinthians would describe themselves, and, in consequence, cannot be taken as a description of the historical situation. It is a reminder that in any debate of consequence control belongs to the one who can define the terms of the debate. GLBTI communities know this only too well. We find ourselves under the scrutiny of medical professionals, psychiatrists, politicians, coalitions in support of 'family values', religious leaders and a host of others each of whom offer some definition of who we are and how we fit – or do not fit – into acceptable social patterns. The result is that we are treated as objects in these debates rather than as subjects who have the capacity to act as moral agents on our own behalf. Paul's description of the Corinthians as 'children' (4.14) indicates that he, too, wants the Corinthians to defer to his better judgement: 'I fed you with milk, not solid food, for you were not ready for solid food. Even now you are still not ready . . .' (3.2). By describing the Corinthians as divided into multiple factions, Paul may be attempting to draw attention away from the source of the conflict, which appears to be between followers of Paul and followers of Apollos (see 3.4–10, where Paul clearly subordinates Apollos, claiming that he built on the foundation which Paul laid) (Wire 1990: 43; Witherington 1994: 83–7).

Paul describes the conflict in Corinth in terms of 'wisdom' versus 'folly' (1.18–2.16). The language of 'wisdom' comes from the Corinthians who claim this wisdom for themselves, but are critical of Paul because he does not, from their perspective, speak 'plausible words of wisdom' (2.4). Paul never gives voice to the 'wisdom' espoused by the Corinthians so that any effort to describe it involves a certain amount of speculation. However, Paul's effort to redefine wisdom in terms of the 'weakness of the cross' suggests that the Corinthians, by contrast, understand wisdom in terms of spiritual power. Paul's praise of their 'speech and knowledge', as well as 'spiritual gifts', in the Thanksgiving (1.5, 7) suggests that these were valued as marks of 'wisdom' by the Corinthians: specifically, God's wisdom 'present in their own hearing and speaking', an understanding of wisdom which may have its source in Hellenistic Jewish traditions (Wisd. 7.27–8; 8.8) (Wire 1990: 53; Horsley 1998: 47). This is supported by the ways in which this wisdom is manifested in the community. Some of the Corinthians who possess knowledge eat meat offered to idols without fear of defiling themselves (8.1–13). The Corinthians value speaking in tongues (*glossolalia*) and prophesying (14.1–32; see Wisd. 7.27), both of which Paul includes in his list of spiritual gifts enjoyed within the community (12.27–31). These displays signal that, for the Corinthians, their life in Christ gives them confidence, rooted in knowledge and experienced as spiritual power.

Members of GLBTI communities who have found their place within spiritual communities may resonate with the experience of the Corinthians. There is a sense of elation that accompanies the realization that we are beloved of God, regardless of whom declares us to be godless. This knowledge gives us the confidence to recognize that, ultimately, social forces and institutions have only limited power over our lives. It also empowers us to exercise our spiritual gifts, whether acting up, extending hospitality within and beyond our communities, speaking prophetic words against all forms of injustice, offering healing to those whose spirits and bodies have been broken, or proclaiming the good news of God's expansive love for creation in all its manifold forms.

There is some indication in the letter that this sense of spiritual power may be fuelled in one way or another by social location. Paul states in 1.16, 'not many of you were wise by human standards, not many were powerful, not many were of noble birth'. This remark points to the socio-economic diversity present in the community (Theissen 1982: 72). Although not many are wise in worldly terms or powerful, some clearly are (for example, Stephanus whose household Paul baptized (1.16; 16.5–18)). Dale Martin proposes that it is the social elite who are laying claim to 'wisdom', since it is these who would have been able to invite a philosopher into their home, providing financial support and other forms of benefaction in return for education in philosophy (1995: 73). In contrast, Anne Wire sees evidence that the 'wisdom' claimed by the Corinthians offered those of low status (slaves, Greeks and women) a 'surge of status in wisdom, power, and honor' resulting in a rise in social location (1990: 62–4). The considerable attention given to women in the letter (see especially 7; 11.2–14; 14.33–6) signals that, whether of high or low socio-economic status, they are among those whom Paul identifies with the 'problem' and, it seems likely, are proponents of 'wisdom'. While the exact relation of socio-economic status to wisdom remains uncertain, it is evident that the status claimed by those who manifest wisdom in the Corinthian community is of concern to Paul. With a voice that, perhaps, borders on sarcasm he declares in 4.10: 'You are held in honour, but we in disrepute.'

Paul calls attention to what he sees as a negative side to the Corinthians' confidence. From his perspective, it leads to behaviour that threatens the health and wholeness of the community: those who, with confidence, eat meat offered to idols undermine those who fear that doing so would be a breach of faith (8.7). Speaking in tongues, because it calls attention to the individual, becomes a mark of status rather than a gift to build up the community (14.2). Other fractures in the community arise from callousness in terms of how individuals relate to the others in the community: at community meals, which are followed by a celebration of the Lord's Supper, those who arrive first (perhaps the social elite who do not work with their hands and whose time is their own, or, alternatively, those who have come to prepare the meal, e.g., slaves and women) eat and drink before the remainder arrive with the result that some go hungry while others have become drunk (11.17–22). Disagreements between individuals are not resolved within the community, but taken to public courts (6.1–11), another indication that social as well as spiritual power is likely to be at play. All of these actions Paul views as arising from a false sense of status among individuals or groups.

GLBTI communities also are not immune to divisions arising from issues related to status and identity. A pervasive patriarchal culture (despite significant changes within the past century) continues to render women of second-class status in many contexts. The earning power of lesbians in the USA, for example, is 75.5 cents to every dollar earned by gay men (figure for 2003; source: US Women's Bureau and the National Committee on Pay Equity). Households of gay men, therefore, may enjoy not only greater economic security, but also the influence, access and leisure that their greater earning power provides. Male-to-female transsexuals and transgendered persons can experience a sudden shift in both economic and social status when they assume a female identity, quite apart from the barriers that arise from their trans identity. Lesbians may feel at odds with some transsexual/gendered male-to-females who adopt a female identity that many lesbians associate with patriarchal definitions of gender. Intersexed persons and bisexuals may find themselves chafing at the rigid gender identities of many gays and lesbians, and find themselves isolated because they seemingly pose a threat to those whose orientation can more nearly be made to conform to heterosexual standards. Race brings to the surface a variety of other issues, among them blatant and subtle forms of racism within GLBTI communities, lack of pay equity, as well as access to and quality of healthcare. While we may pose a united front for PRIDE month, in reality we often find ourselves divided along lines of gender identity, race, class, orientation, politics and religion.

Paul challenges the wisdom professed by the Corinthians by juxtaposing it against the 'folly' of the cross. Surprisingly, references to the cross are rare in the writings of Paul and it is only here in 1 Corinthians that he uses the phrase 'the message about the cross' (1.18), a phrase he does not explicate except in terms of its effect. Anne Wire observes that the 'thing being defined is neither a single object – a wooden cross – nor the past event of Jesus' crucifixion, but the *recurring event of the word of the cross*' (1990: 49, emphasis added). This 'speech-event' is defined in terms of response: for those who are perishing, it is 'foolishness' (1.18), but for those who are being saved it is 'the power of God and the wisdom of God' (1.24). These two responses point to the paradox which Paul views as the power of the cross. From a human perspective, the cross is a sign of ignominy (1.22): an instrument of torture reserved for slaves, traitors and the marginalized, representing the most humiliating form of death. Yet Paul claims it as a sign of God's wisdom and power, precisely because it is through human weakness, transparently displayed in the cross, that God's power is made most evident (1.20–5). The intended effect of this definition is to set at odds the Corinthians' definition of wisdom, which is manifested in displays of power. Paul eschews such wisdom 'so that the cross of Christ might not be emptied of its power' (1.17). To the contrary, Paul declares, it is not through power, status or wisdom that God is made known in the world, but through 'what is low and despised . . . so that no one might boast in the presence of God' (1.28–9).

Paul's argument is evidently rooted in his own experience. Elsewhere, Paul boasts of his prior status (2 Cor. 11.21–3; Phil. 3.4b–6), which, as a follower of Christ, has led to loss: 'To the present hour we are hungry and thirsty, we are poorly clothed and beaten and homeless, and we grow weary from the work of our own hands' (4.11–12; see also 2 Cor. 11.22–30). It is likely, then, that Paul sees in the cross a reflection of his own loss of power and status, which loss has become the means for God's power to be revealed in his life (Phil. 3.7–11). Yet for many of the Corinthians the experience appears to have been the opposite. Those who were previously not powerful, not of noble birth, not considered wise (1.26), who may have initially seen in the crucified Christ a mirror of their own life experience, have experienced a rise in status which begins with the cross and ends in the power Christ's resurrection (Wire 1990: 62–71).

The power that the Corinthians claim for themselves as a sign of wisdom Paul declares a sign of their spiritual immaturity, because it leads to what he describes as jealousy and quarrels arising from status claims (3.3 (2.6–3.4)). It is not that Paul utterly rejects the spiritual gifts exhibited by the Corinthians; rather he is concerned with the effect that these produce. From Paul's perspective, the spiritual gifts that the Corinthians enjoy should be used for the building up of the community of faith, which Paul describes as the 'body of Christ' (12.27): 'For just as the body is one and has many members, and all the members of the body, though many, are one body, so it is with Christ' (12.12). Unless the body works together, for the mutual benefit of all, the body cannot function. In order for this to happen, more than a simple co-ordination of effort is required. Rather, it is dependent upon a spirit of co-operation which Paul identifies with love (13.1–13). The gifts manifested individually by the Corinthians, says Paul, are without value unless they are informed by this spirit of love working for the benefit of the community. Prophecy and knowledge will end, and speaking in tongues will cease, but love, which is patient, kind, not envious, irritable or resentful, and which does not insist on its own way, will endure (13.8, 4–6).

The metaphor of the body as a symbol of social unity is well worn and appealing. Paul's emphasis on interdependence, that is, a unity which is dependent upon a self-conscious recognition of and celebration of diversity, continues to challenge all communities of faith to examine the ways in which they have constructed hierarchies that threaten the life of the body rather than contribute to its health and function. GLBTI communities, often divided in their bid for self-preservation in a hostile environment, are increasingly aware that our unity in the midst of our diversity will not only make us stronger than the sum of our parts, but make us better able to discern where wisdom resides by our listening to and learning from each other. As the dominant culture is better able to recognize GLBTI communities as members of the body, so too will society as a whole be strengthened.

Resisting readers, however, may be suspicious of the image of the body. This suspicion may arise in part because of our propensity to envision bodies in gendered terms. Just what does this body look like? Must we conform to a particular image of the body in order to be a part of the body? Would it make any difference if this were a transgendered or intersexed body? Body image also begs the question of who or what determines the direction in which the body is to go. Paul, himself, seems concerned with this question. Despite his rhetoric of the unity of the body, he breaks it down into its individual parts when he applies it to the Church: 'And God has appointed in the Church first apostles, second prophets, third teachers . . .' (12.28). Although Paul has earlier described apostles as those who are 'last of all . . . a spectacle to the world', there is no question that he views the example set by the apostles as, 'first of all', that which is to be imitated by the 'body'. Yet the impact of this directive will not be experienced equally: those who began with little or no status stand far more to lose by this than those who, like Paul, have the luxury of seeing themselves positively in terms of what they have lost.

Paul returns to the 'body' again in the closing chapters of the letter when he turns to the topic of the resurrection. There is a strategy at work here; Paul nowhere separates the death of Christ from his resurrection (e.g. Rom. 1.3–4; 6.3–4; Phil. 2.6–11; 3.10–11), but in 1 Corinthians he places a vast distance between his discussion of the two because that is, in effect, what he wants the Corinthians to do. In his mind, they have moved too quickly from death to resurrection; he wants them to understand death and resurrection as two distinct, if interrelated, events: one tied to the past with lasting consequences (the death of Christ), and the other inextricably tied to the future (the resurrection). Paul begins with a question, 'Now if Christ is proclaimed raised from the dead, how can some of you say there is no resurrection of the dead?' (15.12). Whether the Corinthians deny the resurrection of the dead because they claim access to resurrection power in the present or because they reject the idea that dead bodies can be raised to eternal life is debated (see Wire 1990; Horsley 1998; Martin 1995; 1996). In either case, the nature of future resurrection is in dispute.

Early in the letter, Paul praises the Corinthians for the abundance of their spiritual gifts, then places his praise in context: 'so that you may be blameless on the day of our Lord Jesus Christ' (1.8). This one phrase clearly establishes Paul's apocalyptic orientation. He understands time to be divided into two great epochs: the present, described by the world, which is passing away; and the future, when the eternal reign of God will be established once for all on the 'day of our Lord'. From Paul's perspective, we stand at the turning point between the two: one foot firmly rooted in that which is passing away and represented by our perishable bodies; the other already established in the future, but as a promise through the resurrection of Christ. The fulfilment of that promise is, from Paul's perspective, dependent upon our remaining embedded (or embodied) in Christ in the present age. Paul restates this idea in a number of ways in chapter 15 (vv. 2, 19, 20, 22, 23, 46, 49, 50, 51), placing emphasis always on the future. He states this openly when he declares, 'flesh and blood cannot inherit the kingdom of God' (15.50). Flesh and blood belong to the perishable, that is, the present age; to the future belongs that which is incorruptible, the spiritual body that we receive through Christ (15.42–9). The Corinthians have, from Paul's perspective, confounded the two by failing to recognize the fragility of their present existence and thereby jeopardizing their future.

GLBTI communities revel in bodies. They know, in a way that heterosexuals can often ignore, that you cannot really know who you are until you come to grips with who you are in your body. Therefore, Paul's emphasis on the continuity of an embodied existence is one with which GLBTI communities can resonate. At the same time, the Aids epidemic and, less often recognized, breast cancer (among other diseases) have reminded GLBTI communities of the fragility of our bodies. Paul's promise of a spiritual body in the life to come, a body that has not been ravaged by drugs or chemotherapy or mutilated in surgery, can be heard as a genuine message of hope by those who are too keenly aware of their present bodies passing away. His view of life in an apocalyptic context can also be a helpful reminder that there are powers and principalities (for example, hate crimes) over which we have no control, and to which we are vulnerable. Yet Paul claims that it is in these moments and places where we are weakest that we can discover we are sustained by the power of God, in part by recognizing that in our own embodied existence we are also embedded in the body of Christ, the community of believers. GLBTI communities might then remind Paul that in God's creative imagination, a body can encompass far more diversity and complexity than he could possibly suppose.

The body, gender and sex

Chapter 5 of the letter begins with a charge against the community for tolerating what Paul calls 'sexual immorality'. The word *porneia* is a general term and does not single out one kind of behaviour over another. Its frequent occurrence in 1 Corinthians sets this letter apart. In the discussion that follows, Paul consistently focuses on how the *porneia* or behaviour of the individual impacts the group – that is, the 'body'. Implicit in his discussion is an understanding of gender that is based on separation and differentiation.

The first instance of *porneia* involves a man who is said to be living with 'his father's wife' (5.1). This phrasing indicates that the woman is the man's step-mother, quite possibly closer in age to the grown son than the father. Both Jewish and Roman law legislated against such a relationship, which was considered incestuous. It is possible that the two persons involved felt guided by a new set of social definitions following their baptism into Christ. Paul's challenge is not to the man, but to the Corinthians, whom he charges to expel the man from the community (see Lev. 18.18, 29). Lack of reference to casting out the woman suggests that she may not be a member of the congregation; in 5.9–13 Paul states that he does not judge the immorality of outsiders, but the immorality of those within the community, who, together, constitute the 'temple of God' (3.16–17; 6.19). The interpretation of 5.5 is disputed: it may refer to literal destruction of the flesh (as a result of being cast out of the 'body' and into the world); however, the Greek reads 'that the spirit might be saved', not '*his* spirit'; thus 'spirit' may refer to the spirit of the community. In either case, Paul's concern is the integrity of the Corinthian body. It is therefore the community that is held accountable for the man's behaviour.

In 6.9, Paul lists those who 'will not inherit the kingdom of God'. Included are two words whose translations are disputed: *malakoi, arsenokoitai*. Elsewhere in the Second Testament, *malakoi* means 'soft' and is used in reference to clothing (Matt. 11.8; Luke 7.25). In moral discourse, it is translated variously to describe those who are 'morally weak', for example men who enjoy luxury and live decadently (Boswell 1980: 341; Martin 1996: 125). In contemporary parlance we might translate *malakoi* as 'metrosexual'. Dale Martin observes that, while it could refer to 'a man who allowed himself to be penetrated' (i.e. to assume the passive role, therefore transgressing the boundary between 'male' and 'female'), to limit the term to this meaning is 'simply wrong' (1996: 125). Whereas *malakoi* is a quite common word, *arsenokoitai* is not. Since the first extant use of the word is probably 1 Corinthians, determining its precise meaning is difficult. The prefix, *arsen,* means 'male' (as opposed to 'female'); *koitē* refers to 'bed' and, by extension, sexual intercourse. Robin Scroggs understands this term to refer to a man who lies with another man (1983: 85–8, 106–8); John Boswell, to a male prostitute, although not necessarily one who engages in sex exclusively with men (noting the absence of this word in reference to homosexual activity in Greek (344–6)). Dale Martin observes that *arsenokoitai* occurs elsewhere in conjunction with not adultery or prostitution, but economic exploitation, and he thus suggests it refers to prostitution or pimping (1996: 119–21).

It is important that these two words be heard in context; they should not be singled out from the other vices in verses 9–10, which include greed, drunkenness, thievery and idolatry. If *malakoi* is understood as decadence and *arsenokoitai* as pimping, then the entire list of vices can be seen to revolve specifically around behaviours that involve excess and exploitation, behaviours that ultimately place one's own interests at odds with God's covenant relationship with humankind. Within the context of 1 Corinthians, this vice list is framed by Paul's complaint against lawsuits between believers and those visiting prostitutes. Both of these activities fall under the heading of excess and exploitation. The list is intended to be illustrative of these moral flaws. It is not *specifically* descriptive of nor directed towards homosexual activity, nor, indeed, sexual activity in general.

Paul does become specific in his critique of men who are visiting prostitutes (6.12–20). Although there is extensive evidence for both male and female prostitutes in the ancient world, Paul's use here of the feminine form of the word indicates that he has female prostitutes in mind. While it would not be unknown for a woman to visit a female prostitute, Paul's concern in chapter 7 with men whose 'passions' may lead them to sin suggests that it is men with whom he is concerned here. Raymond Collins notes that 'visiting prostitutes' was a classical *topos* used by philosophical moralists to introduce topics of morality (1999: 240). Whether Paul is citing an actual practice, therefore, is unclear, although his audience would need to be able to recognize this behaviour in order for his argument to be credible (Wire 1990: 74).

The presenting issue (visiting prostitutes) is, in a sense, secondary to the spiritual issue as far as Paul is concerned. The Corinthians maintain that 'all things are lawful for me' (6.12; 10.23). This has apparently resulted in the belief that if they are embedded in Christ, they are 'protected'; no other power can harm them and they can enjoy a radical freedom. Paul's counter that 'not all things are beneficial' is an effort not to limit their freedom per se, but to challenge their worldview. According to Paul's apocalyptic outlook, the world is divided between competing forces of good and evil; in this cosmic battle, the outcome is sure, but not yet complete. The Corinthians' view that 'all things are lawful' reveals, from Paul's point of view, a lack of sensitivity to powers of corruption still at work in the world (so also 5.6). Paul believes that in this not yet complete apocalyptic epoch, the world continues to be typified by greed, robbers, idolaters and sexual immorality (5.9–10; 6.9–10). To 'be united to a prostitute', then, is to expose oneself to those forces working against God, implicitly violating the presence of God that resides in the believer through the Holy Spirit (6.18). The danger to the believer is that he exposes himself to those things which are, from an apocalyptic viewpoint, passing away and destined for destruction. For this reason, Paul reminds the Corinthians that they (both individually and collectively) are 'not their own' but belong to God and, therefore, should glorify God in their (individual and collective) body (6.19–20).

Paul shows no concern for the prostitutes; they are, apparently, outside the community. He neither condemns them, nor shows any awareness of the socio-economic forces that conspire to entrench their existence. His challenge is to the men whom he sees as exposing the body, not only their own, but also that of the Corinthian community, to the powers of evil which are still at work in the world and to which he believes they are vulnerable.

Paul's concern with 'sexual immorality' continues in chapter 7, where he turns to the subject of marriage. Here he takes up what is widely regarded as a slogan in the Corinthian community: 'it is well for a man not to touch a woman' (7.1). Whatever was originally intended, many members of GLBTI communities will be inclined to heartily agree. In the case of the Corinthian community, this slogan apparently reflected the practice of celibacy. Celibacy was recognized as a spiritual discipline in both Graeco-Roman cults and Judaism. Paul himself advocates celibacy (7.7, 29–31, 38, 40) so that believers might dedicate themselves to 'the affairs of the Lord' while the 'present form of this world is passing away' (7.31b–34). Nonetheless his prevailing ethic is that believers should 'remain as they are' only so long as it is possible to exercise self-control. Those who have a gift other than celibacy should marry (7.7–9), yet not solely for the purpose of self-gratification. Paul emphasizes that the primary concern of those who are married is the pleasure of their partner (7.4, 33, 34). He stresses the mutual obligation that married men and women owe with respect to conjugal relations, proposing that abstinence for the sake of prayer be only for a designated time, jointly determined (7.2–5).

Yet Paul is not wholly consistent. In 7.25 Paul addresses a group of women who appear to hold special status among the unmarried, the 'virgins': women who are 'holy in body and spirit' (7.34). Here Paul reverses strategy, stating that if a virgin marries she does not sin (7.28). Following a lengthy digression on the virtues of remaining unmarried (7.29–35), Paul again addresses the 'virgins', yet his comments are directed not towards the women, but towards those men who would marry them (7.36–8). While Paul ostensibly supports the 'virgins', who share his singular devotion to the service of God, in the end, he leaves the decision of whether or not to marry to the man (Wire 1990: 89). Paul's goal is that the men should avoid sexual immorality (7.36), but he can achieve this only by persuading the 'virgins' to surrender their physical and spiritual autonomy (Wire 1990: 87–97). That he leaves the decision to the man suggests that the women have made their choice – to remain celibate. But this does not solve Paul's problem of sexual immorality. In the face of competing goods, it is the more socially vulnerable women who are asked to compromise.

These verses begin to bring into full view Paul's implicit understanding of gender. Although women are prominent in Pauline churches (1.11; 16.19), assuming distinctive positions of leadership, Paul nonetheless falls back on gender hierarchy to assert his own authority as 'father' over the community (4.14–15) and to order what he views as the disordered life of the community. This is most evident in 11.2–3, where Paul declares that Christ is the head of the man, and the man (or husband – the words are identical in Greek) is the head of the woman (or wife) (see also 11.7–8). The tension with Galatians 3.28 is obvious, and reflects a tension found elsewhere in Paul between status in Christ and functional status in the world (especially slaves (7.21–4)). Paul's arguments in the much contested verses that follow (11.2–16) suggest that gender boundaries were being transgressed by women seeking to live out their status in the risen Christ. The contested 'boundary marker' is a veil, which, Dale Martin has shown, both symbolized and effected a 'protective barrier guarding the woman's head and, by metanymic transfer, her genitals' (1995: 234). Troy Martin, in a study of these verses against the background of ancient physiology, proposes that, in fact, women's hair was understood as a part of female genitalia since women's long hair was thought to assist 'the uterus in drawing semen upward and inward' (2004: 83). In rejecting a head covering while praying and prophesying, then, these women, from Paul's perspective, bring shame upon the community by exposing their genitalia to public view. From the women's perspective, however, this action probably represents their reluctance to be restricted to their 'functional status' within patriarchal social structures and their desire to 'realize their full integration in to Christ, God's image' (Wire 1990: 131).

What is striking in each of these fleeting discussions is the explicit concern to integrate spirituality and sexual practice. In the case of the Corinthians, this means transgressing boundaries in a variety of ways, in each case guided by a particular understanding of what it means to be raised with Christ through whom they enjoy a new identity and status, no longer threatened by the 'powers and principalities' that control the 'world that is passing away'. Paul, driven by an apocalyptic outlook, is keenly aware of the 'powers and principalities' at work in the world and urges the Corinthians to continue to be guided by what he views as functional social structures that will protect them until the 'day of the Lord' is at hand. Between these two, we gain a glimpse of the complex understandings of gender identity and sexuality at work in the ancient world. This should serve as a guard against efforts to over-simplify discussions of sexuality and spirituality, or to lift such conversations out of contexts comprised of specific social settings and spiritual practices.

Reading with Paul, GLBTI communities may be surprised by the fundamentally positive view Paul has of sex. He clearly understands it as an integral part of relationships described by mutual commitment and stability. There is no indication that he relates it to procreation. It has a positive value in itself. Paul also raises the challenge of boundaries: at what point do relationships become exploitive or indulgent to a degree that they violate God's overarching ethic of justice? And by what means do we hold ourselves accountable?

Reading against Paul, GLBTI communities may resist his perpetuation of gender hierarchies and definitions, observing that Paul himself is able to recognize our new status in Christ as transgressing either/or divisions, although Paul is unable to consistently translate this realization into a social reality. The witness of the Corinthians demonstrates that this new status does not result in rigid uniformity, but opens up a variety of ways in which individuals may express coherency in sexuality and spirituality – an enterprise in which GLBTI communities also may see themselves joined. GLBTI communities will also strongly resist Paul's misguided efforts to maintain a 'purity of the body' that requires those who are most vulnerable to surrender their freedom in Christ. Rather, they may see this as an opportunity to challenge all the faithful to examine in what ways they are mutually responsible for maintaining the health of the body of Christ. Going beyond Paul, they will open their doors to those who have been excluded from the body (for example the prostitutes), recognizing that the health of the body suffers when it is defined more by exclusion than inclusion.

14.33–6: A call for radical exclusion

There is considerable debate surrounding the question of whether or not the admonition that 'women should be silent in the churches' comes from Paul's hand. The similarity of these verses to 1 Timothy 2.11–12 leads some to conclude that they were added later in an effort to bring Paul into conformity with more restrictive views on the role of women. Yet all extant manuscripts contain these verses, although where the verses are located varies. A few scholars argue that Paul is, in fact, quoting the Corinthians at this point, as he does elsewhere in the letter. All of these proposals represent, in one way or another, an effort to deal with our obvious discomfort with these words. They are a canonical embarrassment. In the context of this commentary, however, these verses can raise some provocative questions: What happens when we silence a portion of the community? What does such an action say about the community and what is lost from the life of the community when such an action is undertaken? Is such an action ever justified? As people who have been routinely silenced, GLBTI communities may find it helpful to retain the painful witness represented by these verses so that these important questions might be raised.

2 Corinthians

Between the writing of 1 and 2 Corinthians events have occurred which have placed a further strain on Paul's relationship with the Corinthians. In 2 Corinthians we learn that Paul made a second, 'painful' visit to Corinth, during which a public confrontation took place between Paul and an unnamed individual (the issue remains a mystery) (2.1–11). Paul apparently intended to make a third visit to Corinth, then changed his mind, sending in his stead Titus with a letter from Paul (7.6–8, 13). Titus apparently brought back a 'word of consolation' to Paul from the Corinthians (7.5–16). However, the Corinthians also expressed frustration that Paul had said he intended to visit Corinth, both coming and going from Macedonia, then failed to appear (1.16). This led the Corinthians to accuse him of being inconsistent in both his words and his actions (1.15–22). Paul defends himself by claiming that he did not want to cause more pain following his disastrous, earlier visit (1.23–2.5). He again promises a third visit (12.14), sending all or a part of the letter we call 2 Corinthians ahead of him (many scholars consider 2 Corinthians a composite of several letters). It is apparent from this letter that a further complicating factor is involved: other apostles have arrived in Corinth who overshadow Paul's person and efforts. Paul must, therefore, defend himself on two fronts.

Suffering and consolation

Paul begins 2 Corinthians with a benediction ('blessed be . . .') that focuses attention on God, who offers humankind mercy and consolation 'in all our affliction' (1.3–4; cf. 1 Cor. 1.4–9). These opening words constitute a declaration of faith that evokes remembrance of God's saving activity in the past (mercy (Ps. 103.1–4); comfort (Isa. 49.13)), but, written in the present tense, it also is a reminder of God's activity in the 'now'. In view of Paul's tenuous relationship with the Corinthians, these words also represent a strategic move. They orient the Corinthians toward the source of their shared identity with Paul (God), and urge the Corinthians towards the consolation Paul hopes to effect: reconciliation between Paul and the Corinthians (7.5–11).

In order for this reconciliation to be achieved, Paul must persuade the Corinthians of the validity of his apostleship. The threat comes from the presence of other apostles in the community (called 'super-apostles' by Paul (11.5; 12.11)), who differ from Paul in both manner and message. Whether these apostles pose a direct challenge to Paul, or indirect, by having captured the attention of the Corinthians, is uncertain. Everything that can be known about these 'super-apostles' comes from Paul's own words. The result is little indeed and filtered through Paul's own polemical outlook. The experience of GLBTI communities, which are used to being judged according to the descriptions promoted by their opponents, should make us cautious readers.

Because Paul makes a direct comparison between these apostles and himself with respect to ethnic identity, it can be assumed that they, like Paul, are Jewish followers of Jesus ('Are they Hebrews? . . . Israelites? . . . descendants of Abraham? So am I' (11.22)). Where they come from is unknown; there is no reason to assume that they represent the 'Jerusalem faction' mentioned in other letters (Gal. 2.12). Since Paul accuses the Corinthians of too easily submitting to 'a different gospel from the one you received' (meaning his own), it is possible that their proclamation differs from Paul's (11.5). However, since Paul never directly contests the content of their preaching, this may be no more than slander on his part. The primary point of engagement is around how these apostles present themselves to the Corinthians: they bring letters of commendation and compare themselves with others (3.1; 10.12, 18), 'boast in outward appearances' (5.12) and are eloquent in speech (11.6). By comparison, Paul fairs poorly: he has no formal letters of commendation (3.2), his physical stature is weak (10.10), and his speech is 'contemptible' (10.10; 11.6). What is most egregious from Paul's point of view is that these other apostles have insinuated themselves into his congregation, taking advantage of his labours in building up the Corinthians, and claiming credit for work they have not done (10.13–16). Yet he also indicates that at least some among the Corinthians view Paul as claiming more authority for himself than is warranted (10.8). Paul's authority rests on persuasion rather than any prior claim (5.11).

Members of GLBTI communities may feel the edge of this competition keenly. It is not only the 'queens' who are known for their vanity. Appearance, mannerisms, speech and presence are all ways in which we have learned to channel our identities and by which we know one another. They both distinguish us from 'outsiders' and, to a certain degree, protect us from outsiders by restricting access. Within GLBTI communities they can also become a source of competition, a means of ranking one another, or a way of establishing territory. While it is easy to dismiss these markers as superficial, they are a legitimate expression of our self-understanding and reflect, in some cases, a radical reorientation of definitions of gender and gender-typing in the dominant culture. It can be argued that Paul is about something similar.

Paul endeavours to distinguish himself from these 'super-apostles', in part, by drawing his own set of comparisons between them: they are peddlers of God's word, he is sincere (2.14–17); they prey upon the Corinthians, he takes advantage of no one (11.20; 7.2); they proclaim themselves, he proclaims Jesus Christ (4.5). These are standard insults and reflect no more than Paul's efforts to discredit the other apostles. Nonetheless, it may be the particular way in which Paul understands his apostleship in relation to Jesus Christ that sets him apart. In the opening verses, Paul makes an implicit link between his own suffering and the suffering of Christ (1.5–6). It is not Paul's intent in any way to claim a Christ-like status for himself; rather, Paul is saying that as he participates in the suffering of Christ, he also comes to know the consolation that we receive through Christ (1.5, 9–10). His experience of this consolation puts him in a position to offer consolation and hope to others (1.6). Paul is, in effect, building on the 'theology of the cross' of which he speaks in 1 Corinthians. In that letter, Paul claims that the cross is a sign of God's wisdom and power, because it is through human weakness displayed in the cross, that God's power is made most evident (1 Cor. 1.20–5). In 2 Corinthians, Paul draws on this image in defence of his apostleship: it is in his suffering and weakness that the power of God is most present (1.9; 12.9) – just as Christ was crucified in weakness, but now lives by the power of God (13.4).

Paul goes on to describe his apostleship in terms of human weakness, but God's power. In speaking of how God rescued him from death in Asia, he concludes that this was 'so that we would rely not on ourselves but on God who raises the dead' (1.9). This relationship of utter dependence is expressed again in chapter 2. Here Paul speaks of how God, 'in Christ always leads us in triumphal procession' (2.14). This image can be easily misconstrued. Those led in 'triumphal procession' are not the victors, but those captured in war. At the conclusion of the procession, these would be executed as a final act of public humiliation (Matera 2003: 71–3). In taking over this image, it may seem that Paul pushes the image of dependence to an extreme, but he does so in order to emphasize his complete dependence on God in both life and death. The almost macabre description that follows of Paul as an 'aroma of Christ to God' (2.15) may be an allusion to the sacrificial nature of Paul's ministry (twice he offers lists of the many afflictions he has suffered (6.4–10; 11.16–30)) or possibly draw on the image of Wisdom, who exhorts her children to 'send out aromatic fragrance like incense' (Sirach 39.13–14). In this case, Christ takes on the identity of Wisdom, while Paul becomes the aromatic fragrance of Christ to those who are being saved, but the fragrance of death to those who are perishing (Wan 2000: 59–60). It is this image in particular that Paul uses to contrast himself with those whom he calls 'peddlers of God's word' (2.17) and why Paul can claim that 'our competence comes from God, not ourselves' (3.4–6; 5.20).

Colleen Conway writes that the ideology of masculinity in the Graeco-Roman world understood submission to suffering and death on behalf of others as a 'noble and manly act'... 'Thus, what otherwise might be a shameful experience is mitigated by the notion of self sacrifice...' (n.d.: 16). This insight reveals that what Paul describes as human weakness (and which could be read as emasculating Paul) is, at some level, a defence of Paul's masculinity. In order for Paul's defence to be effective, his audience would need to hear and understand his language in this way. The unfortunate effect of this language is that it continues to support the androcentric orientation and patriarchal structure of society rather than challenge it. This will reinforce the frustration of resisting readers within GLBTI communities who recognize that the persistently androcentric orientation of the dominant culture infects our communities as well. The suggestion that the idea of suffering coupled with masculinity has the potential to challenge ideologies of masculinity that focus on domination has some merit. However, it is not wholly satisfying because, ultimately, it does not challenge the notion that male gendered persons are empowered to act in and on behalf of society, while others are positioned to be the passive recipients of their actions.

Those who read with Paul may hear in the text some resistance to this paradigm. The image, in particular, of Paul as a captive of war places emphasis on his extreme vulnerability. In Paul's instance, this is mitigated by the one to whom he is captive, God, and it is this dependence on God that Paul wants to emphasize. Nonetheless, Paul's status evokes real-life images of victims of war, many of whom are women and children. Wars typically also prey on those who in any way sit on the margins of society. Some in GLBTI communities may see in Paul's description, then, not a reinforcing of the masculine paradigm, but a crossing of boundaries into a trans-space, where gender definitions are bent and reconfigured.

For Paul, entering this trans-space allows the power of God to be most visible. It also places the whole of his existence in a larger context. We are, in Paul's words, 'treasure in clay jars', constantly on the verge of being shattered (4.7–12). Yet, he continues, 'we know that if the earthly tent we live in is destroyed, we have a building from God, a house not made with hands, eternal in the heavens' (5.1 (5.1–10)). This reflects more than the expectation of life in the great hereafter. Paul sees the present moment from an apocalyptic perspective, where the continuum of time is divided into two great epochs. We reside in the great moment in between – between that which is passing away and the moment of the new creation, when everything old has passed away and everything has become new (5.16–19). Paul views the whole of existence from the perspective of the 'new', the 'already present, but not yet complete' creative moment that God has begun in Christ.

The promise of a 'new creation' is tantalizing and invites us to stretch the limits of our imagination. The limitations and definitions of the old creation stand poised to be shattered, just like clay jars. GLBTI communities may view themselves as standing with one foot firmly planted in the past, while the other is moving towards the future. The old creation is represented by the divisions that continue to plague us: racism, gender-privilege, internalized homophobia, economic disparity and deprivation; the new by a gender-bending dance in which we explore all the positive, life-giving dimensions of what it means to be human in a way that honours and reflects the mercy and consolation first initiated by God towards us.

Ultimately, Paul's hope in 2 Corinthians is that he and the Corinthians might become a consolation to each other (1.6–7; 7.5–7). In this case, however, mutual consolation does not signal parity. The consolation that Paul seeks from the Corinthians is their submission, once again, to his authority as an apostle. Paul tells them that he feels 'a divine jealousy' for them having promised to present them as a 'chaste virgin' in marriage to Christ (11.2); but he fears that they have been led astray, deceived as was Eve (11.3). Ascribing female gender to the Corinthians is intended to locate them firmly in a subordinate status to Paul and underline both their immaturity and need for dependence. Resisting readers will be troubled by Paul's use of this language to describe the new creation, perpetuating gender dichotomies and a patriarchal social order that belongs to the old. Those who read with Paul will hear in this language Paul's way of indicating that his honour is on the line and is dependent upon what the Corinthians choose to do; as he says elsewhere, '*you* are our letter of commendation' (3.1–3).

Reading with Paul it is possible to hear in 2 Corinthians a genuine message of hope, described by the agency of God who moves on behalf of humankind to bring comfort/consolation in the midst of suffering. Paul is a part of that movement, because he himself has received consolation and therefore is able to console others. Implicit in this is a charge that we, who have been consoled, should likewise console others. This is a particularly hopeful message to GLBTI communities, where multiple oppressions can converge and, more often than not, we are told that God has rejected us. A resisting reader, however, is less likely to find comfort. The inexorable movement towards conformity with Paul may feel too familiar, reminding us of how often we are asked to bend to the norms established by others. A dialogue with Paul, however, may allow us to retain our voices, while listening respectfully to his efforts to persuade us.

12.7–8: Paul's thorn in the flesh

In 12.7–8 Paul speaks of being afflicted with a 'thorn in the flesh'. Many have speculated on the nature of this affliction. Jerome Murphy-O'Connor, noting that 'thorn' and 'messenger of Satan' stand in apposition, and that elsewhere Paul refers to his opponents as 'servants of Satan' (11.14–15), suggests that it refers to opponents of Paul (1991: 119). There is no credible reason to view the 'thorn' as a sexual affliction. Paul himself does not specify what the affliction is, but only refers to it as an example of how God's power is perfected in our weakness (12.9).

A material response to the body

In Galatians 2.10 Paul reports that he was asked by the leaders in Jerusalem to 'remember the poor' as he carried the gospel to the 'uncircumcised'. References in other of his letters indicate that Paul set about taking up a collection among the Gentile churches to deliver to Jerusalem (Rom. 15.25–9; 1 Cor. 16.1–4; 2 Cor. 8–9; 12.14–18). This offering was more than a simple act of charity in response to the needs of the 'saints' or of thanksgiving in response to God (2 Cor. 9.12). It also served as a validation of Paul's ministry. It is evident from Galatians that some called Paul's ministry among the Gentiles into question; specifically, there was concern over whether Paul's gospel was consistent with that proclaimed by the church in Jerusalem, or represented a breakaway movement with Paul at its centre (Gal. 2.1–10). A meeting with the leaders in Jerusalem brought recognition that Paul's ministry, like theirs, reflected the ongoing work of Jesus Christ in the world. The offering then became a means by which Paul could tangibly demonstrate the close, mutual relationship between the churches: since the Gentile churches shared in the spiritual blessings of the Jerusalem church (i.e. the gospel), so the Gentile churches should also be of service to the Jerusalem church in its moment of material need (Rom. 15.27). This reciprocity was the cornerstone for establishing a relationship of mutual need, support and respect between them.

A nearly parallel example exists today, but with a different outcome. For over fifteen years the Universal Fellowship of Metropolitan Community Churches has sought both membership and observer status in the National Council of Churches. These requests have consistently been denied. Although UFMCC continues to maintain dialogue with the NCC, suspicion lingers within the NCC that UFMCC somehow represents a different gospel, one not consistent with the member churches of the NCC. The parallel is an apt one because the controversy surrounding the Gentiles focused on practice rather than belief: should Gentiles be circumcised and adhere to dietary laws as followers of the Jewish Messiah, Jesus? Similarly, the controversy surrounding UFMCC does not focus on belief, but on the question of whether homosexuals should refrain from 'practising' in order to be followers of the assumed-to-be heterosexual Jesus. Paul and the Jerusalem church both came to recognize that the inclusion of the Gentiles was the fulfilment of an eschatological vision lifted up by the prophets, in which all the nations would gather to worship the God of Israel (Isa. 2.2–3; Micah 4.1–2) (Matthews 1994b: 209). The Church today is still waiting to respond to the vision of the prophets (Isa. 56.3–7) and ongoing activity of the Spirit (Acts 10; 15), which calls for the radical inclusion of all people in Christ's body. This inability to establish a relationship of reciprocity, one where there is a mutual sharing of gifts and the benefits of interdependence are recognized and experienced, weakens the witness of the body of Christ. Nonetheless, GLBTI communities continue to demonstrate some of the benefits that can be gained by collaboration through offerings collected by UFMCC, the World Rainbow Fund, and other GLBTI agencies.

The offering for the church in Jerusalem, while helping to resolve one controversy, sparked another. It is evident from 2 Corinthians that the offering had led to suspicion and rumours. Some of the Corinthians apparently suspected Paul of using the offering to support himself, while giving the appearance of taking nothing from the Corinthians for his work among them by refusing direct financial support (11.7, 9; 12.13, 16). The situation is complicated by the fact that Paul did accept direct financial support from the Philippian churches in Macedonia (11.8–9; Phil. 1.5; 4.10). Why, then, did Paul not accept support from the Corinthians? It is possible that he did not want to become co-opted by any one of what he viewed as the several factions within the Corinthian community, but we can never know for certain. In order to avoid all signs of impropriety, Paul says that he would send Titus ahead, along with two others – one known for his proclamation of the good news (8.18) (likely to appeal to the Corinthians' attraction to those who 'speak well'), and another, a brother who had 'proved himself' – to collect the offering (8.22). Earlier, Paul had told the Corinthians also that he would 'send any whom you approve' to take the gift to Jerusalem and 'if it seems advisable' they would travel with him (1 Cor. 16.3–4). His caution on this matter reveals his genuine concern that his actions not be misinterpreted.

This situation points to the entanglements that can arise whenever money is involved. GLBTI communities know the shame that can arise when 'one of our own' mishandles the financial resources entrusted to them. Every marginalized community is susceptible to the pressure to behave as 'model citizens'; to show that they are better than the dominant culture in order to gain acceptance within the dominant culture. We also know the temptation to accept generous and necessary contributions, even when those contributions involve us in obligations that may compromise our ability to act with complete integrity.

A second charge brought against Paul is that he exacted contributions to the Jerusalem offering through extortion (2 Cor. 9.5). Paul backs off what may have been heard as a command (8.8) to stress that all contributions are voluntary, as each has means (8.3, 12). Of greater concern to Paul is that the Corinthians complete what they had begun (8.7), not only as a genuine expression of their love, but also so that Paul himself will not be humiliated by their absence from this effort (9.1–5). While emphasizing that they need not give to the point of adding stress to their own situation (8.12), he challenges them to be sensitive to the balance between 'your present abundance and their need' (8.13–15; 9.7–10). This is always the challenge. It is a challenge within GLBTI communities where there is often lack of awareness of the terrific economic diversity and need that exists within these communities. It is also a challenge for those in marginalized communities who may assume that their need is always greater, not recognizing that they reside merely at *one edge* of the margin.

Galatians

PATRICK S. CHENG

Freedom from the law is the central theme of Paul's letter to the Galatians (5.1). As such, it resonates powerfully with queer Christians who have been oppressed by numerous laws, both religious and secular, that have tried to restrict our sexualities and relationships. In particular, Galatians is a declaration of independence from those modern-day 'false believers' (2.4) – namely, right-wing fundamentalists – who try to impose their own legalistic code of sexual conduct upon LGBT people, instead of proclaiming the true gospel of Jesus Christ – a gospel that is grounded in faith, and not the law.

In this commentary, I read Galatians from the perspective of an openly gay Christian man who understands the epistle to be a critique of those 'false believers' who persecute LGBT people today in the name of God's 'law'. In addition, I also read Galatians from my social location as a queer person of Asian descent – that is, someone who exists as a minority within a minority. For me, Galatians can also be read as a critique of the dominant white queer culture to the extent that it imposes its own implicit code of conduct or 'law' upon those of us who are also from minority ethnic or cultural backgrounds.

Commissioned for Queer Ministry

Paul begins his letter to the Galatians with a clear statement of the authority by which he proclaims the gospel. He notes that he was commissioned directly through Jesus Christ and God the Creator (1.1), and that he received his gospel through a revelation of Jesus Christ (1.12). In other words, Paul was not commissioned by human sources, nor did he receive his gospel from other humans. Paul's special calling was to proclaim the gospel to the Gentiles – that is, the 'uncircumcised' (2.7) – as opposed to the ministry of James, Peter and John, who were entrusted with proclaiming the gospel to the Jewish people.

The question of authority is particularly important for those of us who are queer Christians. Because we remain at the margins of the mainline Christian denominations – most of which refuse to marry us or to ordain us – we, like Paul, must look directly to Jesus Christ and God the Creator for our commissions. As Chris Glaser tells us, we do not need the mainline churches to confirm our ministries. Rather, we are called by God to share in Paul's 'boldness in asserting God's call of us' (Glaser 1994: 9/23). Just as Paul was called to minister to the Gentiles, we are called to proclaim the gospel to our own communities, just as Troy Perry did by founding the Metropolitan Community Churches in 1968.

Some of us, like Paul, may even have persecuted the LGBT community prior to our own coming out of the closet (1.13; Acts 9.1–19; Spong 2005: 137–9). Or, conversely, we may have been out of the closet, but seen Christianity as the 'enemy' and therefore persecuted the Christian community prior to fully integrating our Christian identities with our queer identities. We should not beat ourselves up for this persecution, but rather rejoice in the fact that we cannot grow spiritually unless we recognize our own 'complicity in the sacred forms of the past, with all their violence and victims' (Alison 2001: 34). It is God's direct revelation of the gospel to us that allows us to overcome our prejudices and to witness our vocational callings as queer Christians (1.23).

No Compulsory Heterosexuality

Paul then turns to the central problem that was facing the church at Galatia – false teachers who were insisting that the converts must be circumcised in order to become followers of Jesus Christ. In other words, the false teachers were insisting that one could not become a follower of Jesus Christ without also following the Jewish law, which mandated the circumcision of converts.

By contrast, Paul insisted that circumcision was *not* necessary to become a follower of Jesus Christ. Paul recalls his specific commission to proclaim the gospel to the Gentiles, who were uncircumcised (2.9). He criticizes those, like Peter, who would insist otherwise. Paul recalls Peter's hypocrisy in refusing to break bread publicly with the Gentiles out of fear of the 'circumcision faction' (2.12), even though Peter himself had 'live[d] like a Gentile and not like a Jew' (2.14). Paul uses very strong language against the false teachers. Paul sees these false teachers as proclaiming a 'different gospel' that 'perverts' the gospel of Christ (1.6–7). He also accuses the Galatians for being 'foolish' in being 'bewitched' (3.1) by the false teachers.

This problem of circumcision is analogous to the contemporary debate over whether one can engage in queer sex and be Christian. The right-wing fundamentalists who insist that queer people cannot be Christian unless we renounce our sexualities are akin to the false teachers in Galatia who insisted on circumcision under Jewish law as a requirement for following Jesus Christ. As Tom Bohache writes in his queer reading of Galatians, we LGBT Christians do not have to give up our sexualities to be acceptable to God. In his words, we 'do not have to circumcise the foreskins of our sexual orientation in order to be acceptable to Almighty God' (Bohache 2000: 235).

The good news for LGBT Christians is that '[o]ur status as children of God is not dependent on outside forces or rules or lists of sins created by human beings' (Bohache 2000: 235). Rather, we are loved by God because of the incredible depth of God's grace. The gospel is more than just a code of conduct – it transcends the idea of 'goodness' and its related notions of 'bound consciences' and 'conforming dependency on group approval' (Alison 2003: 113).

As a result, those of us who are queer Christians recognize that neither compulsory circumcision nor compulsory heterosexuality is required in order to be a follower of Jesus Christ. Indeed, as Tom Hanks has written, homophobic individuals who impose 'heterosexual norms on sexual minorities' and ex-gay 'tortures' are in fact proclaiming 'another gospel' (Hanks 2000: 121–2), just like the false teachers in Galatia. Just as Paul confronted Peter over his hypoc-risy over table fellowship, we are called to boldly confront the hypocrisy of so-called Christians who exclude LGBT people from full membership in the Church (Glaser 1994: 9/23). It is important for us to speak up abut this because religious hypocrisy ultimately inhibits the honesty and spiritual growth of others (Truluck 2000: 286).

No Longer Male and Female

In one of the best-known verses in Galatians, Paul proclaims that: 'There is no longer Jew or Greek, there is no longer slave or free, there is no longer male and female; for all of you are one in Christ Jesus' (3.28). In this section of the epistle, Paul warns the Galatians not to be divided over the role of the law in their lives, since they are all united in baptism in Christ Jesus.

In order to counter the divisive arguments of the false teachers about the necessity of the Mosaic law, Paul cites the scriptural example of Abraham and how he and his 'offspring' were blessed by God because he believed in God (3.6), long before the law was even revealed on Mount Sinai (3.17). According to Paul, the Mosaic law was merely designed to serve as a disciplinarian until Jesus Christ, who is Abraham's 'offspring' (3.16), came to justify us by faith (3.24). Thus, *all* who are baptized in Christ Jesus – whether Jew or Greek, slave or free, or male or female – are heirs to the original promise made to Abraham and his offspring (3.29). This is particularly significant for queer Christians, who are freed from the Mosaic prohibitions against male-to-male anal inter-course in Leviticus 18.22 and 20.13.

It is not surprising that the promise of radical equality in Galatians 3.28 resonates strongly with queer Christians and our allies. In other words, not only is there no longer Jew or Greek, slave or free, male and female, but *there is no longer straight or queer* (see, for example, Jennings 2003: 166–9; McNeill 1993: 147–8; Rogers 1999: 37–66; Truluck 2000: 209–10; Tutu 1996: ix). According to Chris Glaser, for example, the promise of equality in Galatians 3.28 transcends the 'bashing' and 'skirmishes' in the mainstream churches over LGBT people (Glaser 1994: 4/19). Indeed, if there is no longer male and female in Christ Jesus, then it 'does not matter to God which gender we love, which gender we are, or which gender we believe ourselves to be' (Glaser 1994: 10/3). Similarly, Kathy Rudy notes that Galatians 3.28 calls us to create a world in which 'Christian faithfulness' – and not gender or sexual orientation – is the 'primary and only measure' (Rudy 1997: 100–1).

Most recently, bisexual and transgender Christians have read Galatians 3.28 as a specific affirmation of their diverse gender identities. For example, Susan Craig, a bisexual pastor, cites Galatians 3.28 in writing about how bisexuals are '[n]either gay nor straight' and yet 'both gay and straight' (Craig 2000: 198). Justin Tanis, a transgender minister, notes that Galatians 3.28 allows us to see ourselves as 'children of God first and foremost'. For Tanis, Galatians 3.28

'paints for us a vision of a world beyond gender, in which there is room for infi-nite variation and infinite grace' (Tanis 2003: 83). Finally, Virginia Mollenkott sees Galatians 3.28 as 'depolarizing' the categories of male and female, and affirming a 'third sex' of intersexed people, transsexuals and transgenderists (Mollenkott 2001: 113–14).

Freedom from Sexual Legalism

Paul then turns to the central theme of Galatians, which is that Jesus Christ has freed us from the yoke of slavery to the law (5.1). Paul draws a scriptural analogy to the two children of Abraham: Ishmael, who was the son of the slave woman Hagar (4.25), and Isaac, who was the son of the free woman Sarah (4.28). In the past, we were more like Ishmael than Isaac. We were enslaved and remained under the authority of guardians and trustees (4.2–3). However, with the coming of Jesus Christ, we have been adopted by God and, like Isaac, are full heirs of God (4.5).

Paul's reference to the 'yoke of slavery' speaks to queer people and our allies on multiple levels. On one level, the yoke of slavery is the 'sexual legalism' of right-wing fundamentalists that keeps LGBT people in their places (Glaser 1994: 7/8; see also Truluck 2000: 28). On another level, the yoke of slavery is the fear of association – held by many of our non-queer allies – that solidar-ity with us will cause their heterosexual identities to be questioned. On still another level, the yoke of slavery is the 'ideological legalism' within the LGBT community that defines what it means to be 'gay, lesbian, and politically or spiritually correct' (Glaser 1994: 7/8) and that prevents us from respecting the true diversity of bodies and perspectives within our community. It is Jesus Christ who sets us free from all of these yokes of slavery.

Paul's various references to adoption and heirs in this section of Galatians also speak to LGBT people. For example, we are a living reminder to Christians of the vocational calling to be hospitable to outsiders. Eugene Rogers notes that our very existence – as people who turn to alternative means of creating our families – are a reminder to all Christians that we are *all* products of adoption as God's children (Rogers 1999: 260). Paradoxically, our status as heirs of God also transforms us from outsiders to a place where there is neither inside nor outside. In the words of James Alison, our status as heirs of God brings us from the margins and the periphery to 'being in on the centre of things without being the centre' (Alison 2003: 72). In short, through God's adoption, we are loved for who we are, period.

Fruits of the Spirit

Even though we have been freed from the law, however, Paul warns us that this freedom should not be seen as an opportunity for self-indulgence (5.13). Rather, we must be guided by living in accordance with the Spirit (5.16). Specifically, we are to become 'slaves' to one another through love (5.13) and to follow the single commandment of loving neighbour as self (5.14).

It is not surprising, therefore, that the fruits of the Spirit are acts that are focused on the neighbour or the 'other': love, joy, peace, patience, kindness, generosity, faithfulness, gentleness and self-control (5.22). The 'works of the flesh', by contrast, are the opposite of these things: acts that focus on the self, such as enmities, strife, jealousy, anger, and so on (5.19–21), and that serve as a barrier to inheriting the commonwealth of God (5.21).

For LGBT people, this means that we are called to avoid both extremes of 'legalism and licence' so that we can 'love one another' (Glaser 1994: 7/9). Chris Glaser cites a number of examples of how we can act responsibly and be 'responsible to our community,' such as respecting how individuals want to name themselves (for example, honouring phrases such as 'African-American' or 'PWA') and by honouring our commitments to our sisters and brothers in the LGBT community (for example, calling someone when we say that we will). As queer Christians, we are called to live – pun intended! – as fruits of the Spirit.

It should be noted that the 'works of the flesh' referred to by Paul in Galatians 5.19–21 – including references to fornication, impurity and licentiousness – should not be read as condemning sexual orientation or queer sexualities *per se*. Rather, they are referring to acts of 'hostility, anger, and hate' and the ways in which we 'use people as things' instead of respecting other people (Truluck 2000: 178). In fact, Rembert Truluck argues that the 'works of the flesh' include precisely the kind of 'legalistic, judgemental religion' that blindly condemns LGBT people and fails to respect us as children of God (Truluck 2000: 178–9; see also Glaser 1994: 8/30).

Neither Queerness nor Unqueerness

Paul concludes his letter by reminding the Galatians that ultimately what matters is not circumcision or uncircumcision, but rather a new creation in Jesus Christ (6.15). That is, one is called to live as if the world has been crucified (6.14). Such countercultural values include communal values such as bearing each others' burdens (6.2) and working for the good of all (6.10).

For queer Christians today, living as if the world has been crucified means affirming our very existence as LGBT people and responding to human needs because we are a 'new creation' and not because of the demands of the law (Truluck 2000: 63). By creating all kinds of new communities and families (including polyamorous and open relationships), we challenge the heteronormative values of the world and engage in a new creation in Jesus Christ. And, paradoxically, what matters ultimately is not queerness or unqueerness, but rather a new discovery of the richness of the commonwealth of God from being 'just as we are' (Alison 2003: xii).

A Queer Asian American Perspective

As noted in the introduction, I read Galatians from the perspective of a queer Christian. Specifically, the letter affirms how Jesus Christ sets us free from the legalistic codes of sexual conduct that are imposed on us by right-wing fundamentalist Christians. These individuals are the modern-day equivalents of the false teachers who insisted upon circumcision for the Galatians.

As a queer person of Asian descent, however, I read Galatians with another lens. That is, I not only read Galatians as critiquing those right-wing fundamentalist Christians who would impose their own legalistic codes of sexual conduct on us, but I also read Galatians as critiquing the ways in which the dominant queer Christian community often imposes its own codes of conduct upon people of colour and other minorities within the community.

Many queer Asians of faith wrestle with issues that are simply not acknowledged by the dominant queer Christian community. Not only do we wrestle with the homophobia of our families and religious communities, we also wrestle with the racism of our churches and the larger LGBT community (Cheng 2002; 2004; Kim 2004; Lee 2004; Lim 1998). Like the Gentiles in Galatia who searched in vain for an affirmation of their uncut penises, those of us who are gay Asian men often search in vain for an affirmation of our penises in a world of 'white men and white male beauty' (Fung 1998: 118). As such, many of us are ashamed of our identities and try to conform to the dominant culture by rejecting our ethnic and cultural heritage. In our desire to be accepted, we take on the language, food, dress, spirituality and customs of the dominant community to such a degree that we sometimes ignore or fail to reach out to our LGBT Asian sisters and brothers, even when we are in the same space such as a coffee shop, dance club, bar or church.

Galatians can speak powerfully to those of us who are of queer Asian descent, as well as other queer Christians of colour. Specifically, it frees us from the yoke of slavery to the implicit codes of conduct that are imposed by the dominant white queer community. We have been commissioned by God to minister to our community (see for example, Queer Asian Spirit, www. queerasianspirit.org, dedicated to the spiritual lives of LGBT people of Asian descent). We are called to engage in the fruits of the Spirit by loving our fellow queer Asian siblings as ourselves.

A recent example of queer Asians ministering to ourselves occurred in April 2005, when the Gay Asian Pacific Islander Men of New York (GAPIMNY) sponsored a ground-breaking workshop on queer Asian erotic spirituality, which was attended by around thirty gay men of Asian descent. During the course of the workshop, the participants engaged in a number of exercises relating to breathing, sharing and connecting body with spirit. By participating in this radically new creation of queer Asian community, we discovered our beauty and the richness of being loved by God, just as we are.

Ephesians

ROBERT E. GOSS

The letter to the Ephesians presents a number of challenges. In the first place, there is a general consensus that Colossians and Ephesians were not written by the hand of Paul and were authored somewhat later than the death of Paul towards the end of the first century CE. It is pseudonymous work, written in the name of Paul. It appears that the author is a Hellenistic Jewish Christian, perhaps a minority in a church community composed of Gentile and Jewish Christians. The language 'you once walked . . .' (2.2) and 'we also once lived in passions according to the flesh' (2.3) makes a case from a Jewish Christian perspective and reflects the genre of Jewish pseudepigraphy (Yee 2005: 35–70; MacDonald 2000: 16–17). The author is probably from a Pauline church or a church heavily influenced by Paul, and he provides a more comprehensive and sustained interpretation of Paul's teachings than Colossians.

The earliest Greek manuscript of Ephesians reads 'to the saints and faithful in Christ Jesus' (1.1). It appears that at a later time some copyist decided to localize the letter and added 'in Ephesus' to 'the saints' (MacDonald 2000: 192) Second, the letter is written in a different style from Paul's letters and unlike Paul's original letters does not address any particular social or communal problem. The original letter was probably sent to a number of congregations in Asia Minor because its scope is for a broader audience than a local church and shares with Colossians a great interest in universal salvation as a present reality. Ephesians takes the form of liturgical prayers, hymns and exhortations like a sermon.

Thematically, the first half of the letter envisions the Church as a new community where Jews and Gentiles share equally in God's blessings while the second half appeals to church unity through household rules (5.21–6.9) and a Christology that supports a patriarchal family and patriarchal church. Household rules (5.21–6.9) are incorporated into the letter. There are other sets of household rules in Colossians 3.18–4.1 and 1 Peter 2.13–3.12. These are patriarchal household duties spelled out for wife and husband, children and father, and slaves and masters.

Towards the end of the first century CE, many churches had to find peaceful accommodation with the Roman empire until the return of Christ. A new vision of Christianity took shape, abandoning the radical elements of Jesus' message of changing the world and Paul's translation of that message. Earlier itinerant preachers like Paul stressed that all Christians were on an equal footing through baptism (Gal. 3.28) and called for sexual restraint or asceticism. Christians were accused of social improprieties by their cultural adversaries, for they disturbed the Graeco-Roman patriarchal order with their egalitarian vision of household relationships. Since the patriarchal household was a microcosm for the state, equal arrangements between wife/husband, children/father, and slaves/master were regarded as subversive of the Roman state. Elisabeth Schüssler Fiorenza writes,

> Patriarchal *familia* was the nucleus of the state. Not enthusiasm but conversion of subordinate members of the house who were supposed to share in the religion of the *paterfamilias* constituted a revolutionary subversive threat. (Schüssler Fiorenza 1983 (2002): 264)

Moreover, patriarchal governance of the household defined masculinity, and the Roman empire was based on a strong affirmation of clearly defined masculinity in the *paterfamilias* and his wielding of strength and power within the household. Jennifer Glancy notes, 'Presiding over a household required the display of women, children, and slaves who manifested appropriate submission, as well as the other virtues that promised individual and social good order' (Glancy 2003: 265).

These household codes in Colossians and Ephesians are second- and third-generation Christian concerns. Generally, these Christians stopped believing that the end was imminent and began to devise rules on how to function in households in the world. These patriarchal household codes, adopted by several Christian letter-writers in Asia Minor, intended to prove that Christians were socially respectable and free from social improprieties in the lack of clearly defined household roles and hierarchy. In the chapter on Colossians, Tom Bohache correctly considers the letter a piece of patriarchal propaganda of second-generation Christianity. Bohache takes a hermeneutics-of-suspicion approach to deflect its patriarchal underpinnings of an exclusive male-dominated church as revealed in Colossians. Ephesians falls in the same genre of Christian patriarchal propaganda, and some textual readings of the household codes have been favourites of fundamentalist Christians propagating a violent and aggressive Christianity such as the Promise-Keepers to assert patriarchal control over their wives, and Roman Catholics to restrict women from ordained ministry. Can the letter speak to the queer Christian communities without such patriarchal toxicity? Or is it irredeemable and should it be excised from the canon as an unfortunate footnote in Christian history?

Personally, I like the first half of the letter to the Ephesians where the author uses Christology to provide a social, theological and liturgical reconciliation of Gentile and Jewish Christians. He employs a high Christology for the purpose of Christian inclusion, though unfortunately he does not speak of the relationship of Christians to non-Christians. It is in the latter part of the letter that I resort to a queer reading to turn the text inside-out and to read at the seams of the texts any messages that might be meaningful to twenty-first-century queer Christians.

Thus, queer Christian communities should not avoid wrestling with this text and its patriarchal difficulties, but read it as a warning when the egalitarian vision of the Jesus movement waned and the desire to fit in with the Roman culture became a paramount strategy and goal. Is there something we can learn in the twenty-first century?

The Social Context of Ephesians

Towards the end of the first century CE, Jesus' message of the reign of God transformed into a spiritual state accessible through rituals and household codes. There are a number of fragments of verses indicating an origin of liturgical practice of Christians. They include hymns, thanksgiving prayers and allusions to baptism and visionary prayer experiences. From these liturgical fragments, the author reflects an emerging Christology that perceives Christ as a cosmic figure who is one with God the Father, universal Saviour, and head of the Church.

For many second- and third-generation Christians, the Roman empire was no longer considered the enemy. With the rise of the Flavian emperors and their administrative reforms, the Roman empire was considered in a positive light. Horsley and Silberman write about the evolutionary change of view of empire:

> so pervasive was the eventual acceptance of the empire that the image of Christ was slowly transformed from that of an alternative king to that of a model emperor presiding over a shadow government in heaven and showing by example how things should be on earth. A new generation of Christian leaders accepted and creatively adapted the main elements of the dominant imperial milieu to their own spiritual ends. (Horsley and Silberman 1997: 225)

The notion of universal ruler became the dominating metaphor for the cosmic Christ whose rule would bring peace and unity. It is a Pax Christi that parallels the Pax Romana. Christ brings reconciliation, unity, love and peace without the force of military might and arms. It is God's grace in the death of Jesus that effects this spiritual creation of the Church.

Ephesians speaks to a situation found in Acts and 1 Peter where communities were comprised of a majority of Gentiles and a dwindling Jewish minority (MacDonald 2000: 19). The evil of the Gentile world is described in strong terms (2.1–3; 4.17–5.20; 6.10–20), and Margaret MacDonald notes the church in Ephesians is an introversionist community, 'displaying a very strong sense of separation from the outside world' (MacDonald 2000: 256). The Church is concerned with communal identity in the world, social boundaries with the Gentiles, and doing battle with the evil of the world. Dwelling in Christ (2.6) allows believers to escape, in part, from the social world into a spiritual realm ruled by Christ, yet their households are integrated into the Graeco-Roman world of Asia Minor. There is simultaneously a strong anxiety, regarding how Christians fit into the cultural world of the Roman empire near the end of the first century CE. John Elliott delineates the social environment in Asia Minor for the community of 1 Peter:

> It was a time when the expansion of the Christian movement in Asia Minor and its growing visibility as a distinct socio-religious entity was being encountered with suspicion, fear, and anxiety. Spread throughout all of the provinces north of Taurus, the sect had attracted rural as well as urban elements of the population, former Jews as well as a predominant number

of pagans. Living on the margin of political and social life, these *paroikoi*, 'resident aliens' no doubt had seen in this new salvation movement new opportunity for social acceptance and improvement in their economic lot. Coming from the already suspect ranks of strangers, resident aliens, and lower classes, however, these 'Christ-lackeys' gained only further disdain for the exotic religion they embraced. Sporadic local outbreaks of slander and abuse had led to the suffering of these Christians here as elsewhere throughout the world. (Elliott 1981: 83–4)

Christians were perceived as atheists, being without God in their refusal to participate in the state cult of worship of the emperor, and subverting the social fabric of the Roman empire by corrupting households. They subverted the patriarchal household in their conversion to Christianity and in not remaining faithful adherents of the religion of the head of the household. Christians preached the equality of all believers before God through baptism. Christianity preached equality between Jews and Gentiles, male and female, slave and master in its baptismal rituals and its proclamation of an inclusive gospel of grace. The vision of Jesus promoted by Paul preached a message of sexual renunciation.

Pax Christi: Peace and Unity between Gentile and Jewish Christians

Tension between Jewish and Gentile believers persisted through the first century, and MacDonald speculates that 2.11–22 addresses a community now dominated by Gentiles and a dwindling Jewish minority (MacDonald 2000: 19). It may reflect the social situation of many Christian communities in Asia Minor towards the end of the first century CE.

The covenanted ethnocentrism of Judaism fleshed otherness in the Gentiles, for the Gentiles lacked the mark of the covenant: circumcision. Through circumcision, Jewishness and Jewish masculinity were self-defined. The author speaks of Gentiles over and against the community and attaches them to powers of the world and to the lower aeons. He harnesses the language of angelology and demonology to describe the relationship and social distance between the covenanted community and the Gentiles, for Christ 'is our peace; in his flesh he has made both groups into one and has broken down the dividing wall, that is, the hostility between us' (2.14). Christ's death has put an end to hostility between Gentile and Jewish Christians, and Gentiles are citizens with the saints and members of the household of God (2.19).

The author uses the earlier Pauline notions of equality in Christ, for Jesus' death has removed the barriers between Jews and Gentiles by bringing together both Jews and Gentiles into a new, unified community. The Jewish law, which previously distinguished and divided Jew from Gentile, was rendered irrelevant by the cross, and Christ thus reconciled both groups to each other and to God (2.14–16). According to Ephesians, human existence is beset by the malevolent influence of demonic beings. Christ has been given power over them, and through God's grace human beings may be freed from their

immoral and deceitful influences. The new life of believers is one of knowledge and spiritual power, and thus there is the recurring contrast of the old
life with the new (2.1–6, 11–13, 19; 4.22–4; 5.8).

At a time when Christian churches exclude folk and are publicly committed to aggressive and violent practices, the writer of Ephesians understands
the gospel as one of peace and inclusion. Jesus' legacy to his community is
non-violence and inclusiveness. This speaks powerfully to me as a queer cleric
ministering to groups marginalized by Christianity: leather folk, queers into
B/D-S/M, transgendered people, cross-dressers, gay and lesbian families,
queer families, and other configurations that do not easily fit into society. I
envision and have worked to create such a diverse community that reflects
Jesus' gospel of peace and the realizations that each of us reflects the image
of the risen Christ. Christ has died to be individually reflected in the infinite
diversity of people, and the gospel does not homogenize but unites all such
non-conformity and diversity in the vision of the cosmic Christ. This may not
be fully the intention of the author of Ephesians, but there is always a sur-
plus of meaning in the text that the author may not have consciously intended.
Christ's non-violent love allows a practice of radical inclusion rooted in a peace
through the death of Jesus the Christ.

Can queer churches become inclusive enough to include heterosexual
Christians? From my own ministry grounded in the gospel of peace and radical inclusion, I would affirm such a possibility for queer churches to open
themselves and become genuinely queer by being thoroughly inclusive. This
is beyond the tokenism of some current churches that welcome queer folk
but will not bless their unions or ordain openly queer candidates. The author
notes, 'In him the whole structure is joined together and grows into a holy temple in the Lord; in whom you also are built together spiritually into a dwelling-
place for God' (2.21).

Fit into Society at What Costs?

Rather than advocating a complete renewal of family relationships based on
life, forgiveness and mutual submission, however, the author's Christology is
used to justify theologically the structure and duties of the ancient Graeco-
Roman patriarchal family (5.22–6.9). It seems that Christian communities
at the end of the first century CE (and the author of Ephesians, in particular)
adopted the Graeco-Roman household codes either as a survival strategy or
at least as defensive strategies against their outside critics (Tanzer 1994b: 330).
Equality and unity of Jews and Gentile Christians in Christ is qualified by
these household codes. The household code instructs Christians 'to lead a life
worthy of the calling to which you have been called' (4.1).

The whole community is perceived as a household, and believers are God's
children (5.1, 8; 1.15). In 5.22ff., the subordinate group (wives, children and
slaves) are highlighted first while the dominant group (husbands, fathers and
masters) are placed in the superordinate position: 'Be subject to one another
out of reverence for Christ' (5.21). This is preliminary advice to a Christian

household. The author of Ephesians adapts the rules of the household to the church, for Christian couples, families, slaves and masters, but he modifies 5.21–33 by 'replacing patriarchal superordination and domination with the Christian command to love to be lived according to the example of Christ' (Schüssler Fiorenza 1983 (2002): 270). Husbands are commanded three times to love their wives (5.25, 28, 33) while wives are instructed to be submissive to their husbands.

The author presents a Graeco-Roman 'traditional family values' platform that would appeal to Graeco-Romans of the late first century CE. The family values in 5.22–33 call Christian believers to match or exceed the household codes in their ethical behaviour. Peter Brown has written how Ephesians abandoned the chilling tone of sexual renunciation in 1 Corinthians but centred marital relations within society and the universe. The image of Christ and the church 'provided Christians with an image of unbreakable order that the pagan world could understand. In the church, as in the city, the concord of a married couple was made to bear the heavy weight of expressing the ideal harmony of a whole society' (Brown 1988: 57). While the author speaks of church apostles, evangelists, prophets, pastors and teachers (4.12), he curiously neither asks the community to be subordinate to the leaders in a patriarchal hierarchy nor does he claim that the leaders represent God. They are exempt from the hierarchical household rules.

What is apparent in Ephesians is the trajectory of Pauline communities, inculturating in the Roman empire. Rather than building on emancipatory notions of women in the Graeco-Roman world or earlier notions of the discipleship of equals, the author of Ephesians chose codes patriarchal and restrictive of women. This is a clear developmental stage in the patriarchalization of Christianity in the second century CE where a male clerical hierarchy started to replace the earlier gender and communal equality.

The author combines the Pauline notion of bride/bridegroom (2 Cor. 11.2) with the household codes and a love ethic. The Christ–Church relationship becomes the model for the husband–wife relationship. Christology is used to reinforce the submission of wives to their husbands. The 'headship' of Christ hearkens to the patriarchal headship of the Roman emperor over the household of the empire. Christ's headship is an oppressive model that has traditionally been used to exalt the leadership of a clerical male caste over the non-ordained laity and male domination over females in marriage. Even though the example of Christ's sacrificial and self-giving love for the Church becomes the model, this deconstructive potential to the model of Christ's paradigmatic love for the Church has never taken a strong interpretative hold in Christianity. The feminist biblical scholar Elisabeth Schüssler Fiorenza evaluates the Christian household code:

> On the whole, however, the author was not able to Christianize the code. The 'gospel of peace' had transformed the relationship of Gentiles and Jews, but not the social roles of wives, children, and slaves within the household of God. On the contrary, the cultural social structures of domination are theologized and thereby reinforced (Schüssler Fiorenza 1983 (2002): 270).

For nineteen hundred years, the patriarchal Church has read this passage to buttress the hierarchical order of husbands over wives and give it theological justification. It glossed over, I believe, the radical potential of the model of Christ's love for the Church. A queer reading can reopen that potential of Christ-love for the church model and undermine the patriarchal domination model.

Queering Christ and the Body of Christ

Virginia Mollenkott notes Ephesians depicts collectively all believers as the bride of Christ (Eph. 5.25–7) and members of the body of Christ. (Eph. 5.30). She writes,

> If the body of Christ is assumed to be male, then women, by putting on Christ like a garment, are imaged as either androgynous he/shes or as transvestites.
>   And if Christ's body is assumed to be a male body (as the power structures of many churches still seem to indicate), yet the church itself is assumed to be female (as the numbers in the pews would still seem to indicate), then the church itself is a he/she, a transgender entity. Furthermore, since the men in Ephesus were called Christ's bride – and by extension, all Christian men were called Christ's bride – then the New Testament has used imagery of a same-sex marriage in which a 'male' Christ marries not only Christian women but millions of male brides. (Mollenkott 2001: 110)

Mollenkott points out the obvious, but Christian gender hierarchies have prevented or even blinded readers recognizing the simple transgender nature of the Church as the bride of Christ or as the body of Christ. She concludes, 'such biblical gender blending ought to encourage those who take scripture seriously to become less rigid about gender identities, roles, and presentations' (Mollenkott 2001: 112). In a similar vein, the lesbian theologian Elizabeth Stuart notes how she used to wince when Ephesians 5.21–3 was read at heterosexual weddings and how a paper from the theologian Gerard Loughlin has transformed her reaction to this passage from tragic to comic. Loughlin writes,

> (the heteropatriarchal readings of this text) . . . undermined and washed away in the deeper waters of Christian symbolic, for insofar as women are members of the body, they too are called to be Christ to others; so that they too must act as 'groom' and 'husband' to the 'bride' and 'wife' of the other, whether it be as actual man or woman. For it cannot be said that within the community only men are called to love as Christ does . . . (Stuart 2000: 32)

Stuart takes the queer images of a transgendered Christ seriously: a male with a female body and the Church represented as a female body with a male head (Stuart 2000: 32; 2003: 111). Mollenkott and Stuart have picked up and highlighted the queer underpinnings of Ephesians 5.21–30 – so easily glossed over for centuries by patriarchal readings. What we have is a text that can be used to justify same-sex and transgendered marriages. Women are expected to act as Christ through the rite of baptism, for they identify as grooms and husbands and love their wives. Men are to act as Christ and love female-to-male transgendered husbands/grooms. The solidity of Christian gender identities is liquefied first through the sacramental rite of baptism where the believer reflects and lives Christ. The parody of a queer reading actually brings out the full intent of the text of Ephesians 5.21–30. Christology realizes its ultimate queer potential in a transgendered Christ – full of fluid identities (Goss 2002: 170–82). With such a queer reading, the exhortation to love your wife as Christ loves the Church may successfully Christianize the household.

Queer Households

Queer households are thoroughly diverse (Goss and Strongheart 1997), from pair-bonded same-sex relationships, extended families, polyamorous relationships, communal relationships, to master/slave families. Certainly, the household rules for marriages have been limited to pair-bonded, heterosexual marriage until recently. A queer reading of the text allows gender fluidity. If the image of the bride as 'holy and without blemish' (5.27) refers to the baptismal rite as many scholars believe, we find a confusion of images. Baptism, from earlier Pauline times, was understood as the identification with the risen Christ for many diverse men and women. Paul stated bluntly, 'It is no longer I who live, but Christ who lives in me' (Gal. 2.20). Similarly, the body of Christ or the Church is a corporate entity, consisting of innumerable male, female, intersexual and transgendered baptized individuals with Christ living in them. With the fluid gender composition of Christ and the body of Christ, bride and bridegroom become thoroughly queer metaphors with incredible gender elasticity and fluidity. The variations of males and females reflecting Christ and the body of Christ allows for multiple queer configurations of relations: same-sex marital relations, polyamorous, and communal relationships.

Mark Jordan has noted how the fear of agapic excess has limited marital theology, and how queer relationship can impact Christian marriage theology:

> Queer relationships, so far as they are presumed to be 'open,' do destroy Christian marriage in this sense, that they destroy cherished fictions about what it has accomplished. The chief theological accomplishment of Christian marriage is supposed to be that it settles the ancient enmity between eros and agape by granting a restricted title for eros within the universal field of agape. 'You can exercise eros so long as you do so with the minimum number of other (!) people – namely one.' To increase the minimum number throws the truce into doubt. (Jordan 2005: 166)

Queer desire and relationships disrupt the tidiness of Christian patriarchal marriage.

Marriage has been a patriarchal institution – a two-gendered, hierarchically ordered relation blessed by churches and legally recognized. With the advent

of same-sex civil unions and marriage, there has been a rush for many queer
folk to take the plunge and to fight for marriage equality rights. The Ephesian
community tried to fit into Graeco-Roman society by adopting patriarchal
household codes. Even the author's attempt to Christianize the household
codes with the model of Christ's love for the Church, patriarchal justification
for the Church and marriage hierarchy, became normative for centuries until
recently. Is there a warning here for the queer Christian community? Can we
adapt the model of marriage and retain mutuality, equality, flexibility and
sometimes the openness in our relationships? Can we succeed in attaining
the legal benefits and privileges for marriage without sacrificing our creative thinking about relationships, families and intimate partnerships? Can
we allow and support other configured-style relationships such as our queer
reading of Ephesians seems to support?

Philippians

JUSTIN TANIS

Scholars agree that Philippians is undoubtedly a genuine letter of Paul's, but do not come to consensus on the question of where it was written. Nevertheless, it is clear that this is a letter composed while Paul was imprisoned, with a sure and reasonable knowledge that his life was in danger as a result of his missionary activities. It is also clear that this is a letter reflecting a faith that sustained him in the face of threats and challenges, a faith that cared deeply for the well-being of others and that he longed to have lived out among the churches.

Christianity of Paul's time was a religion practised in the margins, in the shadows, in the prisons, and not yet a state religion. In fact, to be a member of Christ's Church was explicitly to be allied outside of the regions of the acceptable, outside of the legal and condoned. In addition, Philippi was a Roman colony, and thus both of the empire and outside of it. Roman in mindset and authority, yet it was also a place where different peoples and streams of thought could come together.

The letter to the Philippians only makes sense when viewed with this context actively in mind. It is in this way that it is queer. It is a perspective from the margins and is a letter written by and to those that the larger society viewed as unacceptable and illegitimate, but by and for those who had discovered a joy that the condemnations of society could not dampen.

The challenge of the epistles is that they have been read as doctrine when they are, in fact, personal letters. Paul's literary gift, indeed, is that he allows all of himself to flow through this correspondence – his insecurities, his joys, his patience and his impatience and so on. This is decidedly not a good basis for policy; it does, however, allow us to gain more understanding of who Paul was as a person. Arguably, Paul's ideas and beliefs shaped the reality of what the Christian Church was to become as much as or more than Jesus' own did, and therefore understanding more about him is useful to us as modern-day people of faith.

There are a number of themes to this epistle that readily lend themselves to a queer reading. First is the concept of companionship. This book is one that explores the support that people give one another and how they are together through thick and thin, through danger and rejoicing. We see Paul's reliance on other men as well as his willingness to put their well-being ahead of his own. This letter is, in part, about the importance of people to each other. Queer people know this; we know the ability to come together, to bond, to support and to affirm one another. We value companionship.

This letter is also about community, a community formed both by shared

beliefs and by the crucible of a hostile world. The early Christians shared
their faith in Jesus Christ and they had in common the dangers of living in the
Roman empire which had no love for their kind. For oppressed communities,
it would be a danger to ignore either of these factors – that we come together
out of the commonality of our sexual orientations and gender identities and
because we live in a world that is at times violently opposed to those differences. Who we are shapes how we live; how we live shapes who we are. This
is true for us as individuals and as communities. This was also true for the
Philippians.

Paul also examines what it means to be abased and to be exalted. This is
informed, surely, by his life perspective as both a religious insider and outsider. He separates the things that are valued by the governments of the world
and society from those things exalted by God.

Finally, there are some references to the body. Since queer bodies are treated
differently and live differently in our society, this is of importance to queer
people. It is in this area where queer thought is most sharply in contrast with
Paul's thinking about bodies. Paul has a strong ambivalence toward fleshly
existence and a disdain for the body, whereas queer people have a strong
grounding in the meaning and value of the body, its desires and needs.

Our exploration of Philippians begins with what we know about Paul's previous encounter with the community at Philippi.

Paul's visit to Philippi: Acts 16

Paul's letter to the Philippians is informed by looking at what we know of
Paul's earlier encounters with the people of Philippi. Acts 16 describes Paul
and Silas' visit to the city in some detail. When they first enter the city, they
head for the river, where they seek to find a place of prayer. And, indeed they
find such a place, but not at all in the form that they might have expected.
Instead, they find a group of women gathered, including Lydia, a dealer in
purple cloth. Lydia is from Thyratira, someone who has settled in Philippi and
is a worshipper of God, which meant that she practised many of the aspects
of Judaism but was not a convert. Lydia is so receptive to the preaching of the
missionaries that she is baptized, along with her entire household, and then
persuades Paul and Silas to come and stay in her home.

A little later they encounter a slave, a young woman who we are told has the
gift of telling the future. Her owners make a profit on her skills. After she follows Paul and Silas around for a number of days, they rebuke the spirit in her,
making her now unable to predict the future. This infuriates her owners, who
drag Paul and Silas down to the magistrates. They were severely flogged and
thrown into jail, where they prayed and sang hymns to pass the time. While
in jail, an earthquake struck the city; the prisoners' chains came loose and all
the doors of the prison were thrown open. Just as the jailer was about to commit suicide, thinking that the prisoners had escaped, Paul called out to him to
let him know that they were all still present. This led the jailer to convert to
Christianity as well.

Paul and Silas were released the next day, with the authorities very disturbed that they had beaten and imprisoned Roman citizens without a trial.

The two men went to Lydia's house to leave a last word of encouragement with the believers and then, wisely, left town before more trouble could ensue.

Thus, Paul's previous encounters with the people of Philippi centred around relationships with very different people – two women, one with an independent means of income and the head of a household, the other completely dependent and at the bottom of the social hierarchy, and a man employed by the Romans for whom death was a better option than dealing with the consequences of a natural happening. The examples given in Acts show the Christians reaching people of varying social and economic strata, of different genders, and of multiple ethnic and national backgrounds. Paul and Silas react to their imprisonment with acts of faith and worship, rather than despair and fear.

In Paul's letter to the Philippians, we see the same themes emerging – the importance of human relationships, engagement of both women and men in leadership, and the kind of faith that is sustaining in the face of injustice and oppression.

Relationships

In this letter, Paul talks forthrightly about his affection for those who serve with him, highlighting the contributions and qualities of his companions. This is particularly notable in Philippians 2.19–24, where he writes,

> I hope in the Sovereign Jesus to send Timothy to you soon, so that I may be cheered by news of you. I have no one like him who will be genuinely concerned for your welfare. All of them are seeking their own interests, not those of Jesus Christ. But Timothy's worth you know, how like a son with his father he has served with me in the work of the gospel. I hope therefore to send him as soon as I see how things go with me; and I trust in the Saviour that I will also come soon.
>
> Still, I think it necessary to send to you Epaphroditus – my brother and co-worker and fellow soldier, your messenger and minister to my need; for he has been longing for all of you, and has been distressed because you heard that he was ill. He was indeed so ill that he nearly died. But God had mercy on him, and not only on him but on me also, so I would not have one sorrow after another. I am the more eager to send him, therefore, in order that you may rejoice at seeing him again, and that I may be less anxious. Welcome him then in the Sovereign with all joy, and honour such people, because he came close to death for the work of Christ, risking his life to make up for those services that you could not give me.

This section serves as a reminder to us that this is indeed a letter, exchanging news and information between people separated by distance who deeply care about each other. Here Paul focuses on relationships between the people active in the early Christian movement. We see the level of hardship that they endured in order to do the work they were called to do as well as the reality that some in the movement were self-centred.

Paul's affection for Timothy and Epaphroditus comes through here. One commentator called Paul's use of father/son imagery patronizing and a reflection of the patriarchal culture; it reminds me, however, of the intimacy of Daddy/boy relationships in the queer world (not limited to biological males). Daddies take on parental responsibilities for rearing their boys to become stronger adults. This may well have begun in response to the disconnect experienced between many gay men and their straight fathers, in which the father was unable to provide the kind of parenting a gay boy needed. Thus, as an adult, a gay man might select a father figure, a Daddy, to assist him with the developmental tasks that were left unaddressed in his childhood. These relationships include mentoring, accountability, affection and love. In the same way, Paul has guided and cared deeply about the men with whom he is serving.

Paul is also concerned that Epaphroditus can return to Philippi with his head held high and under no allegations that he is a quitter. He has been ill and homesick and Paul recognizes that and wants him to be reunited with his community. Paul thinks beyond his own needs, as dire as they might be at the moment, to seek the best for both this individual and the community. Therefore, he urges the community to be welcoming to Epaphroditus and is sending him home.

It is clear that Paul relied on his companions for spiritual, emotional and physical support. Yet as important as they are to him, he recognizes the need for them to return to the community at Philippi and to serve there as well. He is grateful for his need for them, but not selfish.

Community

Right from the beginning, Paul makes a statement about the different nature of the new Christian community. He begins the letter with a customary greeting, but Paul combines the Greek forms of opening, 'Grace to you' with the Hebrew, 'Peace from God', showing the kind of synthesis that is possible. Here he shows that the dominion and gospel of Jesus Christ are for more than one nation. It is an inclusive opening. One could also read the concept of peace here as an emphasis that peace comes from divine sources, not from an imperial authority such as the *Pax Romana*.

Note, too, that Philippians 1 starts with the story of two men working together. Right from the beginning, Paul establishes the relational tone by emphasizing that he and Timothy are a team, both slaves of Christ, spreading the gospel together. This is a letter of partners to other partners.

The role of the community is critical because Paul shows his confidence that the work of an individual is confirmed and continued by the community. What matters is not what one of us does alone with a good work, but what we are able to bring to completion together. Given his precarious situation, in prison and possibly facing death, it is certainly a consolation to him that the communities that he has founded will go on to achieve what he has striven so hard for.

We who have lost so many to Aids know the importance of continuing the work of people who are not able to complete their life's work themselves. There is continuity in community. One of the ways in which Aids has impacted us spiritually has been a sense of needing to continue the work begun by those who have died. There is so much beauty in art that they would have created that we'll never see; so many political advances that will take that much longer now; so much living that simply won't happen.

One of us may die, thousands of us, even tens of thousands of us and more may die, but the movement continues. The community is that which embodies the longings, the dreams and the actions of all of us. This is one of the strengths of the queer community. We have had a strong interplay between the efforts of individuals who devote their lives to expanding our civil rights, our social spaces, our sexual freedoms and our culture and the bulk of community who have made those things come to pass. The efforts of one and the efforts of the community work together to achieve what we long for. This is what Paul meant. It is more important what we do together than what a single star can achieve. And yet the efforts of every individual are also important.

Paul also uses words of passion in this passage, words of longing. The Greek words he uses describe the kind of longing that originates in the guts, from the very bowels of our being and of Jesus'. Queer people know about passion. Queer people know what is worth risking for passion, as well. One of the points that Paul is making is that he is passionate about the gospel and filled with longing for this community. He longs for their presence and desires deeply that which is best for them.

Paul recognized the fluid nature of community and also the very human challenges we face in forming and sustaining healthy communities. In Philippians 1.27–30, he writes,

> Only, live your life in a manner worthy of the gospel of Christ, so that, whether I come and see you or am absent and hear about you, I will know that you are standing firm in one spirit, striving side by side with one mind for the faith of the gospel, and are in no way intimidated by your opponents. For them this is evidence of their destruction, but of your salvation. And this is God's doing. For God has graciously granted you the privilege not only of believing in Christ, but of suffering for him as well – since you are having the same struggle you saw I had and now hear that I still have.

For those who genuinely care about one another, being separated doesn't matter in one sense. People still know that they are loved (moments of insecurity aside), whether or not they are together. One of the things I love about queer culture is that we are everywhere. I can be visiting a small town where I know no one and can find my way into a gay bar and people will talk to me. There is a common cultural language and enough of a shared experience that we spot each other and nurture connections with total strangers.

Paul is also advocating a way of living that is open and distinct. Even though people are attempting to intimidate the Philippian church, he does not want them to assimilate or operate in hiding. This is critical for queer people. We know the power of coming out.

The Transgender Day of Remembrance has emerged as an annual event in October to remember those people who were killed because of their gender differences. There was a particularly moving commemoration in Los Angeles last year; there were 30 or so murdered transpeople who had been killed that year and the same number of people had been recruited to represent them. They stood in a long line at the front of an MCC church and read a brief biography of each slain person. An elderly cross-dresser read about a teen who was female bodied and male identified who had been shot; a transman read about a transwoman who had been killed by a police officer; a white sheriff's deputy in uniform spoke with great emotion in the voice of a Brazilian prostitute deliberately run over by a car. Each person a separate story. Then we all got up and marched out into the streets, down to a memorial park named for Matthew Shepard, the young gay man who had been brutally beaten and left to die. Because we would not be intimidated by our opponents, we went back onto the streets. Death and oppression cannot have the last word; we declared the streets safe that night. And this is the dominion of God at work – we are each other, we are working side by side, with one mind, as Paul declares, refusing to give in to the forces of oppression.

Paul goes on to say, 'If then there is any encouragement in Christ, any consolation from love, any sharing in the Spirit, any compassion and sympathy, make my joy complete: be of the same mind, having the same love, being in full accord and of one mind' (2.1–2). He is dealing with the reality of discord that arises within communities. Whenever you gather a group of people together, you will find differences of approach, of attitude, of personality. This seems to be particularly true among oppressed people, perhaps because the stakes feel so high to us that we argue vehemently for the course of action that we believe will keep us safest or make us freer. Yet this leads to disharmony that causes us to do the work of the oppressors for them, creating internal strife that distracts us from the cause at hand.

Paul deals explicitly in chapter 4 with a conflict between two women, Euodia and Syntyche; much has been written on this, mostly speculative. Sadly, quite a bit of it reflects deeply sexist beliefs about women 'squabbling'. Yet, as Carolyn Osiek (2000: 247) points out, the mention of the women and their disagreement shows that they were important enough to the community that their argument was significantly disruptive to the community.

From a queer perspective, we might point out several things. First, it is a reflection of the value of both women and men to a community. Paul notes the work and commitment of these women. In the face of a conflict, Paul urges others to help them and to be in community with them as they seek resolution. He affirms that they have been co-workers who have struggled hard for the gospel. Second, internal discord is common in oppressed communities. Disagreements should not lead to the rupture of relationships but to a renewed commitment and closeness in order to resolve them.

In the queer communities, we could do well to heed Paul's advice. There remain fractures between lesbians and gay men, with both sides perpetuating stereotypes and at times even stooping to very juvenile scorn for the others' bodies. Being in the presence of the others' genitals (seen or unseen) is not a threat to our own sexuality. I still hear gay men and lesbians state quite emphatically that bisexuals won't get 'off the fence' or are afraid of coming out. It is often an uphill battle still to get organizations that use the acronym

'LGBT' to actually consider, much less genuinely include, the needs of bi and trans people. Organizations seeking political respectability argue that the leather community should stay out of sight at gay pride events. To those who oppose our rights, the differences between us are immaterial; we are all freaks and deviants to them. Therefore, we would do better to struggle beside one another rather than fight with each other.

Paul deeply values the experience of community and connection that he has with the Philippian community. There is something about the first community that nurtured us that we hold deeply and dearly. The first summer I came out, I worked in a United Church of Christ summer camp in downtown Philadelphia with four other queer teens and one straight one. We ran around the city, talking our way into gay bars, going to demonstrations, laughing long in the night and revelling in our newly developing understanding of ourselves. I will always remember those days as a kind of Queer Arcadia, a time of innocence and yet a coming out of innocence into a new knowledge of the world. I think this is similar to how Paul understood Philippi.

In addition, he knows he is most likely coming to the end of his life and so he is saying his thank-yous and goodbyes to this community that is so important to him. He is talking about what the community gave to him, both materially and intangibly. It is most likely because of this perspective that this theme of community rings through this letter so clearly.

Power

Immediately as Paul begins this letter, he engages language of power – slaves, overseers, saints and sovereigns. One of the radical ideas that Paul sets forth, one that the secular and religious authorities found objectionable about his preaching, is that the source of power comes from God, not from the principalities of this world. Christ turns the power structures of this world on their heads and thus changes, even queers, how we see authority, responsibility and power. This unfolds throughout this letter.

A number of translations, including the New Revised Standard Version, soften this language in the text to use more ecclesiastical language or words more common to the modern ear (such as servant for slave) while footnoting the more technically correct words. I believe that Paul means exactly what he is saying – he is talking about slavery, about power, about earthly rulers. To shy away from this language, to soften the text, means to erase what it is saying about how we are to relate to each other, what our allegiances are and how we are to understand the choices that our faith accords us.

In addition to referring to himself as a slave, Paul also used this language to reference Christ. In Philippians 2.3–11, he writes,

> Do nothing from selfish ambition or conceit, but in humility regard others as better than yourselves. Let each of you look not to your own interests, but to the interests of others. Let the same mind be in you that was in Christ Jesus,
>   who, though he was in the form of God,
>   did not regard equality with God as something to be exploited,

but emptied himself, taking the form of a slave,
being born in human likeness.
And being found in human form,
he humbled himself and became obedient to the point of death
– even death on a cross.
Therefore God also highly exalted him
and gave him the name that is above every name,
so that at the name of Jesus,
every knee should bend,
in heaven and on earth and under the earth,
and every tongue should confess that Jesus Christ is Sovereign,
to the glory of God the Creator.

This passage, usually understood as a eucharistic hymn, conveys a central paradox of Christianity – that humility leads to exaltation, that the last shall become the first.

Paul's use of the concept of slavery both for himself and for Christ is a challenging one for modern readers, because we view slavery primarily through the lens of the use of African slaves in the Americas in the seventeenth to nineteenth centuries. The late twentieth and early twenty-first centuries have seen a heightened awareness of freedom as an ideal for the world; in fact, President George W. Bush called upon Americans to be willing to 'pay any price' for freedom around the globe, while simultaneously seeking to curtail the freedom of queer people. Freedom seen in this way is not the ideal of all peoples on our planet, of course.

In the modern communities of sex radicals, there are people who live consensually as Master and slave, with the Masters pledging absolute responsibility and authority for the lives of the slaves, while the slaves pledge obedience and fealty to their owners. These relationships, freely entered into, are centred on stability, responsibility and service. A number of households draw directly from the monastic traditions for organization and structure. One way to view this queer phenomenon is to consider that the participants are choosing to turn away from the materialism and individualism of the world to pursue a path of radical relationship and compassion.

Those who identify as slaves eschew the accumulation of material possessions and dedicate themselves to someone else's comforts and pleasures. It is a way of moving beyond the egocentrism of our modern age and cultivating compassion for others. This is a time-honoured technique of many spiritual practices. In doing so, the slave finds a security and peace that she or he does not find in other ways of living. Even for the Master, the choice to accept the service of another person means taking on a higher level of responsibility for the ultimate well-being of the slave. He or she must ensure that the needs of all are being met, including food, shelter, health care, sex, clothing and so on. It is a deliberate act of interdependence that is sustaining and fulfilling for those called to this way of living.

If we were to see Paul's concept of slavery in this light, it helps us to envision it as a choice to live humbly and compassionately, putting aside the values of the larger culture in pursuit of a deeper relationship with both humanity and divinity. When Paul is his servant-self, thinking of himself as a slave, he writes here in deep and wonderful ways about community and thinks in terms of benefiting others. The troubling passages in Paul's writings are where he speaks in dominant and authoritative ways, laying down the law for others to follow. We might say that Paul's spiritual maturity is better seen when he speaks as slave, rather than as master.

In Barclay's commentary, he points out that the Greek word here used for 'form' means the ontological self, not a role that Jesus is playing as a slave, but that he is truly a slave (Barclay 2003: 43). One modern consensual slave explains, 'serving as a slave is the fulfillment of who and what she is within herself. Gender, shape and sexual preferences aside, a slave is only truly happy when in service to one who will master them' (www.masterslaveconference.org/presenters). Being willing to act with selflessness for others is at its core an expression of who we are, not simply an exterior garment that we put on.

This hymn goes on to explain that because Jesus was willing to be a slave and to subject himself to suffering, God then exalts him. This is not a quid pro quo situation. Jesus did not suffer in order to be exalted nor was the exaltation some sort of reward for suffering. Suffering is a fact of human life and the subject of much religious teaching. Awareness of suffering is considered in many religions the starting-point of the spiritual path.

In Jesus' case, Philippians states, Jesus is exalted because he entered into the suffering with humility and obedience as God wished. By following through with the path that was set before him, he is deserving of praise. One possible way to read this hymn is as praise for following one's own course, being true to our own calling, even (or especially) when it diverges from the socially acceptable or even conventionally wise.

I think it is important to separate this passage, and others like it, from the notion that God requires a human sacrifice for salvation or desires suffering for its own sake. Rather, Jesus' obedience and slavery, his willingness to give all that he has and all that he was in the service of God, was what led to the fulfilment of his mission and God's subsequent exalting of him.

Yet even if Paul sees himself spiritually as a slave, this does not mean that he concedes ground to the political authorities. In fact, in his mind his service requires him to be bold in speaking up to power. He writes, 'I want you to know, beloved, that what has happened to me has actually helped to spread the gospel, so that it has become known throughout the whole imperial guard and to everyone else that my imprisonment is for Christ; and most of the brothers and sisters, having been made confident in the Sovereign by my imprisonment dare to speak the word with greater boldness and without fear.'

It is ironic, isn't it, that sometimes the forces of oppression seeking to shut people up just make them louder? It is the ways in which we react to times of great difficulty that are often the very best witness that we can make for what drives us. The things that the authorities did to Paul to try to stop the Christian movement from spreading further actually had the effect of making the members of the imperial guard try to figure out what he was saying.

The assassination of the gay city councilman Harvey Milk in San Francisco in 1978 didn't drive queer people to huddle in their apartments, it made them take to the streets. The hate-fests led by Fred Phelps and his Westborough

Baptist Church have caused many people to rethink their stance on homosexuality. His rhetoric of God's hatred has led people to think about whether,
in fact, hatred is a characteristic of God. The *Washington Post* documented in
its series on 'Young and Gay in America' in 2004 the way in which a little town
in Oklahoma was galvanized in its support for a gay teen in their town when
Phelps came to protest Michael Shackelford's church. Michael reports that the
incidents of harassment that he experienced actually decreased after Phelps's
presence. People saw their prejudice mirrored and expanded in the Phelps
group's signs and turned away from it. This is the action of God in turning
hearts and minds.

At the same time that we are fighting our earthly battles, we have the comfort of knowing that we are full citizens in heaven. As Paul states in verse
3.20, 'our citizenship is in heaven', and in that sense we can know that we have
all the rights and dignities of any human being. It is our birthright from our
Creator. This reminds us, too, that God's realm is infinite while the powers of
the human world will pass away. We are citizens of something bigger than the
oppressive governments and societies in which we find ourselves on earth.
Remembering that in God's eyes we are full citizens empowers us to seek the
same rights here on earth. In this way, the humiliations visited upon us by an
oppressive system are transformed to glory, and submission is the basis for
exultation.

Suffering

Paul goes on to say in chapter 3, verses 10–11, 'I want to know Christ and the
power of his resurrection and the sharing of his sufferings by becoming like
him in his death, if somehow I may attain the resurrection from the dead.' The
'knowing' here refers in the Greek text to a personal knowledge, not just the
intellectual information. It is not knowing *about* God but knowing God. The
word here for 'to know' is the Greek translation of the word used euphemistically in the Hebrew Bible for sexual relations. It is an intimate knowledge, a
knowledge so deep as to be embedded in the body as well as the mind and
spirit. In the same way, the fact that resurrection of the body is important at all
reminds us that the body is important. Bodily knowledge is part of the contribution and development of our queer selves.

We should be careful of the concept of sharing in Christ's suffering that Paul
notes here. This passage has been misused to encourage women to remain
with battering husbands, to justify enforced celibacy on gay people who are
'allowed' by their churches to be gay but not 'avowed and practising homosexuals' and to tell trans people that they should not transition, but remain
in the pain of their birth gender by saying these are opportunities to relate to
Christ's suffering. It is used to justify the derailing of liberation movements.
Yet Christ's suffering is not a goal to be attained or a condition to be maintained; it is, in fact, the result of human systems of oppression. The useful
part of identifying with Christ's suffering is knowing that when we are faced
with hardship, God knows exactly what it is like to be in such a situation and
is present with us in the reality of it. But that in no way means that it is to

be encouraged. It is much easier to say that someone else should be allowed to suffer because it 'builds character' than to endure such suffering. Queer people live in close proximity to the suffering that an oppressive society can impose and therefore should reject such thinking.

The Body

As queer people, we know the importance of the body. We are distinguished from others, in fact, by the same-sex bodies we desire or the gender-queer bodies we inhabit. Paul, of course, is not known for his affirmations of the body; indeed he is a source of much of Christianity's historic dualism of body and spirit.

In Philippians 1.20–6, he writes,

It is my eager expectation and hope that I will not be put to shame in any way, but that by my speaking with boldness, Christ will be exalted now as always in my body, whether by life or by death. For me, living is Christ and dying is gain. If I am to live in the flesh, that means fruitful labour for me; and I do not know which I prefer. I am hard pressed between the two: my desire is to depart and be with Christ, for that is far better; but to remain in the flesh is more necessary for you. Since I am convinced of this, I know that I will remain and continue with all of you for your progress and joy in faith, so that I may share abundantly in your boasting in Christ Jesus when I come to you again.

This passage creates a double-bind: on the one hand, Paul is saying that the body does matter and on the other is highlighting death as the preferable alternative. He knows that the prayers of his friends and co-workers are aiding him, that the Spirit of Christ is with him, that deliverance may come about. And yet he also has ambiguous feelings about continuing the suffering that is in front of him.

I think this can only usefully be read as the thoughts of someone who is face to face with his own mortality, recognizing that his death is a very real possibility in the short term. To do otherwise would be to glorify death. If we read this passage reflecting the kind of faith that people come to in a hospice, accepting and even welcoming the end to suffering, it makes sense. The impending presence of death creates a space where people may see into the next world in ways more clear and more immediately than we usually see.

The Aids epidemic has, unfortunately, given the queer community much experience of living in the face of death. As a pastor in the queer community, I spent a great deal of time with men who were living with Aids. When they were critically ill and facing the real possibility of death, many of the men, like Paul, expressed to me their dilemma that they felt they needed to stay alive for others. They were guilty about the burden that their care was on their lovers. They were worried about the grief they would leave in their wake, not in any egotistic way, but with a realistic knowledge that they were loved and would be missed.

For those left behind, who did and do grieve deeply, painfully, incredibly, we have had to figure out what it means to keep on living. There are times when joining those on the other side, as Paul longs to join Christ, is very tempting to people. And yet, there is also our experience of the value of life. Being around dying people teaches us the value of each and every day.

Certainly our community also suffers deeply from suicides, brought on by the guilt of a homophobic society. The source of that guilt can be laid squarely on the shoulders of the Christian Church (and other religions as well). When newspapers report that queer teens are four times more likely to attempt suicide than their heterosexual counterparts, we should be greatly alarmed.

Paul goes further, however, saying in Philippians 3.2–9,

Beware of the dogs, beware of the evil workers, beware of those who mutilate the flesh! For it is we who are the circumcision, who worship in the spirit of God and boast in Christ Jesus and have no confidence in the flesh – even though I, too, have reason for confidence in the flesh. If anyone has reason to be confident in the flesh, I have more: circumcised on the eighth day, a member of the people of Israel, of the tribe of Benjamin, a Hebrew born of Hebrews; as to the law, a Pharisee; as to zeal, a persecutor of the Church; as to righteousness under the law, blameless.

Yet whatever gains I had I have come to regard as loss because of Christ. More than that, I regard everything as loss because of the surpassing value of knowing Christ Jesus my Saviour. For Christ's sake I have suffered the loss of all things, and I regard them as rubbish, in order that I may gain Christ and be found in him, not having a righteousness of my own that comes from the law, but one that comes through faith in Christ, the righteousness from God based in faith.

Here Paul makes the point that it is neither our external condition nor the circumstances of our birth that make us acceptable to God. Having undergone the ritual of circumcision and having been born into the 'right clan' were not, in and of themselves, enough for Paul. This is an important warning for those who think that conformity is related to holiness. These comments about the Hebrews also serve as a reminder that all nations are acceptable to God, rather than one nation alone. God's interest is not only in one sort of person – straight people or the gender normative – but instead in the whole range of humanity, created and loved by God.

This passage also reminds us that what is important to God is not our outward appearance but our inward condition. Being born straight or gay, living as male, female or transgender – these facts alone are not enough to say anything about our spiritual state. Rather, it is what we do in our lives and with our lives, how our hearts and minds are connected with God and with humanity, whatever our sexual orientation or gender identity might be.

At the same time, we should be careful in reading the body-negativity of this passage. We should not hold our confidence only in external appearance, but, on the other hand, confidence in our bodies is a wonderful thing. One of the powerful messages of the incarnation of Christ is the blessing of the body as a source of salvation and the revelation of God. Queer people know that our bodies are not like other bodies – especially those of us who are transgender. And yet through the revelation of our bodies, we experience liberation and personal salvation. Gay, lesbian and bi people know the power of touching bodies that are like our own, affirming in the flesh of another the goodness of our own gendered, queer bodies, finding beauty in bodies that are like our own and yet different as well. Part of the development of queer sexual culture rests on an enjoyment of bodies for their own sake.

This passage refers to Paul's experiences as a convert, moving from one way of being to another. As queer people, many (if not most) of us had an experience of conversion, shifting our understanding of ourselves from the heterosexual default to our own identities in response to the needs and longings of our bodies. In doing so, many of us moved from the straight world of our parents, spouses, friends or co-workers, to identify with another community. We literally shift from one culture to another one, embedded within the larger society, but often invisible to it. We learn new social cues, new vocabulary, and new modes of dress. This is similar to Paul's experience of moving from Judaism to Christianity. Paul here talks about the personal impact it has had on him to give up everything in order to follow Christ. In the same way, while there may be things we give up in order to live out queer lives, the gains are so incredible that we would not have it any other way.

We might note here Paul's zealous persecution of the early Christians. This is certainly a phenomenon known to queer people. Mayor James West of Spokane, Washington, made headlines this year for allegedly offering jobs to men he met in gay chat rooms and yet has a long track record of opposing gay rights. Often our worst opponents in the political arena are those who fear their own sexuality or its revelation. In this way, queer people can literally be our own worst enemies. Dealing with this phenomenon remains a significant challenge for us.

Finally, Paul writes at the end of chapter 3, in verse 21, 'Christ will transform the body of our humiliation that it may be conformed to the body of glory, by the power that also enables him to make all things subject to himself.' This transformation of the body may speak to some of us as queer people. Our bodies are often what leads us to discover our differences. We may know the humiliations in our bodies of gay bashings, of playground taunts, or of being forced into a gender that does not feel right or good or comfortable for us. While this has been interpreted by some as referring to a spiritual or heavenly transformation, it can also apply to our earthly bodies.

Transformation in our bodies happens when we learn to love and accept them as they are. The bear movement, comprised of men who love large and hairy men, is a wonderful example of queer people choosing to honour bodies that society often discounts. They see beauty, value and sex appeal in their own bodies and in the bodies of the men they court. Instead of humiliation, they see glory.

In the same way, transgender bodies, which are often a source of discomfort and difficulty growing up, may become bodies which we accept and love. Society may see humiliation in a man wearing women's clothing, but a crossdresser or drag queen can be transformed into glory. By wearing the clothes that feel right to her, that express her inner femininity in a way that is gratifying to her, she transforms herself. This is not a question of whether someone passes as female (or male) or is beautiful in a conventional sense, but whether the person is able to be transformed into someone able to love themselves and the image they see in the mirror.

Queer people are amazing alchemists in this way. There are many examples of how we do this – the teased sissy boy becomes the muscular star of the gym, for instance, or the bashed victim becomes the advocate for hate-crime prevention education. Some queer people use the practices of sadomasochism to transform pain into ecstatic pleasure. The difference between humiliation and glory may exist in the eye of the beholder. Our abilities to make this transformation in our lives is indeed a spiritual power.

Love

Paul raises a very interesting point in Philippians 1.9–11 – that love should be knowledgeable. He says, 'And this is my prayer, that your love may overflow more and more with knowledge and full insight to help you determine what is best, so that in the day of Christ you may be pure and blameless, having produced the harvest of righteousness that comes through Jesus Christ for the glory and praise of God.'

The love that we have in Christ should lead us to greater levels of information and insight. Being pure and blameless is not the result of an innocence born out of ignorance, but as a result of good decisions made through a mature faith. Paul is speaking here not of blind love, but of a love of knowingness, a love that reaches into the realms of heart and mind.

One of the things that troubles me is the strength by which some strands of Christianity push an ignorant faith, a 'because I told you so' sort of religion. Thus, they say it is more faithful to believe in a literal version of Genesis than to be awed by a God who can set evolution in motion. Or, rather than looking at what modern research is teaching us about the vast varieties of gender and sexual expression and behaviour, they reduce their version of 'morality' to sex that has the potential for reproduction. But Paul does not encourage the 'shut up and do what you've been told' sort of faith in this passage, although his writings elsewhere have certainly been used to say that. Rather, here he encourages the Philippians to greater knowledge.

This is also a prayer that love grows and that the ways in which we live as a result of love will continue to mature. Love becomes more knowledgeable when we practise it. We can live out the love we have in increasing ways, expanding our sense of compassion, faith and commitment to community. We can love people by knowing more and more about them, not just loving the superficial aspects of those we meet, but loving them more fully as we encounter the quirks, the insecurities, the brilliance, the passion in others.

I was recently talking to a straight man I am close to about the differences in sexual freedom experienced by gay and straight men. In particular, we were discussing the fact that gay men can have sex with each other without the expectation of a relationship necessarily being added on to it. He made a comment about gay men having 'loveless sex', meaning this separation of the expectation of a love relationship from sex. I countered by saying that while gay men can have loveless sex, we have also learned to love for an hour, to literally love the one you are with and then let it go.

This is part of what we as gay men have learned about love and can add to the discourse about it. Love is not just about hearts and roses and living happily ever after. Love can be broader than one person; shorter than an hour and longer than a lifetime. Love is a passionate desire for the well-being of another person – even one whose name you may not know. Loving sex may lead to a commitment or simply a great orgasm. But rather than being willing to take at face value only what we were taught about love in Sunday school, fairy tales and health class, we have explored and learned about love in ways that broaden our knowledge and our individual choices.

Salvation

Paul says a very radical and striking thing in the second chapter of Philippians, verses 12–13. He writes, 'Therefore, my beloved, just as you have always obeyed me, not only in my presence, but much more now in my absence, work out your own salvation with fear and trembling; for it is God who is at work in you, enabling you both to will and to work for God's good pleasure.' I believe that this passage is one that is critical to the maturing of our faith. Revd Troy Perry, founder of Metropolitan Community Churches, has long quoted this scripture as a way of helping people to address their quandaries around sexuality – work out your own salvation, he says to them.

Rather than creating and following laundry lists of sins and acceptable activities, this approach requires us to prayerfully look to our conscience and examine our faith. It necessitates a relationship with God and an application of our beliefs to our relationships with other people. The rule of our salvation might be no more, and certainly no less, than applying what Jesus called the greatest commandments – to love God with all our hearts, all our minds and with all our strength and to love our neighbours as ourselves – to the situations we encounter day by day. Obedience can be to higher principles, and to a Higher Power, rather than to a series of commandments. Following the divine impulse and our own vocation and conscience is the point, rather than blindly obeying rules for their own sake.

Communities of faith would be wise, I believe, to empower people with the tools that they need to make their own decisions about right and wrong in ways much broader than we are currently doing because the current approach has led to dogmatic fundamentalism on the one hand or people simply ignoring religious institutions on the other. To think this way, however, would require us to trust individual people of faith to make their own decisions; something institutional communities are often unwilling to do. One question I have posed to MCC students is this: Which do you find more ethical and why: a couple in a monogamous relationship where domestic violence is present or three people engaged in a sexual relationship in which all are happy and fulfilled? This question forces us to look at to what extent the *form* of the relationship is important to us and to what extent the happiness of those involved is, and to what degree is a religious institution prepared to trust individual choices?

We who are queer have worked out our own sexuality and gender. We were able to listen to the internal voice that spoke to us about who we are, who we desire, and who we love. For many of us, that journey began alone, in the quiet of our bedrooms as teenagers, in our minds, in our hearts. Those first steps weren't in the context of supportive community, but in aloneness. Our hearts knew something, though, and we found the courage to follow them. Salvation can be the same sort of coming out. It means not just following what others have told us about the path, but being willing to look with the same sort of openness at who we might be and who God might be, and then taking the next step. The spiritual quest is not about following the crowd, but about following the divine, and that will take us in unexpected directions. Working out salvation is like coming out; what it meant when I started and what it means to me now are quite different.

In his commentary, Barclay notes that the term 'fear and trembling' means here not an immobilizing terror but rather a sense of awe (2003: 50–1). Our fear should not be about how God might punish or harm us, but the ways in which our actions might bring hurt to God and others. It means, in this context, that we should take very seriously the impact of what we do, and act accordingly.

Rejoicing and Justice

One of the very beautiful themes in Philippians is Paul's affirmation of joy in the face of all that he has endured. In what is probably the most familiar part of Philippians to many readers, Paul says, in Philippians 4.4–9,

> Rejoice in the Sovereign always; again I will say, Rejoice. Let your gentleness be known to everyone. The Saviour is near. Do not worry about anything, but in everything by prayer and supplication with thanksgiving let your requests be made known to God. And the peace of God, which surpasses all understanding, will guard your hearts and minds in Christ Jesus.
>
> Finally beloved, whatever is true, whatever is honourable, whatever is just, whatever is pure, whatever is pleasing, whatever is commendable, if there is any excellence and if there is anything worthy of praise, think about these things. Keep on doing the things that you have learned and received and heard and seen in me, and the God of peace will be with you.

Despite his imprisonment and trials, Paul is able to rejoice and find comfort in Christ's presence with him. This is a hymn of the strength of his conviction.

Of particular note here is the word translated by the NRSV as 'gentleness'. In his commentary, Barclay notes, 'The Greeks themselves explained this word as "justice and something better than justice." They said that *epieikeia* ought to come in when strict justice became unjust because of its generality' (2003: 88). Paul is advocating gentleness here, a gentleness in the application of justice so that it becomes more just.

One hallmark of queer organizing is our passion for justice. While this may at times lead us on a chase in pursuit of the politically correct, it flows from a deep desire for justice and fairness in the world. We fight so vehemently against the forces of oppression and even against each other because it matters to us. We care fiercely about justice and freedom.

Justice is, in this passage, not just a call for keeping all the rules the same, but applying a greater standard of fairness. Everyone is to be treated in a way that is fair, but where the rules are applied with enough flexibility that they matter. We should be reminded, too, to temper our passions with a sense of gentleness and innate fairness for others, living as we ourselves are seeking to be treated.

We are also a people of rejoicing, a gay people. We know how to celebrate what life offers and cherish it, even in the face of illness and oppression. Like for Paul, justice and rejoicing are intertwined for us.

Conclusion

Paul's writings have not been the most liberating for queer people. And yet, there are themes of great faithfulness in Philippians which can inspire us, teach us and even liberate us. His emphasis on companionship, community, justice and an aware and thoughtful faith are things which would serve us well as queer people of faith.

Colossians

THOMAS BOHACHE

Introduction

Throughout most of Christian history, those who have studied the letter to the Colossians (the seventh epistle in the Christian Testament of the Bible) have described it as follows: (1) a letter, (2) by the apostle Paul from prison, (3) to the Christian church at Colossae in Asia Minor. So it appeared to those who were constrained by church tradition and older methods of biblical interpretation; in recent decades, however, literary, historical-critical and social-scientific methods of biblical interpretation have challenged each of these assumptions, so that contemporary students of the Second Testament now learn that Colossians was composed (1) in letter *form*, (2) by a *disciple* of Paul's using his name, (3) to a Christian community *identified with* the ancient town of Colossae.

'What difference could this possibly make?' one might ask; after all, this is a scripture written nearly two thousand years ago. What's important for us is what it tells us about God, right? Who wrote it, in what form and to whom hardly seem relevant issues in today's world. Nothing could be further from the truth, for, as liberation hermeneutics from non-white, non-male, non-privileged and (finally!) non-heterosexual readers continues to demonstrate, the context of a text is of paramount importance in (re)constructing its meaning. Consequently, it matters greatly to any interpretation of Colossians – especially a queer one – whether Paul in fact wrote it, whether it was indeed a letter, and for whom it was intended.

Feminist scholars have demonstrated that second-generation Christians radically altered the direction of incipient Christianity first imaged by Paul in his genuine letters. Paul seemed to have preached a gospel of God's grace that reached beyond social barriers and distinctions; convinced that the world would be coming to an end, he believed that unity amid diversity was more important than allegiance to social and religious rules (Schüssler Fiorenza 1983: 205–41; Bohache 2000). In the next generation, however, as the climactic end of the world failed to materialize and Christians began to realize that they needed to continue to reside in a world dominated by the Roman empire, their leaders began to gradually remould some of the earliest Christian beliefs and to accommodate the surrounding culture so that Christians could coexist in relative peace with non-Christians (Schüssler Fiorenza 1983: 251–333). Thus, scholars have asserted that at least six of the letters in the Second Testament that bear Paul's name were more probably composed by a 'Pauline school' of his followers,[1] who reorganized and reformulated Paul's message for their own context. It was perfectly acceptable and even commonplace in antiquity to ascribe someone else's name to one's own writing in order to honour the person and to claim authority through their name; the modern concern with plagiarism and copyrights was non-existent in the Graeco-Roman milieu that produced the Second Testament (Johnson 1992b: 338).

Turning specifically to the provenance of Colossians, Pauline experts point out that this letter includes 28 words not used in undisputed letters of Paul; that it differs from these genuine letters in theological tone regarding Christology, eschatology and ecclesiology; and that it reflects the overall cultural context existing subsequent to Paul's death (Horgan 1990: 876–7; Lohse 1971: 72, 90–1). Additionally, it resembles the letter to the Ephesians, which is almost certainly deutero-Pauline, more than it does any of the undisputed Pauline letters. Both Colossians and Ephesians, on close inspection, are more like sermons or tracts on Christian devotion and behaviour than letters, leading many scholars to conclude that they are letters 'in name only' and that their purpose (like the books of James and Hebrews) is to teach and uplift the Christian community as it journeyed into the second century CE. Moreover, if one assumes non-Pauline authorship and a composition date subsequent to Paul's death (probably 62 CE; Perkins 1988: 117), this raises the question for whom this letter/treatise was meant: the town of Colossae was destroyed by an earthquake in 60–1 CE, and Colossians is the only extant reference to a Christian community in Colossae; additionally, the names of community members in Colossians is a virtual duplication of those found in Paul's (undisputed) letter to Philemon. Thus, the Second Testament scholar Mary Rose D'Angelo has suggested that the deutero-Pauline author(s) selected a place no longer in existence in order to discuss general matters of relevance to second-century Christianity (D'Angelo 1994b: 316).

Methodology

In this way, by examining issues of authorship, genre and audience, the queer interpreter is able to get a better sense of how to approach the letter to the Colossians; consequently, the following presuppositions will guide this examination of Colossians: (1) This letter is not what it purports to be; (2) therefore, one must approach the text with a 'hermeneutics of suspicion', i.e. the principle that the reader is not receiving the whole story and must dig beneath the surface language for a truer contemporary meaning; (3) authorship was attributed to Paul in order to receive automatic authority for the theological and social propositions addressed; (4) a defunct place was utilized and the names of real first-generation Christians employed in order to create a location that second-generation Christians could relate to in the 'good old days' of Paul's leadership, perhaps in order to convince the new generation that Christian leaders'

---

1 Ephesians, Colossians, 2 Thessalonians, 1 and 2 Timothy and Titus are considered 'deutero-Pauline' by most Second Testament scholars (Fitzmyer 1990: 770; Levine 2003a: 1).

reactions to social conditions were not really changing from what they used to be, but had always been this way. (This is similar to the evoking by patristic authors of an 'apostolic age' of doctrinal unity, when in actuality earliest Christianity was full of diversity and very little orthodoxy. See Bauer 1971.)

In accordance with these presuppositions, this author's guiding thesis is that not only does Colossians *not* reflect the spirit of the Jesus Movement and the earliest Christian communities; moreover, it was instrumental in imposing upon second-generation Christians the heteropatriarchal hierarchy and social mores found in the Roman empire. As a result, socially marginalized people who had felt welcomed as equals in earliest Christianity now were encouraged to assimilate and accept societal relationships and values that supported an oppressive colonial-imperial regime. Theologically, Colossians solicits this encouragement by invoking a Father God and a triumphant Christ who is 'Lord' of all. Because the oppression of sexual minorities such as gay, lesbian, bisexual, transgendered and other queer people has always depended upon the subjugation of women and the advancement of a patriarchal mindset, any biblical text that supports this agenda is bad news for queers. Although I have often found helpful verses in Colossians to use as proof-texts in sermons, upon closer examination of this letter in its entirety, my conclusion is that queer people should beware of Colossians and all that it represents, as we struggle to gain our rightful place in a world that has been perverted by racism, colonialism, classism, misogyny and compulsory heterosexuality. Thus, my treatment of Colossians will not be a 'queering' of the text so much as an argument for jettisoning it entirely from the queer canon of scripture.

What Is Colossians About?

'Paul' begins his 'letter' to 'the Colossians' by noting that he prays for them and commends their faith in the gospel that has been imparted to them. He praises them that this gospel is bearing fruit among them, even as it is bearing fruit throughout the world. He encourages them to remain steadfast in Christ, who has brought redemption to the entire world through his death. In Christ, God's word and wisdom have been revealed. Therefore, the Colossians should persevere in their commitment to Christ as their Head, in whom 'the whole fullness of deity dwells' and not be deceived by 'elemental spirits' or 'human traditions'. The author affirms the traditional Pauline teaching of freedom found in Galatians; however, he narrowly construes this as a freedom from the bonds of Torah observance and not the radical 'discipleship of equals' envisioned in Galatians 3.28. The Colossians have received new life, for they have been 'raised with Christ'; because they have received this new life, they need not be conformed to this world. They need not be concerned with earthly matters if they are truly strong in Christ. This new life in Christ is reflected in community harmony that comes from love and forgiveness of one another; this harmony takes root in and guides traditional relationships between husbands and wives, parents and children, and masters and slaves, allowing all to coexist in peace with one another. Finally, because the Colossian Christians should be intent upon their prayer life and their spiritual foundation in Christ, they need not worry about relations with outsiders. He urges them to 'conduct [them]selves wisely' and 'make the most of the time' ahead of them. However, rather than stressing new types of relationships among community members and the empowerment of gifts and diversity with a view toward the imminent consummation of the age (Christ's second coming or *parousia*), as in Galatians and 1 Corinthians, 'Paul' here counsels moderation and placid acceptance of the ways things are, as though through his rising Christ has already come again and made things as good as can be expected in this earthly life. Throughout the letter there is a stress placed on the spiritual component of our earthly lives; concentration on life 'in Christ' allows Christians to endure 'this world'.

What Is Colossians *Really* About?

Since we know little regarding a Christian community at Colossae, interpreters have had difficulty ascertaining the occasion of this letter. (See e.g. Lohse 1971 and MacDonald 2000.) References to avoiding 'elemental spirits' and 'human traditions' are vague at best; therefore, following D'Angelo's hypothesis noted above that Colossians was written pseudonymously to a community that no longer existed, I believe that one may view Colossians as *general* instruction for *all* Christians rather than a letter written to address a specific situation (as are Galatians and 1 Corinthians): 'elemental spirits', 'human traditions', 'self-abasement' and references to 'angels' and 'visions' could easily summarize the syncretism that the second generation of Christian leaders was trying to eradicate as the Church grew and spread far and wide. Uniformity, hierarchy and right order were seen as necessary controls once Christianity became a worldwide faith; moreover, as the end of the world and Christ's *parousia* failed to materialize, the leaders believed that the Church should conform itself to the status quo of the Roman empire and not 'rock the boat', risking further persecution (reaching its definitive formulation in 1 Peter's directive to submit to the government). References to Paul's imprisonment and Jesus' suffering and execution would have reminded second-generation Christians of their persecution under the emperors Tiberius and Nero (and possibly Domitian, depending upon how one dates Colossians). The leaders, in Paul's name, would have been encouraging compatibility with the forces of empire – saying in effect that, by persevering spiritually and creating harmony no matter what worldly conditions surrounded them, Christians could 'act as if' and endure the world, because until the world did end (whenever that might be) this was as good as it was going to get. This is a far cry from the non-traditional, anti-imperial and counter-cultural vision Jesus referred to as 'the Reign of God'![2]

In light of the foregoing, I propose that the best way to treat Colossians is as a piece of propaganda in the second-generation Christian agenda which Elisabeth Schüssler Fiorenza termed initially the Church's 'patriarchalization' (Schüssler Fiorenza 1983: 288–9) and more recently its 'kyriarchalization'

---

2 See my treatment of Jesus' notion of the Reign of God in my commentary on 'Matthew' in this volume.

(Schüssler Fiorenza 1992a: 117).[3] This propaganda, much like that emanating from the US White House of George W. Bush, had as its aim to inspire a culture of fear and disinformation so that ordinary people would follow the directions of their leaders without question. What better way to get people on board the party line than to put such sentiments into the mouth of St Paul (much as George W. credits divine inspiration[4])? Realizing that a text is propaganda allows the reader to go 'behind' the text to determine what is really being said: in the case of Colossians, I propose that we go behind the text to uncover what the deutero-Pauline author was actually saying to and intending for the Christian Church. In doing so, we will see that Colossians is *not* a liberative text for those who remain oppressed and marginalized in today's world, including queer people.

Image of Christ

The anonymous author of Colossians sets the tone for the entire work in chapter 1, where he[5] puts forth one of the most famous christological portions of the Second Testament – the 'Christ Hymn' of Colossians 1.15–20. Most scholars agree that this was probably a widely used piece of liturgical poetry or song from incipient Christianity, which the author included in the letter because it would have been familiar to his audience (MacDonald 2000: 68). The hymn represents a very 'high' Christology; that is, it portrays Jesus the Christ as a divine figure who is one with God 'the Father', whereas so-called 'low' Christologies stress the humanity of Jesus as Christ (Haight 1999: 178–84). These verses in Colossians have often been compared to another early christological hymn, Philippians 2.6–11, which describes Jesus as emptying his Godhead, taking the form of a 'slave' (i.e. human form), and being rewarded by God with exaltation for his obedience 'even unto death on a cross'.

While these two early Christian hymn fragments are similar, I believe that they may be distinguished: Colossians 1.15–20 does not describe Jesus Christ's humanity as a diminution of his divinity; he is, on the contrary, seen as the firstborn of both the living and the dead; his humanity is referred to not as an emptying, nor his human form as slavery; nor is his death seen as something which God must reward through exaltation, but rather as a unique, intended means by which God reconciled the cosmos to Godself. Thus, even though this fragment may have had early origins, I believe that it was redacted later than Philippians, an undisputedly Pauline letter. Paul in his genuine letters consistently sees the death of Jesus as a shameful event (Greek *skandalon*, 1 Cor. 1.23)

---

3 This concept of 'kyriarchalization' is quite important for a liberative interpretation of Colossians: 'Western society and family are not just male, but they are patriarchal (rule of the father) or, more accurately, *kyriarchal* (rule of the master or lord), because elite propertied men have power over those subordinate to and dependent on them' (Schüssler Fiorenza 1992a: 117).

4 See Alterman and Green 2004, esp. chs 10 and 13.

5 Even though we do not know whether this anonymous author was male or female, I use 'he' because I am extremely doubtful that a woman would have written a text such as this, which depleted the freedom and general equality of Galatians, an authentically Pauline letter.

which God rehabilitated to God's glory through the resurrection. Colossians, on the other hand, matches the later 'divine visitor' Christology of the Gospel of John and other late first- and early second-century Second Testament and Gnostic texts, which enunciate the atonement theology that the pre-existent Christ figure (also called *Logos* and *Sophia*) became human in order to die and rise again in order to mend the creation, which had 'fallen' because of either human sin or misbehaviour on the part of semi-divine emanations (Bultmann 1955: 12, 66). This demonstrates to me that Colossians, while purporting to be a letter from Paul, nevertheless includes a Christology later than Paul's, thus supporting deutero-Pauline provenance.

Moreover, the author employs this high Christology in order to support his agenda of hierarchy, control by leaders, and other manifestations of kyriarchy. The importance of the Christ image as a tool in this propaganda is seen in the way in which a chiasm is formed around Colossians 1.15–20 by the three verses that precede and follow the hymn:

[A] May you be made strong with all the *strength* that comes from [God's] glorious *power,*

[B] and may you be prepared to *endure* everything with *patience,* (1.11)

[C] while joyfully giving thanks to the *Father, who has enabled you to share* in the inheritance of the saints in the light. (1.12)

[D] [God] has rescued us from the *power of darkness* and transferred us into the kingdom of

[E] [the] Beloved Son, in whom we have *redemption,* the *forgiveness* of sins. (1.13)

The Christ Hymn (1.15–20)

[D'] And you who were once *estranged and hostile* in mind, doing evil things, (1.21)

[E'] *[Christ] has now reconciled* in his fleshly body through death,

[C'] so as to present you *holy* and *blameless* and *irreproachable* before him, (1.22)

[B'] provided that you continue securely *established* and *steadfast* in the faith,

[A'] without shifting from the *hope promised by the gospel* that you heard . . . (1.23)

The various balancings of the three verses on either side of the Christ Hymn point to its importance, since Christ's portrayal here will be instrumental in understanding the rest of Colossians. The two phrases immediately preceding and following the hymn detail the human state ('darkness', 'estranged', 'hostile') that has been changed because of God's action in Christ ('redemption', 'forgiveness', 'reconciled'). However, because the Christ portrayed in the Christ Hymn is a pre-existent, cosmic Christ, possessing 'all the fullness of deity', the Christ Hymn causes a shift in how the chiasm is balanced and the first phrases replicated in the last phrases: what was attributed to *God* in 1.11–12 is now 'transferred' to *Christ* in 1.22–3. This then allows the author to concentrate on the supreme Headship of Christ over the Church, whose leaders are over men/masters/fathers, who are over women/slaves/children. Only by submitting to this ecclesial and social hierarchy will Christians be able to live out their salvation in Christ: one must 'endure everything with patience' and 'continue securely established and steadfast' in order to 'share in the inheritance of the saints' and remain 'holy and blameless and irreproachable'. Thus, I submit that the Colossians Christ Hymn, far from being merely a beautiful way of lauding the cosmic Christ, is an intentional injection into second-generation Christianity of a tyrannical, triumphant Christ who will vanquish foes and protect his followers if they remain submissive. This is the authoritative, militaristic Christ who would serve the Roman empire so well once Christianity was officially recognized as the imperial religion under Constantine. The Christ of Colossians is also the universal Saviour without whom there is no salvation (Acts 4.12), and in whose name generations of christofascists have destroyed Muslims, Jews and the indigenous peoples of Africa, Asia and the Americas. As global citizens work for a more inclusive and tolerant world, people of faith – perhaps especially queer communities – need to acknowledge that the 'recognition of other ways to salvation is one of the important distinguishing factors for a christology for the twenty-first century' (Gillis 1998: 89), and in order to do so, we must distance ourselves from the Christology of Colossians 1.15–20.

Freedom in Christ

One of the hallmarks of Pauline Christianity was the notion of freedom in Christ, most passionately represented in Galatians, one of Paul's earliest extant letters. As I have written elsewhere, Galatians stands for the Pauline belief that 'the Christian message, indeed, the very integrity of the gospel, depended upon universality and inclusivity – the welcoming into God's realm of all people through Jesus Christ' (Bohache 2000: 232). Distinctions are eliminated in Christ, leading Paul to assert, 'There is no longer Jew or Greek, no longer slave or free, no more male and female; for you are all one in Christ Jesus' (Gal. 3.28). Elisabeth Schüssler Fiorenza, in her ground-breaking enquiry into Christian origins, has concluded that inclusivity was a staple in earliest Christian mission and the Pauline house-churches (the 'discipleship of equals'), in which women, slaves and others held roles of prominence alongside free, male citizens (Schüssler Fiorenza 1983: 180–3, 213); and I, along with other biblical scholars, believe that this type of freedom and openness may be traced back to the historical ministry of Jesus of Nazareth (Crossan 1991: 341–2). As feminist scholars have noted, this freedom in Christ described by Paul was later modified by the apostle when women prophets in Corinth were becoming a bit 'too free', setting the stage for its virtual abrogation in the deutero-Pauline epistles (Schüssler Fiorenza 1983: 218–32; Standhartinger 2003: 93).

Radical Pauline freedom in Christ is lacking in Colossians. Instead, one sees the 'Headship' of Christ which must overarch all Christian life; but this 'Headship' is a stifling one when it encourages uniformity at the expense of diversity, and compatibility with imperial order instead of countercultural vigilance. In Colossians, Christ's resurrection is an encouragement to tolerate the earthly status quo, rather than the Pauline notion of a foretaste of the blessed freedom from imperial death that can be had by all Christians through God's gracious act in Christ.

Social roles

As noted above, the earliest Christian gatherings were extremely diverse, following the lead of Jesus' own egalitarian practices. While little is certain about Palestinian Christianity, the Pauline house churches of the Hellenistic world have been well documented and researched. Feminist historians of early Christianity have retrieved women's leadership roles by 'reading the silence' of Christian texts and investigating what references to women they do contain; similarly, social historians, anthropologists, sociologists and classical scholars have explored the institution of slavery in the Roman empire. These scholars have concluded that poor people, women of all classes, slaves, and freedmen and -women were attracted to popular and mystery religions rather than traditional or ancestral religions because they were treated democratically in these newly emerging cults, including Christianity (Pomeroy 1975; Martin 1991).

These house churches met in the homes of the wealthy, who lived amid the trappings and privileges of the Roman empire. It is believed that Christian worship took place in an open courtyard, into which would come the various members of the household – men, women, children and slaves, each from their respective quarters – as well as visitors of various social classes from outside the home. All of these disparate elements worshipped side by side, united through Christ in a wonderful democratic experiment. As noted in the previous discussion, Paul reminded the Galatians that distinctions had been erased in baptism (Gal. 3.26–8); he went on to remind the Corinthians that they must not allow distinctions to disturb Christian assembly, especially in the administering of the Lord's Supper (1 Cor. 11.17–34).

The Second Testament scholar Pheme Perkins has pointed out that the vocabulary of the traditional family was adopted by Christians ('all are children of God, brothers and sisters of one another and of Christ'), but she also describes what a typical household in the Roman world looked like:

> The ancient 'household' was considerably more complex than what we think of as a 'family.' Roman law held that all persons, male and female, were ultimately under the authority of the oldest male head of their family. (Women remained part of their paternal family [except in limited circumstances] while their children belonged to the father's family.) In addition, slaves and others dependent upon a wealthy person would be considered part of the latter's household. Even a peasant farmer or a craftsman [sic] in the city might have a number of persons living in his or her household who were not 'family' in the sense in which we use the term. (Perkins 1988: 129)

It is precisely this use of familial and household language that raises troubling questions: In the hierarchical Roman world, did a man's being a Christian negate and supersede his position as father, husband and master? Did the mistress of the house have the right, once Christian, to treat her slaves unfairly? Scholars are not agreed on this issue. Some (usually white and male) believe that Christians would know instinctively that the egalitarian language was simply metaphorical and did not alter the imperial social structure for Christians, while liberation interpreters (black, feminist and womanist) have suggested that this need not be the case. Christianity in its earliest days may have been socially radical and threatening to the imperial status quo, leading to its persecution, just as Jesus' radical egalitarianism contributed to his execution as an imperial criminal (Herzog 2000: 240–1).

I believe it is much more probable that – in keeping with Jesus' radical views – earliest Christian assemblies were egalitarian.[6] If Jesus' primary message of the Reign of God was anti-imperial (and I believe it was), then surely the movement that developed in his wake would have retained at least some of this anti-imperial focus. One way of opposing the Roman empire was to undermine its social hierarchy – the 'glue' that cemented levels of domination, oppression, subservience and servitude. Thus, the Pauline house churches, in worshipping together across class and gender lines, did so in defiance of Caesar and his empire; their very use of familial language flaunted their unorthodox relations in the face of empire. Is it any wonder there were persecutions of the new sect by the imperial power structure?

Nevertheless, this countercultural Christian fervour seems to have abated by the second generation. The texts of this generation – Colossians, Ephesians, the Pastoral Epistles (1 and 2 Timothy, Titus), and 1 Peter – include rules of behaviour that Christians should practise so as to keep order in the churches and demonstrate that they are good Roman citizens. These rules of behaviour are known as 'household codes' (German *haustafeln*), the earliest of which appears in Colossians 3.18–4.1: 'Wives, be subject to your husbands . . . ; children, obey your parents . . . ; slaves, obey your earthly masters in everything . . .' In the Roman patriarchal (or better, kyriarchal) world, the husband/father/master was Caesar in the empire of his household. A peaceful household reflected a peaceful empire; good Christians must be good citizens. Harmony is stressed throughout Colossians, at the price of the social freedom that belief in Christ used to provide. The Jesus who welcomed everyone to his table is now the cosmic Christ who is Head of his Household, the Church. All must fulfil their roles 'wholeheartedly, fearing the Lord' (Col. 3.22).

While some scholars have tried to explain away the 'love patriarchalism' of the deutero-Pauline epistles' household codes (Hays 1996: 64–5), I see them as thinly disguised propaganda to confirm traditional heteropatriarchal cultural roles for women, slaves and children – precisely those for whom incipient Christianity was most attractive (Schüssler Fiorenza 1983: 218, 263–5; Thurston 2003: 162–3). Colossians set the stage for this by first introducing an exalted

---

6 This 'discipleship of equals' comports with images portrayed in the Gospels, which survive as a dangerous memory of Jesus, inasmuch as they were written later in the first century, after the earliest Pauline churches had evolved into the more kyriarchal deutero-Pauline churches. Thus, Schüssler Fiorenza notes: 'The Gospel of Mark was written at approximately the same time as Colossians, which marks the beginnings of the patriarchal household-code trajectory . . . [T]he first writers of Gospels articulate a very different ethos of Christian discipleship and community than that presented by the writers of the injunctions to patriarchal submission . . .' (Schüssler Fiorenza 1983: 316)

and exultant Christ, then further limiting the freedom that Christ was thought to have made possible for humanity, and finally imposing rules of behaviour on those most likely to rock both the imperial boat and the second-generation Christian leadership's dinghy, as it sought to align itself with empire.

How Might We Queer Colossians?

I stated at the outset that my essay would not be a typical queering of this book of scripture, but rather an argument to dispense with Colossians entirely in queer religious sensibility. I agree with Mary Rose D'Angelo when she asserts that 'no portion of Colossians can be read as "the word of God" as if it were detached from the Household Codes, or from the cosmic vision and theological rationale that undergird them' (D'Angelo 1994b: 323). However, lest I prooftext D'Angelo in support of my own argument, I must hasten to point out that she adds the proviso that we cannot solve the problem by excising Colossians from the canon or from Christian memory, since this epistle, even though it is unappealing, is still part of our Christian heritage. Clearly, we must remember how second- and third-generation Christians diluted the early egalitarian messages of Jesus and Paul; however, I believe that we are still able to dispute Colossians' appropriateness as God's revealed word when it can be – and has been – utilized to buttress racism, sexism, classism and compulsory heterosexuality.

Instead, I propose that the best way to queer Colossians is to reject its treatment of three elements I have critiqued above – image of Christ, freedom in Christ, and social roles – and to suggest other, more empowering ways of describing and living out these elements.

Image of Christ

Queer Christians must have an image of Christ that affirms their personhood and the God-givenness of their sexuality. A queer Christology begins with the following presuppositions: that queerness is a part of creation, that it is not a perversion of creation, that it is not in and of itself sinful, and that it does not need to be changed, but rather must be embraced and celebrated if it is to fulfil God's intention for humankind. Christology's two foci – the person of Christ and the work of Christ – must never be used to condemn or diminish any form of sexuality: thus, I do not believe that God sent 'His Son' to die to atone for the sin that was introduced into the world as a result of the fall described in Genesis 3. Such notions of atonement are accompanied by the traditional teaching not only that sex was a result of the fall, but that divinely approved gender roles were also one of its negative manifestations. It is this view of Christ's role in salvation that is buttressed by Colossians' image of the cosmic Christ and his Headship over the Church. When one does not hold such a view of who Jesus is as Christ and what he did as Christ, it opens the discussion to examine more holistic images of Christ.

Both female and male, traditional and liberation scholars have demonstrated that Jesus Christ need not be a 'holy terror' in order to offer health and wholeness (the root meanings of 'salvation') to humanity. Views of Christ that emphasize his divinity at the expense of his humanity (for example the Christologies of Karl Barth, Rudolf Bultmann and Karl Rahner) usually are not helpful to human becoming; in contrast, views of Jesus' humanity as an embracing of his Christ-ness (for example the Christologies of Friedrich Schleiermacher, Matthew Fox, Carter Heyward and Jacquelyn Grant) are extremely helpful to an organic, holistic and cosmic spirituality, for they do not divorce humanness from the rest of creation or rank it according to out-moded notions of Platonic and Manichaean dualism.

One of the most helpful ways of reimaging the cosmic Christ of Colossians is to reclaim its origins in the figure of Divine Wisdom. The Hebrew Bible scholars Silvia Schroer and Asphodel Long have demonstrated that the figure of Wisdom (Hebrew *Hochmah*; Greek *Sophia*) in both the canonical and apoc-ryphal Hebrew scriptures is a female manifestation of the one God, who was present at creation and through whom the creation came into being (Schroer 2000; Long 1993). This is the part of God that travelled with the Israelite refu-gees as cloud and fire and was later invoked in Jewish ritual as the *Shekinah* (Presence). The Second Testament scholars Elisabeth Schüssler Fiorenza and Ben Witherington have shown how this Hebrew figure of Wisdom was used in the Second Testament to apply divine attributes to Jesus as Christ, while Mary Rose D'Angelo has changed the pronouns of the Colossians Christ Hymn to feminine gender to demonstrate that what is said of Christ here could just as easily apply to Sophia (Schüssler Fiorenza 1994b: 139–44; Witherington 1994: 266–72; D'Angelo 1994b: 318). The Asian feminist theologian Grace Ji-Sun Kim has recently suggested that Christ as Sophia can be an interfaith tool for Korean women to embrace the Buddhist notion of *prajna* (wisdom) and thereby import into Christianity elements of Korean culture that have been heretofore denied as syncretistic (Kim 2002: 82–90).

I have written elsewhere that I believe that the incarnation reveals God's blessing of embodiment – including queer bodies (Bohache 2003: 19–20). My notion of Christ is that of 'Anointed One', and each one of us is called to be anointed to serve God in this world. Thus, incarnational embodiment did not happen just once in Jesus but happens over and over again in the diverse persons, bodies and sexualities we see around us. The cosmic Christ who is Divine Wisdom can be a part of each one of us and can empower us to change oppressive realities; She is present whenever we co-create with God, and She accompanies us on our journey. Thus, we can reclaim the Christ Hymn of Colossians for a queer milieu, without also adopting the ways in which Christ was used among second-generation Christians as an authority figure who gave divine approval to systems of hierarchy and domination.

Freedom in Christ

In the same way, queer people can reclaim that initial freedom in Christ that so energized and motivated the earliest Christian groups. We can dis-empower the 'unfreedom' begun in Colossians and continued in the other deutero-Pauline epistles and throughout Christian history. Because a queer Christology acknowledges that we each have Christ in us, this freedom in

Christ is an essential part of our birthright as children of God. In this way, we can edit ourselves back into the family and household of Christ, just as lesbian, gay, bisexual and transgendered people have demanded that we be written back into the entire human story.

But just as is true of every freedom, freedom in the Queer Christ entails some responsibilities: it means that we do not just work for our own freedom, but for the freedom of the entire cosmos, both humankind and otherkind. We do not sell out to the forces of empire, especially the insidious American empire that seeks to rule the world and impose 'American values' and government on other countries. White, well-educated, well-paid gay men have the responsibility to use our privilege to work against intolerance, rather than 'passing' and reaping the benefits that we receive by virtue of an accident of gender and skin colour. White lesbians, though themselves discriminated against, must be in solidarity with their sisters of colour, including straight women, in order to overcome the triple oppression of sexism, racism and classism. Lesbians and gay men, in celebrating our sexualities, must address the rampant biphobia and transphobia in our communities and never hold ourselves out as the new elite who have climbed over the backs of other queer people whom we deem less respectable.

Social roles

Finally, queer people of faith must confront the insidiousness of a society that would impose 'traditional, biblical, family values' on everyone. Those Christians who rely upon a literal reading of scripture to block social equality invariably use the Household Codes of the Second Testament to do their dirty work for them. They fail to see that these *haustafeln* were a tool that male church leadership used in order to cosy up to the Roman empire and demonstrate that good Christians (that is, free, male, propertied Christians) could be good citizens and were not a threat to the status quo. Just as queer Christians face the Religious (un)Right today on the battlefield of fixed gender roles, heteronormativity and compulsory heterosexuality, so the early Christians faced a political regime started by Augustus Caesar that sought to reinvigorate the traditional patriarchal family through such weapons as a tax on 'bachelors' and punishment for childlessness.[7]

Queer Christians must realize that heterosexism and homophobia are rooted in sexism – the disempowerment of women and non-elite men through the reifying of traditional, patriarchal gender roles, accompanied by institutional racism and classism. It is easy for white, heterosexual male biblical interpreters to dismiss criticisms of the *haustafeln* in Colossians as an example of 'love patriarchalism', for they have never been discriminated against because of their position in the socio-sexual hierarchy. As postcolonial theorists have demonstrated, submission and obedience look different to the 'subaltern'

---

7 The census that Luke tells us was the occasion of Mary and Joseph's travel to Bethlehem was in fact an imperial tool used not only for taxing the citizens but for ascertaining who was married, how many children they had, and whether they were 'productive' members of the Roman empire.

among us (Kwok 2005). In describing a holistic ecological theoethics rooted in an appreciation for the erotic in every aspect of creation, the gay ethicist Daniel Spencer has expressed this well:

A social order that depends on women orienting their lives toward men must define lesbians as unnatural and unfeminine. Similarly, gay men who refuse to participate in relationships of compulsory heterosexuality must also be defined as unnatural and unmasculine. . . . 'By living out a definition of femaleness contrary to the accepted norms of naturalness, lesbians expose nature as a social construct, rather than as a biological necessity.' . . . *In social orders that assume heterosexual naturalism, maintaining total silence about the possibility of homosexuality or bisexuality is the most politically effective means of keeping all women oriented toward and subordinate to men, and gay men subordinate to heterosexual men.* (Spencer 1996: 62–3; citation omitted and emphasis added)

Thus, the behaviour of women submitting to their husbands, children obeying their parents and slaves obeying their masters has clear ramifications for queer consciousness; it is when behaviour and roles are coded as masculine or feminine, dominant or submissive, enfranchised or disenfranchised that the political elite are able to enforce the status quo. Colossians' Household Code is a way of coding behaviour that would leave some 'on top' and some 'on bottom', both literally and figuratively. Moreover, the ramifications for queer liberation do not reside exclusively in the husband/wife or male/female dichotomy: slaves (both female and male) in the ancient world were used by their masters sexually both for sexual release and to reinscribe the slaves' subjection; for male slaves this would have also involved their 'feminization' or 'emasculation', relegating them still lower on the social hierarchy with its interlocking oppressions (Spencer 1996: 270). This is yet one more reason why it is unhealthy for queer people to view Colossians as God's revealed word to humanity, then or now. Any 'scripture' whose message is 'keep on being passive!' is not only dangerously anti-human; it is also seriously anti-divine, since it perverts the image of God contained in each of us.

1 and 2 Thessalonians

THEODORE JENNINGS

1 Thessalonians

This is the oldest document of the Second Testament, the first letter of Paul, probably written as early as 43 CE (Richard 1995: 8) or as late as 50 CE, probably not long after Paul had been in Thessalonica for a few months, where he had gone when chased out of Philippi. Thessalonica was the chief city of Macedonia, a seaport, where people of many cultures and religions huddled together in a kind of urban slum drawn by the possibility of gaining some sort of living as labourers, traders and crafts persons (Malherbe 1987: 5; Richard 1995: 2–3).

Plying his (new?)[1] trade as a leatherworker in the rather hard work of a minor tentmaker (Acts 18.3, Ascough 2000: 315), Paul appears to have set up shop in the quarter of other leatherworkers, living and working among them. As was generally the case in ancient (and still in many modern third world) cities, those who had similar trades would live in the same quarter or tenement working in their rooms to sell their products in the tiny shops on the ground floor (Malherbe 1987: 17; Ascough 2000: 318).

Thus living and working as an ordinary manual labourer among them, Paul also would seem to them a kind of moral philosopher like the Cynic preachers who sought the moral betterment of the lower orders of society. Just as today the preponderant literature in ordinary bookstores is of the self-help variety, so also in antiquity it was the wandering philosophers who offered (often illiterate) people advice and admonition about how to live more meaningful or even moral lives (Malherbe 21–8).

It is among some such group of labourers, perhaps predominantly young men, that Paul seeks to form a community of love and hope. If the members of this group are predominantly young men this would not be because Paul is at all averse to working with women but because of the happenstance of his finding here the immediate context of his teaching among them (Ascough 2000: 324, 327).

---

1 Although not mentioned in the standard commentaries it should not be ruled out that Paul as a middle-class Pharisee and citizen of Rome has adopted a low-class manual trade to which he had apprenticed himself in Thessalonica. This would help to account for his self-description as infant and orphan. It would also correspond to his emphasis throughout his correspondence on the downward mobility of the incarnation and on the need for the imitation of this on the part of the adherents of the gospel.

The letter itself portrays a community of rather intense personal feelings, a band of brothers (in this letter they are addressed as brothers more than a dozen times), as it were, who are therefore not in competition with one another (Ascough 2000: 321–2) but living in intense solidarity. Moreover the relationship between them and Paul seems also to be one of intense personal bonding, of great loyalty and an intense desire to be and live together.

The group appears to be largely, perhaps exclusively, pagan or Gentile (in spite of Acts 17.1–8).

While the lifestyle of Paul is that of an ordinary worker and his approach is that of something like a Cynic philosopher his message appears to be of an apocalyptic tone. The horizon of his teaching is formed by the expectation of the cataclysm of society (wrath) from which his hearers have learned to expect deliverance by the returning messiah who had been rejected and executed by the religious and political powers but had been raised from the dead, vindicated and would soon return to redeem those who were loyal to his messianic mission. The apocalyptic horizon however does not have a menacing tone here. Rather Paul seems concerned to offer assurance and consolation.

In reading Paul's letters we should always bear in mind that we cannot obtain absolute certainty about his intentions and meaning. This is true not only because of the enormous linguistic and cultural distance that separates us from his time, but also because Paul makes clear that he adapts his own language to the ideas and language of his addressees (1 Cor. 9.19–23). Thus, many of Paul's phrases and images may depend on the specific ways of speaking and thinking about the world that characterize the particular group to whom he is writing. In addition he and his addressees will have a certain shared experience together that his letters can simply presuppose but which those of us who were not part of that experience can only guess at. Thus the aim of commentary cannot be to 'close the book' on Paul's meaning but to open the book to a fresh generation of readers who are invited to consider a range of possible meanings and intentions.

Greetings

The salutation indicates that the letter comes not only from Paul but from Paul and those of his companions known to the 'assembly' in Thessalonica. That the letter is addressed to the assembly indicates not only that all are equally recipients of this message but that the group of lower-class labourers (Ascough 2000: 315, 317) have been addressed as free citizens of the new polity that Paul is concerned to bring into being. They are assembled as free and responsible citizens in 'God the father and the lord Jesus, messiah'. And as such they receive 'grace and peace'.

The thanksgiving is a standard part of Paul's letters (absent only in Galatians). What Paul recalls in his thanksgiving/prayer is their 'work of faith, labour of love, endurance in hope' (1.3). It is noteworthy that here there is no opposition between faith (loyalty) and work. It is the horizon of hope that enables their steadfastness or endurance and so the labour of love and the work of loyalty. Love and loyalty (faith) are not interior attitudes but modes of engaging the world and one another based upon perseverance in hope.

That these who are God's beloved have (been) chosen is clear from the way in which they have received the glad message of Paul that came to them not only as word but also as power and divine spirit and assurance. As is common for Paul 'spirit' is connected to the announcement and reception of the message (1.5; see Gal. 3.3). It is not only the message but also the reception in the sense of full persuasion. Thus Paul will also point to the affliction (an apocalyptic term) and joy that mark the breakthrough as divine spirit into the mind/heart of the hearers. That is, the message is such that it uproots people from their customary way of being in the world (affliction) and releases that excess which is experienced as joy.

The efficacy of this spirited hearing is demonstrated through a series of imitations. They imitate Paul (and the Lord) (1.6); they are imitated by those in Macedonia and Achaia (1.7). Thus their loyalty to the message that they have received in this way is already well known. As we shall see, this has much to do with steadfastness in the face of opposition, which is the pattern that they have discovered in Paul and the Lord.

The welcome, which is to say the openness to the utterly strange and novel message (and bearer of that message, Paul) which they have extended, goes so far that they have actually left off that which previously allowed meaning to their lives (1.9). It is here (turning from idols) that we discover that Paul's addressees are pagans rather than Judaeans, despite the divergence of this from the composition of the community suggested by Acts 17.1–8 (Gaventa 1998b: 4).

That they turn to a 'living God' makes clear that they have turned to the God of Israel but with the difference that this God is now understood or welcomed in the key of hope as they await the coming of the one who had been raised from the dead. This being raised from the dead is not a mere event of the past but is rather the basis for the hope of deliverance from the world catastrophe here designated as coming 'wrath' (1.10; 5.9). The wrath here is not directly attributed to God but is instead a world-historical collapse that is understood to be inevitable. It is thus not the subject of Paul's preaching but is a shared presupposition with his Gentile hearers on the basis of which it was possible to announce deliverance from this fate. It is a presupposition common to many great urban empires, the subconscious sense that the world is on the verge of complete catastrophe.

The coming of the risen one is a theme to be sounded at several points in the letter and indeed it is this theme that seems to order the much later division of the letter into chapters (1.10; 2.19; 3.13; 4.15).

This introductory address has sounded themes that will be unpacked in the body of the letter that follows. The next two chapters develop the passionate relationship between Paul and this community of 'leather-men'. Chapter 2 expands on themes announced in 1.5–6.

The passionate mission (2.1–16)

Paul rehearses the occasion and manner of his mission in Thessalonica. He came to them 'on the run' from ferocious opposition in Philippi, yet still (hiding out, one supposes, among the leather folk of Thessalonica) he had the courage in God to declare the good news from God in spite of the danger (2.2). (Note that here, as in Romans, it is not just Paul's gospel but God's.) That his motives are pure, that is, not self-interested in the sense of seeking to take advantage of his hearers for selfish advantage, means that he has no need to use deceptive tactics. This is also a way in which Cynic preachers distinguished themselves from the sophists (Malherbe 1987: 23–4; Richard 1995: 98–9).

It is important to Paul that he has not sought to gain favour by flattering his hearers or in order to get money from them. These are of course the very things that preachers are often, not without reason, suspected of doing with their would-be congregations.

It is in this context that Paul expresses his passion for these folk with extraordinary metaphors. It is not just that he does not depend on them for (financial) support but that he becomes a nurse who cherishes the children put into her charge to whom she offers her very soul (and body, as wet nurse) out of longing or desire for them because they are her/his beloved (2.7–8). The tenderness,[2] longing, desire that Paul expresses here is not only transgendering (Gaventa 1998b: 31–4) but also verges on the erotic (Gaventa (1998b: 9, 40) speaks of this as a sort of 'love letter'). It is remarkable, given this earliest metaphor for creating and guiding a congregation that in the post-Pauline church masculinist metaphors like elder, pastor and so on have come to be predominant rather than nurse (or wet nurse).

Paul then returns to the theme of his labouring with them both in the leather trade that he shared with them and in his care of them in other ways, especially his admonishing and guiding them. He now switches to a parental and paternal metaphor, which is, however, corrected by reference to them not as sons but as brothers, and subsequently his self-reference as an orphan longing for them who are then his parents (2.17). The aim of these exhortations is that his hearers should lead a life 'worthy of God' who has summoned them into God's own glory, that is, to belong to God. It is therefore important that Paul himself has behaved in a way that is also worthy of God (as nurse, as father) as holy, just and blameless among them whom he describes as the loyal or faithful ones.

The remarkable deployment of metaphors to describe the relation between Paul and this community – nurse, father, infant, orphan and brother – scrambles not only gender categories but positions or roles of authority and power (Gaventa 1998b: 26–8). Only an extraordinarily passionate love can afford to be so heedless of the categories and roles by which society is governed.

Paul then turns to their reception of the word not as his word but as God's. The divinity of the word is shown by the way it effects among them the courage to endure persecution as well as the inner conflict of radical transformation in worldview. Here Paul points to the example of the assemblies in Judaea that were persecuted by the Judaean authorities, just as those same authorities had persecuted Jesus and the prophets and Paul himself. Thus Paul draws a parallel between the way his Thessalonian community is persecuted by Thessalonian authorities and the way Judaean authorities persecute prophets,

---

2 The 'tenderness' of 2.7 is also rendered as infant in some ancient texts, thereby adding to the dizzying variety of metaphors by which Paul describes his relation to the Thessalonians.

Jesus and Paul himself. This is also the passion of mission, that it endures opposition from the social and religious order within which it seeks to inaugurate new assemblies of hope and love. Thus the leather folk are praised for 'bearing it'.

Unfortunately the phrase that Paul uses here to describe persecution by Judaean authorities changes its meaning dramatically when there is a shift in power such that Christians become the dominant group who then justify their persecution of a minority (the Jews) by reference to Paul's plea against this same persecution at the hands of religious authorities.[3]

The good news of requited love (2.17–3.13)

We turn now from the description of Paul's gentle nurse-like love for these leather folk and their reception of his words to good effect in that they have also endured persecution, to the more recent relation between these people and their now distant friend. Paul finds himself far away from this beloved community of brothers (perhaps in Athens) and unable to come to be with them 'face-to-face'.

The expressions that Paul uses here are remarkably unguarded. He is telling this band of brothers that even though he has been parted from them only a short time, he was as a man in mourning, or an orphaned child – even though this absence was one of the face-to-face only and not of the heart where he remains in intimate presence with them. Still this heart presence is not enough to assuage his deep longing, his eager desire (or, as we shall see, lust) to be physically close to them again. And here Paul quite emphatically steps out from the threesome who have written this letter to speak directly and in his own name, for it is he who has been hindered from consummating his desire for them, by some hindrance which he attributes to 'Satan', most probably some further threat to his ability to be with them, though whether this threat comes from foes who await his return to Thessalonica or those who prevent him from leaving Athens is not clear. Paul explains his eagerness and deep longing to be with them in body as well as heart by telling them that they are his crown, what he has to show for his athletic prowess (crown is here an athletic rather than a regal metaphor) as a missioner at the coming of 'our Lord Jesus' (2.19).

It is the deep longing for direct contact with these leather folk, indeed when he could not bear the separation any longer, that motivates him to remain alone in Athens while Timothy is sent from Paul's side to visit with his dear ones in Thessalonica. The difficulty seems to be that these beloved ones are having to endure persecution. Paul may have feared that they would not be able to bear it, that the affliction would be too much for them, that they would cave in under pressure (3.2–5). It is Timothy's task to strengthen their loyalty to the gospel (and to Paul). This is done by reminding them that affliction and persecution is their unavoidable lot (3.3–4). In some way the community that Paul has formed with these workers is so profoundly counter-cultural that they may expect the same sort of persecution from pagan neighbours and authorities that also has

---

3 Gaventa (1998b: 35–6) and Richard (1995: 17–19) give good reasons for regarding vv. 14–16 as a later interpolation which might then refer to the fall of Jerusalem in 70 CE.

characterized the experience of the decidedly counter-cultural communities in Judaea.

But Timothy has gone and now returned and Paul discovers that the love he had bestowed on these rough labourers was not in vain for they have held fast in their loyalty to the gospel (or to Paul?) and in their love for Paul. Indeed so personally involved has Paul been with them that loyalty to the gospel and the mutual love between this small band and himself are very nearly the same thing. That they reciprocate Paul's own longing for a reunion, that his love for them is not unrequited, is for Paul a source of great comfort and strength as he faces his own afflictions and persecutions. Indeed he speaks of being 'evangelized' by Timothy's good news of the Thessalonians' love for and loyalty to him (Malherbe 1987: 68). It is their mutual yearning for one another that strengthens them in their capacity to endure and to remain faithful to one another and to the gospel. It is their love that enables Paul to endure his own suffering (3.7), it is this which he says keeps him alive (3.8). Thus Paul gives expression to his great gratitude to God, directs to God his own great joy at their love and loyalty. It is this which only strengthens his desire to be with them again in order to give them what he can that will supply whatever may be lacking in their faithfulness. Paul is attempting to deal with certain doubts that weaken their hope and their loyalty – an issue he will address at a later point in this letter.

But first the letter seems to come to a close with a resounding prayer and benediction. In this benediction Paul invokes 'our God and Father' (a terminology that has now been invoked three times), and 'the Lord Jesus', a terminology that is also a distinctive feature of this letter (2.19). Not surprisingly the petition is that Paul will be brought to be with them at last. Moreover he then prays that they will 'abound and exceed' in love. It is the work of the Lord (Jesus) that is especially invoked here when it comes to asking for an excessive or overflowing love that extends itself outward to embrace not only members of the community but 'all'.[4]

It is in this way, through an abundant and excessive love directed to all that their hearts (that is, their wills or desires) are made blameless and holy. That is, holiness is here entirely a matter of an abundant love directed toward one another and to all. This is remarkable since there is sometimes a tendency to think of holiness as a withdrawal from 'all' or as a moralism that can scarcely be characterized as abundant and excessive love. But for Paul holiness means nothing more than this love. It is indeed the excessiveness of this love that makes it distinctive, that makes it counter-cultural and so in that way makes it seem quite at odds with the way the world normally works. There is then something deeply paradoxical about this: a heedless, unguarded love for all is what makes them seem different, even distinct, from the world and in that odd sense separated from it: by being so deeply immersed in love for one another and for all.

It is in any case precisely this unhindered love for all that makes them ready for the coming of the Lord Jesus 'with all the saints' and so ready to stand before 'our God and Father'.

---

4 The NRSV correctly eliminates the term all 'men' which is not in the Greek text.

Although the letter seems to end here with this resounding benediction, in fact Paul's words seem crafted to draw to a close his love song to the community (direct my way to you) while opening to the subsequent themes that have to do precisely with the life of love and with the coming of 'the Lord Jesus'.

Exhortations (4.1–12)

The remainder of the letter appears at first sight to be divided into exhortations regarding the lifestyle of the members of the community (4.1–12; 5.12–22) and a discussion of the eschatological horizon within which they are to live.

The first section (4.1–8) seems in most translations to be concerned with what are today called sexual ethics but this may not be quite what it seems. Translations of the passage, and commentaries, generally suggest through the key verse 4 that what is at stake here is a concern to avoid promiscuity and especially adultery. However, these translations may leave a wrong impression. Thus, for example, when Paul warns his readers 'not in the passion of lust' in verse 5 the unwary reader might not know that the term translated as lust here is the same word that Paul has earlier used to describe his own desire for them: *epithumia* (2.17). If we were to provide a more clear view of what is going on here we would either have to say that Paul has a great lust for the guys in Thessalonica or we would have to say that he is warning them against excessive desire in the matter of their 'wives'. But here is yet another problem. For most translators have basically conjured up wives for these men out of whole cloth. We should notice that if these translators are right then all of Paul's addressees are male who may have wives. But there is no word for wives in the Greek. Instead there is a term (*skeous*) that in other uses is (or may be) translated as instruments (for example, Acts 9.15). At some points it may also be translated as 'vessels' (Rom. 9.21–3) but this is less common. What has happened is that the translators have used vessels here, then have imagined that vessels are women and then that the women are wives. The only possible justification is that 1 Peter 3.7 refers to wives as 'weaker vessels/ instruments'. But the comparative there suggests that males/men/husbands are also 'vessels/instruments'. That is, the idea of instruments/vessels is not a gendered idea. Indeed it is grammatically masculine. Thus the translators have imported into Paul at this point a remarkable bit of sexism, and perhaps heterosexism, of their own invention. If we restore the term to its more likely significance we have 'let each one of you have his own instrument [tool] in holiness and honour'.[5]

What precedes this is a warning against *porneia*. This is often translated as fornication (promiscuity) but it is also the standard term for prostitution. If we suppose that prostitution here is literal rather than the common metaphor for idolatry (about which Paul has already spoken) then the admonition would be to avoid using or being a prostitute. The use of prostitutes would have been one of the main sources of sexual outlet for those men who did not have, or

---

5 The NRSV suggests 'body' as a translation of this metaphor of instrument. Ascough (2000: 325–7) provides an interesting case for understanding *skeuos* as male genitalia or, more precisely, the penis.

could not afford, wives. It was an overwhelmingly common practice, perhaps especially in port towns and cities, and the prostitute quarter was generally at or in the vicinity of temples (though this would not have involved what is commonly imagined as temple prostitution). This venue also helps to explain Paul's rather odd supposition that uniting one's body with a prostitute would mean separating oneself from Christ in 1 Corinthians 6.15–16. Hiring prostitutes and hanging out in pagan temples amounts pretty much to the same thing. Thus the difference between literal and metaphorical prostitution is not so great as might at first be supposed. A possibility that is generally ignored is that the young (male) leatherworkers might also get a bit of spare cash by hiring themselves out as prostitutes (in the same sort of places).

Paul is in any case urging his 'brothers' not to traffic with/as prostitutes and to possess their 'tools' or instruments in honour and holiness, not in the passion of desire like peoples who do not know God. Are these admonitions connected? It is not certain. He continues: no one should go overboard and defraud his brother in 'this matter'. It is most likely that the Greek term here should be translated as business or trade (Richard 1995: 201–2). Of course passion of desire could be connected with the idea of defrauding and so the admonition could have to do with a desire for accumulating property that might lead one to take advantage of one's neighbour or brother and thus to use one's tools (of leather work) honourably rather than dishonourably and so on. In which case the admonition concerning prostitution would have to do with warning folk away from the sort of 'riotous living' that leads one to squander resources and so to use ones tools to defraud one's fellow worker, with whom one is supposed to be sharing all one's goods.

The point of this exercise is to warn unwary readers that translators are quite capable of importing into Paul's thought a preoccupation with sex that may not be there. The erotophobia so often attributed to Paul may, in fact, be more in the eye of the beholder, or the pen of the translator (Richard 1995: 197–202).

That we are called to holiness rather than uncleanness may be understood again in terms of not seeking one's own advantage at the expense of the other, and in this way demonstrating the belonging to the God of love that, for Paul, is holiness. The not seeking one's own advantage is something that plays a very important part in Paul's writing generally (see Phil. 2.3–4; Rom. 15.1–3). Disregarding this is disobedience not simply of Paul or any other authority but is a turning aside from that which empowers the life of community as such: the divine spirit.

That it is this which is of importance to Paul is demonstrated by what follows, namely that what is at stake here is the mutual love of the 'brothers'. It is precisely this that they have learned from God: to love one another. Thus the preceding admonitions are correctly understood as establishing the negative condition of this love: not seeking one's own advantage at the expense of the 'brother'. In keeping with what he has announced earlier Paul indicates that he knows that their love is demonstrated in their solidarity with 'all the brothers in Macedonia'. He only wants this to continue and grow and become even more 'excessive'.

This takes practical form in the daily 'business' of this commune of workers who are urged to attend to their labour in an exemplary fashion so that they shall not be accused falsely of becoming lazy. This may be a danger for those who expect the imminent coming of the Messiah. Thus they should be attentive in their work and not become dependent upon others and so a burden to them. In this of course Paul is encouraging them to do as he has done among them, when he did not depend on their handouts but joined them in their trade. It is, however, important to recall that there are other groups within the Jesus movement who in fact take up, like the Cynics for example, the life of depending on the kindness of strangers (Mark 6.8–12). There is no need to assume direct opposition between these attitudes as they may be situation-specific. That is, Paul's views about labour in this text may be specific to the sort of community (as workers' commune) that has formed in Thessalonica. The difficulty of course is that the concern for the respect of outsiders, while important for the survival of a tiny counter-cultural group, may become, under different social conditions, an excuse for becoming the pillar of the social establishment, temptations not unknown to the GLBT movements.

That the group is not simply to settle down in the world as it is but that it is instead a movement that expects the end of the present social order is the reason for Paul's turn to the question of the return of Jesus, something that has been signalled repeatedly in the letter as the ground of their endurance in hope and so their labour of love.

The coming of the Lord (4.13–)

The teaching of Paul concerning the coming of the Lord may appear as a change of subject but should instead be understood as indicating the ground of the life of love to which he has been attending. Indeed the issue that Paul deals with here is not speculative but rather deals with a pastoral concern: the grief of the community at the death of one or more of their members. Thus he begins with grief (that you may not grieve) and ends with 'comfort one another with these words'.

It is, after all, death that threatens all love, all deep attachment to the other. And it is first of all the death of the other rather than the prospect of one's own death that makes this question most urgent (Levinas 2000: 16–21). Paul has already mentioned his own terrible grief at his separation from his loved ones in Thessalonica and thus knows something about grief, the death that is, above all, separation from the ones that one loves.

That the death of the other does not entail irreparable separation, and thus grief without hope, is signified by the resurrection of Jesus who had died. It is this resurrection of the dead that anticipates the return to us of all 'who have fallen asleep'. Importantly, Paul does not speak of this as our departure to be with them, but of their coming to greet or to welcome us. It is this return of the dead that shatters the barrier and power of death.

Early discussions of this text by Heidegger[6] and Bultmann (1951: 345–52) turn the emphasis to one upon 'mortality' and in particular one's own mortality in

---

6 For a discussion of Heidegger's early reflections on 1 Thessalonians, see Hent de Vries (1999: 181–243).

order to 'demythologize' the apocalyptic of Paul and to effect an emphasis upon one's own anxiety concerning one's own death. In this respect Kasemann, and Beker (1980: 135–81), are right to emphasize the apocalyptic horizon of Paul's thought which also makes more prominent his own concern with love and its vicissitudes. On the other hand it is important not to turn Paul's teaching here into speculative or even sci-fi like depictions of an end time. It is important to recall the presenting issue: grief (rather than curiosity), and the goal, comfort (rather than esoteric knowledge).

That what is at stake is not curiosity and speculation is clear in Paul's insistence that they need no instruction into the times and seasons. Rather their life is to be lived now in the wakefulness (or insomnia) of anticipation. They are not to be like those who drug themselves with sleepiness, even when they think they are awake. The life of faithfulness and love is one of alertness. Others are drowsy with what they think of as peace and security, as if nothing new was to be expected. They lull themselves into taking the structures of their world for granted. But these structures, and so this social and cultural world, cannot endure. For these structures are opposed to the justice of God. And so they will be utterly swept away.

It is noteworthy that in this letter, at least, God is not the agent of destruction or of vengeance. As noted earlier the great wrath, the great catastrophe, is like a fate that hangs over a world that does not know faithfulness and love and hope. The divine action is rather one of deliverance from the deluge that comes. 'For God did not appoint us to wrath but to the reception of salvation through our Lord Jesus messiah.'

That salvation comes through Jesus messiah is clear in that he has himself been victimized by the violent forces of the world but has been raised, thereby making clear the victory of love over violence and death. We should also note here again Paul's basic values of loyalty, love and the hope that makes endurance possible (5.8, recall 1.3). The wakefulness and alertness of those who belong to the dawning of this new day expresses itself precisely therefore in the encouragement and edification of one another that expresses the common destiny of all: to live together with the coming messiah.

Life in community (5.12–)

The admonitions that follow presuppose the importance of life in and as community. They are not addressed to isolated individuals but to persons who share life together. Hence at the end Paul says the letter is to be read to all (5.27) and we recall Paul's audacious claim that these common labourers constitute an *ekklesia* or a coming together of the citizens of a new democratic polity. Within this polity there are those who by common consent and particular gifts have the task of helping to organize the work and life of the group (Ascough 2000: 317–18). We should not think here of a fixed sort of hierarchy at all and still less of those who are in charge of 'spiritual' matters as opposed to the 'secular' business of the commune. Rather the text refers to those who have the nurse-like qualities to which Paul referred at the beginning. Their work is to be respected if the group as a whole is to flourish. The gentleness of Paul's admonitions is remarkable: 'encourage the fainthearted, help the weak, be patient with all'. This is the nurse-like work which all perform (and in this way imitate Paul's way of being among them).

That one should do good to all, even to those who do bad things to one, is an admonition that will have been ascribed to Jesus in Matthew's Sermon on the Mount (Matt. 5.43–8) but its Pauline provenance cannot be doubted (Rom. 12.19–21).

The benediction desires for all of these recipients that they should be made whole and spotless in all respects in anticipation of the coming of the Lord. And it speaks of the faithfulness (*pistos*) of God in accomplishing precisely this. Their faithfulness (to Paul, to one another, to the gospel) is thus a reflection of the divine faithfulness. Thus concluding with faithfulness in the horizon of hope, Paul directs this band of brothers to one another that they may demonstrate their love for one another with a kiss.

2 Thessalonians

2 Thessalonians is remarkable both for its similarity to 1 Thessalonians and for its no less striking differences. Missing from this letter is the passionate warmth of 1 Thessalonians. Instead we have a writer who seems emotionally distant from the community, speaking of commanding rather than yearning, for example. In terms of content, the outline and several themes from 1 Thessalonians are repeated almost verbatim, while several prominent themes are developed in ways that appear to flatly contradict the perspective of 1 Thessalonians. Most scholars suppose that this letter was not written by the same Paul who was responsible for the first letter, in spite (or because) of the fact that the letter betrays an awareness of the possibility of forgery and falsification of Pauline letters. Even if the letter was not written by the same Paul responsible for 1 Thessalonians, this text remains invaluable for the light it sheds on the earliest Christian communities, especially under threat of persecution, and for showing us how a relationship to Paul becomes a relationship to a tradition. It may also offer invaluable insight into the relation between the emerging Christian communities and the way in which 'empire' appears from the standpoint of the 'underside' of history; something not irrelevant to all too many people today in the shadow of an emerging world order that crushes the weak and vulnerable masses of humanity.

Greetings

The salutation (1.1–5) very closely echoes the beginning of 1 Thessalonians. In both cases we note that the cause of gratitude is the growth in faithfulness and in love for one another. Characteristic of the point of view of this letter is the restriction of love to members of the community, which therefore seems far more embattled than in 1 Thessalonians.

At 1.5–12 the imagery of the return or 'revelation' of the Lord has a far more menacing tone. A strong emphasis is placed upon what this will mean for those who have made life difficult for the community, for the appearing of the Lord entails 'vengeance upon those who do not know God and upon those who do not adhere to the good news of our Lord Jesus'. The vengeance here seems to be 'exclusion from the presence of the Lord'. That is, as menacing as this section is, it does not indulge itself in the torments of the opponents. We should read this theme against the background of intense persecution of a minority community by very powerful authorities. For the embattled community the will to endure may be strengthened by holding out for an expected comeuppance for the perpetrators of violence. This may also serve to make clear that it is not the community itself that is to be the agent of any such retribution. The role of the community is simply to hang on and ride out the storm that is breaking over it.

When (2.1–12)

In 1 Thessalonians the presenting issue appeared to be concern at the separation from those who had died. Here the eschatological question appears to be rather more speculative, concerning the timing of the coming or appearing or self-manifestation of the Lord Jesus messiah. (The language of appearing used here may be derived from the language of the emperor cult.) The difficulty appears to be that some have concluded that the end has already come. Thus the writer aims to indicate to them that this is not so, that the time has not yet come (2.2). The manner of doing this is at some variance from the position that appears in 1 Thessalonians. For there we were told that the coming would be in a time of apparent peace and security (1 Thess. 4.3) but now it is placed in the context of a mighty rebellion and flood of wickedness (2.3).

At this point we encounter two figures who are introduced into the apocalyptic scenario: the man of lawlessness (*anomie*) and the 'one who restrains' the lawless one but who will be overcome by him. Here we have a possible three- or four-part scenario: the lawless one, the restrainer, the lawless one again and then 'the Lord Jesus'. The scenario fits roughly with a pattern that we know from contemporary Roman history. For example, Caligula was regarded as a deliverer from the excesses of Tiberius. But Caligula was far worse (he in fact did call himself 'God' and had his own image placed in the temple in Rome and sent it to be placed in the temple in Jerusalem). Indeed he went so far as to deify his own horse. When he was assassinated Claudius became emperor, but the rumours of the return of Caligula abounded. Subsequently when Claudius is overthrown (largely because of the tyrannical excesses of his wife and her paramours) and Nero becomes emperor, the latter is first hailed as a hero who will restore Rome but is soon seen as far worse than Claudius. When he is assassinated, order is restored, but there are constant rumours of his return. The scenario indicated in the letter then might fit roughly with these events in the succession of dictators: a violent dictator has a reign of terror. He is restrained by the uprising of the military/aristocratic classes (and by his death), but his return is nonetheless expected (even from the dead) when he will be even more powerful. The point is not to assign this sort of pattern to particular events (death/return of Caligula or death/return of Nero for example) but to say that a pattern exists in Roman political/social reality which the scenario in 2 Thessalonians seems to echo. To this we may add the perspective on such a 'lawless one' that corresponds fairly well to Jewish views concerning Antiochus Epiphanes (see Daniel 11.36) or to Ptolemy or to

Caligula (Gaventa 1998b: 111–12). Thus while the images employed here may well seem bizarre or arcane to those far removed from the turbulent times of the early Roman empire they would have echoed widely shared perspectives on the course of contemporary history. The task of interpretation then would be not to separate these images from their own time and place in order to absolutize them but to discover similar ways in which Christian preaching might connect vividly to the experience of imperial rule 'from the underside' of contemporary history.

Of particular interest here is the sense that what rules in the turbulent political sphere of the empire is a lie and that many are deceived. Roman pagan observers of these times (Tacitus, Suetonius and so on) would generally agree with that perspective. Oppression and persecution are always characterized by systematic distortions of the truth, whether we think of anti-Semitism in early twentieth-century Europe or white supremacy in the history of the USA, or the myth of the inferiority of colonialized peoples. To this we should also add the tissue of lies and libels that make patriarchy and misogyny possible, or those that underwrite heterosexism and homophobia. In every case it is the reign of deliberate dis-information that makes domination possible. At the same time the author of this letter suggests that people actually collaborate in their own deception, preferring to believe lies rather than discover the truth. The combination of deliberate lies and willing self-deception is the necessary framework for all forms of tyranny, and the only remedy is the simple truth; the truth of the proclamation of the gospel.

Stand firm (2.13–17)

In spite of the somewhat lurid language of the preceding passage, the author's main point is that the community should not be distracted by speculation about the end and should in any case certainly not suppose that the end has already come.

The encouragement to stand firm and the grounding of this in the sure call of God stands in some contrast to the way in which this sort of apocalyptic scenario is sometimes used to terrorize the faithful and to unsettle their minds or to tell them that the time has indeed come.

The reference to traditions communicated to them from Paul (2.15) is one of the indicators that this may be actually from a post-Pauline Paulinist who thinks that he has the spirit or mind of Paul.

If love that extends outward to all and hope that awaits with confidence serve as central values in 1 Thessalonians they are largely absent here, replaced instead with a grim determination to hang on and to close ranks. In both cases we have situations of apparent conflict and even persecution, but the values deemed necessary to the community are importantly different. This is not to say that the values highlighted here are wrong. Indeed there are situations of such severe persecution that minority communities may be able only to close ranks and hang on and be comforted with the thought that their persecutors will one day be finally punished. But hope becomes more hard-bitten (and veers dangerously close to a hope for vengeance) and love becomes less generous, more cramped and confined, and even suspicious.

Work! (3.6–15)

We should notice here first that the role of 'Paul' in relation to this community is certainly not one of brother among brothers, nor is it that he in addition to being father can also describe himself as wet nurse or even as child or orphan. In this letter 'Paul' is only an authority who insists upon being obeyed. 'I command you' he begins (3.6) and concludes with 'if anyone refuses to obey . . .'.

But if Paul has changed so as to be scarcely recognizable from the passionate lover of the first letter, the situation of the community still bears recognizable features. The instructions about work here make particular sense if we suppose, as we did in the case of 1 Thessalonians, that the community is something like a workers' co-op or commune. The text recalls what we also read in 1 Thessalonians, that Paul set an example of working alongside them in the workshop (night and day), rather than seeking to be supported by them (as would be the case with wandering philosophers, or preachers). In the same way those who are a part of the commune should also participate according to their abilities in its labours. The instruction on this point is rather more severe than in 1 Thessalonians (he who does not work should not eat) but would be rather more appropriate to a commune of workers than it would in a world in which this comes to mean something like 'get a job'. In any case it is the community itself that provides the work that is to be done.

The importance of this instruction may owe as well to the mistaken view that the end has already come. In this case there may have been those who decided not to contribute to the welfare or work of the group on the grounds that the end had already come. It is this sort of idleness that Paul's words seek to interdict. We should however remind ourselves of the very different example of the Gospels, in which Jesus' followers leave work (and family) in order to be dependent on the kindness of strangers.

In any case, free-loaders who think they are too good to pitch in with whatever needs to be done in the commune/community may be shunned or given the cold shoulder. However, Paul maintains that even here the shirker is not to be treated as an enemy but rather warned as a brother. That is, the ethos here is not that of 'every man for himself' but rather the ethos of the family. In both of these letters Paul is invoking the ethos of the new family, constituted not by biological ties but by shared commitment. The family here as generally in the Second Testament is 'families we choose' (Gaventa 1998b: 29) rather than a valorization of traditional 'marriage and family values'.

Benediction

The third chapter, like the second, concludes with a brief benediction. Here the theme is peace. Despite the background of conflict in the empire what the author wishes for his readers is peace that comes from the one who is peace. This may be a fitting conclusion to the final admonition concerning work that has had in view the internal 'quietness' of the community which is not to be disrupted by 'busybodies' who have nothing to do but stir up discontent within this band of 'brothers'.

Conclusion

How are we to understand the relation between these two letters? Certainly enough time has elapsed between them that it is possible for the writer of the second letter to suppose that there may have been letters pretending to be from Paul that were forgeries. The second letter certainly seems patterned on the first, both in terms of outline and in terms of the formulation of certain themes. Moreover the features of the community that may be inferred from the letters bear striking resemblance to one another. In each case the community of brothers seems also to be a commune of workers. In each case the community appears in a situation of intense persecution with very powerful forces arrayed against it. And in each case the author points them forward to the coming of their Messiah and Lord in order to bolster their capacity to withstand the sufferings of the present.

Yet something very basic has changed. The sweet wine of mutual longing and loyalty has begun to turn toward the vinegar of a rather grim perseverance. The horizon of love has shrunk from one directed to all, to a love directed to an inner circle. The horizon of hope has shifted from ecstatic reunion with those who have died and with the Lord, to a protracted world drama of violence and fear. The divine love has come to signify not only rescue from impending catastrophe but also vengeance upon the tormentors of the community. And Paul himself has become less a nurse or an orphan longing for reunion with his beloved, than a distant authority figure who issues implacable commands.

Is it Paul who has changed? Is it the situation of the community that has become so much more desperate? Or has another author with a different character and theological perspective written to Paul's beloved community in Paul's name? In the nature of the case historical questions like these admit of no certain answers, only greater and lesser degrees of probability.

In any case the juxtaposition of these two letters gives us invaluable snapshots of a community of faith under dire threat and of the ways in which their leaders sought to strengthen them for the difficult times in which they lived. And they pose for us the question of how we will have negotiated the time of testing and affliction.

The Pastoral Letters: 1 and 2 Timothy, and Titus

ROBERT E. GOSS AND DEBORAH KRAUSE

Queering the Church and Gay Culture

The reading in which we are engaged started in a conversation in which one of us discussed the nature of the rhetoric in the Pastoral Epistles and the other was compelled to think of the quest for hypermasculinity within gay culture. The point of connection was the 'pumped-up' nature of the Pastoral Epistle writer's understanding of the Church and the drive to 'pump up' the body certain gay men have felt within their experience of being gay men. Our purpose is to juxtapose these sites of 'pumpatude' to wonder about the construction of realities within the Church and gay culture and how such constructions have served and can serve to dismember persons and communities within particular quests for an 'ideal' or a space of original blessing and certainty. In both cases the quest for the ideal provides a space within which the vagaries and realities of conflict and complexity are streamlined out of view in the service of establishing the illusion of the unitary, inviolable, pure and potent. In attempting to queer the culture, Church and text in this way we are setting out to break open these spaces, to question what they have streamlined out of view in the service of wondering about the multiple ways we might be able to be gay and the multiple ways we might be able to be church.

The practice of queer reading has emerged as a contextual reading strategy within translesbigay cultural liberation studies. To queer in this regard has been to challenge hegemonic interpretations of tradition and constructions of society and culture in order to expose their heterosexist commitments and assumptions and to offer counter readings that hold those hegemonic interpretations and constructions up for question. In the most basic etymological sense 'to queer' means to make strange – and Queer Interpretation is precisely a practice of making strange that which has been assumed to be familiar. Queer Interpretation challenges domesticated constructions and interpretations purported by Church and culture and wonders about who such constructions and interpretations have closeted. As a strategy of liberation, Queer Interpretation seeks to expose and challenge the violence that such constructions and interpretations have done to people's identities, experiences and bodies. In this sense 'Queer Reading' is reading that both works against the grain of established heterosexist hierarchies, and works for the goal of greater inclusion for translesbigay people within society and culture. In this sense, we

venture this reading of texts and bodies guided by Ken Stone's broad identification of queer biblical interpretation in his edited volume *Queer Commentary
of the Hebrew Bible*: 'a range of approaches to biblical interpretation that take as
their point of departure a critical interrogation and active contestation of the
many ways in which the bible is and has been read to support heteronormative and normalizing configurations of sexual practices and sexual identities'
(Stone 2001: 33).

It is indeed a queer thing to analogize the rhetoric of the Pastoral Epistle
writer with the practice of steroid use and bodybuilding within gay cultures.
Such an intersection of what many consider a sacred text and that which has
been normatively described as 'deviant' social behaviour raises all kinds of
questions about what is sacred and what is profane. To place the pumped-
up rhetoric of the epistle writer and the pumped-up bodies of men next to
one another is to trouble the alleged normalcy of the one with the apparent
abnormality of the other. To analogize the rhetoric and social programme of
the Pastoral Epistle writer with bodybuilding is to hold together two separate quests for the 'ideal'. When these quests are placed within their historical
and social contexts they can be seen as reactions to threats of outside influences, be it heresy or disease. This contextual examination makes strange that
which appears to be familiar and makes more familiar that which may at first
look foreign. Be it the Pastoral Epistle writer's understanding of the 'body'
of the ecclesia or the artificially developed bodies of certain gay men, both
projects are understood as projections of desire for a space that is inviolable,
safe and secure. The question our examination seeks to raise in both contexts
is at what expense such apparent security and safety is built. Ultimately we
seek to explore how such idealization of the Church and the body result in the
disfiguring of individual lives and the shape of community.

The Steroid Church – A Queer Reading of the Pastoral Epistles (PE)

Seeing the 'pumped-up' nature of the rhetoric of the Pastoral Epistle writer
requires a bit of a dressing-down of his letters, or an undressing of his persona as the apostle Paul. In their historical context the letters are understood
by most scholars to be examples of the ancient practice of pseudepigraphy
– which means they are falsely ascribed in their authorship to a venerable historical figure whose authority and legend the letter writer is seeking to extend
and claim. In this light, much of traditional historical critical interpretation
has disparaged the PE as 'late' and inauthentic expressions of a bishop who
seeks to accommodate the Pauline church from its radical egalitarian vision
of Galatians 3.28 ('No Jew or Greek, slave or free, male and female') to a hier-
archal, patriarchal institution that is complicit with the ways of Roman rule
and culture. Roman society was built on the cultural codes that the stronger
dominated the weaker, and women were weaker than men. In this sense, the
infamous dictates of the PE writer for women to be silent (1 Tim. 2.11) and for
slaves to be submissive to their masters (1 Tim. 6.1–2) are understood as a mis-
representation of Graeco-Roman cultural values for the teaching of the apostle
Paul. In this sense, the writer of the PE is understood to be misrepresenting

Paul, using his name to shore up the Church as it faced the challenges of heresy, and the ongoing reality of the delay of the return of Christ. As such the letters are not the 'real Paul', but rather are theologically drained in their vision and applied to the pressures and struggles that the Church faced into the second century as it lived in the world.

We would not argue with the fact that the PE are 'pseudo-Paul', nor would we also argue with the insight that they represent in many ways a diminishing of Paul's theology and social vision in accommodation to Graeco-Roman culture. Where the traditional historical analysis of these letters has gone wanting, however, is in its glossing over the remarkably diverse context of early Christianities in which the PE writer engages in his reading of Paul, and the extent to which this reading is a tremendous power play within the history of the Church. The PE writer is not simply trying to save the Church from heretics or the pressures of the delay of the *parousia*, rather he is presenting his social vision of the Church within the cloak of Paul's authority while disparaging the practices and beliefs of those whom he considered 'other'. When the letters are seen as a discourse of power in this way they are not so much an inevitable diminishing of Paul's radical gospel, as they are their own radical reappropriation of Paul and his authority for the purpose of projecting a particular understanding of the Church, its practices and its organization. In this sense the PE attempt to bring into submission the disparate and troublesome voices of early Christian communities by establishing 'Paul's' vision of the Church on Roman cultural principles of power and gender ideology.

In the light of these issues of power the PE writer's rhetoric is a kind of performance – a performance of 'Paul' and a performance of the ideal of church leadership. In the guise of this performance 'Paul' speaks to his most intimate travelling companions in ministry 'Timothy' and 'Titus' to describe to them the proper order of the Church. As the writer carries out this performance, however, he reveals his insecurities. There are tensions between what he says and how he says it. There are struggles around his language and his meaning. A reading that looks for such insecurities, that brings to light tensions, that enhances the presence of such struggles for 'normalcy' is a practice of queer reading that seeks to open spaces and de-naturalize the Church as it has been constructed and projected by the PE writer.

Unlike the writer of what we call the seven authentic letters (the real Paul), the writer of the PE never uses the phrase the 'body of Christ'. The term appears frequently in Paul's characterization of the Church, but the PE writer uses less organic terms such as 'Household of faith' and 'pillar and bulwark of truth' (1 Tim. 3.15). Paul is comfortable to explore the vagaries and idiosyncrasies of human flesh as it relates to the life of the Church. In fact in Romans 12 and 1 Corinthians 12 he engages the metaphor of the body in all of its limitations and frailty as a means toward exploring the diversity of gifts within the Church. Some are eyes, some are ears, some are tongues, some hands and feet. There the body stands, flabby, wide-ranging, and definitely weird right next to the Church. In contrast to Paul, human flesh is not a metaphor in the PE writer's ecclesiological vocabulary. Flesh for him remains a confessional term associated with Christ's incarnation (1 Tim. 3.16), and with the particularities of instructions about what those in the Church may and may not do with their bodies (e.g. 1 Tim. 4.8).

A central term that represents the PE writer's drive to 'pump up' his particular vision of the Church through the authority of Paul is with the verb *hugiaino* and the adjective *hugies*. The term appears eight times in the PE corpus. It is used to express the physical health and vigour of the PE writer's vision of the Church, its teachings and practices. The term is often translated into English as 'sound', but with its implications of strength and vigour the adjectives 'buff', 'huge' and 'ripped' might better serve. In six different uses the PE writer describes the strength of the 'teaching' or 'doctrine' of the Church, the vigour of the words of Jesus Christ, and the soundness of 'Titus's' own words. In each of these uses the threat of outside teaching, heretical practices or 'other ways' of being church evoke the call for attention to the strength and inviolability of the PE writer's vision of the Church. Such a call on the part of the PE writer reveals his concern to project an image of an impenetrable church, one that is free of the disease of heresy. That such a concern is evident within his rhetoric is a way of illuminating the 'performed' nature of the PE writer's vision of the Church. He is not simply stating the facts, rather he is asserting within a highly charged and competitive context of alternative ecclesiologies that his vision of the Church (as Paul's vision) is solid and will endure forever. His correlation of hard bodies with pastoral power underscores his calls for male ecclesial leadership and control. He conceives the larger, ecclesial organization as an extended family, led by a pumped-up, hardened leadership. He gives instruction to the weaker, 'how one must behave in God's house, which is the church of the living God' (1 Tim. 3.15). The PE writer vests social control in a hierarchy of stronger male bodies who preside over the household, displaying their authority over women, children and slaves.

In counterpoint to the concern for strength in the Church's teachings and beliefs the PE writer reveals another concern for the tendency of some to be 'other' (*heteros*) or to deviate/swerve (*astocheo*). These activities belong to people who seek to wreck the Church and destroy the Church in its strength. 'Otherness' and swerving/deviation are precisely the sensibilities that the pumped-up Church resists. In fact, the inviolable strength of the Church is structured in such a way that women keep silent, slaves keep submissive and the bishop remains in charge. This structure will not allow for deviation and swerve – it is the rigid and pumped structure of a church in which everyone has a place and the speech and vision of the leadership must stand as the word and vision for all.

The PE writer's rhetorical practice of building up the Church is tied to masculinity throughout his correspondence with Timothy and Titus. Nowhere is this more evident than in the idealization of male power as the letter writer encourages Timothy to remain strong in his leadership of the Church and strong in the faith. In this instruction the letter writer promotes three visions of an ideal hypermasculinity – the good soldier, the disciplined athlete and the hard-working farmer (weren't these three of the guys in the Village People?). All three stand as models of how ideal men within the service of the ideal and vigorous Church behave. As the Church is unitary and solid, so is the commitment of these model men to their tasks, and in each case their tasks are to obey the 'rules', and to follow the chain of command. The PE writer's call to Timothy to embody this ideal of manhood represents one part of his construction of an idealized, hypermasculine Church.

> You then my son, be strong in the grace that is in Christ Jesus, and what you have heard from me before many witnesses entrust to faithful men who will be able to teach others also. Share in suffering as a good soldier of Christ Jesus. No soldier on service gets entangled in the practical things of life, since his aim is to satisfy the one who enlisted him. An athlete is not crowned unless he competes according to the rules. It is the hard working farmer who ought to have the first share of the crops. (2 Tim. 2.1–7)

Importantly, scholars of early Christianity have observed that the PE writer's construction of an idealized masculinity for ecclesial leadership is not part of a monolithic tradition or expectation of masculine performance in the early Church. Jennifer Glancy has noted that the PE's notion of masculinity or 'real men' stands in cultural contrast to earlier constructions of masculinity. As much as the PE attempt to provide a unitary example of masculine strength for the purpose of demonstrating the unitary authority of the Church, their canonical context, with other writings that have diverse portrayals of masculinity (for example John the Baptist, Jesus, the Twelve, and Paul), blows their cover. Far from settling the issue of the 'ideal man' such diversity of presentation leaves open the questions of what is strong, what is good and what is male.

> The Christian masculinity prescribed by the Pastor is at odds with the images of possible masculinities. Early Christian writings represent John the Baptist, Jesus, and Paul as anomalous men in their passions, in their eschewal of matrimonial and paternal roles, and, in the case of Jesus, in shameful death. (Glancy 2003: 250)

This queering of the PE has sought to ground the letter writer's insistence to construct a particular kind of Church and to expose his anxieties about the health of the Church. Through a reading of his rhetorical constructions about strength in the Church, and his determination to avoid swerving, straying and deviation, this queering has looked upon his letters as a discourse of power that seeks to build a vision of the Church that is inviolable to difference, and that can withstand diversity. It is a singular church that stands on the solid 'deposit of faith'. Such a construction is an artificial enhancement of the Church that demands the rigid social divisions between men's and women's activities, that exploits the economic agency of certain classes for the power and privilege of a few. The buff nature of the PE writer's Church therefore squelches out the voices and lives of women, slaves, children and others in the service of purity, strength, truth and 'the faith'. This queering has attempted to denaturalize the PE writer's rhetoric and to expose the strong body of his construction – strong indeed, but we wonder, is it healthy?

The Steroid Gay Body: The Steroid Church

We have problematized the 'pumped-up', hypermasculine image of the PE's Church. It is problematic as an image of the Church for its exclusions of women and lesser-status males, and it is connected to heterosexist notions of the masculine body. The cultural historian Thomas Laqueur has detailed how the ancient world constructed the sexual body, not within the two-sex model of our contemporary culture but the one-sex model. Graeco-Roman culture perceived two genders within a continuum of maleness. A contemporary or near-contemporary to the author of 1 Timothy, Galen of Pergamum writes,

> Turn outward, the woman's, turn inward, so to speak, and fold double the man's (genital organs), and you will find the same in both in every respect. (Laqueur 1990: 25)

The ancient Mediterranean model of sex is further comprehended within the notions of penetrability. Penetration expresses a superior status of the hardened body, while soft bodies or bodies of lesser status are penetrated (Williams 1999). These notions still shape segments of contemporary gay male culture. Hard bodies are the dominant expression of masculine status and the ideology of dominance. The impenetrable, hardened becomes the normative ideal while soft, effeminate and flabby bodies of females and lesser males hold a lesser, even despised status.

To construct the body of Christ as masculine, pumped up by ascetic practices may have been a normative strategy to gain wider apologetic acceptance and sustain male hegemony within the PE's Church. It attempted to elide the social roles and voices of Christian women and weaker males. It feared the feminized body and the feminine. Gender codes were the last residue of purity codes within the ancient world.

The biblical scholar Stephen Moore writes, 'Hardcore bodybuilding is a purity system, arguably the most rigorous purity system, to be found in contemporary Western culture' (Moore 1996: 76). Bodybuilding provides a vehicle to secure the gaze of women and gay men. It separates body according to hardness, muscles and buffness. The last decade or so has witnessed the emergence of a Southern-California, steroid-enhanced body aesthetic among young urban gay males. Gay men have used bodybuilding to pump up their muscular, male bodies, often to attract the gaze of other men and to reassure themselves of their masculinity. There have been previous, cloned styles of physical aesthetics; in the 1970s and early 1980s, it was the moustache or beard, hairy clone with a checkered flannel shirt, jeans and boots. In the late 1990s into the twenty-first century, it became large-pecs, tight shirts, close-cropped hair, and hairless or shaved chests.

One certainly could argue that both the mid-1970s and contemporary aesthetics of male beauty within the gay community were produced as counter-cultural movements responding to dominant heterosexist notions of masculinity. There are, however, different cultural factors that contribute to the cult of body worship in the two periods. Both the Graeco-Roman world and dominant American society have stigmatized gay males as less than males or equated gays with the feminine in both the 1970s and 1990s. The contemporary situation of gay males differs from the earlier period. The cultural writer Michelangelo Signorile notes,

> Being healthy and disease-free also began to mean having muscles and strong sturdy body. As the 1990s raced on, we set out to prove we were supermen despite AIDS. (Signorile 1998: 67)

Aids had a devastating impact on the gay male community. It also heightened gay male awareness of body appearance, for the wasting-away syndrome became a signifier of HIV and unhealthy bodies. Physicians treated gay men with HIV wasting syndrome with anabolic steroids to pump up their bodies. The indelible cultural impact became 'muscles equals health'. Now particular pumped-up bodies are often a signifier of HIV+ status.

In addition to the Aids pandemic, muscular bodies also became a signifier for masculinity: 'muscles equals masculinity'. The social stigma of gay propelled the development of the butch bottom, the penetrated male who exuded muscular and buffed body. The missionaries for this new physical aesthetics of masculinity were the gay porn stars of the late 1980s – Jeff Stryker, Jon King, Joey Stefano, Kevin Williams and Ryan Idol. Butch tops and bottoms have queered the traditional codes of penetrator/penetrated within the gay male community that frequently portrays bottoms as lesser males. Gay porn stars modelled a masculinity that was hairless, with pumped-up muscles, tanned and hard-bodied. What emerged within the urban gay male communities was a cult of masculinity that became a religious obsession for many young gay males. Signorile writes, 'Gyms are the cult's temples. Night clubs and sex clubs, its shrines' (Signorile 1998: 75–6). Circuit parties – several days long – where thousands of gay men participate in a marathon orgy of dancing and other embodied activities – become fashion shows where they display their pumped bodies of perfection to one another.

The hypermasculine gay body is built up through the technology of the gym and often through dangerous steroid-enhancements, chest and buttock implants. Body hair is shaved off chests to display hardened muscles. Body hair signified experience, age and a type of masculinity. Experience carried the spectre of HIV while youth and pumped body subverted the images of HIV bodies, wasted away and prematurely aged. The gay cult of ripped bodies attempted to elide the soft, the feminine.

The physical paradigm of masculine beauty demands conformity to a purity code as rigid as any fundamentalist church. It builds upon the desire to be the perfect male and have the perfect male body. Bar papers, internet sex and phone services enforce this image of masculine image in exclusive terms. 'No Fats, no fems need reply.' Straight-appearing, muscled, youthfulness, 'body stats' and hairlessness institutionalize this masculine body code. It becomes a masculinist code, with exclusive ideals that border upon a body fascism. Yet it is culturally contagious among gay youth. Signorile tells of Mark in Chelsea, New York, and he reports Mark saying, 'I would see all of those guys with their muscles, and I wanted to be one of them' (Signorile 1998: 168).

This gay cult of masculinity, like its heterosexual counterpart, defines itself in radical opposition to things feminine though the gay male may soften some of its opposition to things feminine, but not to male bodies that are fat, old and feminine. 'No pecs, no sex' becomes their mode of operating and connecting erotically with one another. 'No pecs, no sex' becomes a ritual chant of exclusion. The gay writer David Nimmons writes about the fierce gay devotion to male beauty: 'the beliefs we share about beauty and bodies work to help us erect barriers between each other. They have become the single most fertile domain where we erect differences and distance' (Nimmons 2002: 196). The gay cult to masculine beauty sets up its ideal of masculine aesthetics as a form of hegemonic masculinity. Size and hardness are the goals of this cult. Stephen Moore observes, 'the bodybuilder is an outsized penis in a state of permanent erection' (Moore 1996: 133). Softness and lack of size are the shadow fears that lurk in the wings of this cult. Soft males and soft bodies are ignored; pumped-up gay ascetics exclude these lesser males.

Ironically, body asceticism in the gyms, combined with steroid use in building up the muscles rapidly, has a downside for men. It leads to breast enhancement and shrinkage of male testicles. By refusing the feminine and its divinization of hypermasculinity, the body begins to move full circle to develop feminine features. What this masculinist cult fears the most is realized: a feminized body. Mark Simpson writes, 'The bodybuilder does not understand that he was destined all along to be a transsexual butterfly' (Simpson 1994: 42). Gay misogyny can be as destructive as heterosexual male misogyny.

Conclusion

In this queer reading of the texts of 1 and 2 Timothy and Titus with the activity of bodybuilding within certain cultures of gay men we have begun to see some connections between them in their performance of hypermasculinity. Within both sites the performance of making either the structures of the Church or the body hard is vested with tremendous desire for purity and fear of violation and disease. While we may have empathy with such desire and fear, what is clear to us in both sites is that the practice of making unified and solid that which is diverse and fluid is a practice that results in the diminishing of individual lives and the full beauty of human community. In the quest of building ideal Church or ideal man we build distorted bodies that can begin to mirror elements of the soft and vulnerable we so wish to repress, the very constructions the PE writer and hypermasculine-identified men seem to find most abject.

We choose to end with some reflections by Gerard Loughlin who has struggled well with the issue of hypermasculinity in the Church and in men's bodies. He proposes that a solution to these virulent purity codes is to rebuild our entire notion of the body of Christ. In an essay, 'Refiguring masculinity in Christ', Loughlin writes,

> It is only in the complex, fecund and fluid matrix of Christ-become-the Church that Christian theology may refigure masculinity . . . since to be

masculine in Christ is surely to become more likely the body of Christ, to be at one and the same time more Christic and more bodily. But since the body of Christ is – in the manifold of the Christian imaginary – both the crucified, risen, and ascended Lord, the mother who nurtures her children, and each and every one of them. (Loughlin 1998: 410)

Loughlin notes that identities are destabilized in Christ, and he explains the appropriateness of conceiving 'Christ hermaphroditic' in medieval Christian theology.

Christ is at one and the same time male and female, masculine and feminine . . . But we can at least see that such an understanding implies a possible refiguring of our sexed identities. For if the male Christ is both feminine and masculine, can we any longer be certain as to what constitutes masculinity and femininity? It could be done only by making appeal to the very thing that Christ's hermaphroditism calls in question: the social forms outside Christ's hermaphroditic body. (Loughlin 1998: 411)

All attempts to elide the feminine disrupt the Church by silencing important voices in the community, and all attempts to elide all the feminine within gay males lead to the re-emergence of the feminine in new transgender, steroid configurations of bodybuilder bodies. The lesson seems to be that human communities and bodies are diverse and fluid. Rhetorical performances of community and identity that seek to repress this diversity and fluidity often result in contortion and violence. And yet these performances are coercions that ultimately do not allay concerns of violability and vulnerability. In fact they create new vulnerabilities. What would it mean in churches and in gay culture to accept soft bodies as well as hard bodies, bodies that mature and lose their muscle-tone, disabled bodies, and different bodies, without the judgement of exclusions?

Philemon

STEPHEN J. MOORE

The only way to imagine a society without slavery [in ancient times] would have been to imagine a different society. (*Horsley 1997: 59*)

However that may be, let each of you lead the life that the Sovereign [Lord] has assigned, to which God called you. This is my rule in all the Churches . . . Were you a slave when called? Do not be concerned about it. Even if you can gain your freedom, make use of your present condition now more than ever. For whoever was called in the Sovereign [Lord] as a slave is a freed person belonging to the Sovereign [Lord], just as whoever was free when called is a slave of Christ. You were bought with a price; do not become slaves of human masters [and mistresses]. In whatever condition you were called, brothers and sisters, there remain with God. (*1 Corinthians 7.17, 21–4, NRSV*)

But now that faith has come, we are no longer subject to a disciplinarian, for in Christ Jesus you are all children of God through faith. As many of you as were baptized into Christ have clothed yourselves with Christ. There is no longer Jew or Greek, there is no longer slave or free, there is no longer male and female; for all of you are one in Christ Jesus. (*Galatians 3.25–8, NRSV*)

The letter of Paul to Philemon represents a transitional place between the praxis of radical egalitarianism of the historical Jesus of Nazareth (Crossan 1991; Funk 1998) and the later deutero-Pauline traditions of some of the early non-Judaean Christian churches; traditions which soon rejected the difficulties and challenge of egalitarian praxis, and accommodated to paternal, patriarchal Graeco-Roman culture (Eph. 6.5–9; Col. 3.22–4.1). What is often overlooked is that *Pax Romana* (Roman *Peace*?) was obtained via systematic violence, war, exploitation and domination. The imperial rule of Rome (in contrast to Jesus' vision of the imperial rule of God) was built and maintained on the backs of what has been termed the largest 'slave society' in the ancient world (Finley 1964: 45–9):

It appears that all who could afford to own a slave did, from the more typical few to as many as hundreds and even thousands. It is estimated that in some places the slave population was more than half the total population. Even conservative estimates place the number of slaves around thirty percent. (Ryan 2005: 170)

The overwhelming majority of slaves were prisoners of war, captives and others who were kidnapped and separated from their families, their homeland, and even other country-men and -women so that they would be less likely to unite and rebel. The slave-based economy provided honour and status to conquerors and ruling classes who, because of their status and power, considered themselves due the tribute and loyalty of slaves in exchange for preserving their lives and providing further protection. Therefore in ancient times slavery was viewed as exclusively linked to revenue and not specifically to race. However, while even Romans could find themselves in bond or debt slavery, the majority of slaves were not citizens, but foreigners, regarded as property [chattel slavery] and having few if any human rights and little access to justice. While there were discussions and debates concerning the treatment of slaves, no genuine legislation protecting slaves apparently existed. Owners had exclusive rights over slaves, which meant that the owners who were responsible for protecting slaves also had the legal right to inflict punishment and even death. Therefore the condition of a slave's life depended to a great extent upon his or her owner as well as the kind of service he or she could provide . . . Ancient writings also show that slaves were stereotyped as useless, lazy and even criminal. Generally . . . flight was the only way for a slave to secure freedom. Subsequently, laws were enacted that made running away a serious crime that could label the offender a fugitive who, when found, would be returned to the owner to face severe punishment and even death. Anyone who harbored such a fugitive could also be charged with theft. A slave could, however, reasonably seek asylum from an abusive owner or could seek mediation from an owner's friend [amicus domini] who could legally provide temporary refuge but might still be responsible for any financial loss to the slave owner. (Ryan 2005: 170–1)

It is in this context that we read Paul's letter to Philemon and the leadership of the Christian community meeting in his home, concerning Onesimus, Philemon's slave. Onesimus has apparently run away (from abuse?) and/or has taken legal asylum and refuge with Paul, who is in prison (at Ephesus?). Paul is returning Onesimus to Philemon, with the accompanying letter. Paul uses considerable rhetorical skills (professed 'love', paternalistic pressure and manipulation, guilt) to encourage Philemon to receive Onesimus back into his community, with a new social status. Onesimus is not to be received back as a returned 'slave'. He is not to be received back as simply a 'freed person' (manumission). Paul's rhetoric requests that Onesimus be received back in a status which is 'equal' to Paul's own social, political, economic and religious status with them (v. 17). Paul seems to be encouraging Philemon and the leadership of the Christian community meeting in his home, to live out the radical egalitarian praxis suggested not only by the historical Jesus, but also by the pre-Pauline Christian baptismal formula found in Paul's letter to the Galatians (Gal. 3.25–8). This pre-Pauline baptismal formula proclaims liberation to a new status for those 'in Christ' from oppressive societal distinctions between people based on gender identification, power, class, religion and culture. Clearly for Philemon (and the Christian community meeting in his home?), such liberation has not yet become a *complete* reality in *praxis*. For this reason Paul has written his letter. We do not know if Philemon and the community meeting in his home followed Paul's suggestions.

The Question of Praxis

In human life and human community, there often exists a gulf between the ideals of theory (what we say, teach and believe) and praxis (what we actually do). Praxis can be understood as a measuring of our ability to 'live out' what we say, teach and believe. In the context of Christian faith and Christian community, praxis can be understood as a measuring of our 'faith' as experienced in our 'actions'. Put simply, it represents our ability to 'practise what we preach'; our ability not only to 'talk-the-talk' but also to 'walk-the-walk' of faith.

It is clear that at least some people in the post-Jesus/pre-Pauline Christian tradition expressed a 'language' of radical egalitarianism in relation to their experiences of faith and personal transformation. It is also clear that this language was remembered, and passed on to Paul in the form of an early Christian baptismal formula (Gal. 3.25–8). Did this *language* of egalitarianism become *praxis* in the lives of these people, and to what extent? Was it simply metaphor and symbol, or was it lived out in daily living?

Is it possible for us, in modern culture, to embrace and follow the teachings and life praxis of liberation found in the pre-Pauline baptismal formula of Galatians 3.25–8, as reflected in the letter to Philemon? If so, how might we arrive at that destination?

Liberation to a new social status for those 'in Christ' from oppressive societal distinctions between people based on gender identification, power, class, religion and culture might be seen by many as clear benefits. However, it may also be seen as a great threat and loss for others.

Should egalitarian language and praxis be extended to the categories of human sexuality? What of queer GLBT people, who seek a sexual praxis of Christian egalitarianism? How should such a one respond to existing paternal, patriarchal sexual language and sexual praxis of 'male-over-female; master-over-slave; top-over-bottom; butch-over-fem'?

Hebrews

THOMAS HANKS

Shortly after my coming out in 1989, after 40 years in the closet and 25 years as an evangelical missionary (Bible professor) in Latin America, I was invited to write the article on 'poor/poverty in the New Testament' for the *Anchor Bible Dictionary* (Doubleday 1992). Having become divorced and unemployed in the coming-out process and brimming with sermon ideas for gay brothers in similar straits, I was free to dedicate some months to figure out, 'Is Hebrews really queer?' God did not just 'speak' but shouted encouragement to me as I studied and wrote about Hebrews! Every chapter seemed to have a powerful message – or several – and I soon had a lengthy and highly edifying manuscript that no publisher seemed to be interested in. André Gide noted, 'It is better to be hated for what one is than loved for what one is not.'

Introduction

Although traditionally known as 'The Epistle of the Apostle Paul to the Hebrews', the book is neither a letter nor from Paul, but anonymous in the earliest Greek manuscripts. Hebrews probably was written around 65–6 CE, shortly after Paul's martyrdom and the great fire in Rome, but before the Roman war and destruction of Jerusalem (67–70 CE). Hebrews thus was penned perhaps less than a decade after Paul's letter to several house churches in Rome (55–8 CE). The author may well have been Apollos (Acts 18.24), apparently an unmarried, subversive, itinerant preacher like Paul and Jesus. The author represents a cultured, educated elite and addresses persons with a degree of education but recently impoverished by discrimination and persecution (10.32–4).

Most likely Hebrews was written to a house church in Rome, where Claudius' edict expelling Jews from Rome (49 CE) and the great fire (64 CE) had led to considerable persecution (10.32–4). Jewish believers in Jesus, when banished from Jewish synagogues, no longer would enjoy even the limited legal protection granted to other Jews (13.12–14). Priscilla (Rom. 16.3–5) or the apostle Junia (Rom. 16.7) may well have been one of the 'leaders' in the house church addressed, so although not written *by* a woman (in Heb. 11.32 the Greek grammar refers to the author as masculine), Hebrews may well have been written *to* a house church in Rome led by women.

The house church members addressed probably were mainly Jewish believers in Jesus who had immigrated back to Rome after Claudius' decree of expulsion (49 CE) was allowed to lapse with the accession of Nero (54–68

CE). The temptation to dishonour marriage (13.4) and fascination with queer Melchizedek (5.6–10; 7.1–28) may reflect that the majority of members were unmarried, sexual minorities. Another significant link between Paul's letter to the Romans and Hebrews may be the emphasis on Jesus' faithfulness unto death (Heb 12.2; see Christ's 'faithfulness as a son over God's house', 3.2, 6) and Paul's disputed references to the 'faithfulness *of* Jesus'.

Of all the Christian scriptures, Hebrews most frequently cites the Hebrew Bible, but continually suggests new interpretations, often Christological, and never simply reflects the original meaning (Attridge 1989). The two texts most featured are Psalm 110 and Jeremiah 31.31–4, both reflecting sexual minority perspectives. Hebrews represents an extreme among the Christian scriptures in the apparent degree of Neoplatonism in its language and theology, evidently reflecting its Hellenistic Jewish roots. However, its emphasis on the Hebrew traditions of creation, the Exodus liberation, Jesus' incarnation in a '*body* prepared', then resurrected and ascended (Heb. 10.5; Ps. 40.6–8), and its apocalyptic hope of a renewed cosmos (Heb. 12) distinguish it from pure Neoplatonism.

'Anti-Semitism' (Anti-Judaism) in Hebrews and Homophobia in Paul?

John Boswell has demonstrated how anti-Semitism and homophobia developed as parallel prejudices, especially in the late Middle Ages (1150–1400 CE):

> Most societies . . . which freely tolerate religious diversity also accept sexual variation, and the fate of Jews and gay people has been almost identical throughout European history, from early Christian hostility to extermination in concentration camps. The same laws which oppressed Jews oppressed gay people ['sodomites']; the same groups bent on eliminating Jews tried to wipe out homosexuality; the same periods of European history which could not make room for Jewish distinctiveness reacted violently against sexual nonconformity; the same countries which insisted on religious uniformity imposed majority standards of sexual conduct ; and even the same methods of propaganda were used against Jews and gay people – picturing them as animals bent on the destruction of the children of the majority (Boswell 1980: 15–16).

Boswell's conclusion is now amply confirmed by Louis Crompton (2003), showing how inquisitional violence promoting the killing of Jews and sodomites remained characteristic of Western 'civilization' well into the twentieth century. In the biblical field, for decades academics of various persuasions have fallen over backwards to defend the Second Testament against any charge or suspicion of anti-Semitism/Judaism, while at the same time blithely propagating the notion that St Paul in particular is responsible for centuries of homophobic violence against sexual minorities, 'sodomites'.

Hebrews provides neither clobber texts nor lesser ammunition for promoting homophobic violence; however, it is commonly assumed to be 'supersessionist', promoting the superiority of the 'Christian religion' to Judaism and advocating the replacement of Judaism by 'Christianity'. For dealing with homophobic recourse to favourite clobber texts in Leviticus and Paul, it is instructive to deal with the conclusion that Hebrews is supersessionist and promotes anti-Semitism/Judaism:

- Hebrews speaks of the superiority of Christ (1.1–4 etc.), not of 'Christianity', which remained a sect of Judaism even into the second century. Jesus' followers are referred to as 'Christians' only three times in the Christian scriptures (Acts 11.26; cf. 26.28; 1 Peter 4.16).
- As Robert Gordon points out, 'both Judaism and Christianity are supersessionist in relation to the Hebrew scriptures, both having turned their backs on forms of worship that involve the satisfaction of the deity by means of animal sacrifices' (2000: 28).
- Like Romans, Hebrews speaks of faith in God, not in Jesus. The strong warnings in Hebrews against apostasy are directed toward followers of Jesus, not the Jews.

1.1–4 Jesus: God's decisive, final revelation (not Leviticus or Paul)

'At many times and in various ways' reminds us of the diversity of biblical teaching in the sexual area. The 'many times' points to the diversity of historical contexts reflected in biblical texts. The decimated population of the Exile needed to hear exhortations to reproduce the species – Genesis 1 etc.; patriarchy presupposed male superiority. Jesus, by his sacrifice, cleanses us from our *sins* (oppression, lack of compassionate solidarity with those in need, intentions and acts that harm neighbour) – not from our sexuality. The loving, responsible expression of our sexuality is not sin and needs no confession or cleansing; sex is not 'dirty', only acts that are unjust, unloving, violent, harmful to neighbour are 'unclean'.

1.5–2.4 Biblical angels as a sexual minority and Jesus' superiority to them.

All of Jesus' followers can expect to have 'enemies' (1.13), but especially the poor, oppressed and sexual minorities. Victory is promised, but is most complete when foes are not humiliated, but transformed into friends. Only those who persist in harming others face humiliation at Jesus' final triumph. Psalm 2.7, cited in Hebrews 1.5, is a royal psalm in which the Judaean king expresses his confidence in God's protection against his enemy oppressors (Attridge 1989: 53). The 'begetting' of the original psalm referred to the king's coronation, but in Hebrews refers to Jesus' ascension (implying his resurrection; Acts 13.33–4). Jesus' reign is fundamentally characterized by freedom, justice, love and joy, but not marriage and procreation (2.8–9; cf. Ps. 45). With the misleading translation 'righteousness' in 2.8–9, modern versions miss the reference to 'justice'. Homophobia and discrimination against sexual minorities are unjust; God 'hates' the wickedness of homophobia, racism, sexism, anti-Judaism, and so on but does not hate sexual minorities nor any loving, responsible expression of our sexuality.

2.5–18 Humanity's glorious origin and destiny (how Jesus' death defeats evil and removes all obstacles)

From the beginning, sexual minorities form part of God's good creation, created in God's image (Ps. 8.5), bearers of full human dignity (Heb. 2.6–8). Behind human agents of oppression and violence, Hebrews discerns other forces of evil (false ideologies that rationalize violence, the calumny of propaganda and lies), and proclaims that by his death Jesus has defeated and destroyed all such forces, including those inspired by ignorance and bigotry regarding sexual minorities (2.14). By his death, Jesus frees us even from the fear of death – and hence from all lesser fears as well (2.15). God 'helps' oppressed people, by taking hold of them to free them, not to stuff them back into 'closets of despair' (2.16, 18; 8.9). The cleansing of sins Jesus offers us through his death applies on the one hand to the sins of sexual minorities: clinging to respectable reputations, lack of courage to leave their closets, failure to love enemies who persecute them. It is applied as well to the sins of oppressors: injustice, bigotry and lack of compassion. Jesus, an unmarried representative of sexual minorities, is especially qualified by his personal testing and suffering to 'help' sexual minorities today in all their suffering and in their special temptations (2.17; 4.14–16).

3.1–6 Moses and Jesus: paradigms of fidelity (vs. warped notions of sexual 'fidelity' today)

In both legal and popular usage today, 'faithful' commonly means one thing only: *negative* avoidance of all sexual activity outside the marriage contract. If a spouse has avoided all sexual activity outside the marriage contract, that person is crowned as 'faithful' (however unfaithful in other areas). In the Bible, 'faithful' has a very different meaning. The Second Testament insists that being faithful to our calling, following Jesus and seeking first God's reign often involve breaking family ties, even with a wife (Luke 14.26; 18.29). Faithful/ness in the Bible is always a positive concept: it refers to what someone does and how it is done; never is it a negative concept such as avoiding or abstaining. In the biblical traditions, marriage commonly was a patriarchal family arrangement and did not involve the intervention of state or clergy, nor did it involve the exchange of vows. Obviously we may apply the concept of 'faithfulness' to the modern institution of marriage and to vows and promises in the sexual area, but to judge a whole person's character as 'faithful/unfaithful' on the basis of sexual abstinence is utterly contrary to the Bible. Even in the sexual area, a person may have failed totally to be a good sexual lover, but be legally and socially approved as 'faithful' simply for having abstained from sexual relationships outside the marriage contract.

3.7–19 Hearing God's voice in the midst of the Aids crisis (God gets angry at oppressors, not the oppressed)

'Synonyms for sin' include: hardening of heart, refusing to listen to God and to collaborate with God in the historical project of full liberation; always straying in heart . . . not knowing God's ways; testing God; unbelief . . . departing from God; disobedience; being led astray by the deceitfulness of sin. Hebrews does not define sin legalistically, nor 'ethically' in universal Greek absolutes, but rather historically in terms of God's project of liberation from oppression (3.16) and guidance towards fuller liberation in the wilderness period (3.17; Num. 14). Israel refused to listen to God, refused further collaboration in the historical project of full liberation, and died (3.17). So today, God's commands are intrinsically related to the historical project of liberation and abundant life for all. When God works to free slaves from oppression, or women from the injustice of an inferior status, or sexual minorities from discrimination and violence – not to listen to God's voice today and work together with God is sin. Sin is so deceitful (3.13) that even divine commands commonly are utilized to justify it, such as Paul's commands to slaves used to justify racism, or his instructions regarding first-century women's head coverings, used to marginalize women from church leadership.

The Hebrew scriptures contain hundreds of references to the 'wrath' of Yahweh. Jesus himself occasionally displayed anger (Mark 3.6), but avoided speaking of God's anger (cf. Luke 21.23; John 3.36). Many Second Testament books follow Jesus in avoiding such terminology; references to divine anger are rare except for Romans and Revelation. In Hebrews, references to divine anger occur especially in the citations from the Hebrew scriptures (3.7–11, 17; Ps. 95.7–11). By ascribing anger to God, certain biblical writers seek to emphasize that God cannot remain passively indifferent in the face of human violence, cruelty, oppression and injustice. Especially, Second Testament writers seek to make clear that God's 'wrath' is always just and rational (Rom. 1.18), and thus to be distinguished from pagan concepts. Hebrews emphasizes that God's anger is provoked when we refuse to listen to God's voice and turn aside from God's liberating purposes, contenting ourselves instead with the poverty and oppression of an unjust status quo (3.10–11, 17).

If the root of sin is refusing to listen, how can we listen to God's voice today? Since Stonewall (1969) we have become aware of the violence suffered by sexual minorities – and have recognized the God of the Exodus at work to liberate. Not to work with God in seeking liberty and justice for sexual minorities is sin (Ps. 103.6–7; Luke 4.18–19). Aids is not 'the wrath of God against homosexuals'; God's wrath works against the injustice of the oppressors, not against the oppressed (Rom. 1.18); failure to show compassionate solidarity is what brings judgement (Matt. 25.31–46). The Church can listen to God's voice by listening to the sexual minorities in our midst (13.3); sexual minorities will grow strong as they avoid divisive bickering over minutiae, learn to listen to God through one another and work with other oppressed groups to create a 'rainbow coalition'.

4.1–13 Out of the closet and into God's rest

God's word is living and active, penetrating the uttermost recesses of human motivations (4.11–13); God's word unmasks the cruel rationalizations of oppressors, but also cowardly, unbelieving rationalizations of the oppressed, who are tempted to remain in bondage instead of trusting God's promise of freedom and responding to God's invitation to construct a new community characterized by freedom, justice and love. Hebrews speaks continually not of 'reading God's book' but of 'hearing God's voice', which often involves careful scrutiny of inspired scripture, but also a sensitivity to the Spirit to discern what God wants to say to us today in a very different historical context, with scientific insights in many areas that far transcend the limited perspectives of biblical writers. Thus, Hebrews frequently cites the Hebrew scriptures, but the later applications the author makes commonly far transcend the meaning of the original texts (Attridge 1989).

God's word is a sword, not a club. Sexual minorities often suffer much from those who use God's word as a 'club' to clobber and to foment 'gay-bashing'. They even speak of the 'clobber texts' – favourite proof-texts commonly mistranslated and misinterpreted to foment hatred and violence against sexual minorities. Hebrews teaches, rather, that God's word is 'sharper than any double-edged sword' – not a 'club' to bash the weak, but a 'sword' to pierce the conscience of the oppressors and call them to repentance. As a sword, God's word does not load us with false guilt, but unmasks real guilt of the oppressors as well as the failures of the oppressed. Real guilt has to do with acts of oppression and lack of solidarity with the oppressed – things that reveal lack of love and result in actual harm to our neighbour (Rom. 13.8–10). Experienced as a 'sword', and not brandished as a 'club', God's word enables sexual minorities to see that God created them and loves them just as they are; their sin does not consist in any sexual orientation, nor in loving, responsible expressions of their sexuality, but in their lack of solidarity with others who suffer oppression, failure of courage to come out of the closet, etc. Proper use of God's word as a 'sword' requires disciplined study, careful interpretation and sensitive application (2 Tim. 2.15); ignorant laying hold of the Bible as a club only advertises the prejudice and bigotry of the assailant (Attridge 1989: 133).

Can we 'rest' inside the 'closet'? Sexual minorities who believe in Jesus experience a kind of 'rest' in the closet (Heb. 3.3), but not the full rest Jesus intends for his followers. Life in the closet is an 'Egyptian bondage', a life of continual subterfuge where one is 'loved for what one is not', a life of continual fear of being 'outed' and 'hated for what one is' (André Gide). In the hostile world outside the closet, sexual minorities experience tribulation – hardly conducive to rest! Nor is unemployment what Jesus meant when he promised 'rest'! Other factors that make rest difficult outside the closet include alienation from family, divorce suits, loss of jobs, inheritances, friends, prestige and health insurance. Such expressions of oppression characterize what the Second Testament calls 'the world'. Outside the closet, sexual minorities can learn to rest in the unique peace Jesus promises (John 14.27); they join hands with others who work to fulfil God's purpose: a world freed from oppression and discrimination.

4.14–5.10 Prayer: bold approach to the throne of a gracious God

In the face of injustice, oppression and persecution, Jesus' followers' first 'line of attack' is always prayer; other action may also prove necessary, as the Spirit leads, but nothing is more important or effective. We may need to demonstrate before the White House or the Pink House in Argentina, but not before we besiege the throne of God; we may need to petition and organize marches – but direct access to the throne of God is our greatest privilege and our greatest source of power for achieving that liberation from all oppression, which is central to God's purpose for humanity. An interview with some president pales into insignificance in comparison with our privilege of Jesus' 'interview' with God the Creator on our behalf as our great high priest.

Jesus' sinlessness and our sinfulness (4.15; 5.1–3). Jesus was 'without sin' (sinless), but not 'sexless'. The Word became 'flesh' (John 1.14), which implies sexuality and the urge to propagate the species (John 1.13), but is characterized by weakness and mortality (5.7, 'flesh . . . death'). Our sinfulness does not reside in our sexuality (unless expressed unlovingly, harming the neighbour), but is especially characterized by 'straying' due to 'ignorance' (5.2). For example, one can mortally harm a neighbour through ignorance by not following carefully medically prescribed guidelines for safer sex, or by loading friends susceptible to heart attacks with too much cholesterol, pushing alcohol or cigarettes on those who need to abstain, contaminating air with our own smoke, driving after drinking, etc. (for 'ignorances,' or sins of ignorance, see also Heb. 9.7; the sacrifices in Lev. 4.2; 22.14). Probably most of the hatred, violence and oppression of sexual minorities also is based on ignorance, false ideologies and 'majority propaganda', coupled with fear. Also, the great harm done to sexual minorities through 'Ex-Gay'-type ministries results from ignorance about both science and the Bible. If so much sin is due to ignorance, then to combat sin effectively we need sound education, not just emotional denunciations and exhortations to repentance.

Jesus' prayer life and ours (5.7; 4.16). In the days of his flesh, Jesus prayed first for himself; in the face of death, Jesus' prayers were characterized by tears, loud cries, urgency and fear (5.7). Hebrews here gives us its only concrete reference to Jesus' earthly ministry – his prayer life, culminating in Gethsemane, but not limited to that intense experience. Because of Jesus' saving work, our prayer life (4.16) can be characterized by 'confidence' or 'bold frankness', freedom of speech in the presence of God. The timely 'help' God promises involves not just sympathy but effective, liberating action.

5.11–6.12 For times of persecution, when solidarity with the oppressed falters

Symptoms of spiritual and psychological immaturity include: being easily distracted from the search for solid truth (5.11), forgetful of basics (5.12); oversensitive to injustices suffered, while insensitive to injustices committed, fleeting pleasures rather than authentic, enduring good (5.14). Commitment to Jesus and solidarity with his followers was publicly expressed in baptism (6.1–8). To abandon pagan temples and banquets (or even modest synagogues) and start assembling with the house churches meant loss of status and public shame and involved a kind of 'option' for the oppressed, persecuted (largely poor) followers of Jesus. 'Coming out' as a disciple of Jesus in first-century Rome was a lot like 'coming out of the closet' for sexual minorities today. Individualism, isolation and a life of subterfuge are rejected as one opts to share the oppression and persecution now commonly suffered by sexual minorities. While gay men and lesbians coming out of the closet may often meet their parents scrambling to get in, it is virtually impossible to return to the closet, once out. Like Christian baptism, it involves a step that normally cannot be repeated. Often we may wish it were otherwise, but as Hebrews reminds us, some decisions in life are irrevocable. God respects our freedom and those irrevocable decisions. Rather than trying to sneak back into the closet, what is called for is a decisive turning from egotistic individualism and a decisive, positive commitment – to building enduring communities characterized by freedom, justice, mutual respect and love.

From stern warning, Hebrews turns to address readers as 'beloved' by the writer (6.9), and expressing 'love' in humble acts of service to poor and needy saints (6.10) – the first references to interpersonal love in the book. Today Aids ministries provide countless opportunities and illustrations of this kind of humble, loving service; also for communicating Jesus' Good News that God's loving embrace encompasses each one, and that the 'salvation' (6.9) Jesus accomplished includes sexual minorities. Jesus' Good News, communicated through appropriate deeds and words, can inspire a 'full assurance of hope until the end' (6.11). Faith (6.12) that is persevering and patient (literally, 'suffering long') inherits all God's covenant promises.

6.13–20 God's promise and oath: hope's anchor when the storms of persecution rage

Faith–hope's basis is: God is faithful and does not lie. Sexual minorities suffer cruelly because of lies and majority propaganda. As children they are brainwashed with a presentation of a world in which sexual minorities do not exist – everyone is expected to marry and become the father/mother of two children. Very early, a process of sexual 'education' may begin, which actually consists of heterosexual 'majority propaganda' (either failing to even mention sexual minorities or portraying them negatively as sinful, criminal or mentally ill). Such majority propaganda, even when not explicitly taught from books, appears omnipresent in the TV, films and public displays of affection legally permitted/approved.

If an adolescent manages to crack through the propaganda barrage to discover that he/she is not alone in feeling 'different', parents commonly rush in to assure that it is only a 'passing phase'. They may find a psychologist still eager to take their money for several years in an effort to 'cure' the wayward, deviant adolescent. If help is sought from religion, the lies multiply: God is said to promise to 'cure' homosexuality, since it is a disease; or God is said to have given all homosexuals the spiritual gift of sexual abstinence, so they can be happy missionaries like the apostle Paul; or God is portrayed as furious with homosexuals for engaging in acts 'contrary to nature', always an unforgivable sin. God is said to have created 'Adam and Eve, not Adam and Steve' – and Steve is not supposed to ask who created him. Classmates and even distant relatives strive to find the 'right girl/boy' who will manage to convince the deviant to go straight. Hebrews reminds us that the lies of majority propaganda do not proceed from God, for God does not lie; Jesus is the truth, and the truth frees us from the lies of majority propaganda (John 14.6; 8.32).

Faith–hope's content is God's promises. God never promised to 'cure homo-sexuality', since it is not a disease and is never even referred to in scripture, much less as a disease to be cured. God never promised to give some spiritual gift of sexual abstinence to all persons of homosexual orientation. The notion of orientation is a nineteenth-century scientific discovery about which biblical writers knew and wrote nothing; neither the word nor concept existed before the nineteenth century. When in the Bible's creation story God says, 'It is not good for man to be alone,' the text does not add 'unless he is homosexual'. To make such an addition is to put a lie in God's mouth. In the biblical covenants God promises to free us from all oppression, forgive us our sins, not our sexu-ality, enable us to know God and practise justice, be guided by the Spirit into all truth, and experience the abundant life Jesus spoke of (John 10.10).

In baptism we promise to seek first God's reign and be faithful to God. Gay men and lesbians may freely commit themselves to a sexually exclusive relationship as a same-sex couple, in which case each will seek to keep that agreement. More complex is the common situation where gay men or lesbians, brainwashed by majority propaganda, fall into the trap of heterosexual 'mar-riage'. The Bible never presents marriage as a covenant with vows. Such vows are mechanisms of oppression for sexual minorities and can even result in blackmail. Sometimes they need to be unmasked and set aside.

7.1–28 Melchizedek, patron saint for queers

To make Jesus priest, God changed the law (7.11–21). The law needed to be 'removed', because the priesthood was unable to perfect anyone (7.11–12; cf. 11.5; 12.27). Jesus did not descend from Levi and Aaron, but from the tribe of Judah, and Moses' law never permitted descendants of Judah to be priests (7.13–14). Jesus' priesthood stems not from anything in Moses' law, but from the power of his indestructible life, and is attested by God's promise of an eternal priesthood (7.15–17, citing Ps. 110.4). God thus annulled Moses' 'fleshly' law and intro-duced a better hope that enables us to draw near to God (7.18–19). Descendants of Levi and Aaron became priests without being authenticated by any such divine oath; but Jesus' priesthood, being established by God's oath (stronger than the law), is not weak and perishable, but eternal (7.20–1).

Hebrews presents *Melchizedek* as the most appropriate patron saint for sexual minorities (7.1–10). Adam was uniquely qualified as sexual minor-ity representative in that he had no human parents, had an incestuous mate taken from his own side/rib, and begat children with his mate according to divine command, but without ever being married. Jesus, too, was uniquely qualified as sexual minority representative, since he had no biological father, legally was 'illegitimate', never married and had no biological descendants. Melchizedek, however, is presented in Hebrews (following Genesis 14) as sur-passing both Adam and Jesus as sexual minority representative: he had nei-ther human parentage nor biological descendants. Nevertheless, he ruled as priest-king in Jerusalem with a reign characterized by both justice and peace (justice, *sedek; salem*, shalom, peace). In many respects he appears to resemble the two-spirited, gay spiritual leaders in Native-American tribes.

8.1–13 Ordination deconstructed: Jesus, a lay minister with a better covenant and better promises

Hebrews describes Jesus' better ministry, affirming that he became perfectly qualified (7.28) to serve as high priest in God's very presence in the authentic (heavenly) sanctuary (8.1–2). Israel's priests, descended from Levi and Aaron, were ordained to offer to God the gifts and sacrifices prescribed by Torah, but while on earth Jesus was but a 'layman' and not qualified by proper descent to minister in the earthly temple (8.3–4; Bruce 1990: 183). The sanctuary where Israel's priests served was but a shadowy copy of the true (authentic) heavenly sanctuary (8.5; Ex. 25.40). The language of Hebrews here is similar to that of Platonic idealism, but the thought is not the same, since the writer avoids any dichotomy between material and non-material (Jesus' resurrected, ascended body is in heaven), and the whole Levitical order historically foreshadows 'the good things to come' (Heb. 10.1).

Sexual minorities, who form part of God's people in every age and under every covenant, can rejoice especially that the fundamental provision of the Exodus covenant (liberation from oppression) is also fundamental in Jesus' mission (Luke 4.18–19) and covenant promises (Mark 14.24), because the same liberating God is at work throughout human history (Ps. 103.6–7). Sexual minorities need no special 'sexual majority' priesthood as mediators, for they too can 'know God' (Heb. 8.11) as they practise justice (Jer. 22.15–16) and solidarity with the needy (Heb. 10.32–4; Matt. 25.31–46).

God's 'better promises' (8.6) expressed in the new covenant never suggest miraculous changes in sexual orientation. Such fraudulent promises and claims are a modern invention in so-called 'Ex-Gay' ministries, which have no basis in scripture and no scientific support. Even Paul's claim to a spiritual gift of sexual abstention is only for a few (1 Cor. 7.7), and he never claimed nor suggested that anyone of homosexual orientation automatically had such a gift.

9.1–28 Jesus' death: earthly defeat, 'heavenly' accomplishment

Christ, the high priest of God's new order, made the perfect sacrifice (9.23–8). However inadequate all human analogies, and however great the mystery of Jesus' cross, Hebrews emphasizes that the decisive effect was the solution to our sin problem: by his death, Jesus 'did away' with sin ('annulment', v. 26) and 'took away' sin ('bear', v. 28). The basic problem was not that the wrath of God needed appeasing, but that sin needed to be eliminated (all that harms individuals and makes human community impossible – oppression and lack of compassionate solidarity). Jesus' redemptive death is the clue to our life: it was not a defeat, but his major accomplishment (on redemption, see Attridge 1989: 249, notes 61–2).

In Hebrews 9, the last word (in Greek) is 'salvation' (v. 28), referring there not to forgiveness of sins (9.22), but to the final decisive liberation from death and all destructive forces at Jesus' second 'coming' (literally, 'appearance', since he is always present and comes continuously by his Spirit; Matt. 28.20; Rev. 1–3). Instead of 'salvation', Hebrews 9 prefers to speak of Jesus' accomplishment as 'redemption' (9.12, 15), using the Exodus analogy of poor slaves who are liberated from their oppressors. However, Hebrews views the more basic human problem as universal (not limited to some wealthy, powerful oppressing class): sin, which defiles every human soul and conscience. Jesus' blood (death) redeems and frees us by accomplishing a decisive purgation, or cleansing from sin (9.22). This cleansing annuls sin and all its effects (v. 26) and ushers in God's long-awaited new order (v. 10). For oppressed groups (sexual minorities, etc.) it is particularly meaningful to remember that salvation brings redemption from slavery, with freedom and dignity; but also to realize that powerful oppressors only manifest in practice the destructive egotistical tendencies that are present in all of us and that need the decisive cleansing resulting from Jesus' sacrifice.

Since sexual minorities commonly are made scapegoats for the evil others suffer, the biblical references to the scapegoat on the day of Atonement may prove more helpful in communicating the mysterious significance and accomplishment of Jesus' death (9.22; Lev. 16.20–2; also Schwager 1987). On the cross Jesus shed little blood and carried none of it to heaven, but he gave his life for us (Mark 10.45; cf. Lev. 17.11) and instituted a bloodless sacrament (Mark 14.24–5). The cross heralds the end of violence.

10.1–18 Jesus' death: how 'filthy' sexual minorities can get a clean conscience (and why Leviticus never really worked)

The Exodus and creation accounts (Gen. 1–Ex. 19) can help create self-esteem and a sense of dignity for oppressed peoples. Torah's legal provisions also are best understood as promoting justice for the oppressed. When misused as a club, however (to protect the powerful and terrorize the weak), Torah's legal provisions became instruments to destroy human dignity and self-esteem. Instead of leaving people with a sense of forgiveness, a clean conscience, a healthy sense of direction, the law became simply an accuser that loaded the weak and poor with false guilt, heightened inferiority complexes and suicidal depression. Jesus blasted the lawyer-theologians (legalistic 'scribes') and pious fundamentalists for using Torah in this cruel and destructive way (Matt. 23; Luke 11.39–48).

Hebrews emphasizes that although Jesus is 'the same' (13.8; unchangeable, like God, 1.12), even during Israel's history God repeatedly introduced radical changes in the law (and modern scientific studies of the Pentateuch underline even more emphatically the dynamic, changing character of Torah, reflecting centuries of diversity in historical conditions). When Jesus inaugurated Jeremiah's promised new covenant, assuming an eternal priesthood quite 'off the map' for Leviticus, the changes became even more radical. The ark of the covenant in Moses' wilderness tabernacle contained the Ten Words/ Commandments written on stone as a summary of Torah's fundamental concerns (Heb. 9.4) – but as Jesus and his followers challenged and set aside the Sabbath law, even the Ten Commandments lost any aura of 'ethical absolutes'. Paul used some of them to illustrate concretely how love avoids harming the neighbour (Rom. 13.8–10), but the 'laws' God promises to write on hearts (Heb. 10.16) are only examples of human love (Lev. 19.18, 33–4). Hospitality to strangers and visiting prisoners may be even better pointers than the Decalogue (Heb. 13.1–6; Matt. 25.31–46)!

10.19–39 *Freedom of speech for sexual minorities*

In 6.4–8 Hebrews warned sternly of God's judgement on members who turned away from God and forsook their commitment to solidarity with Jesus' followers (6.6; cf. 10.25). The sin involved was thus a lack of solidarity with the weak and oppressed in their various needs (Matt. 25.31–46). Even more grave, however, would be active collaboration with the oppressors in their crimes of injustice. Jesus had given his life for them. To abandon his followers in a time of persecution and collaborate with their oppressors was to despise Jesus, and 'trample' his blood under foot. Sexual minorities who step out of the closet are 'enlightened', begin to find one another, and become empowered as they meet together. Like the house churches in Rome, such groups need to multiply, learn to network with one another and other oppressed groups. Returning to the closet to collaborate with oppressors in order to avoid persecution Hebrews portrays as the gravest of sins.

11.1–7 *Faith before the flood: worshipping, walking, building*

Words, like the humans that use them, are dynamic and changing. Hence they cannot be 'defined' in any static sense, but only described in their most characteristic aspects. As a preliminary orientation to its classic exposition of faith, Hebrews 11 gives us a 'snapshot' that focuses on faith's relationship to invisible spheres: (1) the as yet unseen future; and (2) invisible present realities, such as God (freedom, justice, truth, love, etc.). While many moderns profess not to believe in the personal, infinite, triune God revealed decisively and finally in Jesus Christ, probably no one is really a thoroughly consistent materialist. Even purported dialectical 'materialists' make strident demands for 'justice', expound at length about the 'meaning' of 'history' and exhort us to maintain firm our 'hope' as we work to bring in the promised 'utopia'! Hebrews is more up-front in making explicit the conviction that only faith can 'give objective reality to objects of hope', that is make present the desired future. To that end, faith also links us to invisible present realities.

Before speaking of the faith of others, Hebrews first reminds us of our faith that the invisible God spoke an invisible word and thus created everything we see (11.3). Hebrews thus explicitly rejects the notion of Greek philosophers that the existing universe was made out of visible elements – earth, fire and water – along with invisible air. Hebrews approximates the theological concept of creation *ex nihilo*, thus negating any atheistic concept of evolution. Also absent is the modern fundamentalist concern to insist on a recent creation in six literal days.

Abel worshipped God with a superior sacrifice (11.4; Gen. 4.3–5). The superiority of Abel's sacrifice did not consist objectively in its content, but in the inner attitude of Abel's faith, which resulted in his becoming the victim of Cain's murderous violence, the Bible's first 'martyr' (Jesus even describes him as the first 'prophet', Luke 11.50–1; cf. Matt. 23.34–6; 1 John 3.12; Prov. 15.8; Gen. 4.7).

Enoch walked with (translated in the Septuagint as 'pleased') God (1.5–6; Gen. 5.18, 21–4). Hebrews expounds Enoch's faith in terms of the Greek translation ('pleased') instead of the original Hebrew 'walked with'. Enoch's walking with God resulted in his escaping the experience of death. Faith presupposes believing in God's existence and fundamental goodness/justice. The image of life as a path to be trod in God's presence by an individual like Enoch, or in company with God's people is fundamental to biblical teaching. The Bible never speaks of 'morals' or 'ethics'. The Bible prefers to speak of our trustful, obedient relationship to God as 'walking' (Gen. 6.9; 17.1; 24.40; 48.15; Pss. 56.13; 116.9). As we walk, the scenery changes with diverse historical contexts, so the concrete content of obedience may also change, but there is fundamental continuity: 'do justice, love mercy, and walk humbly with your God' (Micah 6.8).

Noah's example lays starkly before us the radical character of faith in God as transcending ordinary human reason. On superficial materialistic presuppositions, nothing could be more unreasonable than constructing a large boat far from all navigable waters. Noah received a divine word of warning and acted on it with a faith that transcended superficial materialism. What he thus 'saved' was his 'house (hold)'. Households included everyone living together, whatever their gender, blood relationships or sexual arrangements; slaves commonly were included. Noah's faith resulted in 'rescue' from the flood for his entire household (and the accompanying animals, as Genesis indicates). Noah's faith was thus quite 'reasonable', and proved thoroughly practical – but it appeared the height of folly to his contemporary 'materialists', who perished in the flood.

11.8–22 Patriarchal faith: salvation by child-abuse?

Abraham: faith of a landless immigrant (11.8–10). As in the case of Noah, Abraham's behaviour is reasonable and sane, given the presupposition that God exists and communicates with human beings, but apart from such an experience it would seem the height of folly. God called Abraham and gave him promises, and by faith–hope in God's faithfulness, Abraham faithfully 'obeyed'. God promised him an unknown earthly 'land' (11.9), but Hebrews transforms the object of Abraham's hope into the heavenly Jerusalem, 'the city with foundations, whose architect and builder is God' (11.10; cf. v. 16; 12.22–4).

Weighty textual evidence supports the idea that Sarah's faith is here celebrated (vv. 11–12). However, literally, the Greek speaks of receiving power for 'deposition of seed'. Nowhere else in ancient Greek literature is such a role assigned to a woman, since the existence of the female egg and its crucial role in human conception was not understood until modern times (Lane 1991: 47b:344–5; van der Horst 1996). Although obviously active in giving birth, women in antiquity were usually considered purely passive in conception, functioning as 'incubators' where the male deposited the seed.

If superficial materialist faith be rejected as impossible, grave dangers also must be faced in the faith that God exists and speaks to us (vv. 17–19)! Abraham became thoroughly convinced that God had commanded him to slaughter Isaac like some animal sacrifice. Although the voice from heaven stopped the killing at the crucial moment, for Isaac it must have been a terrifying experience – a kind of child-abuse far surpassing many episodes of sexual abuse of children. Both Jewish and Christian traditions forget Isaac's perspective and focus exclusively on Abraham as a paragon of obedience in an incomparable situation of testing. For Hebrews, Abraham leaps from primitive belief in a cruel deity who demands child-sacrifice, to mature Christian faith in the God who raises the dead (11.19, perhaps elaborating the 'we shall return . . .' of Gen. 22.5). Like Abraham, sexual minorities tend to be immigrants. As adolescents on farms or in towns, they commonly are rejected and thrown out by homophobic parents and churches, suffer discrimination in employment and rejection by peers. At first they may simply seek the familiar – a more welcoming rural setting, 'another country', only to find that although preparing for them a city, God has not always prepared them for the city. Contrary to popular myth, however, not homosexuals, but heterosexual male relatives like Abraham are the primary abusers of children.

11.23–31 Moses' faith: stepping out of the closet to liberate the oppressed

Moses was stuffed into a 'closet' (basket), thus hiding his Hebrew identity for 40 years. His Hebrew people continued to suffer, serving Pharaoh as slaves, while Moses enjoyed princely privileges of wealth and education in the world's most powerful empire. Had he remained in the closet, possibly he could have had some ameliorating influence on his people's suffering and saved himself immense deprivation. At the age of 40 Moses finally decided to be true to himself and the God who created him: he refused to be called 'the son of Pharaoh's daughter' – his safe, comfortable closet was shattered! He opted to share the lot of oppressed slaves, God's chosen people, and lead them to freedom (11.24–6). Perhaps nowhere in the Bible is the 'preferential option for the poor', advocated by Latin American liberation theologies, so clearly expressed. Hebrews shares with Exodus the perspective that the slaves were not poor due to racial inferiority or laziness (Ex. 5.17), but because of injustice and oppression. The solution was thus not Egyptian band aids of charity, but the 'liberty and justice for all' which God called Moses to establish. Moses' faith-decision to come out of the closet and identify himself as a descendant of Hebrew slaves may appear too delayed to us and to the slaves who could have 'outed him'. Similar decisions by sexual minorities constitute the most powerful political action possible today. Liberation for countless others can result, but is usually accompanied by persecution.

The pagan prostitute Rahab, a sexual minority, made a decisive contribution to the liberation of the poor (11.30–1; Josh. 2). Although shocking to many readers, biblical writers exalt Rahab the harlot: James places her exemplary faith alongside Abraham's (2.25); Matthew in Jesus' geneaology (1.5) shatters Jewish tradition by naming her an ancestress of the Messiah; and Hebrews makes her its first explicit female paradigm of faith. Even more shocking, biblical interpreters now commonly assume that in showing hospitality ('peace' in Heb. 11.31) to the Hebrew spies, Rahab would have included sexual services commonly offered in such situations in the Ancient Near East. She thus expressed her new 'faith' in the God at work to liberate the oppressed (she was Jericho's 'absolute outsider'; Attridge 1989: 344) and avoided the sin of the Sodomites against their angel visitors (inhospitality, attempted gang rape; cf. Gen. 18–19; Heb. 13.2). The harlot's hospitality to spies thus proved decisive in the collapse of the key fortress city of Jericho.

11.32–40 Faith's apparent defeats and the problem of evil

Hebrews' male author continues with a rhetorical summary of seven masculine examples of faith-heroes and ten characteristic acts of faith described in the
Hebrew scriptures (11.32–35a). The seventh example referring to 'the prophets'
could include women like Huldah. The inclusion of Barak – to the exclusion
of Deborah – and Jephthah, whose vow led him to kill his daughter, remind
us of the author's patriarchal cultural context, which only occasionally is transcended. The ten exemplary expressions of faith also are dominated by patriarchal male values. Human history provides abundant examples of women
and sexual minorities manifesting militant faith. Women military heroes – for
example, the gender-benders Deborah and Joan of Arc – and sexual minority rulers and military heroes – Alexander the Great, Frederick the Great,
Lawrence of Arabia – stand as eloquent refutations of modern arguments
against women and homosexuals in the military or political office. Human
history also is replete with examples of oppressed and marginalized groups
and leaders suffering apparent defeat and martyrdom (Heb. 11.35b–38).

12.1–13 How to run by faith (even when no one is chasing you): if God is our parent, is evil only 'discipline'?

Run the race with perseverance: looking to Jesus (12.1–3). Jesus is not so much the
'Lord above us' in a static hierarchy, but rather the leader-pioneer who marches
before us. Without him neither we nor the ancient exemplars could reach matur-
ity/perfection (12.2; 11.40). This may well imply a kind of 'theological critique'
of the ancient heroes, many of whom the scriptures portray as far from perfect (Jacob, Jephthah, Samson!); a corollary might be that military exploits be
admired as examples of faith and courage, but not slavishly imitated by disciples of one who commanded Peter to put up his sword. Exemplary subjects
of faith are innumerable; but for Christians the sole object of saving faith is
the one God supremely revealed in Jesus Christ (1.1–4). Above all in times of
violent persecution, Jesus' disciples will be sorely tempted to 'take the sword'
(11.32–35a) – and 'perish by the sword'. Hence, Hebrews reminds us that in
such circumstances Jesus triumphed by enduring the cross and despising its
shame (12.3).

    Is all human suffering simply parental 'discipline' (12.4–11)? For anyone familiar
with the Hebrew scriptures, the explanation of human suffering (evil) as a
kind of divine parental discipline would be almost axiomatic (Heb. 1.5–6, citing Prov. 3.11–12). C. S. Lewis once wrote: 'God whispers to us in our pleasure,
speaks in our conscience, but shouts in our pains: it is His megaphone to rouse
a deaf world.' Later, however, a harrowing personal tragedy forced Lewis to
recognize the inadequacy of this argument (citations in Bruce 1990: 346). Does
a God of love not also 'shout' in our joys, including sexual pleasure? The context in Hebrews suggests a limited view of 'discipline' as involving stern decisions freely made (12.2), resulting from compassionate solidarity, which can
lead to a martyrdom that defies tyrants (12.4). God's parental 'discipline' in
this context permits us to face and make such painful decisions – the Creator's
supreme tribute to the our freedom (Heb. 6.4–6; 10.26–31). To explain Aids

as mere parental discipline is to portray God as a cruel sadist who tortures humans. Undoubtedly we can all learn something from terrible suffering, but lessons that are the result of suffering do not adequately explain the multiple and complex causes of evil.

As those who commonly suffer persecution, we are exhorted to 'run the race' – even when no one is chasing us. Like the early disciples, we discover that we too can be inspired by a 'great cloud of witnesses' (including many 'bastards', 12.8!) as we explore the riches of our gay and lesbian historical heritage (see the successive contributions resulting from recent advances in African-American, feminist, third-world liberationist, and gay/lesbian historical studies).

'Running the race' also involves looking to love ourselves (12.12–13). The 'justice' of 12.11 is here elaborated with the metaphors of feeble arms and weak knees that are 'straightened' (v. 12) and paths made 'straight/level'. The discipline expounded (12.4–11) produces the twin fruits of justice for the oppressed (12.11) and peace with neighbours (12.11, 14) and God (13.20). Queers demand 'justice' not mere compassion, but neither they nor their 'lifestyles' need to be 'straightened' in the sense of 'conformed to those of the heterosexual majority' (vv. 12–13). Science recognizes that 'homosexuality' is not a sickness, and thus cannot be 'healed'. Homophobia can be healed, and gays can experience inner healing of wounds inflicted by a homophobic society. Thus can we run the race 'marked out for us', looking only to Jesus (12.1).

12.14–29 The heavenly Jerusalem: do we go up, or will it come down?

Esau's forfeiture, for a single meal, of his double inheritance rights as first-born exemplified the kind of short-sighted materialism of a 'secular or profane' person that is not to be imitated (12.16). Readers are said to have arrived at Mount Zion, which, unlike Sinai, can be touched. A five-tiered assembly is gathered thereon: angels, spirits of the departed, the Church consisting of 'firstborn', God and Jesus. The assembly is characterized more by joy than fear. The two references to God remind readers that the living God is immanent (near, present) as well as transcendent (12.22–3). The references to Jesus' blood as 'speaking' prepare readers for the following exhortation to listen.

Having recently survived the great fire in Rome (64 CE), readers would have vivid impressions of the kind of disaster threatened by a God whose holy love resembled fire. Citing Haggai 2.6, Hebrews refers to an earth and material heaven(s) that are both created, and can be 'shaken' and 'removed' by God's mere voice (12.25–7). Only God's 'kingdom' proves unshakeable, apparently descending to earth to be gratefully 'received' (12.28; cf. Attridge 1989: 381). 'Mount Zion' and 'the heavenly Jerusalem' do not refer to an immaterial realm separated eternally from the earthly scene (12.22–4; cf. 11.10, 16). Rather they are 'near' in space as well as time (13.14) and will finally descend to earth to consummate God's realm (Heb. 12.26–8; Rev. 21–2; Matt. 6.10). Although joyful (v. 23), Christian worship of God is also to be ever characterized by reverence and awe (v. 28; cf. vv. 18–21), since God is progressively revealed as holy love.

God speaks today to us also (12.25–9). Many white heterosexual males claim to have a private 'pipeline' to heaven that enables them uniquely to hear God speaking and telling everyone else exactly how they need to behave sexually.

Increasingly, sexual minority representatives are coming to realize that God speaks to us as well. God speaks to us by the word and the Spirit as we worship and as we follow Jesus. Because commonly we are a hidden minority, especially the more affluent sexual minority representatives often are tempted to shrink back from solidarity with other oppressed groups such as women, the poor, people of colour, immigrants and ethnic minorities, Aids sufferers, the physically challenged. God often speaks to us, calling us to repentance and confession for our comfortable indifference and collaboration with those who oppress. 'See that you do not refuse the One speaking' (12.25).

God speaks to us as we work for peace (12.14–21). Authentic peace on earth can only be established as the fruit of justice (12.11, 14), not by seeking to prop up an unjust status quo that rationalizes persecution and discrimination against minorities. In a classic example of 'blaming the victims', one book attacked 'homosexuality' as 'the bond that breaks' the unity of the Church – instead of facing up to the cruel bigotry expressed in homophobia. The peace and unity of the Church are undermined by hatred and fear of sexual minorities, not by the responsible expression of their love.

Homophobia is a noxious root (12.15) that produces bitter fruit: injustice, gay-bashing, parents disowning their adolescent children, throwing them out on the street and even attempting to kill them, teen-suicides, depression, alcoholism, drug addiction. Proper fear of God casts out all lesser fears, including homophobia. The axe must be laid to this noxious root if the Church's peace and unity are to be restored and maintained. Authentic holiness involves us in strenuous opposition: to all injustice, and hypocrisy; to all cowardly shrinking from compassionate solidarity with the weak; to all traitorous collaboration with oppressors. Many religious leaders, following Esau's example, sell out the rights of sexual minorities in order to guarantee promotions and improve their retirement benefits.

God shouts to us in our joys (12.22–4). Sexual minorities stand among the joyful throng that have come to Mount Zion (v. 22) and to Jesus (v. 24), who promised life and peace to all who trust him and obey his love-commands. Worshipping with other impoverished saints in a house church could prove depressing. Hebrews tells us to lift our eyes and contemplate seven spiritual realities that surround us, and which make us part of an innumerable, exuberant throng. God speaks to us in such worship experiences, God whispers in love at times of discouragement and pain – but God also shouts to us in ecstatic moments of sexual love (Song 8.6–7): (1) that God created us the way we are; (2) that God loves and accepts us even when society and church do not; (3) that we can learn to 'see God' (Heb. 12.14) at work in human history to make the heavenly Jerusalem descend to earth (a society characterized by freedom, justice, wisdom, peace and love); (4) that God calls us to worship and solidarity with all who follow Jesus.

God's holy love is a consuming fire. Hate merchants commonly claim to have heard on their private heavenly pipeline that God commands them to terrorize people of colour by burning crosses before their homes and churches. Since Troy Perry founded the Metropolitan Community Church as a place where sexual minorities are welcomed, some 38 MCC places of worship have been burned by religious fanatics, following the late medieval tradition that 'faggots' are to be burned. This scandal has received scant media attention, where bigoted attacks on the dignity of sexual minorities still get free publicity – something never permitted when anti-Semitism or racism is involved.

The Catholic author Ann Patrick Ware writes: 'No longer, I believe, can responsible people get away with deploring violence and acts of violence, while at the same time fueling the fires that cause such acts' (Ware 1988: 31). The scriptures emphasize that not all fire is from God, who warned Israel against playing with 'strange fire' (Lev. 10.1–3). Fire kindled by fear and hate for minority groups is 'strange fire' that has nothing to do with the fire of God's holy love. What the flame of God's holy love consumes are the sins of oppression and idolatry. Flames ignited by bigots in their hatred of minorities are 'strange fire' from evil sources – not from the God supremely revealed in Jesus! When oppressed peoples experience the raging fires of persecution and the deep waters of grief, God promises: 'When you pass through the waters, I will be with you . . . when you walk through fire you shall not be burned, and the flame shall not consume you' (Isa. 43.1–3).

13.1–6 Loving the brothers – and also the sisters

Hebrews 13.1–6 summarizes the Christian 'lifestyle' or 'way of life' (tropos, 13.5; cf. 'conduct', v. 7; 'walking', v. 9); the fundamental focus is on love as manifest in concrete relations. Commentators universally refer here to Christian 'ethics' or 'morality', but these Greek philosophical concepts are totally absent from the Bible (their virtual omnipresence in the discourse of those who pretend to 'take the Bible seriously' clearly indicates that what many 'defenders of the Bible' really take seriously is their addiction to the thought patterns of Greek philosophy). The historical and dialectical connotations of the word 'praxis' make it a more adequate description of the kind of obedience Hebrews here envisions.

Modern readers have great difficulty interpreting biblical teaching in what we call 'sexual' matters, since the modern terms and concepts 'sex'/'sexual' are totally absent from the Bible. Hebrews first critiques the Greek tendency to despise the material, seeking to counter an ideology that is 'marriage/marriage bed'-negative with a more positive attitude ('honour'). Neither sexual abstinence (1 Cor. 7.7) nor marriage and maximum reproduction (Gen 1–2) are advocated as 'absolutes'. Rather Christian freedom is maintained in the focus on a positive attitude. 'Honour' towards marriage replaces the 'honour' for parents in the Ten Commandments. The following prohibition of 'love for money' indicates that the preceding prohibition of adultery and prostitution relates abuses to irresponsible expressions of excessive desire (pornous, recourse to prostitutes etc. – all forms of 'coveting').

An author like Apollos, a bachelor missionary like Paul (13.23), understandably would place hospitality to strangers as the most important expression of Christian love (13.2) – even more basic than any of the Ten Commandments! The Sodom story commonly was misinterpreted in contemporary Jewish literature as condemning the same-gender expressions of love common in Greek and Roman society. Apollos' fascination with the Sodom story may well reflect his own consciousness of being 'different' along with the 'order of

Melchizedek'. Like Jesus (Matt. 10.14–15; Luke 10.10–12), the author of Hebrews corrects contemporary Jewish 'homophobia' by reminding readers that the Sodom story had to do with inhospitality to angels.

Rahab, already singled out for her hospitality, was the only woman explicitly named and honoured in chapter 11. By her hospitality, she expressed not only the love commanded in 13.1–2, but daring 'faith', receiving Israelite spies with 'peace' (11.31). If Rahab performed her expected professional services, sexual love may be viewed as a significant dimension of the biblical concept of 'peace'. By exhorting readers to 'honour' marriage (13.4), Hebrews counteracts 'sex-negative' bias in contemporary platonic philosophy (1 Tim. 4.3). However, by commanding only honour, Hebrews refuses to make marriage an ethical absolute – thus breaking with the Genesis command to reproduce the species. The freedom of queers was thus maintained, as long as harm was avoided. God's promise (Heb. 13.5b, citing Deut. 31.6) to be present with the oppressed is especially meaningful to queers who have been abandoned by family, church or friends and persecuted by society. The expression of faith in God's 'help' in the face of persecution and oppression is likewise relevant to uncloseted sexual minorities who have suffered discrimination in employment, loss of jobs, health insurance, inheritance rights, and more. As elsewhere in Hebrews (8.9; 2.16), God's 'help' refers especially to liberation from oppression.

13.7–25 Following the 'real' leaders: Roman house churches, model for Christian anarchy?

Hebrews 13.7–25 contains three imperatives regarding the house-church leadership in Rome: 'remember' previous leaders, 'obey' present (local house-church) leaders, and 'greet' all the leaders and saints in (perhaps four) other Roman house churches. The implied leadership structure stands in stark contrast with later developments, when authority descended from above: a complex hierarchy.

Hebrews is directed to all the members of a Roman house church in a context where 'leaders' were equals (without even official titles of elder or deacon). By addressing the members, not their leaders, and by writing a letter of 'exhortation' (13.22) rather than orders, Hebrews implies that the real power remains with the entire people of God ('saints', 13.24), who are exhorted willingly to submit to authentic leadership in their house church). Hebrews has swept ecclesial bureaucracy aside with its rejection of the Mosaic order of Levites and Aaronic priesthood (vv. 10–14).

Remember previous leaders who died (13.7–16). By characterizing previous leaders as those of exemplary faith who 'spoke the word of God' (v. 7), Hebrews implies that all church members have a basic knowledge of scripture (5.11–6.3) and a capacity and responsibility for discernment to interpret God's word (not blindly submitting to vast stretches of priestly law in Leviticus, for example). Authentic leadership was constituted now simply by exemplary faith and capacity to discern and speak God's word – not by ordination processes bestowing hierarchical status. The new model for leadership involves educated lay women and men who recognize only 'lay' leaders – who in turn follow the layman Jesus – not a congregation of passive, illiterate 'sheep' who blindly submit to an authoritarian 'pastor'. The upstart layman Jesus has now been constituted the only 'shepherd' (13.8, 20–1), and his 'sheep' include the house-church lay leaders along with the other members (Matt. 23.8–12). Jesus is exalted as 'the same' – not as some static tyrant rigidly imposing an unjust status quo – but as a Moses-like shepherd who faithfully leads his people out of bondage into authentic freedom (13.8, 20).

Obey current church leaders (3.17–21). Lay leaders who had followed Jesus 'outside the camp' exemplified rejection of the old priestly hierarchy and were thus representative of 'subversive' liberating leadership. Their aim was to enhance freedom, not to control; their power line was prevailing intercession ('watch . . . pray', 13.17–18; cf. Jesus, 4.14–16; 7.25). In a house church of some 15–20 members, the leaders to be obeyed would be well known personally and would know each member by name (John 10.1–5) – there were no distant hierarchical heads, and no follower of Jesus was a dog at the end of some lengthy 'chain of command'. Animal sacrifices (though extensively commanded in Leviticus 1–5) are no longer valid, but two kinds of sacrifice are still to be continually offered: *praise* to the God who liberates from all oppression, and *good works* to the poor and oppressed. Prayer is a privilege and responsibility of each lay member, as well as of each lay leader.

Greet the lay leaders and members of other house churches in Rome. Readers are exhorted to listen patiently to leaders in other lands (3.22–3). Hebrews' author and Timothy are leaders with roots in other cultures. They can exhort in writing, or visit personally, but do not claim a superior authority over the local leaders of any house church. Hebrews does not set one congregation over another, but fosters ecumenicity through visits and letters; neither isolation nor domination is the preferred pattern, but a unity in diversity that faithfully reflects the being of the triune God revealed in Jesus. Some call this pattern Christian 'an-*archy*' – enhancing freedom by opposing the development of higher-archies. Women, people of colour and sexual minorities have a common interest in opposing traditional oppressive hierarchies and promoting the kind of anarchy/democracy in church and society that Hebrews advocates. Often, however, one secular organization or church comes to claim monopoly rights over sexual minorities as well. Hebrews provides the pattern for multiplying local house churches, but also for maintaining unity among equals.

James

L. WILLIAM COUNTRYMAN

The letter of James is remarkable both for its collegial and irenic style and for its willingness to confront major wrongdoing by Christians. The letter aims to heal a sickness in the Christian society that extends to many areas of the community's life, but is particularly evident in excessive deference of the faithful to the rich and in a claim on the part of the rich that they are above the 'royal law' of loving one's neighbour as oneself. James carefully sets up his argument to nullify the defences, both internal and public, of those whom he will charge with wrongdoing, even before making the charge itself.

The following treatment of the letter of James combines three primary perspectives. The author is a biblical scholar whose study focuses on the cultural distance between the ancient Mediterranean world and our own. He is also an Anglican Christian who finds the scriptures to be a principal point of encounter with God and with the Good News of Jesus. And he is a gay man, whose spiritual journey has led him to celebrate this fact as a gift from God. He regards exegesis as the task of bringing the complexities of ancient texts and their worlds into conversation with the complexities of our own world.

The letter of James was slow to become part of the Second Testament canon, emerging clearly into the light of day only in the late second or early third century. In the fourth century, Eusebius still categorized it as one of the disputed books. Even after it had acquired a seemingly secure place in the canon, Luther objected to it as denying the principle of justification by faith alone and being too little concerned with the figure of Christ. Other Reformers, however, disagreed with him.

The Greek in which the work is written is, by Second Testament standards, refined; and this raised questions as early as the fourth century as to whether it could really have been written, as was traditionally assumed, by James 'the Brother of the Lord'. Whether this James was the actual author or whether the work was simply ascribed to him, it does appear to have emerged from Jewish Christian circles, which may explain why it was somewhat slow to make its way into a Second Testament canon determined predominantly by the traditions and concerns of Gentile Christianity.

The letter is important, then, partly because it represents the voice of a now obscured element of early Christianity – those followers of Jesus who remained at home in Judaism and formed one of several sects offering interpretations of what true Judaism was about. The addressees appear to be living in settled circumstances, in small towns and villages. There is nothing to suggest that their communities include any Gentiles. The letter has little to say about Christology, but alludes to Jesus' teaching in a form close to that found in the Gospel of Matthew.

Modern scholarship long assigned the letter of James a relatively late date because of doubts about its authorship and the fact that it is never specifically cited before the late second century. On the other hand, there are no concerns expressed in it that are specifically characteristic of the second century. Some elements even suggest an early date, not least the fact that the addressees, while experiencing some disadvantages connected to their profession of faith, do not seem to inhabit a world ravaged by either war or persecution. It would be easiest to find such circumstances in the Eastern Mediterranean world before the First Jewish War (66–70 CE).

Like Pharisaic-Rabbinic Judaism, with its concentration on *halakhah*, James focuses on conduct more than doctrine: 'Religion that is pure and undefiled before God, the Father, is this: to care for orphans and widows in their distress, and to keep oneself unstained by the world' (1.27). The letter is full of wise counsel and admonitions, some rather acerbic, about behaviour. Its similarity to parts of the book of Proverbs in the scriptures of Israel leads some to read it as embodying a kind of Second Testament wisdom literature.

The Greek counterpart of such practical Hebrew wisdom was called *parainesis* (paraenesis, in English). Elements of it often show up as part of the concluding material in Second Testament letters (e.g. Phil. 4.4–9; 1 Thess. 5.12–20), but nowhere else does it dominate an entire writing as it does in James. Such material is apt to seem somewhat formless or even rote to the modern reader; and students of James have always found the letter difficult to summarize or outline in any clear or compelling way. One way of understanding it, then, might be to assume that is has no specific 'occasion' of writing and no particular topic that it wishes to address, but is more interested in handing on the accumulated wisdom of the community or of the author.

On the other hand, the classic use of proverbial wisdom is to cite it for particular purposes; the truly wise person is the one who can identify the right proverb for the occasion. If 'Nothing ventured, nothing gained' is right for one occasion, 'A bird in the hand is worth two in the bush' is better for another. If we note, then, that the wisdom in the letter of James is in fact focused on a relatively small number of topics and that they put in repeated appearances throughout the letter, we may well suspect that there is a particular set of issues in view, which the author is addressing not by composing a step-by-step logical argument, but by circling round the issues in ways that the addressees were better equipped to follow than the more remote reader of later times.

While the letter has little in the way of rhetorical structure or logical progression of the kind one would find in a letter of, say, Paul, there is a striking shift of modality from the seemingly miscellaneous wisdom of the opening chapter to the more sharply defined social vignettes (2.1–26; 4.12–5.6) and the impassioned teaching on the tongue (3.1–4.16) in the centre of the letter and back again to the 'soft focus' of traditional wisdom at the end (5.7–20). Even the opening and closing segments are not entirely miscellaneous, being devoted to a relatively small body of topics, including the meaning of trials, the value of faith and prayer, the generosity of God, the dangers of human speech, the importance of loving acts. All of these would be pertinent to a situation of conflict in a local church or churches.

The more sharply focused materials in 2.1–5.6 tell us something about the specific issues at hand. One would appear to be a tendency to observe social distinctions that James sees as perverting the common life of the Christian community. He gives the example of differential treatment offered to two visitors to the church and condemns it as a display of partiality (2.1–9). This implies to him that the addressees are making distinctions among themselves, not just in regard to outsiders (2.4). Interestingly, he has prepared the hearer or reader of the letter for this issue as early as 1.9–11, where he spoke of poor and rich 'brothers' as being somehow equalized in the context of the Church. This kind of preparation of a topic by mentioning it one or more times in passing before addressing it more directly is typical of James's style.

In connection with the making of social distinctions, James takes up the issue of faith and works in a way suggesting that some of his more prosperous addressees may have been using a kind of half-understood Paulinism to justify their ungenerous treatment of the poor. Modern readers sometimes assume that the early Christians were themselves uniformly poor, but it is clear from other Second Testament writings that, like other voluntary organizations of the time, they came from a variety of social levels. James assumes that this kind of variety is present among his addressees, too. He refers to 'the rich brother' in 1.10 (that, at least, is the least forced way of understanding the Greek phrasing in the passage). He also describes the congregation's meeting place as furnished with seats and footstools (2.3).

James follows up his example of the two visitors and his rejection of the 'faith instead of works' argument with an impassioned discourse on modes of speech, ranging from teaching to 'conflicts and disputes'. The discussion closes with admonitions against speaking ill of a brother or sister, which suggests that the author knows of serious conflicts in the life of the community (4.11–12).

Finally, the central section of the letter concludes with sharp attacks on two specific groups of people, first traders, then rich landowners who have not paid their workers. The first attack (4.13–17) follows naturally on James's concern with speech, for his complaint is that the traders formulate their plans as if they had no need to acknowledge their radical dependence on God. But the second attack, on the landowners (5.1–6), creates a shocking impression through the vehemence of James's language (for example, the rich are like cattle fattened for slaughter, 5.5) and his apparent levelling of a charge of murder against some members of the Christian community (5.6).

Students of James have long debated whether 5.1–6 is addressed to rich Christians or rather, in the rhetorical mode of *apostrophe*, to rich outsiders, who were safely out of earshot, as a way of encouraging and consoling James's addressees. In favour of the latter, one may note that James has already referred to the rich as oppressors (2.6). Moreover, one is at least reluctant to think of the possibility that members of an early Christian community would in fact commit murder.

On the other hand, if we take the passage as addressed to outsiders, then we fail to take seriously the evidence, already noted, that the churches James addressed included rich members. Still more to the point, the reference here to murder, however shocking, has been foreshadowed in two earlier passages, both associating the possibility of murder with the letter's addressees. In one passage (2.11), James has proposed the hypothetical possibility that his auditors might have committed murder, which would then make them guilty as regards the whole law, even those sins they had not specifically committed. In the second (4.2), he apparently accuses the congregation as a whole of committing murder. (There is some difficulty with the text here; see commentary.)

We do not actually have to assume a case of premeditated homicide in the congregation. What James specifies is that the rich have withheld the wages of their field workers (5.4). Given the marginal existence of such persons, this could easily contribute to someone's death. Torah, in fact, twice requires that such wages be paid on a daily basis (Lev. 19.13; Deut. 24.14–15). Even if the withholding of wages was only a contributing factor in someone's death, it is not a light matter.

On this reading of the letter, James's willingness to confront rich Christians stands out as particularly notable. The unwillingness of later readers to acknowledge that Christians are capable of committing this kind of violence against one another or against outsiders, accordingly, becomes the real problem. In a church that has often failed to speak the truth not just to wealth and power but to specifically Christian wealth and power, James becomes a particularly important document, questioning both the use of violence and our frequent denial of it.

The rhetoric James uses to frame his argument is worthy of some discussion in its own right. He is a person of authority, a teacher who counts on his wisdom being acknowledged by his addressees. In the patriarchal context of the ancient Mediterranean world, he is expected to address the assembly of the community (understood as composed of its free adult males) in a way that is both persuasive and commanding. In some respects, he follows the expected pattern. He is willing to give commands. And with frequent use of *aner* ('adult male human being', not always clearly translated in NRSV), he paints his audience as predominantly male. Having done so, he then uses this identification to deliver a staggering insult to them when he calls them 'adulterous women' (a more literal translation of 4.4, where NRSV has simply 'adulterers'). (Some ancient copyists were uncomfortable enough with James's choice of words that they altered it to 'Adulterous men and women'.)

On the other hand, James is also careful to blur or even violate the sharp boundaries of status and gender laid down by patriarchal expectations. He includes women in his address, even though he does not obliterate male privilege. His usual formula of address to his audience is *adelphoi*, appropriately translated in NRSV as 'Brothers and sisters'. He is careful to specify that the person in need might be 'a brother or a sister' (2.14). He parallels his reference to God as 'Father of lights' (1.17) with the claim that God 'gave us birth', using a verb specific to the role of mother (1.18). He sets the figure of Rahab the prostitute alongside that of Abraham the patriarch (2.23–5).

While James writes in a way appropriate to his status as a figure of authority, he is careful, at the same time, to present himself as a part of the community. The addressees are 'brothers and sisters', not 'children' as in 1 John. He uses the first person plural freely to identify himself as one of them. His authority comes from his being 'servant (*or* slave) of God and of the Lord Jesus Christ' (1.1). He is more like his audience than different. He even brings the great Elijah into the common fold as 'a human being like us' (5.17), suggesting that the distance between a teacher like himself and the addressees cannot be very great. None of this abolishes the patriarchal social context of the time. But it does show an early Christian leader who is negotiating it with considerable care and finesse.

There are several critical issues here for the queer reader at the present time. One is James's insistence that authentic Christian faith becomes evident only where there is generous and respectful treatment of others. The severing of faith as belief in certain doctrines from faith as a way of life lived in reliance on the generosity of God and endeavouring to share that generosity with others – too often typical of the social conservatism of the present – has no place in James's thinking. Indeed, in an interesting reversal of the usual image, he describes works as the animating spirit without which faith is merely a dead body (2.17).

Furthermore, the good deeds in question are not restricted to material assistance, though that is included. The critical thing is to treat all people with respect, outsiders as much as insiders, the poor and marginalized as much as the rich and powerful. James rejoices in the egalitarianism of the Christian community, which places rich and poor, in some sense, on a common footing (1.9–11). One notes the inability or unwillingness of some Christians today to do this with sexual minorities, whom they are likely to dismiss as unworthy of their consideration or actively to exile from their communion. This behaviour invalidates, from James's perspective, their claim to speak authentically from a standpoint of faith.

In addition, James offers some important advice on Christian behaviour in times of tension – advice that has been largely ignored ever since it was first written: 'let everyone be quick to listen, slow to speak, slow to anger' (1.19). This standard of behaviour is diametrically opposite to the superior, declamatory, commanding and dismissive rhetoric of much of the self-styled Christian right and would transform current disputes among Christians if it were observed.

Outline

Commentary

1.1 The author's self-designation as 'servant' (better, 'slave') rejects any claim to personal importance, but at the same time presents the author as the agent of God and Jesus, a role often filled in this period by trusted slaves.

1.2–8 The letter begins by stressing the importance of faith/trust as converting trials into an opportunity for growth and even joy. This is addressed to the community as a whole. James acknowledges the possibility that some individuals might fail to enter into the community's faith – but only in the third person, which avoids the implication that this is actually the case (1.6–8).

1.10 the rich in being brought low Even though the words are not actually repeated, the parallelism with v. 9 implies the translation '[and let] the rich [brother rejoice] in being brought low'. This is normal usage in Greek when parallel construction is involved. The rich Christian can rejoice in being brought low because it is a sign of being in the community of the saved. James will return to the subject of rich and poor in 2.1–7 and 5.1–6.

1.17–18 God, as father and mother of the community, stands in sharp contrast to desire (1.14–15), which can give birth only to sin and death.

1.19 be quick to listen, slow to speak, slow to anger The Greek phrase includes rhyme and other devices to render it memorable. It constitutes a prescription for hearing the present letter as it was read aloud, but also, beyond that, for Christian discourse in general.

1.22–4 Human beings can absorb the meaning of the gospel message only as they act on it.

1.25 the perfect law, the law of liberty In Mediterranean antiquity, the law dealt differently with free persons, slaves and freedpersons (emancipated slaves). The basic principle of Christian living is that it acknowledges each person as a free person and therefore sweeps away all claims to privilege based on inequities of power. As James returns to this topic, it emerges that he has in mind the law of loving one's neighbour as oneself.

1.27 religion The Greek word refers specifically to the cultic aspects of religion, which James here redefines in relational and ethical terms.

2.5 Has not God chosen the poor . . . ? James makes use of an identification of the pious as the poor (Hebrew *anawim*) that is found in the Psalms and in Jewish piety of the time. Those reckoned as belonging to this category were not always literally poor.

2.6 Is it not the rich who oppress you? Early Christian converts came from a wide range of social backgrounds. But oppression did come typically from rich and powerful outsiders, who alone had the influence to bring it about.

2.7 the excellent name Presumably the name of Jesus, perhaps as invoked in baptism.

2.8 the royal law The same as 'the perfect law, the law of liberty' in 1.25. It is 'royal law' in the sense that it is the law of God's kingdom. James seems to be recalling Jesus' emphasis on this commandment (cf. Matt. 22.34–40), though the quotation itself comes from Leviticus 19.18.

2.8–13 James's argument is that if the congregation fails by showing partiality toward the rich visitor over against the poor one, it has really failed in respect of the whole law. The specific reference to murder in 2.11 seems extreme and unmotivated; but it foreshadows the confrontation with the rich in 5.1–6.

2.14–26 James does not appear to be attacking Paul directly. (Paul would certainly have agreed with his emphasis on the importance of works of charity.) But he is aware of Paul's arguments as is evident in his use of Paul's favorite text: 'Abraham believed God, and it was reckoned to him as righteousness' (Gen. 15.6). The text, in the present translation, would seem to work better for Paul than for James; but the Greek version as cited by James could also be translated, 'it was reckoned for him for the purpose of righteousness', i.e. 'to give rise to righteousness'. In other words, Abraham's faith led directly to his good works.

3.1 Not many of you should become teachers The multiplicity of teachers in early Christianity must have been a staggering problem at times. Virtually all the Second Testament letters bear witness to divisions that resulted at least partly from the arrival of new itinerant teachers with somewhat different versions of the gospel message. James discourages the multiplication of teachers by emphasizing the danger of the role to its occupants, but quickly moves on to more general wisdom about the dangers of speech, enlarging on the foreshadowing of this topic already offered in 1.19–21. The passionate character of this extended passage (3.1–4.12), however, makes it quite different from the calmer and more general treatment of the topic in chapter 1.

3.5–12 James opposes blessing and cursing to each other and questions how they can come from the same mouth. Paul, of course, was guilty of this charge (cf. Gal. 1.8–9). He was probably by no means unique among early Christians, but the preservation of his anathemas in writing has seemed to authenticate the practice and made it difficult for later Christians to take James's admonition seriously.

3.13–18 Here the topic appears to shift to envy, but James is simply bringing in the social motivations for destructive speech. He will return to 'conflicts and disputes' in 4.1.

4.2 Again, the charge that the community has committed murder.

4.4 Adulterers! Literally, 'adulterous women', which will have posed a double insult to an audience that James's world would conceive as pre-eminently male. The image is based on the long-standing Hebrew use of 'harlotry' as a synonym for the worship of foreign gods, but James quickly shifts to the imagery of friendship, recalling his earlier reference to Abraham as 'the friend of God' (2.23).

4.5–6 Or do you suppose that it is for nothing that scripture says, 'God [literally, he] yearns jealously for the spirit that he has made to dwell in us'? But he gives all the more grace; therefore it says, 'God opposes the proud, but gives grace to the humble.' The source of the first quotation (in v. 5) has never been identified; the second is from the Old Greek Version of Proverbs 3.34. Verse 5 might better be repunctuated and translated, using a slightly different reading of the verb: 'Or do you suppose that the scripture speaks in vain? Jealousy is what the spirit that has taken up residence in us longs for. But he [God] gives more grace.' Then follows the quotation from Proverbs. There is no easy solution to this difficult passage. The NRSV translation, however, does not fit well into the thought of the passage and it is forced to assume a positive sense for *phthonos* (jealousy) – something found nowhere else in the Second Testament or in the Old Greek version of the scriptures of Israel. In my translation, I assume that the appeal to scripture in verse 5 is general. James then characterizes the spirit that is actually dominating the community as envious (cf. 4.1–3) and contrasts it to the kind of behaviour demanded by the law (4.11–12). Still, James promises that God's grace will overcome the spirit of jealousy.

4.13–16 James's complaint is not against the merchants' making of plans, but against their failure to acknowledge that everything in life is a gift of God. In itself, this may seem only to be carelessness of speech; but for James, the deed is what gives life to faith and shows its character for all to see (2.11).

5.6 You have condemned and murdered the righteous one, who does not resist you. It is difficult not to hear an echo of the death of Jesus in this phrasing. It would not be unthinkable for James to accuse these wayward Christian landowners of having, in effect, killed Jesus; the letter to the Hebrews, in fact, addresses similar language to Christian apostates (6.6). This does not contradict the more obvious and practical sense in which their failure to pay their workers may have led to the death of one or more persons. Since James probably knew either Matthew's Gospel or the oral traditions that led to it, he may have had in mind the parable of the Sheep and Goats with its 'just as you did it to one of the least of these who are members of my family, you did it to me' (Matt. 25.31–46).

5.7–11 James turns to an emphasis on patience that matches up with the emphasis on endurance at the beginning of the letter (1.2–3). The last day, which threatened to be a 'day of slaughter' for the rich wrongdoers in the preceding paragraph, now takes the form of 'the coming of the Lord', a sign of hope for the abused faithful.

5.9, 11 Patience involves certain social practices as well: forbearance toward one's sister or brother and a complete honesty that renders oaths meaningless and redundant.

5.13–18 Faith expressed in prayer leads to healing, forgiveness and the restoration of justice – the great theme of Elijah's ministry. James sketches a vision of a community in which all members care for one another.

5.19–20 The parting comments emphasize that the goal is one of restoring communion, not of claiming vindication for oneself.

1 and 2 Peter

ROBIN HAWLEY GORSLINE

Queer people can identify with the 'resident aliens' and 'strangers' of 1 Peter, if not the Christian 'beloved' defended from the attacks of scoffers by 2 Peter – living, as we do, among those who, at best, so often do not understand us and, at worst, actively revile us. The actions of our antagonists may even be said to be in response to faith – heterosupremacy is so powerful it often functions like an article of faith to its practitioners. We who adhere to different sexual practices can seem to be threats to the natural order in which they so fervently believe. I write this essay from Virginia where, as a pastor in Metropolitan Community Church, I spend each day resisting, and helping the queer and queer-friendly community resist, a general climate of fear and antagonism toward queers, which includes state-sponsored hate.

This is not unlike the world inhabited by those Christians to whom 1 Peter, and perhaps 2 Peter, are addressed – opposed not for their sexual lives but because their religious beliefs and practices conflicted with the dominant non-Christian culture in which they lived. While most scholars think that there was little official persecution of Christians by the Roman authorities at the time of the writing of 1 and 2 Peter, it seems clear from the two letters that there was considerable opposition within the dominant social framework to the faith and its adherents. 1 Peter certainly makes it clear that the basis of this opposition rested on the tendency of Christians to upset some of the social arrangements that others believed provided the foundations of social order (a condition of great importance in ancient times, as now). 2 Peter appears to be primarily an apologetic/polemic document, set up as a reply to five critiques, or 'slanders', against beliefs current among the faithful. In 1 Peter, we have evidence that those critical of the Christians believed that if slaves could disobey masters and wives their husbands – something they saw Christians encouraging – then society was headed to disaster. The author of 2 Peter presents arguments against theological errors being advanced by those he saw as hostile to the received tradition of faith, and the author outlines the necessary responses of the faithful. His response includes condemnation of his opponents for their lust, a tactic that makes many queers uneasy.

Moreover, the strategies in response to this opposition adopted by the writers of these two letters – not likely to be the same person or even community – hold questionable appeal to queers today. For example, 1 Peter resorts to strategies that rely on achieving some level of acceptance by those who are most critical of the communities in question. The author of 2 Peter is less interested in winning over the opponents than he is in refuting them through vigorous argumentation, but even here his polemics against sexual pollution and other impurities can create dis-ease among queers. However, there are glimmers of hope, and perhaps even possiblities for rethinking strategies, and certainly for seeing some seeds of liberation in the texts, despite real concerns that they simply do not fit well into contemporary queer life. Thus, in the pages that follow, I explore the question: Can Christian, or other, queers draw upon these two very different books in the Christian scriptures for a word of hope in a hostile world? I examine the books in the order they appear in the canon of scripture, and I close with some summary comments about both texts. All scripture quotations are from the NRSV, unless otherwise indicated.

1 Peter: Who Are These Strangers and Resident Aliens Anyway?

Much debate among biblical scholars interested in this text surrounds the identity of the intended recipients of the letter – arguing over identity politics apparently is not limited to queer theory. Although it may seem to be merely an argument among scholars about arcane questions of textual and sociological evidence, the debate actually constitutes a central issue in assessing the letter's value to pastors and others in queer contexts. If we can discern the identity and actual situation of these people, we will be better able to evaluate what they did in their situation and its utility for us. Of course, no data exists by which a definitive answer can be given, and persuasive cases have been made from a number of different perspectives.

One view, forcefully articulated by John H. Elliott, claims that the Christians of Asia Minor being addressed were literally 'visiting strangers' and 'resident aliens', that is, they were members of a specific legal class in Roman-ruled society. Elliott bases much of his view on the status of *paroikoi* and *paroikia*, a group that has the status neither of full citizenship nor of complete strangers. This gave these Christians a precarious legal standing in the community, and created a form of 'double jeopardy' for them – suspect because of their status as non-citizens and non-permanent residents, they carried the additional stigma of being associated with a suspect brand of religion.

For queers, there can be a sense of considerable shared identity with the *paroikia*, who with the slaves and artisans of the cities constituted the working class of the Roman empire. The identification has less to do with socio-economic status than with the fact that *paroikia* enjoyed only limited legal protection, a condition which queers understand. Elliott's description of their status can sound familiar to queers in the United States: they 'were restricted in regard to intermarriage and the transfer of property, could be pressed into military service, were free to engage in cultic rights but were excluded from priestly offices, and yet shared full responsibility with the citizenry for all financial burdens such as a tribute, taxes and production quotas' (Elliott 1981: 68). Elliott argues that 1 Peter is designed to help its recipients resist assimilation and strengthen group solidarity and identity in order to sustain and empower a compelling witness to their faith in the face of hostility from their neighbours. He thus sees the admonitions to slaves and wives (and others) to behave in socially acceptable ways as a strategy that is focused on the fundamental project of promoting the faith.

Other interpreters reject Elliott's view. David Balch sees the letter as promoting assimilation by the Christians into the behaviours of the larger society in order to silence their critics (Balch 1981: 81–2). He contends that the letter should be read in the light of tension between Roman society and foreign, Eastern religions that upset social harmony. This was particularly so in households led by men who were 'pagan', but whose wives were Christian, and in households where owners were 'pagan' and slaves were Christian. The view that Christianity (and Judaism) changed their converts' religious habits led to accusations that they were 'corrupting and reversing Roman social and household customs'. Balch argues that the author of 1 Peter believes that public perceptions of this disharmony might lead to punishment by the Roman governor (and conversely, praise from the governor for those who accepted their place in the hierarchical Roman framework). Thus, he concludes that the household codes in 1 Peter were intended to encourage 'conduct which would contradict the Roman slanders' (Balch 1981: 119).

Steven R. Bechtler disagrees with Elliott, saying the terms *paroikoi* and *paroikia* 'are figures of speech, metaphors, by which a situation of social alienness is characterized, rather than literal designations of a legally recognized social stratum, whether of the intended audience or of the actual readers' (Bechtler 1998: 81). He also disagrees with Balch, contending that although the letter shows considerable congruence with Roman social customs the author is far from urging assimilation by the Christians. Bechtler also rejects ideas, offered by several others (Talbert 1986; Thurén 1990), that attempt to synthesize Elliott and Balch. Instead, he utilizes Victor Turner's work on liminality in order to show that the Christian faith communities in Asia Minor addressed in the letter were being shown how to live in the border situation of being both slaves and free, to live in the 'social liminality of the people of God in a non-Christian world' (Bechtler 1998: 155). Bechtler contends that the metaphors of the text – including the various terms used to characterize the Christians as 'resident aliens' as well as other terms such as 'temple' (*oikos*) – function together to

> legitimize the addressees' social liminality. They are neither fully integrated members of society nor entirely removed from it. They have made a clean break with the past and yet their obedience to God entails conduct in accordance with certain societal conventions. For those readers who accept 1 Peter's constellation of metaphors as constitutive of their identity, social alienation is valorized as the will of God, as the corollary to their divine election, and as the authentic expression of the vocation to which God has called them as God's own people. Their social liminality, thus, need not be a threat to their personal integrity, as long as they recognize that they are members of an alternative social entity and that this alternative community provides their plausibility structure over against the claims – and threats – of the larger society. (155–6)

Thus, it is possible to see this letter as expressing a reality remarkably similar to that of many queers who so often find ourselves living in two worlds. This 'double consciousness' may especially mark those queers who participate in Christian churches. When I conducted a Bible study on 1 Peter at the church I serve, the students kept remarking on the parallels with their own personal situations; the situation of our church in a conservative, southern community; and the situation of our church in an LGBT community noticeably more hostile to religion than the larger culture. We are, on the one hand, often reviled, or at best treated as questionable members of the body of Christ, by many non-queer co-religionists, while, on the other, we are dismissed as hopelessly anachronistic and misguided by queers who, very understandably, see Christianity as an, if not *the*, enemy of the well-being and survival of queer folk.

There is a fourth view to be raised here, although fuller consideration of it follows below. That view emanates from feminist study of the text, and is most explicitly stated by Elisabeth Schüssler Fiorenza, who claims that 'the majority of the [members of the community in 1 Peter] were slaves of pagan masters and wives of pagan husbands' (Schüssler Fiorenza 1983: 261). She bases this claim largely on the lack of address in 1 Peter (unlike the household code in Colossians) to 'masters', although husbands are mentioned. The reference in 3.1 appears to be to non-Christian husbands, while the reference to the necessity of husbands living 'considerately' with their wives in 3.7 appears to be to Christian husbands. Schüssler Fiorenza is correct in stressing that the largest amount of address directed toward specific groups is that towards slaves and wives. This point carries considerable potential consequence in understanding the letter, some of which will be considered in the next section.

Some Problems at Home

If I stopped here, readers might be drawn to examine 1 Peter, hoping to find not only a sense of shared identification with some early Christian ancestors (the letter was most likely written in the period between 70 and 95 CE) but also some hope for contemporary struggles in a hostile world. However, feminist analysis of this book finds in it 'little that may be appropriated by women, and little that may be appropriated by other individuals suffering under unjust social institutions' (Corley 1994b: 356). Queers of all stripes have learned to be suspicious of any text, or movement, that is unfriendly to women and other oppressed persons and groups.

The household codes in 1 Peter appear not at all liberative, at least as seen from our vantage point. The author urges all who hear and read the letter to accept the authority of (a more full-bodied translation might be for them to 'subordinate themselves to') various human institutions. These superordinate institutions include the Roman state (and therefore the emperor, 2.13–17), masters (for slaves, 2.18–20), and husbands (for wives, 3.1–6). At the same time, some commentators have argued that the author is not arguing for the *rightness*, morally considered, of such subordination, but doing so to serve the cause of silencing those who speak against the faith. Elliott argues, for example, that 1 Peter offers '*distinctly Christian reasons*' in support of his exhortation for the subordination of wives to husbands (Elliott 2000: 596). These reasons include a reverence for God, a desire to convert non-Christian husbands to faith in Christ, and a desire to follow the example of matriarchs in faith (for example

Sarah, who called Abraham 'master'). Elliott, in a strenuous, and sometimes dismissive, critique of Schüssler Fiorenza, claims that the aim of 1 Peter is 'not to encourage conformity to secular society but precisely the opposite: to affirm the holiness and distinctiveness of the reborn family of God and to urge holy non-conformity with Gentile modes of thought and life' (Elliott 2000: 597).

However that may be, one cannot easily dismiss Schüssler Fiorenza's argument that the wives and slaves who have become Christian – thus upsetting the governing social and religious system by claiming equality in the name of Christ – represent the true spirit of a religious consciousness that is being tamped down in this letter, albeit in response to apparent pressure from the larger culture.

The practice in ancient times was that the male head of the household determined the religious affiliation of everyone in the household. Wives and slaves who made these choices for themselves presented a clear challenge to this patriarchal structure. Christian communities often encouraged non-slave women and all slaves to choose for themselves, thus bringing down on the communities criticism from the husbands and slave owners so challenged, and this history seems evident from the letter (see 3.1 for reference to those who 'disobey the word'). Schüssler Fiorenza writes,

> It is apparent that the author conceives of the household code as a form or apologia for the Christian faith. However, unlike Josephus or Philo who write such defenses for the attackers of the Jews, the author addresses Christians, who are powerless and without legal recourse, urging them to adapt to the *politeuma* of Rome and its ancestral customs. In this way, the author does not lessen the tension between the Christian community and the patriarchal society, since this tension is created precisely by the abandonment of the religion of the *paterfamilias*. The author wants to strengthen their rejection of the 'old religion,' but he does so by relinquishing the new freedom of those slaves and women who became members of the new priestly people. (Schüssler Fiorenza 1983: 262)

In Schüssler Fiorenza's understanding, it is precisely the creation of a community of equals, set into motion by the example of Jesus and carried forward by the disciples after his death, that lies at the core of the gospel – and that in 1 Peter this core is being abandoned.

She also argues that 1 Peter stresses a spiritualizing of the faith by seeking to remove behaviour that creates problems with non-Christians and encouraging an inner radiance (for example, wives encouraged in 3.4 to let their adornment 'be the inner self with the lasting beauty of a gentle and quiet spirit') and a deep identification in suffering with the suffering of Jesus (slaves, in 2.19, reminded that 'it is a credit to you if, being aware of God, you endure pain while suffering unjustly'). Others link this spiritualization of the faith to social consequences in history. '[T]he Petrine admonition that both slaves and women should endure unjust or terrifying situations still serves as a scriptural justification for violence against women in the present, in the same way that it gave justification for violence against African Americans under slavery in the past' (Corley 1994b: 349).

There also is the matter of sexual behaviour and beliefs, always present, as queers know, in social situations. Corley points out that

> all slaves were sexually available to their masters or to whomever their masters might give them. This was a hardship in particular for slave women and attractive young boys. Male and female slaves are thus being told to suffer even physical punishment or rape in order to quiet anti-Christian rumors that Christians are a seditious threat to the security of the household. (Corley 1994b: 353)

Feminists also see a hint that wives should submit to sexual abuse by the positive reference to Sarah (who was given to the household of Pharaoh by her husband on account of her great beauty).

Corley argues that 1 Peter relies too much on a 'suffering servant' concept of atonement, and that the idea that women and slaves, by suffering with a smile and dignity, can win over those who reject the faith simply perpetuates cycles of violence and victimization and holds up the victim as a model for women. She contrasts this view with that of others who understand that suffering may be the outcome, but not the purpose, of discipleship. 'Christian suffering should become a vehicle for social change, not a means of social assimilation, as in 1 Peter' (Corley 1994b: 355). This reliance on the suffering Christ as the model for Christian living, and its particular application here to women and slaves – those least able to defend themselves – creates the condition for widespread abuse in the home and elsewhere.

Can This Book Be Saved?

An important principle of historical biblical criticism as it has been practised for more than a century is that texts are to be read in their own context. Readers are cautioned against overlaying contemporary ideas and concerns on the texts. More recently, feminists and others have helped us see that such reading is in reality not a one-way affair. Instead, the conversation between ancient texts and contemporary concerns often can be mutually enriching, and it is always necessary. This certainly is ground on which queers who read the Bible have found we must stand. Our struggle for liberation, and the struggles of those others (some of whom are queer) around us – African Americans, women, differently abled, people of different socio-economic classes, and others – for liberation tell us that if we do not bring our experience to the texts that others have used to oppress us we, and they, will never be free.

We have moved far from the days when a main concern was to disprove allegations that the Bible condemns homosexuality. We know the answer to that charge now, and only those who refuse to listen still proceed as if it does (not that they are without ecclesio-political power in perpetuating their misreadings). Moreover, 1 Peter does not appear to have anything to say about homosexuality, although 2.11 ('abstain from the desires of the flesh that wage war against the soul') probably causes some right-wing religionists to quiver in delight at what would appear to them to be another biblical queer-bashing.

Instead, 1 Peter gives us clear evidence that among the early Christians were enough feisty women and uppity slaves to cause others to be angry and worried. The anger may have come more from those outside the movement and the worry may have come more from the inside, reflecting the precarious social standing of all in the movement, but the main fact is that there were enough of these women and slaves to create problems for those accustomed to being in control (in and out of the movement). This is good news for Christian-identified queers. These women and men can be claimed as ancestors in the faith.

I suggest that we read 1 Peter through a lens that brings together Bechtler's use of liminality and Schüssler Fiorenza's observation that the main addressees of this letter are wives and slaves who had acted against the social structure. Such a reading can provide us with a picture that looks remarkably like the place of many queers in the Church today. Many Christian queers find themselves in churches where they are 'neither fully integrated members of society nor entirely removed from it' (Bechtler 1998: 155). Even those of us in the Universal Fellowship of Metropolitan Community Churches – where being queer is the norm rather than the exception – find that within the larger Church we are neither fully integrated nor entirely removed.

At the same time, Schüssler Fiorenza's observation that the addressees of 1 Peter are primarily the disruptive ones seems accurately to describe many of us who work daily to advance the cause of queer liberation, fighting homophobia on all fronts, including within our own religious ranks. In the MCC church I serve, many of the members register varying levels of discomfort and anger about my community activities, as well as an unhappiness that almost every week, at least once, we mention the words lesbian, gay, bisexual and transgender, or at least refer to 'our community' in a way that evokes LGBT concerns, in worship (and usually in my sermons). The unhappy ones don't want me, or others, to say much about being queer (in our local LGBT community, the word 'queer' is almost a fighting word). They appear to have several fears. The first is that the straight people who come will feel unwelcome (and I agree, we don't want to do what the straight churches do to queers – but then we never bash anyone for their sexuality). The second fear is that the community activities bring attention to the church and endanger those who are not 'out'. The third, unspoken for the most part, is the fear that being a queer Christian actually requires us to bring together that which we – all of us, straight and gay – have been taught for so long to keep apart, namely our sexuality and our spirituality.

It is here that I find the connection between our situation today and that of the addressees in 1 Peter most potent. Of course, 1 Peter is not addressing sexuality in any important way, but the author is addressing the conflict between the liberative, change-making power of faith, on the one hand, and the oppressive, anti-change power of society's non-faith, on the other. In the process of dealing with that conflict, the author pens a powerful message that results in trying to separate the social change inherent in the message and life of Jesus Christ and his disciples from the personal change inherent in the message and life of Jesus Christ and his disciples.

I recognize myself and my sisters and brothers struggling for change, in these wives and slaves who are being told to tone it down, to bear their pain and suffering in patience and silence. I recognize members of the congregation and community I serve, who tell me that it is my activism that is making the 'principalities and powers' angry at queers. I recognize several of the leading politicians of my state, who encourage me not to press so hard for marriage equality because it makes the conservative legislature angry, angry enough to do even more to hurt queers than they have already done.

But I also see myself in the writer of 1 Peter. I recognize myself in the writer when, at times, I lose sight of the liberative message of the gospel and begin to tell anxious, angry queers to remember how much better things are now than they were before. I, a white man, recognize myself in the writer of 1 Peter when I flinch from the angry words of an African American, Latino/a or Asian colleague, when I wish they would not be so angry, making me and others uncomfortable.

This book is about conflict between Christian communities on the one side and non-Christian society on the other – in a way not unlike how Paul's epistles are often about conflict within Christian communities. In both cases, the writers are trying to help their listeners and readers avoid being torn apart by the conflicts that inevitably arise when new faith meets old realities. At the same time, I see a difference between this text and the Pauline ones, and certainly between it and the synoptic Gospels and the Acts of the Apostles, and that difference is in how each treats conflict. Studying this text has resulted in my wanting to study the canonical Gospels in terms of conflict theory – after all, Jesus never shied away from conflict. In fact, he often seemed to seek it out and encourage it. That difference – on the one hand, seeking to avoid conflict, and on the other, seeking it out or at least not avoiding conflict – is a key to understanding this text, and also to understanding how we, as queers, today can relate to it.

The letter opens with words about the addressees being chosen and destined to be obedient to Jesus Christ, and having been the recipients of new birth into a living hope through the resurrection as well as an inheritance 'that is imperishable, undefiled, and unfading, *kept in heaven for you'*. These opening words set the stage for the spiritualization spoken of above by Schüssler Fiorenza. The writer then tells the addressees that although they rejoice in all this 'now for a little while you have had to suffer various trials' that testify to the genuineness of their faith (1.1–7, italics mine).

These words point to an initial understanding that the suffering and trials they are enduring are the result of their faith. Speaking only as one, I can say that I am willing to bear suffering and trials on account of my faith, including that suffering and those trials that occur when others refuse to accept the unity I feel between my faith and my social situation (a queer Christian, living out loud in a homophobic community).

However, subsequent chapters and admonitions – the Household Code – appear to change the nature of the conflict, taking it from one between those who are faithful on the one hand and those who are not on the other, to one between those among the faithful who are most vulnerable (slaves and wives) and those among the faithful who are less vulnerable (the men who are not slaves). Of course, we do not know who actually wrote this letter (other than a clear sense that it was not the apostle Peter), but it is logically iron-clad to assume that it was neither a slave nor a subjugated wife. In queer life, the author of a text such as this is most likely to be a white gay man who does not want to lose his professional or corporate status, his second home on Fire Island, and his entrée into the best (straight and gay) social circles.

Therefore, queers can best use this text to claim some ancestors, while at the same time eschewing the assimilationist-sounding tactics of its author. To say that does not mean that the author wanted only assimilation. Indeed, Bechtler and others are correct in rejecting that view; even Schüssler Fiorenza understands the text as one in which the author wants its recipients to stay true to the faith. However, the practical effect – when you are among the oppressed – is to view this text as a call to avoid further difficulty with the powers-that-are.

Thus, what queers may not do is take this text as a sourcebook for strategy and tactics to achieve liberation. Instead, we may read it with profit if our goal is to learn what not to do, how not to be in alliance or solidarity with the oppressed. Those who complain that Schüssler Fiorenza and others are reading back onto the text concerns that are not part of the text do not understand how the oppressed must read the Bible, and other writings considered sacred. They also do not understand how they, as among the dominant group, read the texts. We, all of us, read texts, at least in part, through lenses made up of where we stand, where we have come from, and how our reading will affect us, and others, today. Queers recognize the author of 1 Peter as one of the 'don't rock the boat' types, but thanks to the author's address to others in his community we also recognize our fellow boat-rockers. Rock on.

2 Peter: Does This Letter Matter?

2 Peter is little read; it appears as a church reading in the three cycles of the Revised Common Lectionary only twice. Of the 449 pages in the Second Testament in the New Oxford Annotated Bible (NRSV) it takes up only four. The arguments appear esoteric to many contemporary Christians; doctrines such as that concerning the Second Coming seem out of date and unscientific. Heresy, schism and false teaching, with which the letter is greatly concerned, seem old-fashioned (Craddock 1995: 85–6; Perkins 1993: 162–3). Additionally, much of the letter, especially chapter 2, appears to have been redacted from the biblical book known as Jude. This matter is not provable with historical finality, but the analysis of Neyrey (1980) and others (Fornberg 1977; Bauckham 1983) has convinced most scholars that the old idea of the chronological primacy of 2 Peter over Jude (based primarily on the idea that a letter 'written by' an apostle would have to come first) is no longer tenable. Nor do most scholars today believe that the reference (3.1) to an earlier letter connects 2 Peter to 1 Peter (Neyrey may be a possible exception); instead, this letter is most likely one of two letters of which we have only the second.

With these factors in mind, the question naturally arises: Why should we care today about such a document? What can it say that is of value in queer contexts? The answer lies in a defensive framework, namely that this letter needs to be known so that its reliance on negative views of sexuality (here called lust or desire) may be understood and countered. It is probably a good thing that

2 Peter appears so little in the lectionary of most churches, and yet if we are to know and understand Christian history this letter carries some importance. That may be especially so because we know so little of its history; it is not addressed to a particular community and might well indicate that the problems it purports to address – and the arguments it offers – were widespread.

Based on a considerable amount of conjecture – which is of course a vital part of historical and redaction criticism – it seems that 2 Peter was most likely written very late in the first century or fairly early in the second, somewhere from 95 CE to 110 CE. This is a time when the original apostles were all gone, and the Christian communities may well have been experiencing considerable conflict about belief and practice, with no strong authorities in place to settle vexing questions. The use of the name of Simeon Peter as author may be an attempt to claim some authority from the mantle of the original Peter, and it purports to be a farewell address of a leader about to die – an attempt to claim the extra authority of a leader leaving important instructions to those who remain. It is also a time, as we shall show below, when popular ideas about theodicy challenged Christian (and much Jewish) orthodoxy about the providence of God.

Neyrey (1993: 112) has identified five 'slanders' to which the author is responding. The criticisms and the defences mounted against them may be listed in this way: prophecy of the parousia defended (1.16–18), prophecy and interpretation defended (1.19–21), divine judgement defended (2.1–3, 4–10a), divine word of judgement defended (3.1–3, 4–7), and delay of divine judgement defended (3.8–9, 10–13). He also has hypothesized that the false teachers and scoffers to whom the author directs the defence are 'either Epicureans, who rejected traditional theodicy, or "scoffers" (*Apikoros*) who espoused a similar deviant theology' (Neyrey 1993: 122).

The space needed to fully outline the Epicurean view of life is not available to us, but it is important for our purposes to know that they rejected ancient ideas of an afterlife and post-mortem retribution by the divine for sins committed on earth. Their rejection of these ideas caused many to see them as immoral persons who encouraged wickedness and vice. However, the Epicurean view became popular over time, becoming generally popular as a theological view of many, including Jews, Christians and non-theistic believers, and causing widespread rejection of more traditional views of theodicy. One way, then, that we can situate the strong views about lust and desire articulated by the author of 2 Peter is in the context of an argument by those who opposed this scepticism – who considered those who held the popular, Epicurean-based view to be immoral persons practising wickedness and vice (Neyrey 1993: 127).

It also is possible to see these strong views by the author of 2 Peter as evidence of internal strife in one or more Christian communities. Eve Kosofsky Sedgwick, among other queer literary theorists, has noted the importance of 'silence' in understanding the queerness of texts (Sedgwick 1993: 79). Marie-Eloise Rosenblatt, offering a feminist reading of 2 Peter, notes the silence about women in the text. From this silence, and other factors, she avers that the letter is designed to maintain male hegemony within a 'heterogeneous Christian community torn by internal dissension' (Rosenblatt 1994b(1): 399). Others (Craddock 1995; Perkins 1993) share her view that this text is addressing internal error. Writing about the book of Jude (from which 2 Peter borrows heavily), Rosenblatt suggests that because the usual way to practise lust involves men and women, 'the reader may deduce that the polemic involves women as well as men' (although the women are never mentioned) (Rosenblatt 1994b(1): 393). Rosenblatt also sees a borrowing from Jude in 'a general line of rhetorical attack: association of rival teachers with sexual immorality' (Rosenblatt 1994b(1): 400).

Sex, Again

Whether we follow Neyrey in seeing the text as a response to a more generalized set of errors in society or Rosenblatt and others in seeing it as a response to internal heresies, what is clear in a queer reading of the text is that alleged sexual misconduct is believed to be the proof of wrong thinking. Echoing a traditional view, Craddock makes this point clearly when he writes, 'At work is a double heresy, theological and ethical. The writer understands that the two are related; that is, corrupt living grows out of erroneous doctrine' (1995: 93).

Thus, the letter opens with a customary greeting and a recitation of God's powerful gifts through Jesus Christ, and continues (1.4), 'Thus he has given us, through these things, his precious and very great promises, so that through them you may escape from the corruption that is in the world because of lust, and may become participants of the divine nature.' Neyrey (1993: 106) translates 'lust' as 'desire'. Either way, we are on notice that the source of turning away from God and Jesus Christ is at least related to what we call sexuality. Two verses later (1.6) self-control is extolled, and a little later it is clearly contrasted with those in Sodom and Gomorrah 'who indulge their flesh in depraved lust and despise authority' (2.10–22). For queers, these passages form the heart of the matter, even though it would be stretching things considerably to claim that this text is speaking only (or even primarily) of same-sex lust.

Neyrey's analysis, drawing on the investigations of Mary Douglas into purity and pollution, is helpful in seeing the focus on lust in larger context. Purity was an important concept in the ancient world, resting on the maintenance of boundaries that supported order in the world, where everything has a place and everything (and everyone) is in its place – and if something or someone is out of place, they are polluted and unclean. The author of 2 Peter shares in this view. Neyrey writes that 'certain people (3.2), places (1.18), and things (2.21; 3.11) are labeled "holy" (*hagios*) because they are associated with or authorized by God' (Neyrey 1993: 136). The truly faithful will be 'spotless, unblemished' and will practise virtue (1.5–7). Similarly, there are references to corruption and defilement in 2 Peter (1.4; 2.12, 19, 20, 22) as well as reference to 'spots and blemishes' (2.13). 'Passion' (2.18; 3.3), 'debauchery' (2.2, 18) and 'adultery' (2.14) are linked with corruption as well.

The writer of 2 Peter draws a sharp differentiation between the faithful and pure, on the one side, and the unfaithful and polluted, on the other. Those who are the former are the insiders – God's favoured – and those who are the latter are the outsiders, those who live wrongly because they do not follow God and Jesus Christ. The writer also shows a strong bent toward authority, both of God and of those who teach the received faith and traditions; the insiders respect it and the outsiders lack knowledge because they show no respect for this authority. The latter are the scoffers, those who belittle important knowledge such as the transfiguration (1.18), disrespecting the gifts of God and the teaching of those who know the value of these gifts.

Neyrey suggests that the sharp line between the pure and the polluted in this system leads not only to intense efforts at social control but also to intense efforts to control the body. He avers that 'self-control' in 2 Peter means 'strong bodily control, in particular, control of the orifices of the body' (Neyrey 1993: 139). The eyes, mouth and genitals are each a contested area in 2 Peter. The contrast between the author's eyes, through which he sees holy visions (1.16) and the eyes of his opponents, through which they see evil (2.14) is stark. As for the mouth, the author speaks inspired words (1.20–1; 3.1–2) while the others scoff at them (3.3–4). The mouths of the opponents share dissipation when they eat and those who follow them are like 'the dog [who] turns back to its own vomit' (2.22). As for the genitals, when the true believers exercise self-control, they will be moral; we have already seen what happens to the others who are sexually out of control (adultery, debauchery and desire/lust).

Queers know about these sorts of boundaries, especially in our sexuality. We put parts of our bodies in what much of society thinks are the wrong places, and share our bodies with the wrong people. We look longingly at the wrong people. We say the wrong words to the wrong people, and we even make so bold as to speak about our lives openly, in contravention of the received social wisdom to keep our lives to ourselves. Our orifices always seem to be doing something wrong!

Thus, this letter appears to have little positive meaning for Christian queers. We can say, as was claimed above about 1 Peter, that this letter reminds us that we have ancestors. It may comfort some to know we have been this way before. However, these ancestors are not acknowledged as part of the community of faith, but rather as the enemies of the faith and its gathered believers. Clearly, a significant portion of right-wing, fundamentalist Christianity sees queers that way yet today, and it may be that this text can function in our lives as a template for what my fellow Virginians – James Dobson, Jerry Falwell, Pat Robertson and their followers – are saying about us now. Alas, it does not seem we need an ancient template of this sort to help us either understand or oppose their contemporaneously virulent claims. Surely, they do not need any more help in perpetuating the hate.

Concluding Remarks

1 and 2 Peter are not among the most important biblical texts for anyone, queer or non-queer. However, each conveys information about the Christian Church in formation, even if that information is only partial and of limited value. We are reminded through these texts that Christians living in community created social disruption in the larger world. We also are reminded that arguments within the communities reveal a more fractured internal existence than may appear from the traditional stories of Christian history.

Often, students in church Bible study classes object to the closing of the scriptural canon long ago, contending that those who did so stopped all the arguing (and of course pretended that revelation had somehow stopped). Analysing these texts demonstrates that although the arguments may be old, they are not really over. The precise points raised in the letters may be *passé*, but the larger issues have not died.

Those of us who are faithful to the God of the Hebrew Bible and the Christian Testament (and who, like me, claim Jesus Christ as Saviour), and who simultaneously stand on the ground of queer consciousness, inhabit a liminal space. It is a strange space that cannot be fixed in one spot, but is nonetheless somewhere to stand that conveys the interlocking authenticity of our sense of self and our faith. We stand 'there' and confront texts like these two letters with a sense of adventure and a sense of foreboding. We feel the excitement of adventure because we realize that the tools we have today – not only historical criticism, but also various particular forms of criticism from feminists and other liberationists – help us and others to construct new relationships with these texts. At the same time, we feel foreboding because we realize just how often others before us have found no help, and often terror or at least negativity, from these texts, and how many others are still using these texts, despite their literary and theological obscurity, to keep people away from the reality of God's love and to maintain a religious torpor that denies the spiritual juiciness of just about everyone in the Bible from Abraham to Jesus, the disciples and Paul.

Thus, it is our task to uncover the richness of life, wherever and whenever we can – knowing that in successive readings of these texts, and many others, we shall continue to uncover the long-hidden spiritual vibrancy of our forebears and their resistance to oppression. In that spirit, I offer this reading of these texts, trusting that others will take it from here.

The Johannine Letters

L. WILLIAM COUNTRYMAN

The Johannine letters are all concerned with maintenance of unity in the Church, a unity which the author or authors see as embedded in the tradition of Jesus' teaching, in the practice of love for one another in the community, and in the hospitality offered by the network of house churches to travelling Christians. 1 and 2 John are combating a spiritual elitism that threatens both to reject the tradition and to dissolve the bonds of love within and among the churches. 3 John is concerned with the behaviour of the patron of a particular house church who is attempting to take that church out of the network over which the author presides.

The following treatment of the three letters of John combines three primary perspectives. The author is a biblical scholar whose study focuses on the cultural distance between the ancient Mediterranean world and our own. He is also an Anglican Christian who finds the scriptures to be a principal point of encounter with God and with the Good News of Jesus. And he is a gay man, whose spiritual journey has led him to celebrate this fact as a gift from God. He regards exegesis as the task of bringing the complexities of ancient texts and their worlds into conversation with the complexities of our own world.

Introduction

The letters of John, particularly the first two, are closely related in terms of language and style to the Gospel of John. They probably came out of the same network of early Christian communities as the Gospel, but it is not easy to specify more exactly the historical connections among these various works. The theology of the letters is not identical to that of the Gospel; and they reflect a different set of social issues within the life of the group. Where the Gospel of John is concerned about the relationship of the Christian community to developing Rabbinic Judaism, the letters are more concerned with internal challenges arising from differences in teaching, rivalry over community leadership and questions about the nature of Christian unity.

It may seem more logical to assume that the division between Jewish Christianity (of which the Johannine communities constituted one variety) and non-Christian Judaism would have taken place first, with the internal fragmentation following. But the reverse is just as possible. We know from the letters of Paul that Christian communities could experience internal divisions quite early in their history. Developing tensions with the larger Jewish community may even have had the effect of encouraging internal cohesion in Johannine churches, which could afford more internal fighting at an earlier time when they were at peace externally.

In the present article, I take my lead from Kenneth Grayston, who argued that the letters come from at least two different writers within the Johannine community, neither of them identical with the author of the Fourth Gospel, and that 1 John, at least, is older than the Gospel (Grayston 1984: 6–22). 1 John is attacking charismatic leaders who minimize the value of the Jesus tradition and rely more on their own experience of the Spirit. The Gospel, in some respects, actually mediates between the position of the author of 1 John and that of the dissidents attacked in the letter. For example, where 1 John knows of only one *paracletos* (advocate, comforter), namely Jesus (2.1), the Gospel is willing to allow for two, the second being the Spirit (14.16).

Many scholars (probably the majority) date the letters after the Gospel, thereby placing them in the early second century. One may then look for evidence of Gnostic tendencies in the dissidents; but there is nothing that clearly marks them as such. The most likely evidence might be the insistence of 1 John on acknowledging Jesus as having 'come in the flesh' (4.2). Rejection of the fleshliness of Jesus could reflect Gnostic suspicion of the physical creation; but, on the other hand, docetism (the teaching that Jesus' earthly, human form was an appearance rather than real flesh) is quite apt to turn up in early Christian piety that is otherwise non-Gnostic. The main issue in 1 John seems to be rather the tension between those who rely on the traditions about Jesus' life and teachings for guidance and those who rely instead on the immediate inspiration of prophetic spirit(s). (Here, as often in the Second Testament, early Christians are a little unclear as to the relationship of the singular Holy Spirit to the plural spirits that were thought to inspire prophets; cf. 1 Cor. 14.32.)

1 John has had a secure place in the Second Testament canon since the late second century, but the two shorter letters were for a long time marginal even in Greek-speaking Christianity and never gained a place in the canon of the East Syrian Christians. 2 John is closely related to 1 John in terms of its concerns and perspective, but it does little more than dictate a conclusion where 1 John argues at length the moral implications of belief. It may, then, come from a writer other than the author of 1 John. 3 John is close in style to 2 John, but deals with issues different from the ones that prompted the writing of the other two letters.

In all three letters, the author writes as a person of authority. In 2 and 3 John, he calls himself 'the Elder'. In 1 John, he assumes a similar quality of seniority by describing himself as part of the corps of oral tradents whose grasp of the Christian message went back to intimate association with Jesus himself. His seniority is also evident in his habit of addressing his hearers/readers as 'children' or, perhaps, 'little children'. (The word *teknia* is a diminutive; but diminutive forms did not always have clear diminutive force in the Greek of the period.) At the same time, the author recognizes the presence of people of all ages in the community and shows appropriate regard for each age group in 1 John 2.12–14.

1 *John* reflects a situation in which the unity of the community is being shattered by tensions between the bearers of the oral tradition about Jesus (note the strong emphasis on this tradition in 1.1–4) and other, more charismatically oriented leaders whose claim to authority is based rather on prophetic inspiration. The author repeatedly encourages his addressees not to be impressed by such claims. They, too, have an 'anointing' (*chrisma*, a pun on *charisma* or 'gift'); they, too have 'knowledge' (2.20, 27). They have the tradition and do not need new teachers to tell them the truth about God and Jesus. Quite the contrary, they must take it on themselves to judge the inspiration of the charismatics by discerning the character of the spirits speaking through them (4.1–6).

The author sees the tension between a more tradition-oriented and a more charismatic-oriented leadership becoming manifest as division in the community, threatened or actually put into effect. Of those who have actually left, the writer says, in effect, to let them go; they were never really a part of the community (2.19). The dissidents who are still within the community are in some sense the more challenging group. The author addresses the issues they raise partly in terms of discernment of spirits, as already noted, but also in terms of care for one another within the Christian community, intimating that there has been some tendency on the part of the charismatics to pull back from involvement in the common fund of the community.

In response, 1 John highlights the community's *koinonia* ('sharing, communion, fellowship'; the word could even denote the common fund itself, though 1 John does not use it in that sense) and the Johannine version of the love-commandment: 'Love one another.' Both are ways of appealing for unity in the congregation. Since the earliest Christian communities were made up of converts, it was relatively easy for them to fragment when they disagreed about the implications of the gospel; other letter writers in the Second Testament are similarly preoccupied with the maintenance of unity. For 1 John, unity is manifest partly in terms of continuity of teaching (sticking with the tradition that comes from Jesus) but also in terms of the mutual care the members of the community exercise toward one another. 1 John demonstrates the centrality of such loving behaviour by anchoring it not only in the love-commandment, but in the very nature of God: 'God is love' (4.8, 16).

The author treats the dissidents harshly in this letter, even referring to them as 'antichrists' (2.18–19). This language, however, is likely to create an exaggerated impression on the modern reader, as we have come to associate the term 'antichrist', without any warrant in the Second Testament texts themselves, with the figure of the Beast in Revelation 13. In 1 and 2 John, the 'antichrists' are teachers, not world-political figures of supernatural evil. Here, *antichristos* has something closer to its etymological meaning of 'anti-anointed'. It seems likely that the dissidents spoke of themselves as *christoi* ('anointed ones'), implying that, like Jesus, they enjoyed the direct inspiration of the Spirit and were therefore in some sense Jesus' equals. 1 and 2 John respond with the otherwise nonsensical epithet 'anti-anointed,' suggesting that they are really the opposite of what they claim to be.

1 John makes no analytical argument against the position of the dissidents. The rhetoric of the letter, like that of some of Jesus' speeches in the Gospel of John, is circular. It makes use of an artificially small Greek vocabulary and

keeps circling back through varying combinations of the principal terms and images to make and reinforce basic points about the nature of two opposed positions or ways of life. Jesus and the tradition that stems from him come to be associated with life, truth and love. The dissidents are associated with false-hood, the fragmenting of the community and failure (or even refusal) to care for the needy in the congregation.

It is safe to say that the author is not merely reporting the situation in unbiased fashion. It does not follow, however, that the rhetoric is therefore entirely baseless or arbitrary. A description of the opponents that was alto-gether unrelated to reality would not have served the author's purpose in a situation where they were known directly to many of the addressees. We do not, however, need to assume that the dissidents were con-artists. They were spiritual elitists who were sceptical of the bonds that connected them to the religiously less advanced members of the community.

Even if the argument of the letter does not move by clear logical steps, there is an overall coherence to the author's basic stance. Connection with Jesus through the oral tradition and its bearers brings with it a command to love one another. Christian community can legitimately be judged by this standard. No claim to connection with Jesus or with God that does not also issue in acts of love can be taken seriously. God is love. You cannot claim to love God if you are not also demonstrating love for your brother or sister (2.9–11). The author's problem with the dissidents is that their spiritual elitism leads them to look down on those sisters and brothers who do not appear to have reached their level of attainment; and this seems to them to justify backing away from com-mitment to the *koinonia* of the whole community.

The ultimate standard for the unity of the Church in 1 John is not doctrinal agreement, but the practice of love. The author is indeed committed to a cer-tain kind of teaching, one that builds on the tradition of Jesus' teaching and insists on Jesus' corporeality. But, far from being an abstract doctrine, to be believed for its own sake, this is important because it is the ground for the author's assertion of the importance of loving one another. Commitment to the Jesus tradition serves to counter the tendency of the dissidents to ignore the needs of those around them and focus only on their own spiritual attainment. For 1 John, the ministry and teaching of Jesus, conveyed through the oral tradi-tion, offer a touchstone by which authentic Christian life can be recognized.

2 *John* seems to address much the same set of issues as 1 John and uses the language of *antichristoi* to describe the opponents. It contains less of an argu-ment than 1 John and is more a simple assertion of the correct position to take. It is perhaps most interesting to us now for its address to 'the elect lady and her children' and the greetings it extends from 'the children of your elect sis-ter'. These were long taken to be allegorical references to churches (the lady and her sister) and to their members (the children). (The Greek *ekklesia* is a feminine noun; and the Church could indeed be presented allegorically in the figure of a woman, as in Revelation 21 or Hermas, *The Shepherd*, Visions 1–2.) More recently, as scholars have recognized the prominence of women in early Judaism and Christianity, it has seemed more appropriate to take the expres-sions literally as referring to two women of social prominence who are both

serving as patrons of their local Christian congregations, with their children as their associates. (Cf. Phoebe in Romans 16.1–2 and the way Paul addresses the triad of Philemon, Apphia and Archippus, presumably husband, wife and son, in Philemon 1–2.) Such patrons were vital to the life of early Christian communities. They provided space for the congregation to assemble, offered hospitality to travelling Christians, and provided other social benefits that only relatively wealthy persons could offer. Like other ancient Mediterranean voluntary associations, the early Christian communities probably depended on the presence of such sponsors.

3 *John* is an intervention in local political problems among Christian house churches. The Elder addresses Gaius, who is probably the patron of one such congregation, and complains of the behaviour of another patron, Diotrephes, who seems to be taking his house church out of the network of churches in communion with the Elder. There are no accusations of false teaching, just the claim that Diotrephes has refused to offer hospitality to the Elder's messengers and tried to keep others from offering it (10). The suggested reason is that Diotrephes 'likes to put himself first'. If he can take his house church out of the network, he will not have to share authority with the Elder. Demetrius, the third figure named, may be the Elder's emissary who has come bearing the letter and asking for the assistance of Gaius in either bringing Diotrephes back into the network or isolating him so that he cannot extend his influence further.

For the modern queer reader, the Johannine correspondence may offer both attractive and unattractive elements. To begin with the latter, we certainly see in this correspondence the play of power and authority at work in the context of early Christian internal politics. This is most obvious in 2 and 3 John, but it is also the case in 1 John, whose author carefully positions himself at the very beginning as one in a tradition of eye witnesses and tradition bearers. While 1 John employs arguments of other kinds as well, the author does insist on an absolute kind of personal authority: 'We are from God. Whoever knows God listens to us, and whoever is not from God does not listen to us' (4.6). This pronouncement may well remind the reader of Jesus' style of speaking in the Gospel of John. It seems to admit of no argument and no dissenting perspective.

Without seeking to make this stance palatable to the modern reader, I think it is worth pointing out that to some extent it was implicit in the nature of the oral tradition which served as the principal means by which Jesus' message was carried out into the larger world. The message and its bearer were intimately connected with one another. The oral tradent must not only retell the stories and teachings of Jesus, but live in accordance with them. Under such circumstances, one could not easily detach authority from identity.

It is important to note, then, that 1 John's principal criterion for belonging to the Christian community is behavioural. While there are indeed a few sentences devoted to the question of testing spirits and to belief, the larger part of the letter is devoted to the subject of love. God is love; and if you actually believe this, it will necessarily show in your behaviour, particularly toward other members of the community. (The Johannine form of the love commandment is 'Love one another', which may or may not relieve the Christian of responsibility for the outsider, but certainly does make an explicit demand about behaviour within the community.)

And it is precisely here that the Johannine correspondence becomes particularly important for members of sexual minorities and queer people generally in the Church today. Love demands caring for the needs of the sister and brother, including most fundamentally the need of basic human respect. The common claim made by self-styled Christians on the right to 'love the sinner' does not measure up to the Johannine standard. The behaviour that goes under this heading is condescending, demeaning and contemptuous. It takes it as axiomatic that the person claiming to love in this way knows more about the 'sinner' who is being loved than the latter can possibly know about herself or himself, that this superior person has no need to learn anything about life or love from the person thus 'befriended', that the superior person owes no respect to the person who is 'loved' in this fashion. None of this has anything to do with love; it merely filches this otherwise sacred word to cover the sins of the right wing. To accept 1 John's insistence on the primacy of love is to see through all this fraud. Indeed, modern experience makes it easy to see why the author of 1 John would characterize the opponents as 'liars'.

The Johannine letters are marked by the situations in which they were written. They cannot escape being political. But the key issue is that they are on the side of an inclusive network of rather ordinary Christians. The rich patron who wishes to isolate one house church from others is up to no good, harming the other members of that house church as much as the wider network. The spiritual elitists that pride themselves on having the inside track with God and therefore being in a position to condescend to other Christians are equally up to no good. When basic respect for one another within the Christian community disappears, the community is in danger. The solution is for ordinary believers to remember that they, too, have an anointing and that their business is to love one another.

Outline of 1 John

Commentary

1 John

1.1 what was from the beginning The author emphasizes the continuity of the letter with the teaching that created the community in the first place. Thus both the author and the letter represent traditional teaching.

what we have looked at and touched with our hands Older translations captured the emphasis on corporeality better: 'which we have looked upon and our hands have handled' (AV). This does not necessarily constitute a claim on the part of the author to have been an immediate disciple of Jesus, though that is not impossible if we date the letters before the Gospel of John. He writes here in the first person plural ('we'), identifying himself as part of the chain of oral tradents who have preserved and disseminated the accounts of Jesus' deeds and teachings.

1.3 so that you also may have fellowship with us Participating in fellowship with the community is how one participates in fellowship with God. This has the effect, further on in the letter, of excluding the dissidents, who are, in effect, creating a separate fellowship around themselves, based on different principles.

1.4 The purpose in writing is the fulfilment of joy. The ancient manuscripts disagree as to whether the joy in question is 'ours' or 'yours'. The problem arose from shifts in the pronunciation of Greek around the beginning of the Common Era, which made the first person plural and second person plural forms homonyms of one another. Because both pronouns are common in 1 John, there are several points at which the text is uncertain. Sometimes, as here, it does not make a great difference, since the centrality of Christian love in this letter means that all joy must eventually be mutual.

1.7 the blood of Jesus his Son cleanses us from all sin The author is not advocating later theories of 'penal substitutionary atonement', although later theologians have interpreted this phrase in that sense. The point rather is that sacrificial rites were assumed, by both Jews and Gentiles in the ancient Mediterranean world, to remove barriers between human and divine beings without there being any one exact explanation of how this worked. The author's point is that this has already happened and that Christians already enjoy the freedom of redeemed status in God's presence. It is not something still to be struggled for.

2.1 so that you may not sin The author seems unclear as to whether the redeemed can continue to sin. In principle, he holds that those born of God do not sin (5.18); but in practice, he recognizes the possibility of it (5.14–17).

2.2 atoning sacrifice Also variously translated as 'expiation' or 'propitiation'. See above on 1.7.

2.3–6 Genuine knowledge of God is evidenced only by a life lived in accordance with it. The following verses (2.7–11) reveal that the author has the command to love one another particularly in mind.

2.12–14 Here the author celebrates the community's past experience of faith in a style reminiscent of Hebrew poetry, replete with parallelism and repetitions that serve to make the passage stand out in the letter as a whole. This reaffirmation of the community confirms what is implied in the introduction

(1.1–4), that the author is recalling them to their earlier faith, not introducing something new. It implies that the opponents, with their spiritual elitism, are placing new demands on the community. The author writes a new commandment, to be sure, but it is also the old one that they have already known and observed (2.7–8).

2.15–17 While it is easy to read the Johannine writings as advocating a dualistic rejection of matter, the love of the 'world', in this context, means simply those behaviours, whether motivated by selfishness or spiritual arrogance, that militate against loving one another in the community.

2.18 the last hour Johannine Christianity, on the whole, was less apocalyptic in its thinking than some other forms of Second Testament Christianity, for example that of Paul. But like their co-religionists, they saw themselves as living not in the normal run of history, but in a new moment that involved decisive choices between good and evil. To say that it is 'the last hour' implies the sharpening of such choices.

2.22 The antichrists here are teachers who claim to be 'anointed' in the same sense as Jesus and therefore deny the importance of the oral tradition stemming from Jesus and represented by the author and by the earlier faith of the community. See the discussion in the introduction to this article.

2.28 confidence The Greek *parrhesia* can also be translated 'boldness, courage'. In the context of ancient philosophy, it refers to the inner confidence that enables a person to speak the truth to power. In 1 John, it refers to the clarity of conscience that enables the Christian to stand in God's presence without fear.

2.29–3.3 Despite the importance attached to confessing Jesus as the Anointed/ Christ, the fundamental criterion of faithfulness here is ethical, not doctrinal. Indeed, the author insists on a certain agnosticism in the presence of ultimate truth; there is much that we cannot fully know until we experience it.

3.4–10 The same point is made even more sharply by claiming that one's behaviour is transparent to one's relationship (or lack thereof) to God.

3.11–24 This ethical contrast begins with Cain and therefore pervades all human history. The author treats generosity to one's sisters and brothers as the opposite of murder.

4.1–6 Testing of spirits seems like an abrupt shift of topic, but the letter will immediately return to the commandment to love one another in 4.7. This suggests that the two topics are part of the same larger issue. The teachers who claim superior authority as prophets are also the people who are dividing the community and ignoring the needs of others. For the author, the maintenance of the community in love is intimately tied to maintenance of its tie to Jesus through the oral tradition. Hence, the discussion is not simply one of principles, whether ethical or doctrinal, but also one of personal authority: 'Whoever knows God listens to us.'

4.7–12 The author again stresses the priority of God's love, the obligation to love one another, and the unknowability of God without this experience of love.

4.13 It is the ordinary members of the community who truly know the Spirit, not the self-proclaimed charismatics.

4.17 Only the experience of God's love coming to expression in their lives can give confidence (*parrhesia*).

5.1–5 Belief in Jesus and the practice of love are seen as implying one another.

5.6–8 The three witnesses to the faith of the community are the Spirit, the water and the blood. 'The water' is probably that of baptism. 'The blood' may well be a reference to Jesus' death, which reunites us to God (1.7) and provides a model for our own love of the sisters and brothers (3.16). The Spirit is the life-force that shapes the community as a community of love and therefore of eternal life – in contrast to the dissident teachers, who think of the Spirit (or their individual prophetic spirits) rather as what gives them superiority over the other members of the congregation.

5.14–17 Given the earlier claim (3.9) that those born of God do not sin, it is necessary for the author to offer some interpretation of the current situation in the community, how to understand its failure to maintain unity, and how to deal with the new situation. The author gives directions about prayer which indicate that the failure is not absolute and that those who have wavered can be welcomed back. Nonetheless, the author continues to insist (5.18) that the community is distinguished by its particular purity of life.

5.21 Idols have not been mentioned up to this point in the letter, and it is surprising to find them the topic of the closing sentence. If we take the reference literally, it is a reminder to Jewish Christians living in a Gentile context that they are still to maintain their separation from Greek religion. Alternatively, the author may be using 'idols' metaphorically in the sense of 'anything that falsely claims the place of the true God'. In that case, the 'idols' in question are a metaphor for everything that the letter stands against.

2 John

4–6 As in 1 John, truth and love are intimately linked with one another. Doctrine cannot serve as the sole criterion of membership in the community. Indeed, truth is something not merely to believe but to 'walk in'. In other words, it is a standard of loving behaviour.

7 Refusal to confess Jesus as having come in the flesh counters the focus on the purely spiritual attributed to the charismatics in 1 John. Spiritual exclusivism results in a certain indifference to the traditions about Jesus, on the one hand, and, on the other, to the corporeal realities of life that affect one's sisters and brothers.

9 Going beyond the teaching of Christ refers to the spiritual elitism of the charismatic teachers, for whom simple membership in the loving community of Jesus' followers seems insufficient. The author insists on the sufficiency of the simple and direct religious faith and praxis that the community has long known.

10–11 The author seeks to close the boundaries of the network of house churches with which he is associated. The fluidity of early Christianity, which began with a heavy dependence on itinerant apostles, prophets and teachers, left the communities open to a great variety of voices, some of whom, inevitably, were teaching things at odds with each other. It is not surprising that boundaries came, in due course, to be more sharply drawn or hospitality more cautiously meted out. Whether one sees this as a good thing or a bad will depend partly on how one evaluates the notion of gospel that was being propagated in any given instance. In this instance, the author seems to be embracing the same emphasis on the commandment to love one another as in 1 John, but is paradoxically protecting this teaching by narrowing the circle to which it applies.

3 John

2 walk in the truth See note on 2 John 4–6.

5 the friends More literally, 'the brothers and sisters', i.e. members of Johannine Christian communities. In this case, they are travellers, perhaps even the Elder's emissaries, since they are described as 'brothers and sisters' who are 'strangers to you'.

9–10 Diotrephes is erecting the same kinds of barriers between his house church and the rest of the Johannine network that the Elder urges the 'elect lady' to put in place in 2 John 10–11 so as to exclude the *antichristoi*. We have no direct evidence, however, as to Diotrephes' reasons for doing this. The Elder imputes it to his desire to be in control.

11 The Elder again emphasizes that behaviour is the critical evidence of belonging to God.

Jude

L. WILLIAM COUNTRYMAN

Over the last two hundred years, scholars have often perceived the letter of Jude as embodying concerns typical of an increasingly patriarchal church, obsessed with orthodoxy and deeply suspicious of sexuality in a way more typical of second-century than of first-century Christianity. Jude's reference to Sodom and Gomorrah has sometimes led to superficial assumptions that the author is attacking homosexual people. The present essay reads Jude rather as defending a relatively simple and straightforward Jewish Christian tradition (probably of the first century) against itinerant teachers who are insisting that true access to God can be attained only through sexual intimacy with (and domination of) angels. Jude's angry rhetoric, unfortunately, undercuts the content of the message, encouraging the quite different reading of the letter that has long been common.

The following treatment of the letter of Jude combines three primary perspectives. The author is a biblical scholar whose study focuses on the cultural distance between the ancient Mediterranean world and our own. He is also an Anglican Christian who finds the scriptures to be a principal point of encounter with God and with the Good News of Jesus. And he is a gay man, whose spiritual journey has led him to celebrate this fact as a gift from God. He regards exegesis as the task of bringing the complexities of ancient texts and their worlds into conversation with the complexities of our own world.

Christians have commonly read the letter of Jude as championing the emergent orthodoxy of the second century – defending it in a way that can be described, without exaggeration, as authoritarian and insulting. Certainly, Jude does not construct any careful theological arguments against the teachers attacked here. In fact, it is not easy to discern what Jude's own theological principles are. Much of the document consists of the citation of scriptural examples of sin and judgement (5–11, 14–15) and another substantial portion is pure invective (12–13, 16).

For those reading from queer perspectives, the letter may also seem to evince serious anxiety about sexuality in general. The author is concerned about 'licentiousness' (4), about scriptural examples of sexual irregularities (6–7), and about issues of impurity, possibly sexual in origin (8, 23). Indeed, people of varying backgrounds have read Jude's citation of the story of Sodom and Gomorrah (7) as making hostile reference specifically to same-gender eroticism, placing Jude squarely on the side of subsequent Christian oppression of queer sexualities.

If Jude does not play a very large role in modern conflicts over sexuality, that may be partly because of its brevity and lack of clarity. But it also owes something to the fact that the letter of Jude is relatively marginal to the canon of the Second Testament. The oldest specific references to it appear only in the later second century; even after that, it was long reckoned among the disputed books. It never entered the canon of East Syrian (sometimes called 'Assyrian') Christians. Jude is also odd in embracing a First Testament canon larger than that of any modern Christian group, including not only *1 Enoch*, which the Ethiopian Church alone regards as scriptural, but also, apparently, the otherwise uncanonical *Assumption of Moses*. (Both works can be found in collections of First Testament Pseudepigrapha, though we have no complete copy of the latter.) Luther considered Jude of marginal value and consigned it to the appendix of his German Second Testament.

Ironically, however, Jude has a kind of double canonical value in that much of its content reappears in the central chapter of 2 Peter. While there is disagreement as to which author copied from which, it is easier, on the whole, to assume that the author of the longer document (2 Peter) used the shorter (Jude) as a source. On that hypothesis, comparison of the two suggests that the author of 2 Peter felt a need to 'regularize' Jude's First Testament canon and to make his citations and insults less sexual.

The origins of the letter are obscure. Given the presupposition that the letter's addressees would share the author's concern for Levitical laws concerning sexual ejaculation (8, 23; cf. Lev. 15.16–18), it is likely that its social context was Jewish Christian. In such communities, the practice of Levitical purity continued, for the most part, as a matter of course, since it simply constituted the ongoing cultural definition of what was clean or dirty.

The name of the author matches that of one of Jesus' brothers (Mark 6.3), and the salutation further defines him as 'servant (*or* slave) of Jesus Christ and brother of James', perhaps a roundabout way of confirming that identification. Most modern scholars have doubted the authenticity of this claim, partly because of reluctance to think that we have anything that old from Jewish Christianity, partly because the author's Greek seems too accomplished for a Galilean of no very high social status, and partly because certain elements in the letter have been seen as pointing to a date in the early second century, too late for it to have been written by the historical Jude.

The question of the letter's date is entangled with issues of its interpretation. Perhaps the most famous line in the letter is from verse 3: 'that ye should earnestly contend for the faith which was once delivered unto the saints' (AV). This seems to many to bespeak the concern, characteristic of second-century Christianity, to define 'orthodoxy' and defend it from 'heresy'. This reading of the passage, in fact, is one of the principal arguments for assigning a second-century date to the letter.

Despite the antiquity of this interpretation of the verse, however, there are good linguistic reasons to translate it quite differently. I suggest this version: 'contend *with the help of the trust* that was once delivered to the saints'. On this translation, the faith is presented as a source of strength, not as something threatened and needing defence. On this interpretation of the verse, the letter falls more comfortably into the first century, when the majority of the addressees would still have been converts and the author, in calling them to rely on their faith, would be reminding them of their earlier experience of conversion and trust in God. I will assume this relatively early dating in what follows.

This interpretation of verse 3 also accords better with Jude's second reference to faith, in verses 20–1, where he tells his audience to 'build yourselves up on your most holy faith'. The word translated 'faith' also means 'trust'. The object of 'faith' here is not doctrine, but the relationship with God. The addressees are to rely on their prior experience of trust in God rather than pursue other rites or religious demands to ensure their standing.

From the perspectives of queer interpretation, this difference of emphasis is potentially very significant. It spells the difference between a conventional interpretation of Jude that places the letter on the side of patriarchal hegemony in the Church and an interpretation that is open to seeing in the letter some appeal to lived spiritual experience.

It seems likely that Jude's interest in issues of sexuality has also been misinterpreted in the past. As noted above, the letter's reference to Sodom and Gomorrah has led some readers (including scholars who should know better) to assume that verse 7 constitutes an attack on same-gender sexual relationships. This interpretation has even affected modern English translations, beginning with the RSV. The NRSV text translates the passage, 'indulged in sexual immorality and pursued unnatural lust'; but it also gives a more literal translation in a footnote. The AV was more exact: 'giving themselves over to fornication, and going after strange flesh'.

'Going after strange flesh' is hardly a natural idiom for same-gender sexual intercourse. And, indeed, the syntax of the passage in Greek and the structure of the larger argument in verses 6–8 both confirm that what is really in question for Jude is not same-gender eroticism, but the desire of humans to have sexual relations with angels. He begins with the story of the angels who 'left their proper dwelling' to have sex with human women – a story told briefly in Genesis 6.1–4 and at greater length in 1 *Enoch*, which Jude regarded as scripture (cf. vv. 14–15). From the latter source, we learn that their misdeed was punished by imprisonment 'in deepest darkness'.

Jude traces a parallel between the angels of verse 6, who had intercourse with human women and were therefore condemned to eternal punishment, and the people of Sodom and Gomorrah, who attempted to have forcible sex with the angelic visitors. While most modern readers of Genesis 19 probably assume that the people of Sodom did not recognize the angelic nature of the two visitors, the Genesis account does not in fact rule out Jude's interpretation.[1]

Once we have recognized that Jude is concerned about sexual relations between human and angelic beings, we can see that the subject pervades the rest of the letter, even if past readers did not generally recognize it. Jude describes the new teachers as defiling the flesh 'in the same way' as the angels who left their place and the people of Sodom and Gomorrah (v. 8), thus

---

1 The men of Sodom refer to the visitors as 'men'; but this does not mean that they were unaware of their angelic status. This way of speaking about supernatural beings is also found elsewhere; e.g. Judg. 13.6; 2 Macc. 3.22–8; Mark 16.5; Luke 24.4 (cf. Matt. 28.2; John 20.12).

underlining his claim that the 'intruders' stand in the same tradition of seeking sexual intercourse with angels.

Jude goes on to say that they 'defile the flesh, reject authority, and slander the glorious ones'. The references to dreaming and the defiling of the flesh suggest a religious praxis that involved visions or dreams of intercourse with angelic beings, presumably resulting in ejaculation, which would cause impurity (cf. Lev. 15.16–18). More importantly, however, the teachers understood this practice to demonstrate their power to command sexual intercourse with an angelic being. This would be an act of domination and would therefore defame the latter. 'Authority' and 'glorious ones' (literally, 'glories') are here terms for various types of angelic beings.

The humiliation of the angelic beings seems to be the graver concern here. Michael is instanced as a counterexample (v. 9). He does not even attempt to exercise personal authority over Satan but calls on the power of God. (Ancient evidence suggests that Jude is here referring to the end of *Assumption of Moses*; unfortunately, we no longer possess a copy of the text that includes the relevant passage.) But Jude is also concerned about impurity. The Levitical system did not treat all impurity as necessarily sinful, but it did want to keep it at a distance from the temple and other sacred rites. Accordingly, a sacred rite that deliberately produced sexual pollution was a conflict in terms.

Such a practice may seem quite strange to most modern readers, but it was not entirely without reason in the context of late Mediterranean antiquity when the angelic orders could be conceived as a kind of bureaucratic barrier between humanity and a God conceived on analogy with the remote Roman emperor. The mystic, for example, who sought to reach the throne of God had to know how to negotiate a path through the angelic orders. Similar concerns surfaced in the church at Colossae, where some teachers apparently maintained that Christians needed to co-operate with angelic beings by observing certain rites and restrictions (Col. 2.8–23).

While neither the early Jewish mystics nor the Colossian teachers apparently spoke in terms of sexual relations with angels, such would be intelligible as one way to imagine exerting control over them, for sexual relations in antiquity were normally conceived as involving a significant difference in social standing and power, whether based on gender, age or the difference in status between free person and slave. The teachers are claiming to have achieved superiority over the angels. Jude, by contrast, charges them with behaving 'like irrational animals' (v. 10), thus turning their claim on its head and categorizing them as being less than human themselves.

Jude's animosity toward these sexual rites or practices pervades the letter and has often been read as a kind of generalized hostility on the author's part toward sexuality as such. This would be readily conceivable if the letter is a second-century document, since the Christianity of that period was beginning to exalt virginity as the ideal state for the faithful. It would be unusual, however, in a first-century document, and Jude can in fact be read as attacking not sexuality as such but one variety of Christian teaching that placed on the faithful a further requirement above and beyond their relationship with Jesus before they could enter the divine presence. This is comparable to the concern that the author of Colossians expresses about the enlarged role being given there to angels.

Jude's salutation and the doxology that closes the letter are both consistent with this concern, emphasizing as they do the intimacy and security of the addressees' relationship with God. The salutation (vv. 1–2) speaks of the addressees not only as beloved in God and called, but also as 'kept safe' for Jesus. The doxology (vv. 24–5) assumes that they are already standing in God's presence – the standing posture, as opposed to kneeling or prostration, reflects confidence in their relationship with God – and speaks of God as the one who will keep them from falling or stumbling. There is no role in either passage for angelic intermediaries. Jude's goal, then, is at least partly that of protecting the simplicity of Christian faith, dependent not on appeasing or controlling a multiplicity of supernatural powers or on complex rites of access to God but on God's own direct intervention, in Christ, to open the way of faith to all.

If later generations have tended to read Jude more as a traditionalist patriarch, hostile to innovation in general and to sex in particular, that owes a good deal to Jude's choice of rhetoric. The style is polemical, even insulting (esp. vv. 12–13). He tells us little about the opponents (his original readers perhaps did not need to be informed about them), and he does not engage them in rational, logical argument. He just says, 'This isn't how we do things!' In this respect, his rhetoric is very tradition-oriented.

He attacks his opponents as 'intruders' (v. 4). This reflects the fact that early Christianity was spread, for the most part, by itinerant preachers, called 'apostles' and 'prophets'. Paul is one example; and we have more detailed description of the problems such figures might occasion in the *Didache* (or *Teaching of the Twelve Apostles*), which dates from about the end of the first century. Jude's language here is certainly pejorative, but the implication that the teachers were relatively recent arrivals is perfectly conceivable.

Whether such missionaries were a good thing or a bad depended, of course, largely on the perspective of the person passing judgement. Jude is never fully explicit about their teaching or praxis, but he says that they 'pervert the grace of our God into licentiousness and deny our only Master and Lord, Jesus Christ' (v. 4). The generalized phrasing here suggests the two elements that we have already seen as primary concerns in the letter. One is a sexual praxis that lay outside the norms of the society. The other is that the opponents' praxis and teaching amounted, from Jude's perspective, to a denial of the addressees' existing trust in God through Jesus.

Jude also lards his letter liberally with insults. In verse 11, Cain (see Gen. 4) and Korah (see Num. 16) are both major sinners, punished in their different ways. Balaam seems an odder choice: Numbers 22–3 actually presents him as having resisted the temptation to curse Israel for pay; but Jude is following extra-biblical tradition, which claimed that he succumbed to the offer of money. By using this example, Jude insinuates that the 'intruders' are only interested in making money from the congregation, a common charge flung at itinerant Christian missionaries – and no doubt sometimes true. (Jude makes the charge explicit in verse 16.)

Verses 12–13 embody an extended string of insults, which return to the motif of sexuality with their reference to 'the foam of their own shame'. 'Foam' (*aphros*) is connected with the name of the goddess of love and sexuality,

Aphrodite (literally 'Gift of the Foam'). She was born of the semen from her father's severed genitals, after they were cast into the sea.

Furthermore, Jude insists (vv. 14–18) that the arrival of these teachers was predicted both in writing (by Enoch) and in oral tradition (by the apostles of Jesus, i.e. the early missionaries, not 'the Twelve'). There is nothing to be surprised about here! For all their bizarre practices, they are old hat.

Jude also condemns the teachers for creating division in the community (v. 19). This is true insofar as they are setting up a new religious elite. Of course, Jude is also doing his part to divide the community by expelling them and their sympathizers; but he lays the blame on them for having introduced a new element into the faith of the community.

For all his bullying, however, Jude does recognize that local Christian communities have to make decisions in these matters. And even though he indicates the direction he wants these decisions to take, his actual prescription (vv. 22–3) is somewhat vague and would have to be worked out in practice by local leaders. The author's patriarchal, authoritarian style, despite indications of a relatively more open polity in the community itself, poses one basic problem for later readers. Another is that Christianity's long subsequent history of suspicion toward sexuality in general and of hostility toward queer people in particular means that we tend to read Second Testament texts through that screen.

The present reading, however, finds that Jude's primary concern is not sex but religious or spiritual elitism. Jude objects to the creation of a new version of Christian praxis open only to the spiritually advanced and involving sexual congress with angelic beings. Such elitism would reverse the tradition of direct access to God that Jude and his audience have inherited and would divide the community into two levels of membership – those who have had sex with angels and those who have not. Ironically, the modern analogues of this elitism include mandatory heterosexual marriage or, alternatively, mandatory celibacy, without which some feel that the rest of us cannot be saved. For the elitists, Jesus just isn't enough.

The challenge of Jude for queer readers is to cultivate the ability to separate his reasoning, which is sound, from his style of argument, which is all too familiar to us in the mouths of modern-day religious tyrants. The substitution of insult for argument is not helpful in our age. Instead, we should be intent on making sure that we work with the help of the trust we have already experienced as a gift from God and refuse to accept the idea that there are additional requirements if we want to stand in God's presence. There are no additional requirements. We already stand there.

Revelation/Apocalypse

TINA PIPPIN AND J. MICHAEL CLARK

Once upon a time there was a world full of imperialism and war. And in this world the majority of people experienced economic deprivation, gender and sexual inequality and violence, and the invention of an all-powerful hetero-masculine religion. This is the world of the Revelation Apocalypse of John, revealing the underside of the first-century CE *Pax Romana*. This world is not unlike our own twenty-first-century world. With these common links, what is a responsible and ethical way to read the Apocalypse of John and face A/apocalypse in our time? Does commentary on this book deserve to be included in a 'queer commentary'? Can this book be reimagined or reconfigured as representing a just future world for all living beings, including lesbian, gay, bisexual, transgendered and queer peoples?

Throughout the nineteenth and twentieth centuries scholars attempted to make sense of this last book of the Bible. The most common interpretive strategies focused on the historical. The dominant readings in commentaries on the Apocalypse of John continue to centre on the answers to questions of date, authorship, recipients and the overarching historical, social and political context for the book. The majority opinion is that an itinerate preacher-prophet named John wrote to seven churches in Western Anatolia at or near the end of the reign of the Emperor Domitian (81–95 CE).

Meanwhile popular culture is making sense of the A/apocalypse like John did in the first century – by exploring the imagination of the End by commenting on the contemporary (perceived and real) horrors of the time. Apocalypse is thus individual and systemic, and the focus in ancient Jewish and Christian apocalypses is on the individual seer and his personal experience of apocalypse (whether it be Ezekiel in the Babylonian Exile or John as a subject in the Roman empire).

Apocalypses are always stunning. The visionaries are generally overwhelmed by the magnitude of the vision, dazzled by the grandness of the sights, deafened by the noise of destruction. Stunned, overwhelmed, dazzled and deafened ourselves – indeed dismayed and horrified by what we find here – the questions we are asking of this book of the Bible are certainly rooted in our own different social locations. One of us is a white, heterosexual feminist 'ally' in search of a more descriptive term than 'ally', and always wary of those in heteroprivileged relationships (as Tina is) who publish on themes dealing with the lived experiences of sexual or racial minorities. The other one of us is a white, HIV-positive pro-feminist gay male who was one of the early organizers of the gay men's theology movement (and a co-founder of the American

Academy of Religion group), but is now living in a rural area and out of the political or social groups he formerly supported as an urbanite. In different ways neither one of us speaks for all or part of the 'gay community'. Each of us is 'scripturephobic' (Michael's term) and also believes that the 'commentary' genre in biblical studies is a modern concept that stymies the biblical text.

Commentaries have historically excluded minority voices in favour of some 'objectifiable' meaning. The subjects of textual oppression are invisible and silent. But this collection turns that traditional notion of commentary on its head by placing gay voices at the centre. Does contributing to a commentary volume necessarily lead to an endorsement of the traditional nature of the genre? Could we be unknowingly repeating some past sins of biblical inter-pretation? We are, after all, dealing with a most volatile, dangerous text. The Apocalypse is not known to be a friendly text, let alone a gay-friendly text. Can we simply dismiss the standard style of commentary and decide to be commentators of a different sort? Out of the mess – of what is considered standard in Apocalypse studies, of the search for hope and good messages in this biblical text – what do we extract or salvage, if anything? We don't even think a positive feminist reading is possible. And while we respect and gen-erally agree with Third World and postcolonial readings of the Apocalypse that focus energy against the US empire, these readings fall short on finding a liberatory strand for sexual minorities in favour of reconstructing the text as part of the sacred Christian canon. With such negative attitudes, why are we unable to walk away from the Apocalypse? Are we suffering from some sort of onlooker syndrome, unable to turn away from the various (textual and interpretive) wrecks of Apocalypse?

Moreover, why are we doing this chapter on a book we both find to be mis-ogynistic, patriarchal, homophobic and heterosexist, violent and, to under-state it, a poor vision of future justice? We are not the likely choices to provide a reconstructed or revisionist reading of this text. We are contrarians; we say a joint, resounding 'No!' to any redemptive project on this text. Nonetheless, we see as our task a counter-reading, a reading against the grain of both main-stream and fundamentalist Christian texts on the Apocalypse of John. We don't walk away because we see some value in 'facing apocalypse'. Perhaps the relevance of the Apocalypse of John in a queer commentary is that it speaks to injustice to the 'Other' and we can use the exclusionary tactics and message of this text as an impetus and catalyst to speak out for justice action.

Lee Quinby points out the dangers of the Apocalypse of John and also any apocalypse vision: 'Apocalypse presents itself as the revelation of absolute Truth' (1999: 66). Quinby wants to dismantle 'masculinist apocalypse' (1999: xxiv). In our 'comments' here we want to do a similar, deconstructive move to reveal the Apocalypse as a cultural text that is masculinist, homophobic *and* homoerotic, and utterly ambiguous. Our task in this chapter is to relate the Apocalypse of John to queer theory and practices. We see and hear the A/ apocalypse everywhere; it slips into our consciousness even (and especially) when we renounce it. Thus we move toward anti (Quinby) and counter (Keller) A/apocalypse. First we must journey into the textual territory and seek our own truths.

The Wonderful World of Apocalyptic Literature

Apocalyptic literature is distinctively exclusivistic and legalistic. The binary nature of apocalyptic provides a perfect space for dividing the world into good and evil, right and wrong. Christians who desire a place in God's heavenly kingdom must obey the strict codes of faith and witnessing. And part of the strict code, according to the current premillennialist interpreters who hold much political clout in the USA, is the exclusion, policing and punishment of LGBTQ peoples. The Defense of Marriage Act (under the Clinton Administration) and the current Marriage Amendment and reactionary state movements set up gay people as the ultimate evildoers. Gay marriage threatens to undermine the very pillars of Western culture, and thus to dismantle the very foundation of American empire. As psychiatrist Robert Jay Lifton relates, an important piece of 'superpower syndrome' is the ultimate victory of good against evil (2003: 120). The premillennial, superpower dream is of a world destroyed during the Rapture and thus made pure by God and the true believers. In this vision the faithful join with God in the violence. The Apocalypse of John leaves the violence in God's hands, with God's angel army bringing destruction to the earth. Yet some members of the radical Christian Right dream, for example, of bringing an American-style democracy to Iraq and of bunker-busting mini-nukes.

Lifton refers to this taking up of apocalyptic violence as 'destroying the world in order to save it' (2003). Gay people are perceived as a threat to world purity; the apocalypse will bring the final hope of a pure Christian nation; 'bring it on' is the battle cry. But more familiar are the millennial groups that turn to violence, either outwardly or through mass suicide (such as Aum Shinrikyō, Jonestown, and Heaven's Gate). Lifton relates the unstable actions of Jim Jones with his members. As he claimed to be 'the only true heterosexual among them', Jones also acted out his power to purify:

> He also engaged in homosexual encounters in which he humiliated his partners, taking pleasure in revealing to them their homosexual inclinations. Such was the 'therapeutic' atmosphere that one of these male partners declared, 'Your fucking me in the ass was, as I see it now, necessary to get me to deal with my deep-seated repression against my homosexuality.... I know beyond doubt that you are the very best sexual partner in the world and I don't think I've ever thought I really could compete with you.' (2000: 288)

Jones was also humiliating married men by having sex with their wives. He acted out his power as an apocalyptic leader through sex, under the cover(s) of purifying the world from the gay menace. But as Lifton reminds us, 'Only exceptional people can resist atrocity-producing situations' (2003: 42).

In the aftermath of the apocalypse, there are no more gay people left. The only sexual relationships are Augustinian ones; women are in their proper place beneath men. At least this is the desire of the Left Behind novels. Heterosexuals only need apply to be members of the 'Tribulation Force' after the Rapture and during the seven-year reign of the Antichrist. Brave men and women lead this Force through the difficult years, living and organizing underground, refusing the Mark of the Beast, but with the women bringing babies into this frightful scenario just the same. When Tim LaHaye and Jerry Jenkins read the Apocalypse of John between the lines, they see the *Left Behind* story (and its prequel, and military offshoot, and children's series, and board games, and on and on into marketing heaven). The world will be cleansed of evildoers and non-Christians and all non-heterosexuals. This is the great hope of much apocalyptic thought. The dangers of these stories are obvious, especially as the militant Christian Right seeks to enact these end-time visions into current political policy. In the either–or world of the Apocalypse, only the strong (read: macho male) survive; the weak (read: feminine) must be eradicated. This 'survival of the fittest' (in God's eyes) is an ironic form of Darwinism brought to us by the proponents of so-called 'intelligent design' and anti-evolutionary actions on local school boards. Some early Christians contested this book's inclusion in the Christian canon, but even by the fourth century this scriptural conclusion functioned as an anchor (in mostly bad ways).

The final battle of good versus evil is also seen as the last fight of the war between God and Satan. The journalist Grace Halsell once heard Jerry Falwell state on one of his Middle East tours, 'Jesus is no sissy!', referring to the violent presence of Jesus at Armageddon (Halsell 1999: 115). Falwell is incorrect, of course, for in the Apocalypse Jesus is not only the all-powerful Son of Man but also the wounded Lamb. Catherine Keller comments:

> Yet the Apocalypse itself runs counter to the idolatry of invulnerable hyper-masculinity. Both the Lamb and Beast display their gynomorphic openings, their wounds. They expose an inevitable mutuality of wounding. In their mimicry they nearly sabotage the dream of superpower, the dream of impassionability. Almost they cry for compassion. (2005: 49)

So in this book that claims so much authority and power there are fissures, cracks in the dominant structures. Do not be fooled; these openings do not lead to a liberatory vision of future human sexuality – in heaven or on earth. There are many openings and reopenings, and each one has been repetitively wounding to LGBTQ peoples.

The Apocalyptic Same-Sex Couple

At best, there are only occasional mentions of same sex love in the Bible. Even the suspected gay or lesbian character has an effective heterosexual cover (e.g. David or Ruth). One similar and similarly ambiguous place where we need to stop and look is in chapter 11 in the Apocalypse of John. The story of the two witnesses is a strange tale of martyrdom. This pair of male prophets wear sackcloth and prophesy for 1,260 days (11.3). The witnesses have great authority and power:

> And if anyone wants to harm them, fire pours from their mouth and consumes their foes; anyone who wants to harm them must be killed in this manner. They have authority to shut the sky, so that no rain may fall during

the days of their prophesying, and they have authority over the waters to turn them into blood, and to strike the earth with every kind of plague, as often as they desire. (Apoc. 11.5–6)

Then the beast comes out of the abyss and kills them and the people rejoice and party over their dead bodies for three and a half days (11.7–10). The prophets brought drought and disease and the people (of the nations) were glad to get rid of them. Then God resurrects the prophetic pair and calls them to heaven (11.11–13): 'And they went to heaven in a cloud while their enemies watched them. At that moment there was a great earthquake, and a tenth of the city fell; seven thousand people were killed in the earthquake, and the rest were terrified and gave glory to the God of heaven' (11.12b–13). All this action takes place in Jerusalem – not the new one but the old one. Here there is a temple to be measured except for the outer courts: 'leave that out, for it is given over to the nations, and they will trample over the holy city for forty-two months' (11.2). The old Jerusalem will be destroyed and replaced with the shining new city/Bride. In the meantime these two prophetic anti-healers strike out at the city's inhabitants 'as often as they desire' (11.60). Their desire is for judgement and vengeance against the nations that attack Jerusalem.

Carpenter discusses this passage using Joseph Wittreich's reading of Blake and Milton. As the two witnesses resurrect, Wittreich interprets this as their coming out of the closet, since for Wittreich all prophecy is a 'closeted litera-ture' (Carpenter 1995: 127). Wittreich sees the testimony of the two witnesses as liberatory rhetoric; in Carpenter's read Wittreich makes this narrative 'into a liberatory testimony against injustice that becomes a visionary coming-out narrative' (1995: 127). As prophets the two witnesses are able to model eternal resurrection from the Beast, even as they are killed by the Beast and mocked by the nations in the earthly city. The Beast (of (homo)sexuality) comes out of the a(by)ss and kills the male couple, but then God resurrects the pair and calls them to heaven. From the heavenly city is the promise of vengeance: 'The nations raged but your wrath has come, and the time for judging the dead, for rewarding your servants, the prophets and saints and all who fear your name, both small and great, and for destroying those who destroy the earth' (Apoc. 11.18). Rather than any 'liberatory testimony against injustice' here, we find that this story of the two witnesses simply heaps violence on violence: on top of a gay apocalypse is a retaliation of cosmic magnitude. How ironic that sexu-ality kills them, but the sacred redeems/validates them as a same-sex couple! Apocalypse is quintessential sadomasochism, whether divinely or humanly generated or encouraged.

Queer Eye for the Apocalypse

As popular media includes more gay-themed shows, there is also the prolifer-ation of stereotypes: of gay men as effete interior and fashion designers and lesbian women as butch construction or security workers. Of course, there have been important exceptions, but shows such as *Queer Eye for the Straight Guy* perpetuate the binary system as it seeks to cross these traditional renderings of sexual orientation. The Apocalypse of John at surface glance seems to be lifting up as normative the strong, silent type of hetero-male in both its deities and the 144,000. John is terrified by this monster among the lampstands:

> When I saw him, I fell at his feet as though dead. But he placed his right hand on me, saying, 'Do not be afraid; I am the first and the last, and the living one. I was dead, and see, I am alive forever and ever; and I have the keys of Death and of Hades. Now write what you have seen, what is, and what is to take place after this.' (Apoc. 1.17–20)

The Son of Man speaks with a two-edged sword in his mouth, sending sharp words to and through his angel messengers. But after the letters to the seven churches (Apoc. 2–3), this warrior deity falls silent until the end of the revelation. His last words before the vision starts to take off are: 'Listen! I am standing at the door, knocking; if you hear my voice and open the door, I will come in to you and eat with you and you with me. To the one who conquers I will give a place with me on my throne, just as I myself conquered and sat down with my Father on his throne' (Apoc. 4.20–1). The promise comes at great cost of conformity to the apocalyptic rule.

The two-edged sword in the mouth of the Son of Man is a scary sight. In the throne room all are bowing down to the One (erect) Phallus, the one who can hold his Phallus (aka sword) in his mouth. The resurrection/re-erection of Christ from the dead takes on new meaning. The phallus-shaped scroll that John eats is sweet, then bitter.

In 22.12–15 Jesus speaks again: 'See, I am coming soon; my reward is with me, to repay according to everyone's work. I am the Alpha and the Omega, the first and the last, the beginning and the end. Blessed are those who wash their robes, so that they will have the tree of life and may enter the city by the gates. Outside are the dogs and sorcerers, and fornicators and murders and idolaters, and everyone who loves and practises falsehood.' Jesus must be seated on the throne, for he refers to himself as the Alpha and Omega in 21.6. And the Lamb is said to be 'at the centre of the throne' in 7.17. The metaphorical creatures that represent the deity are multiple and morph throughout the text.

There are hints at the sexual undertones (overtones?) of the throne room – with the multitudes crying praise, the twenty-four elders on their throne, the 144,000 purified (by not touching women) men singing praises with the elders and the angels and the four living, winged creatures to the One (the Lamb, Son of Man and God) on the Throne: 'At once I was in the spirit, and there in heaven stood a throne, with one seated on the throne! And the one seated there looks like jasper and carnelian, and around the throne is a rainbow that looks like an emerald' (Apoc. 4.2–3). John describes the throne further: 'Coming from the throne are flashes of lightning, and rumblings and peals of thunder, and in front of the throne burn seven flaming torches, which are the seven spirits of God; and in front of the throne there is something like a sea of glass, like crystal' (Apoc. 4.5–6a). Compare Ezekiel's vision of the throne in 1.26–8 in which he sees a human form on the throne: 'Upward from what appeared like the loins I saw something like gleaming amber, something that looked like fire enclosed all around; and downward from what looked like the loins I saw something that looked like fire, and there was a splendour all around. Like the bow in a cloud on a rainy day, such was the appearance of the splendour all around. This was the appearance of the likeness of the glory of the Lord' (Ezek. 1.27–8). Ezekiel focuses on the loins of the deity; John's interest is in the multitudes of men. In both visions there is overwhelming desire and fulfilment.

Accompanying the Lamb in the throne room are the 144,000 singing men, a virtual gay men's chorus! On their foreheads are the tattooed names of Jesus and God. They are singing phalluses, for the name of God is written on the penis at circumcision (see Berger 1999: 15–16). The song, and their penises, are their tickets into the throne room. They are the only ones sealed as holy for God: 'And I heard the number of those who were sealed, one hundred and forty-four thousand, sealed out of every tribe of the people of Israel' (7.4). Only they can learn the mystical song from the thunderous voices of heaven. They sing 'a new song' like the twenty-four elders and four living creatures and angels and 'every creature in heaven and on earth and under the earth and in the sea, and all that is in them' (in 5.8–14). Knowledge of the song gives the 144,000 special status: 'No one could learn that song except the one hundred and forty-four thousand who have been redeemed from the earth. It is these who have not defiled themselves with women, for they are virgins; these follow the Lamb wherever he goes. They have been redeemed from humankind as first fruits for God and the Lamb, and in their mouth no lie was found; they are blameless' (Apoc. 14.3–5). Heaven requires a certain level of musical ability. Like all the numbers in the Apocalypse, 144,000 is symbolic. But this symbol refers to a mess of ambiguity, especially sexual. The most literal interpretation would be that only celibate or gay, Jewish men (coming 12,000 each from each of the twelve tribes of Israel in 7.5–8) are among God's chosen. At least they are the first in a salvation hierarchy, with the great redeemed multitude following 'from every nation, from all tribes and peoples and languages' (7.9). Surely this group includes women, but no specific information is given. The only time the Apocalypse names the female gender is in a story of violence ('Jezebel', the Woman Clothed with the Sun, the Whore of Babylon, and the Bride of Christ/Lamb) (see Pippin 1992 and 1999).

In a chapter heavy with a previous conversation, we decided that the Apocalypse is not liberatory for LGBTQ peoples. Even if the 144,000 men become the Brides of Christ, the Queens of Heaven, Michael Clark stated that 'You can go to the gym with God, but you can't sleep with God' (Pippin 1999: 125). Along these lines Mary Wilson Carpenter refers to an 'apocalyptics of the closet'. She explains, 'The "key" image of apocalyptic marriage is indeed a keystone of male homosocial desire, articulating the incorporation of the feminine with the evacuation of the female body, complying with compulsory heterosexuality but celebrating a union with "nature"' (1995: 124). These 144,000 represent a takeover of the binary system (male/female, nature/culture, etc.) but they remain in ambiguous territory. Women are subsumed into the patriarchal vision, but as Clark reminds us, you really can't have it all, even in heaven: 'The impetus [of this text] is clearly toward a celibate world of saved, but sexless, nonetheless heterosexual men – a movement toward the death of (sexual) desire! A dreary utopia, indeed!' (in Pippin 1999: 119, 121).

In other words, there is a perverse heteronormality on the surface of the

Apocalypse (or maybe given the recent campaign against gay marriage, hetero-normality is just plain perverse?), but it's not much on the surface. The hateful uprising in opposition to gay marriage is an intermediary step. God will punish these homosexual 'sinners' at the end time. As Philip Greven so forcefully argues, Christians who were raised with corporal punishment, and who inflict it on their own children, see the Apocalypse as the logical religious answer: a punishing, authoritarian deity inflicting pain on all and rescue and redemption on a few really obedient children. He states, 'The Apocalypse of the Book of Revelation has been one of the most enduring sadomasochistic fantasies obsessing many Protestants' (1990: 211). Our actions make God enact *His* wrath as a stern father/king figure. If the ultimate sinners are 'fornicators' ('Jezebel', the Whore of Babylon, homosexuals, infidels, etc.), that is, sexual transgressors, then the ultimate punishment will be reserved for them – public humiliation and gruesome death. In the millennial fantasies of American Protestantism, homosexuality is near the top of the list for ushering in the End. In some prophecy belief, especially in the post-Stonewall age, the face of evil is homosexual. Paul Boyer relates: 'Many writers cited a cryptic phrase in the Book of Daniel describing the coming Evil One ("Neither shall he regard . . . the desire of women") to argue that Antichrist himself will be homosexual' (1992: 234). Mostly in the 1970s the Cold War was the main concern of prophecy belief (e.g. Hal Lindsey's *The Late Great Planet Earth*), and homosexuality came in as a way of further objectifying and dissing the enemy.

Sexuality is tightly controlled in the Apocalypse but gender is and is not clearly defined. Catherine Keller offers this solution: 'For if the apocalypse pattern indelibly subjugates women as the bearers of sex, inscribing authority in a virginal masculinity which requires the maintenance of gender boundaries . . . then the rabid dualism of the originative apocalypse pattern presupposes the strict sexual dualism of which heterosexism marks the edges' (Keller 1996: 263). She notes that 'virginity minimizes sex and thus the possibility of male slippage. But if sex, like the primordial serpent, can slither within and between the sacred sex/gender boundaries indiscriminately, the world falls down' (263). The 144,000 slither between these boundaries, slipping between the cracks in the apocalyptic structure.

Adela Yarbro Collins sees the 144,000 as virginal warrior priests (1984: 131). In her discussion of Apocalypse 14.4 she presents the argument that continence is seen as ideal:

> This hypothesis is supported by the fact that continence is not advocated for all, but only for those who would 'follow the Lamb wherever he goes.' Once again, there is evidence of an origin in aggressive feeling. Continence is presented, not so much as a positive good, but rather as the avoidance of a disturbing alternative: 'It is these who have not *defiled* themselves with women.' Such a remark reveals a complex set of emotions, involving perhaps hatred and fear both of women and one's own body. (1984: 159)

It is interesting that Yarbro Collins uses the word 'continence', since it can have several meanings, from sexual abstinence to bladder control. These men are totally pure: no women, no shit. She's right; they really do fear and hate women and even their own bodies.

This fear of pollution factors in with the negative responses to Andres Serrano's apocalyptic art piece, *Piss Christ* (1987). In a section entitled, 'The Passing of Piss Prophets', Lee Quinby remarks that this photograph has connections with Apocalypse 22.1: 'Then the angel showed me the river of the water of life, bright as crystal, flowing from the throne of God and of the Lamb.' Of Serrano's picture of the crucifix in glowing yellow liquid Quinby adds, 'Even apocalypticists might honour such a portrayal – until piss enters the picture. . . . Urine may well be *a* water of life, but it sure can't be *the* water of life' (1999: 119). Serrano creates an anti-apocalyptic image by calling forth the critique of the message (piss) and also the medium (the phallus/penis). Flowing from the throne comes this water of life; the throne and those on it are mimicking a urination scene. Or is the throne a toilet? With so many men in the throne room, there's sure to be a pissing contest – or at least one to gain entrance into the throne room. The winner of this contest is obvious; no one can top the river of life.

To return to the 144,000, Yarbro Collins further considers that this story sets the stage for martyrdom. The focus in the passage on the men not defiling themselves with women 'demands critical assessment because of its potential for injustice toward women and alienation from the body' (1984: 160). More recently she provides a more positive reading:

> The vision of the new creation as a wedding is a counterbalance to Rev. 14.1–5. Because of the present crisis, which John implied was about to intensify, the ideal was to renounce sexual relations and prepare for the end. At the same time, as one of the fundamental characteristics of God's good creation, sexual union is a symbol of the new creation, of wholeness, of the time of salvation. (2003: 213)

The 144,000 represent the whole of those who are faithful and undefiled. But they are also imaged as perfect men, those who have not been made impure by women. They may come, penetrate the throne room. They can 'follow the Lamb wherever he goes' (Apoc. 14.4), since they are the Lamb's virginal slaves. We want to push this argument further to say that such a passage leads to injustice toward LGBTQ peoples. Are heaven and hell so different? Does apocalypse ruin everything, even eternal 'life'?

We want to push these ideas further. Are the 144,000 a choir of anatomically incorrect Ken dolls, or are they a Viagra-infused, permanently erect, yet non-sexual group, saluting (with their erect but non-sexual phalluses) the One God with the symbol of the One phallus, à la Lacan? Or are they homoerotic, but castrated, god-crazed men? They are certainly worshipping a giant phallus – the ever erect, weapon-wielding god of the apocalypse. Only a male God could be engorged with such violent power, dominating any and every other male (and any and every other 'other' too), but disinclined to allow the 144,000 to enjoy (to be orgasmically erect). Only God 'comes', as it were. We suspect the 144,000 are therefore flaccid, not erect, given the sexless nature of the holy city. Perhaps they are even castrated men ('ex-gays') who must settle for a homo-social holy city because they can no longer be homo-sexual (or sexual period).

Nevertheless, the text is itself so sexually ambiguous that there is no way to unravel it to get to 'This is the sexuality of the Apocalypse'. Of course, LaHaye and others have the key and they find a text they can manipulate for hate in ways no less strongly than Romans 1.26–7 and 1 Corinthians 6.9. The radical religious Right can use their exclusivistic eschatology to take a (final) aim at gay people. The conclusion was and is that the Apocalypse is not a liberatory text, no matter which way we read it: 'Thus, ambiguous sexualities as well as terror fill the throne room of God. . . . What remains is the misogyny and exclusion by a powerful, wrathful deity. In the Apocalypse, the Kingdom of God is the kingdom of perversity' (Pippin 1999: 125).

Queer-as-Hell Folk – in Babylon and Beyond

So are gay people present but not present in the Apocalypse? Do they walk the narrative as spectres, haunting the margins and centre and endless retellings? Does the cleansing hoped for by the radical right occur in the biblical vision? What does happen in the heavenly kingdom? Returning to popular culture for clues, we note that, in the popular HBO (Home Box Office) series *Queer as Folk* (or at least in its first season and a half), the fictional gay male characters dwell in the burgh of The Pit (or Abyss), in a fictionalized gay ghetto in Pittsburgh. They flock to a bar named 'Babylon'; here 'Babylon' does not encode an oppressive empire in opposition to the oppressed – as John of Patmos encoded the relationship of ancient Rome to the early Christians – but rather situates the very heart of the ghetto as an ambiguous symbol of liberation and self-oppression.

The theme of self-oppression is ubiquitous here: self-oppression is emphasized, for example, by the men's collective – and again ambiguous – desire and disdain for long-term relationships. Unlike the divinely vindicated apocalyptic same-sex couple, the two witnesses, these men witness to the stereotypical failure of gay male relationships, refusing the very love they appear to seek or shaping relationships with psychological if not physical sadomasochism. Even a violent fag-bashing at the end of the first season does nothing to redirect the anti-relational energy among these gay men (and, stereotypically again, the only really long-term relationship in this drama is a lesbian couple, albeit, too, a relationship not without its own problems). Rather than relationship, the gay male goal is always sex and more sex – to become 'whores of Babylon'.

Self-oppression is further inscribed in the series by the valorization (idolization, idolatry) of the culture of youth by these men for whom gay life is 'over' at the age of 30 (a very Christological age!); thirtieth birthdays are hellaceous occasions. While an earlier, pre-Aids generation of gay male novelists such as Larry Kramer (in *Faggots*) and Andrew Holleran (in *Dancer from the Dance*) depicted gay male characters experiencing 'burn-out' with the bar and bathhouse scene and a resultant transformation (maturity?) at the age of 40 (Clark 1986: 43–52), these HBO queer-as-hell folk have shortened the gay lifespan by a decade, perhaps indicative of the virtual erasure of that earlier generation by the apocalyptic plague of Aids. Wallowing in sex, the HBO men, too, are burnt out by the fires of Babylon, by the passions of desire. Indeed, the passionate heat of desire diminishes the value of each accumulating orgasm: accumulated multiple partnered orgasms = the death of desire.

In his psychological study of American post-apocalypses, James Berger notes the connection between the experience or imagining of trauma and *jouissance*, which he defines, with Kristeva and Žižek, as 'orgasm, the "little death"' (Berger 1999: 17). Berger points to the apocalyptic nature of sex; *jouissance* 'annihilates language' (1999: 15):

> When we come, our personalities disperse, our autobiographies are suspended, we are over, are coming, have come. What is revealed or unveiled in orgasm? Exactly what is revealed in any apocalypse: nothing, or nothing that can be said. That bodies are bodies, or that God is God. Tautologies. That bodies are God, or that God is a body, speaking flesh, dying speech. Nonsense. (1999: 14)

Here Berger is expressing the inexpressible nature of apocalyptic desire, the sexual, orgasmic nature of desiring the divine, desiring the end, and what happens after the end. The imagining of the end is violent, sexual and thrilling. The Apocalypse provides the ultimate cathartic joyride. If one is a true believer in this ending of the world and the deity who constructs and orchestrates the final chaos, then one is in the inner, protected circle – front row seats in the stadium of doom and desire. Such voyeurism is exciting; one can keep one's puritanical purity while vicariously participating in the evildoers' violent sex acts. If anyone has an ear to hear: hear and see Jezebel thrown on a bed, her unrepentant children struck dead (Apoc. 3.22–3)! Watch the Woman Clothed with the Sun give birth to the Messiah (Apoc. 12.2, 5), then disappear into the wilderness, never to be heard from again! Witness the gang rape of the Whore of Babylon; see the nations feast on her flesh and set her on fire so that she burns forever (Apoc. 17.16)! Be present at the marriage of the Lamb and the Bride (Apoc. 19.6–9) and see the Bride turned into the New Jerusalem (Apoc. 21.2, 9–10)! 'The Spirit and the bride say, "Come." And let everyone who hears say, "Come"' (Apoc. 22.17a–b). 'The one who testifies to these things says, "Surely I am coming soon." Amen. Come Lord Jesus!' (Apoc. 22.20). The Apocalypse is beginning to sound like an orgasmic freak side show at a circus. Perhaps that's what draws so many people to gaze upon its many (ultimate) horrors.

Relating this concept of *jouissance* to the Apocalypse of John, Berger points to the regulation of sex: 'To speak about sex is to assume the role of the angel measuring the New Jerusalem, measuring the incommensurable, and this is the function of the term *jouissance* ("bliss," "joy," "orgasm"). . . . *Jouissance* is apocalyptic, in that it annihilates language, replacing it with what previously we were both unable and forbidden to conceptualize' (1999: 15). It remains for us a difficult task to speak about apocalyptic sex.

It's Raining (Reigning) Men!

In premillennialist dispensational Christianity the story of the future is clear and glorious. Jesus will come again in the clouds and take the true believers with him into heaven. The central passage of this belief is 1 Thessalonians 4.16–17:

> For the Lord himself, with a cry of command, with the archangel's call and with the sound of God's trumpet, will descend from heaven, and the dead in Christ will rise first. Then we who are alive, who are left, will be caught up in the clouds together with them to meet the Lord in the air; and so we will be with the Lord forever.

This vision of graves emptying and cars suddenly without drivers has played repeatedly in fiction and film versions. What follows in the apocalyptic time-line is complete chaos, decaying infrastructure and the rise of the Antichrist who leads the one world order during the seven-year Tribulation. Those who repent and believe during this time will experience great persecution, but the survivors will see Jesus throw Satan into the abyss and begin his thousand-year reign in the New Jerusalem. According to Hal Lindsey, Jerry Falwell, Pat Robertson, Tim LaHaye and others, there are definite, identifiable events happening today that are hints of the imminence of the end time. War in the Middle East, the establishment of the European Union, and threats to the structure of the 'American family' are some of the major indicators. The very existence of LGBTQ peoples is a definite symbol of the decline of American empire. Homosexuality is seen as a disease, and homosexuals as capable of being cured (if only they would believe in Jesus in the proper way).

There is an ambiguity in this construction of events. On the one hand, the enemies and evildoers are needed so that Jesus will come soon. Gay marriage has galvanized so many politically right-wing evangelicals because it shows an enemy living out so-called normative family values. It is like children on a playground ending the game when the unpopular child wants to play. The activists against same-sex marriage have created a whole mythology around the sexual perversions (multiple partners, disease-spreading intentions) of homosexuals (see Shorto 2005: 37). The threat is that the patriarchal structure of traditional heterosexual marriage, indeed our very societal structure and democracy itself, will be undermined by the existence of this Other. Could it be that one hierarchical relationship has to feed off another, each one more (or differently) violent than the first? On the other hand, apologetic Christianity desires the conversion of all people. If all converted, then who would be damned? All the fun would be drained from the apocalypse. We believe these anti-gay activists are playing out the end time in the present in some twisted ways. Isn't being a born-again Christian supposed to give one special privileges and status? All that work (for some it doesn't come so easy . . .) performing heterosexuality should lead to some kind of glory. The notion, for example, that a lesbian couple's marriage could also be blessed by God is anathema. But more, one of the top traditional enemies of 'good Christian families' would be included as part of the 'norm' of God's creation.

These themes are discussed in Tony Kushner's two-play sequence *Angels in*

America: A Gay Fantasia on a National Theme, Part One: Millennium Approaches and *Part Two: Peristroika*. The rich cast of characters includes a McCarthy-esque closeted gay lawyer, Roy Cohn, who is trying to convince a promising clerk for an Appeals judge and a closeted, repressed Mormon, Joe Pitt (read: Joe A[by]ss!), to seize the opportunity of working at the Justice Department in Washington DC. Cohn is dying of Aids, which he insists on calling cancer. He insists to his doctor, 'I have sex with men. But unlike nearly every other man of whom this is true, I bring the guy I'm screwing to the White House and President Reagan smiles at us and shakes his hand. Because *what* I am is defined entirely by *who* I am. Roy Cohn is not a homosexual. Roy Cohn is a heterosexual man, Henry, who fucks around with men' (Kushner 1995: 52). Prior Walter, who is dying of Aids and abandoned by his lover, Louis Ironson, has prophetic visions on his sickbed. An angel with eight vaginas appears to him several times and fucks him (e.g. 1995: 174). Eventually, Prior makes it to heaven for a brief visit. There he finds only angels of the Council of Continental Principalities, for God has abandoned heaven.

For Kushner the individual end is not the 'End of It All', the end of history. McCarthyism continues through the Reagan administration and beyond, consistently revived by the radical Christian Right and their anti-gay hate speech and policies, in particular governing relationships and health. In *Angels in America* there is hope in the end – both in community and in the form of AZT and other Aids medications. With the ability for many to manage the disease has come a new form of the Aids plague. The gay male ghetto has increasingly become an apocalyptically suicidal community in new and virtual ways. Michael Specter reports that another drug, crystal methamphetamine (interestingly, for us at least, nicknamed 'Tina'), has changed both Aids education and any growth in safe sex (Specter 2005: 38). Specter points out how crystal meth breaks down inhibitions, and men who meet on websites (such as 'Craig's List') can ask for 'PNP' or 'party and play' indicating drugs and sex (2005: 42). He calls the intersection of '"depression, partner violence, substance abuse"' and HIV a '"syndemics" – a syndrome of interacting epidemics' which leads to risky sex (2005: 44). With 'more than forty thousand new HIV infections each year' in the United States and 20 million dead worldwide to date (Specter 2005: 39), there should be an alarm and a culture of fear like that with the apocalyptic portrayal of the bird flu. Instead, as Specter observes, there is complacency; HIV is seen now not as an epidemic, let alone a plague. There is an increase in unsafe sex practices, particularly 'bare-backing' as unprotected anal sex, another apocalyptic example of taking it up the a(by)ss! Given the equine connection to 'bare-backing', one cannot help but wonder if unsafe anal sex isn't an intentionally dangerous flirtation, an apocalyptic fucking of the four horses of the Apocalypse (compare the sexual overtones of bare-back horse-riding in Peter Shaffer's play *Equus*). Is the rectum a grave? A womb/tomb? Perhaps not, but rather simply the a(by)ss; in fact the spelling of the English word itself gives us a clue that this is sex 'by-ass', as in 'taking it up the a(by)ss'. Especially with the rise in bare-backing (no condoms) by younger gays, it plays out as an interesting place for the sowing of seeds (semen), even if that could also be sowing the seeds of death (HIV/Aids) in the a(by)ss, albeit that too many folk think new medications solve that problem.

Similarly, we find a painting by Jan van Eyck and a workshop assistant entitled, 'The Last Judgement' (ca. 1430). There are three tiers: heaven, judgement and hell. The dead pour head-first from the underneath (rectum?) of a skeleton (representing Death). The skeleton is under the archangel Michael, who wields sword and shield. Is Death giving birth – into death, into eternal death? The passageway of death is the rectum, leading to the grave, to hell itself. There are layers of hell; there is torment under the earth in the a(by)ss – beasts with hell mouths, mouths within mouths, like the famous beast in the film *Alien*. Like the sexual a(by)ss, all these mouths within mouths (not to mention swords in mouths) continue to reflect an erotics of the damned – a perverse fellatio of/with God in the A/apocalypse.

As discussed in detail elsewhere (see Clark 1999), Catherine Keller is in fact keenly aware of both the fluidity and the ambiguity of apocalyptic thinking. The apocalyptic can be a 'double-edged' sword (Keller 1996: 41), for example functioning *both* as prophetic judgement on homophobia and Aids-oppression *and* as a self-fulfilling horror that turns on the victims its genesis meant to liberate. Likewise, apocalyptic 'retaliation . . . affects not just the violators' (1996: 43). As but one example, if Gabriel Rotello is correct – that the fantasy of a heterosexual Aids devastation which would purge our society of its homophobia and nurture non-discriminatory compassion in its stead, if that apocalyptic fantasy is not going to happen (Rotello 1997: 33, cf. 165, 179) – then those who currently oppress will continue to do so and those who currently suffer and die will continue to do so. The Aids-apocalyptic horror continues (cf. Clark 1999). There are new medications called Aids inhibitors; can we create an 'A/apocalypse inhibitor' as well? Or is it impossible to manage the A/apocalypse and live as if it were merely another chronic horror tale?

The apocalyptic habit of mind *is* horrible because, as Keller also points out, it is generally 'destructive, and perhaps first of all self-destructive' (1996: 11). She later explains, 'Apocalypse . . . rages out of the bitter heart of systematic suffering: If history itself must end to staunch the tears, to stop the time of suffering, so be it' (1996: 85). In other words, if one's *personal* history must end to stop the suffering, so be it. Apocalypse is suicidal. Such apocalyptic despair might also explain, at least in part, gay/lesbian suicide rates and, where it occurs, passive acceptance of HIV-progression and Aids-death. As Keller herself has noted, the 'apocalyptic habit' feeds on an 'endist obsession' with the finality of death, in this case the finality of death to Aids (1996: 128). In short, apocalypse tends to backfire: HIV/Aids becomes cataclysmically apocalyptic if it is the only escape from homophobia or the only escape from the vicious cycles of the gay male sexual ghetto (cf. Clark 1999).

In other words, multiple performances of apocalypse abound. In his reading of apocalyptic gay literature Richard Dellamora invokes deconstructive and postmodern theories. He relates, 'The signs of the times register apocalypse as an important aspect of gay existence and cultural practice. Lesbian and gay existence, as much and more than ever, are enmeshed as subject and object in national tropes and obsessions' (Dellamora 1994: 194–5). To illustrate, Dellamora quotes a press account from Madonna's 1993 *The Girlie Show*, in which she reads from the Apocalypse of John in her performance of 'In This Life: . . . the troupe alternately mimes couplings and brawls. It's an ambiguous sequence, mourning the sexual freedom of the pre-Aids 1970's, then hinting at biblical retribution' (in Dellamora 1995: 1). Dellamora observes further: 'The most notable feature of the history of the formation of male sexual minorities has been the repeated catastrophes that have conditioned their emergence and continued existence' (1994: 1).

He adds that 'AIDS has not destroyed the memory of gay existence, but it has made such destruction imaginable' (1994: 28). From Tony Kushner to Trent Lott (who thought unreproductive, white, gay men should be jailed for refusing to add to the race), the gay A/apocalypse has been central. Dellamora points to some reason for this thinking from the radical Right:

> Among dominant groups apocalyptic narratives have often been invoked in order to validate violence done to others. Among subordinate groups apocalyptic thinking is frequently an effect of the pressure of persecution. Apocalyptic narratives have been mobilized to justify the imprisonment, torture, and execution of the subjects of male–male desire. (1994: 3)

Berger relates that homosexuality is an 'apocalyptic sexual discourse'. In Kushner's *Angels in America*, gay men and the county itself are sick. Berger states,

> AIDS is gratuitous, a superfluous apocalypse that nevertheless has happened. The angels? They are forces of stasis and death that render earthly life insignificant in a great cosmic perspective. . . . The angels must be rejected. *Angels in America*, while constantly invoking the apocalypse, finally is about removing the apocalypse from historical catastrophe, about opposing apocalypse with politics. . . . What is there left after the end? Paradise or shit. (Berger 1999: 16)

With Serrano (and his Christ), there's a lot to be pissed about.

Conclusion: The Thousand-Year Rant

The comedian Bill Mayer observed after the 2004 presidential election, 'When homophobia trumps terrorism – wow . . . '. We are writing this 'commentary' in the middle of such insanity in the United States. We are writing on a biblical text in which God gets to play Terrorist. This same God institutes an all-male, sexless heaven. Does terrorism trump homophobia in the Apocalypse, or is it a draw? Is that, the equalizing of terrorism and homophobia, in the end, the divine example and definition of justice?

What service are we doing in this 'commentary'? How is our negative reaction to the Apocalypse helping the cause of LGBTQ rights? What about those evangelical Christians for whom all scripture must hold truth and grace? How can we refuse to 'rework' the Apocalypse into a liberatory narrative, saying that it is just not possible to do so? How can we be saying that the text does not hold liberatory possibilities, except in the act of resisting it? Doesn't that undermine the authority of the Bible, and ultimately of its God? We're arguing that the God of the Apocalypse (and all apocalyptic literature) is a violent, sadomasochistic deity that demands resistance. This theology of mass destruction in the Apocalypse of John cannot be revised, reconstructed or retrofitted for our present context. And we do not wish to loot (as lectionaries tend to do) the text of its heavenly liturgy, streets of gold, or other seemingly more pleasant scenery. There is too much work to be done toward and into a liberatory future that builds upon the concepts of community, love, forgive-ness, compassion and hope. The Apocalypse of John undermines any and all futures for LGBTQ peoples (and their too liberal allies). We are co-conspirators in a plot to overthrow apocalypse. As both contrarians and co-conspirators, we find ourselves asking: Why are some interpretive strategies liberating for some people? Postcolonial readings against empire (e.g. Ernesto Cardenal's 'Apocalypse' poem) are examples of the contemporary connections that cry out to be made. At the same time, in this complex web of a destructive story of the end of the world, the characterizations of women, and men, do not bring redemption or reconciliation.

We took this assignment of writing on this end book of the Bible in order to be able to move forward – through facing what we fear and distrust and then speaking out. In a way we want to speak truth to power, the power of this text in Western Christianity and politics. We don't mean to imply that this text is the 'enemy'. It is not an 'us' versus 'it' or 'us' versus 'homophobe inter-preters of this text' situation. We want to name the power and witness (Gk. *martyr*) to other truths, born of real lives and real injustices, and real suffering. But this text has power, and we're engaging in an endless conversation with the Apocalypse; we'll never get in the last word. This text will live beyond us. Apocalyptic possibilities are very real in the twenty-first century, espe-cially as we've outlined here – with the Aids apocalypse, with continued vio-lence against LGBTQ people, and with the struggle for a just world, and a just God. Ultimately, if anything at all can be said with even a potentially positive LGBTQ spin about this text, it is that, clearly, it is not the LGBTQ community that is perverse. Rather, the perversity lies with the apocalyptic king-dom and its sexually ambivalent and sadomasochistic god.

Bibliography

First Testament

Abba, R., 1978, 'Priests and Levites in Ezekiel', *VT* 8, pp. 1–9.

Ackerman, James S., 1987a, 'Numbers', in Robert Alter and Frank Kermode (eds), *The Literary Guide to the Bible*, Cambridge, Mass.: Belknap Press of Harvard University Press, pp. 78–91.

Ackerman, James S., 1987b, 'Jonah', in Robert Alter and Frank Kermode (eds), *The Literary Guide to the Bible*, Cambridge, Mass.: Belknap Press of Harvard University Press, pp. 234–43.

Ackerman, James S., 1990, 'Knowing good and evil: a literary analysis of the Court History in 2 Samuel 9—20 and 1 Kings 1—2', *JBL* 109 (1), pp. 41–60.

Ackerman, Susan, 1989, '"And the women knead dough": the worship of the Queen of Heaven in sixth-century Judah', in Peggy L. Day (ed.), *Gender and Difference in Ancient Israel*, Minneapolis: Fortress Press, pp. 109–24.

Ackerman, Susan, 1992, *Under Every Green Tree: Popular Religion in Sixth-Century Judah*, Atlanta: Scholars Press.

Ackerman, Susan, 1998, 'Isaiah', in C. A. Newsom and S. H. Ringe (eds), *Women's Bible Commentary*, expanded edition with Apocrypha, Louisville: Westminster John Knox Press, pp. 169–77.

Ackerman, Susan, 1999, '"And the women knead dough": the worship of the Queen of Heaven in sixth-century Judah', in Alice Bach (ed.), *Women in the Hebrew Bible: A Reader*, London: Routledge, pp. 21–32.

Ackroyd, Peter R., 1979, *Israel Under Babylon and Persia*, The New Clarendon Bible Old Testament 4, Oxford: Oxford University Press.

Adorno, Theodor W., 1990, *Negative Dialectics*, trans. E. B. Ashton, London: Routledge.

Adorno, Theodor W., and Max Horkheimer, 1999, *Dialectic of Enlightenment*, trans. John Cumming, New York: Continuum.

Aichele, George (ed.), 2000, *Culture, Entertainment and the Bible*, JSOTSS 309, Sheffield: Sheffield Academic Press.

Albrektson, B., 1963, *Studies in the Text and Theology of the Book of Lamentations with a Critical Edition of the Peshitta Text*, Studia Theologica Lundensia, Lund: Gleerup.

Albright, William F., 1940, *From the Stone Age to Christianity: Monotheism and the Historical Process*, Baltimore: Johns Hopkins University Press.

Ali, Abdullah Yusuf, 1938, *The Holy Qur'an: Text, Translation and Commentary*, Beirut: Dar al Arabia.

Allen, Leslie C., 1983, *Psalms 101–150*, Word Bible Commentary 21, Waco: Word Books.

Allen, Leslie C., 2003, *Ezra, Nehemiah, Esther*, New International Biblical Commentary, Peabody: Hendrickson.

Almond, Philip, 1999, *Adam and Eve in Seventeenth-Century Thought*, Cambridge, New York, Melbourne: Cambridge University Press.

Alonso-Schökel, L., 1961, 'Erzählkunst im buche der Richter', *Bib* 42, pp. 143–72.

Alpert, Rebecca, 1992, 'Challenging male/female complementarity: Jewish lesbians and the Jewish tradition', in Howard Schwartz (ed.), *People of the Body: Jews and Judaism from an Embodied Perspective*, Albany: SUNY Press, pp. 361–77.

Alpert, Rebecca, 1997, *Like Bread on the Seder Plate: Jewish Lesbians and the Transformation of Tradition*, New York: Columbia University Press.

Alpert, Rebecca, 2000, 'Do justice, love mercy, walk humbly: reflections on Micah and gay ethics', in Robert E. Goss and Mona West (eds), *Take Back the Word: A Queer Reading of the Bible*, Cleveland, Ohio: Pilgrim Press, pp. 170–82.

Alter, Robert, 1981, *The Art of Biblical Narrative*, New York: Basic Books.

Amit, Yairah, 1999, *The Book of Judges: The Art of Editing*, trans. Jonathan Chipman, Leiden: Brill.

Amnesty International, 2001, 'Crimes of hate, conspiracy of silence. torture and ill-treatment based on sexual identity', ACT 40/016/2001, Oxford: Alden Press.

Anderson, Cheryl B., 2004, *Women, Ideology, and Violence: Critical Theory and the Construction of Gender in the Book of the Covenant and the Deuteronomic Law*, JSOTSS 394, London and New York: T&T Clark.

Anderson, G. W., 1965/66, 'Enemies and evildoers in the book of Psalms', *BJRL* 48, 18–29.

Andreasen, N. E. A., 1983, 'The role of the Queen Mother in Israelite society', *CBQ* 45 (2), pp. 179–94.

Anonymous, 1939, *Midrash Rabbah: Genesis*, trans. Rabbi Dr Harry Freedman and Maurice Simon, London: Soncino Press.

Anonymous, 1984, *The Zohar*, trans. Harry Sperling and Maurice Simon, London and New York: Soncino Press.

Antonelli, Judith E., 1975, *In the Image of God: A Feminist Commentary on the Torah*, Northvale, N.J.: Jason Aronson.

Armour, Ellen, 1999, *Deconstruction, Feminist Theology and the Problem of Difference*, Chicago: University of Chicago Press.

Aschkenasy, Nehama, 1998, *Woman at the Window: Biblical Tales of Oppression and Escape*, Detroit: Wayne State University Press.

Ateek, Naim, 1995, 'Pentecost and the intifada', in Fernando F. Segovia and Mary Ann Tolbert (eds), *Reading from This Place*, Volume 2: *Social Location and Biblical Interpretation in Global Perspective*, Minneapolis: Fortress Press, pp. 69–81.

Babuscio, Jack, 1977, 'Camp and the gay sensibility', in Richard Dyer (ed.), *Gays and Film*, London: British Film Institute, pp. 40–57.

Bach, Alice, 1994, 'With a song in her heart: listening to scholars listening to Miriam', in A. Brenner (ed.), *A Feminist Companion to Exodus to Deuteronomy*, Feminist Companion to the Bible 6, Sheffield: Sheffield Academic Press, pp. 243–54.

Bach, Alice, 2000, 'Dreaming of Miriam's well', in A. Brenner (ed.), *Exodus to Deuteronomy*, Feminist Companion to the Bible (second series) 5, Sheffield: Sheffield Academic press, pp. 151–8.

Bagemihl, B., 1999, *Biological Exuberance: Animal Homosexuality and Natural Diversity*, New York: St Martin's Press.

Bail, U., 1998, '"O God, hear my prayer": Psalm 55 and violence against women', in A. Brenner and C. Fontaine (eds), *Wisdom and Psalms*, Feminist Companion to the Bible 2, Sheffield: Sheffield Academic Press, pp. 242–63.

Bailey, D. S., 1975, *Homosexuality and the Western Christian Tradition*, Hamden: Archon Books.

Bailey, Randall C., 1995, 'They're nothing but incestuous bastards: the polemical use of sex and sexuality in Hebrew canon narratives', in F. Segovia and M.

A. Tolbert (eds), *Reading from this Place*, Volume 1: *Social Location and Biblical Interpretation in the United States*, Minneapolis: Fortress Press, pp. 121–38.

Bakhtin, Mikhail, 1964, *Rabelais and his World*, Indiana: Indiana University Press.

Bal, Mieke, 1994, *On Meaning-Making: Essays in Semiotics*, Sonoma: Polebridge Press.

Barber, Cyril J., 2004, *The Dynamics of Effective Leadership: Learning From Nehemiah*, Fearn: Christian Focus.

Barker, Margaret, 1987, *The Older Testament: The Survival of Themes from the Ancient Royal Cult in Sectarian Judaism and Early Christianity*, London: SPCK.

Barker, Margaret, 1991, *The Gate of Heaven: The History and Symbolism of the Temple in Jerusalem*, London: SPCK.

Barker, Margaret, 1992, *The Great Angel: A Study of Israel's Second God*, Louisville: Westminster/John Knox Press.

Baskin, Judith R., 1983, *Pharaoh's Counsellors: Job, Jethro and Balaam in Rabbinic and Patristic Tradition*, Chico: Scholars Press.

Bass, Bernard M., 1990, *Bass and Stodgill's Handbook of Leadership: Theory, Research and Managerial Application*, 3rd edn, New York: Free Press.

Bates, S., 2004, *A Church at War: Anglicans and Homosexuality*, New York: St Martin's Press.

Batto, B. F., 1992, *Slaying the Dragon: Mythmaking in the Biblical Tradition*, Louisville: Westminster John Knox Press.

Bauckham, Richard J., 1983, *Jude, 2 Peter*, Word Bible Commentary 50, Waco: Word Books.

Bauer, A., 1998, 'Jeremiah as female impersonator: roles of difference in gender perception and gender perceptivity', in H. Washington *et al.* (eds), *Escaping Eden: New Feminist Perspectives on the Bible*, Biblical Seminar 65, Sheffield: Sheffield Academic Press, pp. 199–207.

Bauer, A., 1999, *Gender in the Book of Jeremiah: A Feminist-Literary Reading*, Studies in Biblical Literature 5, New York and Frankfurt: Peter Lang.

Bauer, A., 2000, 'Das Buch Jeremia: Wenn kluge Klagefrauen und prophetische Pornographie den Weg ins Exil weisen', in Luise Schottroff and Marie-Theres Wacker (eds), *Kompendium Feministische Bibelauslegung*, Gütersloh: Christian Kaiser, Gütersloher Verlagshaus, pp. 258–69.

Bauer-Levesque, A., 2004, 'Roundtable discussion: same-sex marriage – Response', *JFSR*, 20 (2), pp. 112–17.

Beal, Timothy K., 1997, *The Book of Hiding: Gender, Ethnicity, Annihilation, and Esther*, New York and London: Routledge.

Beal, Timothy K., 2002, *Religion and Its Monsters*, New York and London: Routledge.

Becking, Bob, and Meindert Dijkstra (eds), 1996, *On Reading Prophetic Texts: Gender-Specific and Related Studies in Memory of Fokkelien van Dijk-Hemmes*, New York: Brill.

Be'er, Ilana, 1994, 'Blood discharge: on female im/purity in the Priestly code and in biblical literature', in Athalya Brenner (ed.), *A Feminist Companion to Exodus to Deuteronomy*, Feminist Companion to the Bible 6, Sheffield: Sheffield Academic Press.

Bell, Shannon, 1994, *Reading, Writing and Rewriting the Prostitute Body*, Bloomington: Indiana University Press.

Benko, Stephen, 1993, *The Virgin Goddess: Studies in the Pagan and Christian Roots of Mariology*, Leiden and New York: Brill.

Berlant, Lauren, and Elizabeth Freeman, 1993, 'Queer nationality', in Michael Warner (ed.), *Fear of a Queer Planet: Queer Politics and Social Theory*, Minneapolis: University of Minnesota Press, pp. 193–229.

Berlin, Adele, 1983, *Poetics and Interpretation of Biblical Narrative*, Sheffield: Almond Press.

Berlin, Adele, 2001, *The JPS Bible Commentary: Esther*, Philadelphia: Jewish Publication Society.

Berquist, J., 2002, *Controlling Corporeality: The Body and the Household in Ancient Israel*, New Brunswick and London: Rutgers University Press.

Bertholet, Alfred, 1936, *Hesekiel, von Alfred Bertholet, mit einem Beitrag von Kurt Galling*, Tübingen: Mohr.

Bezner, Sharon, 2000, 'A queer reading of the book of Jonah', in Robert E. Goss and Mona West (eds), *Take Back the Word: A Queer Reading of the Bible*, Cleveland, Ohio: Pilgrim Press, pp. 161–9.

Biale, David, 1997, *Eros and the Jews from Biblical Israel to Contemporary America*, Berkeley, Los Angeles, London: University of California Press.

Biale, Rachel, 1984, *Women and Jewish Law: An Exploration of Women's Issues in Halakhic Sources*, New York: Schocken.

Billman, K. D., and D. L. Migliore, 1999, *Rachel's Cry: Prayer of Lament and Rebirth of Hope*, Cleveland: United Church Press.

Binger, Tilde, 1997, *Asherah: Goddesses in Ugarit, Israel and the Old Testament*, JSOTSS 232, Sheffield: Sheffield Academic Press.

Bird, Phyllis A., 1987, 'The place of women in the Israelite cultus', in Patrick D. Miller, Jr, Paul D. Hanson and S. Dean McBride (eds), *Ancient Israelite Religion: Essays in Honour of Frank Moore Cross*, Philadelphia: Fortress Press, pp. 397–419.

Bird, Phyllis A., 1989a, '"To play the harlot": an inquiry into an Old Testament metaphor', in P. L. Day (ed.), *Gender and Difference in Ancient Israel*, Philadelphia: Fortress Press, pp. 75–94.

Bird, Phyllis, 1989b, 'The harlot as heroine: narrative art and social presupposition in three Old Testament texts', *Semeia* 46, pp. 119–39.

Bird, Phyllis A., 1997a, *Missing Persons and Mistaken Identities: Women and Gender in Ancient Israel*, Overtures to Biblical Theology, Minneapolis: Fortress Press.

Bird, Phyllis A., 1997b, 'The end of the male cult prostitute: a literary-historical and sociological analysis of Hebrew *QĀDĒŠ-QĔDĒŠÎM*', in J. A. Emerton (ed.), *Congress Volume: Cambridge 1995*, VTSup 66, Leiden and New York: Brill, pp. 37–80.

Bird, Phyllis A., 2000, 'The Bible in Christian ethical deliberation concerning homosexuality: Old Testament contributions', in David L. Balch (ed.), *Homosexuality, Science, and the 'Plain Sense' of Scripture*, Grand Rapids: Eerdmans.

Birkeland, H., 1955, *The Evildoers in the Book of Psalms*, Oslo: J. Dybwad.

Blenkinsopp, Joseph, 1988, *Ezra-Nehemiah*, OTL, Philadelphia: Westminster Press.

Blenkinsopp, Joseph, 1990, *Ezekiel*, Louisville: John Knox Press.

Blenkinsopp, Joseph, 1996, *A History of Prophecy in Israel*, Louisville: Westminster John Knox Press.

Blenkinsopp, Joseph, 2000, *Isaiah 1–39: A New Translation with Introduction and Commentary*, Anchor Bible, New York: Doubleday.

Blenkinsopp, Joseph, 2002, *Isaiah 40–55: A New Translation with Introduction and Commentary*, Anchor Bible, New York: Doubleday.

Blenkinsopp, Joseph, 2003, *Isaiah 56–66: A New Translation with Introduction and Commentary*, Anchor Bible, New York: Doubleday.

Bloch, Ernst, 1995, *The Principle of Hope*, trans. Neville Plaice, Stephen Plaice and Paul Knight, Cambridge, Mass.: MIT Press.

Bloch, Ernst, and Theodor Adorno, 2001, 'Something's missing: a discussion between Ernst Bloch and Theodor W. Adorno on the contradictions of utopia longing', in *The Utopian Function of Art and Literature: Selected Essays*, trans. Jack Zipes and Frank Mecklenburg, Cambridge, Mass.: MIT Press, pp. 1–17.

Blumenthal, David R., 1993, *Facing the Abusing God: A Theology of Protest*, Louisville, Ky.: Westminster John Knox Press.

Boer, Roland, 1997, *Novel Histories: The Function of Biblical Criticism*, Sheffield: Academic Press.

Boer, Roland, 1999, *Knockin' on Heaven's Door: The Bible and Popular Culture*, New York: Routledge.

Boer, Roland, 2001, 'Yahweh as top: a lost Targum', in K. Stone (ed.), *Queer Commentary and the Hebrew Bible*, JSOTSS 334, London and New York: Sheffield Academic Press, pp. 75–105.

Boling, Robert G., 1975, *Judges*, Anchor Bible 6A, New York: Doubleday.

Boswell, J., 1980, *Christianity, Social Tolerance and Homosexuality: Gay People in Western Europe from the Beginning of the Christian Era to the Fourteenth Century*, Chicago and London: University of Chicago Press.

Botterweck, G. Johannes, and Helmer Ringgren (eds), 1974, *Theological Dictionary of the Old Testament*, vol. 1, trans. J. T. Willis, G. W. Bromiley and D. E. Green, Grand Rapids: Eerdmans.

Botterweck, G. Johannes, and Helmer Ringgren (eds), 1986, *Theological Dictionary of the Old Testament*, vol. 5, trans. David E. Green, Grand Rapids: Eerdmans.

Bowen, Nancy, 1999, 'The daughters of your people: female prophets in Ezekiel 13.17–23', *JBL* 118, pp. 417–33.

Boyarin, Daniel, 1992, 'This we know to be the carnal Israel: circumcision and the erotic life of God and Israel', *Critical Inquiry* 18 (3), pp. 474–505.

Boyarin, Daniel, 1995, 'Are there any Jews in "the History of Sexuality"?', *Journal of the History of Sexuality* 5, pp. 333–55.

Boyarin, Daniel, 1996, '"An imaginary and desirable converse": Moses and monotheism as family romance', in T. K. Beal and David M. Gunn (eds), *Reading Bible, Writing Books: Identity and the Book*, London and New York: Routledge, pp. 184–207.

Boyer, Paul, 1992, *When Time Shall Be No More: Prophecy Belief in Modern American Culture*, Cambridge, Mass.: Harvard University Press.

Bozak, B. A., 1991, *Life 'Anew': A Literary-Theological Study of Jer. 30–31*, AnBib 22, Rome: Editrice Pontificio Istituto Biblico.

Brandscheidt, R., 1988, *Das Buch der Klagelieder*, Düsseldorf: Patmos.

Braun, Roddy, 1979, 'Chronicles, Ezra and Nehemiah: theology and literary history', in J. A. Emerton (ed.), *Studies in the Historical Books of the Old Testament*, VTSup 30, Leiden: Brill, pp. 52–64.

Braun, Roddy, 1986, *1 Chronicles*, Word Biblical Commentaries 14, Waco: Word Books.

Brenner, A., 1986, 'Female social behaviour: two descriptive patterns within the "birth of a hero" paradigm', *VT* 36 (3), pp. 257–73.

Brenner, Athalya, 1993a, 'On "Jeremiah" and the poetics of (prophetic?) pornography', in Athalya Brenner and Fokkelien van Dijk-Hemmes, *On Gendering Texts: Female and Male Voices in the Hebrew Bible*, Biblical Interpretation Series 1, Leiden: Brill, pp. 178–93.

Brenner, Athalya, (ed.), 1993b, *The Feminist Companion to Genesis*, Feminist Companion to the Bible 2, Sheffield: Sheffield Academic Press.

Brenner, Athalya, 1994a [1985], *The Israelite Woman: Social Role and Literary Type in Biblical Narrative*, Sheffield: Sheffield Academic Press.

Brenner, Athalya, 1994b, '"Who's afraid of feminist criticism?" who's afraid of biblical humour? The case of the obtuse foreign ruler in the Hebrew Bible', *JSOT* 63, pp. 38–55.

Brenner, Athalya, 1995, 'On prophetic propaganda and the politics of "love": the case of Jeremiah', in A. Brenner (ed.), *The Feminist Companion to the Latter Prophets*, Feminist Companion to the Bible 8, Sheffield: Sheffield Academic Press, pp. 256–74.

Brenner, Athalya, 1996, 'Pornoprophetics revisited', *JSOT* 70, pp. 63–86.

Brenner, Athalya, 1997, *The Intercourse of Knowledge: On Gendering Desire and 'Sexuality' in the Hebrew Bible*, Biblical Interpretation Series 26, Leiden: Brill.

Brenner, Athalya, (ed.), 2000, *Exodus to Deuteronomy*, Feminist Companion to the Bible (second series) 5, Sheffield: Sheffield Academic Press.

Brenner, Athalya, 2005, *I Am . . . Biblical Women Tell Their Stories*, Minneapolis: Fortress Press.

Brenner, Athalya, and F. van Dijk-Hemmes, 1993, *On Gendering Texts: Female and Male Voices in the Hebrew Bible*, Leiden: Brill.

Brettler, Marc Zvi, 1989, *God is King: Understanding an Israelite Metaphor*, JSOTSS 76, Sheffield: JSOT Press.

Brettler, Marc Zvi, 1995, *The Creation of History in Ancient Israel*, London: Routledge.

Brettler, Marc Zvi, 1998, 'Women and Psalms: towards an understanding of the role of women's prayer in the Israelite cult,' in V. H. Matthews, B. M. Levinson and T. Frymer-Kensky (eds), *Gender and Law in the Hebrew Bible and the Ancient Near East*, JSOTSS 262, Sheffield: Sheffield Academic Press, pp. 25–56.

Breuer, J, 1988, *The Book of Jeremiah*, New York and Jerusalem: P. Feldheim.

Briggs, C. A., 1906, *A Critical and Exegetical Commentary on the Book of Psalms*, 2 vols, ICC, Edinburgh: T&T Clark.

Bright, John, 1981, *A History of Israel*, 5th edn, London: SCM Press.

Brooks, Beatrice, 1997, 'Fertility cult functionaries in the Old Testament', *JBL* 60, pp. 227–53.

Broome, E. C., 1946, 'Ezekiel's abnormal personality', *JBL* 65, pp. 277–92.

Brooten, Bernadette J., 1985, 'Early Christian women and their cultural context', in Adela Yarbro Collins (ed.), *Feminist Perspectives on Biblical Scholarship*, Atlanta: Scholars Press, pp. 65–91.

Brooten, Bernadette J., 1994, 'Paul's view on the nature of women and female homoeroticism', in C. W. Atkinson, C. H. Buchanan, and M. R. Miles (eds), *Immaculate and Powerful: The Female in Sacred Image and Social Reality*, Boston: Beacon Press, pp. 61–87.

Brooten, Bernadette J., 1996, *Love Between Women: Early Christian Responses to Female Homoeroticism*, Chicago and London: University of Chicago Press.

Brown, Francis, S. R. Driver and Charles A. Briggs, 1906, *A Hebrew and English Lexicon of the Old Testament: with an appendix containing the Biblical Aramaic, based on the Lexicon of William Gesenius*, trans. Edward Robinson, Oxford: Clarendon Press.

Brownlee, W. H., 1983, '"Son of Man set your face": Ezekiel the refugee prophet', *Hebrew Union College Annual* 54, pp. 83–110.

Broyles, C. C., 1999, *Psalms*, NIBC, Peabody: Hendrickson.

Brueggemann, Walter, 1984, *The Message of the Psalms: A Theological Commentary*, Minneapolis: Augsburg.

Brueggemann, Walter, 1995, *The Psalms and the Life of Faith*, Düsseldorf: Patmos.

Brueggemann, Walter, 1997, *Theology of the Old Testament: Testimony, Dispute, Advocacy*, Minneapolis: Fortress Press.

Brueggemann, Walter, 1998, *A Commentary on Jeremiah: Exile and Homecoming*, Grand Rapids: Eerdmans.

Brueggemann, Walter, 2003, *An Introduction to the Old Testament: The Canon and Christian Imagination*, Louisville: Westminster John Knox Press.

Brummett, Barry, 1991, *Contemporary Apocalyptic Rhetoric*, New York: Praeger.

Buber, Martin, 1958, *Moses: The Revelation and the Covenant*, New York: Harper & Row.

Buckley, Thomas, and Alma Gottlieb, 1988, *Blood Magic: The Anthropology of Menstruation*, Berkeley: University of California Press.

Budde, K., 1897, *Das Buch der Richter*, KHCAT 7, Freiburg: Mohr.

Burdick, Stuart C., 2001, 'Why take Leviticus seriously', *BR* 17 (3), p. 4.

Burnette-Bletsch, Rhonda, 2001, 'Woman who mutilates a man's genitals', in Carol Meyers (ed.), *Women in Scripture: A Dictionary of Named and Unnamed Women in the Hebrew Bible, The Apocryphal/Deuterocanonical Books, and the New Testament*, Grand Rapids and Cambridge: Eerdmans, p. 234.

Burns, John Barclay, 2000, 'Devotee or deviate: the "dog" (*keleb*) in ancient Israel as a symbol of male passivity and perversion', *Journal of Religion and Society* 2, pp. 1–10.

Butler, Judith, 1990, *Gender Trouble: Feminism and the Subversion of Identity*, New York: Routledge.

Butler, Judith, 1993, *Bodies that Matter*, New York: Routledge.

Butler, Judith, 1999, *Gender Trouble: Feminism and the Subversion of Identity*, 10th anniversary edn, London and New York: Routledge.

Butler, Judith, 2004, *Undoing Gender*, New York and London: Routledge.

Buttenwieser, M., 1938, *The Psalms*, Chicago: University of Chicago Press.

Camp, Claudia V., 1987, 'Female voice, written word: women and authority in Hebrew scripture', in P. M. Cooey, S. A. Farmer and M. E. Ross (eds), *Embodied Love: Sensuality and Relationship as Feminist Values*, San Francisco: Harper & Row, pp. 97–113.

Camp, Claudia V., 1998a, '1 and 2 Kings', in C. A. Newsom and S. H. Ringe (eds), *Women's Bible Commentary*, expanded edition with Apocrypha, Louisville: Westminster/John Knox Press, pp. 102–16.

Camp, Claudia V., 1998b, 'Texts of Terror', *JFSR* 14, pp. 81–104.

Camp, Claudia V., 2000a, 'Huldah', in C. Meyers, T. Craven and R. S. Kraemer (eds), *Women in Scripture: A Dictionary of Named and Unnamed Women in the Hebrew Bible, the Apocryphal/Deuterocanonical Books, and the New Testament*, Boston: Houghton Mifflin, pp. 96–7.

Camp, Claudia V., 2000b, *Wise, Strange, and Holy: The Strange Woman and the Making of the Bible*, Gender, Culture, Theory 9, Sheffield: Sheffield Academic Press.

Carden, Michael, 1999, 'Homophobia and rape in Sodom and Gibeah: a response to Ken Stone', *JSOT* 82, pp. 83–96.

Carden, Michael, 2004, *Sodomy: A History of a Christian Biblical Myth*, London: Equinox.

Carmichael, C. M., 1997, *Law, Legend, and Incest in the Bible*, Ithaca: Cornell University Press.

Carroll, R. P., 1979, *When Prophecy Failed: Reactions and Responses to Failure in the Old Testament Prophetic Tradition*, London: SCM Press.

Carroll, R. P., 1986, *Jeremiah: A Commentary*, Old Testament Library, Philadelphia: Westminster Press.

Carroll, R. P., 1999, 'Something rich and strange: imagining a future for Jeremiah studies', in A. R. P. Diamond *et al.*, *Troubling Jeremiah*, JSOTSS 260, Sheffield: Sheffield Academic Press, pp. 423–43.

Carter, Charles E., and Carol L. Meyers (eds), 1996, *Community, Identity and Ideology: Social Science Approaches to the Hebrew Bible*, Winona Lake: Eisenbrauns.

Ceresko, A., 1980, 'A note on Psalm 63: a psalm of vigil,' *ZAW* 92, pp. 435–6.

Chiel, S., and H. Dreher, 2000, *For Thou Art With Me: The Healing Power of Psalms*, Emmaus: Daybreak.

Children's Hospital St Louis, 2003, 'Parents and kids', s.v. 'New born appearance common questions', http://www.stlouischildrens.org/articles/kids_parents.asp, accessed 28 July 2003.

Childs, Brevard Springs, 1970, *Biblical Theology in Crisis*, Philadelphia: Westminster Press.

Childs, Brevard Springs, 2001, *Isaiah*, Old Testament Library, Louisville: Westminster John Knox Press.

Cholewinski, Alfred, 1976, *Heiligkeitsgesetz und Deuteronomium*, AnBib 66, Rome: Biblical Institute Press.

Circle of Concerned African Women Theologians, 2003, 'A call for well research papers', http://www.thecirclecawt.org/callforpapers.htm, accessed 10 July 2003.

Clark, Michael J., 1989, *A Place to Start: Towards an Unapologetic Gay Liberation Theology*, Dallas: Monument Press.

Clark, Michael J., 1997, *Defying the Darkness: Gay Theology in the Shadows*, Cleveland, Ohio: Pilgrim Press.

Clements, Ronald E., 1996, *Old Testament Prophecy: From Oracles to Canon*, Louisville: Westminster John Knox Press.

Cleto, Fabio, 1999, 'Introduction: queering the camp' in Fabio Cleto (ed.), *Camp: Queer Aesthetics and the Performing Subject*, Ann Arbor: University of Michigan Press, pp. 1–42.

Clines, David J. A., 1984, *Ezra, Nehemiah and Esther*, New Century Bible, Grand Rapids: Eerdmans.

Clines, David J. A., 1995a, 'Why is there a book of Job, and what does it do to you if you read it?', in Clines, *Interested Parties: The Ideology of Writers and Readers of the Hebrew Bible*, Sheffield: Sheffield Academic Press, pp. 122–44.

Clines, David J. A., 1995b, 'The book of Psalms, where men are men: on the gender of Hebrew piety', paper delivered at the SBL Annual Meeting, Philadelphia, http://www.shef.ac.uk/uni/academic/A-C/biblst/DJACcurrres/GenderPiety.html

Clines, David J. A., 1998, 'Reading Esther from left to right: contemporary strategies for reading a biblical text', in Clines, *On the Way to the Postmodern: Old Testament Essays 1967–1998*, vol. 1, JSOTSS 292, Sheffield: Sheffield Academic Press, pp. 3–22.

Clines, David J. A., 2002, 'He-prophets: masculinity as a problem for the Hebrew prophets and their interpreters', in Alastair G. Hunter and Philip R. Davies (eds), *Sense and Sensitivity: Essays on Reading the Bible in Memory of Robert Carroll*, London: Sheffield Academic Press, pp. 311–27.

Coats, George W., 1977, 'The King's loyal opposition', in George W. Coats and Burke O. Long (eds), *Canon and Authority: Essays in Old Testament Religion and Theology*, Philadelphia: Fortress Press, pp. 91–109.

Cogan, M., 2000, *I Kings: A New Translation with Introduction and Commentary*, Anchor Bible 10, Garden City: Doubleday.

Cogan, M., and H. Tadmor, 1988, *II Kings: A New Translation with Introduction and Commentary*, Anchor Bible 11, Garden City: Doubleday.

Coggins, Richard, Anthony Phillips, and Michael Knibb (eds), 1982, *Israel's Prophetic Tradition: Essays in Honour of Peter R. Ackroyd*, New York: Cambridge University Press.

Cohen, A., 1948, *The Twelve Prophets: Hebrew Text, English Translation and Commentary*, Bournemouth: Soncino Press.

Cohen, A. (ed.), 1950, *Joshua and Judges: Hebrew Text and English Translation with Introductions and Commentary*, London: Soncino Press.

Cohen, Mark E., 1988, *The Canonical Lamentations of Ancient Mesopotamia*, vol. 1, Potomac, Md.: Capital Decisions.

Cohn, R. L., 2000, *2 Kings*, Collegeville, Minn.: Liturgical Press.

Cole, R. L., 2000, *The Shape and Message of Book III (Psalms 73–89)*, JSOTSS 307, Sheffield: Sheffield Academic Press.

Collins, John J., 1993, *A Commentary on the Book of Daniel*, Minneapolis: Fortress Press.

Comstock, Gary David, 1991, *Violence Against Lesbians and Gay Men*, New York: University of Columbia Press.

Comstock, Gary David, 1993, *Gay Theology Without Apology*, Cleveland, Ohio: Pilgrim Press.

Comstock, Gary David, 1996, *Unrepentant, Self-Affirming, Practicing: Lesbian/Bisexual/Gay People within Organized Religion*, New York: Continuum.

Conger, Jay A., 1988, 'Theoretical Foundations of Charismatic Leadership,' in Jay A. Conger, Rabindra N. Kanungo, and associates (eds), *Charismatic Leadership: The Elusive Factor in Organizational Effectiveness*, San Francisco: Jossey-Bass, pp. 12–39.

Connolly, W. E., 1993, *The Augustinian Imperative: A Reflection on the Politics of Morality*, London: Sage.

Conrad, Edgar W., 1993, 'Ban', in Bruce M. Metzger and Michael D. Coogan (eds), *The Oxford Companion to the Bible*, New York and Oxford: Oxford University Press, p. 73.

Conrad, Edgar W., 1997, 'The end of prophecy and the appearance of angels/messengers in the book of the Twelve', *JSOT* 73, pp. 65–79.

Conrad, Edgar W., 1999, *Zechariah*, Sheffield: Sheffield Academic Press.

Conrad, Edgar W., 2000, 'Messengers in Isaiah and the Twelve: implications for reading prophetic books', *JSOT* 91, pp. 83–97.

Conrad, Edgar W., 2003a, 'Forming the Twelve and forming canon', in Paul Redditt and Aaron Schart (eds), *Thematic Threads in the Book of the Twelve*, Beihefte zur Zeitschrift für die Alttestamentliche Wissenschaft 325, Berlin: Walter de Gruyter, pp. 90–103.

Conrad, Edgar W., 2003b, *Reading the Latter Prophets: Towards a New Canonical Criticism*, JSOTSS 376, London and New York: T&T Clark International.

Conrad, Edgar W., 2003c, 'Semiotics, scribes and prophetic books', in Roland Boer and Edgar W. Conrad (eds), *Redirected Travel: Alternative Journeys and Places in Biblical Studies*, JSOTSS 382, London and New York: T&T Clark International, pp. 41–9.

Cook, Stephen L., 1995, *Prophecy and Apocalypticism: The Postexilic Social Setting*, Minneapolis: Fortress Press.

Countryman, L. W., 1988, *Dirt, Greed, and Sex: Sexual Ethics in the New Testament and Their Implications for Today*, Philadelphia: Fortress Press.

Countryman, L. W., 2005, *Love Human and Divine: Reflections on Love, Sexuality, and Friendship*, Harrisburg: Morehouse.

Craigie, P. C., 1983, *Psalms 1–50*, Word Bible Commentary 19, Waco: Word Books.

Creekmur, Corey K., and Alexander Doty (eds), 1995, *Out in Culture: Gay, Lesbian, and Queer Essays in Popular Culture*, Series Q, Durham, N.C.: Duke University Press.

Crenshaw, James L., 1988, *Ecclesiastes: A Commentary*, Old Testament Library, London: SCM Press.

Croft, S. J. L., 1987, *The Identity of the Individual in the Psalms*, JSOTSS 44, Sheffield: JSOT Press.

Cross, Frank M., 1973, *Canaanite Myth and Hebrew Epic: Essays in the History of the Religion of Israel*, Cambridge, Mass.: Harvard University Press.

Culley, R. C., 1994, 'The Temple in Psalms 84, 63, and 42–43', in J. C. Petit, A. Charron and A. Myre (eds), *Où demeures-tu? Jn 1,38: la maison depuis le monde biblique: en hommage au professeur Guy Couturier*, Montreal: Fides, pp. 187–97.

Dahood, M., 1965–70, *Psalms: A New Translation with Introduction and Commentary*, 3 vols, Anchor Bible, New York: Doubleday.

Daly, Mary, 1973, *Beyond God the Father: Toward a Philosophy of Women's Liberation*, Boston: Beacon Press.

Darr, Katheryn Pfisterer, 1992, 'Ezekiel', in C. A. Newsom and S. H. Ringe (eds), *The Women's Bible Commentary*, London: SPCK/ Louisville: Westminster John Knox Press, pp. 183–90.

Darr, Katheryn Pfisterer, 1994, *Isaiah's Vision and the Family of God*, Literary Currents in Biblical Interpretation, Louisville: Westminster John Knox Press.

Darr, Katheryn Pfisterer, 1998, 'Ezekiel', in C. A. Newsom and S. H. Ringe (eds), *Women's Bible Commentary Expanded Edition with Apocrypha*, Louisville: Westminster John Knox Press.

Daube, David, 1986, 'The Old Testament prohibitions of homosexuality', *Zeitschrift der Savigny-Stiftung für Reschtsgeschichte: Romanistische Abteilung* 103, pp. 446–8.

Davidson, Robert, 1985, *Jeremiah II with Lamentations*, Daily Study Bible, Edinburgh: St Andrews Press.

Davidson, S., 2002, 'Jeremiah's letter to the exiles: (a)way from home', paper presented at SBL, Bible and Cultural Studies Group, Toronto, 24 November 2002.

Davies, Dominic, 1996a, 'Homophobia and heterosexism', in Dominic Davies and Charles Neal (eds), *Pink Therapy: A Guide for Counsellors and Therapists Working with Lesbian, Gay and Bisexual Clients*, Buckingham and Philadelphia: Open University Press, pp. 41–65.

Davies, Dominic, 1996b, 'Working with people coming out', in Dominic Davies and Charles Neal (eds), *Pink Therapy: A Guide for Counsellors and Therapists Working with Lesbian, Gay and Bisexual Clients*, Buckingham and Philadelphia: Open University Press, pp. 66–85.

Davies, Gordon F., 1999, *Ezra and Nehemiah*, Berit Olam, Collegeville: Liturgical Press.

Davies, Philip R., 1995, *In Search of 'Ancient Israel'*, JSOTSS 148, Sheffield: Sheffield Academic Press.

Davis, L., 1990, *The Courage to Heal Workbook: For Women and Men Survivors of Child*

Sexual Abuse, New York: Perennial.

Day, J., 1985, *God's Conflict with the Dragon and the Sea*, Cambridge: Cambridge University Press.

Décor, Fitzgerald, 1967, 'Two special meanings of the word in biblical Hebrew', *JSS* 12, pp. 230–40.

Delaney, Carol, 1991, *The Seed and the Soil: Gender and Cosmology in Turkish Village Society*, California: University of California Press.

Delekat, L., 1967, *Asylie und Schutzorakel am Zionheiligtum: Eine Untersuchung zu den privaten Feindpsalmen*, Leiden: Brill.

Delitzsch, F., 1880–1, *Biblical Commentary on the Psalms*, trans. Francis Bolton, 3 vols, Edinburgh: T&T Clark.

Dempsey, Carol J., 1998, 'The "whore" of Ezekiel 16: the impact and ramifications of gender-specific metaphors in light of biblical law and divine judgement', in Victor Matthews, Bernard M. Levinson and Tikva Frymer-Kensky (eds), *Gender and Law in the Hebrew Bible and the Ancient Near East*, JSOTSS 262, Sheffield: Sheffield Academic Press, pp. 57–78.

Dempsey, Carol J., 2000, *The Prophets: A Liberation-Critical Reading*, Minneapolis: Fortress Press.

Dever, William G., 1990, *Recent Archaeological Discoveries and Biblical Research*, Seattle and London: University of Washington Press.

Dever, William G., 1993, 'Cultural continuity, ethnicity in the archaeological record and the question of Israelite origins', *Eretz-Israel* 24, pp. 22–33.

Dever, William G., 2005, *Did God Have a Wife? Archaeology and Folk Religion in Ancient Israel*, Grand Rapids: Eerdmans.

DeVries, S. J., 1986, 'The forms of prophetic address in Chronicles', *Hebrew Annual Review* 10, pp. 15–36.

Diamond, A. R. P., and K. M. O'Connor, 1996, 'Unfaithful passions: coding women, coding men in Jeremiah 2–3', *BibInt* 4 (2), pp. 288–310.

Diamond, A. R. P., K. M. O'Connor and L. Stuhlman (eds), 1999, *Troubling Jeremiah*, JSOTSS 260, Sheffield: Sheffield Academic Press.

Dinesen, I., 1934, 'The Dreamers', in *Seven Gothic Tales*, New York: Random House, pp. 271–55.

Dinesen, I., 1942, 'A Consolatory Tale', in *Winter's Tales*, New York: Random House, pp. 286–312 .

Dinesen, I., 1989 [1937, 1960], *Out of Africa and Shadows on the Grass*, New York: Random House.

Dobbs-Allsopp, F. W., 2000, 'Book of Lamentations', in David Noel Freeman (ed.), *Eerdmans Dictionary of the Bible*, Cambridge and Grand Rapids: Eerdmans, pp. 785–7.

Dolev, E., and J. Nerubay, 1982, 'Battle wounds in the Bible', *Koroth* 8 (5–6), pp. 35–7.

Donnelly, Jack, 2003, *Universal Human Rights in Theory and Practice*, Ithaca and London: Cornell University Press.

Douglas, Mary, 1966, *Purity and Danger: An Analysis of the Concepts of Pollution and Taboo*, London: Routledge & Kegan Paul.

Douglas, Mary, 1992, *Purity and Danger: An Analysis of the Concepts of Pollution and Taboo*, London and New York: Routledge.

Douglas, Mary, 1993, 'The forbidden animals in Leviticus', *JSOT* 59, pp 3–23.

Douglas, Mary, 1999, *Leviticus as Literature*, Oxford: Oxford University Press.

Dover, K. J., 1978, *Greek Homosexuality*, London: Gerald Duckworth.

Downton, James V., Jr., 1973, *Rebel Leadership: Commitment and Charisma in the Revolutionary Process*, New York: Free Press.

Duhm, B., 1901, *Das Buch Jeremia*, KHCAT 11, Leipzig: J.C.B. Mohr.

Dynes, W. R., 1998, 'Love in the Ancient Mediterranean', *Journal of Homosexuality* 436 (1), pp. 114–26. (A version is archived at www.indegayforum.org.)

Eaton, John H., 1986 [1976], *Kingship and the Psalms*, 2nd edn, Bible Seminar, Sheffield: JSOT Press.

Edwards, George, 1984, *Gay/Lesbian Liberation: A Biblical Perspective*, New York: Pilgrim Press.

Edwards, Lisa, 2000, 'Shelach-Lecha: the grasshoppers and the giants', in Elyse Goldstein (ed.), *The Women's Torah Commentary*, Woodstock, Vt.: Jewish Lights, pp. 279–85.

Eichler, B. L., 1976, 'Bestiality', in Keith Crim (ed.), *Interpreter's Dictionary of the Bible*, Supplement, Nashville: Abingdon, pp. 96–7.

Eichrodt, Walter, 1970, *Ezekiel: A Commentary*, Philadelphia: Westminster Press.

Eilberg-Schwartz, H., 1990, *The Savage in Judaism: An Anthropology of Israelite Religion and Ancient Judaism*, Bloomington: Indiana University Press.

Eilberg-Schwartz, Howard, 1991, 'People of the body: the problem of the body for the people of the book', *Journal of the History of Sexuality* 2, pp. 1–24.

Eilberg-Schwartz, Howard, 1992, 'The problem of the body for the people of the book', in *People of the Body: Jews and Judaism from an Embodied Perspective*, Albany: State University of New York Press, pp. 17–46.

Eilberg-Schwartz, Howard, 1994, *God's Phallus and Other Problems for Men and Monotheism*, Boston: Beacon Press.

Eissfeldt, Otto, 1966, 'Jahwe Zebaoth', in *Kleine Schriften* III, Tübingen: Mohr, pp. 103–23.

Elliger, Karl, 1966, *Leviticus*, HAT 4, Tübingen: Mohr.

Elwell, Sue Levi, 1997, 'Amid desert's harsh sands, Moses confronts harsh reality', *Philadelphia Jewish Exponent*, 19 June.

Elwes, Catherine, 1990, 'Floating femininity: a look at performance art by women', in Sarah Kent and Jacqueline Morreau (eds), *Women's Images of Men*, London: Pandora Press, pp. 64–93.

Emerson, J., 1996, 'Yang Chu's discovery of the body', *Philosophy East and West* 46 (4), pp. 533–66.

Engberg-Pedersen, T., 2000, *Paul and the Stoics*, Lousiville: Westminster John Knox Press.

Eskenazi, Tamara Cohn, 1988, *In an Age of Prose*, Atlanta: Scholars Press.

Eslinger, Lyle, 1991, 'Freedom or knowledge? Perspective and purpose in the Exodus narrative (Exodus 1–15)', in *JSOT* 52 (1), pp. 43–60.

Evangelical Alliance Policy Commission, 2000, *Transsexuality*, Carlisle: Paternoster Press.

Exum, J. Cheryl, 1983, '"You shall let every daughter live": a study of Exodus 1:8–2:20', *Semeia* 28 (1), pp. 63–82.

Exum, J. Cheryl, 1992, *Tragedy and Biblical Narrative: Arrows of the Almighty*, Cambridge and New York: Cambridge University Press.

Exum, J. Cheryl, 1993, *Fragmented Women: Feminist (Sub)versions of Biblical Narratives*, JSOTSS 163, Sheffield: Sheffield Academic Press.

Exum, J. Cheryl, 1996, *Plotted, Shot and Painted: Cultural Representations of Biblical Women*, JSOTSS 215; Gender, Culture, Theory 3, Sheffield: Sheffield Academic Press.

Farley, W., 1990, *Tragic Vision and Divine Compassion: A Contemporary Theodicy*, Louisville: Westminster John Knox Press.

Fausto-Sterling, Anne, 1993, 'The five sexes: why male and female are not enough', *The Sciences* 33, pp. 20–4.

Fausto-Sterling, Anne, 2000, *Sexing the Body: Gender Politics and the Construction of Sexuality*, New York: Basic Books.

Fewell, Danna Nolan, 1995, 'Deconstructive criticism: Achsah and the (e)razed city of writing', in Gale Yee (ed.), *Judges and Method: New Approaches in Biblical Studies*, Minneapolis: Augsburg Press, pp. 119–45.

Fewell, Danna Nolan, and David M. Gunn, 1990, 'Controlling perspectives: women, men and the authority of violence in Judges 4 and 5', *JAAR* 58, pp. 389–411.

Fewell, Danna Nolan, and David M. Gunn, 1993, *Gender, Power, and Promise: The Subject of the Bible's First Story*, Nashville: Abingdon Press.

Finagan, J., 1950, 'The chronology of Ezekiel', *JBL* 69, pp. 61–6.

Finkelstein, Israel, 1996, 'Ethnicity and origin of the Iron I settlers in the highlands of Canaan: can the real Israel stand up?', *Biblical Archaeology* 59, pp. 198–212.

Finkelstein, Israel, and N. A. Silberman, 2001, *The Bible Unearthed: Archaeology's New Vision of Ancient Israel and the Origin of Its Sacred Texts*, New York and London: Free Press.

Fishbane, Michael, 1984, 'Sin and judgment in the prophecies of Ezekiel', *Interpretation* 38, pp. 131–50.

Flanagan, J., 1981, 'Chiefs in Israel', *JSOT* 20, pp. 47–73.

Flanagan, J., 1992, 'Samuel, book of, 1–2: text, composition, and content', in D. N. Freedman (ed.), *The Anchor Bible Dictionary*, Vol. 5, New York and London: Doubleday, pp. 957–65.

Flint, P. W., 1998, 'The book of Psalms in the light of the Dead Sea Scrolls', *VT* 48, pp. 453–72.

Fohrer, Georg, 1955, *Ezechiel, mit einem Beitrag von Kurt Galling*, Tübingen: Mohr.

Fontaine, Carole R., 1997, 'The abusive Bible: on the use of feminist method in pastoral contexts', in Athalya Brenner and Carole Fontaine (eds), *A Feminist Companion to Reading the Bible: Approaches, Methods and Strategies*, Feminist Companion to the Bible, Sheffield: Sheffield Academic Press, pp. 84–113.

Fortune, M., 1983, *Sexual Violence, the Unmentionable Sin: An Ethical and Pastoral Perspective*, Cleveland, Ohio: Pilgrim Press.

Fortune, M., 1987, *Keeping the Faith: Questions and Answers for the Abused Woman*, San Francisco: Harper & Row.

Foucault, Michel (ed.), 1980, *Herculine Barbin: Being the Recently Discovered Memoirs of a Nineteenth-Century French Hermaphrodite*, New York: Pantheon Books.

Foucault, Michel, 1990, *The History of Sexuality: The Use of Pleasure*, trans. Robert Hurley, New York: Random House.

Foucault, Michel, 1991, 'What is critique', in Sylvère Lotringer and Lisa Hochroth (eds), *The Politics of Truth*, New York: Semiotext(e), pp. 50–8.

Fox, Everett, 1995, *The Five Books of Moses*, New York: Schocken Books.

Frankel, Ellen, 1996, *The Five Books of Miriam: A Woman's Commentary on the Torah*, New York: Putnam.

Frazer, James George, 1990, *The Golden Bough: A Study in Magic and Religion*, New York: St Martin's Press.

Fredrickson, D. E., 2000, 'Natural and unnatural use in Romans 1:24–27', in D. L. Balch (ed.), *Homosexuality, Science, and the 'Plain Sense' of Scripture*, Grand Rapids: Eerdmans, pp. 197-222.

Freedman, D. N., 1950, 'Joshua: introduction and commentary', in A. Cohen (ed.), *Joshua and Judges: Hebrew Text and English Translation with Introductions and Commentary*, London: Soncino Press, pp. xi–151.

Freedman, D. N., 1954, 'The book of Ezekiel', *Interpretation* 8, pp. 446–71.

Freedman, D. N., 1960, 'The Name of the God of Moses', *JBL* 79, pp. 151–6.

Fretheim, T., 1999, *First and Second Kings*, Louisville: Westminster John Knox Press.

Freud, Sigmund, 1946, *Totem and Taboo: Resemblances Between the Psychic Loves of Savages and Neurotics*, trans. A. Brill, New York: Vintage Books.

Friedlander, Gerald, 1916, *Pirke de Rabbi Eliezer (The Chapters of Rabbi Eliezer the Great): According to the Text of the Manuscript Belonging to Abraham Epstein of Vienna*, New York: Sepher-Hermon Press.

Frymer-Kensky, Tikva, 1992, 'Deuteronomy', in C. A. Newsom and S. H. Ringe (eds), *The Women's Bible Commentary*, London: SPCK/Louisville: Westminster John Knox Press, pp. 52–62.

Frymer-Kensky, Tikva, 2002, *Reading the Women of the Bible*, New York: Schocken Books.

Fuchs, Esther, 2003, 'Men in biblical feminist scholarship', *JFSR* 19 (2), pp. 93–114.

Fuchs-Kreimer, Nancy, 2000, 'Mishpatim: what we must do', in E. Goldstein (ed.), *The Women's Torah Commentary: New Insights for Women Rabbis on the 53 Weekly Torah Portions*, Woodstock: Jewish Lights Press, pp. 148–53.

Gadd, C. J., 1963, 'The second Lamentation for Ur', in David Winton Thomas and W. D. McHardy (eds), *Hebrew and Semitic Studies Presented to Godfrey Rolles Driver*, Oxford: Clarendon Press, pp. 59–71.

Gagnon, R. A. J., 2001, *The Bible and Homosexual Practice: Texts and Hermeneutics*, Nashville: Abingdon Press.

Galambush, J., 1992, *Jerusalem in the Book of Ezekiel: The City as Yahweh's Wife*, SBLDS 130, Atlanta: Scholars Press.

Galling, K., 1956, 'Der Ehrenname Elias und die Entrückung Elias,' *Zeitschrift für Theologie und Kirche*, 53, pp. 129–48.

Garber, Marjorie, 1992, *Vested Interests: Cross-Dressing and Cultural Anxiety*, New York: Routledge.

Garscha, Jörg, 1974, *Studien zum Ezechielbuch: eine redaktionskritische Untersuchung von 1-39*, Bern: Herbert Lang.

Gerstenberger, E., 1998, *Psalms: With an Introduction to Cultic Poetry, Part One*, Grand Rapids: Eerdmans.

Gerstenberger, E., 2000, *Psalms and Lamentations, Part Two*, Grand Rapids: Eerdmans.

Gilmore, D., 1987, *Honor and Shame and the Unity of the Mediterranean*, Washington: American Anthropological Association.

Ginsburg, Christian D., 1861 [1970], *Qoheleth and the Song of Songs*, New York: KTAV.

Ginzberg, Louis, 1941, *Legends of the Jews Vol. IV: Bible Times and Characters from Joshua to Esther*, Philadelphia: The Jewish Publication Society of America.

Ginzberg, Louis, 1956, *Legends of the Jews Vol. VI: Notes to Volumes III and IV from Moses in the Wilderness to Esther*, Philadelphia: Jewish Publication Society of America.

Girard, René, 1996, 'The plague in literature and myth', in Robert A. Segal (ed.), *Literary Criticism and Myth*, Theories of Myth 4, London and New York: Garland, pp. 155–72.

Girard, René, 2005, *Violence and the Sacred*, trans. Patrick Gregory, London and New York: Continuum.

Glancy, Jennifer A., 1998, 'House readings and field readings: the discourse of slavery and biblical/cultural studies', in J. Cheryl Exum and Stephen D. Moore (eds), *Biblical Studies/Cultural Studies*, Sheffield: Sheffield Academic Press, pp. 465–82.

Glaser, Chris, 1998, *Coming Out as Sacrament*, Louisville: Westminster John Knox Press.

Glatt, Melvin J., 1986, 'Midrash: the defender of God', *Judaism* 35 (1), pp. 87–97.

Goitein, S. D., 1988, 'Women as creators of biblical genres', *Prooftexts* 8, pp. 1–33.

Gold, V. R., *et al.* (eds), 1995, *The New Testament and Psalms: An Inclusive Version*, Oxford: Oxford University Press.

Goodfriend, Elaine Adler, 1992, 'Prostitution', in D. N. Freedman (ed.) *Anchor Bible Dictionary*, vol. 5, New York: Doubleday, pp. 505–10.

Goodfriend, Elaine Adler, 2001, 'Temple prostitute', in Carol Meyers (ed.), *Women in Scripture: A Dictionary of Named and Unnamed Women in the Hebrew Bible, The Apocryphal/Deuterocanonical Books, and the New Testament*, Grand Rapids and Cambridge: Eerdmans, pp. 231–2.

Gordon, P., and H. Washington, 1993, 'Rape as a military metaphor in the Hebrew Bible', in Athalya Brenner (ed.), *A Feminist Companion to the Latter Prophets*, Feminist Companion to the Bible 8, Sheffield: Sheffield Academic Press, pp. 308–25.

Goss, Robert E., 1993, *Jesus Acted Up: A Gay and Lesbian Manifesto*, New York: Harper SanFrancisco.

Goss, Robert E., 2002, *Queering Christ: Beyond Jesus Acted up*, Cleveland, Ohio: Pilgrim Press.

Goss, Robert E., and Amy Adams Squire Strongheart (eds), 1997, *Our Families, Our Values: Snapshots of Queer Kinship*, New York: Harrington Park Press.

Goss, Robert E., and Mona West (eds), 2000, *Take Back the Word: A Queer Reading of the Bible*, Cleveland, Ohio: Pilgrim Press

Gottwald, Norman K., 1954, *Studies in the Book of Lamentations*, SBT 14, London: SCM Press.

Gottwald, Norman K., 1964, *All the Kingdoms of the Earth; Israelite Prophecy and International Relations in the Ancient Near East*, New York: Harper & Row.

Gottwald, Norman K., 1979, *The Tribes of Yahweh: A Sociology of the Religion of Liberated Israel, 1250–1050 BCE*, London: SCM Press.

Gottwald, Norman K., 1989, *The Future of Liberation Theology*, Maryknoll: Orbis Books.

Goulder, M. D., 1982, *The Psalms of the Sons of Korah*, JSOTSS 20, Sheffield: JSOT Press.

Goulder, M. D., 1990, *The Prayers of David (Psalms 51–72)*, Studies in the Psalter 2; JSOTSS 102, Sheffield: Sheffield Academic Press.

Goulder, M. D., 1996, *The Psalms of Asaph and the Pentateuch*, Studies in the Psalter 3; JSOTSS 233, Sheffield: Sheffield Academic Press.

Goulder, M. D., 1998, *The Psalms of Return (Book V, Psalms 107–150)*, Studies in the Psalter 4; JSOTSS 258, Sheffield: Sheffield Academic Press.

Grabbe, Lester L., 1998, *Ezra-Nehemiah*, New York: Routledge.

Grahn, Judy, 1984, *Another Mother Tongue: Gay Words, Gay Worlds*, Boston: Beacon Press.

Gray, John, 1963, *I and II Kings: A Commentary*, Philadelphia: Westminster Press.

Greenberg, David F., 1988, *The Construction of Homosexuality*, Chicago and London: University of Chicago Press.

Greenberg, Moshe, 1967, *Ezekiel I–II*, Anchor Bible 22a, New York: Doubleday.

Greenberg, Moshe, 1983, 'Ezekiel 17: a holistic interpretation', *Journal of the American Oriental Society* 3, pp. 149–54.

Greenberg, Moshe, 1984, 'The design and themes of Ezekiel's program of restoration', *Interpretation* 38, pp. 181–208.

Greenberg, S., 2004, *Wrestling With God and Men: Homosexuality in the Jewish Tradition*, Madison: University of Wisconsin Press.

Greenstein, E. L., 1999, 'In Job's face/facing Job', in F. C. Black, R. Boer and E. Runions (eds), *The Labour of Reading: Desire, Alienation, and Biblical Interpretation*, Atlanta: Society of Biblical Literature, pp. 301–17.

Gross, Sally, *Intersexuality and Scripture*, http://www.bfpubs.demon.co.uk/sally.htm

Grosz, Elizabeth, 1990, *Lacan and Feminism*, New York: Routledge.

Gruber, Mayer I., 1983, 'The Qadeš in the Book of Kings and in Other Sources', *Tarbiz* 52 (2), pp. 167–76.

Gruber, Mayer I., 1986, 'Hebrew Qedešah and her Canaanite and Akkadian Cognates', *Ugarit-Forschungen* 18, pp. 133–48.

Gruber, Mayer I., 1988, 'The Qedešah: what was her function?', *Be'er Sheva* 3, pp. 45–51.

Guest, P. Deryn, 1997, 'Dangerous liaisons in the book of Judges', *SJOT* 11 (2), pp. 241–69.

Guest, P. Deryn, 1998, 'Can Judges survive without sources? Challenging the consensus', *JSOT* 78, pp. 43–61.

Guest, P. Deryn, 1999, 'Hiding behind the naked woman: a recriminative response', *Biblical Interpretation: A Journal of Contemporary Approaches* 4, (4), pp. 413–48.

Guest, Deryn, P., 2001, 'Battling for the Bible: academy, church and the gay agenda', *Theology and Sexuality* 15, pp. 66–93.

Guest, Deryn P., 2005, *When Deborah Met Jael: Lesbian Biblical Hermeneutics*, London: SCM Press.

Guillaume, Philippe, 2004, *Waiting for Josiah: The Judges*, London and New York: T&T Clark International.

Guindon, André, 1986, *The Sexual Creators*, Lanham, Md.: University Press of America.

Gunkel, H., 1937, *Einleitung in die Psalmen: die Gattungen der religiösen Lyrik Israels*, Göttingen: Vanderhoeck & Ruprecht.

Gunkel, H., 1967, *The Psalms: A Form-Critical Introduction*, trans. Thomas M. Horner, Philadelphia: Fortress Press.

Gunkel, H., *et al.* (eds), 1926–31, *Die Religion in Geschichte und Gegenwart*, 2nd edn, Tübingen: Mohr.

Gunn, David M., 1978, *The Story of King David: Genre and Interpretation*, Sheffield: Sheffield Academic Press.

Gunn, David M., 1987, 'Joshua and Judges', in Robert Alter and Frank Kermode (eds), *The Literary Guide to the Bible*, London: Collins, pp. 102–21.

Gunn, David M., 1998, 'Colonialism and the vagaries of scripture: Te Kooti in Canaan (a story of Bible and dispossession in Aotearoa/New Zealand)', in Tod Linafelt and Timothy K. Beal (eds), *God in the Fray: A Tribute to Walter Brueggemann*, Minneapolis: Fortress Press, pp. 127–42.

Haacker, Klaus, 1994, 'Exegetische Gesichtspunkte zum Thema Homosexualität', *Theologische Beiträge* 25, pp. 173–80.

Haag, Herbert, 1960, '"Offenbaren" in der hebräischen Bibel', *Theologische Zeitschrift*

16, pp, 251–8.

Haak, Robert D., 1992, *Habakkuk*, VTSup 44, Leiden: Brill.

Habel, N. C., 1985, *The Book of Job*, Old Testament Library, Philadelphia: Westminster Press.

Hackbarth, Alexa, 2003, 'Vanity, thy name is Metrosexual', *Washington Post*, 17 November.

Hackett, J., 1989, 'Can a sexist model liberate us? Ancient Near Eastern "Fertility" goddesses', *JFSR* 5 (1), pp. 65–76.

Hackett, J., 1998, '1 and 2 Samuel', in C. A. Newsom and S. H. Ringe (eds), *Women's Bible Commentary: Expanded Edition with Apocrypha*, Louisville: Westminster John Knox Press, pp. 91–101.

Hadley, Judith, 2000, *The Cult of Asherah in Ancient Israel and Judah*, Cambridge: Cambridge University Press.

Haldeman, D. C., 1994, 'The practice and ethics of sexual orientation conversion therapy', *Journal of Consulting and Clinical Psychology* 62, (2), pp. 221–7.

Hallam, Paul, 1993, *The Book of Sodom*, London and New York: Verso.

Hallo, William W., and K. Lawson Younger, Jr. (eds), 1997, *The Context of Scripture*, vol. 1: *Canonical Compositions from the Biblical World*, Leiden: Brill.

Halpern, Baruch, 1996, *The First Historians: The Hebrew Bible and History*, Pennsylvania: Pennsylvania State University Press.

Halpern, Baruch, 2001, *David's Secret Demons: Messiah, Murderer, Traitor, King*, Grand Rapids and Cambridge: Eerdmans.

Hamlin, E. J., 1990, *Judges: At Risk in the Promised Land*, International Theological Commentary, Grand Rapids: Eerdmans.

Handy, Lowell K., 1992, 'Uneasy laughter: Ehud and Eglon as ethnic humour', *SJOT* 6 (2), pp. 223–46.

Hanks, Thomas, 2000, 'Matthew and Mary of Magdala', in Robert E. Goss and Mona West (eds), *Take Back the Word: A Queer Reading of the Bible*, Cleveland, Ohio: Pilgrim Press, pp. 185–95.

Hanson, P. D., 1979, *The Dawn of Apocalyptic: The Historical and Sociological Roots of Jewish Apocalyptic Eschatology*, rev. edn, Philadelphia: Fortress Press.

Hanson, R. S., 1968, *The Psalms in Modern Speech For Public and Private Use*, vol. 2: *Psalms 42–89*, Philadelphia: Fortress Press.

Harman, William. 1989, 'Sacred marriage in the study of religion: a perspective from India on a concept that grew out of the Ancient Near East', *Religion* 19 (4), pp. 353–76.

Harris, S., and G. F. Petrie, 2003, *Bullying: The Bullies, the Victims, the Bystanders*, Lanham: Scarecrow Press.

Hart, D. B., 2003, *The Beauty of the Infinite: The Aesthetics of Christian Truth*, Grand Rapids: Eerdmans.

Hart, D. B., 2005, *The Doors of the Sea: Where Was God in the Tsunami?*, Grand Rapids: Eerdmans.

Hart, Lynda, 1992, 'Karen Finley's dirty work: censorship, homophobia, and the NEA', *Genders* 14, pp. 1–15.

Hart, Lynda, 1998, *Between the Body and the Flesh: Performing Sadomasochism*, New York: Columbia University Press.

Hartley, John E., 1992, *Leviticus 1–27*, Word Bible Commentary 4, Waco: Word Books.

Havea, Jione, 2003, *Elusions of Control: Biblical Law on the Words of Women*, Atlanta: Society of Biblical Literature.

Hawk, Daniel L., 1992, 'Strange house guests: Rahab, Lot and the dynamics of deliverance', in Danna Nolan Fewell (ed.), *Reading Between Texts: Intertextuality and the Hebrew Bible*, Louisville: Westminster John Knox Press, pp. 89–97.

Hawk, Daniel L., 1997, 'The problem with pagans', in Timothy K. Beal and David M. Gunn (eds), *Reading Bibles, Writing Bodies: Identity and the Book*, London and New York: Routledge, pp. 153–63.

Hawk, Daniel L., 2000, *Joshua*, Berit Olam: Studies in Hebrew Narrative and Poetry, Collegeville, Minn.: Liturgical Press.

Hazen, A. L., *20th Century History of New Castle and Lawrence County Pennsylvania and Representative Citizens*, Chicago: Richmond-Arnold, http://www.rootsweb.com/~usgenweb/pa/lawrence/1908/ch1.htm

Hefling, C., 1996, 'By their fruits: a traditionalist argument', in Hefling (ed.), *Our Selves, Our Souls and Bodies*, Boston: Cowley, pp. 157–74.

Helminiak, Daniel, 1994, *What the Bible Really Says About Homosexuality*, San Francisco: Alamo Square Press.

Helminiak, Daniel, 1997, 'Response: Ethics, Biblical and Denominational: A Response to Mark Smith', *Journal of the American Academy of Religion* 54 (4), pp. 855–9.

Henderson, T., 2003, '"What is to prevent me from being baptized?": reading beyond the readily apparent', *Chicago Theological Seminary Register* 93.3, pp. 14–22.

Hens-Piazza, G., 2003, *Nameless, Blameless, and Without Shame: Two Cannibal Mothers Before a King*, Collegeville: Liturgical Press.

Herman, Dianne, 1984, 'The rape culture', in Jo Freeman (ed.), *Women: A Feminist Perspective*, 3rd edn, Palo Alto: Mayfield, pp. 20–44.

Herntrich, Volkmar, 1932, *Ezechielprobleme*, Giessen: A. Töpelmann.

Hertz, Robert, 1960, *Death and the Right Hand*, trans. Rodney and Claudia Needham, Aberdeen: Cohen & West.

Hertzberg, H. W., 1964, *I and II Samuel: A Commentary*, trans. J. S. Bowden, Old Testament Library, London: SCM Press.

Herzfeld, M., 1996, *The Poetics of Manhood: Contest and Identity in a Cretan Mountain Village*, Princeton: Princeton University Press.

Heschel, A. J., 1962, *The Prophets*, vol. 1, New York: Harper & Row.

Heschel, Susannah, 1998, *Abraham Geiger and the Jewish Jesus*, Chicago: University of Chicago Press.

Heschel, Susannah, 2003, 'Orange on the Seder plate', in S. C. Anisfeld (ed.), *The Women's Passover Companion: Women's Reflections on the Festival of Freedom*, Woodstock: Jewish Lights, pp. 70–7.

Hiebert, P., 1989, '"Whence shall help come to me?": the biblical widow', in P. L. Day (ed.), *Gender and Difference in Ancient Israel*, Minneapolis: Fortress Press, pp. 125–41.

Hildebrand, Michael Dean, 1998, 'Structure and theology in the Holiness Code', Ph.D. dissertation, Berkeley: University of California.

Hillers, Delbert R., 1964, *Treaty-Curses and the Old Testament Prophets*, Rome: Pontifical Biblical Institute.

Hillers, Delbert R., 1992, *Lamentations: A New Translation with Introduction and Commentary*, Anchor Bible 7a, New York: Doubleday.

Hirsch, S. R., 1966, *The Psalms*, vol. 2, New York: Philip Feldheim.

Hoffner, Harry A., Jr., 1966, 'Symbols for masculinity and femininity: their uses in Ancient Near Eastern sympathetic magic rituals', *JBL* 85, pp. 326–34.

Hoffner, Harry A., Jr., 1997, *The Laws of the Hittites: A Critical Edition*, Documenta et

Monumenta Orientis Antiqui 23, Leiden: Brill.

Holladay, W. L., 1986, *Jeremiah 1*, Hermeneia, Philadelphia: Fortress Press.

Holladay, W. L., 1989, *Jeremiah 2*, Hermeneia, Minneapolis: Fortress Press.

Holladay, W. L., 1993, *The Psalms through Three Thousand Years: Prayerbook of a Cloud of Witness*, Minneapolis: Fortress Press.

Hölscher, Gustav, 1994, *Hesekiel, der dichter und das buch, eine literarkritische untersuchung*, Giessen: A. Töpelmann.

hooks, bell, 1992, *Black Looks: Race and Representation*, Boston: South End Press.

Horner, T., 1978, *Jonathan Loved David: Homosexuality in Biblical Times*, Philadelphia: Westminster Press.

Hornsby, Teresa J., 1999, '"Israel has become a worthless thing": re-reading Gomer in Hosea 1–3', *JSOT* 82, pp. 115–28.

Hossfeld, F.-L., and E. Zenger, 1993, *Die Psalmen I, Psalm 1–50*, Die Neue Echter Bibel, Würzberg: Echter.

House of Bishops, 2003, *Some Issues in Human Sexuality: A Guide to the Debate*, London: Church House Publishing.

House, Paul R., 1988, *Zephaniah: A Prophetic Drama*, Sheffield: Almond Press.

Huerta, Christian de la, 1999, *Coming Out Spiritually: The Next Step*, New York: Jeremy P. Tarcher/Putnam.

Hulse, E. V., 1975, 'The nature of biblical "leprosy" and the use of alternative medical terms in modern translations of the Bible', *PEQ* 107, pp. 87–105.

Ilan, Tal, 2000, 'The daughters of Zelophehad and women's inheritance: the biblical injunction and its outcome', in Athalya Brenner (ed.), *Exodus to Deuteronomy, Feminist Companion to the Bible*, Second Series 5, Sheffield: Sheffield Academic Press, pp. 176–86.

Irigaray, Luce, 1985a, *Speculum of the Other Women*, trans. Gillian C. Gill, Ithaca: Cornell University Press.

Irigaray, Luce, 1985b, 'The power of discourse and the subordination of the feminine', in Irigaray, *This Sex Which is Not One*, trans. Catherine Porter, Ithaca: Cornell University Press, pp. 68–85.

Irigaray, Luce, 2002, *To Speak is Never Neutral*, trans. Gail Schwab, New York: Routledge.

Irwin, W. A., 1943, *The Problem of Ezekiel*, Chicago: University of Chicago Press.

Jagose, Annamarie, 1996, *Queer Theology: An Introduction*, New York: New York University Press.

Jameson, Fredric, 1981, *The Political Unconscious: Narrative as a Socially Symbolic Act*, Ithaca, NY: Cornell University Press.

Jameson, Fredric, 1982, 'Progress versus Utopia, or, Can we imagine the future', *Science Fiction Studies* 9 (2), pp. 147–58.

Jameson, Fredric, 1988, 'Of islands and trenches: neutralization and the production of utopian discourse', in *The Ideologies of Theory, Essays 1971–1986*, vol. 2, Minneapolis: University of Minnesota Press, pp. 75–101.

Jantzen, Grace, 1992, 'Song of Moses, song of Miriam: who is seconding whom?', *CBQ* 54 (2), pp. 211–20.

Janzen, David, 2000, 'The "mission" of Ezra', *JBL* 119 (4), pp. 619–43.

Jastrow, Marcus, 1989, *A Dictionary of the Targumim, the Talmud Babli and Yerushalmi, and the Midrashic Literature*, New York: Judaica Press.

Jennings, Theodore W., 2001, 'YHWH as Erastes', in K. Stone (ed.), *Queer Commentary and the Hebrew Bible*, JSOTSS 334, Sheffield: Sheffield Academic Press, pp. 36–74.

Jennings, Theodore W., 2003, *The Man Jesus Loved*, Cleveland, Ohio: Pilgrim Press.

Jewett, R., 2000, 'The social context and implications of homoerotic references in Romans 1:24–27', in D. L Balch (ed.) *Homosexuality, Science, and the 'Plain Sense' of Scripture*, Grand Rapids: Eerdmans, pp. 223–41.

Jobling, David, 1998, *1 Samuel*, Berit Olam: Studies in Hebrew Narrative and Poetry, Collegeville, Minn.: Liturgical Press.

Jones, D. W., 2004, *Reforming the Morality of Usury: A Study of Differences that Separated the Protestant Reformers*, Lanham: University Press of America.

Jordan, Mark, 1997, *The Invention of Sodomy in Christian Theology*, Chicago and London: University of Chicago Press.

Jost, R., 1995, *Frauen, Männer und die Himmelskönigin: Exegetische Studien*, Gütersloh: Gütersloher Verlagshaus.

Joüon, Paul, 1947, *Grammaire de l'hébreu biblique*, Rome: Pontifical Biblical Institute.

Joyce, Paul M., 1993, 'Lamentations and the grief process: a psychological reading', *Biblical Interpretation* 1 (3), pp. 304–20.

Jull, Tom A., 1998 '*hrqm* in Judges 3: a scatological reading', *JSOT* 81, pp. 63–75.

Kader, Samuel, 1999, *Openly Gay Openly Christian: How the Bible Really is Gay Friendly*, San Francisco: Leyland.

Kaiser, B. B., 1987, 'Poet as "female impersonator": the image of daughter Zion as speaker in biblical poems of suffering', *JR* 67, pp. 164–82.

Kamionkowski, Tamar S., 2000, 'Gender ambiguity and subversive metaphor in Ezekiel 16', dissertation, Brandeis University.

Kamionkowski, Tamar S., 2003, *Gender Reversal and Cosmic Chaos: A Study on the Book of Ezekiel*, JSOTSS 368, Sheffield: Sheffield Academic Press.

Keefe, A., 1993, 'Rapes of women/wars of men', *Semeia* 61, pp. 79–97.

Keller, C., 2003, *Face of the Deep: A Theology of Becoming*, New York and London: Routledge.

Kelso, Julie, 2003, 'In search of the forgotten mother: engaging with Chronicles in an Irigarayan mode', unpublished Ph.D. thesis, University of Queensland.

Kikawada, Isaac M., 1972, 'Two notes on Eve', *JBL* 91, pp. 331–7.

Kilian, Rudolph, 1963, *Literarkritische und formgeschichtliche Untersuchung des Heiligkeitsgesetzes*, Bonn: Peter Hanstein.

Kinsey, Alfred C., Wardell B. Pomeroy and Clyde E. Martin, 1948, *Sexual Behaviour in the Human Male*, London and Philadelphia: W. B. Saunders.

Kinsey, Alfred C., Wardell B. Pomeroy and Clyde E. Martin, 1953, *Sexual Behaviour in the Human Female*, London and Philadelphia: W. B. Saunders.

Kirk-Duggan, Cheryl, 1994, 'Divine puppeteer: Yahweh of Exodus', in A. Brenner (ed.) *Exodus to Deuteronomy*, Feminist Companion to the Bible, Second Series 5, Sheffield: Sheffield Academic Press, pp. 75–103.

Klein, Lillian R., 1989, *The Triumph of Irony in the Book of Judges*, JSOTSS 68, Sheffield: Almond Press.

Klein, Lillian R. 1993, 'The book of Judges: paradigm and deviation in images of women', in Athalya Brenner (ed.), *A Feminist Companion to Judges*, Feminist Companion to the Bible 4, Sheffield: Sheffield Academic Press, pp. 55–71.

Kleinhans, Chuck, 1994, 'Taking out the trash: camp and the politics of parody', in Moe Moyer (ed.), *The Politics and Poetics of Camp*, London: Routledge, pp. 182–201.

Knobel, Peter S., 1987, 'The Targum of Qohelet', in Martin McNamara (ed.), *The Aramaic Bible*, vol. 15, Collegeville, Minn.: Liturgical Press.

Knohl, Israel, 1995, *The Sanctuary of Silence: The Priestly Torah and the Holiness School*, Minneapolis: Fortress Press.

Knoppers, G. N., 1997, 'The vanishing Solomon: the disappearance of the united monarchy from recent histories of ancient Israel', *JBL* 116 (1), pp. 19–44.

Koch, Timothy R., 2001a, 'Cruising as methodology: homoeroticism and the scriptures', in Ken Stone (ed.), *Queer Commentary and the Hebrew Bible*, JSOTSS 334, New York: Sheffield Academic Press, pp. 169–80.

Koch, Timothy R., 2001b 'Cruising as methodology: homoeroticism and the scriptures', *Theology and Sexuality* 14, pp. 10–22.

Kohn, Risa Levitt, 2002, *Ezekiel, the Exile, and the Torah*, Sheffield: Sheffield Academic Press.

Kolakowski, Victoria S. 1997, 'The concubine and the eunuch: queering up the breeder's Bible', in Robert E. Goss and Amy Adams Squire Strongheart (eds), *Our Families, Our Values: Snapshots of Queer Kinship*, New York: Harrington Park Press, pp. 35–49.

Kolakowski, Victoria S., 2000, 'Throwing a party: patriarchy, gender, and the death of Jezebel', in Robert E. Goss and Mona West (eds), *Take Back the Word: A Queer Reading of the Bible*, Cleveland, Ohio: Pilgrim Press, pp. 103–14.

Kramer, Phyllis Silverman, 2000, 'Rahab: from peshat to pedagogy, or: The many faces of a heroine', in George Aichele (ed.), *Culture, Entertainment and the Bible*, JSOTSS 309, Sheffield: Sheffield Academic Press, pp. 156–72

Kramer, Samuel Noah, 1959, 'Sumerian literature and the Bible', *An Bib* 12, pp. 185–204.

Kramer, Samuel Noah, 1969, *The Sacred Marriage Rite: Aspects of Faith, Myth, and Ritual in Ancient Sumer*, Bloomington: Indiana University Press.

Kraus, H.-J., 1968, *Klagelieder (Threni)*, BKAT 20, Neukirechen-Vluyn: Neukirchener Verlag.

Kraus, H.-J., 1986 [1979], *Theology of the Psalms*, trans. Keith Crim, Minneapolis: Augsburg Press.

Kraus, H.-J., 1988, *Psalms 1–59*, trans. Hilton C. Oswald, Continental Commentaries, Minneapolis: Augsburg Press.

Kraus, H.-J., 1989, *Psalms 60–150*, trans. Hilton C. Oswald, Continental Commentaries, Minneapolis: Augsburg Press.

Kuefler, M., 2001, *The Manly Eunuch: Masculinity, Gender Ambiguity, and Christian Ideology in Late Antiquity*, Chicago: University of Chicago Press.

Kugel, James L., 1998, *Traditions of the Bible*, Cambridge, Mass.: Harvard University Press.

Kunin, Seth, 1996, 'The Bridegroom of Blood: A Structural Analysis', in *JSOT* 70, pp. 3–16.

Kushner, Tony, 1993, *Angels in America, Part One: Millennium Approaches: A Gay Fantasia on National Themes*, New York: Theatre Communications Group.

Kvam, Kristen E., Linda S. Schearing and Valarine H. Ziegler (eds), 1999, *Eve and Adam: Jewish, Christian, and Muslim Readings on Genesis and Gender*, Bloomington: Indiana University Press.

Lachs, Samuel T., 1966, 'The date of Lamentations V', *Jewish Quarterly Review* 57, pp. 46–56.

Lamp, E.-T., 1989, 'Öffentlichkeit als Bedrohung – Ein Beitrag zur Deutung des "Feindes" im Klagepsalm des einzelnen', *BN* 50, pp. 46–57.

Lasine, S., 1991, 'Jehoram and the cannibal mothers (2 Kings 6.24–33): Solomon's judgment in an inverted world', *JSOT* 50, pp.27–53.

La Valley, Al, 1995, 'The great escape', in Corey K. Creekmur and Alexander Doty (eds), *Out in Culture: Gay, Lesbian, and Queer Essays in Popular Culture*, Series Q, Durham, N.C.: Duke University Press, pp. 60–70.

Leibowitz, Nehama, 1980, *Studies in BaMidbar/Numbers*, trans. Aryeh Newman, Jerusalem: World Zionist Organisation.

Lemche, Niels Peter, 1991, *The Canaanites and Their Land: The Tradition of the Canaanites*, JSOTSS 110, Sheffield: Sheffield Academic Press.

Lemke, W. E., 1984, 'Life in the present and hope for the future', *Interpretation* 38, pp. 165–80.

Lerner, Gerda, 1986, *The Creation of Patriarchy*, Women and History 1, Oxford and New York: Oxford University Press.

Leveen, Adriane B., 2002, 'Variations on a theme: differing conceptions of memory in the book of Numbers', *JSOT* 27 (2), pp. 201–21.

Levenson, Jon D., 1976, *Theology of the Program of Restoration in Ezekiel 40-48*, Harvard Semitic Monographs 10, Missoula: Scholars Press.

Levenson, Jon D., 1978, 'I Samuel as literature and history', *CBQ* 40, pp. 11–28.

Levenson, Jon D., 1988, *Creation and the Persistence of Evil: The Jewish Drama of Divine Omnipotence*, San Francisco: Harper & Row.

Levenson, Jon D., and Baruch Halpern, 1980, 'The political import of David's marriages', *JBL* 99, pp. 507–18.

Levine, Baruch A., 1989, *Leviticus*, Philadelphia: Jewish Publication Society.

Levine, Baruch A., 1993, *Numbers 1–20*, Anchor Bible 4, New York: Doubleday.

Levine, Sarra, 2000, 'Naso: inscribing jealousy on the bodies of women', in Elyse Goldstein (ed.), *The Women's Torah Commentary*, Woodstock: Jewish Lights, pp. 261–9.

Lévi-Strauss, Claude, 1969, *The Elementary Structures of Kinship*, Boston: Beacon Press.

L'Hour, Jean, 1964, 'Les interdits To'eba dans le Deutéronome', *RB* 71, pp. 481–503.

Lieber, David, 2001, *Etz Hayim: Torah and Commentary*, Philadelphia: Jewish Publications Society and the Rabbinical Assembly.

Linafelt, Tod, 2000, 'Zion's cause: the presentation of pain in the book of Lamentations' in Tod Linafelt (ed.), *Strange Fire: Reading the Bible after the Holocaust*, New York; New York University Press, pp. 267–79.

Lindars, Barnabas, 1995, *Judges 1–5: A New Translation and Commentary*, Edinburgh: T&T Clark.

Linville, James, 1997, 'Rethinking the "Exilic" book of Kings', *JSOT* 75, pp. 21–42.

Linzey, A., 1993, *Animal Theology*, Urbana: University of Illinois Press; paperback edn 1995.

Linzey, A., 1998, *Animal Gospel*, Louisville: Westminster John Knox Press.

Livingston, Jennie, 1990, *Paris is Burning*, Miramax Films.

Long, B., 1984, *1 Kings with an Introduction to Historical Literature*, Grand Rapids: Eerdmans.

Long, B., 1991, *2 Kings*, Grand Rapids: Eerdmans.

Long, R. E., 2004, *Men, Homosexuality, and the Gods: An Exploration into the Religious Significance of Male Homosexuality in World Perspective*, Binghamton: Haworth Press.

Long, R. E., 2005, 'Of argument and aesthetic distaste: a response to J. Budziszewski', *Philosophia Christi* 2 (1), pp. 53–8.

Lott, Sonia, 1998, 'The menstruation cycle and disorders of menstruation', in *Obstetrics and Gynaecology* 7, pp. 69–79.

Lundbom, Jack R., 2004, *Jeremiah 37–52*, Anchor Bible 21c, New York: Doubleday.

Lust, J., 1986, *Ezekiel and His Book: Textual and Literary Criticism and their Interrelation*, Leuven: Leuven University Press.

Lynch, Bernard, 1996, 'Religious and spiritual conflicts', in Dominic Davies and Charles Neal (eds), *Pink Therapy: A Guide for Counsellors and Therapists Working with Lesbian, Gay and Bisexual Clients*, Buckingham and Philadelphia: Open University Press, pp. 199–208.

MacDonald, Diane L., 1995, *Transgressive Corporeality: The Body, Poststructuralism, and the Theological Imagination*, Albany: State University of New York Press.

Macht, David I., 1933, 'A Scientific Appreciation of Leviticus 12.1–5', *JBL* 52, pp. 253–60.

Maddison, S., 2000, *Fags, Hags and Queer Sisters: Gender Dissent and Heterosocial Bonds in Gay Culture*, New York: St Martin's Press.

Mader, D., 1980, 'The *Entimos Pais* of Matthew 8:5–13 and Luke 7:1–19', in W. R. Dynes and S. Donaldson (eds), *Homosexuality and Religion and Philosophy*, New York: Garland, pp. 223–35.

Magdalene, F. Rachel, 1995, 'Ancient Near Eastern treaty-curses and the ultimate texts of terror: a study of the language of divine sexual abuse in the prophetic corpus', in Athalya Brenner (ed.), *The Feminist Companion to the Latter Prophets*, Feminist Companion to the Bible 8, Sheffield: Sheffield Academic Press, pp. 326–53.

Magonet, Jonathon, 1994, *A Rabbi Reads the Psalms*, London: SCM Press.

Magonet, Jonathon, 1996, '"But if it is a girl she is unclean for twice seven days . . .": the riddle of Leviticus 12', in John F. A. Sawyer (ed.), *Reading Leviticus: A Conversation with Mary Douglas*, Sheffield: Sheffield Academic Press, pp. 144–52.

Maitland, Sara, 1983, 'Of Deborah and Jael', in *Telling Tales*, London: Journeyman Press, pp. 1–4.

Mandolfo, C., 2000, *God in the Dock: Dialogic Tension in the Psalms of Lament*, JSOTSS 357, Sheffield: Sheffield Academic Press.

Marks, Herbert, 1987, 'The Twelve Prophets', in Robert Alter and Frank Kermode (eds), *The Literary Guide to the Bible*, Cambridge, Mass.: Belknap Press of Harvard University Press, pp. 207–33.

Marsman, H. J., 2003, *Women in Ugarit and Israel: Their Social and Religious Position in the Context of the Ancient Near East*, Leiden and Boston: Brill.

Martin, D. B., 1995, *The Corinthian Body*, New Haven: Yale University Press.

Martin, D. B., 1996, '*Arsenokoites* and *Malakos*: meanings and consequences', in R. L. Brawley (ed.), *Biblical Ethics and Homosexuality: Listening to Scripture*, Louisville: Westminster John Knox Press, pp. 117–36.

Martin-Achard, R., and S. P. Re'emi, 1984, *God's People in Crisis: A Commentary on the Book of Amos; A Commentary on the Book of Lamentations*, International Theological Commentary, Grand Rapids: Eerdmans.

Mauss, M., 1967, *The Gift: Forms and Functions of Exchange in Archaic Societies*, New York: W.W. Norton.

Mayes, A. D. H., 1979, *The New Century Bible: Deuteronomy*, Grand Rapids: Eerdmans/London: Marshall, Morgan & Scott.

McCann, J.C., Jr (ed.), 1993, *The Shape and Shaping of the Psalter*, JSOTSS 159, Sheffield: Sheffield Academic Press.

McCarter, P. K., 1980, *I Samuel: A New Translation with Introduction, Notes and Commentary*, Anchor Bible Commentary 8, New York and London: Doubleday.

McCarter, P. K., 1984, *II Samuel: A New Translation with Introduction, Notes and Commentary*, Anchor Bible Commentary 9, New York and London: Doubleday.

McConville, J. G., 1983, 'Priests and Levites in Ezekiel: a crux in the interpretation of Israel's history', *TynBull* 34, pp. 3–31.

McDaniel, T. F., 1968, 'The alleged sumerian influence upon Lamentations', *VT* 18, pp. 198–209.

McFague, S., 1982, *Metaphorical Theology: Models of God in Religious Language*, Philadelphia: Fortress Press.

McFarlane, Linda, 1998, *Diagnosis: Homophobic. The Experiences of Lesbian and Gay Men and Bisexuals in Mental Health Services*, London: Project for Advice, Counselling and Education.

McKay, J. W., 1979, 'Psalms of vigil', *ZAW* 91, pp. 236–7.

McKenzie, John L., 1966, *The World of the Judges*, Englewood Cliffs: Prentice Hall.

McNeill, John J., 1976, *The Church and the Homosexual*, Kansas: Sheed Andrews & McMeel.

Mein, Andrew, 2002, *Ezekiel and the Ethics of Exile*, London: Oxford University Press.

Mendenhall, George E., 1954, 'Covenant forms in Israelite tradition', *BA* 17 (3), pp. 50–76.

Mendenhall, George E., 1962, 'The Hebrew conquest of Palestine', *BA* 25, pp. 66–87.

Mettinger, T. N. D., 1982, *The Dethronement of Sabaoth: Studies in the Shem and Kabod Theologies*, CBOT 18, Lund: C. W. K. Gleerup.

Meyer, Moe, 1994, 'Introduction: reclaiming the discourse of camp', in Moe Meyer (ed.), *The Politics and Poetics of Camp*, London: Routledge, pp. 1–22.

Meyers, Carol, 1983, 'Procreation, production, and protection: male–female balance in early Israel', *JAAR* 51, pp. 569–93.

Meyers, Carol, 1991, 'Of drums and damsels: women's performance in ancient Israel', *BA* 54, pp. 16–27.

Meyers, Carol, 1994a, 'Miriam the musician', in Athalya Brenner (ed.), *Exodus to Deuteronomy*, Feminist Companion to the Bible, Second Series 5, Sheffield: Sheffield Academic Press, pp. 207–30.

Meyers, Carol, 1994b, 'Hannah and her sacrifice: reclaiming women's agency', in Athalya Brenner (ed.), *A Feminist Companion to Samuel and Kings*, Feminist Companion to the Bible 5, Sheffield: Sheffield Academic Press, pp. 93–104.

Meyers, Carol, 1999, '"Women of the neighborhood" (Ruth 4.17): Informal female networks in ancient Israel', in Athalya Brenner (ed.), *Ruth and Esther*, Feminist Companion to the Bible, Second Series 3, Sheffield: Sheffield Academic Press, pp. 110–27.

Meyers, Carol, 2000, 'Female sorcerer (Exod 22:18; Isa 57:3)', in C. Meyers, T. Craven and R. S. Kraemer (eds), *Women in Scripture: A Dictionary of the Named and Unnamed Women in the Hebrew Bible, the Apocryphal/Deuterocanonical Books, and the New Testament*, Boston and New York: Houghton Mifflin, p. 197.

Michasiw, Kim, 1994, 'Camp, masculinity, masquerade', *Differences: A Journal of Feminist Cultural Studies* 6, pp. 146–73.

Milgrom, Jacob, 1970, *Studies in Levitical Terminology, I: The Encroacher and the Levite; the Term Aboda*, Near Eastern Studies 14, Berkeley: University of California Press.

Milgrom, Jacob, 1976, 'Israel's sanctuary: the priestly picture of Dorian Gray', *BR* 83, pp. 390–9.

Milgrom, Jacob, 1990, *The JPS Torah Commentary*, Philadelphia: Jewish Publication Society.

Milgrom, Jacob, 1991, *Leviticus 1–16*, Anchor Bible 3, New York: Doubleday.

Milgrom, Jacob, 1992, 'Book of Numbers', in David Noel Freeman (ed.), *The Anchor Bible Dictionary*, vol. 4, New York: Doubleday, pp. 1146–55.

Milgrom, Jacob, 1993, 'Does the Bible prohibit homosexuality', *BR* 9 (6), pp. 11.

Milgrom, Jacob, 1994, 'How not to read the Bible', *BR* 10 (2), pp. 14, 48.

Milgrom, Jacob, 2000, *Leviticus 17–22*, Anchor Bible 3a, New York: Doubleday.

Milgrom, Jacob, 2001, *Leviticus 23–27*, Anchor Bible 3b, New York: Doubleday.

Millard, M., 1994, *Die Komposition des Psalters: Ein formgeschichtlicher Ansatz*, Forschungen zum alten Testament 9, Tübingen: Mohr-Siebert.

Miller, Alice, 1991, 'The miscreated child in the lamentations of Jeremiah', in Alice Miller (ed.), *Breaking Down the Wall of Silence to Join the Waiting Child*, London: Virago, pp. 114–26.

Miller, D. A., 1989, 'Sontag's urbanity', *October* 49, pp. 91–101.

Miller, J. E., 1997, 'A response: pederasty and Romans 1:27: A response to Mark Smith', *JAAR* 65 (4), pp. 861–6.

Miller, John Wolf, 1955, *Das Verhältnis Jeremias und Hesekiels sprachlich und theologisch Untersucht, mit besonderer Berücksichtigung der Prosareden Jeremias*, Assen: Van Gorcum.

Miller, Patrick D., 1986, *Interpreting the Psalms*, Philadelphia: Fortress Press.

Miller, Patrick D., 1990, *Deuteronomy: Interpretation: A Bible Commentary for Teaching and Preaching*, Louisville: John Knox Press.

Mintz, Alan, 1982, 'The rhetoric of Lamentations and the representation of catastrophe', *Prooftexts* 2, pp. 1–17.

Mitchell, S., 1993, *A Book of Psalms: Selected and Adapted from the Hebrew*, New York: HarperCollins.

Mitulski, Jim, 2000, 'Ezekiel understand AIDS: AIDS understand Ezekiel, or reading the Bible with HIV', in Robert E. Goss and Mona West (eds), *Take Back the Word: A Queer Reading of the Bible*, Cleveland, Ohio: Pilgrim Press, pp. 153–60.

Mollenkott, Virginia Ramey, 2000, 'Reading the Bible from low and outside: lesbitransgay People as God's tricksters', in Robert E. Goss and Mona West (eds), *Take Back the Word: A Queer Reading of the Bible*, Cleveland, Ohio: Pilgrim Press, pp. 13–22.

Mollenkott, Virginia Ramey, 2001, *Omnigender: A trans-Religious Approach*, Cleveland, Ohio: Pilgrim Press.

Moon, Michael, 1989, 'Flaming closets', *October* 51, pp. 19–54.

Moore, G., 2003, *A Question of Truth: Christianity and Homosexuality*, New York: Continuum.

Moore, George Foot, 1895, *A Critical and Exegetical Commentary on Judges*, International Critical Commentary, Edinburgh: T&T Clark.

Moore, Michael S., 1983, 'Human suffering in Lamentations', *Revue Biblique* 90, pp. 534–55.

Moore, Stephen D., 2001, *God's Beauty Parlor and Other Queer Spaces in and Around the Bible*, Stanford: Stanford University Press.

Morgenstern, Julian, 1956, 'Jerusalem – 485 B.C.', *HUCA* 27, pp. 101–179.

Morgenstern, Julian, 1957, 'Jerusalem – 485 B.C.', *HUCA* 28, pp. 15–47.

Morgenstern, Julian, 1963, 'The bloody husband', *Hebrew Union College Annual* 34, pp. 35–70.

Morgenstern, Julian, 1966, 'Jerusalem – 485 B.C.', *HUCA* 31, pp. 1–29.

Morrow, Deana F., 2003, 'Cast into the wilderness: the impact of institutionalized religion on lesbians', *Journal of Lesbian Studies* 7, pp. 109–23.

Mowinckel, Sigmund, 1914, *Zur Komposition des Buches Jeremia*, Kristiana: Dybwad.

Mowinckel, Sigmund, 1962, *The Psalms in Israel's Worship*, vol. 1, Nashville: Abingdon Press.

Moxnes, H., 2003, *Putting Jesus in His Place: A Radical Vision of Household and Kingdom*, Louisville: Westminster John Knox Press.

Moyer, Moe, 1994, 'Introduction: reclaiming the discourse of camp', in Moe Moyer (ed.), *The Politics and Poetics of Camp*, London: Routledge, pp. 1–22.

Mullen, E. T., 1993, *Narrative History and Ethnic Boundaries*, Atlanta: Scholars Press.

Müllner, Ilse, 1999, 'Lethal differences: sexual violence as violence against others in Judges 19', in Athalya Brenner (ed.), *Judges*, Feminist Companion to the Bible, Second Series 4, Sheffield: Sheffield Academic Press, pp. 126–42.

Nelson, Richard D., 1997, *Joshua: A Commentary*, Louisville: Westminster John Knox Press.

Newsom, Carol A., 1984, 'A maker of metaphors – Ezekiel's oracles against Tyre', *Interpretation* 38, pp. 151–64.

Newsom, Carol A., 1989, 'Woman and the discourse of patriarchal wisdom: a study of Proverbs 1–9, in Peggy L. Day (ed.), *Gender and Difference in Ancient Israel*, New York: Fortress Press, pp. 143–60.

Newsom, Carol A., 1996, 'The book of Job', in L. Keck *et al.* (eds), *The New Interpreter's Bible*, vol. 4, Nashville: Abingdon Press, pp. 617–37.

Newsom, Carol A., 1998, 'Job', in C. A. Newsom and S. H. Ringe (eds), *Women's Bible Commentary: Expanded Edition with Apocrypha*, Louisville: Westminster John Knox Press, pp. 130–6.

Newsom, Carol A., 2003, *The Book of Job: A Contest of Moral Imaginations*, Oxford and New York: Oxford University Press.

Niditch, Susan, 1986, 'Ezekiel 40–48 in a visionary context', *CBQ* 48, pp. 208–24.

Niditch, Susan, 1989, 'Eroticism and death in the tale of Jael', in Peggy Day (ed.), *Gender and Difference in Ancient Israel*, Philadelphia: Fortress Press, pp. 43–57.

Niditch, Susan, 1992, 'Genesis', in C. A. Newsom and S. H. Ringe (eds), *Women's Bible Commentary*, Louisville: Westminster John Knox Press, pp. 13–29.

Niditch, Susan, 1993, *War in the Hebrew Bible: A Study in the Ethics of Violence*, New York and Oxford: Oxford University Press.

Nissinen, Marti, 1998, *Homoeroticism in the Biblical World: A Historical Perspective*, trans. Kirsi Stjerna, Minneapolis: Fortress Press.

Noth, Martin, 1960, *The History of Israel*, 2nd edn, trans. P. R. Ackroyd, New York: Harper & Row.

Noth, Martin, 1962, *Exodus: A Commentary*, trans. J. S. Bowden, Philadelphia: Westminster Press.

Noth, Martin, 1991 [1957], *The Deuteronomistic History*, trans. Jane Doull *et al.*, 2nd edn, Sheffield: Sheffield Academic Press.

Nugent, Robert, 1997, 'Homophobia and the U.S. Roman Catholic clergy', in James T. Sears and Walter L. Williams (eds), *Overcoming Heterosexism and Homophobia: Strategies that Work*, New York: Columbia University Press, pp. 345–70.

O'Connell, Robert H., 1996, *The Rhetoric of the Book of Judges*, VTSup 63, Leiden: Brill.

O'Connor, Kathleen M., 1992, 'Jeremiah', in C. A. Newsom and S. H. Ringe (eds), *Women's Bible Commentary*, Louisville: Westminster John Knox Press, pp. 169–77.

O'Donovan, Oliver, 1982, *Transsexualism and Christian Marriage*, Cambridge: Grove Books.

Ollenburger, B. C., 1987, *Zion: The City of the Great King*, JSOTSS 41, Sheffield: Sheffield Academic Press.

Olson, Dennis T., 1997, 'Negotiating boundaries: the old and new generations and the theology of numbers', *Interpretation*, 51 (3), pp. 229–40.

Olyan, Saul M., 1988, *Asherah and the Cult of Yahweh in Israel*, Atlanta: Scholars Press.

Olyan, Saul M.. 1994, '"And with a male you shall not lie the lying down of a woman": on the meaning and significance of Leviticus 18:22 and 20:13', *Journal of the History of Sexuality* 5, pp. 179–206. Reprinted in G. D. Comstock and S. Henking (eds), *Que(e)rying Religion: A Critical Anthology*, New York: Continuum, 1997, pp. 398–414.

Ortner, S. B., and H. Whitehead, 1981, 'Introduction: accounting for sexual meanings', in S. B. Ortner and H. Whitehead (eds), *Sexual Meanings: The Cultural Construction of Gender and Sexuality*, Cambridge and New York: Cambridge University Press, pp. 1–27.

Ostriker, Alicia Suskin, 1994, *The Nakedness of the Fathers: Biblical Visions and Revisions*, New Brunswick: Rutgers University Press.

Ostriker, Alicia Suskin, 2000, 'A holy of holies: The Song of Songs as countertext', in Athalya Brenner and Carole R. Fontaine (eds), *The Song of Songs*, Feminist Companion to the Bible, Second Series 6, Sheffield: Sheffield Academic Press, pp. 36–54.

Oswalt, J. N., 1986, *The Book of Isaiah, Chapters 1–39*, New International Commentary on the Old Testament, Grand Rapids: Eerdmans.

Oswalt, J. N., 1998, *The Book of Isaiah, Chapters 40–66*, New International Commentary on the Old Testament, Grand Rapids: Eerdmans.

Owen, Wilfred, 1999, *War Poems and Manuscripts of Wilfred Owen*, http://www.hcu.ox.ac.uk/jtap/warpoems.htm

Pakkala, Juha, 2004, *Ezra the Scribe: The Development of Ezra 7–10 and Nehemiah 8*, New York: Walter de Gruyter.

Pardes, Ilana, 1992, *Countertraditions in the Bible: A Feminist Approach*, Cambridge, Mass., and London: Harvard University Press.

Patai, Raphael, 1978, *The Hebrew Goddess*, New York: Avon Books; first published by Discus.

Patrick, Dale, 1985, *Old Testament Law*, Atlanta: John Knox Press.

Patte, Daniel, 2002, 'Can one be critical without being autobiographical? The case of Romans 1:26–27', in Ingrid Rosa Kitzberger (ed.), *Autobiographical Biblical Criticism: Between Text and Self*, Leiden: Deo, pp. 34–59.

Pattison, S., 2000, *Shame: Theory, Therapy, Theology*, Cambridge: Cambridge University Press.

Pellegrini, Ann, 1996, *Performance Anxieties*, New York: Routledge.

Person, Hara E., 2000, 'Masa'ei: boundaries and limit', in Elyse Goldstein (ed.), *The Women's Torah Commentary*, Woodstock: Jewish Lights, pp. 321–7.

Pham, Xuan Huong Thi, 1996, 'Lamentations 1 and 2, Isa 51:9—52:2, and Their Mourning Ceremony Setting', dissertation, the Catholic University of America.

Phelan, Peggy, 1993, *Unmarked: The Politics of Performance*, New York: Routledge.

Pippin, Tina, 1994, 'Jezebel re-vamped' in Athalya Brenner (ed.), *A Feminist Companion to Samuel and Kings*, Feminist Companion to the Bible 5, Sheffield: Sheffield Academic Press, pp. 196–206.

Pitzele, Peter, 1996, 'Korah's riddle', *Learn Torah With . . . 2.38* (22 June).

Polish, D. F., 2000, *Bringing the Psalms to Life: How to Understand and Use the Book of Psalms*, Woodstock: Jewish Lights.

Polzin, Robert, 1980, *Moses and the Deuteronomist: A Literary Study of the Deuteronomic History. Part One: Deuteronomy, Joshua, Judges*, Indiana Studies in Biblical Literature, Bloomington and Indianapolis: Indiana University Press.

Pope, M. H., 1973, *Job*, Anchor Bible 15, Garden City, NY: Doubleday.

Pope, M. H., 1977, *Song of Songs: A New Translation with Introduction and Commentary*, Anchor Bible 7c, New York and London: Doubleday.

Prior, Michael, 1997, *The Bible and Colonialism: A Moral Critique*, Biblical Seminar 48, Sheffield: Sheffield Academic Press.

Provan, Iain, 1990, 'Reading texts against a historical background', *SJOT* 1, pp. 130–43.

Pywell, Geoff, 1994, *Staging Real Events: The Performance of Everyday Events*, Lewisburg: Bucknell University Press.

Rahner, Karl, 1999, 'The hiddenness of God', *Theological Investigations*, vol. 16, New York: Crossroad.

Raitt, Thomas, 1977, *A Theology of Exile: Judgment and Deliverance in Jeremiah and Ezekiel*, Philadelphia: Fortress Press.

Rashkow, Ilona, 2000, 'Oedipus wrecks: Moses and God's rod', in Athalya Brenner (ed.), *Exodus to Deuteronomy*, Feminist Companion to the Bible, Second Series 5, Sheffield: Sheffield Academic Press, pp. 59–74.

Rattray, Susan, 1987, 'Marriage rules, kinship terms and family structure in the Bible', in Kent Harold Richards (ed.), *SBL Seminar Papers*, Atlanta: Scholars Press, pp. 537–43.

Raymond, Janice, 1979, *The Transsexual Empire: The Making of the She-Male*, Boston: Beacon Press.

Redditt, Paul L., 2001, 'Recent research on the Book of the Twelve as one book', *Currents in Biblical Research* 9, pp. 47–80.

Redditt, Paul, and Aaron Schart, 2003, *Thematic Threads in the Book of the Twelve*, BZAW 325, Berlin: Walter de Gruyter.

Redford, Donald B., 1992, *Egypt, Canaan, and Israel in Ancient Times*, Princeton: Princeton University Press.

Reid, Stephen, 1986, 'The book of Exodus: a laboratory for hermeneutics', in M. L. Branson and C. Rene Padilla (eds), *Conflict and Context: Hermeneutics in the Americas*, Grand Rapids, Eerdmans, pp. 155–64.

Reineke, Martha J., 1997, *Sacrificed Lives: Kristeva on Women and Violence*, Bloomington: Indiana University Press.

Reis, Pamela T., 1991, 'The bridegroom of blood: a new reading', *Judaism* 40, pp. 324–31.

Rendsburg, G. A., 1990, *Linguistic Evidence for the Northern Origin of Selected Psalms*, SBLMS, 43, Atlanta: Scholars Press.

Rentorff, Rolf, 1996, 'Is it possible to read Leviticus as a separate book?', in John F. A. Sawyer (ed.), *Reading Leviticus: A Conversation with Mary Douglas*, JSOTSS 227, Sheffield: Sheffield Academic Press, pp. 22–35.

Reventlow, Henning Graf, 1961, *Das Heiligkeitsgesetz: Formgeschichtlich Untersucht*, Neukirchen: Neukirchener Verlag.

Rich, Adrienne, 1987, 'Compulsory heterosexuality and lesbian existence', in Rich, *Blood, Bread and Poetry: Selected Prose 1979–1985*, London: Virago, pp. 23–75.

Rienstra, M. V., 1992, *Swallow's Nest: A Feminine Reading of the Psalms*, Grand Rapids: Eerdmans.

Ringrose, Kathryn M., 2003, *The Perfect Servant: Eunuchs and the Social Construction of Gender in Byzantium*, Chicago: University of Chicago Press.

Rivers, Ian, 2000, 'Homophobia and young people', in LGCM *Christian Homophobia: The Churches' Persecution of Gay and Lesbian People*, London: LGCM, pp. 17–19.

Robertson, Pamela, 1996, *Guilty Pleasures: Feminist Camp from Mae West to Madonna*,

Durham, N.C.: Duke University Press.

Roehrs, W. R., 1958, 'The dumb prophet', *Concordia Theological Monthly* 29, pp. 176–86.

Rofé, A., 1988, 'The vineyard of Naboth: the origin and message of the story', *VT* 38 (1), pp. 89–104.

Rogerson, John, 2003, 'Deuteronomy', in James D. G. Dunn and John W. Rogerson (eds), *Eerdmans Commentary on the Bible*, Grand Rapids: Eerdmans, pp. 153–73.

Roscoe, Will, 1997, 'Precursors of Islamic male homosexualities', in Stephen O. Murray and Will Roscoe (eds), *Islamic Homosexualities: Culture, History, and Literature*, New York: New York University Press.

Rose, Rabbi Dawn Robinson, 2000, 'Insider out: unmasking the abusing God', in Robert E. Goss and Mona West (eds), *Take Back the Word: A Queer Reading of the Bible*, Cleveland, Ohio: Pilgrim Press, pp. 143–52.

Rowlett, Lori L., 1992, 'Inclusion, exclusion and marginality in the book of Joshua' *JSOT* 55, pp. 15–23.

Rowlett, Lori L., 1996, *Joshua and the Rhetoric: A New Historicist Analysis*, JSOTSS 226, Sheffield: Sheffield Academic Press.

Rowlett, Lori L., 2000, 'Disney's Pocahontas and Joshua's Rahab in postcolonial perspective', in George Aichele (ed.), *Culture, Entertainment and the Bible*, JSOTSS 309, Sheffield: Sheffield Academic Press, pp. 66–75.

Rowley, H. H., 1953, 'The book of Ezekiel in modern study', *BJRL* 36, pp. 146–90.

Rubin, G., 1974, 'The traffic in women: notes on the political economy of sex', in R. Reiter (ed.), *Toward an Anthropology of Women*, New York and London: Monthly Review Press, pp. 157–210.

Rudolph, Wilhelm, 1962, *Das Buch Ruth, Das Hohe Leid. Die Klagelieder*, KAT, Gütersloh: Gerd Mohn.

Rudolph, Wilhelm, 1968, *Jeremia*, HAT 1 (12), Tübingen: Mohr.

Runions, Erin, 2001, *Changing Subjects: Gender, Nation and future in Micah*, London: Sheffield Academic Press.

Sakenfeld, Katharine Doob, 1992, 'Numbers', in C. A. Newsom and S. H. Ringe (eds), *The Women's Bible Commentary*, Louisville, Ky.: Westminster John Knox Press, pp. 45–51.

Sakenfeld, Katharine Doob, 1995, *Journeying with God: A Commentary on the Book of Numbers*, International Theological Commentary, Grand Rapids: Eerdmans.

Sanders, J. A., 1967, *The Dead Sea Psalms Scroll*, Ithaca: Cornell University Press.

Sarna, N. M., 1993, *On the Book of Psalms: Exploring the Prayers of Ancient Israel*, New York: Schocken.

Sawyer, Deborah F., 2002, *God, Gender and the Bible*, Biblical Limits Series, London and New York: Routledge.

Sawyer, John F. A., 1987, *Prophecy and the Prophets of the Old Testament*, Oxford, New York and Toronto: Oxford University Press.

Scarf, Mimi, 1983, 'Marriages made in heaven? Battered Jewish wives', in Susannah Heschel (ed.), *On Being a Jewish Feminist: A Reader*, New York: Schocken, pp. 51–64.

Schmitt, Arno, and Jehoeda Sofer (eds), 1992, *Sexuality and Eroticism among Males in Muslim Societies*, trans. Peter op't Veld, Haworth Gay and Lesbian Studies, New York: Harrington Park Press.

Schneider, Laurel C., 2001, 'Yahwist desires: imagining divinity queerly', in Ken Stone (ed.), *Queer Commentary and the Hebrew Bible*, JSOTSS 334, London and New

York: Sheffield Academic Press, pp. 210–27.

Schneider, Tammi J., 2000, *Judges*, Berit Olam Studies in Hebrew Narrative and Poetry, Collegeville, Minn.: Liturgical Press.

Scholz, Susanna, 1998, 'Through whose eyes: a "right" reading of Genesis 34', in Athalya Brenner (ed.), *Genesis*, Feminist Companion to the Bible, Second Series 1, Sheffield: Sheffield Academic Press, pp. 150–71.

Schottroff, Luise, 1994, 'The sayings source Q', in Elizabeth Schüssler Fiorenza (ed.), *Searching the Scriptures*, vol. 2: *A Feminist Commentary*, New York: Crossroad, pp. 510–34.

Schroer, S., and T. Staubli, 2000, 'Saul, David and Jonathan: the story of a triangle? A contribution to the issue of homosexuality in the First Testament', in Athalya Brenner (ed.), *Samuel and Kings*, Feminist Companion to the Bible, Second Series 7, Sheffield: Sheffield Academic Press, pp. 22–36.

Schulman, Sarah, 1991, *People in Trouble*, New York: Penguin.

Schüngel-Straumann, Helen, 1995, 'God as mother in Hosea 11', in Athalya Brenner (ed.), *A Feminist Companion to the Latter Prophets*, Feminist Companion to the Bible 8, Sheffield: Sheffield Academic Press, pp. 194–218.

Schwartz, R. M., 1997, *The Curse of Cain: The Violent Legacy of Monotheism*, Chicago and London: University of Chicago Press.

Scott, R. B. Y., 1965, *Proverbs. Ecclesiastes*, Anchor Bible Commentary, Garden City, NY: Doubleday.

Scroggs, Robin, 1983, *The New Testament and Homosexuality: Contextual Background for Contemporary Debate*, Philadelphia: Fortress Press.

Sedgwick, Eve Kosofsky, 1985, *Between Men: English Literature and Male Homosocial Desire*, New York: Columbia University Press.

Sedgwick, Eve Kosofsky, 1990, *Epistemology of the Closet*, Berkeley: University of California Press.

Sedgwick, Eve Kosofsky, 1993, *Tendencies*, Durham, N.C.: Duke University Press.

Sedgwick, Eve Kosofsky, 1994, *The Epistemology of the Closet*, London: Penguin.

Segovia, F. F., and M. A. Tolbert (eds), 1995, *Reading from this Place*, vol. 1: *Social Location and Biblical Interpretation in the United States*, Minneapolis: Fortress Press.

Seidman, Naomi, 1994, 'Burning the book of Lamentations', in C. Büchmann and C. Spiegel (eds), *Out of the Garden: Women Writers on the Bible*, London: Pandora, pp. 278–88.

Seidman, Steven,1996, 'Introduction', in Steven Seidman (ed.), *Queer Theology/ Sociology*, Cambridge and Oxford: Blackwell, pp. 1–29.

Seitz, C. R., 2001, 'The book of Isaiah 40–66' in D. L. Peterson (ed.), *The New Interpreter's Bible*, vol. 6, Nashville: Abingdon Press, pp. 307–552.

Seow, Choon-Leong, 1995, 'Qohelet's autobiography', in A. Beck *et al.* (eds), *Fortunate the Eyes that See*, Grand Rapids: Eerdmans, pp. 257–82.

Seow, Choon-Leong, 1997, *Ecclesiastes*, Anchor Bible Commentary, New York: Doubleday.

Setel, D. T., 1985, 'Prophets and pornography: female sexuality imagery in Hosea', in L. M. Russell (ed.), *Feminist Interpretation of the Bible*, Oxford: Basil Blackwell, pp. 86–95.

Shankman, Ray, 1991, 'The cut that unties: word as covenant in Exodus 4:24–26', *Cross Currents* 41 (2), pp. 168–78.

Sheinkin, David, 1986, *Path of the Kabbalah*, ed. Edward Hoffman, St Paul: Paragon House.

Sheppard, G. T., 1991, '"Enemies" and the politics of prayer in the book of Psalms', in David Jobling, P. L. Day and G. T. Sheppard (eds), *The Bible and the Politics of Exegesis: Essays in Honor of Norman K. Gottwald on His Sixty-Fifth Birthday*, Cleveland, Ohio: Pilgrim Press, pp. 61–82.

Sherlock, C., 1983, 'Ezekiel's dumbness', *ExpTim* 94, pp. 296–8.

Sherman, N., 2005, *Stoic Warriors: The Ancient Philosophy Behind the Military Mind*, New York: Oxford University Press.

Sherwood, Yvonne, 1996, *The Prostitution and the Prophet: Hosea's Marriage in Literary-Theological Perspective*, JSOTSS 212, Sheffield: Sheffield Academic Press.

Sherwood, Yvonne, 2000, *A Biblical Text and Its Afterlives: The Survival of Jonah in Western Culture*, Cambridge and New York: Cambridge University Press.

Shields, Mary, 2000, 'Subverting a man of God, elevating a woman: role and power reversal in 2 Kings 4', in Athalya Brenner (ed.), *Samuel and Kings*, Feminist Companion to the Bible, Second Series 7, Sheffield: Sheffield Academic Press, pp. 115–24.

Shields, Mary, 2001, 'An abusive God? Identity and power/gender and violence in Ezek. 23', in A. K. M. Adam (ed.), *Postmodern Interpretations of the Bible*, St Louis: Chalice Press, pp. 129–51.

Siebert-Hommes, Jopie, 2002, 'The symbolic function of clothing in the book of Esther', *European Electronic Journal for Feminist Exegesis*, www.lectio.unibe.ch/02_1/siebert.htm

Siler-Khodr, Theresa M., 1992, 'Endocrine and paracrine function of the human placenta', in Richard A. Polin and William W. Fox (eds), *Fetal and Neonatal Physiology*, Philadelphia: W.B. Saunders, pp. 74–85.

Simpson, John H., 1997, 'The social construction of plagues', in José Oscar Beozzo and Virgil Elizondo (eds), *The Return of the Plague*, London: SCM Press, pp. 18–23.

Simpson, Mark, 1994, 'Here come the mirror men', *The Independent*, 15 November.

Simpson, Mark, 2002, 'Meet the metrosexual', *Salon.com*, 22 July.

Smith, Mark S., 1988, '"Seeing God in the Psalms": the background to the beatific vision in the Hebrew Bible', *CBQ* 50, pp. 171–83.

Smith, Morton, 1995, *Studies in the Cult of Yahweh*, 2 vols, Leiden: Brill.

Soggin, J. Alberto, 1976, *Introduction to the Old Testament: From its Origins to the Closing of the Alexandrian Canon*, trans. John Bowden, Old Testament Library, London: SCM Press.

Soggin, J. Alberto, 1981, *Judges*, trans. John Bowden, Old Testament Library, London: SCM Press.

Sohn, Ruth, 2000, 'Beha'alotecha: the silencing of Miriam', in Elyse Goldstein (ed.), *The Women's Torah Commentary*, Woodstock, Vt.: Jewish Lights, pp. 270–8.

Sontag, Susan, 1994, *Against Interpretation*, London: Vintage Books.

Sproul, Barbara C., 1979, *Primal Myths: Creating World*, San Francisco: Harper & Row.

Stables, Dot, 1999, *Physiology in Childbearing with Anatomy Related Biosciences*, Edinburgh: Bailliere Tindall.

Stanley, R., 2001, 'Charismatic leadership in ancient Israel: a social-scientific approach', unpublished dissertation, Southwestern Baptist Theological Seminary.

Starbuck, S. R .A., 1999, *Court Oracles in the Psalms: The So-Called Royal Psalms in their Ancient Near Eastern Context*, SBLDS 172, Atlanta: Scholars Press.

Sternberg, Meir, 1985, *The Poetics of Biblical Narrative: Ideological Literature and the Drama of Reading*, Bloomington: Indiana University Press.

Stewart, David Tabb, 2000, 'Ancient sexual laws: text and intertext of the biblical Holiness code and Hittite law', dissertation, Berkeley: University of California.

Steymans, H. U., 1995, *Deuteronomium 28 und die adê zur Thronfolgeregelung Asarhaddons: Segen und Fluch im Alten Orient und in Israel*, OBO 145, Freiburg: Universitätsverlag; Göttingen: Vandenhoeck & Ruprecht.

Stone, Ira F., 2001, 'The precarious ties that bind us', *Cross Currents* 51 (3), pp. 273–87.

Stone, Ken, 1996, *Sex, Honor and Power in the Deuteronomistic History*, JSOTSS 234, Sheffield: Sheffield Academic Press.

Stone, Ken, 1999, 'Safer text: reading biblical laments in the age of AIDS', *Theology and Sexuality* 10, pp. 16–27.

Stone, Ken, 2000, 'The garden of Eden and the heterosexual contract', in Robert Goss and Mona West (eds), *Take Back the Word: A Queer Reading of the Bible*, Cleveland, Ohio: Pilgrim Press, pp. 57–70.

Stone, Ken, 2001a, 'Queer commentary and biblical interpretation: an introduction', in Ken Stone (ed.), *Queer Commentary and the Hebrew Bible*, JSOTSS 334, London and New York: Sheffield Academic Press, pp. 11–34.

Stone, Ken, 2001b, 'Lovers and raisin cakes: food, sex and divine insecurity in Hosea', in Ken Stone (ed.), *Queer Commentary and the Hebrew Bible*, JSOTSS 334, London and New York: Sheffield Academic Press, pp. 116–39.

Stone, Ken, 2002, '"Before the eyes of all Israel": public sex in the Bible', American Academy of Religion Annual Meeting, Toronto, Ontario, November.

Stone, Ken, 2004a, 'Queering the Canaanite', in M. Althaus-Reid and L. Isherwood (eds), *The Sexual Theologian: Essays on Sex, God and Politics*, London: T&T Clark, pp. 110–34.

Stone, Ken, 2004b, '"You seduced me, you overpowered me, and you prevailed": religious experience and homoerotic sadomasochism in Jeremiah', paper presented at the American Academy of Religion, Gay Men's Issues in Religion Group, San Antonio, Texas, 20 November.

Stone, Ken, 2005, *Practising Safer Texts: Food, Sex and Bible in Queer Perspective*, London: T&T Clark.

Stowers, S. K., 1993, *A Rereading of Romans: Justice, Jews, and Gentiles*, New Haven: Yale University Press; paperback edn 1997.

Stuart, Elizabeth (ed.), 1992, *Daring to Speak Love's Name*, London: Hamish Hamilton.

Stuart, Elizabeth, 1997, 'Introduction', in E. Stuart with Andy Braunston, Malcolm Edwards, John MacMahon and Tim Morrison (eds), *Religion is a Queer Thing: A Guide to the Christian Faith for Lesbian, Gay, Bisexual and Transgendered People*, London and Washington: Cassell, pp. 1–5.

Stuart, Elizabeth, 2000, 'Camping around the canon: humor as a hermeneutical tool in queer readings of biblical texts', in Robert Goss and Mona West (eds), *Take Back the Word: A Queer Reading of the Bible*, Cleveland, Ohio: Pilgrim Press, pp. 23–34.

Stuart, Elizabeth, 2003, *Gay and Lesbian Theologies: Repetitions with Critical Difference*, London and New York: Ashgate.

Suvin, Darko, 1979, *Metamorphoses of Science Fiction: On the Poetics and History of Literary Genre*, New Haven, Conn.: Yale University Press.

Sweasey, Peter, 1997, *From Queer to Eternity: Spirituality in the Lives of Lesbian, Gay and Bisexual People*, London and Washington: Cassell.

Sweeney, Marvin A., David W. Cotter, Jerome T. Walsh and Chris Franke (eds), 2000, *The Twelve Prophets*, Berit Olam, Collegeville: Liturgical Press.

al-Tabari, Abū Ja'far Muhammad, 1991, *The History of al-Tabarī (Tar'rīkh al-rusul wa'l mulūk)*, vol. 3: *The Children of Israel*, trans. and annotated William M. Brinner, Albany: State University of New York Press.

Tanakh, 1985, *Tanakh: A New Translation of the Holy Scriptures According to the Traditional Hebrew Text*, Philadelphia: Jewish Publication Society.

Tanis, Justin, 2003, *Trans-gendered: Theology, Ministry and Communities of Faith*, Cleveland, Ohio: Pilgrim Press.

Tanner, B. LaNeel, 2001, *The Book of Psalms through the Lens of Intertextuality*, Studies in Biblical Literature 26, New York: Lang.

Tate, M. E., 1990, *Psalms 51–100*, Word Bible Commentary 20, Waco: Word Books.

Temple, G., 2004, *Gay Unions: In the Light of Scripture, Tradition, and Reason*, New York: Church Publishing.

Thompson, Stith, 1966, *Motif-Index of Folk Literature*, Bloomington and London: Indiana University Press.

Thompson, Thomas L., 1992, *Early History of the Israelite People from the Written and Archaeological Sources*, Studies in the History of the Ancient Near East 4, Leiden: Brill.

Thompson, Thomas L., 2000, *The Bible in History: How Writers Create a Past*, London: Pimlico.

Throntveit, Mark A., 1992, *Ezra-Nehemiah*, Louisville: John Knox Press.

Tombs, D., 2002, 'Honour, shame and conquest: male identity, sexual violence and the body politic', *Journal of Hispanic/Latino Theology* 4 (4), pp. 21–40.

Travis, Irene S. 2000, 'Love your mother: a lesbian womanist reading of scripture', in Robert E. Goss and Mona West (eds), *Take Back the Word: A Queer Reading of the Bible*, Cleveland, Ohio: The Pilgrim Press, pp. 35–42.

Treves, M., 1963, 'Conjectures sur les dates et les sujets des Lamentations', *Bulletin Renan* 95, pp. 1–4.

Trexler, R. C., 1995, *Sex and Conquest: Gendered Violence, Political Order, and the European Conquest of the Americas*, Ithaca: Cornell University Press.

Trible, Phyllis, 1973, 'Depatriarchalizing in biblical interpretation', *JAAR* 41, pp. 30–48.

Trible, Phyllis, 1978, *God and the Rhetoric of Sexuality*, Overtures to Biblical Theology, Philadelphia: Fortress Press.

Trible, Phyllis, 1984, *Texts of Terror: Literary-Feminist Readings of Biblical Narratives*, Philadelphia: Fortress Press.

Trible, Phyllis, 1994, 'Bringing Miriam out of the shadows', in Athalya Brenner, (ed.), *A Feminist Companion to Exodus to Deuteronomy*, Feminist Companion to the Bible 6, Sheffield: Sheffield Academic Press, pp. 166–86.

Tucker, Robert C., 'The Theory of Charismatic Leadership', *Deadalus*, 97, (1968), pp. 731–56.

Truluck Rembert S., 'Steps to recovery from Bible abuse', http://www.truluck.com/index.html

Tucker, G. M., 2001, 'The book of Isaiah 1–39', in D. L. Peterson (ed.), *The New Interpreter's Bible*, vol. 6, Nashville: Abingdon Press, pp. 25–306.

Tulchinsky, Dan, and A. Brian Little, 1994, *Maternal-Fetal Endocrinology*, Philadelphia: W. B. Saunders.

University of Michigan Health System, 2002, *McKesson Clinical Reference System: Pediatric Adviser 2002.1*, s.v. 'The normal newborn's appearance: breast engorgement: genitals, girls', http://www.med.umich.edu/1 libr/pa/pa-newbappe-hhg.htm, accessed 28 July 2003.

Vaid, Urvashi, 1995, *Virtual Equality: The Mainstreaming of Gay and Lesbian Liberation*, New York: Anchor Books.

Van Nuys, K. 1953, 'Evaluating the pathological in prophetic experience (particularly in Ezekiel)', *Journal of the Bible and Religion* 21, pp. 244–51.

Van Seters, John, 1972, 'The Terms "Amorite" and "Hittite" in the Old Testament', *VT* 22, pp. 64–82.

Van Seters, John, 1983, *In Search of History: Historiography in the Ancient World and the Origins of Biblical History*, New Haven and London: Yale University Press.

van Tilborg, Sjef, 1993, *Imaginative Love in John*, Leiden and New York: Brill.

Van der Toorn, Karel, 1992, 'Prostitution (OT): cultic prostitution', in D. N. Freedman (ed.), *The Anchor Bible Dictionary*, vol. 6, New York: Doubleday, pp. 510–13.

Via, D. O., and R. A. J. Gagnon, 2001, *Homosexuality and the Bible: Two Views*, Minneapolis: Fortress Press.

von Rad, Gerhard, 1962, *The Message of the Prophets*, trans. D. M. G. Stalker, San Francisco: HarperCollins.

von Rad, Gerhard, 1965a, *The Problem of the Hexateuch and Other Essays*, trans. E. W. T. Dicken, Edinburgh and London: Oliver & Boyd.

von Rad, Gerhard, 1965b, *Old Testament Theology*, vol. 2, trans: D. M. G. Stalker, London: SCM Press.

von Rad, Gerhard, 1966, *Deuteronomy: A Commentary*, trans. D. Barton, Old Testament Library, London: SCM Press.

Wacker, Marie-Theres, 1995, 'Traces of the Goddess in the book of Hosea', in Athalya Brenner (ed.), *A Feminist Companion to the Latter Prophets*, Feminist Companion to the Bible 8, Sheffield: Sheffield Academic Press, pp. 219–41.

Ward, R.B., 1997, 'Why unnatural? The tradition behind Romans 1:26–27', *Harvard Theological Review* 90 (3), pp. 263–84.

Warner Michael, (ed.), 1993, *Fear of a Queer Planet: Queer Politics and Social Theory*, Minneapolis: University of Minnesota Press.

Warrior, Robert A., 2000, 'Canaanites, cowboys and Indians: deliverance, conquest and liberation theology today', in R. Alpert (ed.), *Voices of the Religious Left: A Contemporary Sourcebook*, Philadelphia: Temple University Press, pp. 51–7.

Washington, Harold C., 1997, 'Violence and the construction of gender in the Hebrew Bible: a new historicist approach', *Biblical Interpretation* 5 (4), pp. 324–63.

Washington, H. C., Susan L. Graham and Pamela Thimmes (eds), 1998, *Escaping Eden: New Feminist Perspectives on the Bible*, The Biblical Seminar 65, Sheffield: Sheffield Academic Press.

Webb, Barry G., 1987, *Judges: An Integrated Reading*, JSOTSS 46, Sheffield: Sheffield Academic Press.

Webster, Alison R., 1995, *Found Wanting: Women, Christianity and Sexuality*, Women on Women, London: Cassell.

Weeks, Jeffrey, 1996, 'The construction of homosexuality', in Steven Seidman (ed.) *Queer Theory/Sociology*, Oxford: Blackwell, pp. 41–63.

Weems, Renita J., 1988, *Just a Sister Away: A Womanist Vision of Women's Relationships in the Bible*, San Diego: LuraMedia.

Weems, Renita J., 1992, 'The Hebrew Women Are Not Like the Egyptian Women', *Semeia* 59 (1), pp. 25–34.

Weems, Renita J., 1995, *Battered Love: Marriage, Sex and Violence in the Hebrew Prophets*, Overtures to Biblical Theology, Philadelphia: Fortress Press.

Weinberg, Tzvi, 1977, 'Tô'beâ', *Beth Mikra*, 69, pp. 230–7.

Weinfeld, Moshe, 1972, *Deuteronomy and the Deuteronomic School*, Oxford:

Clarendon.

Weinfeld, Moshe, 1996, 'Feminine features in the imagery of God in Israel: the sacred marriage and the sacred tree', *VT* 46, pp. 515–29.

Weiser, A., 1962, *The Psalms: A Commentary*, trans. Herbert Hartwell, Old Testament Library, Philadelphia: Westminster Press.

Wellhausen, Julius, 1994 [1883], *Prolegomena to the History of Israel*, Atlanta: Scholars Press.

Wenham, Gordon J., 1979, *The Book of Leviticus*, Grand Rapids: Eerdmans.

West, Donald J., and Richard Green (eds), 1997, *Sociolegal Control of Homosexuality: A Multi-Nation Comparison*, London and New York: Plenum Press.

West, Mona, 1999, 'Reading the Bible as Queer Americans: Social Location and the Hebrew Scriptures', *Theology and Sexuality* 10, pp. 28–42.

West, Mona, 2000, 'Outsiders, aliens, and boundary crossers: a queer reading of the Hebrew Exodus', in Robert E. Goss and Mona West (eds), *Take Back the Word: A Queer Reading of the Bible*, Cleveland, Ohio: The Pilgrim Press, pp. 71–81.

West, Mona, 2001, 'The gift of voice, the gift of tears: a queer reading of Lamentations in the context of AIDS', in Ken Stone (ed.), *Queer Commentary and the Hebrew Bible*, JSOTSS 334, London and New York: Sheffield Academic Press, pp. 140–51.

Westenholz, J. G., 1989, 'Tamar, QĔDĒŠĀ, QADIŠTU, and sacred prostitution in Mesopotamia', *Harvard Theological Review* 82 (3), pp. 245–65.

Westermann, Claus, 1980, *The Psalms: Structure, Content and Message*, trans. Ralph D. Gehrke, Minneapolis: Augsburg.

Westermann, Claus, 1981, *Praise and Lament in the Psalms*, trans. Keith R. Crim and Richard N. Soulen, Atlanta: John Knox Press.

Westermann, Claus, 1994, *Lamentations: Issues and Interpretation*, Edinburgh: T&T Clark.

de Wette, W. M. L., 1805, 'Dissertatio critica exegetica qua Deuteronomium a prioribus Pentateuchi libris diversu, alius cujusdam recentioris actoris opus esse monstratur', Halle.

Whedbee, W., 1977, 'The comedy of Job', in R. Polzin and D. Robertson (eds), *Studies in the Book of Job*, Semeia 7, Missoula: Scholars Press, pp. 1–39.

Wheeler, Brannon M., 2002, *Prophets in the Quran: an Introduction to the Quran and Muslim Exegesis*, London and New York: Continuum.

Whitelam, Keith, 1989, 'Israel's traditions of origin: reclaiming the land', *JSOT* 44, pp. 19–42.

Wiesel, Elie, 2000, 'Konarch', *Bible Review* 16 (3), pp. 12–15.

Williams, Preston, 1987, 'Moses and Afro-Americans', *Religion and Intellectual Life* 4 (2), pp. 11–14.

Williamson, H. G. M., 1977, *Israel in the Book of Chronicles*, Cambridge: Cambridge University Press.

Williamson, H. G. M., 1982, *1 and 2 Chronicles*, New Century Bible Commentary, Grand Rapids: Eerdmans.

Williamson, H. G. M., 1985, *Ezra, Nehemiah*, Word Bible Commentary, Nashville: Thomas Nelson.

Willner, Ann Ruth, 1968, *Charismatic Political Leadership: A Theory*, Princeton: Princeton University Press.

Wilson, G. H., 1985, *The Editing of the Hebrew Psalter*, SBLDS 76, Chico: Scholars Press.

Wilson, Nancy, 1995, *Our Tribe: Queer Folks, God, Jesus, and the Bible*, New York: HarperSanFrancisco.

Wilson, R. R., 1984, 'Prophecy in Crisis: The Call of Ezekiel', *Interpretation*, 38, pp. 117–30.

Wilton, Tamsin, 2000, *Sexualities in Health and Social Care: A Textbook*, Buckingham and Philadelphia: Open University Press.

Wittig, Monique, 1992, *The Straight Mind and Other Essays*, New York, London, Toronto, Sydney, Tokyo, Singapore: Harvester Wheatsheaf.

Wold, Donald J., 1977, 'The meaning of biblical penalty kareth', Ph.D. dissertation, Berkeley: University of California.

Wold, Donald J., 1998, *Out of Order: Homosexuality in the Bible and the Ancient Near East*, Grand Rapids: Baker Books.

Wolde, E. Van, 1995, 'The development of Job: Mrs Job as catalyst', in Athalya Brenner (ed.), *A Feminist Companion to Wisdom Literature*, Feminist Companion to the Bible 9, Sheffield: Sheffield Academic Press, pp. 201–21.

Wolde, Ellen van, 1996, *Stories of the Beginning: Genesis I–II and Other Creation Stories*, trans. John Bowden, London: SCM Press.

Wolfe, Roland Emerson, 1935, 'The Editing of the Book of the Twelve', *ZAW*, 53, pp. 90–129.

Wright, David Pearson, and Richard N. Jones, 1992, 'Discharge', in D. N. Freedman (ed.) *The Anchor Bible Dictionary*, vol. 2, New York: Doubleday, pp. 204–7.

Wyatt, N., 1986, 'Cain's wife', *Folklore* 97 (4), pp. 88–95, 232.

Wyatt, N., 1995, 'Eve', in Karl van der Toorn, Bob Becking and P. W. van der Horst (eds), *Dictionary of Deities and Demons in the Bible*, Leiden: Brill, pp. 599–602.

Wyatt, N., 2005, *The Mythic Mind: Essays on Cosmology and Religion in Ugaritic and Old Testament Literature*, London and Oakville: Equinox.

Yamauchi, Edwin M., 1980a, 'The archaeological background of Nehemiah', *Biblotheca Sacra* 137, pp. 291–309.

Yamauchi, Edwin M., 1980b, 'Was Nehemiah the cupbearer a eunuch?' *ZAW* 92, pp. 132–43.

Yee, Gale A., 1998, 'Hosea', in C. A. Newsom and S. H. Ringe (eds), *Women's Bible Commentary Expanded Edition with Apocrypha*, Louisville: Westminster John Knox Press, pp. 207–15.

Yee, Gale A., 2003, *Poor Banished Children of Eve: Woman as Evil in the Hebrew Bible*, Minneapolis: Fortress Press.

York, A., 1977, 'Ezekiel I: Inaugural and Restoration Visions', *VT*, 27, pp. 82–98.

Zeidman, Reena, 1997, 'Marginal discourse: lesbianism in Jewish law', *Women in Judaism* 1 (1), (e-journal, http://www.utoronto.ca/wjudaism/jouranl/vol1n1/v1n1zeid.htm

Zimmerli, Walter, 1982, *I Am Yahweh*, Atlanta: John Knox Press.

Zimmerli, Walter, 1983, *Ezekiel 1 and 2*, Philadelphia: Fortress Press.

Zimmermann, Frank, 1973, *The Inner World of Qohelet*, New York: KTAV.

Zita, Jacquelyn N., 1998, *Body Talk: Philosophical Reflections on Sex and Gender*, New York: Columbia University Press.

Zlotowitz, M., 1986, *Bereishis: Genesis / A New Translation with a Commentary Anthologized from Talmudic, Midrashic and Rabbinic Sources*, Brooklyn, NY: Mesorah.

Zobel, Hans-Jürgen, 1975, 'galah', in G. Johannes Botterweck and Helmer Ringgren (eds), *Theological Dictionary of the Old Testament*, vol 2, Grand Rapids: Eerdmans, pp. 476–88.

Zobel, Hans-Jürgen, 2003, 'sebaot', in G. Johannes Botterweck and Helmer Ringgren (eds), *Theological Dictionary of the Old Testament*, vol. 12, Grand Rapids:

Eerdmans, pp. 215–32.
Zornberg, Avivah Gottleib, 1996, *The Beginning of Desire: Reflections on Genesis*, New York: Doubleday.
Zornberg, Avivah Gottleib, 2001, *The Particulars of Rapture: Reflections on Exodus*, New York and London: Doubleday.

Second Testament

Achtemeier, Paul, 1985, *Romans*, Atlanta: John Knox Press.

Albright, W. F., and C. S. Mann, 1971, *Matthew: A New Translation with Introduction and Commentary*, Anchor Bible 26, Garden City, NY: Doubleday.

Alison, James, 2001, *Faith Beyond Resentment: Fragments Catholic and Gay*, New York: Crossroad.

Alison, James, 2003, *On Being Liked*, New York: Crossroad.

Alterman, Eric, and Mark Green, 2004, *The Book on Bush: How George W. (Mis)leads America*, New York: Penguin Books.

Althaus-Reid, Marcella, 2001a, *Indecent Theology: Theological Perversions in Sex, Gender and Politics*, New York: Routledge.

Althaus-Reid, Marcella, 2001b, 'The divine exodus of God', in W. Jeanrod and C. Theobald (eds), *God, Experience and Mystery*, comprising *Concilium* 289, pp. 33–41.

Anderson, Janice Capel, 2001, 'Matthew: gender and reading', in Amy Jill Levine (ed.), *A Feminist Companion to Matthew*, Feminist Companion to the New Testament and Early Christian Writings 1, Sheffield: Sheffield Academic Press, pp. 25–51.

Ascough, Richard S., 2000, 'The Thessalonian Christian community as a professional voluntary association', *JBL* 119 (2), pp. 311–28.

Attridge, Harold W., 1989, *A Commentary on the Epistle to the Hebrews*, Hermeneia, Philadelphia: Fortress Press.

Attridge, Harold W., 1992, 'Hebrews, Epistle to the', in *The Anchor Bible Dictionary*, ed. David Noel Freedman, vol. 3, New York: Doubleday, pp. 97–104.

Bailey, D. S., 1975, *Homosexuality and the Western Christian Tradition*, Hamden, Conn.: Archon Books.

Balch, David L., 1981, *Let Wives Be Submissive: The Domestic Code in 1 Peter*, Atlanta: Scholars Press.

Barclay, William, 2003, *The Letters to the Philippians, Colossians, and Thessalonians*, Louisville, Westminster John Knox Press.

Bates, S., 2004, *A Church at War: Anglicans and Homosexuality*, New York: St Martin's Press.

Bauckham, Richard, 1983, *Jude, 2 Peter*, Dallas: Word.

Bauer, Walter, 1971, *Orthodoxy and Heresy in Earliest Christianity*, 2nd edn, trans. and ed. Robert A. Kraft and Gerhard Krodel, Philadelphia: Fortress Press; reprinted Mifflintown, Pa.: Sigler Press, 1996.

Bechtler, Steven Richard, 1998, *Following in His Steps: Suffering, Community, and Christology in 1 Peter*, Atlanta: Scholars Press.

Beker, J. Christiaan, 1980, *Paul the Apostle: The Triumph of God in Life and Thought*, Philadelphia: Fortress Press.

Belo, Fernando, 1981, *A Materialist Reading of the Gospel of Mark*, trans. Matthew O'Connell, Maryknoll: Orbis.

Berger, James, 1999, *After the End: Representations of Post-Apocalypse*, Minneapolis: University of Minnesota Press.

Biale, D., 1992, *Eros and the Jews: From Biblical Israel to Contemporary America*, New York: Basic Books.

Bohache, Thomas, 2000, '"To cut or not to cut?" Is compulsory heterosexuality a prerequisite for Christianity?' in Robert E. Goss and Mona West (eds), *Take Back the Word: A Queer Reading of the Bible*, Cleveland, Ohio: Pilgrim Press, pp.

227–239.

Bohache, Thomas, 2003, 'Embodiment as incarnation: an incipient queer Christology', *Theology and Sexuality* 10 (1), pp. 9–29.

Boisvert, Donald L., 2004, *Sanctity and Male Desire*, Cleveland, Ohio: Pilgrim Press.

Borg, Marcus J., 1984, *Conflict, Holiness, and Politics in the Teachings of Jesus*, Harrisburg, Pa.: Trinity Press International; 2nd edn 1998.

Boswell, John, 1980, *Christianity, Social Tolerance, and Homosexuality*, Chicago: University of Chicago Press.

Boyarin, Daniel, 1995, 'Are There Any Jews in "The History of Sexuality?"' *Journal of the History of Sexuality* 5 (3), pp. 333–55.

Boyer, Paul, 1992, *When Time Shall Be No More: Prophecy Belief in Modern American Culture*, Cambridge, Mass.: Harvard University Press.

Brantley, William F., 1996, 'The thunder of new wings: AIDS – a journey beyond belief', in *Redeeming Men: Religion and Masculinities*, ed. Stephen Boyd, Merle Longwood and Mark Muesse, Louisville: Westminster John Knox Press, pp. 197–208.

Brooten, Bernadette J., 1985a, 'Patristic interpretations of Romans 1:26', in *Studia Patristica XVIII: Papers of the Ninth International Patristics Conference, Oxford, 1983*, vol. 1: *Historica-Theologica-Gnostica-Biblica*, ed. Elizabeth A. Livingstone, Kalamazoo: Cistercian Publications, pp. 287–91.

Brooten, Bernadette J., 1985b, 'Paul's views on the nature of women and female homoeroticism', in *Immaculate and Powerful*, ed. Clarissa W. Atkinson, Constance H. Buchanan, and Margaret R. Miles, Boston: Beacon Press, pp. 61–87.

Brooten, Bernadette J., 1990, 'Paul and the law: how complete was the departure?' *Princeton Seminary Bulletin*, supp. 1, pp. 71–89.

Brooten, Bernadette J., 1996, *Love Between Women: Early Christian Responses to Female Homoeroticism*, Chicago: University of Chicago Press.

Brown, Dan, 2003, *The Da Vinci Code*, New York: Doubleday.

Brown, Peter, 1988, *The Body and Society: Men, Women, and Sexual Renunciation in Early Christianity*, New York: Columbia University Press.

Brown, Raymond E., 1977, *The Birth of the Messiah: A Commentary on the Infancy Narratives in Matthew and Luke*, New York: Doubleday.

Brown, Raymond E., 1997, 'Letter to the Philippians', in *The Anchor Bible Commentary*, New York: Doubleday.

Brown, Raymond E., Joseph A. Fitzmyer and Roland E. Murphy (eds), 1990, *The New Jerome Biblical Commentary*, Englewood Cliffs, NJ: Prentice-Hall.

Bruce, F. F., 1964/90, *La Epístola a los Hebreos*, Buenos Aires: Nueva Creación.

Bruce, F. F., 1987, *The Epistle to the Hebrews*, New London Commentaries, Grand Rapids: Eerdmans.

Bryan, Christopher, 2000, *A Preface to Romans: Notes on the Epistle in Its Literary and Cultural Setting*, Oxford: Oxford University Press.

Bultmann, Rudolf, 1951, *Theology of the New Testament*, vol. 1, trans. Kendrick Grobel, New York: Charles Scribner's Sons.

Bultmann, Rudolf, 1955, *Theology of the New Testament*, vol. 2, trans. Kendrick Grobel, New York: Charles Scribner's Sons.

Butler, Judith, 1999, *Gender Trouble: Feminism and the Subversion of Identity*, New York and London: Routledge.

Byrne, Brendan, SJ, 1996, *Romans*, Sacra Pagina 6, Collegeville, Minn.: Liturgical Press/Michael Glazier.

Capps, Donald E., 1995, *The Child's Song: The Religious Abuse of Children*, Louisville: Westminster John Knox Press.

Carden, Michael, 2004, *Sodomy: A History of a Christian Biblical Myth*, London: Equinox.

Carmichael, C. M., 1997, *Law, Legend, and Incest in the Bible*, Ithaca: Cornell University Press.

Carpenter, Mary Wilson, 1995, 'Representing apocalypse: sexual politics and the violence of revelation', in Richard Dellamora (ed.), *Postmodern Apocalypse: Theory and Cultural Practice at the End*, Philadelphia: University of Pennsylvania Press, pp. 107–35.

Carr, David M., 2003, *The Erotic Word: Sexuality, Spirituality, and the Bible*, New York: Oxford University Press.

Carter, Warren, 2000, *Matthew and the Margins: A Sociopolitical and Religious Reading*. Maryknoll, NY: Orbis Books.

Carter, Warren, 2001, *Matthew and Empire: Initial Explorations*, Harrisburg, Pa.: Trinity Press International.

Carter, Warren, 2002, 'Getting Martha out of the kitchen', in *A Feminist Companion to Luke*, ed. Amy-Jill Levine, New York: Sheffield Academic Press, pp. 214–31.

Castelli, Elizabeth A., 1994b, 'Romans', in *Searching the Scriptures*, vol. 2: *A Feminist Commentary*, ed. Elisabeth Schüssler Fiorenza, New York: Crossroad, pp. 272–300.

Charles, J. Daryl, 1998, *Literary Strategy in the Epistle of Jude*, Scranton, Pa.: University of Scranton Press.

Cheng, Patrick S., 2002, 'Multiplicity and Judges 19: constructing a queer Asian Pacific American biblical hermeneutic', *Semeia* 90/91, pp. 119–33.

Cheng, Patrick S., 2004, 'Response', in 'Roundtable discussion: same-sex marriage', *Journal of Feminist Studies in Religion* 20 (2), pp. 103–7.

Chilton, Bruce, 2004, *Rabbi Paul: An Intellectual Biography*, New York: Doubleday.

Clark, J. Michael, 1986, *Liberation and Disillusionment: The Development of Gay Male Criticism and Popular Fiction a Decade after Stonewall*, Dallas: Liberal Press.

Clark, J. Michael, 1999, 'Queering the apocalypse: reading Catherine Keller's *Apocalypse Now and Then*', *Journal of Men's Studies* 7 (2), pp. 233–44.

Clarke, Andrew D., 2002, 'Jew and Greek, slave and free, male and female: Paul's theology of ethnic, social and gender inclusiveness in Romans 16', in P. Oakes (ed.), *Rome in the Bible and the Early Church*, Grand Rapids: Baker, pp. 103–25.

Coakley, Sarah, 2001, 'The eschatological body: gender, transformation, and God', in James Buckley and L. Gregory Jones (eds), *Theology and Eschatology at the Turn of the Millennium*, Oxford: Blackwell, pp. 59–71.

Collins, Raymond F., 1999, *First Corinthians*, Sacra Pagina, Collegeville: Liturgical Press.

Comstock, G. D., 1993, *Gay Theology Without Apology*, Cleveland, Ohio: Pilgrim Press.

Conway, Colleen, n.d., 'The ideology of masculinity in the Corinthian correspondence', paper delivered to the Catholic Biblical Association (cited with permission).

Conway, Colleen, 2003, 'Behold the man: masculine Christology and the Fourth Gospel', in *New Testament Masculinities*, ed. Stephen D. Moore and Janice Capel Anderson, Atlanta: Society of Biblical Literature, pp. 163–80.

Corley, Kathleen E., 1994b, '1 Peter' in *Searching the Scriptures*, vol. 2: *A Feminist Commentary*, ed. Elisabeth Schüssler Fiorenza, New York: Crossroad, pp.

349–60.

Countryman, L. William, 1988, *Dirt, Greed and Sex*, Philadelphia: Fortress Press.

Countryman, L. William, 2003, *Interpreting the Truth: Changing the Paradigm of Biblical Studies*, Harrisburg, Pa.: Trinity Press International.

Countryman, L. William, 2005, *Love Human and Divine: Reflections on Love, Sexuality, and Friendship*, Harrisburg: Morehouse.

Countryman, L. William and Riley, M. R., 2001, *Gifted by Otherness: Gay and Lesbian Christians in the Church*, Harrisburg: Morehouse.

Craddock, Fred B., 1995, *First and Second Peter and Jude*, Louisville: Westminster John Knox Press.

Craddock, Fred B., 1998, 'Hebrews' in *New Interpreter's Bible*, vol. 12, Nashville: Abingdon Press.

Craig, Susan, 2000, 'Untitled', in Debra R. Kolodny (ed.), *Blessed Bi Spirit: Bisexual People of Faith*, New York: Continuum.

Cranfield, C. E. B., 1975, 1979, *A Critical and Exegetical Commentary on the Epistle to the Romans*, International Critical Commentary, 2 vols, Edinburgh: T&T Clark.

Crompton, Louis, 2003, *Homosexuality and Civilization*, Cambridge, Mass., and London: Harvard University Press.

Crossan, John Dominic, 1991, *The Historical Jesus: The Life of a Jewish Mediterranean Peasant*, New York: HarperCollins.

Crossan, John Dominic, 1995, *Jesus: A Revolutionary Biography*, New York: Harper Collins.

Crossan, John Dominic, and Reed, Jonathan L., 2004, *In Search of Paul: How Jesus's Apostle Opposed Rome's Empire with God's Empire*, San Francisco: HarperSanFrancisco.

Croy, C. N., 1998, *Endurance in Suffering: Hebrews 12:1–3 in Its Rhetorical, Religious and Philosophical Context*, SNTSMS, Cambridge: Cambridge UniversityPress.

D'Angelo, Mary Rose, 1994b, 'Colossians', in Elisabeth Schüssler Fiorenza (ed.), *Searching the Scriptures*, vol. 2: *A Feminist Commentary*, New York: Crossroad, pp. 313–24.

D'Angelo, Mary Rose, 1998, 'Hebrews', in *The Women's Bible Commentary*, ed. Carol A. Newsom and Sharon H. Ringe, Louisville: Westminster John Knox Press, pp. 455–9.

D'Angelo, Mary Rose, 1999, 'Women Partners in the New Testament', in Gary David Comstock and Susan E. Henking (eds), *Que(e)rying Religion: A Critical Anthology*, New York: Continuum, pp. 441–55.

Danker, Frederick William (ed.), 2000, *A Greek–English Lexicon of the New Testament and Other Early Christian Literature*, Chicago: University of Chicago Press.

Davidson, J., 2001, 'Dover, Foucault, and Greek homosexuality: penetration and the truth of sex', *Past and Present* 170, pp. 3–51.

Dellamora, Richard, 1994, *Apocalyptic Overtures: Sexual Politics and the Sense of an Ending*, New Brunswick, N.J.: Rutgers University Press.

Dellamora, Richard (ed.), 1995, *Postmodern Apocalypse: Theory and Cultural Practice at the End*, Philadelphia: University of Pennsylvania Press.

Derida, Jacques and Maurizio Ferraris, 2001, *A Taste for the Secret*, ed. and trans. Giacomo Donis and David Webb, Cambridge: Polity Press.

deSilva, D. A., 1996, *Despising Shame: Honor, Discourse and Community Maintenance in the Epistle to the Hebrews*, SBLDS 152, Atlanta: Scholars Press.

deSilva, D. A., 2000, *Perseverance in Gratitude: A Socio-Rhetorical Commentary on the Epistle to the Hebrews*, Grand Rapids: Eerdmans.

Deutsch, Celia M., 1996, *Lady Wisdom, Jesus, and the Sages: Metaphor and Social Context in Matthew's Gospel*, Valley Forge, Pa.: Trinity Press International.

De Vries, Hent, 1999, *Philosophy and the Turn to Religion*, Baltimore: Johns Hopkins University Press.

Dickinson, Peter, 1995, '"Go-go dancing on the brink of the apocalypse": representing AIDS: an essay in seven epigraphs', in Richard Dellamora (ed.), *Postmodern Apocalypse: Theory and Cultural Practice at the End*, Philadelphia: University of Pensylvania Press, pp. 219–40.

Dibelius, Martin, 1976, *James*, rev. Heinrich Greeven, trans. Michael A. Williams, Hermeneia, Philadelphia: Fortress Press.

Donaldson, Laura E., 2002, 'The breasts of Columbus: a political anatomy of postcolonialism and feminist religious discourse', in L. E. Donaldson and P. Kwok (eds), *Postcolonialism, Feminism, and Religious Discourse*, New York and London: Routledge, pp. 41–61.

Donaldson, Laura E., and Kwok Pui-lan (eds), 2002, *Postcolonialism, Feminism, and Religious Discourse*, New York and London: Routledge.

Douglas, Mary, 1966, *Purity and Danger: An Analysis of the Concepts of Pollution and Taboo*, London: Routledge & Kegan Paul.

Dover, K. J., 1978, *Greek Homosexuality*, New York: Vintage Books.

Dube, Musa W., 2000, *Postcolonial Feminist Interpretation of the Bible*, St. Louis, Mo.: Chalice Press.

Dunn, James D. G., 1988, *Romans 1–8, 9–16*, Word Bible Commentary 38A–B, Dallas: Word Books.

Dunn, J. D. G., 1998, *The Theology of Paul the Apostle*, Grand Rapids: Eerdmans.

Dynes, W. R., 1997, 'Love in the ancient Mediterranean', *Journal of Homosexuality* 36 (1), pp. 114–26; a version is archived at www.indegayforum.org.

Edwards, George R., 1984, *Gay/Lesbian Liberation: A Biblical Perspective*, New York: Pilgrim Press.

Eisenbaum, Pamela, 2004, 'A remedy for having been born of woman: Jesus, gentiles, and genealogy in Romans', *JBL* 123(4), pp. 671–702.

Eller, Vernard, 1987, *Christian Anarchy*, Grand Rapids: Eerdmans.

Ellingworth, Paul, 1993, *Commentary on Hebrews*, New International Greek Testament Commentary, Grand Rapids: Eerdmans.

Elliott, John H., 1981, *Home for the Homeless: A Sociological Exegesis of 1 Peter, Its Situation and Strategy*, Philadelphia: Fortress Press.

Elliott, John H., 2000, *1 Peter: A New Translation with Introduction and Commentary*, The Anchor Bible 37B, New York: Doubleday.

Ellul, Jacques, 1998, *Anarchie et Christianisme*, Lyon: Atelier de Creation Libertaire.

Emerson, J., 1996, 'Yang Chu's Discovery of the Body', *Philosophy East and West* 46 (4), pp. 533–66.

Engberg-Pedersen, Troels, 2000, *Paul and the Stoics*, Louisville: Westminster John Knox Press.

Esler, Philip F., 2003a, *Conflict and Identity in Romans*, Minneapolis: Fortress Press.

Esler, Philip F., 2003b, 'Social identify, the virtues, and the good life: a new approach to Romans 12:1–15:13', *Biblical Theological Bulletin* 33, pp. 51–63.

Esler, Philip F., 2003c, 'The Sodom tradition in Romans 1:18–32', *Biblical Theological Bulletin* 34, pp. 4–16.

Evans, Craig A., and Donald A. Hagner (eds), 1993, *Anti-Semitism and Early Christianity*, Minneapolis: Fortress Press.

Felder, Cain Hope (ed.), 1991, *Stony the Road We Trod: African American Biblical*

Interpretation, Minneapolis: Fortress Press.

Finley, Moses, 1964, 'Roman slavery', in *Slavery in Classical Antiquity: Views and Controversies*, ed. Moses I. Finley, London: Lowe & Brydone, pp. 45–9.

Fitzmyer, Joseph A., 1990, 'Introduction to the New Testament epistles', in Raymond E. Brown, Joseph A. Fitzmyer and Roland E. Murphy (eds), *The New Jerome Bible Commentary*, Englewood Cliffs, N.J.: Prentice-Hall, pp. 768–71.

Fitzmyer, Joseph A., 1993, *Romans*, Anchor Bible 33, New York: Doubleday.

Fitzmyer, Joseph A., 1998, *The Acts of the Apostles: A New Translation with Introduction and Commentary*, Anchor Bible 31, New York: Doubleday.

Fornberg, Tord, 1977, *An Early Church in a Pluralistic Society: A Study of 2 Peter*, Lund: Gleerup.

Foucault, Michel, 1976–86, *The History of Sexuality*, 3 vols, New York: Random House.

Fox, Matthew, 1988, *The Coming of the Cosmic Christ: The Healing of Mother Earth and the Birth of a Global Renaissance*, New York: Harper & Row.

Fredrickson, David E., 2000, 'Natural and unnatural use in Romans 1:24–27: Paul and the philosophic critique of Eros', in *Homosexuality, Science, and the 'Plain Sense' of Scripture*, ed. David L. Balch, Grand Rapids: Eerdmans, pp. 197–222.

Freire, Paulo, 1970, *Pedagogy of the Oppressed*, trans. Myra Bergman Ramos, New York: Crossroad; rev. 20th anniversary edn, 1993.

Freyne, Sean, 2004, *Jesus, a Jewish Galilean: A New Reading of the Jesus-Story*, London and New York: T&T Clark International.

Frilingos, Chris, 2003, 'Sexing the Lamb', in Stephen D. Moore and Janice Capel Anderson (eds), *New Testament Masculinities*, Semeia Studies, Atlanta, Ga.: Society of Biblical Literature, pp. 297–317.

Fung, Richard, 1998, 'Looking for my penis: the eroticized Asian in gay video porn', in David L. Eng and Alice Y. Hom (eds), *Q&A: Queer in Asian America*, Philadelphia: Temple University Press.

Funk, Robert W., 1994, 'Forward', in Robert J. Miller (ed.), *The Complete Gospels*, Annotated Scholars Version, New York: HarperCollins, pp. vii–ix.

Funk, Robert, and the Jesus Seminar, 1998, *The Acts of Jesus: 'What Did Jesus Really Do?'*, Polebridge Press Books, San Francisco: HarperSanFrancisco.

Gagnon, Robert A. J., 2001, *The Bible and Homosexual Practice: Texts and Hermeneutics* Nashville: Abingdon Press.

Gagnon, Robert J., and Dan O. Via, 2003, *Homosexuality and the Bible: Two Views*, Minneapolis: Augsburg Fortress Press.

Gaiser, Frederick J., 1994, 'A new word on homosexuality? Isaiah 56:1–8 as case study', *Word and World* 14 (3), pp. 280–93.

Garland, David E., 1995, *Reading Matthew: A Literary and Theological Commentary on the First Gospel*, New York: Crossroad.

Gathercole, Simon J., 2002, *Where is Boasting? Early Jewish Soteriology and Paul's Response in Romans 1–8*, Grand Rapids: Eerdmans.

Gaventa, Beverly Roberts, 1998a, 'Romans', in *The Women's Bible Commentary*, ed. Carol A. Newsom and Sharon H. Ringe, Louisville: Westminster John Knox Press, pp. 403–10.

Gaventa, Beverly Roberts, 1998b, *First and Second Thessalonians*, Louisville: John Knox Press.

Gillis, Chester, 1998, *Pluralism: A New Paradigm for Theology*, Louvain: Peeters Press; Grand Rapids: Eerdmans.

Glancy, Jennifer A., 1998, 'Obstacles to slaves' participation in the Corinthian church', *JBL* 117 (3), pp. 481–501.

Glancy, Jennifer A., 2002, *Slavery in Early Christianity*, New York and Oxford: Oxford University Press.

Glancy, Jennifer A., 2003, 'Protocols of masculinity in the pastoral epistles', in *New Testament Masculinities*, ed. Stephen D. Moore and Janice Capel Anderson, Semeia Studies 45, Atlanta: Society of Biblical Literature, pp. 235–64.

Glancy, Jennifer A., 2004, 'Boasting of beatings (2 Corinthians 11:23–25)', *JBL* 123 (1), pp. 99–135.

Glaser, Chris, 1994, *The Word Is Out: Daily Reflections on the Bible for Lesbians and Gay Men*, Louisville: Westminster John Knox Press.

Glaser, Chris, 1998, *Coming Out as Sacrament*, Louisville: Westminster John Knox Press.

Goldsmith, Steven, 1993, *Unbuilding Jerusalem: Apocalypse and Romantic Representation*, Ithaca, NY: Cornell University Press.

Gordon, Robert P., 2000, *Hebrews*, Sheffield: Sheffield Academic Press.

Goss, Robert, 1993, *Jesus ACTED UP: A Gay and Lesbian Manifesto*, San Francisco: HarperSanFrancisco.

Goss, Robert, 1997, 'Queering procreative privilege: coming out as families', in Robert Goss and Amy Strongheart (eds), *Our Families, Our Values: Snapshots of Queer Kinship*, New York: Haworth Press, pp. 3–20.

Goss, Robert, 2000, 'The Beloved Disciple: a queer bereavement narrative in a time of AIDS', in *Take Back the Word: A Queer Reading of the Bible*, ed. Robert E. Goss and Mona West, Cleveland, Ohio: Pilgrim Press, pp. 206–18.

Goss, Robert, 2002, *Queering Christ: Beyond Jesus ACTED UP*, Cleveland, Ohio: Pilgrim Press.

Goss, Robert, and Amy Adams Squire Strongheart, 1997, *Our Families, Our Values: Snapshots of Queer Kinship*, Binghampton: Haworth Press.

Goss, Robert E., and Mona West (eds), 2000, *Take Back the Word: A Queer Reading of the Bible*, Cleveland, Ohio: Pilgrim Press.

Grahn, Judy, 1983, *Another Mother Tongue: Gay Words, Gay Worlds*, Boston: Beacon Press.

Grayston, Kenneth, 1984, *The Johannine Epistles*, New Century Bible Commentary, Grand Rapids: Eerdmans.

Greenberg, S., 2004, *Wrestling With God and Men: Homosexuality in the Jewish Tradition*. Madison: University of Wisconsin Press.

Greven, Philip, 1990, *Spare the Child: The Religious Roots of Punishment and the Psychological Impact of Physical Abuse*, New York: Vintage Books.

Grieb, A. Katherine, 2002, *The Story of Romans: A Narrative Defense of God's Righteousness*, Louisville: Westminster John Knox Press.

Guest, Deryn, 2005, *When Deborah Met Jael: Lesbian Biblical Hermeneutics*, London: SCM Press.

Hagner, Donald A., 1983/90, *Hebrews*, NIBC 14, Peabody, Mass.: Hendrickson.

Hagner, Donald A., 2002, *Encountering the Book of Hebrews: An Exposition*, Grand Rapids: Baker.

Haight, Roger, 1999, *Jesus: Symbol of God*, Maryknoll, NY: Orbis Books.

Halperin, David M., 1989, *One Hundred Years of Homosexuality, and Other Essays on Greek Love*, New York: Routledge.

Halperin, David M., 2002, *How To Do the History of Homosexuality*, Chicago: University of Chicago Press.

Halsell, Grace, 1999, *Forcing God's Hand: Why Millions Pray for a Quick Rapture and Destruction of Planet Earth*, Beltsville, Md.: Amana Publications, 1999.

Hanks, Thomas D., 1982/83, *God So Loved the Third World: The Biblical Vocabulary of Oppression*, trans. James C. Dekker, New York: Orbis..

Hanks, Thomas D., 1992, 'Poor/Poverty (New Testament)', in *The Anchor Bible Dictionary*, vol. 5, ed. David Noel Freedman, New York: Doubleday, pp. 414–24.

Hanks, Thomas D., 1997, 'Paul's Letter to the Romans as a source of affirmation for queers and their families, in *Our Families, Our Values*, ed. Robert Goss and Amy Strongheart, New York: Harrington, pp. 137–49.

Hanks, Thomas D., 2000, *The Subversive Gospel: A New Testament Commentary for Liberation*, Cleveland, Ohio: Pilgrim Press.

Harink, Douglas, 2003, *Paul among the Postliberals: Pauline Theology Beyond Christendom and Modernity*, Grand Rapids: Brazos/Baker.

Harrington, Daniel J., 1991, *The Gospel of Matthew*, Sacra Pagina 1, Collegeville: Michael Glazier/Liturgical Press.

Hart, D. B., 2003, *The Beauty of the Infinite: The Aesthetics of Christian Truth*, Grand Rapids: Eerdmans.

Hart, D. B., 2005, *The Doors of the Sea: Where Was God in the Tsunami?* Grand Rapids: Eerdmans.

Harvey, Andrew, 1998, *Son of Man: The Mystical Path to Christ*, New York: Jeremy P. Tarcher/Putnam.

Haughton, Rosemary, 1969, *Beginning Life in Christ*, Westminster, Md., Newman Press.

Havener, Ivan, 1983, *First Thessalonians, Philippians, Philemon, Second Thessalonians, Colossians, Ephesians*, Collegeville Bible Commentary, NT 8, Collegeville: Liturgical Press.

Hays, Richard B., 1996, *The Moral Vision of the New Testament: A Contemporary Introduction to New Testament Ethics*, New York: HarperCollins.

Hefling, Charles, 1997, 'By their fruits: a traditionalist argument', in *Our Selves, Our Souls and Bodies*, ed. C. Hefling, Boston: Cowley, pp. 157–74.

Helminiak, Daniel A., 1995/2000, *What the Bible Really Says about Homosexuality*, Tajique, New Mexico: Alamo Square.

Helminiak, Daniel A., 1997, 'Response: ethics, biblical and denominational: a response to Mark Smith', *JAAR* 54 (4), pp. 855–9.

Herzog II, William R., 1994, *Parables as Subversive Speech: Jesus as Pedagogue of the Oppressed*, Louisville: Westminster John Knox Press.

Herzog II, William R., 2000, *Jesus, Justice, and the Reign of God: A Ministry of Liberation*, Louisville: Westminster John Knox Press.

Heyward, Carter, 1989, *Touching Our Strength: The Erotic as Power and the Love of God*, San Francisco: Harper & Row.

Hill, Craig C., 2001, 'Romans', in *The Oxford Bible Commentary*, ed. John Barton and John Muddiman, New York: Oxford University Press, pp. 1083–1108.

Hill, Jim, and Rand Cheadle, 1995, *The Bible Tells Me So*, Anchor Books, New York: Doubleday.

Hinkelammert, Franz J., 2000, *La Fe de Abraham y el Edipo Occidental*, 3rd edn, San José, Costa Rica: DEI.

Hooker, Morna D., 1960, 'Adam in Romans i', *New Testament Studies* 9, pp. 370–1.

Horgan, Maurya P., 1990, 'The Letter to the Colossians', in Raymond E. Brown, Joseph A. Fitzmyer, and Roland E. Murphy (eds), *The New Jerome Biblical Commentary*, Englewood Cliffs: Prentice-Hall, pp. 876–82.

Horner, Tom, 1978, *Jonathan Loved David: Homosexuality in Biblical Times*, Philadelphia: Westminster Press.

Horsley, Richard A., 1993a, *Jesus and the Spiral of Violence: Popular Jewish Resistance in Roman Palestine*, Minneapolis: Fortress Press.

Horsley, Richard A., 1993b, *The Liberation of Christmas: The Infancy Narratives in Social Context*, New York: Continuum.

Horsley, Richard A. (ed.), 1997, *Paul and Empire: Religion and Power in Roman Imperial Society*, Harrisburg, Pa.: Trinity Press International.

Horsley, Richard A., 1998, *1 Corinthians*, Abingdon New Testament Commentaries, Nashville: Abingdon Press.

Horsley, Richard A., 2000, *Paul and Politics*, Harrisburg, Pa.: Trinity Press International.

Horsley, Richard A., 2001a, 'The gospel of the savior's birth', in Richard A. Horsley and James Tracy (eds), *Christmas Unwrapped: Consumerism, Christ and Culture*, Harrisburg, Pa.: Trinity Press International, pp. 113–38.

Horsley, Richard A., 2001b, 'Messiah, magi, and model imperial king', in Richard A. Horsley and James Tracy (eds), *Christmas Unwrapped: Consumerism, Christ and Culture*, Harrisburg, Pa.: Trinity Press International, pp. 139–161.

Horsley, Richard A., 2003, *Jesus and Empire: The Kingdom of God and the New World Disorder*, Minneapolis: Fortress Press.

Horsley, Richard A., 2004, 'The empire of God and the empire of Rome: re-contextualizing Jesus' proclamation of the kingdom', paper presented at the Society of Biblical Literature Annual Meeting, Jesus Traditions, Gospels, and Negotiating the Roman Imperial World Consultation, 20 November 2004, San Antonio, Tex.

Horsley, Richard A., and Neil Asher Silberman, 1997, *The Message and the Kingdom: How Jesus and Paul Ignited a Revolution and Transformed the Ancient World*, New York: Groset/Putnam.

Horsley, Richard A., and James Tracy (eds), 2001, *Christmas Unwrapped: Consumerism, Christ, and Culture*, Harrisburg, Pa.: Trinity Press International.

Horst, Pieter W. van der, 1996, 'Sarah's seminal emission: Hebrews 11:11 in the light of ancient embryology', in *A Feminist Companion to the Hebrew Bible in the New Testament*, ed. Athalya Brenner, Sheffield: Sheffield Academic Press, pp. 112–34.

Hubbard, Thomas K., 1988, 'Popular perceptions of elite homosexuality in classic Athens', *Arion* ser. 3, 6(1), pp. 48–78.

Hubbard, Thomas K., 2003, *Homosexuality in Greece and Rome: A Sourcebook of Basic Documents*, Berkeley: University of California Press.

Ingebretsen, Edward J., 2001, *At Stake: Monsters and the Rhetoric of Fear in Public Culture*, Chicago and London: University of Chicago Press.

Isasi-Díaz, Ada María, 2003, 'Christ in *mujerista* theology', in Tatha Wiley (ed.), *Thinking of Christ: Proclamation, Explanation, Meaning*, London and New York: Continuum, pp. 157–76.

Jennings, Theodore W., 2003, *The Man Jesus Loved: Homoerotic Narratives from the New Testament*, Cleveland, Ohio: Pilgrim Press.

Jennings, Theodore W., 2005, *Jacob's Wound: Homoerotic Narrative in the Literature of Ancient Israel*, New York and London: Continuum.

Jewett, Robert, 1981, *Letter to Pilgrims: A Commentary on the Epistle to the Hebrews*, New York: Pilgrim Press.

Jewett, Robert, 1982, *Christian Tolerance: Paul's Message to the Modern Church*, Philadelphia: Westminster Press.

Jewett, Robert, 1997, 'Honor and shame in the argument of Romans', in *Putting Body and Soul Together: Essays in Honor of Robin Scroggs*, ed. Virginia Wiles, Alexandra Brown and Gordon F. Snyder, Valley Forge, Pa.: Trinity Press International, pp. 25–73.

Jewett, Robert, 2000, 'The social context and implications of homoerotic references in Romans 1:24–27', in *Homosexuality, Science, and the 'Plain Sense' of Scripture*, ed. David L. Balch, Grand Rapids: Eerdmans, pp. 278–304.

Johnson, E. Elizabeth, 1992a, 'Ephesians', in Carol A. Newsom and Sharon H. Ringe (eds), *The Women's Bible Commentary*, Louisville: Westminster John Knox Press, pp. 338–42.

Johnson, E. Elizabeth, 1992b, 'Colossians', Carol A. Newsom and Sharon H. Ringe (eds), *The Women's Bible Commentary*, Louisville: Westminster John Knox Press, pp. 346–8.

Johnson, Elizabeth, 1992c, *She Who IS: The Mystery of God in Feminist Theological Discourse*, New York: Crossroad.

Johnson, Luke Timothy, 1995, *The Letter of James*, Anchor Bible, New York: Doubleday.

Johnson, Luke Timothy, 1997, *Reading Romans: A Literary and Theological Commentary*, New York: Crossroad.

Johnson, Luke Timothy, 2001, *Reading Romans*, Macon, Ga.: Smyth & Helwys.

Jones, D. W., 2004, *Reforming the Morality of Usury: A Study of Differences that Separated the Protestant Reformers*, Lanham, Md.: University Press of America.

Jordan, Mark D., 2005, *Blessing Same-sex Unions: The Perils of Queer Romance and the Confusions of Christian Marriage*, Chicago: University of Chicago Press.

Keller, Catherine, 1996, *Apocalypse Now and Then: A Feminist Guide to the End of the World*, Boston: Beacon Press, 1996.

Keller, Catherine, 2005, *God and Power: Counter-Apocalyptic Journeys*, Minneapolis: Fortress Press.

Kelly, J. N. D., 1969, *A Commentary on the Epistles of Peter and of Jude*, New York: Harper & Row.

Kelly, Michael, 1994, *The Erotic Contemplative*, vol. 6, video-talk produced by EroSpirit, Oakland.

Kim, Grace Ji-Sun, 2002, *The Grace of Sophia: A Korean North American Women's Christology*, Cleveland, Ohio: Pilgrim Press.

Kim, Michael, 2004, 'Out and about: coming of age in a straight white world', in Arar Han and John Hsu (eds), *Asian American X: An Intersection of 21st Century Asian American Voices*, Ann Arbor: University of Michigan Press.

Kittredge, Cynthia Briggs, 1994b, 'Hebrews', in *Searching the Scriptures*, vol. 2: *A Feminist Commentary*, ed. Elisabeth Schüssler Fiorenza, New York: Crossroad, pp. 428–54.

Koester, Craig C., 2001, *Epistle to the Hebrews*, Anchor Bible, New York: Doubleday.

Koch, Timothy R., 2001, 'Cruising as methodology: homoeroticism and the Scriptures', in Ken Stone (ed.), *Queer Commentary and the Hebrew Bible*, JSOTSS 334, New York: Sheffield Academic Press, pp. 169–80.

Krause, Deborah, 2004, *1 Timothy*, London: T&T Clark.

Kuefler, Matthew, 2001, *The Manly Eunuch: Masculinity, Gender Ambiguity, and Christian Ideology in Late Antiquity*, Chicago: University of Chicago Press.

Kushner, Tony, 1995, *Angels in America: A Gay Fantasia on National Themes: Part One: Millennium Approaches; Part Two: Perestroika*, New York: Theatre Communications Group.

Kwok Pui-lan, 2005, *Postcolonial Imagination and Feminist Theology*, Louisville and London: Westminster John Knox Press.

Lampe, Peter, 1991, 'The Roman Christians of Romans 16', in *The Romans Debate*, ed. Karl P. Donfried, Peabody, Mass.: Hendrickson, pp. 216–30.

Lampe, Peter, 2003, *From Paul to Valentinus: Christians at Rome in the First Two Centuries*, Minneapolis: Fortress Press; first published in German, 1987.

Lane, William L., 1991, *Hebrews 1–8* and *Hebrews 9–13*, Word Biblical Commentary 47A and 47B. Dalla1: Word.

Laqueur, Thomas, 1990, *Making Sex: Body and Gender from the Greeks to Freud*, Cambridge, Mass.: Harvard University Press.

Larson, Jennifer, 2004, 'Paul's masculinity', *JBL* 123 (1), pp. 85–97.

Lawrence, Jr., Raymond J., 1989, *The Poisoning of Eros: Sexual Values in Conflict*, New York: Augustine Moore Press.

Lebacqz, Karen, 1987, *Justice in an Unjust World*, Minneapolis: Augsburg Press.

Lee, Jeanette Mei Gim, 2004, 'Queerly a Good Friday', in Kevin K. Kumashiro (ed.), *Restoried Selves: Autobiographies of Queer Asian/Pacific American Activists*, New York: Harrington Park Press.

Lee, Jung Young, 1995, *Marginality: The Key to Multicultural Theology*, Minneapolis: Fortress Press.

Levinas, Emmanuel, 2000, *God, Death, and Time*, trans. Bettina Bergo, Stanford: Stanford University Press.

Levine, Amy-Jill, 1988, *The Social and Ethnic Dimensions of Matthean Salvation History*, Lewiston, NY: Edwin Mellen Press.

Levine, Amy-Jill, 1992, 'Matthew', in Carol A. Newsom and Sharon H. Ringe (eds), *The Women's Bible Commentary*, Louisville: Westminster John Knox Press, pp. 252–62.

Levine, Amy-Jill, 2001a, 'Discharging responsibility: Matthean Jesus, biblical law, and hemorrhaging woman', in Amy-Jill Levine (ed.), *A Feminist Companion to Matthew*, Sheffield: Sheffield Academic Press, pp. 70–87.

Levine, Amy-Jill (ed.), 2001b, *A Feminist Companion to Matthew*, Feminist Companion to the New Testament and Early Christian Writings 1, Sheffield: Sheffield Academic Press.

Levine, Amy-Jill (ed.), 2002, *A Feminist Companion to Luke*, New York: Sheffield Academic Press.

Levine, Amy-Jill, 2003a, 'Introduction,' in Amy-Jill Levine (ed.), *A Feminist Companion to the Deutero-Pauline Epistles*, Cleveland, Ohio: Pilgrim Press, pp. 1–13.

Levine, Amy-Jill (ed.), 2003b, *A Feminist Companion to the Deutero-Pauline Epistles*. Feminist Companion to the New Testament and Early Christian Writings 6, Cleveland, Ohio: The Pilgrim Press.

Lifton, Robert Jay, 2000, *Destroying the World in Order to Save It: Aum Shinrikyō, Apocalyptic Violence, and the New Global Terrorism*, New York: Henry Holt & Company.

Lifton, Robert Jay, 2003, *Superpower Syndrome: America's Apocalyptic Confrontation with the World*, New York: Thunder's Mouth Press/Nation Books.

Lim, You-Leng Leroy, 1998, 'Webs of betrayal, webs of blessing', in David L. Eng and Alice Y. Hom (eds), *Q&A: Queer in Asian America*, Philadelphia: Temple University Press.

Linzey, A., 1993, *Animal Theology*, Urbana: University of Illinois Press.

Linzey, A., 1998, *Animal Gospel*, Lousiville: Westminster John Knox Press.

Lohse, Eduard, 1971, *Colossians and Philemon*, trans. William R. Poehlmann and Robert J. Karris, Hermeneia: a Critical and Historical Commentary on the Bible, Philadelphia: Fortress Press.

Lohse, Eduard, 2003, *Der Brief an die Römer*, KEK 4, 15th edn, Göttingen: Vanderhoeck & Ruprecht.

Long, Asphodel P., 1993, *In a Chariot Drawn by Lions: The Search for the Female in Deity*, Freedom, Calif.: The Crossing Press.

Long, Ron, 2004, *Men, Gods and Homosexuality*, New York: Haworth.

Long, Ron, 2005, 'Of argument and aesthetic distaste: a response to J. Budziszewski', *Philosophia Christi* 2 (1), pp. 53–8.

Long, Thomas G., 1997, *Hebrews*, Interpretation, Louisville: Westminster John Knox Press.

Lopez, Davina C., 2004, 'The Roman imperial impact on women in Galilee', slide lecture accompanying a paper presented by Richard A. Horsley at the Society of Biblical Literature Annual Meeting, Women in the Biblical World Section, 20 November 2004, San Antonio, Tex.

Loughlin, Gerard, 1998, 'Refiguring masculinity in Christ', in *Religion and Sexuality*, ed. Michael Hayes, Wendy Porter and David Tombs, Sheffield: Sheffield Academic Press, pp. 405–14.

MacDonald, Margaret Y., 2000, *Colossians and Ephesians*, Sacra Pagina 17, Collegeville, Minn.: Liturgical Press/Michael Glazier.

Mader, Donald, 1992, 'The *Entimos Pais* of Matthew 8:5–13 and Luke 7:1–19', in *Homosexuality and Religion and Philosophy*, ed. Wayne R. Dynes and Stephen Donaldson, New York: Garland Publications, pp. 223–35.

Malherbe, Abraham J., 1987, *Paul and the Thessalonians: The Philosophic Tradition of Pastoral Care*, Philadelphia: Fortress Press.

Martin, Clarice J., 1991, 'The *Haustafeln* (household codes) in African American biblical interpretation: "free slaves" and "subordinate women"', in Cain Hope Felder (ed.), *Stony the Road We Trod: African American Biblical Interpretation*, Minneapolis: Fortress Press, pp. 206–31.

Martin, Dale B., 1990, *Slavery as Salvation: The Metaphor of Slavery in Pauline Christianity*, New Haven: Yale University Press.

Martin, Dale B., 1995, *The Corinthian Body*, New Haven: Yale University Press.

Martin, Dale B., 1996, '*Aresonokoitês and Malakos*: meanings and consequences', in *Biblical Ethics and Homosexuality: Listening to Scripture*, ed. Robert L. Brawley, Louisville: Westminster John Knox Press, pp. 117–36.

Martin, James, 2000, 'And then he kissed me: an Easter love story', in Robert E. Goss and Mona West (eds), *Take Back the Word: A Queer Reading of the Bible*, Cleveland, Ohio: Pilgrim Press, pp. 219–26.

Martin, Troy, 2004, 'Paul's argument from nature for the veil in 1 Corinthians 11: 13–15: a testical instead of a head covering', *JBL* 123, pp. 75–84.

Martyn, J. Louis, 1968, *History and Theology in the Fourth Gospel*, Nashville: Abingdon Press; 2nd edn, 1979.

Matera, Frank J., 2003, *II Corinthians: A Commentary*, New Testament Library, Louisville: Westminster John Knox Press.

Matthews, Shelley, 1994b, '2 Corinthians', in *Searching the Scriptures*, vol. 2: *A Feminist Commentary*, ed. Elisabeth Schüssler Fiorenza, New York: Crossroad.

McGinn, Bernard, John J. Collins and Stephen J. Stein (eds), 2003, *The Continuum History of Apocalypticism*, New York and London: Continuum.

McNally, Terrence, 1998, *Corpus Christi: A Play*, New York: Grove Press.

McNeill, John J., 1988, *Taking a Chance on God*, Boston: Beacon Press.

McNeill, John J., 1993, *The Church and the Homosexual*, 4th edn, Boston: Beacon Press.

McNeill, John J., 1995, *Freedom, Glorious Freedom*, Boston: Beacon Press.

Meier, John P., 1979, *The Vision of Matthew: Christ, Church, and Morality in the First Gospel*, New York: Paulist Press.

Mendelson, Edward, 1999, *Later Auden*, New York: Farrar, Straus & Giroux.

Milgrom, Jacob, 1991, *Leviticus 1–16*, Anchor Bible, New York: Doubleday.

Milgrom, Jacob, 2000, *Leviticus 17–22*, Anchor Bible, New York: Doubleday.

Miller, James E., 1995, 'The practices of Rom. 1:26: Homosexual or heterosexual', *Novum Testamentum* 37 (1), pp. 1–11.

Miller, James E., 1997, 'A response: pederasty and Romans 1:27: a response to Mark Smith', *JAAR* 65 (4), pp. 861–6.

Miller, Robert J. (ed.), 1994, *The Complete Gospels*, Annotated Scholars Version, 3rd edn, New York: HarperCollins.

Milton, John, 1968, *Paradise Lost*, ed. Alastair Fowler, London: Longman.

Miranda, José P., 1971/74, *Marx and the Bible: A Critique of the Philosophy of Oppression*, Maryknoll: Orbis.

Mollenkott, Virginia Ramey, 2001, *Omnigender: A Trans-Religious Approach*, Cleveland, Ohio: Pilgrim Press.

Moltmann, Jürgen, 1998, *The Crucified God: The Cross of Christ as the Foundation and Criticism of Christian Theology*, trans. R. A. Wilson and John Bowden, London: SCM Press; Eng. trans. first published 1974.

Moo, Douglas, 1996, *The Epistle to the Romans*, NICNT, Grand Rapids: Eerdmans.

Moo, Douglas, 2002, *Encountering the Book of Romans*, Grand Rapids: Baker Academic.

Moore, Gareth, OP, 2001, *The Body in Context: Sex and Catholicism*, New York: Continuum.

Moore, Stephen D., 1996, *God's Gym: Divine Male Bodies of the Bible*, New York and London: Routledge.

Moore, Stephen D., 2001, *God's Beauty Parlor: And Other Queer Spaces In and Around the Bible*, Stanford: Stanford University. See 'Sex and the single apostle', pp. 133–72, 253–68.

Moxnes, Halvor, 1988a, *The Economy of the Kingdom: Social Conflict and Economic Relations in Luke's Gospel*, Philadelphia: Fortress Press.

Moxnes, Halvor, 1988b, 'Honor, shame, and the outside world in Paul's letter to the Romans', in *The Social World of Formative Christianity and Judaism*, ed. Jacob Neusner *et al.*, Philadelphia: Fortress Press, pp. 207–18.

Moxnes, Halvor, 2003, *Putting Jesus in His Place: A Radical Vision of Household and Kingdom*, Louisville and London: Westminster John Knox Press.

Munt, Sally (ed.), 1992, *New Lesbian Criticism: Literary and Cultural Readings*, New York: Columbia University Press.

Murphy-O'Connor, Jerome, 1991, *The Theology of the Second Letter to the Corinthians*, New Testament Theology, Cambridge: Cambridge University Press.

Murphy O'Connor, Jerome, 1996, *Paul: A Critical Life*, Oxford: Clarendon Press.

Nelson-Pallmeyer, Jack, 2001, *Jesus Against Christianity: Reclaiming the Missing Jesus*, Harrisburg, Pa.: Trinity Press International.

Newsom, Carol A. and Sharon H. Ringe (eds), 1992, *The Women's Bible Commentary*, Louisville: Westminster John Knox Press.

Neyrey, Jerome H., 1980, 'The form and background of the polemic in 2 Peter', *JBL*

99, pp. 407–31.

Neyrey, Jerome H. (ed.), 1991, *The Social World of Luke–Acts: Models for Interpretation*, Peabody: Hendrickson.

Neyrey, Jerome H., 1993, *2 Peter, Jude: A New Translation with Introduction and Commentary*, Anchor Bible 37C, New York: Doubleday.

Nimmons, David, 2002, *Soul Beneath the Skin: The Unseen Hearts and Habits of Gay Men*, New York: St Martin's Press.

Nissinen, Martti, 1998, *Homoeroticism in the Biblical World: A Historical Perspective*, trans. Kirsi Stjerna, Minneapolis: Fortress Press.

Noth, Martin, 1960, *The History of Israel*, 2nd edn, trans. P. R. Ackroyd, New York: Harper & Row.

O'Day, Gail, 2001, 'The Gospel of John: reading the incarnate Word', in Robert Fortna and Tom Thatcher (eds), *Jesus in Johannine Tradition*, Louisville: Westminster John Knox Press, pp. 25–34.

Olyan, Saul M., 1994, "And with a male you shall not lie the lying down of a woman": on the meaning and significance of Leviticus 18:22 and 20:13', *Journal of the History of Sexuality* 5, pp. 179–206.

Osiek, Carolyn, 2000, *Philippians, Philemon*, Abingdon New Testament Commentaries, Nashville: Abingdon Press.

Pagels, Elaine, 1995, *The Origin of Satan*, New York: Random House.

Perkins, Benjamin, 2000, 'Coming out, Lazarus's and ours: queer reflections of a psychospiritual, political journey', in *Take Back the Word: A Queer Reading of the Bible*, ed. Robert E. Goss and Mona West, Cleveland, Ohio: The Pilgrim Press, pp. 196–205.

Perkins, Pheme, 1988, *Reading the New Testament*, 2nd edn, New York and Mahwah: Paulist Press.

Perkins, Pheme, 1993, *First and Second Peter, James, and Jude*, Louisville: Westminister John Knox Press.

Perkins, Pheme, 1998, 'Philippians', in *The Women's Bible Commentary*, ed. Carol A. Newsom and Sharon H. Ringe, Louisville: Westminster John Knox Press.

Perlongher, Néstor, 1997, *Matan a una Marica*.

Perry, Troy D., 1991, 'A meditation on religion and leatherspace', in *Leatherfolk: Radical Sex, People, Politics, and Practice*, ed. Mark Thompson, Boston: Alyson, pp. 247–51.

Pfitzner, V. C., 1997, *Hebrews*, Nashville: Abingdon Press.

Pippin, Tina, 1992, *Death and Desire: The Rhetoric of Gender in the Apocalypse of John*, Louisville: Westminister John Knox Press.

Pippin, Tina, 1999, *Apocalyptic Bodies: The Biblical End of the World in Text and Image*, New York and London: Routledge.

Pomeroy, Sarah B., 1975, *Goddesses, Whores, Wives, and Slaves: Women in Classical Antiquity*, New York: Schocken Books.

Pope, Harrison G., Katherine Phillips and Roberto Olverardo, 2000, *The Adonis Complex: The Secret Crisis of Male Body Obsessions*, New York: The Free Press.

Portefaix, Lilian, 2003. '"Good citizenship" in the household of God: women's position in the pastorals reconsidered in the light of Roman rule', in Amy-Jill Levine (ed.), *A Feminist Companion to the Deutero-Pauline Epistles*, Feminist Companion to the New Testament and Early Christian Writings 6, Cleveland, Ohio: Pilgrim Press, pp. 147–58.

Queen, Carol, and Lawrence Schimel (eds), 1997, *PoMoSexuals: Challenging Assumptions about Gender and Sexuality*, San Francisco: Cleis Press.

Quinby, Lee, 1999, *Millennial Seduction: A Skeptic Confronts Apocalyptic Culture*, Ithaca, NY and London: Cornell University Press.

Reese, Ruth Anne, 2000, *Writing Jude: The Reader, the Text, and the Author in Constructs of Power and Desire*, Leiden: Brill.

Reid, Marty L., 1995, 'Paul's rhetoric of mutuality: a rhetorical reading of Romans', in *Society of Biblical Literature 1995 Seminar Papers*, Atlanta: Scholars Press, pp. 117–39.

Reinhartz, Adele, 1994b, 'The Gospel of John', in *Searching the Scriptures*, vol. 2: *A Feminist Commentary*, ed. Elisabeth Schüssler Fiorenza, New York: Crossroad, pp. 561–600.

Reumann, John, 2003, 'Romans', in *Eerdmans Bible Commentary*, ed. James D. G. Dunn, Grand Rapids: Eerdmans, pp. 1277–313.

Rich, Adrienne, 1987, 'Compulsory heterosexuality and lesbian existence', in *Blood, Bread and Poetry: Selected Prose 1979–1985*, New York: W.W. Norton & Co, pp. 23–75.

Richard, Earl J., 1995, *First and Second Thessalonians*, Sacra Pagina Series 11, Collegeville, Minn.: Liturgical Press.

Ridderbos, Simon Jan, 1963, 'Bibel und Homosexualität', in Hermanus Bianchi *et al.*, *Der homosexuelle Nächste: Ein Symposion*, Hamburg: Furche, pp. 50–73, 274.

Ringe, Sharon H., 1985, *Jesus, Liberation, and the Biblical Jubilee: Images for Ethics and Christology*, Philadelphia: Fortress Press.

Ringrose, Katherine M., 2003, *The Perfect Servant: Eunuchs and the Social Construction of Gender in Byzantium*, Chicago: University of Chicago Press.

Rivkin, Ellis, 1991, 'What crucified Jesus?', in *Jesus' Jewishness: Exploring the Place of Jesus within Early Judaism*, ed. James H. Charlesworth, New York: Crossroad, pp. 226–57.

Rogers, Eugene F., Jr., 1999, *Sexuality and the Christian Body: Their Way into the Triune God*, Oxford: Blackwell.

Rolheiser, Ronald, 1996, *Against the Infinite Horizons*, New York: Crossroad.

Rosenblatt, Marie Eloise, 1994b(1), '2 Peter', in *Searching the Scriptures*, vol. 2: *A Feminist Commentary*, ed. Elisabeth Schüssler Fiorenza, New York: Crossroad, pp. 399–405.

Rosenblatt, Marie Eloise, 1994b(2), 'Jude', in *Searching the Scriptures*, vol. 2: *A Feminist Commentary*, ed. Elisabeth Schüssler Fiorenza, New York: Crossroad, pp. 392–8.

Rotello, Gabriel, 1997, *Sexual Ecology: AIDS and the Destiny of Gay Men*, New York: Dutton/Penguin.

Roy, Arundhati, 2003, *War Talk*, Cambridge, Mass.: South End Press.

Rudy, Kathy, 1997, *Sex and the Church: Gender, Homosexuality, and the Transformation of Christian Ethics*, Boston: Beacon Press.

Ruether, Rosemary Radford, 2000, *Christianity and the Making of the Modern Family: Ruling Ideologies, Diverse Realities*, Boston: Beacon Press.

Russo, Vito, 1987, *The Celluloid Closet: Homosexuality in the Movies*, rev. edn, Perennial Library, New York: Harper & Row.

Ryan, Judith M., 2005, *Philippians and Philemon*, Sacra Pagina, Collegeville: Liturgical Press.

Saldarini, Anthony J., 1994, *Matthew's Christian-Jewish Community*, Chicago and London: University of Chicago Press.

Saunders, Stanley P., 2001, *Philippians and Galatians*, Louisville: Geneva Press.

Schaberg, Jane, 1987, *The Illegitimacy of Jesus: A Feminist Theological Interpretation of the Infancy Narratives*, San Francisco: Harper & Row.

Schaberg, Jane, 1992, 'Luke', in *The Women's Bible Commentary*, expanded edition, ed. Carol A. Newsom and Sharon H. Ringe, Louisville: Westminster John Knox Press, 363–80.

Schaberg, Jane, 2004, *The Resurrection of Mary Magdalene: Legends, Apocrypha, and the Christian Testament*, New York: Continuum.

Schaeffer, Francis A., 1998, *The Finished Work of Christ: The Truth of Romans 1–8*, Wheaton: Crossway.

Schmidt, Thomas E., 1995, *Straight and Narrow: Compassion and Clarity in the Homosexuality Debate*, Downers Grove: InterVarsity Press.

Schnackenburg, Rudolf, 1992, *The Johannine Epistles: Introduction and Commentary*, New York: Crossroad.

Schneemelcher, Wilhelm (ed.), 1992, *New Testament Apocrypha*, 2 vols, Louisville: Westminster John Knox Press.

Schoedel, W. R., 1997, 'Same-sex Eros: Paul and the Graeco-Roman tradition', in *Homosexuality, Science, and the 'Plain Sense' of Scripture*, ed. D. L. Balch, Grand Rapids: Eerdmans, pp. 43–72.

Schottroff, Luise, and Wolfgang Stegemann, 1986, *Jesus and the Hope of the Poor*, trans. Matthew O'Connell, Maryknoll: Orbis Books.

Schreiner, Thomas R., 1998, *Romans*, Baker Exegetical Commentary on the New Testament, Grand Rapids: Baker Books.

Schroer, Silvia, 2000, *Wisdom Has Built Her House: Studies on the Figure of Sophia in the Bible*, trans. Linda M. Maloney and William McDonough, Collegeville: Liturgical Press/Michael Glazier.

Schüssler Fiorenza, Elisabeth, 1983, *In Memory of Her: A Feminist Theological Reconstruction of Christian Origins*, New York: Crossroad; 10th anniversary edn 2002.

Schüssler Fiorenza, Elisabeth, 1992a, *But She Said: Feminist Practices of Biblical Interpretation*, Boston: Beacon Press.

Schüssler Fiorenza, Elisabeth, 1992b, 'Feminist Hermeneutics', in D. N. Freedman et al. (eds), *The Anchor Bible Dictionary*, vol. 2, New York: Doubleday, pp. 783–92.

Schüssler Fiorenza, Elisabeth, 1994a, *Jesus: Miriam's Child, Sophia's Prophet: Critical Issues in Feminist Christology*, New York: Continuum.

Schüssler Fiorenza, Elisabeth (ed.), 1994b, *Searching the Scriptures*, vol. 2: *A Feminist Commentary*, New York: Crossroad.

Schwager, Raymund, 1987, *Must there be Scapegoats? Violence and Redemption in the Bible*, San Francisco: Harper & Row.

Scott, Martin, 1992, *Sophia and the Johannine Jesus*, Sheffield: JSOT Press.

Scroggs, Robin, 1983, *The New Testament and Homosexuality: Contextual Background for Contemporary Debate*, Philadelphia: Fortress Press.

Sedgwick, Eve Kosofsky, 1993, *Tendencies*, Durham, N.C.: Duke University Press.

Seltzer, Robert M., 1980, *Jewish People, Jewish Thought: The Jewish Experience in History*, New York: Macmillan.

Sherman, N., 2003, *Stoic Warriors: The Ancient Philosophy Behind the Military Mind*, New York: Oxford University Press.

Shorto, Russell, 2005, 'What's their real problem with gay marriage?', *New York Times Magazine*, 19 June, pp. 34–41, 64–7.

Signorile, Michelangelo, 1998, *Life Outside: The Signorile Report on Gay Men: Sex, Drugs, Muscles, and the Passages of Life*, New York: Harper Perennial.

Siker, Jeffrey S., 1994, 'How to decide? homosexual Christians, the Bible, and Gentile inclusion', *Theology Today* 31 (2), pp. 223–34.

Siker, Jeffrey S., 1996, 'Gentile wheat and homosexual Christians: New Testament directions for the heterosexual Church', in *Biblical Ethics and Homosexuality: Listening to Scripture*, ed. Robert L. Brawley, Louisville: Westminster John Knox Press, pp. 137–51.

Simpson, Mark, 1994, *Male Impersonators: Men Performing Masculinity*, New York: Routledge.

Simpson, Robert Hamilton, 2005, 'How to be fashionably queer: reminding the Church of the importance of sexual stories', *Theology and Sexuality* 11 (2), pp. 97–108.

Smith, Mark D., 1985, 'Ancient bisexuality and the interpretation of Romans 1: 26–27', *JAAR* 64 (2), pp. 223–56.

Smith, Mark D., 1997, 'Paul and ancient bisexuality: a rejoinder', *JAAR* 65 (4), pp. 867–70.

Specter, Michael, 2005, 'Higher risk: crystal meth, the internet, and dangerous choices about AIDS', *The New Yorker*, 23 May, pp. 38–45.

Spencer, Daniel T., 1996, *Gay and Gaia: Ethics, Ecology, and the Erotic*, Cleveland, Ohio: Pilgrim Press.

Spong, John Shelby, 1991, *Rescuing the Bible from Fundamentalism*, San Francisco: HarperSanFrancisco.

Spong, John Shelby, 1992, *Born of a Woman: A Bishop Rethinks the Birth of Jesus*, New York: HarperCollins.

Spong, John Shelby, 2005, *The Sins of Scripture: Exposing the Bible's Texts of Hate to Reveal the God of Love*, San Francisco: HarperSanFrancisco.

Standhartinger, Angela, 2003, 'The epistle to the congregation in Colossae and the invention of the "household code"', in Amy-Jill Levine (ed.), *A Feminist Companion to the Deutero-Pauline Epistles*, Feminist Companion to the New Testament and Early Christian Writings 6, Cleveland, Ohio: Pilgrim Press, pp. 88–97.

Starbird, Margaret, 1993, *The Woman with the Alabaster Jar: Mary Magdalene and the Holy Grail*, New York: Bear and Company.

Stone, Ken, 2001, 'Introduction', in *Queer Commentary and the Hebrew Bible*, Cleveland, Ohio: Pilgrim Press.

Stowasser, Martin, 1997, 'Homosexualität und Bibel, exegetische une herme-neutishe Überlegungen zu einem schwierigen Thema', *New Testament Studies* 43, pp. 503–26.

Stowers, Stanley K., 1994, *A Rereading of Romans*, New Haven: Yale University Press; paperback edn 1996.

Stuart, Elizabeth, 1995, *Just Good Friends*, New York: Mowbray.

Stuart, Elizabeth, 2000, 'Camping around the canon: humour as hermeneutical tool for queer readings of biblical texts', in Robert E. Goss and Mona West (eds), *Take Back the Word: A Queer Reading of the Bible*, Cleveland, Ohio: Pilgrim Press, pp. 23–34.

Stuart, Elizabeth, 2003, *Gay and Lesbian Theologies: Repetitions with a Critical Difference*, Burlington, Vt.: Ashgate.

Sugirtharajah, R. S., 2003, *Postcolonial Reconfigurations: An Alternative Way of Reading the Bible and Doing Theology*, St Louis, Mo.: Chalice Press.

Swancutt, Diana M., 2003, '"The disease of effemination": the charge of effemi-nacy and the verdict of God (Romans 1:18–2:16)', in Stephen D. Moore and Janice Capel Anderson (eds), *New Testament Masculinities*, Semeia Studies 45, Atlanta: Society of Biblical Literature, pp. 193–233.

Swancutt, Diana M., 2004, 'Sexy Stoics and the rereading of Romans 1:18–2:16', in

A Feminist Companion to Paul, ed. Amy-Jill Levine, Cleveland, Ohio: Pilgrim Press, pp. 42–73.

Talbert, Charles H., 1986, 'Once again: the plan of 1 Peter', in *Perspectives on First Peter*, ed. Charles H. Talbert, Macon, Ga.: Mercer University Press, pp. 141–51.

Talbert, Charles H., 2002, *Romans*, Smith & Helwys Bible Commentary, Macon, Ga.: Smyth & Helwys.

Tamez, Elsa, 1991, *Contra Toda Condena: La justificación por la fe desde los excluidos*, San José, Costa Rica: DEI/SEBILA.

Tamez, Elsa, 1998/99, 'Der Brief an die gemeinde in Rom: Eine feministische Lektüre', in *Kompendium Feministische Bibelauslegung*, ed. Luise Schottroff and Marie-Theres Wacker, Gütersloh: Chr. Kaiser/Gütersloher, pp. 557–73.

Tanis, Justin, 2003, *Trans-Gendered: Theology, Ministry, and Communities of Faith*, Cleveland, Ohio: Pilgrim Press.

Tanzer, Sarah J., 1994b, 'Ephesians', in *Searching the Scriptures*, vol. 2: *A Feminist Commentary*, ed. Elisabeth Schüssler Fiorenza, New York: Crossroad, pp. 325–48.

Tarachow, Sidney, 1955, 'St. Paul and early Christianity: a pyschoanalysis and historical study', *Pyschoanalysis and Social Science* 4, pp. 223–81.

Temple, G., 2003, *Gay Unions: In the Light of Scripture, Tradition, and Reason*, New York: Church Publishing.

Theissen, Gerd, 1982, *The Social Setting of Pauline Christianity: Essays on Corinth*, Philadelphia: Fortress Press.

Theissen, Gerd, 1983/87, *Psychological Aspects of Pauline Theology*. Philadelphia: Fortress Press.

Theissen, Gerd, 1987, *The Shadow of the Galilean*, Philadelphia, Fortress Press.

Theissen, Gerd, 1999, *The Religion of the Earliest Churches: Creating a Symbolic World*, Minneapolis: Fortress Press.

Thistleton, Anthony C., 2003, 'Hebrews', in *Eerdmans Commentary on the Bible*, ed. James D. G. Dunn and John W. Rogerson, Grand Rapids: Eerdmans, pp. 1451–82.

Thompson, James W., 1982, *The Beginnings of Christian Philosophy: The Epistle to the Hebrews*, CBQMS 13, Washington, DC: Catholic Biblical Association of America.

Thurén, Lauri, 1990, *The Rhetorical Strategy of 1 Peter, with Special Regard to Ambiguous Expressions*, Abo, Finland: Abo Academy Press.

Thurston, Bonnie, 2003, '1 Timothy 5.3–16 and the leadership of women in the early Church', in Amy-Jill Levine (ed.), *A Feminist Companion to the Deutero-Pauline Epistles*, Feminist Companion to the New Testament and Early Christian Writings 6, Cleveland, Ohio: Pilgrim Press, pp. 159–74.

Tombs, D., 2002, 'Honour, shame and conquest: male identity, sexual violence and the body politic', *Journal of Hispanic/Latino Theology* 4 (4), pp. 21–40.

Tomson, Peter J., 1990, *Paul and the Jewish Law*, Minneapolis: Fortress Press.

Trexler, R. C., 1995, *Sex and Conquest: Gendered Violence, Political Order, and the European Conquest of the Americas*, Ithaca: Cornell University Press.

Truluck, Rembert, 2000, *Steps to Recovery from Bible Abuse*, Gaithersburg, Md.: Chi Rho Press.

Tutu, Desmond M., 1996, 'Foreword', in Marilyn Bennett Alexander and James Preston (eds), *We Were Baptized Too: Claiming God's Grace for Lesbians and Gays*, Louisville: Westminster John Knox Press.

Vanhoye, Albert, 1992, *Sacerdotes antiguos, Sacerdote nuevo según el Nuevo Testamento*, Salamanca: Biblioteca de Estudios Bíblicos.

Vanhoye, Albert, 1999, 'Hebreos', in *Comentario Bíblico Internacional*, ed. William R.

Farmer, Estella (Navarra): Verbo Divino. Excellent bibliography in Spanish.

Van de Spijker, Herman, 1968, *Die gleichgeschlechtliche Zuneigung: Homotropie: Homosexualität, Homoerotik, Homophilie – und die katholische Moraltheologie*, Olten: Walter.

Van Tilborg, Sjef, 1993, *Imaginative Love in John*, Leiden: Brill.

Verstraete, Beert, 1980, 'Slavery and the dynamics of male homosexual relationships in ancient Rome', *Journal of Homosexuality* 5, pp. 227–36.

Wagener, Ulrike, 1999, 'Der Brief an de HebräerInnen: Fremde in der Welt', in *Kompendium Feministische Bibelauslegung*, ed. Luise Schottroff and Marie-Theres Wacker, Gütersloh: Gütersloher/Chr. Kaiser, pp. 683–93.

Wahlberg, Rachel Conrad, 1986, *Jesus According to a Woman*, New York: Paulist Press.

von Wahlde, Urban C., 1990, *The Johannine Commandments: 1 John and the Struggle for the Johannine Tradition*, New York: Paulist Press.

Wainwright, Elaine M., 1994b, 'The Gospel of Matthew', in Elisabeth Schüssler Fiorenza (ed.), *Searching the Scriptures*, vol. 2: *A Feminist Commentary*, New York: Crossroad, pp. 635–77.

Wainwright, Elaine M., 1998, *Shall We Look for Another? A Feminist Rereading of the Matthean Jesus*, Maryknoll, NY: Orbis Books.

Wainwright, Elaine M., 2001, 'Not without my daughter: gender and demon possession in Matthew 15.21–28', in Amy-Jill Levine (ed.), *A Feminist Companion to the Deutero-Pauline Epistles*, Feminist Companion to the New Testament and Early Christian Writings 6, Cleveland, Ohio: Pilgrim Press, pp. 126–37.

Wall, Robert W., 1997, *Community of the Wise: The Letter of James*, New Testament in Context, Valley Forge, Pa.: Trinity Press International.

Walters, Jonathan, 1993, '"No more than a boy": The shifting construction of masculinity from ancient Greece to the Middle Ages', *Gender and History* 5 (1), pp. 20–33.

Wan, Sze-kar, 2000, *Power in Weakness: The Second Letter of Paul to the Corinthians*, The New Testament in Context, Harrisburg, Pa.: Trinity Press International.

Ward, Graham, 2000, *Cities of God*, New York: Routledge.

Ward, Roy Bowen, 1997, 'Why unnatural? the tradition behind Romans 1:26–27', *Harvard Theological Review* 90, pp. 263–84.

Ware, Ann Patrick, 1988, 'The Vatican letter: presuppositions and objections', in Jeannine Gramick and Pat Furey (eds), *The Vatican and Homosexuality*, New York: Crossroad, pp. 28–32.

Warner, Michael, 1993, 'Introduction', in *Fear of a Queer Planet*, ed. Michael Warner, Minneapolis: University of Minnesota Press.

Warner, Michael, 1999, *The Trouble with Normal: Sex, Politics, and the Ethics of Queer Life*, New York: Free Press/Simon & Schuster.

West, Mona, 2003, 'The raising of Lazarus: a lesbian coming out story', in *A Feminist Companion to John*, vol. 1, ed. Amy-Jill Levine with Marianne Blickenstaff, Cleveland, Ohio: Pilgrim Press, pp. 143–58.

West, Mona, 2005, 'Coming out as sacrament', UFMCC website, http://www.mccchurch.org/AM/Template.cfm?Section=Resources&Template=/CM/HTMLDisplay.cfm&ContentID=578.

Westerholm, Stephen, 2004, *Perspectives Old and New on Paul: The 'Lutheran' Paul and His Critics*, Grand Rapids: Eerdmans.

Wiley, Tatha (ed.), 2003, *Thinking of Christ: Proclamation, Explanation, Meaning*, New York and London: Continuum.

Williams, Craig A., 1999, *Roman Homosexuality: Ideologies of Masculinity in Classical Antiquity*, Oxford and New York: Oxford University Press.

Williams, Robert, 1992, *Just As I Am*, New York: Crown.

Wilson, Nancy L., 1995, *Our Tribe: Queer Folks, God, Jesus, and the Bible*, New York: HarperCollins.

Wink, Walter, 2002, *The Human Being: Jesus and the Enigma of the Son of the Man*, Minneapolis: Fortress Press.

Winkler, John J., 1990, *The Constraints of Desire*. New York: Routledge.

Wire, Antoinette Clark, (1990), *The Corinthian Women Prophets: A Reconstruction Through Paul's Rhetoric*, Minneapolis: Fortress Press.

Witherington III, Ben, 1994, *Jesus the Sage: The Pilgrimage of Wisdom*, Minneapolis: Fortress Press.

Witherington III, Ben, 1995, *Conflict and Community in Corinth: A Socio-Rhetorical Commentary on 1 and 2 Corinthians*, Grand Rapids: Eerdmans.

Wold, Donald, 1998, *Out of Order: Homosexuality in the Bible and the Ancient Near East*, Grand Rapids: Baker Books.

Wright, N. T., 1996, 'The Laws in Romans 2', in James D. G. Dunn (ed.), *Paul and the Mosaic Law*, Tübingen: Mohr, pp. 131–50.

Wright, N. T., 2002, 'The letter to the Romans', in *The New Interpreter's Bible*, ed. Leander E. Keck, vol. 10, Nashville: Abingdon Press, pp. 393–770.

Wright, Tom, 2004, *Paul for Everyone: The Prison Letters*, Louisville: Westminster John Knox Press.

Yarbro Collins, Adela, 1984, *Crisis and Catharsis: The Power of the Apocalypse*, Philadelphia, Pa.: Westminster Press.

Yarbro Collins, Adela, 2003, 'The book of Revelation', in Bernard McGinn, John J. Collins, and Stephen J. Stein (eds), *The Continuum History of Apocalypticism*, New York and London: Continuum, pp. 195–217.

Yee, Tet-Lim N., 2005, *Jews, Gentiles, and Ethnic Reconciliation: Paul's Jewish Identity and Ephesians*, New York: Cambridge University Press.

Name and Subject Index